TO

HAVE YOU SEEN
MY BASEBALL??

☆ PHIL ☆

XXX .

Collins

Mini
Thesaurus

Collins

An Imprint of HarperCollins*Publishers*

second edition 1999

© HarperCollins Publishers 1993, 1999

latest reprint 2004

HarperCollins Publishers
Westerhill Road, Bishopbriggs, Glasgow G64 2QT
Great Britain

www.collinsdictionaries.com

Collins® and Bank of English® are registered trademarks
of HarperCollins Publishers Limited

ISBN 0-00-472379-1

A catalogue record for this book
is available from the British Library.

Typeset by Ann Rautenbach

Printed and bound in Great Britain by
Charles Letts & Company Ltd

EDITORIAL STAFF

FOREWORD

Collins Mini Thesaurus, which was first published in 1993, has proved to be an immensely popular language resource. It allows you to look up a word and find a wide selection of alternatives that can replace it. It is, therefore, tremendously helpful when you are trying to find different ways of expressing yourself, as well as being an invaluable aid for crosswords and puzzles.

The A-Z arrangement of main entry words lets you go straight to any word without having to use an index, just as if you were looking up a word in a dictionary. In addition, all main entry words are printed in colour so that they are quick and easy to find. In the new **Mini Thesaurus**, the number of entries has been increased, thus giving you an even greater chance of finding the word you want. At the same time, the list of alternative words (synonyms) for each main entry word has been reviewed to give the widest possible choice of the most helpful alternatives. The new edition also takes account of recent changes in the language, with new terms like *gridlock*, *nerd* and *Internet* included as main entries, and words and idioms like *gut-wrenching*, *in the loop*, *big hitter* and *go pear-shaped* being found among the synonyms.

The **Collins Mini Thesaurus** also includes lists of antonyms at many of the main entry words. These lists provide a range of opposites which give you another way of expressing yourself. For instance, if you want to say that something is *difficult*, you may find it effective to take a word from the antonym list and use a phrase like "*by no means easy.*"

As part of an innovative design, key synonyms have been underlined and placed first in each list. This layout lets you see immediately which sense of the word is referred to. It also gives you an idea of which synonym is the closest alternative to the word you have looked up. Where helpful, the key synonym is also underlined at the start of the relevant list of antonyms in the entry, allowing you to identify at once the particular sense for which these can be used as opposites.

These innovations mean that the **Collins Mini Thesaurus** provides the user with a treasury of useful words arranged in the most helpful format possible.

FEATURES OF THE THESAURUS

Main entry words
in colour

Synonyms
words, listed in
alphabetical order, that
can be used in place of
the main entry word

Key synonym
given first and
underlined

Sense numbers
synonyms divided
according to meaning
to help you find the
sense you want

Antonyms
words, listed in
alphabetical order,
that mean the
opposite of the main
entry word

Labels
show the context in
which it is appropriate
to use the word

cramp

(*slang*), revise, swot

cramp[1] *noun* spasm, ache, contraction, convulsion, pain, pang, stitch, twinge

cramp[2] *verb* restrict, constrain, hamper, handicap, hinder, impede, inhibit, obstruct

cramped *adjective* closed in, confined, congested, crowded, hemmed in, overcrowded, packed, uncomfortable

➤ **Antonyms**
capacious, commodious, large, open, roomy, sizable *or* sizeable, spacious, uncongested, uncrowded

cranny *noun* crevice, chink, cleft, crack, fissure, gap, hole, opening

crash *noun* **1** collision, accident, bump, pile-up (*informal*), prang (*informal*), smash, wreck **2** smash, bang, boom, clang, clash, clatter, din, racket, thunder **3** collapse, debacle, depression, downfall, failure, ruin ♦ *verb* **4** collide, hit, crash-land (*an aircraft*), drive into, have an accident, plough into, wreck **5** collapse, be ruined, fail, fold, fold up, go belly up (*informal*), go bust (*informal*), go to the wall, go under **6** hurtle, fall headlong, give way, lurch, overbalance, plunge, topple

crass *adjective* insensitive, boorish, gross, indelicate, oafish, stupid, unrefined, witless

➤ **Antonyms**
bright, clever, intelligent, refined, sensitive, sharp, smart

crate *noun* container, box, case, packing case, tea chest

crater *noun* hollow, depression, dip

crave *verb* **1** long for, desire, hanker after, hope for, lust after, want, yearn for **2** *Informal* beg, ask, beseech, entreat, implore, petition, plead for, pray for, seek, solicit, supplicate

craving *noun* longing, appetite, desire, hankering, hope, hunger, thirst, yearning, yen (*informal*)

FEATURES OF THE THESAURUS

create

crawl *verb* **1** <u>creep</u>, advance slowly, inch, slither, worm one's way, wriggle, writhe **2** <u>grovel</u>, creep, fawn, humble oneself, toady **3** <u>be full of</u>, be alive, be overrun (*slang*), swarm, teem

➤ **Antonyms**
≠*creep*: dart, dash, fly, race, run

craze *noun* <u>fad</u>, enthusiasm, fashion, infatuation, mania, rage, trend, vogue

crazy *adjective* **1** *Informal* <u>ridiculous</u>, absurd, foolish, idiotic, ill-conceived, ludicrous, nonsensical, preposterous, senseless **2** <u>fanatical</u>, devoted, enthusiastic, infatuated, mad, passionate, wild (*informal*) **3** <u>insane</u>, crazed, demented, deranged, mad, nuts (*slang*), out of one's mind, unbalanced

➤ **Antonyms**
≠*ridiculous*: brilliant, feasible, practicable, prudent, realistic, sensible, wise, workable ≠*fanatical*: cool, indifferent, uncaring, unenthusiastic, uninterested ≠*insane*: in one's right mind, mentally sound, rational, sane, sensible

creak *verb* <u>squeak</u>, grate, grind, groan, scrape, scratch, screech

cream *noun* **1** <u>lotion</u>, cosmetic, emulsion, essence, liniment, oil, ointment, paste, salve, unguent **2** <u>best</u>, crème de la crème, elite, flower, pick, prime ♦ *adjective* **3** <u>off-white</u>, yellowish-white

creamy *adjective* <u>smooth</u>, buttery, milky, rich, soft, velvety

crease *noun* **1** <u>line</u>, corrugation, fold, groove, ridge, wrinkle ♦ *verb* **2** <u>wrinkle</u>, corrugate, crumple, double up, fold, rumple, screw up

create *verb* **1** <u>make</u>, compose, devise, formulate, invent, originate, produce, spawn **2** <u>cause</u>, bring about, lead to, occasion **3** <u>appoint</u>, constitute, establish, install, invest, make, set up

➤ **Antonyms**
≠*make*: annihilate, demolish, destroy

Labels
a label in brackets applies only to the word before it

a label which is not in brackets applies to the whole of that particular sense

Antonym senses
where there is more than one synonym sense, its corresponding antonym list is introduced by the key synonym with a ≠ sign to show which sense the antonym list refers to

Foreign words and phrases

Phrases and idioms

vii

A a

abandon verb **1** <u>leave</u>, desert, forsake, strand **2** <u>give up</u>, relinquish, surrender, yield ♦ noun **3** <u>wildness</u>, recklessness

➤ **Antonyms**

verb ≠<u>give up</u>: claim, hold, keep, take ♦ noun ≠<u>wildness</u>: control, moderation, restraint

abandonment noun <u>leaving</u>, dereliction, desertion, forsaking

abashed adjective <u>embarrassed</u>, ashamed, chagrined, disconcerted, dismayed, humiliated, mortified, shamefaced, taken aback

➤ **Antonyms**

at ease, composed, confident, unabashed, unashamed, undismayed

abate verb <u>decrease</u>, decline, diminish, dwindle, fade, lessen, let up, moderate, relax, slacken, subside, weaken

➤ **Antonyms**

amplify, escalate, increase, intensify, magnify

abbey noun <u>monastery</u>, convent, friary, nunnery, priory

abbreviate verb <u>shorten</u>, abridge, compress, condense, contract, cut, reduce, summarize

➤ **Antonyms**

amplify, draw out, elongate, expand, extend, increase, lengthen, prolong, protract, spin out, stretch out

abbreviation noun <u>shortening</u>, abridgment, contraction, reduction, summary, synopsis

abdicate verb <u>give up</u>, abandon, quit, relinquish, renounce, resign, step down (informal)

abdication noun <u>giving up</u>, abandonment, quitting, renunciation, resignation, retirement, surrender

abduct verb <u>kidnap</u>, carry off, seize, snatch (slang)

abduction noun <u>kidnapping</u>, carrying off, seizure

aberration noun <u>oddity</u>, abnormality, anomaly, defect, irregularity, lapse, peculiarity, quirk

abet verb <u>help</u>, aid, assist, connive at, support

abeyance noun in abeyance <u>shelved</u>, hanging fire, on ice (informal), pending, suspended

abhor verb <u>hate</u>, abominate, detest, loathe, shrink from, shudder at

➤ **Antonyms**

admire, adore, cherish, delight in, desire, enjoy, like, love, relish

abhorrent adjective <u>hateful</u>, abominable, disgusting, distasteful, hated, horrid, loathsome, offensive, repulsive

abide verb <u>tolerate</u>, accept, bear, endure, put up with, stand, suffer

abide by verb **1** <u>obey</u>, agree to, comply with, conform to, follow, observe, submit to **2** <u>carry out</u>, adhere to, discharge, fulfil, keep to

abiding adjective <u>everlasting</u>, continuing, enduring, lasting, permanent, persistent, unchanging

➤ **Antonyms**

brief, ephemeral, evanescent, fleeting, momentary, passing, short, short-lived, temporary, transitory

ability noun <u>skill</u>, aptitude, capability, competence, expertise, proficiency, talent

➤ **Antonyms**

inability, incapability, incapacity, incompetence, weakness

abject adjective **1** <u>miserable</u>, deplorable, forlorn, hopeless, pitiable, wretched **2** <u>servile</u>, cringing, degraded, fawning, grovelling, submissive

➤ **Antonyms**

≠<u>servile</u>: dignified, distinguished, exalted, grand, great, high, lofty, noble

ablaze adjective <u>on fire</u>, aflame, alight, blazing, burning, fiery, flaming, ignited, lighted

able *adjective* <u>capable</u>, accomplished, competent, efficient, proficient, qualified, skilful

➤ **Antonyms**

amateurish, incapable, incompetent, inefficient, inept, mediocre, unskilful

able-bodied *adjective* <u>strong</u>, fit, healthy, robust, sound, sturdy

➤ **Antonyms**

ailing, debilitated, feeble, frail, sickly, weak

abnormal *adjective* <u>unusual</u>, atypical, exceptional, extraordinary, irregular, odd, peculiar, strange, uncommon

➤ **Antonyms**

common, conventional, customary, normal, ordinary, regular, unexceptional, usual

abnormality *noun* <u>oddity</u>, deformity, exception, irregularity, peculiarity, singularity, strangeness

abode *noun* <u>home</u>, domicile, dwelling, habitat, habitation, house, lodging, pad (*slang*), quarters, residence

abolish *verb* <u>do away with</u>, annul, cancel, destroy, eliminate, end, eradicate, put an end to, quash, rescind, revoke, stamp out

➤ **Antonyms**

continue, create, establish, found, institute, introduce, legalize, promote, sustain

abolition *noun* <u>ending</u>, cancellation, destruction, elimination, end, extermination, termination, wiping out

abominable *adjective* <u>terrible</u>, despicable, detestable, disgusting, hateful, horrible, horrid, repulsive, revolting, vile

➤ **Antonyms**

admirable, agreeable, charming, delightful, desirable, good, likable *or* likeable, pleasant, pleasing, wonderful

abort *verb* **1** <u>terminate</u> (*a pregnancy*), miscarry **2** <u>stop</u>, arrest, axe (*informal*), call off, check, end, fail, halt, terminate

abortion *noun* <u>termination</u>, deliberate miscarriage, miscarriage

abortive *adjective* <u>failed</u>, fruitless, futile, ineffectual, miscarried, unsuccessful, useless, vain

abound *verb* <u>be plentiful</u>, flourish, proliferate, swarm, swell, teem, thrive

abounding *adjective* <u>plentiful</u>, abundant, bountiful, copious, full, profuse, prolific, rich

about *preposition* **1** <u>regarding</u>, as regards, concerning, dealing with, on, referring to, relating to **2** <u>near</u>, adjacent to, beside, circa (*used with dates*), close to, nearby ◆ *adverb* **3** <u>nearly</u>, almost, approaching, approximately, around, close to, more or less, roughly

above *preposition* <u>over</u>, beyond, exceeding, higher than, on top of, upon

➤ **Antonyms**

below, beneath, under, underneath

abrasion *noun* *Medical* <u>graze</u>, chafe, scrape, scratch, scuff, surface injury

abrasive *adjective* **1** <u>unpleasant</u>, caustic, cutting, galling, grating, irritating, rough, sharp **2** <u>rough</u>, chafing, grating, scraping, scratchy

abreast *adjective* **1** <u>alongside</u>, beside, side by side **2** <u>abreast of</u> <u>informed about</u>, acquainted with, *au courant* with, *au fait* with, conversant with, familiar with, in the picture about, in touch with, keeping one's finger on the pulse of, knowledgeable about, up to date with, up to speed with

abridge *verb* <u>shorten</u>, abbreviate, condense, cut, decrease, reduce, summarize

➤ **Antonyms**

enlarge, expand, extend, lengthen, prolong

abroad *adverb* <u>overseas</u>, in foreign lands, out of the country

abrupt *adjective* **1** <u>sudden</u>, precipitate, quick, surprising, unexpected **2** curt, brusque, gruff, impatient, rude, short, terse

➤ **Antonyms**

≠sudden: easy, leisurely, slow, unhurried ≠curt: civil, courteous, gracious, polite

abscond *verb* flee, clear out, disappear, escape, make off, run off, steal away

absence *noun* **1** nonattendance, absenteeism, truancy **2** lack, deficiency, need, omission, unavailability, want

absent *adjective* **1** missing, away, elsewhere, gone, nonexistent, out, unavailable **2** absent-minded, blank, distracted, inattentive, oblivious, preoccupied, vacant, vague ♦ *verb* **3** absent oneself stay away, keep away, play truant, withdraw

➤ **Antonyms**

adjective ≠missing: in attendance, present ≠absent-minded: alert, attentive, aware, conscious ♦ *verb* ≠stay away: attend, show up (informal)

absent-minded *adjective* vague, distracted, dreaming, forgetful, inattentive, preoccupied, unaware

➤ **Antonyms**

alert, awake, observant, perceptive, quick, wary, wide-awake

absolute *adjective* **1** total, complete, outright, perfect, pure, sheer, thorough, utter **2** supreme, full, sovereign, unbounded, unconditional, unlimited, unrestricted

absolutely *adverb* totally, completely, entirely, fully, one hundred per cent, perfectly, utterly, wholly

➤ **Antonyms**

fairly, probably, reasonably, somewhat

absolution *noun* forgiveness, deliverance, exculpation, exoneration, mercy, pardon, release

absolve *verb* forgive, deliver, exculpate, excuse, let off, pardon, release, set free

➤ **Antonyms**

blame, censure, charge, condemn, convict, sentence

absorb *verb* **1** soak up, consume, digest, imbibe, incorporate, receive, suck up, take in **2** preoccupy, captivate, engage, engross, fascinate, rivet

absorbed *adjective* **1** preoccupied, captivated, engrossed, fascinated, immersed, involved, lost, rapt, riveted, wrapped up **2** digested, assimilated, incorporated, received, soaked up

absorbent *adjective* permeable, porous, receptive, spongy

absorbing *adjective* fascinating, captivating, engrossing, gripping, interesting, intriguing, riveting, spellbinding

➤ **Antonyms**

boring, dreary, dull, humdrum, mind-numbing, tedious, tiresome, unexciting

absorption *noun* **1** soaking up, assimilation, consumption, digestion, incorporation, sucking up **2** concentration, fascination, immersion, intentness, involvement, preoccupation

abstain *verb* refrain, avoid, decline, deny (oneself), desist, fast, forbear, forgo, give up, keep from

➤ **Antonyms**

abandon oneself, give in, indulge, partake, yield

abstemious *adjective* self-denying, ascetic, austere, frugal, moderate, sober, temperate

➤ **Antonyms**

gluttonous, greedy, immoderate, incontinent, intemperate, self-indulgent

abstention *noun* refusal, abstaining, abstinence, avoidance, forbearance, refraining, self-control, self-denial, self-restraint

abstinence *noun* self-denial, abstemiousness, avoidance, forbearance, moderation, self-restraint, soberness, teetotalism, temperance

➤ **Antonyms**

abandon, excess, gluttony, greediness, indulgence, self-indulgence

abstinent *adjective* <u>self-denying</u>, abstaining, abstemious, forbearing, moderate, self-controlled, sober, temperate

abstract *adjective* **1** <u>theoretical</u>, abstruse, general, hypothetical, indefinite, notional, recondite ♦ *noun* **2** <u>summary</u>, abridgment, digest, epitome, outline, précis, résumé, synopsis ♦ *verb* **3** <u>summarize</u>, abbreviate, abridge, condense, digest, epitomize, outline, précis, shorten **4** <u>remove</u>, detach, extract, isolate, separate, take away, take out, withdraw

➤ **Antonyms**

adjective actual ≠<u>theoretical</u>: concrete, definite, factual, material, real, specific ♦ *noun* ≠<u>summary</u>: enlargement, expansion ♦ *verb* ≠<u>remove</u>: add, combine, inject

abstraction *noun* **1** <u>idea</u>, concept, formula, generalization, hypothesis, notion, theorem, theory, thought **2** <u>absentmindedness</u>, absence, dreaminess, inattention, pensiveness, preoccupation, remoteness, woolgathering

abstruse *adjective* <u>obscure</u>, arcane, complex, deep, enigmatic, esoteric, recondite, unfathomable, vague

➤ **Antonyms**

apparent, clear, evident, manifest, patent, perceptible, plain, self-evident

absurd *adjective* <u>ridiculous</u>, crazy (*informal*), dumb-ass (*slang*), farcical, foolish, idiotic, illogical, inane, incongruous, irrational, ludicrous, nonsensical, preposterous, senseless, silly, stupid, unreasonable

➤ **Antonyms**

intelligent, logical, prudent, rational, reasonable, sensible, smart, wise

absurdity *noun* <u>ridiculousness</u>, farce, folly, foolishness, incongru-

ity, joke, nonsense, silliness, stupidity

abundance *noun* <u>plenty</u>, affluence, bounty, copiousness, exuberance, fullness, profusion

➤ **Antonyms**

dearth, deficiency, lack, need, paucity, scantiness, scarcity, sparseness

abundant *adjective* <u>plentiful</u>, ample, bountiful, copious, exuberant, filled, full, luxuriant, profuse, rich, teeming

➤ **Antonyms**

few, inadequate, in short supply, insufficient, lacking, rare, scant, scarce, short, sparse

abuse *noun* **1** <u>ill-treatment</u>, damage, exploitation, harm, hurt, injury, maltreatment, manhandling **2** <u>insults</u>, blame, castigation, censure, defamation, derision, disparagement, invective, reproach, scolding, vilification **3** <u>misuse</u>, misapplication ♦ *verb* **4** <u>ill-treat</u>, damage, exploit, harm, hurt, injure, maltreat, misuse, take advantage of **5** <u>insult</u>, castigate, curse, defame, disparage, malign, scold, vilify

➤ **Antonyms**

verb ≠<u>ill-treat</u>: care for, protect ≠<u>insult</u>: acclaim, commend, compliment, flatter, praise, respect

abusive *adjective* **1** <u>insulting</u>, censorious, defamatory, disparaging, libellous, offensive, reproachful, rude, scathing **2** <u>harmful</u>, brutal, cruel, destructive, hurtful, injurious, rough

➤ **Antonyms**

≠<u>insulting</u>: approving, complimentary, flattering

abysmal *adjective* <u>terrible</u>, appalling, awful, bad, dire, dreadful

abyss *noun* <u>pit</u>, chasm, crevasse, fissure, gorge, gulf, void

academic *adjective* **1** <u>scholarly</u>, bookish, erudite, highbrow, learned, literary, studious **2** <u>hypothetical</u>, abstract, conjectural, impractical, notional, speculative, theoretical ♦ *noun* **3** <u>scholar</u>, academician, don, fellow, lecturer, master, professor, tutor

accede verb **1** <u>agree</u>, accept, acquiesce, admit, assent, comply, concede, concur, consent, endorse, grant **2** <u>inherit</u>, assume, attain, come to, enter upon, succeed, succeed to (as heir)

accelerate verb <u>speed up</u>, advance, expedite, further, hasten, hurry, quicken

➤ **Antonyms**
decelerate, delay, hinder, impede, obstruct, slow down

acceleration noun <u>speeding up</u>, hastening, hurrying, quickening, stepping up (informal)

accent noun **1** <u>pronunciation</u>, articulation, brogue, enunciation, inflection, intonation, modulation, tone **2** <u>emphasis</u>, beat, cadence, force, pitch, rhythm, stress, timbre ◆ verb **3** <u>emphasize</u>, accentuate, stress, underline, underscore

accentuate verb <u>emphasize</u>, accent, draw attention to, foreground, highlight, stress, underline, underscore

➤ **Antonyms**
gloss over, make light or little of, minimize, play down, underplay

accept verb **1** <u>receive</u>, gain, get, obtain, secure, take **2** <u>agree to</u>, admit, approve, believe, concur with, consent to, cooperate with, recognize

➤ **Antonyms**
≠<u>agree to</u>: decline, deny, disown, rebut, refuse, reject, repudiate, spurn

acceptable adjective <u>satisfactory</u>, adequate, admissible, all right, fair, moderate, passable, suitable, tolerable

➤ **Antonyms**
unacceptable, unsatisfactory, unsuitable

acceptance noun **1** <u>accepting</u>, acquiring, gaining, getting, obtaining, receipt, securing, taking **2** <u>agreement</u>, acknowledgment, acquiescence, admission, adoption, approval, assent, concur-

rence, consent, cooperation, recognition

accepted adjective <u>agreed</u>, acknowledged, approved, common, conventional, customary, established, normal, recognized, traditional

➤ **Antonyms**
abnormal, irregular, strange, unconventional, uncustomary, unorthodox, unusual, unwonted

access noun <u>entrance</u>, admission, admittance, approach, entry, passage, path, road

accessibility noun **1** <u>handiness</u>, availability, nearness, possibility, readiness **2** <u>approachability</u>, affability, cordiality, friendliness, informality **3** <u>openness</u>, susceptibility

accessible adjective **1** <u>handy</u>, achievable, at hand, attainable, available, near, nearby, obtainable, reachable **2** <u>approachable</u>, affable, available, cordial, friendly, informal **3** <u>open</u>, exposed, liable, susceptible, vulnerable, wide-open

➤ **Antonyms**
≠<u>handy</u>: far-off, inaccessible, unavailable, unobtainable, unreachable

accessory noun **1** <u>addition</u>, accompaniment, adjunct, adornment, appendage, attachment, decoration, extra, supplement, trimming **2** <u>accomplice</u>, abettor, assistant, associate (in crime), colleague, confederate, helper, partner

accident noun **1** <u>misfortune</u>, calamity, collision, crash, disaster, misadventure, mishap **2** <u>chance</u>, fate, fluke, fortuity, fortune, hazard, luck

accidental adjective <u>unintentional</u>, casual, chance, fortuitous, haphazard, inadvertent, incidental, random, unexpected, unforeseen, unlooked-for, unplanned

➤ **Antonyms**
calculated, designed, expected, foreseen, intended, intentional, planned

accidentally *adverb* unintentionally, by accident, by chance, fortuitously, haphazardly, inadvertently, incidentally, randomly, unwittingly

► **Antonyms**

by design, consciously, deliberately, on purpose, wilfully

acclaim *verb* **1** praise, applaud, approve, celebrate, cheer, clap, commend, exalt, hail, honour, salute ♦ *noun* **2** praise, acclamation, applause, approval, celebration, commendation, honour, kudos

► **Antonyms**

noun ≠praise: bad press, censure, criticism, disparagement, fault-finding, flak (*informal*)

acclamation *noun* praise, acclaim, adulation, approval, ovation, plaudit, tribute

acclimatization *noun* adaptation, adjustment, habituation, inurement, naturalization

acclimatize *verb* adapt, accommodate, accustom, adjust, get used to, habituate, inure, naturalize

accolade *noun* praise, acclaim, applause, approval, commendation, compliment, ovation, recognition, tribute

accommodate *verb* **1** house, cater for, entertain, lodge, put up, shelter **2** help, aid, assist, oblige, serve **3** adapt, adjust, comply, conform, fit, harmonize, modify, reconcile, settle

accommodating *adjective* helpful, considerate, cooperative, friendly, hospitable, kind, obliging, polite, unselfish, willing

► **Antonyms**

disobliging, inconsiderate, rude, uncooperative, unhelpful

accommodation *noun* housing, board, digs (*Brit. informal*), house, lodging(s), quarters, shelter

accompaniment *noun* **1** supplement, accessory, companion, complement **2** backing music, backing

accompany *verb* **1** go with, attend, chaperon, conduct, convoy, escort, hold (someone's) hand **2** occur with, belong to, come with, follow, go together with, supplement

accompanying *adjective* additional, associated, attached, attendant, complementary, related, supplementary

accomplice *noun* helper, abettor, accessory, ally, assistant, associate, collaborator, colleague, henchman, partner

accomplish *verb* do, achieve, attain, bring about, carry out, complete, effect, execute, finish, fulfil, manage, perform, produce

► **Antonyms**

fail, fall short

accomplished *adjective* skilled, expert, gifted, masterly, polished, practised, proficient, talented

► **Antonyms**

amateurish, incapable, incompetent, inexpert, unskilled, untalented

accomplishment *noun* **1** completion, bringing about, carrying out, conclusion, execution, finishing, fulfilment, performance **2** achievement, act, coup, deed, exploit, feat, stroke, triumph

accord *noun* **1** agreement, conformity, correspondence, harmony, rapport, sympathy, unison ♦ *verb* **2** agree, conform, correspond, fit, harmonize, match, suit, tally

► **Antonyms**

noun ≠agreement: conflict, contention, disagreement, discord ≠agree: conflict, contrast, differ, disagree

accordingly *adverb* **1** appropriately, correspondingly, fitly, properly, suitably **2** consequently, as a result, ergo, hence, in consequence, so, therefore, thus

according to *adverb* **1** as stated by, as believed by, as maintained by, in the light of, on the authority of, on the report of **2**

in keeping with, after, after the manner of, consistent with, in accordance with, in compliance with, in line with, in the manner of

accost verb <u>approach</u>, buttonhole, confront, greet, hail

account noun **1** <u>description</u>, explanation, narrative, report, statement, story, tale, version **2** Commerce <u>statement</u>, balance, bill, books, charge, invoice, reckoning, register, score, tally **3** <u>importance</u>, consequence, honour, note, significance, standing, value, worth ◆ verb **4** <u>consider</u>, count, estimate, judge, rate, reckon, regard, think, value

accountability noun <u>responsibility</u>, answerability, chargeability, culpability, liability

accountable adjective <u>responsible</u>, amenable, answerable, charged with, liable, obligated, obliged

accountant noun <u>auditor</u>, bean counter (informal), book-keeper

account for verb <u>explain</u>, answer for, clarify, clear up, elucidate, illuminate, justify, rationalize

accredited adjective <u>authorized</u>, appointed, certified, empowered, endorsed, guaranteed, licensed, official, recognized

accrue verb <u>increase</u>, accumulate, amass, arise, be added, build up, collect, enlarge, flow, follow, grow

accumulate verb <u>collect</u>, accrue, amass, build up, gather, hoard, increase, pile up, store

➤ **Antonyms**

diffuse, disperse, dissipate, scatter

accumulation noun <u>collection</u>, build-up, gathering, heap, hoard, increase, mass, pile, stack, stock, stockpile, store

accuracy noun <u>exactness</u>, accurateness, authenticity, carefulness, closeness, correctness, fidelity, precision, strictness, truthfulness, veracity

➤ **Antonyms**

carelessness, erroneousness, im-

precision, inaccuracy, incorrectness, inexactitude, laxness

accurate adjective <u>exact</u>, authentic, careful, close, correct, faithful, precise, scrupulous, spot-on (Brit. informal), strict, true, unerring

➤ **Antonyms**

careless, imperfect, imprecise, inaccurate, incorrect, inexact, wrong

accurately adverb <u>exactly</u>, authentically, closely, correctly, faithfully, precisely, scrupulously, strictly, to the letter, truly, unerringly

accursed adjective **1** <u>cursed</u>, bewitched, condemned, damned, doomed, hopeless, ill-fated, ill-omened, jinxed, unfortunate, unlucky, wretched **2** <u>hateful</u>, abominable, despicable, detestable, execrable, hellish, horrible

➤ **Antonyms**

≠cursed: blessed, charmed, favoured, fortunate, lucky

accusation noun <u>charge</u>, allegation, complaint, denunciation, incrimination, indictment, recrimination

accuse verb <u>charge</u>, blame, censure, denounce, impeach, impute, incriminate, indict

➤ **Antonyms**

absolve, defend, exonerate

accustom verb <u>adapt</u>, acclimatize, acquaint, discipline, exercise, familiarize, train

accustomed adjective **1** <u>usual</u>, common, conventional, customary, established, everyday, expected, habitual, normal, ordinary, regular, traditional **2** <u>used</u>, acclimatized, acquainted, adapted, familiar, familiarized, given to, in the habit of, trained

➤ **Antonyms**

≠usual: abnormal, odd, peculiar, rare, strange, unaccustomed, uncommon, unfamiliar, unusual ≠used: unaccustomed, unfamiliar, unused

ace noun **1** Cards, dice, etc. <u>one</u>, single point **2** Informal <u>expert</u>, champion, dab hand (*Brit. informal*), master, star, virtuoso, wizard (*informal*) ♦ *adjective* **3** *Informal* **excellent**, awesome (*slang*), brilliant, fine, great, outstanding, superb

ache *verb* **1** hurt, pain, pound, smart, suffer, throb, twinge ♦ *noun* **2** pain, hurt, pang, pounding, soreness, suffering, throbbing

achieve *verb* attain, accomplish, acquire, bring about, carry out, complete, do, execute, fulfil, gain, get, obtain, perform

achievement *noun* accomplishment, act, deed, effort, exploit, feat, feather in one's cap, stroke

acid *adjective* **1** sour, acerbic, acrid, pungent, tart, vinegary **2** sharp, biting, bitter, caustic, cutting, harsh, trenchant, vitriolic

► **Antonyms**

≠sour: alkaline, bland, mild, pleasant, sweet ≠sharp: bland, gentle, kindly, mild, pleasant, sweet

acidity *noun* **1** sourness, acerbity, pungency, tartness **2** sharpness, bitterness, harshness

acknowledge *verb* **1** accept, admit, allow, concede, confess, declare, grant, own, profess, recognize, yield **2** greet, address, hail, notice, recognize, salute **3** reply to, answer, notice, react to, recognize, respond to, return

► **Antonyms**

≠accept: deny, disclaim, discount, reject, renounce, repudiate ≠greet: disdain, disregard, ignore, reject, snub, spurn ≠reply to: disregard, ignore

acknowledged *adjective* accepted, accredited, approved, confessed, declared, professed, recognized, returned

acknowledgment *noun* **1** acceptance, admission, allowing, confession, declaration, profession, realization, yielding **2** greeting, addressing, hail, hailing, notice, recognition, salutation, salute **3** appreciation, answer, credit, gratitude, reaction, recognition, reply, response, return, thanks

acquaint *verb* tell, disclose, divulge, enlighten, familiarize, inform, let (someone) know, notify, reveal

acquaintance *noun* **1** associate, colleague, contact **2** knowledge, awareness, experience, familiarity, fellowship, relationship, understanding

► **Antonyms**

≠associate: buddy, good friend ≠knowledge: ignorance, unfamiliarity

acquainted with *adjective* familiar with, alive to, apprised of, *au fait with*, aware of, conscious of, experienced in, informed of, knowledgeable about, versed in

acquiesce *verb* agree, accede, accept, allow, approve, assent, comply, concur, conform, consent, give in, go along with, submit, yield

► **Antonyms**

balk at, contest, demur, disagree, dissent, fight, object, protest, refuse, resist, veto

acquiescence *noun* agreement, acceptance, approval, assent, compliance, conformity, consent, giving in, obedience, submission, yielding

acquire *verb* get, amass, attain, buy, collect, earn, gain, gather, obtain, receive, secure, win

► **Antonyms**

be deprived of, forgo, give up, lose, relinquish, renounce, surrender

acquisition *noun* **1** possession, buy, gain, prize, property, purchase **2** acquiring, attainment, gaining, procurement

acquisitive *adjective* greedy, avaricious, avid, covetous, grabbing, grasping, predatory, rapacious

► **Antonyms**

bounteous, bountiful, generous, lavish, liberal, munificent, openhanded, unselfish, unstinting

acquit verb **1** <u>clear</u>, discharge, free, liberate, release, vindicate **2** <u>behave</u>, bear, comport, conduct, perform

➤ **Antonyms**

≠<u>clear</u>: charge, condemn, convict, damn, find guilty

acquittal noun <u>clearance</u>, absolution, deliverance, discharge, exoneration, liberation, release, relief, vindication

acrid adjective <u>pungent</u>, bitter, caustic, harsh, sharp, vitriolic

acrimonious adjective <u>bitter</u>, caustic, irascible, petulant, rancorous, spiteful, splenetic, testy

➤ **Antonyms**

affable, benign, forgiving, good-tempered

acrimony noun <u>bitterness</u>, harshness, ill will, irascibility, rancour, virulence

➤ **Antonyms**

amity, friendliness, friendship, good feelings, goodwill, liking, warmth

act noun **1** <u>deed</u>, accomplishment, achievement, action, exploit, feat, performance, undertaking **2** <u>law</u>, bill, decree, edict, enactment, measure, ordinance, resolution, statute **3** <u>performance</u>, routine, show, sketch, turn **4** <u>pretence</u>, affectation, attitude, front, performance, pose, posture, show ♦ verb **5** <u>do</u>, carry out, enact, execute, function, operate, perform, take effect, work **6** <u>perform</u>, act out, impersonate, mimic, play, play or take the part of, portray, represent

act for verb <u>stand in for</u>, cover for, deputize for, fill in for, replace, represent, substitute for, take the place of

acting noun **1** <u>performance</u>, characterization, impersonation, performing, playing, portrayal, stagecraft, theatre ♦ adjective **2** <u>temporary</u>, interim, pro tem, provisional, substitute, surrogate

action noun **1** <u>deed</u>, accomplishment, achievement, act, exploit, feat, performance **2** <u>lawsuit</u>, case, litigation, proceeding, prosecution, suit **3** <u>energy</u>, activity, force, liveliness, spirit, vigour, vim, vitality **4** <u>movement</u>, activity, functioning, motion, operation, process, working **5** <u>battle</u>, clash, combat, conflict, contest, encounter, engagement, fight, skirmish, sortie

activate verb <u>start</u>, arouse, energize, galvanize, initiate, mobilize, move, rouse, set in motion, stir

➤ **Antonyms**

arrest, check, deactivate, halt, impede, stop, turn off

active adjective **1** <u>busy</u>, bustling, hard-working, involved, occupied, on the go (informal), on the move, strenuous **2** <u>energetic</u>, alert, animated, industrious, lively, quick, sprightly, spry, vigorous **3** <u>in operation</u>, acting, at work, effectual, in action, in force, operative, working

➤ **Antonyms**

dormant, dull, idle, inactive, inoperative, lazy, sedentary, slow, sluggish, torpid, unimaginative, unoccupied

activist noun <u>militant</u>, organizer, partisan

activity noun **1** <u>action</u>, animation, bustle, exercise, exertion, hustle, labour, motion, movement **2** <u>pursuit</u>, hobby, interest, pastime, project, scheme

➤ **Antonyms**

≠<u>action</u>: dullness, idleness, immobility, inaction, inactivity, indolence, inertia, lethargy, passivity, sluggishness, torpor

actor noun <u>performer</u>, actress, luvvie (informal), player, Thespian

actress noun <u>performer</u>, actor, leading lady, player, starlet, Thespian

actual adjective <u>definite</u>, concrete, factual, physical, positive, real, substantial, tangible

➤ **Antonyms**

fictitious, hypothetical, made-up, probable, supposed, theoretical, unreal, untrue

actually *adverb* <u>really</u>, as a matter of fact, indeed, in fact, in point of fact, in reality, in truth, literally, truly

acumen *noun* <u>judgment</u>, astuteness, cleverness, ingenuity, insight, intelligence, perspicacity, shrewdness

acute *adjective* **1** <u>serious</u>, critical, crucial, dangerous, grave, important, severe, urgent **2** <u>sharp</u>, excruciating, fierce, intense, piercing, powerful, severe, shooting, violent **3** <u>perceptive</u>, astute, clever, insightful, keen, observant, sensitive, sharp, smart

➤ **Antonyms**
≠<u>perceptive</u>: dense, dim, dim-witted, dull, obtuse, slow, stupid, unintelligent

acuteness *noun* **1** <u>seriousness</u>, gravity, importance, severity, urgency **2** <u>perceptiveness</u>, astuteness, cleverness, discrimination, insight, perspicacity, sharpness

adamant *adjective* <u>determined</u>, firm, fixed, obdurate, resolute, stubborn, unbending, uncompromising

➤ **Antonyms**
compliant, compromising, easy-going, flexible, lax, receptive, responsive, susceptible, tractable, yielding

adapt *verb* <u>adjust</u>, acclimatize, accommodate, alter, change, conform, convert, modify, remodel, tailor

adaptability *noun* <u>flexibility</u>, changeability, resilience, versatility

adaptable *adjective* <u>flexible</u>, adjustable, changeable, compliant, easy-going, plastic, pliant, resilient, versatile

adaptation *noun* **1** <u>acclimatization</u>, familiarization, naturalization **2** <u>conversion</u>, adjustment, alteration, change, modification, transformation, variation, version

add *verb* **1** <u>count up</u>, add up, compute, reckon, total, tot up **2** <u>include</u>, adjoin, affix, append, attach, augment, supplement

➤ **Antonyms**
deduct, diminish, lessen, reduce, remove, subtract, take away, take from

addendum *noun* <u>addition</u>, appendage, appendix, attachment, extension, extra, postscript, supplement

addict *noun* **1** <u>junkie</u> (*informal*), fiend (*informal*), freak (*informal*) **2** <u>fan</u>, adherent, buff (*informal*), devotee, enthusiast, follower, nut (*slang*)

addicted *adjective* <u>hooked</u> (*slang*), absorbed, accustomed, dedicated, dependent, devoted, habituated

addiction *noun* <u>dependence</u>, craving, enslavement, habit, obsession

addition *noun* **1** <u>inclusion</u>, adding, amplification, attachment, augmentation, enlargement, extension, increasing **2** <u>extra</u>, addendum, additive, appendage, appendix, extension, gain, increase, increment, supplement **3** <u>counting up</u>, adding up, computation, totalling, totting up **4** in addition (to) <u>as well (as)</u>, additionally, also, besides, into the bargain, moreover, over and above, to boot, too

➤ **Antonyms**
≠<u>inclusion</u>, <u>counting up</u>: deduction, detachment, diminution, lessening, reduction, removal, subtraction

additional *adjective* <u>extra</u>, added, fresh, further, new, other, spare, supplementary

address *noun* **1** <u>location</u>, abode, dwelling, home, house, residence, situation, whereabouts **2** <u>speech</u>, discourse, dissertation, lecture, oration, sermon, talk ♦ *verb* **3** <u>speak to</u>, approach, greet, hail, talk to **4** address (oneself) to <u>concentrate on</u>, apply (oneself) to, attend to, devote (oneself) to, engage in, focus on, take care of

add up *verb* <u>count up</u>, add, compute, count, reckon, total, tot up

adept *adjective* **1** <u>skilful</u>, able, accomplished, adroit, expert, practised, proficient, skilled, versed ♦ *noun* **2** <u>expert</u>, dab hand (*Brit. informal*), genius, hotshot (*informal*), master

➤ **Antonyms**

adjective ≠<u>skilful</u>: amateurish, awkward, clumsy, inept, unskilled

adequacy *noun* <u>sufficiency</u>, capability, competence, fairness, suitability, tolerability

adequate *adjective* <u>enough</u>, competent, fair, satisfactory, sufficient, tolerable, up to scratch (*informal*)

➤ **Antonyms**

deficient, inadequate, insufficient, lacking, meagre, scant, unsatisfactory

adhere *verb* <u>stick</u>, attach, cleave, cling, fasten, fix, glue, hold fast, paste

adherent *noun* <u>supporter</u>, admirer, devotee, disciple, fan, follower, upholder

➤ **Antonyms**

adversary, antagonist, enemy, foe, opponent, opposer, rival

adhesive *adjective* **1** <u>sticky</u>, clinging, cohesive, gluey, glutinous, tenacious ♦ *noun* **2** <u>glue</u>, cement, gum, paste

adieu *noun* <u>goodbye</u>, farewell, leave-taking, parting, valediction

adjacent *adjective* <u>next</u>, adjoining, beside, bordering, cheek by jowl, close, near, neighbouring, next door, touching

➤ **Antonyms**

distant, far away, remote, separated

adjoin *verb* <u>connect</u>, border, join, link, touch

adjoining *adjective* <u>connecting</u>, abutting, adjacent, bordering, neighbouring, next door, touching

adjourn *verb* <u>postpone</u>, defer, delay, discontinue, interrupt, put off, suspend

➤ **Antonyms**

assemble, continue, convene, gather

adjournment *noun* <u>postponement</u>, delay, discontinuation, interruption, putting off, recess, suspension

adjudicate *verb* <u>judge</u>, adjudge, arbitrate, decide, determine, mediate, referee, settle, umpire

adjudication *noun* <u>judgment</u>, arbitration, conclusion, decision, finding, pronouncement, ruling, settlement, verdict

adjust *verb* <u>alter</u>, accustom, adapt, make conform, modify

adjustable *adjective* <u>alterable</u>, adaptable, flexible, malleable, modifiable, movable

adjustment *noun* **1** <u>alteration</u>, adaptation, modification, redress, regulation, tuning **2** <u>acclimatization</u>, orientation, settling in

ad-lib *verb* <u>improvise</u>, busk, extemporize, make up, speak off the cuff, wing it (*informal*)

administer *verb* **1** <u>manage</u>, conduct, control, direct, govern, handle, oversee, run, supervise **2** <u>give</u>, apply, dispense, impose, mete out, perform, provide

administration *noun* <u>management</u>, application, conduct, control, direction, government, running, supervision

administrative *adjective* <u>managerial</u>, directorial, executive, governmental, organizational, regulatory, supervisory

administrator *noun* <u>manager</u>, bureaucrat, executive, official, organizer, supervisor

admirable *adjective* <u>excellent</u>, commendable, exquisite, fine, laudable, praiseworthy, wonderful, worthy

➤ **Antonyms**

bad, deplorable, disappointing, mediocre, no great shakes (*informal*), worthless

admiration *noun* <u>regard</u>, amazement, appreciation, approval, esteem, praise, respect, wonder

admire *verb* **1** <u>respect</u>, appreciate, approve, esteem, look up to, praise, prize, think highly of, value **2** <u>marvel at</u>, appreciate, delight in, take pleasure in, wonder at

➤ **Antonyms**
despise, look down on, scorn, sneer at, undervalue

admirer noun **1** <u>suitor</u>, beau, boyfriend, lover, sweetheart, wooer **2** <u>fan</u>, devotee, disciple, enthusiast, follower, partisan, supporter

admissible adjective <u>permissible</u>, acceptable, allowable, passable, tolerable

➤ **Antonyms**
disallowed, inadmissible, intolerable, unacceptable

admission noun **1** <u>entrance</u>, acceptance, access, admittance, entrée, entry, initiation, introduction **2** <u>confession</u>, acknowledgment, allowance, declaration, disclosure, divulgence, revelation

admit verb **1** <u>confess</u>, acknowledge, declare, disclose, divulge, own, reveal **2** <u>allow</u>, agree, grant, let, permit, recognize **3** <u>let in</u>, accept, allow, give access, initiate, introduce, receive, take in

➤ **Antonyms**
≠allow: deny, dismiss, forbid, negate, prohibit, reject ≠<u>let in</u>: exclude, keep out

admonish verb <u>reprimand</u>, berate, chide, rebuke, scold, slap on the wrist, tell off (informal)

➤ **Antonyms**
commend, praise

adolescence noun **1** <u>youth</u>, boyhood, girlhood, minority, teens **2** <u>youthfulness</u>, childishness, immaturity

adolescent adjective **1** <u>young</u>, boyish, girlish, immature, juvenile, puerile, teenage, youthful ♦ noun **2** <u>youth</u>, juvenile, minor, teenager, youngster

adopt verb **1** <u>foster</u>, take in **2** <u>choose</u>, assume, espouse, follow, maintain, take up

➤ **Antonyms**
≠<u>choose</u>: abandon, disclaim, disown, give up, reject, renounce,

repudiate, spurn, wash one's hands of

adoption noun **1** <u>fostering</u>, adopting, taking in **2** <u>choice</u>, appropriation, assumption, embracing, endorsement, espousal, selection, taking up

adorable adjective <u>lovable</u>, appealing, attractive, charming, cute, dear, delightful, fetching, pleasing, sweet

➤ **Antonyms**
despicable, displeasing, hateful, unlikable or unlikeable, unlovable

adore verb <u>love</u>, admire, cherish, dote on, esteem, exalt, glorify, honour, idolize, revere, worship

➤ **Antonyms**
abhor, abominate, despise, detest, hate, loathe

adoring adjective <u>loving</u>, admiring, affectionate, devoted, doting, fond

➤ **Antonyms**
despising, detesting, hating, loathing

adorn verb <u>decorate</u>, array, embellish, festoon

adornment noun <u>decoration</u>, accessory, embellishment, festoon, frill, frippery, ornament, supplement, trimming

adrift adjective **1** <u>drifting</u>, afloat, unanchored, unmoored **2** <u>aimless</u>, directionless, goalless, purposeless ♦ adverb **3** <u>wrong</u>, amiss, astray, off course

adroit adjective <u>skilful</u>, adept, clever, deft, dexterous, expert, masterful, neat, proficient, skilled

➤ **Antonyms**
awkward, blundering, bungling, cack-handed (informal), clumsy, ham-fisted or ham-handed (informal), inept, inexpert, maladroit, uncoordinated, unskilful

adulation noun <u>worship</u>, fawning, fulsome praise, servile flattery, sycophancy

➤ **Antonyms**
abuse, censure, condemnation, disparagement, revilement, ridicule, vilification

adult noun **1** <u>grown-up</u>, grown or

grown-up person (man *or* woman), person of mature age ♦ *adjective* **2** fully grown, full grown, fully developed, grown-up, mature, of age, ripe

advance *verb* **1** progress, come forward, go on, make inroads, proceed **2** promote, accelerate, bring forward, elevate, hasten, speed, upgrade **3** benefit, further, improve, prosper **4** suggest, offer, present, proffer, put forward, submit **5** lend, pay beforehand, supply on credit ♦ *noun* **6** progress, advancement, development, forward movement, headway, inroads, onward movement **7** improvement, breakthrough, gain, growth, progress, promotion, step **8** loan, credit, deposit, down payment, prepayment, retainer **9** advances overtures, approach, approaches, moves, proposals, proposition ♦ *adjective* **10** prior, beforehand, early, forward, in front **11 in advance** beforehand, ahead, earlier, previously

➤ **Antonyms**
verb ≠underlined progress: decrease, diminish, lessen, move back, regress, retreat, weaken ≠underlined promote: demote, hold back, impede, retard, set back ≠underlined suggest: hide, hold back, suppress, withhold ≠underlined lend: defer payment, withhold payment

advanced *adjective* foremost, ahead, avant-garde, forward, higher, leading, precocious, progressive

➤ **Antonyms**
backward, behind, late, retarded, underdeveloped, undeveloped

advancement *noun* promotion, betterment, gain, improvement, preferment, progress, rise

advantage *noun* benefit, ascendancy, dominance, good, help, lead, precedence, profit, superiority, sway

➤ **Antonyms**
curse, difficulty, disadvantage, downside, drawback, handicap, hindrance, inconvenience, snag

advantageous *adjective* **1** beneficial, convenient, expedient, helpful, of service, profitable, useful, valuable, worthwhile **2** superior, dominant, dominating, favourable

➤ **Antonyms**
≠underlined beneficial: detrimental, unfavourable, unfortunate, unhelpful, useless

adventure *noun* escapade, enterprise, experience, exploit, incident, occurrence, undertaking, venture

adventurer *noun* **1** mercenary, charlatan, fortune-hunter, gambler, opportunist, rogue, speculator **2** hero, daredevil, heroine, knight-errant, traveller, voyager

adventurous *adjective* underlined daring, bold, daredevil, enterprising, intrepid, reckless

➤ **Antonyms**
careful, cautious, circumspect, hesitant, prudent, safe, tentative, timid, timorous, unadventurous, wary

adversary *noun* opponent, antagonist, competitor, contestant, enemy, foe, rival

➤ **Antonyms**
accomplice, ally, associate, confederate, friend, helper, partner, supporter

adverse *adjective* unfavourable, contrary, detrimental, hostile, inopportune, negative, opposing

➤ **Antonyms**
advantageous, auspicious, beneficial, favourable, fortunate, helpful, lucky, opportune, propitious, suitable

adversity *noun* hardship, affliction, bad luck, disaster, distress, hard times, misfortune, reverse, trouble

advert *noun* *Brit. informal* advertisement, ad (*informal*), announcement, blurb, commercial, notice, plug (*informal*), poster

advertise *verb* publicize, announce, inform, make known, notify, plug (*informal*), promote, tout

advertisement *noun* **advert** (*Brit. informal*), ad (*informal*), announcement, blurb, commercial, notice, plug (*informal*), poster

advice *noun* guidance, counsel, help, opinion, recommendation, suggestion

advisability *noun* wisdom, appropriateness, aptness, desirability, expediency, fitness, propriety, prudence, suitability

advisable *adjective* wise, appropriate, desirable, expedient, fitting, politic, prudent, recommended, seemly, sensible

➤ **Antonyms**
ill-advised, impolitic, improper, imprudent, inappropriate, inexpedient, silly, stupid, undesirable, unfitting, unseemly, unwise

advise *verb* **1** recommend, admonish, caution, command, counsel, prescribe, suggest, urge **2** notify, acquaint, apprise, inform, let (someone) know, make known, report, tell, warn

adviser *noun* guide, aide, confidant, consultant, counsellor, guru, helper, mentor, right-hand man

advisory *adjective* advising, consultative, counselling, helping, recommending

advocate *verb* **1** recommend, advise, argue for, campaign for, champion, commend, encourage, promote, propose, support, uphold ♦ *noun* **2** supporter, campaigner, champion, counsellor, defender, promoter, proponent, spokesman, upholder **3** *Law* lawyer, attorney, barrister, counsel, solicitor

➤ **Antonyms**
verb ≠recommend: contradict, oppose, resist, speak against

affable *adjective* friendly, amiable, amicable, approachable, congenial, cordial, courteous, genial, pleasant, sociable, urbane

➤ **Antonyms**
brusque, cold, discourteous, dis-

tant, haughty, rude, standoffish, surly, unapproachable, unfriendly, unpleasant, unsociable

affair *noun* **1** event, activity, business, episode, happening, incident, matter, occurrence **2** relationship, amour, intrigue, liaison, romance

affect[1] *verb* **1** influence, act on, alter, bear upon, change, concern, impinge upon, relate to **2** move, disturb, overcome, perturb, stir, touch, upset

affect[2] *verb* put on, adopt, aspire to, assume, contrive, feign, imitate, pretend, simulate

affectation *noun* pretence, act, artificiality, assumed manners, façade, insincerity, pose, pretentiousness, show

affected *adjective* pretended, artificial, contrived, feigned, insincere, mannered, phoney *or* phony (*informal*), put-on, unnatural

➤ **Antonyms**
genuine, natural, real, unaffected

affecting *adjective* moving, pathetic, pitiful, poignant, sad, touching

affection *noun* fondness, attachment, care, feeling, goodwill, kindness, liking, love, tenderness, warmth

affectionate *adjective* fond, attached, caring, devoted, doting, friendly, kind, loving, tender, warm-hearted

➤ **Antonyms**
cold, cool, indifferent, uncaring, undemonstrative, unfeeling, unresponsive

affiliate *verb* join, ally, amalgamate, associate, band together, combine, incorporate, link, unite

affinity *noun* **1** attraction, fondness, inclination, leaning, liking, partiality, rapport, sympathy **2** similarity, analogy, closeness, connection, correspondence, kinship, likeness, relationship, resemblance

➤ **Antonyms**
≠attraction: abhorrence, animosity, antipathy, aversion, dislike,

hatred, hostility, loathing, repugnance, revulsion ≠similarity: difference, disparity, dissimilarity

affirm verb declare, assert, certify, confirm, maintain, pronounce, state, swear, testify

► Antonyms

deny, rebut, refute, reject, renounce, repudiate

affirmation noun declaration, assertion, certification, confirmation, oath, pronouncement, statement, testimony

affirmative adjective agreeing, approving, assenting, concurring, confirming, consenting, corroborative, favourable, positive

► Antonyms

denying, disagreeing, disapproving, dissenting, negating, negative

afflict verb torment, distress, grieve, harass, hurt, oppress, pain, plague, trouble

affliction noun suffering, adversity, curse, disease, hardship, misfortune, ordeal, plague, scourge, torment, trial, trouble, woe

affluence noun wealth, abundance, fortune, opulence, plenty, prosperity, riches

affluent adjective wealthy, loaded (slang), moneyed, opulent, prosperous, rich, well-heeled (informal), well-off, well-to-do

► Antonyms

broke (informal), destitute, down at heel, hard-up (informal), impecunious, impoverished, penniless, poor, poverty-stricken, skint (Brit. slang), stony-broke (Brit. slang)

afford verb 1 As in can afford spare, bear, manage, stand, sustain 2 give, offer, produce, provide, render, supply, yield

affordable adjective inexpensive, cheap, economical, low-cost, moderate, modest, reasonable

► Antonyms

beyond one's means, costly, dear, exorbitant, expensive, unaffordable, uneconomical

affront noun 1 insult, offence, outrage, provocation, slap in the face (informal), slight, slur ♦ verb 2 offend, anger, annoy, displease, insult, outrage, provoke, slight

aflame adjective burning, ablaze, alight, blazing, fiery, flaming, lit, on fire

afoot adjective going on, abroad, brewing, current, happening, in preparation, in progress, on the go (informal), up (informal)

afraid adjective 1 scared, apprehensive, cowardly, faint-hearted, fearful, frightened, nervous 2 sorry, regretful, unhappy

► Antonyms

≠scared: bold, fearless, unafraid ≠sorry: happy, pleased

afresh adverb again, newly, once again, once more, over again

after adverb following, afterwards, behind, below, later, subsequently, succeeding, thereafter

► Antonyms

before, earlier, in advance, in front, previously, prior to, sooner

aftermath noun effects, aftereffects, consequences, end result, outcome, results, sequel, upshot, wake

again adverb 1 once more, afresh, anew, another time 2 also, besides, furthermore, in addition, moreover

against preposition 1 beside, abutting, facing, in contact with, on, opposite to, touching, upon 2 opposed to, anti (informal), averse to, hostile to, in defiance of, in opposition to, resisting, versus 3 in preparation for, in anticipation of, in expectation of, in provision for

age noun 1 time, date, day(s), duration, epoch, era, generation, lifetime, period, span 2 old age, advancing years, decline (of life), majority, maturity, senescence, senility, seniority ♦ verb 3 grow old, decline, deteriorate, mature, mellow, ripen

► Antonyms

noun ≠old age: adolescence, boyhood or girlhood, childhood, immaturity, young days, youth

aged adjective old, ancient, antiquated, antique, elderly, getting on, grey

➤ **Antonyms**

adolescent, boyish or girlish, childish, immature, juvenile, young, youthful

agency noun 1 business, bureau, department, office, organization 2 Old-fashioned medium, activity, means, mechanism

agenda noun list, calendar, diary, plan, programme, schedule, timetable

agent noun 1 representative, envoy, go-between, negotiator, rep (informal), surrogate 2 worker, author, doer, mover, operator, performer 3 force, agency, cause, instrument, means, power, vehicle

aggravate verb 1 make worse, exacerbate, exaggerate, increase, inflame, intensify, magnify, worsen 2 Informal annoy, bother, get on one's nerves (informal), irritate, nettle, provoke

➤ **Antonyms**

≠make worse: alleviate, assuage, calm, diminish, ease, improve, lessen, mitigate ≠annoy: assuage, calm, pacify, please

aggravation noun 1 worsening, exacerbation, exaggeration, heightening, increase, inflaming, intensification, magnification 2 Informal annoyance, exasperation, gall, grief (informal), hassle (informal), irritation, provocation

aggregate noun 1 total, accumulation, amount, body, bulk, collection, combination, mass, pile, sum, whole ♦ adjective 2 total, accumulated, collected, combined, composite, cumulative, mixed ♦ verb 3 combine, accumulate, amass, assemble, collect, heap, mix, pile

aggression noun 1 hostility, antagonism, belligerence, destructiveness, pugnacity 2 attack, assault, injury, invasion, offensive,

onslaught, raid

aggressive adjective 1 hostile, belligerent, destructive, offensive, pugnacious, quarrelsome 2 forceful, assertive, bold, dynamic, energetic, enterprising, militant, pushy (informal), vigorous

➤ **Antonyms**

≠hostile: friendly, peaceful ≠forceful: mild, quiet, retiring, submissive

aggressor noun attacker, assailant, assaulter, invader

aggrieved adjective hurt, afflicted, distressed, disturbed, harmed, injured, unhappy, wronged

aghast adjective horrified, amazed, appalled, astonished, astounded, awestruck, confounded, shocked, startled, stunned

agile adjective 1 nimble, active, brisk, lithe, quick, sprightly, spry, supple, swift 2 acute, alert, bright (informal), clever, lively, quick-witted, sharp

➤ **Antonyms**

≠nimble: awkward, clumsy, heavy, lumbering, ponderous, slow, slow-moving, stiff, ungainly, unsupple

agility noun nimbleness, litheness, liveliness, quickness, suppleness, swiftness

agitate verb 1 upset, disconcert, distract, excite, fluster, perturb, trouble, unnerve, worry 2 stir, beat, convulse, disturb, rouse, shake, toss

➤ **Antonyms**

≠upset: appease, assuage, calm, calm down, mollify, pacify, placate, quiet, quieten, soothe, still

agitation noun 1 turmoil, clamour, commotion, confusion, disturbance, excitement, ferment, trouble, upheaval 2 turbulence, convulsion, disturbance, shaking, stirring, tossing

agitator noun troublemaker, agent provocateur, firebrand, instigator, rabble-rouser, revolutionary, stirrer (informal)

agog adjective eager, avid, curious, enthralled, enthusiastic, excited, expectant, impatient, in suspense

➤ **Antonyms**

apathetic, incurious, indifferent, unconcerned, uninterested

agonize *verb* suffer, be distressed, be in agony, be in anguish, go through the mill, labour, strain, struggle, worry

agony *noun* suffering, anguish, distress, misery, pain, throes, torment, torture

agree *verb* **1** concur, assent, be of the same opinion, comply, consent, see eye to eye **2** get on (together), coincide, conform, correspond, match, tally

➤ **Antonyms**

≠concur: contradict, deny, differ, disagree, dispute, dissent

agreeable *adjective* **1** pleasant, delightful, enjoyable, gratifying, likable *or* likeable, pleasing, satisfying, to one's taste **2** consenting, amenable, approving, complying, concurring, in accord, onside (*informal*), sympathetic, well-disposed, willing

➤ **Antonyms**

≠pleasant: disagreeable, displeasing, horrid, offensive, unlikable *or* unlikeable, unpleasant

agreement *noun* **1** concurrence, agreeing, assent, compliance, concord, consent, harmony, union, unison **2** correspondence, compatibility, conformity, congruity, consistency, similarity **3** contract, arrangement, bargain, covenant, deal (*informal*), pact, settlement, treaty, understanding

➤ **Antonyms**

≠concurrence: argument, clash, conflict, discord, dispute, dissent, division, falling-out, quarrel, row, squabble ≠correspondence: difference, discrepancy, disparity, dissimilarity, diversity, incompatibility, incongruity

agricultural *adjective* farming, agrarian, country, rural, rustic

agriculture *noun* farming, cultiva-

tion, culture, husbandry, tillage

aground *adverb* beached, ashore, foundered, grounded, high and dry, on the rocks, stranded, stuck

ahead *adverb* in front, at an advantage, at the head, before, in advance, in the lead, leading, to the fore, winning

aid *noun* **1** help, assistance, benefit, encouragement, favour, promotion, relief, service, support ♦ *verb* **2** help, assist, encourage, favour, promote, serve, subsidize, support, sustain

➤ **Antonyms**

noun ≠help: hindrance ♦ *verb* ≠help: harm, hinder, hurt, impede, obstruct, oppose, thwart

aide *noun* assistant, attendant, helper, right-hand man, second, supporter

ailing *adjective* ill, indisposed, infirm, poorly, sick, under the weather (*informal*), unwell, weak

ailment *noun* illness, affliction, complaint, disease, disorder, infirmity, malady, sickness

aim *verb* **1** intend, attempt, endeavour, mean, plan, point, propose, seek, set one's sights on, strive, try ♦ *noun* **2** intention, ambition, aspiration, desire, goal, objective, plan, purpose, target

aimless *adjective* purposeless, directionless, pointless, random, stray

➤ **Antonyms**

deliberate, purposeful

air *noun* **1** atmosphere, heavens, sky **2** wind, breeze, draught, zephyr **3** manner, appearance, atmosphere, aura, demeanour, impression, look, mood **4** tune, aria, lay, melody, song ♦ *verb* **5** publicize, circulate, display, exhibit, express, give vent to, make known, make public, reveal, voice **6** ventilate, aerate, expose, freshen

airborne *adjective* flying, floating, gliding, hovering, in flight, in the air, on the wing

airing *noun* **1** ventilation, aeration, drying, freshening **2** exposure, circulation, display, dissemination, expression, publicity, utterance, vent

airless adjective <u>stuffy</u>, close, heavy, muggy, oppressive, stifling, suffocating, sultry

➤ **Antonyms**
airy, breezy, fresh, light, open, spacious, well-ventilated

airs plural noun <u>affectation</u>, arrogance, haughtiness, hauteur, pomposity, pretensions, superciliousness, swank (informal)

airy adjective **1** <u>well-ventilated</u>, fresh, light, open, spacious, uncluttered **2** <u>light-hearted</u>, blithe, cheerful, high-spirited, jaunty, lively, sprightly

➤ **Antonyms**
≠<u>well-ventilated</u>: airless, close, heavy, muggy, oppressive, stale, stifling, stuffy, suffocating, unventilated ≠<u>light-hearted</u>: dismal, gloomy, glum, melancholy, miserable, morose, sad

aisle noun <u>passageway</u>, alley, corridor, gangway, lane, passage, path

alacrity noun <u>eagerness</u>, alertness, enthusiasm, promptness, quickness, readiness, speed, willingness, zeal

➤ **Antonyms**
apathy, lethargy, reluctance, unwillingness

alarm noun **1** <u>fear</u>, anxiety, apprehension, consternation, fright, nervousness, panic, scare, trepidation **2** <u>danger signal</u>, alarm bell, alert, bell, distress signal, hooter, siren, warning ♦ verb **3** <u>frighten</u>, daunt, dismay, distress, give (someone) a turn (informal), panic, scare, startle, unnerve

➤ **Antonyms**
noun ≠<u>fear</u>: calm, calmness, composure, sang-froid ♦ verb ≠<u>frighten</u>: assure, calm, comfort, reassure, relieve

alarming adjective <u>frightening</u>, daunting, distressing, disturbing, scaring, shocking, startling, unnerving

alcoholic noun **1** <u>drunkard</u>, dipso-

maniac, drinker, drunk, inebriate, tippler, toper, wino (informal) ♦ adjective **2** <u>intoxicating</u>, brewed, distilled, fermented, hard, strong

alcove noun <u>recess</u>, bay, compartment, corner, cubbyhole, cubicle, niche, nook

alert adjective **1** <u>watchful</u>, attentive, awake, circumspect, heedful, observant, on guard, on one's toes, on the lookout, vigilant, wide-awake ♦ noun **2** <u>warning</u>, alarm, alert, signal, siren ♦ verb **3** <u>warn</u>, alarm, forewarn, inform, notify, signal

➤ **Antonyms**
adjective ≠<u>watchful</u>: careless, heedless, unaware, unconcerned, unwary ♦ noun ≠<u>warning</u>: all clear ♦ verb ≠<u>warn</u>: lull

alertness noun <u>watchfulness</u>, attentiveness, heedfulness, liveliness, vigilance

alias adverb **1** <u>also known as</u>, also called, otherwise, otherwise known as ♦ noun **2** <u>pseudonym</u>, assumed name, nom de guerre, nom de plume, pen name, stage name

alibi noun <u>excuse</u>, defence, explanation, justification, plea, pretext, reason

alien adjective **1** <u>strange</u>, exotic, foreign, incongruous, unfamiliar ♦ noun **2** <u>foreigner</u>, newcomer, outsider, stranger

➤ **Antonyms**
adjective ≠<u>strange</u>: akin, alike, connected, kindred, like, related, similar ♦ noun ≠<u>foreigner</u>: citizen, countryman, dweller, inhabitant, national, resident

alienate verb <u>set against</u>, disaffect, estrange, make unfriendly, turn away

alienation noun <u>setting against</u>, disaffection, estrangement, remoteness, separation, turning away

alight[1] verb **1** <u>get off</u>, descend, disembark, dismount, get down **2** <u>land</u>, come down, come to rest, descend, light, perch, settle, touch down

➤ **Antonyms**

≠**land**: ascend, fly up, go up, lift off, move up, rise, soar, take off

alight² *adjective* **1** on fire, ablaze, aflame, blazing, burning, fiery, flaming, lighted, lit **2** lit up, bright, brilliant, illuminated, shining

align *verb* **1** ally, affiliate, agree, associate, cooperate, join, side, sympathize **2** line up, even up, order, range, regulate, straighten

alignment *noun* **1** alliance, affiliation, agreement, association, cooperation, sympathy, union **2** lining up, adjustment, arrangement, evening up, order, straightening up

alike *adjective* **1** similar, akin, analogous, corresponding, identical, of a piece, parallel, resembling, the same ♦ *adverb* **2** similarly, analogously, correspondingly, equally, evenly, identically, uniformly

➤ **Antonyms**

adjective ≠**similar**: different, dissimilar, diverse, separate, unlike ♦ *adverb* ≠**similarly**: differently, distinctly, unequally

alive *adjective* **1** living, animate, breathing, in the land of the living (*informal*), subsisting **2** in existence, active, extant, functioning, in force, operative **3** lively, active, alert, animated, energetic, full of life, vital, vivacious

➤ **Antonyms**

≠**living**: dead, deceased, departed, expired, inanimate, lifeless ≠**in existence**: extinct, inactive, inoperative, lost ≠**lively**: apathetic, dull, inactive, lifeless, spiritless

all *adjective* **1** the whole of, every bit of, the complete, the entire, the sum of, the totality of, the total of **2** every, each, each and every, every one of, every single **3** complete, entire, full, greatest, perfect, total, utter ♦ *adverb* **4** completely, altogether, entirely, fully, totally, utterly, wholly

♦ *noun* **5** whole amount, aggregate, entirety, everything, sum total, total, totality, utmost

allegation *noun* claim, accusation, affirmation, assertion, charge, declaration, statement

allege *verb* claim, affirm, assert, charge, declare, maintain, state

➤ **Antonyms**

contradict, deny, disagree with, disclaim, oppose, refute, renounce, repudiate

alleged *adjective* **1** stated, affirmed, asserted, declared, described, designated **2** supposed, doubtful, dubious, ostensible, professed, purported, so-called, unproved

allegiance *noun* loyalty, constancy, devotion, faithfulness, fidelity, obedience

➤ **Antonyms**

disloyalty, faithlessness, inconstancy, infidelity, treachery

allegorical *adjective* symbolic, emblematic, figurative, symbolizing

allegory *noun* symbol, fable, myth, parable, story, symbolism, tale

allergic *adjective* sensitive, affected by, hypersensitive, susceptible

allergy *noun* sensitivity, antipathy, hypersensitivity, susceptibility

alleviate *verb* ease, allay, lessen, lighten, moderate, reduce, relieve, soothe

alley *noun* passage, alleyway, backstreet, lane, passageway, pathway, walk

alliance *noun* union, affiliation, agreement, association, coalition, combination, confederation, connection, federation, league, marriage, pact, partnership, treaty

➤ **Antonyms**

breach, break, dissociation, disunion, disunity, division, rupture, separation, split, split-up

allied *adjective* united, affiliated, associated, combined, connected, in league, linked, related

allocate *verb* <u>assign</u>, allot, allow, apportion, budget, designate, earmark, mete, set aside, share out

allocation *noun* <u>assignment</u>, allotment, allowance, lot, portion, quota, ration, share

allot *verb* <u>assign</u>, allocate, apportion, budget, designate, earmark, mete, set aside, share out

allotment *noun* **1** <u>plot</u>, kitchen garden, patch, tract **2** <u>assignment</u>, allowance, grant, portion, quota, ration, share, stint

all-out *adjective* <u>total</u>, complete, exhaustive, full, full-scale, maximum, thoroughgoing, undivided, unremitting, unrestrained

▶ **Antonyms**
careless, cursory, half-hearted, negligent, off-hand, perfunctory, unenthusiastic

allow *verb* **1** <u>permit</u>, approve, authorize, enable, endure, let, sanction, stand, suffer, tolerate **2** <u>give</u>, allocate, allot, assign, grant, provide, set aside, spare **3** <u>acknowledge</u>, admit, concede, confess, grant, own

▶ **Antonyms**
≠<u>permit</u>: ban, disallow, forbid, prohibit, proscribe, refuse ≠<u>give</u>: deny, forbid, refuse ≠<u>acknowledge</u>: contradict, deny, disagree with, oppose

allowable *adjective* <u>permissible</u>, acceptable, admissible, all right, appropriate, suitable, tolerable

allowance *noun* **1** <u>portion</u>, allocation, amount, grant, lot, quota, ration, share, stint **2** <u>concession</u>, deduction, discount, rebate, reduction

allow for *verb* <u>take into account</u>, consider, make allowances for, make concessions for, make provision for, plan for, provide for, take into consideration

alloy *noun* **1** <u>mixture</u>, admixture, amalgam, blend, combination, composite, compound, hybrid ♦ *verb* **2** <u>mix</u>, amalgamate, blend, combine, compound, fuse

all right *adjective* **1** <u>satisfactory</u>, acceptable, adequate, average, fair, O.K. or okay (*informal*), standard, up to scratch (*informal*) **2** <u>well</u>, healthy, O.K. or okay (*informal*), safe, sound, unharmed, uninjured, whole

▶ **Antonyms**
≠<u>satisfactory</u>: bad, inadequate, not good enough, not up to scratch (*informal*), poor, unacceptable, unsatisfactory ≠<u>well</u>: ailing, bad, ill, injured, off colour, poorly, sick, sickly, unhealthy, unwell

allude *verb* <u>refer</u>, hint, imply, intimate, mention, suggest, touch upon

allure *noun* **1** <u>attractiveness</u>, appeal, attraction, charm, enchantment, enticement, glamour, lure, persuasion, seductiveness, temptation ♦ *verb* **2** <u>attract</u>, captivate, charm, enchant, entice, lure, persuade, seduce, tempt, win over

alluring *adjective* <u>attractive</u>, beguiling, captivating, come-hither, fetching, glamorous, seductive, tempting

▶ **Antonyms**
off-putting (*Brit. informal*), repellent, repugnant, repulsive, unattractive

allusion *noun* <u>reference</u>, casual remark, hint, implication, innuendo, insinuation, intimation, mention, suggestion

ally *noun* **1** <u>partner</u>, accomplice, associate, collaborator, colleague, friend, helper ♦ *verb* **2** <u>unite</u>, associate, collaborate, combine, join, join forces, unify

▶ **Antonyms**
noun ≠<u>partner</u>: adversary, antagonist, competitor, enemy, foe, opponent, rival ♦ *verb* ≠<u>unite</u>: alienate, disunite, divide, drive apart, separate

almighty *adjective* **1** <u>all-powerful</u>, absolute, invincible, omnipotent, supreme, unlimited **2** *Informal* <u>great</u>, enormous, excessive, intense, loud, severe, terrible

➤ **Antonyms**

≠all-powerful: helpless, impotent, powerless, weak ≠great: feeble, insignificant, paltry, poor, slight, tame, weak

almost *adverb* nearly, about, approximately, close to, just about, not quite, on the brink of, practically, virtually

alone *adjective* by oneself, apart, detached, isolated, lonely, only, on one's tod (*slang*), separate, single, solitary, unaccompanied

➤ **Antonyms**

accompanied, aided, among others, assisted, escorted, helped, joint, together

aloof *adjective* distant, detached, haughty, remote, standoffish, supercilious, unapproachable, unfriendly

➤ **Antonyms**

friendly, gregarious, neighbourly, open, warm

aloud *adverb* out loud, audibly, clearly, distinctly, intelligibly, plainly

already *adverb* before now, at present, before, by now, by then, even now, heretofore, just now, previously

also *adverb* too, additionally, and, as well, besides, further, furthermore, in addition, into the bargain, moreover, to boot

alter *verb* adapt, adjust, amend, convert, modify, reform, revise, transform, turn, vary

alteration *noun* change, adaptation, adjustment, amendment, conversion, difference, modification, reformation, revision, transformation, variation

alternate *verb* **1** change, act reciprocally, fluctuate, interchange, oscillate, rotate, substitute, take turns ♦ *adjective* **2** every other, alternating, every second, interchanging, rotating

alternative *noun* **1** choice, option, other (of two), preference, recourse, selection, substitute ♦ *adjective* **2** different, alternate, another, other, second, substitute

alternatively *adverb* or, as an alternative, if not, instead, on the other hand, otherwise

although *conjunction* though, albeit, despite the fact that, even if, even though, notwithstanding, while

altogether *adverb* **1** completely, absolutely, fully, perfectly, quite, thoroughly, totally, utterly, wholly **2** on the whole, all in all, all things considered, as a whole, collectively, generally, in general **3** in total, all told, everything included, in all, in sum, taken together

➤ **Antonyms**

≠completely: halfway, incompletely, in part, not fully, partially, relatively, slightly, somewhat, to a certain degree or extent

altruistic *adjective* selfless, benevolent, charitable, generous, humanitarian, philanthropic, public-spirited, self-sacrificing, unselfish

➤ **Antonyms**

egotistic(al), looking out for number one (*informal*), self-centred, self-interested, selfish, self-seeking, ungenerous

always *adverb* continually, consistently, constantly, eternally, evermore, every time, forever, invariably, perpetually, repeatedly, without exception

➤ **Antonyms**

hardly, hardly ever, infrequently, once in a blue moon, once in a while, rarely, scarcely ever, seldom

amalgamate *verb* combine, ally, blend, fuse, incorporate, integrate, merge, mingle, unite

➤ **Antonyms**

disunite, divide, part, separate, split, split up

amalgamation *noun* combination, blend, coalition, compound, fusion, joining, merger, mixture, union

amass *verb* collect, accumulate, assemble, compile, gather, hoard, pile up

amateur noun <u>nonprofessional</u>, dabbler, dilettante, layman

amateurish adjective <u>unprofessional</u>, amateur, bungling, clumsy, crude, inexpert, unaccomplished

➤ **Antonyms**
experienced, expert, practised, professional, skilled

amaze verb <u>astonish</u>, alarm, astound, bewilder, dumbfound, shock, stagger, startle, stun, surprise

amazement noun <u>astonishment</u>, admiration, bewilderment, confusion, perplexity, shock, surprise, wonder

amazing adjective <u>astonishing</u>, astounding, breathtaking, eye-opening, jaw-dropping, overwhelming, staggering, startling, stunning, surprising

ambassador noun <u>representative</u>, agent, consul, deputy, diplomat, envoy, legate, minister

ambiguity noun <u>vagueness</u>, doubt, dubiousness, equivocation, obscurity, uncertainty

ambiguous adjective <u>unclear</u>, dubious, enigmatic, equivocal, inconclusive, indefinite, indeterminate, obscure, vague

➤ **Antonyms**
clear, definite, explicit, obvious, plain, simple, specific, unequivocal, unmistakable, unquestionable

ambition noun **1** <u>enterprise</u>, aspiration, desire, drive, eagerness, longing, striving, yearning, zeal **2** <u>goal</u>, aim, aspiration, desire, dream, hope, intent, objective, purpose, wish

ambitious adjective <u>enterprising</u>, aspiring, avid, eager, hopeful, intent, purposeful, striving, zealous

➤ **Antonyms**
apathetic, good-for-nothing, lazy, unambitious, unaspiring

ambivalent adjective <u>undecided</u>, contradictory, doubtful, equivocal, in two minds, uncertain, unsure, wavering

➤ **Antonyms**
certain, clear, decided, definite, positive, sure, unwavering

amble verb <u>stroll</u>, dawdle, meander, mosey (informal), ramble, saunter, walk, wander

ambush noun **1** <u>trap</u>, lying in wait, waylaying ◆ verb **2** <u>trap</u>, attack, bushwhack (U.S.), ensnare, surprise, waylay

amenable adjective <u>receptive</u>, able to be influenced, acquiescent, agreeable, compliant, open, persuadable, responsive, susceptible

➤ **Antonyms**
inflexible, intractable, obdurate, obstinate, pig-headed, stubborn

amend verb <u>change</u>, alter, correct, fix, improve, mend, modify, reform, remedy, repair, revise

amendment noun **1** <u>change</u>, alteration, correction, emendation, improvement, modification, reform, remedy, repair, revision **2** <u>alteration</u>, addendum, addition, attachment, clarification

amends plural noun As in **make amends for** <u>compensation</u>, atonement, recompense, redress, reparation, restitution, satisfaction

amenity noun <u>facility</u>, advantage, comfort, convenience, service

amiable adjective <u>pleasant</u>, affable, agreeable, charming, congenial, engaging, friendly, genial, likable or likeable, lovable

➤ **Antonyms**
disagreeable, hostile, unfriendly, unpleasant

amicable adjective <u>friendly</u>, amiable, civil, cordial, courteous, harmonious, neighbourly, peaceful, sociable

➤ **Antonyms**
antagonistic, belligerent, hostile, pugnacious, quarrelsome, uncivil, unfriendly, unkind, unsociable

amid, amidst preposition <u>in the middle of</u>, among, amongst, in the midst of, in the thick of, surrounded by

amiss adverb **1** <u>wrongly</u>, erroneously, improperly, inappropriately, incorrectly, mistakenly, unsuitably **2** *As in* take (something) amiss <u>as an insult</u>, as offensive, out of turn, wrongly ◆ *adjective* **3** <u>wrong</u>, awry, faulty, incorrect, mistaken, untoward

➤ **Antonyms**

adverb ≠<u>wrongly</u>: appropriately, correctly, properly, rightly, suitably, well ◆ *adjective* ≠<u>wrong</u>: accurate, correct, O.K. or okay (*informal*), proper, right

ammunition *noun* <u>munitions</u>, armaments, explosives, powder, rounds, shells, shot

amnesty *noun* <u>general pardon</u>, absolution, dispensation, forgiveness, immunity, remission (*of penalty*), reprieve

amok, amuck *adverb* *As in* run amok <u>madly</u>, berserk, destructively, ferociously, in a frenzy, murderously, savagely, uncontrollably, violently, wildly

among, amongst *preposition* **1** <u>in the midst of</u>, amid, amidst, in the middle of, in the thick of, surrounded by, together with, with **2** <u>in the group of</u>, in the class of, in the company of, in the number of, out of **3** <u>to each of</u>, between

amorous *adjective* <u>loving</u>, erotic, impassioned, in love, lustful, passionate, tender

➤ **Antonyms**

aloof, cold, distant, frigid, passionless, undemonstrative, unfeeling, unloving

amount *noun* <u>quantity</u>, expanse, extent, magnitude, mass, measure, number, supply, volume

amount to *verb* <u>add up to</u>, become, come to, develop into, equal, mean, total

ample *adjective* <u>plenty</u>, abundant, bountiful, copious, expansive, extensive, full, generous, lavish, plentiful, profuse

➤ **Antonyms**

inadequate, insufficient, little, meagre, restricted, scant, skimpy, small, sparse, unsatisfactory

amplify *verb* **1** <u>go into detail</u>, develop, elaborate, enlarge, expand, explain, flesh out **2** <u>expand</u>, enlarge, extend, heighten, increase, intensify, magnify, strengthen, widen

➤ **Antonyms**

≠<u>go into detail</u>: abbreviate, abridge, simplify ≠<u>expand</u>: boil down, condense, curtail, cut down, decrease, reduce

amply *adverb* <u>fully</u>, abundantly, completely, copiously, generously, profusely, richly

➤ **Antonyms**

inadequately, insufficiently, meagrely, poorly, sparsely, thinly

amputate *verb* <u>cut off</u>, curtail, lop, remove, separate, sever, truncate

amuck *see* AMOK

amuse *verb* <u>entertain</u>, charm, cheer, delight, interest, please, tickle

➤ **Antonyms**

be tedious, bore, pall on, tire, weary

amusement *noun* **1** <u>entertainment</u>, cheer, enjoyment, fun, merriment, mirth, pleasure **2** <u>pastime</u>, diversion, entertainment, game, hobby, joke, recreation, sport

➤ **Antonyms**

≠<u>entertainment</u>: boredom, monotony, tedium

amusing *adjective* <u>funny</u>, comical, droll, enjoyable, entertaining, humorous, interesting, witty

➤ **Antonyms**

boring, dull, flat, humdrum, monotonous, tedious, tiresome, unamusing, unexciting, unfunny, uninteresting

anaemic *adjective* <u>pale</u>, ashen, colourless, feeble, pallid, sickly, wan, weak

➤ **Antonyms**

blooming, florid, glowing, radiant, rosy, rosy-cheeked, ruddy

anaesthetic *noun* **1** <u>painkiller</u>, analgesic, anodyne, narcotic, opiate, sedative, soporific ◆ *adjective* **2** <u>pain-killing</u>, analgesic, anodyne, deadening, dulling, numbing, sedative, soporific

analogy noun <u>similarity</u>, comparison, correlation, correspondence, likeness, parallel, relation, resemblance

analyse verb **1** <u>examine</u>, evaluate, investigate, research, test, work over **2** <u>break down</u>, dissect, divide, resolve, separate, think through

analysis noun <u>examination</u>, breakdown, dissection, inquiry, investigation, scrutiny, sifting, test

analytic, analytical adjective <u>rational</u>, inquiring, inquisitive, investigative, logical, organized, problem-solving, systematic

anarchic adjective <u>lawless</u>, chaotic, disorganized, rebellious, riotous, ungoverned

➤ **Antonyms**
controlled, disciplined, law-abiding, ordered, peaceful, restrained, well-behaved

anarchist noun <u>revolutionary</u>, insurgent, nihilist, rebel, terrorist

anarchy noun <u>lawlessness</u>, chaos, confusion, disorder, disorganization, revolution, riot

➤ **Antonyms**
control, discipline, government, law, law and order, order, peace, rule

anatomy noun **1** <u>examination</u>, analysis, dissection, division, inquiry, investigation, study **2** <u>structure</u>, build, composition, frame, framework, make-up

ancestor noun <u>forefather</u>, forebear, forerunner, precursor, predecessor

➤ **Antonyms**
descendant, issue, offspring, progeny, successor

ancient adjective <u>old</u>, aged, antique, archaic, old-fashioned, primeval, primordial, timeworn

➤ **Antonyms**
current, fresh, in vogue, modern, new, newfangled, recent, state-of-the-art, up-to-date

ancillary adjective <u>supplementa-</u>

<u>ry</u>, additional, auxiliary, extra, secondary, subordinate, subsidiary, supporting

➤ **Antonyms**
cardinal, chief, main, major, premier, primary, prime, principal

and conjunction <u>also</u>, along with, as well as, furthermore, in addition to, including, moreover, plus, together with

anecdote noun <u>story</u>, reminiscence, short story, sketch, tale, urban legend, urban myth, yarn

angel noun **1** <u>divine messenger</u>, archangel, cherub, seraph **2** *Informal* <u>dear</u>, beauty, darling, gem, jewel, paragon, saint, treasure

angelic adjective **1** <u>pure</u>, adorable, beautiful, entrancing, lovely, saintly, virtuous **2** <u>heavenly</u>, celestial, cherubic, ethereal, seraphic

➤ **Antonyms**
≠heavenly: demonic, devilish, diabolic, diabolical, fiendish, hellish, infernal, satanic

anger noun **1** <u>rage</u>, annoyance, displeasure, exasperation, fury, ire, outrage, resentment, temper, wrath ♦ verb **2** <u>enrage</u>, annoy, displease, exasperate, gall, incense, infuriate, madden, outrage, rile, vex

➤ **Antonyms**
noun ≠rage: acceptance, calmness, forgiveness, goodwill, patience, peace, pleasure ♦ verb ≠enrage: appease, calm, pacify, placate, please, soothe

angle¹ noun **1** <u>intersection</u>, bend, corner, crook, edge, elbow, nook, point **2** <u>point of view</u>, approach, aspect, outlook, perspective, position, side, slant, standpoint, viewpoint

angle² verb <u>fish</u>, cast

angry adjective <u>furious</u>, annoyed, cross, displeased, enraged, exasperated, incensed, infuriated, irate, mad (*informal*), outraged, resentful

➤ **Antonyms**
amiable, calm, friendly, happy,

mild, peaceful, pleasant

angst noun <u>anxiety</u>, apprehension, unease, worry

▶ **Antonyms**

calmness, composure, contentment, ease, peace of mind

anguish noun <u>suffering</u>, agony, distress, grief, heartache, misery, pain, sorrow, torment, woe

animal noun **1** <u>creature</u>, beast, brute **2** *Applied to a person* <u>brute</u>, barbarian, beast, monster, savage, wild man ♦ *adjective* **3** <u>physical</u>, bestial, bodily, brutish, carnal, gross, sensual

animate verb **1** <u>enliven</u>, energize, excite, fire, inspire, invigorate, kindle, move, stimulate ♦ *adjective* **2** <u>living</u>, alive, alive and kicking, breathing, live, moving

▶ **Antonyms**

verb ≠<u>enliven</u>: check, curb, deaden, deter, discourage, dull, inhibit, kill, put a damper on, restrain

animated adjective <u>lively</u>, ebullient, energetic, enthusiastic, excited, passionate, spirited, vivacious

▶ **Antonyms**

apathetic, boring, dull, inactive, lethargic, lifeless, listless, passive

animation noun <u>liveliness</u>, ebullience, energy, enthusiasm, excitement, fervour, passion, spirit, verve, vivacity, zest

animosity noun <u>hostility</u>, acrimony, antipathy, bitterness, enmity, hatred, ill will, malevolence, malice, rancour, resentment

▶ **Antonyms**

amity, benevolence, congeniality, friendliness, friendship, goodwill, harmony, kindness, love, rapport, sympathy

annals plural noun <u>records</u>, accounts, archives, chronicles, history

annex verb **1** <u>seize</u>, acquire, appropriate, conquer, occupy, take over **2** <u>join</u>, add, adjoin, attach, connect, fasten

▶ **Antonyms**

≠<u>join</u>: detach, disconnect, separate, unfasten

annihilate verb <u>destroy</u>, abolish, eradicate, exterminate, extinguish, obliterate, wipe out

announce verb <u>make known</u>, advertise, broadcast, declare, disclose, proclaim, report, reveal, tell

▶ **Antonyms**

conceal, cover up, hide, hold back, hush (up), keep back, keep quiet, keep secret, suppress, withhold

announcement noun <u>statement</u>, advertisement, broadcast, bulletin, communiqué, declaration, proclamation, report, revelation

announcer noun <u>presenter</u>, broadcaster, commentator, master of ceremonies, newscaster, newsreader, reporter

annoy verb <u>irritate</u>, anger, bother, displease, disturb, exasperate, get on one's nerves (*informal*), hassle (*informal*), madden, molest, pester, plague, trouble, vex

▶ **Antonyms**

appease, calm, comfort, mollify, soothe

annoyance noun **1** <u>irritation</u>, anger, bother, hassle (*informal*), nuisance, trouble **2** <u>nuisance</u>, bore, bother, drag (*informal*), pain (*informal*)

annoying adjective <u>irritating</u>, disturbing, exasperating, maddening, troublesome

▶ **Antonyms**

agreeable, amusing, charming, delightful, enjoyable, entertaining, gratifying, pleasant

annual adjective <u>yearly</u>, once a year, yearlong

annually adverb <u>yearly</u>, by the year, every year, once a year, per annum, per year

annul verb <u>invalidate</u>, abolish, cancel, declare or render null and void, negate, nullify, repeal, retract

▶ **Antonyms**

bring back, re-enforce, re-establish, reimpose, reinstate, re-introduce, restore

anoint verb <u>consecrate</u>, bless, hallow, sanctify

anomalous adjective <u>unusual</u>, abnormal, eccentric, exceptional, incongruous, inconsistent, irregular, odd, peculiar

➤ Antonyms

common, customary, familiar, natural, normal, ordinary, regular, typical, usual

anomaly noun <u>irregularity</u>, abnormality, eccentricity, exception, incongruity, inconsistency, oddity, peculiarity

anonymous adjective <u>unnamed</u>, incognito, nameless, unacknowledged, uncredited, unidentified, unknown, unsigned

➤ Antonyms

acknowledged, credited, identified, known, named, signed

answer verb 1 <u>reply</u>, explain, react, resolve, respond, retort, return, solve ♦ noun 2 <u>reply</u>, comeback, defence, explanation, reaction, rejoinder, response, retort, return, riposte, solution

➤ Antonyms

verb ≠<u>reply</u>: ask, inquire, interrogate, query, question ♦ noun ≠<u>reply</u>: inquiry, interrogation, query, question

answerable adjective, usually with for or to <u>responsible</u>, accountable, amenable, chargeable, liable, subject, to blame

answer for verb <u>be responsible for</u>, be accountable for, be answerable for, be chargeable for, be liable for, be to blame for

antagonism noun <u>hostility</u>, antipathy, conflict, discord, dissension, friction, opposition, rivalry

➤ Antonyms

accord, agreement, amity, friendship, harmony, love, peacefulness, sympathy

antagonist noun <u>opponent</u>, adversary, competitor, contender, enemy, foe, rival

antagonistic adjective <u>hostile</u>, at odds, at variance, conflicting, incompatible, in dispute, opposed, unfriendly

antagonize verb <u>annoy</u>, anger, get on one's nerves (informal), hassle (informal), irritate, offend

➤ Antonyms

appease, calm, mollify, pacify, placate, propitiate, soothe, win over

anthem noun 1 <u>hymn</u>, canticle, carol, chant, chorale, psalm 2 <u>song of praise</u>, paean

anthology noun <u>collection</u>, compendium, compilation, miscellany, selection, treasury

anticipate verb <u>expect</u>, await, foresee, foretell, hope for, look forward to, predict, prepare for

anticipation noun <u>expectation</u>, expectancy, foresight, forethought, premonition, prescience

anticlimax noun <u>disappointment</u>, bathos, comedown (informal), letdown

➤ Antonyms

climax, culmination, height, highlight, high point, peak

antics plural noun <u>clowning</u>, escapades, horseplay, mischief, playfulness, pranks, tomfoolery, tricks

antidote noun <u>cure</u>, countermeasure, remedy

antipathy noun <u>hostility</u>, aversion, bad blood, dislike, enmity, hatred, ill will

➤ Antonyms

affection, affinity, attraction, empathy, fellow-feeling, goodwill, rapport, sympathy

antiquated adjective <u>obsolete</u>, antique, archaic, dated, old-fashioned, out-of-date, passé

➤ Antonyms

all-singing, all-dancing, current, fashionable, modern, modish, new, state-of-the-art, up-to-date

antique noun 1 <u>period piece</u>, bygone, heirloom, relic ♦ adjective 2 <u>vintage</u>, antiquarian, classic, olden 3 <u>old-fashioned</u>, archaic, obsolete, outdated

antiquity noun 1 <u>old age</u>, age, ancientness, elderliness, oldness 2 <u>distant past</u>, ancient times, olden days, time immemorial

antiseptic adjective 1 <u>hygienic</u>,

clean, germ-free, pure, sanitary, sterile, uncontaminated ♦ *noun* **2** <u>disinfectant</u>, germicide, purifier

➤ **Antonyms**
adjective ≠<u>hygienic</u>: contaminated, dirty, impure, infected, insanitary, polluted, septic, unhygienic

antisocial *adjective* **1** <u>unsociable</u>, alienated, misanthropic, reserved, retiring, uncommunicative, unfriendly, withdrawn **2** <u>disruptive</u>, antagonistic, belligerent, disorderly, hostile, menacing, rebellious, uncooperative

➤ **Antonyms**
≠<u>unsociable</u>: companionable, friendly, gregarious, philanthropic, sociable, social

antithesis *noun* <u>opposite</u>, contrary, contrast, converse, inverse, reverse

anxiety *noun* <u>uneasiness</u>, angst, apprehension, concern, foreboding, misgiving, nervousness, tension, trepidation, worry

➤ **Antonyms**
assurance, calmness, confidence, serenity

anxious *adjective* **1** <u>uneasy</u>, apprehensive, concerned, fearful, in suspense, nervous, on tenterhooks, tense, troubled, worried **2** <u>eager</u>, desirous, impatient, intent, itching, keen, yearning

➤ **Antonyms**
≠<u>uneasy</u>: assured, calm, certain, composed, confident, cool, nonchalant, unfazed *(informal)*, unperturbed ≠<u>eager</u>: disinclined, hesitant, loath, reluctant

apart *adverb* **1** <u>to pieces</u>, asunder, in bits, in pieces, to bits **2** <u>separate</u>, alone, aside, away, by oneself, isolated, to one side **3** **apart from** <u>except for</u>, aside from, besides, but, excluding, not counting, other than, save

apartment *noun* <u>room</u>, accommodation, flat, living quarters, penthouse, quarters, rooms, suite

apathetic *adjective* <u>uninterested</u>, cool, indifferent, passive, phlegmatic, unconcerned

➤ **Antonyms**
anxious, caring, concerned, enthusiastic, excited, interested, worried, zealous

apathy *noun* <u>lack of interest</u>, coolness, indifference, inertia, nonchalance, passivity, torpor, unconcern

➤ **Antonyms**
anxiety, concern, enthusiasm, feeling, interest, zeal

apex *noun* <u>highest point</u>, crest, crown, culmination, peak, pinnacle, point, summit, top

➤ **Antonyms**
base, bottom, depths, lowest point, nadir

apiece *adverb* <u>each</u>, for each, from each, individually, respectively, separately, to each

➤ **Antonyms**
all together, as a group, collectively, en masse, overall, together

aplomb *noun* <u>self-possession</u>, calmness, composure, confidence, level-headedness, poise, sang-froid, self-assurance, self-confidence

➤ **Antonyms**
awkwardness, confusion, discomfiture, discomposure, embarrassment, self-consciousness

apocryphal *adjective* <u>dubious</u>, doubtful, legendary, mythical, questionable, unauthenticated, unsubstantiated

➤ **Antonyms**
attested, authentic, authenticated, authorized, factual, substantiated, true, undisputed, unquestionable

apologetic *adjective* <u>regretful</u>, contrite, penitent, remorseful, rueful, sorry

apologize *verb* <u>say sorry</u>, ask forgiveness, beg pardon, express regret

apology *noun* **1** <u>defence</u>, acknowledgment, confession, excuse, explanation, justification, plea **2** *As in* **an apology for** <u>mockery</u>, caricature, excuse, imitation, travesty

apostle *noun* **1** <u>evangelist</u>, her-aid, messenger, missionary, preacher **2** supporter, advocate, champion, pioneer, propagandist, proponent

apotheosis noun deification, elevation, exaltation, glorification, idealization, idolization

appal verb horrify, alarm, daunt, dishearten, dismay, frighten, outrage, shock, unnerve

appalling adjective horrifying, alarming, awful, daunting, dreadful, fearful, frightful, horrible, shocking, terrifying

➤ **Antonyms**
encouraging, heartening, reassuring

apparatus noun **1** equipment, appliance, contraption (informal), device, gear, machinery, mechanism, tackle, tools **2** organization, bureaucracy, chain of command, hierarchy, network, setup (informal), structure, system

apparent adjective **1** obvious, discernible, distinct, evident, manifest, marked, unmistakable, visible **2** seeming, ostensible, outward, superficial

➤ **Antonyms**
≠obvious: doubtful, dubious, hazy, indefinite, uncertain, unclear, vague ≠seeming: actual, genuine, real, sincere, true

apparently adverb it appears that, it seems that, on the face of it, ostensibly, outwardly, seemingly, superficially

apparition noun ghost, chimera, phantom, spectre, spirit, wraith

appeal verb **1** plead, ask, beg, call upon, entreat, pray, request **2** attract, allure, charm, entice, fascinate, interest, please, tempt ♦ noun **3** plea, application, entreaty, petition, prayer, request, supplication **4** attraction, allure, beauty, charm, fascination

➤ **Antonyms**
verb ≠plead: deny, refuse, reject, repudiate, repulse ≠attract: alienate, repulse, revolt ♦ noun ≠plea: denial, refusal, rejection, repudiation ≠attraction: repulsiveness

appealing adjective attractive, alluring, charming, desirable, engaging, winsome

➤ **Antonyms**
repellent, repugnant, repulsive, unalluring, unappealing, unattractive, undesirable

appear verb **1** come into view, be present, come out, coming to light, crop up (informal), emerge, materialize (informal), surface, turn up **2** look (like or as if), occur, seem, strike one as

➤ **Antonyms**
≠come into view: disappear, vanish

appearance noun **1** arrival, coming, emergence, introduction, presence **2** look, demeanour, expression, figure, form, looks, manner, mien (literary) **3** impression, front, guise, illusion, image, outward show, pretence, semblance

appease verb **1** pacify, calm, conciliate, mollify, placate, quiet, satisfy, soothe **2** ease, allay, alleviate, calm, relieve, soothe

➤ **Antonyms**
≠pacify: aggravate (informal), anger, annoy, antagonize, arouse, enrage, irritate, madden, provoke

appeasement noun **1** pacification, accommodation, compromise, concession, conciliation, mollification, placation **2** easing, alleviation, lessening, relieving, soothing

appendage noun attachment, accessory, addition, supplement

appendix noun supplement, addendum, addition, adjunct, appendage, postscript

appetite noun desire, craving, demand, hunger, liking, longing, passion, relish, stomach, taste, yearning

➤ **Antonyms**
abhorrence, aversion, disgust, disinclination, dislike, distaste, loathing, repugnance, revulsion

appetizing adjective delicious, appealing, inviting, mouthwatering, palatable, succulent, tasty, tempting

➤ **Antonyms**

distasteful, nauseating, unappetizing, unpalatable, unsavoury

applaud verb praise, acclaim, approve, cheer, clap, commend, compliment, encourage, extol

➤ **Antonyms**

boo, censure, condemn, criticize, deride, disparage, hiss, ridicule, run down, slag (off) (slang)

applause noun ovation, accolade, approval, big hand, cheers, clapping, hand, praise

appliance noun device, apparatus, gadget, implement, instrument, machine, mechanism, tool

applicable adjective appropriate, apt, fitting, pertinent, relevant, suitable, useful

➤ **Antonyms**

inapplicable, inappropriate, irrelevant, unsuitable, wrong

applicant noun candidate, claimant, inquirer

application noun 1 request, appeal, claim, inquiry, petition, requisition 2 effort, commitment, dedication, diligence, hard work, industry, perseverance

apply verb 1 request, appeal, claim, inquire, petition, put in, requisition 2 use, bring to bear, carry out, employ, exercise, exert, implement, practise, utilize 3 put on, cover with, lay on, paint, place, smear, spread on 4 be relevant, be applicable, be appropriate, bear upon, be fitting, fit, pertain, refer, relate 5 apply oneself try, be diligent, buckle down (informal), commit oneself, concentrate, dedicate oneself, devote oneself, persevere, work hard

appoint verb 1 assign, choose, commission, delegate, elect, name, nominate, select 2 decide, allot, arrange, assign, choose, designate, establish, fix, set 3 equip, fit out, furnish, provide, supply

➤ **Antonyms**

≠assign: discharge, dismiss, fire, give the sack (informal), sack (informal) ≠decide: cancel ≠equip: dismantle, divest, strip

appointed adjective 1 assigned, chosen, delegated, elected, named, nominated, selected 2 decided, allotted, arranged, assigned, chosen, designated, established, fixed, set 3 equipped, fitted out, furnished, provided, supplied

appointment noun 1 meeting, arrangement, assignation, date, engagement, interview, rendezvous 2 selection, assignment, choice, election, naming, nomination 3 job, assignment, office, place, position, post, situation 4 appointments fittings, fixtures, furnishings, gear, outfit, paraphernalia, trappings

apportion verb divide, allocate, allot, assign, dispense, distribute, dole out, give out, ration out, share

apportionment noun division, allocation, allotment, assignment, dispensing, distribution, doling out, rationing out, sharing

apposite adjective appropriate, applicable, apt, fitting, pertinent, relevant, suitable, to the point

➤ **Antonyms**

inapplicable, inappropriate, inapt, irrelevant, unsuitable

appraisal noun assessment, estimate, estimation, evaluation, judgment, opinion

appraise verb assess, estimate, evaluate, gauge, judge, rate, review, value

appreciable adjective significant, considerable, definite, discernible, evident, marked, noticeable, obvious, pronounced, substantial

➤ **Antonyms**

inappreciable, indiscernible, insignificant, minor, minute, negligible, small, trivial, unnoticeable, unsubstantial

appreciate verb **1** <u>value</u>, admire, enjoy, like, prize, rate highly, respect, treasure **2** <u>be aware of</u>, perceive, realize, recognize, sympathize with, take account of, understand **3** <u>be grateful for</u>, be appreciative, be indebted, be obliged, be thankful for, give thanks for **4** <u>increase</u>, enhance, gain, grow, improve, rise

► **Antonyms**

≠<u>value</u>: belittle, disdain, disparage, scorn ≠<u>be aware of</u>: be unaware of, misunderstand, underrate ≠<u>be grateful for</u>: be ungrateful for ≠<u>increase</u>: deflate, depreciate, devaluate, fall

appreciation noun **1** <u>gratitude</u>, acknowledgment, gratefulness, indebtedness, obligation, thankfulness, thanks **2** <u>awareness</u>, admiration, comprehension, enjoyment, perception, realization, recognition, sensitivity, sympathy, understanding **3** <u>increase</u>, enhancement, gain, growth, improvement, rise

► **Antonyms**

≠<u>gratitude</u>: ingratitude ≠<u>awareness</u>: ignorance, incomprehension ≠<u>increase</u>: decline, depreciation, devaluation, fall

appreciative adjective **1** <u>grateful</u>, beholden, indebted, obliged, thankful **2** <u>aware</u>, admiring, enthusiastic, respectful, responsive, sensitive, sympathetic, understanding

apprehend verb **1** <u>arrest</u>, capture, catch, nick (slang, chiefly Brit.), seize, take prisoner **2** <u>understand</u>, comprehend, conceive, get the picture, grasp, perceive, realize, recognize

► **Antonyms**

≠<u>arrest</u>: discharge, free, let go, liberate, release ≠<u>understand</u>: be at cross-purposes, be unaware of, be unconscious of, get one's lines crossed, misapprehend, misconceive, misunderstand

apprehension noun **1** <u>anxiety</u>, alarm, concern, dread, fear, foreboding, suspicion, trepidation,

worry **2** <u>arrest</u>, capture, catching, seizure, taking **3** <u>awareness</u>, comprehension, grasp, perception, understanding

► **Antonyms**

≠<u>anxiety</u>: assurance, composure, confidence, nonchalance, serenity, unconcern ≠<u>arrest</u>: discharge, liberation, release ≠<u>awareness</u>: incomprehension

apprehensive adjective <u>anxious</u>, concerned, foreboding, nervous, uneasy, worried

► **Antonyms**

assured, at ease, composed, confident, nonchalant, unafraid

apprentice noun <u>trainee</u>, beginner, learner, novice, probationer, pupil, student

► **Antonyms**

ace (informal), adept, dab hand (Brit. informal), expert, master, past master, pro

approach verb **1** <u>move towards</u>, come close, come near, draw near, near, reach **2** <u>make a proposal to</u>, appeal to, apply to, make overtures to, sound out **3** <u>set about</u>, begin work on, commence, embark on, enter upon, make a start, undertake ♦ noun **4** <u>coming</u>, advance, arrival, drawing near, nearing **5** often plural <u>proposal</u>, advance, appeal, application, invitation, offer, overture, proposition **6** <u>access</u>, avenue, entrance, passage, road, way **7** <u>way</u>, manner, means, method, style, technique **8** <u>likeness</u>, approximation, semblance

approachable adjective **1** <u>friendly</u>, affable, congenial, cordial, open, sociable **2** <u>accessible</u>, attainable, reachable

► **Antonyms**

≠<u>friendly</u>: aloof, cool, distant, remote, reserved, standoffish, unfriendly, withdrawn ≠<u>accessible</u>: inaccessible, out of reach, out-of-the-way, remote, unreachable

appropriate adjective **1** <u>suitable</u>, apt, befitting, fitting, pertinent, relevant, to the point, well-suited ♦ verb **2** <u>seize</u>, commandeer, confiscate, impound, take possession of, usurp **3** <u>steal</u>, embezzle, filch, misappropriate, pilfer, pocket **4** <u>allocate</u>, allot, apportion, assign, devote, earmark, set aside

➤ **Antonyms**

adjective ≠<u>suitable</u>: inappropriate, irrelevant, unfitting, unsuitable ♦ *verb* ≠<u>seize</u>: cede, donate, give, relinquish ≠<u>allocate</u>: withhold

approval *noun* **1** <u>consent</u>, agreement, assent, authorization, blessing, endorsement, permission, recommendation, sanction **2** <u>favour</u>, acclaim, admiration, applause, appreciation, esteem, good opinion, praise, respect

➤ **Antonyms**

≠<u>favour</u>: disapproval, dislike, disparagement, dissatisfaction

approve *verb* **1** <u>favour</u>, admire, commend, have a good opinion of, like, praise, regard highly, respect **2** <u>agree to</u>, allow, assent to, authorize, consent to, endorse, pass, permit, recommend, sanction

➤ **Antonyms**

≠<u>favour</u>: censure, condemn, deplore, disapprove, find unacceptable, frown on, object to, take exception to ≠<u>agree to</u>: disallow, veto

approximate *adjective* **1** <u>close</u>, near **2** <u>rough</u>, estimated, inexact, loose ♦ *verb* **3** <u>come close</u>, approach, border on, come near, reach, resemble, touch, verge on

➤ **Antonyms**

adjective ≠<u>close</u>, <u>rough</u>: accurate, correct, definite, exact, precise, specific

approximately *adverb* <u>almost</u>, about, around, circa (*used with dates*), close to, in the region of, just about, more or less, nearly, roughly

approximation *noun* <u>guess</u>, conjecture, estimate, estimation, guesswork, rough calculation, rough idea

apron *noun* <u>pinny</u> (*informal*), pinafore

apt *adjective* **1** <u>inclined</u>, disposed, given, liable, likely, of a mind, prone, ready **2** <u>appropriate</u>, fitting, pertinent, relevant, suitable, to the point **3** <u>gifted</u>, clever, quick, sharp, smart, talented

➤ **Antonyms**

≠<u>appropriate</u>: ill-fitted, ill-suited, ill-timed, inappropriate, inopportune, irrelevant, unsuitable ≠<u>gifted</u>: awkward, clumsy, incompetent, inept, inexpert, slow, stupid

aptitude *noun* **1** <u>tendency</u>, inclination, leaning, predilection, proclivity, propensity **2** <u>gift</u>, ability, capability, faculty, intelligence, proficiency, talent

arable *adjective* <u>productive</u>, farmable, fertile, fruitful

arbiter *noun* **1** <u>judge</u>, adjudicator, arbitrator, referee, umpire **2** <u>authority</u>, controller, dictator, expert, governor, lord, master, pundit, ruler

arbitrary *adjective* <u>random</u>, capricious, chance, erratic, inconsistent, personal, subjective, whimsical

➤ **Antonyms**

consistent, logical, rational, reasonable, reasoned, sensible, sound

arbitrate *verb* <u>settle</u>, adjudicate, decide, determine, judge, mediate, pass judgment, referee, umpire

arbitration *noun* <u>settlement</u>, adjudication, decision, determination, judgment

arbitrator *noun* <u>judge</u>, adjudicator, arbiter, referee, umpire

arc *noun* <u>curve</u>, arch, bend, bow, crescent, half-moon

arcade *noun* <u>gallery</u>, cloister, colonnade, portico

arcane *adjective* <u>mysterious</u>, esoteric, hidden, occult, recondite, secret

arch[1] *noun* **1** <u>archway</u>, curve, dome, span, vault **2** <u>curve</u>, arc, bend, bow, hump, semicircle ♦ *verb* **3** <u>curve</u>, arc, bend, bow, bridge, span

arch² *adjective* <u>playful</u>, frolicsome, mischievous, pert, roguish, saucy, sly, waggish

archaic *adjective* **1** <u>old</u>, ancient, antique, bygone, olden (*archaic*), primitive **2** <u>old-fashioned</u>, antiquated, behind the times, obsolete, outmoded, out of date, passé

➤ **Antonyms**

≠<u>old</u>: contemporary, current, modern, new, present, recent ≠<u>old-fashioned</u>: latest, modern, new, newfangled, state-of-the-art, up-to-date, up-to-the-minute

archetypal *adjective* **1** <u>typical</u>, classic, ideal, model, standard **2** <u>original</u>, prototypical *or* prototypical

archetype *noun* **1** <u>standard</u>, model, paradigm, pattern, prime example **2** <u>original</u>, prototype

architect *noun* **1** <u>designer</u>, master builder, planner

architecture *noun* **1** <u>design</u>, building, construction, planning **2** <u>structure</u>, construction, design, framework, make-up, style

archive *noun* **1** <u>record office</u>, museum, registry, repository **2** *archives* <u>records</u>, annals, chronicles, documents, papers, rolls

arctic *adjective Informal* <u>freezing</u>, chilly, cold, frigid, frozen, glacial, icy

Arctic *adjective* <u>polar</u>, far-northern, hyperborean

ardent *adjective* **1** <u>passionate</u>, amorous, hot-blooded, impassioned, intense, lusty **2** <u>enthusiastic</u>, avid, eager, keen, zealous

➤ **Antonyms**

≠<u>passionate</u>: cold, cool, impassive ≠<u>enthusiastic</u>: apathetic, indifferent, lukewarm, unenthusiastic

ardour *noun* **1** <u>passion</u>, fervour, intensity, spirit, vehemence, warmth **2** <u>enthusiasm</u>, avidity, eagerness, keenness, zeal

arduous *adjective* <u>difficult</u>, exhausting, fatiguing, gruelling, laborious, onerous, punishing, rig-

orous, strenuous, taxing, tiring

➤ **Antonyms**

child's play (*informal*), easy, easy-peasy (*slang*), effortless, light, simple, undemanding

area *noun* **1** <u>region</u>, district, locality, neighbourhood, zone **2** <u>part</u>, portion, section, sector **3** <u>field</u>, department, domain, province, realm, sphere, territory

arena *noun* **1** <u>ring</u>, amphitheatre, bowl, enclosure, field, ground, stadium **2** <u>sphere</u>, area, domain, field, province, realm, sector, territory

argue *verb* **1** <u>discuss</u>, assert, claim, debate, dispute, maintain, reason, remonstrate **2** <u>quarrel</u>, bicker, disagree, dispute, fall out (*informal*), fight, squabble

argument *noun* **1** <u>quarrel</u>, clash, controversy, disagreement, dispute, feud, fight, row, squabble **2** <u>discussion</u>, assertion, claim, debate, dispute, plea, questioning, remonstration **3** <u>reason</u>, argumentation, case, defence, dialectic, ground(s), line of reasoning, logic, polemic, reasoning

➤ **Antonyms**

≠<u>quarrel</u>: accord, agreement, concurrence

argumentative *adjective* <u>quarrelsome</u>, belligerent, combative, contentious, contrary, disputatious, litigious, opinionated

➤ **Antonyms**

accommodating, amenable, complaisant, compliant, conciliatory, easy-going, obliging

arid *adjective* **1** <u>dry</u>, barren, desert, parched, sterile, torrid, waterless **2** <u>boring</u>, dreary, dry, dull, tedious, tiresome, uninspired, uninteresting

➤ **Antonyms**

≠<u>dry</u>: fertile, fruitful, lush, rich, verdant ≠<u>boring</u>: exciting, interesting, lively, sexy (*informal*), stimulating

arise *verb* **1** <u>happen</u>, begin, emerge, ensue, follow, occur, result, start, stem **2** *Old-fashioned* <u>get up</u>, get to one's feet, go up, rise, stand up, wake up

aristocracy noun <u>upper class</u>, elite, gentry, nobility, patricians, peerage, ruling class
➤ **Antonyms**
commoners, common people, hoi polloi, lower classes, masses, plebeians, proletariat, working classes

aristocrat noun <u>noble</u>, aristo (informal), grandee, lady, lord, patrician, peer, peeress

aristocratic adjective <u>upper-class</u>, blue-blooded, elite, gentlemanly, lordly, noble, patrician, titled
➤ **Antonyms**
common, lower-class, plebeian, proletarian, working-class

arm[1] noun <u>upper limb</u>, appendage, limb

arm[2] verb Especially with weapons <u>equip</u>, accoutre, array, deck out, furnish, issue with, provide, supply

armada noun <u>fleet</u>, flotilla, navy, squadron

armaments plural noun <u>weapons</u>, ammunition, arms, guns, materiel, munitions, ordnance, weaponry

armed adjective <u>carrying weapons</u>, equipped, fitted out, primed, protected

armistice noun <u>truce</u>, ceasefire, peace, suspension of hostilities

armour noun <u>protection</u>, armour plate, covering, sheathing, shield

armoured adjective <u>protected</u>, armour-plated, bombproof, bulletproof, ironclad, mailed, steel-plated

arms plural noun 1 <u>weapons</u>, armaments, firearms, guns, instruments of war, ordnance, weaponry 2 <u>heraldry</u>, blazonry, crest, escutcheon, insignia

army noun 1 <u>soldiers</u>, armed force, legions, military, military force, soldiery, troops 2 <u>vast number</u>, array, horde, host, multitude, pack, swarm, throng

aroma noun <u>scent</u>, bouquet, fragrance, odour, perfume, redolence, savour, smell

aromatic adjective <u>fragrant</u>, balmy, perfumed, pungent, redolent, savoury, spicy, sweet-scented, sweet-smelling
➤ **Antonyms**
acrid, fetid, foul, foul-smelling, malodorous, offensive, rank, smelly, stinking

around preposition 1 <u>surrounding</u>, about, encircling, enclosing, encompassing, on all sides of, on every side of 2 <u>approximately</u>, about, circa (used with dates), roughly ♦ adverb 3 <u>everywhere</u>, about, all over, here and there, in all directions, on all sides, throughout, to and fro 4 <u>near</u>, at hand, close, close at hand, nearby, nigh (archaic or dialect)

arouse verb 1 <u>stimulate</u>, excite, incite, instigate, provoke, spur, stir up, summon up, whip up 2 <u>awaken</u>, rouse, waken, wake up
➤ **Antonyms**
≠stimulate: allay, calm, dampen, quell, quench, still

arrange verb 1 <u>plan</u>, construct, contrive, devise, fix up, organize, prepare 2 <u>agree</u>, adjust, come to terms, compromise, determine, settle 3 <u>put in order</u>, classify, group, line up, order, organize, position, sort 4 <u>adapt</u>, instrument, orchestrate, score
➤ **Antonyms**
≠put in order: disarrange, disorganize, disturb, mess up, scatter

arrangement noun 1 often plural <u>plan</u>, organization, planning, preparation, provision, schedule 2 <u>agreement</u>, adjustment, compact, compromise, deal, settlement, terms 3 <u>order</u>, alignment, classification, form, organization, structure, system 4 <u>adaptation</u>, instrumentation, interpretation, orchestration, score, version

array noun 1 <u>arrangement</u>, collection, display, exhibition, formation, line-up, parade, show, supply 2 Poetic <u>clothing</u>, apparel, attire, clothes, dress, finery, garments, regalia ♦ verb 3 <u>arrange</u>, display, exhibit, group, parade, range, show 4 <u>dress</u>, adorn, attire, clothe, deck, decorate, festoon

arrest *verb* **1** <u>capture</u>, apprehend, catch, detain, nick (*slang, chiefly Brit.*), seize, take prisoner **2** <u>stop</u>, block, delay, end, inhibit, interrupt, obstruct, slow, suppress **3** <u>grip</u>, absorb, engage, engross, fascinate, hold, intrigue, occupy ♦ *noun* **4** <u>capture</u>, bust (*informal*), cop (*slang*), detention, seizure **5** <u>stopping</u>, blockage, delay, end, hindrance, interruption, obstruction, suppression

➤ **Antonyms**
verb ≠<u>capture</u>: free, let go, release, set free ≠<u>stop</u>: accelerate, promote, quicken, speed up ♦ *noun* ≠<u>capture</u>: freeing, release ≠<u>stopping</u>: acceleration, promotion, quickening

arresting *adjective* <u>striking</u>, engaging, impressive, noticeable, outstanding, remarkable, stunning, surprising

➤ **Antonyms**
inconspicuous, unimpressive, unnoticeable, unremarkable

arrival *noun* **1** <u>coming</u>, advent, appearance, arriving, entrance, happening, occurrence, taking place **2** <u>newcomer</u>, caller, entrant, incomer, visitor

arrive *verb* **1** <u>come</u>, appear, enter, get to, reach, show up (*informal*), turn up **2** *Informal* <u>succeed</u>, become famous, make good, make it (*informal*), make the grade (*informal*)

➤ **Antonyms**
≠<u>come</u>: depart, disappear, exit, go, go away, leave, vanish, withdraw

arrogance *noun* <u>conceit</u>, disdainfulness, haughtiness, highhandedness, insolence, pride, superciliousness, swagger

➤ **Antonyms**
bashfulness, diffidence, humility, meekness, modesty, shyness

arrogant *adjective* <u>conceited</u>, disdainful, haughty, high-handed, overbearing, proud, scornful, supercilious

➤ **Antonyms**
bashful, deferential, diffident, humble, modest, servile, shy, unassuming

arrow *noun* **1** <u>dart</u>, bolt, flight, quarrel, shaft (*archaic*) **2** <u>pointer</u>, indicator

arsenal *noun* <u>armoury</u>, ammunition dump, arms depot, ordnance depot, stockpile, store, storehouse, supply

art *noun* <u>skill</u>, craft, expertise, ingenuity, mastery, virtuosity

artful *adjective* <u>cunning</u>, clever, crafty, shrewd, sly, smart, wily

➤ **Antonyms**
artless, frank, ingenuous, open, simple, straightforward

article *noun* **1** <u>piece</u>, composition, discourse, essay, feature, item, paper, story, treatise **2** <u>thing</u>, commodity, item, object, piece, substance, unit **3** <u>clause</u>, item, paragraph, part, passage, point, portion, section

articulate *adjective* **1** <u>expressive</u>, clear, coherent, eloquent, fluent, lucid, well-spoken ♦ *verb* **2** <u>express</u>, enunciate, pronounce, say, speak, state, talk, utter, voice

➤ **Antonyms**
adjective ≠<u>expressive</u>: faltering, incoherent, incomprehensible, mute, silent, speechless, stammering, tongue-tied, unclear, unintelligible

artifice *noun* **1** <u>trick</u>, contrivance, device, machination, manoeuvre, stratagem, subterfuge, tactic **2** <u>cleverness</u>, ingenuity, inventiveness, skill

artificial *adjective* **1** <u>synthetic</u>, man-made, manufactured, nonnatural, plastic **2** <u>fake</u>, bogus, counterfeit, imitation, mock, sham, simulated **3** <u>insincere</u>, affected, contrived, false, feigned, forced, phoney *or* phony (*informal*), unnatural

➤ **Antonyms**
≠<u>fake</u>: authentic ≠<u>insincere</u>: frank, genuine, honest, natural, sincere, true, unaffected

artillery noun big guns, battery, cannon, cannonry, gunnery, ordnance

artisan noun craftsman, journeyman, mechanic, skilled workman, technician

artistic adjective creative, aesthetic, beautiful, cultured, elegant, refined, sophisticated, stylish, tasteful

➤ Antonyms

inartistic, inelegant, tasteless, unattractive

artistry noun skill, brilliance, craftsmanship, creativity, finesse, mastery, proficiency, virtuosity

artless adjective 1 straightforward, frank, guileless, open, plain 2 natural, plain, pure, simple, unadorned, unaffected, unpretentious

➤ Antonyms

≠straightforward: artful, crafty, cunning, false ≠natural: affected, artificial, unnatural

as conjunction 1 when, at the time that, during the time that, just as, while 2 in the way that, in the manner that, like 3 what, that which 4 since, because, considering that, seeing that 5 for instance, like, such as ♦ preposition 6 being, in the character of, in the role of, under the name of

ascend verb move up, climb, go up, mount, scale

➤ Antonyms

descend, drop, fall, go down, move down, sink

ascent noun 1 rise, ascending, ascension, climb, mounting, rising, scaling, upward movement 2 upward slope, gradient, incline, ramp, rise, rising ground

ascertain verb find out, confirm, determine, discover, establish, learn

ascetic noun 1 monk, abstainer, hermit, nun, recluse ♦ adjective 2 self-denying, abstinent, austere, celibate, frugal, puritanical, self-disciplined

➤ Antonyms

noun ≠monk: hedonist, sensual-

ist, voluptuary ♦ adjective ≠self-denying: abandoned, luxurious, self-indulgent, sensuous, voluptuous

ascribe verb attribute, assign, charge, credit, impute, put down, refer, set down

ashamed adjective embarrassed, distressed, guilty, humiliated, mortified, remorseful, shamefaced, sheepish, sorry

➤ Antonyms

pleased, proud, satisfied, unashamed

ashen adjective pale, colourless, grey, leaden, like death warmed up (informal), pallid, wan, white

➤ Antonyms

blooming, blushing, florid, flushed, glowing, red, rosy, rosy-cheeked, ruddy

ashore adverb on land, aground, landwards, on dry land, on the beach, on the shore, shorewards, to the shore

aside adverb 1 to one side, apart, beside, on one side, out of the way, privately, separately, to the side ♦ noun 2 interpolation, parenthesis

asinine adjective stupid, dumb-ass (slang), fatuous, foolish, idiotic, imbecilic, moronic, senseless

➤ Antonyms

bright, clever, intelligent, quick-witted, sensible, smart, wise

ask verb 1 inquire, interrogate, query, question, quiz 2 request, appeal, beg, demand, plead, seek 3 invite, bid, summon

➤ Antonyms

≠inquire: answer, reply, respond

askew adverb 1 crookedly, aslant, awry, obliquely, off-centre, to one side ♦ adjective 2 crooked, awry, cockeyed (informal), lopsided, oblique, off-centre, skewwhiff (Brit. informal)

➤ Antonyms

adverb ≠crookedly: aligned, evenly, in line, level, right, squarely, straight, true ♦ adjective ≠crooked: aligned, even, in line, level, right, square, straight, true

asleep *adjective* <u>sleeping</u>, dormant, dozing, fast asleep, napping, slumbering, snoozing (*informal*), sound asleep

aspect *noun* **1** <u>feature</u>, angle, facet, side **2** <u>position</u>, outlook, point of view, prospect, scene, situation, view **3** <u>appearance</u>, air, attitude, bearing, condition, demeanour, expression, look, manner

asphyxiate *verb* <u>suffocate</u>, choke, smother, stifle, strangle, strangulate, throttle

aspiration *noun* <u>aim</u>, ambition, desire, dream, goal, hope, objective, wish

aspire *verb* <u>aim</u>, desire, dream, hope, long, seek, set one's heart on, wish

aspiring *adjective* <u>hopeful</u>, ambitious, eager, longing, wannabe (*informal*), would-be

ass *noun* **1** <u>donkey</u>, moke (*slang*) **2** <u>fool</u>, blockhead, halfwit, idiot, jackass, numbskull or numskull, oaf, twit (*informal, chiefly Brit.*)

assail *verb* <u>attack</u>, assault, fall upon, lay into (*informal*), set upon

assailant *noun* <u>attacker</u>, aggressor, assailer, assaulter, invader

assassin *noun* <u>murderer</u>, executioner, hatchet man (*slang*), hit man (*slang*), killer, liquidator, slayer

assassinate *verb* <u>murder</u>, eliminate (*slang*), hit (*slang*), kill, liquidate, slay, take out (*slang*)

assault *noun* **1** <u>attack</u>, charge, invasion, offensive, onslaught ◆ *verb* **2** <u>attack</u>, beset, fall upon, lay into (*informal*), set about, set upon, strike at

➤ **Antonyms**
noun ≠<u>attack</u>: defence, protection, resistance ◆ *verb* ≠<u>attack</u>: defend, protect, resist

assemble *verb* **1** <u>gather</u>, amass, bring together, call together, collect, come together, congregate, meet, muster, rally **2** <u>put together</u>, build up, connect, construct, fabricate, fit together, join, piece together, set up

➤ **Antonyms**
≠<u>gather</u>: adjourn, break up (*informal*), disband, dismiss, disperse, scatter ≠<u>put together</u>: disassemble, divide, take apart

assembly *noun* **1** <u>gathering</u>, collection, company, conference, congress, council, crowd, group, mass, meeting **2** <u>putting together</u>, building up, connecting, construction, piecing together, setting up

assent *noun* **1** <u>agreement</u>, acceptance, approval, compliance, concurrence, consent, permission, sanction ◆ *verb* **2** <u>agree</u>, allow, approve, consent, grant, permit

➤ **Antonyms**
noun ≠<u>agreement</u>: denial, disagreement, disapproval, dissension, dissent, objection, refusal ◆ *verb* ≠<u>agree</u>: deny, disagree, dissent, object, protest

assert *verb* **1** <u>state</u>, affirm, declare, maintain, profess, pronounce, swear **2** <u>insist upon</u>, claim, defend, press, put forward, stand up for, stress, uphold **3** assert oneself <u>be forceful</u>, exert one's influence, make one's presence felt, put oneself forward, put one's foot down (*informal*)

➤ **Antonyms**
≠<u>state</u>, <u>insist upon</u>: deny, disclaim, rebut, refute, retract

assertion *noun* **1** <u>statement</u>, claim, declaration, pronouncement **2** <u>insistence</u>, maintenance, stressing

assertive *adjective* <u>confident</u>, aggressive, domineering, emphatic, feisty (*informal, chiefly U.S. & Canad.*), forceful, insistent, positive, pushy (*informal*), strong-willed

➤ **Antonyms**
bashful, diffident, hesitant, meek, reserved, retiring, self-conscious, self-effacing, shrinking, shy, timid, unassertive

assess *verb* **1** <u>judge</u>, appraise, estimate, evaluate, rate, size up (*informal*), value, weigh **2** <u>evaluate</u>, fix, impose, levy, rate, tax, value

assessment *noun* **1** <u>judgment</u>, appraisal, estimate, evaluation, rating, valuation **2** <u>evaluation</u>, charge, fee, levy, rating, toll, valuation

asset *noun* **1** <u>benefit</u>, advantage, aid, blessing, boon, feather in one's cap, help, resource, service **2** <u>assets</u> <u>property</u>, capital, estate, funds, goods, money, possessions, resources, wealth

➤ **Antonyms**
≠<u>benefit</u>: burden, disadvantage, drag, drawback, encumbrance, handicap, hindrance, impediment, liability

assiduous *adjective* <u>diligent</u>, hardworking, indefatigable, industrious, persevering, persistent, unflagging

➤ **Antonyms**
careless, idle, inattentive, indolent, lax, lazy, negligent, slack

assign *verb* **1** <u>select</u>, appoint, choose, delegate, designate, name, nominate **2** <u>give</u>, allocate, allot, apportion, consign, distribute, give out, grant **3** <u>attribute</u>, accredit, ascribe, put down

assignation *noun* **1** <u>secret meeting</u>, clandestine meeting, illicit meeting, rendezvous, tryst (*archaic*) **2** <u>selection</u>, appointment, assignment, choice, delegation, designation, nomination

assignment *noun* <u>task</u>, appointment, commission, duty, job, mission, position, post, responsibility

assimilate *verb* **1** <u>learn</u>, absorb, digest, incorporate, take in **2** <u>adjust</u>, adapt, blend in, mingle

assist *verb* <u>help</u>, abet, aid, cooperate, lend a helping hand, serve, support

➤ **Antonyms**
frustrate, hamper, handicap, hinder, hold back, hold up, impede, obstruct

assistance *noun* <u>help</u>, aid, back-ing, cooperation, helping hand, support

➤ **Antonyms**
hindrance, obstruction, opposition

assistant *noun* <u>helper</u>, accomplice, aide, ally, colleague, right-hand man, second, supporter

associate *verb* **1** <u>connect</u>, ally, combine, identify, join, link, lump together **2** <u>mix</u>, accompany, consort, hobnob, mingle, socialize ♦ *noun* **3** <u>partner</u>, collaborator, colleague, confederate, co-worker **4** <u>friend</u>, ally, companion, comrade, mate (*informal*)

➤ **Antonyms**
verb ≠<u>connect</u>: detach, disconnect, distinguish, isolate, segregate, separate, set apart ≠<u>mix</u>: avoid, be estranged, part company

association *noun* **1** <u>group</u>, alliance, band, club, coalition, federation, league, organization, society **2** <u>connection</u>, blend, combination, joining, juxtaposition, mixture, pairing, union

assorted *adjective* <u>various</u>, different, diverse, miscellaneous, mixed, motley, sundry, varied

➤ **Antonyms**
alike, identical, like, same, similar, uniform, unvaried

assortment *noun* <u>variety</u>, array, choice, collection, jumble, medley, mixture, selection

assume *verb* **1** <u>take for granted</u>, believe, expect, fancy, imagine, infer, presume, suppose, surmise, think **2** <u>take on</u>, accept, enter upon, put on, shoulder, take over **3** <u>put on</u>, adopt, affect, feign, imitate, impersonate, mimic, pretend to, simulate **4** <u>take over</u>, appropriate, commandeer, seize, take

➤ **Antonyms**
≠<u>take for granted</u>: know, prove ≠<u>take on</u>, <u>take over</u>: give up, hand over, leave, put aside, relinquish

assumed *adjective* **1** <u>false</u>, bogus, counterfeit, fake, fictitious, made-up, make-believe **2** <u>taken for granted</u>, accepted, expected, hypothetical, presumed, presupposed, supposed, surmised

▶ Antonyms

≠<u>false</u>: actual, authentic, natural, real ≠<u>taken for granted</u>: known, positive, true

assumption noun **1** <u>presumption</u>, belief, conjecture, guess, hypothesis, inference, supposition, surmise **2** <u>taking on</u>, acceptance, acquisition, adoption, entering upon, putting on, shouldering, takeover, taking up **3** <u>taking</u>, acquisition, appropriation, seizure, takeover

assurance noun **1** <u>assertion</u>, declaration, guarantee, oath, pledge, promise, statement, vow, word **2** <u>confidence</u>, boldness, certainty, conviction, faith, nerve, poise, self-confidence

▶ Antonyms

≠<u>assertion</u>: falsehood, lie ≠<u>confidence</u>: diffidence, doubt, self-doubt, shyness, timidity, uncertainty

assure verb **1** <u>promise</u>, certify, confirm, declare confidently, give one's word to, guarantee, pledge, swear, vow **2** <u>convince</u>, comfort, embolden, encourage, hearten, persuade, reassure **3** <u>make certain</u>, clinch, complete, confirm, ensure, guarantee, make sure, seal, secure

assured adjective **1** <u>confident</u>, certain, poised, positive, self-assured, self-confident, sure of oneself **2** <u>certain</u>, beyond doubt, confirmed, ensured, fixed, guaranteed, in the bag (slang), secure, settled, sure

▶ Antonyms

≠<u>confident</u>: bashful, diffident, hesitant, self-conscious, timid ≠<u>certain</u>: doubtful, uncertain, unconfirmed, unsettled, unsure

astonish verb <u>amaze</u>, astound, bewilder, confound, daze, dumbfound, stagger, stun, surprise

astonishing adjective <u>amazing</u>, astounding, bewildering, breath-

taking, brilliant, jaw-dropping, sensational (informal), staggering, stunning, surprising

astonishment noun <u>amazement</u>, awe, bewilderment, confusion, consternation, surprise, wonder, wonderment

astounding adjective <u>amazing</u>, astonishing, bewildering, breathtaking, brilliant, impressive, jaw-dropping, sensational (informal), staggering, stunning, surprising

astray adjective, adverb <u>off the right track</u>, adrift, amiss, lost, off, off course, off the mark, off the subject

astute adjective <u>intelligent</u>, canny, clever, crafty, cunning, perceptive, sagacious, sharp, shrewd, subtle

▶ Antonyms

dull, naive, slow, stupid, unintelligent

asylum noun **1** <u>refuge</u>, harbour, haven, preserve, retreat, safety, sanctuary, shelter **2** Old-fashioned <u>mental hospital</u>, hospital, institution, madhouse (informal), psychiatric hospital

*atheism noun <u>nonbelief</u>, disbelief, godlessness, heathenism, infidelity, irreligion, paganism, scepticism, unbelief

atheist noun <u>nonbeliever</u>, disbeliever, heathen, infidel, pagan, sceptic, unbeliever

athlete noun <u>sportsperson</u>, competitor, contestant, gymnast, player, runner, sportsman, sportswoman

athletic adjective <u>fit</u>, active, energetic, muscular, powerful, strapping, strong, sturdy

▶ Antonyms

delicate, feeble, frail, puny, sickly, weedy (informal)

athletics plural noun <u>sports</u>, contests, exercises, gymnastics, races, track and field events

atmosphere noun **1** <u>air</u>, aerosphere, heavens, sky **2** <u>feeling</u>, ambience, character, climate, environment, mood, spirit, surroundings, tone

atom noun particle, bit, dot, molecule, speck, spot, trace

atone verb, usually with for make amends, compensate, do penance, make redress, make reparation, make up for, pay for, recompense, redress

atonement noun amends, compensation, penance, recompense, redress, reparation, restitution

atrocious adjective 1 cruel, barbaric, brutal, fiendish, infernal, monstrous, savage, vicious, wicked 2 Informal shocking, appalling, detestable, grievous, horrible, horrifying, terrible

➤ Antonyms
≠cruel: generous, gentle, good, honourable, humane, kind, merciful ≠shocking: admirable, fine, tasteful

atrocity noun 1 cruelty, barbarity, brutality, fiendishness, horror, savagery, viciousness, wickedness 2 act of cruelty, abomination, crime, evil, horror, outrage

attach verb 1 connect, add, couple, fasten, fix, join, link, secure, stick, tie 2 put, ascribe, assign, associate, attribute, connect

➤ Antonyms
≠connect: detach, disconnect, dissociate, loosen, remove, separate, untie

attached adjective 1 spoken for, accompanied, engaged, married, partnered 2 attached to fond of, affectionate towards, devoted to, full of regard for

attachment noun 1 fondness, affection, affinity, attraction, liking, regard 2 accessory, accoutrement, extension, extra, fitting, fixture, supplement

➤ Antonyms
≠fondness: animosity, antipathy, aversion, disinclination, distaste, hatred, hostility, loathing

attack verb 1 assault, invade, lay into (informal), raid, set upon, storm, strike (at) 2 criticize, abuse, blame, censure, have a go (at) (informal), put down, vili-

fy ♦ noun 3 assault, campaign, charge, foray, incursion, invasion, offensive, onslaught, raid, strike 4 criticism, abuse, blame, censure, denigration, stick (slang), vilification 5 bout, convulsion, fit, paroxysm, seizure, spasm, stroke

➤ Antonyms
verb ≠assault: defend, guard, protect, support, sustain ♦ noun ≠assault: defence, support

attacker noun assailant, aggressor, assaulter, intruder, invader, raider

attain verb achieve, accomplish, acquire, complete, fulfil, gain, get, obtain, reach

attainment noun achievement, accomplishment, completion, feat

attempt verb 1 try, endeavour, seek, strive, undertake, venture ♦ noun 2 try, bid, crack (informal), effort, go (informal), shot (informal), stab (informal), trial

attend verb 1 be present, appear, frequent, go to, haunt, put in an appearance, show oneself, turn up, visit 2 look after, care for, mind, minister to, nurse, take care of, tend 3 pay attention, hear, heed, listen, mark, note, observe, pay heed 4 attend to apply oneself to, concentrate on, devote oneself to, get to work on, look after, occupy oneself with, see to, take care of

➤ Antonyms
≠be present: be absent, miss, play truant ≠look after, apply oneself to: neglect ≠pay attention: discount, disregard, ignore, neglect

attendance noun 1 presence, appearance, attending, being there 2 turnout, audience, crowd, gate, house, number present

attendant noun 1 assistant, aide, companion, escort, follower, guard, helper, servant ♦ adjective 2 accompanying, accessory, associated, concomitant, consequent, related

attention noun **1** <u>concentration</u>, deliberation, heed, intentness, mind, scrutiny, thinking, thought **2** <u>notice</u>, awareness, consciousness, consideration, observation, recognition, regard **3** <u>care</u>, concern, looking after, ministration, treatment **4**

➤ **Antonyms**

≠<u>concentration</u>, <u>notice</u>: carelessness, disregard, disrespect, distraction, inattention, laxity, laxness, thoughtlessness, unconcern ≠<u>care</u>: negligence

attentive adjective **1** <u>intent</u>, alert, awake, careful, concentrating, heedful, mindful, observant, studious, watchful **2** <u>considerate</u>, courteous, helpful, kind, obliging, polite, respectful, thoughtful

➤ **Antonyms**

≠<u>intent</u>: absent-minded, careless, distracted, dreamy, heedless, inattentive, preoccupied, unheeding, unmindful ≠<u>considerate</u>: neglectful, negligent, remiss, thoughtless

attic noun <u>loft</u>, garret

attire noun <u>clothes</u>, apparel, costume, dress, garb, garments, outfit, robes, wear

attitude noun **1** <u>disposition</u>, approach, frame of mind, mood, opinion, outlook, perspective, point of view, position, stance **2** <u>position</u>, pose, posture, stance

attract verb <u>appeal to</u>, allure, charm, draw, enchant, entice, lure, pull (informal), tempt

➤ **Antonyms**

disgust, give one the creeps (informal), put one off, repel, repulse, revolt, turn one off (informal)

attraction noun <u>appeal</u>, allure, charm, enticement, fascination, lure, magnetism, pull (informal), temptation

attractive adjective <u>appealing</u>, alluring, charming, fair, fetching, good-looking, handsome, inviting, lovely, pleasant, pretty, tempting

➤ **Antonyms**

disagreeable, displeasing, distasteful, offensive, repulsive, ugly, unappealing, unbecoming, uninviting, unlikable or unlikeable, unpleasant, unsightly

attribute verb **1** <u>ascribe</u>, assign, charge, credit, put down to, refer, set down to, trace to ♦ noun **2** <u>quality</u>, aspect, character, characteristic, facet, feature, peculiarity, property, trait

attune verb <u>accustom</u>, adapt, adjust, familiarize, harmonize, regulate

audacious adjective **1** <u>daring</u>, bold, brave, courageous, fearless, intrepid, rash, reckless **2** <u>cheeky</u>, brazen, defiant, impertinent, impudent, insolent, presumptuous, shameless

➤ **Antonyms**

≠<u>daring</u>: careful, cautious, guarded, prudent, timid, unadventurous, unenterprising ≠<u>cheeky</u>: deferential, tactful, unassuming

audacity noun **1** <u>daring</u>, boldness, bravery, courage, fearlessness, nerve, rashness, recklessness **2** <u>cheek</u>, chutzpah (U.S. & Canad. informal), effrontery, impertinence, impudence, insolence, nerve

audible adjective <u>clear</u>, detectable, discernible, distinct, hearable, perceptible

➤ **Antonyms**

faint, imperceptible, inaudible, indistinct, low, out of earshot

audience noun **1** <u>spectators</u>, assembly, crowd, gathering, gathering, listeners, onlookers, turnout, viewers **2** <u>interview</u>, consultation, hearing, meeting, reception

aura noun <u>air</u>, ambience, atmosphere, feeling, mood, quality, tone

auspicious adjective <u>favourable</u>, bright, encouraging, felicitous, hopeful, promising

➤ **Antonyms**

bad, discouraging, ill-omened, inauspicious, infelicitous, ominous, unfavourable, unlucky, unpromising, unpropitious

austere adjective **1** stern, forbidding, formal, serious, severe, solemn, strict **2** ascetic, abstemious, puritanical, self-disciplined, sober, solemn, strait-laced, strict **3** plain, bleak, harsh, simple, spare, Spartan, stark

➤ **Antonyms**
≠stern: cheerful, free-and-easy, genial, indulgent, kindly ≠ascetic: abandoned, free-and-easy, indulgent, loose, permissive ≠plain: comfortable, indulgent, luxurious

austerity noun **1** sternness, formality, inflexibility, rigour, seriousness, severity, solemnity, stiffness, strictness **2** asceticism, puritanism, self-denial, self-discipline, sobriety **3** plainness, simplicity, starkness

authentic adjective genuine, actual, authoritative, bona fide, legitimate, pure, real, true-to-life, valid

➤ **Antonyms**
counterfeit, fake, false, fraudulent, imitation, mock, pseudo (informal), synthetic, unreal, untrue

authenticity noun genuineness, accuracy, certainty, faithfulness, legitimacy, purity, truthfulness, validity

author noun **1** writer, composer, creator **2** creator, architect, designer, father, founder, inventor, originator, producer

authoritarian adjective **1** strict, autocratic, dictatorial, doctrinaire, dogmatic, severe, tyrannical ♦ noun **2** disciplinarian, absolutist, autocrat, despot, dictator, tyrant

➤ **Antonyms**
adjective ≠strict: broad-minded, democratic, flexible, indulgent, lenient, liberal, permissive, tolerant

authoritative adjective **1** reliable, accurate, authentic, definitive, dependable, trustworthy, valid **2** commanding, assertive, imperi-

ous, imposing, masterly, self-assured

➤ **Antonyms**
≠reliable: undependable, unreliable ≠commanding: humble, subservient

authority noun **1** power, command, control, direction, influence, supremacy, sway, weight **2** usually plural powers that be, administration, government, management, officialdom, police, the Establishment **3** expert, connoisseur, guru, judge, master, professional, specialist

authorization noun permission, a blank cheque, approval, leave, licence, permit, warrant

authorize verb **1** empower, accredit, commission, enable, entitle, give authority **2** permit, allow, approve, give authority for, license, sanction, warrant

➤ **Antonyms**
ban, debar, disallow, exclude, forbid, outlaw, prohibit, proscribe, rule out, veto

autocracy noun dictatorship, absolutism, despotism, tyranny

autocrat noun dictator, absolutist, despot, tyrant

autocratic adjective dictatorial, absolute, all-powerful, despotic, domineering, imperious, tyrannical

automatic adjective **1** mechanical, automated, mechanized, push-button, self-propelling **2** involuntary, instinctive, mechanical, natural, reflex, spontaneous, unconscious, unwilled

➤ **Antonyms**
≠mechanical: done by hand, hand-operated, human, manual, physical ≠involuntary: conscious, deliberate, intentional, voluntary

autonomous adjective self-ruling, free, independent, self-determining, self-governing, sovereign

autonomy noun independence, freedom, home rule, self-determination, self-government,

self-rule, sovereignty
➤ **Antonyms**
dependency, foreign rule, subjection

auxiliary adjective **1** supplementary, back-up, emergency, fallback, reserve, secondary, subsidiary, substitute **2** supporting, accessory, aiding, ancillary, assisting, helping ◆ noun **3** backup, reserve **4** helper, assistant, associate, companion, subordinate, supporter
➤ **Antonyms**
adjective ≠supplementary, supporting: cardinal, chief, essential, first, leading, main, primary, prime, principal

avail verb **1** benefit, aid, assist, be of advantage, be useful, help, profit ◆ noun **2** benefit, advantage, aid, good, help, profit, use

availability noun accessibility, attainability, handiness, readiness

available adjective accessible, at hand, at one's disposal, free, handy, on tap, ready, to hand
➤ **Antonyms**
busy, engaged, inaccessible, in use, occupied, spoken for, taken, unattainable, unavailable, unobtainable

avalanche noun **1** snow-slide, landslide, landslip **2** flood, barrage, deluge, inundation, torrent

avant-garde adjective progressive, experimental, groundbreaking, innovative, pioneering, unconventional
➤ **Antonyms**
conservative, conventional, traditional

avarice noun greed, covetousness, meanness, miserliness, niggardliness, parsimony, stinginess
➤ **Antonyms**
generosity, liberality

avaricious adjective grasping, covetous, greedy, mean, miserly, niggardly, parsimonious, stingy

avenge verb get revenge for, get even for (informal), get one's own back, hit back, punish, repay, retaliate

avenue noun street, approach, boulevard, course, drive, passage, path, road, route, way

average noun **1** usual, mean, medium, midpoint, norm, normal, par, standard **2** on average usually, as a rule, for the most part, generally, normally, typically ◆ adjective **3** usual, commonplace, fair, general, normal, ordinary, regular, standard, typical **4** mean, intermediate, medium, medium, middle ◆ verb **5** make on average, balance out to, be on average, do on average, even out to
➤ **Antonyms**
adjective ≠usual: abnormal, awful, bad, exceptional, great, notable, outstanding, remarkable, special, terrible, unusual ≠mean: maximum, minimum

averse adjective opposed, disinclined, hostile, ill-disposed, loath, reluctant, unwilling
➤ **Antonyms**
agreeable, amenable, inclined, keen, sympathetic, willing

aversion noun hatred, animosity, antipathy, disinclination, dislike, hostility, revulsion, unwillingness
➤ **Antonyms**
desire, inclination, liking, love, willingness

avert verb **1** turn away, turn aside **2** ward off, avoid, fend off, forestall, frustrate, preclude, prevent, stave off

aviator noun pilot, aeronaut, airman, flyer

avid adjective **1** enthusiastic, ardent, devoted, eager, fanatical, intense, keen, passionate, zealous **2** insatiable, grasping, greedy, hungry, rapacious, ravenous, thirsty, voracious
➤ **Antonyms**
≠enthusiastic: apathetic, impassive, indifferent, lukewarm, unenthusiastic

avoid verb **1** refrain from, dodge, duck (out of) (informal), eschew, fight shy of, shirk **2** prevent, avert **3** keep away from, bypass, dodge, elude, escape, evade, shun, steer clear of

➤ **Antonyms**

≠keep away from: approach, confront, contact, face, face up to, find, pursue, seek out

avoidance *noun* evasion, dodging, eluding, escape, keeping away, shunning, steering clear

avowed *adjective* **1** declared, open, professed, self-proclaimed, sworn **2** confessed, acknowledged, admitted

await *verb* **1** wait for, abide, anticipate, expect, look for, look forward to, stay for **2** be in store for, attend, be in readiness for, be prepared for, be ready for, wait for

awake *adjective* **1** not sleeping, aroused, awakened, aware, conscious, wakeful, wide-awake **2** alert, alive, attentive, aware, heedful, observant, on the lookout, vigilant, watchful ◆ *verb* **3** wake up, awaken, rouse, wake **4** alert, arouse, kindle, provoke, revive, stimulate, stir up

➤ **Antonyms**

adjective ≠not sleeping: asleep, dozing, napping, sleeping, unconscious ≠alert: inattentive, unaware

awaken *verb* **1** awake, arouse, revive, rouse, wake **2** alert, kindle, provoke, stimulate, stir up

awakening *noun* waking up, arousal, revival, rousing, stimulation, stirring up

award *verb* **1** give, bestow, confer, endow, grant, hand out, present ◆ *noun* **2** prize, decoration, gift, grant, trophy

aware *adjective* **1** aware of knowing about, acquainted with, conscious of, conversant with, familiar with, mindful of **2** informed, enlightened, in the loop, in the picture, knowledgeable

➤ **Antonyms**

ignorant, insensible, oblivious, unaware, unfamiliar with, unknowledgeable

awareness *noun* knowledge,

consciousness, familiarity, perception, realization, recognition, understanding

away *adverb* **1** off, abroad, elsewhere, from here, from home, hence **2** at a distance, apart, far, remote **3** aside, out of the way, to one side **4** continuously, incessantly, interminably, relentlessly, repeatedly, uninterruptedly, unremittingly ◆ *adjective* **5** not present, abroad, absent, elsewhere, gone, not at home, not here, out

awe *noun* **1** wonder, admiration, amazement, astonishment, dread, fear, horror, respect, reverence, terror ◆ *verb* **2** impress, amaze, astonish, frighten, horrify, intimidate, stun, terrify

➤ **Antonyms**

noun ≠wonder: contempt, disrespect, irreverence, scorn

awesome *adjective* awe-inspiring, amazing, astonishing, breathtaking, formidable, impressive, intimidating, stunning

awful *adjective* **1** terrible, abysmal, appalling, deplorable, dreadful, frightful, ghastly, horrendous **2** *Obsolete* awe-inspiring, awesome, fearsome, majestic, solemn

➤ **Antonyms**

≠terrible: amazing, brilliant, excellent, fabulous, great (*informal*), fantastic, great (*informal*), magnificent, marvellous, miraculous, sensational (*informal*), smashing (*informal*), super (*informal*), superb, terrific, tremendous, wonderful

awfully *adverb* **1** badly, disgracefully, dreadfully, reprehensibly, unforgivably, unpleasantly, woefully, wretchedly **2** *Informal* very, dreadfully, exceedingly, exceptionally, extremely, greatly, immensely, terribly

awkward *adjective* **1** clumsy, gauche, gawky, inelegant, lumbering, uncoordinated, ungainly **2** inconvenient, clunky (*informal*), cumbersome, difficult, troublesome, unmanageable, unwieldy **3** embarrassing, delicate, difficult, ill at ease, inconvenient, uncomfortable

> ➤ **Antonyms**

≠*clumsy*: adept, adroit, dexterous, graceful, skilful ≠*inconvenient*: convenient, easy, handy ≠*embarrassing*: comfortable, pleasant

awkwardness noun **1** clumsiness, gawkiness, inelegance, ungainliness **2** unwieldiness, difficulty, inconvenience **3** embarrassment, delicacy, difficulty, inconvenience

axe noun **1** hatchet, adze, chopper **2** for the axe *Informal* the sack (*informal*), dismissal, termination, the boot (*slang*), the chop (*slang*) ♦ verb **3** *Informal* cut back, cancel, dismiss, dispense with, eliminate, fire (*informal*), get rid of, remove, sack (*informal*)

axiom noun principle, adage, aphorism, dictum, maxim, precept, truism

axiomatic adjective self-evident, accepted, assumed, certain, given, granted, manifest, understood

axis noun pivot, axle, centre line, shaft, spindle

axle noun shaft, axis, pin, pivot, rod, spindle

B b

babble verb **1** gabble, burble, chatter, jabber, prattle, waffle (*informal, chiefly Brit.*) **2** gibber, gurgle ♦ noun **3** gabble, burble, drivel, gibberish, waffle (*informal, chiefly Brit.*)

baby noun **1** infant, babe, babe in arms, bairn (*Scot.*), child, newborn child ♦ adjective **2** small, little, mini, miniature, minute, teeny-weeny, tiny, wee

babyish adjective childish, foolish, immature, infantile, juvenile,

puerile, sissy, spoiled

> ➤ **Antonyms**

adult, grown-up, mature, of age

back noun **1** rear, end, far end, hind part, hindquarters, reverse, stern, tail end **2** behind one's back secretly, covertly, deceitfully, sneakily, surreptitiously ♦ verb **3** move back, back off, backtrack, go back, retire, retreat, reverse, turn tail, withdraw **4** support, advocate, assist, champion, endorse, promote, sponsor ♦ adjective **5** rear, end, hind, hindmost, posterior, tail **6** previous, delayed, earlier, elapsed, former, overdue, past

> ➤ **Antonyms**

noun ≠*rear*: face, fore, front, head ♦ verb ≠*move back*: advance, approach, move forward, progress ≠*support*: attack, combat, hinder, thwart, undermine, weaken ♦ adjective ≠*rear*: advance, fore, front ≠*previous*: future, late

backbiting noun slander, bitchiness (*slang*), cattiness (*informal*), defamation, disparagement, gossip, malice, scandalmongering, spitefulness

backbone noun **1** *Medical* spinal column, spine, vertebrae, vertebral column **2** strength of character, character, courage, determination, fortitude, grit, nerve, pluck, resolution

backbreaking adjective exhausting, arduous, crushing, gruelling, hard, laborious, punishing, strenuous

back down verb give in, accede, admit defeat, back-pedal, cave in (*informal*), concede, surrender, withdraw, yield

backer noun supporter, advocate, angel (*informal*), benefactor, patron, promoter, second, sponsor, subscriber

backfire verb fail, boomerang, disappoint, flop (*informal*), miscarry, rebound, recoil

background noun history, circumstances, culture, education, environment, grounding, tradition, upbringing

backing noun <u>support</u>, aid, assistance, encouragement, endorsement, moral support, patronage, sponsorship

backlash noun <u>reaction</u>, counteraction, recoil, repercussion, resistance, response, retaliation

backlog noun <u>build-up</u>, accumulation, excess, hoard, reserve, stock, supply

back out verb, often with of <u>withdraw</u>, abandon, cancel, give up, go back on, resign, retreat

backslide verb <u>relapse</u>, go astray, go wrong, lapse, revert, slip, stray, weaken

backslider noun <u>relapser</u>, apostate, deserter, recidivist, recreant, renegade, turncoat

back up verb <u>support</u>, aid, assist, bolster, confirm, corroborate, reinforce, second, stand by, substantiate

backward adjective <u>slow</u>, behind, dull, retarded, subnormal, underdeveloped, undeveloped

backwards, backward adverb <u>towards the rear</u>, behind, in reverse, rearward

bacteria plural noun <u>microorganisms</u>, bacilli, bugs (slang), germs, microbes, pathogens, viruses

bad adjective 1 <u>inferior</u>, defective, faulty, imperfect, inadequate, poor, substandard, unsatisfactory 2 <u>harmful</u>, damaging, dangerous, deleterious, detrimental, hurtful, ruinous, unhealthy 3 <u>wicked</u>, corrupt, criminal, evil, immoral, mean, sinful, wrong 4 <u>naughty</u>, disobedient, mischievous, unruly 5 <u>rotten</u>, decayed, mouldy, off, putrid, rancid, sour, spoiled 6 <u>unfavourable</u>, adverse, distressing, gloomy, grim, troubled, unfortunate, unpleasant

► **Antonyms**

≠<u>inferior</u>: adequate, fair, satisfactory ≠<u>harmful</u>: agreeable, beneficial, good, healthful, safe, sound, wholesome ≠<u>wicked</u>:

ethical, fine, first-rate, good, moral, righteous, virtuous ≠<u>naughty</u>: biddable, docile, good, obedient, well-behaved

badge noun <u>mark</u>, brand, device, emblem, identification, insignia, sign, stamp, token

badger verb <u>pester</u>, bully, goad, harass, hound, importune, nag, plague, torment

badinage noun <u>wordplay</u>, banter, mockery, pleasantry, repartee, teasing

badly adverb 1 <u>poorly</u>, carelessly, imperfectly, inadequately, incorrectly, ineptly, wrongly 2 <u>unfavourably</u>, unfortunately, unsuccessfully 3 <u>severely</u>, deeply, desperately, exceedingly, extremely, greatly, intensely, seriously

► **Antonyms**

≠<u>poorly</u>: ably, competently, correctly, properly, rightly, satisfactorily, splendidly, well

baffle verb <u>puzzle</u>, bewilder, confound, confuse, flummox, mystify, nonplus, perplex, stump

► **Antonyms**

clarify, clear up, elucidate, explain, interpret, make plain, spell out

bag noun 1 <u>container</u>, receptacle, sac, sack ♦ verb 2 <u>catch</u>, acquire, capture, kill, land, shoot, trap

baggage noun <u>luggage</u>, accoutrements, bags, belongings, equipment, gear, paraphernalia, suitcases, things

baggy adjective <u>loose</u>, bulging, droopy, floppy, ill-fitting, oversize, roomy, sagging, slack

► **Antonyms**

close, close-fitting, snug, stretched, taut, tight, tight-fitting

bail noun Law <u>security</u>, bond, guarantee, pledge, surety, warranty

bail out see BALE OUT

bait noun 1 <u>lure</u>, allurement, attraction, decoy, enticement, incentive, inducement, snare, temptation ♦ verb 2 <u>tease</u>, annoy, bother, harass, hassle (informal), hound, irritate, persecute, torment, wind up (Brit. slang)

baked adjective <u>dry</u>, arid, desiccated, parched, scorched, seared, sun-baked, torrid

balance noun **1** <u>stability</u>, composure, equanimity, poise, self-control, self-possession, steadiness **2** <u>equilibrium</u>, correspondence, equity, equivalence, evenness, parity, symmetry **3** <u>remainder</u>, difference, residue, rest, surplus ♦ verb **4** <u>stabilize</u>, level, match, parallel, steady **5** <u>compare</u>, assess, consider, deliberate, estimate, evaluate, weigh **6** Accounting <u>calculate</u>, compute, settle, square, tally, total

➤ **Antonyms**
noun ≠<u>equilibrium</u>: disproportion, instability, unbalance ♦ verb ≠<u>stabilize</u>: outweigh, overbalance, upset

balcony noun **1** <u>terrace</u>, veranda **2** <u>upper circle</u>, gallery, gods

bald adjective **1** <u>hairless</u>, bald-headed, depilated **2** <u>plain</u>, blunt, direct, forthright, straightforward, unadorned, unvarnished

balderdash noun <u>nonsense</u>, claptrap (informal), drivel, garbage (informal), gibberish, hogwash, hot air (informal), rubbish

baldness noun **1** <u>hairlessness</u>, alopecia (Pathology), bald-headedness **2** <u>plainness</u>, austerity, bluntness, severity, simplicity

bale out, bail out verb **1** Informal <u>help</u>, aid, relieve, rescue, save (someone's) bacon (informal, chiefly Brit.) **2** <u>escape</u>, quit, retreat, withdraw

balk, baulk verb **1** <u>recoil</u>, evade, flinch, hesitate, jib, refuse, resist, shirk, shrink from **2** <u>foil</u>, check, counteract, defeat, frustrate, hinder, obstruct, prevent, thwart

➤ **Antonyms**
≠<u>recoil</u>: accede, accept, acquiesce, comply, relent, submit, yield ♦ ≠<u>foil</u>: abet, advance, aid, assist, further, help, promote, support, sustain

ball noun <u>sphere</u>, drop, globe, globule, orb, pellet, spheroid

ballast noun <u>counterbalance</u>, balance, counterweight, equilibrium, sandbag, stability, stabilizer, weight

balloon verb <u>swell</u>, billow, blow up, dilate, distend, expand, grow rapidly, inflate, puff out

ballot noun <u>vote</u>, election, poll, polling, voting

ballyhoo noun Informal <u>fuss</u>, babble, commotion, hubbub, hue and cry, hullabaloo, noise, racket, to-do

balm noun **1** <u>ointment</u>, balsam, cream, embrocation, emollient, lotion, salve, unguent **2** <u>comfort</u>, anodyne, consolation, curative, palliative, restorative, solace

balmy adjective **1** <u>mild</u>, clement, pleasant, summery, temperate **2** see BARMY

➤ **Antonyms**
≠<u>mild</u>: harsh, inclement, intense, rough, stormy

bamboozle verb Informal **1** <u>cheat</u>, con (informal), deceive, dupe, fool, hoodwink, swindle, trick **2** <u>puzzle</u>, baffle, befuddle, confound, confuse, mystify, perplex, stump

ban verb **1** <u>prohibit</u>, banish, bar, block, boycott, disallow, disqualify, exclude, forbid, outlaw ♦ noun **2** <u>prohibition</u>, boycott, disqualification, embargo, restriction, taboo

➤ **Antonyms**
verb ≠<u>prohibit</u>: allow, approve, authorize, enable, let, permit, sanction ♦ noun ≠<u>prohibition</u>: allowance, approval, permission, sanction

banal adjective <u>unoriginal</u>, hackneyed, humdrum, mundane, pedestrian, stale, stereotyped, trite, unimaginative

➤ **Antonyms**
fresh, imaginative, interesting, new, novel, original, stimulating, unique, unusual

band[1] noun **1** <u>ensemble</u>, combo, group, orchestra **2** <u>gang</u>, body, company, group, party, posse (informal)

band² noun **strip**, belt, bond, chain, cord, ribbon, strap

bandage noun **1** dressing, compress, gauze, plaster ♦ verb **2** dress, bind, cover, swathe

bandit noun robber, brigand, desperado, highwayman, marauder, outlaw, thief

bane noun plague, bête noire, curse, nuisance, pest, ruin, scourge, torment

➤ **Antonyms**

blessing, comfort, consolation, joy, pleasure, relief, solace, support

bang noun **1** explosion, clap, clash, pop, slam, thud, thump **2** blow, bump, cuff, knock, punch, smack, stroke, whack ♦ verb **3** hit, belt (informal), clatter, knock, slam, strike, thump **4** explode, boom, clang, resound, thump, thunder ♦ adverb **5** hard, abruptly, headlong, noisily, suddenly **6** straight, precisely, slap, smack

banish verb **1** expel, deport, eject, evict, exile, outlaw **2** get rid of, ban, cast out, discard, dismiss, oust, remove

➤ **Antonyms**

≠expel: accept, admit, receive, welcome

banishment noun expulsion, deportation, exile, expatriation, transportation

banisters plural noun railing, balusters, balustrade, handrail, rail

bank¹ noun **1** storehouse, depository, repository **2** store, accumulation, fund, hoard, reserve, reservoir, savings, stock, stockpile ♦ verb **3** save, deposit, keep

bank² noun **1** mound, banking, embankment, heap, mass, pile, ridge **2** side, brink, edge, margin, shore ♦ verb **3** pile, amass, heap, mass, mound, stack **4** tilt, camber, cant, heel, incline, pitch, slant, slope, tip

bank³ noun row, array, file, group, line, rank, sequence, series, succession

bankrupt adjective insolvent,

broke (informal), destitute, impoverished, in queer street, in the red, ruined, wiped out (informal)

➤ **Antonyms**

in the money (informal), solvent, sound, wealthy

bankruptcy noun insolvency, disaster, failure, liquidation, ruin

banner noun flag, colours, ensign, pennant, placard, standard, streamer

banquet noun feast, dinner, meal, repast, revel, treat

banter verb **1** joke, jest, kid (informal), rib (informal), taunt, tease ♦ noun **2** joking, badinage, jesting, kidding (informal), repartee, teasing, wordplay

baptism noun Christianity christening, immersion, purification, sprinkling

baptize verb Christianity purify, cleanse, immerse

bar noun **1** rod, paling, palisade, pole, rail, shaft, stake, stick **2** obstacle, barricade, barrier, block, deterrent, hindrance, impediment, obstruction, stop **3** public house, boozer (Brit., Austral. & N.Z. informal), canteen, counter, inn, pub (informal, chiefly Brit.), saloon, tavern, watering hole (facetious slang) ♦ verb **4** fasten, barricade, bolt, latch, lock, secure **5** obstruct, hinder, prevent, restrain **6** exclude, ban, black, blackball, forbid, keep out, prohibit

➤ **Antonyms**

noun ≠obstacle: aid, benefit, help ♦ verb ≠exclude: accept, admit, allow, let, permit, receive

Bar noun the Bar Law barristers, body of lawyers, counsel, court, judgment, tribunal

barb noun **1** dig, affront, cut, gibe, insult, sarcasm, scoff, sneer **2** point, bristle, prickle, prong, quill, spike, spur, thorn

barbarian noun **1** savage, brute, yahoo **2** lout, bigot, boor, philistine

barbaric adjective **1** uncivilized,

primitive, rude, wild **2** <u>brutal</u>, barbarous, coarse, crude, cruel, fierce, inhuman, savage

➤ **Antonyms**

civilized, cultivated, cultured, gentlemanly, gracious, humane, refined, sophisticated, urbane

barbarism noun **1** <u>savagery</u>, coarseness, crudity

barbarous adjective **1** <u>uncivilized</u>, barbarian, brutish, primitive, rough, rude, savage, uncouth, wild **2** <u>brutal</u>, barbaric, cruel, ferocious, heartless, inhuman, monstrous, ruthless, vicious

barbed adjective **1** <u>cutting</u>, critical, hostile, hurtful, nasty, pointed, scathing, unkind **2** <u>spiked</u>, hooked, jagged, prickly, spiny, thorny

bare adjective **1** <u>naked</u>, nude, stripped, unclad, unclothed, uncovered, undressed, without a stitch on (informal) **2** <u>plain</u>, bald, basic, sheer, simple, stark, unembellished **3** <u>simple</u>, austere, spare, spartan, unadorned, unembellished

➤ **Antonyms**

≠<u>naked</u>: attired, clad, clothed, concealed, covered, dressed, hidden ≠<u>simple</u>: adorned

barefaced adjective **1** <u>obvious</u>, blatant, flagrant, open, transparent, unconcealed **2** <u>shameless</u>, audacious, bold, brash, brazen, impudent, insolent

➤ **Antonyms**

≠<u>obvious</u>: concealed, covered, hidden, inconspicuous, masked, obscured, secret

barely adverb <u>only just</u>, almost, at a push, by the skin of one's teeth, hardly, just, scarcely

➤ **Antonyms**

amply, completely, fully, profusely

bargain noun **1** <u>agreement</u>, arrangement, contract, pact, pledge, promise **2** <u>good buy</u>, (cheap) purchase, discount, giveaway, good deal, reduction, snip (informal), steal (informal) ◆ verb **3** <u>negotiate</u>, agree, contract, cov-

enant, cut a deal, promise, stipulate, transact

barge noun <u>canal boat</u>, flatboat, lighter, narrow boat

bark[1] noun, verb <u>yap</u>, bay, growl, howl, snarl, woof, yelp

bark[2] noun <u>covering</u>, casing, cortex (Anatomy, botany), crust, husk, rind, skin

barmy adjective Also **balmy** Slang <u>insane</u>, crazy, daft (informal), foolish, idiotic, nuts (slang), out of one's mind, stupid

➤ **Antonyms**

all there (informal), in one's right mind, of sound mind, rational, reasonable, sane, sensible

barracks plural noun <u>camp</u>, billet, encampment, garrison, quarters

barrage noun **1** <u>torrent</u>, burst, deluge, hail, mass, onslaught, plethora, stream **2** Military <u>bombardment</u>, battery, cannonade, fusillade, gunfire, salvo, shelling, volley

barren adjective **1** <u>infertile</u>, childless, sterile **2** <u>unproductive</u>, arid, desert, desolate, dry, empty, unfruitful, waste

➤ **Antonyms**

≠<u>unproductive</u>: fecund, fertile, fruitful, lush, productive, profitable, rich, useful

barricade noun **1** <u>barrier</u>, blockade, bulwark, fence, obstruction, palisade, rampart, stockade ◆ verb **2** <u>bar</u>, block, blockade, defend, fortify, obstruct, protect, shut in

barrier noun **1** <u>barricade</u>, bar, blockade, boundary, fence, obstacle, obstruction, wall **2** <u>hindrance</u>, difficulty, drawback, handicap, hurdle, obstacle, restriction, stumbling block

barter verb <u>trade</u>, bargain, drive a hard bargain, exchange, haggle, sell, swap, traffic

base[1] noun **1** <u>bottom</u>, bed, foot, foundation, pedestal, rest, stand, support **2** <u>basis</u>, core, essence, heart, key, origin, root, source **3** <u>centre</u>, camp, headquarters, home, post, settlement, starting point, station ♦ verb **4** <u>found</u>, build, construct, depend, derive, establish, ground, hinge **5** <u>place</u>, locate, post, station

➤ **Antonyms**

noun ≠<u>bottom</u>: apex, crest, crown, peak, summit, top, vertex

base² adjective **1** <u>dishonourable</u>, contemptible, despicable, disreputable, evil, immoral, shameful, sordid, wicked **2** <u>counterfeit</u>, alloyed, debased, fake, forged, fraudulent, impure

➤ **Antonyms**

≠<u>dishonourable</u>: admirable, good, honest, honourable, just, moral, noble, pure, rare, righteous, upright, valuable, virtuous ≠<u>counterfeit</u>: pure, unalloyed

baseless adjective <u>unfounded</u>, groundless, unconfirmed, uncorroborated, ungrounded, unjustified, unsubstantiated, unsupported

➤ **Antonyms**

authenticated, confirmed, corroborated, proven, substantiated, supported, validated, verified, well-founded

bash verb **1** Informal <u>hit</u>, belt (informal), smash, sock (slang), strike, wallop (informal) ♦ noun **2** Informal <u>attempt</u>, crack (informal), go (informal), shot (informal), stab (informal), try

bashful adjective <u>shy</u>, blushing, coy, diffident, reserved, reticent, retiring, timid

➤ **Antonyms**

bold, brash, confident, egoistic, fearless, forward, impudent, pushy (informal), self-assured

basic adjective <u>essential</u>, elementary, fundamental, key, necessary, primary, vital

➤ **Antonyms**

minor, secondary, supplementary, trivial, unessential

basically adverb <u>essentially</u>, at heart, fundamentally, inherently, in substance, intrinsically, mostly, primarily

basics plural noun <u>essentials</u>, brass tacks (informal), fundamentals, nitty-gritty (informal), nuts and bolts (informal), principles, rudiments

basis noun <u>foundation</u>, base, bottom, footing, ground, groundwork, support

bask verb <u>lie in</u>, laze, loll, lounge, relax, sunbathe, swim in

bass adjective <u>deep</u>, deep-toned, low, low-pitched, resonant, sonorous

bastard noun **1** Informal, offensive <u>rogue</u>, blackguard, miscreant, reprobate, scoundrel, villain, wretch **2** <u>illegitimate child</u>, love child, natural child

bastion noun <u>stronghold</u>, bulwark, citadel, defence, fortress, mainstay, prop, rock, support, tower of strength

bat noun, verb <u>hit</u>, bang, smack, strike, swat, thump, wallop (informal), whack

batch noun <u>group</u>, amount, assemblage, bunch, collection, crowd, lot, pack, quantity, set

bath noun **1** <u>wash</u>, cleansing, douche, scrubbing, shower, soak, tub ♦ verb **2** <u>wash</u>, bathe, clean, douse, scrub down, shower, soak

bathe verb **1** <u>swim</u> **2** <u>wash</u>, cleanse, rinse **3** <u>cover</u>, flood, immerse, steep, suffuse

baton noun <u>stick</u>, club, crook, mace, rod, sceptre, staff, truncheon, wand

batten verb, usually with **down** <u>fasten</u>, board up, clamp down, cover up, fix, nail down, secure, tighten

batter verb <u>beat</u>, buffet, clobber (slang), pelt, pound, pummel, thrash, wallop (informal)

battery noun <u>artillery</u>, cannon, cannonry, gun emplacements, guns

battle noun **1** <u>fight</u>, action, attack, combat, encounter, engagement, hostilities, skirmish **2** <u>conflict</u>, campaign, contest, crusade, dispute, struggle ♦ verb **2** <u>struggle</u>, argue, clamour, dispute, fight, lock horns, strive, war

> **► Antonyms**

noun ≠fight, conflict: accord, agreement, armistice, ceasefire, concord, entente, peace, suspension of hostilities, truce

battlefield noun battleground, combat zone, field, field of battle, front

battleship noun warship, gunboat, man-of-war

batty adjective crazy, daft (informal), dotty (slang, chiefly Brit.), eccentric, mad, odd, peculiar, potty (Brit. informal), touched

bauble noun trinket, bagatelle, gewgaw, gimcrack, knick-knack, plaything, toy, trifle

baulk see BALK

bawdy adjective rude, coarse, dirty, indecent, lascivious, lecherous, lewd, ribald, salacious, smutty

> **► Antonyms**

chaste, clean, decent, good, modest, respectable, seemly, virtuous

bawl verb 1 cry, blubber, sob, wail, weep 2 shout, bellow, call, clamour, howl, roar, yell

bay[1] noun inlet, bight, cove, gulf, natural harbour, sound

bay[2] noun recess, alcove, compartment, niche, nook, opening

bay[3] verb, noun howl, bark, clamour, cry, growl, yelp

bazaar noun 1 fair, bring-and-buy, fête, sale of work 2 market, exchange, marketplace

be verb exist, be alive, breathe, inhabit, live

beach noun shore, coast, sands, seashore, seaside, water's edge

beached adjective stranded, abandoned, aground, ashore, deserted, grounded, high and dry, marooned, wrecked

beacon noun signal, beam, bonfire, flare, lighthouse, sign, watchtower

bead noun drop, blob, bubble, dot, droplet, globule, pellet, pill

beady adjective bright, gleaming,

glinting, glittering, sharp, shining

beak noun 1 bill, mandible, neb (archaic or dialect), nib 2 Slang nose, proboscis, snout

beam noun 1 smile, grin 2 ray, gleam, glimmer, glint, glow, shaft, streak, stream 3 rafter, girder, joist, plank, spar, support, timber ♦ verb 4 smile, grin 5 radiate, glare, gleam, glitter, glow, shine 6 send out, broadcast, emit, transmit

bear verb 1 support, have, hold, maintain, possess, shoulder, sustain, uphold 2 carry, bring, convey, hump (Brit. slang), move, take, transport 3 produce, beget, breed, bring forth, engender, generate, give birth to, yield 4 tolerate, abide, allow, brook, endure, permit, put up with (informal), stomach, suffer

> **► Antonyms**

≠support: abandon, cease, desert, discontinue, drop, give up, leave, quit, relinquish ≠carry: drop, put down, shed

bearable adjective tolerable, admissible, endurable, manageable, passable, sufferable, supportable, sustainable

> **► Antonyms**

insufferable, insupportable, intolerable, oppressive, too much (informal), unacceptable, unbearable, unendurable

bearer noun carrier, agent, conveyor, messenger, porter, runner, servant

bearing noun 1 usually with on or upon relevance, application, connection, import, pertinence, reference, relation, significance 2 manner, air, aspect, attitude, behaviour, demeanour, deportment, posture

> **► Antonyms**

≠relevance: inappositeness, inappropriateness, irrelevance

bearings plural noun position, aim, course, direction, location, orientation, situation, track, way, whereabouts

bear out verb support, confirm,

beast noun **1** animal, brute, creature **2** brute, barbarian, fiend, monster, ogre, sadist, savage, swine

beastly adjective unpleasant, awful, disagreeable, horrid, mean, nasty, rotten

➤ **Antonyms**

agreeable, fine, good, pleasant

beat verb **1** hit, bang, batter, buffet, knock, pound, strike, thrash **2** flap, flutter **3** throb, palpitate, pound, pulsate, quake, thump, vibrate **4** defeat, conquer, outdo, overcome, surpass, vanquish ♦ noun **5** throb, palpitation, pulsation, pulse **6** route, circuit, course, path, rounds, way **7** rhythm, accent, cadence, metre, stress, time

beaten adjective **1** stirred, blended, foamy, frothy, mixed, whipped, whisked **2** defeated, cowed, overcome, overwhelmed, thwarted, vanquished

beat up verb Informal assault, attack, batter, beat the living daylights out of (informal), knock about or around, thrash

beau noun **1** Chiefly U.S. boyfriend, admirer, fiancé, lover, suitor, sweetheart **2** dandy, coxcomb, fop, gallant, ladies' man

beautiful adjective attractive, charming, delightful, exquisite, fair, fine, gorgeous, handsome, lovely, pleasing

➤ **Antonyms**

awful, bad, hideous, repulsive, terrible, ugly, unattractive, unpleasant, unsightly

beautify verb make beautiful, adorn, decorate, embellish, festoon, garnish, glamorize, ornament

beauty noun **1** attractiveness, charm, comeliness, elegance, exquisiteness, glamour, grace, handsomeness, loveliness **2** belle, good-looker, lovely (slang), stunner (informal)

➤ **Antonyms**

≠attractiveness: repulsiveness, ugliness, unpleasantness

becalmed adjective still, motionless, settled, stranded, stuck

because conjunction since, as, by reason of, in that, on account of, owing to, thanks to

beckon verb gesture, bid, gesticulate, motion, nod, signal, summon, wave at

become verb **1** come to be, alter to, be transformed into, change into, develop into, grow into, mature into, ripen into **2** suit, embellish, enhance, fit, flatter, set off

becoming adjective **1** appropriate, compatible, fitting, in keeping, proper, seemly, suitable, worthy **2** flattering, attractive, comely, enhancing, graceful, neat, pretty, tasteful

➤ **Antonyms**

≠appropriate: improper, inappropriate, unfit, unsuitable, unworthy ≠flattering: ugly, unattractive, unbecoming, unflattering

bed noun **1** bedstead, berth, bunk, cot, couch, divan **2** plot, area, border, garden, patch, row, strip **3** bottom, base, foundation, groundwork

bedevil verb **1** torment, afflict, distress, harass, plague, trouble, vex, worry **2** confuse, confound

bedlam noun pandemonium, chaos, commotion, confusion, furore, tumult, turmoil, uproar

bedraggled adjective messy, dirty, dishevelled, disordered, muddied, unkempt, untidy

bedridden adjective confined to bed, confined, flat on one's back, incapacitated, laid up (informal)

bedrock noun **1** bottom, bed, foundation, rock bottom, substratum, substructure **2** basics, basis, core, essentials, fundamentals, nuts and bolts (informal), roots

beefy adjective Informal brawny, bulky, hulking, muscular, stocky,

strapping, sturdy, thickset
➤ **Antonyms**
frail, puny, scrawny, skinny

befall *verb* Archaic or literary <u>happen</u>, chance, come to pass, fall, occur, take place, transpire (*informal*)

befitting *adjective* <u>appropriate</u>, apposite, becoming, fit, fitting, proper, right, seemly, suitable
➤ **Antonyms**
improper, inappropriate, irrelevant, unbecoming, unfit, unsuitable, wrong

before *preposition* **1** <u>ahead of</u>, in advance of, in front of **2** <u>earlier than</u>, in advance of, prior to **3** <u>in the presence of</u>, in front of ◆ *adverb* **4** <u>previously</u>, ahead, earlier, formerly, in advance, sooner **5** <u>in front</u>, ahead
➤ **Antonyms**
preposition ≠<u>ahead of</u>: <u>earlier than</u>: after, behind, following, succeeding ◆ *adverb* ≠<u>previously</u>, <u>in front</u>: after, afterwards, behind, later, subsequently, thereafter

beforehand *adverb* <u>in advance</u>, ahead of time, already, before, earlier, in anticipation, previously, sooner

befriend *verb* <u>help</u>, aid, assist, back, encourage, side with, stand by, support, welcome

beg *verb* **1** <u>scrounge</u>, cadge, seek charity, solicit charity, sponge on, touch (someone) for (*slang*) **2** <u>implore</u>, beseech, entreat, petition, plead, request, solicit
➤ **Antonyms**
≠<u>scrounge</u>: claim, demand, exact, extort, insist on ≠<u>implore</u>: award, bestow, confer, contribute, donate, give, grant, impart, present

beggar *noun* <u>tramp</u>, bag lady (*chiefly U.S.*), bum (*informal*), down-and-out, pauper, vagrant

beggarly *adjective* <u>poor</u>, destitute, impoverished, indigent, needy, poverty-stricken

begin *verb* **1** <u>start</u>, commence, embark on, initiate, instigate, institute, prepare, set about **2** <u>happen</u>, appear, arise, come into being, emerge, originate, start
➤ **Antonyms**
cease, complete, end, finish, stop, terminate

beginner *noun* <u>novice</u>, amateur, apprentice, learner, neophyte, starter, trainee, tyro
➤ **Antonyms**
authority, expert, master, old hand, past master *or* past mistress, pro (*informal*), professional, veteran

beginning *noun* **1** <u>start</u>, birth, commencement, inauguration, inception, initiation, onset, opening, origin, outset **2** <u>seed</u>, fount, germ, root
➤ **Antonyms**
≠<u>start</u>: closing, completion, conclusion, end, ending, finish, termination

begrudge *verb* <u>resent</u>, be jealous, be reluctant, be stingy, envy, grudge

beguile *verb* **1** <u>fool</u>, cheat, deceive, delude, dupe, hoodwink, mislead, take for a ride (*informal*), trick **2** <u>charm</u>, amuse, distract, divert, engross, entertain, occupy
➤ **Antonyms**
≠<u>fool</u>: alert, enlighten, put right

beguiling *adjective* <u>charming</u>, alluring, attractive, bewitching, captivating, enchanting, enthralling, intriguing

behave *verb* **1** <u>act</u>, function, operate, perform, run, work **2** <u>conduct oneself properly</u>, act correctly, keep one's nose clean, mind one's manners
➤ **Antonyms**
≠<u>conduct oneself properly</u>: act up (*informal*), be bad, be naughty, carry on (*informal*), get up to mischief (*informal*), misbehave, muck about (*Brit. slang*)

behaviour *noun* **1** <u>conduct</u>, actions, bearing, demeanour, deportment, manner, manners, ways **2** <u>action</u>, functioning, operation, performance

behind *preposition* **1** <u>after</u>, at the back of, at the heels of, in the rear of, following, later than **2** <u>causing</u>, at the bottom of, initiating, instigating, responsible for **3** <u>supporting</u>, backing, for, in agreement, on the side of ♦ *adverb* **4** <u>after</u>, afterwards, following, in the wake (of), next, subsequently **5** <u>overdue</u>, behindhand, in arrears, in debt ♦ *noun* **6** *Informal* <u>bottom</u>, butt (*U.S. & Canad. informal*), buttocks, posterior

➤ **Antonyms**

adverb ≠<u>after</u>: earlier than, in advance of, in front of, in the presence of, prior to ≠<u>overdue</u>: ahead, earlier, formerly, in advance, previously, sooner

behold *verb Archaic or literary* <u>look at</u>, observe, perceive, regard, survey, view, watch, witness

beholden *adjective* <u>indebted</u>, bound, grateful, obliged, owing, under obligation

being *noun* **1** <u>existence</u>, life, reality **2** <u>nature</u>, entity, essence, soul, spirit, substance **3** <u>creature</u>, human being, individual, living thing

➤ **Antonyms**

≠<u>existence</u>: nonbeing, nonexistence, nothingness, oblivion

belated *adjective* <u>late</u>, behindhand, behind time, delayed, late in the day, overdue, tardy

belch *verb* **1** <u>burp</u> (*informal*), hiccup **2** <u>emit</u>, discharge, disgorge, erupt, give off, spew forth, vent

beleaguered *adjective* **1** <u>harassed</u>, badgered, hassled (*informal*), persecuted, pestered, plagued, put upon, vexed **2** <u>besieged</u>, assailed, beset, blockaded, hemmed in, surrounded

belief *noun* **1** <u>trust</u>, assurance, confidence, conviction, feeling, impression, judgment, notion, opinion **2** <u>faith</u>, credo, creed, doctrine, dogma, ideology, principles, tenet

➤ **Antonyms**

≠<u>trust</u>: disbelief, distrust, doubt,

dubiety, incredulity, mistrust, scepticism

believable *adjective* <u>credible</u>, authentic, imaginable, likely, plausible, possible, probable, trustworthy

➤ **Antonyms**

doubtful, dubious, implausible, incredible, questionable, unacceptable, unbelievable

believe *verb* **1** <u>accept</u>, be certain of, be convinced of, credit, depend on, have faith in, rely on, swear by, trust **2** <u>think</u>, assume, gather, imagine, judge, presume, reckon, speculate, suppose

➤ **Antonyms**

disbelieve, distrust, doubt, know, question

believer *noun* <u>follower</u>, adherent, convert, devotee, disciple, supporter, upholder, zealot

➤ **Antonyms**

agnostic, atheist, disbeliever, doubting Thomas, infidel, sceptic, unbeliever

belittle *verb* <u>disparage</u>, decry, denigrate, deprecate, deride, scoff at, scorn, sneer at

➤ **Antonyms**

boast about, exalt, praise, vaunt

belligerent *adjective* **1** <u>aggressive</u>, bellicose, combative, hostile, pugnacious, unfriendly, warlike, warring ♦ *noun* **2** <u>fighter</u>, combatant, warring nation

➤ **Antonyms**

adjective ≠<u>aggressive</u>: amicable, conciliatory, friendly, nonviolent

bellow *noun, verb* <u>shout</u>, bawl, cry, howl, roar, scream, shriek, yell

belly *noun* **1** <u>stomach</u>, abdomen, corporation (*informal*), gut, insides (*informal*), paunch, potbelly, tummy ♦ *verb* **2** <u>swell out</u>, billow, bulge, fill, spread, swell

bellyful *noun* <u>surfeit</u>, enough, excess, glut, plateful, plenty, satiety, too much

belonging *noun* <u>relationship</u>, acceptance, affinity, association, attachment, fellowship, inclusion, loyalty, rapport

belongings plural noun possessions, accoutrements, chattels, effects, gear, goods, paraphernalia, personal property, stuff, things

belong to verb **1** be the property of, be at the disposal of, be held by, be owned by **2** be a member of, be affiliated to, be allied to, be associated with, be included in

beloved adjective dear, admired, adored, darling, loved, pet, precious, prized, treasured, valued, worshipped

below preposition **1** lesser, inferior, subject, subordinate **2** less than, lower than ♦ adverb **3** lower, beneath, down, under, underneath

belt noun **1** waistband, band, cummerbund, girdle, girth, sash **2** Geography zone, area, district, layer, region, stretch, strip, tract

bemoan verb lament, bewail, deplore, grieve for, mourn, regret, rue, weep for

bemused adjective puzzled, at sea, bewildered, confused, flummoxed, muddled, nonplussed, perplexed

bench noun **1** seat, form, pew, settle, stall **2** worktable, board, counter, table, trestle table, workbench **3** the bench court, courtroom, judges, judiciary, magistrates, tribunal

benchmark noun reference point, criterion, gauge, level, measure, model, norm, par, standard, yardstick

bend verb **1** curve, arc, arch, bow, lean, turn, twist, veer ♦ noun **2** curve, angle, arc, arch, bow, corner, loop, turn, twist

beneath preposition **1** under, below, lower than, underneath **2** inferior to, below, less than **3** unworthy of, unbefitting ♦ adverb **4** underneath, below, in a lower place

► **Antonyms**

preposition ≠under: above, atop,

higher than, on top of, over, upon ≠inferior to: higher than, over

benefactor noun supporter, backer, donor, helper, patron, philanthropist, sponsor, well-wisher

beneficial adjective helpful, advantageous, benign, favourable, profitable, useful, valuable, wholesome

► **Antonyms**

detrimental, disadvantageous, harmful, pernicious, useless

beneficiary noun recipient, heir, inheritor, payee, receiver

benefit noun **1** help, advantage, aid, asset, assistance, favour, good, profit ♦ verb **2** help, aid, assist, avail, enhance, further, improve, profit

► **Antonyms**

noun ≠help: damage, detriment, disadvantage, downside, harm, impairment, injury ♦ verb ≠help: damage, harm, impair, injure, worsen

benevolent adjective kind, altruistic, benign, caring, charitable, generous, philanthropic

benign adjective **1** kindly, amiable, friendly, genial, kind, obliging, sympathetic **2** Medical harmless, curable, remediable

► **Antonyms**

≠kindly: harsh, severe, stern, unfavourable, unkind, unsympathetic ≠harmless: malignant

bent adjective **1** curved, angled, arched, bowed, crooked, hunched, stooped, twisted **2** bent on determined to, disposed to, fixed on, inclined to, insistent on, predisposed to, resolved on, set on ♦ noun **3** inclination, ability, aptitude, leaning, penchant, preference, propensity, tendency

► **Antonyms**

adjective ≠curved: erect, even, in line, level, straight, true, upright

bequeath verb leave, bestow, endow, entrust, give, grant, hand down, impart, pass on, will

bequest noun legacy, bestowal,

endowment, estate, gift, inheritance, settlement

berate *verb* scold, castigate, censure, chide, criticize, harangue, rebuke, reprimand, reprove, tell off (*informal*), upbraid

➤ **Antonyms**
applaud, approve, commend, compliment, congratulate, praise

bereavement *noun* loss, affliction, death, deprivation, misfortune, tribulation

bereft *adjective* deprived, devoid, lacking, parted from, robbed of, wanting

berserk *adverb* crazy, amok, enraged, frantic, frenzied, mad, raging, wild

berth *noun* 1 bunk, bed, billet, hammock 2 *Nautical* anchorage, dock, harbour, haven, pier, port, quay, wharf ♦ *verb* 3 *Nautical* anchor, dock, drop anchor, land, moor, tie up

beseech *verb* beg, ask, call upon, entreat, implore, plead, pray, solicit

beset *verb* plague, bedevil, harass, pester, trouble

beside *preposition* 1 next to, abreast of, adjacent to, alongside, at the side of, close to, near, nearby, neighbouring 2 **beside oneself** distraught, apoplectic, at the end of one's tether, demented, desperate, frantic, frenzied, out of one's mind, unhinged

besides *adverb* 1 too, also, as well, further, furthermore, in addition, into the bargain, moreover, otherwise, what's more ♦ *preposition* 2 apart from, barring, excepting, excluding, in addition to, other than, over and above, without

besiege *verb* 1 surround, blockade, encircle, hem in, lay siege to, shut in 2 harass, badger, harry, hassle (*informal*), hound, nag, pester, plague

besotted *adjective* infatuated, doting, hypnotized, smitten, spellbound

best *adjective* 1 finest, foremost, leading, most excellent, outstanding, pre-eminent, principal, supreme, unsurpassed ♦ *adverb* 2 most highly, extremely, greatly, most deeply, most fully ♦ *noun* 3 finest, cream, *crème de la crème*, elite, flower, pick, prime, top

bestial *adjective* brutal, barbaric, beastly, brutish, inhuman, savage, sordid

bestow *verb* present, award, commit, give, grant, hand out, impart, lavish

➤ **Antonyms**
acquire, attain, come by, gain, get, obtain, procure

bet *noun* 1 gamble, long shot, risk, speculation, stake, venture, wager ♦ *verb* 2 gamble, chance, hazard, risk, speculate, stake, venture, wager

betoken *verb* indicate, bode, denote, promise, represent, signify, suggest

betray *verb* 1 be disloyal, be treacherous, be unfaithful, break one's promise, double-cross (*informal*), inform on or against, sell out (*informal*), stab in the back 2 give away, disclose, divulge, expose, let slip, reveal, uncover, unmask

betrayal *noun* 1 disloyalty, deception, double-cross (*informal*), sellout (*informal*), treachery, treason, trickery 2 giving away, disclosure, divulgence, revelation

➤ **Antonyms**
≠disloyalty: constancy, devotion, faithfulness, fidelity, loyalty, steadfastness, trustworthiness
≠giving away: keeping, keeping secret

better *adjective* 1 superior, excelling, finer, greater, higher-quality, more desirable, preferable, surpassing 2 well, cured, fully recovered, on the mend (*informal*), recovering, stronger ♦ *adverb* 3 in a more excellent manner, in a superior way, more advantageously, more attractively, more competently, more effectively **4** <u>to a greater degree</u>, more completely, more thoroughly ♦ *verb* **5** <u>improve</u>, enhance, further, raise

➤ **Antonyms**

adjective ≠<u>superior</u>: inferior, lesser, smaller, worse ≠<u>well</u>: worse ♦ *adverb* ≠<u>in a more excellent manner</u>: worse ≠*verb* ≠<u>improve</u>: go downhill, lessen, lower, weaken, worsen

between *preposition* <u>amidst</u>, among, betwixt, in the middle of, mid

beverage *noun* <u>drink</u>, liquid, liquor, refreshment

bevy *noun* <u>group</u>, band, bunch (*informal*), collection, company, crowd, gathering, pack, troupe

bewail *verb* <u>lament</u>, bemoan, cry over, deplore, grieve for, moan, mourn, regret

beware *verb* <u>be careful</u>, be cautious, be wary, guard against, heed, look out, mind, take heed, watch out

bewilder *verb* <u>confound</u>, baffle, bemuse, confuse, flummox, mystify, nonplus, perplex, puzzle

bewildered *adjective* <u>confused</u>, at a loss, at sea, baffled, flummoxed, mystified, nonplussed, perplexed, puzzled

bewitch *verb* <u>enchant</u>, beguile, captivate, charm, enrapture, entrance, fascinate, hypnotize

➤ **Antonyms**

disgust, give one the creeps (*informal*), repel, repulse, turn off (*informal*)

bewitched *adjective* <u>enchanted</u>, charmed, entranced, fascinated, mesmerized, spellbound, under a spell

beyond *preposition* **1** <u>past</u>, above, apart from, at a distance, away from, over **2** <u>exceeding</u>, out of reach of, superior to, surpassing

bias *noun* **1** <u>prejudice</u>, favouritism, inclination, leaning, partiality, tendency ♦ *verb* **2** <u>prejudice</u>, distort, influence, predispose, slant, sway, twist, warp, weight

➤ **Antonyms**

noun ≠<u>prejudice</u>: equality, equity, fairness, impartiality, neutrality, objectivity, open-mindedness

biased *adjective* <u>prejudiced</u>, distorted, one-sided, partial, slanted, weighted

bicker *verb* <u>quarrel</u>, argue, disagree, dispute, fight, row (*informal*), squabble, wrangle

➤ **Antonyms**

agree, assent, concur, cooperate, get on

bid *verb* **1** <u>offer</u>, proffer, propose, submit, tender **2** <u>say</u>, call, greet, tell, wish **3** <u>tell</u>, ask, command, direct, instruct, order, require ♦ *noun* **4** <u>offer</u>, advance, amount, price, proposal, sum, tender **5** <u>attempt</u>, crack (*informal*), effort, go (*informal*), stab (*informal*), try

bidding *noun* <u>order</u>, beck and call, command, direction, instruction, request, summons

big *adjective* **1** <u>large</u>, enormous, extensive, great, huge, immense, massive, substantial, vast **2** <u>important</u>, eminent, influential, leading, main, powerful, prominent, significant **3** <u>grown-up</u>, adult, elder, grown, mature **4** <u>generous</u>, altruistic, benevolent, gracious, magnanimous, noble, unselfish

➤ **Antonyms**

≠<u>large</u>: diminutive, insignificant, little, miniature, petite, pygmy or pigmy, small, tiny, wee ≠<u>important</u>: humble, ignoble, insignificant, minor, modest, ordinary, unimportant, unknown ≠<u>grown-up</u>: immature, young

bighead *noun* *Informal* <u>boaster</u>, braggart, know-all (*informal*)

bigheaded *adjective* <u>boastful</u>, arrogant, cocky, conceited, egotistic, immodest, overconfident, swollen-headed

bigot *noun* <u>fanatic</u>, racist, sectarian, zealot

bigoted *adjective* <u>intolerant</u>, biased, dogmatic, narrow-minded, opinionated, prejudiced, sectarian

➤ **Antonyms**

broad-minded, equitable, open-minded, tolerant, unbiased, unbigoted, unprejudiced

bigotry noun intolerance, bias, discrimination, dogmatism, fanaticism, narrow-mindedness, prejudice, sectarianism

➤ **Antonyms**

broad-mindedness, open-mindedness, permissiveness, tolerance

bigwig noun Informal important person, big hitter (informal), big shot (informal), celebrity, dignitary, mogul, personage, somebody, V.I.P.

➤ **Antonyms**

nobody, nonentity, nothing

bill[1] noun 1 charges, account, invoice, reckoning, score, statement, tally 2 proposal, measure, piece of legislation, projected law 3 advertisement, bulletin, circular, handbill, handout, leaflet, notice, placard, poster 4 list, agenda, card, catalogue, inventory, listing, programme, roster, schedule ♦ verb 5 charge, debit, invoice 6 advertise, announce, give advance notice of, post

bill[2] noun beak, mandible, neb (archaic or dialect), nib

billet verb 1 quarter, accommodate, berth, station ♦ noun 2 quarters, accommodation, barracks, lodging

billow noun 1 wave, breaker, crest, roller, surge, swell, tide ♦ verb 2 surge, balloon, belly, puff up, rise up, roll, swell

bind verb 1 tie, fasten, hitch, lash, secure, stick, strap, wrap 2 oblige, compel, constrain, engage, force, necessitate, require ♦ noun 3 Informal nuisance, bore, difficulty, dilemma, drag (informal), pain in the neck (informal), quandary, spot (informal)

➤ **Antonyms**

verb ≠tie: free, loosen, release, unbind, undo, unfasten, untie

binding adjective compulsory, indissoluble, irrevocable, mandatory, necessary, obligatory, unalterable

➤ **Antonyms**

noncompulsory, optional, unforced, voluntary

binge noun Informal bout, bender (informal), feast, fling, orgy, spree

biography noun life story, account, curriculum vitae, CV, life, memoir, profile, record

birth noun 1 childbirth, delivery, nativity, parturition 2 ancestry, background, blood, breeding, lineage, parentage, pedigree, stock

➤ **Antonyms**

≠childbirth: death, demise, end, extinction, passing, passing away or on

bisect verb cut in two, cross, cut across, divide in two, halve, intersect, separate, split

bit[1] noun piece, crumb, fragment, grain, morsel, part, scrap, speck

bit[2] noun curb, brake, check, restraint, snaffle

bitchy adjective Informal spiteful, backbiting, catty (informal), mean, nasty, snide, vindictive

➤ **Antonyms**

charitable, generous, kindly, magnanimous, nice

bite verb 1 cut, chew, gnaw, nip, pierce, pinch, snap, tear, wound ♦ noun 2 wound, nip, pinch, prick, smarting, sting, tooth marks 3 snack, food, light meal, morsel, mouthful, piece, refreshment, taste

biting adjective 1 piercing, bitter, cutting, harsh, penetrating, sharp 2 sarcastic, caustic, cutting, incisive, mordant, scathing, stinging, trenchant, vitriolic

bitter adjective 1 sour, acid, acrid, astringent, harsh, sharp, tart, unsweetened, vinegary 2 resentful, acrimonious, begrudging, hostile, sore, sour, sullen 3 freezing, biting, fierce, intense, severe, stinging

➤ **Antonyms**

≠*sour*: bland, mellow, mild, pleasant, sugary, sweet ≠*resentful*: appreciative, grateful, happy, mellow, pleasant, sweet, thankful ≠*freezing*: balmy, gentle, mild, pleasant

bitterness noun **1** sourness, acerbity, acidity, sharpness, tartness **2** resentment, acrimony, animosity, asperity, grudge, hostility, rancour, sarcasm

bizarre adjective strange, eccentric, extraordinary, fantastic, freakish, ludicrous, outlandish, peculiar, unusual, weird, zany

➤ **Antonyms**

common, customary, normal, ordinary, regular, routine, standard, typical

blab verb tell, blurt out, disclose, divulge, give away, let slip, let the cat out of the bag, reveal, spill the beans (*informal*)

black adjective **1** dark, dusky, ebony, jet, pitch-black, raven, sable, swarthy **2** gloomy, depressing, dismal, foreboding, hopeless, ominous, sad, sombre **3** angry, furious, hostile, menacing, resentful, sullen, threatening **4** wicked, bad, evil, iniquitous, nefarious, villainous ♦ verb **5** boycott, ban, bar, blacklist

➤ **Antonyms**

adjective ≠*dark*: bright, illuminated, light, lighted, lit, sunny ≠*gloomy*: cheerful, happy, warm ≠*angry*: amicable, cheerful, friendly, happy, pleased, warm ≠*wicked*: good, honourable, moral, pure

blacken verb **1** darken, befoul, begrime, cloud, dirty, make black, smudge, soil **2** discredit, defame, denigrate, malign, slander, smear, smirch, vilify

blackguard noun scoundrel, bastard (*offensive*), bounder (*old-fashioned Brit. slang*), rascal, rogue, swine, villain

blacklist verb exclude, ban, bar, boycott, debar, expel, reject, snub

black magic noun witchcraft, black art, diabolism, necromancy, sorcery, voodoo, wizardry

blackmail noun **1** threat, extortion, hush money (*slang*), intimidation, ransom ♦ verb **2** threaten, coerce, compel, demand, extort, hold to ransom, intimidate, squeeze

blackness noun darkness, duskiness, gloom, murkiness, swarthiness

➤ **Antonyms**

brightness, brilliance, light, lightness, luminescence, luminosity, phosphorescence, radiance

blackout noun **1** unconsciousness, coma, faint, loss of consciousness, oblivion, swoon **2** noncommunication, censorship, radio silence, secrecy, suppression, withholding news

black sheep noun disgrace, bad egg (*old-fashioned informal*), dropout, ne'er-do-well, outcast, prodigal, renegade, reprobate, wastrel

blame verb **1** hold responsible, accuse **2** criticize, censure, chide, condemn, find fault with, reproach ♦ noun **3** responsibility, accountability, accusation, culpability, fault, guilt, liability, onus

➤ **Antonyms**

verb ≠*hold responsible*: absolve, acquit, clear, excuse, exonerate, forgive, vindicate ≠*criticize*: approve of, commend, compliment, praise ♦ noun ≠*responsibility*: absolution, excuse, exoneration, vindication

blameless adjective innocent, above suspicion, clean, faultless, guiltless, immaculate, impeccable, irreproachable, perfect, unblemished, virtuous

➤ **Antonyms**

at fault, culpable, guilty, responsible, to blame

blameworthy adjective reprehensible, discreditable, disreputable, indefensible, inexcusable, iniquitous, reproachable, shameful

bland adjective dull, boring, flat,

humdrum, insipid, tasteless, unexciting, uninspiring, vapid

➤ **Antonyms**

distinctive, exciting, interesting, stimulating

blank adjective **1** unmarked, bare, clean, clear, empty, plain, void, white **2** expressionless, deadpan, empty, impassive, poker-faced (informal), vacant, vague ♦ noun **3** empty space, emptiness, gap, nothingness, space, vacancy, vacuum, void

➤ **Antonyms**

adjective ≠unmarked: completed, filled in, full, marked ≠expressionless: alert, expressive, intelligent, interested, lively

blanket noun **1** cover, coverlet, rug **2** covering, carpet, cloak, coat, layer, mantle, sheet ♦ verb **3** cover, cloak, coat, conceal, hide, mask, obscure, suppress

blare verb sound out, blast, clamour, clang, resound, roar, scream, trumpet

blarney noun flattery, blandishment, cajolery, coaxing, soft soap (informal), spiel, sweet talk (informal), wheedling

blasé adjective indifferent, apathetic, lukewarm, nonchalant, offhand, unconcerned

➤ **Antonyms**

enthusiastic, excited, interested

blaspheme verb curse, abuse, damn, desecrate, execrate, profane, revile, swear

blasphemous adjective irreverent, godless, impious, irreligious, profane, sacrilegious, ungodly

➤ **Antonyms**

devout, God-fearing, godly, pious, religious, respectful, reverent, reverential

blasphemy noun irreverence, cursing, desecration, execration, impiety, profanity, sacrilege, swearing

blast noun **1** explosion, bang, burst, crash, detonation, discharge, eruption, outburst, salvo, volley **2** gust, gale, squall, storm, strong breeze, tempest **3**

blare, blow, clang, honk, peal, scream, toot, wail ♦ verb **4** blow up, break up, burst, demolish, destroy, explode, put paid to, ruin, shatter

blastoff noun launch, discharge, expulsion, firing, launching, lift-off, projection, shot

blatant adjective obvious, brazen, conspicuous, flagrant, glaring, obtrusive, ostentatious, overt

➤ **Antonyms**

hidden, inconspicuous, quiet, subtle, tasteful, unnoticeable, unobtrusive

blaze noun **1** fire, bonfire, conflagration, flames **2** glare, beam, brilliance, flare, flash, gleam, glitter, glow, light, radiance ♦ verb **3** burn, fire, flame **4** shine, beam, flare, flash, glare, gleam, glow

bleach verb whiten, blanch, fade, grow pale, lighten, wash out

bleak adjective **1** exposed, bare, barren, desolate, unsheltered, weather-beaten, windswept **2** dismal, cheerless, depressing, discouraging, dreary, gloomy, grim, hopeless, joyless, sombre

➤ **Antonyms**

≠exposed: protected, sheltered, shielded ≠dismal: cheerful, cosy, encouraging, promising

bleary adjective dim, blurred, blurry, foggy, fuzzy, hazy, indistinct, misty, murky

bleed verb **1** lose blood, flow, gush, ooze, run, shed blood, spurt **2** draw or take blood, extract, leech **3** Informal extort, drain, exhaust, fleece, milk, squeeze

blemish noun **1** mark, blot, defect, disfigurement, fault, flaw, imperfection, smudge, stain, taint ♦ verb **2** mark, damage, disfigure, impair, injure, mar, spoil, stain, sully, taint, tarnish

➤ **Antonyms**

noun ≠mark: enhancement, improvement, ornament, refinement ♦ verb ≠mark: correct, enhance, improve, perfect, purify, refine, restore

blend *verb* **1** mix, amalgamate, combine, compound, merge, mingle, unite **2** go well, complement, fit, go with, harmonize, suit ♦ *noun* **3** mixture, alloy, amalgamation, combination, compound, concoction, mix, synthesis, union

bless *verb* **1** sanctify, anoint, consecrate, dedicate, exalt, hallow, ordain **2** endow, bestow, favour, give, grace, grant, provide

➤ **Antonyms**

≠sanctify: anathematize, curse, damn, excommunicate ≠endow: afflict, blight, burden, curse, plague, torment, trouble

blessed *adjective* **1** holy, adored, beatified, divine, hallowed, revered, sacred, sanctified

blessing *noun* **1** benediction, benison, commendation, consecration, dedication, grace, invocation, thanksgiving **2** approval, backing, consent, favour, good wishes, leave, permission, sanction, support **3** benefit, favour, gift, godsend, good fortune, help, kindness, service, windfall

➤ **Antonyms**

≠benediction: condemnation, curse, malediction ≠approval: disapproval, disfavour, objection, reproof ≠benefit: damage, disadvantage, drawback, harm, misfortune

blight *noun* **1** curse, affliction, bane, contamination, corruption, evil, plague, pollution, scourge, woe **2** disease, canker, decay, fungus, infestation, mildew, pest, pestilence, rot ♦ *verb* **3** frustrate, crush, dash, disappoint, mar, ruin, spoil, undo, wreck

➤ **Antonyms**

noun ≠curse: benefaction, blessing, boon, bounty, favour, godsend, help

blind *adjective* **1** sightless, eyeless, unseeing, unsighted, visionless **2** unaware of, careless, heedless, ignorant, inattentive, inconsider-

ate, indifferent, insensitive, oblivious, unconscious of **3** unreasoning, indiscriminate, prejudiced ♦ *noun* **4** cover, camouflage, cloak, façade, feint, front, mask, masquerade, screen, smoke screen

➤ **Antonyms**

adjective ≠sightless: seeing, sighted ≠unaware of: alive to, aware, conscious, heedful, knowledgeable, observant

blindly *adverb* **1** thoughtlessly, carelessly, heedlessly, inconsiderately, recklessly, senselessly **2** aimlessly, at random, indiscriminately, instinctively

blink *verb* **1** wink, bat, flutter **2** flicker, flash, gleam, glimmer, shine, twinkle, wink ♦ *noun* **3 on the blink** *Slang* not working (properly), faulty, malfunctioning, out of action, out of order, playing up

bliss *noun* joy, beatitude, blessedness, blissfulness, ecstasy, euphoria, felicity, gladness, happiness, heaven, nirvana, paradise, rapture

➤ **Antonyms**

anguish, distress, grief, heartbreak, misery, sadness, sorrow, unhappiness, woe, wretchedness

blissful *adjective* joyful, ecstatic, elated, enraptured, euphoric, happy, heavenly (*informal*), rapturous

blister *noun* sore, abscess, boil, carbuncle, cyst, pimple, pustule, swelling

blithe *adjective* heedless, careless, casual, indifferent, nonchalant, thoughtless, unconcerned, untroubled

➤ **Antonyms**

concerned, preoccupied, thoughtful

blitz *noun* attack, assault, blitzkrieg, bombardment, campaign, offensive, onslaught, raid, strike

blizzard *noun* snowstorm, blast, gale, squall, storm, tempest

bloat *verb* puff up, balloon, blow up, dilate, distend, enlarge, expand, inflate, swell

► **Antonyms**

contract, deflate, shrink, shrivel, wither, wrinkle

blob noun <u>drop</u>, ball, bead, bubble, dab, droplet, globule, lump, mass

bloc noun <u>group</u>, alliance, axis, coalition, faction, league, union

block noun 1 <u>piece</u>, bar, brick, chunk, hunk, ingot, lump, mass 2 <u>obstruction</u>, bar, barrier, blockage, hindrance, impediment, jam, obstacle ♦ verb 3 <u>obstruct</u>, bung up (informal), choke, clog, close, plug, stem the flow, stop up 4 <u>stop</u>, bar, check, halt, hinder, impede, obstruct, thwart

► **Antonyms**

verb ≠<u>obstruct</u>: clear, open, unblock, unclog ≠<u>stop</u>: advance, aid, facilitate, further, lend support to, promote, push, support

blockade noun <u>stoppage</u>, barricade, barrier, block, hindrance, impediment, obstacle, obstruction, restriction, siege

blockage noun <u>obstruction</u>, block, impediment, occlusion, stoppage

blockhead noun <u>idiot</u>, chump (informal), dunce, fool, nitwit, numbskull or numskull, thickhead, twit (informal, chiefly Brit.)

bloke noun Informal <u>man</u>, chap, character (informal), fellow, guy (informal), individual, person

blond, blonde adjective <u>fair</u>, fair-haired, fair-skinned, flaxen, golden-haired, light, tow-headed

blood noun 1 <u>lifeblood</u>, gore, vital fluid 2 <u>family</u>, ancestry, birth, descent, extraction, kinship, lineage, relations

bloodcurdling adjective <u>terrifying</u>, appalling, chilling, dreadful, fearful, frightening, hair-raising, horrendous, horrifying, scaring, spine-chilling

bloodshed noun <u>killing</u>, blood bath, blood-letting, butchery, carnage, gore, massacre, murder, slaughter, slaying

bloodthirsty adjective <u>cruel</u>, bar-

barous, brutal, cut-throat, ferocious, gory, murderous, savage, vicious, warlike

bloody adjective 1 <u>bloodstained</u>, bleeding, blood-soaked, blood-spattered, gaping, gory 2 <u>cruel</u>, ferocious, fierce, sanguinary, savage

bloom noun 1 <u>flower</u>, blossom, blossoming, bud, efflorescence, opening (of flowers) 2 <u>prime</u>, beauty, flourishing, health, heyday, vigour 3 <u>glow</u>, freshness, lustre, radiance ♦ verb 4 <u>blossom</u>, blow, bud, burgeon, open, sprout 5 <u>flourish</u>, develop, fare well, grow, prosper, succeed, thrive, wax

► **Antonyms**

noun ≠<u>glow</u>: bloodlessness, paleness, pallor, wanness, whiteness ♦ verb ≠<u>blossom</u>, <u>flourish</u>: decay, decline, die, fade, fail, perish, wane, wither

blossom noun 1 <u>flower</u>, bloom, bud, floret, flowers ♦ verb 2 <u>flower</u>, bloom, burgeon 3 <u>grow</u>, bloom, develop, flourish, mature, progress, prosper, thrive

blot noun 1 <u>spot</u>, blotch, mark, patch, smear, smudge, speck, splodge 2 <u>stain</u>, blemish, defect, fault, flaw, scar, spot, taint ♦ verb 3 <u>stain</u>, disgrace, mark, smirch, smudge, spoil, spot, sully, tarnish 4 <u>soak up</u>, absorb, dry, take up 5 <u>blot out</u>: a <u>obliterate</u>, darken, destroy, eclipse, efface, obscure, shadow b <u>erase</u>, cancel, expunge

blow[1] verb 1 <u>carry</u>, buffet, drive, fling, flutter, move, sweep, waft 2 <u>exhale</u>, breathe, pant, puff 3 <u>play</u>, blare, mouth, pipe, sound, toot, trumpet, vibrate

blow[2] noun 1 <u>knock</u>, bang, clout (informal), punch, smack, sock (slang), stroke, thump, wallop (informal), whack 2 <u>setback</u>, bombshell, calamity, catastrophe, disappointment, disaster, misfortune, reverse, shock

blow out verb 1 <u>put out</u>, extinguish, snuff 2 <u>burst</u>, erupt, explode, rupture, shatter

blow up verb 1 <u>explode</u>, blast, blow sky-high, bomb, burst, detonate, rupture, shatter 2 <u>inflate</u>, bloat, distend, enlarge, expand, fill, puff up, pump up, swell 3 Informal <u>lose one's temper</u>, become angry, erupt, fly off the handle (informal), hit the roof (informal), rage, see red (informal)

bludgeon noun 1 <u>club</u>, cosh (Brit.), cudgel, truncheon ♦ verb 2 <u>club</u>, beat up, cosh (Brit.), cudgel, knock down, strike 3 <u>bully</u>, bulldoze (informal), coerce, force, railroad (informal), steamroller

blue adjective 1 <u>azure</u>, cerulean, cobalt, cyan, navy, sapphire, sky-coloured, ultramarine 2 <u>depressed</u>, dejected, despondent, downcast, low, melancholy, sad, unhappy 3 <u>smutty</u>, indecent, lewd, obscene, risqué, X-rated (informal)

➤ **Antonyms**
≠depressed: blithe, cheerful, cheery, chirpy (informal), happy, jolly, merry, optimistic, sunny ≠smutty: decent, respectable

blueprint noun <u>plan</u>, design, draft, outline, pattern, pilot scheme, prototype, sketch

blues plural noun <u>depression</u>, doldrums, dumps (informal), gloom, low spirits, melancholy, unhappiness

bluff¹ verb 1 <u>deceive</u>, con, delude, fake, feign, mislead, pretend, pull the wool over someone's eyes ♦ noun 2 <u>deception</u>, bluster, bravado, deceit, fraud, humbug, pretence, sham, subterfuge

bluff² noun 1 <u>precipice</u>, bank, cliff, crag, escarpment, headland, peak, promontory, ridge ♦ adjective 2 <u>hearty</u>, blunt, blustering, genial, good-natured, open, outspoken, plain-spoken

➤ **Antonyms**
adjective ≠hearty: delicate, diplomatic, discreet, sensitive, tactful, thoughtful

blunder noun 1 <u>mistake</u>, bloomer (Brit. informal), clanger (informal), faux pas, gaffe, howler (informal), indiscretion 2 <u>error</u>, fault, inaccuracy, mistake, oversight, slip, slip-up (informal) ♦ verb 3 <u>make a mistake</u>, botch, bungle, err, put one's foot in it (informal), slip up (informal) 4 <u>stumble</u>, bumble, flounder

➤ **Antonyms**
noun ≠error: accuracy, correctness ♦ verb ≠make a mistake: be correct, be exact, get it right

blunt adjective 1 <u>dull</u>, dulled, edgeless, pointless, rounded, unsharpened 2 <u>forthright</u>, bluff, brusque, frank, outspoken, plain-spoken, rude, straightforward, tactless ♦ verb 3 <u>dull</u>, dampen, deaden, numb, soften, take the edge off, water down, weaken

➤ **Antonyms**
adjective ≠dull: keen, pointed, sharp ≠forthright: courteous, diplomatic, sensitive, subtle, tactful ♦ verb ≠dull: sharpen, stimulate

blur verb 1 <u>make indistinct</u>, cloud, darken, make hazy, make vague, mask, obscure ♦ noun 2 <u>indistinctness</u>, confusion, fog, haze, obscurity

blurt out verb <u>exclaim</u>, disclose, let the cat out of the bag, reveal, spill the beans (informal), tell all, utter suddenly

blush verb 1 <u>turn red</u>, colour, flush, go red (as a beetroot), redden, turn scarlet ♦ noun 2 <u>reddening</u>, colour, flush, glow, pink tinge, rosiness, rosy tint, ruddiness

➤ **Antonyms**
verb ≠turn red: blanch, blench, drain, fade, pale, turn pale, whiten

bluster verb 1 <u>roar</u>, bully, domineer, hector, rant, storm ♦ noun 2 <u>hot air</u> (informal), bluff, bombast, bravado

blustery adjective <u>gusty</u>, boisterous, inclement, squally, stormy, tempestuous, violent, wild, windy

board noun **1** plank, panel, piece of timber, slat, timber **2** directors, advisers, committee, conclave, council, panel, trustees **3** meals, daily meals, provisions, victuals ♦ verb **4** get on, embark, enter, mount **5** lodge, put up, quarter, room

➤ **Antonyms**

verb ≠get on: alight, arrive, disembark, dismount, get off, go ashore, land

boast verb **1** brag, blow one's own trumpet, crow, strut, swagger, talk big (slang), vaunt **2** possess, be proud of, congratulate oneself, exhibit, flatter oneself, pride oneself on, show off ♦ noun **3** brag, avowal

➤ **Antonyms**

verb ≠brag: cover up, disavow ♦ noun ≠brag: disavowal

boastful adjective bragging, cocky, conceited, crowing, egotistical, full of oneself, swaggering, swollen-headed, vaunting

➤ **Antonyms**

deprecating, humble, modest, self-effacing, unassuming

bob verb duck, bounce, hop, nod, oscillate, waggle, wobble

bode verb portend, augur, be an omen of, forebode, foretell, predict, signify, threaten

bodily adjective physical, actual, carnal, corporal, corporeal, material, substantial, tangible

body noun **1** physique, build, figure, form, frame, shape **2** torso, trunk **3** corpse, cadaver, carcass, dead body, remains, stiff (slang) **4** organization, association, band, bloc, collection, company, confederation, congress, corporation, society **5** main part, bulk, essence, mass, material, matter, substance

boffin noun Brit. informal expert, brainbox, egghead, genius, intellectual, inventor, mastermind

bog noun marsh, fen, mire, morass, quagmire, slough, swamp, wetlands

bogey noun bugbear, bête noire,

bugaboo, nightmare

bogus adjective fake, artificial, counterfeit, false, forged, fraudulent, imitation, phoney or phony (informal), sham

➤ **Antonyms**

actual, authentic, genuine, real, true

bohemian adjective **1** unconventional, alternative, artistic, arty (informal), left bank, nonconformist, offbeat, unorthodox ♦ noun **2** nonconformist, beatnik, dropout, hippy, iconoclast

➤ **Antonyms**

adjective ≠unconventional: bourgeois, conservative, conventional, square (informal), straight (slang), straight-laced, stuffy

boil¹ verb bubble, effervesce, fizz, foam, froth, seethe

boil² noun pustule, blister, carbuncle, gathering, swelling, tumour, ulcer

boisterous adjective unruly, disorderly, loud, noisy, riotous, rollicking, rowdy, unrestrained, vociferous, wild

➤ **Antonyms**

calm, controlled, peaceful, quiet, restrained, self-controlled, subdued

bold adjective **1** fearless, adventurous, audacious, brave, courageous, daring, enterprising, heroic, intrepid, valiant **2** impudent, barefaced, brazen, cheeky, confident, forward, insolent, rude, shameless

➤ **Antonyms**

≠fearless: cowardly, fainthearted, fearful, timid, timorous ≠impudent: courteous, meek, modest, polite, retiring, shy, tactful

bolster verb support, augment, boost, help, reinforce, shore up, strengthen

bolt noun **1** bar, catch, fastener, latch, lock, sliding bar **2** pin, peg, rivet, rod ♦ verb **3** run away, abscond, dash, escape, flee, fly, make a break (for it), run for it **4** lock, bar, fasten, latch, secure **5** gobble, cram, devour, gorge, gulp, guzzle, stuff, swallow whole, wolf

bomb noun **1** explosive, device, grenade, mine, missile, projectile, rocket, shell, torpedo ♦ verb **2** blow up, attack, blow sky-high, bombard, destroy, shell, strafe, torpedo

bombard verb **1** bomb, assault, blitz, fire upon, open fire, pound, shell, strafe **2** attack, assail, beset, besiege, harass, hound, pester

bombardment noun bombing, assault, attack, barrage, blitz, fusillade, shelling

bombastic adjective grandiloquent, grandiose, high-flown, inflated, pompous, verbose, wordy

bona fide adjective genuine, actual, authentic, honest, kosher (informal), legitimate, real, true

➤ **Antonyms**
bogus, counterfeit, ersatz, fake, false, imitation, phoney or phony (informal), sham

bond noun **1** fastening, chain, cord, fetter, ligature, manacle, shackle, tie **2** tie, affiliation, affinity, attachment, connection, link, relation, union **3** agreement, contract, covenant, guarantee, obligation, pledge, promise, word ♦ verb **4** hold together, bind, connect, fasten, fix together, glue, paste

bondage noun slavery, captivity, confinement, enslavement, imprisonment, subjugation

bonus noun extra, dividend, gift, icing on the cake, plus, premium, prize, reward

bony adjective thin, emaciated, gaunt, lean, scrawny, skin and bone, skinny

book noun **1** work, publication, title, tome, tract, volume **2** notebook, album, diary, exercise book, jotter, pad ♦ verb **3** reserve, arrange for, charter, engage, make reservations, organize, programme, schedule **4** note, enter, list, log, mark

down, put down, record, register, write down

booklet noun brochure, leaflet, pamphlet

boom verb **1** bang, blast, crash, explode, resound, reverberate, roar, roll, rumble, thunder **2** flourish, develop, expand, grow, increase, intensify, prosper, strengthen, swell, thrive ♦ noun **3** bang, blast, burst, clap, crash, explosion, roar, rumble, thunder **4** expansion, boost, development, growth, improvement, increase, jump, upsurge, upswing, upturn

➤ **Antonyms**
verb ≠flourish: crash, fail, fall, slump ♦ noun ≠expansion: collapse, crash, decline, depression, downturn, failure, recession, slump

boon noun benefit, advantage, blessing, favour, gift, godsend, manna from heaven, windfall

boorish adjective loutish, churlish, coarse, crude, oafish, uncivilized, uncouth, vulgar

➤ **Antonyms**
cultured, genteel, polite, refined, sophisticated, urbane

boost noun **1** help, encouragement, gee-up, praise, promotion **2** rise, addition, expansion, improvement, increase, increment, jump ♦ verb **3** increase, add to, amplify, develop, enlarge, expand, heighten, raise **4** promote, advertise, encourage, foster, further, gee up, hype, plug (informal), praise

➤ **Antonyms**
noun ≠help: condemnation, criticism ≠rise: cut-back, decline, decrease, deterioration, fall, reduction ♦ verb ≠increase: cut, decrease, diminish, drop, lessen, lower, moderate, reduce, scale down ≠promote: condemn, criticize, hinder, hold back

boot noun kick, drive, drop-kick, knock, punt, put the boot in(to) (slang), shove

booty noun plunder, gains, haul,

loot, prey, spoils, swag (*slang*), takings, winnings

border *noun* **1** frontier, borderline, boundary, line, march **2** edge, bounds, brink, limits, margin, rim, verge ♦ *verb* **3** edge, bind, decorate, fringe, hem, rim, trim

bore[1] *verb* drill, burrow, gouge out, mine, penetrate, perforate, pierce, sink, tunnel

bore[2] *verb* **1** tire, be tedious, fatigue, jade, pall on, send to sleep, wear out, weary ♦ *noun* **2** nuisance, anorak (*informal*), pain (*informal*), yawn (*informal*)

► **Antonyms**
verb ≠tire: amuse, engross, excite, fascinate, hold the attention of, interest, stimulate

bored *adjective* fed up, listless, tired, uninterested, wearied

boredom *noun* tedium, apathy, ennui, flatness, monotony, sameness, tediousness, weariness, world-weariness

► **Antonyms**
amusement, entertainment, excitement, interest, stimulation

boring *adjective* uninteresting, dull, flat, humdrum, mind-numbing, monotonous, tedious, tiresome

borrow *verb* **1** take on loan, cadge, scrounge (*informal*), touch (someone) for (*slang*), use temporarily **2** steal, adopt, copy, obtain, plagiarize, take, usurp

► **Antonyms**
≠take on loan: advance, give, lend, loan, provide, return

bosom *noun* **1** breast, bust, chest ♦ *adjective* **2** intimate, boon, cherished, close, confidential, dear, very dear

boss[1] *noun* head, chief, director, employer, gaffer (*informal, chiefly Brit.*), leader, manager, master, supervisor

boss[2] *noun* stud, knob, point, protuberance, tip

boss around *verb Informal* domineer, bully, dominate, oppress, order, push around (*slang*)

bossy *adjective Informal* domineering, arrogant, authoritarian, autocratic, dictatorial, hectoring, high-handed, imperious, overbearing, tyrannical

botch *verb* **1** spoil, blunder, bungle, cock up (*Brit. slang*), make a pig's ear of (*informal*), mar, mess up, screw up (*informal*) ♦ *noun* **2** mess, blunder, bungle, cock-up (*Brit. slang*), failure, hash, pig's ear (*informal*)

bother *verb* **1** trouble, alarm, concern, disturb, harass, hassle (*informal*), inconvenience, pester, plague, worry ♦ *noun* **2** trouble, difficulty, fuss, hassle (*informal*), inconvenience, irritation, nuisance, problem, worry

► **Antonyms**
verb ≠trouble: aid, assist, help, relieve, succour, support ♦ *noun* ≠trouble: advantage, aid, benefit, comfort, convenience, help

bottleneck *noun* hold-up, block, blockage, congestion, impediment, jam, obstacle, obstruction, snarl-up (*informal, chiefly Brit.*)

bottle up *verb* suppress, check, contain, curb, keep back, restrict, shut in, trap

bottom *noun* **1** lowest part, base, bed, depths, floor, foot, foundation **2** underside, lower side, sole, underneath **3** buttocks, backside, behind (*informal*), posterior, rear, rump, seat ♦ *adjective* **4** lowest, last

► **Antonyms**
noun ≠lowest part: cover, crown, height, lid, peak, summit, surface, top ♦ *adjective* ≠lowest: higher, highest, top, upper

bottomless *adjective* unlimited, boundless, deep, fathomless, immeasurable, inexhaustible, infinite, unfathomable

bounce *verb* **1** rebound, bob, bound, jump, leap, recoil, ricochet, spring ♦ *noun* **2** life, dynamism, energy, go (*informal*), liveliness, vigour, vivacity, zip (*informal*) **3** springiness, elasticity, give, recoil, resilience, spring

bound[1] *adjective* **1** tied, cased, fastened, fixed, pinioned, secured, tied up **2** certain, destined, doomed, fated, sure **3** obliged, beholden, committed, compelled, constrained, duty-bound, forced, pledged, required

bound[2] *verb* limit, confine, demarcate, encircle, enclose, hem in, restrain, restrict, surround

bound[3] *verb, noun* leap, bob, bounce, gambol, hurdle, jump, skip, spring, vault

boundary *noun* limits, barrier, border, borderline, brink, edge, extremity, fringe, frontier, margin

boundless *adjective* unlimited, endless, immense, incalculable, inexhaustible, infinite, unconfined, untold, vast

> **Antonyms**

bounded, confined, limited, little, restricted, small

bounds *plural noun* boundary, border, confine, edge, extremity, limit, rim, verge

bountiful *adjective Literary* **1** plentiful, abundant, ample, bounteous, copious, exuberant, lavish, luxuriant, prolific **2** generous, liberal, magnanimous, open-handed, prodigal, unstinting

bounty *noun Literary* **1** generosity, benevolence, charity, kindness, largesse *or* largess, liberality, philanthropy **2** reward, bonus, gift, present

bouquet *noun* **1** bunch of flowers, buttonhole, corsage, garland, nosegay, posy, spray, wreath **2** aroma, fragrance, perfume, redolence, savour, scent

bourgeois *adjective* middle-class, conventional, hidebound, materialistic, traditional

bout *noun* **1** period, fit, spell, stint, term, turn **2** fight, boxing match, competition, contest, encounter, engagement, match, set-to, struggle

bow[1] *verb* **1** bend, bob, droop, genuflect, nod, stoop **2** give in,

acquiesce, comply, concede, defer, kowtow, relent, submit, succumb, surrender, yield ♦ *noun* **3** bending, bob, genuflexion, kowtow, nod, obeisance

bow[2] *noun Nautical* prow, beak, fore, head, stem

bowels *plural noun* **1** guts, entrails, innards (*informal*), insides (*informal*), intestines, viscera, vitals **2** depths, belly, core, deep, hold, inside, interior

bowl[1] *noun* basin, dish, vessel

bowl[2] *verb* throw, fling, hurl, pitch

box[1] *noun* **1** container, carton, case, casket, chest, pack, package, receptacle, trunk ♦ *verb* **2** pack, package, wrap

box[2] *verb* fight, exchange blows, spar

boxer *noun* fighter, prizefighter, pugilist, sparring partner

boy *noun* lad, fellow, junior, schoolboy, stripling, youngster, youth

boycott *verb* embargo, ban, bar, black, exclude, outlaw, prohibit, refuse, reject

> **Antonyms**

accept, advocate, back, defend, help, patronize, promote, support, welcome

boyfriend *noun* sweetheart, admirer, beau, date, lover, man, suitor

boyish *adjective* youthful, adolescent, childish, immature, juvenile, puerile, young

brace *noun* **1** support, bolster, bracket, buttress, prop, reinforcement, stay, strut, truss ♦ *verb* **2** support, bolster, buttress, fortify, reinforce, steady, strengthen

bracing *adjective* refreshing, brisk, crisp, exhilarating, fresh, invigorating, stimulating

> **Antonyms**

debilitating, draining, enervating, exhausting, fatiguing, sapping, soporific, taxing, tiring, weakening

brag *verb* boast, blow one's own trumpet, bluster, crow, swagger, talk big (*slang*), vaunt

braggart *noun* <u>boaster</u>, big-mouth (*slang*), bragger, show-off (*informal*)

braid *verb* <u>interweave</u>, entwine, interlace, intertwine, lace, plait, twine, weave

brainless *adjective* <u>stupid</u>, dumb-ass (*slang*), foolish, idiotic, inane, mindless, senseless, thoughtless, witless

brains *plural noun* <u>intelligence</u>, intellect, sense, understanding

brainwave *noun* <u>idea</u>, bright idea, stroke of genius, thought

brainy *adjective* *Informal* <u>intelligent</u>, bright, brilliant, clever, smart

brake *noun* 1 <u>control</u>, check, constraint, curb, rein, restraint ♦ *verb* 2 <u>slow</u>, check, decelerate, halt, moderate, reduce speed, slacken, stop

branch *noun* 1 <u>bough</u>, arm, limb, offshoot, shoot, spray, sprig 2 <u>division</u>, chapter, department, office, part, section, subdivision, subsection, wing

brand *noun* 1 <u>label</u>, emblem, hallmark, logo, mark, marker, sign, stamp, symbol, trademark 2 <u>kind</u>, cast, class, grade, make, quality, sort, species, type, variety ♦ *verb* 3 <u>mark</u>, burn, burn in, label, scar, stamp 4 <u>stigmatize</u>, censure, denounce, discredit, disgrace, expose, mark

brandish *verb* <u>wave</u>, display, exhibit, flaunt, flourish, parade, raise, shake, swing, wield

brash *adjective* <u>bold</u>, audacious, cocky, impertinent, impudent, insolent, pushy (*informal*), rude

► **Antonyms**
careful, cautious, polite, prudent, reserved, respectful, timid, uncertain

bravado *noun* <u>swagger</u>, bluster, boastfulness, boasting, bombast, swashbuckling, vaunting

brave *adjective* 1 <u>courageous</u>, bold, daring, fearless, heroic, intrepid, plucky, resolute, valiant ♦ *verb* 2 <u>confront</u>, defy, endure,

face, stand up to, suffer, tackle, withstand

► **Antonyms**
adjective ≠<u>courageous</u>: afraid, cowardly, craven, faint-hearted, fearful, frightened, scared, shrinking, timid ♦ *verb* ≠<u>confront</u>: give in to, retreat from, surrender to

bravery *noun* <u>courage</u>, boldness, daring, fearlessness, fortitude, heroism, intrepidity, mettle, pluck, spirit, valour

► **Antonyms**
cowardice, faint-heartedness, fearfulness, fright, timidity

brawl *noun* 1 <u>fight</u>, affray (*Law*), altercation, clash, dispute, fracas, fray, melee *or* mêlée, punch-up (*Brit. informal*), rumpus, scuffle, skirmish ♦ *verb* 2 <u>fight</u>, scrap (*informal*), scuffle, tussle, wrestle

brawn *noun* <u>muscle</u>, beef (*informal*), might, muscles, power, strength, vigour

brawny *adjective* <u>muscular</u>, beefy (*informal*), hefty (*informal*), lusty, powerful, strapping, strong, sturdy, well-built

► **Antonyms**
frail, scrawny, skinny, thin, undeveloped, weak, weakly, weedy (*informal*), wimpish *or* wimpy (*informal*)

brazen *adjective* <u>bold</u>, audacious, barefaced, brash, defiant, impudent, insolent, shameless, unabashed, unashamed

► **Antonyms**
cautious, diffident, modest, reserved, shy, timid

breach *noun* 1 <u>nonobservance</u>, contravention, infraction, infringement, noncompliance, transgression, trespass, violation 2 <u>crack</u>, cleft, fissure, gap, opening, rift, rupture, split

► **Antonyms**
≠<u>nonobservance</u>: adherence to, compliance, fulfilment, honouring, observation, performance

bread *noun* 1 <u>food</u>, fare, nourishment, sustenance 2 *Slang* <u>money</u>, cash, dough (*slang*)

breadth *noun* 1 <u>width</u>, broadness, latitude, span, spread, wideness **2** extent, compass, expanse, range, scale, scope

break verb **1** separate, burst, crack, destroy, disintegrate, fracture, fragment, shatter, smash, snap, split, tear **2** disobey, breach, contravene, disregard, infringe, renege on, transgress, violate **3** reveal, announce, disclose, divulge, impart, inform, let out, make public, proclaim, tell **4** stop, abandon, cut, discontinue, give up, interrupt, pause, rest, suspend **5** weaken, demoralize, dispirit, subdue, tame, undermine **6** Of a record, etc. beat, better, exceed, excel, go beyond, outdo, outstrip, surpass, top ♦ noun **7** division, crack, fissure, fracture, gap, hole, opening, split, tear **8** rest, breather (informal), hiatus, interlude, intermission, interruption, interval, let-up (informal), lull, pause, respite **9** Informal stroke of luck, advantage, chance, fortune, opening, opportunity

▶ **Antonyms**

verb ≠ separate: attach, bind, connect, fasten, join, repair, unite ≠ disobey: abide by, adhere to, conform, follow, obey, observe

breakable adjective fragile, brittle, crumbly, delicate, flimsy, frail, frangible, friable

▶ **Antonyms**

durable, indestructible, lasting, nonbreakable, shatterproof, solid, strong, toughened, unbreakable

breakdown noun collapse, disintegration, disruption, failure, mishap, stoppage

break down verb **1** collapse, come unstuck, fail, seize up, stop, stop working **2** be overcome, crack up (informal), go to pieces

break-in noun burglary, breaking and entering, robbery

break off verb **1** detach, divide, part, pull off, separate, sever, snap off, splinter **2** stop, cease, desist, discontinue, end, finish,

halt, pull the plug on, suspend, terminate

break out verb begin, appear, arise, commence, emerge, happen, occur, set in, spring up, start

breakthrough noun development, advance, discovery, find, invention, leap, progress, quantum leap, step forward

break up verb **1** separate, dissolve, divide, divorce, part, scatter, sever, split **2** stop, adjourn, disband, dismantle, end, suspend, terminate

breast noun bosom, bust, chest, front, teat, udder

breath noun respiration, breathing, exhalation, gasp, gulp, inhalation, pant, wheeze

breathe verb **1** inhale and exhale, draw in, gasp, gulp, pant, puff, respire, wheeze **2** whisper, murmur, sigh

breather noun Informal rest, break, breathing space, halt, pause, recess, respite

breathless adjective **1** out of breath, gasping, gulping, panting, short-winded, spent, wheezing **2** excited, eager, on tenterhooks, open-mouthed, with bated breath

breathtaking adjective amazing, astonishing, awe-inspiring, exciting, impressive, magnificent, sensational, stunning (informal), thrilling

breed verb **1** reproduce, bear, bring forth, hatch, multiply, procreate, produce, propagate **2** bring up, cultivate, develop, nourish, nurture, raise, rear **3** produce, arouse, bring about, cause, create, generate, give rise to, stir up ♦ noun **4** variety, pedigree, race, species, stock, strain, type **5** kind, brand, sort, stamp, type, variety

breeding noun **1** upbringing, ancestry, cultivation, development, lineage, nurture, raising, rearing, reproduction, training **2** refinement, conduct, courtesy, cultivation, culture, manners, polish, sophistication, urbanity

breeze noun 1 light wind, air, breath of wind, current of air, draught, gust, waft, zephyr ♦ verb 2 move briskly, flit, glide, hurry, pass, sail, sweep

breezy adjective 1 windy, airy, blowy, blustery, fresh, gusty, squally 2 carefree, blithe, casual, easy-going, free and easy, jaunty, light-hearted, lively, sprightly

➤ **Antonyms**
≠windy: calm, heavy, oppressive, windless ≠carefree: calm, dull, heavy, lifeless, sad, serious

brevity noun 1 shortness, briefness, impermanence, transience, transitoriness 2 conciseness, crispness, curtness, economy, pithiness, succinctness, terseness

➤ **Antonyms**
≠conciseness: discursiveness, long-windedness, rambling, tautology, verbiage, verbosity, wordiness

brew verb 1 make (beer), boil, ferment, infuse (tea), soak, steep, stew 2 develop, foment, form, gather, start, stir up ♦ noun 3 drink, beverage, blend, concoction, infusion, liquor, mixture, preparation

bribe verb 1 buy off, corrupt, grease the palm or hand of (slang), pay off (informal), reward, suborn ♦ noun 2 inducement, allurement, backhander (slang), enticement, kickback (U.S.), pay-off (informal), sweetener (slang)

bribery noun buying off, corruption, inducement, palm-greasing (slang), payola (informal)

bric-a-brac noun knick-knacks, baubles, curios, ornaments, trinkets

bridal adjective matrimonial, conjugal, connubial, marital, marriage, nuptial, wedding

bridge noun 1 arch, flyover, overpass, span, viaduct ♦ verb 2 connect, join, link, span

➤ **Antonyms**
verb ≠connect: cleave, disjoin, divide, keep apart, separate, sever, split, sunder

bridle noun 1 curb, check, control, rein, restraint ♦ verb 2 get angry, be indignant, bristle, draw (oneself) up, get one's back up, raise one's hackles, rear up

brief adjective 1 short, ephemeral, fleeting, momentary, quick, short-lived, swift, transitory ♦ noun 2 summary, abridgment, abstract, digest, epitome, outline, précis, sketch, synopsis ♦ verb 3 inform, advise, explain, fill in (informal), instruct, keep posted, prepare, prime, put (someone) in the picture (informal)

➤ **Antonyms**
adjective ≠short: extensive, lengthy, long, protracted

briefing noun instructions, conference, directions, guidance, information, preparation, priming, rundown

briefly adverb shortly, concisely, hastily, hurriedly, in a nutshell, in brief, momentarily, quickly

brigade noun group, band, company, corps, force, organization, outfit, squad, team, troop, unit

brigand noun bandit, desperado, freebooter, gangster, highwayman, marauder, outlaw, plunderer, robber

bright adjective 1 shining, brilliant, dazzling, gleaming, glowing, luminous, lustrous, radiant, shimmering, vivid 2 intelligent, astute, aware, clever, inventive, quick-witted, sharp, smart, wide-awake 3 sunny, clear, cloudless, fair, limpid, lucid, pleasant, translucent, transparent, unclouded

➤ **Antonyms**
≠intelligent: dense, dim, dim-witted (informal), dull, dumb (informal), foolish, idiotic, simple, slow, stupid, thick, unintelligent ≠sunny: cloudy, dark, dim, dusky, gloomy, grey, overcast

brighten *verb* light up, gleam, glow, illuminate, lighten, make brighter, shine

➤ **Antonyms**

blacken, cloud over *or* up, dim, dull, obscure, overshadow, shade, shadow

brightness *noun* **1** shine, brilliance, glare, incandescence, intensity, light, luminosity, radiance, vividness **2** intelligence, acuity, cleverness, quickness, sharpness, smartness

➤ **Antonyms**

≠shine: dimness, dullness

brilliance, brilliancy *noun* **1** brightness, dazzle, intensity, luminosity, lustre, radiance, sparkle, vividness **2** cleverness, distinction, excellence, genius, greatness, inventiveness, talent, wisdom **3** splendour, éclat, glamour, grandeur, illustriousness, magnificence

➤ **Antonyms**

≠brightness: darkness, dimness, dullness ≠cleverness: idiocy, inanity, incompetence, ineptitude, silliness, simple-mindedness, stupidity

brilliant *adjective* **1** shining, bright, dazzling, glittering, intense, luminous, radiant, sparkling, vivid **2** splendid, celebrated, famous, glorious, illustrious, magnificent, notable, outstanding, superb **3** intelligent, clever, expert, gifted, intellectual, inventive, masterly, penetrating, profound, talented

➤ **Antonyms**

≠shining: dark, dim, dull, gloomy ≠splendid: dull, ordinary, run-of-the-mill, unaccomplished, unexceptional, untalented ≠intelligent: dim, simple, slow, stupid

brim *noun* **1** rim, border, brink, edge, lip, margin, skirt, verge ♦ *verb* **2** be full, fill, fill up, hold no more, overflow, run over, spill, well over

bring *verb* **1** take, bear, carry, conduct, convey, deliver, escort, fetch, guide, lead, transfer, transport **2** cause, contribute to, create, effect, inflict, occasion, produce, result in, wreak

bring about *verb* cause, accomplish, achieve, create, effect, generate, give rise to, make happen, produce

bring off *verb* accomplish, achieve, carry off, execute, perform, pull off, succeed

bring up *verb* **1** rear, breed, develop, educate, form, nurture, raise, support, teach, train **2** mention, allude to, broach, introduce, move, propose, put forward, raise

brink *noun* edge, border, boundary, brim, fringe, frontier, limit, lip, margin, rim, skirt, threshold, verge

brisk *adjective* lively, active, bustling, busy, energetic, quick, sprightly, spry, vigorous

➤ **Antonyms**

heavy, lazy, lethargic, slow, sluggish, unenergetic

briskly *adverb* quickly, actively, apace, efficiently, energetically, promptly, rapidly, readily, smartly

bristle *noun* **1** hair, barb, prickle, spine, stubble, thorn, whisker ♦ *verb* **2** stand up, rise, stand on end **3** be angry, bridle, flare up, rage, see red, seethe

bristly *adjective* hairy, prickly, rough, stubbly

brittle *adjective* fragile, breakable, crisp, crumbling, crumbly, delicate, frail, frangible, friable

➤ **Antonyms**

durable, nonbreakable, shatterproof, strong, sturdy, toughened

broach *verb* **1** bring up, introduce, mention, open up, propose, raise the subject, speak of, suggest, talk of, touch on **2** open, crack, draw off, pierce, puncture, start, tap, uncork

broad *adjective* **1** wide, ample, expansive, extensive, generous, large, roomy, spacious, vast, voluminous, widespread **2** general, all-embracing, comprehensive, encyclopedic, inclusive, overarching, sweeping, wide, wide-ranging

► **Antonyms**

≠wide: close, confined, constricted, cramped, limited, meagre, narrow, restricted, tight

broadcast noun **1** transmission, programme, show, telecast ♦ verb **2** transmit, air, beam, cable, put on the air, radio, relay, show, televise **3** make public, advertise, announce, circulate, proclaim, publish, report, spread

broaden verb expand, develop, enlarge, extend, increase, spread, stretch, supplement, swell, widen

► **Antonyms**

constrain, diminish, narrow, reduce, restrict, tighten

broad-minded adjective tolerant, free-thinking, indulgent, liberal, open-minded, permissive, unbiased, unbigoted, unprejudiced

► **Antonyms**

biased, bigoted, dogmatic, inflexible, intolerant, narrow-minded, prejudiced

broadside noun attack, assault, battering, bombardment, censure, criticism, denunciation, diatribe, swipe

brochure noun booklet, advertisement, circular, folder, handbill, hand-out, leaflet, mailshot, pamphlet

broke adjective Informal penniless, bankrupt, bust (informal), down and out, impoverished, insolvent, in the red, ruined, short, skint (Brit. slang)

► **Antonyms**

affluent, comfortable, prosperous, rich, solvent, wealthy, well-to-do

broken adjective **1** smashed, burst, fractured, fragmented, ruptured, separated, severed, shattered **2** interrupted, discontinuous, erratic, fragmentary, incomplete, intermittent, spasmodic **3** not working, defective, im-

perfect, kaput (informal), on the blink (slang), out of order **4** imperfect, disjointed, halting, hesitating, stammering

brokenhearted adjective heartbroken, desolate, devastated, disconsolate, grief-stricken, inconsolable, miserable, sorrowful, wretched

broker noun dealer, agent, factor, go-between, intermediary, middleman, negotiator

bronze adjective reddish-brown, brownish, chestnut, copper, rust, tan

brood noun **1** offspring, clutch, family, issue, litter, progeny ♦ verb **2** think upon, agonize, dwell upon, mope, mull over, muse, obsess, ponder, ruminate

brook noun stream, beck, burn, rill, rivulet, watercourse

brother noun **1** sibling, blood brother, kin, kinsman, relation, relative **2** monk, cleric, friar

brotherhood noun **1** fellowship, brotherliness, camaraderie, companionship, comradeship, friendliness, kinship **2** association, alliance, community, fraternity, guild, league, order, society, union

brotherly adjective kind, affectionate, altruistic, amicable, benevolent, cordial, fraternal, friendly, neighbourly, philanthropic, sympathetic

browbeat verb bully, badger, coerce, dragoon, hector, intimidate, ride roughshod over, threaten, tyrannize

► **Antonyms**

beguile, cajole, coax, entice, inveigle, lure, seduce, sweet-talk (informal), tempt, wheedle

brown adjective **1** brunette, auburn, bay, bronze, chestnut, chocolate, coffee, dun, hazel, sunburnt, tan, tanned, tawny, umber ♦ verb **2** fry, cook, grill, sauté, seal, sear

browse verb **1** skim, dip into, examine cursorily, flip through, glance at, leaf through, look round, look through, peruse, scan, survey **2** graze, eat, feed, nibble

bruise verb **1** discolour, damage, injure, mar, mark, pound ♦ noun **2** discoloration, black mark, blemish, contusion, injury, mark, swelling

brunt noun full force, burden, force, impact, pressure, shock, strain, stress, thrust, violence

brush[1] noun **1** broom, besom, sweeper **2** encounter, clash, conflict, confrontation, skirmish, tussle ♦ verb **3** clean, buff, paint, polish, sweep, wash **4** touch, flick, glance, graze, kiss, scrape, stroke, sweep

brush[2] noun shrubs, brushwood, bushes, copse, scrub, thicket, undergrowth

brush off verb Slang ignore, disdain, dismiss, disregard, reject, repudiate, scorn, snub, spurn

brush up verb revise, bone up (informal), cram, go over, polish up, read up, refresh one's memory, relearn, study

brusque adjective curt, abrupt, discourteous, gruff, impolite, sharp, short, surly, terse

➤ **Antonyms**

civil, courteous, polite, well-mannered

brutal adjective **1** cruel, bloodthirsty, heartless, inhuman, ruthless, savage, uncivilized, vicious **2** harsh, callous, gruff, impolite, insensitive, rough, rude, severe

➤ **Antonyms**

≠cruel: civilized, gentle, humane, kind, merciful, softhearted ≠harsh: polite, sensitive

brutality noun cruelty, atrocity, barbarism, bloodthirstiness, ferocity, inhumanity, ruthlessness, savagery, viciousness

brute noun **1** savage, barbarian, beast, devil, fiend, monster, sadist, swine **2** animal, beast, creature, wild animal ♦ adjective **3** mindless, bodily, carnal, fleshly, instinctive, physical, senseless, unthinking

bubble noun **1** air ball, bead, blister, blob, drop, droplet, globule ♦ verb **2** foam, boil, effervesce, fizz, froth, percolate, seethe, sparkle **3** gurgle, babble, burble, murmur, ripple, trickle

bubbly adjective **1** lively, animated, bouncy, elated, excited, happy, merry, sparky **2** frothy, carbonated, effervescent, fizzy, foamy, sparkling

buccaneer noun pirate, corsair, freebooter, privateer, sea-rover

buckle noun **1** fastener, catch, clasp, clip, hasp ♦ verb **2** fasten, clasp, close, hook, secure **3** distort, bend, bulge, cave in, collapse, contort, crumple, fold, twist, warp

bud noun **1** shoot, embryo, germ, sprout ♦ verb **2** develop, burgeon, burst forth, grow, shoot, sprout

budding adjective developing, beginning, burgeoning, embryonic, fledgling, growing, incipient, nascent, potential, promising

budge verb move, dislodge, push, shift, stir

budget noun **1** allowance, allocation, cost, finances, funds, means, resources ♦ verb **2** plan, allocate, apportion, cost, estimate, ration

buff[1] adjective **1** yellowish-brown, sandy, straw, tan, yellowish ♦ verb **2** polish, brush, burnish, rub, shine, smooth

buff[2] noun Informal expert, addict, admirer, aficionado, connoisseur, devotee, enthusiast, fan

buffer noun safeguard, bulwark, bumper, cushion, fender, intermediary, screen, shield, shock absorber

buffet[1] noun snack bar, brasserie, café, cafeteria, refreshment counter, sideboard

buffet[2] verb batter, beat, bump, knock, pound, pummel, strike, thump, wallop (informal)

buffoon noun clown, comedian, comic, fool, harlequin, jester, joker, wag

bug noun **1** Informal illness, disease, infection, lurgy (informal), virus **2** fault, defect, error, flaw, glitch, gremlin ♦ verb **3** Informal annoy, bother, disturb, get on one's nerves (informal), hassle (informal), irritate, pester, vex **4** tap, eavesdrop, listen in, spy

bugbear noun pet hate, bane, bête noire, bogey, dread, horror, nightmare

build verb **1** construct, assemble, erect, fabricate, form, make, put up, raise ♦ noun **2** physique, body, figure, form, frame, shape, structure

➤ **Antonyms**
verb ≠construct: demolish, dismantle, tear down

building noun structure, domicile, dwelling, edifice, house

build-up noun increase, accumulation, development, enlargement, escalation, expansion, gain, growth

bulbous adjective bulging, bloated, convex, rounded, swelling, swollen

bulge noun **1** swelling, bump, hump, lump, projection, protrusion, protuberance **2** increase, boost, intensification, rise, surge ♦ verb **3** swell out, dilate, distend, expand, project, protrude, puff out, stick out

➤ **Antonyms**
noun ≠swelling: cavity, concavity, crater, dent, depression, hole, hollow, indentation, pit

bulk noun **1** size, dimensions, immensity, largeness, magnitude, substance, volume, weight **2** main part, better part, body, lion's share, majority, mass, most, nearly all, preponderance

bulky adjective large, big, cumbersome, heavy, hulking, massive, substantial, unwieldy, voluminous, weighty

➤ **Antonyms**
convenient, handy, manageable, neat, slim, small

bulldoze verb demolish, flatten, level, raze

bullet noun projectile, ball, missile, pellet, shot, slug

bulletin noun announcement, account, communication, communiqué, dispatch, message, news flash, notification, report, statement

bully noun **1** persecutor, browbeater, bully boy, coercer, intimidator, oppressor, ruffian, tormentor, tough ♦ verb **2** persecute, browbeat, coerce, domineer, hector, intimidate, oppress, push around (slang), terrorize, tyrannize

bulwark noun **1** fortification, bastion, buttress, defence, embankment, partition, rampart **2** defence, buffer, guard, mainstay, safeguard, security, support

bumbling adjective clumsy, awkward, blundering, bungling, incompetent, inefficient, inept, maladroit, muddled

➤ **Antonyms**
able, capable, competent, efficient, fit

bump verb **1** knock, bang, collide (with), crash, hit, slam, smash into, strike **2** jerk, bounce, jolt, rattle, shake ♦ noun **3** knock, bang, blow, collision, crash, impact, jolt, thud, thump **4** lump, bulge, contusion, hump, nodule, protuberance, swelling

bumper adjective exceptional, abundant, bountiful, excellent, jumbo (informal), massive, whopping (informal)

bumpkin noun yokel, country bumpkin, hillbilly, peasant, rustic

bumptious adjective cocky, arrogant, brash, conceited, forward, full of oneself, overconfident, pushy (informal), self-assertive

bumpy adjective rough, bouncy, choppy, jarring, jerky, jolting, rutted, uneven

bunch noun **1** number, assortment, batch, bundle, clump, cluster, collection, heap, lot, mass, pile **2** group, band, crowd, flock, gang, gathering, party, team ◆ verb **3** group, assemble, bundle, cluster, collect, huddle, mass, pack

bundle noun **1** bunch, assortment, batch, collection, group, heap, mass, pile, stack ◆ verb **2** with out, off, into, etc. push, hurry, hustle, rush, shove, throw, thrust

bundle up verb wrap up, swathe

bungle verb mess up, blow (slang), blunder, botch, foul up, make a mess of, muff, ruin, spoil

► **Antonyms**

accomplish, achieve, carry off, fulfil, succeed

bungling adjective incompetent, blundering, cack-handed (informal), clumsy, ham-fisted (informal), inept, maladroit

bunk, bunkum noun Informal nonsense, balderdash, baloney (informal), garbage (informal), hogwash, hot air (informal), moonshine, poppycock (informal), rubbish, stuff and nonsense, twaddle

buoy noun **1** marker, beacon, float, guide, signal ◆ verb **2** buoy up encourage, boost, cheer, cheer up, hearten, keep afloat, lift, raise, support, sustain

buoyancy noun **1** lightness, weightlessness **2** cheerfulness, animation, bounce (informal), good humour, high spirits, liveliness

buoyant adjective **1** floating, afloat, light, weightless **2** cheerful, carefree, chirpy (informal), happy, jaunty, light-hearted, upbeat

► **Antonyms**

≠cheerful: cheerless, depressed, despairing, gloomy, glum, melancholy, moody, morose, pessimistic, sad, unhappy

burden noun **1** load, encumbrance, weight **2** trouble, affliction, millstone, onus, responsibility, strain, weight, worry ◆ verb **3** weigh down, bother, encumber, handicap, load, oppress,

saddle with, tax, worry

bureau noun **1** office, agency, branch, department, division, service **2** desk, writing desk

bureaucracy noun **1** government, administration, authorities, civil service, corridors of power, officials, the system **2** red tape, officialdom, regulations

bureaucrat noun official, administrator, civil servant, functionary, mandarin, officer, public servant

burglar noun housebreaker, cat burglar, filcher, pilferer, robber, sneak thief, thief

burglary noun breaking and entering, break-in, housebreaking, larceny, robbery, stealing, theft, thieving

burial noun interment, entombment, exequies, funeral, obsequies

buried adjective **1** interred, entombed, laid to rest **2** hidden, concealed, private, sequestered, tucked away

burlesque noun **1** parody, caricature, mockery, satire, send-up (Brit. informal), spoof (informal), takeoff (informal), travesty ◆ verb **2** satirize, ape, caricature, exaggerate, imitate, lampoon, make a monkey out of, make fun of, mock, parody, ridicule, send up (Brit. informal), spoof (informal), take off (informal), take the piss out of (taboo slang), travesty

burly adjective brawny, beefy (informal), big, bulky, hefty, hulking, stocky, stout, sturdy, thickset, well-built

► **Antonyms**

lean, puny, scraggy, scrawny, slight, spare, thin, weak, weedy (informal), wimpish or wimpy (informal), wussy (slang)

burn verb **1** be on fire, be ablaze, blaze, flame, flare, glow, go up in flames, smoke **2** set on fire, char, ignite, incinerate, kindle, light, parch, scorch, sear, singe, toast **3** be passionate, be angry, be aroused, be inflamed, fume, seethe, simmer, smoulder

burning *adjective* **1** <u>intense</u>, ardent, eager, fervent, impassioned, passionate, vehement **2** <u>crucial</u>, acute, compelling, critical, essential, important, pressing, significant, urgent, vital **3** <u>blazing</u>, fiery, flaming, flashing, gleaming, glowing, illuminated, scorching, smouldering

➤ **Antonyms**
≠*intense*: apathetic, calm, cool, faint, indifferent, mild

burnish *verb* <u>polish</u>, brighten, buff, furbish, glaze, rub up, shine, smooth

➤ **Antonyms**
abrade, graze, scratch, scuff

burrow *noun* **1** <u>hole</u>, den, lair, retreat, shelter, tunnel ♦ *verb* **2** <u>dig</u>, delve, excavate, hollow out, scoop out, tunnel

burst *verb* **1** <u>explode</u>, blow up, break, crack, puncture, rupture, shatter, split, tear apart **2** <u>rush</u>, barge, break, break out, erupt, gush forth, run, spout ♦ *noun* **3** <u>explosion</u>, bang, blast, blowout, break, crack, discharge, rupture, split **4** <u>rush</u>, gush, gust, outbreak, outburst, outpouring, spate, spurt, surge, torrent ♦ *adjective* **5** <u>ruptured</u>, flat, punctured, rent, split

bury *verb* **1** <u>inter</u>, consign to the grave, entomb, inhume, lay to rest **2** <u>embed</u>, engulf, submerge **3** <u>hide</u>, conceal, cover, enshroud, secrete, stow away

➤ **Antonyms**
≠*inter, hide*: bring to light, dig up, discover, disinter, dredge up, exhume, expose, find, reveal, turn up, uncover, unearth

bush *noun* **1** <u>shrub</u>, hedge, plant, shrubbery, thicket **2 the bush** <u>the wild</u>, backwoods, brush, scrub, scrubland, woodland

bushy *adjective* <u>thick</u>, bristling, fluffy, fuzzy, luxuriant, rough, shaggy, unruly

busily *adverb* <u>actively</u>, assiduously, briskly, diligently, energetically, industriously, purposefully, speedily, strenuously

business *noun* **1** <u>trade</u>, bargaining, commerce, dealings, industry, manufacturing, selling, transaction **2** <u>establishment</u>, company, concern, corporation, enterprise, firm, organization, venture **3** <u>profession</u>, career, employment, function, job, line, occupation, trade, vocation, work **4** <u>concern</u>, affair, assignment, duty, pigeon (*informal*), problem, responsibility, task

businesslike *adjective* <u>efficient</u>, methodical, orderly, organized, practical, professional, systematic, thorough, well-ordered

➤ **Antonyms**
careless, disorderly, disorganized, impractical, inefficient, irregular, sloppy, unprofessional, unsystematic

businessman *noun* <u>executive</u>, capitalist, employer, entrepreneur, financier, industrialist, merchant, tradesman, tycoon

bust [1] *noun* <u>bosom</u>, breast, chest, front, torso

bust [2] *Informal* ♦ *verb* **1** <u>break</u>, burst, fracture, rupture **2** <u>arrest</u>, catch, raid, search ♦ *adjective* **3 go bust** <u>go bankrupt</u>, become insolvent, be ruined, fail

bustle *verb* **1** <u>hurry</u>, fuss, hasten, rush, scamper, scurry, scuttle ♦ *noun* **2** <u>activity</u>, ado, commotion, excitement, flurry, fuss, hurly-burly, stir, to-do

➤ **Antonyms**
verb ≠*hurry*: idle, laze, lie around, loaf, loiter, loll, relax, rest, take it easy ♦ *noun* ≠*activity*: inaction, inactivity, quiet, quietness, stillness, tranquillity

bustling *adjective* <u>busy</u>, active, buzzing, crowded, full, humming, lively, swarming, teeming

busy *adjective* **1** <u>occupied</u>, active, employed, engaged, hard at work, industrious, on duty, rushed off one's feet, working **2** <u>lively</u>, energetic, exacting, full, hectic, hustling ♦ *verb* **3** <u>occupy</u>, absorb, employ, engage, engross, immerse, interest

busybody 76 **cabin**

➤ **Antonyms**

adjective ≠<u>occupied</u>, <u>lively</u>: idle, inactive, indolent, lackadaisical, lazy, relaxed, slothful, unoccupied

busybody *noun* <u>nosey parker</u> (*informal*), gossip, meddler, snooper, stirrer (*informal*), troublemaker

but *conjunction* **1** <u>however</u>, further, moreover, nevertheless, on the contrary, on the other hand, still, yet ♦ *preposition* **2** <u>except</u>, bar, barring, excepting, excluding, notwithstanding, save, with the exception of ♦ *adverb* **3** <u>only</u>, just, merely, simply, singly, solely

butcher *noun* **1** <u>murderer</u>, destroyer, killer, slaughterer, slayer ♦ *verb* **2** <u>slaughter</u>, carve, clean, cut, cut up, dress, joint, prepare **3** <u>kill</u>, assassinate, cut down, destroy, exterminate, liquidate, massacre, put to the sword, slaughter, slay

butt[1] *noun* **1** <u>end</u>, haft, handle, hilt, shaft, shank, stock **2** <u>stub</u>, fag end (*informal*), leftover, tip

butt[2] *noun* <u>target</u>, Aunt Sally, dupe, laughing stock, victim

butt[3] *verb, noun* **1** With or of the head or horns <u>knock</u>, bump, poke, prod, push, ram, shove, thrust ♦ *verb* **2** butt in <u>interfere</u>, chip in (*informal*), cut in, interrupt, intrude, meddle, put one's oar in, stick one's nose in

butt[4] *noun* <u>cask</u>, barrel

buttonhole *verb* <u>detain</u>, accost, bore, catch, grab, importune, take aside, waylay

buttress *noun* **1** <u>support</u>, brace, mainstay, prop, reinforcement, stanchion, strut ♦ *verb* **2** <u>support</u>, back up, bolster, prop up, reinforce, shore up, strengthen, sustain, uphold

buxom *adjective* <u>plump</u>, ample, bosomy, busty, curvaceous, healthy, voluptuous, well-rounded

➤ **Antonyms**

delicate, slender, slight, slim, svelte, thin, trim

buy *verb* **1** <u>purchase</u>, acquire, get, invest in, obtain, pay for, procure, shop for ♦ *noun* **2** <u>purchase</u>, acquisition, bargain, deal

➤ **Antonyms**

verb ≠<u>purchase</u>: auction, barter, retail, sell

by *preposition* **1** <u>via</u>, by way of, over **2** <u>through</u>, through the agency of **3** <u>near</u>, along, beside, close to, next to, past ♦ *adverb* **4** <u>near</u>, at hand, close, handy, in reach **5** <u>past</u>, aside, away, to one side

bygone *adjective* <u>past</u>, antiquated, extinct, forgotten, former, lost, of old, olden

➤ **Antonyms**

coming, forthcoming, future, prospective, to be, to come

bypass *verb* <u>go round</u>, avoid, circumvent, depart from, detour round, deviate from, get round, give a wide berth to, pass round

➤ **Antonyms**

come together, connect, converge, cross, intersect, join, link, meet, touch, unite

bystander *noun* <u>onlooker</u>, eyewitness, looker-on, observer, passer-by, spectator, viewer, watcher, witness

➤ **Antonyms**

contributor, participant

byword *noun* <u>saying</u>, adage, maxim, motto, precept, proverb, slogan

C c

cab *noun* <u>taxi</u>, hackney carriage, minicab, taxicab

cabal *noun* **1** <u>clique</u>, caucus, conclave, faction, league, party, set **2** <u>plot</u>, conspiracy, intrigue, machination, scheme

cabin *noun* **1** <u>room</u>, berth, compartment, quarters **2** <u>hut</u>, chalet, cottage, lodge, shack, shanty, shed

cabinet noun cupboard, case, chiffonier, closet, commode, dresser, escritoire, locker

Cabinet noun council, administration, assembly, counsellors, ministry

cad noun Old-fashioned, informal scoundrel, bounder (old-fashioned Brit. slang), heel (slang), rat (informal), rotter (slang, chiefly Brit.)

caddish adjective ungentlemanly, despicable, ill-bred, low, unmannerly

➤ Antonyms
gentlemanly, honourable, mannerly

café noun snack bar, brasserie, cafeteria, coffee bar, coffee shop, eatery or eaterie, lunchroom, restaurant, tearoom

cage noun enclosure, pen, pound

cagey, cagy adjective Informal wary, careful, cautious, chary, discreet, guarded, noncommittal, shrewd, wily

➤ Antonyms
careless, imprudent, indiscreet, reckless, unthinking, unwary

cajole verb persuade, coax, flatter, seduce, sweet-talk (informal), wheedle

cake noun 1 block, bar, cube, loaf, lump, mass, slab ♦ verb 2 encrust, bake, coagulate, congeal, solidify

calamitous adjective disastrous, cataclysmic, catastrophic, deadly, devastating, dire, fatal, ruinous, tragic

➤ Antonyms
advantageous, beneficial, favourable, fortunate, good, helpful

calamity noun disaster, cataclysm, catastrophe, misadventure, misfortune, mishap, ruin, tragedy, tribulation

➤ Antonyms
advantage, benefit, blessing, boon, good fortune, good luck, help

calculate verb 1 work out, compute, count, determine, enumerate, estimate, figure, reckon 3 2 plan, aim, design, intend

calculated adjective deliberate, considered, intended, intentional, planned, premeditated, purposeful

➤ Antonyms
hasty, impetuous, impulsive, spontaneous, unintentional, unplanned, unpremeditated

calculating adjective scheming, crafty, cunning, devious, Machiavellian, manipulative, sharp, shrewd, sly

➤ Antonyms
direct, downright, frank, guileless, honest, open

calculation noun 1 working out, answer, computation, estimate, forecast, judgment, reckoning, result 2 planning, contrivance, deliberation, discretion, foresight, forethought, precaution

calibre noun 1 worth, ability, capacity, distinction, merit, quality, stature, talent 2 diameter, bore, gauge, measure

call verb 1 name, christen, describe as, designate, dub, entitle, label, style, term 2 cry, arouse, hail, rouse, shout, yell 3 phone, ring up (informal, chiefly Brit.), telephone 4 summon, assemble, convene, gather, muster, rally ♦ noun 5 cry, hail, scream, shout, signal, whoop, yell 6 summons, appeal, command, demand, invitation, notice, order, plea, request 7 need, cause, excuse, grounds, justification, occasion, reason

➤ Antonyms
verb ≠cry: be quiet, be silent, murmur, mutter, speak softly, whisper ≠summon: call off, cancel, dismiss, disperse ♦ noun ≠cry: murmur, mutter, whisper ≠summons: dismissal

call for verb 1 require, demand, entail, involve, necessitate, need, occasion, suggest 2 fetch, collect, pick up

calling noun profession, career, life's work, mission, trade, vocation

call on verb visit, drop in on,

look in on, look up, see

callous adjective heartless, cold, hard-bitten, hardened, hard-hearted, insensitive, uncaring, unfeeling

➤ **Antonyms**

caring, compassionate, considerate, gentle, sensitive, soft, sympathetic, tender, understanding

callow adjective inexperienced, green, guileless, immature, naive, raw, unsophisticated

calm adjective 1 cool, collected, composed, dispassionate, relaxed, sedate, self-possessed, unemotional 2 still, balmy, mild, quiet, serene, smooth, tranquil, windless ♦ noun 3 peacefulness, hush, peace, quiet, repose, serenity, stillness ♦ verb 4 quieten, hush, mollify, placate, relax, soothe

➤ **Antonyms**

adjective ≠cool: agitated, disturbed, emotional, excited, frantic, perturbed, shaken, troubled, worried ≠still: rough, stormy, wild ♦ noun ≠peacefulness: agitation, disturbance, wildness ♦ verb ≠quieten: aggravate, agitate, arouse, disturb, excite, irritate, stir

calmness noun 1 coolness, composure, cool (slang) equanimity, impassivity, poise, sang-froid, self-possession 2 peacefulness, calm, hush, quiet, repose, restfulness, serenity, stillness, tranquillity

camouflage noun 1 disguise, blind, cloak, concealment, cover, mask, masquerade, screen, subterfuge ♦ verb 2 disguise, cloak, conceal, cover, hide, mask, obfuscate, obscure, screen, veil

➤ **Antonyms**

verb ≠disguise: bare, display, exhibit, expose, reveal, show, uncover, unmask, unveil

camp[1] noun camp site, bivouac, camping ground, encampment, tents

camp[2] adjective Informal effemi-
nate, affected, artificial, mannered, ostentatious, posturing

campaign noun operation, attack, crusade, drive, expedition, movement, offensive, push

canal noun waterway, channel, conduit, duct, passage, watercourse

cancel verb 1 call off, abolish, abort, annul, delete, do away with, eliminate, erase, expunge, obliterate, repeal, revoke 2 cancel out make up for, balance out, compensate for, counterbalance, neutralize, nullify, offset

cancellation noun abandonment, abolition, annulment, deletion, elimination, repeal, revocation

cancer noun growth, corruption, malignancy, pestilence, sickness, tumour

candid adjective honest, blunt, forthright, frank, open, outspoken, plain, straightforward, truthful

➤ **Antonyms**

biased, complimentary, diplomatic, flattering, kind, subtle

candidate noun contender, applicant, claimant, competitor, contestant, entrant, nominee, runner

candour noun honesty, directness, forthrightness, frankness, openness, outspokenness, straightforwardness, truthfulness

➤ **Antonyms**

bias, cunning, deceit, diplomacy, dishonesty, flattery, insincerity, prejudice, subtlety

canker noun disease, bane, blight, cancer, corruption, infection, rot, scourge, sore, ulcer

cannon noun gun, big gun, field gun, mortar

canny adjective shrewd, astute, careful, cautious, clever, judicious, prudent, wise

➤ **Antonyms**

inept, obtuse, unskilled

canon noun 1 rule, criterion, dictate, formula, precept, principle, regulation, standard, statute, yardstick 2 list, catalogue, roll

canopy *noun* awning, covering, shade, sunshade

cant[1] *noun* **1** hypocrisy, humbug, insincerity, lip service, pretence, pretentiousness, sanctimoniousness **2** jargon, argot, lingo, patter, slang, vernacular

cant[2] *verb* tilt, angle, bevel, incline, rise, slant, slope

cantankerous *adjective* bad-tempered, choleric, contrary, disagreeable, grumpy, irascible, irritable, testy, waspish

➤ **Antonyms**
amiable, cheerful, genial, good-natured, happy, merry, pleasant

canter *noun* **1** jog, amble, dog-trot, lope ◆ *verb* **2** jog, amble, lope

canvass *verb* **1** campaign, electioneer, solicit, solicit votes **2** poll, examine, inspect, investigate, scrutinize, study ◆ *noun* **3** poll, examination, investigation, scrutiny, survey, tally

cap *verb* *Informal* beat, better, crown, eclipse, exceed, outdo, outstrip, surpass, top, transcend

capability *noun* ability, capacity, competence, means, potential, power, proficiency, qualification(s), wherewithal

➤ **Antonyms**
inability, incompetence, inefficiency, ineptitude, powerlessness

capable *adjective* able, accomplished, competent, efficient, gifted, proficient, qualified, talented

➤ **Antonyms**
incapable, incompetent, ineffective, inept, inexpert, unqualified, unskilled

capacious *adjective* spacious, broad, commodious, expansive, extensive, roomy, sizable *or* sizeable, substantial, vast, voluminous, wide

➤ **Antonyms**
confined, constricted, cramped, enclosed, incommodious, insubstantial, limited, narrow, poky, restricted, small, tight, tiny, uncomfortable

capacity *noun* **1** size, amplitude, compass, dimensions, extent, magnitude, range, room, scope, space, volume **2** ability, aptitude, aptness, capability, competence, facility, genius, gift **3** function, office, position, post, province, role, sphere

cape *noun* headland, head, peninsula, point, promontory

caper *noun* **1** escapade, antic, high jinks, jape, lark (*informal*), mischief, practical joke, prank, stunt ◆ *verb* **2** dance, bound, cavort, frolic, gambol, jump, skip, spring, trip

capital *noun* **1** money, assets, cash, finances, funds, investment(s), means, principal, resources, wealth, wherewithal ◆ *adjective* **2** principal, cardinal, major, prime, vital **3** *Old-fashioned* first-rate, excellent, fine, splendid, sterling, superb

capitalism *noun* private enterprise, free enterprise, laissez faire *or* laisser faire, private ownership

capitalize on *verb* take advantage of, benefit from, cash in on (*informal*), exploit, gain from, make the most of, profit from

capitulate *verb* give in, cave in (*informal*), come to terms, give up, relent, submit, succumb, surrender, yield

➤ **Antonyms**
beat, conquer, crush, defeat, subdue, subjugate, vanquish

caprice *noun* whim, fad, fancy, fickleness, impulse, inconstancy, notion, whimsy

capricious *adjective* unpredictable, changeful, erratic, fickle, fitful, impulsive, inconsistent, inconstant, mercurial, variable, wayward, whimsical

➤ **Antonyms**
consistent, constant, firm, immovable, resolute, stable, unchangeable, unwavering

capsize *verb* overturn, invert, keel over, tip over, turn over, turn turtle, upset

capsule noun **1** pill, lozenge, tablet **2** Botany pod, case, receptacle, seed case, sheath, shell, vessel

captain noun leader, boss, chief, commander, head, master, skipper

captivate verb charm, allure, attract, beguile, bewitch, enchant, enrapture, enthral, entrance, fascinate, infatuate, mesmerize

➤ **Antonyms**

alienate, disenchant, disgust, repel, repulse

captive noun **1** prisoner, convict, detainee, hostage, internee, prisoner of war, slave ♦ adjective **2** confined, caged, enslaved, ensnared, imprisoned, incarcerated, locked up, penned, restricted, subjugated

captivity noun confinement, bondage, custody, detention, imprisonment, incarceration, internment, slavery

capture verb **1** catch, apprehend, arrest, bag, collar (informal), secure, seize, take, take prisoner ♦ noun **2** catching, apprehension, arrest, imprisonment, seizure, taking, taking captive, trapping

➤ **Antonyms**

verb ≠catch: free, let go, let out, liberate, release, set free, turn loose

car noun **1** vehicle, auto (U.S.), automobile, jalopy (informal), machine, motor, motorcar, wheels (informal) **2** U.S. & Canad. (railway) carriage, buffet car, cable car, coach, dining car, sleeping car, van

carcass noun body, cadaver (Medical), corpse, dead body, framework, hulk, remains, shell, skeleton

cardinal adjective principal, capital, central, chief, essential, first, fundamental, key, leading, main, paramount, primary

➤ **Antonyms**

inessential, least important, low-

est, secondary, subordinate

care verb **1** be concerned, be bothered, be interested, mind ♦ noun **2** caution, attention, carefulness, consideration, forethought, heed, management, pains, prudence, vigilance, watchfulness **3** protection, charge, control, custody, guardianship, keeping, management, supervision **4** worry, anxiety, concern, disquiet, perplexity, pressure, responsibility, stress, trouble

➤ **Antonyms**

noun ≠caution: abandon, carelessness, heedlessness, inattention, indifference, laxness, neglect, negligence, unconcern ≠worry: pleasure, relaxation

career noun **1** occupation, calling, employment, life's work, livelihood, pursuit, vocation ♦ verb **2** rush, barrel (along) (informal, chiefly U.S. & Canad.), bolt, dash, hurtle, race, speed, tear

care for verb **1** look after, attend, foster, mind, minister to, nurse, protect, provide for, tend, watch over **2** like, be fond of, desire, enjoy, love, prize, take to, want

carefree adjective untroubled, blithe, breezy, cheerful, easygoing, halcyon, happy-go-lucky, light-hearted

➤ **Antonyms**

careworn, dejected, depressed, despondent, gloomy, low, melancholy, miserable, sad, unhappy, worried

careful adjective **1** cautious, chary, circumspect, discreet, prudent, scrupulous, thoughtful, thrifty **2** thorough, conscientious, meticulous, painstaking, particular, precise

➤ **Antonyms**

abandoned, careless, casual, inexact, neglectful, negligent, reckless, remiss, slovenly, thoughtless, unconcerned, untroubled

careless adjective **1** slapdash, cavalier, inaccurate, irresponsible, lackadaisical, neglectful, off-hand, slipshod, sloppy (*informal*) **2** negligent, absent-minded, forgetful, hasty, remiss, thoughtless, unthinking **3** nonchalant, artless, casual, unstudied

► **Antonyms**

≠ slapdash: accurate, careful, neat, orderly, painstaking, tidy ≠ negligent: attentive, careful, wary, watchful

carelessness noun negligence, indiscretion, irresponsibility, laxity, neglect, omission, slackness, sloppiness (*informal*), thoughtlessness

caress verb **1** stroke, cuddle, embrace, fondle, hug, kiss, neck (*informal*), nuzzle, pet ♦ noun **2** stroke, cuddle, embrace, fondling, hug, kiss, pat

caretaker noun warden, concierge, curator, custodian, janitor, keeper, porter, superintendent, watchman

cargo noun load, baggage, consignment, contents, freight, goods, merchandise, shipment

caricature noun **1** parody, burlesque, cartoon, distortion, farce, lampoon, satire, send-up (*Brit. informal*), takeoff (*informal*), travesty ♦ verb **2** parody, burlesque, distort, lampoon, mimic, mock, ridicule, satirize, send up (*Brit. informal*), take off (*informal*)

carnage noun slaughter, blood bath, bloodshed, butchery, havoc, holocaust, massacre, mass murder, murder, shambles

carnal adjective sexual, erotic, fleshly, lascivious, lewd, libidinous, lustful, sensual

carnival noun festival, celebration, fair, fête, fiesta, gala, holiday, jamboree, jubilee, merrymaking, revelry

carol noun song, chorus, ditty, hymn, lay

carp verb find fault, cavil, complain, criticize, pick holes, quibble, reproach

► **Antonyms**

admire, applaud, approve, com-

mend, pay tribute to, praise, speak highly of

carpenter noun joiner, cabinet-maker, woodworker

carriage noun **1** vehicle, cab, coach, conveyance **2** bearing, air, behaviour, comportment, conduct, demeanour, deportment, gait, manner, posture

carry verb **1** transport, bear, bring, conduct, convey, fetch, haul, lug, move, relay, take, transfer **2** win, accomplish, capture, effect, gain, secure

carry on verb **1** continue, endure, keep going, last, maintain, perpetuate, persevere, persist **2** *Informal* make a fuss, create (*slang*) misbehave, raise Cain

carry out verb perform, accomplish, achieve, carry through, effect, execute, fulfil, implement, realize

carton noun box, case, container, pack, package, packet

cartoon noun **1** drawing, caricature, comic strip, lampoon, parody, satire, sketch, takeoff (*informal*) **2** animation, animated cartoon, animated film

cartridge noun **1** shell, charge, round **2** container, capsule, case, cassette, cylinder, magazine

carve verb cut, chip, chisel, engrave, etch, hew, mould, sculpt, slice, whittle

cascade noun **1** waterfall, avalanche, cataract, deluge, downpour, falls, flood, fountain, outpouring, shower, torrent ♦ verb **2** flow, descend, fall, flood, gush, overflow, pitch, plunge, pour, spill, surge, teem, tumble

case¹ noun **1** instance, example, illustration, occasion, occurrence, specimen **2** situation, circumstance(s), condition, context, contingency, event, position, state **3** *Law* lawsuit, action, dispute, proceedings, suit, trial

case² noun **1** container, box, canister, carton, casket, chest, crate, holder, receptacle, suitcase, tray **2** covering, capsule, casing, envelope, jacket, sheath, shell, wrapper

cash noun money, brass (North English dialect), coinage, currency, dough (slang), funds, notes, ready money, silver

cashier[1] noun teller, bank clerk, banker, bursar, clerk, purser, treasurer

cashier[2] verb dismiss, discard, discharge, drum out, expel, give the boot to (slang)

casket noun box, case, chest, coffer, jewel box

cast noun 1 actors, characters, company, dramatis personae, players, troupe 2 type, complexion, manner, stamp, style ♦ verb 3 choose, allot, appoint, assign, name, pick, select 4 give out, bestow, deposit, diffuse, distribute, emit, radiate, scatter, shed, spread 5 form, found, model, mould, set, shape 6 throw, fling, hurl, launch, pitch, sling, thrust, toss

caste noun class, estate, grade, order, rank, social order, status, stratum

castigate verb reprimand, berate, censure, chastise, criticize, lambast(e), rebuke, scold

cast-iron adjective certain, copper-bottomed, definite, established, fixed, guaranteed, settled

castle noun fortress, chateau, citadel, keep, palace, stronghold, tower

cast-off adjective 1 unwanted, discarded, rejected, scrapped, surplus to requirements, unneeded, useless ♦ noun 2 reject, discard, failure, outcast, second

castrate verb neuter, emasculate, geld

casual adjective 1 careless, blasé, cursory, lackadaisical, nonchalant, offhand, relaxed, unconcerned 2 chance, accidental, incidental, irregular, occasional, random, unexpected 3 informal, non-dressy, sporty

► **Antonyms**

≠careless: committed, con-

cerned, enthusiastic, passionate, serious ≠chance: arranged, deliberate, expected, fixed, foreseen, intentional, planned, premeditated ≠informal: ceremonial, dressy, formal

casualty noun victim, death, fatality, loss, sufferer, wounded

cat noun feline, kitty (informal), moggy (slang), puss (informal), pussy (informal), tabby

catacombs plural noun vault, crypt, tomb

catalogue noun 1 list, directory, gazetteer, index, inventory, record, register, roll, roster, schedule ♦ verb 2 list, accession, alphabetize, classify, file, index, inventory, register, tabulate

catapult noun 1 sling, slingshot (U.S.) ♦ verb 2 shoot, heave, hurl, pitch, plunge, propel

catastrophe noun disaster, adversity, calamity, cataclysm, fiasco, misfortune, tragedy, trouble

catcall noun jeer, boo, gibe, hiss, raspberry, whistle

catch verb 1 seize, clutch, get, grab, grasp, grip, lay hold of, snatch, take 2 capture, apprehend, arrest, ensnare, entrap, snare, trap 3 discover, catch in the act, detect, expose, find out, surprise, take unawares, unmask 4 contract, develop, get, go down with, incur, succumb to, suffer from 5 make out, comprehend, discern, get, grasp, hear, perceive, recognize, sense, take in ♦ noun 6 fastener, bolt, clasp, clip, latch 7 Informal drawback, disadvantage, fly in the ointment, hitch, snag, stumbling block, trap, trick

► **Antonyms**

verb ≠seize: drop, free, give up, liberate, loose, release ≠contract: avert, avoid, escape, ward off ♦ noun ≠drawback: advantage, benefit, bonus, boon

catching adjective infectious, communicable, contagious, transferable, transmittable

➤ **Antonyms**

incommunicable, non-catching, non-contagious, non-infectious, non-transmittable

catch on verb Informal understand, comprehend, find out, get the picture, grasp, see, see through, twig (Brit. informal)

catchword noun slogan, byword, motto, password, watchword

catchy adjective memorable, captivating, haunting, popular

categorical adjective absolute, downright, emphatic, explicit, express, positive, unambiguous, unconditional, unequivocal, unqualified, unreserved

➤ **Antonyms**

conditional, indefinite, qualified, uncertain, vague

category noun class, classification, department, division, grade, grouping, heading, section, sort, type

cater verb provide, furnish, outfit, purvey, supply

cattle plural noun cows, beasts, bovines, livestock, stock

catty adjective spiteful, backbiting, bitchy (informal), malevolent, malicious, rancorous, shrewish, snide, venomous

➤ **Antonyms**

benevolent, charitable, generous, kind, pleasant

cause noun 1 origin, agent, beginning, creator, genesis, mainspring, maker, producer, root, source, spring 2 reason, basis, grounds, incentive, inducement, justification, motivation, motive, purpose 3 aim, belief, conviction, enterprise, ideal, movement, principle ♦ verb 4 produce, bring about, create, generate, give rise to, incite, induce, lead to, result in

➤ **Antonyms**

noun ≠origin: consequence, effect, end, outcome, result ♦ verb ≠produce: deter, foil, inhibit, prevent, stop

caustic adjective 1 burning, acrid,

astringent, biting, corroding, corrosive, mordant, vitriolic 2 sarcastic, acrimonious, cutting, pungent, scathing, stinging, trenchant, virulent, vitriolic

➤ **Antonyms**

≠sarcastic: gentle, kind, mild, pleasant, soft, soothing, sweet

caution noun 1 care, alertness, carefulness, circumspection, deliberation, discretion, forethought, heed, prudence, vigilance, watchfulness 2 warning, admonition, advice, counsel, injunction ♦ verb 3 warn, admonish, advise, tip off, urge

➤ **Antonyms**

noun ≠care: carelessness, daring, imprudence, rashness, recklessness ♦ verb ≠warn: dare

cautious adjective careful, cagey (informal), chary, circumspect, guarded, judicious, prudent, tentative, wary

➤ **Antonyms**

adventurous, bold, careless, daring, foolhardy, impetuous, inattentive, incautious, rash, reckless, unguarded

cavalcade noun parade, array, march-past, procession, spectacle, train

cavalier adjective haughty, arrogant, disdainful, lofty, lordly, offhand, scornful, supercilious

cavalry noun horsemen, horse, mounted troops

➤ **Antonyms**

foot soldiers, infantrymen

cave noun hollow, cavern, cavity, den, grotto

cavern noun cave, hollow, pothole

cavernous adjective deep, hollow, sunken, yawning

cavity noun hollow, crater, dent, gap, hole, pit

cease verb stop, break off, conclude, discontinue, end, finish, halt, leave off, refrain, terminate

➤ **Antonyms**

begin, commence, continue, initiate, start

ceaseless adjective continual,

constant, endless, eternal, everlasting, incessant, interminable, never-ending, nonstop, perpetual, unremitting

➤ **Antonyms**

intermittent, irregular, occasional, periodic, spasmodic, sporadic

cede *verb* surrender, concede, hand over, make over, relinquish, renounce, resign, transfer, yield

celebrate *verb* **1** rejoice, commemorate, drink to, keep, kill the fatted calf, observe, put the flags out, toast **2** perform, bless, honour, solemnize

celebrated *adjective* well-known, acclaimed, distinguished, eminent, famous, illustrious, notable, popular, prominent, renowned

➤ **Antonyms**

forgotten, insignificant, obscure, unacclaimed, undistinguished, unknown

celebration *noun* **1** party, festival, festivity, gala, jubilee, merrymaking, red-letter day, revelry **2** performance, anniversary, commemoration, honouring, observance, remembrance, solemnization

celebrity *noun* **1** personality, big name, big shot (*informal*), dignitary, luminary, star, superstar, V.I.P. **2** fame, distinction, notability, prestige, prominence, renown, reputation, repute, stardom

➤ **Antonyms**

≠personality: has-been, nobody, unknown ≠fame: obscurity

celestial *adjective* heavenly, angelic, astral, divine, ethereal, spiritual, sublime, supernatural

celibacy *noun* chastity, continence, purity, virginity

cell *noun* **1** room, cavity, chamber, compartment, cubicle, dungeon, stall **2** unit, caucus, core, coterie, group, nucleus

cement *noun* **1** mortar, adhesive, glue, gum, paste, plaster, sealant ◆ *verb* **2** stick together, attach, bind, bond, combine, glue, join, plaster, seal, unite, weld

cemetery *noun* graveyard, burial ground, churchyard, God's acre, necropolis

censor *verb* cut, blue-pencil, bowdlerize, expurgate

censorious *adjective* critical, captious, carping, cavilling, condemnatory, disapproving, disparaging, fault-finding, hypercritical, scathing, severe

censure *noun* **1** disapproval, blame, condemnation, criticism, obloquy, rebuke, reprimand, reproach, reproof, stick (*slang*) ◆ *verb* **2** criticize, blame, castigate, condemn, denounce, rap over the knuckles, rebuke, reprimand, reproach, scold, slap on the wrist

➤ **Antonyms**

noun ≠disapproval: approval, commendation, encouragement ◆ *verb* ≠criticize: applaud, commend, compliment

central *adjective* **1** middle, inner, interior, mean, median, mid **2** main, chief, essential, focal, fundamental, key, primary, principal

➤ **Antonyms**

≠middle: exterior, outer, outermost ≠main: minor, secondary, subordinate, subsidiary

centralize *verb* unify, concentrate, condense, incorporate, rationalize, streamline

centre *noun* **1** middle, core, focus, heart, hub, kernel, midpoint, nucleus, pivot ◆ *verb* **2** focus, cluster, concentrate, converge, revolve

➤ **Antonyms**

noun ≠middle: border, boundary, brim, circumference, edge, fringe, lip, margin, perimeter, periphery, rim

ceremonial *adjective* **1** ritual, formal, liturgical, ritualistic, solemn, stately ◆ *noun* **2** ritual, ceremony, formality, rite, solemnity

ceremonious

➤ **Antonyms**

adjective ≠*ritual*: casual, informal, relaxed, simple

ceremonious *adjective* formal, civil, courteous, deferential, dignified, punctilious, solemn, stately, stiff

ceremony *noun* 1 ritual, commemoration, function, observance, parade, rite, service, show, solemnities 2 formality, ceremonial, decorum, etiquette, niceties, pomp, propriety, protocol

certain *adjective* 1 sure, assured, confident, convinced, positive, satisfied 2 known, conclusive, incontrovertible, irrefutable, true, undeniable, unequivocal 3 inevitable, bound, definite, destined, fated, inescapable, sure 4 fixed, decided, definite, established, settled

➤ **Antonyms**

disputable, doubtful, dubious, equivocal, indefinite, questionable, uncertain, unconvinced, undecided, unlikely, unreliable, unsettled, unsure

certainly *adverb* definitely, assuredly, indisputably, indubitably, surely, truly, undeniably, undoubtedly, without doubt

certainty *noun* 1 sureness, assurance, confidence, conviction, faith, positiveness, trust, validity 2 fact, banker, reality, sure thing (*informal*), truth

➤ **Antonyms**

≠*sureness*: disbelief, doubt, indecision, scepticism, uncertainty, unsureness

certificate *noun* document, authorization, credential(s), diploma, licence, testimonial, voucher, warrant

certify *verb* confirm, assure, attest, authenticate, declare, guarantee, testify, validate, verify

chafe *verb* 1 rub, abrade, rasp, scrape, scratch 2 be annoyed, be impatient, fret, fume, rage, worry

chaff[1] *noun* waste, dregs, husks,

refuse, remains, rubbish, trash

chaff[2] *verb* tease, mock, rib (*informal*), ridicule, scoff, taunt

chain *noun* 1 link, bond, coupling, fetter, manacle, shackle 2 series, progression, sequence, set, string, succession, train ◆ *verb* 3 bind, confine, enslave, fetter, handcuff, manacle, restrain, shackle, tether

chairman *noun* director, chairperson, chairwoman, master of ceremonies, president, speaker, spokesman

challenge *noun* 1 test, confrontation, provocation, question, trial, ultimatum ◆ *verb* 2 test, confront, defy, dispute, object to, question, tackle, throw down the gauntlet

chamber *noun* 1 room, apartment, bedroom, compartment, cubicle, enclosure, hall 2 council, assembly, legislative body, legislature

champion *noun* 1 winner, conqueror, hero, title holder, victor 2 defender, backer, guardian, patron, protector, upholder ◆ *verb* 3 support, advocate, back, commend, defend, encourage, espouse, fight for, promote, uphold

chance *noun* 1 probability, likelihood, odds, possibility, prospect 2 opportunity, occasion, opening, time 3 luck, accident, coincidence, destiny, fate, fortune, providence 4 risk, gamble, hazard, jeopardy, speculation, uncertainty ◆ *verb* 5 risk, endanger, gamble, hazard, jeopardize, stake, try, venture, wager

➤ **Antonyms**

noun ≠*probability*: certainty, design, impossibility, improbability, intention, surety, unlikelihood

change *noun* 1 alteration, difference, innovation, metamorphosis, modification, mutation, revolution, transformation, transition 2 variety, break (*informal*), departure, diversion, novelty, variation 3 exchange, conversion, interchange, substitution, swap, trade ◆ verb 4 alter, convert, modify, mutate, reform, reorganize, restyle, shift, transform, vary 5 exchange, barter, convert, interchange, replace, substitute, swap, trade

► Antonyms

noun ≠alteration, variety: constancy, invariability, monotony, permanence, stability, uniformity ◆ verb ≠alter: hold, keep, remain, stay

changeable adjective variable, erratic, fickle, inconstant, irregular, mobile, mutable, protean, shifting, unsettled, unstable, volatile, wavering

► Antonyms

constant, invariable, irreversible, regular, reliable, stable, steady, unchangeable

channel noun 1 route, approach, artery, avenue, course, means, medium, path, way 2 passage, canal, conduit, duct, furrow, groove, gutter, route, strait ◆ verb 3 direct, conduct, convey, guide, transmit

chant verb 1 sing, carol, chorus, descant, intone, recite, warble ◆ noun 2 song, carol, chorus, melody, psalm

chaos noun disorder, anarchy, bedlam, confusion, disorganization, lawlessness, mayhem, pandemonium, tumult

► Antonyms

neatness, orderliness, organization, tidiness

chaotic adjective disordered, anarchic, confused, deranged, disorganized, lawless, riotous, topsy-turvy, tumultuous, uncontrolled

chap noun Informal fellow, bloke (Brit. informal), character, guy (informal), individual, man, person

chaperone noun 1 escort, companion ◆ verb 2 escort, accompany, attend, protect, safeguard, shepherd, watch over

chapter noun section, clause, division, episode, part, period, phase, stage, topic

character noun 1 nature, attributes, calibre, complexion, disposition, personality, quality, temperament, type 2 reputation, honour, integrity, rectitude, strength, uprightness 3 role, part, persona, portrayal 4 eccentric, card (informal), oddball (informal), original 5 symbol, device, figure, hieroglyph, letter, mark, rune, sign

characteristic noun 1 feature, attribute, faculty, idiosyncrasy, mark, peculiarity, property, quality, quirk, trait ◆ adjective 2 typical, distinctive, distinguishing, idiosyncratic, individual, peculiar, representative, singular, special, symbolic, symptomatic

► Antonyms

adjective ≠typical: rare, uncharacteristic, unrepresentative, unusual

characterize verb identify, brand, distinguish, indicate, mark, represent, stamp, typify

charade noun pretence, fake, farce, pantomime, parody, travesty

charge verb 1 accuse, arraign, blame, impeach, incriminate, indict 2 attack, assail, assault, rush, stampede, storm 3 fill, load 4 Formal command, bid, commit, demand, entrust, instruct, order, require ◆ noun 5 price, amount, cost, expenditure, expense, outlay, payment, rate, toll 6 accusation, allegation, imputation, indictment 7 attack, assault, onset, onslaught, rush, sortie, stampede 8 care, custody, duty, office, responsibility, safekeeping, trust 9 ward 10 instruction, command, demand, direction, injunction, mandate, order, precept

► Antonyms

verb ≠accuse: absolve, acquit, clear, exonerate, pardon ≠attack: back off, retreat, withdraw ◆ noun ≠accusation: absolution, acquittal, clearance, exoneration, pardon, reprieve ≠attack: retreat, withdrawal

charisma noun charm, allure, attraction, lure, magnetism, personality

charismatic *adjective* <u>charming</u>, alluring, attractive, enticing, influential, magnetic

charitable *adjective* **1** <u>kind</u>, considerate, favourable, forgiving, humane, indulgent, lenient, magnanimous, sympathetic, tolerant, understanding **2** <u>generous</u>, beneficent, benevolent, bountiful, kind, lavish, liberal, philanthropic

➤ **Antonyms**

≠<u>kind</u>: inconsiderate, mean, strict, uncharitable, unforgiving, unkind, unsympathetic ≠<u>generous</u>: mean, stingy, ungenerous

charity *noun* **1** <u>donations</u>, assistance, benefaction, contributions, endowment, fund, gift, hand-out, help, largesse *or* largess, philanthropy, relief **2** <u>kindness</u>, altruism, benevolence, compassion, fellow feeling, generosity, goodwill, humanity, indulgence

➤ **Antonyms**

≠<u>donations</u>: meanness, miserliness, selfishness, stinginess ≠<u>kindness</u>: hatred, ill will, intolerance, malice

charlatan *noun* <u>fraud</u>, cheat, con man (*informal*), fake, impostor, phoney *or* phony (*informal*), pretender, quack, sham, swindler

charm *noun* **1** <u>attraction</u>, allure, appeal, fascination, magnetism **2** <u>spell</u>, enchantment, magic, sorcery **3** <u>talisman</u>, amulet, fetish, trinket ✦ *verb* **4** <u>attract</u>, allure, beguile, bewitch, captivate, delight, enchant, enrapture, entrance, fascinate, mesmerize, win over

➤ **Antonyms**

noun ≠<u>attraction</u>: repulsiveness, unattractiveness ✦ *verb* ≠<u>attract</u>: alienate, repel, repulse

charming *adjective* <u>attractive</u>, appealing, captivating, cute, delightful, fetching, likable *or* likeable, pleasing, seductive, winsome

➤ **Antonyms**

disgusting, horrid, repulsive, unappealing, unattractive, unlikable *or* unlikeable, unpleasant, unpleasing

chart *noun* **1** <u>table</u>, blueprint, diagram, graph, map, plan ✦ *verb* **2** <u>plot</u>, delineate, draft, map out, outline, shape, sketch

charter *noun* **1** <u>document</u>, contract, deed, licence, permit, prerogative ✦ *verb* **2** <u>hire</u>, commission, employ, lease, rent **3** <u>authorize</u>, sanction

chase *verb* **1** <u>pursue</u>, course, follow, hunt, run after, track **2** <u>drive away</u>, drive, expel, hound, put to flight ✦ *noun* **3** <u>pursuit</u>, hunt, hunting, race

chasm *noun* <u>gulf</u>, abyss, crater, crevasse, fissure, gap, gorge, ravine

chaste *adjective* <u>pure</u>, immaculate, innocent, modest, simple, unaffected, undefiled, virtuous

➤ **Antonyms**

corrupt, dirty, immoral, impure, promiscuous, unchaste, unclean, wanton

chasten *verb* <u>subdue</u>, chastise, correct, discipline, humble, humiliate, put in one's place, tame

chastise *verb* **1** <u>scold</u>, berate, castigate, censure, correct, discipline, upbraid **2** *Old-fashioned* <u>beat</u>, flog, lash, lick (*informal*), punish, scourge, whip

➤ **Antonyms**

≠<u>scold</u>: commend, compliment, congratulate, praise, reward ≠<u>beat</u>: caress, cuddle, embrace, fondle, hug

chastity *noun* <u>purity</u>, celibacy, continence, innocence, maidenhood, modesty, virginity, virtue

➤ **Antonyms**

debauchery, immorality, lewdness, licentiousness, promiscuity, wantonness

chat *noun* **1** <u>talk</u>, chatter, chinwag (*Brit. informal*), conversation, gossip, heart-to-heart, natter, tête-à-tête ✦ *verb* **2** <u>talk</u>, chatter, gossip, jaw (*slang*), natter

chatter noun 1 prattle, babble, blather, chat, gab (informal), gossip, natter ◆ verb 2 prattle, babble, blather, chat, gab (informal), gossip, natter, rabbit (on) (Brit. informal), schmooze (slang)

cheap adjective 1 inexpensive, bargain, cut-price, economical, keen, low-cost, low-priced, reasonable, reduced 2 inferior, common, poor, second-rate, shoddy, tatty, tawdry, two a penny, worthless 3 Informal despicable, contemptible, mean

➤ **Antonyms**
≠inexpensive: costly, dear, expensive, pricey (informal), steep ≠inferior: admirable, decent, elegant, good, high-class, superior, tasteful, valuable ≠despicable: admirable, decent, generous, good, honourable

cheapen verb degrade, belittle, debase, demean, denigrate, depreciate, devalue, discredit, disparage, lower

cheat verb 1 deceive, beguile, con (informal), defraud, doublecross (informal), dupe, fleece, fool, mislead, rip off (slang), swindle, trick ◆ noun 2 deceiver, charlatan, con man (informal), double-crosser (informal), shark, sharper, swindler, trickster 3 deception, deceit, fraud, rip-off (slang), scam (slang), swindle, trickery

check verb 1 examine, inquire into, inspect, investigate, look at, make sure, monitor, research, scrutinize, study, test, vet 2 stop, delay, halt, hinder, impede, inhibit, limit, obstruct, restrain, retard ◆ noun 3 examination, inspection, investigation, onceover (informal), research, scrutiny, test 4 stoppage, constraint, control, curb, damper, hindrance, impediment, limitation, obstacle, obstruction, restraint

➤ **Antonyms**
verb ≠examine: disregard, ignore, neglect, overlook, pass over, pay no attention to ≠stop: accelerate, advance, begin, encourage, further, give free rein, help, release, start

cheek noun Informal impudence, audacity, chutzpah (U.S. & Canad. informal), disrespect, effrontery, impertinence, insolence, lip (slang), nerve, temerity

cheeky adjective impudent, audacious, disrespectful, forward, impertinent, insolent, insulting, pert, saucy

➤ **Antonyms**
civil, courteous, deferential, mannerly, polite, respectful, well-behaved, well-mannered

cheer verb 1 applaud, acclaim, clap, hail 2 cheer up, brighten, buoy up, comfort, encourage, gladden, hearten, uplift ◆ noun 3 applause, acclamation, ovation, plaudits

➤ **Antonyms**
verb ≠applaud: blow a raspberry, boo, hiss, jeer, ridicule ≠cheer up: depress, discourage, dishearten, sadden

cheerful adjective happy, buoyant, cheery, chirpy (informal), enthusiastic, jaunty, jolly, light-hearted, merry, optimistic, upbeat (informal)

➤ **Antonyms**
cheerless, dejected, depressed, depressing, despondent, dismal, down, downcast, dull, gloomy, low, melancholy, miserable, morose, pensive, sad, unhappy

cheerfulness noun happiness, buoyancy, exuberance, gaiety, geniality, good cheer, good humour, high spirits, jauntiness, light-heartedness

cheerless adjective gloomy, bleak, desolate, dismal, drab, dreary, forlorn, miserable, sombre, woeful

➤ **Antonyms**
cheerful, cheery, happy, jolly, joyful, light-hearted, merry

cheer up verb 1 comfort, encourage, enliven, gee up, gladden, hearten, jolly along (informal) 2 take heart, buck up (informal), perk up, rally

cheery *adjective* <u>cheerful</u>, breezy, carefree, chirpy (*informal*), genial, good-humoured, happy, jovial, upbeat (*informal*)

chemist *noun* <u>pharmacist</u>, apothecary (*obsolete*), dispenser

cherish *verb* <u>cling to</u>, cleave to, encourage, entertain, foster, harbour, hold dear, nurture, prize, sustain, treasure 2 <u>care for</u>, comfort, hold dear, love, nurse, shelter, support

➤ **Antonyms**

abandon, desert, despise, disdain, dislike, forsake, hate, neglect

chest *noun* <u>box</u>, case, casket, coffer, crate, strongbox, trunk

chew *verb* <u>bite</u>, champ, chomp, crunch, gnaw, grind, masticate, munch

chewy *adjective* <u>tough</u>, as tough as old boots, leathery

chic *adjective* <u>stylish</u>, elegant, fashionable, smart, trendy (*Brit. informal*)

➤ **Antonyms**

inelegant, old-fashioned, outmoded, out-of-date, unfashionable

chide *verb* Old-fashioned <u>scold</u>, admonish, berate, censure, criticize, lecture, rebuke, reprimand, reproach, reprove, tell off (*informal*), tick off (*informal*)

chief *noun* 1 <u>head</u>, boss (*informal*), captain, commander, director, governor, leader, manager, master, principal, ruler ♦ *adjective* 2 <u>primary</u>, foremost, highest, key, leading, main, predominant, pre-eminent, premier, prime, principal, supreme, uppermost

➤ **Antonyms**

noun ≠<u>head</u>: follower, subject, subordinate ♦ *adjective* ≠<u>primary</u>: least, minor, subordinate, subsidiary

chiefly *adverb* 1 <u>especially</u>, above all, essentially, primarily, principally 2 <u>mainly</u>, in general, in the main, largely, mostly, on the whole, predominantly, usually

child *noun* <u>youngster</u>, babe, baby, bairn (*Scot.*), infant, juvenile, kid (*informal*), offspring, toddler, tot

childbirth *noun* <u>child-bearing</u>, confinement, delivery, labour, lying-in, parturition, travail

childhood *noun* <u>youth</u>, boyhood *or* girlhood, immaturity, infancy, minority, schooldays

childish *adjective* <u>immature</u>, boyish *or* girlish, foolish, infantile, juvenile, puerile, young

➤ **Antonyms**

adult, grown-up, manly *or* womanly, mature, sensible, sophisticated

childlike *adjective* <u>innocent</u>, artless, guileless, ingenuous, naive, simple, trusting

chill *noun* 1 <u>cold</u>, bite, coldness, coolness, crispness, frigidity, nip, rawness, sharpness ♦ *verb* 2 <u>cool</u>, freeze, refrigerate 3 <u>dishearten</u>, dampen, deject, depress, discourage, dismay ♦ *adjective* 4 <u>cold</u>, biting, bleak, chilly, freezing, frigid, raw, sharp, wintry

chilly *adjective* 1 <u>cool</u>, brisk, crisp, draughty, fresh, nippy, penetrating, sharp 2 <u>unfriendly</u>, frigid, hostile, unresponsive, unsympathetic, unwelcoming

➤ **Antonyms**

≠<u>cool</u>: balmy, hot, mild, scorching, sunny, sweltering, warm ≠<u>unfriendly</u>: congenial, cordial, friendly, sympathetic, warm, welcoming

chime *verb, noun* <u>ring</u>, clang, jingle, peal, sound, tinkle, toll

china *noun* <u>pottery</u>, ceramics, crockery, porcelain, service, tableware, ware

chink *noun* <u>opening</u>, aperture, cleft, crack, cranny, crevice, fissure, gap

chip *noun* 1 <u>scratch</u>, fragment, nick, notch, shard, shaving, sliver, wafer ♦ *verb* 2 <u>nick</u>, chisel, damage, gash, whittle

chirp *verb* <u>chirrup</u>, cheep, peep, pipe, tweet, twitter, warble

chivalrous *adjective* <u>courteous</u>,

bold, brave, courageous, gallant, gentlemanly, honourable, valiant

➤ **Antonyms**

boorish, cowardly, dishonourable, disloyal, rude, uncourtly, ungallant, unmannerly

chivalry noun <u>courtesy</u>, courage, gallantry, gentlemanliness, knight-errantry, knighthood, politeness

choice noun **1** <u>option</u>, alternative, pick, preference, say **2** <u>selection</u>, range, variety ♦ adjective **3** <u>best</u>, elite, excellent, exclusive, prime, rare, select

choke verb **1** <u>strangle</u>, asphyxiate, gag, overpower, smother, stifle, suffocate, suppress, throttle **2** <u>block</u>, bar, bung, clog, congest, constrict, obstruct, stop

choose verb <u>pick</u>, adopt, designate, elect, opt for, prefer, select, settle upon

➤ **Antonyms**

decline, dismiss, exclude, forgo, leave, refuse, reject, throw aside

choosy adjective Informal <u>fussy</u>, discriminating, faddy, fastidious, finicky, particular, picky (informal), selective

➤ **Antonyms**

easy to please, undemanding, unselective

chop verb <u>cut</u>, cleave, fell, hack, hew, lop, sever

chore noun <u>task</u>, burden, duty, errand, job

chortle verb, noun <u>chuckle</u>, cackle, crow, guffaw

chorus noun **1** <u>choir</u>, choristers, ensemble, singers, vocalists **2** <u>refrain</u>, burden, response, strain **3** <u>unison</u>, accord, concert, harmony

christen verb **1** <u>baptize</u> **2** <u>name</u>, call, designate, dub, style, term, title

Christmas noun <u>festive season</u>, Noel, Xmas (informal), Yule (archaic), Yuletide (archaic)

chronicle noun **1** <u>record</u>, account, annals, diary, history, journal, narrative, register, story ♦ verb **2** <u>record</u>, enter, narrate, put on record, recount, register,

relate, report, set down, tell

chubby adjective <u>plump</u>, buxom, flabby, podgy, portly, roly-poly, rotund, round, stout, tubby

➤ **Antonyms**

lean, skinny, slender, slight, slim, thin

chuck verb Informal <u>throw</u>, cast, fling, heave, hurl, pitch, sling, toss

chuckle verb <u>laugh</u>, chortle, crow, exult, giggle, snigger, titter

chum noun Informal <u>friend</u>, companion, comrade, crony, mate (informal), pal (informal)

chunk noun <u>piece</u>, block, dollop (informal), hunk, lump, mass, nugget, portion, slab

churlish adjective <u>rude</u>, brusque, harsh, ill-tempered, impolite, sullen, surly, uncivil

➤ **Antonyms**

amiable, civil, courteous, good-tempered, pleasant, polite

churn verb <u>stir up</u>, agitate, beat, convulse, swirl, toss

cinema noun <u>films</u>, big screen (informal), flicks (slang), motion pictures, movies, pictures

cipher noun **1** <u>code</u>, cryptograph **2** <u>nobody</u>, nonentity

circle noun **1** <u>ring</u>, disc, globe, orb, sphere **2** <u>group</u>, clique, club, company, coterie, set, society ♦ verb **3** <u>go round</u>, circumnavigate, circumscribe, encircle, enclose, envelop, ring, surround, wheel

circuit noun <u>course</u>, journey, lap, orbit, revolution, route, tour, track

circuitous adjective <u>indirect</u>, labyrinthine, meandering, oblique, rambling, roundabout, tortuous, winding

➤ **Antonyms**

as the crow flies, direct, straight, undeviating, unswerving

circular adjective **1** <u>round</u>, ring-shaped, rotund, spherical **2** <u>orbital</u>, circuitous, cyclical ♦ noun **3** <u>advertisement</u>, notice

circulate verb **1** <u>spread</u>, broadcast, disseminate, distribute, issue, make known, promulgate, publicize, publish 2 flow, gyrate, radiate, revolve, rotate

circulation noun 1 bloodstream 2 flow, circling, motion, rotation 3 distribution, currency, dissemination, spread, transmission

circumference noun boundary, border, edge, extremity, limits, outline, perimeter, periphery, rim

circumstance noun event, accident, condition, contingency, happening, incident, occurrence, particular, respect, situation

circumstances plural noun situation, means, position, state, state of affairs, station, status

cistern noun tank, basin, reservoir, sink, vat

citadel noun fortress, bastion, fortification, keep, stronghold, tower

cite verb quote, adduce, advance, allude to, enumerate, extract, mention, name, specify

citizen noun inhabitant, denizen, dweller, resident, subject, townsman

city noun town, conurbation, metropolis, municipality

civic adjective public, communal, local, municipal

civil adjective 1 civic, domestic, municipal, political 2 polite, affable, courteous, obliging, refined, urbane, well-mannered

➤ Antonyms

≠civic: military, religious, state ≠polite: discourteous, ill-mannered, impolite, rude, uncivil, ungracious

civilization noun 1 culture, advancement, cultivation, development, education, enlightenment, progress, refinement, sophistication 2 society, community, nation, people, polity

civilize verb cultivate, educate, enlighten, refine, sophisticate, tame

civilized adjective cultured, educated, enlightened, humane, polite, sophisticated, tolerant, urbane

➤ Antonyms

ignorant, naive, primitive, simple, uncivilized, uncultivated, uncultured, undeveloped, unenlightened, unsophisticated, wild

claim verb 1 assert, allege, challenge, insist, maintain, profess, uphold 2 demand, ask, call for, insist, need, require ♦ noun 2 assertion, affirmation, allegation, pretension, privilege, protestation 4 demand, application, call, petition, request, requirement 5 right, title

clairvoyant noun 1 psychic, diviner, fortune-teller, visionary ♦ adjective 2 psychic, extrasensory, second-sighted, telepathic, visionary

clamber verb climb, claw, scale, scrabble, scramble, shin

clammy adjective moist, close, damp, dank, sticky, sweaty

clamour noun noise, commotion, din, hubbub, outcry, racket, shouting, uproar

clamp noun 1 vice, bracket, fastener, grip, press ♦ verb 2 fasten, brace, fix, make fast, secure

clan noun family, brotherhood, faction, fraternity, group, society, tribe

clandestine adjective secret, cloak-and-dagger, concealed, covert, furtive, private, stealthy, surreptitious, underground

clap verb applaud, acclaim, cheer

➤ Antonyms

blow a raspberry, boo, catcall, hiss, jeer

clarification noun explanation, elucidation, exposition, illumination, interpretation, simplification

clarify verb explain, clear up, elucidate, illuminate, interpret, make plain, simplify, throw or shed light on

clarity noun clearness, definition, limpidity, lucidity, precision, simplicity, transparency

➤ Antonyms

cloudiness, complexity, haziness, imprecision, intricacy, obscurity

clash verb 1 conflict, cross

swords, feud, grapple, lock horns, quarrel, war, wrangle **2** <u>crash</u>, bang, clang, clank, clatter, jangle, jar, rattle ♦ noun **2** <u>conflict</u>, brush, collision, confrontation, difference of opinion, disagreement, fight, showdown (informal)

clasp noun **1** <u>fastening</u>, brooch, buckle, catch, clip, fastener, grip, hook, pin **2** <u>grasp</u>, embrace, grip, hold, hug ♦ verb **3** <u>grasp</u>, clutch, embrace, grip, hold, hug, press, seize, squeeze **4** <u>fasten</u>, connect

class noun **1** <u>group</u>, category, division, genre, kind, set, sort, type ♦ verb **2** <u>classify</u>, brand, categorize, designate, grade, group, label, rank, rate

classic adjective **1** <u>definitive</u>, archetypal, exemplary, ideal, model, quintessential, standard **2** <u>typical</u>, characteristic, regular, standard, time-honoured, usual **3** <u>best</u>, consummate, finest, first-rate, masterly, world-class **4** <u>lasting</u>, abiding, ageless, deathless, enduring, immortal, undying ♦ noun **5** <u>standard</u>, exemplar, masterpiece, model, paradigm, prototype

► **Antonyms**

adjective ≠<u>best</u>: inferior, modern, poor, second-rate, terrible

classical adjective <u>pure</u>, elegant, harmonious, refined, restrained, symmetrical, understated, well-proportioned

classification noun <u>categorization</u>, analysis, arrangement, grading, sorting, taxonomy

classify verb <u>categorize</u>, arrange, catalogue, grade, pigeonhole, rank, sort, systematize, tabulate

classy adjective Informal <u>high-class</u>, elegant, exclusive, posh (informal, chiefly Brit.), stylish, superior, top-drawer, up-market

clause noun <u>section</u>, article, chapter, condition, paragraph, part, passage

claw noun **1** <u>nail</u>, pincer, talon, tentacle ♦ verb **2** <u>scratch</u>, dig, lacerate, maul, rip, scrape, tear

clean adjective **1** <u>pure</u>, flawless, fresh, immaculate, impeccable, spotless, unblemished, unsullied **2** <u>hygienic</u>, antiseptic, decontaminated, purified, sterile, sterilized, uncontaminated, unpolluted **3** <u>moral</u>, chaste, decent, good, honourable, innocent, pure, respectable, upright, virtuous **4** <u>complete</u>, conclusive, decisive, entire, final, perfect, thorough, total, unimpaired, whole ♦ verb **5** <u>cleanse</u>, disinfect, launder, purge, purify, rinse, sanitize, scour, scrub, wash

► **Antonyms**

adjective ≠<u>pure</u>: dirty, filthy, mucky, soiled, sullied, unwashed ≠<u>hygienic</u>: adulterated, contaminated, infected, polluted ≠<u>moral</u>: dishonourable, immoral, impure, indecent, unchaste ♦ verb ≠<u>cleanse</u>: adulterate, defile, dirty, infect, mess up, pollute, soil, stain

cleanse verb <u>clean</u>, absolve, clear, purge, purify, rinse, scour, scrub, wash

cleanser noun <u>detergent</u>, disinfectant, purifier, scourer, soap, solvent

clear adjective **1** <u>certain</u>, convinced, decided, definite, positive, resolved, satisfied, sure **2** <u>obvious</u>, apparent, blatant, comprehensible, conspicuous, distinct, evident, manifest, palpable, plain, pronounced, recognizable, unmistakable **3** <u>transparent</u>, crystalline, glassy, limpid, pellucid, see-through, translucent **4** <u>bright</u>, cloudless, fair, fine, light, luminous, shining, sunny, unclouded **5** <u>unobstructed</u>, empty, free, open, smooth, unhindered, unimpeded **6** <u>unblemished</u>, clean, immaculate, innocent, pure, untarnished ♦ verb **7** <u>unblock</u>, disentangle, extricate, free, loosen, open, rid, unload **8** <u>pass over</u>, jump, leap, miss, vault **9** <u>brighten</u>, break up, lighten **10** <u>clean</u>, cleanse, erase, purify, refine, sweep away, tidy (up), wipe **11** absolve, acquit, excuse, exonerate, justify, vindicate **12** gain, acquire, earn, make, reap, secure

➤ **Antonyms**
adjective ≠obvious: confused, doubtful, hidden, indistinct, obscured, unrecognizable ≠transparent: cloudy, muddy, nontransparent, opaque, turbid ≠bright: cloudy, dark, dull, foggy, hazy, misty, murky, overcast, stormy ≠unobstructed: barricaded, blocked, closed, hampered, impeded, obstructed ♦ *verb* ≠absolve: accuse, blame, charge, condemn, convict, find guilty

clear-cut *adjective* straightforward, black-and-white, cut-and-dried (*informal*), definite, explicit, plain, precise, specific, unambiguous, unequivocal

clearly *adverb* obviously, beyond doubt, distinctly, evidently, markedly, openly, overtly, undeniably, undoubtedly

clergy *noun* priesthood, churchmen, clergymen, clerics, holy orders, ministry, the cloth

clergyman *noun* minister, chaplain, cleric, man of God, man of the cloth, padre, parson, pastor, priest, vicar

clever *adjective* intelligent, bright, gifted, ingenious, knowledgeable, quick-witted, resourceful, shrewd, smart, talented

➤ **Antonyms**
awkward, clumsy, dense, dull, dumb (*informal*), inept, inexpert, maladroit, slow, stupid, thick, unaccomplished, witless

cleverness *noun* intelligence, ability, brains, ingenuity, quick wits, resourcefulness, shrewdness, smartness

cliché *noun* platitude, banality, commonplace, hackneyed phrase, stereotype, truism

client *noun* customer, applicant, buyer, consumer, patient, patron, shopper

clientele *noun* customers, business, clients, following, market,

patronage, regulars, trade

cliff *noun* rock face, bluff, crag, escarpment, overhang, precipice, scar, scarp

climactic *adjective* crucial, critical, decisive, paramount, peak

climate *noun* weather, temperature

climax *noun* culmination, height, highlight, high point, peak, summit, top, zenith

climb *verb* ascend, clamber, mount, rise, scale, shin up, soar, top

climb down *verb* **1** descend, dismount **2** back down, eat one's words, retract, retreat

clinch *verb* settle, conclude, confirm, decide, determine, seal, secure, set the seal on, sew up (*informal*)

cling *verb* stick, adhere, clasp, clutch, embrace, grasp, grip, hug

clinical *adjective* unemotional, analytic, cold, detached, dispassionate, impersonal, objective, scientific

clip¹ *verb* **1** trim, crop, curtail, cut, pare, prune, shear, shorten, snip ♦ *noun, verb* **2** *Informal* smack, clout (*informal*), cuff, knock, punch, strike, thump, wallop (*informal*), whack

clip² *verb* attach, fasten, fix, hold, pin, staple

clique *noun* group, cabal, circle, coterie, faction, gang, set

cloak *noun* **1** cape, coat, mantle, wrap ♦ *verb* **2** cover, camouflage, conceal, disguise, hide, mask, obscure, screen, veil

clog *verb* obstruct, block, congest, hinder, impede, jam

close¹ *verb* **1** shut, bar, block, lock, plug, seal, secure, stop up **2** end, cease, complete, conclude, finish, shut down, terminate, wind up **3** connect, come together, couple, fuse, join, unite ♦ *noun* **4** end, completion, conclusion, culmination, denouement, ending, finale, finish

➤ **Antonyms**
verb ≠shut: clear, free, open, re-

lease, unblock, unclog, uncork, unstop, widen ≠**end**: begin, commence, initiate, open, start ≠**connect**: disconnect, disjoin, disunite, divide, part, separate, split, uncouple

close² adjective **1** <u>near</u>, adjacent, adjoining, at hand, cheek by jowl, handy, impending, nearby, neighbouring, nigh **2** <u>intimate</u>, attached, confidential, dear, devoted, familiar, inseparable, loving **3** <u>careful</u>, detailed, intense, minute, painstaking, rigorous, thorough **4** <u>compact</u>, congested, crowded, dense, impenetrable, jam-packed, packed, tight **5** <u>stifling</u>, airless, heavy, humid, muggy, oppressive, stuffy, suffocating, sweltering **6** <u>secretive</u>, private, reticent, secret, taciturn, uncommunicative **7** <u>mean</u>, miserly, stingy

► **Antonyms**

≠**near**: distant, far, far away, far off, outlying, remote ≠**intimate**: alienated, aloof, chilly, cold, cool, distant, indifferent, standoffish, unfriendly ≠**compact**: dispersed, free, loose, uncongested, uncrowded ≠**stifling**: airy, fresh ≠**mean**: charitable, extravagant, generous, lavish, liberal, magnanimous, unstinting

closed adjective **1** <u>shut</u>, fastened, locked, out of service, sealed **2** <u>exclusive</u>, restricted **3** <u>finished</u>, concluded, decided, ended, over, resolved, settled, terminated

► **Antonyms**

≠**shut**: ajar, open, unclosed, unfastened, unlocked, unsealed

cloth noun <u>fabric</u>, material, textiles

clothe verb <u>dress</u>, array, attire, cover, drape, equip, fit out, garb, robe, swathe

► **Antonyms**

disrobe, divest, expose, strip, strip off, unclothe, uncover, undress

clothes plural noun <u>clothing</u>, apparel, attire, costume, dress, garb, garments, gear (informal), outfit, wardrobe, wear

clothing noun <u>clothes</u>, apparel, attire, costume, dress, garb, garments, gear (informal), outfit, wardrobe, wear

cloud noun **1** <u>mist</u>, gloom, haze, murk, vapour **2** <u>obscure</u>, becloud, darken, dim, eclipse, obfuscate, overshadow, shade, shadow, veil **3** <u>confuse</u>, disorient, distort, impair, muddle, muddy the waters

cloudy adjective **1** <u>dull</u>, dim, gloomy, leaden, louring or lowering, overcast, sombre, sunless **2** <u>opaque</u>, muddy, murky

► **Antonyms**

≠**dull**: bright, clear, fair, sunny, uncloudy

clout Informal ♦ noun **1** <u>influence</u>, authority, power, prestige, pull, weight ♦ verb **2** <u>hit</u>, clobber (slang), punch, sock (slang), strike, thump, wallop (informal)

clown noun **1** <u>comedian</u>, buffoon, comic, fool, harlequin, jester, joker, prankster ♦ verb **2** <u>play the fool</u>, act the fool, jest, mess about

club noun **1** <u>association</u>, company, fraternity, group, guild, lodge, set, society, union **2** <u>stick</u>, bat, bludgeon, cosh (Brit.), cudgel, truncheon ♦ verb **3** <u>beat</u>, bash, batter, bludgeon, cosh (Brit.), hammer, pummel, strike

clue noun <u>indication</u>, evidence, hint, lead, pointer, sign, suggestion, suspicion, trace

clueless adjective <u>stupid</u>, dim, dozy (Brit. informal), dull, halfwitted, simple, slow, thick, unintelligent, witless

clump noun **1** <u>cluster</u>, bunch, bundle, group, mass ♦ verb **2** <u>stomp</u>, lumber, plod, thud, thump, tramp

clumsy adjective <u>awkward</u>, bumbling, gauche, gawky, ham-fisted (informal), lumbering, maladroit, ponderous, uncoordinated, ungainly, unwieldy

► **Antonyms**

adept, adroit, competent, deft,

dexterous, expert, graceful, handy, proficient, skilful

cluster noun 1 <u>gathering</u>, assemblage, batch, bunch, clump, collection, group, knot ◆ verb 2 <u>gather</u>, assemble, bunch, collect, flock, group

clutch verb <u>seize</u>, catch, clasp, cling to, embrace, grab, grasp, grip, snatch

clutches plural noun <u>power</u>, claws, control, custody, grasp, grip, hands, keeping, possession, sway

clutter verb 1 <u>litter</u>, scatter, strew ◆ noun 2 <u>untidiness</u>, confusion, disarray, disorder, hotchpotch, jumble, litter, mess, muddle

► **Antonyms**
verb ≠<u>litter</u>: order, organize, tidy ◆ noun ≠<u>untidiness</u>: neatness, order, organization, tidiness

coach noun 1 <u>bus</u>, car, carriage, charabanc, vehicle 2 <u>instructor</u>, handler, teacher, trainer, tutor ◆ verb 3 <u>instruct</u>, drill, exercise, prepare, train, tutor

coalesce verb <u>blend</u>, amalgamate, combine, fuse, incorporate, integrate, merge, mix, unite

coalition noun <u>alliance</u>, amalgamation, association, bloc, combination, confederation, conjunction, fusion, merger, union

coarse adjective 1 <u>rough</u>, crude, homespun, impure, unfinished, unpolished, unprocessed, unpurified, unrefined 2 <u>vulgar</u>, earthy, improper, indecent, indelicate, ribald, rude, smutty

► **Antonyms**
≠<u>rough</u>: fine-grained, polished, purified, refined, smooth, soft ≠<u>vulgar</u>: inoffensive, polite, proper

coarseness noun 1 <u>roughness</u>, crudity, unevenness 2 <u>vulgarity</u>, bawdiness, crudity, earthiness, indelicacy, ribaldry, smut, uncouthness

coast noun 1 <u>shore</u>, beach, border, coastline, seaboard, seaside ◆ verb 2 <u>cruise</u>, drift, freewheel, glide, sail, taxi

coat noun 1 <u>fur</u>, fleece, hair, hide, pelt, skin, wool 2 <u>layer</u>, coating, covering, overlay ◆ verb 3 <u>cover</u>, apply, plaster, smear, spread

coax verb <u>persuade</u>, allure, cajole, entice, prevail upon, sweet-talk (informal), talk into, wheedle

► **Antonyms**
browbeat, bully, coerce, force, harass, intimidate, pressurize, threaten

cocktail noun <u>mixture</u>, blend, combination, mix

cocky adjective <u>overconfident</u>, arrogant, brash, cocksure, conceited, egotistical, full of oneself, swaggering, vain

► **Antonyms**
hesitant, lacking confidence, modest, self-effacing, uncertain, unsure

code noun 1 <u>cipher</u>, cryptograph 2 <u>principles</u>, canon, convention, custom, ethics, etiquette, manners, maxim, regulations, rules, system

cogent adjective <u>convincing</u>, compelling, effective, forceful, influential, potent, powerful, strong, weighty

cogitate verb <u>think</u>, consider, contemplate, deliberate, meditate, mull over, muse, ponder, reflect, ruminate

coherent adjective 1 <u>consistent</u>, logical, lucid, meaningful, orderly, organized, rational, reasoned, systematic 2 <u>intelligible</u>, articulate, comprehensible

► **Antonyms**
≠<u>consistent</u>: confusing, disjointed, illogical, inconsistent, meaningless, rambling, vague ≠<u>intelligible</u>: incomprehensible, unintelligible

coil verb <u>wind</u>, curl, loop, snake, spiral, twine, twist, wreathe, writhe

coin noun 1 <u>money</u>, cash, change, copper, silver, specie ◆ verb 2 <u>invent</u>, create, fabricate, forge, make up, mint, mould, originate

coincide verb **1** <u>occur simultaneously</u>, be concurrent, coexist, synchronize **2** <u>agree</u>, accord, concur, correspond, harmonize, match, square, tally

➤ Antonyms

≠agree: be inconsistent, be unlike, contradict, differ, disagree, part, separate

coincidence noun **1** <u>chance</u>, accident, fluke, happy accident, luck, stroke of luck **2** <u>coinciding</u>, concurrence, conjunction, correlation, correspondence

coincidental adjective <u>chance</u>, accidental, casual, fluky (informal), fortuitous, unintentional, unplanned

➤ Antonyms

calculated, deliberate, done on purpose, intentional, planned, prearranged

cold adjective **1** <u>chilly</u>, arctic, bleak, cool, freezing, frigid, frosty, frozen, icy, wintry **2** <u>unfriendly</u>, aloof, distant, frigid, indifferent, reserved, standoffish ♦ noun **3** <u>coldness</u>, chill, frigidity, frostiness, iciness

➤ Antonyms

adjective ≠chilly: balmy, heated, hot, mild, sunny, warm ≠unfriendly: caring, compassionate, emotional, friendly, loving, passionate, warm

cold-blooded adjective <u>callous</u>, dispassionate, heartless, ruthless, steely, stony-hearted, unemotional, unfeeling

➤ Antonyms

caring, emotional, feeling, friendly, humane, kind, passionate, warm

collaborate verb **1** <u>work together</u>, cooperate, join forces, participate, play ball (informal), team up **2** <u>conspire</u>, collude, cooperate, fraternize

collaboration noun <u>teamwork</u>, alliance, association, cooperation, partnership

collaborator noun **1** <u>co-worker</u>, associate, colleague, confederate, partner, team-mate **2** <u>traitor</u>, fraternizer, quisling, turncoat

collapse verb **1** <u>fall down</u>, cave in, crumple, fall, fall apart at the seams, give way, subside **2** <u>fail</u>, come to nothing, fold, founder, go belly-up (informal) ♦ noun **3** <u>falling down</u>, cave-in, disintegration, falling apart, ruin, subsidence **4** <u>failure</u>, downfall, flop, slump **5** <u>faint</u>, breakdown, exhaustion, prostration

collar verb Informal <u>seize</u>, apprehend, arrest, capture, catch, grab, nab (informal), nail (informal)

colleague noun <u>fellow worker</u>, ally, assistant, associate, collaborator, comrade, helper, partner, team-mate, workmate

collect verb **1** <u>assemble</u>, cluster, congregate, convene, converge, flock together, rally **2** <u>gather</u>, accumulate, amass, assemble, heap, hoard, save, stockpile

➤ Antonyms

≠gather: disperse, distribute, scatter, spread, strew

collected adjective <u>calm</u>, composed, cool, poised, self-possessed, serene, unperturbed, unruffled

➤ Antonyms

agitated, distressed, emotional, excitable, nervous, perturbed, ruffled, troubled

collection noun **1** <u>accumulation</u>, anthology, compilation, heap, hoard, mass, pile, set, stockpile, store **2** <u>group</u>, assembly, assortment, cluster, company, crowd **3** <u>contribution</u>, alms, offering, offertory

collective adjective <u>combined</u>, aggregate, composite, corporate, cumulative, joint, shared, unified, united

➤ Antonyms

divided, individual, split, uncombined

collide verb **1** <u>crash</u>, clash, come into collision, meet head-on **2** <u>conflict</u>, clash

collision noun **1** <u>crash</u>, accident, bump, impact, pile-up (infor-

mal), prang (_informal_), smash **2** conflict, clash, confrontation, encounter, opposition, skirmish

colloquial _adjective_ informal, conversational, demotic, everyday, familiar, idiomatic, vernacular

colony _noun_ settlement, community, dependency, dominion, outpost, possession, province, satellite state, territory

colossal _adjective_ huge, enormous, gigantic, immense, mammoth, massive, monumental, prodigious, vast

➤ **Antonyms**
average, diminutive, little, miniature, minute, ordinary, pygmy or pigmy, small, tiny, weak, wee

colour _noun_ **1** hue, colorant, dye, paint, pigment, shade, tint ♦ _verb_ **2** paint, dye, stain, tinge, tint **3** blush, flush, redden

colourful _adjective_ **1** bright, brilliant, multicoloured, psychedelic, variegated **2** interesting, distinctive, graphic, lively, picturesque, rich, vivid

➤ **Antonyms**
≠bright: colourless, dark, drab, dreary, dull, faded ≠interesting: boring, characterless, dull, flat, lifeless, monotonous, unexciting, uninteresting, unvaried

colourless _adjective_ **1** drab, achromatic, anaemic, ashen, bleached, faded, wan, washed out **2** uninteresting, characterless, dreary, dull, insipid, lacklustre, vapid

➤ **Antonyms**
≠drab: blooming, flushed, glowing, healthy, radiant, robust, ruddy ≠uninteresting: animated, bright, colourful, compelling, distinctive, exciting, interesting, unusual

column _noun_ **1** pillar, obelisk, post, shaft, support, upright **2** line, cavalcade, file, procession, rank, row

coma _noun_ unconsciousness, oblivion, stupor, trance

comb _verb_ **1** untangle, arrange, dress, groom **2** search, forage,

hunt, rake, ransack, rummage, scour, sift

combat _noun_ **1** fight, action, battle, conflict, contest, encounter, engagement, skirmish, struggle, war, warfare ♦ _verb_ **2** fight, defy, do battle with, oppose, resist, withstand

➤ **Antonyms**
noun ≠fight: agreement, armistice, peace, surrender, truce ♦ _verb_ ≠fight: accept, acquiesce, declare a truce, give up, make peace, support, surrender

combatant _noun_ fighter, adversary, antagonist, enemy, opponent, soldier, warrior

combination _noun_ **1** mixture, amalgamation, blend, coalescence, composite, connection, mix **2** association, alliance, coalition, confederation, consortium, federation, syndicate, union

combine _verb_ join together, amalgamate, blend, connect, integrate, link, merge, mix, pool, unite

➤ **Antonyms**
detach, dissociate, divide, part, separate, sever

come _verb_ **1** move towards, advance, approach, draw near, near **2** arrive, appear, enter, materialize, reach, show up (_informal_), turn up (_informal_) **3** happen, fall, occur, take place **4** result, arise, emanate, emerge, flow, issue, originate **5** reach, extend **6** be available, be made, be offered, be on offer, be produced

come about _verb_ happen, arise, befall, come to pass, occur, result, take place, transpire (_informal_)

come across _verb_ find, bump into (_informal_), chance upon, discover, encounter, meet, notice, stumble upon, unearth

comeback _noun_ **1** _Informal_ return, rally, rebound, recovery, resurgence, revival, triumph **2** response, rejoinder, reply, retaliation, retort, riposte

come back *verb* return, reappear, recur, re-enter

comedian *noun* comic, card (*informal*), clown, funny man, humorist, jester, joker, wag, wit

comedown *noun* **1** decline, deflation, demotion, reverse **2** *Informal* disappointment, anticlimax, blow, humiliation, letdown

comedy *noun* humour, farce, fun, hilarity, jesting, joking, light entertainment

➤ **Antonyms**

high drama, melancholy, melodrama, sadness, seriousness, solemnity, tragedy

comeuppance *noun* *Informal* punishment, chastening, deserts, due reward, recompense, retribution

comfort *noun* **1** luxury, cosiness, ease, opulence, snugness, well-being **2** relief, compensation, consolation, help, succour, support ♦ *verb* **3** console, commiserate with, hearten, reassure, soothe

➤ **Antonyms**

noun ≠relief: aggravation, annoyance, hassle (*informal*), inconvenience, irritation ♦ *verb* ≠console: aggravate (*informal*), agitate, annoy, bother, depress, distress, hassle (*informal*), irk, irritate, sadden, trouble

comfortable *adjective* **1** pleasant, agreeable, convenient, cosy, homely, relaxing, restful **2** happy, at ease, at home, contented, gratified, relaxed, serene **3** *Informal* well-off, affluent, in clover (*informal*), prosperous, well-to-do

➤ **Antonyms**

≠pleasant: inadequate, uncomfortable, unpleasant ≠happy: distressed, ill at ease, like a fish out of water, miserable, nervous, tense, troubled, uncomfortable, uneasy

comforting *adjective* consoling, cheering, consolatory, encouraging, heart-warming, reassuring, soothing

➤ **Antonyms**

alarming, dismaying, disturbing, upsetting, worrying

comic *adjective* **1** funny, amusing, comical, droll, farcical, humorous, jocular, witty ♦ *noun* **2** comedian, buffoon, clown, funny man, humorist, jester, wag, wit

➤ **Antonyms**

adjective ≠funny: depressing, melancholy, pathetic, sad, serious, solemn, touching, tragic

comical *adjective* funny, amusing, comic, droll, farcical, hilarious, humorous, priceless, side-splitting

coming *adjective* **1** approaching, at hand, forthcoming, imminent, impending, in store, near, nigh ♦ *noun* **2** arrival, advent, approach

command *verb* **1** order, bid, charge, compel, demand, direct, require **2** have authority over, control, dominate, govern, handle, head, lead, manage, rule, supervise ♦ *noun* **3** order, commandment, decree, demand, directive, instruction, requirement, ultimatum **4** authority, charge, control, government, management, mastery, power, rule, supervision

➤ **Antonyms**

verb ≠order: appeal (to), ask, beg, beseech, plead, request, supplicate ≠have authority over: be inferior, be subordinate, follow

commandeer *verb* seize, appropriate, confiscate, requisition, sequester, sequestrate

commander *noun* officer, boss, captain, chief, commanding officer, head, leader, ruler

commanding *adjective* controlling, advantageous, decisive, dominant, dominating, superior

commemorate *verb* remember, celebrate, honour, immortalize, pay tribute to, recognize, salute

➤ **Antonyms**

disregard, forget, ignore, overlook

commemoration noun <u>remembrance</u>, ceremony, honouring, memorial service, tribute

commence verb <u>begin</u>, embark on, enter upon, initiate, open, originate, start

► **Antonyms**
bring or come to an end, cease, complete, conclude, end, finish, halt, stop, terminate

commend verb <u>praise</u>, acclaim, applaud, approve, compliment, extol, recommend, speak highly of

► **Antonyms**
censure, condemn, criticize, disapprove

commendable adjective <u>praiseworthy</u>, admirable, creditable, deserving, estimable, exemplary, laudable, meritorious, worthy

commendation noun <u>praise</u>, acclaim, acclamation, approbation, approval, credit, encouragement, good opinion, panegyric, recommendation

comment noun 1 <u>remark</u>, observation, statement 2 <u>note</u>, annotation, commentary, explanation, exposition, illustration ◆ verb 3 <u>remark</u>, mention, note, observe, point out, say, utter 4 <u>annotate</u>, elucidate, explain, interpret

commentary noun 1 <u>narration</u>, description, voice-over 2 <u>notes</u>, analysis, critique, explanation, review, treatise

commentator noun 1 <u>reporter</u>, special correspondent, sportscaster 2 <u>critic</u>, annotator, interpreter

commerce noun <u>trade</u>, business, dealing, exchange, traffic

commercial adjective 1 <u>mercantile</u>, trading 2 <u>materialistic</u>, mercenary, profit-making

commiserate verb <u>sympathize</u>, console, feel for, pity

commission noun 1 <u>duty</u>, errand, mandate, mission, task 2 <u>fee</u>, cut, percentage, rake-off (slang), royalties 3 <u>committee</u>, board, commissioners, delegation, deputation, representatives

◆ verb 4 <u>appoint</u>, authorize, contract, delegate, depute, empower, engage, nominate, order, select

commit verb 1 <u>do</u>, carry out, enact, execute, perform, perpetrate 2 <u>put in custody</u>, confine, imprison

► **Antonyms**
≠<u>do</u>: omit ≠<u>put in custody</u>: free, let out, release, set free

commitment noun 1 <u>dedication</u>, devotion, involvement, loyalty 2 <u>responsibility</u>, duty, engagement, liability, obligation, tie

► **Antonyms**
≠<u>dedication</u>: indecisiveness, vacillation, wavering

common adjective 1 <u>average</u>, commonplace, conventional, customary, everyday, familiar, frequent, habitual, ordinary, regular, routine, standard, stock, usual 2 <u>popular</u>, accepted, general, prevailing, prevalent, universal, widespread 3 <u>collective</u>, communal, popular, public, social 4 <u>vulgar</u>, coarse, inferior, plebeian

► **Antonyms**
≠<u>average</u>: abnormal, outstanding, rare, scarce, strange, uncommon, unusual ≠<u>collective</u>: personal, private ≠<u>vulgar</u>: cultured, refined, sensitive

commonplace adjective 1 <u>everyday</u>, banal, common, humdrum, mundane, obvious, ordinary, run-of-the-mill, widespread ◆ noun 2 <u>cliché</u>, banality, platitude, truism

► **Antonyms**
adjective ≠<u>everyday</u>: exciting, extraordinary, ground-breaking, interesting, new, novel, original, rare, strange, uncommon, unique, unusual

common sense noun <u>good sense</u>, gumption (Brit. informal), horse sense, level-headedness, native intelligence, prudence, sound judgment, wit

commotion noun <u>disturbance</u>, disorder, excitement, furore, fuss, hue and cry, rumpus, tumult, turmoil, upheaval, uproar

communal *adjective* public, collective, general, joint, shared

► **Antonyms**

exclusive, individual, personal, private, single, unshared

commune *noun* community, collective, cooperative, kibbutz

commune with *verb* contemplate, meditate on, muse on, ponder, reflect on

communicate *verb* make known, convey, declare, disclose, impart, inform, pass on, proclaim, transmit

► **Antonyms**

conceal, cover up, hold back, hush up, keep secret, suppress, withhold

communication *noun* 1 passing on, contact, conversation, correspondence, dissemination, link, transmission 2 message, announcement, disclosure, dispatch, information, news, report, statement, word

communicative *adjective* talkative, chatty, expansive, forthcoming, frank, informative, loquacious, open, outgoing, voluble

► **Antonyms**

quiet, reserved, reticent, secretive, taciturn, uncommunicative, uninformative, untalkative

Communism *noun* socialism, Bolshevism, collectivism, Marxism, state socialism

Communist *noun* socialist, Bolshevik, collectivist, Marxist, Red (*informal*)

community *noun* society, brotherhood, commonwealth, company, general public, people, populace, public, residents, state

commuter *noun* daily traveller, straphanger (*informal*), suburbanite

compact[1] *adjective* 1 closely packed, compressed, condensed, dense, pressed together, solid, thick 2 brief, compendious, concise, succinct, terse, to the point ♦ *verb* 3 pack closely, compress, condense, cram, stuff, tamp

► **Antonyms**

adjective ≠closely packed: dispersed, loose, roomy, scattered, spacious, sprawling ≠brief: lengthy, long-winded, rambling, verbose, wordy ♦ *verb* ≠pack closely: disperse, loosen, separate

compact[2] *noun* agreement, arrangement, bargain, bond, contract, covenant, deal, pact, treaty, understanding

companion *noun* 1 friend, accomplice, ally, associate, colleague, comrade, consort, mate (*informal*), partner 2 escort, aide, assistant, attendant, chaperon, squire

companionship *noun* fellowship, camaraderie, company, comradeship, conviviality, esprit de corps, friendship, rapport, togetherness

company *noun* 1 business, association, concern, corporation, establishment, firm, house, partnership, syndicate 2 group, assembly, band, collection, community, crowd, gathering, party, set 3 companionship, fellowship, presence, society 4 guests, callers, party, visitors

comparable *adjective* 1 on a par, a match for, as good as, commensurate, equal, equivalent, in a class with, proportionate, tantamount 2 similar, akin, alike, analogous, cognate, corresponding, cut from the same cloth, of a piece, related

► **Antonyms**

different, dissimilar, incomparable, unequal

comparative *adjective* relative, by comparison, qualified

compare *verb* 1 weigh, balance, contrast, juxtapose, set against 2 *usually with* with be on a par with, approach, bear comparison, be in the same class as, be the equal of, compete with, equal, hold a candle to, match 3 compare to liken to, correlate to, equate to, identify with, mention in the same breath as, parallel, resemble

comparison noun **1** contrast, distinction, juxtaposition **2** similarity, analogy, comparability, correlation, likeness, resemblance

compartment noun section, alcove, bay, berth, booth, carriage, cubbyhole, cubicle, locker, niche, pigeonhole

compass noun range, area, boundary, circumference, extent, field, limit, reach, realm, scope

compassion noun sympathy, condolence, fellow feeling, humanity, kindness, mercy, pity, sorrow, tender-heartedness, tenderness, understanding

➤ **Antonyms**
apathy, cold-heartedness, indifference, mercilessness, unconcern

compassionate adjective sympathetic, benevolent, charitable, humane, humanitarian, kindhearted, merciful, pitying, tender-hearted, understanding

➤ **Antonyms**
callous, harsh, heartless, inhumane, pitiless, uncaring, unfeeling, unmerciful, unsympathetic

compatibility noun harmony, affinity, agreement, concord, empathy, like-mindedness, rapport, sympathy

compatible adjective harmonious, adaptable, congruous, consistent, in harmony, in keeping, suitable

➤ **Antonyms**
contradictory, inappropriate, inapt, incompatible, unfitting, unharmonious, unsuitable

compel verb force, coerce, constrain, dragoon, impel, make, oblige, railroad (informal)

compelling adjective **1** fascinating, enchanting, enthralling, gripping, hypnotic, irresistible, mesmeric, spellbinding **2** pressing, binding, coercive, imperative, overriding, peremptory, unavoidable, urgent **3** convincing, cogent, conclusive, forceful, irrefutable, powerful, telling, weighty

➤ **Antonyms**
≠fascinating: boring, dull, humdrum, ordinary, uninteresting

compensate verb **1** recompense, atone, make amends, make good, refund, reimburse, remunerate, repay **2** cancel (out), balance, counteract, counterbalance, make up for, offset, redress

compensation noun recompense, amends, atonement, damages, reimbursement, remuneration, reparation, restitution, satisfaction

compete verb contend, be in the running, challenge, contest, fight, strive, struggle, vie

competence noun ability, capability, capacity, expertise, fitness, proficiency, skill, suitability

➤ **Antonyms**
inability, inadequacy, incompetence

competent adjective able, adequate, capable, fit, proficient, qualified, suitable

➤ **Antonyms**
inadequate, incapable, incompetent, unqualified, unskilled

competition noun **1** rivalry, opposition, strife, struggle **2** contest, championship, event, head-to-head, puzzle, quiz, tournament **3** opposition, challengers, field, rivals

competitive adjective **1** cut-throat, aggressive, antagonistic, at odds, dog-eat-dog, opposing, rival **2** ambitious, combative

competitor noun contestant, adversary, antagonist, challenger, opponent, rival

compilation noun collection, accumulation, anthology, assemblage, assortment, treasury

compile verb put together, accumulate, amass, collect, cull, garner, gather, marshal, organize

complacency noun self-satisfaction, contentment, satisfaction, smugness

complacent adjective self-satisfied, contented, pleased with oneself, resting on one's laurels, satisfied, serene, smug, unconcerned

➤ **Antonyms**

discontent, dissatisfied, troubled, uneasy, unsatisfied

complain verb find fault, bemoan, bewail, carp, deplore, groan, grouse, grumble, lament, moan, whine, whinge (informal)

complaint noun 1 criticism, charge, grievance, gripe (informal), grouse, grumble, lament, moan, protest 2 illness, affliction, ailment, disease, disorder, malady, sickness, upset

complement noun 1 completion, companion, consummation, counterpart, finishing touch, rounding-off, supplement 2 total, aggregate, capacity, entirety, quota, totality, wholeness ◆ verb 3 complete, cap (informal), crown, round off, set off

complementary adjective completing, companion, corresponding, interdependent, interrelating, matched, reciprocal

➤ **Antonyms**

contradictory, different, incompatible, incongruous, uncomplementary

complete adjective 1 total, absolute, consummate, outright, perfect, thorough, thoroughgoing, utter 2 finished, accomplished, achieved, concluded, ended 3 entire, all, faultless, full, intact, plenary, unbroken, whole ◆ verb 4 finish, close, conclude, crown, end, finalize, round off, settle, wrap up (informal)

➤ **Antonyms**

adjective ≠total: partial ≠finished: inconclusive, unaccomplished, unfinished, unsettled ≠entire: deficient, imperfect, incomplete, spoilt ◆ verb ≠finish: begin, commence, initiate, start

completely adverb totally, absolutely, altogether, entirely, every inch, fully, hook, line and sinker, in full, lock, stock and barrel, one hundred per cent, perfectly, thoroughly, utterly, wholly

completion noun finishing, bitter end, close, conclusion, culmination, end, fruition, fulfilment

complex adjective 1 compound, composite, heterogeneous, manifold, multifarious, multiple 2 complicated, convoluted, elaborate, intricate, involved, labyrinthine, tangled, tortuous ◆ noun 3 structure, aggregate, composite, network, organization, scheme, system 4 Informal obsession, fixation, fixed idea, idée fixe, phobia, preoccupation

➤ **Antonyms**

adjective ≠complicated: clear, easy, elementary, obvious, simple, straightforward, uncomplicated

complexion noun 1 skin, colour, colouring, hue, pigmentation, skin tone 2 nature, appearance, aspect, character, guise, light, look, make-up

complexity noun complication, elaboration, entanglement, intricacy, involvement, ramification

complicate verb make difficult, confuse, entangle, involve, muddle, ravel

➤ **Antonyms**

clarify, clear up, disentangle, explain, simplify, spell out

complicated adjective 1 difficult, involved, perplexing, problematic, puzzling, troublesome 2 involved, complex, convoluted, elaborate, intricate, labyrinthine

➤ **Antonyms**

≠difficult: clear, easy, undemanding, understandable ≠involved: simple, straightforward, uncomplicated, uninvolved

complication noun 1 complexity, confusion, entanglement, intricacy, web 2 problem, difficulty, drawback, embarrassment, obstacle, snag

compliment noun 1 praise, bouquet, commendation, congratulations, eulogy, flattery, honour, tribute ◆ verb 2 praise, commend, congratulate, extol, flatter, pay tribute to, salute, speak highly of

➤ **Antonyms**

noun ≠<u>praise</u>: condemnation, criticism, disparagement, insult ◆ verb ≠<u>praise</u>: condemn, criticize, disparage, insult, put down

complimentary adjective **1** <u>flattering</u>, appreciative, approving, commendatory, congratulatory, laudatory **2** <u>free</u>, courtesy, donated, gratis, gratuitous, honorary, on the house

➤ **Antonyms**

≠<u>flattering</u>: abusive, critical, disparaging, insulting, uncomplimentary, unflattering

compliments plural noun <u>greetings</u>, good wishes, regards, remembrances, respects, salutation

comply verb <u>obey</u>, abide by, acquiesce, adhere to, conform to, follow, observe, submit, toe the line

➤ **Antonyms**

defy, disobey, disregard, ignore, oppose, resist

component noun **1** <u>part</u>, constituent, element, ingredient, item, piece, unit ◆ adjective **2** <u>constituent</u>, inherent, intrinsic

compose verb **1** <u>put together</u>, build, comprise, constitute, construct, fashion, form, make, make up **2** <u>create</u>, contrive, devise, invent, produce, write **3** <u>calm</u>, collect, control, pacify, placate, quiet, soothe **4** <u>arrange</u>, adjust

➤ **Antonyms**

≠<u>put together</u>: bulldoze, demolish, destroy, dismantle ≠<u>calm</u>: agitate, disturb, excite, perturb, trouble, unsettle, upset

composed adjective <u>calm</u>, at ease, collected, cool, levelheaded, poised, relaxed, sedate, self-possessed, serene, unflappable

➤ **Antonyms**

agitated, antsy (informal), anxious, disturbed, excited, nervous, twitchy (informal), uneasy, upset

composition noun **1** <u>creation</u>,

compilation, fashioning, formation, formulation, making, production, putting together **2** <u>design</u>, arrangement, configuration, formation, layout, make-up, organization, structure **3** <u>essay</u>, exercise, literary work, opus, piece, treatise, work

composure noun <u>calmness</u>, aplomb, equanimity, poise, sangfroid, self-assurance, self-possession, serenity

➤ **Antonyms**

agitation, discomposure, excitability, nervousness, uneasiness

compound noun **1** <u>combination</u>, alloy, amalgam, blend, composite, fusion, medley, mixture, synthesis ◆ verb **2** <u>combine</u>, amalgamate, blend, intermingle, mix, synthesize, unite **3** <u>intensify</u>, add to, aggravate, augment, complicate, exacerbate, heighten, magnify, worsen ◆ adjective **4** <u>complex</u>, composite, intricate, multiple

➤ **Antonyms**

noun ≠<u>combination</u>: element ◆ verb ≠<u>combine</u>: divide, part, segregate ≠<u>intensify</u>: decrease, lessen, minimize, moderate, modify ◆ adjective ≠<u>complex</u>: pure, simple, single, unmixed

comprehend verb <u>understand</u>, apprehend, conceive, fathom, grasp, know, make out, perceive, see, take in

➤ **Antonyms**

get (it) wrong, misapprehend, misconceive, misconstrue, misinterpret, mistake, misunderstand

comprehensible adjective <u>understandable</u>, clear, coherent, conceivable, explicit, intelligible, plain

comprehension noun <u>understanding</u>, conception, discernment, grasp, intelligence, perception, realization

➤ **Antonyms**

incomprehension, misapprehension, misunderstanding, unawareness

comprehensive adjective <u>broad</u>,

all-embracing, all-inclusive, blanket, complete, encyclopedic, exhaustive, full, inclusive, overarching, thorough

► **Antonyms**
incomplete, limited, narrow, restricted, specialized, specific

compress verb 1 <u>squeeze</u>, abbreviate, concentrate, condense, contract, crush, press, shorten, squash

comprise verb 1 <u>be composed of</u>, consist of, contain, embrace, encompass, include, take in 2 <u>make up</u>, compose, constitute, form

compromise noun 1 <u>give-and-take</u>, accommodation, adjustment, agreement, concession, settlement, trade-off ♦ verb 2 <u>meet halfway</u>, adjust, agree, concede, give and take, go fifty-fifty (informal), settle, strike a balance 3 <u>weaken</u>, discredit, dishonour, embarrass, expose, jeopardize, prejudice

► **Antonyms**
noun ≠<u>give-and-take</u>: contention, controversy, difference, disagreement, dispute, quarrel ♦ verb ≠<u>meet halfway</u>: argue, contest, differ, disagree ≠<u>weaken</u>: boost, enhance, support

compulsion noun 1 <u>urge</u>, force, necessity, need, obsession, preoccupation 2 <u>force</u>, coercion, constraint, demand, duress, obligation, pressure, urgency

compulsive adjective <u>irresistible</u>, compelling, driving, neurotic, obsessive, overwhelming, uncontrollable, urgent

compulsory adjective <u>obligatory</u>, binding, de rigueur, forced, imperative, mandatory, required, requisite

► **Antonyms**
discretionary, non-obligatory, optional, voluntary

compute verb <u>calculate</u>, add up, count, enumerate, figure out, reckon, tally, total

comrade noun <u>companion</u>, ally, associate, colleague, co-worker,

fellow, friend, partner

con Informal ♦ noun 1 <u>swindle</u>, deception, fraud, scam (slang), sting (informal), trick ♦ verb 2 <u>swindle</u>, cheat, deceive, defraud, double-cross (informal), dupe, hoodwink, rip off (slang), trick

concave adjective <u>hollow</u>, indented

► **Antonyms**
bulging, convex, curving, protuberant, rounded

conceal verb <u>hide</u>, bury, camouflage, cover, disguise, mask, obscure, screen

► **Antonyms**
disclose, display, divulge, expose, lay bare, reveal, show, uncover, unmask, unveil

concede verb 1 <u>admit</u>, accept, acknowledge, allow, confess, grant, own 2 <u>give up</u>, cede, hand over, relinquish, surrender, yield

► **Antonyms**
≠<u>admit</u>: contest, deny, disclaim, dispute, protest, refute, reject ≠<u>give up</u>: beat, conquer, defeat, fight to the bitter end, make a stand

conceit noun 1 <u>self-importance</u>, arrogance, egotism, narcissism, pride, swagger, vanity 2 Archaic <u>fancy</u>, fantasy, image, whim, whimsy

conceited adjective <u>self-important</u>, arrogant, bigheaded (informal), cocky, egotistical, full of oneself, immodest, narcissistic, too big for one's boots or breeches, vain

► **Antonyms**
humble, modest, self-effacing, unassuming

conceivable adjective <u>imaginable</u>, believable, credible, possible, thinkable

► **Antonyms**
inconceivable, incredible, unbelievable, unimaginable, unthinkable

conceive verb 1 <u>imagine</u>, believe, comprehend, envisage, fancy, suppose, think, understand 2

think up, contrive, create, design, devise, formulate 3 <u>become pregnant</u>, become impregnated

concentrate verb 1 <u>focus one's attention on</u>, be engrossed in, put one's mind to, rack one's brains 2 <u>focus</u>, bring to bear, centre, cluster, converge 3 <u>gather</u>, accumulate, cluster, collect, congregate, huddle

► Antonyms

≠<u>focus one's attention on</u>: disregard, let one's mind wander, lose concentration, pay no attention to, pay no heed to ≠<u>focus, gather</u>: diffuse, disperse, dissipate, scatter, spread out

concentrated adjective 1 <u>intense</u>, all-out (informal), deep, hard, intensive 2 <u>condensed</u>, boiled down, evaporated, reduced, rich, thickened, undiluted

concentration noun 1 <u>single-mindedness</u>, absorption, application, heed 2 <u>focusing</u>, bringing to bear, centralization, centring, consolidation, convergence, intensification 3 <u>convergence</u>, accumulation, aggregation, cluster, collection, horde, mass

► Antonyms

≠<u>single-mindedness</u>: absent-mindedness, disregard, distraction, inattention ≠<u>focusing</u>, <u>convergence</u>: diffusion, dispersal, scattering, spreading-out

concept noun <u>idea</u>, conception, conceptualization, hypothesis, image, notion, theory, view

conception noun 1 <u>idea</u>, concept, design, image, notion, plan 2 <u>impregnation</u>, fertilization, germination, insemination

concern noun 1 <u>worry</u>, anxiety, apprehension, burden, care, disquiet, distress 2 <u>importance</u>, bearing, interest, relevance 3 <u>business</u>, affair, interest, job, responsibility, task 4 <u>business</u>, company, corporation, enterprise, establishment, firm, organization
♦ verb 5 <u>worry</u>, bother, disquiet, distress, disturb, make anxious,

perturb, trouble 6 <u>be relevant to</u>, affect, apply to, bear on, interest, involve, pertain to, regard, touch

concerned adjective 1 <u>involved</u>, active, implicated, interested, mixed up, privy to 2 <u>worried</u>, anxious, bothered, distressed, disturbed, troubled, uneasy, upset

► Antonyms

aloof, carefree, detached, indifferent, neglectful, unconcerned, uninterested, untroubled, without a care

concerning preposition <u>regarding</u>, about, apropos of, as regards, on the subject of, re, relating to, respecting, touching, with reference to

concession noun 1 <u>grant</u>, adjustment, allowance, boon, compromise, indulgence, permit, privilege, sop 2 <u>conceding</u>, acknowledgment, admission, assent, confession, surrender, yielding

conciliate verb <u>pacify</u>, appease, clear the air, mediate, mollify, placate, reconcile, soothe, win over

conciliation noun <u>pacification</u>, appeasement, mollification, placation, reconciliation, soothing

conciliatory adjective <u>pacifying</u>, appeasing, mollifying, pacific, peaceable, placatory

concise adjective <u>brief</u>, compendious, condensed, laconic, pithy, short, succinct, terse

► Antonyms

discursive, garrulous, lengthy, long-winded, rambling, verbose, wordy

conclude verb 1 <u>decide</u>, assume, deduce, gather, infer, judge, surmise, work out 2 <u>end</u>, cease, close, complete, finish, round off, terminate, wind up 3 <u>accomplish</u>, bring about, carry out, effect, pull off

► Antonyms

≠<u>end</u>: begin, commence, initiate, open, start

conclusion noun 1 <u>decision</u>, conviction, deduction, inference, judgment, opinion, verdict **2** end, bitter end, close, completion, ending, finale, finish, result, termination **3** outcome, consequence, culmination, end result, result, upshot

conclusive *adjective* decisive, clinching, convincing, definite, final, irrefutable, ultimate, unanswerable

▶ **Antonyms**

contestable, disputable, doubtful, dubious, inconclusive, indecisive, indefinite, questionable, unconvincing, vague

concoct *verb* make up, brew, contrive, devise, formulate, hatch, invent, prepare, think up

concoction *noun* mixture, blend, brew, combination, compound, creation, preparation

concrete *adjective* **1** specific, definite, explicit **2** real, actual, factual, material, sensible, substantial, tangible

▶ **Antonyms**

≠specific: indefinite, unspecified, vague ≠real: abstract, immaterial, insubstantial, intangible, notional, theoretical

concur *verb* agree, acquiesce, assent, consent

condemn *verb* **1** disapprove, blame, censure, criticize, damn, denounce, reproach, reprove, upbraid **2** sentence, convict, damn, doom, pass sentence on

▶ **Antonyms**

≠disapprove: acclaim, applaud, approve, commend, compliment, condone, praise ≠sentence: acquit, free, liberate

condemnation *noun* **1** disapproval, blame, censure, denunciation, reproach, reproof, stricture **2** sentence, conviction, damnation, doom, judgment

condensation *noun* **1** distillation, liquefaction, precipitate, precipitation **2** abridgment, contraction, digest, précis, synopsis **3** concentration, compression, consolidation, crystallization, cur-

tailment, reduction

condense *verb* **1** abridge, abbreviate, compress, concentrate, epitomize, shorten, summarize **2** concentrate, boil down, reduce, thicken

▶ **Antonyms**

≠abridge: elaborate, enlarge, expand, lengthen ≠concentrate: dilute, make thinner, thin (out), water down, weaken

condensed *adjective* **1** abridged, compressed, concentrated, shortened, shrunken, slimmed-down, summarized **2** concentrated, boiled down, reduced, thickened

condescend *verb* **1** patronize, talk down to **2** lower oneself, bend, deign, humble *or* demean oneself, see fit, stoop

condescending *adjective* patronizing, disdainful, lofty, lordly, snobbish, snooty (*informal*), supercilious, superior, toffee-nosed (*slang, chiefly Brit.*)

condition *noun* **1** state, circumstances, lie of the land, position, shape, situation, state of affairs **2** requirement, limitation, prerequisite, proviso, qualification, restriction, rider, stipulation, terms **3** health, fettle, fitness, kilter, order, shape, state of health, trim **4** ailment, complaint, infirmity, malady, problem, weakness ♦ *verb* **5** accustom, adapt, equip, prepare, ready, tone up, train, work out

conditional *adjective* dependent, contingent, limited, provisional, qualified, subject to, with reservations

▶ **Antonyms**

absolute, categorical, unconditional, unrestricted

conditions *plural noun* circumstances, environment, milieu, situation, surroundings, way of life

condone *verb* overlook, excuse, forgive, let pass, look the other way, make allowance for, pardon, turn a blind eye to

➤ **Antonyms**

censure, condemn, denounce, disapprove, punish

conduct noun **1** behaviour, attitude, bearing, demeanour, deportment, manners, ways **2** management, administration, control, direction, guidance, handling, organization, running, supervision ♦ verb **3** carry out, administer, control, direct, handle, manage, organize, preside over, run, supervise **4** behave, acquit, act, carry, comport, deport **5** accompany, convey, escort, guide, lead, steer, usher

confederacy noun union, alliance, coalition, confederation, federation, league

confer verb **1** discuss, consult, converse, deliberate, discourse, talk **2** grant, accord, award, bestow, give, hand out, present

conference noun meeting, colloquium, congress, consultation, convention, discussion, forum, seminar, symposium

confess verb **1** admit, acknowledge, come clean (informal), concede, confide, disclose, divulge, own up **2** declare, affirm, assert, confirm, profess, reveal

➤ **Antonyms**

≠admit: conceal, cover, deny, hide, hush up, keep secret, suppress, withhold

confession noun admission, acknowledgment, disclosure, exposure, revelation, unbosoming

confidant, confidante noun close friend, alter ego, bosom friend, crony, familiar, intimate

confide verb **1** tell, admit, confess, disclose, divulge, impart, reveal, whisper **2** Formal entrust, commend, commit, consign

confidence noun **1** trust, belief, credence, dependence, faith, reliance **2** self-assurance, aplomb, assurance, boldness, courage, firmness, nerve, self-possession **3** in confidence in secrecy, between you and me (and the gatepost), confidentially, privately

➤ **Antonyms**

≠trust: disbelief, distrust, doubt, misgiving, mistrust ≠self-assurance: apprehension, fear, self-doubt, shyness, uncertainty

confident adjective **1** certain, convinced, counting on, positive, satisfied, secure, sure **2** self-assured, assured, bold, dauntless, fearless, self-reliant

➤ **Antonyms**

≠certain: doubtful, dubious, not sure, tentative, uncertain, unconvinced, unsure ≠self-assured: afraid, hesitant, insecure, lacking confidence, nervous, scared, unsure

confidential adjective secret, classified, hush-hush (informal), intimate, off the record, private, privy

confidentially adverb in secret, behind closed doors, between ourselves, in camera, in confidence, personally, privately, sub rosa

confine verb restrict, cage, enclose, hem in, hold back, imprison, incarcerate, intern, keep, limit, shut up

confinement noun **1** imprisonment, custody, detention, incarceration, internment, porridge (slang) **2** childbirth, childbed, labour, lying-in, parturition

confines plural noun limits, boundaries, bounds, circumference, edge, precincts

confirm verb **1** prove, authenticate, bear out, corroborate, endorse, ratify, substantiate, validate, verify **2** strengthen, buttress, establish, fix, fortify, reinforce

confirmation noun **1** proof, authentication, corroboration, evidence, substantiation, testimony, validation, verification **2** sanction, acceptance, agreement, approval, assent, endorsement, ratification

➤ **Antonyms**

≠proof: contradiction, denial, repudiation ≠sanction: annulment, cancellation, disapproval, refusal, rejection

confirmed *adjective* long-established, chronic, dyed-in-the-wool, habitual, hardened, ingrained, inveterate, seasoned

confiscate *verb* seize, appropriate, commandeer, impound, sequester, sequestrate

► **Antonyms**

free, give, give back, hand back, release, restore, return

confiscation *noun* seizure, appropriation, forfeiture, impounding, sequestration, takeover

conflict *noun* 1 opposition, antagonism, difference, disagreement, discord, dissension, friction, hostility, strife 2 battle, clash, combat, contest, encounter, fight, strife, war ♦ *verb* 3 be incompatible, be at variance, clash, collide, differ, disagree, interfere

► **Antonyms**

noun ≠opposition, battle: accord, agreement, harmony, peace, treaty, truce ♦ *verb* ≠be incompatible: agree, coincide, harmonize, reconcile

conflicting *adjective* incompatible, antagonistic, clashing, contradictory, contrary, discordant, inconsistent, opposing, paradoxical

► **Antonyms**

accordant, agreeing, compatible, congruous, consistent, harmonious, similar, unopposing

conform *verb* 1 comply, adapt, adjust, fall in with, follow, obey, toe the line 2 agree, accord, correspond, harmonize, match, suit, tally

conformist *noun* traditionalist, stick-in-the-mud (*informal*), yes man

conformity *noun* compliance, conventionality, observance, orthodoxy, traditionalism

confound *verb* bewilder, astound, baffle, confuse, dumbfound, flummox, mystify, nonplus, perplex

confront *verb* face, accost, challenge, defy, encounter, oppose, stand up to, tackle

► **Antonyms**

avoid, circumvent, dodge, evade, flee, keep *or* steer clear of, sidestep

confrontation *noun* conflict, contest, encounter, fight, head-to-head, set-to (*informal*), showdown (*informal*)

confuse *verb* 1 mix up, disarrange, disorder, jumble, mingle, muddle, ravel 2 bewilder, baffle, bemuse, faze, flummox, mystify, nonplus, perplex, puzzle 3 disconcert, discompose, disorient, fluster, rattle (*informal*), throw off balance, unnerve, upset

confused *adjective* 1 bewildered, at sea, baffled, disorientated, flummoxed, muddled, nonplussed, perplexed, puzzled, taken aback 2 disordered, chaotic, disorganized, higgledy-piggledy (*informal*), in disarray, jumbled, mixed up, topsy-turvy, untidy

► **Antonyms**

≠bewildered: aware, enlightened, informed ≠disordered: arranged, in order, ordered, orderly, organized, tidy

confusing *adjective* bewildering, baffling, contradictory, disconcerting, misleading, perplexing, puzzling, unclear

► **Antonyms**

clear, definite, explicit, plain, simple, straightforward, uncomplicated, understandable

confusion *noun* 1 bewilderment, disorientation, mystification, perplexity, puzzlement 2 disorder, chaos, commotion, jumble, mess, muddle, shambles, turmoil, untidiness, upheaval

► **Antonyms**

≠bewilderment: clarification, enlightenment, explanation, solution ≠disorder: arrangement, neatness, order, organization, tidiness

congenial *adjective* 1 pleasant, affable, agreeable, companionable, favourable, friendly, genial, kindly **2** compatible, kindred, like-minded, sympathetic, well-suited

congenital *adjective* inborn, immanent, inbred, inherent, innate, natural

congested *adjective* **1** overcrowded, crowded, teeming **2** clogged, blocked-up, crammed, jammed, overfilled, overflowing, packed, stuffed

➤ **Antonyms**

≠overcrowded: empty, half-full, uncrowded ≠clogged: clear, free, uncongested, unobstructed

congestion *noun* **1** overcrowding, crowding **2** clogging, bottleneck, jam, surfeit

congratulate *verb* compliment, pat on the back, wish joy to

congratulations *plural noun, interjection* good wishes, best wishes, compliments, felicitations, greetings

congregate *verb* come together, assemble, collect, convene, converge, flock, gather, mass, meet

➤ **Antonyms**

break up, dispel, disperse, dissipate, part, scatter, separate, split up

congregation *noun* assembly, brethren, crowd, fellowship, flock, multitude, throng

congress *noun* meeting, assembly, conclave, conference, convention, council, legislature, parliament

conjecture *noun* **1** guess, hypothesis, shot in the dark, speculation, supposition, surmise, theory ♦ *verb* **2** guess, hypothesize, imagine, speculate, suppose, surmise, theorize

conjugal *adjective* marital, bridal, connubial, married, matrimonial, nuptial, wedded

conjure *verb* perform tricks, juggle

conjure up *verb* bring to mind, contrive, create, evoke, produce as if by magic, recall, recollect

conjuror, conjurer *noun* magi-

cian, illusionist, sorcerer, wizard

connect *verb* link, affix, attach, couple, fasten, join, unite

➤ **Antonyms**

detach, disconnect, dissociate, divide, part, separate, sever, unfasten

connected *adjective* linked, affiliated, akin, allied, associated, combined, coupled, joined, related, united

connection *noun* **1** association, affinity, bond, liaison, link, relationship, relevance, tie-in **2** link, alliance, association, attachment, coupling, fastening, junction, tie, union **3** contact, acquaintance, ally, associate, friend, sponsor

connivance *noun* collusion, abetting, complicity, conspiring, tacit consent

connive *verb* **1** conspire, collude, cook up (*informal*), intrigue, plot, scheme **2 connive at** turn a blind eye to, abet, disregard, let pass, look the other way, overlook, wink at

connoisseur *noun* expert, aficionado, appreciator, authority, buff (*informal*), devotee, judge

conquer *verb* **1** defeat, beat, crush, get the better of, master, overcome, overpower, overthrow, quell, subjugate, vanquish **2** seize, acquire, annex, obtain, occupy, overrun, win

➤ **Antonyms**

≠defeat: be defeated, capitulate, give in, give up, lose, quit, submit, surrender, yield

conqueror *noun* winner, conquistador, defeater, master, subjugator, vanquisher, victor

conquest *noun* **1** defeat, mastery, overthrow, rout, triumph, victory **2** takeover, annexation, coup, invasion, occupation, subjugation

conscience *noun* principles, moral sense, scruples, sense of right and wrong, still small voice

conscientious *adjective* thorough, careful, diligent, exact, faithful, meticulous, painstaking, particular, punctilious

➤ **Antonyms**

careless, irresponsible, negligent, remiss, slack, thoughtless, unconscientious

conscious adjective **1** <u>aware</u>, alert, alive to, awake, responsive, sensible, sentient **2** <u>deliberate</u>, calculated, intentional, knowing, premeditated, self-conscious, studied, wilful

➤ **Antonyms**

≠<u>aware</u>: ignorant, insensible, oblivious, unaware, unconscious ≠<u>deliberate</u>: accidental, uncalculated, unintended, unintentional, unplanned, unpremeditated, unwitting

consciousness noun <u>awareness</u>, apprehension, knowledge, realization, recognition, sensibility

consecrate verb <u>sanctify</u>, dedicate, devote, hallow, ordain, set apart, venerate

consecutive adjective <u>successive</u>, in sequence, in turn, running, sequential, succeeding, uninterrupted

consensus noun <u>agreement</u>, assent, common consent, concord, general agreement, harmony, unanimity, unity

consent noun **1** <u>agreement</u>, acquiescence, approval, assent, compliance, go-ahead (informal), O.K. or okay (informal), permission, sanction ♦ verb **2** <u>agree</u>, acquiesce, allow, approve, assent, concur, permit

➤ **Antonyms**

noun ≠<u>agreement</u>: disagreement, disapproval, dissent, refusal, unwillingness ♦ verb ≠<u>agree</u>: decline, demur, disagree, disapprove, dissent, refuse, resist

consequence noun **1** <u>result</u>, effect, end result, issue, outcome, repercussion, sequel, upshot **2** <u>importance</u>, account, concern, import, moment, significance, value, weight

consequent adjective <u>following</u>, ensuing, resultant, resulting, sub-

sequent, successive

consequently adverb <u>as a result</u>, accordingly, ergo, hence, subsequently, therefore, thus

conservation noun <u>protection</u>, guardianship, husbandry, maintenance, preservation, safeguarding, safekeeping, saving, upkeep

conservative adjective **1** <u>traditional</u>, cautious, conventional, diehard, hidebound, reactionary, sober ♦ noun **2** <u>traditionalist</u>, diehard, reactionary, stick-in-the-mud (informal)

➤ **Antonyms**

adjective ≠<u>traditional</u>: imaginative, innovative, liberal, progressive, radical ♦ noun ≠<u>traditionalist</u>: changer, innovator, progressive, radical

Conservative adjective **1** <u>Tory</u>, right-wing ♦ noun **2** <u>Tory</u>, right-winger

conserve verb <u>protect</u>, hoard, husband, keep, nurse, preserve, save, store up, take care of, use sparingly

➤ **Antonyms**

be extravagant, blow (slang), dissipate, fritter away, misspend, spend, squander, use up, waste

consider verb **1** <u>think</u>, believe, deem, hold to be, judge, rate, regard as **2** <u>think about</u>, cogitate, contemplate, deliberate, meditate, ponder, reflect, ruminate, turn over in one's mind, weigh **3** <u>bear in mind</u>, keep in view, make allowance for, reckon with, remember, respect, take into account

considerable adjective <u>large</u>, appreciable, goodly, great, marked, noticeable, plentiful, sizable or sizeable, substantial

➤ **Antonyms**

insignificant, insubstantial, meagre, paltry, small

considerably adverb <u>greatly</u>, appreciably, markedly, noticeably, remarkably, significantly, substantially, very much

considerate adjective <u>thoughtful</u>, attentive, concerned, kindly, mindful, obliging, patient, tactful, unselfish

► **Antonyms**
heedless, inconsiderate, selfish, thoughtless

consideration noun **1** thought, analysis, deliberation, discussion, examination, reflection, review, scrutiny **2** factor, concern, issue, point **3** thoughtfulness, concern, considerateness, kindness, respect, tact **4** payment, fee, recompense, remuneration, reward, tip

considering preposition taking into account, in the light of, in view of

consignment noun shipment, batch, delivery, goods

consist verb **1 consist of** be made up of, amount to, be composed of, comprise, contain, embody, include, incorporate, involve **2 consist in** lie in, be expressed by, be found or contained in, inhere in, reside in

consistency noun **1** texture, compactness, density, firmness, thickness, viscosity **2** constancy, evenness, regularity, steadfastness, steadiness, uniformity

consistent adjective **1** unchanging, constant, dependable, persistent, regular, steady, true to type, undeviating **2** agreeing, coherent, compatible, congruous, consonant, harmonious, logical

► **Antonyms**
≠unchanging: changing, deviating, erratic, inconsistent, irregular ≠agreeing: contradictory, contrary, discordant, incompatible, incongruous, inconsistent, inharmonious

consolation noun comfort, cheer, encouragement, help, relief, solace, succour, support

console verb comfort, calm, cheer, encourage, express sympathy for, soothe

► **Antonyms**
agitate, discomfort, distress, hurt, sadden, torment, trouble, upset

consolidate verb **1** strengthen, fortify, reinforce, secure, stabilize **2** combine, amalgamate, federate, fuse, join, unite

consort verb **1** associate, fraternize, go around with, hang about, around or out with, keep company, mix ♦ noun **2** spouse, companion, husband, partner, wife

conspicuous adjective **1** obvious, blatant, clear, evident, noticeable, patent, salient **2** noteworthy, illustrious, notable, outstanding, prominent, remarkable, salient, signal, striking

► **Antonyms**
≠obvious: concealed, hidden, imperceptible, inconspicuous, obscure, unnoticeable ≠noteworthy: humble, inconspicuous, insignificant, ordinary, undistinguished, unmemorable, unnotable

conspiracy noun plot, collusion, intrigue, machination, scheme, treason

conspirator noun plotter, conspirer, intriguer, schemer, traitor

conspire verb **1** plot, contrive, intrigue, machinate, manoeuvre, plan, scheme **2** work together, combine, concur, contribute, cooperate, tend

constant adjective **1** continuous, ceaseless, incessant, interminable, nonstop, perpetual, sustained, unrelenting **2** unchanging, even, fixed, invariable, permanent, stable, steady, uniform, unvarying **3** faithful, devoted, loyal, stalwart, staunch, true, trustworthy, trusty

► **Antonyms**
≠continuous: erratic, inconstant, intermittent, irregular, occasional, random, unsustained ≠unchanging: changeable, changing, deviating, uneven, unstable, variable ≠faithful: disloyal, fickle, irresolute, undependable

constantly adverb continuously, all the time, always, continually, endlessly, incessantly, interminably, invariably, nonstop, perpetually

► **Antonyms**

(every) now and then, every so often, from time to time, intermittently, irregularly, now and again, occasionally, periodically, sometimes

consternation noun <u>dismay</u>, alarm, anxiety, distress, dread, fear, trepidation

constituent noun **1** <u>voter</u>, elector **2** <u>component</u>, element, factor, ingredient, part, unit ♦ *adjective* **3** <u>component</u>, basic, elemental, essential, integral

constitute verb <u>make up</u>, compose, comprise, establish, form, found, set up

constitution noun **1** <u>health</u>, build, character, disposition, physique **2** <u>structure</u>, composition, form, make-up, nature

constitutional adjective **1** <u>statutory</u>, chartered, vested ♦ *noun* **2** <u>walk</u>, airing, stroll, turn

constrain verb **1** <u>force</u>, bind, coerce, compel, impel, necessitate, oblige, pressurize **2** <u>restrict</u>, check, confine, constrict, curb, restrain, straiten

constraint noun **1** <u>restriction</u>, check, curb, deterrent, hindrance, limitation, rein **2** <u>force</u>, coercion, compulsion, necessity, pressure, restraint

construct verb <u>build</u>, assemble, compose, create, fashion, form, make, manufacture, put together, shape

► **Antonyms**

bulldoze, demolish, destroy, dismantle, flatten, knock down, level, pull down, tear down

construction noun **1** <u>building</u>, composition, creation, edifice **2** *Formal* <u>interpretation</u>, explanation, inference, reading, rendering

constructive adjective <u>helpful</u>, positive, practical, productive, useful, valuable

► **Antonyms**

negative, unhelpful, unproductive, useless, worthless

consult verb <u>ask</u>, compare notes, confer, pick (someone's) brains, question, refer to, take counsel, turn to

consultant noun <u>specialist</u>, adviser, authority

consultation noun <u>seminar</u>, appointment, conference, council, deliberation, dialogue, discussion, examination, hearing, interview, meeting, session

consume verb **1** <u>eat</u>, devour, eat up, gobble (up), put away, swallow **2** <u>use up</u>, absorb, dissipate, exhaust, expend, spend, squander, waste **3** <u>destroy</u>, annihilate, demolish, devastate, lay waste, ravage **4** *often passive* <u>obsess</u>, absorb, dominate, eat up, engross, monopolize, preoccupy

consumer noun <u>buyer</u>, customer, purchaser, shopper, user

consummate verb **1** <u>complete</u>, accomplish, conclude, crown, end, finish, fulfil ♦ *adjective* **2** <u>skilled</u>, accomplished, matchless, perfect, polished, practised, superb, supreme **3** <u>complete</u>, absolute, conspicuous, extreme, supreme, total, utter

► **Antonyms**

verb ≠<u>complete</u>: begin, commence, inaugurate, initiate, originate, start

consumption noun **1** <u>using up</u>, depletion, diminution, dissipation, exhaustion, expenditure, loss, waste **2** *Old-fashioned* <u>tuberculosis</u>, T.B.

contact noun **1** <u>communication</u>, association, connection **2** <u>touch</u>, contiguity **3** <u>acquaintance</u>, connection ♦ *verb* **4** <u>get or be in touch with</u>, approach, call, communicate with, reach, speak to, write to

contagious adjective <u>infectious</u>, catching, communicable, spreading, transmissible

contain verb **1** <u>hold</u>, accommodate, enclose, have capacity for, incorporate, seat **2** <u>include</u>, comprehend, comprise, consist of, embody, embrace, involve **3 restrain**, control, curb, hold back, hold in, keep a tight rein on, repress, stifle

container noun **holder**, receptacle, repository, vessel

contaminate verb **pollute**, adulterate, befoul, corrupt, defile, infect, stain, taint, tarnish

➤ **Antonyms**
clean, cleanse, decontaminate, disinfect, fumigate, purify, sanitize, sterilize

contamination noun **pollution**, contagion, corruption, defilement, impurity, infection, poisoning, taint

contemplate verb **1 think about**, consider, deliberate, meditate, muse over, ponder, reflect upon, ruminate (upon) **2 consider**, envisage, expect, foresee, intend, plan, think of **3 look at**, examine, eye up, gaze at, inspect, regard, stare at, study, survey, view

contemporary adjective **1 coexisting**, concurrent, contemporaneous **2 modern**, à la mode, current, newfangled, present, present-day, recent, up-to-date ◆ noun **3 peer**, fellow

➤ **Antonyms**
adjective ≠modern: antecedent, antique, early, obsolete, old, old-fashioned, out-of-date, passé

contempt noun **scorn**, derision, disdain, disregard, disrespect, mockery, neglect, slight

➤ **Antonyms**
admiration, esteem, honour, liking, regard, respect

contemptible adjective **despicable**, detestable, ignominious, measly, paltry, pitiful, shameful, worthless

➤ **Antonyms**
admirable, honourable, laudable, praiseworthy

contemptuous adjective **scornful**, arrogant, condescending, derisive, disdainful, haughty, sneering, supercilious, withering

➤ **Antonyms**
civil, courteous, deferential, gracious, mannerly, obsequious, polite, respectful

contend verb **1 compete**, clash, contest, fight, jostle, strive, struggle, vie **2 argue**, affirm, allege, assert, dispute, hold, maintain

content[1] noun **1 meaning**, essence, gist, significance, substance **2 amount**, capacity, load, measure, size, volume

content[2] adjective **1 satisfied**, agreeable, at ease, comfortable, contented, fulfilled, willing to accept ◆ verb **2 satisfy**, appease, humour, indulge, mollify, placate, please ◆ noun **3 satisfaction**, comfort, contentment, ease, gratification, peace of mind, pleasure

contented adjective **satisfied**, comfortable, content, glad, gratified, happy, pleased, serene, thankful

➤ **Antonyms**
annoyed, discontented, displeased, dissatisfied, troubled, uncomfortable, uneasy

contentious adjective **argumentative**, bickering, captious, cavilling, disputatious, quarrelsome, querulous, wrangling

contentment noun **satisfaction**, comfort, content, ease, equanimity, fulfilment, happiness, peace, pleasure, serenity

➤ **Antonyms**
discomfort, discontent, discontentment, displeasure, dissatisfaction, uneasiness, unhappiness

contents plural noun **constituents**, elements, ingredients, load

contest noun **1 competition**, game, match, tournament, trial **2 struggle**, battle, combat, conflict, controversy, dispute, fight ◆ verb **3 dispute**, argue, call in or into question, challenge, debate, doubt, object to, oppose, question **4 compete**, contend, fight, strive, vie

contestant noun **competitor**, candidate, contender, entrant, participant, player

context noun **1 circumstances**, ambience, conditions, situation

2 <u>frame of reference</u>, background, connection, framework, relation

contingency noun <u>possibility</u>, accident, chance, emergency, event, eventuality, happening, incident

continual adjective <u>constant</u>, frequent, incessant, interminable, recurrent, regular, repeated, unremitting

➤ **Antonyms**
erratic, fluctuating, infrequent, intermittent, irregular, occasional, periodic, spasmodic, sporadic

continually adverb <u>constantly</u>, all the time, always, forever, incessantly, interminably, nonstop, persistently, repeatedly

continuation noun **1** <u>continuing</u>, perpetuation, prolongation, resumption **2** <u>addition</u>, extension, furtherance, postscript, sequel, supplement

continue verb **1** <u>remain</u>, abide, carry on, endure, last, live on, persist, stay, survive **2** <u>keep on</u>, carry on, go on, maintain, persevere, persist in, stick at, sustain **3** <u>resume</u>, carry on, pick up where one left off, proceed, recommence, return to, take up

➤ **Antonyms**
≠remain: abdicate, leave, quit, resign, retire, step down ≠keep on, resume: break off, discontinue, give up, leave off, pack in (Brit. informal), quit, stop

continuing adjective <u>lasting</u>, enduring, in progress, ongoing, sustained

continuity noun <u>sequence</u>, cohesion, connection, flow, progression, succession

continuous adjective <u>constant</u>, extended, prolonged, unbroken, unceasing, undivided, uninterrupted

➤ **Antonyms**
broken, ending, inconstant, intermittent, interrupted, occasional, spasmodic

contraband noun **1** <u>smuggling</u>, black-marketing, bootlegging,

trafficking ◆ adjective **2** <u>smuggled</u>, banned, bootleg, forbidden, hot (informal), illegal, illicit, prohibited, unlawful

contract noun **1** <u>agreement</u>, arrangement, bargain, commitment, covenant, pact, settlement ◆ verb **2** <u>agree</u>, bargain, come to terms, commit oneself, covenant, negotiate, pledge **3** <u>shorten</u>, abbreviate, curtail, diminish, dwindle, lessen, narrow, reduce, shrink, shrivel **4** <u>catch</u>, acquire, be afflicted with, develop, get, go down with, incur

➤ **Antonyms**
verb ≠agree: decline, disagree, refuse, turn down ≠shorten: broaden, distend, enlarge, expand, grow, increase, multiply, spread, stretch, swell, widen ≠catch: avert, avoid, escape, ward off

contraction noun <u>shortening</u>, abbreviation, compression, narrowing, reduction, shrinkage, shrivelling, tightening

contradict verb <u>deny</u>, be at variance with, belie, challenge, controvert, fly in the face of, negate, rebut

➤ **Antonyms**
affirm, agree, authenticate, confirm, defend, endorse, support, verify

contradiction noun <u>denial</u>, conflict, contravention, incongruity, inconsistency, negation, opposite

contradictory adjective <u>inconsistent</u>, conflicting, contrary, incompatible, opposed, opposite, paradoxical

contraption noun Informal <u>device</u>, apparatus, contrivance, gadget, instrument, mechanism

contrary noun **1** <u>opposite</u>, antithesis, converse, reverse ◆ adjective **2** <u>opposed</u>, adverse, clashing, contradictory, counter, discordant, hostile, inconsistent, opposite, paradoxical **3** <u>perverse</u>, awkward, cantankerous, difficult, disobliging, intractable, obstinate, stroppy (*Brit. slang*), unaccommodating

➤ **Antonyms**

adjective ≠ opposed: accordant, congruous, consistent, harmonious, in agreement, unopposed ≠ perverse: accommodating, agreeable, cooperative, eager to please, helpful, obliging, willing

contrast *noun* **1** difference, comparison, disparity, dissimilarity, distinction, divergence, foil, opposition ◆ *verb* **2** differentiate, compare, differ, distinguish, oppose, set in opposition, set off

contribute *verb* **1** give, add, bestow, chip in (*informal*), donate, provide, subscribe, supply **2** contribute to be partly responsible for, be conducive to, be instrumental in, help, lead to, tend to

contribution *noun* gift, addition, donation, grant, input, offering, subscription

contributor *noun* giver, donor, patron, subscriber, supporter

contrite *adjective* sorry, chastened, conscience-stricken, humble, penitent, regretful, remorseful, repentant, sorrowful

contrivance *noun* **1** device, apparatus, appliance, contraption, gadget, implement, instrument, invention, machine, mechanism **2** plan, intrigue, machination, plot, ruse, scheme, stratagem, trick

contrive *verb* **1** bring about, arrange, effect, manage, manoeuvre, plan, plot, scheme, succeed **2** devise, concoct, construct, create, design, fabricate, improvise, invent, manufacture

contrived *adjective* forced, artificial, elaborate, laboured, overdone, planned, strained, unnatural

➤ **Antonyms**

genuine, natural, relaxed, spontaneous, unfeigned, unforced

control *noun* **1** power, authority, charge, command, guidance, management, oversight, supervision, supremacy **2** restraint,

brake, check, curb, limitation, regulation ◆ *verb* **3** have power over, administer, command, direct, govern, handle, have charge of, manage, manipulate, supervise **4** restrain, check, constrain, contain, curb, hold back, limit, repress, subdue

controls *plural noun* instruments, console, control panel, dash, dashboard, dials

controversial *adjective* disputed, at issue, contentious, debatable, disputable, open to question, under discussion

controversy *noun* argument, altercation, debate, dispute, quarrel, row, squabble, wrangling

convalescence *noun* recovery, improvement, recuperation, rehabilitation, return to health

convalescent *adjective* recovering, getting better, improving, mending, on the mend, recuperating

convene *verb* gather, assemble, bring together, call, come together, congregate, convoke, meet, summon

convenience *noun* **1** usefulness, accessibility, advantage, appropriateness, availability, benefit, fitness, suitability, utility **2** appliance, amenity, comfort, facility, help, labour-saving device

➤ **Antonyms**

≠ usefulness: inconvenience, uselessness

convenient *adjective* **1** useful, appropriate, fit, handy, helpful, labour-saving, serviceable, suitable, timely **2** nearby, accessible, at hand, available, close at hand, handy, just round the corner, within reach

➤ **Antonyms**

≠ useful: awkward, inconvenient, unsuitable, useless ≠ nearby: distant, inaccessible, inconvenient, out-of-the-way

convention *noun* **1** custom, code, etiquette, practice, propriety, protocol, tradition, usage **2** agreement, bargain, contract, pact, protocol, treaty **3** assembly, conference, congress, convocation, council, meeting

conventional *adjective* **1** ordinary, accepted, customary, normal, orthodox, regular, standard, traditional, usual **2** unoriginal, banal, hackneyed, prosaic, routine, run-of-the-mill, stereotyped

➤ **Antonyms**

abnormal, off-the-wall (*slang*), uncommon, unconventional, unorthodox

converge *verb* come together, coincide, combine, gather, join, meet, merge

conversation *noun* talk, chat, conference, dialogue, discourse, discussion, gossip, tête-à-tête

converse[1] *verb* talk, chat, commune, confer, discourse, exchange views

converse[2] *noun* **1** opposite, antithesis, contrary, obverse, other side of the coin, reverse ♦ *adjective* **2** opposite, contrary, counter, reverse, reversed, transposed

conversion *noun* **1** change, metamorphosis, transformation **2** adaptation, alteration, modification, reconstruction, remodelling, reorganization

convert *verb* **1** change, alter, transform, transpose, turn **2** adapt, apply, customize, modify, remodel, reorganize, restyle, revise **3** reform, convince, proselytize ♦ *noun* **4** neophyte, disciple, proselyte

convex *adjective* rounded, bulging, gibbous, protuberant

➤ **Antonyms**

concave, cupped, hollowed, indented, sunken

convey *verb* **1** communicate, disclose, impart, make known, relate, reveal, tell **2** carry, bear, bring, conduct, fetch, guide, move, send, transport

convict *verb* **1** find guilty, condemn, imprison, pronounce guilty, sentence ♦ *noun* **2** prisoner, criminal, culprit, felon, jail-

bird, lag (*slang*)

conviction *noun* **1** belief, creed, faith, opinion, persuasion, principle, tenet, view **2** confidence, assurance, certainty, certitude, firmness, reliance

convince *verb* persuade, assure, bring round, prevail upon, satisfy, sway, win over

convincing *adjective* persuasive, cogent, conclusive, credible, impressive, plausible, powerful, telling

➤ **Antonyms**

beyond belief, dubious, far-fetched, implausible, improbable, incredible, unconvincing, unlikely

convulse *verb* shake, agitate, churn up, derange, disorder, disturb, twist, work

convulsion *noun* spasm, contraction, cramp, fit, paroxysm, seizure

cool *adjective* **1** cold, chilled, chilly, nippy, refreshing **2** calm, collected, composed, relaxed, sedate, self-controlled, self-possessed, unemotional, unruffled **3** unfriendly, aloof, distant, indifferent, lukewarm, offhand, standoffish, unenthusiastic, unwelcoming ♦ *verb* **4** chill, cool off, freeze, lose heat, refrigerate ♦ *noun* **5** *Slang* calmness, composure, control, poise, self-control, self-discipline, self-possession, temper

➤ **Antonyms**

adjective ≠cold: lukewarm, sunny, tepid, warm ≠calm: agitated, excited, impassioned, nervous, overwrought, tense ≠unfriendly: amiable, cordial, friendly, outgoing, warm ♦ *verb* ≠chill: heat, reheat, thaw, warm (up)

cooperate *verb* work together, collaborate, combine, conspire, coordinate, join forces, pool resources, pull together

➤ **Antonyms**

conflict, contend with, fight, hamper, hamstring, hinder, impede, obstruct, oppose, prevent, resist, struggle against

cooperation noun **1** teamwork, collaboration, combined effort, esprit de corps, give-and-take, unity

➤ **Antonyms**

discord, dissension, hindrance, opposition, rivalry

cooperative adjective **1** helpful, accommodating, obliging, onside (informal), responsive, supportive **2** shared, collective, combined, joint

coordinate verb bring together, harmonize, integrate, match, organize, synchronize, systematize

cope verb **1** manage, carry on, get by (informal), hold one's own, make the grade, struggle through, survive **2** cope with deal with, contend with, grapple with, handle, struggle with, weather, wrestle with

copious adjective abundant, ample, bountiful, extensive, full, lavish, plentiful, profuse

copy noun **1** reproduction, counterfeit, duplicate, facsimile, forgery, imitation, likeness, model, replica ◆ verb **2** reproduce, counterfeit, duplicate, replicate, transcribe **3** imitate, act like, ape, behave like, emulate, follow, mimic, mirror, repeat

➤ **Antonyms**

noun ≠reproduction: model, original, pattern, prototype, the real thing ◆ verb ≠reproduce: create, originate

cord noun rope, line, string, twine

cordial adjective warm, affable, agreeable, cheerful, congenial, friendly, genial, hearty, sociable

➤ **Antonyms**

aloof, cold, distant, formal, frigid, reserved, unfriendly

cordon noun **1** chain, barrier, line, ring ◆ verb **2** cordon off surround, close off, encircle, enclose, fence off, isolate, picket, separate

core noun centre, crux, essence, gist, heart, kernel, nub, nucleus, pith

corner noun **1** angle, bend, crook, joint **2** space, hideaway, hide-out, nook, retreat ◆ verb **3** trap, run to earth **4** As in corner the market monopolize, dominate, engross, hog (slang)

corny adjective Slang unoriginal, hackneyed, old-fashioned, old hat, stale, stereotyped, trite

corporation noun **1** business, association, corporate body, society **2** town council, civic authorities, council, municipal authorities **3** Informal paunch, beer belly (informal), middle-age spread (informal), potbelly, spare tyre (Brit. slang), spread (informal)

corps noun team, band, company, detachment, division, regiment, squadron, troop, unit

corpse noun body, cadaver, carcass, remains, stiff (slang)

correct adjective **1** true, accurate, exact, faultless, flawless, O.K. or okay (informal), precise, right **2** proper, acceptable, appropriate, fitting, kosher (informal), O.K. or okay (informal), seemly, standard ◆ verb **3** rectify, adjust, amend, cure, emend, redress, reform, remedy, right **4** punish, admonish, chasten, chastise, chide, discipline, rebuke, reprimand, reprove

➤ **Antonyms**

adjective ≠true: false, inaccurate, incorrect, untrue, wrong ≠proper: improper, inappropriate, unacceptable, unfitting, unsuitable ◆ verb ≠rectify: damage, harm, impair, ruin, spoil ≠punish: compliment, excuse, praise

correction noun **1** rectification, adjustment, alteration, amendment, emendation, improvement, modification **2** punishment, admonition, castigation, chastisement, discipline, reformation, reproof

correctly adverb rightly, accurately, perfectly, precisely, properly, right

correctness noun **1** truth, accuracy, exactitude, exactness, faultlessness, fidelity, preciseness, precision, regularity **2** decorum, civility, good breeding, propriety, seemliness

correspond *verb* **1** be consistent, accord, agree, conform, fit, harmonize, match, square, tally **2** communicate, exchange letters, keep in touch, write

➤ **Antonyms**

≠be consistent: be at variance, be dissimilar, be inconsistent, be unlike, differ, disagree, diverge, vary

correspondence *noun* **1** letters, communication, mail, post, writing **2** relation, agreement, coincidence, comparison, conformity, correlation, harmony, match, similarity

correspondent *noun* **1** letter writer, pen friend *or* pal **2** reporter, contributor, journalist

corresponding *adjective* related, analogous, answering, complementary, equivalent, matching, reciprocal, similar

corridor *noun* passage, aisle, alley, hallway, passageway

corroborate *verb* support, authenticate, back up, bear out, confirm, endorse, ratify, substantiate, validate

➤ **Antonyms**

contradict, disprove, invalidate, negate, rebut, refute

corrode *verb* eat away, consume, corrupt, erode, gnaw, oxidize, rust, wear away

corrosive *adjective* corroding, caustic, consuming, erosive, virulent, vitriolic, wasting, wearing

corrupt *adjective* **1** dishonest, bent (*slang*), bribable, crooked (*informal*), fraudulent, unprincipled, unscrupulous, venal **2** depraved, debased, degenerate, dissolute, profligate, vicious **3** distorted, altered, doctored, falsified ♦ *verb* **4** bribe, buy off, entice, fix (*informal*), grease (someone's) palm (*slang*), lure, suborn **5** deprave, debauch, pervert, subvert **6** distort, doctor, tamper with

➤ **Antonyms**

adjective ≠dishonest, depraved: ethical, honest, honourable, moral, noble, principled, righteous, scrupulous, straight, upright, virtuous ♦ *verb* ≠deprave: correct, reform

corruption *noun* **1** dishonesty, bribery, extortion, fraud, shady dealings (*informal*), unscrupulousness, venality **2** depravity, decadence, evil, immorality, perversion, vice, wickedness **3** distortion, doctoring, falsification

corset *noun* girdle, belt, bodice

cosmetic *adjective* beautifying, nonessential, superficial, surface

cosmic *adjective* universal, stellar

cosmopolitan *adjective* **1** sophisticated, broad-minded, catholic, open-minded, universal, urbane, well-travelled, worldly-wise ♦ *noun* **2** man *or* woman of the world, jet-setter, sophisticate

➤ **Antonyms**

adjective ≠sophisticated: insular, limited, narrow-minded, parochial, provincial, unsophisticated

cost *noun* **1** price, amount, charge, damage (*informal*), expense, outlay, payment, worth **2** loss, damage, detriment, penalty, sacrifice, suffering ♦ *verb* **3** sell at, come to, command a price of, set (someone) back (*informal*) **4** lose, do disservice to, harm, hurt, injure

costly *adjective* **1** expensive, dear, exorbitant, extortionate, highly-priced, steep **2** damaging, catastrophic, deleterious, disastrous, harmful, loss-making, ruinous

➤ **Antonyms**

≠expensive: cheap, cheapo (*informal*), dirt-cheap, economical, fair, inexpensive, low-priced, reasonable, reduced

costs *plural noun* expenses, budget, outgoings, overheads

costume *noun* outfit, apparel, attire, clothing, dress, ensemble, garb, livery, uniform

cosy adjective <u>snug</u>, comfortable, comfy (informal), homely, intimate, sheltered, tucked up, warm

cottage noun <u>cabin</u>, chalet, hut, lodge, shack

cough noun 1 <u>frog or tickle in one's throat</u>, bark, hack ♦ verb 2 <u>clear one's throat</u>, bark, hack

council noun <u>governing body</u>, assembly, board, cabinet, committee, conference, congress, convention, panel, parliament

counsel noun 1 <u>advice</u>, direction, guidance, information, recommendation, suggestion, warning 2 <u>legal adviser</u>, advocate, attorney, barrister, lawyer, solicitor ♦ verb 3 <u>advise</u>, advocate, exhort, instruct, recommend, urge, warn

count verb 1 <u>add (up)</u>, calculate, compute, enumerate, number, reckon, tally, tot up 2 <u>matter</u>, be important, carry weight, rate, signify, tell, weigh 3 <u>consider</u>, deem, judge, look upon, rate, regard, think 4 <u>take into account or consideration</u>, include, number among ♦ noun 5 <u>calculation</u>, computation, enumeration, numbering, poll, reckoning, sum, tally

counter verb 1 <u>retaliate</u>, answer, hit back, meet, oppose, parry, resist, respond, ward off ♦ adverb 2 <u>opposite to</u>, against, at variance with, contrariwise, conversely, in defiance of, versus

➤ **Antonyms**

verb ≠<u>retaliate</u>: accept, cave in (informal), give in, surrender, take, yield ♦ adverb ≠<u>opposite to</u>: in agreement, parallel

counteract verb <u>act against</u>, foil, frustrate, negate, neutralize, offset, resist, thwart

counterbalance verb <u>offset</u>, balance, compensate, make up for, set off

counterfeit adjective 1 <u>fake</u>, bogus, faked, forged, imitation, phoney or phony (informal), sham, simulated ♦ noun 2 <u>fake</u>, copy, forgery, fraud, imitation, phoney or phony (informal), reproduction, sham ♦ verb 3 <u>fake</u>, copy, fabricate, feign, forge, imitate, impersonate, pretend, sham, simulate

➤ **Antonyms**

adjective ≠<u>fake</u>: authentic, genuine, original, real, the real thing

countermand verb <u>cancel</u>, annul, override, repeal, rescind, retract, reverse, revoke

counterpart noun <u>opposite number</u>, complement, equal, fellow, match, mate, supplement, tally, twin

countless adjective <u>innumerable</u>, endless, immeasurable, incalculable, infinite, legion, limitless, myriad, numberless, untold

➤ **Antonyms**

finite, limited, restricted

count on or **upon** verb <u>depend on</u>, bank on, believe (in), lean on, pin one's faith on, reckon on, rely on, take for granted, take on trust, trust

country noun 1 <u>nation</u>, commonwealth, kingdom, people, realm, state 2 <u>territory</u>, land, region, terrain 3 <u>people</u>, citizens, community, inhabitants, nation, populace, public, society 4 <u>countryside</u>, backwoods, farmland, green belt, outback (Austral. & N.Z.), provinces, sticks (informal)

➤ **Antonyms**

≠<u>countryside</u>: city, metropolis, town

countryside noun <u>country</u>, farmland, green belt, outback (Austral. & N.Z.), outdoors, sticks (informal)

count up verb <u>add</u>, reckon up, sum, tally, total

county noun <u>province</u>, shire

coup noun <u>masterstroke</u>, accomplishment, action, deed, exploit, feat, manoeuvre, stunt

couple noun 1 <u>pair</u>, brace, duo, two, twosome ♦ verb 2 <u>link</u>, connect, hitch, join, marry, pair, unite, wed, yoke

coupon noun <u>slip</u>, card, certificate, ticket, token, voucher

courage noun bravery, daring, fearlessness, gallantry, heroism, mettle, nerve, pluck, resolution, valour

➤ Antonyms

cowardice, cravenness, faint-heartedness, fear, timidity

courageous adjective brave, bold, daring, fearless, gallant, gritty, intrepid, lion-hearted, stouthearted, valiant

➤ Antonyms

chicken (slang), cowardly, craven, faint-hearted, gutless (informal), lily-livered, scared, spineless, timid, timorous, yellow (informal)

courier noun 1 guide, representative 2 messenger, bearer, carrier, envoy, runner

course noun 1 classes, curriculum, lectures, programme, schedule 2 progression, development, flow, movement, order, progress, sequence, unfolding 3 route, direction, line, passage, path, road, track, trajectory, way 4 racecourse, cinder track, circuit 5 procedure, behaviour, conduct, manner, method, mode, plan, policy, programme 6 period, duration, lapse, passage, passing, sweep, term, time 7 of course naturally, certainly, definitely, indubitably, needless to say, obviously, undoubtedly, without a doubt ♦ verb 8 run, flow, gush, race, speed, stream, surge 9 hunt, chase, follow, pursue

court noun 1 law court, bar, bench, tribunal 2 courtyard, cloister, piazza, plaza, quad (informal), quadrangle, square, yard 3 palace, hall, manor 4 royal household, attendants, cortege, entourage, retinue, suite, train ♦ verb 5 woo, date, go (out) with, run after, serenade, set one's cap at, take out, walk out with 6 cultivate, curry favour with, fawn upon, flatter, pander to, seek, solicit 7 invite, attract, bring about, incite, prompt, provoke, seek

courteous adjective polite, affable, attentive, civil, gallant, gracious, refined, respectful, urbane, well-mannered

➤ Antonyms

discourteous, disrespectful, ill-mannered, impolite, insolent, rude, uncivil, ungracious, unkind

courtesy noun 1 politeness, affability, civility, courteousness, gallantry, good manners, graciousness, urbanity 2 favour, indulgence, kindness

courtier noun attendant, follower, squire

courtly adjective ceremonious, chivalrous, dignified, elegant, formal, gallant, polished, refined, stately, urbane

courtyard noun yard, enclosure, quad, quadrangle

cove noun bay, anchorage, inlet, sound

covenant noun 1 promise, agreement, arrangement, commitment, contract, pact, pledge ♦ verb 2 promise, agree, contract, pledge, stipulate, undertake

cover verb 1 clothe, dress, envelop, put on, wrap 2 overlay, coat, daub, encase, envelop 3 submerge, engulf, flood, overrun, wash over 4 conceal, cloak, disguise, enshroud, hide, mask, obscure, shroud, veil 5 travel over, cross, pass through or over, traverse 6 protect, defend, guard, shield 7 report, describe, investigate, narrate, relate, tell of, write up ♦ noun 8 covering, canopy, case, coating, envelope, jacket, lid, top, wrapper 9 disguise, façade, front, mask, pretext, screen, smoke screen, veil 10 protection, camouflage, concealment, defence, guard, shelter, shield 11 insurance, compensation, indemnity, protection, reimbursement

➤ Antonyms

verb ≠conceal: exhibit, expose, reveal, show, unclothe, uncover, unmask, unwrap ♦ noun ≠covering: base, bottom

covering adjective 1 explanatory, accompanying, descriptive, introductory ♦ noun 2 cover, blanket, casing, coating, layer, wrapping

cover-up noun concealment, complicity, conspiracy, front, smoke screen, whitewash (informal)

cover up verb conceal, draw a veil over, hide, hush up, suppress, sweep under the carpet, whitewash (informal)

covet verb long for, aspire to, crave, desire, envy, lust after, set one's heart on, yearn for

covetous adjective envious, acquisitive, avaricious, close-fisted, grasping, greedy, jealous, rapacious, yearning

coward noun wimp (informal), chicken (slang), scaredy-cat (informal), yellow-belly (slang)

cowardice noun faint-heartedness, fearfulness, spinelessness, weakness

cowardly adjective faint-hearted, chicken (slang), craven, fearful, scared, soft, spineless, timorous, weak, yellow (informal)

➤ **Antonyms**
audacious, bold, brave, courageous, daring, dauntless, intrepid, plucky, valiant

cowboy noun cowhand, cattleman, drover, gaucho (S. American), herdsman, rancher, stockman

cower verb cringe, draw back, flinch, grovel, quail, shrink, tremble

coy adjective shy, bashful, demure, modest, reserved, retiring, shrinking, timid

➤ **Antonyms**
bold, brash, brazen, forward, impertinent, impudent, pert, pushy (informal), saucy, shameless

crack verb 1 break, burst, cleave, fracture, snap, splinter, split 2 snap, burst, crash, detonate, explode, pop, ring 3 give in, break down, collapse, give way, go to pieces, lose control, succumb, yield 4 Informal hit, clip (infor-

mal), clout (informal), cuff, slap, smack, whack 5 solve, decipher, fathom, get the answer to, work out ♦ noun 6 snap, burst, clap, crash, explosion, pop, report 7 break, chink, cleft, cranny, crevice, fissure, fracture, gap, rift 8 Informal blow, clip (informal), clout (informal), cuff, slap, smack, whack 9 Informal joke, dig, funny remark, gag (informal), jibe, quip, wisecrack, witticism ♦ adjective 10 Slang first-class, ace, choice, elite, excellent, first-rate, hand-picked, superior, world-class

crackdown noun suppression, clampdown, crushing, repression

cracked adjective broken, chipped, damaged, defective, faulty, flawed, imperfect, split

cradle noun 1 crib, bassinet, cot, Moses basket 2 birthplace, beginning, fount, fountainhead, origin, source, spring, wellspring ♦ verb 3 hold, lull, nestle, nurse, rock, support

craft noun 1 occupation, business, employment, handicraft, pursuit, trade, vocation, work 2 skill, ability, aptitude, art, artistry, expertise, ingenuity, know-how (informal), technique, workmanship 3 vessel, aircraft, boat, plane, ship, spacecraft

craftsman noun skilled worker, artisan, maker, master, smith, technician, wright

craftsmanship noun workmanship, artistry, expertise, mastery, technique

crafty adjective cunning, artful, calculating, devious, sharp, shrewd, sly, subtle, wily

➤ **Antonyms**
frank, honest, ingenuous, innocent, naive, open, simple

crag noun rock, bluff, peak, pinnacle, tor

cram verb 1 stuff, compress, force, jam, pack in, press, shove, squeeze 2 overeat, glut, gorge, satiate, stuff 3 study, bone up (informal), mug up (slang), revise, swot

cramp[1] noun spasm, ache, contraction, convulsion, pain, pang, stitch, twinge

cramp[2] verb restrict, constrain, hamper, handicap, hinder, impede, inhibit, obstruct

cramped adjective closed in, confined, congested, crowded, hemmed in, overcrowded, packed, uncomfortable

➤ **Antonyms**

capacious, commodious, large, open, roomy, sizable or sizeable, spacious, uncongested, uncrowded

cranny noun crevice, chink, cleft, crack, fissure, gap, hole, opening

crash noun 1 collision, accident, bump, pile-up (informal), prang (informal), smash, wreck 2 smash, bang, boom, clang, clash, clatter, din, racket, thunder 3 collapse, debacle, depression, downfall, failure, ruin ◆ verb 4 collide, bump (into), crash-land (an aircraft), drive into, have an accident, hit, plough into, wreck 5 collapse, be ruined, fail, fold, fold up, go belly up (informal), go bust (informal), go to the wall, go under 6 hurtle, fall headlong, give way, lurch, overbalance, plunge, topple

crass adjective insensitive, boorish, gross, indelicate, oafish, stupid, unrefined, witless

➤ **Antonyms**

bright, clever, intelligent, refined, sensitive, sharp, smart

crate noun container, box, case, packing case, tea chest

crater noun hollow, depression, dip

crave verb 1 long for, desire, hanker after, hope for, lust after, want, yearn for 2 Informal beg, ask, beseech, entreat, implore, petition, plead for, pray for, seek, solicit, supplicate

craving noun longing, appetite, desire, hankering, hope, hunger, thirst, yearning, yen (informal)

crawl verb 1 creep, advance slowly, inch, slither, worm one's way, wriggle, writhe 2 grovel, creep, fawn, humble oneself, toady 3 be full of, be alive, overrun (slang), swarm, teem

➤ **Antonyms**

≠creep: dart, dash, fly, race, run

craze noun fad, enthusiasm, fashion, infatuation, mania, rage, trend, vogue

crazy adjective 1 Informal ridiculous, absurd, foolish, idiotic, ill-conceived, ludicrous, nonsensical, preposterous, senseless 2 fanatical, devoted, enthusiastic, infatuated, mad, passionate, wild (informal) 3 insane, crazed, demented, deranged, mad, nuts (slang), out of one's mind, unbalanced

➤ **Antonyms**

≠ridiculous: brilliant, feasible, practicable, prudent, realistic, sensible, wise, workable ≠fanatical: cool, indifferent, uncaring, unenthusiastic, uninterested ≠insane: in one's right mind, mentally sound, rational, sane, sensible

creak verb squeak, grate, grind, groan, scrape, scratch, screech

cream noun 1 lotion, cosmetic, emulsion, essence, liniment, oil, ointment, paste, salve, unguent 2 best, crème de la crème, elite, flower, pick, prime ◆ adjective 3 off-white, yellowish-white

creamy adjective smooth, buttery, milky, rich, soft, velvety

crease noun 1 line, corrugation, fold, groove, ridge, wrinkle ◆ verb 2 wrinkle, corrugate, crumple, double up, fold, rumple, screw up

create verb 1 make, compose, devise, formulate, invent, originate, produce, spawn 2 cause, bring about, lead to, occasion 3 appoint, constitute, establish, install, invest, make, set up

➤ **Antonyms**

≠make: annihilate, demolish, destroy

creation noun **1** making, conception, formation, generation, genesis, procreation **2** setting up, development, establishment, formation, foundation, inception, institution, production **3** invention, achievement, brainchild (informal), concoction, handiwork, magnum opus, pièce de résistance, production **4** universe, cosmos, nature, world

creative adjective imaginative, artistic, clever, gifted, ingenious, inspired, inventive, original, visionary

creativity noun imagination, cleverness, ingenuity, inspiration, inventiveness, originality

creator noun maker, architect, author, designer, father, inventor, originator, prime mover

creature noun **1** living thing, animal, beast, being, brute **2** person, human being, individual, man, mortal, soul, woman

credentials plural noun certification, authorization, document, licence, papers, passport, reference(s), testimonial

credibility noun believability, integrity, plausibility, reliability, trustworthiness

credible adjective **1** believable, conceivable, imaginable, likely, plausible, possible, probable, reasonable, thinkable **2** reliable, dependable, honest, sincere, trustworthy, trusty

► **Antonyms**

≠believable: doubtful, implausible, inconceivable, incredible, questionable, unbelievable, unlikely ≠reliable: dishonest, insincere, not dependable, unreliable, untrustworthy

credit noun **1** praise, acclaim, acknowledgment, approval, commendation, honour, kudos, recognition, tribute **2** As in be a credit to source of satisfaction or pride, feather in one's cap, honour **3** prestige, esteem, good name, influence, position, regard, reputation, repute, standing, status **4** belief, confidence, credence, faith, reliance, trust **5** on credit on account, by deferred payment, by instalments, on hire-purchase, on (the) H.P., on the slate (informal), on tick (informal) ♦ verb **6** believe, accept, have faith in, rely on, trust **7** credit with attribute to, ascribe to, assign to, impute to

creditable adjective praiseworthy, admirable, commendable, honourable, laudable, reputable, respectable, worthy

credulity noun gullibility, blind faith, credulousness, naïveté

creed noun belief, articles of faith, catechism, credo, doctrine, dogma, principles

creek noun **1** inlet, bay, bight, cove, firth or frith (Scot.) **2** U.S., Canad., Austral., & N.Z. stream, bayou, brook, rivulet, runnel, tributary, watercourse

creep verb **1** sneak, approach unnoticed, skulk, slink, steal, tiptoe **2** crawl, glide, slither, squirm, wriggle, writhe ♦ noun **3** Slang bootlicker (informal), crawler (slang), sneak, sycophant, toady

creeper noun climbing plant, rambler, runner, trailing plant, vine (chiefly U.S.)

creeps plural noun give one the creeps Informal disgust, frighten, make one's hair stand on end, make one squirm, repel, repulse, scare

creepy adjective Informal disturbing, eerie, frightening, hairraising, macabre, menacing, scary (informal), sinister

crescent noun meniscus, new moon, sickle

crest noun **1** top, apex, crown, highest point, peak, pinnacle, ridge, summit **2** tuft, comb, crown, mane, plume **3** emblem, badge, bearings, device, insignia, symbol

crestfallen adjective disappointed, dejected, depressed, despondent, discouraged, disheartened, downcast, downhearted

➤ **Antonyms**

cock-a-hoop, elated, encouraged, exuberant, joyful, on cloud nine (informal), over the moon (informal)

crevice noun gap, chink, cleft, crack, cranny, fissure, hole, opening, slit

crew noun **1** (ship's) company, hands, (ship's) complement **2** team, corps, gang, posse, squad **3** Informal crowd, band, bunch (informal), gang, horde, mob, pack, set

crib noun **1** Informal translation, key **2** cradle, bassinet, bed, cot **3** manger, rack, stall ◆ verb **4** Informal copy, cheat, pirate, plagiarize, purloin, steal

crime noun **1** offence, felony, misdeed, misdemeanour, transgression, trespass, unlawful act, violation **2** lawbreaking, corruption, illegality, misconduct, vice, wrongdoing

criminal noun **1** lawbreaker, convict, crook (informal), culprit, felon, offender, sinner, villain ◆ adjective **2** unlawful, corrupt, crooked (informal), illegal, illicit, immoral, lawless, wicked, wrong **3** Informal disgraceful, deplorable, foolish, preposterous, ridiculous, scandalous, senseless

➤ **Antonyms**

adjective ≠unlawful: honest, honourable, innocent, law-abiding, lawful, legal, right

cringe verb **1** shrink, cower, draw back, flinch, recoil, shy, wince **2** grovel, bootlick (informal), crawl, creep, fawn, kowtow, pander to, toady

cripple verb **1** disable, hamstring, incapacitate, lame, maim, paralyse, weaken **2** damage, destroy, impair, put out of action, put paid to, ruin, spoil

➤ **Antonyms**

≠damage: aid, assist, ease, facilitate, further, help, promote

crippled adjective disabled, handicapped, incapacitated, laid up (informal), lame, paralysed

crisis noun **1** critical point, climax, crunch (informal), crux, culmination, height, moment of truth, turning point **2** emergency, deep water, dire straits, meltdown (informal), panic stations (informal), plight, predicament, trouble

crisp adjective **1** firm, brittle, crispy, crumbly, crunchy, fresh **2** clean, neat, smart, spruce, tidy, trim, well-groomed, well-pressed **3** bracing, brisk, fresh, invigorating, refreshing

➤ **Antonyms**

≠firm: drooping, droopy, flaccid, floppy, limp, soft ≠bracing: balmy, clement, mild, pleasant, warm

criterion noun standard, bench mark, gauge, measure, principle, rule, test, touchstone, yardstick

critic noun **1** judge, analyst, authority, commentator, connoisseur, expert, pundit, reviewer **2** fault-finder, attacker, detractor, knocker (informal)

critical adjective **1** crucial, all-important, decisive, pivotal, precarious, pressing, serious, urgent, vital **2** disparaging, captious, censorious, derogatory, disapproving, fault-finding, nagging, nit-picking (informal), scathing **3** analytical, discerning, discriminating, fastidious, judicious, penetrating, perceptive

➤ **Antonyms**

≠crucial: safe, secure, unimportant ≠disparaging: appreciative, approving, complimentary, uncritical ≠analytical: undiscriminating

criticism noun **1** fault-finding, bad press, censure, character assassination, disapproval, disparagement, flak (informal), stick (slang) **2** analysis, appraisal, appreciation, assessment, comment, commentary, critique, evaluation, judgment

criticize verb find fault with, carp, censure, condemn, disapprove of, disparage, knock (informal), put down, slate (informal)

> ➤ **Antonyms**
commend, compliment, extol, praise

croak verb squawk, caw, grunt, utter or speak huskily, wheeze

crook noun Informal criminal, cheat, racketeer, robber, rogue, shark, swindler, thief, villain

crooked adjective **1** bent, curved, deformed, distorted, hooked, irregular, misshapen, out of shape, twisted, warped, zigzag **2** at an angle, askew, awry, lopsided, off-centre, skewwhiff (Brit. informal), slanting, squint, uneven **3** Informal dishonest, bent (slang), corrupt, criminal, fraudulent, illegal, shady (informal), underhand, unlawful

> ➤ **Antonyms**
≠bent: flat, straight ≠dishonest: ethical, fair, honest, honourable, lawful, legal, straight

croon verb sing, hum, purr, warble

crop noun **1** produce, fruits, gathering, harvest, reaping, vintage, yield ◆ verb **2** cut, clip, lop, pare, prune, shear, snip, trim **3** graze, browse, nibble

crop up verb Informal happen, appear, arise, emerge, occur, spring up, turn up

cross verb **1** go across, bridge, cut across, extend over, move across, pass over, span, traverse **2** intersect, crisscross, intertwine **3** oppose, block, impede, interfere, obstruct, resist **4** interbreed, blend, crossbreed, crossfertilize, cross-pollinate, hybridize, intercross, mix, mongrelize ◆ noun **5** crucifix, rood **6** crossroads, crossing, intersection, junction **7** mixture, amalgam, blend, combination **8** trouble, affliction, burden, grief, load, misfortune, trial, tribulation, woe, worry ◆ adjective **9** angry, annoyed, grumpy, ill-tempered, in a bad mood, irascible, put out, short **10** transverse, crosswise, diagonal, intersecting, oblique

> ➤ **Antonyms**
adjective ≠angry: affable, cheerful, even-tempered, genial, good-humoured, good-natured

cross-examine verb question, grill (informal), interrogate, pump, quiz

cross out or **off** verb strike off or out, blue-pencil, cancel, delete, eliminate, score off or out

crouch verb bend down, bow, duck, hunch, kneel, squat, stoop

crow verb gloat, blow one's own trumpet, boast, brag, exult, strut, swagger, triumph

crowd noun **1** multitude, army, horde, host, mass, mob, pack, swarm, throng **2** group, bunch (informal), circle, clique, lot, set **3** audience, attendance, gate, house, spectators ◆ verb **4** flock, congregate, gather, mass, stream, surge, swarm, throng **5** squeeze, bundle, congest, cram, pack, pile

crowded adjective packed, busy, congested, cramped, full, jam-packed, swarming, teeming

crown noun **1** coronet, circlet, diadem, tiara **2** laurel wreath, garland, honour, laurels, prize, trophy, wreath **3** high point, apex, crest, pinnacle, summit, tip, top ◆ verb **4** honour, adorn, dignify, festoon **5** cap, be the climax or culmination of, complete, finish, perfect, put the finishing touch to, round off, top **6** Slang strike, belt (informal), biff (slang), box, cuff, hit over the head, punch

Crown noun **1** monarchy, royalty, sovereignty **2** monarch, emperor or empress, king or queen, ruler, sovereign

crucial adjective **1** Informal vital, essential, high-priority, important, momentous, pressing, urgent **2** critical, central, decisive, pivotal

crucify verb execute, persecute, torment, torture

crude adjective **1** primitive, clumsy, makeshift, rough, rough-and-ready, rudimentary, unpolished **2** <u>vulgar</u>, coarse, dirty, gross, indecent, obscene, smutty, tasteless, uncouth **3** <u>unrefined</u>, natural, raw, unprocessed

► **Antonyms**

≠<u>vulgar</u>: genteel, polished, refined, subtle, tasteful ≠<u>unrefined</u>: fine, fine-grained, processed, refined

crudely *adverb* vulgarly, bluntly, coarsely, impolitely, roughly, rudely, tastelessly

crudity *noun* **1** <u>roughness</u>, clumsiness, crudeness **2** <u>vulgarity</u>, coarseness, impropriety, indecency, indelicacy, obscenity, smuttiness

cruel *adjective* **1** <u>brutal</u>, barbarous, callous, hard-hearted, heartless, inhumane, malevolent, sadistic, spiteful, unkind, vicious **2** <u>merciless</u>, pitiless, ruthless, unrelenting

► **Antonyms**

benevolent, caring, compassionate, gentle, humane, kind, merciful, sympathetic, warm-hearted

cruelly *adverb* **1** <u>brutally</u>, barbarously, callously, heartlessly, in cold blood, mercilessly, pitilessly, sadistically, spitefully **2** <u>bitterly</u>, deeply, fearfully, grievously, monstrously, severely

cruelty *noun* <u>brutality</u>, barbarity, callousness, depravity, fiendishness, inhumanity, mercilessness, ruthlessness, spitefulness

cruise *noun* **1** <u>sail</u>, boat trip, sea trip, voyage ♦ *verb* **2** <u>sail</u>, coast, voyage **3** <u>travel along</u>, coast, drift, keep a steady pace

crumb *noun* <u>bit</u>, fragment, grain, morsel, scrap, shred, soupçon

crumble *verb* **1** <u>disintegrate</u>, collapse, decay, degenerate, deteriorate, fall apart, go to pieces, go to wrack and ruin, tumble down **2** <u>crush</u>, fragment, granulate, grind, pound, powder, pulverize

crumple *verb* **1** <u>crush</u>, crease, rumple, screw up, scrumple, wrinkle **2** <u>collapse</u>, break down,

cave in, fall, give way, go to pieces

crunch *verb* **1** <u>chomp</u>, champ, chew noisily, grind, munch ♦ *noun* **2** *Informal* <u>critical point</u>, crisis, crux, emergency, moment of truth, test

crusade *noun* <u>campaign</u>, cause, drive, movement, push

crush *verb* **1** <u>squash</u>, break, compress, press, pulverize, squeeze **2** <u>overcome</u>, conquer, overpower, overwhelm, put down, quell, stamp out, subdue **3** <u>humiliate</u>, abash, mortify, put down (*slang*), quash, shame ♦ *noun* **4** <u>crowd</u>, huddle, jam

crust *noun* <u>layer</u>, coating, covering, shell, skin, surface

crusty *adjective* **1** <u>crispy</u>, hard **2** <u>irritable</u>, cantankerous, cross, gruff, prickly, short-tempered, testy

cry *verb* **1** <u>weep</u>, blubber, shed tears, snivel, sob **2** <u>shout</u>, bawl, bellow, call out, exclaim, howl, roar, scream, shriek, yell ♦ *noun* **3** <u>weeping</u>, blubbering, snivelling, sob, sobbing, weep **4** <u>shout</u>, bellow, call, exclamation, howl, roar, scream, screech, shriek, yell **5** <u>appeal</u>, plea

► **Antonyms**

verb ≠<u>weep</u>: chortle, chuckle, giggle, laugh, snicker, snigger ≠<u>shout</u>: mumble, murmur, mutter, whisper

cry off *verb Informal* <u>back out</u>, excuse oneself, quit, withdraw

cub *noun* <u>young</u>, offspring, whelp

cuddle *verb* <u>hug</u>, bill and coo, cosset, embrace, fondle, pet, snuggle

cudgel *noun* <u>club</u>, baton, bludgeon, cosh (*Brit.*), stick, truncheon

cue *noun* <u>signal</u>, catchword, hint, key, prompting, reminder, sign, suggestion

cul-de-sac *noun* <u>dead end</u>, blind alley

culminate *verb* <u>end up</u>, climax, close, come to a climax, come to a head, conclude, finish, wind up

culmination noun climax, acme, conclusion, consummation, finale, peak, pinnacle, zenith

culpable adjective blameworthy, at fault, found wanting, guilty, in the wrong, to blame, wrong

➤ **Antonyms**
blameless, clean (slang), guiltless, innocent, not guilty, squeaky-clean

culprit noun offender, criminal, evildoer, felon, guilty party, miscreant, transgressor, wrongdoer

cult noun 1 sect, clique, faction, religion, school 2 devotion, idolization, worship

cultivate verb 1 farm, plant, plough, tend, till, work 2 develop, foster, improve, promote, refine 3 court, dance attendance upon, run after, seek out

cultivation noun 1 farming, gardening, husbandry, planting, ploughing, tillage 2 development, encouragement, fostering, furtherance, nurture, patronage, promotion, support

cultural adjective artistic, civilizing, edifying, educational, enlightening, enriching, humane, liberal

culture noun 1 civilization, customs, lifestyle, mores, society, way of life 2 refinement, education, enlightenment, good taste, sophistication, urbanity 3 farming, cultivation, husbandry

cultured adjective refined, educated, enlightened, highbrow, sophisticated, urbane, well-informed, well-read

➤ **Antonyms**
coarse, uncultivated, uneducated, unrefined, vulgar

culvert noun drain, channel, conduit, gutter, watercourse

cumbersome adjective awkward, bulky, burdensome, heavy, unmanageable, unwieldy, weighty

➤ **Antonyms**
convenient, easy to use, handy, manageable, practical

cunning adjective 1 crafty, artful, devious, Machiavellian, sharp, shifty, sly, wily 2 skilful, imaginative, ingenious ♦ noun 3 craftiness, artfulness, deviousness, guile, slyness, trickery 4 skill, artifice, cleverness, ingenuity, subtlety

➤ **Antonyms**
adjective ≠crafty: artless, frank, honest, ingenuous ≠skilful: maladroit ♦ noun ≠craftiness: candour, ingenuousness, sincerity ≠skill: clumsiness

cup noun 1 mug, beaker, bowl, chalice, goblet, teacup 2 trophy

cupboard noun cabinet, press

curb noun 1 restraint, brake, bridle, check, control, deterrent, limitation, rein ♦ verb 2 restrain, check, control, hinder, impede, inhibit, restrict, retard, suppress

cure verb 1 make better, correct, ease, heal, mend, relieve, remedy, restore 2 preserve, dry, pickle, salt, smoke ♦ noun 3 remedy, antidote, medicine, nostrum, panacea, treatment

curiosity noun 1 inquisitiveness, interest, nosiness (informal), prying, snooping (informal) 2 oddity, freak, novelty, phenomenon, rarity, sight, spectacle, wonder

curious adjective 1 inquiring, inquisitive, interested, questioning, searching 2 inquisitive, meddling, nosy (informal), prying 3 unusual, bizarre, extraordinary, mysterious, novel, odd, peculiar, rare, strange, unexpected

➤ **Antonyms**
≠inquiring: incurious, indifferent, uninquisitive, uninterested ≠unusual: common, everyday, familiar, ordinary

curl verb 1 twirl, bend, coil, curve, loop, spiral, turn, twist, wind ♦ noun 2 twist, coil, kink, ringlet, spiral, whorl

curly adjective curling, crinkly, curled, frizzy, fuzzy, wavy, winding

currency noun 1 money, coinage, coins, notes 2 acceptance, circulation, exposure, popularity, prevalence, vogue

current *adjective* **1** present, contemporary, fashionable, in fashion, in vogue, present-day, trendy (*Brit. informal*), up-to-date **2** prevalent, accepted, common, customary, in circulation, popular, topical, widespread ♦ *noun* **3** flow, course, draught, jet, progression, river, stream, tide, undertow **4** mood, atmosphere, feeling, tendency, trend, undercurrent

➤ **Antonyms**

adjective ≠present: archaic, obsolete, old-fashioned, outmoded, out-of-date, passé, past

curse *verb* **1** swear, blaspheme, cuss (*informal*), take the Lord's name in vain **2** damn, anathematize, excommunicate ♦ *noun* **3** oath, blasphemy, expletive, obscenity, swearing, swearword **4** denunciation, anathema, ban, excommunication, hoodoo (*informal*), jinx **5** affliction, bane, hardship, plague, scourge, torment, trouble

cursed *adjective* damned, accursed, bedevilled, doomed, ill-fated

curt *adjective* short, abrupt, blunt, brief, brusque, gruff, monosyllabic, succinct, terse

curtail *verb* cut short, cut back, decrease, diminish, dock, lessen, reduce, shorten, truncate

curtain *noun* hanging, drape (*chiefly U.S.*)

curve *noun* **1** bend, arc, curvature, loop, trajectory, turn ♦ *verb* **2** bend, arc, arch, coil, hook, spiral, swerve, turn, twist, wind

curved *adjective* bent, arched, bowed, rounded, serpentine, sinuous, twisted

cushion *noun* **1** pillow, beanbag, bolster, hassock, headrest, pad ♦ *verb* **2** soften, dampen, deaden, muffle, stifle, suppress

cushy *adjective* *Informal* easy, comfortable, soft, undemanding

custody *noun* **1** safekeeping, care, charge, keeping, protection, supervision **2** imprisonment, confinement, detention, incarceration

custom *noun* **1** tradition, convention, policy, practice, ritual, rule, usage **2** habit, practice, procedure, routine, way, wont **3** customers, patronage, trade

customary *adjective* usual, accepted, accustomed, common, conventional, established, normal, ordinary, routine, traditional

➤ **Antonyms**

exceptional, infrequent, irregular, occasional, rare, uncommon, unusual

customer *noun* client, buyer, consumer, patron, purchaser, regular (*informal*), shopper

customs *plural noun* duty, import charges, tariff, tax, toll

cut *verb* **1** penetrate, chop, pierce, score, sever, slash, slice, slit, wound **2** divide, bisect, dissect, slice, split **3** trim, clip, hew, lop, mow, pare, prune, shave, snip **4** abridge, abbreviate, condense, curtail, delete, shorten **5** reduce, contract, cut back, decrease, diminish, lower, slash, slim (down) **6** shape, carve, chisel, engrave, fashion, form, sculpt, whittle **7** hurt, insult, put down, snub, sting, wound **8** *Informal* ignore, avoid, cold-shoulder, slight, spurn, turn one's back on ♦ *noun* **9** incision, gash, laceration, nick, slash, slit, stroke, wound **10** reduction, cutback, decrease, fall, lowering, saving **11** *Informal* share, percentage, piece, portion, section, slice **12** style, fashion, look, shape

➤ **Antonyms**

verb ≠abridge, reduce: add to, augment, enlarge, expand, increase ≠ignore: accept gladly, embrace, greet, hail, receive, welcome with open arms

cutback *noun* reduction, cut, decrease, economy, lessening, retrenchment

cut down *verb* **1** fell, hew, level, lop **2** reduce, decrease, lessen, lower

cute *adjective* appealing, attractive, charming, delightful, engaging, lovable, sweet, winning, winsome

cut in *verb* interrupt, break in, butt in, intervene, intrude

cut off *verb* 1 separate, isolate, sever 2 interrupt, disconnect, intercept

cut out *verb* stop, cease, give up, refrain from

cutthroat *adjective* 1 competitive, dog-eat-dog, fierce, relentless, ruthless, unprincipled ♦ *noun* 2 murderer, assassin, butcher, executioner, hit man (*slang*), killer

cutting *adjective* hurtful, acrimonious, barbed, bitter, caustic, malicious, sarcastic, scathing, vitriolic, wounding

➤ **Antonyms**
consoling, flattering, kind, mild

cycle *noun* era, circle, period, phase, revolution, rotation

cynic *noun* sceptic, doubter, misanthrope, misanthropist, pessimist, scoffer

cynical *adjective* sceptical, contemptuous, derisive, distrustful, misanthropic, mocking, pessimistic, scoffing, scornful, unbelieving

➤ **Antonyms**
credulous, gullible, hopeful, optimistic, trustful, trusting, unsceptical, unsuspecting

cynicism *noun* scepticism, disbelief, doubt, misanthropy, pessimism

D d

dab *verb* 1 pat, daub, stipple, tap, touch ♦ *noun* 2 spot, bit, drop, pat, smudge, speck 3 pat, flick, stroke, tap, touch

dabble *verb* 1 play at, dip into, potter, tinker, trifle (with) 2 splash, dip

daft *adjective Informal, chiefly Brit.* 1 foolish, absurd, asinine, crackpot (*informal*), crazy, dumb-ass (*slang*), idiotic, silly, stupid, witless 2 crazy, crackers (*Brit. slang*), demented, deranged, insane, nuts (*slang*), touched, unhinged

dagger *noun* knife, bayonet, dirk, stiletto

daily *adjective* 1 everyday, diurnal, quotidian ♦ *adverb* 2 every day, day by day, once a day

dainty *adjective* delicate, charming, elegant, exquisite, fine, graceful, neat, petite, pretty

➤ **Antonyms**
awkward, clumsy, coarse, gauche, inelegant, maladroit, uncouth, ungainly

dam *noun* 1 barrier, barrage, embankment, obstruction, wall ♦ *verb* 2 block up, barricade, hold back, obstruct, restrict

damage *verb* 1 harm, hurt, impair, injure, ruin, spoil, weaken, wreck ♦ *noun* 2 harm, destruction, detriment, devastation, hurt, injury, loss, suffering 3 *Informal* cost, bill, charge, expense

➤ **Antonyms**
verb ≠harm: better, fix, improve, mend, repair ♦ *noun* ≠harm: gain, improvement, reparation

damages *plural noun Law* compensation, fine, reimbursement, reparation, satisfaction

damaging *adjective* harmful, deleterious, detrimental, disadvantageous, hurtful, injurious, ruinous

➤ **Antonyms**
advantageous, favourable, helpful, profitable, useful, valuable

dame *noun* noblewoman, baroness, dowager, *grande dame*, lady, peeress

damn *verb* 1 criticize, blast, censure, condemn, denounce, put down 2 sentence, condemn, doom

➤ **Antonyms**
≠criticize: acclaim, applaud, approve, congratulate, honour, praise

damnation noun Theology <u>condemnation</u>, anathema, damning, denunciation, doom

damned adjective 1 <u>doomed</u>, accursed, condemned, lost 2 Slang <u>detestable</u>, confounded, hateful, infernal, loathsome

damp adjective 1 <u>moist</u>, clammy, dank, dewy, drizzly, humid, soggy, sopping, wet ♦ noun 2 <u>moisture</u>, dampness, dankness, drizzle ♦ verb 3 <u>moisten</u>, dampen, wet 4 damp down <u>curb</u>, allay, check, diminish, inhibit, pour cold water on, reduce, stifle

➤ Antonyms

adjective ≠<u>moist</u>: arid, dry, watertight ♦ noun ≠<u>moisture</u>: aridity, dryness ♦ verb ≠<u>curb</u>: encourage, gee up, hearten, inspire

dampen verb 1 <u>reduce</u>, check, dull, lessen, moderate, restrain, stifle 2 <u>moisten</u>, make damp, spray, wet

damper noun As in put a damper on <u>discouragement</u>, cold water (informal), hindrance, restraint, wet blanket (informal)

dance verb 1 <u>prance</u>, hop, jig, skip, sway, trip, whirl ♦ noun 2 <u>ball</u>, disco, discotheque, hop (informal), knees-up (Brit. informal), social

dancer noun <u>ballerina</u>, Terpsichorean

danger noun <u>peril</u>, hazard, jeopardy, menace, pitfall, risk, threat, vulnerability

dangerous adjective <u>perilous</u>, breakneck, chancy (informal), hazardous, insecure, precarious, risky, unsafe, vulnerable

➤ Antonyms

harmless, innocuous, O.K. or okay (informal), out of danger, out of harm's way, safe, safe and sound, secure

dangerously adverb <u>perilously</u>, alarmingly, hazardously, precariously, recklessly, riskily, unsafely

dangle verb 1 <u>hang</u>, flap, flap down, sway, swing, trail 2 <u>wave</u>, brandish, flaunt, flourish

dapper adjective <u>neat</u>, natty (informal), smart, soigné or soignée, spruce, spry, trim, wellgroomed, well turned out

➤ Antonyms

dishevelled, dowdy, ill-groomed, rumpled, sloppy (informal), slovenly, unkempt, untidy

dare verb 1 <u>risk</u>, hazard, make bold, presume, venture 2 <u>challenge</u>, defy, goad, provoke, taunt, throw down the gauntlet ♦ noun 3 <u>challenge</u>, provocation, taunt

daredevil noun 1 <u>adventurer</u>, desperado, exhibitionist, madcap, show-off (informal), stunt man ♦ adjective 2 <u>daring</u>, adventurous, audacious, bold, deathdefying, madcap, reckless

daring adjective 1 <u>brave</u>, adventurous, audacious, bold, daredevil, fearless, intrepid, reckless, venturesome ♦ noun 2 <u>bravery</u>, audacity, boldness, bottle (Brit. slang), courage, fearlessness, nerve (informal), pluck, temerity

➤ Antonyms

adjective ≠<u>brave</u>: anxious, careful, cautious, cowardly, fainthearted, fearful, timid, wary ♦ noun ≠<u>bravery</u>: anxiety, caution, cowardice, fear, timidity

dark adjective 1 <u>dim</u>, dingy, murky, shadowy, shady, sunless, unlit 2 <u>brunette</u>, black, darkskinned, dusky, ebony, sable, swarthy 3 <u>gloomy</u>, bleak, dismal, grim, morose, mournful, sad, sombre 4 <u>evil</u>, foul, infernal, sinister, vile, wicked 5 <u>secret</u>, concealed, hidden, mysterious ♦ noun 6 <u>darkness</u>, dimness, dusk, gloom, murk, obscurity, semi-darkness 7 <u>night</u>, evening, nightfall, night-time, twilight

➤ Antonyms

adjective ≠<u>brunette</u>: blond, blonde, fair, fair-haired, flaxenhaired, light, light-complexioned, towheaded ≠<u>gloomy</u>: bright, cheerful, clear, genial, glad, hopeful, pleasant, sunny

darken verb <u>make dark</u>, blacken, dim, obscure, overshadow

➤ **Antonyms**

brighten, illuminate, lighten, light up, make bright, shine

darkness noun dark, blackness, duskiness, gloom, murk, nightfall, shade, shadows

darling noun 1 beloved, dear, dearest, love, sweetheart, truelove ◆ adjective 2 beloved, adored, cherished, dear, precious, treasured

darn verb 1 mend, cobble up, patch, repair, sew up, stitch ◆ noun 2 mend, invisible repair, patch, reinforcement

dart verb dash, fly, race, run, rush, shoot, spring, sprint, tear

dash verb 1 rush, bolt, fly, hurry, race, run, speed, sprint, tear 2 throw, cast, fling, hurl, slam, sling 3 crash, break, destroy, shatter, smash, splinter 4 frustrate, blight, foil, ruin, spoil, thwart, undo ◆ noun 5 rush, dart, race, run, sortie, sprint, spurt 6 little, bit, drop, hint, pinch, soupçon, sprinkling, tinge, touch 7 style, brio, élan, flair, flourish, panache, spirit, verve

➤ **Antonyms**

verb ≠rush: crawl, dawdle, walk ≠frustrate: enhance, improve ◆ noun ≠little: lot, much

dashing adjective 1 bold, debonair, gallant, lively, spirited, swashbuckling 2 stylish, elegant, flamboyant, jaunty, showy, smart, sporty

➤ **Antonyms**

≠bold: boring, dreary, dull, lacklustre, stolid, unexciting, uninteresting

data noun information, details, facts, figures, statistics

date noun 1 time, age, epoch, era, period, stage 2 appointment, assignation, engagement, meeting, rendezvous, tryst 3 partner, escort, friend ◆ verb 4 put a date on, assign a date to, fix the period of 5 become oldfashioned, be dated, show one's age 6 date from or date back to, come from, bear a date of, belong to, exist from, originate in

dated adjective old-fashioned, obsolete, old hat, outdated, outmoded, out of date, passé, unfashionable

➤ **Antonyms**

à la mode, all the rage, current, in vogue, latest, modern, stylish, trendy (Brit. informal), up-to-date

daub verb smear, coat, cover, paint, plaster, slap on (informal)

daunting adjective intimidating, alarming, demoralizing, disconcerting, discouraging, disheartening, frightening, off-putting (Brit. informal), unnerving

➤ **Antonyms**

cheering, comforting, encouraging, heartening, reassuring

dauntless adjective fearless, bold, doughty, gallant, indomitable, intrepid, resolute, stouthearted, undaunted, unflinching

dawdle verb waste time, dally, delay, drag one's feet or heels, hang about, idle, loaf, loiter, trail

➤ **Antonyms**

fly, get a move on (informal), hasten, hurry, lose no time, make haste, rush

dawn noun 1 daybreak, aurora (poetic), cockcrow, crack of dawn, daylight, morning, sunrise, sunup 2 beginning, advent, birth, emergence, genesis, origin, rise, start ◆ verb 3 grow light, break, brighten, lighten 4 begin, appear, develop, emerge, originate, rise, unfold 5 dawn on or upon hit, become apparent, come into one's head, come to mind, occur, register (informal), strike

day noun 1 twenty-four hours, daylight, daytime 2 point in time, date, time 3 time, age, epoch, era, heyday, period, zenith

daybreak noun dawn, break of day, cockcrow, crack of dawn, first light, morning, sunrise, sunup

daydream noun 1 fantasy,

dream, fancy, imagining, pipe dream, reverie, wish ♦ *verb 2* fantasize, dream, envision, fancy, imagine, muse

daylight *noun* sunlight, light of day, sunshine

daze *verb 1* stun, benumb, numb, paralyse, shock, stupefy ♦ *noun 2* shock, bewilderment, confusion, distraction, stupor, trance, trancelike state

dazed *adjective* shocked, bewildered, confused, disorientated, dizzy, muddled, punch-drunk, staggered, stunned

dazzle *verb 1* impress, amaze, astonish, bowl over (*informal*), overpower, overwhelm, take one's breath away *2* blind, bedazzle, blur, confuse, daze ♦ *noun 3* splendour, brilliance, glitter, magnificence, razzmatazz (*slang*), sparkle

dazzling *adjective* splendid, brilliant, glittering, glorious, scintillating, sensational (*informal*), sparkling, stunning, virtuoso

➤ **Antonyms**

dull, ordinary, tedious, unexceptional, unexciting, uninspiring, uninteresting, unremarkable

dead *adjective 1* deceased, defunct, departed, extinct, late, passed away, perished *2* not working, inactive, inoperative, stagnant, unemployed, useless *3* numb, inert, paralysed *4* total, absolute, complete, outright, thorough, unqualified, utter *5* *Informal* exhausted, dead beat (*informal*), spent, tired, worn out *6* boring, dull, flat, uninteresting ♦ *noun 7* middle, depth, midst ♦ *adverb 8* *Informal* exactly, absolutely, completely, directly, entirely, totally

➤ **Antonyms**

adjective ≠deceased: alive, alive and kicking, animate, existing, living ≠not working: active, alive, effective, in use, operative, productive, working

deaden *verb* reduce, alleviate, blunt, cushion, diminish, dull,

lessen, muffle, smother, stifle, suppress, weaken

deadline *noun* time limit, cutoff point, limit, target date

deadlock *noun 1* impasse, dead heat, draw, gridlock, stalemate, standoff, standstill, tie

deadlocked *adjective* even, equal, level, neck and neck

deadly *adjective 1* lethal, dangerous, death-dealing, deathly, fatal, malignant, mortal *2* *Informal* boring, dull, mind-numbing, monotonous, tedious, tiresome, uninteresting, wearisome

deadpan *adjective* expressionless, blank, impassive, inexpressive, inscrutable, poker-faced, straight-faced

deaf *adjective 1* hard of hearing, stone deaf, without hearing *2* oblivious, indifferent, unconcerned, unhearing, unmoved

deafen *verb* make deaf, din, drown out, split *or* burst the eardrums

deafening *adjective* ear-piercing, booming, ear-splitting, overpowering, piercing, resounding, ringing, thunderous

deal *noun 1* *Informal* agreement, arrangement, bargain, contract, pact, transaction, understanding *2* amount, degree, extent, portion, quantity, share ♦ *verb 3* sell, bargain, buy and sell, do business, negotiate, stock, trade, traffic

dealer *noun* trader, merchant, purveyor, supplier, tradesman, wholesaler

deal out *verb* distribute, allot, apportion, assign, dispense, dole out, give, mete out, share

deal with *verb 1* handle, attend to, cope with, get to grips with, manage, see to, take care of, treat *2* be concerned with, consider

dear *noun 1* beloved, angel, darling, loved one, precious, treasure ♦ *adjective 2* beloved, cherished, close, favourite, intimate, precious, prized, treasured *3* expensive, at a premium, costly, high-priced, overpriced, pricey (*informal*)

➤ **Antonyms**

adjective ≠<u>beloved</u>: disliked, hated ≠<u>expensive</u>: cheap, common, inexpensive, worthless

dearly *adverb* **1** <u>very much</u>, extremely, greatly, profoundly **2** <u>at great cost</u>, at a high price

dearth *noun* <u>scarcity</u>, deficiency, inadequacy, insufficiency, lack, paucity, poverty, shortage, want

death *noun* **1** <u>dying</u>, demise, departure, end, exit, passing **2** <u>destruction</u>, downfall, extinction, finish, ruin, undoing

➤ **Antonyms**

≠<u>dying</u>: birth ≠<u>destruction</u>: beginning, emergence, genesis, growth, rise

deathly *adjective* <u>deathlike</u>, ghastly, grim, pale, pallid, wan

debacle *noun* <u>disaster</u>, catastrophe, collapse, defeat, fiasco, reversal, rout

debase *verb* <u>degrade</u>, cheapen, devalue, lower, reduce

➤ **Antonyms**

elevate, enhance, exalt, improve, uplift

debatable *adjective* <u>doubtful</u>, arguable, controversial, dubious, moot, problematical, questionable, uncertain

debate *noun* **1** <u>discussion</u>, argument, contention, controversy, dispute ◆ *verb* **2** <u>discuss</u>, argue, dispute, question **3** <u>consider</u>, deliberate, ponder, reflect, ruminate, weigh

debauchery *noun* <u>depravity</u>, dissipation, dissoluteness, excess, indulgence, intemperance, lewdness, overindulgence

debonair *adjective* <u>elegant</u>, charming, courteous, dashing, refined, smooth, suave, urbane, well-bred

debrief *verb* <u>interrogate</u>, cross-examine, examine, probe, question, quiz

debris *noun* <u>remains</u>, bits, detritus, fragments, rubble, ruins,

waste, wreckage

debt *noun* **1** <u>debt</u>, commitment, liability, obligation **2 in debt** <u>owing</u>, in arrears, in the red (*informal*), liable

debtor *noun* <u>borrower</u>, mortgagor

debunk *verb Informal* <u>expose</u>, cut down to size, deflate, disparage, mock, ridicule, show up

debut *noun* <u>introduction</u>, beginning, bow, coming out, entrance, first appearance, initiation, presentation

decadence *noun* <u>degeneration</u>, corruption, decay, decline, deterioration, dissipation, dissolution

decadent *adjective* <u>degenerate</u>, abandoned, corrupt, decaying, declining, dissolute, immoral, self-indulgent

➤ **Antonyms**

decent, good, high-minded, honourable, incorruptible, moral, principled, proper, upright, upstanding, virtuous

decapitate *verb* <u>behead</u>, execute, guillotine

decay *verb* **1** <u>decline</u>, crumble, deteriorate, disintegrate, dwindle, shrivel, wane, waste away, wither **2** <u>rot</u>, corrode, decompose, perish, putrefy ◆ *noun* **3** <u>decline</u>, collapse, degeneration, deterioration, fading, failing, wasting, withering **4** <u>rot</u>, caries, decomposition, gangrene, putrefaction

➤ **Antonyms**

verb ≠<u>decline</u>: expand, flourish, flower, grow, increase ◆ *noun* ≠<u>decline</u>: growth

decease *noun Formal* <u>death</u>, demise, departure, dying, release

deceased *adjective* <u>dead</u>, defunct, departed, expired, former, late, lifeless

deceit *noun* <u>dishonesty</u>, cheating, chicanery, deception, fraud, lying, pretence, treachery, trickery

➤ **Antonyms**

candour, frankness, honesty, openness, sincerity, truthfulness

deceitful *adjective* <u>dishonest</u>, deceptive, false, fraudulent, sneaky, treacherous, two-faced, untrustworthy

deceive verb take in (informal), cheat, con (informal), dupe, fool, hoodwink, mislead, swindle, trick

deceiver noun liar, cheat, con man (informal), double-dealer, fraud, impostor, swindler, trickster

decency noun respectability, civility, correctness, courtesy, decorum, etiquette, modesty, propriety

decent adjective **1** satisfactory, adequate, ample, fair, passable, reasonable, sufficient, tolerable **2** respectable, chaste, decorous, modest, proper, pure **3** proper, appropriate, becoming, befitting, fitting, seemly, suitable **4** Informal kind, accommodating, courteous, friendly, generous, gracious, helpful, obliging, thoughtful

➤ **Antonyms**

≠satisfactory: clumsy, inept, unsatisfactory ≠proper: awkward, immodest, improper, incorrect, indecent, unseemly, unsuitable ≠kind: awkward, discourteous

deception noun **1** trickery, cunning, deceit, fraud, guile, legerdemain, treachery **2** trick, bluff, decoy, hoax, illusion, lie, ruse, subterfuge

➤ **Antonyms**

≠trickery: candour, frankness, honesty, openness, truthfulness

deceptive adjective misleading, ambiguous, deceitful, dishonest, false, fraudulent, illusory, unreliable

decide verb reach or come to a decision, adjudge, adjudicate, choose, conclude, determine, make up one's mind, resolve

➤ **Antonyms**

be indecisive, be unable to decide, blow hot and cold (informal), dither (chiefly Brit.), hesitate, hum and haw, shillyshally (informal), swither (Scot.), vacillate

decidedly adverb definitely, clearly, distinctly, downright, positively, unequivocally, unmistakably

decimate verb devastate, ravage, wreak havoc on

decipher verb figure out (informal), crack, decode, deduce, interpret, make out, read, solve

decision noun **1** judgment, arbitration, conclusion, finding, resolution, ruling, sentence, verdict **2** decisiveness, determination, firmness, purpose, resolution, resolve, strength of mind or will

decisive adjective **1** crucial, conclusive, critical, fateful, influential, momentous, significant **2** resolute, decided, determined, firm, forceful, incisive, strong-minded, trenchant

➤ **Antonyms**

≠crucial: doubtful, indecisive, uncertain, undecided ≠resolute: hesitant, hesitating, indecisive, in two minds (informal), irresolute, uncertain, undecided, vacillating

deck verb decorate, adorn, array, beautify, clothe, dress, embellish, festoon

declaim verb **1** orate, harangue, hold forth, lecture, proclaim, rant, recite, speak **2** declaim against protest against, attack, decry, denounce, inveigh, rail

declaration noun **1** statement, acknowledgment, affirmation, assertion, avowal, disclosure, protestation, revelation, testimony **2** announcement, edict, notification, proclamation, profession, pronouncement

declare verb **1** state, affirm, announce, assert, claim, maintain, proclaim, profess, pronounce, swear, utter **2** make known, confess, disclose, reveal, show

decline verb **1** lessen, decrease, diminish, dwindle, ebb, fade, fall off, shrink, sink, wane **2** deteriorate, decay, degenerate, droop, languish, pine, weaken, worsen **3** refuse, abstain, avoid, reject, say 'no', turn down ♦ noun **4**

lessening, downturn, drop, dwindling, falling off, recession, slump **5** deterioration, decay, degeneration, failing, weakening, worsening

➤ **Antonyms**

verb ≠lessen: increase, rise ≠deteriorate: improve ≠refuse: accept, agree, consent ♦ noun ≠lessening: rise, upswing ≠deterioration: improvement

decode verb decipher, crack, decrypt, interpret, solve, unscramble, work out

➤ **Antonyms**

encode, encrypt, scramble

decompose verb rot, break up, crumble, decay, fall apart, fester, putrefy

decor noun decoration, colour scheme, furnishing style, ornamentation

decorate verb **1** adorn, beautify, embellish, festoon, grace, ornament, trim **2** do up (informal), colour, furbish, paint, paper, renovate, wallpaper **3** pin a medal on, cite, confer an honour on or upon

decoration noun **1** adornment, beautification, elaboration, embellishment, enrichment, ornamentation, trimming **2** ornament, bauble, frill, garnish, trimmings **3** medal, award, badge, ribbon, star

decorative adjective ornamental, beautifying, fancy, nonfunctional, pretty

decorous adjective proper, becoming, correct, decent, dignified, fitting, polite, seemly, well-behaved

➤ **Antonyms**

out of keeping, unbefitting, unseemly

decorum noun propriety, decency, dignity, etiquette, good manners, politeness, protocol, respectability

➤ **Antonyms**

bad manners, impoliteness, impropriety, indecorum, rudeness, unseemliness

decoy noun **1** lure, bait, enticement, inducement, pretence, trap ♦ verb **2** lure, deceive, ensnare, entice, entrap, seduce, tempt

decrease verb **1** lessen, cut down, decline, diminish, drop, dwindle, lower, reduce, shrink, subside ♦ noun **2** lessening, contraction, cutback, decline, dwindling, falling off, loss, reduction, subsidence

➤ **Antonyms**

verb ≠lessen: enlarge, expand, extend, increase ♦ noun ≠lessening: expansion, extension, growth

decree noun **1** law, act, command, edict, order, proclamation, ruling, statute ♦ verb **2** order, command, demand, ordain, prescribe, proclaim, pronounce, rule

decrepit adjective **1** weak, aged, doddering, feeble, frail, infirm **2** worn-out, battered, beat-up (informal), broken-down, dilapidated, ramshackle, rickety, run-down, tumbledown, weather-beaten

decry verb condemn, belittle, criticize, denigrate, denounce, discredit, disparage, put down, run down

dedicate verb **1** devote, commit, give over to, pledge, surrender **2** inscribe, address

dedicated adjective devoted, committed, enthusiastic, purposeful, single-minded, whole-hearted, zealous

➤ **Antonyms**

indifferent, uncaring, uncommitted, unconcerned, uninterested

dedication noun **1** devotion, adherence, allegiance, commitment, faithfulness, loyalty, single-mindedness, wholeheartedness **2** inscription, address, message

➤ **Antonyms**

≠devotion: apathy, coolness, indifference, unconcern

deduce verb conclude, draw, gather, glean, infer, reason, take to mean, understand

deduct verb <u>subtract</u>, decrease by, knock off (informal), reduce by, remove, take away, take off
➤ **Antonyms**
add, add to, enlarge

deduction noun **1** <u>subtraction</u>, decrease, diminution, discount, reduction, withdrawal **2** <u>conclusion</u>, assumption, finding, inference, reasoning, result

deed noun **1** <u>action</u>, achievement, act, exploit, fact, feat, performance **2** Law <u>document</u>, contract, title

deep adjective **1** <u>wide</u>, bottomless, broad, far, profound, unfathomable, yawning **2** <u>mysterious</u>, abstract, abstruse, arcane, esoteric, hidden, obscure, recondite, secret **3** <u>intense</u>, extreme, grave, great, profound, serious (informal), unqualified **4** <u>absorbed</u>, engrossed, immersed, lost, preoccupied, rapt **5** <u>dark</u>, intense, rich, strong, vivid **6** <u>low</u>, bass, booming, low-pitched, resonant, sonorous ◆ noun **7** <u>middle</u>, dead **8** the deep Poetic <u>ocean</u>, briny (informal), high seas, main, sea
➤ **Antonyms**
adjective ≠<u>wide</u>: shallow ≠<u>mysterious</u>: shallow ≠<u>intense</u>: shallow, superficial ≠<u>dark</u>: light, pale ≠<u>low</u>: high, sharp

deepen verb **1** <u>dig out</u>, excavate, hollow, scoop out **2** <u>intensify</u>, grow, increase, magnify, reinforce, strengthen

deeply adverb **1** <u>thoroughly</u>, completely, gravely, profoundly, seriously, severely, to the core, to the heart, to the quick **2** <u>intensely</u>, acutely, affectingly, distressingly, feelingly, mournfully, movingly, passionately, sadly

deface verb <u>vandalize</u>, damage, deform, disfigure, mar, mutilate, spoil, tarnish

de facto adverb **1** <u>in fact</u>, actually, in effect, in reality, really ◆ adjective **2** <u>actual</u>, existing, real

defame verb <u>slander</u>, bad-mouth

(slang, chiefly U.S. & Canad.), cast aspersions on, denigrate, discredit, disparage, knock (informal), libel, malign, smear

default noun **1** <u>failure</u>, deficiency, dereliction, evasion, lapse, neglect, nonpayment, omission ◆ verb **2** <u>fail</u>, dodge, evade, neglect

defeat verb **1** <u>beat</u>, conquer, crush, master, overwhelm, rout, trounce, vanquish, wipe the floor with (informal) **2** <u>frustrate</u>, baffle, balk, confound, foil, get the better of, ruin, thwart ◆ noun **3** <u>conquest</u>, beating, overthrow, pasting (slang), rout **4** <u>frustration</u>, failure, rebuff, reverse, setback, thwarting
➤ **Antonyms**
verb ≠<u>beat</u>: bow, cave in (informal), lose, submit, succumb, surrender, yield ◆ noun ≠<u>conquest</u>: success, triumph, victory

defeatist noun **1** <u>pessimist</u>, prophet of doom, quitter ◆ adjective **2** <u>pessimistic</u>

defect noun **1** <u>imperfection</u>, blemish, blotch, error, failing, fault, flaw, spot, taint ◆ verb **2** <u>desert</u>, abandon, change sides, go over, rebel, revolt, walk out on (informal)

defection noun <u>desertion</u>, apostasy, rebellion

defective adjective <u>faulty</u>, broken, deficient, flawed, imperfect, not working, on the blink (slang), out of order
➤ **Antonyms**
adequate, intact, perfect, whole, working

defector noun <u>deserter</u>, apostate, renegade, turncoat

defence noun **1** <u>protection</u>, cover, guard, immunity, resistance, safeguard, security, shelter **2** <u>shield</u>, barricade, bulwark, buttress, fortification, rampart **3** <u>argument</u>, excuse, explanation, justification, plea, vindication **4** Law <u>plea</u>, alibi, denial, rebuttal, testimony

defenceless adjective <u>helpless</u>, exposed, naked, powerless, unarmed, unguarded, unprotected, vulnerable, wide open

➤ **Antonyms**

free from harm, guarded, out of harm's way, protected, safe, safe and sound, secure

defend verb 1 <u>protect</u>, cover, guard, keep safe, preserve, safeguard, screen, shelter, shield 2 <u>support</u>, champion, endorse, justify, speak up for, stand up for, stick up for (*informal*), uphold, vindicate

defendant noun <u>the accused</u>, defence, offender, prisoner at the bar, respondent

defender noun 1 <u>protector</u>, bodyguard, escort, guard 2 <u>supporter</u>, advocate, champion, sponsor

defensive adjective <u>on guard</u>, on the defensive, protective, uptight (*informal*), watchful

defer¹ verb <u>postpone</u>, delay, hold over, procrastinate, put off, put on ice (*informal*), shelve, suspend

defer² verb <u>comply</u>, accede, bow, capitulate, give in, give way to, submit, yield

deference noun <u>respect</u>, attention, civility, consideration, courtesy, honour, politeness, regard, reverence

➤ **Antonyms**

contempt, discourtesy, dishonour, disregard, disrespect, impertinence, impoliteness, impudence, incivility, insolence, irreverence, lack of respect, rudeness

deferential adjective <u>respectful</u>, ingratiating, obedient, obeisant, obsequious, polite, reverential, submissive

defiance noun <u>resistance</u>, confrontation, contempt, disobedience, disregard, insolence, insubordination, opposition, rebelliousness

➤ **Antonyms**

accordance, acquiescence, compliance, deference, obedience, observance, regard, respect, subservience

defiant adjective <u>resisting</u>, audacious, bold, daring, disobedient, insolent, insubordinate, mutinous, provocative, rebellious

➤ **Antonyms**

cowardly, meek, obedient, respectful, submissive

deficiency noun 1 <u>lack</u>, absence, dearth, deficit, scarcity, shortage 2 <u>failing</u>, defect, demerit, fault, flaw, frailty, imperfection, shortcoming, weakness

➤ **Antonyms**

≠lack: abundance, adequacy, sufficiency, surfeit

deficient adjective 1 <u>lacking</u>, inadequate, insufficient, meagre, scant, scarce, short, skimpy, wanting 2 <u>unsatisfactory</u>, defective, faulty, flawed, impaired, imperfect, incomplete, inferior, weak

deficit noun <u>shortfall</u>, arrears, deficiency, loss, shortage

define verb 1 <u>describe</u>, characterize, designate, explain, expound, interpret, specify, spell out 2 <u>mark out</u>, bound, circumscribe, delineate, demarcate, limit, outline

definite adjective 1 <u>clear</u>, black-and-white, cut-and-dried (*informal*), exact, fixed, marked, particular, precise, specific 2 <u>certain</u>, assured, decided, guaranteed, positive, settled, sure

➤ **Antonyms**

≠clear: confused, fuzzy, general, hazy, imprecise, indefinite, indistinct, inexact, unclear, undetermined, vague ≠certain: uncertain, undecided

definitely adverb <u>certainly</u>, absolutely, categorically, clearly, positively, surely, undeniably, unmistakably, unquestionably, without doubt

definition noun 1 <u>explanation</u>, clarification, elucidation, exposition, statement of meaning 2 <u>sharpness</u>, clarity, contrast, distinctness, focus, precision

definitive adjective 1 <u>final</u>, absolute, complete, conclusive, decisive 2 <u>authoritative</u>, exhaustive, perfect, reliable, ultimate

deflate verb **1** <u>collapse</u>, empty, exhaust, flatten, puncture, shrink **2** <u>humiliate</u>, chasten, disconcert, dispirit, humble, mortify, put down (slang), squash **3** Economics <u>reduce</u>, depress, devalue, diminish

▶ **Antonyms**

≠<u>collapse</u>: balloon, bloat, blow up, dilate, distend, expand, increase, inflate, puff up or out, swell ≠<u>humiliate</u>: boost, expand, increase, inflate

deflect verb <u>turn aside</u>, bend, deviate, diverge, glance off, ricochet, swerve, veer

deflection noun <u>deviation</u>, bend, divergence, swerve

deform verb **1** <u>distort</u>, buckle, contort, gnarl, mangle, misshape, twist, warp **2** <u>disfigure</u>, deface, maim, mar, mutilate, ruin, spoil

deformity noun <u>abnormality</u>, defect, disfigurement, malformation

defraud verb <u>cheat</u>, con (informal), diddle (informal), embezzle, fleece, pilfer, rip off (slang), swindle, trick

deft adjective <u>skilful</u>, adept, adroit, agile, dexterous, expert, neat, nimble, proficient

▶ **Antonyms**

awkward, bumbling, cack-handed (informal), clumsy, gauche, inept, maladroit, unskilful

defunct adjective **1** <u>dead</u>, deceased, departed, extinct, gone **2** <u>obsolete</u>, bygone, expired, inoperative, invalid, nonexistent, out of commission

defy verb <u>resist</u>, brave, confront, disregard, flout, scorn, slight, spurn

degenerate adjective **1** <u>depraved</u>, corrupt, debauched, decadent, dissolute, immoral, low, perverted ◆ verb **2** <u>worsen</u>, decay, decline, decrease, deteriorate, fall off, lapse, sink, slip

degradation noun **1** <u>disgrace</u>, discredit, dishonour, humiliation, ignominy, mortification, shame **2** <u>deterioration</u>, decline, degeneration, demotion, downgrading

degrade verb **1** <u>demean</u>, debase, discredit, disgrace, dishonour, humble, humiliate, shame **2** <u>demote</u>, downgrade, lower

▶ **Antonyms**

≠<u>demean</u>: dignify, enhance, ennoble, honour, improve ≠<u>demote</u>: elevate, promote, raise

degrading adjective <u>demeaning</u>, dishonourable, humiliating, infra dig (informal), shameful, undignified, unworthy

degree noun <u>stage</u>, grade, notch, point, rung, step, unit

deity noun <u>god</u>, divinity, goddess, godhead, idol, immortal, supreme being

dejected adjective <u>downhearted</u>, crestfallen, depressed, despondent, disconsolate, disheartened, downcast, glum, miserable, sad

▶ **Antonyms**

blithe, cheerful, chirpy (informal), happy, joyous, light-hearted, upbeat (informal)

dejection noun <u>low spirits</u>, depression, despair, despondency, doldrums, downheartedness, gloom, melancholy, sadness, sorrow, unhappiness

de jure adverb <u>legally</u>, by right, rightfully

delay verb **1** <u>put off</u>, defer, hold over, postpone, procrastinate, shelve, suspend **2** <u>hold up</u>, bog down, detain, hinder, hold back, impede, obstruct, set back, slow up ◆ noun **3** <u>putting off</u>, deferment, postponement, procrastination, suspension **4** <u>hold-up</u>, hindrance, impediment, interruption, interval, setback, stoppage, wait

▶ **Antonyms**

verb ≠<u>hold up</u>: accelerate, advance, facilitate, hasten, hurry, precipitate, quicken, rush, speed (up)

delegate noun **1** <u>representative</u>, agent, ambassador, commissioner, deputy, envoy, legate ◆ verb

2 <u>entrust</u>, assign, consign, devolve, give, hand over, pass on, transfer 3 <u>appoint</u>, accredit, authorize, commission, depute, designate, empower, mandate

delegation noun 1 <u>deputation</u>, commission, contingent, embassy, envoys, legation, mission 2 <u>devolution</u>, assignment, commissioning, committal

delete verb <u>remove</u>, cancel, cross out, efface, erase, expunge, obliterate, rub out, strike out

deliberate adjective 1 <u>intentional</u>, calculated, conscious, planned, prearranged, premeditated, purposeful, wilful 2 <u>unhurried</u>, careful, cautious, circumspect, measured, methodical, ponderous, slow, thoughtful ♦ verb 3 <u>consider</u>, cogitate, consult, debate, discuss, meditate, ponder, reflect, think, weigh

➤ **Antonyms**
adjective ≠<u>intentional</u>: accidental, inadvertent, unconscious, unintended, unpremeditated, unthinking ≠<u>unhurried</u>: fast, hasty, hurried, impetuous, impulsive, rash

deliberately adverb <u>intentionally</u>, by design, calculatingly, consciously, in cold blood, knowingly, on purpose, wilfully, wittingly

deliberation noun 1 <u>consideration</u>, calculation, circumspection, forethought, meditation, reflection, thought 2 <u>discussion</u>, conference, consultation, debate

delicacy noun 1 <u>fineness</u>, accuracy, daintiness, elegance, exquisiteness, lightness, precision, subtlety 2 <u>fragility</u>, flimsiness, frailty, slenderness, tenderness, weakness 3 <u>treat</u>, dainty, luxury, savoury, titbit 4 <u>fastidiousness</u>, discrimination, finesse, purity, refinement, sensibility, taste 5 <u>sensitivity</u>, sensitiveness, tact

delicate adjective 1 <u>fine</u>, deft, elegant, exquisite, graceful, precise, skilled, subtle 2 <u>subtle</u>, choice, dainty, delicious, fine, savoury, tender 3 <u>fragile</u>, flimsy, frail, slender, slight, tender,

weak 4 <u>considerate</u>, diplomatic, discreet, sensitive, tactful

➤ **Antonyms**
≠<u>fine</u>: coarse, crude, indelicate, unrefined ≠<u>subtle</u>: harsh, strong ≠<u>considerate</u>: harsh, inconsiderate, indelicate, insensitive, rough

delicately adverb 1 <u>finely</u>, daintily, deftly, elegantly, exquisitely, gracefully, precisely, skilfully, subtly 2 <u>tactfully</u>, diplomatically, sensitively

delicious adjective <u>delectable</u>, appetizing, choice, dainty, mouthwatering, savoury, scrumptious (informal), tasty, toothsome

➤ **Antonyms**
disagreeable, distasteful, unpleasant

delight noun 1 <u>pleasure</u>, ecstasy, enjoyment, gladness, glee, happiness, joy, rapture ♦ verb 2 <u>please</u>, amuse, charm, cheer, enchant, gratify, thrill 3 **delight in** <u>take pleasure in</u>, appreciate, enjoy, feast on, like, love, relish, revel in, savour

➤ **Antonyms**
noun ≠<u>pleasure</u>: disfavour, dislike, displeasure, distaste ♦ verb ≠<u>please</u>: disgust, displease, gall, irk, offend, upset, vex

delighted adjective <u>pleased</u>, ecstatic, elated, enchanted, happy, joyous, jubilant, overjoyed, thrilled

delightful adjective <u>pleasant</u>, agreeable, charming, delectable, enchanting, enjoyable, pleasurable, rapturous, thrilling

➤ **Antonyms**
disagreeable, displeasing, distasteful, horrid, nasty, unpleasant

delinquent noun <u>criminal</u>, culprit, lawbreaker, miscreant, offender, villain, wrongdoer

delirious adjective 1 <u>mad</u>, crazy, demented, deranged, incoherent, insane, raving, unhinged 2 <u>ecstatic</u>, beside oneself, carried away, excited, frantic, frenzied, hysterical, wild

➤ **Antonyms**
calm, clear-headed, coherent,

compos mentis, in one's right mind, lucid, rational, sane, sensible

delirium noun **1** <u>madness</u>, derangement, hallucination, insanity, raving **2** <u>frenzy</u>, ecstasy, fever, hysteria, passion

deliver verb **1** <u>carry</u>, bear, bring, cart, convey, distribute, transport **2** <u>hand over</u>, commit, give up, grant, make over, relinquish, surrender, transfer, turn over, yield **3** <u>give</u>, announce, declare, present, read, utter **4** <u>release</u>, emancipate, free, liberate, loose, ransom, rescue, save **5** <u>strike</u>, administer, aim, deal, direct, give, inflict, launch

deliverance noun <u>release</u>, emancipation, escape, liberation, ransom, redemption, rescue, salvation

delivery noun **1** <u>handing over</u>, consignment, conveyance, dispatch, distribution, surrender, transfer, transmission **2** <u>speech</u>, articulation, elocution, enunciation, intonation, utterance **3** <u>childbirth</u>, confinement, labour, parturition

delude verb <u>deceive</u>, beguile, dupe, fool, hoodwink, kid (*informal*), mislead, take in (*informal*), trick

deluge noun **1** <u>flood</u>, cataclysm, downpour, inundation, overflowing, spate, torrent **2** <u>rush</u>, avalanche, barrage, flood, spate, torrent ♦ verb **3** <u>flood</u>, douse, drench, drown, inundate, soak, submerge, swamp **4** <u>overwhelm</u>, engulf, inundate, overload, overrun, swamp

delusion noun <u>misconception</u>, error, fallacy, false impression, fancy, hallucination, illusion, misapprehension, mistake

de luxe adjective <u>luxurious</u>, costly, exclusive, expensive, grand, opulent, select, special, splendid, superior

delve verb <u>research</u>, burrow, explore, ferret out, forage, investigate, look into, probe, rummage, search

demagogue noun <u>agitator</u>, firebrand, rabble-rouser

demand verb **1** <u>request</u>, ask, challenge, inquire, interrogate, question **2** <u>require</u>, call for, cry out for, entail, involve, necessitate, need, want **3** <u>claim</u>, exact, expect, insist on, order ♦ noun **4** <u>request</u>, inquiry, order, question, requisition **5** <u>need</u>, call, claim, market, requirement, want

► **Antonyms**

verb ≠require, <u>claim</u>: come up with, contribute, furnish, give, grant, produce, provide, supply, yield

demanding adjective <u>difficult</u>, challenging, exacting, hard, taxing, tough, trying, wearing

► **Antonyms**

a piece of cake (*informal*), child's play (*informal*), easy, easy-peasy (*slang*), effortless, simple, straightforward, undemanding

demarcation noun <u>delimitation</u>, differentiation, distinction, division, separation

demean verb <u>lower</u>, abase, debase, degrade, descend, humble, stoop

demeanour noun <u>behaviour</u>, air, bearing, carriage, comportment, conduct, deportment, manner

demented adjective <u>mad</u>, crazed, crazy, deranged, frenzied, insane, maniacal, unbalanced, unhinged

► **Antonyms**

all there (*informal*), compos mentis, in one's right mind, lucid, mentally sound, normal, of sound mind, rational, reasonable, sensible, sound

demise noun **1** <u>failure</u>, collapse, downfall, end, fall, ruin **2** *Euphemistic* <u>death</u>, decease, departure

democracy noun <u>self-government</u>, commonwealth, republic

democratic adjective <u>self-governing</u>, autonomous, egalitarian, popular, populist, representative

demolish verb 1 knock down, bulldoze, destroy, dismantle, flatten, level, raze, tear down 2 defeat, annihilate, destroy, overthrow, overturn, undo, wreck

➤ Antonyms

≠knock down: build, construct, create, repair, restore, strengthen

demolition noun knocking down, bulldozing, destruction, explosion, levelling, razing, tearing down, wrecking

demon noun 1 evil spirit, devil, fiend, ghoul, goblin, malignant spirit 2 wizard, ace (informal), fiend, master

demonic, demoniac, demoniacal adjective 1 devilish, diabolic, diabolical, fiendish, hellish, infernal, satanic 2 frenzied, crazed, frantic, frenetic, furious, hectic, maniacal, manic

demonstrable adjective provable, evident, irrefutable, obvious, palpable, self-evident, unmistakable, verifiable

demonstrate verb 1 prove, display, exhibit, indicate, manifest, show, testify to 2 show how, describe, explain, illustrate, make clear, teach 3 march, parade, picket, protest, rally

demonstration noun 1 march, mass lobby, parade, picket, protest, rally, sit-in 2 explanation, description, exposition, presentation, test, trial 3 proof, confirmation, display, evidence, exhibition, expression, illustration, testimony

demoralize verb dishearten, deject, depress, discourage, dispirit, undermine, unnerve, weaken

➤ Antonyms

boost, cheer, egg on, encourage, gee up, hearten, spur

demote verb downgrade, degrade, kick downstairs (slang), lower in rank, relegate

➤ Antonyms

advance, promote, raise, upgrade

demur verb 1 object, balk, dispute, hesitate, protest, refuse, take exception, waver ◆ noun 2

As in without demur objection, compunction, dissent, hesitation, misgiving, protest, qualm

demure adjective shy, diffident, modest, reserved, reticent, retiring, sedate, unassuming

➤ Antonyms

brash, brazen, forward, immodest, impudent, shameless

den noun 1 lair, cave, cavern, haunt, hide-out, hole, shelter 2 Chiefly U.S. study, cubbyhole, hideaway, retreat, sanctuary, sanctum

denial noun 1 negation, contradiction, dissent, renunciation, repudiation, retraction 2 refusal, prohibition, rebuff, rejection, repulse, veto

➤ Antonyms

≠negation: acknowledgment, admission, affirmation, avowal, confession, declaration, profession

denigrate verb disparage, badmouth (slang, chiefly U.S. & Canad.), belittle, knock (informal), malign, rubbish (informal), run down, slander, vilify

➤ Antonyms

acclaim, approve, compliment, extol, honour, laud, praise

denomination noun 1 religious group, belief, creed, persuasion, school, sect 2 unit, grade, size, value

denote verb indicate, betoken, designate, express, imply, mark, mean, show, signify

denounce verb condemn, accuse, attack, censure, denunciate, revile, stigmatize, vilify

dense adjective 1 thick, close-knit, compact, condensed, heavy, impenetrable, opaque, solid 2 Informal stupid, dozy (Brit. informal), dull, dumb (informal), obtuse, slow-witted, stolid, thick

➤ Antonyms

≠thick: light, scattered, sparse, thin, transparent ≠stupid: alert, bright, clever, intelligent, quick

density noun tightness, bulk, compactness, consistency, denseness, impenetrability, mass, solidity, thickness

dent noun **1** <u>hollow</u>, chip, crater, depression, dimple, dip, impression, indentation, pit ♦ verb **2** <u>make a dent in</u>, gouge, hollow, press in, push in

deny verb **1** <u>contradict</u>, disagree with, disprove, rebuff, rebut, refute **2** <u>refuse</u>, begrudge, disallow, forbid, reject, turn down, withhold **3** <u>renounce</u>, disclaim, disown, recant, repudiate, retract

▶ **Antonyms**
≠<u>contradict</u>: accept, acknowledge, admit, affirm, agree, allow, concede, confirm ≠<u>refuse</u>: accept, grant, let, permit, receive

depart verb **1** <u>leave</u>, absent (oneself), disappear, exit, go, go away, quit, retire, retreat, withdraw **2** <u>deviate</u>, differ, digress, diverge, stray, swerve, turn aside, vary, veer

▶ **Antonyms**
≠<u>leave</u>: arrive, remain, show up (informal), stay, turn up

department noun <u>section</u>, branch, bureau, division, office, station, subdivision, unit

departure noun **1** <u>leaving</u>, exit, exodus, going, going away, leave-taking, removal, retirement, withdrawal **2** <u>divergence</u>, deviation, digression, variation **3** <u>shift</u>, change, difference, innovation, novelty, whole new ball game (informal)

▶ **Antonyms**
≠<u>leaving</u>: advent, appearance, arrival, coming, entrance, return

depend verb **1** <u>trust in</u>, bank on, count on, lean on, reckon on, rely upon, turn to **2** <u>be determined by</u>, be based on, be contingent on, be subject to, be subordinate to, hang on, hinge on, rest on, revolve around

dependable adjective <u>reliable</u>, faithful, reputable, responsible, staunch, steady, sure, trustworthy, trusty, unfailing

▶ **Antonyms**
irresponsible, undependable, un-

reliable, untrustworthy

dependant noun <u>relative</u>, child, minor, protégé, subordinate

dependent adjective **1** <u>reliant</u>, defenceless, helpless, relying on, vulnerable, weak **2** **dependent on** or **upon** <u>determined by</u>, conditional on, contingent on, depending on, influenced by, subject to

▶ **Antonyms**
≠<u>reliant</u>: autonomous, independent, self-reliant

depict verb **1** <u>draw</u>, delineate, illustrate, outline, paint, picture, portray, sketch **2** <u>describe</u>, characterize, narrate, outline, represent

depiction noun <u>representation</u>, delineation, description, picture, portrayal, sketch

deplete verb <u>use up</u>, consume, drain, empty, exhaust, expend, impoverish, lessen, reduce

▶ **Antonyms**
add to, augment, enhance, expand, increase, raise

deplorable adjective **1** <u>terrible</u>, grievous, lamentable, pitiable, regrettable, sad, unfortunate, wretched **2** <u>disgraceful</u>, dishonourable, reprehensible, scandalous, shameful

▶ **Antonyms**
≠<u>terrible</u>: brilliant, excellent, fantastic, great (informal), marvellous, outstanding, super (informal), superb ≠<u>disgraceful</u>: admirable, laudable, notable, praiseworthy

deplore verb <u>disapprove of</u>, abhor, censure, condemn, denounce, object to, take a dim view of

deploy verb <u>position</u>, arrange, set out, station, use, utilize

deployment noun <u>position</u>, arrangement, organization, spread, stationing, use, utilization

deport verb **1** <u>expel</u>, banish, exile, expatriate, extradite, oust **2** **deport oneself** <u>behave</u>, acquit oneself, act, bear oneself, carry oneself, comport oneself, conduct oneself, hold oneself

depose verb **1** remove from office, demote, dethrone, dismiss, displace, oust **2** Law testify, avouch, declare, make a deposition

deposit verb **1** put, drop, lay, locate, place **2** store, bank, consign, entrust, lodge ♦ noun **3** down payment, instalment, part payment, pledge, retainer, security, stake **4** sediment, accumulation, dregs, lees, precipitate, silt

depot noun **1** storehouse, depository, repository, warehouse **2** Chiefly U.S. & Canad. bus station, garage, terminus

depraved adjective corrupt, degenerate, dissolute, evil, immoral, sinful, vicious, vile, wicked

➤ **Antonyms**
chaste, decent, good, honourable, innocent, pure, upright, virtuous, wholesome

depravity noun corruption, debauchery, evil, immorality, sinfulness, vice, wickedness

depreciate verb **1** decrease, deflate, devalue, lessen, lose value, lower, reduce **2** disparage, belittle, denigrate, deride, detract, run down, scorn, sneer at

➤ **Antonyms**
≠decrease: add to, appreciate, augment, enhance, enlarge, expand, grow, increase, rise ≠disparage: admire, appreciate, cherish, esteem, like, prize, rate highly, regard, respect, value

depreciation noun **1** devaluation, deflation, depression, drop, fall, slump **2** disparagement, belittlement, denigration, deprecation, detraction

depress verb **1** sadden, deject, discourage, dishearten, dispirit, make despondent, oppress, weigh down **2** lower, cheapen, depreciate, devalue, diminish, downgrade, lessen, reduce **3** press down, flatten, level, lower, push down

➤ **Antonyms**
≠sadden: cheer, elate, hearten,

lift, raise, uplift ≠lower: heighten, increase, raise, strengthen

depressed adjective **1** low-spirited, blue, dejected, despondent, discouraged, dispirited, downcast, downhearted, fed up, sad, unhappy **2** poverty-stricken, deprived, disadvantaged, needy, poor, run-down **3** lowered, cheapened, depreciated, devalued, weakened **4** sunken, concave, hollow, indented, recessed

depressing adjective bleak, discouraging, disheartening, dismal, dispiriting, gloomy, harrowing, sad, saddening

depression noun **1** low spirits, dejection, despair, despondency, downheartedness, dumps (informal), gloominess, melancholy, sadness, the blues **2** recession, economic decline, hard or bad times, inactivity, slump, stagnation **3** hollow, bowl, cavity, dent, dimple, dip, indentation, pit, valley

deprivation noun **1** withholding, denial, dispossession, expropriation, removal, withdrawal **2** want, destitution, distress, hardship, need, privation

deprive verb withhold, bereave, despoil, dispossess, rob, strip

deprived adjective poor, bereft, destitute, disadvantaged, down at heel, in need, lacking, needy

➤ **Antonyms**
favoured, fortunate, lucky, prosperous, successful, well-off

depth noun **1** deepness, drop, extent, measure **2** profoundness, astuteness, discernment, insight, penetration, profundity, sagacity, wisdom

➤ **Antonyms**
≠deepness: height, peak, pinnacle, top ≠profoundness: emptiness, lack of depth or substance, superficiality, triviality

deputation noun delegation, commission, embassy, envoys, legation

deputize verb stand in for, act for, take the place of, understudy

deputy *noun* substitute, delegate, legate, lieutenant, number two, proxy, representative, second-in-command, surrogate

deranged *adjective* mad, crazed, crazy, demented, distracted, insane, irrational, unbalanced, unhinged

▶ **Antonyms**
all there (*informal*), calm, *compos mentis*, in one's right mind, lucid, mentally sound, normal, of sound mind

derelict *adjective* **1** abandoned, deserted, dilapidated, discarded, forsaken, neglected, ruined ♦ *noun* **2** tramp, bag lady, down-and-out, outcast, vagrant

deride *verb* mock, disdain, disparage, insult, jeer, ridicule, scoff, scorn, sneer, taunt

derisory *adjective* ridiculous, contemptible, insulting, laughable, ludicrous, outrageous, preposterous

derivation *noun* origin, beginning, foundation, root, source

derive from *verb* come from, arise from, emanate from, flow from, issue from, originate from, proceed from, spring from, stem from

derogatory *adjective* disparaging, belittling, defamatory, offensive, slighting, uncomplimentary, unfavourable, unflattering

▶ **Antonyms**
appreciative, complimentary, flattering, fulsome

descend *verb* **1** move down, drop, fall, go down, plummet, plunge, sink, subside, tumble **2** slope, dip, incline, slant **3** lower oneself, degenerate, deteriorate, stoop **4** be descended originate, be handed down, be passed down, derive, issue, proceed, spring **5** descend on attack, arrive, invade, raid, swoop

▶ **Antonyms**
≠move down: ascend, climb, go up, mount, rise, scale, soar

descent *noun* **1** coming down, drop, fall, plunge, swoop **2**

slope, declivity, dip, drop, incline, slant **3** ancestry, extraction, family tree, genealogy, lineage, origin, parentage **4** decline, degeneration, deterioration

describe *verb* **1** relate, depict, explain, express, narrate, portray, recount, report, tell **2** trace, delineate, draw, mark out, outline

description *noun* **1** account, depiction, explanation, narrative, portrayal, report, representation, sketch **2** kind, brand, category, class, order, sort, type, variety

descriptive *adjective* graphic, detailed, explanatory, expressive, illustrative, pictorial, picturesque, vivid

desert[1] *noun* wilderness, solitude, waste, wasteland, wilds

desert[2] *verb* abandon, abscond, forsake, jilt, leave, leave stranded, maroon, quit, strand, walk out on (*informal*)

▶ **Antonyms**
look after, provide for, take care of

deserted *adjective* abandoned, derelict, desolate, empty, forsaken, neglected, unoccupied, vacant

deserter *noun* defector, absconder, escapee, fugitive, renegade, runaway, traitor, truant

desertion *noun* abandonment, absconding, apostasy, betrayal, defection, dereliction, escape, evasion, flight, relinquishment

deserve *verb* merit, be entitled to, be worthy of, earn, justify, rate, warrant

deserved *adjective* well-earned, due, earned, fitting, justified, merited, proper, rightful, warranted

deserving *adjective* worthy, commendable, estimable, laudable, meritorious, praiseworthy, righteous

▶ **Antonyms**
not deserving of, not good enough, not worth, undeserving, unworthy

design *verb* **1** plan, draft, draw,

outline, sketch, trace **2** create, conceive, fabricate, fashion, invent, originate, think up **3** intend, aim, mean, plan, propose, purpose ♦ noun **4** plan, blueprint, draft, drawing, model, outline, scheme, sketch **5** arrangement, construction, form, organization, pattern, shape, style **6** intention, aim, end, goal, object, objective, purpose, target

designate verb **1** name, call, dub, entitle, label, style, term **2** appoint, assign, choose, delegate, depute, nominate, select

designation noun name, description, label, mark, title

designer noun creator, architect, deviser, inventor, originator, planner

desirable adjective **1** agreeable, advantageous, advisable, beneficial, good, preferable, profitable, worthwhile **2** attractive, adorable, alluring, fetching, glamorous, seductive, sexy (informal)

> **Antonyms**

≠agreeable: disagreeable, distasteful, unacceptable, unappealing, unattractive, undesirable, unpleasant, unpopular ≠attractive: unappealing, unattractive, undesirable, unsexy (informal)

desire verb **1** want, crave, hanker after, hope for, long for, set one's heart on, thirst for, wish for, yearn for ♦ noun **2** wish, aspiration, craving, hankering, hope, longing, thirst, want **3** lust, appetite, libido, passion

desist verb stop, break off, cease, discontinue, end, forbear, leave off, pause, refrain from

desolate adjective **1** uninhabited, bare, barren, bleak, dreary, godforsaken, solitary, wild **2** miserable, dejected, despondent, disconsolate, downcast, forlorn, gloomy, wretched ♦ verb **3** lay waste, depopulate, despoil, destroy, devastate, lay low, pillage, plunder, ravage, ruin **4** deject, depress, discourage, dishearten, dismay, distress, grieve

> **Antonyms**

adjective ≠uninhabited: inhabited, populous ≠miserable: cheerful, happy, joyous, light-hearted ♦ verb ≠lay waste: develop ≠deject: cheer, encourage, hearten

desolation noun **1** ruin, destruction, devastation, havoc **2** bleakness, barrenness, isolation, solitude **3** misery, anguish, dejection, despair, distress, gloom, sadness, woe, wretchedness

despair noun **1** despondency, anguish, dejection, depression, desperation, gloom, hopelessness, misery, wretchedness ♦ verb **2** lose hope, give up, lose heart

despairing adjective hopeless, dejected, desperate, despondent, disconsolate, frantic, griefstricken, inconsolable, miserable, wretched

despatch see DISPATCH

desperado noun criminal, bandit, lawbreaker, outlaw, villain

desperate adjective **1** reckless, audacious, daring, frantic, furious, risky **2** grave, drastic, extreme, urgent

desperately adverb **1** gravely, badly, dangerously, perilously, seriously, severely **2** hopelessly, appallingly, fearfully, frightfully, shockingly

desperation noun **1** recklessness, foolhardiness, frenzy, impetuosity, madness, rashness **2** misery, agony, anguish, despair, hopelessness, trouble, unhappiness, worry

despicable adjective contemptible, detestable, disgraceful, hateful, mean, shameful, sordid, vile, worthless, wretched

> **Antonyms**

admirable, ethical, good, honest, honourable, moral, noble, praiseworthy, righteous, upright, virtuous, worthy

despise verb look down on, abhor, detest, loathe, revile, scorn

> **Antonyms**

admire, adore, be fond of, be keen on, cherish, esteem, love

despite *preposition* in spite of, against, even with, in the face of, in the teeth of, notwithstanding, regardless of, undeterred by

despondency *noun* dejection, depression, despair, desperation, gloom, low spirits, melancholy, misery, sadness

despondent *adjective* dejected, depressed, disconsolate, disheartened, dispirited, downhearted, glum, in despair, sad, sorrowful

➤ **Antonyms**
buoyant, cheerful, cheery, chirpy (*informal*), glad, happy, hopeful, joyful, light-hearted, optimistic, upbeat (*informal*)

despot *noun* tyrant, autocrat, dictator, oppressor

despotic *adjective* tyrannical, authoritarian, autocratic, dictatorial, domineering, imperious, oppressive

despotism *noun* tyranny, autocracy, dictatorship, oppression, totalitarianism

destination *noun* journey's end, haven, resting-place, station, stop, terminus

destined *adjective* fated, bound, certain, doomed, intended, meant, predestined

destiny *noun* fate, doom, fortune, karma, kismet, lot, portion

destitute *adjective* penniless, down and out, impoverished, indigent, insolvent, moneyless, penurious, poor, poverty-stricken

destroy *verb* ruin, annihilate, crush, demolish, devastate, eradicate, shatter, wipe out, wreck

destruction *noun* ruin, annihilation, demolition, devastation, eradication, extermination, havoc, slaughter, wreckage

destructive *adjective* damaging, calamitous, catastrophic, deadly, devastating, fatal, harmful, lethal, ruinous

detach *verb* separate, cut off, disconnect, disengage, divide, remove, sever, tear off, unfasten

➤ **Antonyms**
attach, bind, connect, fasten

detached *adjective* **1** separate, disconnected, discrete, unconnected **2** uninvolved, disinterested, dispassionate, impartial, impersonal, neutral, objective, reserved, unbiased

➤ **Antonyms**
≠ uninvolved: biased, concerned, interested, involved

detachment *noun* **1** indifference, aloofness, coolness, nonchalance, remoteness, unconcern **2** impartiality, fairness, neutrality, objectivity **3** *Military* unit, body, force, party, patrol, squad, task force

detail *noun* **1** point, aspect, component, element, fact, factor, feature, particular, respect **2** fine point, nicety, particular, triviality **3** *Military* party, assignment, body, detachment, duty, fatigue, force, squad ♦ *verb* **4** list, catalogue, enumerate, itemize, recite, recount, rehearse, relate, tabulate **5** appoint, allocate, assign, charge, commission, delegate, send

detailed *adjective* comprehensive, blow-by-blow, exhaustive, full, intricate, minute, particular, thorough

➤ **Antonyms**
brief, compact, concise, condensed, short, succinct, summary, superficial

detain *verb* **1** delay, check, hinder, hold up, impede, keep back, retard, slow up (*or* down) **2** hold, arrest, confine, intern, restrain

detect *verb* **1** notice, ascertain, identify, note, observe, perceive, recognize, spot **2** discover, find, track down, uncover, unmask

detective *noun* investigator, cop (*slang*), gumshoe (*U.S. slang*), private eye, private investigator, sleuth (*informal*)

detention *noun* imprisonment, confinement, custody, incarceration, quarantine

➤ **Antonyms**
acquittal, discharge, emancipa-

tion, freedom, liberation, liberty, release

deter verb discourage, dissuade, frighten, inhibit from, intimidate, prevent, put off, stop, talk out of

detergent noun cleaner, cleanser

deteriorate verb decline, degenerate, go downhill (informal), lower, slump, worsen

➤ **Antonyms**
advance, ameliorate, get better, improve

determination noun resolution, dedication, doggedness, fortitude, perseverance, persistence, resolve, single-mindedness, steadfastness, tenacity, willpower

➤ **Antonyms**
doubt, hesitancy, hesitation, indecision, irresolution, vacillation

determine verb 1 settle, conclude, decide, end, finish, ordain, regulate 2 find out, ascertain, detect, discover, establish, learn, verify, work out 3 decide, choose, elect, make up one's mind, resolve

determined adjective resolute, dogged, firm, intent, persevering, persistent, single-minded, steadfast, tenacious, unwavering

deterrent noun discouragement, check, curb, disincentive, hindrance, impediment, obstacle, restraint

➤ **Antonyms**
bait, carrot (informal), enticement, incentive, inducement, lure, motivation, spur, stimulus

detest verb hate, abhor, abominate, despise, dislike intensely, loathe, recoil from

➤ **Antonyms**
adore, cherish, dote on, love, relish

detonate verb explode, blast, blow up, discharge, set off, trigger

detour noun diversion, bypass, indirect course, roundabout way

detract verb lessen, devaluate, di

minish, lower, reduce, take away from

➤ **Antonyms**
add to, augment, boost, complement, enhance, improve, reinforce, strengthen

detriment noun damage, disadvantage, disservice, harm, hurt, impairment, injury, loss

detrimental adjective damaging, adverse, deleterious, destructive, disadvantageous, harmful, prejudicial, unfavourable

➤ **Antonyms**
advantageous, beneficial, efficacious, favourable, good, helpful

devastate verb destroy, demolish, lay waste, level, ravage, raze, ruin, sack, wreck

devastating adjective overwhelming, cutting, overpowering, savage, trenchant, vitriolic, withering

devastation noun destruction, demolition, desolation, havoc, ruin

develop verb 1 advance, evolve, flourish, grow, mature, progress, prosper, ripen 2 form, breed, establish, generate, invent, originate 3 expand, amplify, augment, broaden, elaborate, enlarge, unfold, work out

development noun 1 growth, advance, evolution, expansion, improvement, increase, progress, spread 2 event, happening, incident, occurrence, result, turn of events, upshot

deviant adjective 1 perverted, kinky (slang), sick (informal), twisted, warped ♦ noun 2 pervert, freak, misfit

➤ **Antonyms**
adjective ≠perverted: conventional, normal, orthodox, straight, straightforward

deviate verb differ, depart, diverge, stray, swerve, veer, wander

deviation noun departure, digression, discrepancy, disparity, divergence, inconsistency, irregularity, shift, variation

device *noun* **1** gadget, apparatus, appliance, contraption, implement, instrument, machine, tool **2** ploy, gambit, manoeuvre, plan, scheme, stratagem, trick, wile

devil *noun* **1 the Devil** Satan, Beelzebub, Evil One, Lucifer, Mephistopheles, Old Nick (*informal*), Prince of Darkness **2** brute, beast, demon, fiend, monster, ogre, terror **3** scamp, rascal, rogue, scoundrel **4** person, beggar, creature, thing, wretch

devilish *adjective* fiendish, atrocious, damnable, detestable, diabolical, hellish, infernal, satanic, wicked

devious *adjective* **1** sly, calculating, deceitful, dishonest, double-dealing, insincere, scheming, surreptitious, underhand, wily **2** indirect, circuitous, rambling, roundabout

▶ **Antonyms**
≠sly: blunt, candid, direct, downright, forthright, frank, honest, straight, straightforward ≠indirect: direct, straight, straightforward

devise *verb* work out, conceive, construct, contrive, design, dream up, formulate, invent, think up

devoid *adjective* lacking, bereft, deficient, destitute, empty, free from, wanting, without

devote *verb* dedicate, allot, apply, assign, commit, give, pledge, reserve, set apart

devoted *adjective* dedicated, ardent, committed, constant, devout, faithful, loyal, staunch, steadfast, true

▶ **Antonyms**
disloyal, inconstant, indifferent, uncommitted, undedicated, unfaithful

devotee *noun* enthusiast, adherent, admirer, aficionado, buff (*informal*), disciple, fan, fanatic, follower, supporter

devotion *noun* **1** dedication, adherence, allegiance, commit-

ment, constancy, faithfulness, fidelity, loyalty **2** love, affection, attachment, fondness, passion **3** devoutness, godliness, holiness, piety, reverence, spirituality **4 devotions** prayers, church service, divine office, religious observance

▶ **Antonyms**
≠dedication: carelessness, disregard, inattention, indifference, laxity, laxness, neglect, thoughtlessness ≠devoutness: derision, disrespect, impiety, irreverence

devour *verb* **1** eat, consume, gobble, gulp, guzzle, polish off (*informal*), swallow, wolf **2** destroy, annihilate, consume, ravage, waste, wipe out **3** enjoy, read compulsively or voraciously, take in

devout *adjective* religious, godly, holy, orthodox, pious, prayerful, pure, reverent, saintly

▶ **Antonyms**
impious, irreligious, irreverent, sacrilegious

dexterity *noun* **1** skill, adroitness, deftness, expertise, finesse, nimbleness, proficiency, touch **2** cleverness, ability, aptitude, ingenuity

▶ **Antonyms**
clumsiness, gaucheness, inability, incapacity, incompetence, ineptitude, uselessness

diabolical *adjective* *Informal* dreadful, abysmal, appalling, atrocious, hellish, outrageous, shocking, terrible

diagnose *verb* identify, analyse, determine, distinguish, interpret, pinpoint, pronounce, recognize

diagnosis *noun* **1** examination, analysis, investigation, scrutiny **2** opinion, conclusion, interpretation, pronouncement

diagonal *adjective* slanting, angled, cross, crossways, crosswise, oblique

diagonally *adverb* aslant, at an angle, cornerwise, crosswise, obliquely

diagram *noun* plan, chart, drawing, figure, graph, representation, sketch

dialect noun <u>language</u>, brogue, idiom, jargon, patois, provincialism, speech, vernacular

dialogue noun <u>conversation</u>, communication, conference, discourse, discussion, exchange

diary noun <u>journal</u>, appointment book, chronicle, daily record, engagement book, Filofax (Trademark)

dicky adjective Brit. informal <u>weak</u>, fluttery, shaky, unreliable, unsound, unsteady

dictate verb 1 <u>speak</u>, read out, say, utter 2 <u>order</u>, command, decree, demand, direct, impose, lay down the law, pronounce
♦ noun 3 <u>command</u>, decree, demand, direction, edict, fiat, injunction, order 4 <u>principle</u>, code, law, rule

dictator noun <u>absolute ruler</u>, autocrat, despot, oppressor, tyrant

dictatorial adjective 1 <u>absolute</u>, arbitrary, autocratic, despotic, totalitarian, tyrannical, unlimited, unrestricted 2 <u>domineering</u>, authoritarian, bossy (informal), imperious, oppressive, overbearing

► Antonyms
≠<u>absolute</u>: constitutional, democratic, egalitarian, restricted ≠<u>domineering</u>: humble, servile

dictatorship noun <u>absolute rule</u>, absolutism, authoritarianism, autocracy, despotism, totalitarianism, tyranny

diction noun <u>pronunciation</u>, articulation, delivery, elocution, enunciation, fluency, inflection, intonation, speech

dictionary noun <u>wordbook</u>, glossary, lexicon, vocabulary

die verb 1 <u>pass away</u>, breathe one's last, croak (slang), expire, give up the ghost, kick the bucket (slang), peg out (informal), perish, snuff it (slang) 2 <u>dwindle</u>, decay, decline, fade, sink, subside, wane, wilt, wither 3 <u>stop</u>,

break down, fade out or away, fail, fizzle out, halt, lose power, peter out, run down 4 be dying for <u>long for</u>, ache for, be eager for, desire, hunger for, pine for, yearn for

► Antonyms
≠<u>pass away</u>: be born, begin, come to life, exist, live, survive ≠<u>dwindle</u>, <u>stop</u>: flourish, grow, increase

die-hard noun <u>reactionary</u>, fanatic, old fogey, stick-in-the-mud (informal)

diet[1] noun 1 <u>food</u>, fare, nourishment, nutriment, provisions, rations, sustenance, victuals 2 <u>regime</u>, abstinence, fast, regimen
♦ verb 3 <u>slim</u>, abstain, eat sparingly, fast, lose weight

► Antonyms
verb ≠<u>slim</u>: get fat, guzzle, overindulge, pig out (slang), stuff oneself

diet[2] noun <u>council</u>, chamber, congress, convention, legislature, meeting, parliament

differ verb 1 <u>be dissimilar</u>, contradict, contrast, depart from, diverge, run counter to, stand apart, vary 2 <u>disagree</u>, clash, contend, debate, demur, dispute, dissent, oppose, take exception, take issue

► Antonyms
≠<u>be dissimilar</u>: accord, coincide, harmonize ≠<u>disagree</u>: accord, acquiesce, agree, assent, concur

difference noun 1 <u>dissimilarity</u>, alteration, change, contrast, discrepancy, disparity, diversity, variation, variety 2 <u>disagreement</u>, argument, clash, conflict, contretemps, debate, dispute, quarrel 3 <u>remainder</u>, balance, rest, result

► Antonyms
≠<u>dissimilarity</u>: comparability, conformity, congruence, likeness, relation, resemblance, sameness, similarity ≠<u>disagreement</u>: agreement

different adjective 1 <u>unlike</u>, altered, changed, contrasting, disparate, dissimilar, divergent, inconsistent, opposed **2** various, assorted, diverse, miscellaneous, sundry, varied **3** unusual, atypical, distinctive, extraordinary, peculiar, singular, special, strange, uncommon

differentiate verb **1** distinguish, contrast, discriminate, make a distinction, mark off, separate, set off or apart, tell apart **2** make different, adapt, alter, change, convert, modify, transform

difficult adjective **1** hard, arduous, demanding, formidable, laborious, onerous, strenuous, uphill **2** problematical, abstruse, baffling, complex, complicated, intricate, involved, knotty, obscure **3** troublesome, demanding, fastidious, fussy, hard to please, perverse, refractory, unaccommodating

➤ **Antonyms**

≠hard: easy, light, manageable, simple, straightforward, uncomplicated ≠troublesome: accommodating, amenable, cooperative, pleasant

difficulty noun **1** laboriousness, arduousness, awkwardness, hardship, strain, strenuousness, tribulation **2** predicament, dilemma, embarrassment, hot water (informal), jam (informal), mess, plight, quandary, trouble **3** problem, complication, hindrance, hurdle, impediment, obstacle, pitfall, snag, stumbling block

diffidence noun shyness, bashfulness, hesitancy, insecurity, modesty, reserve, self-consciousness, timidity

➤ **Antonyms**

assurance, boldness, confidence, courage, self-confidence, self-possession

diffident adjective shy, bashful, doubtful, hesitant, insecure, modest, reserved, self-conscious, timid, unassertive, unassuming

dig verb **1** excavate, burrow, delve, hollow out, mine, quarry, scoop, tunnel **2** investigate, delve, dig down, go into, probe,

research, search **3** with out or up find, discover, expose, uncover, unearth, uproot **4** poke, drive, jab, prod, punch, thrust ◆ noun **5** poke, jab, prod, punch, thrust **6** cutting remark, barb, crack (slang), gibe, insult, jeer, sneer, taunt, wisecrack (informal)

digest verb **1** ingest, absorb, assimilate, dissolve, incorporate **2** take in, absorb, consider, contemplate, grasp, study, understand ◆ noun **3** summary, abridgment, abstract, epitome, précis, résumé, synopsis

digestion noun ingestion, absorption, assimilation, conversion, incorporation, transformation

dignified adjective distinguished, formal, grave, imposing, noble, reserved, solemn, stately

➤ **Antonyms**

crass, unbecoming, undignified, unseemly, vulgar

dignitary noun public figure, bigwig (informal), high-up (informal), notable, personage, pillar of society, V.I.P., worthy

dignity noun **1** decorum, courtliness, grandeur, gravity, loftiness, majesty, nobility, solemnity, stateliness **2** honour, eminence, importance, rank, respectability, standing, status **3** self-importance, pride, self-esteem, self-respect

digress verb wander, depart, deviate, diverge, drift, get off the point or subject, go off at a tangent, ramble, stray

digression noun departure, aside, detour, deviation, divergence, diversion, straying, wandering

dilapidated adjective ruined, broken-down, crumbling, decrepit, in ruins, ramshackle, rickety, run-down, tumbledown

dilate verb enlarge, broaden, expand, puff out, stretch, swell, widen

➤ **Antonyms**

compress, constrict, contract, narrow, shrink

dilatory *adjective* <u>time-wasting</u>, delaying, lingering, procrastinating, slow, sluggish, tardy, tarrying

➤ **Antonyms**

prompt, punctual, sharp (*informal*)

dilemma *noun* <u>predicament</u>, difficulty, mess, plight, problem, puzzle, quandary, spot (*informal*)

dilettante *noun* <u>amateur</u>, aesthete, dabbler, trifler

diligence *noun* <u>application</u>, attention, care, industry, laboriousness, perseverance

diligent *adjective* <u>hard-working</u>, assiduous, attentive, careful, conscientious, industrious, painstaking, persistent, studious, tireless

➤ **Antonyms**

careless, dilatory, good-for-nothing, indifferent, lazy

dilute *verb* 1 <u>water down</u>, adulterate, cut, make thinner, thin (out), weaken 2 <u>reduce</u>, attenuate, decrease, diffuse, diminish, lessen, mitigate, temper, weaken

➤ **Antonyms**

≠<u>water down</u>: concentrate, condense, strengthen, thicken ≠<u>reduce</u>: intensify, strengthen

dim *adjective* 1 <u>poorly lit</u>, cloudy, dark, grey, overcast, shadowy, tenebrous 2 <u>unclear</u>, bleary, blurred, faint, fuzzy, ill-defined, indistinct, obscured, shadowy 3 *Informal* <u>stupid</u>, dense, dozy (*Brit. informal*), dull, dumb (*informal*), obtuse, slow on the uptake (*informal*), thick 4 <u>take a dim view</u> <u>disapprove</u>, be displeased, be sceptical, look askance, reject, suspect, take exception, view with disfavour ♦ *verb* 5 <u>dull</u>, blur, cloud, darken, fade, obscure

➤ **Antonyms**

adjective ≠<u>poorly lit</u>: bright, clear, cloudless, fair ≠<u>unclear</u>: bright, brilliant, clear, distinct ≠<u>stupid</u>: acute, astute, bright, clever, intelligent, keen, quick-witted, sharp, smart

dimension *noun, often plural* <u>measurement</u>, amplitude, bulk, capacity, extent, proportions, size, volume

diminish *verb* 1 <u>decrease</u>, curtail, cut, lessen, lower, reduce, shrink 2 <u>dwindle</u>, decline, die out, recede, subside, wane

➤ **Antonyms**

≠<u>decrease</u>: amplify, augment, enhance, enlarge, expand, grow, heighten, increase

diminutive *adjective* <u>small</u>, little, mini, miniature, minute, petite, tiny, undersized

➤ **Antonyms**

big, colossal, enormous, giant, gigantic, great, immense, jumbo (*informal*), king-size, massive (*informal*)

din *noun* 1 <u>noise</u>, clamour, clatter, commotion, crash, pandemonium, racket, row, uproar ♦ *verb* 2 <u>din (something) into (someone)</u> instil, drum into, go on at, hammer into, inculcate, instruct, teach

➤ **Antonyms**

noun ≠<u>noise</u>: calm, calmness, hush, peace, quiet, quietness, silence, tranquillity

dine *verb* <u>eat</u>, banquet, feast, lunch, sup

dingy *adjective* <u>dull</u>, dark, dim, drab, dreary, gloomy, murky, obscure, sombre

dinner *noun* <u>meal</u>, banquet, feast, main meal, repast, spread (*informal*)

dip *verb* 1 <u>plunge</u>, bathe, douse, duck, dunk, immerse 2 <u>slope</u>, decline, descend, drop (down), fall, lower, sink, subside ♦ *noun* 3 <u>plunge</u>, douche, drenching, ducking, immersion, soaking 4 <u>bathe</u>, dive, plunge, swim 5 <u>hollow</u>, basin, concavity, depression, hole, incline, slope 6 <u>drop</u>, decline, fall, lowering, sag, slip, slump

dip into *verb* 1 <u>draw upon</u>, reach into 2 <u>sample</u>, browse, glance at, peruse, skim

diplomacy *noun* 1 <u>statesman-</u>

ship, international negotiation, statecraft **2** tact, artfulness, craft, delicacy, discretion, finesse, savoir-faire, skill, subtlety

➤ **Antonyms**

≠ tact: awkwardness, clumsiness, tactlessness, thoughtlessness

diplomat noun negotiator, conciliator, go-between, mediator, moderator, politician, tactician

diplomatic adjective tactful, adept, discreet, polite, politic, prudent, sensitive, subtle

➤ **Antonyms**

impolitic, insensitive, rude, tactless, thoughtless, undiplomatic, unsubtle

dire adjective **1** disastrous, awful, calamitous, catastrophic, horrible, ruinous, terrible, woeful **2** desperate, critical, crucial, drastic, extreme, now or never, pressing, urgent **3** grim, dismal, dreadful, fearful, gloomy, ominous, portentous

direct adjective **1** straight, nonstop, not crooked, shortest, through, unbroken, uninterrupted **2** first-hand, face-to-face, head-on, immediate, personal **3** straightforward, candid, frank, honest, open, plain-spoken, straight, upfront (informal) **4** explicit, absolute, blunt, categorical, downright, express, plain, point-blank, unambiguous, unequivocal ♦ verb **5** control, conduct, guide, handle, lead, manage, oversee, run, supervise **6** order, bid, charge, command, demand, dictate, instruct **7** guide, indicate, lead, point in the direction of, point the way, show **8** address, label, mail, route, send **9** aim, focus, level, point, train

➤ **Antonyms**

adjective ≠ straight: circuitous, crooked, indirect ≠ first-hand: indirect, mediated ≠ straightforward: circuitous, crooked, devious, indirect, sly, subtle ≠ explicit: ambiguous, circuitous, indirect

direction noun **1** way, aim, bearing, course, line, path, road, route, track **2** management, administration, charge, command, control, guidance, leadership, order, supervision

directions plural noun instructions, briefing, guidance, guidelines, plan, recommendation, regulations

directive noun order, command, decree, edict, injunction, instruction, mandate, regulation, ruling

directly adverb **1** straight, by the shortest route, exactly, in a beeline, precisely, unswervingly, without deviation **2** honestly, openly, plainly, point-blank, straightforwardly, truthfully, unequivocally **3** at once, as soon as possible, forthwith, immediately, promptly, right away, straightaway

director noun controller, administrator, chief, executive, governor, head, leader, manager, supervisor

dirge noun lament, dead march, elegy, funeral song, requiem, threnody

dirt noun **1** filth, dust, grime, impurity, muck, mud **2** soil, clay, earth, loam **3** obscenity, indecency, pornography, sleaze, smut

dirty adjective **1** filthy, foul, grimy, grubby, messy, mucky, muddy, polluted, soiled, unclean **2** dishonest, crooked, fraudulent, illegal, treacherous, unfair, unscrupulous, unsporting **3** obscene, blue, indecent, pornographic, salacious, sleazy, smutty **4** As in a dirty look angry, annoyed, bitter, choked, indignant, offended, resentful, scorching ♦ verb **5** soil, blacken, defile, foul, muddy, pollute, smirch, spoil, stain

➤ **Antonyms**

adjective ≠ filthy: clean, pure ≠ dishonest: decent, honest, moral, reputable, respectable, upright ≠ obscene: clean, decent ♦ verb ≠ soil: clean, tidy up

disability noun **1** handicap, affliction, ailment, complaint, defect, disorder, impairment, infirmity, malady **2** incapacity, inability, unfitness

disable verb **1** handicap, cripple, damage, enfeeble, immobilize, impair, incapacitate, paralyse **2** disqualify, invalidate, render or declare incapable

disabled adjective handicapped, crippled, incapacitated, infirm, lame, paralysed, weakened

► **Antonyms**
able-bodied, fit, hale, healthy, hearty, robust, sound, strong, sturdy

disadvantage noun **1** harm, damage, detriment, disservice, hurt, injury, loss, prejudice **2** drawback, downside, handicap, inconvenience, nuisance, snag, trouble

► **Antonyms**
≠harm, drawback: advantage, aid, benefit, convenience, gain, help, merit, profit

disagree verb **1** differ (in opinion), argue, clash, cross swords, dispute, dissent, object, quarrel, take issue with **2** conflict, be dissimilar, contradict, counter, differ, diverge, run counter to, vary **3** make ill, bother, discomfort, distress, hurt, nauseate, sicken, trouble, upset

► **Antonyms**
≠differ (in opinion): agree, concur, get on (together) ≠conflict: accord, coincide, harmonize

disagreeable adjective **1** nasty, disgusting, displeasing, distasteful, objectionable, obnoxious, offensive, repugnant, repulsive, unpleasant **2** ill-natured, badtempered, churlish, difficult, disobliging, irritable, rude, surly, unpleasant

► **Antonyms**
≠nasty: agreeable, delightful, enjoyable, lovely, nice, pleasant ≠ill-natured: agreeable, congenial, delightful, friendly, goodnatured, lovely, nice, pleasant

disagreement noun **1** incompatibility, difference, discrepancy, disparity, dissimilarity, divergence, incongruity, variance **2** argument, altercation, clash, conflict, dispute, dissent, quarrel, row, squabble

► **Antonyms**
≠incompatibility: correspondence, harmony, similarity ≠argument: accord, agreement, assent, consensus, unison, unity

disallow verb reject, disavow, dismiss, disown, rebuff, refuse, repudiate

disappear verb **1** vanish, evanesce, fade away, pass, recede **2** cease, die out, dissolve, evaporate, leave no trace, melt away, pass away, perish

► **Antonyms**
appear, arrive, materialize, reappear

disappearance noun vanishing, departure, eclipse, evanescence, evaporation, going, melting, passing

disappoint verb let down, disenchant, disgruntle, dishearten, disillusion, dismay, dissatisfy, fail

disappointed adjective let down, cast down, despondent, discouraged, disenchanted, disgruntled, dissatisfied, downhearted, frustrated

► **Antonyms**
content, contented, fulfilled, happy, pleased, satisfied

disappointing adjective unsatisfactory, depressing, disconcerting, discouraging, inadequate, insufficient, sad, sorry

disappointment noun **1** frustration, chagrin, discontent, discouragement, disenchantment, disillusionment, dissatisfaction, regret **2** letdown, blow, calamity, choker (informal), misfortune, setback

disapproval noun displeasure, censure, condemnation, criticism, denunciation, dissatisfaction, objection, reproach

disapprove verb condemn, deplore, dislike, find unacceptable, frown on, look down one's nose at (*informal*), object to, reject, take a dim view of, take exception to

➤ **Antonyms**

applaud, approve, like

disarm *verb* **1** <u>render defenceless</u>, disable **2** <u>win over</u>, persuade, set at ease **3** <u>demilitarize</u>, deactivate, demobilize, disband

disarmament *noun* <u>arms reduction</u>, arms limitation, de-escalation, demilitarization, demobilization

disarming *adjective* <u>charming</u>, irresistible, likable or likeable, persuasive, winning

disarrange *verb* <u>disorder</u>, confuse, disorganize, disturb, jumble (up), mess (up), scatter, shake (up), shuffle

disarray *noun* **1** <u>confusion</u>, disorder, disorganization, disunity, indiscipline, unruliness **2** <u>untidiness</u>, chaos, clutter, hotchpotch, jumble, mess, muddle, shambles

➤ **Antonyms**

arrangement, harmony, method, neatness, order, orderliness, organization, pattern, plan, regularity, symmetry, system, tidiness

disaster *noun* <u>catastrophe</u>, adversity, calamity, cataclysm, misfortune, ruin, tragedy, trouble

disastrous *adjective* <u>terrible</u>, calamitous, cataclysmic, catastrophic, devastating, fatal, ruinous, tragic

disbelief *noun* <u>scepticism</u>, distrust, doubt, dubiety, incredulity, mistrust, unbelief

➤ **Antonyms**

belief, credence, credulity, faith, trust

discard *verb* <u>get rid of</u>, abandon, cast aside, dispense with, dispose of, drop, dump (*informal*), jettison, reject, throw away or out

➤ **Antonyms**

hang or hold on to, hold back, keep, reserve, retain, save

discharge *verb* **1** <u>release</u>, allow to go, clear, free, liberate, pardon, set free **2** <u>dismiss</u>, cashier,

discard, expel, fire (*informal*), oust, remove, sack (*informal*) **3** <u>fire</u>, detonate, explode, let loose (*informal*), let off, set off, shoot **4** <u>pour forth</u>, dispense, emit, exude, give off, leak, ooze, release **5** <u>carry out</u>, accomplish, do, execute, fulfil, observe, perform **6** <u>pay</u>, clear, honour, meet, relieve, satisfy, settle, square up ◆ *noun* **7** <u>release</u>, acquittal, clearance, liberation, pardon **8** <u>dismissal</u>, demobilization, ejection **9** <u>firing</u>, blast, burst, detonation, explosion, report, salvo, shot, volley **10** <u>emission</u>, excretion, ooze, pus, secretion, seepage, suppuration

disciple *noun* <u>follower</u>, adherent, apostle, devotee, pupil, student, supporter

➤ **Antonyms**

guru, leader, master, teacher

disciplinarian *noun* <u>authoritarian</u>, despot, martinet, stickler, taskmaster, tyrant

discipline *noun* **1** <u>training</u>, drill, exercise, method, practice, regimen, regulation **2** <u>punishment</u>, castigation, chastisement, correction **3** <u>self-control</u>, conduct, control, orderliness, regulation, restraint, strictness **4** <u>field of study</u>, area, branch of knowledge, course, curriculum, speciality, subject ◆ *verb* **5** <u>train</u>, bring up, drill, educate, exercise, prepare **6** <u>punish</u>, bring to book, castigate, chasten, chastise, correct, penalize, reprimand, reprove

disclose *verb* **1** <u>make known</u>, broadcast, communicate, confess, divulge, let slip, publish, relate, reveal **2** <u>show</u>, bring to light, expose, lay bare, reveal, uncover, unveil

➤ **Antonyms**

conceal, cover, hide, keep dark, keep secret, mask, obscure, veil

disclosure *noun* <u>revelation</u>, acknowledgment, admission, announcement, confession, declaration, divulgence, leak, publication

discolour *verb* <u>stain</u>, fade, mark,

soil, streak, tarnish, tinge

discomfort noun **1** pain, ache, hurt, irritation, malaise, soreness **2** uneasiness, annoyance, distress, hardship, irritation, nuisance, trouble

► **Antonyms**

≠pain: comfort, ease ≠uneasiness: ease, reassurance, solace

disconcert verb disturb, faze, fluster, perturb, rattle (informal), take aback, unsettle, upset, worry

disconcerting adjective disturbing, alarming, awkward, bewildering, confusing, distracting, embarrassing, off-putting (Brit. informal), perplexing, upsetting

disconnect verb cut off, detach, disengage, divide, part, separate, sever, take apart, uncouple

disconnected adjective illogical, confused, disjointed, incoherent, jumbled, mixed-up, rambling, unintelligible

disconsolate adjective inconsolable, crushed, dejected, desolate, forlorn, grief-stricken, heartbroken, miserable, wretched

discontent noun dissatisfaction, displeasure, envy, regret, restlessness, uneasiness, unhappiness

discontented adjective dissatisfied, disaffected, disgruntled, displeased, exasperated, fed up, unhappy, vexed

► **Antonyms**

cheerful, content, contented, happy, pleased, satisfied

discontinue verb stop, abandon, break off, cease, drop, end, give up, quit, suspend, terminate

discord noun **1** disagreement, conflict, dissension, disunity, division, friction, incompatibility, strife **2** disharmony, cacophony, din, dissonance, harshness, jarring, racket, tumult

► **Antonyms**

≠disagreement: accord, agreement, concord, friendship, harmony, peace, understanding, unison, unity ≠disharmony: concord, harmony, melody, tunefulness

discordant adjective **1** disagreeing, at odds, clashing, conflicting, contradictory, contrary, different, incompatible **2** inharmonious, cacophonous, dissonant, grating, harsh, jarring, shrill, strident

discount verb **1** leave out, brush off (slang), disbelieve, disregard, ignore, overlook, pass over **2** deduct, lower, mark down, reduce, take off ♦ noun **3** deduction, concession, cut, rebate, reduction

discourage verb **1** dishearten, dampen, deject, demoralize, depress, dispirit, intimidate, overawe, put a damper on **2** put off, deter, dissuade, inhibit, prevent, talk out of

► **Antonyms**

≠dishearten: embolden, encourage, gee up, hearten, inspire ≠put off: encourage, urge

discouraged adjective put off, crestfallen, deterred, disheartened, dismayed, dispirited, downcast, down in the mouth, glum

discouragement noun **1** loss of confidence, dejection, depression, despair, despondency, disappointment, dismay, downheartedness **2** deterrent, damper, disincentive, hindrance, impediment, obstacle, opposition, setback

discouraging adjective disheartening, dampening, daunting, depressing, disappointing, dispiriting, off-putting (Brit. informal), unfavourable

discourse noun **1** conversation, chat, communication, dialogue, discussion, seminar, speech, talk **2** speech, dissertation, essay, homily, lecture, oration, sermon, treatise ♦ verb **3** hold forth, expatiate, speak, talk

discourteous adjective rude, bad-mannered, boorish, disrespectful, ill-mannered, impolite, insolent, offhand, ungentlemanly, ungracious

➤ **Antonyms**

civil, courteous, courtly, gracious, mannerly, polite, respectful, well-mannered

discourtesy noun **1** <u>rudeness</u>, bad manners, disrespectfulness, impertinence, impoliteness, incivility, insolence **2** <u>insult</u>, affront, cold shoulder, kick in the teeth (slang), rebuff, slight, snub

discover verb **1** <u>find</u>, come across, come upon, dig up, locate, turn up, uncover, unearth **2** <u>find out</u>, ascertain, detect, learn, notice, perceive, realize, recognize, uncover

discovery noun **1** <u>finding</u>, detection, disclosure, exploration, location, revelation, uncovering **2** <u>breakthrough</u>, find, innovation, invention, secret

discredit verb **1** <u>disgrace</u>, bring into disrepute, defame, dishonour, disparage, slander, smear, vilify **2** <u>doubt</u>, challenge, deny, disbelieve, discount, dispute, distrust, mistrust, question ♦ noun **3** <u>disgrace</u>, dishonour, disrepute, ignominy, ill-repute, scandal, shame, stigma

➤ **Antonyms**

verb ≠<u>disgrace</u>: acclaim, applaud, commend, honour, laud, pay tribute to, praise ♦ noun ≠<u>disgrace</u>: acclaim, acknowledgment, approval, commendation, credit, honour, merit, praise

discreditable adjective <u>disgraceful</u>, dishonourable, ignominious, reprehensible, scandalous, shameful, unworthy

discreet adjective <u>tactful</u>, careful, cautious, circumspect, considerate, diplomatic, guarded, judicious, prudent, wary

➤ **Antonyms**

incautious, indiscreet, injudicious, rash, tactless, undiplomatic, unthinking, unwise

discrepancy noun <u>disagreement</u>, conflict, contradiction, difference, disparity, divergence, incongruity, inconsistency, variation

discretion noun **1** <u>tact</u>, carefulness, caution, consideration, diplomacy, judiciousness, prudence, wariness **2** <u>choice</u>, inclination, pleasure, preference, volition, will

➤ **Antonyms**

≠<u>tact</u>: carelessness, indiscretion, insensitivity, rashness, tactlessness, thoughtlessness

discriminate verb **1** <u>show prejudice</u>, favour, show bias, single out, treat as inferior, treat differently, victimize **2** <u>differentiate</u>, distinguish, draw a distinction, segregate, separate, tell the difference

discriminating adjective <u>discerning</u>, cultivated, fastidious, particular, refined, selective, tasteful

➤ **Antonyms**

careless, general, indiscriminate, random, undiscriminating, unselective

discrimination noun **1** <u>prejudice</u>, bias, bigotry, favouritism, intolerance, unfairness **2** <u>discernment</u>, judgment, perception, refinement, subtlety, taste

discuss verb <u>talk about</u>, argue, confer, consider, converse, debate, deliberate, examine

discussion noun <u>talk</u>, analysis, argument, conference, consultation, conversation, debate, deliberation, dialogue, discourse

disdain noun **1** <u>contempt</u>, arrogance, derision, haughtiness, scorn, superciliousness ♦ verb **2** <u>scorn</u>, deride, disregard, look down on, reject, slight, sneer at, spurn

disdainful adjective <u>contemptuous</u>, aloof, arrogant, derisive, haughty, proud, scornful, sneering, supercilious, superior

disease noun <u>illness</u>, affliction, ailment, complaint, condition, disorder, infection, infirmity, malady, sickness

diseased adjective <u>sick</u>, ailing, infected, rotten, sickly, unhealthy, unsound, unwell, unwholesome

disembark verb <u>land</u>, alight, arrive, get off, go ashore, step out of

disenchanted adjective disillusioned, cynical, disappointed, indifferent, jaundiced, let down, sick of, soured

disenchantment noun disillusionment, disappointment, disillusion, rude awakening

disengage verb release, disentangle, extricate, free, loosen, set free, unloose, untie

disentangle verb untangle, disconnect, disengage, extricate, free, loose, unravel

disfavour noun disapproval, disapprobation, dislike, displeasure

disfigure verb damage, blemish, deface, deform, distort, mar, mutilate, scar

disgorge verb vomit, discharge, eject, empty, expel

disgrace noun 1 shame, degradation, dishonour, disrepute, ignominy, infamy, odium, opprobrium 2 stain, blemish, blot, reproach, scandal, slur, stigma
♦ verb 3 bring shame upon, degrade, discredit, dishonour, humiliate, shame, sully, taint

➤ **Antonyms**
noun ≠shame: credit, esteem, favour, grace, honour, repute
♦ verb ≠bring shame upon: credit, grace, honour

disgraceful adjective shameful, contemptible, detestable, dishonourable, disreputable, ignominious, scandalous, shocking, unworthy

disgruntled adjective discontented, annoyed, displeased, dissatisfied, grumpy, irritated, peeved, put out, vexed

disguise verb 1 hide, camouflage, cloak, conceal, cover, mask, screen, shroud, veil 2 misrepresent, fake, falsify ♦ noun 3 costume, camouflage, cover, mask, screen, veil 4 façade, deception, dissimulation, front, pretence, semblance, trickery, veneer

disguised adjective in disguise, camouflaged, covert, fake, false, feigned, incognito, masked, undercover

disgust noun 1 loathing, abhorrence, aversion, dislike, distaste, hatred, nausea, repugnance, repulsion, revulsion ♦ verb 2 sicken, displease, nauseate, offend, put off, repel, revolt

➤ **Antonyms**
noun ≠loathing: liking, love, pleasure, satisfaction, taste
♦ verb ≠sicken: delight, impress, please

disgusted adjective sickened, appalled, nauseated, offended, repulsed, scandalized

disgusting adjective sickening, foul, gross, loathsome, nauseating, offensive, repellent, repugnant, revolting

dish noun 1 bowl, plate, platter, salver 2 food, fare, recipe

dishearten verb discourage, cast down, deject, depress, deter, dismay, dispirit, put a damper on

➤ **Antonyms**
cheer up, encourage, gee up, hearten, lift

dishevelled adjective untidy, bedraggled, disordered, messy, ruffled, rumpled, tousled, uncombed, unkempt

➤ **Antonyms**
chic, dapper, neat, smart, soigné or soignée, spick-and-span, spruce, tidy, trim, well-groomed

dishonest adjective deceitful, bent (slang), cheating, corrupt, crooked (informal), disreputable, double-dealing, false, lying, treacherous

➤ **Antonyms**
honest, honourable, law-abiding, lawful, principled, true, trustworthy, upright

dishonesty noun deceit, cheating, chicanery, corruption, fraud, treachery, trickery, unscrupulousness

dishonour verb 1 disgrace, debase, debauch, defame, degrade, discredit, shame, sully
♦ noun 2 disgrace, discredit, dis-

repute, ignominy, infamy, obloquy, reproach, scandal, shame **3** insult, abuse, affront, discourtesy, indignity, offence, outrage, sacrilege, slight

➤ **Antonyms**

verb ≠disgrace: esteem, exalt, respect, revere, worship ♦ noun ≠disgrace: decency, goodness, honour, integrity, morality

dishonourable adjective **1** shameful, contemptible, despicable, discreditable, disgraceful, ignominious, infamous, scandalous **2** untrustworthy, blackguardly, corrupt, disreputable, shameless, treacherous, unprincipled, unscrupulous

disillusioned adjective disenchanted, disabused, disappointed, enlightened, undeceived

disinclination noun reluctance, aversion, dislike, hesitance, objection, opposition, repugnance, resistance, unwillingness

disinclined adjective reluctant, averse, hesitating, loath, not in the mood, opposed, resistant, unwilling

disinfect verb sterilize, clean, cleanse, decontaminate, deodorize, fumigate, purify, sanitize

➤ **Antonyms**

contaminate, defile, infect, poison, pollute, taint

disinfectant noun antiseptic, germicide, sterilizer

disinherit verb Law cut off, disown, dispossess, oust, repudiate

disintegrate verb break up, break apart, crumble, fall apart, go to pieces, separate, shatter, splinter

disinterest noun impartiality, detachment, fairness, neutrality

disinterested adjective impartial, detached, dispassionate, even-handed, impersonal, neutral, objective, unbiased, unprejudiced

➤ **Antonyms**

biased, involved, partial, prejudiced

disjointed adjective incoherent, confused, disconnected, disordered, rambling

dislike verb **1** be averse to, despise, detest, disapprove, hate, loathe, not be able to bear or abide or stand, object to, take a dim view of ♦ noun **2** aversion, animosity, antipathy, disapproval, disinclination, displeasure, distaste, enmity, hostility, repugnance

➤ **Antonyms**

verb ≠be averse to: esteem, favour, like ♦ noun ≠aversion: admiration, attraction, delight, esteem, inclination, liking

dislodge verb displace, disturb, extricate, force out, knock loose, oust, remove, uproot

disloyal adjective treacherous, faithless, false, subversive, traitorous, two-faced, unfaithful, untrustworthy

➤ **Antonyms**

constant, dependable, dutiful, faithful, loyal, steadfast, true, trustworthy, trusty

disloyalty noun treachery, breach of trust, deceitfulness, double-dealing, falseness, inconstancy, infidelity, treason, unfaithfulness

dismal adjective gloomy, bleak, cheerless, dark, depressing, discouraging, dreary, forlorn, sombre, wretched

➤ **Antonyms**

bright, cheerful, cheery, glad, happy, joyful, light-hearted

dismantle verb take apart, demolish, disassemble, strip, take to pieces

dismay verb **1** alarm, appal, distress, frighten, horrify, paralyse, scare, terrify, unnerve **2** disappoint, daunt, discourage, dishearten, disillusion, dispirit, put off ♦ noun **3** alarm, anxiety, apprehension, consternation, dread, fear, horror, trepidation **4** disappointment, chagrin, discouragement, disillusionment

dismember verb cut into pieces, amputate, dissect, mutilate, sever

dismiss verb **1** sack (informal),

axe (*informal*), cashier, discharge, fire (*informal*), give notice to, give (someone) their marching orders, lay off, remove **2** let go, disperse, dissolve, free, release, send away **3** put out of one's mind, banish, discard, dispel, disregard, lay aside, reject, set aside

dismissal *noun* the sack (*informal*), expulsion, marching orders (*informal*), notice, removal, the boot (*slang*), the push (*slang*)

disobedience *noun* defiance, indiscipline, insubordination, mutiny, noncompliance, nonobservance, recalcitrance, revolt, unruliness, waywardness

disobedient *adjective* defiant, contrary, disorderly, insubordinate, intractable, naughty, refractory, undisciplined, unruly, wayward

➤ **Antonyms**

compliant, dutiful, manageable, obedient, submissive, well-behaved

disobey *verb* refuse to obey, contravene, defy, disregard, flout, ignore, infringe, rebel, violate

disorder *noun* **1** untidiness, chaos, clutter, confusion, disarray, jumble, mess, muddle, shambles **2** disturbance, commotion, riot, turmoil, unrest, unruliness, uproar **3** illness, affliction, ailment, complaint, disease, malady, sickness

disorderly *adjective* **1** untidy, chaotic, confused, disorganized, higgledy-piggledy (*informal*), jumbled, messy, shambolic (*informal*) **2** unruly, disruptive, indisciplinate, lawless, riotous, rowdy, tumultuous, turbulent, ungovernable

➤ **Antonyms**

≠untidy: arranged, neat, orderly, organized, tidy

disorganized *adjective* muddled, chaotic, confused, disordered, haphazard, jumbled, unsystematic

disown *verb* deny, cast off, disavow, disclaim, reject, renounce, repudiate

disparage *verb* run down, belittle, denigrate, deprecate, deride, malign, put down, ridicule, slander, vilify

dispassionate *adjective* **1** unemotional, calm, collected, composed, cool, imperturbable, serene, unruffled **2** objective, detached, disinterested, fair, impartial, impersonal, neutral, unbiased, unprejudiced

➤ **Antonyms**

≠unemotional: ablaze, ardent, emotional, excited, fervent, impassioned, intense, passionate
≠objective: biased, concerned, interested, involved, partial, prejudiced

dispatch, despatch *verb* **1** send, consign, dismiss, hasten **2** carry out, discharge, dispose of, finish, perform, settle **3** murder, assassinate, execute, kill, slaughter, slay ◆ *noun* **4** message, account, bulletin, communication, communiqué, news, report, story

dispel *verb* drive away, banish, chase away, dismiss, disperse, eliminate, expel

dispense *verb* **1** distribute, allocate, allot, apportion, assign, deal out, dole out, share **2** prepare, measure, mix, supply **3** administer, apply, carry out, discharge, enforce, execute, implement, operate **4** dispense with: **a** do away with, abolish, brush aside, cancel, dispose of, get rid of **b** do without, abstain from, forgo, give up, relinquish

disperse *verb* **1** scatter, broadcast, diffuse, disseminate, distribute, spread, strew **2** break up, disband, dissolve, scatter, separate

➤ **Antonyms**

amass, assemble, collect, concentrate, congregate, convene, gather, muster

dispirited *adjective* disheartened, crestfallen, dejected, depressed, despondent, discouraged, downcast, gloomy, glum, sad

displace *verb* **1** <u>move</u>, disturb, misplace, shift, transpose **2** <u>replace</u>, oust, succeed, supersede, supplant, take the place of

display *verb* **1** <u>show</u>, demonstrate, disclose, exhibit, expose, manifest, present, reveal **2** <u>show off</u>, flash (*informal*), flaunt, flourish, parade, vaunt ♦ *noun* **3** <u>exhibition</u>, array, demonstration, presentation, revelation, show **4** <u>show</u>, flourish, ostentation, pageant, parade, pomp, spectacle

➤ Antonyms

verb ≠<u>show</u>: conceal, cover, hide, keep dark, keep secret, mask, veil

displease *verb* <u>annoy</u>, anger, irk, irritate, offend, pique, put out, upset, vex

displeasure *noun* <u>annoyance</u>, anger, disapproval, dissatisfaction, distaste, indignation, irritation, resentment

➤ Antonyms

approval, pleasure, satisfaction

disposable *adjective* **1** <u>throwaway</u>, biodegradable, nonreturnable **2** <u>available</u>, consumable, expendable

disposal *noun* **1** <u>throwing away</u>, discarding, dumping (*informal*), ejection, jettisoning, removal, riddance, scrapping **2** *at one's disposal* <u>available</u>, at one's service, consumable, expendable, free for use

dispose *verb* <u>arrange</u>, array, distribute, group, marshal, order, place, put

dispose of *verb* **1** <u>get rid of</u>, destroy, discard, dump (*informal*), jettison, scrap, throw out or away, unload **2** <u>deal with</u>, decide, determine, end, finish with, settle

disposition *noun* **1** <u>character</u>, constitution, make-up, nature, spirit, temper, temperament **2** <u>tendency</u>, bent, bias, habit, inclination, leaning, proclivity, propensity **3** <u>arrangement</u>, classifica-

tion, distribution, grouping, ordering, organization, placement

disproportion *noun* <u>inequality</u>, asymmetry, discrepancy, disparity, imbalance, lopsidedness, unevenness

➤ Antonyms

balance, congruity, harmony, proportion, symmetry

disproportionate *adjective* <u>unequal</u>, excessive, inordinate, out of proportion, unbalanced, uneven, unreasonable

disprove *verb* <u>prove false</u>, contradict, discredit, expose, give the lie to, invalidate, negate, rebut, refute

➤ Antonyms

ascertain, bear out, confirm, prove, show, substantiate, verify

dispute *noun* **1** <u>disagreement</u>, altercation, argument, conflict, feud, quarrel **2** <u>argument</u>, contention, controversy, debate, discussion, dissension ♦ *verb* **3** <u>doubt</u>, challenge, contest, contradict, deny, impugn, question, rebut **4** <u>argue</u>, clash, cross swords, debate, quarrel, squabble

disqualification *noun* <u>ban</u>, elimination, exclusion, ineligibility, rejection

disqualified *adjective* <u>ineligible</u>, debarred, eliminated, knocked out, out of the running

disqualify *verb* <u>ban</u>, debar, declare ineligible, preclude, prohibit, rule out

disquiet *noun* **1** <u>uneasiness</u>, alarm, anxiety, concern, disturbance, foreboding, nervousness, trepidation, worry ♦ *verb* **2** <u>make uneasy</u>, bother, concern, disturb, perturb, trouble, unsettle, upset, worry

disregard *verb* **1** <u>ignore</u>, brush aside or away, discount, make light of, neglect, overlook, pass over, pay no heed to, turn a blind eye to ♦ *noun* **2** <u>inattention</u>, contempt, disdain, disrespect, indifference, neglect, negligence, oversight

➤ **Antonyms**

verb ≠<u>ignore</u>: attend, heed, listen to, mind, note, pay attention to, regard, respect, take into consideration, take notice of

disrepair *noun* <u>dilapidation</u>, collapse, decay, deterioration, ruination

disreputable *adjective* <u>discreditable</u>, dishonourable, ignominious, infamous, louche, notorious, scandalous, shady (*informal*), shameful

➤ **Antonyms**

decent, reputable, respectable, respected, upright, worthy

disrepute *noun* <u>discredit</u>, disgrace, dishonour, ignominy, ill repute, infamy, obloquy, shame, unpopularity

disrespect *noun* <u>contempt</u>, cheek, impertinence, impoliteness, impudence, insolence, irreverence, lack of respect, rudeness, sauce

➤ **Antonyms**

esteem, regard, respect

disrespectful *adjective* <u>contemptuous</u>, cheeky, discourteous, impertinent, impolite, impudent, insolent, insulting, irreverent, rude

disrupt *verb* **1** <u>disturb</u>, confuse, disorder, disorganize, spoil, upset **2** <u>interrupt</u>, break up or into, interfere with, intrude, obstruct, unsettle, upset

disruption *noun* <u>disturbance</u>, interference, interruption, stoppage

disruptive *adjective* <u>disturbing</u>, disorderly, distracting, troublesome, unruly, unsettling, upsetting

➤ **Antonyms**

compliant, cooperative, docile, obedient, well-behaved

dissatisfaction *noun* <u>discontent</u>, annoyance, chagrin, disappointment, displeasure, frustration, irritation, resentment, unhappiness

dissatisfied *adjective* <u>discontented</u>, disappointed, disgruntled, displeased, fed up, frustrated, unhappy, unsatisfied

➤ **Antonyms**

content, contented, pleased, satisfied

dissect *verb* **1** <u>cut up or apart</u>, anatomize, dismember, lay open **2** <u>analyse</u>, break down, explore, inspect, investigate, research, scrutinize, study

disseminate *verb* <u>spread</u>, broadcast, circulate, disperse, distribute, publicize, scatter

dissension *noun* <u>disagreement</u>, conflict, discord, dispute, dissent, friction, quarrel, row, strife

dissent *verb* **1** <u>disagree</u>, differ, object, protest, refuse, withhold assent or approval ♦ *noun* **2** <u>disagreement</u>, discord, dissension, objection, opposition, refusal, resistance

➤ **Antonyms**

verb ≠<u>disagree</u>: agree, assent, concur ♦ *noun* ≠<u>disagreement</u>: accord, agreement, assent, concurrence, consensus

dissenter *noun* <u>objector</u>, dissident, nonconformist

dissertation *noun* <u>thesis</u>, critique, discourse, disquisition, essay, exposition, treatise

disservice *noun* <u>bad turn</u>, harm, injury, injustice, unkindness, wrong

➤ **Antonyms**

courtesy, good turn, kindness, service

dissident *adjective* **1** <u>dissenting</u>, disagreeing, discordant, heterodox, nonconformist ♦ *noun* **2** <u>protester</u>, agitator, dissenter, rebel

dissimilar *adjective* <u>different</u>, disparate, divergent, diverse, heterogeneous, unlike, unrelated, various

➤ **Antonyms**

alike, comparable, congruous, corresponding, in agreement, much the same, resembling, uniform

dissipate *verb* **1** <u>squander</u>, consume, deplete, expend, fritter away, run through, spend, waste **2** <u>disperse</u>, disappear, dispel, dissolve, drive away, evaporate, scatter, vanish

dissipation noun **1** dispersal, disappearance, disintegration, dissolution, scattering, vanishing **2** debauchery, dissoluteness, excess, extravagance, indulgence, intemperance, prodigality, profligacy, wantonness, waste

dissociate verb **1** break away, break off, part company, quit **2** separate, detach, disconnect, distance, divorce, isolate, segregate, set apart

dissolute adjective immoral, debauched, degenerate, depraved, dissipated, profligate, rakish, wanton, wild

➤ **Antonyms**

chaste, clean-living, good, moral, upright, virtuous

dissolution noun **1** breaking up, disintegration, division, parting, separation **2** adjournment, discontinuation, end, finish, suspension, termination

➤ **Antonyms**

≠breaking up: alliance, amalgamation, coalition, combination, unification, union

dissolve verb **1** melt, deliquesce, fuse, liquefy, soften, thaw **2** end, break up, discontinue, suspend, terminate, wind up

dissuade verb deter, advise against, discourage, put off, remonstrate, talk out of, warn

➤ **Antonyms**

bring round (informal), coax, convince, persuade, sway, talk into

distance noun **1** space, extent, gap, interval, length, range, span, stretch **2** reserve, aloofness, coldness, coolness, remoteness, restraint, stiffness **3 in the distance** far off, afar, far away, on the horizon, yonder ♦ verb **4 distance oneself** separate oneself, be distanced from, dissociate oneself

distant adjective **1** far-off, abroad, far, faraway, far-flung, outlying, out-of-the-way, remote **2** apart,

dispersed, distinct, scattered, separate **3** reserved, aloof, cool, reticent, standoffish, unapproachable, unfriendly, withdrawn

➤ **Antonyms**

≠far-off: adjacent, adjoining, at hand, close, handy, near, nearby, neighbouring, nigh ≠reserved: close, friendly, intimate, warm

distaste noun dislike, aversion, disgust, horror, loathing, odium, repugnance, revulsion

distasteful adjective unpleasant, disagreeable, objectionable, offensive, repugnant, repulsive, uninviting, unpalatable, unsavoury

➤ **Antonyms**

agreeable, charming, enjoyable, pleasing, pleasurable

distil verb extract, condense, purify, refine

distinct adjective **1** different, detached, discrete, individual, separate, unconnected **2** definite, clear, decided, evident, marked, noticeable, obvious, palpable, unmistakable, well-defined

➤ **Antonyms**

≠different: common, connected, identical, indistinct, similar ≠definite: fuzzy, indefinite, indistinct, obscure, unclear, vague

distinction noun **1** differentiation, discernment, discrimination, perception, separation **2** feature, characteristic, distinctiveness, individuality, mark, particularity, peculiarity, quality **3** difference, contrast, differential, division, separation **4** excellence, eminence, fame, greatness, honour, importance, merit, prominence, repute

distinctive adjective characteristic, idiosyncratic, individual, original, peculiar, singular, special, typical, unique

➤ **Antonyms**

common, ordinary, run-of-the-mill, typical

distinctly adverb definitely, clearly, decidedly, markedly, noticeably, obviously, patently, plainly, unmistakably

distinguish verb **1** <u>differentiate</u>, ascertain, decide, determine, discriminate, judge, tell apart, tell the difference **2** <u>characterize</u>, categorize, classify, mark, separate, set apart, single out **3** <u>make out</u>, discern, know, perceive, pick out, recognize, see, tell

distinguished adjective <u>eminent</u>, acclaimed, celebrated, famed, famous, illustrious, noted, renowned, well-known

➤ **Antonyms**

common, inferior, undistinguished, unknown

distort verb **1** <u>misrepresent</u>, bias, colour, falsify, pervert, slant, twist **2** <u>deform</u>, bend, buckle, contort, disfigure, misshape, twist, warp

distortion noun **1** <u>misrepresentation</u>, bias, falsification, perversion, slant **2** <u>deformity</u>, bend, buckle, contortion, crookedness, malformation, twist, warp

distract verb **1** <u>divert</u>, draw away, sidetrack, turn aside **2** <u>amuse</u>, beguile, engross, entertain, occupy

distracted adjective <u>agitated</u>, at sea, flustered, harassed, in a flap (informal), perplexed, puzzled, troubled

distraction noun **1** <u>diversion</u>, disturbance, interference, interruption **2** <u>entertainment</u>, amusement, diversion, pastime, recreation **3** <u>agitation</u>, bewilderment, commotion, confusion, discord, disorder, disturbance

distraught adjective <u>frantic</u>, agitated, beside oneself, desperate, distracted, distressed, out of one's mind, overwrought, worked-up

distress noun **1** <u>worry</u>, grief, heartache, misery, pain, sorrow, suffering, torment, wretchedness **2** <u>need</u>, adversity, difficulties, hardship, misfortune, poverty, privation, trouble ♦ verb **3** <u>upset</u>, disturb, grieve, harass, sadden,

torment, trouble, worry

distressed adjective **1** <u>upset</u>, agitated, distracted, distraught, tormented, troubled, worried, wretched **2** <u>poverty-stricken</u>, destitute, down at heel, indigent, needy, poor, straitened

distressing adjective <u>upsetting</u>, disturbing, harrowing, heartbreaking, painful, sad, worrying

distribute verb **1** <u>hand out</u>, circulate, convey, deliver, pass round **2** <u>share</u>, allocate, allot, apportion, deal, dispense, dole out

distribution noun **1** <u>delivery</u>, dealing, handling, mailing, transportation **2** <u>sharing</u>, allocation, allotment, apportionment, division **3** <u>classification</u>, arrangement, grouping, organization, placement

district noun <u>area</u>, locale, locality, neighbourhood, parish, quarter, region, sector, vicinity

distrust verb **1** <u>suspect</u>, be suspicious of, be wary of, disbelieve, doubt, mistrust, question, smell a rat (informal) ♦ noun **2** <u>suspicion</u>, disbelief, doubt, misgiving, mistrust, question, scepticism, wariness

➤ **Antonyms**

verb ≠<u>suspect</u>: believe, depend, have confidence, have faith, trust ♦ noun ≠<u>suspicion</u>: confidence, faith, reliance, trust

disturb verb **1** <u>interrupt</u>, bother, butt in on, disrupt, interfere with, intrude on, pester **2** <u>upset</u>, alarm, distress, fluster, harass, perturb, trouble, unnerve, unsettle, worry **3** <u>muddle</u>, disarrange, disorder

➤ **Antonyms**

≠<u>upset</u>: calm, compose, lull, pacify, quiet, quieten, reassure, relax, relieve, settle, soothe

disturbance noun **1** <u>interruption</u>, annoyance, bother, distraction, intrusion **2** <u>disorder</u>, brawl, commotion, fracas, fray, rumpus

disturbed adjective **1** Psychiatry <u>unbalanced</u>, disordered, maladjusted, neurotic, troubled, upset

2 worried, anxious, apprehensive, bothered, concerned, nervous, troubled, uneasy, upset

➤ **Antonyms**

≠unbalanced: balanced, untroubled ≠worried: calm, collected, self-possessed, unfazed (informal), untroubled

disturbing adjective worrying, alarming, disconcerting, distressing, frightening, harrowing, startling, unsettling, upsetting

disuse noun neglect, abandonment, decay, idleness

➤ **Antonyms**

application, employment, practice, service, usage, use

ditch noun **1** channel, drain, dyke, furrow, gully, moat, trench, watercourse ♦ verb **2** Slang get rid of, abandon, discard, dispose of, drop, dump (informal), jettison, scrap, throw out or overboard

dither verb **1** Chiefly Brit. vacillate, faff about (Brit. informal), hesitate, hum and haw, shillyshally (informal), teeter, waver ♦ noun **2** Chiefly Brit. flutter, flap (informal), fluster, tizzy (informal)

➤ **Antonyms**

verb ≠vacillate: come to a conclusion, decide, make a decision, make up one's mind, reach or come to a decision

dive verb **1** plunge, descend, dip, drop, duck, nose-dive, plummet, swoop ♦ noun **2** plunge, jump, leap, lunge, nose dive, spring

diverge verb **1** separate, branch, divide, fork, part, split, spread **2** deviate, depart, digress, meander, stray, turn aside, wander

diverse adjective **1** various, assorted, manifold, miscellaneous, of every description, several, sundry, varied **2** different, discrete, disparate, dissimilar, distinct, divergent, separate, unlike, varying

diversify verb vary, branch out, change, expand, have a finger in every pie, spread out

diversion noun **1** Chiefly Brit. detour, departure, deviation, di-

gression **2** pastime, amusement, distraction, entertainment, game, recreation, relaxation, sport

diversity noun difference, distinctiveness, diverseness, heterogeneity, multiplicity, range, variety

divert verb **1** redirect, avert, deflect, switch, turn aside **2** distract, draw or lead away from, lead astray, sidetrack **3** entertain, amuse, beguile, delight, gratify, regale

diverting adjective entertaining, amusing, beguiling, enjoyable, fun, humorous, pleasant

divide verb **1** separate, bisect, cut (up), part, partition, segregate, split **2** share, allocate, allot, deal out, dispense, distribute **3** cause to disagree, break up, come between, estrange, split

➤ **Antonyms**

≠separate: combine, join, unite

dividend noun bonus, cut (informal), divvy (informal), extra, gain, plus, portion, share, surplus

divine adjective **1** heavenly, angelic, celestial, godlike, holy, spiritual, superhuman, supernatural **2** sacred, consecrated, holy, religious, sanctified, spiritual **3** Informal wonderful, beautiful, excellent, glorious, marvellous, perfect, splendid, superlative ♦ verb **4** infer, apprehend, deduce, discern, guess, perceive, suppose, surmise

divinity noun **1** theology, religion, religious studies **2** god or goddess, deity, guardian spirit, spirit **3** godliness, deity, divine nature, holiness, sanctity

divisible adjective dividable, separable, splittable

division noun **1** separation, cutting up, dividing, partition, splitting up **2** sharing, allotment, apportionment, distribution **3** part, branch, category, class, department, group, section **4** disagreement, difference of opinion, discord, rupture, split, variance

➤ **Antonyms**

≠**disagreement:** accord, agreement, concord, harmony, peace, union, unity

divorce noun 1 separation, annulment, dissolution, split-up ♦ verb 2 separate, disconnect, dissociate, dissolve (marriage), divide, part, sever, split up

divulge verb make known, confess, declare, disclose, let slip, proclaim, reveal, tell

➤ **Antonyms**

conceal, hide, keep secret

dizzy adjective 1 giddy, faint, light-headed, off balance, reeling, shaky, swimming, wobbly, woozy (informal) 2 confused, at sea, befuddled, bemused, bewildered, dazed, dazzled, muddled

do verb 1 perform, accomplish, achieve, carry out, complete, execute 2 be adequate, be sufficient, cut the mustard, pass muster, satisfy, suffice 3 get ready, arrange, fix, look after, prepare, see to 4 solve, decipher, decode, figure out, puzzle out, resolve, work out 5 cause, bring about, create, effect, produce ♦ noun 6 Informal, chiefly Brit. & N.Z. event, affair, function, gathering, occasion, party

do away with verb 1 kill, exterminate, murder, slay 2 get rid of, abolish, discard, discontinue, eliminate, put an end to, put paid to, remove

docile adjective submissive, amenable, biddable, compliant, manageable, obedient, pliant

➤ **Antonyms**

difficult, intractable, troublesome, trying, uncooperative, unmanageable

docility noun submissiveness, compliance, manageability, meekness, obedience

dock[1] noun 1 wharf, harbour, pier, quay, waterfront ♦ verb 2 moor, anchor, berth, drop anchor, land, put in, tie up 3 Of spacecraft link up, couple, hook up, join, rendezvous, unite

dock[2] verb 1 deduct, decrease, diminish, lessen, reduce, subtract, withhold 2 cut off, clip, crop, curtail, cut short, shorten

➤ **Antonyms**

≠**deduct:** augment, boost, increase, raise

doctor noun 1 G.P., general practitioner, medic (informal), medical practitioner, physician ♦ verb 2 change, alter, disguise, falsify, misrepresent, pervert, tamper with 3 add to, adulterate, cut, dilute, mix with, spike, water down

doctrinaire adjective dogmatic, biased, fanatical, inflexible, insistent, opinionated, rigid

doctrine noun teaching, article of faith, belief, conviction, creed, dogma, opinion, precept, principle, tenet

document noun 1 paper, certificate, record, report ♦ verb 2 support, authenticate, certify, corroborate, detail, substantiate, validate, verify

dodge verb 1 duck, dart, sidestep, swerve, turn aside 2 evade, avoid, elude, get out of, shirk ♦ noun 3 trick, device, ploy, ruse, scheme, stratagem, subterfuge, wheeze (Brit. slang)

dog noun 1 hound, canine, cur, man's best friend, pooch (slang) 2 go to the dogs Informal go to ruin, degenerate, deteriorate, go down the drain, go to pot ♦ verb 3 trouble, follow, haunt, hound, plague, pursue, track, trail

dogged adjective determined, indefatigable, obstinate, persistent, resolute, steadfast, stubborn, tenacious, unflagging, unshakable

➤ **Antonyms**

doubtful, half-hearted, hesitant, irresolute, undetermined

dogma noun doctrine, belief, credo, creed, opinion, teachings

dogmatic adjective opinionated, arrogant, assertive, doctrinaire, emphatic, obdurate, overbearing

doldrums noun the doldrums inactivity, depression, dumps (*informal*), gloom, listlessness, malaise

dole noun **1** *Brit. & Austral. informal* benefit, allowance, gift, grant, handout ♦ *verb* **2 dole out** give out, allocate, allot, apportion, assign, dispense, distribute, hand out

dollop noun lump, helping, portion, scoop, serving

dolt noun idiot, ass, blockhead, chump (*informal*), clot (*Brit. informal*), dope (*informal*), dumb-ass (*slang*), dunce, fool, oaf

domestic *adjective* **1** home, family, household, private **2** homeloving, domesticated, homely, housewifely, stay-at-home **3** domesticated, house-trained, pet, tame, trained **4** native, indigenous, internal ♦ *noun* **5** servant, char (*informal*), charwoman, daily, help, maid

dominant *adjective* **1** controlling, assertive, authoritative, commanding, governing, ruling, superior, supreme **2** main, chief, predominant, pre-eminent, primary, principal, prominent

➤ **Antonyms**

ancillary, auxiliary, inferior, junior, lesser, lower, minor, secondary, subservient, subsidiary

dominate *verb* **1** control, direct, govern, have the whip hand over, monopolize, rule, tyrannize **2** tower above, loom over, overlook, stand head and shoulders above, stand over, survey

domination *noun* control, ascendancy, authority, command, influence, power, rule, superiority, supremacy

domineering *adjective* overbearing, arrogant, authoritarian, bossy (*informal*), dictatorial, highhanded, imperious, oppressive, tyrannical

➤ **Antonyms**

meek, servile, shy, submissive, subservient

dominion noun **1** control, authority, command, jurisdiction, power, rule, sovereignty, supremacy

2 kingdom, country, domain, empire, realm, territory

don *verb* put on, clothe oneself in, dress in, get into, pull on, slip on or into

donate *verb* give, contribute, make a gift of, present, subscribe

donation noun contribution, gift, grant, hand-out, offering, present, subscription

donor *noun* giver, benefactor, contributor, donator, philanthropist

➤ **Antonyms**

beneficiary, receiver, recipient

doom noun **1** destruction, catastrophe, downfall, fate, fortune, ruin ♦ *verb* **2** condemn, consign, damn, destine, sentence

doomed *adjective* condemned, bewitched, cursed, fated, hopeless, ill-fated, ill-omened, luckless, star-crossed

door noun opening, doorway, entrance, entry, exit

dope noun **1** *Slang* drug, narcotic, opiate **2** *Informal* idiot, dimwit (*informal*), dumb-ass (*slang*), dunce, fool, nitwit (*informal*), numbskull or numbskull, simpleton, twit (*informal, chiefly Brit.*) ♦ *verb* **3** drug, anaesthetize, knock out, narcotize, sedate, stupefy

dormant *adjective* inactive, asleep, hibernating, inert, inoperative, latent, sleeping, slumbering, suspended

➤ **Antonyms**

active, alert, aroused, awake, awakened, conscious, wideawake

dose noun quantity, dosage, draught, measure, portion, potion, prescription

dot noun **1** spot, fleck, jot, mark, point, speck, speckle **2** on the dot on time, exactly, on the button (*informal*), precisely, promptly, punctually, to the minute ♦ *verb* **3** spot, dab, dabble, fleck, speckle, sprinkle, stipple, stud

dotage noun senility, decrepitude, feebleness, imbecility, old age, second childhood, weakness

dote on or **upon** verb <u>adore</u>, admire, hold dear, idolize, lavish affection on, prize, treasure

doting adjective <u>adoring</u>, devoted, fond, foolish, indulgent, lovesick

double adjective **1** <u>twice</u>, coupled, dual, duplicate, in pairs, paired, twin, twofold ♦ verb **2** <u>multiply</u>, duplicate, enlarge, grow, increase, magnify ♦ noun **3** <u>twin</u>, clone, dead ringer (slang), Doppelgänger, duplicate, lookalike, replica, spitting image (informal) **4** at or on the **double** <u>quickly</u>, at full speed, briskly, immediately, posthaste, without delay

double-cross verb <u>betray</u>, cheat, defraud, hoodwink, mislead, swindle, trick, two-time (informal)

doubt noun **1** <u>uncertainty</u>, hesitancy, hesitation, indecision, irresolution, lack of conviction, suspense **2** <u>suspicion</u>, apprehension, distrust, misgiving, mistrust, qualm, scepticism ♦ verb **3** <u>be uncertain</u>, be dubious, demur, fluctuate, hesitate, scruple, vacillate, waver **4** <u>suspect</u>, discredit, distrust, fear, lack confidence in, mistrust, query, question

➤ **Antonyms**

noun ≠<u>uncertainty</u>: belief, certainty, confidence, conviction ≠<u>suspicion</u>: confidence, trust ♦ verb ≠<u>suspect</u>: accept, believe, buy (slang), have faith in, trust

doubtful adjective **1** <u>unlikely</u>, debatable, dubious, equivocal, improbable, problematic(al), questionable, unclear **2** <u>unsure</u>, distrustful, hesitating, in two minds (informal), sceptical, suspicious, tentative, uncertain, unconvinced, wavering

➤ **Antonyms**

≠<u>unlikely</u>: certain, definite, indubitable ≠<u>unsure</u>: certain, decided, positive, resolute

doubtless adverb **1** <u>certainly</u>, assuredly, indisputably, of course,

surely, undoubtedly, unquestionably, without doubt **2** <u>probably</u>, apparently, most likely, ostensibly, presumably, seemingly, supposedly

dour adjective <u>gloomy</u>, dismal, dreary, forbidding, grim, morose, sour, sullen, unfriendly

➤ **Antonyms**

carefree, cheerful, cheery, goodhumoured, happy, jovial, pleasant, sunny

dowdy adjective <u>frumpy</u>, dingy, drab, frowzy, old-fashioned, shabby, unfashionable

➤ **Antonyms**

chic, dressy, fashionable, neat, smart, spruce, trim, well-dressed

do without verb <u>manage without</u>, abstain from, dispense with, forgo, get along without, give up, kick (informal)

down adjective **1** <u>depressed</u>, dejected, disheartened, downcast, low, miserable, sad, unhappy ♦ verb **2** Informal <u>swallow</u>, drain, drink (down), gulp, put away, toss off ♦ noun **3** have a down on Informal <u>be antagonistic</u> or hostile to, bear a grudge towards, be prejudiced against, be set against, have it in for (slang)

down-and-out noun **1** <u>tramp</u>, bag lady, beggar, derelict, dosser (Brit. slang), pauper, vagabond, vagrant ♦ adjective **2** <u>destitute</u>, derelict, impoverished, on one's uppers (informal), penniless, short, without two pennies to rub together (informal)

downcast adjective <u>dejected</u>, crestfallen, depressed, despondent, disappointed, disconsolate, discouraged, disheartened, dismayed, dispirited

➤ **Antonyms**

cheerful, cheery, chirpy (informal), elated, happy, joyful, lighthearted

downfall noun <u>ruin</u>, collapse, comeuppance (slang), destruction, disgrace, fall, overthrow, undoing

downgrade verb <u>demote</u>, degrade, humble, lower *or* reduce in rank, take down a peg (*informal*)

➤ **Antonyms**

advance, better, elevate, enhance, improve, promote, raise, upgrade

downhearted *adjective* dejected, crestfallen, depressed, despondent, discouraged, disheartened, dispirited, downcast, sad, unhappy

downpour *noun* rainstorm, cloudburst, deluge, flood, inundation, torrential rain

downright *adjective* complete, absolute, out-and-out, outright, plain, thoroughgoing, total, undisguised, unqualified, utter

down-to-earth *adjective* sensible, matter-of-fact, nononsense, plain-spoken, practical, realistic, sane, unsentimental

downtrodden *adjective* oppressed, exploited, helpless, subjugated, subservient, tyrannized

downward *adjective* descending, declining, earthward, heading down, sliding, slipping

doze *verb* 1 nap, kip (*Brit. slang*), nod off (*informal*), sleep, slumber, snooze (*informal*) ♦ *noun* 2 nap, catnap, forty winks (*informal*), kip (*Brit. slang*), shuteye (*slang*), siesta, snooze (*informal*)

drab *adjective* dull, dingy, dismal, dreary, flat, gloomy, shabby, sombre

➤ **Antonyms**

bright, cheerful, colourful, jazzy (*informal*), vibrant, vivid

draft *noun* 1 outline, abstract, plan, rough, sketch, version 2 order, bill (*of exchange*), cheque, postal order ♦ *verb* 3 outline, compose, design, draw, draw up, formulate, plan, sketch

drag *verb* 1 pull, draw, haul, lug, tow, trail, tug 2 drag on *or* out last, draw out, extend, keep going, lengthen, persist, prolong, protract, spin out, stretch out ♦ *noun* 3 Slang nuisance, annoyance, bore, bother, pain (*informal*), pest

dragoon *verb* force, browbeat, bully, coerce, compel, constrain, drive, impel, intimidate, railroad (*informal*)

drain *noun* 1 pipe, channel, conduit, culvert, ditch, duct, sewer, sink, trench 2 reduction, depletion, drag, exhaustion, sap, strain, withdrawal ♦ *verb* 3 remove, bleed, draw off, dry, empty, pump off *or* out, tap, withdraw 4 flow out, effuse, exude, leak, ooze, seep, trickle, well out 5 drink up, finish, gulp down, quaff, swallow 6 exhaust, consume, deplete, dissipate, empty, sap, strain, use up

drama *noun* 1 play, dramatization, show, stage show 2 theatre, acting, dramaturgy, stagecraft 3 excitement, crisis, histrionics, scene, spectacle, turmoil

dramatic *adjective* 1 theatrical, dramaturgical, Thespian 2 powerful, expressive, impressive, moving, striking, vivid 3 exciting, breathtaking, climactic, electrifying, melodramatic, sensational, suspenseful, tense, thrilling

➤ **Antonyms**

≠powerful: ordinary, run-of-the-mill, undramatic, unexceptional, unmemorable

dramatist *noun* playwright, dramaturge, screenwriter, scriptwriter

dramatize *verb* exaggerate, lay it on (thick) (*slang*), overdo, overstate, play to the gallery

drape *verb* cover, cloak, fold, swathe, wrap

drastic *adjective* extreme, desperate, dire, forceful, harsh, radical, severe, strong

draught *noun* 1 breeze, current, flow, movement, puff 2 drink, cup, dose, potion, quantity

draw *verb* 1 sketch, depict, design, map out, mark out, outline, paint, portray, trace 2 pull, drag, haul, tow, tug 3 take out, extract, pull out 4 attract, allure, elicit, entice, evoke, induce, influence, invite, persuade 5 deduce, derive, infer, make, take ♦ *noun* 6 *Informal* attraction, enticement, lure, pull (*informal*) 7 tie, dead heat, deadlock, impasse, stalemate

drawback *noun* disadvantage, deficiency, difficulty, downside, flaw, handicap, hitch, snag, stumbling block

➤ **Antonyms**
advantage, asset, benefit, gain, help, service, use

drawing *noun* picture, cartoon, depiction, illustration, outline, portrayal, representation, sketch, study

drawn *adjective* tense, haggard, pinched, stressed, tired, worn

draw on *verb* make use of, employ, exploit, extract, fall back on, have recourse to, rely on, take from, use

draw out *verb* extend, drag out, lengthen, make longer, prolong, protract, spin out, stretch, string out

➤ **Antonyms**
curtail, cut, cut short, dock, reduce, shorten, trim, truncate

draw up *verb* 1 draft, compose, formulate, frame, prepare, write out 2 halt, bring to a stop, pull up, stop

dread *verb* 1 fear, cringe at, have cold feet (*informal*), quail, shrink from, shudder, tremble ♦ *noun* 2 fear, alarm, apprehension, dismay, fright, horror, terror, trepidation

dreadful *adjective* terrible, abysmal, appalling, atrocious, awful, fearful, frightful, hideous, horrible, shocking

dream *noun* 1 vision, delusion, hallucination, illusion, imagination, trance 2 daydream, fantasy, pipe dream 3 ambition, aim, aspiration, desire, goal, hope, wish 4 delight, beauty, gem, joy, marvel, pleasure, treasure ♦ *verb* 5 have dreams, conjure up, envisage, fancy, hallucinate, imagine, think, visualize 6 daydream, build castles in the air or

in Spain, fantasize, stargaze

dreamer *noun* idealist, daydreamer, escapist, fantasist, utopian, visionary, Walter Mitty

dreamy *adjective* 1 vague, absent, abstracted, daydreaming, faraway, pensive, preoccupied, with one's head in the clouds 2 impractical, airy-fairy, fanciful, imaginary, quixotic, speculative

➤ **Antonyms**
common-sense, down-to-earth, feet-on-the-ground, practical, pragmatic, realistic, unromantic

dreary *adjective* dull, boring, drab, humdrum, monotonous, tedious, tiresome, uneventful, wearisome

➤ **Antonyms**
bright, interesting

dregs *plural noun* 1 sediment, deposit, dross, grounds, lees, residue, residuum, scum, waste 2 scum, good-for-nothings, rabble, ragtag and bobtail, riffraff

drench *verb* soak, drown, flood, inundate, saturate, souse, steep, swamp, wet

dress *noun* 1 frock, gown, outfit, robe 2 clothing, apparel, attire, clothes, costume, garb, garments, togs ♦ *verb* 4 put on, attire, change, clothe, don, garb, robe, slip on or into 4 bandage, bind up, plaster, treat 5 arrange, adjust, align, get ready, prepare, straighten

➤ **Antonyms**
verb ≠put on: disrobe, shed, strip, take off one's clothes

dressmaker *noun* seamstress, couturier, tailor

dribble *verb* 1 run, drip, drop, fall in drops, leak, ooze, seep, trickle 2 drool, drivel, slaver, slobber

drift *verb* 1 float, be carried along, coast, go (aimlessly), meander, stray, waft, wander 2 pile up, accumulate, amass, bank up, drive, gather ♦ *noun* 3 pile, accumulation, bank, heap, mass, mound 4 meaning, direction, gist, import, intention, purport, significance, tendency, thrust

drifter noun <u>wanderer</u>, beachcomber, bum (*informal*), hobo (*U.S.*), itinerant, rolling stone, vagrant

drill noun **1** <u>boring tool</u>, bit, borer, gimlet **2** <u>training</u>, discipline, exercise, instruction, practice, preparation, repetition ♦ verb **3** <u>bore</u>, penetrate, perforate, pierce, puncture, sink in **4** <u>train</u>, coach, discipline, exercise, instruct, practise, rehearse, teach

drink verb **1** <u>swallow</u>, gulp, guzzle, imbibe, quaff, sip, suck, sup **2** <u>booze</u> (*informal*), hit the bottle (*informal*), tipple, tope ♦ noun **3** <u>beverage</u>, liquid, potion, refreshment **4** <u>alcohol</u>, booze (*informal*), hooch or hootch (*informal, chiefly U.S. & Canad.*), liquor, spirits, the bottle (*informal*) **5** <u>glass</u>, cup, draught

drip verb **1** <u>drop</u>, dribble, exude, plop, splash, sprinkle, trickle ♦ noun **2** <u>drop</u>, dribble, leak, trickle **3** *Informal* <u>weakling</u>, mummy's boy (*informal*), namby-pamby, softie (*informal*), weed (*informal*), wet (*Brit. informal*)

drive verb **1** <u>operate</u>, direct, guide, handle, manage, motor, ride, steer, travel **2** <u>goad</u>, coerce, constrain, force, press, prod, prompt, spur **3** <u>push</u>, herd, hurl, impel, propel, send, urge **4** <u>thrust</u>, hammer, push, ram ♦ noun **5** <u>run</u>, excursion, jaunt, journey, outing, ride, spin (*informal*), trip **6** <u>campaign</u>, action, appeal, crusade, effort, push (*informal*) **7** <u>initiative</u>, ambition, energy, enterprise, get-up-and-go (*informal*), motivation, vigour, zip (*informal*)

drivel noun **1** <u>nonsense</u>, garbage (*informal*), gibberish, hogwash, hot air (*informal*), poppycock (*informal*), rubbish, trash, twaddle, waffle (*informal, chiefly Brit.*) ♦ verb **2** <u>babble</u>, blether, gab (*informal*), prate, ramble, waffle (*informal, chiefly Brit.*)

driving adjective <u>forceful</u>, compelling, dynamic, energetic, storm-ing (*informal*), sweeping, vigorous, violent

drizzle noun **1** <u>fine rain</u>, Scotch mist ♦ verb **2** <u>rain</u>, shower, spot or spit with rain, spray, sprinkle

droll adjective <u>amusing</u>, comical, entertaining, funny, humorous, jocular, waggish, whimsical

drone verb **1** <u>hum</u>, buzz, purr, thrum, vibrate, whirr **2 drone on** <u>speak monotonously</u>, be boring, chant, intone, spout, talk interminably ♦ noun **3** <u>hum</u>, buzz, murmuring, purr, thrum, vibration, whirring

drool verb **1** <u>dribble</u>, drivel, salivate, slaver, slobber, water at the mouth **2 drool over** <u>gloat over</u>, dote on, gush, make much of, rave about (*informal*)

droop verb **1** <u>sag</u>, bend, dangle, drop, fall down, hang (down), sink

drop verb **1** <u>fall</u>, decline, descend, diminish, plummet, plunge, sink, tumble **2** <u>drip</u>, dribble, fall in drops, trickle **3** <u>discontinue</u>, axe (*informal*), give up, kick (*informal*), quit, relinquish ♦ noun **4** <u>droplet</u>, bead, bubble, drip, globule, pearl, tear **5** <u>dash</u>, mouthful, shot (*informal*), sip, spot, tot, trace, trickle **6** <u>decrease</u>, cut, decline, deterioration, downturn, fall-off, lowering, reduction, slump **7** <u>fall</u>, descent, plunge

drop off verb **1** <u>set down</u>, deliver, leave, let off **2** *Informal* <u>fall asleep</u>, doze (off), have forty winks (*informal*), nod (off), snooze (*informal*) **3** <u>decrease</u>, decline, diminish, dwindle, fall off, lessen, slacken

drop out verb <u>leave</u>, abandon, fall by the wayside, give up, quit, stop, withdraw

drought noun <u>dry spell</u>, aridity, dehydration, dryness

➤ **Antonyms**

deluge, downpour, flood

drove noun <u>herd</u>, collection, company, crowd, flock, horde, mob, multitude, swarm, throng

drown verb 1 drench, deluge, engulf, flood, go under, immerse, inundate, sink, submerge, swamp 2 overpower, deaden, muffle, obliterate, overcome, overwhelm, stifle, swallow up, wipe out

drowsy adjective sleepy, dopey (slang), dozy, half asleep, heavy, lethargic, somnolent, tired, torpid

► Antonyms

alert, awake, lively, perky

drudge noun menial, dogsbody (informal), factotum, servant, skivvy (chiefly Brit.), slave, toiler, worker

drudgery noun menial labour, donkey-work, fag (informal), grind (informal), hard work, labour, skivvying (Brit.), slog, toil

drug noun 1 medication, medicament, medicine, physic, poison, remedy 2 dope (slang), narcotic, opiate, stimulant ♦ verb 3 dose, administer a drug, dope (slang), medicate, treat 4 knock out, anaesthetize, deaden, numb, poison, stupefy

drum verb 1 beat, pulsate, rap, reverberate, tap, tattoo, throb 2 **drum into** drive home, din into, hammer away, harp on, instil into, reiterate

drunk adjective 1 intoxicated, drunken, inebriated, legless (informal), merry (Brit. informal), plastered (slang), tipsy, under the influence (informal) ♦ noun 2 drunkard, alcoholic, boozer (informal), inebriate, lush (slang), wino (informal)

drunkard noun drinker, alcoholic, dipsomaniac, drunk, lush (slang), tippler, wino (informal)

drunkenness noun intoxication, alcoholism, bibulousness, dipsomania, inebriation, insobriety, intemperance

dry adjective 1 dehydrated, arid, barren, desiccated, dried up, parched, thirsty 2 dull, boring, dreary, monotonous, plain, tedious, tiresome, uninteresting 3

sarcastic, deadpan, droll, lowkey, sly ♦ verb 4 dehydrate, dehumidify, desiccate, drain, make dry, parch, sear

► Antonyms

adjective ≠dehydrated: damp, humid, moist, wet ≠dull: entertaining, interesting, lively ♦ verb ≠dehydrate: moisten, wet

dry out or **up** verb become dry, harden, shrivel up, wilt, wither, wizen

dual adjective twofold, binary, double, duplex, duplicate, matched, paired, twin

dubious adjective 1 suspect, fishy (informal), questionable, suspicious, unreliable, untrustworthy 2 unsure, doubtful, hesitant, sceptical, uncertain, unconvinced, undecided, wavering

► Antonyms

≠suspect: dependable, reliable, trustworthy ≠unsure: certain, definite, positive, sure

duck verb 1 bob, bend, bow, crouch, dodge, drop, lower, stoop 2 plunge, dip, dive, douse, dunk, immerse, souse, submerge, wet 3 Informal dodge, avoid, escape, evade, shirk, shun, sidestep

dud Informal ♦ noun 1 failure, flop (informal), washout (informal) ♦ adjective 2 useless, broken, duff (Brit. informal), failed, inoperative, worthless

dudgeon noun in high dudgeon indignant, angry, choked, fuming, offended, resentful, vexed

due adjective 1 expected, scheduled 2 payable, in arrears, outstanding, owed, owing, unpaid 3 fitting, appropriate, deserved, justified, merited, proper, rightful, suitable, well-earned ♦ noun 4 right(s), comeuppance (slang), deserts, merits, privilege ♦ adverb 5 directly, dead, exactly, straight, undeviatingly

duel noun 1 single combat, affair of honour 2 contest, clash, competition, encounter, engagement, fight, head-to-head, rivalry ♦ *verb* **3** fight, clash, compete, contend, contest, lock horns, rival, struggle, vie with

dues *plural noun* membership fee, charge, charges, contribution, fee, levy

dull *adjective* **1** boring, dreary, flat, humdrum, monotonous, plain, run-of-the-mill, tedious, uninteresting **2** stupid, dense, dim-witted (*informal*), dozy (*Brit. informal*), slow, thick, unintelligent **3** cloudy, dim, dismal, gloomy, leaden, overcast **4** lifeless, apathetic, blank, indifferent, listless, passionless, unresponsive **5** blunt, blunted, unsharpened ♦ *verb* **6** relieve, allay, alleviate, blunt, lessen, moderate, soften, take the edge off

➤ **Antonyms**
adjective ≠boring: exciting, interesting ≠stupid: bright, clever, intelligent, sharp ≠cloudy: bright ≠lifeless: active, full of beans (*informal*), lively ≠blunt: sharp

duly *adverb* **1** properly, accordingly, appropriately, befittingly, correctly, decorously, deservedly, fittingly, rightfully, suitably **2** on time, at the proper time, punctually

dumb *adjective* **1** mute, mum, silent, soundless, speechless, tongue-tied, voiceless, wordless **2** *Informal* stupid, asinine, dense, dim-witted (*informal*), dull, foolish, thick, unintelligent

➤ **Antonyms**
≠mute: articulate ≠stupid: bright, clever, intelligent, quick-witted, smart

dumbfounded *adjective* amazed, astonished, astounded, flabbergasted (*informal*), lost for words, nonplussed, overwhelmed, speechless, staggered, stunned

dummy *noun* **1** model, figure, form, manikin, mannequin **2** copy, counterfeit, duplicate, imitation, sham, substitute **3** *Slang* fool, blockhead, dumb-ass (*slang*), dunce, idiot, nitwit (*informal*), numbskull or numskull, oaf, simpleton ♦ *adjective* **4** imita-

tion, artificial, bogus, fake, false, mock, phoney or phony (*informal*), sham, simulated

dump *verb* **1** drop, deposit, fling down, let fall, throw down **2** get rid of, dispose of, ditch (*slang*), empty out, jettison, scrap, throw away or out, tip, unload ♦ *noun* **3** rubbish tip, junkyard, refuse heap, rubbish heap, tip **4** *Informal* pigsty, hole (*informal*), hovel, mess, slum

dunce *noun* simpleton, blockhead, duffer (*informal*), dunderhead, ignoramus, moron, nincompoop, numbskull or numskull, thickhead

dungeon *noun* prison, cage, cell, oubliette, vault

duplicate *adjective* **1** identical, corresponding, matched, matching, twin, twofold ♦ *noun* **2** copy, carbon copy, clone, double, facsimile, photocopy, replica, reproduction ♦ *verb* **3** copy, clone, double, repeat, replicate, reproduce

durability *noun* durableness, constancy, endurance, imperishability, permanence, persistence

durable *adjective* long-lasting, dependable, enduring, hard-wearing, persistent, reliable, resistant, strong, sturdy, tough

➤ **Antonyms**
breakable, brittle, delicate, fragile, perishable, weak

duration *noun* length, extent, period, span, spell, stretch, term, time

duress *noun* pressure, coercion, compulsion, constraint, threat

dusk *noun* twilight, dark, evening, eventide, gloaming (*Scot. or poetic*), nightfall, sundown, sunset

➤ **Antonyms**
cockcrow, dawn, daybreak, daylight, morning

dusky *adjective* **1** dark, dark-complexioned, sable, swarthy **2** dim, cloudy, gloomy, murky, obscure, shadowy, shady, tenebrous, twilit

dust noun **1** grime, grit, particles, powder ♦ verb **2** sprinkle, cover, dredge, powder, scatter, sift, spray, spread

dusty adjective dirty, grubby, sooty, unclean, unswept

dutiful adjective conscientious, devoted, obedient, respectful, reverential, submissive

➤ Antonyms
disobedient, disrespectful, insubordinate, remiss

duty noun **1** responsibility, assignment, function, job, obligation, role, task, work **2** loyalty, allegiance, deference, obedience, respect, reverence, toll **3** tax, excise, levy, tariff, toll **4 on duty** at work, busy, engaged; on active service

dwarf verb **1** tower above or over, diminish, dominate, overshadow ♦ adjective **2** miniature, baby, bonsai, diminutive, small, tiny, undersized ♦ noun **3** midget, Lilliputian, pygmy or pigmy, Tom Thumb

dwell verb Formal, literary live, abide, inhabit, lodge, reside

dwelling noun Formal, literary home, abode, domicile, habitation, house, lodging, quarters, residence

dwindle verb lessen, decline, decrease, die away, diminish, fade, peter out, shrink, subside, taper off, wane

➤ Antonyms
enlarge, expand, grow, heighten, increase, magnify, multiply

dye noun **1** colouring, colorant, colour, pigment, stain, tinge, tint ♦ verb **2** colour, pigment, stain, tinge, tint

dying adjective expiring, at death's door, failing, in extremis, moribund, not long for this world

dynamic adjective energetic, forceful, go-ahead, go-getting (informal), high-powered, lively, powerful, storming (informal), vital

➤ Antonyms
apathetic, inactive, listless, sluggish, torpid, undynamic, unenergetic

dynasty noun empire, government, house, regime, rule, sovereignty

E e

each adjective **1** every ♦ pronoun **2** every one, each and every one, each one, one and all ♦ adverb **3** apiece, for each, individually, per capita, per head, per person, respectively, to each

eager adjective keen, agog, anxious, athirst, avid, enthusiastic, fervent, hungry, impatient, longing

➤ Antonyms
apathetic, blasé, impassive, indifferent, lazy, nonchalant, unenthusiastic, uninterested

eagerness noun keenness, ardour, enthusiasm, fervour, hunger, impatience, thirst, yearning, zeal

ear noun sensitivity, appreciation, discrimination, taste

early adjective **1** premature, advanced, forward, untimely **2** primitive, primeval, primordial, undeveloped, young ♦ adverb **3** too soon, ahead of time, beforehand, in advance, in good time, prematurely

➤ Antonyms
adjective ≠primitive: developed, mature, ripe, seasoned ♦ adverb ≠too soon: behind, belated, late, overdue, tardy

earmark verb set aside, allocate, designate, flag, label, mark out, reserve

earn verb **1** make, bring in, collect, gain, get, gross, net, receive **2** deserve, acquire, attain, be entitled to, be worthy of, merit, rate, warrant, win

earnest adjective **1** <u>serious</u>, grave, intent, resolute, resolved, sincere, solemn, thoughtful ♦ noun **2** As in **in earnest** <u>seriousness</u>, sincerity, truth

➤ **Antonyms**

adjective ≠<u>serious</u>: flippant, frivolous, insincere ♦ noun ≠<u>seriousness</u>: apathy, indifference, unconcern

earnings plural noun <u>income</u>, pay, proceeds, profits, receipts, remuneration, salary, takings, wages

earth noun **1** <u>world</u>, globe, orb, planet, sphere **2** <u>soil</u>, clay, dirt, ground, land, turf

earthenware noun <u>crockery</u>, ceramics, pots, pottery, terracotta

earthly adjective **1** <u>worldly</u>, human, material, mortal, secular, temporal **2** Informal <u>possible</u>, conceivable, feasible, imaginable, likely, practical

➤ **Antonyms**

≠<u>worldly</u>: ethereal, heavenly, immaterial, immortal, otherworldly, spiritual, supernatural, unearthly

earthy adjective <u>crude</u>, bawdy, coarse, raunchy (slang), ribald, robust, uninhibited, unsophisticated

ease noun **1** <u>effortlessness</u>, easiness, facility, readiness, simplicity **2** <u>peace of mind</u>, comfort, content, happiness, peace, quiet, serenity, tranquillity **3** <u>leisure</u>, relaxation, repose, rest, restfulness ♦ verb **4** <u>relieve</u>, alleviate, calm, comfort, lessen, lighten, relax, soothe **5** <u>move carefully</u>, edge, inch, manoeuvre, slide, slip

➤ **Antonyms**

≠<u>effortlessness</u>: arduousness, awkwardness, clumsiness, difficulty, effort, exertion ≠<u>peace of mind</u>: agitation, discomfort, disturbance, tension noun ≠<u>leisure</u>: difficulty, discomfort, hardship, pain ♦ verb ≠<u>relieve</u>: aggravate, exacerbate, irritate, worsen

easily adverb <u>without difficulty</u>, comfortably, effortlessly, readily, smoothly, with ease, with one hand tied behind one's back

easy adjective **1** <u>not difficult</u>, a piece of cake (informal), child's play (informal), effortless, no trouble, painless, plain sailing, simple, straightforward, uncomplicated, undemanding **2** <u>carefree</u>, comfortable, cushy (informal), leisurely, peaceful, quiet, relaxed, serene, tranquil, untroubled **3** <u>tolerant</u>, easy-going, indulgent, lenient, mild, permissive, unoppressive

➤ **Antonyms**

≠<u>not difficult</u>: arduous, complex, demanding, difficult, exacting, exhausting, hard, impossible, stiff ≠<u>carefree</u>: difficult, stressful, uncomfortable, worried ≠<u>tolerant</u>: dictatorial, exacting, hard, harsh, inflexible, intolerant, rigid, stern, strict

easy-going adjective <u>relaxed</u>, carefree, casual, easy, even-tempered, happy-go-lucky, laid-back (informal), nonchalant, placid, tolerant, undemanding

➤ **Antonyms**

anxious, edgy, fussy, intolerant, neurotic, on edge, tense, uptight (informal)

eat verb **1** <u>consume</u>, chew, devour, gobble, ingest, munch, scoff (slang), swallow **2** <u>have a meal</u>, dine, feed, take nourishment **3** <u>destroy</u>, corrode, decay, dissolve, erode, rot, waste away, wear away

eavesdrop verb <u>listen in</u>, earwig (informal), monitor, overhear, snoop (informal), spy

ebb verb **1** <u>flow back</u>, go out, recede, retire, retreat, subside, wane, withdraw **2** <u>decline</u>, decrease, diminish, dwindle, fade away, fall away, flag, lessen, peter out ♦ noun **2** <u>flowing back</u>, going out, low tide, low water, retreat, subsidence, wane, withdrawal

eccentric adjective **1** <u>odd</u>, freakish, idiosyncratic, irregular, outlandish, peculiar, quirky, strange, unconventional ♦ *noun* **2** <u>crank</u> (*informal*), character (*informal*), nonconformist, oddball (*informal*), weirdo or weirdie (*informal*)

► **Antonyms**

adjective ≠*odd*: average, conventional, normal, ordinary, regular, run-of-the-mill, straightforward, typical

eccentricity *noun* <u>oddity</u>, abnormality, caprice, capriciousness, foible, idiosyncrasy, irregularity, peculiarity, quirk

ecclesiastic *noun* **1** <u>clergyman</u>, churchman, cleric, holy man, man of the cloth, minister, parson, pastor, priest ♦ *adjective* **2** *Also* **ecclesiastical** <u>clerical</u>, divine, holy, pastoral, priestly, religious, spiritual

echo *noun* **1** <u>repetition</u>, answer, reverberation **2** <u>copy</u>, imitation, mirror image, parallel, reflection, reiteration, reproduction ♦ *verb* **3** <u>repeat</u>, resound, reverberate **4** <u>copy</u>, ape, imitate, mirror, parallel, recall, reflect, resemble

eclipse *noun* **1** <u>obscuring</u>, darkening, dimming, extinction, shading ♦ *verb* **2** <u>surpass</u>, exceed, excel, outdo, outshine, put in the shade (*informal*), transcend

economic *adjective* **1** <u>financial</u>, commercial, industrial **2** <u>profitable</u>, money-making, productive, profit-making, remunerative, viable **3** *Informal Also* **economical** <u>inexpensive</u>, cheap, low-priced, modest, reasonable

economical *adjective* **1** <u>thrifty</u>, careful, frugal, prudent, scrimping, sparing **2** <u>cost-effective</u>, efficient, money-saving, sparing, time-saving

► **Antonyms**

≠*thrifty*: extravagant, generous, imprudent, lavish, profligate, spendthrift, uneconomical, unthrifty, wasteful ≠*cost-effective*: loss-making, uneconomical, unprofitable, wasteful

economize *verb* <u>cut back</u>, be

economical, be frugal, draw in one's horns, retrench, save, scrimp, tighten one's belt

► **Antonyms**

be extravagant, push the boat out (*informal*), spend, splurge, squander

economy *noun* <u>thrift</u>, frugality, husbandry, parsimony, prudence, restraint

ecstasy *noun* <u>rapture</u>, bliss, delight, elation, euphoria, fervour, joy, seventh heaven

► **Antonyms**

affliction, agony, anguish, distress, hell, misery, pain, suffering, torment, torture

ecstatic *adjective* <u>rapturous</u>, blissful, elated, enraptured, entranced, euphoric, in seventh heaven, joyous, on cloud nine (*informal*), overjoyed

eddy *noun* **1** <u>swirl</u>, countercurrent, counterflow, undertow, vortex, whirlpool ♦ *verb* **2** <u>swirl</u>, whirl

edge *noun* **1** <u>border</u>, boundary, brink, fringe, limit, outline, perimeter, rim, side, verge **2** <u>sharpness</u>, bite, effectiveness, force, incisiveness, keenness, point **3** *As in* **have the edge on** <u>advantage</u>, ascendancy, dominance, lead, superiority, upper hand **4** *As in* **on edge** <u>nervous</u>, apprehensive, edgy, ill at ease, impatient, irritable, keyed up, on tenterhooks, tense ♦ *verb* **5** <u>border</u>, fringe, hem **6** <u>inch</u>, creep, ease, sidle, steal

edgy *adjective* <u>nervous</u>, anxious, ill at ease, irritable, keyed up, on edge, on tenterhooks, restive, tense

edible *adjective* <u>eatable</u>, digestible, fit to eat, good, harmless, palatable, wholesome

► **Antonyms**

harmful, indigestible, inedible, poisonous, uneatable

edict *noun* <u>decree</u>, act, command, injunction, law, order, proclamation, ruling

edifice *noun* <u>building</u>, construction, erection, house, structure

edify verb instruct, educate, enlighten, guide, improve, inform, nurture, school, teach

edit verb revise, adapt, condense, correct, emend, polish, rewrite

edition noun version, copy, impression, issue, number, printing, programme (*TV, Radio*), volume

educate verb teach, civilize, develop, discipline, enlighten, improve, inform, instruct, school, train, tutor

educated adjective **1** taught, coached, informed, instructed, nurtured, schooled, tutored **2** cultured, civilized, cultivated, enlightened, knowledgeable, learned, refined, sophisticated

➤ **Antonyms**

≠taught: ignorant, illiterate, uneducated, unlettered, unread, unschooled, untaught ≠cultured: lowbrow, philistine, uncultivated, uncultured, uneducated

education noun teaching, development, discipline, enlightenment, instruction, nurture, schooling, training, tuition

educational adjective instructive, cultural, edifying, educative, enlightening, improving, informative

eerie adjective frightening, creepy (*informal*), ghostly, mysterious, scary (*informal*), spooky (*informal*), strange, uncanny, unearthly, weird

efface verb obliterate, blot out, cancel, delete, destroy, eradicate, erase, rub out, wipe out

effect noun **1** result, conclusion, consequence, end result, event, outcome, upshot **2** operation, action, enforcement, execution, force, implementation **3** impression, essence, impact, sense, significance, tenor ◆ verb **4** bring about, accomplish, achieve, complete, execute, fulfil, perform, produce

effective adjective **1** efficient, active, adequate, capable, competent, productive, serviceable, useful **2** in operation, active, current, in effect, in force, operative **3** powerful, cogent, compelling, convincing, forceful, impressive, persuasive, telling

➤ **Antonyms**

≠efficient: futile, inadequate, incompetent, ineffective, inefficient, insufficient, unproductive, useless, vain, worthless ≠in operation: inactive, inoperative ≠powerful: feeble, ineffectual, pathetic, powerless, tame, weak

effects plural noun belongings, gear, goods, paraphernalia, possessions, property, things

effeminate adjective womanly, camp (*informal*), feminine, sissy, soft, tender, unmanly, weak, womanish

➤ **Antonyms**

butch (*slang*), macho, manly, virile

effervescent adjective **1** bubbling, carbonated, fizzy, foaming, frothy, sparkling **2** lively, animated, bubbly, ebullient, enthusiastic, exuberant, irrepressible, vivacious

➤ **Antonyms**

≠bubbling: flat, stale, watery ≠lively: boring, dull, flat, insipid, lacklustre, lifeless, stale, unexciting

effete adjective decadent, dissipated, enfeebled, feeble, ineffectual, spoiled, weak

efficacious adjective effective, adequate, efficient, operative, potent, powerful, productive, successful, useful

➤ **Antonyms**

futile, ineffective, ineffectual, inefficacious, unproductive, unsuccessful, useless

efficiency noun competence, adeptness, capability, economy, effectiveness, power, productivity, proficiency

efficient adjective competent, businesslike, capable, economic, effective, organized, productive, proficient, well-organized, workmanlike

> **Antonyms**

disorganized, incompetent, inefficient, inept, slipshod, sloppy, unbusinesslike, unproductive, wasteful

effigy noun likeness, dummy, figure, guy, icon, idol, image, picture, portrait, representation, statue

effluent noun waste, effluvium, pollutant, sewage

effort noun 1 exertion, application, elbow grease (*facetious*), endeavour, energy, pains, struggle, toil, trouble, work 2 attempt, endeavour, essay, go (*informal*), shot (*informal*), stab (*informal*), try

effortless adjective easy, painless, plain sailing, simple, smooth, uncomplicated, undemanding

> **Antonyms**

demanding, difficult, formidable, hard, onerous, uphill

effrontery noun insolence, arrogance, audacity, brazenness, cheek (*informal*), impertinence, impudence, nerve, presumption, temerity

effusive adjective demonstrative, ebullient, expansive, exuberant, gushing, lavish, unreserved, unrestrained

egg on verb encourage, exhort, goad, incite, prod, prompt, push, spur, urge

> **Antonyms**

deter, discourage, dissuade, hold back, put off, talk out of

egocentric adjective self-centred, egoistic, egoistical, egotistic, egotistical, selfish

egotism, egoism noun self-centredness, conceitedness, narcissism, self-absorption, self-esteem, self-importance, self-interest, selfishness, vanity

egotist, egoist noun egomaniac, bighead (*informal*), boaster, braggart, narcissist

egotistic, egotistical, egoistic or **egoistical** adjective self-centred, boasting, conceited, egocentric, full of oneself, narcis-

sistic, self-absorbed, self-important, vain

egress noun Formal exit, departure, exodus, way out, withdrawal

eject verb throw out, banish, drive out, evict, expel, oust, remove, turn out

ejection noun expulsion, banishment, deportation, eviction, exile, removal

eke out verb be sparing with, economize on, husband, stretch out

elaborate adjective 1 detailed, intricate, minute, painstaking, precise, studied, thorough 2 complicated, complex, fancy, fussy, involved, ornamented, ornate ◆ verb 3 expand (upon), add detail, amplify, develop, embellish, enlarge, flesh out

> **Antonyms**

adjective ≠complicated: basic, minimal, modest, plain, severe, simple, unadorned, unembellished, unfussy ◆ verb ≠expand (upon): abbreviate, condense, simplify, summarize

elapse verb pass, glide by, go by, lapse, roll by, slip away

elastic adjective 1 flexible, plastic, pliable, pliant, resilient, rubbery, springy, stretchy, supple, tensile 2 adaptable, accommodating, adjustable, compliant, flexible, supple, tolerant, variable, yielding

> **Antonyms**

≠flexible: firm, immovable, inflexible, rigid, set, stiff, unyielding ≠adaptable: firm, immovable, inflexible, intractable, obdurate, resolute, rigid, set, stiff, strict, unyielding

elated adjective joyful, cock-a-hoop, delighted, ecstatic, euphoric, exhilarated, gleeful, jubilant, overjoyed

> **Antonyms**

dejected, depressed, discouraged, dispirited, downcast, miserable, sad, unhappy

elation noun joy, bliss, delight,

ecstasy, euphoria, exhilaration, glee, high spirits, jubilation, rapture

elbow noun 1 joint, angle ◆ verb 2 push, jostle, knock, nudge, shove

elbow room noun scope, freedom, latitude, leeway, play, room, space

elder adjective 1 older, first-born, senior ◆ noun 2 older person, senior

elect verb choose, appoint, determine, opt for, pick, prefer, select, settle on, vote

election noun voting, appointment, choice, judgment, preference, selection, vote

elector noun voter, constituent, selector

electric adjective charged, dynamic, exciting, rousing, stimulating, stirring, tense, thrilling

electrify verb startle, astound, excite, galvanize, invigorate, jolt, shock, stir, thrill

➤ **Antonyms**
be tedious, bore, exhaust, jade, tire, weary

elegance noun style, dignity, exquisiteness, grace, gracefulness, grandeur, luxury, refinement, taste

elegant adjective stylish, chic, delicate, exquisite, fine, graceful, handsome, polished, refined, tasteful

➤ **Antonyms**
clumsy, graceless, inelegant, plain, tasteless, tawdry, ugly, ungraceful, unrefined

element noun 1 component, constituent, factor, ingredient, part, section, subdivision, unit 2 As in **in one's element** environment, domain, field, habitat, medium, milieu, sphere

elementary adjective simple, clear, easy, plain, rudimentary, straightforward, uncomplicated

➤ **Antonyms**
complex, complicated, sophisticated

elements plural noun 1 basics, es-

sentials, foundations, fundamentals, nuts and bolts (informal), principles, rudiments 2 weather conditions, atmospheric conditions, powers of nature

elevate verb 1 raise, heighten, hoist, lift, lift up, uplift 2 promote, advance, aggrandize, exalt, prefer, upgrade

elevated adjective high-minded, dignified, exalted, grand, high-flown, inflated, lofty, noble, sublime

➤ **Antonyms**
humble, lowly, modest, simple

elevation noun 1 promotion, advancement, aggrandizement, exaltation, preferment, upgrading 2 altitude, height

elicit verb 1 bring about, bring forth, bring out, bring to light, call forth, cause, derive, evolve, give rise to 2 obtain, draw out, evoke, exact, extort, extract, wrest

eligible adjective qualified, acceptable, appropriate, desirable, fit, preferable, proper, suitable, worthy

➤ **Antonyms**
inappropriate, ineligible, unacceptable, unqualified, unsuitable

eliminate verb get rid of, cut out, dispose of, do away with, eradicate, exterminate, remove, stamp out, take out

elite noun best, aristocracy, cream, crème de la crème, flower, nobility, pick, upper class

➤ **Antonyms**
dregs, hoi polloi, rabble, riffraff

elitist adjective snobbish, exclusive, selective

elixir noun panacea, nostrum

elocution noun diction, articulation, declamation, delivery, enunciation, oratory, pronunciation, speech, speechmaking

elongate verb make longer, draw out, extend, lengthen, prolong, protract, stretch

elope verb run away, abscond, bolt, decamp, disappear, escape, leave, run off, slip away, steal away

eloquence noun expressiveness, expression, fluency, forcefulness, oratory, persuasiveness, rhetoric, way with words

eloquent adjective **1** silver-tongued, articulate, fluent, forceful, moving, persuasive, stirring, well-expressed **2** expressive, meaningful, suggestive, telling, vivid

➤ **Antonyms**

≠ silver-tongued: faltering, halting, hesitant, inarticulate, speechless, stumbling, tongue-tied, wordless

elsewhere adverb in or to another place, abroad, away, hence (archaic), not here, somewhere else

elucidate verb clarify, clear up, explain, explicate, expound, illuminate, illustrate, make plain, shed or throw light upon, spell out

elude verb **1** escape, avoid, dodge, duck (informal), evade, flee, get away from, outrun **2** baffle, be beyond (someone), confound, escape, foil, frustrate, puzzle, stump, thwart

elusive adjective **1** difficult to catch, shifty, slippery, tricky **2** indefinable, fleeting, intangible, subtle, transient, transitory

emaciated adjective skeletal, cadaverous, gaunt, haggard, lean, pinched, scrawny, thin, undernourished, wasted

emanate verb flow, arise, come forth, derive, emerge, issue, originate, proceed, spring, stem

emancipate verb free, deliver, liberate, release, set free, unchain, unfetter

➤ **Antonyms**

bind, capture, enchain, enslave, fetter, subjugate, yoke

emancipation noun freedom, deliverance, liberation, liberty, release

➤ **Antonyms**

bondage, captivity, confine-

ment, imprisonment, servitude, slavery

embalm verb preserve, mummify

embargo noun **1** ban, bar, boycott, interdiction, prohibition, restraint, restriction, stoppage ♦ verb **2** ban, bar, block, boycott, prohibit, restrict, stop

embark verb **1** go aboard, board ship, take ship **2** embark on or upon begin, commence, enter, launch, plunge into, set about, set out, start, take up

➤ **Antonyms**

≠ go aboard: alight, arrive, get off, go ashore, land, step out of

embarrass verb shame, discomfit, disconcert, distress, fluster, humiliate, mortify, show up (informal)

embarrassed adjective ashamed, awkward, blushing, discomfited, disconcerted, humiliated, mortified, red-faced, self-conscious, sheepish

embarrassing adjective humiliating, awkward, compromising, discomfiting, disconcerting, mortifying, sensitive, shameful, toe-curling (slang), uncomfortable

embarrassment noun **1** shame, awkwardness, bashfulness, distress, humiliation, mortification, self-consciousness, showing up (informal) **2** predicament, bind (informal), difficulty, mess, pickle (informal), scrape (informal)

embellish verb decorate, adorn, beautify, elaborate, embroider, enhance, enrich, festoon, ornament

embellishment noun decoration, adornment, elaboration, embroidery, enhancement, enrichment, exaggeration, ornament, ornamentation

embezzle verb misappropriate, appropriate, filch, misuse, pilfer, purloin, rip off (slang), steal

embezzlement noun misappropriation, appropriation, filching, fraud, misuse, peculation, pilfering, stealing, theft

embittered *adjective* <u>resentful</u>, angry, bitter, disaffected, disillusioned, rancorous, soured, with a chip on one's shoulder (*informal*)

emblem *noun* <u>symbol</u>, badge, crest, image, insignia, mark, sign, token

embodiment *noun* <u>personification</u>, epitome, example, exemplar, expression, incarnation, representation, symbol

embody *verb* **1** <u>personify</u>, exemplify, manifest, represent, stand for, symbolize, typify **2** <u>incorporate</u>, collect, combine, comprise, contain, include

embolden *verb* <u>encourage</u>, fire, inflame, invigorate, rouse, stimulate, stir, strengthen

embrace *verb* **1** <u>hug</u>, clasp, cuddle, envelop, hold, seize, squeeze, take *or* hold in one's arms **2** <u>accept</u>, adopt, espouse, seize, take on board, take up, welcome **3** <u>include</u>, comprehend, comprise, contain, cover, encompass, involve, take in ♦ *noun* **4** <u>hug</u>, clasp, clinch (*slang*), cuddle, squeeze

embroil *verb* <u>involve</u>, enmesh, ensnare, entangle, implicate, incriminate, mire, mix up

embryo *noun* <u>germ</u>, beginning, nucleus, root, rudiment

emend *verb* <u>revise</u>, amend, correct, edit, improve, rectify

emendation *noun* <u>revision</u>, amendment, correction, editing, improvement, rectification

emerge *verb* **1** <u>come into view</u>, appear, arise, come forth, emanate, issue, rise, spring up, surface **2** <u>become apparent</u>, become known, come out, come out in the wash, come to light, crop up, transpire

► **Antonyms**

≠ <u>come into view</u>: depart, disappear, fade, sink, submerge, vanish from sight, wane, withdraw

emergence *noun* <u>coming</u>, advent, appearance, arrival, development, materialization, rise

emergency *noun* <u>crisis</u>, danger, difficulty, extremity, necessity, plight, predicament, quandary, scrape (*informal*)

emigrate *verb* <u>move abroad</u>, migrate, move

emigration *noun* <u>departure</u>, exodus, migration

eminence *noun* <u>prominence</u>, distinction, esteem, fame, greatness, importance, note, prestige, renown, repute

eminent *adjective* <u>prominent</u>, celebrated, distinguished, esteemed, famous, high-ranking, illustrious, noted, renowned, well-known

► **Antonyms**

anonymous, commonplace, lowly, ordinary, undistinguished, unheard-of, unimportant, unknown, unremarkable

emission *noun* <u>giving off *or* out</u>, discharge, ejaculation, ejection, exhalation, radiation, shedding, transmission

emit *verb* <u>give off</u>, cast out, discharge, eject, emanate, exude, radiate, send out, transmit

► **Antonyms**

absorb, assimilate, incorporate, ingest, receive, soak up, take in

emotion *noun* <u>feeling</u>, ardour, excitement, fervour, passion, sensation, sentiment, vehemence, warmth

emotional *adjective* **1** <u>sensitive</u>, demonstrative, excitable, hot-blooded, passionate, sentimental, temperamental **2** <u>moving</u>, affecting, emotive, heart-warming, poignant, sentimental, stirring, touching

► **Antonyms**

≠ <u>sensitive</u>: cold, detached, insensitive, undemonstrative, unemotional, unfeeling, unmoved, unsentimental

emotive *adjective* <u>sensitive</u>, controversial, delicate, touchy

emphasis *noun* <u>stress</u>, accent, attention, force, importance, priority, prominence, significance, weight

emphasize verb stress, accentuate, dwell on, give priority to, highlight, lay stress on, play up, press home, underline

➤ **Antonyms**
gloss over, make light of, make little of, minimize, play down, underplay

emphatic adjective forceful, categorical, definite, insistent, positive, pronounced, resounding, unequivocal, unmistakable, vigorous

➤ **Antonyms**
equivocal, hesitant, tentative, uncertain, undecided, unsure

empire noun kingdom, commonwealth, domain, realm

empirical, empiric adjective firsthand, experiential, experimental, observed, practical, pragmatic

➤ **Antonyms**
academic, assumed, conjectural, hypothetical, putative, speculative, theoretic(al)

employ verb 1 hire, commission, engage, enlist, retain, take on 2 keep busy, engage, fill, make use of, occupy, take up, use up 3 use, apply, bring to bear, exercise, exert, make use of, ply, put to use, utilize ♦ noun 4 As in **in the employ of** service, employment, engagement, hire

employed adjective working, active, busy, engaged, in a job, in employment, in work, occupied

➤ **Antonyms**
idle, jobless, laid off, on the dole (Brit. informal), out of a job, out of work, redundant, unoccupied

employee noun worker, hand, job-holder, staff member, wage-earner, workman

employer noun boss (informal), company, firm, gaffer (informal, chiefly Brit.), owner, patron, proprietor

employment noun 1 taking on, engagement, enlistment, hire, retaining 2 use, application, exercise, exertion, utilization 3 job, line, occupation, profession, trade, vocation, work

emporium noun Old-fashioned shop, bazaar, market, mart, store, warehouse

empower verb enable, allow, authorize, commission, delegate, entitle, license, permit, qualify, sanction, warrant

emptiness noun 1 bareness, blankness, desolation, vacancy, vacuum, void, waste 2 purposelessness, banality, futility, hollowness, inanity, meaninglessness, senselessness, vanity, worthlessness 3 insincerity, cheapness, hollowness, idleness

empty adjective 1 bare, blank, clear, deserted, desolate, hollow, unfurnished, uninhabited, unoccupied, vacant, void 2 purposeless, banal, fruitless, futile, hollow, inane, meaningless, senseless, vain, worthless 3 insincere, cheap, hollow, idle ♦ verb 4 evacuate, clear, drain, exhaust, pour out, unload, vacate, void

➤ **Antonyms**
adjective ≠bare: full, inhabited, occupied, packed, stuffed ≠purposeless: busy, fulfilled, full, interesting, meaningful, occupied, purposeful, satisfying, significant, useful, valuable, worthwhile ♦ verb ≠evacuate: cram, fill, pack, replenish, stock, stuff

empty-headed adjective scatter-brained, brainless, dizzy (informal), featherbrained, harebrained, silly, vacuous

emulate verb imitate, compete with, copy, echo, follow, mimic, rival

enable verb allow, authorize, empower, entitle, license, permit, qualify, sanction, warrant

➤ **Antonyms**
bar, block, hinder, impede, obstruct, prevent, stop, thwart

enact verb 1 establish, authorize, command, decree, legislate, ordain, order, proclaim, sanction 2 perform, act out, depict, play, play the part of, portray, represent

enamoured adjective in love, captivated, charmed, enraptured, fond, infatuated, smitten, taken

encampment noun camp, base, bivouac, camping ground, campsite, cantonment, quarters, tents

encapsulate verb sum up, abridge, compress, condense, digest, epitomize, précis, summarize

enchant verb fascinate, beguile, bewitch, captivate, charm, delight, enrapture, enthral, ravish

enchanter noun sorcerer, conjuror, magician, magus, necromancer, warlock, witch, wizard

enchanting adjective fascinating, alluring, attractive, bewitching, captivating, charming, delightful, entrancing, lovely, pleasant

enclose, inclose verb 1 surround, bound, encase, encircle, fence, hem in, shut in, wall in 2 send with, include, insert, put in

encompass verb 1 surround, circle, encircle, enclose, envelop, ring 2 include, admit, comprise, contain, cover, embrace, hold, incorporate, take in

encounter verb 1 meet, bump into (informal), chance upon, come upon, confront, experience, face, run across ♦ noun 2 meeting, brush, confrontation, rendezvous 3 battle, clash, contest, head-to-head, run-in (informal)

encourage verb 1 inspire, buoy up, cheer, comfort, console, embolden, hearten, reassure 2 spur, advocate, egg on, foster, promote, prompt, support, urge

▶ Antonyms

daunt, depress, deter, discourage, dishearten, dispirit, dissuade, hinder, inhibit, intimidate, prevent, retard, scare, throw cold water on (informal)

encouragement noun inspiration, cheer, incitement, promotion, reassurance, stimulation, stimulus, support

encouraging adjective promising, bright, cheerful, comforting,

good, heartening, hopeful, reassuring, rosy

▶ Antonyms

daunting, depressing, disappointing, discouraging, disheartening, dispiriting, off-putting (informal), unfavourable, unpropitious

encroach verb intrude, impinge, infringe, invade, make inroads, overstep, trespass, usurp

encumber verb burden, hamper, handicap, hinder, impede, inconvenience, obstruct, saddle, weigh down

end noun 1 extremity, boundary, edge, extent, extreme, limit, point, terminus, tip 2 finish, cessation, close, closure, ending, expiration, expiry, stop, termination 3 conclusion, culmination, denouement, ending, finale, resolution 4 remnant, butt, fragment, leftover, oddment, remainder, scrap, stub 5 destruction, death, demise, doom, extermination, extinction, ruin 6 purpose, aim, goal, intention, object, objective, point, reason ♦ verb 7 finish, cease, close, conclude, culminate, stop, terminate, wind up

▶ Antonyms

noun ≠finish: beginning, birth, commencement, opening, origin, outset, source, start ♦ verb ≠finish: begin, come into being, commence, initiate, launch, originate, start

endanger verb put at risk, compromise, imperil, jeopardize, put in danger, risk, threaten

▶ Antonyms

defend, guard, preserve, protect, safeguard, save, secure

endearing adjective attractive, captivating, charming, cute, engaging, lovable, sweet, winning

endearment noun loving word, sweet nothing

endeavour Formal ♦ verb 1 try, aim, aspire, attempt, labour, make an effort, strive, struggle, take pains ♦ noun 2 effort, attempt, enterprise, trial, try, undertaking, venture

ending *noun* <u>finish</u>, cessation, close, completion, conclusion, culmination, denouement, end, finale

➤ **Antonyms**
birth, commencement, onset, opening, origin, source, start, starting point

endless *adjective* <u>eternal</u>, boundless, continual, everlasting, incessant, infinite, interminable, unlimited

➤ **Antonyms**
brief, finite, passing, temporary, transient, transitory

endorse *verb* **1** <u>approve</u>, advocate, authorize, back, champion, promote, ratify, recommend, support **2** <u>sign</u>, countersign

endorsement *noun* **1** <u>approval</u>, advocacy, approbation, authorization, backing, favour, ratification, recommendation, seal of approval, support **2** <u>signature</u>, countersignature

endow *verb* <u>provide</u>, award, bequeath, bestow, confer, donate, finance, fund, give

endowment *noun* <u>provision</u>, award, benefaction, bequest, donation, gift, grant, legacy

endurable *adjective* <u>bearable</u>, acceptable, sufferable, sustainable, tolerable

➤ **Antonyms**
insufferable, intolerable, too much (*informal*), unbearable, unendurable

endurance *noun* **1** <u>staying power</u>, fortitude, patience, perseverance, persistence, resolution, stamina, strength, tenacity, toleration **2** <u>permanence</u>, continuity, durability, duration, longevity, stability

endure *verb* **1** <u>bear</u>, cope with, experience, stand, suffer, sustain, undergo, withstand **2** <u>last</u>, continue, live on, persist, remain, stand, stay, survive

enduring *adjective* <u>long-lasting</u>, abiding, continuing, lasting, perennial, persistent, steadfast, unfaltering, unwavering

➤ **Antonyms**
brief, ephemeral, fleeting, momentary, passing, short, short-lived, temporary, transient, transitory

enemy *noun* <u>foe</u>, adversary, antagonist, competitor, opponent, rival, the opposition, the other side

➤ **Antonyms**
ally, confederate, friend, supporter

energetic *adjective* <u>vigorous</u>, active, animated, dynamic, forceful, indefatigable, lively, strenuous, tireless

➤ **Antonyms**
dull, inactive, lazy, lethargic, lifeless, listless, slow, sluggish, torpid, weak

energy *noun* <u>vigour</u>, drive, forcefulness, get-up-and-go (*informal*), liveliness, pep, stamina, verve, vitality

enforce *verb* <u>impose</u>, administer, apply, carry out, execute, implement, insist on, prosecute, put into effect

engage *verb* **1** <u>participate</u>, embark on, enter into, join, set about, take part, undertake **2** <u>occupy</u>, absorb, engross, grip, involve, preoccupy **3** <u>captivate</u>, arrest, catch, fix, gain **4** <u>employ</u>, appoint, enlist, enrol, hire, retain, take on **5** *Military* <u>begin battle with</u>, assail, attack, encounter, fall on, join battle with, meet, take on **6** <u>set going</u>, activate, apply, bring into operation, energize, switch on

➤ **Antonyms**
≠employ: discharge, dismiss, fire (*informal*), give notice to, lay off, sack (*informal*)

engaged *adjective* **1** <u>betrothed</u> (*archaic*), affianced, pledged, promised, spoken for **2** <u>occupied</u>, busy, employed, in use, tied up, unavailable

➤ **Antonyms**
≠betrothed: available, free, unattached, unengaged ≠occupied:

available, free, uncommitted, unengaged

engagement *noun* **1** appointment, arrangement, commitment, date, meeting **2** betrothal,
troth (*archaic*) **3** battle, action,
combat, conflict, encounter, fight

engaging *adjective* charming,
agreeable, fetching (*in-
formal*), likable or likeable, pleasing, winning, winsome

► **Antonyms**

disagreeable, objectionable, obnoxious, offensive, repulsive, unattractive, unlikable or unlikeable

engender *verb* produce, breed,
cause, create, generate, give rise
to, induce, instigate, lead to

engine *noun* machine, mechanism, motor

engineer *verb* bring about, contrive, create, devise, effect,
mastermind, plan, plot, scheme

engrave *verb* **1** carve, chisel, cut,
etch, inscribe **2** fix, embed, impress, imprint, ingrain, lodge

engraving *noun* carving, etching, inscription, plate, woodcut

engross *verb* absorb, engage, immerse, involve, occupy, preoccupy

engrossed *adjective* absorbed,
caught up, enthralled, fascinated, gripped, immersed, lost, preoccupied, rapt, riveted

engulf *verb* immerse, envelop, inundate, overrun, overwhelm,
submerge, swallow up, swamp

enhance *verb* improve, add to,
boost, heighten, increase, lift, reinforce, strengthen, swell

► **Antonyms**

debase, decrease, depreciate, devalue, diminish, lower, minimize,
reduce, spoil

enigma *noun* mystery, conundrum, problem, puzzle, riddle,
teaser

enigmatic *adjective* mysterious,
ambiguous, cryptic, equivocal,
inscrutable, obscure, puzzling,
unfathomable

► **Antonyms**

clear, comprehensible, simple,

straightforward, uncomplicated

enjoy *verb* **1** take pleasure in or
from, appreciate, be entertained
by, be pleased with, delight in,
like, relish **2** have, be blessed or
favoured with, experience, have
the benefit of, own, possess,
reap the benefits of, use

► **Antonyms**

≠take pleasure in or from: abhor,
despise, detest, dislike, hate,
have no taste or stomach for,
loathe

enjoyable *adjective* pleasurable,
agreeable, delightful, entertaining, gratifying, pleasant, satisfying, to one's liking

► **Antonyms**

despicable, disagreeable, displeasing, hateful, loathsome, obnoxious, offensive, repugnant,
unenjoyable, unpleasant, unsatis-
fying

enjoyment *noun* pleasure,
amusement, delectation, delight,
entertainment, fun, gratification,
happiness, joy, relish

enlarge *verb* **1** increase, add to,
amplify, broaden, expand, ex-
tend, grow, magnify, swell, wid-
en **2** enlarge on expand on, descant on, develop, elaborate on,
expatiate on, give further details
about

► **Antonyms**

≠increase: compress, condense,
curtail, decrease, diminish, less-
en, reduce, shorten ≠expand
on: abbreviate, abridge, condense, shorten

enlighten *verb* inform, advise,
cause to understand, counsel,
edify, educate, instruct, make
aware, teach

enlightened *adjective* informed,
aware, civilized, cultivated, educated, knowledgeable, open-
minded, reasonable, sophisticated

► **Antonyms**

ignorant, short-sighted, small-
minded, unaware, uneducated,
unenlightened

enlightenment *noun* understanding, awareness, comprehension, education, insight, instruction, knowledge, learning, wisdom

enlist verb 1 join up, enrol, enter (into), join, muster, register, sign up, volunteer 2 obtain, engage, procure, recruit

enliven verb cheer up, animate, excite, inspire, invigorate, pep up, rouse, spark, stimulate, vitalize

➤ Antonyms

chill, dampen, deaden, depress, put a damper on, repress, subdue

enmity noun hostility, acrimony, animosity, bad blood, bitterness, hatred, ill will, malice

➤ Antonyms

affection, cordiality, friendliness, friendship, goodwill, harmony, love, warmth

ennoble verb dignify, aggrandize, elevate, enhance, exalt, glorify, honour, magnify, raise

enormity noun 1 wickedness, atrocity, depravity, monstrousness, outrageousness, vileness, villainy 2 atrocity, abomination, crime, disgrace, evil, horror, monstrosity, outrage 3 Informal hugeness, greatness, immensity, magnitude, vastness

enormous adjective huge, colossal, gigantic, gross, immense, mammoth, massive, mountainous, tremendous, vast

➤ Antonyms

diminutive, dwarf, infinitesimal, insignificant, Lilliputian, little, meagre, microscopic, midget, minute, petite, pint-sized (informal), small, tiny, wee

enough adjective 1 sufficient, abundant, adequate, ample, plenty ♦ noun 2 sufficiency, abundance, adequacy, ample supply, plenty, right amount ♦ adverb 3 sufficiently, abundantly, adequately, amply, reasonably, satisfactorily, tolerably

enquire see INQUIRE

enquiry see INQUIRY

enrage verb anger, exasperate, in-

cense, inflame, infuriate, madden

➤ Antonyms

appease, assuage, calm, conciliate, mollify, pacify, placate, soothe

enrich verb 1 enhance, augment, develop, improve, refine, supplement 2 make rich, make wealthy

enrol verb enlist, accept, admit, join up, recruit, register, sign up or on, take on

enrolment noun enlistment, acceptance, admission, engagement, matriculation, recruitment, registration

en route adverb on or along the way, in transit, on the road

ensemble noun 1 whole, aggregate, collection, entirety, set, sum, total, totality 2 outfit, costume, get-up (informal), suit 3 group, band, cast, chorus, company, troupe

ensign noun flag, banner, colours, jack, pennant, pennon, standard, streamer

ensue verb follow, arise, come next, derive, flow, issue, proceed, result, stem

➤ Antonyms

come first, go ahead of, go before, precede

ensure verb 1 make certain, certify, confirm, effect, guarantee, make sure, secure, warrant 2 protect, guard, make safe, safeguard, secure

entail verb involve, bring about, call for, demand, give rise to, necessitate, occasion, require

entangle verb 1 tangle, catch, embroil, enmesh, ensnare, entrap, implicate, snag, snare, trap 2 mix up, complicate, confuse, jumble, muddle, perplex, puzzle

➤ Antonyms

≠tangle: disentangle, extricate, free, loose, unravel, unsnarl, untangle, untwist ≠mix up: clarify, clear (up), resolve

enter verb 1 come or go in or into, arrive, make an entrance, pass into, penetrate, pierce **2** join, commence, embark upon, enlist, enrol, set out on, start, take up **3** record, inscribe, list, log, note, register, set down, take down

➤ **Antonyms**

≠come or go in or into: depart, exit, go, leave, take one's leave, withdraw ≠join: drop out, go, leave, pull out, resign, retire, withdraw

enterprise noun **1** firm, business, company, concern, establishment, operation **2** undertaking, adventure, effort, endeavour, operation, plan, programme, project, venture **3** initiative, adventurousness, boldness, daring, drive, energy, enthusiasm, resourcefulness

enterprising adjective resourceful, adventurous, bold, daring, energetic, enthusiastic, go-ahead, intrepid, spirited

entertain verb **1** amuse, charm, cheer, delight, please, regale **2** show hospitality to, accommodate, be host to, harbour, have company, lodge, put up, treat **3** consider, conceive, contemplate, imagine, keep in mind, think about

entertaining adjective enjoyable, amusing, cheering, diverting, funny, humorous, interesting, pleasant, pleasurable

entertainment noun enjoyment, amusement, fun, leisure activity, pastime, pleasure, recreation, sport, treat

enthral verb fascinate, captivate, charm, enchant, enrapture, entrance, grip, mesmerize

enthusiasm noun keenness, eagerness, fervour, interest, passion, relish, zeal, zest

enthusiast noun lover, aficionado, buff (informal), devotee, fan, fanatic, follower, supporter

enthusiastic adjective keen, avid, eager, fervent, passionate, vigorous, wholehearted, zealous

➤ **Antonyms**

apathetic, blasé, bored, dispassionate, half-hearted, indifferent, nonchalant, unconcerned, unenthusiastic, uninterested

entice verb attract, allure, cajole, coax, lead on, lure, persuade, seduce, tempt

entire adjective whole, complete, full, gross, total

entirely adverb completely, absolutely, altogether, fully, in every respect, thoroughly, totally, utterly, wholly

➤ **Antonyms**

incompletely, moderately, partially, partly, piecemeal, slightly, somewhat, to a certain extent or degree

entitle verb **1** give the right to, allow, authorize, empower, enable, license, permit **2** call, christen, dub, label, name, term, title

entity noun thing, being, creature, individual, object, organism, substance

entourage noun retinue, associates, attendants, company, court, escort, followers, staff, train

entrails plural noun intestines, bowels, guts, innards (informal), insides (informal), offal, viscera

entrance[1] noun **1** way in, access, door, doorway, entry, gate, opening, passage **2** appearance, arrival, coming in, entry, introduction **3** admission, access, admittance, entrée, entry, permission to enter

➤ **Antonyms**

≠way in: exit, outlet, way out ≠appearance: departure, exit, leave-taking

entrance[2] verb **1** enchant, bewitch, captivate, charm, delight, enrapture, enthral, fascinate **2** mesmerize, hypnotize, put in a trance

➤ **Antonyms**

≠enchant: bore, disenchant, put off, turn off (informal)

entrant noun competitor, candidate, contestant, entry, participant, player

entreaty noun plea, appeal, earnest request, exhortation, petition, prayer, request, supplication

entrenched adjective fixed, deep-rooted, deep-seated, ineradicable, ingrained, rooted, set, unshakable, well-established

entrepreneur noun businessman or businesswoman, impresario, industrialist, magnate, tycoon

entrust verb give custody of, assign, commit, confide, delegate, deliver, hand over, turn over

entry noun **1** way in, access, door, doorway, entrance, gate, opening, passage **2** coming in, appearance, entering, entrance, initiation, introduction **3** admission, access, entrance, entrée, permission to enter **4** record, account, item, listing, note

➤ **Antonyms**

≠way in: exit, way out ≠coming in: departure, exit, leave, leave-taking, withdrawal

entwine verb twist, interlace, interweave, knit, plait, twine, weave, wind

➤ **Antonyms**

disentangle, extricate, free, undo, unravel, untangle, unwind

enumerate verb list, cite, itemize, mention, name, quote, recite, recount, relate, spell out

enunciate verb **1** pronounce, articulate, enounce, say, sound, speak, utter, vocalize, voice **2** state, declare, proclaim, promulgate, pronounce, propound, publish

envelop verb enclose, cloak, cover, encase, encircle, engulf, shroud, surround, wrap

envelope noun wrapping, case, casing, cover, covering, jacket, wrapper

enviable adjective desirable, advantageous, favoured, fortunate, lucky, privileged, to die for (informal)

➤ **Antonyms**

disagreeable, painful, thankless, undesirable, unenviable, unpleasant

envious adjective covetous, green with envy, grudging, jealous, resentful

environment noun surroundings, atmosphere, background, conditions, habitat, medium, setting, situation

environmental adjective ecological, green

environmentalist noun conservationist, ecologist, green

environs plural noun surrounding area, district, locality, neighbourhood, outskirts, precincts, suburbs, vicinity

envisage verb **1** imagine, conceive (of), conceptualize, contemplate, fancy, picture, think up, visualize **2** foresee, anticipate, envision, predict, see

envoy noun messenger, agent, ambassador, courier, delegate, diplomat, emissary, intermediary, representative

envy noun **1** covetousness, enviousness, jealousy, resentfulness, resentment ♦ verb **2** covet, be envious (of), begrudge, be jealous (of), grudge, resent

ephemeral adjective brief, fleeting, momentary, passing, short-lived, temporary, transient, transitory

➤ **Antonyms**

abiding, enduring, eternal, immortal, lasting, long-lasting

epidemic noun spread, contagion, growth, outbreak, plague, rash, upsurge, wave

epigram noun witticism, aphorism, bon mot, quip

epilogue noun conclusion, coda, concluding speech, postscript

➤ **Antonyms**

foreword, introduction, preamble, preface, prelude, prologue

episode noun **1** event, adventure, affair, escapade, experience, happening, incident, matter, occurrence **2** part, chapter, instalment, passage, scene, section

epistle noun letter, communication, message, missive, note

epitaph noun <u>monument</u>, inscription

epithet noun <u>name</u>, appellation, description, designation, moniker or monicker (*slang*), nickname, sobriquet, tag, title

epitome noun <u>personification</u>, archetype, embodiment, essence, quintessence, representation, type, typical example

epitomize verb <u>typify</u>, embody, exemplify, illustrate, personify, represent, symbolize

epoch noun <u>era</u>, age, date, period, time

equable adjective <u>even-tempered</u>, calm, composed, easy-going, imperturbable, level-headed, placid, serene, unflappable (*informal*)

➤ **Antonyms**
excitable, nervous, temperamental

equal adjective **1** <u>identical</u>, alike, corresponding, equivalent, the same, uniform **2** <u>regular</u>, symmetrical, uniform, unvarying **3** <u>even</u>, balanced, evenly matched, fifty-fifty (*informal*), level pegging (*Brit. informal*) **4** <u>fair</u>, egalitarian, even-handed, impartial, just, unbiased **5** **equal to** <u>capable of</u>, competent to, fit for, good enough for, ready for, strong enough, suitable for, up to ◆ noun **6** <u>match</u>, counterpart, equivalent, rival, twin ◆ verb **7** <u>match</u>, amount to, be tantamount to, correspond to, equate, level, parallel, tie with

➤ **Antonyms**
adjective ≠<u>identical</u>: different, disproportionate, dissimilar, diverse, unequal, unlike ≠<u>regular</u>: irregular ≠<u>even</u>: unbalanced, unequal, uneven, unmatched ≠<u>fair</u>: biased, inequitable, partial, unequal, unfair, unjust ≠<u>capable of</u>: inadequate, incapable, incompetent, not good enough, not up to, unequal, unfit ◆ verb ≠<u>match</u>: be different, be unequal, disagree

equality noun **1** <u>sameness</u>, balance, correspondence, equiva-

lence, evenness, identity, likeness, similarity, uniformity **2** <u>fairness</u>, egalitarianism, equal opportunity, parity

➤ **Antonyms**
≠<u>sameness</u>: disparity, lack of balance, unevenness ≠<u>fairness</u>: bias, discrimination, imparity, inequality, prejudice, unfairness

equalize verb <u>make equal</u>, balance, equal, even up, level, match, regularize, smooth, square, standardize

equate verb <u>make or be equal</u>, be commensurate, compare, correspond with or to, liken, mention in the same breath, parallel

equation noun <u>equating</u>, comparison, correspondence, parallel

equilibrium noun <u>stability</u>, balance, equipoise, evenness, rest, steadiness, symmetry

equip verb <u>supply</u>, arm, array, fit out, furnish, kit out, provide, stock

equipment noun <u>apparatus</u>, accoutrements, gear, paraphernalia, stuff, supplies, tackle, tools

equitable adjective <u>fair</u>, even-handed, honest, impartial, just, proper, reasonable, unbiased

equivalence noun <u>equality</u>, correspondence, evenness, likeness, parity, sameness, similarity

equivalent noun **1** <u>equal</u>, counterpart, match, opposite number, parallel, twin ◆ adjective **2** <u>equal</u>, alike, commensurate, comparable, corresponding, interchangeable, of a piece, same, similar, tantamount

➤ **Antonyms**
adjective ≠<u>equal</u>: different, dissimilar, incomparable, unequal, unlike

equivocal adjective <u>ambiguous</u>, evasive, indefinite, indeterminate, misleading, oblique, obscure, uncertain, vague

➤ **Antonyms**
absolute, certain, clear, clear-cut, definite, explicit, plain, straight, unambiguous, unequivocal

era noun age, date, day or days, epoch, generation, period, time

eradicate verb wipe out, annihilate, destroy, eliminate, erase, exterminate, extinguish, get rid of, obliterate, remove, root out

erase verb wipe out, blot, cancel, delete, expunge, obliterate, remove, rub out

erect verb 1 build, construct, put up, raise, set up 2 found, create, establish, form, initiate, institute, organize, set up ♦ adjective 3 upright, elevated, perpendicular, pricked-up, stiff, straight, vertical
> ▶ Antonyms
verb ≠build: demolish, destroy, dismantle, tear down ♦ adjective ≠upright: bent, flaccid, horizontal, limp, prone

erode verb wear down or away, abrade, consume, corrode, destroy, deteriorate, disintegrate, eat away, grind down

erosion noun deterioration, abrasion, attrition, destruction, disintegration, eating away, grinding down, wearing down or away

erotic adjective sexual, amatory, carnal, lustful, seductive, sensual, sexy (informal), voluptuous

err verb make a mistake, blunder, go wrong, miscalculate, misjudge, mistake, slip up (informal)

errand noun job, charge, commission, message, mission, task

erratic adjective unpredictable, changeable, inconsistent, irregular, uneven, unreliable, unstable, variable, wayward
> ▶ Antonyms
certain, consistent, constant, dependable, invariable, predictable, regular, stable, steady

erroneous adjective incorrect, fallacious, false, faulty, flawed, invalid, mistaken, unsound, wrong
> ▶ Antonyms
accurate, correct, factual, faultless, flawless, precise, right, true, veracious

error noun mistake, bloomer (Brit. informal), blunder, howler (informal), miscalculation, oversight,

slip, solecism

erstwhile adjective former, bygone, late, old, once, one-time, past, previous, sometime

erudite adjective learned, cultivated, cultured, educated, knowledgeable, scholarly, welleducated, well-read
> ▶ Antonyms
ignorant, illiterate, uneducated, unschooled, untaught

erupt verb 1 explode, belch forth, blow up, burst out, gush, pour forth, spew forth or away, spout, throw off 2 Medical break out, appear

eruption noun 1 explosion, discharge, ejection, flare-up, outbreak, outburst 2 Medical inflammation, outbreak, rash

escalate verb increase, expand, extend, grow, heighten, intensify, mount, rise
> ▶ Antonyms
decrease, diminish, fall, lessen, lower, wane

escapade noun adventure, antic, caper, prank, scrape (informal), stunt

escape verb 1 get away, abscond, bolt, break free or out, flee, fly, make one's getaway, run away or off, slip away 2 avoid, dodge, duck, elude, evade, pass, shun, slip 3 leak, emanate, exude, flow, gush, issue, pour forth, seep ♦ noun 4 getaway, break, break-out, flight 5 avoidance, circumvention, evasion 6 relaxation, distraction, diversion, pastime, recreation 7 leak, emanation, emission, seepage

escort noun 1 guard, bodyguard, convoy, cortege, entourage, retinue, train 2 companion, attendant, beau, chaperon, guide, partner ♦ verb 3 accompany, chaperon, conduct, guide, lead, partner, shepherd, usher

especial adjective Formal exceptional, noteworthy, outstanding, principal, special, uncommon, unusual

especially adverb exceptionally, conspicuously, markedly, notably, outstandingly, remarkably, specially, strikingly, uncommonly, unusually

espionage noun spying, counter-intelligence, intelligence, surveillance, undercover work

espousal noun support, adoption, advocacy, backing, championing, defence, embracing, promotion, taking up

espouse verb support, adopt, advocate, back, champion, embrace, promote, stand up for, take up, uphold

essay noun 1 composition, article, discourse, dissertation, paper, piece, tract, treatise ♦ verb 2 Formal attempt, aim, endeavour, try, undertake

essence noun 1 fundamental nature, being, core, heart, nature, quintessence, soul, spirit, substance 2 concentrate, distillate, extract, spirits, tincture

essential adjective 1 vital, crucial, important, indispensable, necessary, needed, requisite 2 fundamental, basic, cardinal, elementary, innate, intrinsic, main, principal ♦ noun 3 prerequisite, basic, fundamental, must, necessity, rudiment, sine qua non

➤ **Antonyms**

adjective ≠vital, fundamental: dispensable, expendable, extra, incidental, inessential, lesser, minor, nonessential, optional, secondary, superfluous, surplus, trivial, unimportant, unnecessary

establish verb 1 create, constitute, form, found, ground, inaugurate, institute, settle, set up 2 prove, authenticate, certify, confirm, corroborate, demonstrate, substantiate, verify

establishment noun 1 creation, formation, foundation, founding, inauguration, installation, institution, organization, setting up 2 organization, business, company, concern, corporation, enterprise, firm, institution, outfit

(informal) 3 the Establishment the authorities, ruling class, the powers that be, the system

estate noun 1 lands, area, domain, holdings, manor, property 2 Law property, assets, belongings, effects, fortune, goods, possessions, wealth

esteem noun 1 respect, admiration, credit, estimation, good opinion, honour, regard, reverence, veneration ♦ verb 2 respect, admire, love, prize, regard highly, revere, think highly of, treasure, value 3 Formal consider, believe, deem, estimate, judge, reckon, regard, think, view

estimate verb 1 calculate roughly, assess, evaluate, gauge, guess, judge, number, reckon, value 2 form an opinion, believe, conjecture, consider, judge, rank, rate, reckon, surmise ♦ noun 3 approximate calculation, assessment, ballpark figure (informal), guess, guesstimate (informal), judgment, valuation 4 opinion, appraisal, assessment, belief, estimation, judgment

estimation noun opinion, appraisal, appreciation, assessment, belief, consideration, considered opinion, judgment, view

estuary noun inlet, creek, firth, fjord, mouth

et cetera adverb 1 and so on, and so forth ♦ noun 2 and the rest, and others, and the like, et al.

etch verb cut, carve, eat into, engrave, impress, imprint, inscribe, stamp

etching noun print, carving, engraving, impression, imprint, inscription

eternal adjective 1 everlasting, endless, immortal, infinite, never-ending, perpetual, timeless, unceasing, unending 2 permanent, deathless, enduring, immutable, imperishable, indestructible, lasting, unchanging

➤ **Antonyms**

≠everlasting: finite, fleeting,

rare, temporal ≠<u>permanent</u>: changing, ephemeral, evanescent, transient, transitory

eternity noun **1** <u>infinity</u>, ages, endlessness, immortality, perpetuity, timelessness **2** *Theology* the <u>afterlife</u>, heaven, paradise, the hereafter, the next world

ethical adjective <u>moral</u>, conscientious, fair, good, honourable, just, principled, proper, right, upright, virtuous

► **Antonyms**

dishonourable, immoral, improper, low-down (*informal*), underhand, unethical, unfair, unscrupulous

ethics plural noun <u>moral code</u>, conscience, morality, moral philosophy, moral values, principles, rules of conduct, standards

ethnic, ethnical adjective <u>cultural</u>, folk, indigenous, national, native, racial, traditional

etiquette noun <u>good or proper behaviour</u>, civility, courtesy, decorum, formalities, manners, politeness, propriety, protocol

euphoria noun <u>elation</u>, ecstasy, exaltation, exhilaration, intoxication, joy, jubilation, rapture

► **Antonyms**

depression, despair, despondency, gloominess, hopelessness, low spirits, melancholy, melancholy, sadness, the blues

evacuate verb <u>clear</u>, abandon, desert, forsake, leave, move out, pull out, quit, vacate, withdraw

evade verb **1** <u>avoid</u>, dodge, duck, elude, escape, get away from, sidestep, steer clear of **2** <u>avoid answering</u>, equivocate, fend off, fudge, hedge, parry

► **Antonyms**

≠<u>avoid</u>: brave, confront, encounter, face, meet, meet face to face

evaluate verb <u>assess</u>, appraise, calculate, estimate, gauge, judge, rate, reckon, size up (*informal*), weigh

evaporate verb **1** <u>dry up</u>, dehydrate, desiccate, dry, vaporize **2** <u>disappear</u>, dematerialize, dis-

solve, fade away, melt away, vanish

evasion noun **1** <u>avoidance</u>, dodging, escape **2** <u>deception</u>, equivocation, evasiveness, prevarication

evasive adjective <u>deceptive</u>, cagey (*informal*), equivocating, indirect, oblique, prevaricating, shifty, slippery

► **Antonyms**

candid, direct, frank, guileless, honest, open, straight, straightforward, truthful, unequivocating

eve noun **1** <u>night before</u>, day before, vigil **2** <u>brink</u>, edge, point, threshold, verge

even adjective **1** <u>level</u>, flat, horizontal, parallel, smooth, steady, straight, true, uniform **2** <u>regular</u>, constant, smooth, steady, unbroken, uniform, uninterrupted, unvarying, unwavering **3** <u>equal</u>, comparable, fifty-fifty (*informal*), identical, level, like, matching, neck and neck, on a par, similar, tied **4** <u>calm</u>, composed, cool, even-tempered, imperturbable, placid, unruffled, well-balanced **5** <u>get even (with)</u> *Informal* <u>pay back</u>, get one's own back, give tit for tat, reciprocate, repay, requite

► **Antonyms**

≠<u>level</u>: bumpy, curving, rough, twisting, undulating, uneven, wavy ≠<u>regular</u>: broken, fluctuating, irregular, uneven, variable ≠<u>equal</u>: disproportionate, illmatched, imbalanced, irregular, unequal, uneven ≠<u>calm</u>: agitated, changeable, emotional, excitable, quick-tempered, unpredictable

evening noun <u>dusk</u>, gloaming (*Scot. or poetic*), twilight

event noun **1** <u>incident</u>, affair, business, circumstance, episode, experience, happening, occasion, occurrence **2** <u>competition</u>, bout, contest, game, tournament

even-tempered adjective <u>calm</u>, composed, cool, imperturbable, level-headed, placid, tranquil, unexcitable, unruffled

> **Antonyms**

emotional, excitable, highly-strung, hot-headed, hot-tempered, irascible, quick-tempered, temperamental, touchy, volatile

eventful *adjective* exciting, active, busy, dramatic, full, lively, memorable, remarkable

> **Antonyms**

commonplace, dull, humdrum, insignificant, ordinary, trivial, uneventful, unexceptional, unexciting, unimportant, uninteresting, unremarkable

eventual *adjective* final, concluding, overall, ultimate

eventuality *noun* possibility, case, chance, contingency, event, likelihood, probability

eventually *adverb* in the end, after all, at the end of the day, finally, one day, some time, ultimately, when all is said and done

ever *adverb* **1** at any time, at all, at any period, at any point, by any chance, in any case, on any occasion **2** always, at all times, constantly, continually, evermore, for ever, perpetually

everlasting *adjective* eternal, endless, immortal, indestructible, never-ending, perpetual, timeless, undying

> **Antonyms**

brief, ephemeral, fleeting, impermanent, passing, short-lived, temporary, transient, transitory

evermore *adverb* for ever, always, eternally, ever, to the end of time

every *adjective* each, all, each one

everybody *pronoun* everyone, all and sundry, each one, each person, every person, one and all, the whole world

everyday *adjective* ordinary, common, customary, mundane, routine, run-of-the-mill, stock, usual, workaday

> **Antonyms**

exceptional, extraordinary, occasional, special, uncommon, unusual

everyone *pronoun* everybody, all and sundry, each one, each person, every person, one and all, the whole world

everything *pronoun* all, each thing, the lot, the whole lot

everywhere *adverb* to or in every place, all around, all over, far and wide or near, high and low, in every nook and cranny, the world over, ubiquitously

evict *verb* expel, boot out (*informal*), eject, kick out (*informal*), oust, remove, throw out, turf out (*informal*), turn out

evidence *noun* **1** proof, confirmation, corroboration, demonstration, grounds, indication, sign, substantiation, testimony ♦ *verb* **2** show, demonstrate, display, exhibit, indicate, prove, reveal, signify, witness

evident *adjective* obvious, apparent, clear, manifest, noticeable, perceptible, plain, unmistakable, visible

> **Antonyms**

doubtful, imperceptible, obscure, uncertain, unclear, unknown, vague

evidently *adverb* **1** obviously, clearly, manifestly, plainly, undoubtedly, unmistakably, without question **2** apparently, ostensibly, outwardly, seemingly, to all appearances

evil *noun* **1** wickedness, badness, depravity, malignity, sin, vice, villainy, wrongdoing **2** harm, affliction, disaster, hurt, ill, injury, mischief, misfortune, suffering, woe ♦ *adjective* **3** wicked, bad, depraved, immoral, malevolent, malicious, sinful, villainous **4** harmful, calamitous, catastrophic, destructive, dire, disastrous, pernicious, ruinous **5** offensive, foul, noxious, pestilential, unpleasant, vile

evoke *verb* arouse, awaken, call, give rise to, induce, recall, rekindle, stir up, summon up

> **Antonyms**

hold in check, inhibit, repress, restrain, smother, stifle, suppress

evolution noun <u>development</u>, expansion, growth, increase, maturation, progress, unfolding, working out

evolve verb <u>develop</u>, expand, grow, increase, mature, progress, unfold, work out

exact adjective **1** <u>accurate</u>, correct, definite, faultless, precise, right, specific, true, unerring ♦ verb **2** <u>demand</u>, claim, command, compel, extort, extract, force

► **Antonyms**

adjective ≠<u>accurate</u>: approximate, imprecise, inaccurate, incorrect, indefinite, inexact, loose, rough

exacting adjective <u>demanding</u>, difficult, hard, harsh, rigorous, severe, strict, stringent, taxing, tough

► **Antonyms**

easy, easy-peasy (slang), effortless, no bother, simple, undemanding

exactly adverb **1** <u>precisely</u>, accurately, correctly, explicitly, faithfully, scrupulously, truthfully, unerringly **2** <u>in every respect</u>, absolutely, indeed, precisely, quite, specifically, to the letter

exactness noun <u>precision</u>, accuracy, correctness, exactitude, rigorousness, scrupulousness, strictness, veracity

► **Antonyms**

imprecision, inaccuracy, incorrectness, inexactness

exaggerate verb <u>overstate</u>, amplify, embellish, embroider, enlarge, overemphasize, overestimate

exaggeration noun <u>overstatement</u>, amplification, embellishment, enlargement, hyperbole, overemphasis, overestimation

► **Antonyms**

restraint, underplaying, understatement

exalt verb **1** <u>praise</u>, acclaim, extol, glorify, idolize, set on a pedestal, worship **2** <u>raise</u>, advance, elevate, ennoble, honour,

promote, upgrade

exaltation noun **1** <u>praise</u>, acclaim, glorification, idolization, reverence, tribute, worship **2** <u>rise</u>, advancement, elevation, ennoblement, promotion, upgrading

exalted adjective <u>high-ranking</u>, dignified, eminent, grand, honoured, lofty, prestigious

examination noun **1** <u>inspection</u>, analysis, exploration, interrogation, investigation, research, scrutiny, study, test **2** <u>questioning</u>, inquiry, inquisition, probe, quiz, test

examine verb **1** <u>inspect</u>, analyse, explore, investigate, peruse, scrutinize, study, survey **2** <u>question</u>, cross-examine, grill (informal), inquire, interrogate, quiz, test

example noun **1** <u>specimen</u>, case, illustration, instance, sample **2** <u>model</u>, archetype, ideal, paradigm, paragon, prototype, standard **3** <u>warning</u>, caution, lesson

exasperate verb <u>irritate</u>, anger, annoy, enrage, incense, inflame, infuriate, madden, pique

► **Antonyms**

appease, assuage, calm, conciliate, mollify, pacify, placate, soothe

exasperation noun <u>irritation</u>, anger, annoyance, fury, pique, provocation, rage, wrath

excavate verb <u>dig out</u>, burrow, delve, dig up, mine, quarry, tunnel, uncover, unearth

exceed verb **1** <u>surpass</u>, beat, better, cap (informal), eclipse, outdo, outstrip, overtake, pass, top **2** <u>go over the limit of</u>, go over the top, overstep

exceedingly adverb <u>extremely</u>, enormously, exceptionally, extraordinarily, hugely, superlatively, surpassingly, unusually, very

excel verb **1** <u>be superior</u>, beat, eclipse, outdo, outshine, surpass, transcend **2** <u>excel in</u> or at <u>be good at</u>, be proficient in, be skilful at, be talented at, shine at, show talent in

excellence noun high quality, distinction, eminence, goodness, greatness, merit, pre-eminence, superiority, supremacy

excellent adjective outstanding, brilliant, exquisite, fine, first-class, first-rate, good, great, superb, superlative, world-class

➤ **Antonyms**

abysmal, bad, dreadful, inferior, lousy (slang), mediocre, no great shakes (informal), poor, rotten (informal), second-class, second-rate, substandard, terrible

except preposition 1 Also **except for** apart from, barring, besides, but, excepting, excluding, omitting, other than, saving, with the exception of ✦ verb 2 exclude, leave out, omit, pass over

exception noun 1 special case, anomaly, deviation, freak, inconsistency, irregularity, oddity, peculiarity 2 exclusion, leaving out, omission, passing over

exceptional adjective 1 unusual, abnormal, atypical, extraordinary, irregular, odd, peculiar, special, strange 2 remarkable, excellent, extraordinary, marvellous, outstanding, phenomenal, prodigious, special, superior

➤ **Antonyms**

≠unusual: average, common, customary, normal, ordinary, regular, typical, unexceptional, unremarkable, usual ≠remarkable: average, awful, bad, no great shakes (slang), mediocre, no great shakes (informal), second-rate

excerpt noun extract, fragment, part, passage, piece, quotation, section, selection

excess noun 1 surfeit, glut, overload, superabundance, superfluity, surplus, too much 2 overindulgence, debauchery, dissipation, dissoluteness, extravagance, intemperance, prodigality

➤ **Antonyms**

≠surfeit: dearth, deficiency, insufficiency, lack, shortage, want

≠overindulgence: moderation, restraint, self-control, self-discipline, self-restraint, temperance

excessive adjective immoderate, disproportionate, exaggerated, extreme, inordinate, overmuch, superfluous, too much, undue, unfair, unreasonable

exchange verb 1 interchange, barter, change, convert into, swap, switch, trade ✦ noun 2 interchange, barter, quid pro quo, reciprocity, substitution, swap, switch, tit for tat, trade

excitable adjective nervous, emotional, highly strung, hotheaded, mercurial, quicktempered, temperamental, volatile

➤ **Antonyms**

calm, cool, cool-headed, even-tempered, imperturbable, laidback (informal), placid, unexcitable, unruffled

excite verb 1 arouse, animate, galvanize, inflame, inspire, provoke, rouse, stir up 2 thrill, electrify, titillate

excitement noun agitation, action, activity, animation, commotion, furore, passion, thrill

exciting adjective stimulating, dramatic, electrifying, exhilarating, rousing, sensational, stirring, thrilling

➤ **Antonyms**

boring, dreary, dull, flat, humdrum, mind-numbing, monotonous, unexciting, uninspiring, uninteresting

exclaim verb cry out, call out, declare, proclaim, shout, utter, yell

exclamation noun cry, call, interjection, outcry, shout, utterance, yell

exclude verb 1 keep out, ban, bar, boycott, disallow, forbid, prohibit, refuse, shut out 2 leave out, count out, eliminate, ignore, omit, pass over, reject, rule out, set aside

➤ **Antonyms**

≠keep out, remove: accept, admit, allow, let in, permit, receive, welcome ≠leave out: count, include

exclusion noun **1** ban, bar, boycott, disqualification, embargo, prohibition, veto **2** elimination, omission, rejection

exclusive adjective **1** sole, absolute, complete, entire, full, total, undivided, whole **2** limited, confined, peculiar, restricted, unique **3** select, chic, cliquish, fashionable, posh (informal, chiefly Brit.), restricted, snobbish, up-market

► **Antonyms**
≠sole, limited: inclusive, nonexclusive, partial, shared ≠select: common, communal, open, popular, unrestricted

excommunicate verb expel, anathematize, ban, banish, cast out, denounce, exclude, repudiate

excruciating adjective agonizing, harrowing, insufferable, intense, piercing, severe, unbearable, violent

exculpate verb absolve, acquit, clear, discharge, excuse, exonerate, pardon, vindicate

excursion noun trip, day trip, expedition, jaunt, journey, outing, pleasure trip, ramble, tour

excusable adjective forgivable, allowable, defensible, justifiable, pardonable, permissible, understandable, warrantable

excuse noun **1** justification, apology, defence, explanation, grounds, mitigation, plea, reason, vindication ♦ verb **2** justify, apologize for, defend, explain, mitigate, vindicate **3** forgive, acquit, exculpate, exonerate, make allowances for, overlook, pardon, tolerate, turn a blind eye to **4** free, absolve, discharge, exempt, let off, release, relieve, spare

► **Antonyms**
noun ≠justification: accusation, charge, imputation, indictment ♦ verb ≠justify: accuse, blame, censure, chasten, chastise, compel, condemn, correct, criticize, hold responsible, oblige, point a or the finger at, punish ≠free: arraign, charge, convict, indict, sentence

execute verb **1** put to death, behead, electrocute, guillotine, hang, kill, shoot **2** carry out, accomplish, administer, discharge, effect, enact, implement, perform, prosecute

execution noun **1** carrying out, accomplishment, administration, enactment, enforcement, implementation, operation, performance, prosecution **2** killing, capital punishment, hanging

executioner noun **1** hangman, headsman **2** killer, assassin, exterminator, hit man (slang), liquidator, murderer, slayer

executive noun **1** administrator, director, manager, official **2** administration, directorate, directors, government, hierarchy, leadership, management ♦ adjective **3** administrative, controlling, decision-making, directing, governing, managerial

exemplary adjective **1** ideal, admirable, commendable, excellent, fine, good, model, praiseworthy **2** warning, cautionary

exemplify verb show, demonstrate, display, embody, exhibit, illustrate, represent, serve as an example of

exempt adjective **1** immune, excepted, excused, free, not liable, released, spared ♦ verb **2** grant immunity, absolve, discharge, excuse, free, let off, release, relieve, spare

► **Antonyms**
adjective ≠immune: accountable, answerable, chargeable, liable, obligated, responsible, subject

exemption noun immunity, absolution, discharge, dispensation, exception, exoneration, freedom, release

exercise noun **1** exertion, activity, effort, labour, toil, training, work, work-out **2** task, drill, lesson, practice, problem **3** use, application, discharge, fulfilment, implementation, practice, utilization ♦ verb **4** put to use, apply, bring to bear, employ, exert, use, utilize **5** train, practise, work out

exert verb **1** use, apply, bring to bear, employ, exercise, make use of, utilize, wield **2 exert oneself** make an effort, apply oneself, do one's best, endeavour, labour, strain, strive, struggle, toil, work

exertion noun effort, elbow grease (facetious), endeavour, exercise, industry, strain, struggle, toil

exhaust verb **1** tire out, debilitate, drain, enervate, enfeeble, fatigue, sap, weaken, wear out **2** use up, consume, deplete, dissipate, expend, run through, spend, squander, waste

exhausted adjective **1** worn out, all in (slang), debilitated, done in (informal), drained, fatigued, knackered (slang), spent, tired out **2** used up, consumed, depleted, dissipated, expended, finished, spent, squandered, wasted

► **Antonyms**

≠worn out: active, alive and kicking, animated, enlivened, invigorated, refreshed, rejuvenated, restored, revived, stimulated ≠used up: conserved, kept, preserved, replenished, restored

exhausting adjective tiring, backbreaking, debilitating, gruelling, laborious, punishing, sapping, strenuous, taxing

exhaustion noun **1** tiredness, debilitation, fatigue, weariness **2** depletion, consumption, emptying, using up

exhaustive adjective thorough, all-embracing, complete, comprehensive, extensive, full-scale, in-depth, intensive

► **Antonyms**

casual, cursory, incomplete, perfunctory, sketchy, superficial

exhibit verb display, demonstrate, express, indicate, manifest, parade, put on view, reveal, show

exhibition noun display, demonstration, exposition, performance, presentation, representation, show, spectacle

exhilarating adjective exciting, breathtaking, enlivening, invigorating, stimulating, thrilling

exhort verb Formal urge, advise, beseech, call upon, entreat, persuade, press, spur

exhume verb Formal dig up, disentomb, disinter, unearth

► **Antonyms**

bury, entomb, inter

exigency, exigence noun need, constraint, demand, necessity, requirement

exile noun **1** banishment, deportation, expatriation, expulsion **2** expatriate, deportee, émigré, outcast, refugee ♦ verb **3** banish, deport, drive out, eject, expatriate, expel

exist verb **1** be, be present, endure, live, occur, survive **2** survive, eke out a living, get along or by, keep one's head above water, stay alive, subsist

existence noun being, actuality, life, subsistence

existent adjective in existence, alive, existing, extant, living, present, standing, surviving

exit noun **1** way out, door, gate, outlet **2** departure, exodus, farewell, going, goodbye, leave-taking, retreat, withdrawal ♦ verb **3** depart, go away, go offstage (Theatre), go out, leave, make tracks, retire, retreat, take one's leave, withdraw

► **Antonyms**

noun ≠way out: entrance, entry, inlet, opening, way in ♦ verb ≠depart: arrive, come or go in or into, enter, make an entrance

exodus noun departure, evacuation, exit, flight, going out, leaving, migration, retreat, withdrawal

exonerate verb <u>clear</u>, absolve, acquit, discharge, exculpate, excuse, justify, pardon, vindicate

exorbitant adjective <u>excessive</u>, extortionate, extravagant, immoderate, inordinate, outrageous, preposterous, unreasonable

► **Antonyms**

cheap, fair, moderate, reasonable

exorcise verb <u>drive out</u>, cast out, deliver (from), expel, purify

exotic adjective 1 <u>unusual</u>, colourful, fascinating, glamorous, mysterious, strange, striking, unfamiliar 2 <u>foreign</u>, alien, external, imported, naturalized

► **Antonyms**

≠<u>unusual</u>: conventional, familiar, ordinary, run-of-the-mill, unremarkable

expand verb 1 <u>increase</u>, amplify, broaden, develop, enlarge, extend, grow, magnify, swell, widen 2 <u>spread (out)</u>, diffuse, stretch (out), unfold, unfurl, unravel, unroll 3 **expand on** <u>go into detail about</u>, amplify, develop, elaborate on, embellish, enlarge on, expatiate on, expound on, flesh out

► **Antonyms**

≠<u>increase</u>: condense, contract, decrease, reduce, shorten, shrink ≠<u>go into detail about</u>: abbreviate, condense, shorten

expanse noun <u>area</u>, breadth, extent, range, space, stretch, sweep, tract

expansion noun <u>increase</u>, amplification, development, enlargement, growth, magnification, opening, spread

expansive adjective 1 <u>wide</u>, broad, extensive, far-reaching, voluminous, wide-ranging, widespread 2 <u>talkative</u>, affable, communicative, effusive, friendly, loquacious, open, outgoing, sociable, unreserved

expatriate adjective 1 <u>exiled</u>, banished, emigrant, émigré 2 <u>noun</u> 2 <u>exile</u>, emigrant, émigré, refugee

expect verb 1 <u>think</u>, assume, believe, imagine, presume, reckon, suppose, surmise, trust 2 <u>look forward to</u>, anticipate, await, contemplate, envisage, hope for, predict, watch for 3 <u>require</u>, call for, demand, insist on, want

expectant adjective 1 <u>expecting</u>, anticipating, apprehensive, eager, hopeful, in suspense, ready, watchful 2 <u>pregnant</u>, expecting (informal), gravid

expectation noun 1 <u>probability</u>, assumption, belief, conjecture, forecast, likelihood, presumption, supposition 2 <u>anticipation</u>, apprehension, expectancy, hope, promise, suspense

expediency noun <u>suitability</u>, advisability, benefit, convenience, pragmatism, profitability, prudence, usefulness, utility

expedient noun 1 <u>means</u>, contrivance, device, makeshift, measure, method, resort, scheme, stopgap ◆ adjective 2 <u>advantageous</u>, appropriate, beneficial, convenient, effective, helpful, opportune, practical, suitable, useful

► **Antonyms**

adjective ≠<u>advantageous</u>: detrimental, disadvantageous, harmful, ill-advised, impractical, imprudent, inadvisable, inexpedient, unwise, wrong

expedition noun <u>journey</u>, excursion, mission, quest, safari, tour, trek, voyage

expel verb 1 <u>drive out</u>, belch, cast out, discharge, eject, remove, spew 2 <u>dismiss</u>, ban, banish, drum out, evict, exclude, exile, throw out, turf out (informal)

► **Antonyms**

≠<u>dismiss</u>: admit, allow to enter, give access, let in, receive, take in, welcome

expend verb Formal <u>spend</u>, consume, dissipate, exhaust, go through, pay out, use (up)

expendable adjective <u>dispensable</u>, inessential, nonessential, replaceable, unimportant, unnecessary

➤ **Antonyms**

crucial, essential, indispensable, key, necessary, vital

expenditure noun spending, consumption, cost, expense, outgoings, outlay, output, payment

expense noun cost, charge, expenditure, loss, outlay, payment, spending

expensive adjective dear, costly, exorbitant, extravagant, high-priced, lavish, overpriced, steep (informal), stiff

➤ **Antonyms**

bargain, budget, cheap, cut-price, economical, inexpensive, low-cost, low-priced, reasonable

experience noun 1 knowledge, contact, exposure, familiarity, involvement, participation, practice, training 2 event, adventure, affair, encounter, episode, happening, incident, occurrence ♦ verb 3 undergo, encounter, endure, face, feel, go through, live through, sample, taste

experienced adjective knowledgeable, accomplished, expert, practised, seasoned, tested, tried, veteran, well-versed

➤ **Antonyms**

green, incompetent, inexperienced, new, unqualified, unskilled, untrained, untried

experiment noun 1 test, examination, experimentation, investigation, procedure, proof, research, trial, trial run ♦ verb 2 test, examine, investigate, put to the test, research, sample, try, verify

experimental adjective test, exploratory, pilot, preliminary, probationary, provisional, speculative, tentative, trial, trial-and-error

expert noun 1 master, authority, connoisseur, dab hand (Brit. informal), guru, past master, professional, specialist, virtuoso ♦ adjective 2 skilful, adept, adroit, experienced, masterly, practised, professional, proficient, qualified, virtuoso

➤ **Antonyms**

noun ≠master: amateur, dabbler, layman, nonprofessional, novice ♦ adjective ≠skilful: amateurish, clumsy, incompetent, inexperienced, unpractised, unqualified, unskilled, untrained

expertise noun skill, adroitness, command, facility, judgment, know-how (informal), knowledge, mastery, proficiency

expire verb 1 finish, cease, close, come to an end, conclude, end, lapse, run out, stop, terminate 2 breathe out, emit, exhale, expel 3 die, depart, kick the bucket (informal), pass away or on, perish

explain verb 1 make clear or plain, clarify, clear up, define, describe, elucidate, expound, resolve, teach 2 account for, excuse, give a reason for, justify

explanation noun 1 reason, account, answer, excuse, justification, motive, vindication 2 description, clarification, definition, elucidation, illustration, interpretation

explanatory adjective descriptive, illustrative, interpretive

explicit adjective clear, categorical, definite, frank, precise, specific, straightforward, unambiguous

➤ **Antonyms**

ambiguous, implied, indefinite, indirect, obscure, vague

explode verb 1 blow up, burst, detonate, discharge, erupt, go off, set off, shatter 2 disprove, debunk, discredit, give the lie to, invalidate, refute, repudiate

exploit verb 1 take advantage of, abuse, manipulate, milk, misuse, play on or upon 2 make the best use of, capitalize on, cash in on (informal), profit by or from, use, utilize ♦ noun 3 feat, accomplishment, achievement, adventure, attainment, deed, escapade, stunt

exploitation noun misuse, abuse, manipulation, using

exploration noun 1 investigation, analysis, examination, inquiry, inspection, research, scrutiny, search 2 expedition, reconnaissance, survey, tour, travel, trip

exploratory adjective investigative, experimental, fact-finding, probing, searching, trial

explore verb 1 investigate, examine, inquire into, inspect, look into, probe, research, search 2 travel, reconnoitre, scout, survey, tour

explosion noun 1 bang, blast, burst, clap, crack, detonation, discharge, report 2 outburst, eruption, fit, outbreak

explosive adjective 1 unstable, volatile 2 violent, fiery, stormy, touchy, vehement

exponent noun 1 advocate, backer, champion, defender, promoter, proponent, supporter, upholder 2 performer, player

expose verb 1 uncover, display, exhibit, present, reveal, show, unveil 2 make vulnerable, endanger, imperil, jeopardize, lay open, leave open, subject

► **Antonyms**

≠uncover: conceal, cover, hide, mask, protect, screen, shelter, shield

exposed adjective 1 unconcealed, bare, on display, on show, on view, revealed, uncovered 2 unsheltered, open, unprotected 3 vulnerable, in peril, laid bare, susceptible, wide open

exposure noun publicity, display, exhibition, presentation, revelation, showing, uncovering, unveiling

expound verb explain, describe, elucidate, interpret, set forth, spell out, unfold

express verb 1 state, articulate, communicate, declare, phrase, put into words, say, utter, voice, word 2 show, convey, exhibit, indicate, intimate, make known, represent, reveal, signify, stand for, symbolize ♦ adjective 3 explicit, categorical, clear, definite, distinct, plain, unambiguous 4 specific, clear-cut, especial, particular, singular, special 5 fast, direct, high-speed, nonstop, rapid, speedy, swift

expression noun 1 statement, announcement, communication, declaration, utterance 2 indication, demonstration, exhibition, manifestation, representation, show, sign, symbol, token 3 look, air, appearance, aspect, countenance, face 4 phrase, idiom, locution, remark, term, turn of phrase, word

expressive adjective vivid, eloquent, moving, poignant, striking, telling

► **Antonyms**

blank, dead-pan, dull, empty, impassive, inscrutable, vacuous

expressly adverb 1 definitely, categorically, clearly, distinctly, explicitly, in no uncertain terms, plainly, unambiguously 2 specifically, especially, particularly, specially

expulsion noun ejection, banishment, dismissal, eviction, exclusion, removal

exquisite adjective 1 beautiful, attractive, charming, comely, lovely, pleasing, striking 2 fine, beautiful, dainty, delicate, elegant, lovely, precious 3 intense, acute, keen, sharp

► **Antonyms**

≠beautiful: ill-favoured, ugly, unattractive, unlovely, unsightly

extempore adjective impromptu, ad lib, freely, improvised, offhand, off the cuff (informal), spontaneously, unpremeditated, unprepared

extend verb 1 make longer, drag out, draw out, lengthen, prolong, spin out, spread out, stretch 2 last, carry on, continue, go on 3 widen, add to, augment, broaden, enhance, enlarge, expand, increase, supplement 4 offer, confer, impart, present, proffer

> ➤ **Antonyms**

≠make longer: condense, contract, curtail, cut, decrease, limit, reduce, restrict, shorten ≠widen: abbreviate, abridge, condense, contract, cut, decrease, reduce, restrict, shorten ≠offer: take back, withdraw

extension noun 1 annexe, addition, appendage, appendix, supplement 2 lengthening, broadening, development, enlargement, expansion, increase, spread, widening

extensive adjective wide, broad, far-flung, far-reaching, large-scale, pervasive, spacious, vast, voluminous, widespread

> ➤ **Antonyms**

circumscribed, confined, constricted, limited, narrow, restricted, tight

extent noun size, amount, area, breadth, expanse, length, stretch, volume, width

extenuating adjective mitigating, justifying, moderating, qualifying

exterior noun 1 outside, coating, covering, façade, face, shell, skin, surface ♦ adjective 2 outside, external, outer, outermost, outward, surface

> ➤ **Antonyms**

noun ≠outside: inner, inside, interior ♦ adjective ≠outside: inside, interior, internal

exterminate verb destroy, abolish, annihilate, eliminate, eradicate

external adjective 1 outer, exterior, outermost, outside, outward, surface 2 outside, alien, extrinsic, foreign

> ➤ **Antonyms**

≠outer: inner, inside, interior, internal, intrinsic ≠outside: inside, interior, intrinsic

extinct adjective dead, defunct, gone, lost, vanished

> ➤ **Antonyms**

existing, living, surviving

extinction noun dying out, abolition, annihilation, destruction, eradication, extermination, obliteration, oblivion

extinguish verb 1 put out, blow out, douse, quench, smother, snuff out, stifle 2 destroy, annihilate, eliminate, end, eradicate, exterminate, remove, wipe out

extol verb praise, acclaim, commend, eulogize, exalt, glorify, sing the praises of

extort verb force, blackmail, bully, coerce, extract, squeeze

extortionate adjective exorbitant, excessive, extravagant, inflated, outrageous, preposterous, sky-high, unreasonable

> ➤ **Antonyms**

fair, inexpensive, moderate, modest, reasonable

extra adjective 1 additional, added, ancillary, auxiliary, further, more, supplementary 2 surplus, excess, leftover, redundant, spare, superfluous, unused ♦ noun 3 addition, accessory, attachment, bonus, extension, supplement ♦ adverb 4 exceptionally, especially, extraordinarily, extremely, particularly, remarkably, uncommonly, unusually

> ➤ **Antonyms**

adjective ≠additional: compulsory, essential, mandatory, necessary, needed, obligatory, required, requisite, vital ♦ noun ≠addition: essential, must, necessity, precondition, prerequisite, requirement, requisite

extract verb 1 pull out, draw, pluck out, pull, remove, take out, uproot, withdraw 2 derive, draw, elicit, glean, obtain ♦ noun 3 passage, citation, clipping, cutting, excerpt, quotation, selection 4 essence, concentrate, distillation, juice

extraneous adjective irrelevant, beside the point, immaterial, inappropriate, off the subject, unconnected, unrelated

extraordinary adjective unusual, amazing, exceptional, fantastic, outstanding, phenomenal, remarkable, strange, uncommon

➤ **Antonyms**
banal, common, commonplace, customary, everyday, ordinary, unexceptional, unremarkable, usual

extravagance noun **1** waste, lavishness, overspending, prodigality, profligacy, squandering, wastefulness **2** excess, exaggeration, outrageousness, preposterousness, wildness

extravagant adjective **1** wasteful, lavish, prodigal, profligate, spendthrift **2** excessive, outrageous, over the top (slang), preposterous, reckless, unreasonable

➤ **Antonyms**
≠wasteful: careful, close, economical, frugal, miserly, moderate, prudent, sensible, sparing, thrifty, tight-fisted (informal) ≠excessive: conservative, moderate, realistic, reasonable, restrained, sober

extreme adjective **1** maximum, acute, great, highest, intense, severe, supreme, ultimate, utmost **2** severe, drastic, harsh, radical, rigid, strict, uncompromising **3** excessive, fanatical, immoderate, radical **4** farthest, far-off, most distant, outermost, remotest ◆ noun **5** limit, boundary, edge, end, extremity, pole

➤ **Antonyms**
adjective ≠maximum: average, mild, moderate, modest, ordinary, reasonable ≠farthest: nearest

extremely adverb very, awfully (informal), exceedingly, exceptionally, extraordinarily, severely, terribly, uncommonly, unusually

extremist noun fanatic, die-hard, radical, zealot

extremity noun **1** limit, border, boundary, edge, extreme, frontier, pinnacle, tip **2** crisis, adversity, dire straits, disaster, emergency, exigency, trouble **3** extremities hands and feet, fingers and toes, limbs

extricate verb free, disengage, disentangle, get out, release, remove, rescue, wriggle out of

extrovert adjective outgoing, exuberant, gregarious, sociable

➤ **Antonyms**
introspective, introverted, inward-looking, withdrawn

exuberance noun **1** high spirits, cheerfulness, ebullience, enthusiasm, liveliness, spirit, vitality, vivacity, zest **2** luxuriance, abundance, copiousness, lavishness, profusion

exuberant adjective **1** high-spirited, animated, cheerful, ebullient, energetic, enthusiastic, lively, spirited, vivacious **2** luxuriant, abundant, copious, lavish, plentiful, profuse

➤ **Antonyms**
≠high-spirited: apathetic, dull, lifeless, subdued, unenthusiastic

exult verb be joyful, be overjoyed, celebrate, jump for joy, rejoice

eye noun **1** eyeball, optic (informal) **2** appreciation, discernment, discrimination, judgment, perception, recognition, taste ◆ verb **3** look at, check out (informal), contemplate, inspect, study, survey, view, watch

eyesight noun vision, perception, sight

eyesore noun mess, blemish, blot, disfigurement, horror, monstrosity, sight (informal)

eyewitness noun observer, bystander, onlooker, passer-by, spectator, viewer, witness

F f

fable noun **1** story, allegory, legend, myth, parable, tale **2** fiction, fabrication, fantasy, invention, tall story (informal), urban legend, urban myth, yarn (informal)

> ➤ **Antonyms**

actuality, certainty, fact, reality, truth, verity

fabric noun **1** <u>cloth</u>, material, stuff, textile, web **2** <u>framework</u>, constitution, construction, foundations, make-up, organization, structure

fabricate verb **1** <u>make up</u>, concoct, devise, fake, falsify, feign, forge, invent, trump up **2** <u>build</u>, assemble, construct, erect, form, make, manufacture, shape

fabrication noun **1** <u>forgery</u>, concoction, fake, falsehood, fiction, invention, lie, myth **2** <u>construction</u>, assembly, building, erection, manufacture, production

fabulous adjective **1** Informal <u>wonderful</u>, brilliant, fantastic (informal), marvellous, out-of-this-world (informal), sensational (informal), spectacular, superb **2** <u>astounding</u>, amazing, breathtaking, inconceivable, incredible, phenomenal, unbelievable **3** <u>legendary</u>, apocryphal, fantastic, fictitious, imaginary, invented, made-up, mythical, unreal

> ➤ **Antonyms**

actual, common, commonplace, credible, genuine, natural, ordinary, real

façade noun <u>appearance</u>, exterior, face, front, guise, mask, pretence, semblance, show

face noun **1** <u>countenance</u>, features, mug (slang), visage **2** <u>expression</u>, appearance, aspect, look **3** <u>scowl</u>, frown, grimace, pout, smirk **4** <u>side</u>, exterior, front, outside, surface **5** As in save or lose face <u>self-respect</u>, authority, dignity, honour, image, prestige, reputation, standing, status **6** As in put a good face on <u>façade</u>, appearance, display, exterior, front, mask, show ♦ verb **7** <u>look onto</u>, be opposite, front onto, overlook **8** <u>confront</u>, brave, come up against, deal with, encounter, experience, meet, oppose, tackle **9** <u>coat</u>, clad, cover, dress, finish

faceless adjective <u>impersonal</u>, anonymous, remote

facet noun <u>aspect</u>, angle, face, part, phase, plane, side, slant, surface

facetious adjective <u>funny</u>, amusing, comical, droll, flippant, frivolous, humorous, jocular, playful, tongue in cheek

> ➤ **Antonyms**

earnest, genuine, grave, serious, sincere, sober

face up to verb <u>accept</u>, acknowledge, come to terms with, confront, cope with, deal with, meet head-on, tackle

facile adjective <u>superficial</u>, cursory, glib, hasty, shallow, slick

facilitate verb <u>promote</u>, expedite, forward, further, help, make easy, pave the way for, speed up

> ➤ **Antonyms**

delay, frustrate, hamper, handicap, hinder, hold up or back, impede, obstruct, prevent, restrain, thwart

facility noun **1** often plural <u>equipment</u>, advantage, aid, amenity, appliance, convenience, means, opportunity, resource **2** <u>ease</u>, ability, adroitness, dexterity, efficiency, effortlessness, fluency, proficiency, skill

> ➤ **Antonyms**

≠ease: awkwardness, clumsiness, difficulty, ineptness, maladroitness

facsimile noun <u>copy</u>, carbon copy, duplicate, fax, photocopy, print, replica, reproduction, transcript

fact noun **1** <u>event</u>, act, deed, fait accompli, happening, incident, occurrence, performance **2** <u>truth</u>, certainty, reality

> ➤ **Antonyms**

≠truth: fabrication, falsehood, fiction, invention, lie, tall story, untruth

faction noun **1** <u>group</u>, bloc, cabal, clique, contingent, coterie, gang, party, set, splinter group **2** <u>dissension</u>, conflict, disagreement, discord, disunity, division, infighting, rebellion

➤ **Antonyms**

≠<u>dissension</u>: accord, agreement, assent, concord, consensus, peace, rapport, unanimity, unity

factor noun <u>element</u>, aspect, cause, component, consideration, influence, item, part

factory noun <u>works</u>, mill, plant

factual adjective <u>true</u>, authentic, correct, exact, genuine, precise, real, true-to-life

➤ **Antonyms**

fanciful, fictitious, figurative, imaginary, unreal

faculties plural noun <u>powers</u>, capabilities, intelligence, reason, senses, wits

faculty noun **1** <u>ability</u>, aptitude, capacity, facility, power, propensity, skill **2** <u>department</u>, school

➤ **Antonyms**

≠<u>ability</u>: failing, inability, shortcoming, weakness, weak point

fad noun <u>craze</u>, fashion, mania, rage, trend, vogue, whim

fade verb **1** <u>pale</u>, bleach, discolour, lose colour, wash out **2** As in fade away or out <u>dwindle</u>, decline, die away, disappear, dissolve, melt away, vanish, wane

faded adjective <u>discoloured</u>, bleached, dull, indistinct, pale, washed out

fading adjective <u>declining</u>, decreasing, disappearing, dying, on the decline, vanishing

fail verb **1** <u>be unsuccessful</u>, bite the dust, break down, come to grief, come unstuck, fall, fizzle out (informal), flop (informal), founder, miscarry, misfire **2** <u>give out</u>, conk out (informal), cut out, die, peter out, stop working **3** <u>disappoint</u>, abandon, desert, forget, forsake, let down, neglect, omit **4** <u>go bankrupt</u>, become insolvent, close down, fold (informal), go broke (informal), go bust (informal), go into receivership, go out of business, go to the wall, go under ◆ noun **5** without fail <u>regularly</u>, conscientiously, constantly, dependably,

like clockwork, punctually, religiously, without exception

➤ **Antonyms**

verb ≠<u>be unsuccessful</u>: bloom, flourish, grow, pass, prosper, succeed, thrive, triumph

failing noun **1** <u>weakness</u>, blemish, defect, deficiency, drawback, fault, flaw, imperfection, shortcoming ◆ preposition **2** <u>in the absence of</u>, in default of, lacking

➤ **Antonyms**

noun ≠<u>weakness</u>: advantage, asset, forte, metier, speciality, strength

failure noun **1** <u>lack of success</u>, breakdown, collapse, defeat, downfall, fiasco, miscarriage, overthrow **2** <u>loser</u>, black sheep, dead duck (slang), disappointment, dud (informal), flop (informal), nonstarter, washout (informal) **3** <u>bankruptcy</u>, crash, downfall, insolvency, liquidation, ruin

➤ **Antonyms**

≠<u>lack of success</u>: effectiveness, success, triumph ≠<u>bankruptcy</u>: fortune, prosperity

faint adjective **1** <u>dim</u>, distant, faded, indistinct, low, muted, soft, subdued, vague **2** <u>dizzy</u>, exhausted, giddy, light-headed, muzzy, weak, woozy (informal) **3** <u>slight</u>, feeble, remote, unenthusiastic, weak ◆ verb **4** <u>pass out</u>, black out, collapse, flake out (informal), keel over (informal), lose consciousness, swoon (literary) ◆ noun **5** <u>blackout</u>, collapse, swoon (literary), unconsciousness

➤ **Antonyms**

adjective ≠<u>dim</u>: bright, clear, conspicuous, distinct, loud, powerful, strong ≠<u>dizzy</u>: energetic, fresh, hearty, vigorous

faintly adverb **1** <u>softly</u>, feebly, in a whisper, indistinctly, weakly **2** <u>slightly</u>, a little, dimly, somewhat

fair[1] adjective **1** <u>unbiased</u>, above board, equitable, even-handed, honest, impartial, just, lawful, legitimate, proper, unprejudiced **2** <u>light</u>, blond, blonde, fair-haired, flaxen-haired, towheaded **3** <u>beau-</u>

tiful, bonny, comely, handsome, lovely, pretty 4 <u>respectable</u>, adequate, average, decent, moderate, O.K. or okay (*informal*), passable, reasonable, satisfactory, tolerable 5 <u>fine</u>, bright, clear, cloudless, dry, sunny, unclouded

➤ **Antonyms**

≠<u>unbiased</u>: biased, bigoted, inequitable, one-sided, partial, partisan, prejudiced, unfair, unjust ≠<u>beautiful</u>: homely, plain, ugly

fair² *noun* <u>carnival</u>, bazaar, festival, fête, gala, show

fairly *adverb* 1 <u>moderately</u>, adequately, pretty well, quite, rather, reasonably, somewhat, tolerably 2 <u>positively</u>, absolutely, really 3 <u>deservedly</u>, equitably, honestly, impartially, justly, objectively, properly, without fear or favour

fairness *noun* <u>impartiality</u>, decency, disinterestedness, equitableness, equity, justice, legitimacy, rightfulness

fairy *noun* <u>sprite</u>, brownie, elf, leprechaun, peri, pixie, Robin Goodfellow

fairy tale *or* **fairy story** *noun* 1 <u>folk tale</u>, romance 2 <u>lie</u>, cock-and-bull story (*informal*), fabrication, fiction, invention, tall story, untruth, urban legend, urban myth

faith *noun* 1 <u>confidence</u>, assurance, conviction, credence, credit, dependence, reliance, trust 2 <u>religion</u>, belief, church, communion, creed, denomination, dogma, persuasion 3 <u>allegiance</u>, constancy, faithfulness, fidelity, loyalty

➤ **Antonyms**

≠<u>confidence</u>: disbelief, distrust, doubt, misgiving, mistrust, scepticism, suspicion, uncertainty ≠<u>religion</u>: agnosticism ≠<u>allegiance</u>: infidelity

faithful *adjective* 1 <u>loyal</u>, constant, dependable, devoted, reliable, staunch, steadfast, true, trusty 2 <u>accurate</u>, close, exact, precise, strict, true

➤ **Antonyms**

≠<u>loyal</u>: disloyal, faithless, false, false-hearted, inconstant, traitorous, treacherous, unfaithful, unreliable, untrue, untrustworthy

faithless *adjective* <u>disloyal</u>, false, fickle, inconstant, traitorous, treacherous, unfaithful, unreliable

fake *verb* 1 <u>sham</u>, copy, counterfeit, fabricate, feign, forge, pretend, put on, simulate ◆ *noun* 2 <u>impostor</u>, charlatan, copy, forgery, fraud, hoax, imitation, reproduction, sham ◆ *adjective* 3 <u>artificial</u>, counterfeit, false, forged, imitation, mock, phoney *or* phony (*informal*), sham

➤ **Antonyms**

adjective ≠<u>artificial</u>: actual, authentic, bona fide, faithful, genuine, honest, legitimate, real, true, veritable

fall *verb* 1 <u>descend</u>, cascade, collapse, dive, drop, plummet, plunge, sink, subside, tumble 2 <u>decrease</u>, decline, diminish, drop, dwindle, go down, lessen, slump, subside 3 <u>slope</u>, fall away, incline 4 <u>die</u>, be killed, meet one's end, perish 5 <u>be overthrown</u>, capitulate, pass into enemy hands, succumb, surrender 6 <u>occur</u>, befall, chance, come about, come to pass, happen, take place 7 <u>lapse</u>, err, go astray, offend, sin, transgress, trespass ◆ *noun* 8 <u>descent</u>, dive, drop, nose dive, plummet, plunge, slip, tumble 9 <u>decrease</u>, cut, decline, dip, drop, lessening, lowering, reduction, slump 10 <u>collapse</u>, capitulation, defeat, destruction, downfall, overthrow, ruin 11 <u>lapse</u>, sin, transgression

➤ **Antonyms**

verb ≠<u>descend</u>: ascend, climb, go up, increase, mount, rise, scale, soar ≠<u>decrease</u>: advance, appreciate, climb, escalate, extend, heighten, increase ≠<u>die</u>: endure, hold out, survive ≠<u>be overthrown</u>: prevail, triumph

fallacy *noun* <u>error</u>, delusion, falsehood, flaw, misapprehension, misconception, mistake, untruth

fallible *adjective* imperfect, erring, frail, ignorant, uncertain, weak

➤ **Antonyms**

divine, faultless, impeccable, infallible, perfect, superhuman, unerring

fall out *verb Informal* argue, clash, come to blows, differ, disagree, fight, quarrel, squabble

fallow *adjective* uncultivated, dormant, idle, inactive, resting, unplanted, unused

false *adjective* **1** incorrect, erroneous, faulty, inaccurate, inexact, invalid, mistaken, wrong **2** artificial, bogus, counterfeit, fake, forged, imitation, sham, simulated **3** untrue, lying, unreliable, unsound, untruthful **4** deceptive, deceitful, fallacious, fraudulent, hypocritical, misleading, trumped up

➤ **Antonyms**

≠incorrect: correct, exact, right, sound, valid ≠artificial: authentic, bona fide, genuine, honest, real, sincere ≠untrue: reliable, true

falsehood *noun* **1** untruthfulness, deceit, deception, dishonesty, dissimulation, mendacity **2** lie, fabrication, fib, fiction, story, untruth

falsify *verb* alter, counterfeit, distort, doctor, fake, forge, misrepresent, tamper with

falter *verb* hesitate, stammer, stumble, stutter, totter, vacillate, waver

➤ **Antonyms**

continue, endure, keep going, last, persevere, persist, proceed

faltering *adjective* hesitant, broken, irresolute, stammering, tentative, timid, uncertain, weak

fame *noun* prominence, celebrity, glory, honour, renown, reputation, repute, stardom

➤ **Antonyms**

disgrace, dishonour, disrepute, ignominy, infamy, oblivion, obscurity, shame

familiar *adjective* **1** well-known, accustomed, common, customary, frequent, ordinary, recognizable, routine **2** friendly, amicable, close, easy, intimate, relaxed **3** disrespectful, bold, forward, impudent, intrusive, presumptuous

➤ **Antonyms**

≠well-known: infrequent, unaccustomed, uncommon, unfamiliar, unknown, unusual ≠friendly: aloof, cold, detached, distant, formal, unfriendly

familiarity *noun* **1** acquaintance, awareness, experience, grasp, understanding **2** friendliness, ease, informality, intimacy, openness, sociability **3** disrespect, boldness, forwardness, presumption

➤ **Antonyms**

≠acquaintance: ignorance, inexperience, unfamiliarity ≠friendliness: distance, formality, reserve ≠disrespect: constraint, decorum, propriety, respect

familiarize *verb* accustom, habituate, instruct, inure, school, season, train

family *noun* **1** relations, folk (*informal*), household, kin, kith and kin, one's nearest and dearest, one's own flesh and blood, relatives **2** clan, dynasty, house, race, tribe **3** group, class, genre, network, subdivision, system

famine *noun* hunger, dearth, scarcity, starvation

famished *adjective* starving, ravenous, voracious

famous *adjective* well-known, acclaimed, celebrated, distinguished, eminent, illustrious, legendary, noted, prominent, renowned

➤ **Antonyms**

forgotten, mediocre, obscure, undistinguished, unexceptional, unknown, unremarkable

fan¹ *noun* **1** blower, air conditioner, ventilator ◆ *verb* **2** blow, air-condition, cool, refresh, ventilate

fan² *noun* supporter, admirer, aficionado, buff (*informal*), devotee, enthusiast, lover

fanatic *noun* extremist, activist, bigot, militant, zealot

fanatical *adjective* obsessive, bigoted, extreme, fervent, frenzied, immoderate, overenthusiastic, passionate, wild, zealous

fanciful *adjective* unreal, imaginary, mythical, romantic, visionary, whimsical, wild

➤ **Antonyms**
down-to-earth, literal, matter of fact

fancy *adjective* **1** elaborate, baroque, decorative, embellished, extravagant, intricate, ornamental, ornate ◆ *noun* **2** whim, caprice, desire, humour, idea, impulse, inclination, notion, thought, urge **3** delusion, chimera, daydream, dream, fantasy, vision ◆ *verb* **4** *Informal* be attracted to, be captivated by, like, lust after, take a liking to, take to **5** wish for, crave, desire, hanker after, hope for, long for, thirst for, yearn for **6** suppose, believe, conjecture, imagine, reckon, think, think likely

➤ **Antonyms**
adjective ≠elaborate: basic, cheap, common, inferior, ordinary, plain, simple, unadorned, undecorated, unfussy

fantasize *verb* daydream, dream, envision, imagine

fantastic *adjective* **1** *Informal* wonderful, awesome (*slang*), excellent, first-rate, marvellous, sensational (*informal*), superb **2** strange, fanciful, grotesque, outlandish **3** unrealistic, extravagant, far-fetched, ludicrous, ridiculous, wild **4** implausible, absurd, cock-and-bull (*informal*), incredible, preposterous, unlikely

➤ **Antonyms**
≠wonderful: common, everyday, normal, ordinary, poor, typical ≠unrealistic, implausible: credible, moderate, rational, realistic, sensible

fantasy *noun* **1** imagination, crea-

tivity, fancy, invention, originality **2** daydream, dream, flight of fancy, illusion, mirage, pipe dream, reverie, vision

far *adverb* **1** a long way, afar, a good way, a great distance, deep, miles **2** much, considerably, decidedly, extremely, greatly, incomparably, very much ◆ *adjective* **3** remote, distant, faraway, far-flung, far-off, outlying, out-of-the-way

➤ **Antonyms**
adjective ≠remote: adjacent, adjoining, beside, close, near, nearby, neighbouring

farce *noun* **1** comedy, buffoonery, burlesque, satire, slapstick **2** mockery, joke, nonsense, parody, sham, travesty

farcical *adjective* ludicrous, absurd, comic, derisory, laughable, nonsensical, preposterous, ridiculous, risible

fare *noun* **1** charge, price, ticket money **2** food, provisions, rations, sustenance, victuals ◆ *verb* **3** get on, do, get along, make out, manage, prosper

farewell *noun* goodbye, adieu, departure, leave-taking, parting, sendoff (*informal*), valediction

far-fetched *adjective* unconvincing, cock-and-bull (*informal*), fantastic, implausible, incredible, preposterous, unbelievable, unlikely, unrealistic

➤ **Antonyms**
acceptable, authentic, believable, credible, feasible, imaginable, likely, plausible, possible, probable, realistic, reasonable

farm *noun* **1** smallholding, croft (*Scot.*), farmstead, grange, homestead, plantation, ranch (*chiefly North American*) ◆ *verb* **2** cultivate, plant, work

fascinate *verb* entrance, absorb, beguile, captivate, engross, enthral, hold spellbound, intrigue, rivet, transfix

➤ **Antonyms**
bore, disenchant, disgust, put

one off, sicken, turn one off (informal)

fascinating adjective captivating, alluring, compelling, engaging, engrossing, enticing, gripping, intriguing, irresistible, riveting

➤ **Antonyms**
boring, dull, mind-numbing, unexciting, uninteresting

fascination noun attraction, allure, charm, enchantment, lure, magic, magnetism, pull

fashion noun 1 style, craze, custom, fad, look, mode, rage, trend, vogue 2 method, manner, mode, style, way ♦ verb 3 make, construct, create, forge, form, manufacture, mould, shape

fashionable adjective popular, à la mode, chic, in, (informal), in vogue, modern, stylish, trendy (Brit. informal), up-to-date, with it (informal)

➤ **Antonyms**
behind the times, dated, frumpy, obsolete, old-fashioned, outmoded, out of date, unfashionable, unpopular, unstylish

fast¹ adjective 1 quick, brisk, fleet, flying, hasty, nippy (Brit. informal), rapid, speedy, swift 2 dissipated, dissolute, extravagant, loose, profligate, reckless, self-indulgent, wanton, wild 3 fixed, close, fastened, firm, immovable, secure, sound, steadfast, tight ♦ adverb 4 quickly, hastily, hurriedly, in haste, like lightning, rapidly, speedily, swiftly 5 soundly, deeply, firmly, fixedly, securely, tightly

➤ **Antonyms**
adjective ≠quick: leisurely, plodding, slow, slow moving, unhurried ≠fixed: inconstant, unreliable, unstable, wavering, weak ♦ adverb ≠quickly: at a snail's pace, at one's leisure, gradually, leisurely, slowly, steadily, unhurriedly

fast² verb 1 go hungry, abstain, deny oneself, go without food ♦ noun 2 fasting, abstinence

fasten verb fix, affix, attach, bind, connect, join, link, secure, tie

fat adjective 1 overweight, corpulent, heavy, obese, plump, podgy, portly, rotund, stout, tubby 2 fatty, adipose, greasy, oily, oleaginous ♦ noun 3 fatness, blubber, bulk, corpulence, flab, flesh, obesity, paunch

➤ **Antonyms**
adjective ≠overweight: angular, bony, gaunt, lank, lean, scrawny, skinny, slender, slight, slim, spare, thin ≠fatty: lean

fatal adjective 1 lethal, deadly, final, incurable, killing, malignant, mortal, terminal 2 disastrous, baleful, baneful, calamitous, catastrophic, ruinous

➤ **Antonyms**
≠lethal: beneficial, benign, harmless, innocuous, non-lethal, nontoxic, wholesome ≠disastrous: inconsequential, minor

fatality noun death, casualty, loss, mortality

fate noun 1 destiny, chance, divine will, fortune, kismet, nemesis, predestination, providence 2 fortune, cup, horoscope, lot, portion, stars

fated adjective destined, doomed, foreordained, inescapable, inevitable, predestined, preordained, sure, written

fateful adjective 1 crucial, critical, decisive, important, portentous, significant 2 disastrous, deadly, destructive, fatal, lethal, ominous, ruinous

➤ **Antonyms**
≠crucial: inconsequential, insignificant, ordinary, unimportant

father noun 1 daddy (informal), dad (informal), old man (informal), pa (informal), pa (old-fashioned informal), pater, pop (informal) 2 forefather, ancestor, forebear, predecessor, progenitor 3 founder, architect, author, creator, inventor, maker, originator, prime mover 4 priest, padre (informal), pastor ♦ verb 5 sire, beget, get, procreate

fatherland *noun* homeland, motherland, native land

fatherly *adjective* paternal, affectionate, benevolent, benign, kindly, patriarchal, protective, supportive

fathom *verb* understand, comprehend, get to the bottom of, grasp, interpret

fatigue *noun* **1** tiredness, heaviness, languor, lethargy, listlessness ♦ *verb* **2** tire, drain, exhaust, knacker (*slang*), take it out of (*informal*), weaken, wear out, weary

➤ **Antonyms**

noun ≠tiredness: alertness, animation, energy, freshness, get-up-and-go (*informal*), go, life, vigour, zest ♦ *verb* ≠tire: refresh, rejuvenate, relieve, rest, revive, stimulate

fatten *verb* **1** grow fat, expand, gain weight, put on weight, spread, swell, thicken **2** *often with* **up** feed up, build up, feed, nourish, overfeed, stuff

fatty *adjective* greasy, adipose, fat, oily, oleaginous, rich

fatuous *adjective* foolish, brainless, dumb-ass (*slang*), idiotic, inane, ludicrous, mindless, moronic, silly, stupid, witless

fault *noun* **1** responsibility, accountability, culpability, liability **2** mistake, blunder, error, indiscretion, lapse, oversight, slip **3** flaw, blemish, defect, deficiency, failing, imperfection, shortcoming, weakness, weak point **4** at fault guilty, answerable, blamable, culpable, in the wrong, responsible, to blame **5** find fault with criticize, carp at, complain, pick holes in, pull to pieces, quibble, take to task **6** to a fault excessively, immoderately, in the extreme, overmuch, unduly ♦ *verb* **7** criticize, blame, censure, find fault with, hold (someone) responsible, impugn

➤ **Antonyms**

noun ≠flaw: asset, attribute, credit, merit, strength, virtue

faultless *adjective* flawless, correct, exemplary, foolproof, impeccable, model, perfect, unblemished

faulty *adjective* defective, broken, damaged, flawed, impaired, imperfect, incorrect, malfunctioning, out of order, unsound

favour *noun* **1** approval, approbation, backing, good opinion, goodwill, patronage, support **2** good turn, benefit, boon, courtesy, indulgence, kindness, service **3** prefer, incline towards **4** indulge, reward, side with, smile upon **5** support, advocate, champion, commend, encourage

➤ **Antonyms**

noun ≠approval: animosity, antipathy, disapproval, disfavour, ill will, malevolence ≠good turn: disservice, harm, injury, wrong ♦ *verb* ≠prefer: disapprove, disdain, dislike, object to ≠support: oppose

favourable *adjective* **1** advantageous, auspicious, beneficial, encouraging, helpful, opportune, promising, propitious, suitable **2** positive, affirmative, agreeable, approving, encouraging, enthusiastic, reassuring, sympathetic

➤ **Antonyms**

≠advantageous: disadvantageous, inauspicious, unfavourable, unhelpful, unpromising ≠positive: disapproving, ill-disposed, unfavourable, unsympathetic

favourably *adverb* **1** advantageously, auspiciously, conveniently, fortunately, opportunely, profitably, to one's advantage, well **2** positively, approvingly, enthusiastically, helpfully, with approval

favourite *adjective* **1** preferred, best-loved, choice, dearest, esteemed, fave (*informal*), favoured ♦ *noun* **2** darling, beloved, blue-eyed boy (*informal*), fave (*informal*), idol, pet, teacher's pet, the apple of one's eye

fawn[1] *verb*, *often with* **on** *or* **upon**

ingratiate oneself, crawl, creep, cringe, curry favour, dance attendance, flatter, grovel, kowtow, pander to

fawn² *adjective* beige, buff, greyish-brown, neutral

fawning *adjective* obsequious, crawling, cringing, deferential, flattering, grovelling, servile, sycophantic

fear *noun* **1** dread, alarm, apprehensiveness, fright, horror, panic, terror, trepidation **2** bugbear, bête noire, bogey, horror, nightmare, spectre ◆ *verb* **3** be afraid, dread, shake in one's shoes, shudder at, take fright, tremble at **4** fear for worry about, be anxious about, feel concern for

fearful *adjective* **1** scared, afraid, alarmed, frightened, jumpy, nervous, timid, timorous, uneasy **2** frightful, awful, dire, dreadful, gruesome, hair-raising, horrendous, horrific, terrible

➤ **Antonyms**
≠scared: bold, brave, confident, courageous, daring, gutsy (*slang*), intrepid, plucky, unafraid

fearfully *adverb* **1** nervously, apprehensively, diffidently, timidly, timorously, uneasily **2** very, awfully, exceedingly, excessively, frightfully, terribly, tremendously

fearless *adjective* brave, bold, courageous, dauntless, indomitable, intrepid, plucky, unafraid, undaunted, valiant

fearsome *adjective* terrifying, awe-inspiring, daunting, formidable, frightening, horrifying, menacing, unnerving

feasible *adjective* possible, achievable, attainable, likely, practicable, reasonable, viable, workable

➤ **Antonyms**
impossible, impracticable, inconceivable, unreasonable, untenable, unviable, unworkable

feast *noun* **1** banquet, dinner, repast, spread (*informal*), treat **2** treat, delight, enjoyment, gratification, pleasure **3** festival, celebration, fête, holiday, holy day, red-letter day, saint's day ◆ *verb* **4** eat one's fill, gorge, gormandize, indulge, overindulge, pig out (*slang*), wine and dine

feat *noun* accomplishment, achievement, act, attainment, deed, exploit, performance

feathers *plural noun* plumage, down, plumes

feature *noun* **1** aspect, characteristic, facet, factor, hallmark, peculiarity, property, quality, trait **2** highlight, attraction, main item, speciality **3** article, column, item, piece, report, story ◆ *verb* **4** spotlight, emphasize, foreground, give prominence to, play up, present, star

features *plural noun* face, countenance, lineaments, physiognomy

feckless *adjective* irresponsible, good-for-nothing, hopeless, incompetent, ineffectual, shiftless, worthless

federation *noun* union, alliance, amalgamation, association, coalition, combination, league, syndicate

fed up *adjective* dissatisfied, bored, brassed off (*Brit. slang*), depressed, discontented, down in the mouth, glum, sick and tired (*informal*), tired

fee *noun* charge, bill, payment, remuneration, toll

feeble *adjective* **1** weak, debilitated, doddering, effete, frail, infirm, puny, sickly, weedy (*informal*) **2** flimsy, inadequate, insufficient, lame, paltry, pathetic, poor, tame, thin, unconvincing

➤ **Antonyms**
≠weak: energetic, hale, healthy, hearty, lusty, robust, stalwart, strong, sturdy, vigorous ≠flimsy: effective, forceful, successful

feebleness *noun* weakness, effeteness, frailty, infirmity, languor, lassitude, sickliness

feed *verb* **1** cater for, nourish, provide for, provision, supply, sustain, victual, wine and dine **2** sometimes with on eat, devour,

exist on, live on, partake of
♦ *noun* **3** food, fodder, pastur-
age, provender **4** *Informal* meal,
feast, handle, nosh (*slang*), repast,
spread (*informal*)

feel *verb* **1** touch, caress, finger,
fondle, handle, manipulate,
paw, stroke **2** experience, be
aware of, notice, observe, perceive **3** sense, be convinced, in-
tuit **4** believe, consider, deem,
hold, judge, think ♦ *noun* **5** texture, finish, surface, touch **6** impression, air, ambience, atmosphere, feeling, quality, sense

feeler *noun* **1** antenna, tentacle,
whisker **2** *As in* put out feelers
approach, advance, probe

feeling *noun* **1** emotion, ardour,
fervour, intensity, passion, sentiment, warmth **2** impression,
hunch, idea, inkling, notion, presentiment, sense, suspicion **3**
opinion, inclination, instinct,
point of view, view **4** sympathy,
compassion, concern, empathy,
pity, sensibility, sensitivity, understanding **5** sense of touch, perception, sensation **6** atmosphere, air, ambience, aura, feel,
mood, quality

fell *verb* cut down, cut, demolish,
hew, knock down, level

fellow *noun* **1** *Old-fashioned* man,
bloke (*Brit. informal*), chap (*informal*), character, guy (*informal*),
individual, person **2** associate,
colleague, companion, comrade,
partner, peer

fellowship *noun* **1** camaraderie,
brotherhood, companionship, sociability **2** society, association,
brotherhood, club, fraternity,
guild, league, order

feminine *adjective* womanly, delicate, gentle, ladylike, soft, tender

► **Antonyms**

butch, indelicate, manly, mannish, masculine, rough, unfemi-
nine, unladylike, unwomanly, virile

femme fatale *noun* seductress,
enchantress, siren, vamp (*informal*)

fen *noun* marsh, bog, morass,
quagmire, slough, swamp

fence *noun* **1** barrier, barricade,
defence, hedge, palisade, rail-
ings, rampart, wall ♦ *verb* **2** *often
with* in or off enclose, bound,
confine, encircle, pen, protect,
surround **3** evade, dodge,
equivocate, flannel (*Brit. informal*), parry

ferment *noun* commotion, disruption, excitement, frenzy, furore, stir, tumult, turmoil, unrest,
uproar

► **Antonyms**

calmness, hush, peacefulness,
quiet, restfulness, stillness, tranquillity

ferocious *adjective* **1** fierce, predatory, rapacious, ravening, sav-
age, violent, wild **2** cruel, bloodthirsty, brutal, ruthless, vicious

► **Antonyms**

≠**fierce:** calm, docile, gentle,
mild, subdued, submissive, tame

ferocity *noun* savagery, bloodthirstiness, brutality, cruelty,
fierceness, viciousness, wildness

ferret *verb* track down, dig
up, discover, elicit, root out,
search out, trace, unearth

ferry *noun* **1** ferry boat, packet,
packet boat ♦ *verb* **2** carry, chauf-
feur, convey, run, ship, shuttle,
transport

fertile *adjective* productive, abundant, fecund, fruitful, luxuriant,
plentiful, prolific, rich, teeming

► **Antonyms**

barren, dry, impotent, infertile,
poor, sterile, unfruitful, unproductive

fertility *noun* fruitfulness, abundance, fecundity, luxuriance, pro-
ductiveness, richness

fertilizer *noun* compost, dressing, dung, manure

fervent, fervid *adjective* intense,
ardent, devout, earnest, enthusiastic, heartfelt, impassioned, passionate, vehement

► **Antonyms**

apathetic, cold, cool, detached,
dispassionate, frigid, impassive,

unfeeling, unimpassioned

fervour noun <u>intensity</u>, ardour, enthusiasm, excitement, passion, vehemence, warmth, zeal

fester verb 1 <u>intensify</u>, aggravate, smoulder 2 <u>putrefy</u>, decay, suppurate, ulcerate

festival noun 1 <u>celebration</u>, carnival, entertainment, fête, gala, jubilee 2 <u>holy day</u>, anniversary, commemoration, feast, fête, fiesta, holiday, red-letter day, saint's day

festive adjective <u>celebratory</u>, cheery, convivial, happy, jovial, joyful, joyous, jubilant, merry

► **Antonyms**
depressing, drab, dreary, funereal, gloomy, mournful, sad

festivity noun often plural <u>celebration</u>, entertainment, festival, party

festoon verb <u>decorate</u>, array, deck, drape, garland, hang, swathe, wreathe

fetch verb 1 <u>bring</u>, carry, convey, deliver, get, go for, obtain, retrieve, transport 2 <u>sell for</u>, bring in, earn, go for, make, realize, yield

fetching adjective <u>attractive</u>, alluring, captivating, charming, cute, enticing, winsome

fetish noun 1 <u>fixation</u>, mania, obsession, thing (informal) 2 <u>talisman</u>, amulet

feud noun 1 <u>hostility</u>, argument, conflict, disagreement, enmity, quarrel, rivalry, row, vendetta ♦ verb 2 <u>quarrel</u>, bicker, clash, contend, dispute, fall out, row, squabble, war

fever noun <u>excitement</u>, agitation, delirium, ferment, fervour, frenzy, restlessness

feverish or **fevered** adjective 1 <u>hot</u>, febrile, fevered, flushed, inflamed, pyretic (Medical) 2 <u>excited</u>, agitated, frantic, frenetic, frenzied, overwrought, restless

► **Antonyms**
≠<u>excited</u>: calm, collected, composed, cool, dispassionate, nonchalant, tranquil, unemotional,

unfazed (informal), unruffled

few adjective <u>not many</u>, meagre, negligible, rare, scanty, scarcely any, sparse, sporadic

fiasco noun <u>flop</u> (informal), catastrophe, cock-up (Brit. slang), debacle, disaster, failure, mess, washout (informal)

fib noun <u>lie</u>, fiction, story, untruth, white lie

fibre noun 1 <u>thread</u>, filament, pile, strand, texture, wisp 2 As in moral fibre <u>strength of character</u>, resolution, stamina, strength, toughness 3 <u>essence</u>, nature, quality, spirit, substance

fickle adjective <u>changeable</u>, capricious, faithless, inconstant, irresolute, temperamental, unfaithful, variable, volatile

► **Antonyms**
changeless, constant, faithful, firm, loyal, resolute, steadfast, true

fiction noun 1 <u>tale</u>, fantasy, legend, myth, novel, romance, story, yarn (informal) 2 <u>lie</u>, cock and bull story (informal), fabrication, falsehood, invention, tall story, untruth, urban legend, urban myth

fictional adjective <u>imaginary</u>, invented, legendary, made-up, nonexistent, unreal

fictitious adjective <u>false</u>, bogus, fabricated, imaginary, invented, make-believe, mythical, untrue

► **Antonyms**
actual, authentic, genuine, legitimate, real, true, truthful, veracious, veritable

fiddle noun 1 <u>violin</u> 2 Brit. informal <u>fraud</u>, fix, racket, scam (slang), swindle 3 fit as a fiddle Informal <u>healthy</u>, blooming, hale and hearty, in fine fettle, in good form, in good shape, in rude health, in the pink, sound, strong ♦ verb 4 Informal <u>cheat</u>, cook the books (informal), diddle (informal), fix, swindle, wangle (informal) 5 <u>fidget</u>, finger, interfere with, mess about or around, play, tamper with, tinker

fiddling adjective trivial, futile, insignificant, pettifogging, petty, trifling

fidelity noun **1** loyalty, allegiance, constancy, dependability, devotion, faithfulness, staunchness, trustworthiness **2** accuracy, closeness, correspondence, exactness, faithfulness, precision, scrupulousness

> **Antonyms**

≠loyalty: disloyalty, faithlessness, falseness, infidelity, treachery, unfaithfulness, untruthfulness ≠accuracy: inaccuracy, inexactness

fidget verb **1** move restlessly, fiddle (informal), fret, squirm, twitch ◆ noun **2 the fidgets** restlessness, fidgetiness, jitters (informal), nervousness, unease, uneasiness

fidgety adjective restless, antsy (informal), impatient, jittery (informal), jumpy, nervous, on edge, restive, twitchy (informal), uneasy

field noun **1** meadow, grassland, green, lea (poetic), pasture **2** competitors, applicants, candidates, competition, contestants, entrants, possibilities, runners **3** speciality, area, department, discipline, domain, line, province, territory ◆ verb **4** Sport retrieve, catch, pick up, return, stop **5** Informal deal with, deflect, handle, turn aside

fiend noun **1** demon, devil, evil spirit **2** brute, barbarian, beast, ghoul, monster, ogre, savage **3** Informal enthusiast, addict, fanatic, freak (informal), maniac

fiendish adjective wicked, cruel, devilish, diabolical, hellish, infernal, malignant, monstrous, satanic, unspeakable

fierce adjective **1** wild, brutal, cruel, dangerous, ferocious, fiery, menacing, savage, vicious **3** stormy, furious, howling, inclement, powerful, raging, strong, tempestuous, violent **3** intense, cut-throat, keen, relentless, strong

> **Antonyms**

≠wild: docile, domesticated, gentle, harmless, mild, tame ≠stormy: temperate, tranquil

fiercely adverb ferociously, furiously, passionately, savagely, tempestuously, tigerishly, tooth and nail, viciously, with no holds barred

fiery adjective **1** burning, ablaze, afire, aflame, blazing, flaming, on fire **2** excitable, fierce, hot-headed, impetuous, irascible, irritable, passionate

fight verb **1** battle, box, clash, combat, do battle, grapple, spar, struggle, tussle, wrestle **2** oppose, contest, defy, dispute, make a stand against, resist, stand up to, withstand **3** engage in, carry on, conduct, prosecute, wage ◆ noun **4** battle, clash, conflict, contest, dispute, duel, encounter, struggle, tussle **5** resistance, belligerence, militancy, pluck, spirit

fighter noun **1** boxer, prize fighter, pugilist **2** soldier, fighting man, man-at-arms, warrior

fight off verb repel, beat off, drive away, keep or hold at bay, repress, repulse, resist, stave off, ward off

figure noun **1** number, character, digit, numeral, symbol **2** amount, cost, price, sum, total, value **3** shape, body, build, frame, physique, proportions **4** character, big name, celebrity, dignitary, personality **5** diagram, design, drawing, illustration, pattern, representation, sketch ◆ verb **6** calculate, compute, count, reckon, tally, tot up, work out **7** usually with in feature, act, appear, be featured, contribute to, play a part

figurehead noun front man, mouthpiece, puppet, titular or nominal head

figure out verb **1** calculate, compute, reckon, work out **2** understand, comprehend, decipher, fathom, make out, see

filch verb <u>steal</u>, embezzle, misappropriate, pilfer, pinch (*informal*), take, thieve, walk off with

file[1] noun 1 <u>folder</u>, case, data, documents, dossier, information, portfolio 2 <u>line</u>, column, queue, row ◆ verb 3 <u>register</u>, document, enter, pigeonhole, put in place, record 7 <u>march</u>, parade, troop

file[2] verb <u>smooth</u>, abrade, polish, rasp, rub, scrape, shape

fill verb 1 <u>stuff</u>, cram, crowd, glut, pack, stock, supply, swell 2 <u>saturate</u>, charge, imbue, impregnate, pervade, suffuse 3 <u>plug</u>, block, bung, close, cork, seal, stop 4 <u>perform</u>, carry out, discharge, execute, fulfil, hold, occupy ◆ noun 5 **one's fill** <u>sufficient</u>, all one wants, ample, enough, plenty

> **Antonyms**

verb ≠<u>stuff</u>: drain, empty, exhaust, vacate, void

filler noun <u>padding</u>, makeweight, stopgap

fill in verb 1 <u>complete</u>, answer, fill out (*U.S.*), fill up 2 <u>replace</u>, deputize, represent, stand in, sub, substitute, take the place of 3 *Informal* <u>inform</u>, acquaint, apprise, bring up to date, give the facts or background

filling noun <u>stuffing</u>, contents, filler, inside, insides, padding, wadding ◆ adjective <u>satisfying</u>, ample, heavy, square, substantial

film noun 1 <u>movie</u>, flick (*slang*), motion picture 2 <u>layer</u>, coating, covering, dusting, membrane, skin, tissue ◆ verb 3 <u>photograph</u>, shoot, take, video, videotape

filter noun 1 <u>sieve</u>, gauze, membrane, mesh, riddle, strainer ◆ verb 2 <u>purify</u>, clarify, filtrate, refine, screen, sieve, sift, strain, winnow 3 <u>trickle</u>, dribble, escape, exude, leak, ooze, penetrate, percolate, seep

filth noun 1 <u>dirt</u>, excrement, grime, muck, refuse, sewage, slime, sludge, squalor 2 <u>obscenity</u>, impurity, indecency, pornography, smut, vulgarity

filthy adjective 1 <u>dirty</u>, polluted, putrid, slimy, squalid, unclean 2 <u>muddy</u>, begrimed, blackened, grimy, grubby 3 <u>obscene</u>, corrupt, depraved, impure, indecent, lewd, licentious, pornographic, smutty

final adjective 1 <u>last</u>, closing, concluding, latest, terminal, ultimate 2 <u>conclusive</u>, absolute, decided, definite, definitive, incontrovertible, irrevocable, settled

> **Antonyms**

≠<u>last</u>: earliest, first, initial, introductory, opening

finale noun <u>ending</u>, climax, close, conclusion, culmination, denouement, epilogue

> **Antonyms**

commencement, intro (*informal*), lead-in, opening, overture, preamble, preface, preliminaries, prelude

finalize verb <u>complete</u>, clinch, conclude, decide, settle, tie up, work out, wrap up (*informal*)

finally adverb 1 <u>eventually</u>, at last, at length, at long last, in the end, lastly, ultimately 2 <u>in conclusion</u>, in summary, lastly, to conclude

finance verb 1 <u>fund</u>, back, bankroll (*U.S.*), guarantee, pay for, subsidize, support, underwrite ◆ noun 2 <u>economics</u>, accounts, banking, business, commerce, investment, money

finances plural noun <u>resources</u>, affairs, assets, capital, cash, funds, money, wherewithal

financial adjective <u>economic</u>, fiscal, monetary, pecuniary

find verb 1 <u>discover</u>, come across, encounter, hit upon, locate, meet, recognize, spot, uncover 2 <u>realise</u>, detect, discover, learn, note, notice, observe, perceive ◆ noun 3 <u>discovery</u>, acquisition, asset, bargain, catch, good buy

> **Antonyms**

verb ≠<u>discover</u>: lose, mislay, misplace, miss, overlook

find out verb 1 <u>learn</u>, detect, discover, note, observe, perceive, realize **2** detect, catch, disclose, expose, reveal, uncover, unmask

fine[1] *adjective* **1** excellent, accomplished, exceptional, exquisite, first-rate, magnificent, masterly, outstanding, splendid, superior **2** sunny, balmy, bright, clear, clement, cloudless, dry, fair, pleasant **3** satisfactory, acceptable, all right, convenient, good, O.K. or okay (*informal*), suitable **4** delicate, dainty, elegant, expensive, exquisite, fragile, quality **5** subtle, abstruse, acute, hairsplitting, minute, nice, precise, sharp **6** slender, diaphanous, flimsy, gauzy, gossamer, light, sheer, thin

➤ **Antonyms**

≠excellent: indifferent, inferior, poor, second rate, substandard ≠sunny: cloudy, dull, overcast, unpleasant ≠delicate: blunt, coarse, crude, rough

fine[2] *noun* **1** penalty, damages, forfeit, punishment ♦ *verb* **2** penalize, mulct, punish

finery *noun* splendour, frippery, gear (*informal*), glad rags (*informal*), ornaments, showiness, Sunday best, trappings, trinkets

finesse *noun* skill, adeptness, adroitness, craft, delicacy, diplomacy, discretion, savoir-faire, sophistication, subtlety, tact

finger *verb* touch, feel, fiddle with (*informal*), handle, manipulate, maul, paw (*informal*), toy with

finish *verb* **1** stop, cease, close, complete, conclude, end, round off, terminate, wind up, wrap up (*informal*) **2** consume, devour, dispose of, eat, empty, exhaust, use up **3** perfect, polish, refine **4** coat, gild, lacquer, polish, stain, texture, veneer, wax **5** destroy, bring down, defeat, dispose of, exterminate, overcome, put an end to, put paid to, rout, ruin ♦ *noun* **6** end, cessation, close, completion, conclusion, culmination, denouement, finale, run-in **7** defeat, annihilation, curtains (*informal*), death, end, end of

the road, ruin **8** surface, lustre, patina, polish, shine, smoothness, texture

➤ **Antonyms**

verb ≠stop: begin, commence, create, embark on, instigate, start, undertake ♦ *noun* ≠end: beginning, birth, commencement, inception

finished *adjective* **1** over, closed, complete, done, ended, finalized, through **2** spent, drained, empty, exhausted, used up **3** polished, accomplished, perfected, professional, refined **4** ruined, defeated, done for (*informal*), doomed, lost, through, undone, wiped out

➤ **Antonyms**

≠over: begun, incomplete ≠polished: basic, coarse, crude, imperfect, rough, unfinished, unrefined

finite *adjective* limited, bounded, circumscribed, delimited, demarcated, restricted

➤ **Antonyms**

boundless, endless, eternal, everlasting, immeasurable, infinite, limitless, perpetual, unbounded

fire *noun* **1** flames, blaze, combustion, conflagration, inferno **2** bombardment, barrage, cannonade, flak, fusillade, hail, salvo, shelling, sniping, volley **3** passion, ardour, eagerness, enthusiasm, excitement, fervour, intensity, sparkle, spirit, verve, vigour ♦ *verb* **4** shoot, detonate, discharge, explode, let off, pull the trigger, set off, shell **5** *Informal* dismiss, cashier, discharge, make redundant, sack (*informal*), show the door **6** inspire, animate, enliven, excite, galvanize, impassion, inflame, rouse, stir

firebrand *noun* rabble-rouser, agitator, demagogue, incendiary, instigator, tub-thumper

fireworks *plural noun* **1** pyrotechnics, illuminations **2** *Informal* trouble, hysterics, rage, row, storm, uproar

firm[1] *adjective* **1** hard, dense, inflexible, rigid, set, solid, solidified, stiff, unyielding **2** secure, embedded, fast, fixed, immovable, rooted, stable, steady, tight, unshakable **3** determined, adamant, definite, inflexible, resolute, resolved, set on, unbending, unshakable, unyielding

► **Antonyms**

≠hard: flabby, flaccid, limp, soft ≠secure: flimsy, insecure, loose, shaky, unreliable, unstable, unsteady ≠determined: inconstant, irresolute, wavering

firm² noun **1** company, association, business, concern, conglomerate, corporation, enterprise, organization, partnership

firmly adverb **1** securely, immovably, like a rock, steadily, tightly, unflinchingly, unshakably **2** resolutely, staunchly, steadfastly, unchangeably, unwaveringly

firmness noun **1** hardness, inelasticity, inflexibility, resistance, rigidity, solidity, stiffness **2** resolve, constancy, inflexibility, resolution, staunchness, steadfastness

first adjective **1** earliest, initial, introductory, maiden, opening, original, premier, primordial **2** elementary, basic, cardinal, fundamental, key, primary, rudimentary **3** foremost, chief, head, highest, leading, pre-eminent, prime, principal, ruling ♦ noun **4** As in **from the first** start, beginning, commencement, inception, introduction, outset, starting point ♦ adverb **5** to begin with, at the beginning, at the outset, beforehand, firstly, initially, in the first place, to start with

first-rate adjective excellent, crack (slang), elite, exceptional, first class, outstanding, superb, superlative, top-notch (informal), world-class

fishy adjective **1** Informal suspicious, dodgy (Brit., Austral., & N.Z. informal), dubious, funny (informal), implausible, odd, questionable, suspect, unlikely **2** fishlike, piscatorial, piscatory, piscine

fissure noun crack, breach, cleft, crevice, fault, fracture, opening, rift, rupture, split

fit¹ verb **1** suit, accord, belong, conform, correspond, match, meet, tally **2** adapt, adjust, alter, arrange, customize, modify, shape, tweak (informal) **3** equip, arm, fit out, kit out, prepare, provide ♦ adjective **4** appropriate, apt, becoming, correct, fitting, proper, right, seemly, suitable **5** healthy, able-bodied, hale, in good shape, robust, strapping, trim, well

► **Antonyms**

adjective ≠appropriate: amiss, ill-fitted, ill-suited, improper, inappropriate, unfit, unseemly, unsuitable ≠healthy: flabby, in poor condition, out of shape, out of trim, unfit, unhealthy

fit² noun **1** seizure, attack, bout, convulsion, paroxysm, spasm **2** outbreak, bout, burst, outburst, spell

fitful adjective irregular, broken, desultory, disturbed, inconstant, intermittent, spasmodic, sporadic, uneven

► **Antonyms**

constant, even, regular, steady, uniform

fitness noun **1** appropriateness, aptness, competence, eligibility, propriety, readiness, suitability **2** health, good condition, good health, robustness, strength, vigour, wellness

fitting adjective **1** appropriate, apposite, becoming, correct, decent, proper, right, seemly, suitable ♦ noun **2** accessory, attachment, component, part, piece, unit

► **Antonyms**

adjective ≠appropriate: ill-suited, improper, unfitting, unseemly, unsuitable

fix verb **1** place, embed, establish, implant, install, locate, plant, position, set **2** repair, correct, mend, patch up, put to rights, see to **3** fasten, attach, bind, connect, link, secure, stick, tie **4** decide, agree on, arrange, arrive at, determine, establish, set, settle, specify **5** focus, direct **6** *Informal* rig, fiddle (*informal*), influence, manipulate ♦ *noun* **7** *Informal* predicament, difficulty, dilemma, embarrassment, mess, pickle (*informal*), plight, quandary

fixation *noun* obsession, complex, hang-up (*informal*), idée fixe, infatuation, mania, preoccupation, thing (*informal*)

fixed *adjective* **1** immovable, established, permanent, rigid, rooted, secure, set **2** steady, intent, resolute, unwavering **3** agreed, arranged, decided, definite, established, planned, resolved, settled

➤ **Antonyms**

≠immovable: bending, mobile, moving, pliant, unfixed ≠steady: inconstant, varying, wavering

fix up *verb* **1** arrange, agree on, fix, organize, plan, settle, sort out **2** *often with* provide, arrange for, bring about, lay on

fizz *verb* bubble, effervesce, fizzle, froth, hiss, sparkle, sputter

fizzy *adjective* bubbly, bubbling, carbonated, effervescent, gassy, sparkling

flabbergasted *adjective* astonished, amazed, astounded, dumbfounded, lost for words, overwhelmed, speechless, staggered, stunned

flabby *adjective* limp, baggy, drooping, flaccid, floppy, loose, pendulous, sagging

➤ **Antonyms**

firm, hard, solid, taut, tight

flag [1] *noun* **1** banner, colours, ensign, pennant, pennon, standard, streamer ♦ *verb* **2** mark, indicate, label, note **3** *sometimes with* down hail, signal, warn, wave

flag [2] *verb* weaken, abate, droop, fade, languish, peter out, sag, wane, weary, wilt

flagging *adjective* weakening, declining, deteriorating, fading, faltering, waning, wilting

flagrant *adjective* outrageous, barefaced, blatant, brazen, glaring, heinous, scandalous, shameless

➤ **Antonyms**

faint, implied, indirect, insinuated, slight, subtle, understated

flagstone *noun* paving stone, block, flag, slab

flail *verb* thrash, beat, thresh, windmill

flair *noun* **1** ability, aptitude, faculty, feel, genius, gift, knack, mastery, talent **2** style, chic, dash, discernment, elegance, panache, stylishness, taste

flake *noun* **1** chip, layer, peeling, scale, shaving, sliver, wafer ♦ *verb* **2** chip, blister, peel (off)

flake out *verb* collapse, faint, keel over, pass out

flamboyant *adjective* **1** showy, dashing, elaborate, extravagant, florid, ornate, ostentatious, swashbuckling, theatrical **2** colourful, brilliant, dazzling, glamorous, glitzy (*slang*)

flame *noun* **1** fire, blaze, brightness, light **2** *Informal* sweetheart, beau, boyfriend, girlfriend, heart-throb (*Brit.*), lover ♦ *verb* **3** burn, blaze, flare, flash, glare, glow, shine

flaming *adjective* burning, ablaze, blazing, fiery, glowing, raging, red-hot

flank *noun* **1** side, hip, loin, thigh **2** wing, side

flap *verb* **1** flutter, beat, flail, shake, thrash, vibrate, wag, wave ♦ *noun* **2** flutter, beating, shaking, swinging, swish, waving **3** *Informal* panic, agitation, commotion, fluster, state (*informal*), sweat (*informal*), tizzy (*informal*)

flare *verb* **1** blaze, burn up, flicker, glare **2** widen, broaden, spread out ♦ *noun* **3** flame, blaze, burst, flash, flicker, glare

flare up *verb* lose one's temper, blow one's top (*informal*), boil over, explode, fly off the handle (*informal*), throw a tantrum

flash noun **1** <u>blaze</u>, burst, dazzle, flare, flicker, gleam, shimmer, spark, streak **2** <u>moment</u>, instant, jiffy (informal), second, split second, trice, twinkling of an eye ♦ adjective **3** Informal <u>ostentatious</u>, tacky (informal), tasteless, vulgar ♦ verb **4** <u>blaze</u>, flare, flicker, glare, gleam, shimmer, sparkle, twinkle **5** <u>speed</u>, dart, dash, fly, race, shoot, streak, whistle, zoom **6** Informal <u>show</u>, display, exhibit, expose, flaunt, flourish

flashy adjective <u>showy</u>, flamboyant, garish, gaudy, glitzy (slang), jazzy (informal), ostentatious, snazzy (informal)

➤ Antonyms

downbeat, low-key, modest, natural, plain, unaffected, understated

flat¹ adjective **1** <u>even</u>, horizontal, level, levelled, low, smooth **2** <u>punctured</u>, blown out, burst, collapsed, deflated, empty **3** <u>absolute</u>, categorical, downright, explicit, out-and-out, positive, unequivocal, unqualified **4** <u>dull</u>, boring, dead, lacklustre, lifeless, monotonous, tedious, tiresome, uninteresting ♦ adverb **5** <u>completely</u>, absolutely, categorically, exactly, point blank, precisely, utterly **6 flat out** Informal <u>at full speed</u>, all out, at full tilt, for all one is worth, hell for leather (informal)

➤ Antonyms

adjective ≠<u>even</u>: hilly, rough, rugged, sloping, uneven ≠<u>dull</u>: exciting

flat² noun <u>apartment</u>, rooms

flatly adverb <u>absolutely</u>, categorically, completely, positively, unhesitatingly

flatness noun **1** <u>evenness</u>, smoothness, uniformity **2** <u>dullness</u>, monotony, tedium

flatten verb <u>level</u>, compress, even out, iron out, raze, smooth off, squash, trample

flatter verb **1** <u>praise</u>, butter up, compliment, pander to, soft-soap (informal), sweet-talk (informal), wheedle **2** <u>suit</u>, become, do something for, enhance, set off, show to advantage

flattering adjective **1** <u>ingratiating</u>, adulatory, complimentary, fawning, fulsome, laudatory **2** <u>becoming</u>, effective, enhancing, kind, well-chosen

➤ Antonyms

≠ingratiating: blunt, candid, honest, straight; uncomplimentary ≠becoming: unattractive, unbecoming, unflattering

flattery noun <u>obsequiousness</u>, adulation, blandishment, fawning, servility, soft-soap (informal), sweet-talk (informal), sycophancy

flaunt ›verb <u>show off</u>, brandish, display, exhibit, flash, flash about, flourish, parade, sport (informal)

flavour noun **1** <u>taste</u>, aroma, flavouring, piquancy, relish, savour, seasoning, smack, tang, zest **2** <u>quality</u>, character, essence, feel, feeling, style, tinge, tone ♦ verb **3** <u>season</u>, ginger up, imbue, infuse, leaven, spice

➤ Antonyms

noun ≠taste: blandness, flatness, insipidity, tastelessness

flaw noun <u>weakness</u>, blemish, chink in one's armour, defect, failing, fault, imperfection, weak spot

flawed adjective <u>damaged</u>, blemished, defective, erroneous, faulty, imperfect, unsound

flawless adjective <u>perfect</u>, faultless, impeccable, spotless, unblemished, unsullied

flee verb <u>run away</u>, bolt, depart, escape, fly, make one's getaway, scarper (Brit. slang), take flight, take off (informal), take to one's heels, turn tail

fleet noun <u>navy</u>, armada, flotilla, task force

fleeting adjective <u>momentary</u>, brief, ephemeral, passing, short-lived, temporary, transient, transitory

➤ Antonyms

abiding, continuing, durable, enduring, eternal, lasting, long-lasting, long-lived, permanent

flesh noun 1 <u>meat</u>, brawn, fat, tissue, weight 2 <u>physical nature</u>, carnality, flesh and blood, human nature 3 one's own flesh and blood <u>family</u>, blood, kin, kinsfolk, kith and kin, relations, relatives

flexibility noun 1 <u>pliancy</u>, elasticity, give (informal), pliability, resilience, springiness 2 <u>adaptability</u>, adjustability

flexible adjective 1 <u>pliable</u>, elastic, lithe, plastic, pliant, springy, stretchy, supple 2 <u>adaptable</u>, adjustable, discretionary, open, variable

➤ **Antonyms**

≠<u>pliable</u>: fixed, immovable, inflexible, rigid, stiff, tough, unyielding ≠<u>adaptable</u>: absolute, inflexible

flick verb 1 <u>strike</u>, dab, flip, hit, tap, touch 2 <u>flick through</u> <u>browse</u>, flip through, glance at, skim, skip, thumb

flicker verb 1 <u>twinkle</u>, flare, flash, glimmer, gutter, shimmer, sparkle 2 <u>flutter</u>, quiver, vibrate, waver ♦ noun 3 <u>glimmer</u>, flare, flash, gleam, spark 4 <u>trace</u>, breath, glimmer, iota, spark

flight[1] noun 1 Of air travel <u>journey</u>, trip, voyage 2 <u>aviation</u>, aeronautics, flying 3 <u>flock</u>, cloud, formation, squadron, swarm, unit

flight[2] noun <u>escape</u>, departure, exit, exodus, fleeing, getaway, retreat, running away

flimsy adjective 1 <u>fragile</u>, delicate, frail, gimcrack, insubstantial, makeshift, rickety, shaky, shallow 2 <u>thin</u>, gauzy, gossamer, light, sheer, transparent 3 <u>unconvincing</u>, feeble, implausible, inadequate, pathetic, poor, unsatisfactory, weak

➤ **Antonyms**

≠<u>fragile</u>: durable, heavy, robust, solid, sound, stout, strong, sturdy, substantial

flinch verb <u>recoil</u>, cower, cringe, draw back, quail, shirk, shrink, shy away, wince

fling verb 1 <u>throw</u>, cast, catapult, heave, hurl, propel, sling, toss ♦ noun 2 <u>binge</u> (informal), bash, good time, party, rave-up (Brit. slang), spree

flip verb, noun <u>toss</u>, flick, snap, spin, throw

flippancy noun <u>frivolity</u>, impertinence, irreverence, levity, pertness, sauciness

flippant adjective <u>frivolous</u>, cheeky, disrespectful, glib, impertinent, irreverent, offhand, superficial

➤ **Antonyms**

mannerly, polite, respectful, serious, well-mannered

flirt verb 1 <u>chat up</u> (informal), lead on, make advances, make eyes at, make sheep's eyes at, philander 2 usually with with <u>toy with</u>, consider, dabble in, entertain, expose oneself to, give a thought to, play with, trifle with ♦ noun 3 <u>tease</u>, coquette, heartbreaker, philanderer

flirtatious adjective <u>teasing</u>, amorous, come-hither, coquettish, coy, enticing, flirty, provocative, sportive

float verb 1 <u>be buoyant</u>, hang, hover 2 <u>glide</u>, bob, drift, move gently, sail, slide, slip along 3 <u>launch</u>, get going, promote, set up

➤ **Antonyms**

≠<u>be buoyant</u>: dip, drown, founder, go down, settle, sink, submerge ≠<u>launch</u>: abolish, annul, cancel, dissolve, terminate

floating adjective <u>free</u>, fluctuating, movable, unattached, variable, wandering

flock noun 1 <u>herd</u>, colony, drove, flight, gaggle, skein 2 <u>crowd</u>, collection, company, congregation, gathering, group, herd, host, mass ♦ verb 3 <u>gather</u>, collect, congregate, converge, crowd, herd, huddle, mass, throng

flog verb <u>beat</u>, flagellate, flay, lash, scourge, thrash, trounce, whack, whip

flood noun 1 <u>deluge</u>, downpour,

inundation, overflow, spate, tide, torrent 2 **torrent** abundance, flow, glut, profusion, rush, stream ♦ verb 3 **immerse**, drown, inundate, overflow, pour over, submerge, swamp 4 **engulf**, overwhelm, surge, swarm, sweep 5 **oversupply**, choke, fill, glut, saturate

floor noun 1 **tier**, level, stage, storey ♦ verb 2 **knock down**, deck (slang), prostrate 3 Informal **disconcert**, baffle, bewilder, confound, defeat, dumbfound, perplex, puzzle, stump, throw (informal)

flop verb 1 **fail**, collapse, dangle, droop, drop, sag, slump 2 Informal **fail**, come unstuck, fall, fold (informal), founder, go belly-up (slang), misfire ♦ noun 3 Informal **failure**, debacle, disaster, fiasco, nonstarter, washout (informal)

> **Antonyms**

verb ≠**fail**: flourish, make a hit, make it (informal), prosper, succeed, triumph, work ♦ noun ≠**failure**: hit, success, triumph

floppy adjective **droopy**, baggy, flaccid, limp, loose, pendulous, sagging, soft

floral adjective **flowery**, flower-patterned

florid adjective 1 **flushed**, blowsy, high-coloured, rubicund, ruddy 2 **ornate**, baroque, flamboyant, flowery, fussy, high-flown, over-elaborate

> **Antonyms**

≠**flushed**: anaemic, bloodless, pale, pallid, pasty, wan, washed out ≠**ornate**: bare, dull, plain, unadorned

flotsam noun **debris**, detritus, jetsam, junk, odds and ends, wreckage

flounder verb **struggle**, fumble, grope, stumble, thrash, toss

flourish verb 1 **thrive**, bloom, blossom, boom, flower, grow, increase, prosper, succeed 2 **wave**, brandish, display, flaunt, shake, wield ♦ noun 3 **wave**, display,

fanfare, parade, show 4 **ornamentation**, curlicue, decoration, embellishment, plume, sweep

> **Antonyms**

verb ≠**thrive**: decline, diminish, dwindle, fade, fail, grow less, shrink, wane

flourishing adjective **successful**, blooming, going places, in the pink, luxuriant, prospering, rampant, thriving

flout verb **defy**, laugh in the face of, mock, scoff at, scorn, sneer at, spurn

> **Antonyms**

heed, honour, mind, pay attention to, respect

flow verb 1 **run**, circulate, course, move, roll 2 **pour**, cascade, flood, gush, rush, stream, surge, sweep 3 **issue**, arise, emanate, emerge, proceed, result, spring ♦ noun 4 **stream**, course, current, drift, flood, flux, outpouring, spate, tide

flower noun 1 **bloom**, blossom, efflorescence 2 **elite**, best, cream, crème de la crème, pick ♦ verb 3 **bloom**, blossom, flourish, mature, open, unfold

flowery adjective **ornate**, baroque, embellished, fancy, florid, high-flown

> **Antonyms**

bare, basic, plain, simple, unadorned, unembellished

flowing adjective 1 **streaming**, falling, gushing, rolling, rushing, smooth, sweeping 2 **fluent**, continuous, easy, smooth, unbroken, uninterrupted

fluctuate verb **change**, alternate, oscillate, seesaw, shift, swing, vary, veer, waver

fluency noun **ease**, articulateness, assurance, command, control, facility, readiness, slickness, smoothness

fluent adjective **effortless**, articulate, easy, flowing, natural, smooth, voluble, well-versed

> **Antonyms**

faltering, halting, hesitant, hesitating, inarticulate, stammering, stumbling, tongue-tied

fluff noun 1 <u>fuzz</u>, down, nap, pile ◆ verb 2 Informal <u>mess up</u> (informal), bungle, make a mess off, muddle, spoil

fluffy adjective <u>soft</u>, downy, feathery, fleecy, fuzzy

fluid noun 1 <u>liquid</u>, liquor, solution ◆ adjective 2 <u>liquid</u>, flowing, liquefied, melted, molten, runny, watery

➤ **Antonyms**
adjective ≠<u>liquid</u>: firm, hard, rigid, set, solid

fluke noun 1 <u>stroke of luck</u>, accident, chance, coincidence, lucky break, quirk of fate, serendipity

flurry noun 1 <u>commotion</u>, ado, bustle, disturbance, excitement, flutter, fuss, stir 2 <u>gust</u>, squall

flush¹ verb 1 <u>blush</u>, colour, glow, go red, redden 2 <u>rinse out</u>, cleanse, flood, hose down, wash out ◆ noun 3 <u>blush</u>, colour, glow, redness, rosiness

flush² adjective 1 <u>level</u>, even, flat, square, true 2 Informal <u>wealthy</u>, in the money (informal), moneyed, rich, well-heeled (informal), well-off

flushed adjective <u>blushing</u>, crimson, embarrassed, glowing, hot, red, rosy, ruddy

fluster verb 1 <u>upset</u>, agitate, bother, confuse, disturb, perturb, rattle (informal), ruffle, unnerve ◆ noun 2 <u>turmoil</u>, disturbance, dither (chiefly Brit.), flap (informal), flurry, flutter, furore, state (informal)

flutter verb 1 <u>beat</u>, flap, palpitate, quiver, ripple, tremble, vibrate, waver ◆ noun 2 <u>vibration</u>, palpitation, quiver, shiver, shudder, tremble, tremor, twitching 3 <u>agitation</u>, commotion, confusion, dither (chiefly Brit.), excitement, fluster, state (informal)

fly¹ verb 1 <u>take wing</u>, flit, flutter, hover, sail, soar, wing 2 <u>pilot</u>, control, manoeuvre, operate 3 <u>display</u>, flap, float, flutter, show, wave 4 <u>rush</u>, career, dart, dash, hurry, race, shoot, speed, sprint,

tear 5 <u>pass</u>, elapse, flit, glide, pass swiftly, roll on, run its course, slip away 6 <u>flee</u>, escape, get away, run for it, skedaddle (informal), take to one's heels

flying adjective <u>hurried</u>, brief, fleeting, hasty, rushed, short-lived, transitory

foam noun 1 <u>froth</u>, bubbles, head, lather, spray, spume, suds ◆ verb 2 <u>bubble</u>, boil, effervesce, fizz, froth, lather

focus verb 1 <u>concentrate</u>, aim, centre, direct, fix, pinpoint, spotlight, zoom in ◆ noun 2 <u>centre</u>, focal point, heart, hub, target

foe noun <u>enemy</u>, adversary, antagonist, opponent, rival

➤ **Antonyms**
ally, companion, comrade, friend, partner

fog noun <u>mist</u>, gloom, miasma, murk, peasouper (informal), smog

foggy adjective <u>misty</u>, cloudy, dim, hazy, indistinct, murky, smoggy, vaporous

➤ **Antonyms**
bright

foil¹ verb <u>thwart</u>, balk, counter, defeat, disappoint, frustrate, nullify, stop

foil² noun <u>contrast</u>, antithesis, complement

foist verb <u>impose</u>, fob off, palm off, pass off, sneak in, unload

fold verb 1 <u>bend</u>, crease, double over 2 Informal <u>go bankrupt</u>, collapse, crash, fail, go bust (informal), go to the wall, go under, shut down ◆ noun 3 <u>crease</u>, bend, furrow, overlap, pleat, wrinkle

folder noun <u>file</u>, binder, envelope, portfolio

folk noun <u>people</u>, clan, family, kin, kindred, race, tribe

follow verb 1 <u>come after</u>, come next, succeed, supersede, supplant, take the place of 2 <u>accompany</u>, attend, escort, tag along 3 <u>pursue</u>, chase, dog, hound, hunt, shadow, stalk, track, trail 4 <u>result</u>, arise, develop, ensue, flow, issue, proceed, spring 5 obey, be guided by, conform, heed, observe **6** understand, appreciate, catch on (informal), comprehend, fathom, grasp, realize, take in **7** be interested in, cultivate, keep abreast of, support

➤ **Antonyms**

≠come after: guide, lead, precede ≠pursue: avoid, elude, escape ≠obey: abandon, desert, disobey, flout, forsake, give up, ignore, reject, renounce, shun

follower noun supporter, adherent, apostle, devotee, disciple, fan, pupil

➤ **Antonyms**

guru, leader, mentor, svengali, swami, teacher, tutor

following adjective **1** next, consequent, ensuing, later, subsequent, succeeding, successive ♦ noun **2** supporters, clientele, coterie, entourage, fans, retinue, suite, train

folly noun foolishness, imprudence, indiscretion, lunacy, madness, nonsense, rashness, stupidity

➤ **Antonyms**

judgment, level-headedness, prudence, rationality, reason, sanity, sense, wisdom

fond adjective **1** loving, adoring, affectionate, amorous, caring, devoted, doting, indulgent, tender, warm **2** foolish, deluded, delusive, empty, naive, overoptimistic, vain **3** fond of keen on, addicted to, attached to, enamoured of, having a soft spot for, hooked on, into (informal), partial to

➤ **Antonyms**

≠loving: aloof, averse, disinterested, indifferent, unaffectionate, unconcerned, undemonstrative ≠foolish: rational, sensible

fondle verb caress, cuddle, dandle, pat, pet, stroke

fondly adverb **1** lovingly, affectionately, dearly, indulgently, possessively, tenderly, with affection **2** foolishly, credulously, na-ively, stupidly, vainly

fondness noun **1** liking, attachment, fancy, love, partiality, penchant, soft spot, taste, weakness **2** devotion, affection, attachment, kindness, love, tenderness

➤ **Antonyms**

abhorrence, animosity, antagonism, antipathy, aversion, dislike, enmity, hatred, hostility, loathing, repugnance

food noun nourishment, cuisine, diet, fare, grub (slang), nutrition, rations, refreshment

fool noun **1** simpleton, blockhead, dunce, halfwit, idiot, ignoramus, imbecile (informal), numbskull or numskull, twit (informal, chiefly Brit.) **2** dupe, fall guy (informal), laughing stock, mug (Brit. slang), stooge (slang), sucker (slang) **3** clown, buffoon, harlequin, jester ♦ verb **4** deceive, beguile, con (informal), delude, dupe, hoodwink, mislead, take in, trick

➤ **Antonyms**

noun ≠simpleton: expert, genius, master, sage, savant, scholar, wise man

foolhardy adjective rash, hot-headed, impetuous, imprudent, irresponsible, reckless

➤ **Antonyms**

careful, cautious, prudent, shrewd, thoughtful, wary

foolish adjective unwise, absurd, ill-judged, imprudent, injudicious, senseless, silly

➤ **Antonyms**

bright, clever, commonsensical, intelligent, prudent, rational, sane, sensible, smart, wise

foolishly adverb unwisely, idiotically, ill-advisedly, imprudently, injudiciously, mistakenly, stupidly

foolishness noun stupidity, absurdity, folly, imprudence, indiscretion, irresponsibility, silliness, weakness

foolproof adjective infallible, certain, guaranteed, safe, sure-fire (informal), unassailable, unbreakable

footing noun **1** basis, foundation, groundwork **2** relationship, grade, position, rank, standing, status

footling adjective trivial, fiddling, hairsplitting, insignificant, minor, petty, silly, trifling, unimportant

footstep noun step, footfall, tread

forage verb **1** search, cast about, explore, hunt, rummage, scour, seek ♦ noun **2** Cattle, etc. fodder, feed, food, provender

foray noun raid, incursion, inroad, invasion, sally, sortie, swoop

forbear verb refrain, abstain, cease, desist, hold back, keep from, restrain oneself, stop

forbearance noun patience, long-suffering, resignation, restraint, self-control, temperance, tolerance

➤ Antonyms

impatience, impetuosity, intolerance, irritability, shortness

forbearing adjective patient, forgiving, indulgent, lenient, long-suffering, merciful, moderate, tolerant

forbid verb prohibit, ban, disallow, exclude, outlaw, preclude, rule out, veto

➤ Antonyms

allow, approve, authorize, endorse, grant, let, O.K. or okay (informal), permit, sanction

forbidden adjective prohibited, banned, outlawed, out of bounds, proscribed, taboo, vetoed

forbidding adjective threatening, daunting, frightening, hostile, menacing, ominous, sinister, unfriendly

➤ Antonyms

alluring, attractive, beguiling, enticing, inviting, tempting, welcoming

force noun **1** power, energy, impulse, might, momentum, pressure, strength, vigour **2** compulsion, arm-twisting (informal), coercion, constraint, duress, pressure, violence **3** intensity, empha-

sis, fierceness, vehemence, vigour **4** army, host, legion, patrol, regiment, squad, troop, unit **5** in force: **a** valid, binding, current, effective, in operation, operative, working **b** in great numbers, all together, in full strength ♦ verb **6** compel, coerce, constrain, dragoon, drive, impel, make, oblige, press, pressurize **7** push, propel, thrust **8** break open, blast, prise, wrench, wrest

➤ Antonyms

noun ≠power: debility, feebleness, frailty, impotence, ineffectiveness, powerlessness, weakness

forced adjective **1** compulsory, conscripted, enforced, involuntary, mandatory, obligatory **2** false, affected, artificial, contrived, insincere, laboured, stiff, strained, unnatural, wooden

➤ Antonyms

≠compulsory: spontaneous, voluntary ≠false: easy, natural, simple, sincere, spontaneous, unforced

forceful adjective powerful, cogent, compelling, convincing, dynamic, effective, persuasive

➤ Antonyms

faint, feeble, frail, powerless, weak

forcible adjective **1** violent, aggressive, armed, coercive, compulsory **2** compelling, energetic, forceful, potent, powerful, strong, weighty

forebear noun ancestor, father, forefather, forerunner, predecessor

foreboding noun dread, anxiety, apprehension, apprehensiveness, chill, fear, misgiving, premonition, presentiment

forecast verb **1** predict, anticipate, augur, divine, foresee, foretell, prophesy ♦ noun **2** prediction, conjecture, guess, prognosis, prophecy

forefather noun ancestor, father, forebear, forerunner, predecessor

forefront noun lead, centre, fore, foreground, front, prominence, spearhead, vanguard

forego see FORGO

foregoing adjective preceding, above, antecedent, anterior, former, previous, prior

foreign adjective alien, exotic, external, imported, remote, strange, unfamiliar, unknown

➤ **Antonyms**
customary, domestic, familiar, native, well-known

foreigner noun alien, immigrant, incomer, stranger

foremost adjective leading, chief, highest, paramount, pre-eminent, primary, prime, principal, supreme

forerunner noun precursor, harbinger, herald, prototype

foresee verb predict, anticipate, envisage, forecast, foretell, prophesy

foreshadow verb predict, augur, forebode, indicate, portend, prefigure, presage, promise, signal

foresight noun forethought, anticipation, far-sightedness, precaution, preparedness, prescience, prudence

➤ **Antonyms**
carelessness, imprudence, inconsideration, lack of foresight, thoughtlessness

foretell verb predict, forecast, forewarn, presage, prognosticate, prophesy

forethought noun anticipation, far-sightedness, foresight, precaution, providence, provision, prudence

➤ **Antonyms**
carelessness, imprudence, impulsiveness, unpreparedness

forever adverb **1** evermore, always, for all time, for keeps, in perpetuity, till Doomsday, till the cows come home (informal) **2** constantly, all the time, continually, endlessly, eternally, incessantly, interminably, perpetually, unremittingly

forewarn verb caution, advise, alert, apprise, give fair warning, put on guard, tip off

forfeit noun **1** penalty, damages, fine, forfeiture, loss, mulct ♦ verb **2** lose, be deprived of, be stripped of, give up, relinquish, renounce, say goodbye to, surrender

forge verb **1** create, construct, devise, fashion, form, frame, make, mould, shape, work **2** fake, copy, counterfeit, falsify, feign, imitate

forgery noun **1** fake, counterfeit, falsification, imitation, phoney or phony (informal), sham **2** falsification, coining, counterfeiting, fraudulence, fraudulent imitation

forget verb neglect, leave behind, lose sight of, omit, overlook

➤ **Antonyms**
bring to mind, mind, recall, recollect, remember

forgetful adjective absentminded, careless, inattentive, neglectful, oblivious, unmindful, vague

➤ **Antonyms**
attentive, careful, mindful, unforgetful, unforgetting

forgive verb excuse, absolve, acquit, condone, exonerate, let bygones be bygones, let off (informal), pardon

➤ **Antonyms**
blame, censure, charge, condemn, find fault with, reproach, reprove

forgiveness noun pardon, absolution, acquittal, amnesty, exoneration, mercy, remission

forgiving adjective lenient, clement, compassionate, forbearing, magnanimous, merciful, softhearted, tolerant

forgo verb give up, abandon, do without, relinquish, renounce, resign, surrender, waive, yield

forgotten adjective unremembered, bygone, left behind, lost, omitted, past, past recall

fork verb branch, bifurcate, diverge, divide, part, split

forked adjective branching, angled, bifurcate(d), branched, divided, pronged, split, zigzag

forlorn adjective **1** <u>miserable</u>, disconsolate, down in the dumps (*informal*), helpless, hopeless, pathetic, pitiful, unhappy, woebegone, wretched

➤ **Antonyms**

cheerful, happy

form noun **1** <u>shape</u>, appearance, configuration, formation, pattern, structure **2** <u>type</u>, kind, sort, style, variety **3** <u>condition</u>, fettle, fitness, health, shape, trim **4** <u>document</u>, application, paper, sheet **5** <u>class</u>, grade, rank **6** <u>procedure</u>, convention, custom, etiquette, protocol ♦ verb **7** <u>make</u>, build, construct, create, fashion, forge, mould, produce, shape **8** <u>arrange</u>, combine, draw up, organize **9** <u>take shape</u>, appear, become visible, come into being, crystallize, grow, materialize, rise **10** <u>develop</u>, acquire, contract, cultivate, pick up **11** <u>constitute</u>, compose, comprise, make up

formal adjective **1** <u>official</u>, ceremonial, ritualistic, solemn **2** <u>conventional</u>, affected, correct, precise, stiff, unbending

➤ **Antonyms**

casual, easy-going, informal, laid-back (*informal*), relaxed, unceremonious, unofficial

formality noun **1** <u>convention</u>, custom, procedure, red tape, rite, ritual **2** <u>correctness</u>, decorum, etiquette, protocol

format noun <u>arrangement</u>, appearance, construction, form, layout, look, make-up, plan, style, type

formation noun **1** <u>development</u>, constitution, establishment, forming, generation, genesis, manufacture, production **2** <u>arrangement</u>, configuration, design, grouping, pattern, structure

formative adjective <u>developmental</u>, influential

former adjective <u>previous</u>, earlier, erstwhile, one-time, prior

➤ **Antonyms**

coming, current, following, fu-ture, latter, subsequent, succeeding

formerly adverb <u>previously</u>, at one time, before, lately, once

formidable adjective **1** <u>intimidating</u>, daunting, dismaying, fearful, frightful, menacing, terrifying, threatening **2** <u>impressive</u>, awesome, great, mighty, powerful, redoubtable, terrific, tremendous

➤ **Antonyms**

≠<u>intimidating</u>: comforting, encouraging, heartening, pleasant, reassuring

formula noun <u>method</u>, blueprint, precept, principle, procedure, recipe, rule

formulate verb **1** <u>define</u>, detail, express, frame, give form to, set down, specify, systematize **2** <u>devise</u>, develop, forge, invent, map out, originate, plan, work out

forsake verb **1** <u>desert</u>, abandon, disown, leave in the lurch, strand **2** <u>give up</u>, forgo, relinquish, renounce, set aside, surrender, yield

forsaken adjective <u>deserted</u>, abandoned, disowned, forlorn, left in the lurch, marooned, outcast, stranded

fort noun **1** <u>fortress</u>, blockhouse, camp, castle, citadel, fortification, garrison, stronghold **2** <u>hold the fort</u> *Informal* <u>carry on</u>, keep things on an even keel, stand in, take over the reins

forte noun <u>speciality</u>, gift, long suit (*informal*), métier, strength, strong point, talent

➤ **Antonyms**

Achilles heel, chink in one's armour, defect, failing, imperfection, shortcoming, weak point

forth adverb *Formal* or old-fashioned <u>forward</u>, ahead, away, onward, out, outward

forthcoming adjective **1** <u>approaching</u>, coming, expected, future, imminent, impending, prospective, upcoming **2** <u>available</u>, accessible, at hand, in evidence, obtainable, on tap (*informal*) ready **3** <u>communicative</u>, chatty, expansive, free, informative, open, sociable, talkative, unreserved

forthright *adjective* <u>outspoken</u>, blunt, candid, direct, frank, open, plain-spoken, straightforward, upfront (*informal*)

➤ **Antonyms**

dishonest, furtive, secret, secretive, sneaky, underhand, untruthful

forthwith *adverb* <u>at once</u>, directly, immediately, instantly, quickly, right away, straightaway, without delay

fortification *noun* **1** <u>strengthening</u>, reinforcement **2** <u>defence</u>, bastion, fastness, fort, fortress, protection, stronghold

fortify *verb* <u>protect</u>, augment, buttress, reinforce, shore up, strengthen, support

➤ **Antonyms**

debilitate, demoralize, dishearten, impair, reduce, sap the strength of, weaken

fortitude *noun* <u>courage</u>, backbone, bravery, fearlessness, grit, perseverance, resolution, strength, valour

fortress *noun* <u>castle</u>, citadel, fastness, fort, redoubt, stronghold

fortunate *adjective* **1** <u>lucky</u>, favoured, in luck, jammy (*Brit. slang*), successful, well-off **2** <u>providential</u>, advantageous, convenient, expedient, favourable, felicitous, fortuitous, helpful, opportune, timely

➤ **Antonyms**

hapless, ill-fated, ill-starred, miserable, poor, unfortunate, unhappy, unlucky, unsuccessful, wretched

fortunately *adverb* <u>luckily</u>, by a happy chance, by good luck, happily, providentially

fortune *noun* **1** <u>luck</u>, chance, destiny, fate, kismet, providence **2** <u>fortunes</u> <u>destiny</u>, adventures, experiences, history, lot, success **3** <u>wealth</u>, affluence, opulence, possessions, property, prosperity,

riches, treasure

➤ **Antonyms**

≠<u>wealth</u>: destitution, hardship, indigence, penury, poverty, privation

forward *adjective* **1** <u>leading</u>, advance, first, foremost, front, head **2** <u>presumptuous</u>, bold, brash, brazen, cheeky, familiar, impertinent, impudent, pushy (*informal*) **3** <u>well-developed</u>, advanced, precocious, premature ◆ *adverb* **4** <u>forth</u>, ahead, on, onward ◆ *verb* **5** <u>send</u>, dispatch, post, send on **6** <u>promote</u>, advance, assist, expedite, further, hasten, hurry

➤ **Antonyms**

adjective ≠<u>presumptuous</u>: backward, diffident, modest, regressive, retiring, shy ◆ *adverb* ≠<u>forth</u>: backward(s) ◆ *verb* ≠<u>promote</u>: bar, block, hinder, hold up, impede, obstruct

foster *verb* **1** <u>bring up</u>, mother, nurse, raise, rear, take care of **2** <u>promote</u>, cultivate, encourage, feed, nurture, stimulate, support, uphold

➤ **Antonyms**

≠<u>promote</u>: combat, curb, curtail, inhibit, oppose, resist, suppress, withstand

foul *adjective* **1** <u>offensive</u>, abhorrent, despicable, detestable, disgraceful, scandalous, shameful, wicked **2** <u>dirty</u>, fetid, filthy, malodorous, nauseating, putrid, repulsive, squalid, stinking, unclean **3** <u>obscene</u>, abusive, blue, coarse, indecent, lewd, profane, scurrilous, vulgar **4** <u>unfair</u>, crooked, dishonest, fraudulent, shady (*informal*), underhand, unscrupulous ◆ *verb* **5** <u>dirty</u>, besmirch, contaminate, defile, pollute, stain, sully, taint

➤ **Antonyms**

adjective ≠<u>offensive</u>: admirable, attractive, decent, pleasant, respectable ≠<u>dirty</u>: clean, clear, fair, fragrant, fresh, pure, spotless, undefiled ◆ *verb* ≠<u>dirty</u>: clean, cleanse, clear, purify, sanitize

found verb establish, constitute, create, inaugurate, institute, organize, originate, set up, start

foundation noun 1 basis, base, bedrock, bottom, footing, groundwork, substructure, underpinning 2 setting up, endowment, establishment, inauguration, institution, organization, settlement

founder[1] noun initiator, architect, author, beginner, father, inventor, originator

founder[2] verb 1 fail, break down, collapse, come to grief, come unstuck, fall through, miscarry, misfire 2 sink, be lost, go down, go to the bottom, submerge 3 stumble, lurch, sprawl, stagger, trip

foundling noun orphan, outcast, stray, waif

fountain noun 1 jet, font, fount, reservoir, spout, spray, spring, well 2 source, cause, derivation, fount, fountainhead, origin, wellspring

foyer noun entrance hall, antechamber, anteroom, lobby, reception area, vestibule

fracas noun brawl, affray (Law), disturbance, melee or mêlée, riot, rumpus, scuffle, skirmish

fraction noun piece, part, percentage, portion, section, segment, share, slice

fractious adjective irritable, captious, cross, petulant, querulous, refractory, testy, tetchy, touchy

➤ **Antonyms**

affable, agreeable, amiable, genial, good-natured, good-tempered

fracture noun 1 break, cleft, crack, fissure, opening, rift, rupture, split ♦ verb 2 break, crack, rupture, splinter, split

fragile adjective delicate, breakable, brittle, dainty, fine, flimsy, frail, frangible, weak

➤ **Antonyms**

durable, elastic, hardy, resilient, robust, strong, sturdy, tough

fragment noun 1 piece, bit, chip, particle, portion, scrap, shred, sliver ♦ verb 2 break, break up, come apart, come to pieces, crumble, disintegrate, shatter, splinter, split up

➤ **Antonyms**

verb ≠break: bond, combine, compound, fuse, join together, link, merge, unify

fragmentary adjective incomplete, bitty, broken, disconnected, incoherent, partial, piecemeal, scattered, scrappy, sketchy

fragrance noun scent, aroma, bouquet, perfume, redolence, smell, sweet odour

➤ **Antonyms**

miasma, niff (Brit. slang), pong (Brit. informal), reek, smell, stink

fragrant adjective aromatic, balmy, odorous, perfumed, redolent, sweet-scented, sweet-smelling

➤ **Antonyms**

fetid, foul-smelling, malodorous, noisome, pongy (Brit. informal), reeking, smelling, smelly, stinking

frail adjective weak, delicate, feeble, flimsy, fragile, infirm, insubstantial, puny, vulnerable

➤ **Antonyms**

hale, healthy, robust, sound, stalwart, strong, sturdy, substantial, tough, vigorous

frailty noun weakness, fallibility, feebleness, frailness, infirmity, susceptibility

➤ **Antonyms**

fortitude, might, robustness, strength

frame noun 1 casing, construction, framework, shell, structure 2 physique, anatomy, body, build, carcass 3 frame of mind mood, attitude, disposition, humour, outlook, state, temper ♦ verb 4 construct, assemble, build, make, manufacture, put together 5 devise, compose, draft, draw up, formulate, map out, sketch 6 mount, case, enclose, surround

framework noun structure, foundation, frame, groundwork, plan, shell, skeleton, the bare bones

frank *adjective* <u>honest</u>, blunt, candid, direct, forthright, open, outspoken, plain-spoken, sincere, straightforward, truthful

➤ **Antonyms**

artful, crafty, cunning, evasive, indirect, secretive, shifty, underhand

frankly *adverb* 1 <u>honestly</u>, candidly, in truth, to be honest 2 <u>openly</u>, bluntly, directly, freely, plainly, without reserve

frankness *noun* <u>outspokenness</u>, bluntness, candour, forthrightness, openness, plain speaking, truthfulness

frantic *adjective* 1 <u>distraught</u>, at the end of one's tether, berserk, beside oneself, distracted, furious, wild 2 <u>hectic</u>, desperate, fraught (*informal*), frenetic, frenzied

➤ **Antonyms**

calm, collected, composed, cool, laid-back, poised, self-possessed, together (*slang*), unfazed (*informal*), unruffled

fraternity *noun* 1 <u>association</u>, brotherhood, circle, club, company, guild, league, union 2 <u>companionship</u>, brotherhood, camaraderie, fellowship, kinship

fraternize *verb* <u>associate</u>, consort, cooperate, hobnob, keep company, mingle, mix, socialize

➤ **Antonyms**

avoid, eschew, keep away from, shun, steer clear of

fraud *noun* 1 <u>deception</u>, chicanery, deceit, double-dealing, duplicity, sharp practice, swindling, treachery, trickery 2 *Informal* <u>impostor</u>, charlatan, fake, fraudster, hoaxer, phoney *or* phony (*informal*), pretender, swindler

➤ **Antonyms**

≠deception: fairness, good faith, honesty, integrity, probity, rectitude, trustworthiness, virtue

fraudulent *adjective* <u>deceitful</u>, crooked (*informal*), dishonest, double-dealing, duplicitous,

sham, swindling, treacherous

➤ **Antonyms**

above board, genuine, honest, true

fray *verb* <u>wear thin</u>, chafe, rub, wear

freak *noun* 1 <u>oddity</u>, aberration, anomaly, malformation, monstrosity, weirdo *or* weirdie (*informal*) 2 *Informal* <u>enthusiast</u>, addict, aficionado, buff (*informal*), devotee, fan, fanatic, fiend (*informal*), nut (*slang*) ♦ *adjective* 3 <u>abnormal</u>, exceptional, unparalleled, unusual

free *adjective* 1 <u>at liberty</u>, at large, footloose, independent, liberated, loose, on the loose, unfettered 2 <u>allowed</u>, able, clear, permitted, unimpeded, unrestricted 3 <u>complimentary</u>, for free (*informal*), for nothing, free of charge, gratis, gratuitous, on the house, unpaid, without charge 4 <u>available</u>, empty, idle, spare, unemployed, unoccupied, unused, vacant 5 <u>generous</u>, lavish, liberal, unsparing, unstinting ♦ *verb* 6 <u>release</u>, deliver, let out, liberate, loose, set free, turn loose, unchain, untie 7 <u>clear</u>, cut loose, disengage, disentangle, extricate, rescue

➤ **Antonyms**

adjective ≠at liberty: bound, captive, confined, fettered, incarcerated, restrained, restricted ≠generous: close, mean, mingy (*informal*), stingy, tight, ungenerous ♦ *verb* ≠release: confine, imprison, incarcerate, inhibit, limit, restrain, restrict, strain

freedom *noun* 1 <u>liberty</u>, deliverance, emancipation, independence, release 2 <u>licence</u>, blank cheque, carte blanche, discretion, free rein, latitude, opportunity

➤ **Antonyms**

≠liberty: bondage, captivity, imprisonment, servitude, slavery ≠licence: limitation, restriction

free-for-all *noun* *Informal* <u>fight</u>, brawl, dust-up (*informal*), fracas, melee *or* mêlée, riot, row, scrimmage

freely adverb **1** willingly, of one's own accord, of one's own free will, spontaneously, voluntarily, without prompting **2** openly, candidly, frankly, plainly, unreservedly, without reserve **3** abundantly, amply, copiously, extravagantly, lavishly, liberally, unstintingly

freeze verb **1** chill, harden, ice over or up, stiffen **2** suspend, fix, hold up, inhibit, stop

freezing adjective icy, arctic, biting, bitter, chill, frosty, glacial, raw, wintry

freight noun **1** transportation, carriage, conveyance, shipment **2** cargo, burden, consignment, goods, load, merchandise, payload

French adjective Gallic

frenzied adjective uncontrolled, distracted, feverish, frantic, frenetic, furious, rabid, wild

frenzy noun fury, derangement, hysteria, paroxysm, passion, rage, seizure

► **Antonyms**
calm, collectedness, composure, coolness, sanity

frequent adjective **1** common, customary, everyday, familiar, habitual, persistent, recurrent, repeated, usual ♦ verb **2** visit, attend, be found at, hang out at (informal), haunt, patronize

► **Antonyms**
adjective ≠common: few, few and far between, infrequent, occasional, rare, scanty, sporadic ♦ verb ≠visit: avoid, keep away, shun

frequently adverb often, commonly, habitually, many times, much, not infrequently, repeatedly

► **Antonyms**
hardly ever, infrequently, occasionally, once in a blue moon (informal), rarely, seldom

fresh adjective **1** new, different, modern, novel, original, recent, up-to-date **2** additional, added, auxiliary, extra, further, more, other, supplementary **3** natural, unprocessed **4** invigorating, bracing, brisk, clean, cool, crisp, pure, refreshing, unpolluted **5** lively, alert, energetic, keen, refreshed, sprightly, spry, vigorous **6** Informal cheeky, disrespectful, familiar, forward, impudent, insolent, presumptuous

► **Antonyms**
≠new: dull, old, ordinary, stereotyped, trite ≠natural: frozen, pickled, preserved, salted, tinned ≠invigorating: impure, musty, stale, warm ≠lively: exhausted, weary ≠cheeky: well-mannered

freshen verb refresh, enliven, freshen up, liven up, restore, revitalize

freshness noun **1** novelty, inventiveness, newness, originality **2** cleanness, brightness, clearness, glow, shine, sparkle, vigour, wholesomeness

fret verb worry, agonize, brood, lose sleep over, obsess about, upset or distress oneself

fretful adjective irritable, crotchety (informal), edgy, fractious, querulous, short-tempered, testy, touchy, uneasy

friction noun **1** rubbing, abrasion, chafing, grating, rasping, resistance, scraping **2** hostility, animosity, bad blood, conflict, disagreement, discord, dissension, resentment

friend noun **1** companion, buddy (informal), chum (informal), comrade, mate (informal), pal, playmate **2** supporter, ally, associate, patron, well-wisher

► **Antonyms**
adversary, antagonist, competitor, enemy, foe, opponent, rival

friendliness noun amiability, affability, congeniality, conviviality, geniality, kindliness, neighbourliness, sociability, warmth

friendly adjective amiable, affectionate, amicable, close, cordial, familiar, helpful, intimate, neighbourly, on good terms, pally (informal), sociable, sympathetic, welcoming

► **Antonyms**

antagonistic, belligerent, cold, distant, uncongenial, unfriendly

friendship noun friendliness, affection, amity, attachment, concord, familiarity, goodwill, harmony, intimacy

► **Antonyms**

animosity, antagonism, antipathy, aversion, enmity, hatred, hostility, unfriendliness

fright noun fear, alarm, consternation, dread, horror, panic, scare, shock, trepidation

► **Antonyms**

boldness, bravery, courage, pluck, valor

frighten verb scare, alarm, intimidate, petrify, shock, startle, terrify, terrorize, unnerve

► **Antonyms**

allay, assuage, calm, comfort, encourage, hearten, reassure, soothe

frightened adjective afraid, alarmed, petrified, scared, scared stiff, startled, terrified, terrorized, terror-stricken

frightening adjective terrifying, alarming, fearful, fearsome, horrifying, menacing, scary (informal), shocking, unnerving

frightful adjective terrifying, alarming, awful, dreadful, fearful, ghastly, horrendous, horrible, terrible, traumatic

► **Antonyms**

attractive, beautiful, lovely, nice, pleasant

frigid adjective 1 unresponsive, aloof, austere, forbidding, formal, unapproachable, unfeeling 2 cold, arctic, frosty, frozen, glacial, icy, wintry

► **Antonyms**

≠unresponsive: friendly, passionate, responsive, warm ≠cold: hot, stifling, sweltering, warm

frills plural noun trimmings, additions, bells and whistles, embellishments, extras, frippery, fuss, ornamentation, ostentation

fringe noun 1 border, edging, hem, trimming 2 edge, borderline, limits, margin, outskirts, perimeter, periphery ♦ adjective 3 unofficial, unconventional, unorthodox

frisk verb 1 frolic, caper, cavort, gambol, jump, play, prance, skip, trip 2 Informal search, check, inspect, run over, shake down (U.S. slang)

frisky adjective lively, coltish, frolicsome, high-spirited, kittenish, playful, sportive

► **Antonyms**

dull, lacklustre, sedate, stodgy

fritter away verb waste, dissipate, idle away, misspend, run through, spend like water, squander

frivolity noun flippancy, frivolousness, fun, gaiety, levity, lightheartedness, silliness, superficiality, triviality

► **Antonyms**

earnestness, gravity, seriousness, soberness

frivolous adjective 1 flippant, childish, foolish, idle, juvenile, puerile, silly, superficial 2 trivial, footling (informal), minor, petty, shallow, trifling, unimportant

► **Antonyms**

≠flippant: earnest, sensible, serious, solemn ≠trivial: important, serious, vital

frolic verb 1 play, caper, cavort, frisk, gambol, lark, make merry, romp, sport ♦ noun 2 revel, antic, game, lark, romp, spree

frolicsome adjective playful, coltish, frisky, kittenish, lively, merry, sportive

front noun 1 exterior, façade, face, foreground, frontage 2 forefront, front line, head, lead, vanguard 3 Informal disguise, blind, cover, cover-up, façade, mask, pretext, show ♦ adjective 4 foremost, first, head, lead, leading, topmost ♦ verb 5 face onto, look over or onto, overlook

► **Antonyms**

adjective ≠foremost: aft, back,

back end, behind, hindmost, nethermost, rear

frontier noun <u>boundary</u>, borderline, edge, limit, perimeter, verge

frost noun <u>hoarfrost</u>, freeze, rime

frosty adjective **1** <u>cold</u>, chilly, frozen, icy, wintry **2** <u>unfriendly</u>, discouraging, frigid, off-putting (Brit. informal), standoffish, unenthusiastic, unwelcoming

froth noun **1** <u>foam</u>, bubbles, effervescence, head, lather, scum, spume, suds ♦ verb **2** <u>fizz</u>, bubble over, come to a head, effervesce, foam, lather

frothy adjective <u>foamy</u>, foaming, sudsy

frown verb **1** <u>scowl</u>, glare, glower, knit one's brows, look daggers, lour or lower **2** frown on <u>disapprove of</u>, discourage, dislike, look askance at, take a dim view of

frozen adjective <u>icy</u>, arctic, chilled, frigid, frosted, icebound, ice-cold, ice-covered, numb

frugal adjective <u>thrifty</u>, abstemious, careful, economical, niggardly, parsimonious, prudent, sparing

➤ Antonyms

excessive, extravagant, imprudent, lavish, prodigal, profligate, spendthrift, wasteful

fruit noun **1** <u>produce</u>, crop, harvest, product, yield **2** plural <u>result</u>, advantage, benefit, consequence, effect, end result, outcome, profit, return, reward

fruitful adjective <u>useful</u>, advantageous, beneficial, effective, productive, profitable, rewarding, successful, worthwhile

➤ Antonyms

fruitless, futile, ineffectual, pointless, unfruitful, unproductive, useless, vain

fruition noun <u>fulfilment</u>, attainment, completion, materialization, maturity, perfection, realization, ripeness

fruitless adjective <u>useless</u>, futile, ineffectual, pointless, profitless, unavailing, unproductive, unprof-

itable, unsuccessful, vain

➤ Antonyms

effective, fruitful, productive, profitable, useful

frustrate verb <u>thwart</u>, balk, block, check, counter, defeat, disappoint, foil, forestall, nullify, stymie

➤ Antonyms

advance, encourage, forward, further, promote

frustrated adjective <u>disappointed</u>, discouraged, disheartened, embittered, resentful

frustration noun **1** <u>annoyance</u>, disappointment, dissatisfaction, grievance, irritation, resentment, vexation **2** <u>obstruction</u>, blocking, circumvention, foiling, thwarting

fuddy-duddy noun Informal <u>conservative</u>, (old) fogey, square (informal), stick-in-the-mud (informal), stuffed shirt (informal)

fudge verb <u>misrepresent</u>, equivocate, flannel (Brit. informal), hedge, stall

fuel noun <u>incitement</u>, ammunition, provocation

fugitive noun **1** <u>runaway</u>, deserter, escapee, refugee ♦ adjective **2** <u>momentary</u>, brief, ephemeral, fleeting, passing, short-lived, temporary, transient, transitory

fulfil verb **1** <u>achieve</u>, accomplish, carry out, complete, perform, realise, satisfy **2** <u>comply with</u>, answer, conform to, fill, meet, obey, observe

➤ Antonyms

disappoint, dissatisfy, fail in, fail to meet, fall short of, neglect

fulfilment noun <u>achievement</u>, accomplishment, attainment, completion, consummation, implementation, realization

full adjective **1** <u>filled</u>, brimming, complete, loaded, replete, satiated, saturated, stocked **2** <u>extensive</u>, abundant, adequate, ample, comprehensive, exhaustive, generous, plentiful **3** <u>plump</u>, buxom, curvaceous, rounded, voluptuous **4** <u>rich</u>, clear, deep, distinct, loud, resonant, rounded **5**

voluminous, baggy, capacious, large, loose, puffy ◆ *noun* **6** in full completely, in its entirety, in total, without exception

➤ **Antonyms**

adjective ≠filled: blank, devoid, empty, vacant, void ≠extensive: abridged, incomplete, limited, partial ≠rich: faint, thin ≠voluminous: restricted, tight

full-blooded *adjective* vigorous, hearty, lusty, red-blooded, virile

fullness *noun* **1** plenty, abundance, adequateness, ampleness, copiousness, fill, profusion, satiety, saturation, sufficiency **2** richness, clearness, loudness, resonance, strength

full-scale *adjective* major, all-out, comprehensive, exhaustive, in-depth, sweeping, thorough, thoroughgoing, wide-ranging

fully *adverb* totally, altogether, completely, entirely, in all respects, one hundred per cent, perfectly, thoroughly, utterly, wholly

fulsome *adjective* extravagant, excessive, immoderate, inordinate, insincere, sycophantic, unctuous

fumble *verb* grope, feel around, flounder, scrabble

fume *verb* rage, get hot under the collar (*informal*), rant, see red (*informal*), seethe, smoulder, storm

fumes *noun* smoke, exhaust, gas, pollution, smog, vapour

fumigate *verb* disinfect, clean out *or* up, cleanse, purify, sanitize, sterilize

fuming *adjective* furious, angry, enraged, in a rage, incensed, on the warpath (*informal*), raging, seething, up in arms

fun *noun* **1** enjoyment, amusement, entertainment, jollity, merriment, mirth, pleasure, recreation, sport **2 make fun of** mock, lampoon, laugh at, parody, poke fun at, ridicule, satirize, send up (*Brit. informal*) ◆ *adjective* **3** enjoyable, amusing, conviv-ial, diverting, entertaining, lively, witty

➤ **Antonyms**

noun ≠enjoyment: depression, despair, distress, gloom, grief, melancholy, misery, sadness, sorrow, unhappiness

function *noun* **1** purpose, business, duty, job, mission, *raison d'être*, responsibility, role, task **2** reception, affair, do (*informal*), gathering, social occasion ◆ *verb* **3** work, act, behave, do duty, go, operate, perform, run

functional *adjective* **1** practical, hard-wearing, serviceable, useful, utilitarian **2** working, operative

fund *noun* **1** reserve, kitty, pool, stock, store, supply ◆ *verb* **2** finance, pay for, subsidize, support

fundamental *adjective* **1** essential, basic, cardinal, central, elementary, key, primary, principal, rudimentary, underlying ◆ *noun* **2** principle, axiom, cornerstone, law, rudiment, rule

➤ **Antonyms**

adjective ≠essential: incidental, lesser, secondary, subsidiary, superfluous

fundamentally *adverb* essentially, at bottom, at heart, basically, intrinsically, primarily, radically

funds *plural noun* money, capital, cash, finance, ready money, resources, savings, the wherewithal

funeral *noun* burial, cremation, interment, obsequies

funnel *verb* channel, conduct, convey, direct, filter, move, pass, pour

funny *adjective* **1** humorous, amusing, comic, comical, droll, entertaining, hilarious, riotous, side-splitting, witty **2** peculiar, curious, mysterious, odd, queer, strange, suspicious, unusual, weird

➤ **Antonyms**

≠humorous: grave, humourless, melancholy, serious, sober, solemn, stern, unfunny

furious *adjective* **1** angry, beside

oneself, enraged, fuming, incensed, infuriated, livid (*informal*), raging, up in arms 2 *violent*, fierce, intense, savage, turbulent, unrestrained, vehement

➤ **Antonyms**

≠*angry*: calm, dispassionate, impassive, imperturbable, mild, placated, pleased, serene, tranquil

furnish verb 1 *decorate*, equip, fit out, stock 2 *supply*, give, grant, hand out, offer, present, provide

furniture noun *household goods*, appliances, fittings, furnishings, goods, possessions, things (*informal*)

furore noun *commotion*, disturbance, hullabaloo, outcry, stir, to-do, uproar

furrow noun 1 *groove*, channel, crease, hollow, line, rut, seam, trench, wrinkle ◆ verb 2 *wrinkle*, corrugate, crease, draw together, knit

further adverb 1 *in addition*, additionally, also, besides, furthermore, into the bargain, moreover, to boot 2 *adjective* 2 *additional*, extra, fresh, more, new, other, supplementary ◆ verb 3 *promote*, advance, assist, encourage, forward, help, lend support to, work for

➤ **Antonyms**

verb ≠*promote*: foil, frustrate, hinder, impede, obstruct, oppose, prevent, retard, stop, thwart

furthermore adverb *besides*, additionally, as well, further, in addition, into the bargain, moreover, to boot, too

furthest adjective *most distant*, extreme, farthest, furthermost, outmost, remotest, ultimate

furtive adjective *sly*, clandestine, conspiratorial, secretive, sneaky, stealthy, surreptitious, underhand, under-the-table

➤ **Antonyms**

above-board, candid, forthright, frank, open, straightforward, undisguised

fury noun 1 *anger*, frenzy, impetuosity, madness, passion, rage, wrath 2 *violence*, ferocity, fierceness, force, intensity, savagery, severity, vehemence

➤ **Antonyms**

≠*anger*: calm, calmness, composure, equanimity ≠*violence*: hush, peace, peacefulness, serenity, stillness, tranquillity

fuss noun 1 *bother*, ado, commotion, excitement, hue and cry, palaver, stir, to-do 2 *argument*, complaint, furore, objection, row, squabble, trouble ◆ verb 3 *worry*, fidget, flap (*informal*), fret, get worked up, take pains

fussy adjective 1 *particular*, choosy (*informal*), difficult, fastidious, finicky, hard to please, nitpicking (*informal*), pernickety, picky (*informal*) 2 *overelaborate*, busy, cluttered, overworked, rococo

fusty adjective *stale*, airless, damp, mildewed, mouldering, mouldy, musty, stuffy

futile adjective *useless*, fruitless, ineffectual, unavailing, unprofitable, unsuccessful, vain, worthless

➤ **Antonyms**

constructive, effective, fruitful, profitable, successful, useful, valuable, worthwhile

futility noun *uselessness*, emptiness, hollowness, ineffectiveness

future noun 1 *time to come*, hereafter 2 *prospect*, expectation, outlook ◆ adjective 3 *forthcoming*, approaching, coming, fated, impending, later, subsequent, to come

➤ **Antonyms**

adjective ≠*forthcoming*: bygone, erstwhile, ex-, former, late, past, preceding, previous

fuzzy adjective 1 *fluffy*, downy, frizzy, woolly 2 *indistinct*, bleary, blurred, distorted, ill-defined, out of focus, unclear, vague

➤ **Antonyms**

≠*indistinct*: clear, defined, detailed, distinct, in focus, precise

G g

gabble verb 1 prattle, babble, blabber, gibber, gush, jabber, spout ◆ noun 2 gibberish, babble, blabber, chatter, drivel, prattle, twaddle

gadabout noun pleasure-seeker, gallivanter, rambler, rover, wanderer

gadget noun device, appliance, contraption (informal), contrivance, gizmo (slang, chiefly U.S.), instrument, invention, thing, tool

gaffe noun blunder, bloomer (informal), clanger (informal), faux pas, howler, indiscretion, lapse, mistake, slip, solecism

gaffer noun 1 Informal manager, boss (informal), foreman, overseer, superintendent, supervisor 2 old man, granddad, greybeard, old boy (informal), old fellow, old-timer (U.S.)

gag¹ verb 1 retch, heave, puke (slang), spew, throw up (informal), vomit 2 suppress, curb, muffle, muzzle, quiet, silence, stifle, stop up

gag² noun joke, crack (slang), funny (informal), hoax, jest, wisecrack (informal), witticism

gaiety noun 1 cheerfulness, blitheness, exhilaration, glee, high spirits, jollity, lightheartedness, merriment, mirth 2 merrymaking, conviviality, festivity, fun, jollification, revelry

► **Antonyms**

≠cheerfulness: despondency, gloom, melancholy, misery, sadness

gaily adverb 1 cheerfully, blithely, gleefully, happily, joyfully, lightheartedly, merrily 2 colourfully, brightly, brilliantly, flamboyantly, flashily, gaudily, showily

gain verb 1 acquire, attain, cap- ture, collect, gather, get, land, secure 2 improve, advance, increase, pick up, profit 3 reach, arrive at, attain, come to, get to 4 gain on get nearer, approach, catch up with, close, narrow the gap, overtake ◆ noun 5 profit, advantage, benefit, dividend, return, yield 6 increase, advance, growth, improvement, progress, rise

► **Antonyms**

verb ≠acquire: forfeit, lose ≠improve: fail, worsen ◆ noun ≠profit: forfeiture, loss ≠increase: damage, injury

gainful adjective profitable, advantageous, beneficial, fruitful, lucrative, productive, remunerative, rewarding, useful, worthwhile

gains plural noun profits, earnings, prize, proceeds, revenue, takings, winnings

gainsay verb contradict, contravene, controvert, deny, disagree with, dispute, rebut, retract

► **Antonyms**

agree with, back, confirm, support

gait noun walk, bearing, carriage, pace, step, stride, tread

gala noun festival, carnival, celebration, festivity, fête, jamboree, pageant

gale noun 1 storm, blast, cyclone, hurricane, squall, tempest, tornado, typhoon 2 Informal outburst, burst, eruption, explosion, fit, howl, outbreak, paroxysm, peal, shout, shriek, storm

gall¹ noun 1 Informal impudence, brazenness, cheek (informal), chutzpah (U.S. & Canad. informal), effrontery, impertinence, insolence, nerve (informal) 2 bitterness, acrimony, animosity, bile, hostility, rancour

gall² verb 1 annoy, exasperate, irk, irritate, provoke, rankle, vex 2 scrape, abrade, chafe, irritate

gallant adjective 1 brave, bold, courageous, heroic, honourable, intrepid, manly, noble, valiant 2 courteous, attentive, chivalrous, gentlemanly, gracious, noble, polite

➤ **Antonyms**

≠**brave:** cowardly, fearful, ignoble ≠**courteous:** churlish, discourteous, ill-mannered, impolite, rude

gallantry noun **1** courtesy, attentiveness, chivalry, courteousness, gentlemanliness, graciousness, nobility, politeness **2** bravery, boldness, courage, heroism, intrepidity, manliness, spirit, valour

➤ **Antonyms**

≠**courtesy:** churlishness, discourtesy, rudeness, ungraciousness ≠**bravery:** cowardice, irresolution

galling adjective annoying, bitter, exasperating, irksome, irritating, provoking, vexatious

gallivant verb wander, gad about, ramble, roam, rove

gallop verb run, bolt, career, dash, hurry, race, rush, speed, sprint

galore adverb in abundance, all over the place, aplenty, everywhere, in great quantity, in numbers, in profusion, to spare

galvanize verb stimulate, electrify, excite, inspire, invigorate, jolt, provoke, spur, stir

gamble verb **1** bet, game, have a flutter (informal), play, punt, wager **2** risk, chance, hazard, speculate, stick one's neck out (informal), take a chance ♦ noun **3** bet, flutter (informal), punt, wager **4** risk, chance, leap in the dark, lottery, speculation, uncertainty, venture

➤ **Antonyms**

noun ≠**risk:** banker, certainty, foregone conclusion, safe bet, sure thing

gambol verb **1** frolic, caper, cavort, frisk, hop, jump, prance, skip ♦ noun **2** frolic, caper, hop, jump, prance, skip

game noun **1** pastime, amusement, distraction, diversion, entertainment, lark, recreation, sport **2** match, competition, contest, event, head-to-head, meeting, tournament **3** wild animals, prey, quarry **4** scheme, design, plan, plot, ploy, stratagem, tactic, trick ♦ adjective **5** brave, courageous, gallant, gritty, intrepid, persistent, plucky, spirited **6** willing, desirous, eager, interested, keen, prepared, ready

➤ **Antonyms**

noun ≠**pastime:** business, chore, duty, job, labour, toil, work ♦ adjective ≠**brave:** cowardly, fearful, irresolute

gamut noun range, area, catalogue, compass, field, scale, scope, series, sweep

gang noun group, band, clique, club, company, coterie, crowd, mob, pack, squad, team

gangling adjective tall, angular, awkward, lanky, rangy, rawboned, spindly

gangster noun racketeer, crook (informal), hood (U.S. slang), hoodlum (chiefly U.S.), mobster (U.S. slang)

gap noun **1** opening, break, chink, cleft, crack, hole, space **2** interval, breathing space, hiatus, interlude, intermission, interruption, lacuna, lull, pause, respite **3** difference, disagreement, disparity, divergence, inconsistency

gape verb **1** stare, gawk, gawp (Brit. slang), goggle, wonder **2** open, crack, split, yawn

gaping adjective wide, broad, cavernous, great, open, vast, wide open, yawning

garbage noun waste, refuse, rubbish, trash (chiefly U.S.)

garbled adjective jumbled, confused, distorted, double-Dutch, incomprehensible, mixed up, unintelligible

garish adjective gaudy, brash, brassy, flashy, loud, showy, tacky (informal), tasteless, vulgar

➤ **Antonyms**

conservative, elegant, modest, plain, refined, sombre, unobtrusive

garland noun **1** wreath, bays,

chaplet, crown, festoon, honours, laurels ♦ *verb* **2** adorn, crown, deck, festoon, wreathe

garments *plural noun* clothes, apparel, attire, clothing, costume, dress, garb, gear (*slang*), outfit, uniform

garner *verb* collect, accumulate, amass, gather, hoard, save, stockpile, store, stow away

garnish *verb* **1** decorate, adorn, embellish, enhance, ornament, set off, trim ♦ *noun* **2** decoration, adornment, embellishment, enhancement, ornamentation, trimming

➤ **Antonyms**

verb ≠decorate: denude, spoil, strip

garrison *noun* **1** troops, armed force, command, detachment, unit **2** fort, base, camp, encampment, fortification, fortress, post, station, stronghold ♦ *verb* **3** station, assign, position, post, put on duty

garrulous *adjective* talkative, chatty, gossiping, loquacious, prattling, verbose, voluble

➤ **Antonyms**

reserved, reticent, taciturn, tight-lipped, uncommunicative

gash *verb* **1** cut, gouge, lacerate, slash, slit, split, tear, wound ♦ *noun* **2** cut, gouge, incision, laceration, slash, slit, split, tear, wound

gasp *verb* **1** gulp, blow, catch one's breath, choke, pant, puff ♦ *noun* **2** gulp, exclamation, pant, puff, sharp intake of breath

gate *noun* barrier, door, entrance, exit, gateway, opening, passage, portal

gather *verb* **1** assemble, accumulate, amass, collect, garner, mass, muster, stockpile **2** intensify, deepen, expand, grow, heighten, increase, rise, swell, thicken **3** learn, assume, conclude, deduce, hear, infer, surmise, understand **4** fold, pleat, tuck **5** pick, cull, garner, glean, harvest, pluck, reap, select

➤ **Antonyms**

≠assemble: diffuse, disperse, dissipate, scatter, separate

gathering *noun* assembly, company, conclave, congress, convention, crowd, group, meeting

gauche *adjective* awkward, clumsy, ill-mannered, inelegant, tactless, unsophisticated

➤ **Antonyms**

elegant, gracious, refined, sophisticated, urbane, well-mannered

gaudy *adjective* garish, bright, flashy, loud, showy, tacky (*informal*), tasteless, vulgar

➤ **Antonyms**

colourless, conservative, dull, modest, quiet, refined, subtle, tasteful

gauge *verb* **1** judge, adjudge, appraise, assess, estimate, evaluate, guess, rate, reckon, value **2** measure, ascertain, calculate, check, compute, count, determine, weigh ♦ *noun* **3** indicator, criterion, guide, guideline, measure, meter, standard, test, touchstone, yardstick

gaunt *adjective* thin, angular, bony, haggard, lean, pinched, scrawny, skinny, spare

➤ **Antonyms**

chubby, corpulent, fat, lush, obese, plump, stout, well-fed

gawky *adjective* awkward, clumsy, gauche, loutish, lumbering, maladroit, ungainly

➤ **Antonyms**

elegant, graceful

gay *adjective* **1** homosexual, lesbian, queer (*informal, derogatory*) **2** cheerful, blithe, carefree, jovial, light-hearted, lively, merry, sparkling **3** colourful, bright, brilliant, flamboyant, flashy, rich, showy, vivid ♦ *noun* **4** homosexual, lesbian

➤ **Antonyms**

adjective, noun ≠homosexual: heterosexual, straight ♦ *adjective* ≠cheerful: cheerless, down in the dumps (*informal*), grave, grim, melancholy, miserable, sad, sedate, serious, sober, solemn, sombre, unhappy ≠**colourful**: colourless, conservative, drab, dull, sombre

gaze verb 1 <u>stare</u>, gape, look, regard, view, watch, wonder ♦ noun 2 <u>stare</u>, fixed look, look

gazette noun <u>newspaper</u>, journal, news-sheet, paper, periodical

gear noun 1 <u>cog</u>, cogwheel, gearwheel 2 <u>mechanism</u>, cogs, machinery, works 3 <u>clothing</u>, clothes, costume, dress, garments, outfit, togs, wear 4 <u>equipment</u>, accoutrements, apparatus, instruments, paraphernalia, supplies, tackle, tools ♦ verb 5 <u>equip</u>, adapt, adjust, fit

gelatinous adjective <u>jelly-like</u>, glutinous, gummy, sticky, viscous

gem noun 1 <u>precious stone</u>, jewel, stone 2 <u>prize</u>, jewel, masterpiece, pearl, treasure

general adjective 1 <u>common</u>, accepted, broad, extensive, popular, prevalent, public, universal, widespread 2 <u>universal</u>, across-the-board, blanket, collective, comprehensive, indiscriminate, miscellaneous, overall, overarching, sweeping, total 3 <u>imprecise</u>, approximate, ill-defined, indefinite, inexact, loose, unspecific, vague

► **Antonyms**

≠**common**, <u>universal</u>: distinctive, exceptional, extraordinary, individual, peculiar, special, unusual ≠**imprecise**: definite, exact, particular, precise, specific

generally adverb 1 <u>usually</u>, as a rule, by and large, customarily, normally, on the whole, ordinarily, typically 2 <u>commonly</u>, extensively, popularly, publicly, universally, widely

► **Antonyms**

≠**usually**: especially, occasionally, rarely, unusually ≠**commonly**: individually, particularly

generate verb <u>produce</u>, breed, cause, create, engender, give rise to, make, propagate

► **Antonyms**

annihilate, crush, destroy, end,

extinguish, kill, terminate

generation noun 1 <u>age group</u>, breed, crop 2 <u>age</u>, epoch, era, period, time 3 <u>production</u>, creation, formation, genesis, propagation, reproduction

generic adjective <u>collective</u>, blanket, common, comprehensive, general, inclusive, universal, wide

► **Antonyms**

individual, particular, precise, specific

generosity noun 1 <u>liberality</u>, beneficence, bounty, charity, kindness, largesse or largess, munificence, open-handedness 2 <u>unselfishness</u>, goodness, high-mindedness, magnanimity, nobleness

generous adjective 1 <u>liberal</u>, beneficent, bountiful, charitable, hospitable, kind, lavish, open-handed, unstinting 2 <u>unselfish</u>, big-hearted, good, high-minded, lofty, magnanimous, noble 3 <u>plentiful</u>, abundant, ample, copious, full, lavish, liberal, rich, unstinting

► **Antonyms**

≠**liberal**: avaricious, close-fisted, greedy, mean, miserly, parsimonious, selfish, stingy, tight ≠**plentiful**: cheap, minimal, scanty, small, tiny

genesis noun <u>beginning</u>, birth, creation, formation, inception, origin, start

► **Antonyms**

completion, conclusion, end, finish, termination

genial adjective <u>cheerful</u>, affable, agreeable, amiable, congenial, friendly, good-natured, jovial, pleasant, warm

► **Antonyms**

cheerless, cool, unfriendly, ungracious, unpleasant

geniality noun <u>cheerfulness</u>, affability, agreeableness, amiability, conviviality, cordiality, friendliness, good cheer, joviality, warmth

genius noun 1 <u>master</u>, brainbox,

expert, hotshot (*informal*), maestro, mastermind, virtuoso, whiz (*informal*) **2** brilliance, ability, aptitude, bent, capacity, flair, gift, knack, talent

➤ **Antonyms**

≠master: dolt, dunce, fool, halfwit, idiot, imbecile, nincompoop, simpleton

genre *noun* type, category, class, group, kind, sort, species, style

genteel *adjective* refined, courteous, cultured, elegant, gentlemanly, ladylike, polite, respectable, urbane, well-mannered

➤ **Antonyms**

discourteous, ill-bred, impolite, low-bred, uncultured, unrefined

gentle *adjective* **1** mild, compassionate, humane, kindly, meek, placid, sweet-tempered, tender **2** moderate, light, mild, muted, slight, soft, soothing **3** gradual, easy, imperceptible, light, mild, moderate, slight, slow **4** tame, biddable, broken, docile, manageable, placid, tractable

➤ **Antonyms**

≠mild: aggressive, cruel, fierce, hard, harsh, rough, savage, unkind ≠tame: fierce, savage, unmanageable, wild ≠moderate: powerful, strong, violent, wild ≠gradual: sudden

gentlemanly *adjective* polite, civil, courteous, gallant, genteel, honourable, refined, urbane, well-mannered

gentleness *noun* tenderness, compassion, kindness, mildness, softness, sweetness

gentry *noun* nobility, aristocracy, elite, upper class, upper crust (*informal*)

genuine *adjective* **1** authentic, actual, bona fide, legitimate, real, the real McCoy, true, veritable **2** sincere, candid, earnest, frank, heartfelt, honest, unaffected, unfeigned

➤ **Antonyms**

≠authentic: artificial, bogus, counterfeit, fake, false, fraudulent, imitation, phoney, pseudo

(*informal*), sham, simulated ≠sincere: affected, false, feigned, hypocritical, insincere, phoney

germ *noun* **1** microbe, bacterium, bug (*informal*), microorganism, virus **2** beginning, embryo, origin, root, rudiment, seed, source, spark

germane *adjective* relevant, apposite, appropriate, apropos, connected, fitting, material, pertinent, related, to the point or purpose

➤ **Antonyms**

immaterial, inappropriate, irrelevant, unrelated

germinate *verb* sprout, bud, develop, generate, grow, originate, shoot, swell, vegetate

gesticulate *verb* signal, gesture, indicate, make a sign, motion, sign, wave

gesture *noun* **1** signal, action, gesticulation, indication, motion, sign ♦ *verb* **2** signal, gesticulate, indicate, motion, sign, wave

get *verb* **1** obtain, acquire, attain, fetch, gain, land, net, pick up, procure, receive, secure, win **2** contract, catch, come down with, fall victim to, take **3** become, come to be, grow, turn **4** understand, catch, comprehend, fathom, follow, perceive, see, take in, work out **5** persuade, convince, induce, influence, prevail upon **6** *Informal* annoy, bug (*informal*), gall, irritate, upset, vex **7** capture, grab, lay hold of, nab (*informal*), seize, take

get across *verb* **1** cross, ford, negotiate, pass over, traverse **2** communicate, bring home to, convey, impart, make clear or understood, put over, transmit

get at *verb* **1** gain access to, acquire, attain, come to grips with, get hold of, reach **2** imply, hint, intend, lead up to, mean, suggest **3** criticize, attack, blame, find fault with, nag, pick on

getaway *noun* escape, break, break-out, flight

get by *verb* <u>manage</u>, cope, exist, fare, get along, keep one's head above water, make both ends meet, survive

get off *verb* <u>leave</u>, alight, depart, descend, disembark, dismount, escape, exit

get on *verb* **1** <u>board</u>, ascend, climb, embark, mount **2** <u>be friendly</u>, be compatible, concur, get along, hit it off (*informal*)

get over *verb* <u>recover from</u>, come round, get better, mend, pull through, rally, revive, survive

ghastly *adjective* <u>horrible</u>, dreadful, frightful, gruesome, hideous, horrendous, loathsome, shocking, terrible, terrifying

► **Antonyms**
appealing, attractive, beautiful, charming, lovely, pleasing

ghost *noun* **1** <u>spirit</u>, apparition, phantom, soul, spectre, spook (*informal*), wraith **2** <u>trace</u>, glimmer, hint, possibility, semblance, shadow, suggestion

ghostly *adjective* <u>supernatural</u>, eerie, ghostlike, phantom, spectral, spooky (*informal*), unearthly, wraithlike

ghoulish *adjective* <u>macabre</u>, disgusting, grisly, gruesome, morbid, sick (*informal*), unwholesome

giant *noun* **1** <u>ogre</u>, colossus, monster, titan ♦ *adjective* **2** <u>huge</u>, colossal, enormous, gargantuan, gigantic, immense, mammoth, titanic, vast

► **Antonyms**
adjective ≠*huge*: dwarf, Lilliputian, miniature, pygmy *or* pigmy, tiny

gibberish *noun* <u>nonsense</u>, babble, drivel, gobbledegook (*informal*), mumbo jumbo, twaddle

gibe, jibe *noun* **1** <u>taunt</u>, barb, crack (*slang*), dig, jeer, sarcasm, scoffing, sneer ♦ *verb* **2** <u>taunt</u>, jeer, make fun of, mock, poke fun at, ridicule, scoff, scorn, sneer

giddiness *noun* <u>dizziness</u>, faintness, light-headedness, vertigo

giddy *adjective* <u>dizzy</u>, dizzying, faint, light-headed, reeling, unsteady, vertiginous

gift *noun* **1** <u>donation</u>, bequest, bonus, contribution, grant, handout, legacy, offering, present **2** <u>talent</u>, ability, capability, capacity, flair, genius, knack, power

gifted *adjective* <u>talented</u>, able, accomplished, brilliant, capable, clever, expert, ingenious, masterly, skilled

► **Antonyms**
amateur, incapable, inept, slow, talentless, unskilled

gigantic *adjective* <u>enormous</u>, colossal, giant, huge, immense, mammoth, stupendous, titanic, tremendous

► **Antonyms**
diminutive, little, miniature, small, tiny

giggle *verb, noun* <u>laugh</u>, cackle, chortle, chuckle, snigger, titter, twitter

gild *verb* <u>embellish</u>, adorn, beautify, brighten, coat, dress up, embroider, enhance, ornament

gimmick *noun* <u>stunt</u>, contrivance, device, dodge, ploy, scheme

gingerly *adverb* <u>cautiously</u>, carefully, charily, circumspectly, hesitantly, reluctantly, suspiciously, timidly, warily

► **Antonyms**
boldly, carelessly, confidently, rashly

gird *verb* <u>surround</u>, encircle, enclose, encompass, enfold, hem in, ring

girdle *noun* **1** <u>belt</u>, band, cummerbund, sash, waistband ♦ *verb* **2** <u>surround</u>, bound, encircle, enclose, encompass, gird, ring

girl *noun* <u>female child</u>, damsel (*archaic*), daughter, lass, lassie (*informal*), maid (*archaic*), maiden (*archaic*), miss

girth *noun* <u>circumference</u>, bulk, measure, size

gist *noun* <u>point</u>, core, essence, force, idea, meaning, sense, significance, substance

give *verb* **1** <u>present</u>, award, contribute, deliver, donate, grant, hand over *or* out, provide, supply **2** <u>announce</u>, communicate, issue, notify, pronounce, transmit, utter **3** <u>produce</u>, cause, engender, make, occasion **4** <u>surrender</u>, devote, hand over, lend, relinquish, yield **5** <u>concede</u>, allow, grant

► **Antonyms**

≠*present*: accept, get, hold, keep, receive, take, withdraw

give away *verb* <u>reveal</u>, betray, disclose, divulge, expose, leak, let out, let slip, uncover

give in *verb* <u>admit defeat</u>, capitulate, cave in (*informal*), collapse, concede, quit, submit, succumb, surrender, yield

give off *verb* <u>emit</u>, discharge, exude, produce, release, send out, throw out

give out *verb* <u>emit</u>, discharge, exude, produce, release, send out, throw out

give up *verb* <u>abandon</u>, call it a day *or* night, cave in (*informal*), cease, desist, leave off, quit, relinquish, renounce, stop, surrender

glad *adjective* **1** <u>happy</u>, contented, delighted, gratified, joyful, overjoyed, pleased **2** *Archaic* <u>pleasing</u>, cheerful, cheering, gratifying, pleasant

► **Antonyms**

≠*happy*: depressed, melancholy, miserable, sad, sorrowful, unhappy

gladden *verb* <u>please</u>, cheer, delight, gratify, hearten

gladly *adverb* <u>happily</u>, cheerfully, freely, gleefully, readily, willingly, with pleasure

► **Antonyms**

dolefully, grudgingly, reluctantly, sadly, unenthusiastically, unwillingly

gladness *noun* <u>happiness</u>, cheerfulness, delight, gaiety, glee, high spirits, joy, mirth, pleasure

glamorous *adjective* <u>elegant</u>, attractive, dazzling, exciting, fascinating, glittering, glossy, prestigious, smart

► **Antonyms**

colourless, dull, plain, unattractive, unexciting, unglamorous

glamour *noun* <u>charm</u>, allure, appeal, attraction, beauty, enchantment, fascination, prestige

glance *noun* **1** <u>peek</u>, dekko (*slang*), glimpse, look, peep, view ♦ *verb* **2** <u>peek</u>, glimpse, look, peep, scan, view **3** <u>gleam</u>, flash, glimmer, glint, glisten, glitter, reflect, shimmer, shine, twinkle

► **Antonyms**

noun ≠*peek*: examination, good look, inspection, perusal ♦ *verb* ≠*peek*: peruse, scrutinize, study

glare *verb* **1** <u>scowl</u>, frown, glower, look daggers, lour *or* lower **2** <u>dazzle</u>, blaze, flame, flare ♦ *noun* **3** <u>scowl</u>, black look, dirty look, frown, glower, lour *or* lower **4** <u>dazzle</u>, blaze, brilliance, flame, glow

glaring *adjective* **1** <u>conspicuous</u>, blatant, flagrant, gross, manifest, obvious, outrageous, unconcealed **2** <u>dazzling</u>, blazing, bright, garish, glowing

► **Antonyms**

≠*conspicuous*: concealed, hidden, inconspicuous, obscure ≠*dazzling*: soft, subdued, subtle

glassy *adjective* **1** <u>transparent</u>, clear, glossy, shiny, slippery, smooth **2** <u>expressionless</u>, blank, cold, dull, empty, fixed, glazed, lifeless, vacant

glaze *verb* **1** <u>coat</u>, enamel, gloss, lacquer, polish, varnish ♦ *noun* **2** <u>coat</u>, enamel, finish, gloss, lacquer, lustre, patina, polish, shine, varnish

gleam *noun* **1** <u>glow</u>, beam, flash, glimmer, ray, sparkle **2** <u>trace</u>, flicker, glimmer, hint, inkling, suggestion ♦ *verb* **3** <u>shine</u>, flash, glimmer, glint, glisten, glitter, glow, shimmer, sparkle

glee *noun* <u>delight</u>, elation, exhilaration, exuberance, exultation, joy, merriment, triumph

gleeful *adjective* <u>delighted</u>, cock-a-hoop, elated, exuberant, exultant, joyful, jubilant, overjoyed, triumphant

glib *adjective* <u>smooth</u>, easy, fluent, insincere, plausible, quick, ready, slick, suave, voluble

➤ **Antonyms**

halting, hesitant, implausible, sincere, tongue-tied

glide *verb* <u>slide</u>, coast, drift, float, flow, roll, run, sail, skate, slip

glimmer *verb* **1** <u>flicker</u>, blink, gleam, glisten, glitter, glow, shimmer, shine, sparkle, twinkle ♦ *noun* **2** <u>trace</u>, flicker, gleam, hint, inkling, suggestion **3** <u>gleam</u>, blink, flicker, glow, ray, shimmer, sparkle, twinkle

glimpse *noun* **1** <u>look</u>, glance, peek, peep, sight, sighting ♦ *verb* **2** <u>catch sight of</u>, espy, sight, spot, spy, view

glint *verb* **1** <u>gleam</u>, flash, glimmer, glitter, shine, sparkle, twinkle ♦ *noun* **2** <u>gleam</u>, flash, glimmer, glitter, shine, sparkle, twinkle, twinkling

glisten *verb* <u>gleam</u>, flash, glance, glare, glimmer, glint, glitter, shimmer, shine, sparkle, twinkle

glitch *noun* <u>problem</u>, blip, difficulty, gremlin, hitch, interruption, malfunction, snag

glitter *verb* **1** <u>shine</u>, flash, glare, gleam, glimmer, glint, glisten, shimmer, sparkle, twinkle ♦ *noun* **2** <u>shine</u>, brightness, flash, glare, gleam, radiance, sheen, shimmer, sparkle **3** <u>glamour</u>, display, gaudiness, pageantry, show, showiness, splendour, tinsel

gloat *verb* <u>relish</u>, crow, drool, exult, glory, revel in, rub it in (*informal*), triumph

global *adjective* **1** <u>worldwide</u>, international, universal, world **2** <u>comprehensive</u>, all-inclusive, exhaustive, general, total, unlimited

➤ **Antonyms**

≠<u>comprehensive</u>: limited, nar-

row, parochial, restricted

globe *noun* <u>sphere</u>, ball, earth, orb, planet, world

globule *noun* <u>droplet</u>, bead, bubble, drop, particle, pearl, pellet

gloom *noun* **1** <u>depression</u>, dejection, despondency, low spirits, melancholy, sorrow, unhappiness, woe **2** <u>darkness</u>, blackness, dark, dusk, murk, obscurity, shade, shadow, twilight

➤ **Antonyms**

≠<u>depression</u>: brightness, cheerfulness, happiness, high spirits, jollity, joy, mirth ≠<u>darkness</u>: daylight, light, radiance

gloomy *adjective* **1** <u>miserable</u>, crestfallen, dejected, dispirited, downcast, downhearted, glum, melancholy, morose, pessimistic, sad **2** <u>depressing</u>, bad, cheerless, disheartening, dispiriting, dreary, sad, sombre **3** <u>dark</u>, black, dim, dismal, dreary, dull, grey, murky, sombre

➤ **Antonyms**

≠<u>miserable</u>: blithe, bright, cheerful, happy, high-spirited, jolly, merry ≠<u>dark</u>: brilliant, light, radiant, sunny

glorify *verb* **1** <u>enhance</u>, aggrandize, dignify, elevate, ennoble, magnify **2** <u>praise</u>, celebrate, eulogize, extol, sing or sound the praises of **3** <u>worship</u>, adore, bless, exalt, honour, idolize, pay homage to, revere, venerate

➤ **Antonyms**

≠<u>enhance</u>: debase, defile, degrade ≠<u>praise</u>: condemn, humiliate, mock ≠<u>worship</u>: desecrate, dishonour

glorious *adjective* **1** <u>splendid</u>, beautiful, brilliant, dazzling, gorgeous, shining, superb **2** <u>delightful</u>, excellent, fine, gorgeous, marvellous, wonderful **3** <u>famous</u>, celebrated, distinguished, eminent, honoured, illustrious, magnificent, majestic, renowned

➤ **Antonyms**

≠<u>splendid</u>, <u>delightful</u>: awful, dreary, dull, gloomy, horrible, unimpressive, unpleasant ≠<u>fa-</u>

glory noun **1** honour, dignity, distinction, eminence, fame, praise, prestige, renown **2** splendour, grandeur, greatness, magnificence, majesty, nobility, pageantry, pomp ♦ verb **3** triumph, boast, exult, pride oneself, relish, revel, take delight

➤ **Antonyms**

noun ≠honour: condemnation, disgrace, dishonour, disrepute, infamy, shame ≠splendour: triviality

gloss[1] noun shine, brightness, gleam, lustre, patina, polish, sheen, veneer

gloss[2] noun **1** comment, annotation, commentary, elucidation, explanation, footnote, interpretation, note, translation ♦ verb **2** interpret, annotate, comment, elucidate, explain, translate

glossy adjective shiny, bright, glassy, glazed, lustrous, polished, shining, silky

➤ **Antonyms**

drab, dull, mat or matt

glow noun **1** light, burning, gleam, glimmer, luminosity, phosphorescence **2** radiance, brightness, brilliance, effulgence, splendour, vividness ♦ verb **3** shine, brighten, burn, gleam, glimmer, redden, smoulder

➤ **Antonyms**

noun ≠radiance: dullness, greyness

glower verb **1** scowl, frown, give a dirty look, glare, look daggers, lour or lower ♦ noun **2** scowl, black look, dirty look, frown, glare, lour or lower

glowing adjective **1** bright, aglow, flaming, luminous, radiant **2** complimentary, adulatory, ecstatic, enthusiastic, laudatory, rave (informal), rhapsodic

➤ **Antonyms**

≠bright: colourless, dull, grey, pale, wan ≠complimentary: scathing, unenthusiastic

glue noun **1** adhesive, cement,

gum, paste ♦ verb **2** stick, affix, cement, fix, gum, paste, seal

glum adjective gloomy, crestfallen, dejected, doleful, low, morose, pessimistic, sullen

➤ **Antonyms**

cheerful, cheery, chirpy (informal), jolly, joyful, merry, upbeat (informal)

glut noun **1** surfeit, excess, oversupply, plethora, saturation, superfluity, surplus ♦ verb **2** saturate, choke, clog, deluge, flood, inundate, overload, oversupply

➤ **Antonyms**

noun ≠surfeit: dearth, lack, paucity, scarcity, shortage, want

glutton noun gourmand, gannet (slang), pig (informal)

gluttonous adjective greedy, gormandizing, insatiable, piggish, ravenous, voracious

gluttony noun greed, gormandizing, greediness, voracity

gnarled adjective twisted, contorted, knotted, knotty, rough, rugged, weather-beaten, wrinkled

gnaw verb bite, chew, munch, nibble

go verb **1** move, advance, journey, make for, pass, proceed, set off, travel **2** leave, depart, make tracks, move out, slope off, withdraw **3** function, move, operate, perform, run, work **4** elapse, expire, flow, lapse, pass, slip away **5** contribute, lead to, serve, tend, work towards **6** harmonize, agree, blend, chime, complement, correspond, fit, match, suit ♦ noun **7** attempt, bid, crack (informal), effort, shot (informal), try, turn **8** Informal energy, drive, force, life, spirit, verve, vigour, vitality, vivacity

➤ **Antonyms**

verb ≠move: arrive, halt, reach, remain, stay, stop ≠function: break (down), fail, malfunction, stop

goad verb **1** provoke, drive, egg on, exhort, incite, prod, prompt, spur ♦ noun **2** provocation, impetus, incentive, incitement, irritation, spur, stimulus, urge

goal noun aim, ambition, end, intention, object, objective, purpose, target

gobble verb devour, bolt, cram, gorge, gulp, guzzle, stuff, swallow, wolf

gobbledegook noun nonsense, babble, cant, gabble, gibberish, hocus-pocus, jargon, mumbo jumbo, twaddle

go-between noun intermediary, agent, broker, dealer, mediator, medium, middleman

godforsaken adjective desolate, abandoned, bleak, deserted, dismal, dreary, forlorn, gloomy, lonely, remote, wretched

godlike adjective divine, celestial, heavenly, superhuman, transcendent

godly adjective devout, god-fearing, good, holy, pious, religious, righteous, saintly

godsend noun blessing, boon, manna, stroke of luck, windfall

go for verb 1 favour, admire, be attracted to, be fond of, choose, like, prefer 2 attack, assail, assault, launch oneself at, rush upon, set about or upon, spring upon

golden adjective 1 yellow, blond or blonde, flaxen 2 successful, flourishing, glorious, halcyon, happy, prosperous, rich 3 promising, excellent, favourable, opportune

➤ **Antonyms**
≠yellow: black, brunette, dark, dull ≠successful: poorest, sad, unfavourable, worst ≠promising: black, dark, unfavourable

gone adjective 1 past, elapsed, ended, finished, over 2 missing, absent, astray, away, lacking, lost, vanished

good adjective 1 excellent, acceptable, admirable, fine, first-class, first-rate, great, pleasing, satisfactory, splendid, superior 2 honourable, admirable, ethical, honest, moral, praiseworthy, righteous, trustworthy, upright, virtu-

ous, worthy 3 favourable, advantageous, beneficial, convenient, fitting, helpful, profitable, suitable, useful, wholesome 4 kind, altruistic, benevolent, charitable, friendly, humane, kind-hearted, kindly, merciful, obliging 5 expert, able, accomplished, adept, adroit, clever, competent, proficient, skilled, talented 6 well-behaved, dutiful, obedient, orderly, polite, well-mannered 7 valid, authentic, bona fide, genuine, legitimate, proper, real, true 8 full, adequate, ample, complete, considerable, extensive, large, substantial, sufficient ◆ noun 9 benefit, advantage, gain, interest, profit, use, usefulness, welfare, wellbeing 10 virtue, excellence, goodness, merit, morality, rectitude, right, righteousness, worth 11 for good permanently, finally, for ever, irrevocably, once and for all

➤ **Antonyms**
adjective ≠excellent: awful, bad, disagreeable, inadequate, rotten, unpleasant ≠honourable: bad, base, corrupt, dishonest, dishonourable, evil, immoral, improper, sinful ≠favourable: inappropriate, pathetic, unbecoming, unfavourable, unfitting, unsuitable, useless ≠kind: cruel, evil, mean (informal), selfish, unkind, vicious, wicked ≠expert: bad, incompetent, inefficient, unsatisfactory, unskilled ≠well-behaved: ill-mannered, mischievous, naughty, rude ≠valid: counterfeit, false, fraudulent, invalid, phoney ≠full: scant, short ◆ noun ≠benefit: detriment, disadvantage, failure, ill-fortune, loss ≠virtue: badness, baseness, corruption, cruelty, dishonesty, evil, immorality, meanness, wickedness

goodbye noun farewell, adieu, leave-taking, parting

good-for-nothing noun 1 layabout, black sheep, idler, ne'er-do-well, skiver (Brit. slang), slacker (informal), waster, wastrel ◆ adjective 2 worthless, feckless, idle, irresponsible, useless

goodly adjective considerable, ample, large, significant, sizable or sizeable, substantial, tidy (informal)

goodness noun 1 excellence, merit, quality, superiority, value, worth 2 virtue, honesty, honour, integrity, merit, morality, probity, rectitude, righteousness, uprightness 3 benefit, advantage, salubriousness, wholesomeness 4 kindness, benevolence, friendliness, generosity, goodwill, humaneness, kind-heartedness, kindliness, mercy

► **Antonyms**

≠virtue: badness, corruption, dishonesty, evil, immorality, wickedness, worthlessness ≠benefit: detriment, disadvantage

goods plural noun 1 merchandise, commodities, stock, stuff, wares 2 property, belongings, chattels, effects, gear, paraphernalia, possessions, things, trappings

goodwill noun friendliness, amity, benevolence, friendship, heartiness, kindliness

go off verb 1 leave, decamp, depart, go away, move out, part, quit, slope off 2 explode, blow up, detonate, fire 3 Informal rot, go bad, go stale

go out verb 1 leave, depart, exit 2 be extinguished, die out, expire, fade out

go over verb 1 examine, inspect, rehearse, reiterate, review, revise, study, work over

gore[1] noun blood, bloodshed, butchery, carnage, slaughter

gore[2] verb pierce, impale, transfix, wound

gorge noun 1 ravine, canyon, chasm, cleft, defile, fissure, pass ♦ verb 2 overeat, cram, devour, feed, glut, gobble, gulp, guzzle, stuff, wolf

gorgeous adjective 1 beautiful, dazzling, elegant, magnificent, ravishing, splendid, stunning (informal), sumptuous, superb 2 Informal pleasing, delightful, enjoy-

able, exquisite, fine, glorious, good, lovely

► **Antonyms**

cheap, dismal, dreary, dull, homely, plain, repulsive, shabby, shoddy, ugly, unattractive, unsightly

gory adjective bloodthirsty, bloodsoaked, bloodstained, bloody, murderous, sanguinary

gospel noun 1 doctrine, credo, creed, message, news, revelation, tidings 2 truth, certainty, fact, the last word

gossip noun 1 idle talk, blether, chinwag (Brit. informal), chitchat, hearsay, scandal, small talk, tittletattle 2 busybody, chatterbox (informal), chatterer, gossipmonger, scandalmonger, tattler, telltale ♦ verb 3 chat, blether, gabble, jaw (slang), prate, prattle, tattle

go through verb 1 suffer, bear, brave, endure, experience, tolerate, undergo, withstand 2 examine, check, explore, forage, hunt, look, search

gouge verb 1 scoop, chisel, claw, cut, dig (out), hollow (out) ♦ noun 2 gash, cut, furrow, groove, hollow, scoop, scratch, trench

gourmet noun connoisseur, bon vivant, epicure, foodie (informal), gastronome

govern verb 1 rule, administer, command, control, direct, guide, handle, lead, manage, order 2 restrain, check, control, curb, discipline, hold in check, master, regulate, subdue, tame

government noun 1 executive, administration, ministry, powers-that-be, regime 2 rule, administration, authority, governance, sovereignty, statecraft

governor noun leader, administrator, chief, commander, controller, director, executive, head, manager, ruler

gown noun dress, costume, frock, garb, garment, habit, robe

grab verb snatch, capture, catch,

catch *or* take hold of, clutch, grasp, grip, pluck, seize, snap up

grace *noun* **1** elegance, attractiveness, beauty, charm, comeliness, ease, gracefulness, poise, polish, refinement, tastefulness **2** manners, consideration, decency, decorum, etiquette, propriety, tact **3** indulgence, mercy, pardon, reprieve **4** goodwill, benefaction, benevolence, favour, generosity, goodness, kindliness, kindness **5** prayer, benediction, blessing, thanks, thanksgiving ♦ *verb* **6** honour, adorn, decorate, dignify, embellish, enhance, enrich, favour, ornament, set off

➤ **Antonyms**

noun ≠elegance: awkwardness, clumsiness, inelegance, stiffness, tastelessness, ugliness, ungainliness ≠manners: bad manners, tactlessness ≠goodwill: disfavour, ill will ♦ *verb* ≠honour: desecrate, dishonour, insult, ruin, spoil

graceful *adjective* elegant, beautiful, charming, comely, easy, pleasing, tasteful

➤ **Antonyms**

awkward, clumsy, gawky, inelegant, ponderous, stiff, ugly, ungainly, ungraceful

gracious *adjective* kind, charitable, civil, considerate, cordial, courteous, friendly, polite, well-mannered

➤ **Antonyms**

brusque, cold, discourteous, haughty, impolite, rude, surly, unfriendly, ungracious, unpleasant

grade *noun* **1** level, category, class, degree, echelon, group, rank, stage ♦ *verb* **2** classify, arrange, class, group, order, range, rank, rate, sort

gradient *noun* slope, bank, declivity, grade, hill, incline, rise

gradual *adjective* steady, gentle, graduated, piecemeal, progressive, regular, slow, unhurried

➤ **Antonyms**

abrupt, broken, instantaneous,

overnight, sudden

gradually *adverb* steadily, by degrees, gently, little by little, progressively, slowly, step by step, unhurriedly

graduate *verb* **1** mark off, calibrate, grade, measure out, proportion, regulate **2** classify, arrange, grade, group, order, rank, sort

graft *noun* **1** shoot, bud, implant, scion, splice, sprout ♦ *verb* **2** transplant, affix, implant, ingraft, insert, join, splice

grain *noun* **1** seed, grist, kernel **2** cereals, corn **3** bit, fragment, granule, modicum, morsel, particle, piece, scrap, speck, trace **4** texture, fibre, nap, pattern, surface, weave **5** *As in* go against the grain inclination, character, disposition, humour, make-up, temper

grand *adjective* **1** impressive, dignified, grandiose, great, imposing, large, magnificent, regal, splendid, stately, sublime **2** excellent, fine, first-class, great (*informal*), outstanding, smashing (*informal*), splendid, wonderful

➤ **Antonyms**

≠impressive: undignified, unimposing ≠excellent: awful, bad, common, contemptible, mean, petty, poor, terrible, worthless

grandeur *noun* splendour, dignity, magnificence, majesty, nobility, pomp, stateliness, sublimity

➤ **Antonyms**

commonness, inferiority, insignificance, lowliness, triviality, unimportant

grandiose *adjective* **1** imposing, grand, impressive, lofty, magnificent, majestic, monumental, stately **2** pretentious, affected, bombastic, extravagant, flamboyant, high-flown, ostentatious, pompous, showy

➤ **Antonyms**

≠imposing: humble, modest, small-scale ≠pretentious: down-to-earth, unpretentious

grant verb **1** <u>give</u>, allocate, allot, assign, award, donate, hand out, present **2** <u>consent to</u>, accede to, agree to, allow, permit **3** <u>admit</u>, acknowledge, concede ♦ noun **4** <u>award</u>, allowance, donation, endowment, gift, handout, present, subsidy

granule noun <u>grain</u>, atom, crumb, fragment, molecule, particle, scrap, speck

graphic adjective **1** <u>vivid</u>, clear, detailed, explicit, expressive, lively, lucid, striking **2** <u>pictorial</u>, diagrammatic, visual

➤ **Antonyms**
≠<u>vivid</u>: generalized, imprecise, unspecific, vague, woolly

grapple verb **1** <u>deal with</u>, address oneself to, confront, get to grips with, struggle, tackle, take on **2** <u>grip</u>, clutch, grab, grasp, seize, wrestle

grasp verb **1** <u>grip</u>, catch, clasp, clinch, clutch, grab, grapple, hold, lay or take hold of, seize, snatch **2** <u>understand</u>, catch on, catch or get the drift of, comprehend, get, realize, see, take in ♦ noun **3** <u>grip</u>, clasp, clutches, embrace, hold, possession, tenure **4** <u>understanding</u>, awareness, comprehension, grip, knowledge, mastery **5** <u>control</u>, power, reach, scope

grasping adjective <u>greedy</u>, acquisitive, avaricious, covetous, rapacious

➤ **Antonyms**
altruistic, generous, unselfish

grate verb **1** <u>shred</u>, mince, pulverize, triturate **2** <u>scrape</u>, creak, grind, rasp, rub, scratch **3** <u>annoy</u>, exasperate, get on one's nerves (informal), irritate, jar, rankle, set one's teeth on edge

grateful adjective <u>thankful</u>, appreciative, beholden, indebted, obliged

gratification noun <u>satisfaction</u>, delight, enjoyment, fulfilment, indulgence, pleasure, relish, reward, thrill

➤ **Antonyms**
denial, disappointment, frustration, pain

gratify verb <u>please</u>, delight, give pleasure, gladden, humour, requite, satisfy

grating[1] noun <u>grille</u>, grate, grid, gridiron, lattice, trellis

grating[2] adjective <u>irritating</u>, annoying, discordant, displeasing, harsh, jarring, offensive, raucous, strident, unpleasant

➤ **Antonyms**
agreeable, calming, mellifluous, musical, pleasing, soft, soothing

gratitude noun <u>thankfulness</u>, appreciation, gratefulness, indebtedness, obligation, recognition, thanks

➤ **Antonyms**
ingratitude, ungratefulness, unthankfulness

gratuitous adjective **1** <u>unjustified</u>, baseless, causeless, groundless, needless, superfluous, uncalled-for, unmerited, unnecessary, unwarranted, wanton **2** <u>voluntary</u>, complimentary, free, gratis, spontaneous, unasked-for, unpaid, unrewarded

➤ **Antonyms**
≠<u>unjustified</u>: justifiable, provoked, well-founded ≠<u>voluntary</u>: compulsory, involuntary, paid

gratuity noun <u>tip</u>, bonus, donation, gift, largesse or largess, reward

grave[1] adjective **1** <u>important</u>, acute, critical, dangerous, pressing, serious, severe, threatening, urgent **2** <u>solemn</u>, dignified, dour, earnest, serious, sober, sombre, unsmiling

➤ **Antonyms**
≠<u>important</u>: frivolous, insignificant, mild, trifling, unimportant ≠<u>solemn</u>: carefree, exciting, flippant, happy, joyous, merry

grave[2] noun <u>tomb</u>, burying place, crypt, mausoleum, pit, sepulchre, vault

graveyard noun <u>cemetery</u>, burial ground, charnel house, churchyard, necropolis

gravity noun **1** importance, acuteness, momentousness, perilousness, seriousness, severity, significance, urgency, weightiness **2** solemnity, dignity, earnestness, gravitas, seriousness, sobriety

➤ **Antonyms**

≠importance: inconsequentiality, insignificance, triviality, unimportance ≠solemnity: flippancy, frivolity, gaiety, happiness, joy, levity, merriment

graze¹ verb feed, browse, crop, pasture

graze² verb **1** scratch, abrade, chafe, scrape, skin **2** touch, brush, glance off, rub, scrape, shave, skim ◆ noun **1** scratch, abrasion, scrape

greasy adjective fatty, oily, oleaginous, slimy, slippery

great adjective **1** large, big, enormous, gigantic, huge, immense, prodigious, vast, voluminous **2** important, critical, crucial, momentous, serious, significant **3** famous, eminent, illustrious, noteworthy, outstanding, prominent, remarkable, renowned **4** Informal excellent, fantastic (informal), fine, marvellous (informal), superb, terrific (informal), tremendous (informal), wonderful

➤ **Antonyms**

≠large: diminutive, little, small ≠important: inconsequential, inconsiderable, insignificant, petty, trivial, unimportant ≠excellent: average, inferior, poor, secondary, second-rate, undistinguished

greatly adverb very much, considerably, enormously, exceedingly, hugely, immensely, remarkably, tremendously, vastly

greatness noun **1** immensity, enormity, hugeness, magnitude, prodigiousness, size, vastness **2** importance, gravity, momentousness, seriousness, significance, urgency, weight **3** fame, celebrity, distinction, eminence, glory, grandeur, illustriousness, note, renown

greed, greediness noun **1** gluttony, edacity, esurience, gormandizing, hunger, voracity **2** avarice, acquisitiveness, avidity, covetousness, craving, desire, longing, selfishness

➤ **Antonyms**

≠avarice: altruism, benevolence, generosity, munificence, self-restraint, unselfishness

greedy adjective **1** gluttonous, gormandizing, hungry, insatiable, piggish, ravenous, voracious **2** grasping, acquisitive, avaricious, avid, covetous, craving, desirous, rapacious, selfish

➤ **Antonyms**

≠grasping: altruistic, benevolent, generous, munificent, self-restrained, unselfish

green adjective **1** leafy, grassy, verdant **2** ecological, conservationist, environment-friendly, non-polluting, ozone-friendly **3** inexperienced, gullible, immature, naive, new, raw, untrained, wet behind the ears (informal) **4** jealous, covetous, envious, grudging, resentful ◆ noun **5** lawn, common, sward, turf

greet verb welcome, accost, address, compliment, hail, meet, receive, salute

greeting noun welcome, address, reception, salutation, salute

gregarious adjective outgoing, affable, companionable, convivial, cordial, friendly, sociable, social

➤ **Antonyms**

antisocial, reserved, solitary, standoffish, unsociable, withdrawn

grey adjective **1** pale, ashen, pallid, wan **2** dismal, dark, depressing, dim, drab, dreary, dull, gloomy **3** characterless, anonymous, colourless, dull

gridlock noun standstill, deadlock, impasse, stalemate

grief noun sadness, anguish, distress, heartache, misery, regret, remorse, sorrow, suffering, woe

➤ **Antonyms**

cheer, comfort, consolation, delight, gladness, happiness, joy, rejoicing, solace

grievance noun <u>complaint</u>, axe to grind, gripe (informal), injury, injustice

grieve verb **1** <u>mourn</u>, complain, deplore, lament, regret, rue, suffer, weep **2** <u>sadden</u>, afflict, distress, hurt, injure, pain, wound

➤ Antonyms

≠sadden: cheer, comfort, console, ease, gladden, please, rejoice, solace

grievous adjective **1** <u>severe</u>, dreadful, grave, harmful, painful **2** <u>deplorable</u>, atrocious, dreadful, monstrous, offensive, outrageous, shameful, shocking

➤ Antonyms

≠severe: insignificant, mild, trivial, unimportant ≠deplorable: delightful, pleasant

grim adjective <u>forbidding</u>, formidable, harsh, merciless, ruthless, severe, sinister, stern, terrible

➤ Antonyms

benign, cheerful, genial, gentle, kind, pleasant, sympathetic

grimace noun **1** <u>scowl</u>, face, frown, sneer ♦ verb **2** <u>scowl</u>, frown, lour or lower, make a face or faces, sneer

grime noun <u>dirt</u>, filth, grot (slang), smut, soot

grimy adjective <u>dirty</u>, filthy, foul, grubby, soiled, sooty, unclean

grind verb **1** <u>crush</u>, abrade, granulate, grate, mill, pound, powder, pulverize, triturate **2** <u>smooth</u>, polish, sand, sharpen, whet **3** <u>scrape</u>, gnash, grate ♦ noun **4** Informal <u>hard work</u>, chore, drudgery, labour, sweat (informal), toil

grip noun **1** <u>clasp</u>, hold **2** <u>control</u>, clutches, domination, influence, possession, power **3** <u>understanding</u>, command, comprehension, grasp, mastery ♦ verb **4** <u>grasp</u>, clasp, clutch, hold, seize, take hold of **5** <u>engross</u>, absorb, enthral, entrance, fascinate, hold, mesmerize, rivet

gripping adjective <u>fascinating</u>, compelling, engrossing, enthralling, entrancing, exciting, riveting, spellbinding, thrilling

grisly adjective <u>gruesome</u>, appalling, awful, dreadful, ghastly, horrible, macabre, shocking, terrifying

➤ Antonyms

agreeable, attractive, charming, innocuous, nice, pleasant

grit noun **1** <u>gravel</u>, dust, pebbles, sand **2** <u>courage</u>, backbone, determination, fortitude, guts (informal), perseverance, resolution, spirit, tenacity ♦ verb **3** <u>grind</u>, clench, gnash, grate

gritty adjective **1** <u>courageous</u>, brave, determined, dogged, plucky, resolute, spirited, steadfast, tenacious **2** <u>rough</u>, dusty, granular, gravelly, rasping, sandy

groan noun **1** <u>moan</u>, cry, sigh, whine **2** Informal <u>complaint</u>, gripe (informal), grouse, grumble, objection, protest ♦ verb **3** <u>moan</u>, cry, sigh, whine **4** Informal <u>complain</u>, bemoan, gripe (informal), grouse, grumble, lament, object

groggy adjective <u>dizzy</u>, confused, dazed, faint, shaky, unsteady, weak, wobbly

groom noun **1** <u>stableman</u>, hostler or ostler (archaic), stableboy ♦ verb **2** <u>rub down</u>, brush, clean, curry, tend **3** <u>smarten up</u>, clean, preen, primp, spruce up, tidy **4** <u>train</u>, coach, drill, educate, make ready, nurture, prepare, prime, ready

groove noun <u>indentation</u>, channel, cut, flute, furrow, hollow, rut, trench, trough

grope verb <u>feel</u>, cast about, fish, flounder, forage, fumble, scrabble, search

gross adjective **1** <u>blatant</u>, flagrant, grievous, heinous, rank, sheer, unmitigated, utter **2** <u>vulgar</u>, coarse, crude, indelicate, obscene, offensive **3** <u>fat</u>, corpulent, hulking, obese, overweight **4** <u>total</u>, aggregate, before deductions, before tax, entire, whole ♦ verb **5** <u>earn</u>, bring in, make, rake in (informal), take

> **Antonyms**

≠<u>blatant</u>: partial, qualified ≠<u>vulgar</u>: decent, delicate, proper, pure *adjective* ≠<u>fat</u>: delicate, little, petite, slim, small, svelte, thin ≠<u>total</u>: net

grotesque *adjective* <u>unnatural</u>, bizarre, deformed, distorted, fantastic, freakish, outlandish, preposterous, strange

> **Antonyms**

natural, normal

ground *noun* 1 <u>earth</u>, dry land, land, soil, terra firma, terrain, turf 2 <u>stadium</u>, arena, field, park (*informal*), pitch 3 *often plural* <u>land</u>, estate, fields, gardens, terrain, territory 4 *usually plural* <u>dregs</u>, deposit, lees, sediment 5 **grounds** <u>reason</u>, basis, cause, excuse, foundation, justification, motive, occasion, pretext, rationale ◆ *verb* 6 <u>instruct</u>, acquaint with, familiarize with, initiate, teach, train, tutor 7 <u>base</u>, establish, fix, found, set, settle

groundless *adjective* <u>unjustified</u>, baseless, empty, idle, uncalled-for, unfounded, unwarranted

> **Antonyms**

justified, logical, proven, real, reasonable, substantial, supported, true, well-founded

groundwork *noun* <u>preliminaries</u>, foundation, fundamentals, preparation, spadework, underpinnings

group *noun* 1 <u>set</u>, band, bunch, cluster, collection, crowd, gang, pack, party ◆ *verb* 2 <u>arrange</u>, bracket, class, classify, marshal, order, sort

grouse *verb* 1 <u>complain</u>, bellyache (*slang*), carp, gripe (*informal*), grumble, moan, whine, whinge (*informal*) ◆ *noun* 2 <u>complaint</u>, grievance, gripe (*informal*), grouch (*informal*), grumble, moan, objection, protest

grove *noun* <u>wood</u>, coppice, copse, covert, plantation, spinney, thicket

grovel *verb* <u>humble oneself</u>, abase oneself, bow and scrape, crawl, creep, cringe, demean oneself, fawn, kowtow, toady

> **Antonyms**

be proud, domineer, hold one's head high

grow *verb* 1 <u>increase</u>, develop, enlarge, expand, get bigger, multiply, spread, stretch, swell 2 <u>cultivate</u>, breed, farm, nurture, produce, propagate, raise 3 <u>improve</u>, advance, flourish, progress, prosper, succeed, thrive 4 <u>originate</u>, arise, issue, spring, stem 5 <u>become</u>, come to be, get, turn

> **Antonyms**

≠<u>increase</u>: decline, decrease, die, diminish, dwindle, fail, lessen, shrink, subside, wane

grown-up *adjective* 1 <u>mature</u>, adult, fully-grown, of age ◆ *noun* 2 <u>adult</u>, man, woman

growth *noun* 1 <u>increase</u>, development, enlargement, expansion, multiplication, proliferation, stretching 2 <u>progress</u>, advance, expansion, improvement, prosperity, rise, success 3 *Medical* <u>tumour</u>, lump

> **Antonyms**

≠<u>increase</u>: decline, decrease, drop, dwindling, failure, fall, lessening, shrinkage, slackening, subsiding

grub *noun* 1 *Slang* <u>food</u>, nosh (*slang*), rations, sustenance, victuals 2 <u>larva</u>, caterpillar, maggot ◆ *verb* 3 <u>search</u>, ferret, forage, hunt, rummage, scour, uncover, unearth 4 <u>dig up</u>, burrow, pull up, root (*informal*)

grubby *adjective* <u>dirty</u>, filthy, grimy, messy, mucky, scruffy, seedy, shabby, sordid, squalid, unwashed

grudge *noun* 1 <u>resentment</u>, animosity, antipathy, bitterness, dislike, enmity, grievance, rancour ◆ *verb* 2 <u>resent</u>, begrudge, complain, covet, envy, mind

> **Antonyms**

noun ≠<u>resentment</u>: appreciation, goodwill, thankfulness ◆ *verb* ≠<u>resent</u>: be glad for, celebrate, welcome

gruelling adjective <u>exhausting</u>, arduous, backbreaking, demanding, laborious, punishing, severe, strenuous, taxing, tiring

➤ **Antonyms**

cushy (informal), easy, enjoyable, light, pleasant, undemanding

gruesome adjective <u>horrific</u>, ghastly, grim, grisly, horrible, macabre, shocking, terrible

➤ **Antonyms**

appealing, cheerful, pleasant, sweet

gruff adjective **1** <u>surly</u>, bad-tempered, brusque, churlish, grumpy, rough, rude, sullen, ungracious **2** <u>hoarse</u>, croaking, guttural, harsh, husky, low, rasping, rough, throaty

➤ **Antonyms**

≠<u>surly</u>: courteous, good-tempered, gracious, kind, pleasant, polite ≠<u>hoarse</u>: mellifluous, smooth, sweet

grumble verb **1** <u>complain</u>, bleat, carp, gripe (informal), grouch (informal), grouse, moan, whine, whinge (informal) **2** <u>rumble</u>, growl, gurgle, murmur, mutter, roar ♦ noun **3** <u>complaint</u>, grievance, gripe (informal), grouch (informal), grouse, moan, objection, protest **4** <u>rumble</u>, growl, gurgle, murmur, muttering, roar

grumpy adjective <u>irritable</u>, bad-tempered, cantankerous, crotchety (informal), peevish, sulky, sullen, surly, testy

guarantee noun **1** <u>assurance</u>, bond, certainty, pledge, promise, security, surety, warranty, word of honour ♦ verb **2** <u>ensure</u>, assure, certify, make certain, pledge, promise, secure, vouch for, warrant

guard verb **1** <u>watch over</u>, defend, mind, preserve, protect, safeguard, secure, shield ♦ noun **2** <u>protector</u>, custodian, defender, lookout, picket, sentinel, sentry, warder, watch, watchman **3** <u>protection</u>, buffer, defence, safeguard, screen, security, shield **4** off guard <u>unprepared</u>, napping,

unready, unwary **5** on guard <u>prepared</u>, alert, cautious, circumspect, on the alert, on the lookout, ready, vigilant, wary, watchful

guarded adjective <u>cautious</u>, cagey (informal), careful, circumspect, noncommittal, prudent, reserved, reticent, suspicious, wary

guardian noun <u>keeper</u>, champion, curator, custodian, defender, guard, protector, warden

guerrilla noun <u>freedom fighter</u>, partisan, underground fighter

guess verb **1** <u>estimate</u>, conjecture, hypothesize, predict, speculate, work out **2** <u>suppose</u>, believe, conjecture, fancy, imagine, judge, reckon, suspect, think ♦ noun **3** <u>supposition</u>, conjecture, hypothesis, prediction, shot in the dark, speculation, theory

➤ **Antonyms**

verb ≠<u>estimate</u>, <u>suppose</u>: be certain, be sure, know, prove, show ♦ noun ≠<u>supposition</u>: certainty, fact

guesswork noun <u>speculation</u>, conjecture, estimation, supposition, surmise, theory

guest noun <u>visitor</u>, boarder, caller, company, lodger, visitant

guidance noun <u>advice</u>, counselling, direction, help, instruction, leadership, management, teaching

guide noun **1** <u>escort</u>, adviser, conductor, counsellor, guru, leader, mentor, teacher, usher **2** <u>pointer</u>, beacon, guiding light, landmark, lodestar, marker, sign, signpost **3** <u>guidebook</u>, Baedeker, catalogue, directory, handbook, instructions, key, manual **4** <u>model</u>, example, ideal, inspiration, paradigm, standard ♦ verb **5** <u>lead</u>, accompany, conduct, direct, escort, shepherd, show the way, usher **6** <u>steer</u>, command, control, direct, handle, manage, manoeuvre **7** <u>supervise</u>, advise, counsel, influence, instruct, oversee, superintend, teach, train

guild noun <u>society</u>, association,

brotherhood, club, company, corporation, fellowship, fraternity, league, lodge, order, organization, union

guile noun **1** <u>cunning</u>, artifice, cleverness, craft, deceit, slyness, trickery, wiliness

➤ **Antonyms**

candour, frankness, honesty, sincerity, truthfulness

guilt noun **1** <u>culpability</u>, blame, guiltiness, misconduct, responsibility, sinfulness, wickedness, wrongdoing **2** <u>remorse</u>, contrition, guilty conscience, regret, self-reproach, shame, stigma

➤ **Antonyms**

≠culpability: blamelessness, innocence, righteousness, sinlessness, virtue ≠remorse: pride, self-respect

guiltless adjective <u>innocent</u>, blameless, clean (slang), irreproachable, pure, sinless, spotless, squeaky-clean, untainted

guilty adjective **1** <u>culpable</u>, at fault, blameworthy, reprehensible, responsible, sinful, to blame, wrong **2** <u>remorseful</u>, ashamed, conscience-stricken, contrite, regretful, rueful, shamefaced, sheepish, sorry

➤ **Antonyms**

≠culpable: blameless, innocent, moral, righteous, virtuous ≠remorseful: proud

guise noun **1** <u>form</u>, appearance, aspect, demeanour, disguise, mode, pretence, semblance, shape

gulf noun **1** <u>bay</u>, bight, sea inlet **2** <u>chasm</u>, abyss, gap, opening, rift, separation, split, void

gullibility noun <u>credulity</u>, innocence, naïveté, simplicity

gullible adjective <u>naive</u>, born yesterday, credulous, innocent, simple, trusting, unsuspecting, wet behind the ears (informal)

➤ **Antonyms**

cynical, sophisticated, suspicious, untrusting, worldly

gully noun <u>channel</u>, ditch, gutter, watercourse

gulp verb **1** <u>swallow</u>, devour, gobble, guzzle, quaff, swig (informal), swill, wolf **2** <u>gasp</u>, choke, swallow ◆ noun **3** <u>swallow</u>, draught, mouthful, swig (informal)

gum noun **1** <u>glue</u>, adhesive, cement, paste, resin ◆ verb **2** <u>stick</u>, affix, cement, glue, paste

gumption noun <u>resourcefulness</u>, acumen, astuteness, common sense, enterprise, initiative, mother wit, savvy (slang), wit(s)

gun noun <u>firearm</u>, handgun, piece (slang), shooter (slang)

gunman noun <u>terrorist</u>, bandit, gunslinger (U.S. slang), killer

gurgle verb **1** <u>murmur</u>, babble, bubble, lap, plash, purl, ripple, splash ◆ noun **2** <u>murmur</u>, babble, purl, ripple

guru noun <u>teacher</u>, authority, leader, master, mentor, sage, Svengali, tutor

gush verb **1** <u>flow</u>, cascade, flood, pour, run, rush, spout, spurt, stream **2** <u>enthuse</u>, babble, chatter, effervesce, effuse, overstate, spout ◆ noun **3** <u>stream</u>, cascade, flood, flow, jet, rush, spout, spurt, torrent

gust noun **1** <u>blast</u>, blow, breeze, puff, rush, squall ◆ verb **2** <u>blow</u>, blast, squall

gusto noun <u>relish</u>, delight, enjoyment, enthusiasm, fervour, pleasure, verve, zeal

➤ **Antonyms**

apathy, coolness, disinterest, distaste

gut noun **1** Informal <u>paunch</u>, belly, potbelly, spare tyre (Brit. slang) **2** guts: **a** <u>intestines</u>, belly, bowels, entrails, innards (informal), insides (informal), stomach, viscera **b** Informal <u>courage</u>, audacity, backbone, bottle (slang), daring, mettle, nerve, pluck, spirit ◆ verb **3** <u>disembowel</u>, clean **4** <u>ravage</u>, clean out, despoil, empty ◆ adjective **5** As in **gut reaction** <u>instinctive</u>, basic, heartfelt, intuitive, involuntary, natural, spontaneous, unthinking, visceral

gutsy adjective <u>brave</u>, bold, courageous, determined, gritty, indomitable, plucky, resolute, spirited

gutter noun <u>drain</u>, channel, conduit, ditch, sluice, trench, trough

guttural adjective <u>throaty</u>, deep, gravelly, gruff, hoarse, husky, rasping, rough, thick

guy noun Informal <u>man</u>, bloke (Brit. informal), chap, fellow, lad, person

guzzle verb <u>devour</u>, bolt, cram, drink, gobble, stuff (oneself), swill, wolf

Gypsy, Gipsy noun <u>traveller</u>, Bohemian, nomad, rambler, roamer, Romany, rover, wanderer

H h

habit noun 1 <u>mannerism</u>, custom, practice, proclivity, propensity, quirk, tendency, way 2 <u>addiction</u>, dependence

habitation noun 1 <u>occupation</u>, inhabitance, occupancy, tenancy 2 Formal <u>dwelling</u>, abode, domicile, home, house, living quarters, lodging, quarters, residence

habitual adjective <u>customary</u>, accustomed, familiar, normal, regular, routine, standard, traditional, usual

➤ **Antonyms**

abnormal, exceptional, extraordinary, irregular, rare, strange, uncommon, unusual

hack[1] verb <u>cut</u>, chop, hew, lacerate, mangle, mutilate, slash

hack[2] noun 1 <u>scribbler</u>, literary hack 2 <u>horse</u>, crock, nag

hackneyed adjective <u>unoriginal</u>, clichéd, commonplace, overworked, stale, stereotyped, stock, threadbare, tired, trite

➤ **Antonyms**

fresh, new, novel, original, unusual

hag noun <u>witch</u>, crone, harridan

haggard adjective <u>gaunt</u>, careworn, drawn, emaciated, pinched, thin, wan

➤ **Antonyms**

bright-eyed, brisk, energetic, fresh, vigorous

haggle verb <u>bargain</u>, barter, beat down

hail[1] noun 1 <u>shower</u>, barrage, bombardment, downpour, rain, storm, volley ♦ verb 2 <u>shower</u>, batter, beat down upon, bombard, pelt, rain, rain down on

hail[2] verb 1 <u>salute</u>, greet, welcome 2 <u>acclaim</u>, acknowledge, applaud, cheer, honour 3 <u>flag down</u>, signal to, wave down 4 <u>hail from</u> <u>come from</u>, be a native of, be born in, originate in

➤ **Antonyms**

≠salute: avoid, cut (informal), ignore, snub ≠acclaim: boo, condemn, criticize, hiss, insult, jeer

hair noun <u>locks</u>, head of hair, mane, mop, shock, tresses

hairdresser noun <u>stylist</u>, barber, coiffeur or coiffeuse

hair-raising adjective <u>frightening</u>, alarming, bloodcurdling, horrifying, scary, shocking, spine-chilling, terrifying

hairstyle noun <u>haircut</u>, coiffure, cut, hairdo, style

hairy adjective 1 <u>shaggy</u>, bushy, furry, hirsute, stubbly, unshaven, woolly 2 Slang <u>dangerous</u>, difficult, hazardous, perilous, risky

halcyon adjective 1 <u>peaceful</u>, calm, gentle, quiet, serene, tranquil, undisturbed 2 As in halcyon days <u>happy</u>, carefree, flourishing, golden, palmy, prosperous

hale adjective <u>healthy</u>, able-bodied, fit, flourishing, in the pink, robust, sound, strong, vigorous, well

half noun 1 <u>equal part</u>, fifty per cent, hemisphere, portion, section ♦ adjective 2 <u>partial</u>, halved, limited, moderate ♦ adverb 3 <u>partially</u>, in part, partly

half-baked adjective Informal <u>poorly planned</u>, ill-conceived, ill-judged, impractical, short-sighted, unformed, unthought out or through

half-hearted *adjective* unenthusiastic, apathetic, indifferent, lacklustre, listless, lukewarm, perfunctory, tame

➤ **Antonyms**

avid, eager, energetic, enthusiastic, spirited, wholehearted, zealous

halfway *adverb* 1 midway, to or in the middle ♦ *adjective* 2 midway, central, equidistant, intermediate, mid, middle

halfwit *noun* fool, airhead (*slang*), dunderhead, idiot, imbecile (*informal*), moron, numbskull or numskull, simpleton, twit (*informal, chiefly Brit.*)

hall *noun* 1 entrance hall, corridor, entry, foyer, hallway, lobby, passage, passageway, vestibule 2 meeting place, assembly room, auditorium, chamber, concert hall

hallmark *noun* 1 indication, sure sign, telltale sign 2 *Brit.* seal, device, endorsement, mark, sign, stamp, symbol

hallucination *noun* illusion, apparition, delusion, dream, fantasy, figment of the imagination, mirage, vision

halo *noun* ring of light, aura, corona, nimbus, radiance

halt *verb* 1 stop, break off, cease, come to an end, desist, rest, stand still, wait 2 hold back, block, bring to an end, check, curb, cut short, end, nip in the bud, terminate ♦ *noun* 3 stop, close, end, pause, standstill, stoppage

➤ **Antonyms**

verb ≠stop: begin, commence, continue, go ahead, maintain, proceed, resume, start ≠hold back: aid, boost, encourage, forward ♦ *noun* ≠stop: beginning, commencement, continuation, resumption, start

halting *adjective* faltering, awkward, hesitant, laboured, stammering, stumbling, stuttering

halve *verb* bisect, cut in half, divide equally, share equally, split in two

hammer *verb* 1 hit, bang, beat, drive, knock, strike, tap 2 *Informal* defeat, beat, drub, run rings around (*informal*), thrash, trounce, wipe the floor with (*informal*)

hamper *verb* hinder, frustrate, hamstring, handicap, impede, interfere with, obstruct, prevent, restrict

➤ **Antonyms**

aid, assist, boost, encourage, forward, further, help, promote, speed

hand *noun* 1 palm, fist, mitt (*slang*), paw (*informal*) 2 penmanship, calligraphy, handwriting, script 3 worker, artisan, craftsman, employee, hired man, labourer, operative, workman 4 round of applause, clap, ovation 5 at or on hand nearby, at one's fingertips, available, close, handy, near, ready, within reach ♦ *verb* 6 give, deliver, hand over, pass

handbook *noun* guidebook, guide, instruction book, manual

handcuff *verb* shackle, fetter, manacle

handcuffs *plural noun* shackles, cuffs (*informal*), fetters, manacles

handful *noun* few, small number, smattering, sprinkling

➤ **Antonyms**

a lot, heaps, large number, large quantity, loads (*informal*), masses (*informal*), plenty

handicap *noun* 1 disability, defect, impairment 2 disadvantage, barrier, drawback, hindrance, impediment, limitation, obstacle, restriction, stumbling block 3 advantage, head start ♦ *verb* 4 hinder, burden, encumber, hamper, hamstring, hold back, impede, limit, restrict

➤ **Antonyms**

noun ≠disadvantage: advantage, asset, benefit, boost, edge ♦ *verb*

≠hinder: aid, assist, benefit, boost, forward, further, help, promote

handicraft noun craftsmanship, art, craft, handiwork, skill, workmanship

handiwork noun creation, achievement, design, invention, product, production

handle noun 1 grip, haft, hilt, stock ♦ verb 2 hold, feel, finger, grasp, pick up, touch 3 control, direct, guide, manage, manipulate, manoeuvre 4 deal with, cope with, manage

hand-out noun 1 charity, alms, dole 2 leaflet, bulletin, circular, literature (informal), mailshot, press release

handsome adjective 1 good-looking, attractive, comely, dishy (informal, chiefly Brit.), elegant, gorgeous, personable 2 generous, abundant, ample, considerable, large, liberal, plentiful, sizable or sizeable

► Antonyms

≠good-looking: inelegant, tasteless, ugly, unattractive, unprepossessing, unsightly ≠generous: cheap, meagre, mean, miserly, small, stingy, ungenerous

handwriting noun penmanship, calligraphy, hand, scrawl, script

handy adjective 1 convenient, accessible, at hand, at one's fingertips, available, close, nearby, on hand, within reach 2 useful, convenient, easy to use, helpful, manageable, neat, practical, serviceable, user-friendly 3 skilful, adept, adroit, deft, dexterous, expert, proficient, skilled

► Antonyms

≠convenient: awkward, inaccessible, inconvenient, out of the way, unavailable ≠useful: awkward, inconvenient, unwieldy, useless ≠skilful: clumsy, ham-fisted, incompetent, inexpert, maladroit, unskilful, unskilled, useless

hang verb 1 suspend, dangle, droop 2 execute, lynch, string

up (informal) ♦ noun 3 get the hang of grasp, comprehend, understand

hang back verb be reluctant, demur, hesitate, hold back, recoil

hangdog adjective guilty, cowed, cringing, defeated, downcast, furtive, shamefaced, wretched

hangover noun aftereffects, morning after (informal)

hang-up noun Informal preoccupation, block, difficulty, inhibition, obsession, problem, thing (informal)

hank noun coil, length, loop, piece, roll, skein

hanker verb, with for or after desire, crave, hunger, itch, long, lust, pine, thirst, yearn

haphazard adjective unsystematic, aimless, casual, disorganized, hit or miss (informal), indiscriminate, slapdash

► Antonyms

careful, considered, methodical, orderly, organized, systematic, thoughtful

happen verb 1 occur, come about, come to pass, develop, result, take place, transpire (informal) 2 chance, turn out

happening noun event, affair, episode, experience, incident, occurrence, proceeding

happily adverb 1 joyfully, blithely, cheerfully, gaily, gleefully, joyously, merrily 2 luckily, fortunately, opportunely, providentially 3 willingly, freely, gladly, with pleasure

happiness noun joy, bliss, cheerfulness, contentment, delight, ecstasy, elation, jubilation, pleasure, satisfaction

► Antonyms

depression, despondency, distress, grief, low spirits, misery, sadness, sorrow, unhappiness

happy adjective 1 joyful, blissful, cheerful, content, delighted, ecstatic, elated, glad, jubilant, merry, overjoyed, pleased, thrilled 2 fortunate, advantageous, auspicious, favourable, lucky, timely

➤ **Antonyms**

≠joyful: depressed, despondent, down in the dumps (informal), gloomy, low, melancholy, miserable, sad, sombre, sorrowful, unhappy ≠fortunate: unfortunate, unhappy, unlucky

happy-go-lucky adjective carefree, blithe, easy-going, lighthearted, nonchalant, unconcerned, untroubled

➤ **Antonyms**

gloomy, melancholy, morose, sad, serious, unhappy

harangue verb **1** rant, address, declaim, exhort, hold forth, lecture, spout (informal) ♦ noun **2** speech, address, declamation, diatribe, exhortation, tirade

harass verb annoy, bother, harry, hassle (informal), hound, persecute, pester, plague, trouble, vex

harassed adjective hassled (informal), careworn, distraught, strained, tormented, troubled, under pressure, vexed, worried

harassment noun hassle (informal), annoyance, bother, irritation, nuisance, persecution, pestering, trouble

harbour noun **1** port, anchorage, haven ♦ verb **2** maintain, cling to, entertain, foster, hold, nurse, nurture, retain **3** shelter, hide, protect, provide refuge, shield

hard adjective **1** tough, firm, inflexible, rigid, rocklike, solid, stiff, strong, unyielding **2** strenuous, arduous, backbreaking, exacting, exhausting, laborious, rigorous, tough **3** difficult, complicated, intricate, involved, knotty, perplexing, puzzling, thorny **4** harsh, callous, cold, cruel, hardhearted, pitiless, stern, unfeeling, unkind, unsympathetic **5** grim, disagreeable, distressing, grievous, intolerable, painful, unpleasant ♦ adverb **6** energetically, fiercely, forcefully, forcibly, heavily, intensely, powerfully, severely, sharply, strongly, vigorously, violently, with all one's might, with might and main **7** intently,

diligently, doggedly, industriously, persistently, steadily, untiringly

➤ **Antonyms**

adjective ≠tough: flexible, malleable, pliable, soft, weak ≠strenuous: easy, easy-peasy (slang), light, soft ≠difficult: clear, direct, easy, easy-peasy (slang), simple, straightforward, uncomplicated ≠harsh: flexible, gentle, humane, kind, lenient, merciful, mild ♦ adverb ≠energetically: lazily, lightly, loosely, softly, weakly ≠intently: easily, gently, softly

hard-bitten or **hard-boiled** adjective Informal tough, cynical, hard-nosed (informal), matter-of-fact, practical, realistic, unsentimental

➤ **Antonyms**

gentle, idealistic, mild

harden verb **1** solidify, bake, cake, freeze, set, stiffen **2** accustom, habituate, inure, season, train

hardened adjective **1** habitual, chronic, incorrigible, inveterate, shameless **2** seasoned, accustomed, habituated, inured, toughened

➤ **Antonyms**

infrequent, irregular, occasional, rare, unaccustomed

hard-headed adjective shrewd, level-headed, practical, pragmatic, realistic, sensible, tough, unsentimental

➤ **Antonyms**

idealistic, impractical, sentimental, unrealistic

hardhearted adjective unsympathetic, callous, cold, hard, heartless, insensitive, uncaring, unfeeling

➤ **Antonyms**

compassionate, gentle, humane, kind, soft-hearted, sympathetic, understanding, warm, warmhearted

hardiness noun resilience, resolution, robustness, ruggedness, sturdiness, toughness

hardly adverb barely, just, only

just, scarcely, with difficulty

➤ **Antonyms**
abundantly, amply, completely, easily, fully, really, truly, undoubtedly

hardship noun suffering, adversity, difficulty, misfortune, need, privation, tribulation

➤ **Antonyms**
comfort, ease, good fortune, happiness, prosperity

hard up adjective poor, broke (informal), impecunious, impoverished, on the breadline, out of pocket, penniless, short, skint (Brit. slang), strapped for cash (informal)

➤ **Antonyms**
affluent, comfortable (informal), fortunate, loaded (slang), rich, wealthy, well-heeled (informal), well-off

hardy adjective strong, robust, rugged, sound, stout, sturdy, tough

➤ **Antonyms**
delicate, feeble, fragile, frail, sickly, soft, weak, weedy

harm verb 1 injure, abuse, damage, hurt, ill-treat, maltreat, ruin, spoil, wound ◆ noun 2 injury, abuse, damage, hurt, ill, loss, mischief, misfortune

➤ **Antonyms**
verb ≠injure: benefit, cure, heal, help, improve, repair ◆ noun ≠injury: benefit, good, help, improvement

harmful adjective injurious, damaging, deleterious, destructive, detrimental, hurtful, noxious, pernicious

➤ **Antonyms**
beneficial, good, harmless, healthy, safe, wholesome

harmless adjective innocuous, gentle, innocent, inoffensive, nontoxic, safe, unobjectionable

➤ **Antonyms**
dangerous, destructive, harmful, unhealthy, unsafe, unwholesome

harmonious adjective 1 compatible, agreeable, consonant 2 friendly, agreeable, amicable, compatible, congenial, cordial, sympathetic 3 melodious, concordant, dulcet, mellifluous, musical, sweet-sounding, tuneful

➤ **Antonyms**
≠compatible: contrasting, discordant, incompatible, inconsistent, unlike ≠friendly: unfriendly ≠melodious: cacophonous, discordant, grating, harsh, unmelodious

harmonize verb go together, agree, blend, coordinate, correspond, match, tally, tone in with

harmony noun 1 agreement, accord, amicability, compatibility, concord, cooperation, friendship, peace, rapport, sympathy 2 tunefulness, euphony, melody, tune, unison

➤ **Antonyms**
≠agreement: antagonism, conflict, contention, disagreement, dissension, hostility, opposition ≠tunefulness: cacophony

harness noun 1 equipment, gear, tack, tackle ◆ verb 2 exploit, channel, control, employ, mobilize, utilize

harrowing adjective distressing, agonizing, disturbing, gut-wrenching, heart-rending, nerve-racking, painful, terrifying, tormenting, traumatic

harry verb pester, badger, bother, chivvy, harass, hassle (informal), plague

harsh adjective 1 severe, austere, cruel, Draconian, drastic, hard, pitiless, punitive, ruthless, stern, tough 2 raucous, discordant, dissonant, grating, guttural, rasping, rough, strident

➤ **Antonyms**
≠severe: agreeable, gentle, kind, loving, merciful, mild, pleasant, sweet ≠raucous: harmonious, mellifluous, smooth, soft, soothing, sweet

harshly adverb severely, brutally, cruelly, roughly, sternly, strictly

harshness noun severity, asperity, brutality, rigour, roughness, sternness

harvest noun 1 <u>gathering</u>, harvesting, harvest-time, reaping 2 <u>crop</u>, produce, yield ♦ verb 3 <u>gather</u>, mow, pick, pluck, reap

hash noun **make a hash of** Informal <u>mess up</u>, botch, bungle, make a pig's ear of (informal), mishandle, mismanage, muddle

hassle Informal ♦ noun 1 <u>trouble</u>, bother, difficulty, grief (informal), inconvenience, problem 2 <u>argument</u>, bickering, disagreement, dispute, fight, quarrel, row, squabble ♦ verb 3 <u>bother</u>, annoy, badger, bug (informal), harass, hound, pester

haste noun 1 <u>speed</u>, alacrity, quickness, rapidity, swiftness, urgency, velocity 2 <u>rush</u>, hurry, hustle, impetuosity

➤ Antonyms
≠<u>speed</u>: slowness, sluggishness ≠<u>rush</u>: calmness, deliberation, leisureliness

hasten verb <u>rush</u>, dash, fly, hurry (up), make haste, race, scurry, speed

➤ Antonyms
crawl, creep, dawdle, move slowly

hastily adverb 1 <u>quickly</u>, promptly, rapidly, speedily 2 <u>hurriedly</u>, impetuously, precipitately, rashly

hasty adjective 1 <u>speedy</u>, brisk, hurried, prompt, rapid, swift, urgent 2 <u>rash</u>, impetuous, impulsive, precipitate, thoughtless

➤ Antonyms
≠<u>speedy</u>: leisurely, slow ≠<u>rash</u>: careful, cautious, thorough, thoughtful

hatch verb 1 <u>incubate</u>, breed, bring forth, brood 2 <u>devise</u>, conceive, concoct, contrive, cook up (informal), design, dream up (informal), think up

hate verb 1 <u>detest</u>, abhor, despise, dislike, loathe, recoil from 2 <u>be unwilling</u>, be loath, be reluctant, be sorry, dislike, feel disinclined, shrink from ♦ noun 3 <u>dislike</u>, animosity, antipathy, aversion, detestation, enmity, hatred, hostility, loathing

➤ Antonyms
verb ≠<u>detest</u>: be fond of, dote on, enjoy, like, love, relish, treasure ♦ noun ≠<u>dislike</u>: affection, fondness, liking, love

hateful adjective <u>despicable</u>, abhorrent, detestable, horrible, loathsome, obnoxious, odious, offensive, repellent, repugnant, repulsive

➤ Antonyms
attractive, beautiful, charming, desirable, good, likable or likeable, lovable, pleasant, wonderful

hatred noun <u>dislike</u>, animosity, antipathy, aversion, detestation, enmity, hate, repugnance, revulsion

➤ Antonyms
affection, attachment, devotion, fondness, friendliness, goodwill, liking, love

haughty adjective <u>proud</u>, arrogant, conceited, contemptuous, disdainful, imperious, scornful, snooty (informal), stuck-up (informal), supercilious

➤ Antonyms
humble, meek, mild, modest, self-effacing

haul verb 1 <u>drag</u>, draw, heave, lug, pull, tug ♦ noun 2 <u>yield</u>, booty, catch, gain, harvest, loot, spoils, takings

haunt verb 1 <u>plague</u>, obsess, possess, prey on, recur, stay with, torment, trouble, weigh on ♦ noun 2 <u>meeting place</u>, hangout (informal), rendezvous, stamping ground

haunted adjective 1 <u>possessed</u>, cursed, eerie, ghostly, jinxed, spooky (informal) 2 <u>preoccupied</u>, obsessed, plagued, tormented, troubled, worried

haunting adjective <u>evocative</u>, nostalgic, persistent, poignant, unforgettable

have verb 1 <u>possess</u>, hold, keep, obtain, own, retain 2 <u>receive</u>, accept, acquire, gain, get, obtain, procure, secure, take 3 <u>experience</u>, endure, enjoy, feel, meet with, suffer, sustain, undergo 4

Slang cheat, deceive, dupe, fool, outwit, swindle, take in (*informal*), trick **5** give birth to, bear, beget, bring forth, deliver **5** have to be obliged, be bound, be compelled, be forced, have got to, must, ought, should

haven *noun* sanctuary, asylum, refuge, retreat, sanctum, shelter

have on *verb* **1** wear, be clothed in, be dressed in **2** *Informal* tease, deceive, kid (*informal*), pull someone's leg, take the mickey, trick, wind up (*Brit. slang*)

havoc *noun Informal* disorder, chaos, confusion, disruption, mayhem, shambles

haywire *adjective* As in **go haywire** chaotic, confused, disordered, disorganized, mixed up, out of order, shambolic (*informal*), topsy-turvy

hazard *noun* **1** danger, jeopardy, peril, pitfall, risk, threat ◆ *verb* **2** jeopardize, endanger, expose, imperil, risk, threaten **3** As in **hazard a guess** conjecture, advance, offer, presume, throw out, venture, volunteer

hazardous *adjective* dangerous, dicey (*informal, chiefly Brit.*), difficult, insecure, perilous, precarious, risky, unsafe

➤ **Antonyms**
reliable, safe, secure, sound, stable, sure

haze *noun* mist, cloud, fog, obscurity, vapour

hazy *adjective* **1** misty, cloudy, dim, dull, foggy, overcast **2** vague, fuzzy, ill-defined, indefinite, indistinct, muddled, nebulous, uncertain, unclear

➤ **Antonyms**
≠misty: bright, clear, light, sunny ≠vague: certain, clear, detailed, well-defined

head *noun* **1** skull, crown, loaf (*slang*), nut (*slang*), pate **2** mind, brain, brains (*informal*), intellect, intelligence, thought, understanding **3** top, crest, crown, peak, pinnacle, summit, tip **4** leader, boss (*informal*), captain, chief, commander, director, manager, master, principal, supervisor **5** go to one's head excite, intoxicate, make conceited, puff up **6** head over heels completely, intensely, thoroughly, uncontrollably, utterly, wholeheartedly ◆ *adjective* **7** chief, arch, first, leading, main, pre-eminent, premier, prime, principal, supreme ◆ *verb* **8** lead, be or go first, cap, crown, lead the way, precede, top **9** be in charge of, command, control, direct, govern, guide, lead, manage, run **10** make for, aim, go to, make a beeline for, point, set off for, set out, start towards, steer, turn

headache *noun* **1** migraine, head (*informal*), neuralgia **2** *Informal* problem, bane, bother, inconvenience, nuisance, trouble, vexation, worry

heading *noun* title, caption, headline, name, rubric

headlong *adverb, adjective* **1** headfirst, head-on ◆ *adverb* **2** hastily, heedlessly, helter-skelter, hurriedly, pell-mell, precipitately, rashly, thoughtlessly ◆ *adjective* **3** hasty, breakneck, dangerous, impetuous, impulsive, inconsiderate, precipitate, reckless, thoughtless

headstrong *adjective* obstinate, foolhardy, heedless, impulsive, perverse, pig-headed, self-willed, stubborn, unruly, wilful

➤ **Antonyms**
manageable, pliant, subservient, tractable

headway *noun* advance, improvement, progress, progression, way

heady *adjective* **1** exciting, exhilarating, intoxicating, stimulating, thrilling **2** intoxicating, inebriating, potent, strong

heal *verb* cure, make well, mend, regenerate, remedy, restore, treat aggravate, exacerbate, harm, hurt, injure, make worse, wound

health noun **1** <u>condition</u>, constitution, fettle, shape, state **2** <u>wellbeing</u>, fitness, good condition, healthiness, robustness, soundness, strength, vigour

➤ **Antonyms**
≠<u>wellbeing</u>: debility, disease, frailty, illness, sickness, weakness

healthy adjective **1** <u>well</u>, active, fit, hale and hearty, in fine fettle, in good shape (informal), in the pink, robust, strong **2** <u>wholesome</u>, beneficial, hygienic, invigorating, nourishing, nutritious, salubrious, salutary

➤ **Antonyms**
≠<u>well</u>: ailing, delicate, diseased, frail, ill, infirm, poorly (informal), sick, sickly, unfit, unhealthy, unwell ≠<u>wholesome</u>: unhealthy, unwholesome

heap noun **1** <u>pile</u>, accumulation, collection, hoard, lot, mass, mound, stack **2** often plural Informal <u>a lot</u>, great deal, load(s) (informal), lots (informal), mass, plenty, pot(s) (informal), stack(s), tons ♦ verb **3** <u>pile</u>, accumulate, amass, collect, gather, hoard, stack **4** <u>confer</u>, assign, bestow, load, shower upon

hear verb **1** <u>listen to</u>, catch, overhear **2** <u>learn</u>, ascertain, discover, find out, gather, get wind of (informal), pick up **3** Law <u>try</u>, examine, investigate, judge

hearing noun <u>inquiry</u>, industrial tribunal, investigation, review, trial

hearsay noun <u>rumour</u>, gossip, idle talk, report, talk, tittle-tattle, word of mouth

heart noun **1** <u>nature</u>, character, disposition, soul, temperament **2** <u>courage</u>, bravery, fortitude, pluck, purpose, resolution, spirit, will **3** <u>centre</u>, core, hub, middle, nucleus, quintessence **4** <u>by heart</u> <u>by memory</u>, by rote, off pat, parrot-fashion (informal), pat, word for word

heartache noun <u>sorrow</u>, agony, anguish, despair, distress, grief, heartbreak, pain, remorse, suffering, torment, torture

heartbreak noun <u>grief</u>, anguish, desolation, despair, misery, pain, sorrow, suffering

heartbreaking adjective <u>sad</u>, agonizing, distressing, gutwrenching, harrowing, heartrending, pitiful, poignant, tragic

➤ **Antonyms**
cheerful, cheery, happy, jolly, joyful, joyous, light-hearted

heartbroken adjective <u>miserable</u>, brokenhearted, crushed, desolate, despondent, disconsolate, dispirited, heartsick

➤ **Antonyms**
cheerful, elated, happy, in seventh heaven, joyful, on cloud nine, over the moon (informal)

heartfelt adjective <u>sincere</u>, deep, devout, earnest, genuine, honest, profound, unfeigned, wholehearted

➤ **Antonyms**
false, feigned, hypocritical, insincere, phoney or phony (informal), pretended, put on

heartily adverb <u>enthusiastically</u>, eagerly, earnestly, resolutely, vigorously, zealously

heartless adjective <u>cruel</u>, callous, cold, hard, hardhearted, merciless, pitiless, uncaring, unfeeling

➤ **Antonyms**
compassionate, humane, kind, merciful, sympathetic, warmhearted

heart-rending adjective <u>moving</u>, affecting, distressing, gutwrenching, harrowing, heartbreaking, poignant, sad, tragic

hearty adjective **1** <u>friendly</u>, backslapping, ebullient, effusive, enthusiastic, genial, jovial, warm **2** <u>substantial</u>, ample, filling, nourishing, sizable or sizeable, solid, square

➤ **Antonyms**
≠<u>friendly</u>: cold, cool, unfriendly

heat verb **1** <u>warm up</u>, make hot, reheat ♦ noun **2** <u>hotness</u>, high temperature, warmth **3** <u>passion</u>, excitement, fervour, fury, intensity, vehemence

➤ **Antonyms**

verb ≠<u>warm up</u>: chill, cool, cool off, freeze ◆ noun ≠<u>hotness</u>: cold, coldness, coolness ≠<u>passion</u>: calmness, composure, coolness

heated adjective <u>impassioned</u>, angry, excited, fierce, frenzied, furious, intense, passionate, stormy, vehement

➤ **Antonyms**

calm, dispassionate, mild, quiet, rational, unemotional

heathen noun Old-fashioned **1** <u>pagan</u>, infidel, unbeliever ◆ adjective **2** <u>pagan</u>, godless, idolatrous, irreligious

heave verb **1** <u>lift</u>, drag (up), haul (up), hoist, pull (up), raise, tug **2** <u>throw</u>, cast, fling, hurl, pitch, send, sling, toss **3** <u>sigh</u>, groan, puff **4** <u>vomit</u>, be sick, gag, retch, spew, throw up (informal)

heaven noun **1** <u>paradise</u>, bliss, Elysium or Elysian fields (Greek myth), hereafter, life everlasting, next world, nirvana (Buddhism, Hinduism), Zion (Christianity) **2** <u>happiness</u>, bliss, ecstasy, paradise, rapture, seventh heaven, utopia **3** the heavens <u>sky</u>, ether, firmament

heavenly adjective **1** Informal <u>wonderful</u>, beautiful, blissful, delightful, divine (informal), exquisite, lovely, ravishing, sublime **2** <u>celestial</u>, angelic, blessed, divine, holy, immortal

➤ **Antonyms**

≠<u>wonderful</u>: abominable, abysmal, appalling, awful, bad, dire, dreadful, frightful, horrible, horrid, lousy (slang), rotten (informal), terrible, unpleasant, vile ≠<u>celestial</u>: earthly, human, secular, worldly

heavily adverb **1** <u>densely</u>, closely, compactly, thickly **2** <u>considerably</u>, a great deal, copiously, excessively, to excess, very much **3** <u>ponderously</u>, awkward-ly, clumsily, weightily

heaviness noun <u>weight</u>, gravity, heftiness, ponderousness

heavy adjective **1** <u>weighty</u>, bulky, hefty, massive, ponderous **2** <u>considerable</u>, abundant, copious, excessive, large, profuse

➤ **Antonyms**

≠<u>weighty</u>: compact, handy, light, slight, small ≠<u>considerable</u>: light, moderate, slight, sparse

heckle verb <u>jeer</u>, barrack (informal), boo, disrupt, interrupt, shout down, taunt

hectic adjective <u>frantic</u>, animated, chaotic, feverish, frenetic, heated, turbulent

➤ **Antonyms**

calm, peaceful, relaxing, tranquil

hedge noun **1** <u>hedgerow</u> **2** <u>barrier</u>, boundary, screen, windbreak ◆ verb **3** <u>dodge</u>, duck, equivocate, evade, flannel (Brit. informal), prevaricate, sidestep, temporize **4** <u>enclose</u>, cover, guard, protect, safeguard, shield

heed Formal ◆ noun **1** <u>care</u>, attention, caution, mind, notice, regard, respect, thought ◆ verb **2** <u>pay attention to</u>, bear in mind, consider, follow, listen to, note, obey, observe, take notice of

➤ **Antonyms**

noun ≠<u>care</u>: carelessness, disregard, inattention, laxity, laxness, neglect, thoughtlessness ◆ verb ≠<u>pay attention to</u>: be inattentive to, discount, disobey, disregard, flout, ignore, neglect, reject

heedless adjective <u>careless</u>, foolhardy, inattentive, oblivious, thoughtless, unmindful

➤ **Antonyms**

attentive, aware, careful, cautious, heedful, mindful, thoughtful, wary

heel [1] noun Slang <u>swine</u>, bounder (old-fashioned Brit. slang), cad (Brit. informal), rotter (slang, chiefly Brit.)

heel [2] verb <u>lean over</u>, keel over, list, tilt

hefty adjective Informal <u>big</u>, burly,

hulking, massive, muscular, robust, strapping, strong

➤ **Antonyms**

diminutive, little, minute, slight, slim, small, tiny

height noun 1 altitude, elevation, highness, loftiness, stature, tallness 2 peak, apex, crest, crown, pinnacle, summit, top, zenith 3 culmination, climax, limit, maximum, ultimate

➤ **Antonyms**

≠altitude: depth, lowness, shortness, smallness ≠peak: abyss, base, bottom, chasm, depth, nadir ≠culmination: low point, minimum, nadir

heighten verb intensify, add to, amplify, enhance, improve, increase, magnify, sharpen, strengthen

heir noun successor, beneficiary, heiress (fem.), inheritor, next in line

hell noun 1 underworld, abyss, fire and brimstone, Hades (Greek myth), hellfire, inferno, nether world 2 Informal torment, agony, anguish, misery, nightmare, ordeal, suffering, wretchedness

hellish adjective devilish, damnable, diabolical, fiendish, infernal

hello interjection hi (Informal), good afternoon, good evening, good morning, greetings, how do you do?, welcome

helm noun 1 Nautical tiller, rudder, wheel 2 at the helm in charge, at the wheel, in command, in control, in the driving seat, in the saddle

help verb 1 aid, abet, assist, co-operate, lend a hand, succour, support 2 improve, alleviate, ameliorate, ease, facilitate, mitigate, relieve 3 refrain from, avoid, keep from, prevent, resist ♦ noun 4 assistance, advice, aid, cooperation, guidance, helping hand, support

➤ **Antonyms**

verb ≠aid: bar, block, discourage, hinder, impede, obstruct

≠improve: aggravate, harm, hurt, injure, irritate, make worse ♦ noun ≠assistance: block, discouragement, hindrance, obstruction

helper noun assistant, aide, ally, attendant, collaborator, helpmate, mate, right-hand man, second, supporter

helpful adjective 1 useful, advantageous, beneficial, constructive, practical, profitable, timely 2 co-operative, accommodating, considerate, friendly, kind, neighbourly, supportive, sympathetic

helping noun portion, dollop (informal), piece, plateful, ration, serving

helpless adjective powerless, disabled, impotent, incapable, infirm, paralysed, weak

➤ **Antonyms**

able, capable, fit, powerful, robust, strong, sturdy

helter-skelter adjective 1 haphazard, confused, disordered, higgledy-piggledy (informal), hit-or-miss, jumbled, muddled, random, topsy-turvy ♦ adverb 2 carelessly, anyhow, hastily, headlong, hurriedly, pell-mell, rashly, recklessly, wildly

hem noun edge, border, fringe, margin, trimming

hem in verb surround, beset, circumscribe, confine, enclose, restrict, shut in

hence conjunction therefore, ergo, for this reason, on that account, thus

henchman noun attendant, associate, bodyguard, follower, minder (slang), right-hand man, sidekick (slang), subordinate, supporter

henpecked adjective dominated, browbeaten, bullied, meek, subjugated, timid

➤ **Antonyms**

assertive, domineering, forceful, macho, self-assertive

herald noun 1 messenger, crier 2 Often literary forerunner, harbinger, indication, omen, precursor, sign, signal, token ♦ *verb* **3** indicate, foretoken, portend, presage, promise, show, usher in

herd *noun* **1** flock, collection, crowd, drove, horde, mass, mob, multitude, swarm, throng ♦ *verb* **2** congregate, assemble, collect, flock, gather, huddle, muster, rally

hereafter *adverb* **1** in future, from now on, hence, henceforth, henceforward ♦ *noun* **2 the hereafter** afterlife, life after death, next world

hereditary *adjective* **1** genetic, inborn, inbred, inheritable, transmissible **2** *Law* inherited, ancestral, traditional

heredity *noun* genetics, constitution, genetic make-up, inheritance

heresy *noun* unorthodoxy, apostasy, dissidence, heterodoxy, iconoclasm

heretic *noun* nonconformist, apostate, dissenter, dissident, renegade, revisionist

heretical *adjective* unorthodox, heterodox, iconoclastic, idolatrous, impious, revisionist

heritage *noun* inheritance, bequest, birthright, endowment, legacy, tradition

hermit *noun* recluse, anchorite, loner (*informal*), monk

hero *noun* **1** leading man, protagonist **2** idol, champion, conqueror, star, superstar, victor

heroic *adjective* courageous, brave, daring, fearless, gallant, intrepid, lion-hearted, valiant

➤ **Antonyms**
chicken (*slang*), cowardly, craven, faint-hearted, timid

heroine *noun* leading lady, diva, prima donna, protagonist

heroism *noun* bravery, courage, courageousness, fearlessness, gallantry, intrepidity, spirit, valour

hesitant *adjective* uncertain, diffident, doubtful, half-hearted, halting, irresolute, reluctant, unsure, vacillating, wavering

➤ **Antonyms**
confident, definite, firm, forceful, positive, resolute, self-assured, unhesitating, unwavering

hesitate *verb* **1** waver, delay, dither (*chiefly Brit.*), doubt, hum and haw, pause, vacillate, wait **2** be reluctant, balk, be unwilling, demur, hang back, scruple, shrink from, think twice

➤ **Antonyms**
≠waver: be confident, be decisive, be firm ≠be reluctant: be determined, resolve, welcome

hesitation *noun* **1** indecision, delay, doubt, hesitancy, irresolution, uncertainty, vacillation **2** reluctance, misgiving(s), qualm(s), scruple(s), unwillingness

hew *verb* **1** cut, axe, chop, hack, lop, split **2** carve, fashion, form, make, model, sculpt, sculpture, shape, smooth

heyday *noun* prime, bloom, pink, prime of life, salad days

hiatus *noun* pause, break, discontinuity, gap, interruption, interval, respite, space

hidden *adjective* concealed, clandestine, covert, latent, secret, under wraps, unseen, veiled

hide¹ *verb* **1** conceal, secrete, stash (*informal*) **2** go into hiding, go to ground, go underground, hole up, lie low, take cover **3** suppress, draw a veil over, hush up, keep dark, keep secret, keep under one's hat, withhold **4** disguise, camouflage, cloak, conceal, cover, mask, obscure, shroud, veil

➤ **Antonyms**
admit, bare, confess, disclose, display, divulge, exhibit, expose, find, flaunt, reveal, show, uncover, unveil

hide² *noun* skin, pelt

hidebound *adjective* conventional, narrow-minded, rigid, set in one's ways, strait-laced, ultraconservative

➤ **Antonyms**
broad-minded, flexible, liberal, open, receptive, tolerant

hideous *adjective* ugly, ghastly, grim, grisly, grotesque, gruesome, monstrous, repulsive, revolting, unsightly

➤ **Antonyms**
appealing, beautiful, captivating, charming, entrancing, lovely, pleasant, pleasing

hide-out *noun* hiding place, den, hideaway, lair, shelter

hiding *noun* beating, drubbing, licking (*informal*), spanking, thrashing, walloping (*informal*), whipping

hierarchy *noun* grading, pecking order, ranking

high *adjective* 1 tall, elevated, lofty, soaring, steep, towering 2 extreme, excessive, extraordinary, great, intensified, sharp, strong 3 high-pitched, acute, penetrating, piercing, piping, sharp, shrill, strident 4 important, arch, chief, eminent, exalted, powerful, superior 5 *Informal* intoxicated, stoned (*slang*), tripping (*informal*) ♦ *adverb* 6 aloft, at great height, far up, way up

➤ **Antonyms**
adjective ≠tall: dwarfed, low, short, stunted ≠extreme: average, low, mild, moderate ≠high-pitched: alto, bass, deep, gruff, low, low-pitched ≠important: average, insignificant, low, lowly, low-ranking, secondary, undistinguished, unimportant

highbrow *Often disparaging* ♦ *adjective* 1 intellectual, bookish, cultivated, cultured, sophisticated ♦ *noun* 2 intellectual, aesthete, egghead (*informal*), scholar

➤ **Antonyms**
adjective ≠intellectual: ignorant, lowbrow, philistine, uncultivated, unintellectual, unlearned, unsophisticated ♦ *noun* ≠intellectual: idiot, ignoramus, illiterate, imbecile (*informal*), lowbrow, moron, philistine

high-flown *adjective* extravagant, elaborate, exaggerated, florid, grandiose, inflated, lofty, overblown, pretentious

➤ **Antonyms**
down-to-earth, modest, pragmatic, realistic, reasonable, restrained, simple, straightforward, unpretentious

high-handed *adjective* dictatorial, despotic, domineering, imperious, oppressive, overbearing, tyrannical, wilful

highlight *noun* 1 high point, climax, feature, focal point, focus, high spot, peak ♦ *verb* 2 emphasize, accent, accentuate, bring to the fore, show up, spotlight, stress, underline

➤ **Antonyms**
noun ≠high point: disappointment, lowlight, low point ♦ *verb* ≠emphasize: de-emphasize, gloss over, neglect, overlook, play down

highly *adverb* extremely, exceptionally, greatly, immensely, tremendously, vastly, very, very much

highly strung *adjective* nervous, edgy, excitable, neurotic, sensitive, stressed, temperamental, tense

➤ **Antonyms**
calm, collected, easy-going, even-tempered, laid-back (*informal*), placid, relaxed, serene, unfazed (*informal*)

hijack *verb* seize, commandeer, expropriate, take over

hike *noun* 1 walk, march, ramble, tramp, trek ♦ *verb* 2 walk, backpack, ramble, tramp 3 hike up raise, hitch up, jack up, lift, pull up

hilarious *adjective* funny, amusing, comical, entertaining, humorous, rollicking, side-splitting, uproarious

➤ **Antonyms**
gloomy, sad, serious

hilarity *noun* merriment, amusement, exhilaration, glee, high spirits, jollity, laughter, mirth

hill *noun* mount, fell, height, hillock, hilltop, knoll, mound, tor

hillock *noun* mound, hummock, knoll

hilly *adjective* <u>mountainous</u>, rolling, undulating

hilt *noun* <u>handle</u>, grip, haft, handgrip

hinder *verb* <u>obstruct</u>, block, check, delay, encumber, frustrate, hamper, handicap, hold up *or* back, impede, interrupt, stop

➤ **Antonyms**
accelerate, aid, benefit, encourage, expedite, facilitate, further, help, promote, quicken, speed

hindmost *adjective* <u>last</u>, furthest, furthest behind, rearmost, trailing

hindrance *noun* <u>obstacle</u>, barrier, deterrent, difficulty, drawback, handicap, hitch, impediment, obstruction, restriction, snag, stumbling block

➤ **Antonyms**
advantage, aid, asset, assistance, benefit, boon, boost, encouragement, help, support

hinge *verb* **hinge on** <u>depend on</u>, be contingent on, hang on, pivot on, rest on, revolve around, turn on

hint *noun* **1** <u>indication</u>, allusion, clue, implication, innuendo, insinuation, intimation, suggestion **2** <u>advice</u>, help, pointer, suggestion, tip **3** <u>trace</u>, dash, suggestion, suspicion, tinge, touch, undertone ◆ *verb* **4** <u>suggest</u>, imply, indicate, insinuate, intimate

hippy *noun* <u>bohemian</u>, beatnik, dropout

hire *verb* **1** <u>employ</u>, appoint, commission, engage, sign up, take on **2** <u>rent</u>, charter, engage, lease, let ◆ *noun* **3** <u>rental</u>, charge, cost, fee, price, rent

hiss *noun* **1** <u>sibilation</u>, buzz, hissing **2** <u>catcall</u>, boo, jeer ◆ *verb* **3** <u>whistle</u>, sibilate, wheeze, whirr, whiz **4** <u>jeer</u>, boo, deride, hoot, mock

historic *adjective* <u>significant</u>, epoch-making, extraordinary, famous, ground-breaking, momentous, notable, outstanding, remarkable

➤ **Antonyms**
ordinary, unimportant, unknown

historical *adjective* <u>factual</u>, actual, attested, authentic, documented, real

➤ **Antonyms**
fabulous, fictional, legendary, mythical

history *noun* **1** <u>chronicle</u>, account, annals, narrative, recital, record, story **2** <u>the past</u>, antiquity, olden days, yesterday, yesteryear

hit *verb* **1** <u>strike</u>, bang, beat, clout (*informal*), knock, slap, smack, thump, wallop (*informal*), whack **2** <u>collide with</u>, bang into, bump, clash with, crash against, run into, smash into **3** <u>affect</u>, damage, devastate, impact on, influence, leave a mark on, overwhelm, touch **4** <u>reach</u>, accomplish, achieve, arrive at, attain, gain **5 hit it off** *Informal* <u>get on (well) with</u>, be on good terms, click (*slang*), get on like a house on fire (*informal*) ◆ *noun* **6** <u>stroke</u>, belt (*informal*), blow, clout (*informal*), knock, rap, slap, smack, wallop (*informal*) **7** <u>success</u>, sensation, smash (*informal*), triumph, winner

hitch *noun* **1** <u>problem</u>, catch, difficulty, drawback, hindrance, hold-up, impediment, obstacle, snag ◆ *verb* **2** *Informal* <u>hitchhike</u>, thumb a lift **3** <u>fasten</u>, attach, connect, couple, harness, join, tether, tie **4** <u>hitch up</u> <u>pull up</u>, jerk, tug, yank

hitherto *adverb* *Formal* <u>previously</u>, heretofore, so far, thus far, until now

hit on *verb* <u>think up</u>, arrive at, discover, invent, light upon, strike upon, stumble on

hit-or-miss *or* **hit-and-miss** *adjective* <u>haphazard</u>, aimless, casual, disorganized, indiscriminate, random, undirected, uneven

➤ **Antonyms**
arranged, deliberate, organized, planned, systematic

hoard *noun* **1** <u>store</u>, accumulation, cache, fund, pile, reserve, stash, stockpile, supply, treasure-trove ♦ *verb* **2** <u>save</u>, accumulate, amass, collect, gather, lay up, put by, stash away (*informal*), stockpile, store

hoarse *adjective* <u>rough</u>, croaky, grating, gravelly, gruff, guttural, husky, rasping, raucous, throaty

▶ **Antonyms**
harmonious, mellifluous, mellow, melodious, smooth

hoax *noun* **1** <u>trick</u>, con (*informal*), deception, fraud, practical joke, prank, spoof (*informal*), swindle ♦ *verb* **2** <u>deceive</u>, con (*slang*), dupe, fool, hoodwink, swindle, take in (*informal*), trick

hobby *noun* <u>pastime</u>, diversion, (leisure) activity, leisure pursuit, relaxation

hobnob *verb* <u>socialize</u>, associate, consort, fraternize, hang about, hang out (*informal*), keep company, mingle, mix

hoist *verb* **1** <u>raise</u>, elevate, erect, heave, lift ♦ *noun* **2** <u>lift</u>, crane, elevator, winch

hold *verb* **1** <u>grasp</u>, clasp, cling, clutch, cradle, embrace, enfold, grip **2** <u>accommodate</u>, contain, have a capacity for, seat, take **3** <u>restrain</u>, confine, detain, impound, imprison **4** <u>own</u>, have, keep, maintain, occupy, possess, retain **5** <u>consider</u>, assume, believe, deem, judge, presume, reckon, regard, think **6** <u>convene</u>, call, conduct, preside over, run ♦ *noun* **7** <u>grip</u>, clasp, grasp **8** <u>foothold</u>, footing, support **9** <u>control</u>, influence, mastery

▶ **Antonyms**
verb ≠<u>restrain</u>: free, let go, let loose, release ≠<u>own</u>: bestow, give, give away, give up, hand over, offer, turn over ≠<u>consider</u>: deny, disavow, disclaim, refute, reject ≠<u>convene</u>: call off, cancel, postpone

holder *noun* **1** <u>case</u>, container, cover **2** <u>owner</u>, bearer, keeper, possessor, proprietor

hold forth *verb* <u>speak</u>, declaim,

discourse, go on, lecture, preach, spiel (*informal*), spout (*informal*)

hold-up *noun* **1** <u>robbery</u>, mugging (*informal*), stick-up (*slang, chiefly U.S.*), theft **2** <u>delay</u>, bottleneck, hitch, setback, snag, stoppage, traffic jam, wait

hold up *verb* **1** <u>delay</u>, detain, hinder, retard, set back, slow down, stop **2** <u>support</u>, prop, shore up, sustain **3** <u>rob</u>, mug (*informal*), waylay

hold with *verb* <u>approve of</u>, agree to or with, be in favour of, countenance, subscribe to, support

▶ **Antonyms**
be against, disagree with, disapprove of, hold out against, oppose

hole *noun* **1** <u>cavity</u>, cave, cavern, chamber, hollow, pit **2** <u>opening</u>, aperture, breach, crack, fissure, gap, orifice, perforation, puncture, tear, vent **3** <u>burrow</u>, den, earth, lair, shelter **4** *Informal* <u>hovel</u>, dive (*slang*), dump (*informal*), slum **5** *Informal* <u>predicament</u>, dilemma, fix (*informal*), hot water (*informal*), jam (*informal*), mess, scrape (*informal*), spot (*informal*), tight spot

holiday *noun* **1** <u>vacation</u>, break, leave, recess, time off **2** <u>festival</u>, celebration, feast, fête, gala

holiness *noun* <u>sanctity</u>, divinity, godliness, piety, purity, righteousness, sacredness, saintliness, spirituality

hollow *adjective* **1** <u>empty</u>, unfilled, vacant, void **2** <u>toneless</u>, deep, dull, low, muted, reverberant **3** <u>worthless</u>, fruitless, futile, meaningless, pointless, useless, vain ♦ *noun* **4** <u>cavity</u>, basin, bowl, crater, depression, hole, pit, trough **5** <u>valley</u>, dale, dell, dingle, glen ♦ *verb* **6** <u>scoop</u>, dig, excavate, gouge

▶ **Antonyms**
adjective ≠<u>empty</u>: full, occupied, solid ≠<u>toneless</u>: expressive, vibrant ≠<u>worthless</u>: gratifying, meaningful, pleasing, satisfying,

valuable, worthwhile ♦ *noun* ≠*cavity*: bump, mound, projection ≠*valley*: bluff, height, hill, knoll, mountain, rise

holocaust *noun* genocide, annihilation, conflagration, destruction, devastation, massacre

holy *adjective* **1** sacred, blessed, consecrated, hallowed, sacrosanct, sanctified, venerable **2** devout, god-fearing, godly, pious, pure, religious, righteous, saintly, virtuous

➤ **Antonyms**
≠*sacred*: desecrated, unconsecrated, unhallowed, unholy, unsanctified ≠*devout*: blasphemous, corrupt, evil, impious, irreligious, sacrilegious, sinful, unholy, wicked

homage *noun* respect, adoration, adulation, deference, devotion, honour, reverence, worship

➤ **Antonyms**
contempt, disdain, disregard, disrespect, irreverence, scorn

home *noun* **1** dwelling, abode, domicile, habitation, house, pad (*slang*), residence **2** birthplace, home town **3 at home b** a in, available, present **b** at ease, comfortable, familiar, relaxed **4 bring home to** make clear, drive home, emphasize, impress upon, press home ♦ *adjective* **5** domestic, familiar, internal, local, native

homeland *noun* native land, country of origin, fatherland, mother country, motherland

homeless *adjective* **1** destitute, displaced, dispossessed, down-and-out ♦ *noun* **2 the homeless** vagrants, squatters

homely *adjective* comfortable, cosy, friendly, homespun, modest, ordinary, plain, simple, welcoming

➤ **Antonyms**
affected, elaborate, elegant, grand, ostentatious, pretentious, refined, splendid

homespun *adjective* unsophisticated, coarse, homely, home-

made, plain, rough

homicidal *adjective* murderous, deadly, lethal, maniacal, mortal

homicide *noun* **1** murder, bloodshed, killing, manslaughter, slaying **2** murderer, killer, slayer

homily *noun* sermon, address, discourse, lecture, preaching

homogeneity *noun* uniformity, consistency, correspondence, sameness, similarity

homogeneous *adjective* uniform, akin, alike, analogous, comparable, consistent, identical, similar, unvarying

➤ **Antonyms**
different, dissimilar, diverse, heterogeneous, manifold, mixed, unlike, unrelated, varied, various, varying

hone *verb* sharpen, edge, file, grind, point, polish, whet

honest *adjective* **1** trustworthy, ethical, honourable, law-abiding, reputable, scrupulous, truthful, upright, virtuous **2** open, candid, direct, forthright, frank, plain, sincere, upfront (*informal*)

➤ **Antonyms**
≠*trustworthy*: crooked, deceitful, dishonest, immoral, unprincipled, unreliable, unscrupulous, untrustworthy, untruthful ≠*open*: disguised, false, insincere, secretive

honestly *adverb* **1** frankly, candidly, in all sincerity, plainly, straight (out), to one's face, truthfully **2** ethically, by fair means, cleanly, honourably, lawfully, legally

honesty *noun* **1** integrity, honour, incorruptibility, morality, probity, rectitude, scrupulousness, trustworthiness, truthfulness, uprightness, virtue **2** frankness, bluntness, candour, openness, outspokenness, sincerity, straightforwardness

honorary *adjective* nominal, complimentary, in name or title only, titular, unofficial, unpaid

honour *noun* **1** integrity, decency, fairness, goodness, honesty, morality, probity, rectitude **2** <u>prestige</u>, credit, dignity, distinction, fame, glory, renown, reputation **3** <u>tribute</u>, accolade, commendation, homage, praise, recognition **4** <u>privilege</u>, compliment, credit, pleasure ♦ verb **5** <u>respect</u>, adore, appreciate, esteem, prize, value **6** <u>acclaim</u>, commemorate, commend, decorate, praise **7** <u>pay</u>, accept, acknowledge, pass, take **8** <u>fulfil</u>, be true to, carry out, discharge, keep, live up to, observe

➤ **Antonyms**

noun ≠<u>integrity</u>: degradation, dishonesty, dishonour, insincerity ≠<u>prestige</u>: disgrace, dishonour, disrepute, disrespect, infamy, shame ≠<u>tribute</u>: condemnation, contempt, disfavour, insult, scorn, slight ♦ verb ≠<u>respect</u>, ac-<u>claim</u>: condemn, defame, degrade, dishonour, insult, offend, scorn, slight ≠<u>pay</u>: refuse

honourable adjective <u>respected</u>, creditable, estimable, reputable, respectable, virtuous

hoodwink verb <u>deceive</u>, con (informal), delude, dupe, fool, mislead, swindle, trick

hook noun **1** <u>fastener</u>, catch, clasp, link, peg ♦ verb **2** <u>fasten</u>, clasp, fix, secure **3** <u>catch</u>, ensnare, entrap, snare, trap

hooked adjective **1** <u>bent</u>, aquiline, curved, hook-shaped **2** Slang <u>addicted</u>, devoted, enamoured, obsessed, taken, turned on (slang)

hooligan noun <u>delinquent</u>, lager lout, ruffian, vandal, yob or yobbo (Brit. slang)

hooliganism noun <u>delinquency</u>, disorder, loutishness, rowdiness, vandalism, violence

hoop noun <u>ring</u>, band, circlet, girdle, loop, round, wheel

hoot noun **1** <u>toot</u> **2** <u>cry</u>, call **3** <u>catcall</u>, boo, hiss, jeer ♦ verb **4** <u>jeer</u>, boo, hiss, howl down

hop verb **1** <u>jump</u>, bound, caper, leap, skip, spring, trip, vault ♦ noun **2** <u>jump</u>, bounce, bound, leap, skip, spring, step, vault

hope verb **1** <u>desire</u>, aspire, cross one's fingers, long, look forward to, set one's heart on ♦ noun **2** <u>belief</u>, ambition, assumption, confidence, desire, dream, expectation, longing

➤ **Antonyms**

noun ≠<u>belief</u>: despair, distrust, doubt, dread, hopelessness

hopeful adjective **1** <u>optimistic</u>, buoyant, confident, expectant, looking forward to, sanguine **2** <u>promising</u>, auspicious, bright, encouraging, heartening, reassuring, rosy

➤ **Antonyms**

≠<u>optimistic</u>: cheerless, dejected, despairing, hopeless, pessimistic ≠<u>promising</u>: depressing, discouraging, disheartening, unpromising

hopefully adverb <u>optimistically</u>, confidently, expectantly

hopeless adjective impossible, futile, no-win, pointless, unattainable, useless, vain

horde noun <u>crowd</u>, band, drove, gang, host, mob, multitude, pack, swarm, throng

horizon noun <u>skyline</u>, vista

horizontal adjective <u>level</u>, flat, parallel

horrible adjective **1** <u>dreadful</u>, awful, cruel, disagreeable, horrid, mean, nasty, terrible, unpleasant **2** <u>terrifying</u>, appalling, dreadful, frightful, ghastly, grim, grisly, gruesome, hideous, repulsive, revolting, shocking

➤ **Antonyms**

agreeable, appealing, attractive, charming, delightful, enchanting, lovely, pleasant, wonderful

horrid adjective **1** <u>unpleasant</u>, awful, disagreeable, dreadful, horrible, terrible **2** Informal <u>unkind</u>, beastly (informal), cruel, mean, nasty

horrific adjective <u>horrifying</u>, appalling, awful, dreadful, frightful, ghastly, grisly, horrendous, shocking, terrifying

horrify verb **1** <u>terrify</u>, alarm, frighten, intimidate, make one's hair stand on end, petrify, scare **2** shock, appal, dismay, outrage, sicken

➤ **Antonyms**
comfort, delight, enchant, gladden, please, soothe

horror noun **1** terror, alarm, consternation, dread, fear, fright, panic **2** hatred, aversion, detestation, disgust, loathing, odium, repugnance, revulsion

➤ **Antonyms**
≠hatred: affinity, attraction, delight, liking, love

horse noun nag, colt, filly, geegee (slang), mare, mount, stallion, steed (archaic or literary)

horseman noun rider, cavalier, cavalryman, dragoon, equestrian, knight

horseplay noun rough-and-tumble, buffoonery, clowning, fooling around, high jinks, pranks, romping, skylarking (informal)

hospitable adjective welcoming, cordial, friendly, generous, gracious, kind, liberal, sociable

➤ **Antonyms**
inhospitable, parsimonious

hospitality noun welcome, conviviality, cordiality, friendliness, neighbourliness, sociability, warmth

host[1] noun **1** master of ceremonies, entertainer, innkeeper, landlord or landlady, proprietor **2** presenter, anchorman or anchorwoman, compere (Brit.) ♦ verb **3** present, compere (Brit.), front (informal), introduce

host[2] noun multitude, army, array, drove, horde, legion, myriad, swarm, throng

hostage noun prisoner, captive, pawn

hostile adjective **1** unfriendly, antagonistic, belligerent, contrary, ill-disposed, opposed, rancorous **2** inhospitable, adverse, unsympathetic, unwelcoming

➤ **Antonyms**
≠unfriendly: amiable, cordial, friendly, kind, peaceful ≠inhospi-

table: congenial

hostilities plural noun warfare, conflict, fighting, war

➤ **Antonyms**
alliance, ceasefire, peace, treaty, truce

hostility noun unfriendliness, animosity, antipathy, enmity, hatred, ill will, malice, opposition, resentment

➤ **Antonyms**
agreement, amity, approval, congeniality, cordiality, friendliness, goodwill, sympathy

hot adjective **1** heated, boiling, roasting, scalding, scorching, searing, steaming, sultry, sweltering, torrid, warm **2** spicy, biting, peppery, piquant, pungent, sharp **3** passionate, fierce, fiery, intense, raging, stormy, violent **4** new, fresh, just out, latest, recent, up to the minute **5** popular, approved, favoured, in demand, in vogue, sought-after

➤ **Antonyms**
≠heated: chilly, cold, cool, freezing, frigid, frosty, icy ≠spicy: mild ≠passionate: apathetic, calm, dispassionate, halfhearted, indifferent, mild, moderate ≠new: old, stale, trite ≠popular: out of favour, unpopular

hot air noun empty talk, bombast, claptrap (informal), guff (slang), verbiage, wind

hot-blooded adjective passionate, ardent, excitable, fiery, impulsive, spirited, temperamental, wild

➤ **Antonyms**
apathetic, calm, cold, cool, frigid, impassive

hotchpotch noun mixture, farrago, jumble, medley, mélange, mess, mishmash, potpourri

hot-headed adjective rash, fiery, foolhardy, hasty, hot-tempered, impetuous, quick-tempered, reckless, volatile

hound verb harass, badger, goad, harry, impel, persecute, pester, provoke

house *noun* **1** <u>home</u>, abode, domicile, dwelling, habitation, homestead, pad (*slang*), residence **2** <u>household</u>, family **3** <u>dynasty</u>, clan, tribe **4** <u>firm</u>, business, company, organization, outfit (*informal*) **5** <u>assembly</u>, Commons, legislative body, parliament **6 on the house** <u>free</u>, for nothing, gratis ◆ *verb* **7** <u>accommodate</u>, billet, harbour, lodge, put up, quarter, take in **8** <u>contain</u>, cover, keep, protect, sheathe, shelter, store

household *noun* <u>family</u>, home, house

householder *noun* <u>occupant</u>, homeowner, resident, tenant

housing *noun* **1** <u>accommodation</u>, dwellings, homes, houses **2** <u>case</u>, casing, container, cover, covering, enclosure, sheath

hovel *noun* <u>hut</u>, cabin, den, hole, shack, shanty, shed

hover *verb* **1** <u>float</u>, drift, flutter, fly, hang **2** <u>linger</u>, hang about **3** <u>waver</u>, dither (*chiefly Brit.*), fluctuate, oscillate, vacillate

however *adverb* <u>nevertheless</u>, after all, anyhow, but, nonetheless, notwithstanding, still, though, yet

howl *noun* **1** <u>cry</u>, bawl, bay, clamour, groan, roar, scream, shriek, wail ◆ *verb* **2** <u>cry</u>, bawl, bellow, roar, scream, shriek, wail, weep, yell

howler *noun Informal* <u>mistake</u>, bloomer (*Brit. informal*), blunder, boob (*Brit. slang*), clanger (*informal*), error, malapropism

hub *noun* <u>centre</u>, core, focal point, focus, heart, middle, nerve centre

huddle *noun* **1** *Informal* <u>conference</u>, confab (*informal*), discussion, meeting, powwow ◆ *verb* **2** <u>crowd</u>, cluster, converge, flock, gather, press, throng **3** <u>curl up</u>, crouch, hunch up

hue *noun* <u>colour</u>, dye, shade, tinge, tint, tone

hug *verb* **1** <u>clasp</u>, cuddle, embrace, enfold, hold close, squeeze, take in one's arms ◆ *noun* **2** <u>embrace</u>, bear hug, clasp, clinch (*slang*), squeeze

huge *adjective* <u>enormous</u>, colossal, gigantic, immense, large, mammoth, massive, monumental, tremendous, vast

▶ **Antonyms**

insignificant, little, microscopic, minute, small, tiny

hulk *noun* **1** <u>wreck</u>, frame, hull, shell, shipwreck **2** *Disparaging* <u>oaf</u>, lout, lubber, lump (*informal*)

hull *noun* <u>frame</u>, body, casing, covering, framework

hum *verb* **1** <u>drone</u>, buzz, murmur, purr, throb, thrum, vibrate, whir **2** *Informal* <u>be busy</u>, bustle, buzz, pulsate, pulse, stir

human *adjective* **1** <u>mortal</u>, manlike ◆ *noun* **2** <u>human being</u>, creature, individual, man *or* woman, mortal, person, soul

▶ **Antonyms**

adjective ≠<u>mortal</u>: animal, nonhuman ◆ *noun* ≠<u>human being</u>: animal, god, nonhuman

humane *adjective* <u>kind</u>, benign, compassionate, forgiving, good-natured, merciful, sympathetic, tender, understanding

▶ **Antonyms**

barbarous, brutal, cruel, inhuman, inhumane, ruthless, unkind, unmerciful, unsympathetic

humanitarian *adjective* **1** <u>philanthropic</u>, altruistic, benevolent, charitable, compassionate, humane, public-spirited ◆ *noun* **2** <u>philanthropist</u>, altruist, benefactor, Good Samaritan

humanity *noun* **1** <u>human race</u>, Homo sapiens, humankind, man, mankind, people **2** <u>human nature</u>, mortality **3** <u>kindness</u>, charity, compassion, fellow feeling, kind-heartedness, mercy, philanthropy, sympathy

humanize *verb* <u>civilize</u>, educate, enlighten, improve, soften, tame

humble *adjective* **1** <u>modest</u>, meek, self-effacing, unassuming, unostentatious, unpretentious **2** <u>lowly</u>, mean, modest, obscure, ordinary, plebeian, poor, simple, undistinguished ♦ *verb* **3** humiliate, chasten, crush, disgrace, put (someone) in their place, subdue, take down a peg (*informal*)

➤ **Antonyms**

adjective ≠modest: arrogant, conceited, haughty, overbearing, proud, snobbish, superior ≠lowly: aristocratic, distinguished, glorious, high, important, superior ♦ *verb* ≠humiliate: elevate, exalt, magnify, raise

humbug *noun* **1** nonsense, baloney (*informal*), cant, claptrap (*informal*), hypocrisy, quackery, rubbish **2** fraud, charlatan, con man (*informal*), faker, impostor, phoney *or* phony (*informal*), swindler, trickster

humdrum *adjective* dull, banal, boring, dreary, monotonous, mundane, ordinary, tedious, tiresome, uneventful

➤ **Antonyms**

dramatic, entertaining, exciting, extraordinary, interesting, lively, stimulating

humid *adjective* damp, clammy, dank, moist, muggy, steamy, sticky, sultry, wet

➤ **Antonyms**

arid, dry, sunny, torrid

humidity *noun* damp, clamminess, dampness, dankness, moistness, moisture, mugginess, wetness

humiliate *verb* embarrass, bring low, chasten, crush, degrade, humble, mortify, put down, put (someone) in their place, shame

➤ **Antonyms**

elevate, honour, magnify, make proud

humiliating *adjective* embarrassing, crushing, degrading, humbling, ignominious, mortifying, shaming

humiliation *noun* embarrassment, degradation, disgrace, dishonour, humbling, ignominy, indignity, loss of face, mortification, put-down, shame

humility *noun* modesty, humble-

ness, lowliness, meekness, submissiveness, unpretentiousness

➤ **Antonyms**

arrogance, conceit, haughtiness, presumption, pretentiousness, pride, snobbishness, superciliousness, superiority

humorist *noun* comedian, card (*informal*), comic, funny man, jester, joker, wag, wit

humorous *adjective* funny, amusing, comic, comical, droll, entertaining, jocular, playful, waggish, witty

➤ **Antonyms**

earnest, grave, sad, serious, sober, solemn

humour *noun* **1** funniness, amusement, comedy, drollery, facetiousness, fun, jocularity, ludicrousness **2** joking, comedy, farce, jesting, pleasantry, wisecracks (*informal*), wit, witticisms **3** mood, disposition, frame of mind, spirits, temper ♦ *verb* **4** indulge, accommodate, flatter, go along with, gratify, mollify, pander to

➤ **Antonyms**

noun ≠funniness: gravity, melancholy, sadness, seriousness, sobriety, solemnity ♦ *verb* ≠indulge: oppose, stand up to

hump *noun* **1** lump, bulge, bump, mound, projection, protrusion, protuberance, swelling ♦ *verb* **2** *Slang* carry, heave, hoist, lug, shoulder

hunch *noun* **1** feeling, idea, impression, inkling, intuition, premonition, presentiment, suspicion ♦ *verb* **2** draw in, arch, bend, curve

hunger *noun* **1** appetite, emptiness, hungriness, ravenousness **2** starvation, famine **3** desire, ache, appetite, craving, itch, lust, thirst, yearning ♦ *verb* **4** want, ache, crave, desire, hanker, itch, long, thirst, wish, yearn

hungry *adjective* **1** empty, famished, peckish (*informal, chiefly Brit.*), ravenous, starved, starving, voracious **2** eager, athirst, avid, covetous, craving, desirous, greedy, keen, yearning

hunk noun lump, block, chunk, mass, nugget, piece, slab, wedge

hunt verb 1 stalk, chase, hound, pursue, track, trail 2 search, ferret about, forage, look, scour, seek ♦ noun 3 search, chase, hunting, investigation, pursuit, quest

hurdle noun 1 fence, barricade, barrier 2 obstacle, barrier, difficulty, handicap, hazard, hindrance, impediment, obstruction, stumbling block

hurl verb throw, cast, fling, heave, launch, let fly, pitch, propel, sling, toss

hurricane noun storm, cyclone, gale, tempest, tornado, twister (U.S. informal), typhoon

hurried adjective hasty, brief, cursory, perfunctory, quick, rushed, short, speedy, swift

hurry verb 1 rush, dash, fly, get a move on (informal), make haste, scoot, scurry, step on it (informal) ♦ noun 2 haste, flurry, quickness, rush, speed, urgency

➤ **Antonyms**
verb ≠rush: crawl, creep, dawdle, drag one's feet, move slowly ♦ noun ≠haste: calmness, slowness

hurt verb 1 harm, bruise, damage, disable, impair, injure, mar, spoil, wound 2 ache, be sore, be tender, burn, smart, sting, throb 3 upset, annoy, distress, grieve, pain, sadden, wound ♦ noun 4 distress, discomfort, pain, pang, soreness, suffering ♦ adjective 5 injured, bruised, cut, damaged, harmed, scarred, wounded 6 upset, aggrieved, crushed, offended, wounded

➤ **Antonyms**
verb ≠harm: alleviate, cure, heal, relieve, repair, restore, soothe ♦ noun ≠distress: delight, joy, pleasure ♦ adjective ≠injured: alleviated, assuaged, healed, relieved, repaired, restored,

soothed ≠upset: calmed, consoled, placated

hurtful adjective unkind, cruel, cutting, damaging, destructive, malicious, nasty, spiteful, upsetting, wounding

hurtle verb rush, charge, crash, fly, plunge, race, shoot, speed, stampede, tear

husband noun 1 partner, better half (humorous), mate, spouse ♦ verb 2 economize, budget, conserve, hoard, save, store

➤ **Antonyms**
verb ≠economize: be extravagant, fritter away, spend, splash out (informal, chiefly Brit.), squander

husbandry noun 1 farming, agriculture, cultivation, tillage 2 thrift, economy, frugality

hush verb 1 quieten, mute, muzzle, shush, silence ♦ noun 2 quiet, calm, peace, silence, stillness, tranquillity

hush-hush adjective secret, classified, confidential, restricted, top-secret, under wraps

husky adjective 1 hoarse, croaky, gruff, guttural, harsh, raucous, rough, throaty 2 Informal muscular, burly, hefty, powerful, rugged, stocky, strapping, thickset

hustle verb jostle, elbow, force, jog, push, shove

hut noun shed, cabin, den, hovel, lean-to, shanty, shelter

hybrid noun crossbreed, amalgam, composite, compound, cross, half-breed, mixture, mongrel

hygiene noun cleanliness, sanitation

hygienic adjective clean, aseptic, disinfected, germ-free, healthy, pure, sanitary, sterile

➤ **Antonyms**
dirty, filthy, germ-ridden, insanitary, polluted, unhealthy, unhygienic, unwholesome

hymn noun song of praise, anthem, carol, chant, paean, psalm

hype noun Slang publicity, ballyhoo (informal), brouhaha, plug-

hypnotic *adjective* <u>mesmerizing</u>, mesmeric, sleep-inducing, soothing, soporific, spellbinding

hypnotize *verb* <u>mesmerize</u>, put in a trance, put to sleep

hypocrisy *noun* <u>insincerity</u>, cant, deceitfulness, deception, duplicity, pretence

➤ **Antonyms**
honesty, sincerity, truthfulness

hypocrite *noun* <u>fraud</u>, charlatan, deceiver, impostor, phoney *or* phony (*informal*), pretender

hypocritical *adjective* <u>insincere</u>, canting, deceitful, duplicitous, false, fraudulent, phoney *or* phony (*informal*), sanctimonious, two-faced

hypothesis *noun* <u>assumption</u>, postulate, premise, proposition, supposition, theory, thesis

hypothetical *adjective* <u>theoretical</u>, academic, assumed, conjectural, imaginary, putative, speculative, supposed

➤ **Antonyms**
actual, confirmed, established, known, proven, real, true

hysteria *noun* <u>frenzy</u>, agitation, delirium, hysterics, madness, panic

hysterical *adjective* **1** <u>frenzied</u>, crazed, distracted, distraught, frantic, overwrought, raving **2** *Informal* <u>hilarious</u>, comical, side-splitting, uproarious

➤ **Antonyms**
≠<u>frenzied</u>: calm, composed, poised, self-possessed, unfazed (*informal*) ≠<u>hilarious</u>: grave, melancholy, sad, serious

I i

icy *adjective* **1** <u>cold</u>, biting, bitter, chill, chilly, freezing, frosty, ice-cold, raw **2** <u>slippery</u>, glassy, slip-py (*informal or dialect*) **3** <u>unfriend-ly</u>, aloof, cold, distant, frigid, frosty, unwelcoming

➤ **Antonyms**
≠<u>cold</u>: blistering, boiling, hot, sizzling, warm ≠<u>unfriendly</u>: cordial, friendly, gracious, warm

idea *noun* **1** <u>thought</u>, concept, impression, perception **2** <u>belief</u>, conviction, notion, opinion, teaching, view **3** <u>intention</u>, aim, object, objective, plan, purpose

ideal *noun* **1** <u>model</u>, last word, paradigm, paragon, pattern, perfection, prototype, standard ♦ *adjective* **2** <u>perfect</u>, archetypal, classic, complete, consummate, model, quintessential, supreme

➤ **Antonyms**
adjective ≠<u>perfect</u>: deficient, flawed, impaired, imperfect, unsuitable

idealist *noun* <u>romantic</u>, dreamer, Utopian, visionary

idealistic *adjective* <u>perfectionist</u>, impracticable, optimistic, romantic, starry-eyed, Utopian, visionary

➤ **Antonyms**
down-to-earth, practical, pragmatic, realistic, sensible

idealize *verb* <u>romanticize</u>, apotheosize, ennoble, exalt, glorify, magnify, put on a pedestal, worship

ideally *adverb* <u>in a perfect world</u>, all things being equal, if one had one's way

identical *adjective* <u>alike</u>, duplicate, indistinguishable, interchangeable, matching, twin

➤ **Antonyms**
different, disparate, distinct, diverse, separate, unlike

identification *noun* **1** <u>recognition</u>, naming, pinpointing **2** <u>sympathy</u>, association, connection, empathy, fellow feeling, involvement, rapport, relationship

identify *verb* **1** <u>recognize</u>, diagnose, make out, name, pick out, pinpoint, place, put one's finger on (*informal*), spot **2** <u>identify with</u> <u>relate to</u>, associate with, empathize with, feel for, respond to

identity noun **1** <u>existence</u>, individuality, personality, self **2** <u>sameness</u>, correspondence, unity

idiocy noun <u>foolishness</u>, asininity, fatuousness, imbecility, inanity, insanity, lunacy, senselessness

➤ **Antonyms**

sanity, sense, soundness, wisdom

idiom noun **1** <u>phrase</u>, expression, turn of phrase **2** <u>language</u>, jargon, parlance, style, vernacular

idiosyncrasy noun <u>peculiarity</u>, characteristic, eccentricity, mannerism, oddity, quirk, trick

idiot noun <u>fool</u>, chump, cretin, dumb-ass (slang), dunderhead, halfwit, imbecile, moron, nincompoop, numbskull or numskull, simpleton, twit (informal, chiefly Brit.)

idiotic adjective <u>foolish</u>, asinine, crazy, daft (informal), dumb-ass (slang), foolhardy, harebrained, insane, moronic, senseless, stupid

➤ **Antonyms**

brilliant, intelligent, sensible, thoughtful, wise

idle adjective **1** <u>inactive</u>, redundant, unemployed, unoccupied, unused, vacant **2** <u>lazy</u>, good-for-nothing, indolent, lackadaisical, shiftless, slothful, sluggish **3** <u>useless</u>, fruitless, futile, groundless, ineffective, pointless, unavailing, unsuccessful, vain, worthless ♦ verb **4** often with away laze, dally, dawdle, kill time, loaf, loiter, lounge, potter

➤ **Antonyms**

adjective ≠<u>inactive</u>, <u>lazy</u>: active, busy, employed, energetic, industrious, occupied, working ≠<u>useless</u>: advantageous, effective, fruitful, profitable, useful, worthwhile

idleness noun **1** <u>inactivity</u>, inaction, leisure, time on one's hands, unemployment **2** <u>laziness</u>, inertia, shiftlessness, sloth, sluggishness, torpor

idol noun **1** <u>hero</u>, beloved, dar-

ling, fave (informal), favourite, pet, pin-up (slang) **2** <u>graven image</u>, deity, god

idolatry noun <u>adoration</u>, adulation, exaltation, glorification

idolize verb <u>worship</u>, adore, dote upon, exalt, glorify, hero-worship, look up to, love, revere, venerate

idyllic adjective <u>idealized</u>, charming, halcyon, heavenly, ideal, picturesque, unspoiled

if conjunction <u>provided</u>, assuming, on condition that, providing, supposing

ignite verb **1** <u>catch fire</u>, burn, burst into flames, flare up, inflame, take fire **2** <u>set fire to</u>, kindle, light, set alight, torch

ignominious adjective <u>humiliating</u>, discreditable, disgraceful, dishonourable, indecorous, inglorious, shameful, sorry, undignified

➤ **Antonyms**

creditable, honourable, worthy

ignominy noun <u>disgrace</u>, discredit, dishonour, disrepute, humiliation, infamy, obloquy, shame, stigma

➤ **Antonyms**

credit, honour, repute

ignorance noun <u>unawareness</u>, inexperience, innocence, unconsciousness, unfamiliarity

➤ **Antonyms**

comprehension, enlightenment, insight, intelligence, knowledge, understanding, wisdom

ignorant adjective **1** <u>uninformed</u>, benighted, inexperienced, innocent, oblivious, unaware, unconscious, unenlightened, uninitiated, unwitting **2** <u>uneducated</u>, illiterate **3** <u>insensitive</u>, crass, half-baked (informal), rude

➤ **Antonyms**

≠<u>uninformed</u>: aware, conscious, informed, in the loop ≠<u>uneducated</u>: brilliant, cultured, educated, knowledgeable, learned, literate

ignore verb <u>overlook</u>, discount, disregard, neglect, pass over, reject, take no notice of, turn a blind eye to

➤ **Antonyms**

acknowledge, heed, note, pay attention to, recognize, regard

ill *adjective* ♦ **1** unwell, ailing, diseased, indisposed, infirm, off-colour, poorly (*informal*), sick, under the weather (*informal*), unhealthy **2** harmful, bad, damaging, deleterious, detrimental, evil, foul, injurious, unfortunate ♦ *noun* **3** harm, affliction, hardship, hurt, injury, misery, misfortune, trouble, unpleasantness, woe ♦ *adverb* **4** badly, inauspiciously, poorly, unfavourably, unfortunately, unluckily **5** hardly, barely, by no means, scantily

➤ **Antonyms**

adjective ≠unwell: hale, healthy, strong, well ≠harmful: favourable, good ♦ *noun, adverb* ≠hardly: easily, well

ill-advised *adjective* misguided, foolhardy, ill-considered, ill-judged, imprudent, incautious, injudicious, rash, reckless, thoughtless, unwise

➤ **Antonyms**

appropriate, cautious, discreet, judicious, politic, prudent, seemly, sensible, wise

ill-disposed *adjective* unfriendly, antagonistic, disobliging, hostile, inimical, uncooperative, unwelcoming

➤ **Antonyms**

amicable, cooperative, friendly, obliging, welcoming, well-disposed

illegal *adjective* unlawful, banned, criminal, felonious, forbidden, illicit, outlawed, prohibited, unauthorized, unlicensed

➤ **Antonyms**

lawful, legal, licit, permissible

illegality *noun* crime, felony, illegitimacy, lawlessness, wrong

illegible *adjective* indecipherable, obscure, scrawled, unreadable

➤ **Antonyms**

clear, decipherable, legible, plain, readable

illegitimate *adjective* **1** born out of wedlock, bastard **2** unlawful, illegal, illicit, improper, unauthorized

➤ **Antonyms**

≠unlawful: authorized, lawful, legal, legitimate, proper

ill-fated *adjective* doomed, hapless, ill-omened, ill-starred, luckless, star-crossed, unfortunate, unhappy, unlucky

illicit *adjective* **1** illegal, criminal, felonious, illegitimate, prohibited, unauthorized, unlawful, unlicensed **2** forbidden, clandestine, furtive, guilty, immoral, improper

➤ **Antonyms**

≠illegal: above-board, lawful, legal, legitimate, licit, permissible

illiterate *adjective* uneducated, ignorant, uncultured, untaught, untutored

➤ **Antonyms**

cultured, educated, literate, taught, tutored

ill-mannered *adjective* rude, badly behaved, boorish, churlish, discourteous, impolite, insolent, loutish, uncouth

➤ **Antonyms**

civil, courteous, mannerly, polite, well-mannered

illness *noun* sickness, affliction, ailment, disease, disorder, infirmity, malady

illogical *adjective* irrational, absurd, inconsistent, invalid, meaningless, senseless, unreasonable, unscientific, unsound

➤ **Antonyms**

consistent, logical, rational, reasonable, scientific, sound, valid

ill-treat *verb* abuse, damage, harm, injure, maltreat, mishandle, misuse, oppress

illuminate *verb* **1** light up, brighten **2** clarify, clear up, elucidate, enlighten, explain, interpret, make clear, shed light on

➤ **Antonyms**

≠light up: black out, darken, dim, obscure, overshadow ≠clarify: befog, cloud, veil

illuminating *adjective* informative, enlightening, explanatory, helpful, instructive, revealing

➤ **Antonyms**
confusing, puzzling, unhelpful

illumination *noun* 1 light, brightness, lighting, radiance 2 enlightenment, clarification, insight, revelation

illusion *noun* 1 fantasy, chimera, daydream, figment of the imagination, hallucination, mirage, will-o'-the-wisp 2 misconception, deception, delusion, error, fallacy, misapprehension

➤ **Antonyms**
actuality, fact, reality, truth

illusory *adjective* unreal, chimerical, deceptive, delusive, fallacious, false, hallucinatory, mistaken, sham

➤ **Antonyms**
authentic, down-to-earth, factual, genuine, real, reliable, solid, true

illustrate *verb* demonstrate, bring home, elucidate, emphasize, explain, point up, show

illustrated *adjective* pictorial, decorated, graphic

illustration *noun* 1 picture, decoration, figure, plate, sketch 2 example, case, instance, specimen

illustrious *adjective* famous, celebrated, distinguished, eminent, glorious, great, notable, prominent, renowned

➤ **Antonyms**
humble, ignoble, lowly, meek, obscure

ill will *noun* hostility, animosity, bad blood, dislike, enmity, hatred, malice, rancour, resentment, venom

➤ **Antonyms**
amiability, congeniality, cordiality, friendship, goodwill

image *noun* 1 concept, idea, impression, mental picture, perception 2 figure 3 representation, effigy, figure, icon, idol, likeness, picture, portrait, statue 4 replica, counterpart, (dead) ringer (*slang*), Doppelgänger, double, facsimi-

le, spitting image (*informal*)

imaginable *adjective* possible, believable, comprehensible, conceivable, credible, likely, plausible

➤ **Antonyms**
impossible, incomprehensible, inconceivable, incredible, unbelievable, unimaginable, unlikely

imaginary *adjective* fictional, fictitious, hypothetical, illusory, imagined, invented, made-up, nonexistent, unreal

➤ **Antonyms**
actual, factual, genuine, known, proven, real, true

imagination *noun* 1 unreality, illusion, supposition 2 creativity, enterprise, ingenuity, invention, inventiveness, originality, resourcefulness, vision

imaginative *adjective* creative, clever, enterprising, ingenious, inspired, inventive, original

➤ **Antonyms**
literal, uncreative, unimaginative, uninspired, unoriginal

imagine *verb* 1 envisage, conceive, conceptualize, conjure up, picture, plan, think of, think up, visualize 2 believe, assume, conjecture, fancy, guess (*informal, chiefly U.S. & Canad.*), infer, suppose, surmise, suspect, take it, think

imbecile *noun* 1 idiot, chump, cretin, dumb-ass (*slang*), fool, halfwit, moron, numbskull *or* numskull, thickhead, twit (*informal, chiefly Brit.*) ♦ *adjective* 2 stupid, asinine, dumb-ass (*slang*), fatuous, feeble-minded, foolish, idiotic, moronic, thick, witless

imbibe *verb Formal* 1 drink, consume, knock back (*informal*), quaff, sink (*informal*), swallow, swig (*informal*) 2 absorb, acquire, assimilate, gain, gather, ingest, receive, take in

imbroglio *noun* complication, embarrassment, entanglement, involvement, misunderstanding, quandary

imitate *verb* copy, ape, echo,

emulate, follow, mimic, mirror, repeat, simulate

imitation noun **1** replica, fake, forgery, impersonation, impression, reproduction, sham, substitution **2** mimicry, counterfeiting, duplication, likeness, resemblance, simulation ♦ adjective **3** artificial, dummy, ersatz, man-made, mock, phoney or phony (informal), reproduction, sham, simulated, synthetic

➤ **Antonyms**
adjective ≠artificial: authentic, genuine, original, real, true

imitative adjective derivative, copycat (informal), mimetic, parrot-like, second-hand, simulated, unoriginal

imitator noun impersonator, copier, copycat (informal), impressionist, mimic, parrot

immaculate adjective **1** clean, neat, spick-and-span, spotless, spruce, squeaky-clean **2** pure, above reproach, faultless, flawless, impeccable, perfect, unblemished, unexceptionable, untarnished

➤ **Antonyms**
≠clean: dirty, filthy, unclean
≠pure: contaminated, corrupt, impure, stained, tainted

immaterial adjective irrelevant, extraneous, inconsequential, inessential, insignificant, of no importance, trivial, unimportant

➤ **Antonyms**
crucial, essential, germane, important, relevant, significant

immature adjective **1** young, adolescent, undeveloped, unformed, unripe **2** childish, callow, inexperienced, infantile, juvenile, puerile

➤ **Antonyms**
adult, developed, fully-fledged, mature, mellow, ripe

immaturity noun **1** unripeness, greenness, imperfection, rawness, unpreparedness **2** childishness, callowness, inexperience, puerility

immediate adjective **1** instant, in-

stantaneous **2** nearest, close, direct, near, next

➤ **Antonyms**
≠instant: delayed, late, later, leisurely, postponed, slow, tardy
≠nearest: distant, far, remote

immediately adverb at once, directly, forthwith, instantly, now, promptly, right away, straight away, this instant, without delay

immense adjective huge, colossal, enormous, extensive, gigantic, great, massive, monumental, stupendous, tremendous, vast

➤ **Antonyms**
infinitesimal, little, microscopic, minuscule, minute, puny, small, tiny

immensity noun size, bulk, enormity, expanse, extent, greatness, hugeness, magnitude, vastness

immerse verb **1** plunge, bathe, dip, douse, duck, dunk, sink, submerge **2** engross, absorb, busy, engage, involve, occupy, take up

immersion noun **1** dipping, dousing, ducking, dunking, plunging, submerging **2** involvement, absorption, concentration, preoccupation

immigrant noun settler, incomer, newcomer

imminent adjective near, at hand, close, coming, forthcoming, gathering, impending, in the pipeline, looming

➤ **Antonyms**
delayed, distant, far-off, remote

immobile adjective stationary, at a standstill, at rest, fixed, immovable, motionless, rigid, rooted, static, still, stock-still, unmoving

➤ **Antonyms**
active, mobile, movable, on the move

immobility noun stillness, fixity, inertness, motionlessness, stability, steadiness

immobilize verb paralyse, bring to a standstill, cripple, disable, freeze, halt, stop, transfix

immoderate adjective excessive, exaggerated, exorbitant, extravagant, extreme, inordinate, over the top (*slang*), undue, unjustified, unreasonable

➤ **Antonyms**

controlled, judicious, mild, moderate, reasonable, restrained, temperate

immoral *adjective* <u>wicked</u>, bad, corrupt, debauched, depraved, dissolute, indecent, sinful, unethical, unprincipled, wrong

➤ **Antonyms**

good, honourable, law-abiding, moral, pure, upright, virtuous

immorality *noun* <u>wickedness</u>, corruption, debauchery, depravity, dissoluteness, sin, vice, wrong

➤ **Antonyms**

goodness, honesty, lawfulness, morality, purity

immortal *adjective* **1** <u>eternal</u>, deathless, enduring, everlasting, imperishable, lasting, perennial, undying ◆ *noun* **2** <u>great</u>, genius, hero **3** <u>god</u>, goddess

➤ **Antonyms**

adjective ≠<u>eternal</u>: ephemeral, fading, fleeting, mortal, passing, perishable, temporary, transitory

immortality *noun* **1** <u>eternity</u>, everlasting life, perpetuity **2** <u>fame</u>, celebrity, glory, greatness, renown

immortalize *verb* <u>commemorate</u>, celebrate, exalt, glorify

immovable *adjective* **1** <u>fixed</u>, firm, immutable, jammed, secure, set, stable, stationary, stuck **2** <u>inflexible</u>, adamant, obdurate, resolute, steadfast, unshakable, unwavering, unyielding

➤ **Antonyms**

≠<u>inflexible</u>: changeable, flexible, movable, wavering, yielding

immune *adjective* <u>exempt</u>, clear, free, invulnerable, proof (against), protected, resistant, safe, unaffected

➤ **Antonyms**

exposed, liable, prone, susceptible, unprotected, vulnerable

immunity *noun* **1** <u>resistance</u>, im-

munization, protection **2** <u>exemption</u>, amnesty, freedom, indemnity, invulnerability, licence, release

➤ **Antonyms**

≠<u>resistance</u>: exposure, liability, openness, proneness, susceptibility, vulnerability

immunize *verb* <u>vaccinate</u>, inoculate, protect, safeguard

imp *noun* **1** <u>demon</u>, devil, sprite **2** <u>rascal</u>, brat, minx, rogue, scamp

impact *noun* **1** <u>effect</u>, consequences, impression, influence, repercussions, significance **2** <u>collision</u>, blow, bump, contact, crash, jolt, knock, smash, stroke, thump ◆ *verb* **3** <u>hit</u>, clash, collide, crash, crush, strike

impair *verb* <u>worsen</u>, blunt, damage, decrease, diminish, harm, hinder, injure, lessen, reduce, undermine, weaken

➤ **Antonyms**

ameliorate, enhance, improve, strengthen

impaired *adjective* <u>damaged</u>, defective, faulty, flawed, imperfect, unsound

impart *verb* **1** <u>communicate</u>, convey, disclose, divulge, make known, pass on, relate, reveal, tell **2** <u>give</u>, accord, afford, bestow, confer, grant, lend, yield

impartial *adjective* <u>neutral</u>, detached, disinterested, equitable, even-handed, fair, just, objective, open-minded, unbiased, unprejudiced

➤ **Antonyms**

biased, bigoted, partial, prejudiced, unfair, unjust

impartiality *noun* <u>neutrality</u>, detachment, disinterestedness, dispassion, equity, even-handedness, fairness, objectivity, openmindedness

➤ **Antonyms**

bias, favouritism, partiality, partisanship, subjectivity, unfairness

impassable *adjective* <u>blocked</u>, closed, impenetrable, obstructed

impasse *noun* <u>deadlock</u>, dead

end, stalemate, standoff, standstill

impassioned *adjective* intense, animated, fervent, fiery, heated, inspired, passionate, rousing, stirring

➤ **Antonyms**

apathetic, cool, impassive, indifferent, objective

impatience *noun* 1 irritability, intolerance, quick temper, shortness, snappiness 2 restlessness, agitation, anxiety, eagerness, edginess, fretfulness, nervousness, uneasiness

➤ **Antonyms**

≠irritability: control, forbearance, patience, restraint, tolerance ≠restlessness: calm, composure

impatient *adjective* 1 irritable, demanding, hot-tempered, intolerant, quick-tempered, snappy, testy 2 restless, eager, edgy, fretful, straining at the leash

➤ **Antonyms**

≠irritable: easy-going, tolerant ≠restless: calm, composed, cool, imperturbable, patient, quiet

impeach *verb* charge, accuse, arraign, indict

impeccable *adjective* faultless, blameless, flawless, immaculate, irreproachable, perfect, squeaky-clean, unblemished, unimpeachable

➤ **Antonyms**

blameworthy, defective, deficient, faulty, flawed, shallow

impecunious *adjective* poor, broke (*informal*), destitute, down and out, indigent, insolvent, penniless, poverty-stricken

➤ **Antonyms**

affluent, prosperous, rich, wealthy, well-off, well-to-do

impede *verb* hinder, block, check, disrupt, hamper, hold up, obstruct, slow (down), thwart

➤ **Antonyms**

advance, aid, assist, further, help, promote

impediment *noun* obstacle, barrier, difficulty, encumbrance, hindrance, obstruction, snag, stumbling block

➤ **Antonyms**

advantage, aid, assistance, benefit, encouragement, relief, support

impel *verb* force, compel, constrain, drive, induce, oblige, push, require

➤ **Antonyms**

check, discourage, dissuade

impending *adjective* looming, approaching, coming, forthcoming, gathering, imminent, in the pipeline, near, upcoming

impenetrable *adjective* 1 impassable, dense, impermeable, impervious, inviolable, solid, thick 2 incomprehensible, arcane, enigmatic, inscrutable, mysterious, obscure, unfathomable, unintelligible

➤ **Antonyms**

≠impassable: accessible, passable, penetrable ≠incomprehensible: clear, obvious, understandable

imperative *adjective* urgent, crucial, essential, pressing, vital

➤ **Antonyms**

nonessential, unimportant, unnecessary

imperceptible *adjective* undetectable, faint, indiscernible, invisible, microscopic, minute, slight, small, subtle, tiny

➤ **Antonyms**

audible, detectable, discernible, distinguishable, noticeable, perceptible, visible

imperfect *adjective* flawed, damaged, defective, faulty, impaired, incomplete, limited, unfinished

➤ **Antonyms**

complete, finished, flawless, perfect

imperfection *noun* fault, blemish, defect, deficiency, failing, flaw, frailty, shortcoming, taint, weakness

➤ **Antonyms**

excellence, faultlessness, flawlessness, perfection

imperial *adjective* royal, kingly,

majestic, princely, queenly, regal, sovereign

imperil *verb* endanger, expose, jeopardize, risk

➤ **Antonyms**

care for, guard, protect, safeguard, secure

impersonal *adjective* detached, aloof, cold, dispassionate, formal, inhuman, neutral, remote

➤ **Antonyms**

friendly, intimate, outgoing, personal, warm

impersonate *verb* imitate, ape, do (*informal*), masquerade as, mimic, pass oneself off as, pose as (*informal*), take off (*informal*)

impersonation *noun* imitation, caricature, impression, mimicry, parody, takeoff (*informal*)

impertinence *noun* rudeness, brazenness, cheek (*informal*), disrespect, effrontery, front, impudence, insolence, nerve (*informal*), presumption

impertinent *adjective* rude, brazen, cheeky (*informal*), disrespectful, impolite, impudent, insolent, presumptuous

➤ **Antonyms**

mannerly, polite, respectful

imperturbable *adjective* calm, collected, composed, cool, nerveless, self-possessed, serene, unexcitable, unflappable (*informal*), unruffled

➤ **Antonyms**

agitated, excitable, frantic, jittery (*informal*), nervous, panicky, ruffled, touchy, upset

impervious *adjective* **1** sealed, impassable, impenetrable, impermeable, resistant **2** unaffected, immune, invulnerable, proof against, unmoved, untouched

impetuosity *noun* haste, impulsiveness, precipitateness, rashness

impetuous *adjective* rash, hasty, impulsive, precipitate, unthinking

➤ **Antonyms**

cautious, leisurely, slow, wary

impetus *noun* **1** incentive, catalyst, goad, impulse, motivation,

push, spur, stimulus **2** force, energy, momentum, power

impinge *verb* **1** encroach, infringe, invade, obtrude, trespass, violate **2** affect, bear upon, have a bearing on, impact, influence, relate to, touch

impious *adjective* sacrilegious, blasphemous, godless, irreligious, irreverent, profane, sinful, ungodly, unholy, wicked

➤ **Antonyms**

devout, godly, holy, pious, religious, reverent

impish *adjective* mischievous, devilish, puckish, rascally, roguish, sportive, waggish

implacable *adjective* unyielding, inflexible, intractable, merciless, pitiless, unbending, uncompromising, unforgiving

➤ **Antonyms**

flexible, lenient, merciful, tolerant, yielding

implant *verb* **1** instil, inculcate, infuse **2** insert, fix, graft

implement *verb* **1** carry out, bring about, complete, effect, enforce, execute, fulfil, perform, realize ♦ *noun* **2** tool, apparatus, appliance, device, gadget, instrument, utensil

➤ **Antonyms**

verb ≠carry out: delay, hamper, hinder, impede

implicate *verb* incriminate, associate, embroil, entangle, include, inculpate, involve

➤ **Antonyms**

disentangle, dissociate, eliminate, exclude, rule out

implication *noun* suggestion, inference, innuendo, meaning, overtone, presumption, significance

implicit *adjective* **1** implied, inferred, latent, tacit, taken for granted, undeclared, understood, unspoken **2** absolute, constant, firm, fixed, full, steadfast, unqualified, unreserved, wholehearted

➤ **Antonyms**

≠implied: declared, explicit, expressed, obvious, patent, spoken, stated

implied *adjective* unspoken, hinted at, implicit, indirect, suggested, tacit, undeclared, unexpressed, unstated

implore *verb* beg, beseech, entreat, importune, plead with, pray

imply *verb* 1 hint, insinuate, intimate, signify, suggest 2 entail, indicate, involve, mean, point to, presuppose

impolite *adjective* bad-mannered, discourteous, disrespectful, ill-mannered, insolent, loutish, rude, uncouth

➤ **Antonyms**
courteous, mannerly, polite, refined, respectful

impoliteness *noun* bad manners, boorishness, churlishness, discourtesy, disrespect, insolence, rudeness

➤ **Antonyms**
civility, courtesy, delicacy, politeness, respect

import *verb* 1 bring in, introduce ♦ *noun* 2 *Formal* importance, consequence, magnitude, moment, significance, substance, weight 3 meaning, drift, gist, implication, intention, sense, significance, thrust

importance *noun* 1 significance, concern, consequence, import, interest, moment, substance, usefulness, value, weight 2 prestige, distinction, eminence, esteem, influence, prominence, standing, status

important *adjective* 1 significant, far-reaching, momentous, seminal, serious, substantial, urgent, weighty 2 powerful, eminent, high-ranking, influential, noteworthy, pre-eminent, prominent

➤ **Antonyms**
inconsequential, insignificant, minor, needless, negligible, secondary, trivial, undistinctive, unimportant, unnecessary

importunate *adjective Formal* persistent, demanding, dogged, insistent, pressing, urgent

impose *verb* 1 establish, decree, fix, institute, introduce, levy, ordain 2 inflict, appoint, enforce, saddle (someone) with

imposing *adjective* impressive, commanding, dignified, grand, majestic, stately, striking

➤ **Antonyms**
insignificant, mean, modest, ordinary, poor, unimposing

imposition *noun* 1 application, introduction, levying 2 intrusion, liberty, presumption

impossibility *noun* hopelessness, impracticability, inability

impossible *adjective* 1 inconceivable, impracticable, out of the question, unachievable, unattainable, unobtainable, unthinkable 2 absurd, ludicrous, outrageous, preposterous, unreasonable

➤ **Antonyms**
≠inconceivable: conceivable, imaginable, likely, plausible, possible, reasonable

impostor *noun* impersonator, charlatan, deceiver, fake, fraud, phoney or phony (*informal*), pretender, sham, trickster

impotence *noun* powerlessness, feebleness, frailty, helplessness, inability, incapacity, incompetence, ineffectiveness, paralysis, uselessness, weakness

➤ **Antonyms**
ability, adequacy, competence, effectiveness, efficacy, efficiency, powerfulness, strength, usefulness

impotent *adjective* powerless, feeble, frail, helpless, incapable, incapacitated, incompetent, ineffective, paralysed, weak

➤ **Antonyms**
able, capable, competent, effective, potent, powerful, strong

impoverish *verb* 1 bankrupt, beggar, break, ruin 2 diminish, deplete, drain, exhaust, reduce, sap, use up, wear out

impoverished *adjective* poor, bankrupt, destitute, impecunious, needy, on one's uppers, penurious, poverty-stricken

➤ **Antonyms**

affluent, rich, wealthy, well-off

impracticable *adjective* unfeasible, impossible, out of the question, unachievable, unattainable, unworkable

➤ **Antonyms**

feasible, possible, practicable

impractical *adjective* **1** unworkable, impossible, impracticable, inoperable, nonviable, unrealistic, wild **2** idealistic, romantic, starry-eyed, unrealistic

➤ **Antonyms**

≠unworkable: possible, practical, viable, workable ≠idealistic: down-to-earth, realistic, sensible

imprecise *adjective* indefinite, equivocal, hazy, ill-defined, inaccurate, indeterminate, inexact, inexplicit, loose, rough, vague, woolly

➤ **Antonyms**

accurate, definite, exact, explicit, precise

impregnable *adjective* invulnerable, impenetrable, indestructible, invincible, secure, unassailable, unbeatable, unconquerable

➤ **Antonyms**

exposed, insecure, open, vulnerable

impregnate *verb* **1** saturate, infuse, permeate, soak, steep, suffuse **2** fertilize, inseminate, make pregnant

impress *verb* **1** excite, affect, inspire, make an impression, move, stir, strike, touch **2** stress, bring home to, emphasize, fix, inculcate, instil into **3** imprint, emboss, engrave, indent, mark, print, stamp

impression *noun* **1** effect, feeling, impact, influence, reaction **2** idea, belief, conviction, feeling, hunch, notion, sense, suspicion **3** imitation, impersonation, parody, send-up (*Brit. informal*), takeoff (*informal*) **4** mark, dent, hollow, imprint, indentation, outline, stamp

impressionable *adjective* suggestible, gullible, ingenuous, open, receptive, responsive, sensitive, susceptible, vulnerable

➤ **Antonyms**

blasé, hardened, insensitive, jaded, unresponsive

impressive *adjective* grand, awesome, dramatic, exciting, moving, powerful, stirring, striking

➤ **Antonyms**

ordinary, unimposing, unimpressive, uninspiring, unmemorable

imprint *noun* **1** mark, impression, indentation, sign, stamp ♦ *verb* **2** fix, engrave, etch, impress, print, stamp

imprison *verb* jail, confine, detain, incarcerate, intern, lock up, put away, send down (*informal*)

➤ **Antonyms**

emancipate, free, liberate, release

imprisoned *adjective* jailed, behind bars, captive, confined, incarcerated, in jail, inside (*slang*), locked up, under lock and key

imprisonment *noun* custody, confinement, detention, incarceration, porridge (*slang*)

improbability *noun* doubt, dubiety, uncertainty, unlikelihood

improbable *adjective* doubtful, dubious, fanciful, far-fetched, implausible, questionable, unconvincing, unlikely, weak

➤ **Antonyms**

certain, convincing, doubtless, likely, plausible, probable, reasonable

impromptu *adjective* unprepared, ad-lib, extemporaneous, improvised, offhand, off the cuff (*informal*), spontaneous, unrehearsed, unscripted

➤ **Antonyms**

considered, planned, premeditated, prepared, rehearsed

improper *adjective* **1** indecent, risqué, smutty, suggestive, unbecoming, unseemly, untoward, vulgar **2** inappropriate, out of place, uncalled-for, unfit, unsuitable, unwarranted

➤ **Antonyms**

≠indecent: becoming, decent,

proper, seemly ≠inappropriate: apposite, appropriate, suitable

impropriety noun Formal indecency, bad taste, incongruity, vulgarity

➤ **Antonyms**

decency, decorum, delicacy, propriety

improve verb 1 enhance, ameliorate, better, correct, help, rectify, touch up, upgrade 2 progress, advance, develop, make strides, pick up, rally, rise

➤ **Antonyms**

≠enhance: damage, harm, impair, injure, mar, worsen

improvement noun 1 enhancement, advancement, betterment 2 progress, advance, development, rally, recovery, upswing

improvident adjective imprudent, careless, negligent, prodigal, profligate, reckless, shortsighted, spendthrift, thoughtless, wasteful

➤ **Antonyms**

careful, economical, provident, prudent, thrifty

improvisation noun 1 spontaneity, ad-libbing, extemporizing, invention 2 makeshift, ad-lib, expedient

improvise verb 1 concoct, contrive, devise, throw together 2 extemporize, ad-lib, busk, invent, play it by ear (informal), speak off the cuff (informal), wing it (informal)

imprudent adjective unwise, careless, foolhardy, ill-advised, ill-considered, ill-judged, injudicious, irresponsible, rash, reckless

➤ **Antonyms**

careful, judicious, prudent, responsible, wise

impudence noun boldness, audacity, brazenness, cheek (informal), effrontery, impertinence, insolence, nerve (informal), presumption, shamelessness

impudent adjective bold, audacious, brazen, cheeky (informal), impertinent, insolent, presumptuous, rude, shameless

➤ **Antonyms**

courteous, polite, respectful, well-behaved

impulse noun urge, caprice, feeling, inclination, notion, whim, wish

impulsive adjective instinctive, devil-may-care, hasty, impetuous, intuitive, passionate, precipitate, rash, spontaneous

➤ **Antonyms**

cautious, deliberate, planned, premeditated, rehearsed

impunity noun security, dispensation, exemption, freedom, immunity, liberty, licence, permission

impure adjective 1 unrefined, adulterated, debased, mixed 2 immoral, corrupt, indecent, lascivious, lewd, licentious, obscene, unchaste 3 unclean, contaminated, defiled, dirty, infected, polluted, tainted

➤ **Antonyms**

≠immoral: chaste, decent, delicate, modest, moral, pure, wholesome ≠unclean: clean, maculate, spotless, squeaky-clean, undefiled, unsullied

impurity noun contamination, defilement, dirtiness, infection, pollution, taint

imputation noun blame, accusation, aspersion, censure, insinuation, reproach, slander, slur

inability noun incapability, disability, disqualification, impotence, inadequacy, incapacity, incompetence, ineptitude, powerlessness

➤ **Antonyms**

ability, adequacy, capability, capacity, competence, potential, power, talent

inaccessible adjective out of reach, impassable, out of the way, remote, unapproachable, unattainable, unreachable

➤ **Antonyms**

accessible, approachable, attainable, reachable

inaccuracy noun error, defect, erratum, fault, lapse, mistake

inaccurate adjective incorrect, defective, erroneous, faulty, imprecise, mistaken, out, unreliable, unsound, wrong

➤ **Antonyms**
accurate, correct, exact, precise, reliable, sound

inactive adjective unused, dormant, idle, inoperative, unemployed, unoccupied

➤ **Antonyms**
employed, occupied, operative, running, used, working

inactivity noun immobility, dormancy, hibernation, inaction, passivity, unemployment

➤ **Antonyms**
action, activeness, bustle, employment, exertion, mobility, movement

inadequacy noun **1** shortage, dearth, insufficiency, meagreness, paucity, poverty, scantiness **2** incompetence, deficiency, inability, incapacity, ineffectiveness **3** shortcoming, defect, failing, imperfection, weakness

inadequate adjective **1** insufficient, meagre, scant, sketchy, sparse **2** incapable, deficient, faulty, found wanting, incompetent, not up to scratch (informal), unqualified

➤ **Antonyms**
≠insufficient: adequate, ample, satisfactory, sufficient ≠incapable: apt, capable, competent, equal, fit, qualified

inadmissible adjective unacceptable, inappropriate, irrelevant, unallowable

inadvertently adverb unintentionally, accidentally, by accident, by mistake, involuntarily, mistakenly, unwittingly

➤ **Antonyms**
carefully, consciously, deliberately, heedfully, intentionally

inadvisable adjective unwise, illadvised, impolitic, imprudent, inexpedient, injudicious

inane adjective senseless, empty, fatuous, frivolous, futile, idiotic,

mindless, silly, stupid, vacuous

➤ **Antonyms**
meaningful, profound, sensible, serious, significant, weighty

inanimate adjective lifeless, cold, dead, defunct, extinct, inert

➤ **Antonyms**
alive, animate, lively, living

inapplicable adjective irrelevant, inappropriate, unsuitable

➤ **Antonyms**
applicable, appropriate, fitting, relevant, suitable

inappropriate adjective unsuitable, improper, incongruous, out of place, unbecoming, unbefitting, unfitting, unseemly, untimely

➤ **Antonyms**
appropriate, becoming, fitting, proper, seemly, suitable, timely

inarticulate adjective faltering, halting, hesitant

inattention noun neglect, absentmindedness, carelessness, daydreaming, inattentiveness, preoccupation, thoughtlessness

inattentive adjective preoccupied, careless, distracted, dreamy, negligent, unobservant, vague

➤ **Antonyms**
attentive, aware, careful, observant

inaudible adjective indistinct, low, mumbling, out of earshot, stifled, unheard

➤ **Antonyms**
audible, clear, discernible, distinct, perceptible

inaugural adjective first, initial, introductory, maiden, opening

inaugurate verb **1** invest, induct, install **2** launch, begin, commence, get under way, initiate, institute, introduce, set in motion

inauguration noun **1** investiture, induction, installation **2** launch, initiation, institution, opening, setting up

inauspicious adjective unpromising, bad, discouraging, illomened, ominous, unfavourable, unfortunate, unlucky, unpropitious

inborn *adjective* natural, congenital, hereditary, inbred, ingrained, inherent, innate, instinctive, intuitive, native

inbred *adjective* innate, constitutional, deep-seated, ingrained, inherent, native, natural

incalculable *adjective* countless, boundless, infinite, innumerable, limitless, numberless, untold, vast

incantation *noun* chant, charm, formula, invocation, spell

incapable *adjective* **1** incompetent, feeble, inadequate, ineffective, inept, inexpert, insufficient, unfit, unqualified, weak **2** unable, helpless, impotent, powerless

➤ **Antonyms**
≠incompetent: adequate, capable, competent, efficient, expert, fit, qualified, sufficient

incapacitate *verb* disable, cripple, immobilize, lay up (*informal*), paralyse, put out of action (*informal*)

incapacitated *adjective* indisposed, hors de combat, immobilized, laid up (*informal*), out of action (*informal*), unfit

incapacity *noun* inability, impotence, inadequacy, incapability, incompetency, ineffectiveness, powerlessness, unfitness, weakness

incarcerate *verb* imprison, confine, detain, impound, intern, jail *or* gaol, lock up, throw in jail

incarceration *noun* imprisonment, captivity, confinement, detention, internment

incarnate *adjective* personified, embodied, typified

incarnation *noun* embodiment, epitome, manifestation, personification, type

incense *verb* anger, enrage, inflame, infuriate, irritate, madden, make one's hackles rise, rile (*informal*)

incensed *adjective* angry, enraged, fuming, furious, indignant, infuriated, irate, maddened, steamed up (*slang*), up in arms

incentive *noun* encouragement, bait, carrot (*informal*), enticement, inducement, lure, motivation, spur, stimulus

➤ **Antonyms**
deterrent, discouragement, disincentive, dissuasion

inception *noun* beginning, birth, commencement, dawn, initiation, origin, outset, start

➤ **Antonyms**
completion, conclusion, end, ending, finish, termination

incessant *adjective* endless, ceaseless, constant, continual, eternal, interminable, never-ending, nonstop, perpetual, unceasing, unending

➤ **Antonyms**
infrequent, intermittent, occasional, periodic, rare, sporadic

incessantly *adverb* endlessly, ceaselessly, constantly, continually, eternally, interminably, nonstop, perpetually, persistently

incident *noun* **1** happening, adventure, episode, event, fact, matter, occasion, occurrence **2** disturbance, clash, commotion, confrontation, contretemps, scene

incidental *adjective* secondary, ancillary, minor, nonessential, occasional, subordinate, subsidiary

➤ **Antonyms**
crucial, essential, important, necessary, vital

incidentally *adverb* parenthetically, by the bye, by the way, in passing

incinerate *verb* burn up, carbonize, char, cremate, reduce to ashes

incipient *adjective* beginning, commencing, developing, embryonic, inchoate, nascent, starting

incision *noun* cut, gash, notch, opening, slash, slit

incisive *adjective* penetrating, acute, keen, perspicacious, piercing, trenchant

➤ **Antonyms**
dense, dull, vague, woolly

incite *verb* provoke, encourage, foment, inflame, instigate, spur, stimulate, stir up, urge, whip up

➤ **Antonyms**
dampen, deter, discourage, dissuade, restrain

incitement *noun* provocation, agitation, encouragement, impetus, instigation, prompting, spur, stimulus

incivility *noun* rudeness, bad manners, boorishness, discourteousness, discourtesy, disrespect, ill-breeding, impoliteness

➤ **Antonyms**
civility, courteousness, courtesy, good manners, politeness, respect

inclement *adjective* *Formal* stormy, foul, harsh, intemperate, rough, severe, tempestuous

➤ **Antonyms**
balmy, calm, clement, fine, mild, pleasant, temperate

inclination *noun* 1 tendency, disposition, liking, partiality, penchant, predilection, predisposition, proclivity, proneness, propensity 2 slope, angle, gradient, incline, pitch, slant, tilt

➤ **Antonyms**
≠tendency: antipathy, aversion, disinclination, dislike, revulsion

incline *verb* 1 slope, lean, slant, tilt, tip, veer 2 predispose, influence, persuade, prejudice, sway ♦ *noun* 3 slope, ascent, descent, dip, grade, gradient, rise

inclined *adjective* disposed, apt, given, liable, likely, minded, predisposed, prone, willing

inclose *see* ENCLOSE

include *verb* 1 contain, comprise, cover, embrace, encompass, incorporate, involve, subsume, take in 2 introduce, add, enter, insert

➤ **Antonyms**
eliminate, exclude, leave out, omit, rule out

inclusion *noun* addition, incorporation, insertion

➤ **Antonyms**
exception, exclusion, omission, rejection

inclusive *adjective* comprehensive, across-the-board, all-embracing, blanket, general, global, overarching, sweeping, umbrella

➤ **Antonyms**
confined, exclusive, limited, narrow, restricted

incognito *adjective* in disguise, disguised, under an assumed name, unknown, unrecognized

incoherence *noun* unintelligibility, disjointedness, inarticulateness

incoherent *adjective* unintelligible, confused, disjointed, disordered, inarticulate, inconsistent, jumbled, muddled, rambling, stammering, stuttering

➤ **Antonyms**
coherent, intelligible, logical, rational

income *noun* revenue, earnings, pay, proceeds, profits, receipts, salary, takings, wages

incoming *adjective* arriving, approaching, entering, homeward, landing, new, returning

➤ **Antonyms**
departing, exiting, leaving, outgoing

incomparable *adjective* unequalled, beyond compare, inimitable, matchless, peerless, superlative, supreme, transcendent, unmatched, unparalleled, unrivalled

incompatible *adjective* inconsistent, conflicting, contradictory, incongruous, mismatched, unsuited

➤ **Antonyms**
compatible, consistent, harmonious, suited

incompetence *noun* ineptitude, inability, inadequacy, incapability, incapacity, ineffectiveness, unfitness, uselessness

incompetent *adjective* inept, bungling, floundering, incapable, ineffectual, inexpert, unfit, useless

➤ **Antonyms**
able, capable, competent, expert, fit, proficient, skilful

incomplete *adjective* unfinished, deficient, fragmentary, imperfect, partial, wanting

➤ **Antonyms**
complete, finished, perfect, whole

incomprehensible *adjective* unintelligible, baffling, beyond one's grasp, impenetrable, obscure, opaque, perplexing, puzzling, unfathomable

➤ **Antonyms**
apparent, clear, comprehensible, evident, intelligible, manifest, obvious, understandable

inconceivable *adjective* unimaginable, beyond belief, incomprehensible, incredible, mindboggling (*informal*), out of the question, unbelievable, unheard-of, unthinkable

➤ **Antonyms**
believable, comprehensible, conceivable, credible, imaginable, likely, plausible, possible, reasonable

inconclusive *adjective* indecisive, ambiguous, indeterminate, open, unconvincing, undecided, up in the air (*informal*), vague

incongruity *noun* inappropriateness, conflict, discrepancy, disparity, incompatibility, inconsistency, unsuitability

incongruous *adjective* inappropriate, discordant, improper, incompatible, out of keeping, out of place, unbecoming, unsuitable

➤ **Antonyms**
appropriate, becoming, compatible, harmonious, suitable

inconsiderable *adjective* insignificant, inconsequential, minor, negligible, slight, small, trifling, trivial, unimportant

inconsiderate *adjective* selfish, indelicate, insensitive, rude, tactless, thoughtless, unkind, unthinking

➤ **Antonyms**
considerate, kind, sensitive, tactful, thoughtful

inconsistency *noun* **1** unreliability, fickleness, instability, unpredictability, unsteadiness **2** incompatibility, disagreement, discrepancy, disparity, divergence, incongruity, variance

inconsistent *adjective* **1** changeable, capricious, erratic, fickle, inconstant, unpredictable, unstable, unsteady, variable **2** incompatible, at odds, conflicting, contradictory, discordant, incongruous, irreconcilable, out of step

➤ **Antonyms**
≠changeable: consistent, constant, predictable, reliable, stable, steady, unchanging ≠incompatible: compatible, homogeneous, reconcilable, uniform

inconsolable *adjective* heartbroken, brokenhearted, desolate, despairing

inconspicuous *adjective* unobtrusive, camouflaged, hidden, insignificant, ordinary, plain, unassuming, unnoticeable, unostentatious

➤ **Antonyms**
bold, conspicuous, noticeable, obtrusive, obvious, significant, visible

incontrovertible *adjective* indisputable, certain, established, incontestable, indubitable, irrefutable, positive, sure, undeniable, unquestionable

inconvenience *noun* **1** trouble, awkwardness, bother, difficulty, disadvantage, disruption, disturbance, fuss, hindrance, nuisance ♦ *verb* **2** trouble, bother, discommode, disrupt, disturb, put out, upset

inconvenient *adjective* troublesome, awkward, bothersome, disadvantageous, disturbing, inopportune, unsuitable, untimely

> **Antonyms**

convenient, handy, opportune, suitable, timely

incorporate *verb* <u>include</u>, absorb, assimilate, blend, combine, integrate, merge, subsume

incorrect *adjective* <u>false</u>, erroneous, faulty, flawed, inaccurate, mistaken, untrue, wrong

> **Antonyms**

accurate, correct, exact, faultless, flawless, right, suitable, true

incorrigible *adjective* <u>incurable</u>, hardened, hopeless, intractable, inveterate, irredeemable, unreformed

incorruptible *adjective* **1** <u>honest</u>, above suspicion, straight, trustworthy, upright **2** <u>imperishable</u>, everlasting, undecaying

increase *verb* **1** <u>grow</u>, advance, boost, develop, enlarge, escalate, expand, extend, multiply, raise, spread, swell ♦ *noun* **2** <u>growth</u>, development, enlargement, escalation, expansion, extension, gain, increment, rise, upturn

> **Antonyms**

verb ≠<u>grow</u>: abate, abbreviate, abridge, condense, curtail, decline, decrease, diminish, dwindle, lessen, reduce, shorten, shrink

increasingly *adverb* <u>progressively</u>, more and more

incredible *adjective* **1** <u>implausible</u>, beyond belief, far-fetched, improbable, inconceivable, preposterous, unbelievable, unimaginable, unthinkable **2** *Informal* <u>amazing</u>, astonishing, astounding, extraordinary, prodigious, sensational (*informal*), wonderful

incredulity *noun* <u>disbelief</u>, distrust, doubt, scepticism

incredulous *adjective* <u>disbelieving</u>, distrustful, doubtful, dubious, sceptical, suspicious, unbelieving, unconvinced

> **Antonyms**

believing, credulous, gullible, naive, trusting, unsuspecting

increment *noun* <u>increase</u>, accrual, addition, advancement, augmentation, enlargement, gain, step up, supplement

incriminate *verb* <u>implicate</u>, accuse, blame, charge, impeach, inculpate, involve

incumbent *adjective Formal* <u>obligatory</u>, binding, compulsory, mandatory, necessary

incur *verb* <u>earn</u>, arouse, bring (upon oneself), draw, expose oneself to, gain, meet with, provoke

incurable *adjective* <u>fatal</u>, inoperable, irremediable, terminal

indebted *adjective* <u>grateful</u>, beholden, in debt, obligated, obliged, under an obligation

indecency *noun* <u>obscenity</u>, immodesty, impropriety, impurity, indelicacy, lewdness, licentiousness, pornography, vulgarity

> **Antonyms**

decency, delicacy, modesty, propriety, purity

indecent *adjective* **1** <u>lewd</u>, crude, dirty, filthy, immodest, improper, impure, licentious, pornographic, salacious **2** <u>unbecoming</u>, in bad taste, indecorous, unseemly, vulgar

> **Antonyms**

decent, decorous, delicate, modest, proper, pure, respectable, seemly, tasteful

indecipherable *adjective* <u>illegible</u>, indistinguishable, unintelligible, unreadable

indecision *noun* <u>hesitation</u>, dithering (*chiefly Brit.*), doubt, indecisiveness, shilly-shallying (*informal*), uncertainty, vacillation, wavering

indecisive *adjective* <u>hesitating</u>, dithering (*chiefly Brit.*), faltering, in two minds (*informal*), tentative, uncertain, undecided, vacillating, wavering

> **Antonyms**

certain, decided, determined, positive, resolute, unhesitating

indeed *adverb* <u>really</u>, actually, certainly, in truth, truly, undoubtedly

indefensible *adjective* unforgivable, inexcusable, unjustifiable, unpardonable, untenable, unwarrantable, wrong

➤ **Antonyms**
defensible, excusable, forgivable, justifiable, legitimate, pardonable, tenable, warrantable

indefinable *adjective* inexpressible, impalpable, indescribable

indefinite *adjective* unclear, doubtful, equivocal, ill-defined, imprecise, indeterminate, inexact, uncertain, unfixed, vague

➤ **Antonyms**
certain, clear, definite, exact, fixed, specific

indefinitely *adverb* endlessly, ad infinitum, continually, for ever

indelible *adjective* permanent, enduring, indestructible, ineradicable, ingrained, lasting

➤ **Antonyms**
eradicable, erasable, impermanent, removable, temporary, washable

indelicate *adjective* offensive, coarse, crude, embarrassing, immodest, risqué, rude, suggestive, tasteless, vulgar

➤ **Antonyms**
delicate, modest

indemnify *verb* **1** insure, guarantee, protect, secure, underwrite **2** compensate, reimburse, remunerate, repair, repay

indemnity *noun* **1** insurance, guarantee, protection, security **2** compensation, redress, reimbursement, remuneration, reparation, restitution

independence *noun* freedom, autonomy, liberty, self-reliance, self-rule, self-sufficiency, sovereignty

➤ **Antonyms**
bondage, dependence, subjection, subjugation, subordination, subservience

independent *adjective* **1** free, liberated, separate, unconstrained, uncontrolled **2** self-governing, autonomous, non-aligned, self-determining, sover-

eign **3** self-sufficient, liberated, self-contained, self-reliant, self-supporting

➤ **Antonyms**
≠free: controlled, dependent, restrained, subject ≠self-governing: dependent, subject, submissive, subordinate, subservient, subsidiary

independently *adverb* separately, alone, autonomously, by oneself, individually, on one's own, solo, unaided

indescribable *adjective* unutterable, beyond description, beyond words, indefinable, inexpressible

indestructible *adjective* permanent, enduring, everlasting, immortal, imperishable, incorruptible, indelible, indissoluble, lasting, unbreakable

➤ **Antonyms**
breakable, corruptible, destructible, impermanent, mortal, perishable

indeterminate *adjective* uncertain, imprecise, indefinite, inexact, undefined, unfixed, unspecified, unstipulated, vague

➤ **Antonyms**
certain, clear, conclusive, definite, determinate, exact, fixed, precise, specified, stipulated

indicate *verb* **1** signify, betoken, denote, imply, manifest, point to, reveal, suggest **2** point out, designate, specify **3** show, display, express, read, record, register

indication *noun* sign, clue, evidence, hint, inkling, intimation, manifestation, mark, suggestion, symptom

indicative *adjective* suggestive, pointing to, significant, symptomatic

indicator *noun* sign, gauge, guide, mark, meter, pointer, signal, symbol

indict *verb* charge, accuse, arraign, impeach, prosecute, summon

indictment *noun* charge, accusation, allegation, impeachment, prosecution, summons

indifference noun disregard, aloofness, apathy, coldness, coolness, detachment, inattention, negligence, nonchalance, unconcern

➤ **Antonyms**

attention, concern, enthusiasm, interest, regard

indifferent adjective 1 uncon-cerned, aloof, callous, cold, cool, detached, impervious, inattentive, uninterested, unmoved, unsympathetic 2 mediocre, moderate, no great shakes (informal), ordinary, passable, so-so (informal), undistinguished

➤ **Antonyms**

≠unconcerned: avid, concerned, eager, enthusiastic, interested, keen, sympathetic ≠mediocre: excellent, exceptional, fine, first-class, notable, remarkable

indigestion noun heartburn, dyspepsia, upset stomach

indignant adjective resentful, angry, disgruntled, exasperated, incensed, irate, peeved (informal), riled, scornful, up in arms (informal)

indignation noun resentment, anger, exasperation, pique, rage, scorn, umbrage

indignity noun humiliation, affront, dishonour, disrespect, injury, insult, opprobrium, slight, snub

indirect adjective 1 incidental, secondary, subsidiary, unintended 2 circuitous, long-drawn-out, meandering, oblique, rambling, roundabout, tortuous, wandering

➤ **Antonyms**

≠circuitous: direct, straight, straightforward

indiscreet adjective tactless, impolitic, imprudent, incautious, injudicious, naive, rash, reckless, unwise

➤ **Antonyms**

cautious, discreet, judicious, politic, prudent, tactful, wise

indiscretion noun mistake, error, faux pas, folly, gaffe, lapse, slip

indiscriminate adjective random, careless, desultory, general, uncritical, undiscriminating, unsystematic, wholesale

➤ **Antonyms**

deliberate, discriminating, exclusive, systematic

indispensable adjective essential, crucial, imperative, key, necessary, needed, requisite, vital

➤ **Antonyms**

dispensable, nonessential, superfluous, unimportant, unnecessary

indisposed adjective ill, ailing, poorly (informal), sick, under the weather, unwell

➤ **Antonyms**

fine, fit, hardy, healthy, sound, well

indisposition noun illness, ailment, ill health, sickness

indisputable adjective undeniable, beyond doubt, certain, incontestable, incontrovertible, indubitable, irrefutable, unquestionable

➤ **Antonyms**

disputable, doubtful, indefinite, questionable, refutable, uncertain, vague

indistinct adjective unclear, blurred, faint, fuzzy, hazy, ill-defined, indeterminate, shadowy, undefined, vague

➤ **Antonyms**

clear, defined, determinate, distinct, evident

individual adjective 1 personal, characteristic, distinctive, exclusive, idiosyncratic, own, particular, peculiar, singular, special, specific, unique ♦ noun 2 person, being, character, creature, soul, unit

➤ **Antonyms**

adjective ≠personal: collective, common, conventional, general, indistinct, universal

individualist noun maverick, freethinker, independent, loner, lone wolf, nonconformist, original

individuality noun distinctiveness, character, originality, personality, separateness, singularity, uniqueness

individually adverb separately, apart, independently, one at a time, one by one, singly

indoctrinate verb train, brainwash, drill, ground, imbue, initiate, instruct, school, teach

indoctrination noun training, brainwashing, drilling, grounding, inculcation, instruction, schooling

indolent adjective lazy, idle, inactive, inert, languid, lethargic, listless, slothful, sluggish, workshy
► Antonyms
active, assiduous, busy, conscientious, diligent, energetic, industrious, vigorous

indomitable adjective invincible, bold, resolute, staunch, steadfast, unbeatable, unconquerable, unflinching, unyielding
► Antonyms
weak, yielding

indubitable adjective certain, incontestable, incontrovertible, indisputable, irrefutable, obvious, sure, undeniable, unquestionable

induce verb 1 persuade, convince, encourage, incite, influence, instigate, prevail upon, prompt, talk into 2 cause, bring about, effect, engender, generate, give rise to, lead to, occasion, produce
► Antonyms
curb, deter, discourage, dissuade, hinder, prevent, restrain, stop, suppress

inducement noun incentive, attraction, bait, carrot (informal), encouragement, incitement, lure, reward

indulge verb 1 gratify, feed, give way to, pander to, satisfy, yield to 2 spoil, cosset, give in to, go along with, humour, mollycoddle, pamper

indulgence noun 1 luxury, extravagance, favour, privilege, treat 2 gratification, appease-

ment, fulfilment, satiation, satisfaction 3 tolerance, forbearance, patience, understanding

indulgent adjective lenient, compliant, easy-going, forbearing, kindly, liberal, permissive, tolerant, understanding
► Antonyms
austere, demanding, harsh, intolerant, rigorous, stern, strict, stringent, unmerciful

industrialist noun capitalist, big businessman, captain of industry, magnate, manufacturer, tycoon

industrious adjective hardworking, busy, conscientious, diligent, energetic, persistent, purposeful, tireless, zealous
► Antonyms
good-for-nothing, idle, indolent, lackadaisical, lazy, shiftless, slothful

industry noun 1 business, commerce, manufacturing, production, trade 2 effort, activity, application, diligence, labour, tirelessness, toil, zeal

inebriated adjective drunk, halfcut (informal), intoxicated, legless (informal), merry (Brit. informal), paralytic (informal), plastered (slang), tight (informal), tipsy, under the influence (informal)

ineffective adjective useless, fruitless, futile, idle, impotent, inefficient, unavailing, unproductive, vain, worthless
► Antonyms
effective, efficacious, efficient, fruitful, potent, productive, useful, worthwhile

ineffectual adjective weak, feeble, impotent, inadequate, incompetent, ineffective, inept

inefficiency noun incompetence, carelessness, disorganization, muddle, slackness, sloppiness

inefficient adjective incompetent, disorganized, ineffectual, inept, wasteful, weak
► Antonyms
able, capable, competent, effec-

tive, efficient, expert, organized, skilled

ineligible *adjective* <u>unqualified</u>, disqualified, ruled out, unacceptable, unfit, unsuitable

inept *adjective* <u>incompetent</u>, bumbling, bungling, clumsy, inexpert, maladroit

➤ Antonyms

able, adroit, competent, dexterous, efficient, skilful, talented

ineptitude *noun* <u>incompetence</u>, clumsiness, inexpertness, unfitness

inequality *noun* <u>disparity</u>, bias, difference, disproportion, diversity, irregularity, prejudice, unevenness

inequitable *adjective* <u>unfair</u>, biased, discriminatory, one-sided, partial, partisan, preferential, prejudiced, unjust

➤ Antonyms

even-handed, fair, impartial, just, unbiased, unprejudiced

inert *adjective* <u>inactive</u>, dead, dormant, immobile, lifeless, motionless, static, still, unreactive, unresponsive

➤ Antonyms

active, alive, animated, energetic, living, mobile, moving, reactive, responsive

inertia *noun* <u>inactivity</u>, apathy, immobility, lethargy, listlessness, passivity, sloth, unresponsiveness

➤ Antonyms

action, activity, animation, energy, liveliness, vigour, vitality

inescapable *adjective* <u>unavoidable</u>, certain, destined, fated, ineluctable, inevitable, inexorable, sure

inestimable *adjective* <u>incalculable</u>, immeasurable, invaluable, precious, priceless, prodigious

inevitable *adjective* <u>unavoidable</u>, assured, certain, destined, fixed, ineluctable, inescapable, inexorable, sure

➤ Antonyms

avoidable, escapable, evadable, preventable, uncertain

inevitably *adverb* <u>unavoidably</u>,

as a result, automatically, certainly, necessarily, of necessity, perforce, surely, willy-nilly

inexcusable *adjective* <u>unforgivable</u>, indefensible, outrageous, unjustifiable, unpardonable, unwarrantable

➤ Antonyms

defensible, excusable, forgivable, justifiable, pardonable

inexorable *adjective* <u>unrelenting</u>, inescapable, relentless, remorseless, unbending, unyielding

➤ Antonyms

bending, flexible, lenient, relenting, yielding

inexpensive *adjective* <u>cheap</u>, bargain, budget, economical, modest, reasonable

➤ Antonyms

costly, dear, exorbitant, expensive, high-priced, pricey, uneconomical

inexperience *noun* <u>unfamiliarity</u>, callowness, greenness, ignorance, newness, rawness

inexperienced *adjective* <u>immature</u>, callow, green, new, raw, unpractised, untried, unversed

➤ Antonyms

experienced, knowledgeable, practised, seasoned, versed

inexpert *adjective* <u>amateurish</u>, bungling, cack-handed (*informal*), clumsy, inept, maladroit, unpractised, unprofessional, unskilled

inexplicable *adjective* <u>unaccountable</u>, baffling, enigmatic, incomprehensible, insoluble, mysterious, mystifying, strange, unfathomable, unintelligible

➤ Antonyms

comprehensible, explainable, explicable, fathomable, intelligible

inextricably *adverb* <u>inseparably</u>, indissolubly, indistinguishably, intricately, irretrievably, totally

infallibility *noun* <u>perfection</u>, impeccability, omniscience, supremacy, unerringness

infallible *adjective* <u>sure</u>, certain, dependable, foolproof, reliable, sure-fire (*informal*), trustworthy, unbeatable, unfailing

➤ **Antonyms**
doubtful, dubious, uncertain, undependable, unreliable, unsure

infamous adjective notorious, disreputable, ignominious, ill-famed

➤ **Antonyms**
esteemed, glorious, honourable, noble, reputable

infancy noun beginnings, cradle, dawn, inception, origins, outset, start

➤ **Antonyms**
close, conclusion, death, end, finish, termination

infant noun baby, babe, bairn (Scot.), child, toddler, tot

infantile adjective childish, babyish, immature, puerile

➤ **Antonyms**
adult, developed, mature

infatuate verb obsess, besot, bewitch, captivate, enchant, enrapture, fascinate

infatuated adjective obsessed, besotted, bewitched, captivated, carried away, damnable, enamoured, enraptured, fascinated, possessed, smitten (informal), spellbound

infatuation noun obsession, crush (informal), fixation, madness, passion, thing (informal)

infect verb contaminate, affect, blight, corrupt, defile, poison, pollute, taint

infection noun contamination, contagion, corruption, defilement, poison, pollution, virus

infectious adjective catching, communicable, contagious, spreading, transmittable, virulent

infer verb deduce, conclude, derive, gather, presume, surmise, understand

inference noun deduction, assumption, conclusion, presumption, reading, surmise

inferior adjective 1 lower, lesser, menial, minor, secondary, subordinate, subsidiary ♦ noun 2 underling, junior, menial, subordinate

➤ **Antonyms**
adjective ≠lower: greater, higher,

senior, superior, top

inferiority noun 1 inadequacy, deficiency, imperfection, insignificance, mediocrity, shoddiness, worthlessness 2 subservience, abasement, lowliness, subordination

➤ **Antonyms**
≠inadequacy: eminence, excellence, superiority ≠subservience: ascendancy, dominance, superiority

infernal adjective devilish, accursed, damnable, damned, diabolical, fiendish, hellish, satanic

➤ **Antonyms**
angelic, glorious, godlike, seraphic

infertile adjective barren, sterile, unfruitful, unproductive

➤ **Antonyms**
fecund, fertile, fruitful, productive

infertility noun sterility, barrenness, infecundity, unproductiveness

infest verb overrun, beset, invade, penetrate, permeate, ravage, swarm, throng

infested adjective overrun, alive, crawling, ravaged, ridden, swarming, teeming

infiltrate verb penetrate, filter through, insinuate oneself, make inroads (into), percolate, permeate, pervade, sneak in (informal)

infinite adjective never-ending, boundless, eternal, everlasting, illimitable, immeasurable, inexhaustible, limitless, measureless, unbounded

➤ **Antonyms**
bounded, finite, limited, measurable, restricted

infinitesimal adjective microscopic, insignificant, minuscule, minute, negligible, teeny, tiny, unnoticeable

➤ **Antonyms**
enormous, great, huge, infinite, large, vast

infinity noun eternity, boundlessness, endlessness, immensity, vastness

infirm adjective frail, ailing, debilitated, decrepit, doddering, enfeebled, failing, feeble, weak

➤ **Antonyms**

healthy, robust, sound, strong, sturdy, vigorous

infirmity noun <u>frailty</u>, decrepitude, ill health, sickliness, vulnerability

➤ **Antonyms**

health, soundness, stability, strength, vigour, wellness

inflame verb <u>enrage</u>, anger, arouse, excite, incense, infuriate, madden, provoke, rouse, stimulate

➤ **Antonyms**

allay, calm, cool, discourage, pacify, quiet, soothe, suppress

inflamed adjective <u>sore</u>, fevered, hot, infected, red, swollen

inflammable adjective <u>flammable</u>, combustible, incendiary

inflammation noun <u>soreness</u>, painfulness, rash, redness, tenderness

inflammatory adjective <u>provocative</u>, explosive, fiery, intemperate, like a red rag to a bull, rabble-rousing

inflate verb <u>expand</u>, bloat, blow up, dilate, distend, enlarge, increase, puff up or out, pump up, swell

➤ **Antonyms**

collapse, compress, contract, deflate, diminish, lessen, shrink

inflated adjective <u>exaggerated</u>, ostentatious, overblown, swollen

inflation noun <u>expansion</u>, enlargement, escalation, extension, increase, rise, spread, swelling

inflexibility noun <u>obstinacy</u>, intransigence, obduracy

inflexible adjective **1** <u>obstinate</u>, implacable, intractable, obdurate, resolute, set in one's ways, steadfast, stubborn, unbending, uncompromising **2** <u>inelastic</u>, hard, rigid, stiff, taut

➤ **Antonyms**

≠obstinate: flexible, irresolute, yielding ≠inelastic: elastic, flexible, pliable, pliant, supple, yielding

inflict verb <u>impose</u>, administer,

apply, deliver, levy, mete or deal out, visit, wreak

infliction noun <u>imposition</u>, administration, perpetration, wreaking

influence noun **1** <u>effect</u>, hold, magnetism, power, spell, sway, weight **2** <u>control</u>, ascendancy, authority, direction, domination, mastery **3** <u>power</u>, clout (informal), importance, leverage, prestige, pull (informal) ♦ verb **4** <u>affect</u>, control, direct, guide, manipulate, sway **5** <u>persuade</u>, incite, induce, instigate, prompt

influential adjective <u>important</u>, authoritative, instrumental, leading, potent, powerful, significant, telling, weighty

➤ **Antonyms**

impotent, ineffective, ineffectual, powerless, unimportant, uninfluential, weak

influx noun <u>arrival</u>, incursion, inrush, inundation, invasion, rush

inform verb **1** <u>tell</u>, advise, communicate, enlighten, instruct, notify, teach, tip off **2** <u>betray</u>, blow the whistle on (informal), denounce, grass (Brit. slang), incriminate, inculcate, shop (slang, chiefly Brit.), squeal (slang)

informal adjective <u>relaxed</u>, casual, colloquial, cosy, easy, familiar, natural, simple, unofficial

➤ **Antonyms**

ceremonious, conventional, formal, official, stiff

informality noun <u>familiarity</u>, casualness, ease, naturalness, relaxation, simplicity

information noun <u>facts</u>, data, intelligence, knowledge, message, news, notice, report

informative adjective <u>instructive</u>, chatty, communicative, edifying, educational, enlightening, forthcoming, illuminating, revealing

informed adjective <u>knowledgeable</u>, enlightened, erudite, expert, familiar, in the picture, learned, up to date, versed, well-read

informer noun <u>betrayer</u>, accuser,

Judas, sneak, stool pigeon

infrequent *adjective* occasional, few and far between, once in a blue moon, rare, sporadic, uncommon, unusual

➤ Antonyms

common, customary, frequent, habitual, often, regular, usual

infringe *verb* break, contravene, disobey, transgress, violate

infringement *noun* contravention, breach, infraction, transgression, trespass, violation

infuriate *verb* enrage, anger, exasperate, incense, irritate, madden, provoke, rile

➤ Antonyms

appease, calm, mollify, pacify, placate, propitiate, soothe

infuriating *adjective* annoying, exasperating, galling, irritating, maddening, mortifying, provoking, vexatious

ingenious *adjective* creative, bright, brilliant, clever, crafty, inventive, original, resourceful, shrewd

➤ Antonyms

unimaginative, uninventive, unoriginal, unresourceful

ingenuity *noun* originality, cleverness, flair, genius, gift, inventiveness, resourcefulness, sharpness, shrewdness

➤ Antonyms

dullness, incompetence, ineptitude, ineptness

ingenuous *adjective* naive, artless, guileless, honest, innocent, open, plain, simple, sincere, trusting, unsophisticated

➤ Antonyms

artful, crafty, devious, insincere, sly, sophisticated, subtle, wily

inglorious *adjective* dishonourable, discreditable, disgraceful, disreputable, ignoble, ignominious, infamous, shameful, unheroic

ingratiate *verb* pander to, crawl, curry favour, fawn, flatter, grovel, insinuate oneself, toady

ingratiating *adjective* sycophantic, crawling, fawning, flattering,

humble, obsequious, servile, toadying, unctuous

ingratitude *noun* ungratefulness, thanklessness

➤ Antonyms

appreciation, gratefulness, gratitude, thankfulness, thanks

ingredient *noun* component, constituent, element, part

inhabit *verb* live, abide, dwell, occupy, populate, reside

inhabitant *noun* dweller, citizen, denizen, inmate, native, occupant, occupier, resident, tenant

inhabited *adjective* populated, colonized, developed, occupied, peopled, settled, tenanted

inhale *verb* breathe in, draw in, gasp, respire, suck in

➤ Antonyms

blow, breathe out, exhale, expire

inherent *adjective* innate, essential, hereditary, inborn, inbred, inbuilt, ingrained, inherited, intrinsic, native, natural

➤ Antonyms

alien, extraneous, extrinsic, imposed

inherit *verb* be left, come into, fall heir to, succeed to

inheritance *noun* legacy, bequest, birthright, heritage, patrimony

inhibit *verb* restrain, check, constrain, curb, discourage, frustrate, hinder, hold back *or* in, impede, obstruct

➤ Antonyms

allow, enable, encourage, further, let, permit

inhibited *adjective* shy, constrained, guarded, repressed, reserved, reticent, self-conscious, subdued

➤ Antonyms

free, natural, outgoing, relaxed, spontaneous, uninhibited, unreserved

inhibition *noun* shyness, block, hang-up (*informal*), reserve, restraint, reticence, self-consciousness

inhospitable *adjective* **1** unfriendly, cool, uncongenial, unreceptive, unsociable, unwelcoming, xenophobic **2** bleak, barren, desolate, forbidding, godforsaken, hostile

> ► **Antonyms**

≠unfriendly: friendly, generous, genial, gracious, hospitable, sociable, welcoming

inhuman *adjective* cruel, barbaric, brutal, cold-blooded, heartless, merciless, pitiless, ruthless, savage, unfeeling

> ► **Antonyms**

charitable, compassionate, humane, merciful, tender, warmhearted

inhumane *adjective* cruel, brutal, heartless, pitiless, unfeeling, unkind, unsympathetic

inhumanity *noun* cruelty, atrocity, barbarism, brutality, heartlessness, pitilessness, ruthlessness, unkindness

inimical *adjective* hostile, adverse, antagonistic, ill-disposed, opposed, unfavourable, unfriendly, unwelcoming

> ► **Antonyms**

amicable, favourable, friendly, helpful, kindly, welcoming

inimitable *adjective* unique, consummate, incomparable, matchless, peerless, unparalleled, unrivalled

iniquitous *adjective* wicked, criminal, evil, immoral, reprehensible, sinful, unjust

iniquity *noun* wickedness, abomination, evil, injustice, sin, wrong

> ► **Antonyms**

goodness, honesty, integrity, morality, uprightness, virtue

initial *adjective* first, beginning, incipient, introductory, opening, primary

> ► **Antonyms**

closing, concluding, ending, final, last, ultimate

initially *adverb* at first, at or in the beginning, first, firstly, originally, primarily

initiate *verb* **1** begin, commence, get under way, kick off (*informal*), launch, open, originate,

set in motion, start **2** induct, indoctrinate, introduce, invest **3** instruct, acquaint with, coach, familiarize with, teach, train ♦ *noun* **4** novice, beginner, convert, entrant, learner, member, probationer

initiation *noun* introduction, debut, enrolment, entrance, inauguration, induction, installation, investiture

initiative *noun* **1** first step, advantage, first move, lead **2** resourcefulness, ambition, drive, dynamism, enterprise, get-up-and-go (*informal*), leadership

inject *verb* **1** vaccinate, inoculate **2** introduce, bring in, infuse, insert, instil

injection *noun* **1** vaccination, inoculation, jab (*informal*), shot (*informal*) **2** introduction, dose, infusion, insertion

injudicious *adjective* unwise, foolish, ill-advised, ill-judged, impolitic, imprudent, incautious, inexpedient, rash, unthinking

> ► **Antonyms**

cautious, expedient, judicious, prudent, wise

injunction *noun* order, command, exhortation, instruction, mandate, precept, ruling

injure *verb* hurt, damage, harm, impair, ruin, spoil, undermine, wound

injured *adjective* hurt, broken, damaged, disabled, undermined, weakened, wounded

injury *noun* harm, damage, detriment, disservice, hurt, ill, trauma (*Pathology*), wound, wrong

injustice *noun* unfairness, bias, discrimination, inequality, inequity, iniquity, oppression, partisanship, prejudice, wrong

> ► **Antonyms**

equality, equity, fairness, impartiality, justice, right

inkling *noun* suspicion, clue, conception, hint, idea, indication, intimation, notion, suggestion, whisper

inland *adjective* interior, domestic, internal, upcountry

inlet noun bay, bight, creek, firth or frith (Scot.), fjord, passage

inmost or **innermost** adjective deepest, basic, central, essential, intimate, personal, private, secret

innate adjective inborn, congenital, constitutional, essential, inbred, ingrained, inherent, instinctive, intuitive, native, natural

➤ **Antonyms**
acquired, affected, assumed, cultivated, fostered, learned, nurtured, unnatural

inner adjective **1** inside, central, interior, internal, inward, middle **2** hidden, intimate, personal, private, repressed, secret, unrevealed

➤ **Antonyms**
≠inside: exterior, external, outer, outside, outward ≠hidden: obvious, overt, revealed, unconcealed

innkeeper noun publican, host or hostess, hotelier, landlord or landlady, mine host

innocence noun **1** guiltlessness, blamelessness, clean hands, incorruptibility, probity, purity, uprightness, virtue **2** naïveté, artlessness, credulousness, gullibility, inexperience, ingenuousness, simplicity, unworldliness **3** harmlessness, innocuousness, inoffensiveness

➤ **Antonyms**
≠guiltlessness: corruption, guilt, impurity, sinfulness, wrongness ≠naïveté: artfulness, cunning, disingenuousness, guile, wiliness, worldliness

innocent adjective **1** not guilty, blameless, guiltless, honest, in the clear, uninvolved **2** harmless, innocuous, inoffensive, unobjectionable, well-intentioned, well-meant **3** naive, artless, childlike, credulous, gullible, ingenuous, open, simple, unworldly

➤ **Antonyms**
≠not guilty: blameworthy, culpable, guilty, responsible ≠harmless: evil, harmful, wicked ≠na-

ive: artful, disingenuous, sophisticated, worldly

innovation noun modernization, alteration, change, departure, introduction, newness, novelty, variation

innuendo noun insinuation, aspersion, hint, implication, imputation, intimation, overtone, suggestion, whisper

innumerable adjective countless, beyond number, incalculable, infinite, multitudinous, myriad, numberless, numerous, unnumbered, untold

➤ **Antonyms**
calculable, computable, finite, limited, measurable, numbered

inoffensive adjective harmless, innocent, innocuous, mild, quiet, retiring, unobjectionable, unobtrusive

➤ **Antonyms**
harmful, irksome, irritating, malicious, objectionable, offensive

inoperative adjective out of action, broken, defective, ineffective, invalid, null and void, out of order, out of service, useless

inopportune adjective inconvenient, ill-chosen, ill-timed, inappropriate, unfavourable, unfortunate, unpropitious, unseasonable, unsuitable, untimely

➤ **Antonyms**
appropriate, convenient, favourable, fortunate, opportune, seasonable, suitable, timely, well-timed

inordinate adjective excessive, disproportionate, extravagant, immoderate, intemperate, preposterous, unconscionable, undue, unreasonable, unwarranted

➤ **Antonyms**
moderate, reasonable, restrained, sensible

inorganic adjective artificial, chemical, man-made

inquest noun inquiry, inquisition, investigation, probe

inquire, enquire verb **1** ask, query, question **2** investigate, examine, explore, look into, make inquiries, probe, research

inquiry, enquiry *noun* **1** <u>question</u>, query **2** <u>investigation</u>, examination, exploration, inquest, interrogation, probe, research, study, survey

inquisition *noun* <u>investigation</u>, cross-examination, examination, grilling (*informal*), inquest, inquiry, questioning, third degree (*informal*)

inquisitive *adjective* <u>curious</u>, inquiring, nosy (*informal*), probing, prying, questioning

➤ **Antonyms**
apathetic, incurious, indifferent, unconcerned, uninterested, unquestioning

insane *adjective* **1** <u>mad</u>, crazed, crazy, demented, deranged, mentally ill, out of one's mind **2** <u>stupid</u>, daft (*informal*), dumb-ass (*slang*), foolish, idiotic, impractical, irrational, irresponsible, preposterous, senseless

➤ **Antonyms**
logical, lucid, normal, practical, rational, reasonable, reasoned, sane, sensible, sound

insanitary *adjective* <u>unhealthy</u>, dirty, disease-ridden, filthy, infested, insalubrious, polluted, unclean, unhygienic

➤ **Antonyms**
clean, healthy, hygienic, pure, salubrious, unpolluted

insanity *noun* **1** <u>madness</u>, delirium, dementia, mental disorder, mental illness **2** <u>stupidity</u>, folly, irresponsibility, lunacy, senselessness

➤ **Antonyms**
logic, lucidity, normality, rationality, reason, sanity, sense, soundness, wisdom

insatiable *adjective* <u>unquenchable</u>, greedy, intemperate, rapacious, ravenous, voracious

➤ **Antonyms**
limited, quenchable, satiable, temperate

inscribe *verb* <u>carve</u>, cut, engrave, etch, impress, imprint

inscription *noun* <u>engraving</u>, dedication, legend, words

inscrutable *adjective* **1** <u>enigmatic</u>, blank, deadpan, impenetrable, poker-faced (*informal*), unreadable **2** <u>mysterious</u>, hidden, incomprehensible, inexplicable, unexplainable, unfathomable, unintelligible

➤ **Antonyms**
≠enigmatic: open, penetrable, readable, revealing, transparent ≠mysterious: clear, comprehensible, evident, explainable, explicable, intelligible, manifest, obvious, patent, plain

insecure *adjective* **1** <u>anxious</u>, afraid, uncertain, unsure **2** <u>unsafe</u>, defenceless, exposed, unguarded, unprotected, vulnerable, wide-open

➤ **Antonyms**
≠anxious: assured, certain, confident, decisive, secure ≠unsafe: protected, safe, secure

insecurity *noun* <u>anxiety</u>, fear, uncertainty, worry

➤ **Antonyms**
assurance, certainty, confidence, security

insensible *adjective* <u>unaware</u>, impervious, oblivious, unaffected, unconscious, unmindful

➤ **Antonyms**
affected, aware, conscious, mindful, sensible

insensitive *adjective* <u>unfeeling</u>, callous, hardened, indifferent, thick-skinned, tough, uncaring, unconcerned

➤ **Antonyms**
caring, concerned, sensitive, sympathetic

inseparable *adjective* **1** <u>devoted</u>, bosom, close, intimate **2** <u>indivisible</u>, indissoluble

insert *verb* <u>enter</u>, embed, implant, introduce, place, put, stick in

➤ **Antonyms**
delete, extract, pull out, remove, take out, withdraw

insertion *noun* <u>inclusion</u>, addition, implant, interpolation, introduction, supplement

inside adjective **1** inner, interior, internal, inward **2** confidential, classified, exclusive, internal, private, restricted, secret ♦ adverb **3** indoors, under cover, within ♦ noun **4** interior, contents **5** insides Informal stomach, belly, bowels, entrails, guts, innards (informal), viscera, vitals

► Antonyms
adjective ≠inner: exterior, external, outer, outermost, outside, outward

insidious adjective stealthy, deceptive, sly, smooth, sneaking, subtle, surreptitious

► Antonyms
artless, conspicuous, forthright, honest, obvious, open, sincere, straightforward

insight noun understanding, awareness, comprehension, discernment, judgment, observation, penetration, perception, perspicacity, vision

insignia noun badge, crest, emblem, symbol

insignificance noun unimportance, inconsequence, irrelevance, meaninglessness, pettiness, triviality, worthlessness

► Antonyms
consequence, importance, meaningfulness, relevance, significance, weight, worth

insignificant adjective unimportant, inconsequential, irrelevant, meaningless, minor, nondescript, paltry, petty, trifling, trivial

► Antonyms
consequential, considerable, essential, important, meaningful, momentous, relevant, significant, substantial, vital, weighty

insincere adjective deceitful, dishonest, disingenuous, duplicitous, false, hollow, hypocritical, lying, two-faced, untruthful

► Antonyms
direct, earnest, genuine, honest, sincere, straightforward, truthful

insincerity noun deceitfulness, dishonesty, dissimulation, duplicity, hypocrisy, pretence, untruthfulness

► Antonyms
directness, honesty, sincerity, truthfulness

insinuate verb **1** imply, allude, hint, indicate, intimate, suggest **2** ingratiate, curry favour, get in with, worm or work one's way in

insinuation noun implication, allusion, aspersion, hint, innuendo, slur, suggestion

insipid adjective **1** bland, anaemic, characterless, colourless, prosaic, uninteresting, vapid, wishy-washy (informal) **2** tasteless, bland, flavourless, appetizing, watery

► Antonyms
≠bland: colourful, exciting, interesting, lively, stimulating ≠tasteless: appetizing, palatable, piquant, pungent, savoury, tasty

insist verb **1** demand, lay down the law, put one's foot down (informal), require **2** assert, aver, claim, maintain, reiterate, repeat, swear, vow

insistence noun persistence, emphasis, importunity, stress

insistent adjective persistent, dogged, emphatic, importunate, incessant, persevering, unrelenting, urgent

insolence noun rudeness, boldness, cheek (informal), disrespect, effrontery, impertinence, impudence

► Antonyms
civility, courtesy, deference, mannerliness, politeness, respect

insolent adjective rude, bold, contemptuous, impertinent, impudent, insubordinate, insulting

► Antonyms
courteous, deferential, mannerly, polite, respectful

insoluble adjective inexplicable, baffling, impenetrable, indecipherable, mysterious, unaccountable, unfathomable, unsolvable

► Antonyms
comprehensible, explicable, fathomable, solvable

insolvency noun bankruptcy, failure, liquidation, ruin

insolvent adjective bankrupt, broke (informal), failed, gone bust (informal), gone to the wall, in receivership, ruined

insomnia noun sleeplessness, wakefulness

inspect verb examine, check, go over or through, investigate, look over, scrutinize, survey, vet

inspection noun examination, check, checkup, investigation, once-over (informal), review, scrutiny, search, survey

inspector noun examiner, auditor, censor, investigator, overseer, scrutinizer, superintendent, supervisor

inspiration noun 1 revelation, creativity, illumination, insight 2 influence, muse, spur, stimulus
➤ **Antonyms**
deterrent, discouragement

inspire verb 1 stimulate, animate, encourage, enliven, galvanize, gee up, influence, spur 2 arouse, enkindle, excite, give rise to, produce
➤ **Antonyms**
≠stimulate: daunt, depress, discourage, dishearten, dispirit

inspired adjective 1 brilliant, dazzling, impressive, memorable, outstanding, superlative, thrilling, wonderful 2 uplifted, elated, enthused, exhilarated, stimulated

inspiring adjective uplifting, exciting, exhilarating, heartening, moving, rousing, stimulating, stirring
➤ **Antonyms**
depressing, disheartening, dispiriting, dull, uninspiring

instability noun unpredictability, changeableness, fickleness, fluctuation, impermanence, inconstancy, insecurity, unsteadiness, variability, volatility
➤ **Antonyms**
balance, constancy, equilibrium, permanence, predictability, security, stability, steadiness

install verb 1 set up, fix, lay, lodge, place, position, put in, station 2 induct, establish, inaugurate, institute, introduce, invest 3 settle, ensconce, position, plant, system

installation noun 1 setting up, establishment, fitting, instalment, placing, positioning 2 induction, inauguration, investiture 3 equipment, machinery, plant, system

instalment noun portion, chapter, division, episode, part, repayment, section

instance noun 1 example, case, illustration, occasion, occurrence, situation ♦ verb 2 quote, adduce, cite, mention, name, specify

instant noun 1 second, flash, jiffy (informal), moment, split second, trice, twinkling of an eye (informal) 2 juncture, moment, occasion, point, time ♦ adjective 3 immediate, direct, instantaneous, on-the-spot, prompt, quick, split-second 4 precooked, convenience, fast, ready-mixed

instantaneous adjective immediate, direct, instant, on-the-spot, prompt

instantaneously adverb immediately, at once, instantly, in the twinkling of an eye (informal), on the spot, promptly, straight away

instantly adverb immediately, at once, directly, instantaneously, now, right away, straight away, this minute

instead adverb 1 rather, alternatively, in lieu, in preference, on second thoughts, preferably 2 instead of in place of, in lieu of, rather than

instigate verb provoke, bring about, incite, influence, initiate, prompt, set off, start, stimulate, trigger
➤ **Antonyms**
discourage, repress, restrain, stop, suppress

instigation noun prompting, behest, bidding, encouragement, incitement, urging

instigator noun ringleader, agitator, leader, motivator, prime mover, troublemaker

instil verb <u>introduce</u>, engender, imbue, implant, inculcate, infuse, insinuate

instinct noun <u>intuition</u>, faculty, gift, impulse, knack, predisposition, proclivity, talent, tendency

instinctive adjective <u>inborn</u>, automatic, inherent, innate, intuitive, involuntary, natural, reflex, spontaneous, unpremeditated, visceral

➤ **Antonyms**
acquired, considered, premeditated, thinking, voluntary

instinctively adverb <u>intuitively</u>, automatically, by instinct, involuntarily, naturally, without thinking

institute noun 1 <u>society</u>, academy, association, college, foundation, guild, institution, school ♦ verb 2 <u>establish</u>, fix, found, initiate, introduce, launch, organize, originate, pioneer, set up, start

➤ **Antonyms**
verb ≠<u>establish</u>: abandon, abolish, cancel, cease, discontinue, end, stop, suspend, terminate

institution noun 1 <u>establishment</u>, academy, college, foundation, institute, school, society 2 <u>custom</u>, convention, law, practice, ritual, rule, tradition

institutional adjective <u>conventional</u>, accepted, established, formal, orthodox

instruct verb 1 <u>order</u>, bid, charge, command, direct, enjoin, tell 2 <u>teach</u>, coach, drill, educate, ground, school, train, tutor

instruction noun 1 <u>order</u>, command, demand, directive, injunction, mandate, ruling 2 <u>teaching</u>, coaching, education, grounding, guidance, lesson(s), schooling, training, tuition

instructions plural noun <u>orders</u>, advice, directions, guidance, information, key, recommendations, rules

instructive adjective <u>informative</u>, edifying, educational, enlightening, helpful, illuminating, revealing, useful

instructor noun <u>teacher</u>, adviser, coach, demonstrator, guide, mentor, trainer, tutor

instrument noun 1 <u>tool</u>, apparatus, appliance, contraption (informal), device, gadget, implement, mechanism 2 <u>means</u>, agency, agent, mechanism, medium, organ, vehicle

instrumental adjective <u>active</u>, contributory, helpful, influential, involved, useful

insubordinate adjective <u>disobedient</u>, defiant, disorderly, mutinous, rebellious, recalcitrant, refractory, undisciplined, ungovernable, unruly

➤ **Antonyms**
compliant, deferential, disciplined, docile, obedient, submissive, subservient

insubordination noun <u>disobedience</u>, defiance, indiscipline, insurrection, mutiny, rebellion, recalcitrance, revolt

➤ **Antonyms**
acquiescence, compliance, deference, discipline, docility, obedience, submission

insubstantial adjective <u>flimsy</u>, feeble, frail, poor, slight, tenuous, thin, weak

➤ **Antonyms**
firm, solid, strong, substantial, weighty

insufferable adjective <u>unbearable</u>, detestable, dreadful, impossible, insupportable, intolerable, unendurable

➤ **Antonyms**
appealing, attractive, bearable, charming, pleasant

insufficient adjective <u>inadequate</u>, deficient, incapable, lacking, scant, short

➤ **Antonyms**
adequate, ample, enough, plentiful, sufficient

insular adjective <u>narrow-minded</u>, blinkered, circumscribed, inward-looking, limited, narrow, parochial, petty, provincial

➤ **Antonyms**

broad-minded, cosmopolitan, liberal, open-minded, tolerant, worldly

insulate verb <u>isolate</u>, close off, cocoon, cushion, cut off, protect, sequester, shield

insult verb 1 <u>offend</u>, abuse, affront, call names, put down, slander, slight, snub ♦ noun 2 <u>abuse</u>, affront, aspersion, insolence, offence, put-down, slap in the face (informal), slight, snub

➤ **Antonyms**

verb ≠<u>offend</u>: flatter, please, praise ♦ noun ≠<u>abuse</u>: compliment, flattery, honour

insulting adjective <u>offensive</u>, abusive, contemptuous, degrading, disparaging, insolent, rude, scurrilous

➤ **Antonyms**

complimentary, flattering, respectful

insuperable adjective <u>insurmountable</u>, impassable, invincible, unconquerable

➤ **Antonyms**

conquerable, surmountable

insupportable adjective 1 <u>intolerable</u>, insufferable, unbearable, unendurable 2 <u>unjustifiable</u>, indefensible, untenable

insurance noun <u>protection</u>, assurance, cover, guarantee, indemnity, safeguard, security, warranty

insure verb <u>protect</u>, assure, cover, guarantee, indemnify, underwrite, warrant

insurgent adjective 1 <u>rebellious</u>, disobedient, insubordinate, mutinous, revolting, revolutionary, riotous, seditious ♦ noun 2 <u>rebel</u>, insurrectionist, mutineer, revolutionary, rioter

insurmountable adjective <u>insuperable</u>, hopeless, impassable, impossible, invincible, overwhelming, unconquerable

insurrection noun <u>rebellion</u>, coup, insurgency, mutiny, revolt, revolution, riot, uprising

intact adjective <u>undamaged</u>, complete, entire, perfect, sound, unbroken, unharmed, unimpaired, unscathed, whole

➤ **Antonyms**

broken, damaged, harmed, impaired, injured

integral adjective <u>essential</u>, basic, component, constituent, fundamental, indispensable, intrinsic, necessary

➤ **Antonyms**

inessential, unimportant, unnecessary

integrate verb <u>join</u>, amalgamate, assimilate, blend, combine, fuse, incorporate, merge, unite

➤ **Antonyms**

disperse, divide, segregate, separate

integration noun <u>assimilation</u>, amalgamation, blending, combining, fusing, incorporation, mixing, unification

integrity noun 1 <u>honesty</u>, goodness, honour, incorruptibility, principle, probity, purity, rectitude, uprightness, virtue 2 <u>soundness</u>, coherence, cohesion, completeness, unity, wholeness

➤ **Antonyms**

≠<u>honesty</u>: corruption, deceit, dishonesty, immorality

intellect noun <u>intelligence</u>, brains (informal), judgment, mind, reason, sense, understanding

intellectual adjective 1 <u>scholarly</u>, bookish, cerebral, highbrow, intelligent, studious, thoughtful ♦ noun 2 <u>academic</u>, egghead (informal), highbrow, thinker

➤ **Antonyms**

adjective ≠<u>scholarly</u>: ignorant, illiterate, stupid, unintellectual, unlearned ♦ noun ≠<u>academic</u>: idiot, moron

intelligence noun 1 <u>understanding</u>, acumen, brain power, brains (informal), cleverness, comprehension, intellect, perception, sense 2 <u>information</u>, data, facts, findings, knowledge, news, notification, report

➤ **Antonyms**

≠<u>understanding</u>: dullness, ignorance, stupidity ≠<u>information</u>: concealment, misinformation

intelligent *adjective* <u>clever</u>, brainy (*informal*), bright, enlightened, perspicacious, quick-witted, sharp, smart, well-informed

➤ **Antonyms**

dim-witted, dull, foolish, ignorant, obtuse, stupid, unintelligent

intelligentsia *noun* <u>intellectuals</u>, highbrows, literati

intelligible *adjective* <u>understandable</u>, clear, comprehensible, distinct, lucid, open, plain

➤ **Antonyms**

confused, garbled, incomprehensible, puzzling, unclear, unintelligible

intemperate *adjective* <u>excessive</u>, extreme, immoderate, profligate, self-indulgent, unbridled, unrestrained, wild

➤ **Antonyms**

moderate, restrained, self-controlled, temperate

intend *verb* <u>plan</u>, aim, have in mind *or* view, mean, propose, purpose

intense *adjective* 1 <u>extreme</u>, acute, deep, excessive, fierce, great, powerful, profound, severe 2 <u>passionate</u>, ardent, fanatical, fervent, fierce, heightened, impassioned, vehement

➤ **Antonyms**

≠<u>extreme</u>: easy, gentle, mild, moderate, slight ≠<u>passionate</u>: casual, cool, indifferent, subdued, weak

intensify *verb* <u>increase</u>, add to, aggravate, deepen, escalate, heighten, magnify, redouble, reinforce, sharpen, strengthen

➤ **Antonyms**

damp down, decrease, dilute, diminish, dull, lessen, minimize, weaken

intensity *noun* <u>force</u>, ardour, emotion, fanaticism, fervour, fierceness, passion, strength, vehemence

intensive *adjective* <u>concentrated</u>, comprehensive, demanding, exhaustive, in-depth, thorough, thoroughgoing

intent *noun* 1 <u>intention</u>, aim, design, end, goal, meaning, object, objective, plan, purpose ◆ *adjective* 2 <u>intense</u>, absorbed, attentive, engrossed, preoccupied, rapt, steadfast, watchful

➤ **Antonyms**

noun ≠<u>intention</u>: chance, fortune ◆ *adjective* ≠<u>intense</u>: casual, indifferent

intention *noun* <u>purpose</u>, aim, design, end, goal, idea, object, objective, point, target

intentional *adjective* <u>deliberate</u>, calculated, intended, meant, planned, premeditated, wilful

➤ **Antonyms**

accidental, inadvertent, unintentional, unplanned

intentionally *adverb* <u>deliberately</u>, designedly, on purpose, wilfully

inter *verb* <u>bury</u>, entomb, lay to rest

intercede *verb* <u>mediate</u>, arbitrate, intervene, plead

intercept *verb* <u>seize</u>, block, catch, cut off, head off, interrupt, obstruct, stop

interchange *verb* 1 <u>switch</u>, alternate, exchange, reciprocate, swap ◆ *noun* 2 <u>junction</u>, intersection

interchangeable *adjective* <u>identical</u>, equivalent, exchangeable, reciprocal, synonymous

intercourse *noun* 1 <u>sexual intercourse</u>, carnal knowledge, coitus, copulation, sex (*informal*) 2 <u>communication</u>, commerce, contact, dealings

interest *noun* 1 <u>curiosity</u>, attention, concern, notice, regard 3 <u>hobby</u>, activity, diversion, pastime, preoccupation, pursuit 3 *often plural* <u>advantage</u>, benefit, good, profit 4 <u>stake</u>, claim, investment, right, share ◆ *verb* 5 <u>arouse one's curiosity</u>, attract, catch one's eye, divert, engross, fascinate, intrigue

➤ **Antonyms**

noun ≠curiosity: boredom, coolness, disinterest, dispassion, disregard, unconcern ♦ verb ≠arouse one's curiosity: bore, tire, weary

interested adjective **1** curious, attracted, drawn, excited, fascinated, keen **2** involved, concerned, implicated

➤ **Antonyms**

≠curious: apathetic, bored, detached, indifferent, unconcerned, uninterested

interesting adjective intriguing, absorbing, appealing, attractive, compelling, engaging, engrossing, gripping, stimulating, thought-provoking

➤ **Antonyms**

boring, dull, mind-numbing, tedious, tiresome, uninteresting

interface noun connection, border, boundary, frontier, link

interfere verb **1** intrude, butt in, intervene, meddle, stick one's oar in (informal), tamper **2** often with with conflict, clash, hamper, handicap, hinder, impede, inhibit, obstruct

interference noun **1** intrusion, intervention, meddling, prying **2** conflict, clashing, collision, obstruction, opposition

interim adjective temporary, acting, caretaker, improvised, makeshift, provisional, stopgap

interior noun **1** inside, centre, core, heart ♦ adjective **2** inside, inner, internal, inward **3** mental, hidden, inner, intimate, personal, private, secret, spiritual

➤ **Antonyms**

adjective ≠inside: exterior, external, outer, outside, outward

interloper noun trespasser, gate-crasher (informal), intruder, meddler

interlude noun interval, break, breathing space, delay, hiatus, intermission, pause, respite, rest, spell, stoppage

intermediary noun mediator, agent, broker, go-between, middleman

intermediate adjective middle, halfway, in-between (informal), intervening, mid, midway, transitional

interment noun burial, funeral

interminable adjective endless, ceaseless, everlasting, infinite, long-drawn-out, long-winded, never-ending, perpetual, protracted

➤ **Antonyms**

finite, limited, restricted

intermingle verb mix, blend, combine, fuse, interlace, intermix, interweave, merge

intermission noun interval, break, interlude, pause, recess, respite, rest, stoppage

intermittent adjective periodic, broken, fitful, irregular, occasional, spasmodic, sporadic

➤ **Antonyms**

continuous, steady, unceasing

intern verb imprison, confine, detain, hold, hold in custody

internal adjective **1** inner, inside, interior **2** domestic, civic, home, in-house, intramural

➤ **Antonyms**

≠inner: exterior, external, outer, outermost, outside

international adjective universal, cosmopolitan, global, intercontinental, worldwide

Internet noun information superhighway, cyberspace, the net (informal), the web (informal), World Wide Web

interpose verb interrupt, insert, interject, put one's oar in

interpret verb explain, construe, decipher, decode, elucidate, make sense of, render, translate

interpretation noun explanation, analysis, clarification, elucidation, exposition, portrayal, rendition, translation, version

interpreter noun translator, commentator

interrogate verb question, cross-examine, examine, grill (informal), investigate, pump, quiz

interrogation noun questioning, cross-examination, examination, grilling (informal), inquiry, inquisition, third degree (informal)

interrupt verb 1 intrude, barge in (informal), break in, butt in, disturb, heckle, interfere (with) 2 suspend, break off, cut short, delay, discontinue, hold up, lay aside, stop

interruption noun stoppage, break, disruption, disturbance, hitch, intrusion, pause, suspension

intersection noun junction, crossing, crossroads, interchange

interval noun break, delay, gap, interlude, intermission, pause, respite, rest, space, spell

intervene verb 1 step in (informal), arbitrate, intercede, interfere, intrude, involve oneself, mediate, take a hand (informal) 2 happen, befall, come to pass, ensue, occur, take place

intervention noun mediation, agency, interference, intrusion

interview noun 1 meeting, audience, conference, consultation, dialogue, press conference, talk ♦ verb 2 question, examine, interrogate, talk to

interviewer noun questioner, examiner, interrogator, investigator, reporter

intestines plural noun guts, bowels, entrails, innards (informal), insides (informal), viscera

intimacy noun familiarity, closeness, confidentiality

➤ **Antonyms**

aloofness, coldness, detachment, distance, remoteness

intimate[1] adjective 1 close, bosom, confidential, dear, near, thick (informal) 2 private, confidential, personal, secret 3 detailed, deep, exhaustive, firsthand, immediate, in-depth, profound, thorough 4 snug, comfy (informal), cosy, friendly, warm ♦ noun 5 friend, close friend, confidant or confidante, (constant) companion, crony

➤ **Antonyms**

adjective ≠close: distant, remote, superficial ≠private: known, open, public ♦ noun ≠friend: enemy, foe, stranger

intimate[2] verb 1 suggest, hint, imply, indicate, insinuate 2 announce, communicate, declare, make known, state

intimately adverb 1 confidingly, affectionately, confidentially, familiarly, personally, tenderly, warmly 2 in detail, fully, inside out, thoroughly, very well

intimation noun 1 hint, allusion, indication, inkling, insinuation, reminder, suggestion, warning 2 announcement, communication, declaration, notice

intimidate verb frighten, browbeat, bully, coerce, daunt, overawe, scare, subdue, terrorize, threaten

intimidation noun bullying, armtwisting (informal), browbeating, coercion, menaces, pressure, terrorization, threat(s)

intolerable adjective unbearable, excruciating, impossible, insufferable, insupportable, painful, unendurable

➤ **Antonyms**

bearable, endurable, painless, possible, sufferable, supportable, tolerable

intolerance noun narrow-mindedness, bigotry, chauvinism, discrimination, dogmatism, fanaticism, illiberality, prejudice

➤ **Antonyms**

broad-mindedness, liberality, open-mindedness, tolerance, understanding

intolerant adjective narrow-minded, bigoted, chauvinistic, dictatorial, dogmatic, fanatical, illiberal, prejudiced, small-minded

➤ **Antonyms**

broad-minded, liberal, open-minded, tolerant, understanding

intone verb recite, chant

intoxicated adjective 1 drunk, drunken, inebriated, legless (informal), paralytic (informal), plastered (slang), tipsy, under the influence 2 euphoric, dizzy, ecstatic, elated, enraptured, excited, exhilarated, high (informal)

intoxicating adjective 1 alcoholic, strong 2 exciting, exhilarating, heady, thrilling

intoxication noun 1 drunkenness, inebriation, insobriety, tipsiness 2 excitement, delirium, elation, euphoria, exhilaration

intransigent adjective uncompromising, hardline, intractable, obdurate, obstinate, stiff-necked, stubborn, unbending, unyielding

➤ **Antonyms**
acquiescent, compliant, compromising, flexible, open-minded

intrepid adjective fearless, audacious, bold, brave, courageous, daring, gallant, plucky, stout-hearted, valiant

➤ **Antonyms**
afraid, cautious, cowardly, craven, faint-hearted, fearful, timid

intricacy noun complexity, complication, convolutions, elaborateness

intricate adjective complicated, complex, convoluted, elaborate, fancy, involved, labyrinthine, tangled, tortuous

➤ **Antonyms**
clear, easy, obvious, plain, simple, straightforward

intrigue verb 1 interest, attract, fascinate, rivet, titillate 2 plot, connive, conspire, machinate, manoeuvre, scheme ◆ noun 3 plot, chicanery, collusion, conspiracy, machination, manoeuvre, scheme, stratagem, wile 4 affair, amour, intimacy, liaison, romance

intriguing adjective interesting, beguiling, compelling, diverting, exciting, fascinating, tantalizing, titillating

intrinsic adjective inborn, basic, built-in, congenital, constitutional, essential, fundamental, inbred, inherent, native, natural

➤ **Antonyms**
acquired, extraneous, extrinsic

introduce verb 1 present, acquaint, familiarize, make known 2 bring up, advance, air, broach, moot, put forward, submit 3 bring in, establish, found, initiate, institute, launch, pioneer, set up, start 4 insert, add, inject, put in, throw in (informal)

introduction noun 1 launch, establishment, inauguration, institution, pioneering 2 opening, foreword, intro (informal), lead-in, preamble, preface, prelude, prologue

➤ **Antonyms**
≠launch: completion, elimination, termination ≠opening: conclusion, end, epilogue

introductory adjective preliminary, first, inaugural, initial, opening, preparatory

➤ **Antonyms**
closing, concluding, final, last, terminating

introspective adjective inward-looking, brooding, contemplative, introverted, meditative, pensive

introverted adjective introspective, inner-directed, inward-looking, self-contained, withdrawn

intrude verb interfere, butt in, encroach, infringe, interrupt, meddle, push in, trespass

intruder noun trespasser, gatecrasher (informal), infiltrator, interloper, invader, prowler

intrusion noun invasion, encroachment, infringement, interference, interruption, trespass

intrusive adjective interfering, impertinent, importunate, meddlesome, nosy (informal), presumptuous, pushy (informal), uncalled-for, unwanted

intuition noun instinct, hunch, insight, perception, presentiment, sixth sense

intuitive adjective instinctive, innate, spontaneous, untaught

inundate verb flood, drown, engulf, immerse, overflow, overrun, overwhelm, submerge, swamp

invade *verb* **1** <u>attack</u>, assault, burst in, descend upon, encroach, infringe, make inroads, occupy, raid, violate **2** <u>infest</u>, overrun, permeate, pervade, swarm over

invader *noun* <u>attacker</u>, aggressor, plunderer, raider, trespasser

invalid[1] *noun* **1** <u>patient</u>, convalescent, valetudinarian ♦ *adjective* **2** <u>disabled</u>, ailing, bedridden, frail, ill, infirm, sick

invalid[2] *adjective* <u>null and void</u>, fallacious, false, illogical, inoperative, irrational, unfounded, unsound, void, worthless

➤ **Antonyms**

logical, operative, rational, sound, true, valid, viable

invalidate *verb* <u>nullify</u>, annul, cancel, overthrow, undermine, undo

➤ **Antonyms**

authorize, empower, ratify, sanction, validate

invaluable *adjective* <u>precious</u>, inestimable, priceless, valuable, worth one's *or* its weight in gold

➤ **Antonyms**

cheap, rubbishy, valueless, worthless

invariably *adverb* <u>consistently</u>, always, customarily, day in, day out, habitually, perpetually, regularly, unfailingly, without exception

invasion *noun* **1** <u>attack</u>, assault, campaign, foray, incursion, inroad, offensive, onslaught, raid **2** <u>intrusion</u>, breach, encroachment, infraction, infringement, usurpation, violation

invective *noun* <u>abuse</u>, censure, denunciation, diatribe, tirade, tongue-lashing, vilification, vituperation

invent *verb* **1** <u>create</u>, coin, conceive, design, devise, discover, formulate, improvise, originate, think up **2** <u>make up</u>, concoct, cook up (*informal*), fabricate, feign, forge, manufacture, trump up

invention *noun* **1** <u>creation</u>, brain-child (*informal*), contraption, contrivance, design, device, discovery, gadget, instrument **2** <u>creativity</u>, genius, imagination, ingenuity, inventiveness, originality, resourcefulness **3** <u>fiction</u>, falsehood, fantasy, forgery, lie, untruth, yarn

inventive *adjective* <u>creative</u>, fertile, imaginative, ingenious, innovative, inspired, original, resourceful

➤ **Antonyms**

imitative, trite, unimaginative, uninspired, uninventive

inventor *noun* <u>creator</u>, architect, author, coiner, designer, maker, originator

inventory *noun* <u>list</u>, account, catalogue, file, record, register, roll, roster

inverse *adjective* <u>opposite</u>, contrary, converse, reverse, reversed, transposed

invert *verb* <u>overturn</u>, reverse, transpose, upset, upturn

invest *verb* **1** <u>spend</u>, advance, devote, lay out, put in, sink **2** <u>empower</u>, authorize, charge, license, sanction, vest

investigate *verb* <u>examine</u>, explore, go into, inquire into, inspect, look into, probe, research, study

investigation *noun* <u>examination</u>, exploration, inquest, inquiry, inspection, probe, review, search, study, survey

investigator *noun* <u>examiner</u>, inquirer, (private) detective, private eye (*informal*), researcher, sleuth

investiture *noun* <u>installation</u>, enthronement, inauguration, induction, ordination

investment *noun* **1** <u>transaction</u>, speculation, venture **2** <u>stake</u>, ante (*informal*), contribution

inveterate *adjective* <u>long-standing</u>, chronic, confirmed, deep-seated, dyed-in-the-wool, entrenched, habitual, hardened, incorrigible, incurable

invidious *adjective* <u>undesirable</u>,

hateful, thankless, unpleasant

➤ **Antonyms**

desirable, pleasant

invigilate verb <u>watch over</u>, conduct, keep an eye on, oversee, preside over, run, superintend, supervise

invigorate verb <u>refresh</u>, energize, enliven, exhilarate, fortify, galvanize, liven up, revitalize, stimulate

invincible adjective <u>unbeatable</u>, impregnable, indestructible, indomitable, insuperable, invulnerable, unassailable, unconquerable

➤ **Antonyms**

beatable, conquerable, defenceless, powerless, unprotected, vulnerable, weak

inviolable adjective <u>sacrosanct</u>, hallowed, holy, inalienable, sacred, unalterable

inviolate adjective <u>intact</u>, entire, pure, unbroken, undefiled, unhurt, unpolluted, unsullied, untouched, whole

➤ **Antonyms**

broken, defiled, polluted, sullied, touched, violated

invisible adjective <u>unseen</u>, imperceptible, indiscernible

➤ **Antonyms**

discernible, perceptible, seen, visible

invitation noun <u>request</u>, call, invite (informal), summons

invite verb <u>request</u>, ask, beg, bid, summon 2 <u>encourage</u>, ask for (informal), attract, court, entice, provoke, tempt, welcome

inviting adjective <u>tempting</u>, alluring, appealing, attractive, enticing, mouthwatering, seductive, welcoming

➤ **Antonyms**

offensive, off-putting (Brit. informal), repellent, unappealing, unattractive, undesirable, uninviting, unpleasant

invocation noun <u>appeal</u>, entreaty, petition, prayer, supplication

invoke verb 1 <u>apply</u>, implement,

initiate, put into effect, resort to, use 2 <u>call upon</u>, appeal to, beg, beseech, entreat, implore, petition, pray, supplicate

involuntary adjective <u>unintentional</u>, automatic, instinctive, reflex, spontaneous, unconscious, uncontrolled, unthinking

➤ **Antonyms**

calculated, deliberate, intentional, planned, purposed, voluntary, wilful

involve verb 1 <u>entail</u>, imply, mean, necessitate, presuppose, require 2 <u>concern</u>, affect, draw in, implicate, touch

involved adjective 1 <u>complicated</u>, complex, confusing, convoluted, elaborate, intricate, labyrinthine, tangled, tortuous 2 <u>concerned</u>, caught up, implicated, mixed up in or with, participating, taking part

➤ **Antonyms**

≠<u>complicated</u>: easy, easy-peasy (slang), elementary, simple, simplified, straightforward, uncomplicated

involvement noun <u>connection</u>, association, commitment, interest, participation

invulnerable adjective <u>safe</u>, impenetrable, indestructible, insusceptible, invincible, proof against, secure, unassailable

➤ **Antonyms**

defenceless, insecure, susceptible, unprotected, vulnerable, weak

inward adjective 1 <u>incoming</u>, entering, inbound, ingoing 2 <u>internal</u>, inner, inside, interior 3 <u>private</u>, confidential, hidden, inmost, innermost, personal, secret

➤ **Antonyms**

≠<u>internal</u>: exterior, external, outer, outermost, outside, outward
≠<u>private</u>: open, public

inwardly adverb <u>privately</u>, at heart, deep down, inside, secretly

irate adjective <u>angry</u>, annoyed, cross, enraged, furious, incensed, indignant, infuriated, livid

irksome *adjective* irritating, annoying, bothersome, disagreeable, exasperating, tiresome, troublesome, trying, vexing, wearisome

➤ **Antonyms**
agreeable, enjoyable, gratifying, pleasant, pleasing

iron *adjective* **1** ferrous, chalybeate, ferric **2** inflexible, adamant, hard, implacable, indomitable, rigid, steely, strong, tough, unbending, unyielding

➤ **Antonyms**
≠inflexible: bending, easy, flexible, light, malleable, pliable, soft, weak, yielding

ironic, ironical *adjective* **1** sarcastic, double-edged, mocking, sardonic, satirical, with tongue in cheek, wry **2** paradoxical, incongruous

iron out *verb* settle, clear up, get rid of, put right, reconcile, resolve, smooth over, sort out, straighten out

irony *noun* **1** sarcasm, mockery, satire **2** paradox, incongruity

irrational *adjective* illogical, absurd, crazy, nonsensical, preposterous, unreasonable

➤ **Antonyms**
judicious, logical, rational, reasonable, sensible, sound, wise

irrefutable *adjective* undeniable, certain, incontestable, incontrovertible, indisputable, indubitable, sure, unquestionable

irregular *adjective* **1** uneven, asymmetrical, bumpy, crooked, jagged, lopsided, ragged, rough **2** variable, erratic, fitful, haphazard, occasional, random, spasmodic, sporadic, unsystematic **3** unconventional, abnormal, exceptional, extraordinary, peculiar, unofficial, unorthodox, unusual

➤ **Antonyms**
≠uneven: balanced, equal, even, regular, smooth, symmetrical, ≠variable: certain, invariable, methodical, reliable, steady, systematic ≠unconventional: conventional, normal, orthodox, proper, regular, standard, usual

irregularity *noun* **1** unevenness, asymmetry, bumpiness, jaggedness, lopsidedness, raggedness, roughness **2** uncertainty, desultoriness, disorganization, haphazardness **3** abnormality, anomaly, oddity, peculiarity, unorthodoxy

irrelevant *adjective* unconnected, beside the point, extraneous, immaterial, impertinent, inapplicable, inappropriate, neither here nor there, unrelated

➤ **Antonyms**
applicable, appropriate, connected, pertinent, related, relevant

irreparable *adjective* beyond repair, incurable, irremediable, irretrievable, irreversible

irrepressible *adjective* ebullient, boisterous, buoyant, effervescent, unstoppable

irreproachable *adjective* blameless, beyond reproach, faultless, impeccable, innocent, perfect, pure, unimpeachable

irresistible *adjective* overwhelming, compelling, compulsive, overpowering, urgent

irresponsible *adjective* thoughtless, careless, immature, reckless, scatterbrained, shiftless, unreliable, untrustworthy

➤ **Antonyms**
careful, dependable, levelheaded, mature, reliable, responsible, sensible, trustworthy

irreverent *adjective* disrespectful, cheeky (*informal*), flippant, iconoclastic, impertinent, impudent, mocking, tongue-in-cheek

➤ **Antonyms**
deferential, pious, respectful, reverent

irreversible *adjective* irrevocable, final, incurable, irreparable, unalterable

irrevocable *adjective* fixed, fated, immutable, irreversible, predestined, predetermined, settled, unalterable

irrigate verb <u>water</u>, flood, inundate, moisten, wet

irritability noun <u>bad temper</u>, ill humour, impatience, irascibility, prickliness, testiness, tetchiness, touchiness

► **Antonyms**
cheerfulness, good humour, patience

irritable adjective <u>bad-tempered</u>, cantankerous, crotchety (*informal*), ill-tempered, irascible, oversensitive, prickly, testy, tetchy, touchy

► **Antonyms**
calm, cheerful, composed, even-tempered, good-natured, patient

irritate verb **1** <u>annoy</u>, anger, bother, exasperate, get on one's nerves (*informal*), infuriate, needle (*informal*), nettle, rankle with, try one's patience **2** <u>rub</u>, chafe, inflame, pain

► **Antonyms**
≠<u>annoy</u>: calm, mollify, placate, please, soothe

irritated adjective <u>annoyed</u>, angry, bothered, cross, exasperated, nettled, piqued, put out, vexed

irritating adjective <u>annoying</u>, disturbing, infuriating, irksome, maddening, nagging, troublesome, trying

► **Antonyms**
agreeable, calming, mollifying, pleasant, pleasing, soothing

irritation noun **1** <u>annoyance</u>, anger, displeasure, exasperation, indignation, resentment, testiness, vexation **2** <u>nuisance</u>, drag (*informal*), irritant, pain in the neck (*informal*), thorn in one's flesh

► **Antonyms**
≠<u>annoyance</u>: calm, composure, pleasure, serenity, tranquillity

island noun <u>isle</u>, ait or eyot (*dialect*), atoll, cay or key, islet

isolate verb <u>separate</u>, cut off, detach, disconnect, insulate, segregate, set apart

isolated adjective <u>remote</u>, hidden, lonely, off the beaten track, outlying, out-of-the-way, secluded

isolation noun <u>separation</u>, detachment, remoteness, seclusion, segregation, solitude

issue noun **1** <u>topic</u>, bone of contention, matter, point, problem, question, subject **2** <u>edition</u>, copy, number, printing **3** <u>outcome</u>, consequence, effect, end result, result, upshot **4** <u>children</u>, descendants, heirs, offspring, progeny **5** **take issue** <u>disagree</u>, challenge, dispute, object, oppose, raise an objection, take exception ♦ verb **6** <u>give out</u>, announce, broadcast, circulate, deliver, distribute, publish, put out, release

► **Antonyms**
noun ≠<u>outcome</u>: beginning, cause, inception, start ≠<u>children</u>: parent, sire ♦ verb ≠<u>give out</u>: revoke, withdraw

isthmus noun <u>strip</u>, spit

itch noun **1** <u>irritation</u>, itchiness, prickling, tingling **2** <u>desire</u>, craving, hankering, hunger, longing, lust, passion, yearning, yen (*informal*) ♦ verb **3** <u>prickle</u>, irritate, tickle, tingle **4** <u>long</u>, ache, crave, hanker, hunger, lust, pine, yearn

itching adjective <u>longing</u>, avid, eager, impatient, mad keen (*informal*), raring, spoiling for

itchy adjective <u>impatient</u>, eager, edgy, fidgety, restive, restless, unsettled

item noun **1** <u>detail</u>, article, component, entry, matter, particular, point, thing **2** <u>report</u>, account, article, bulletin, dispatch, feature, note, notice, paragraph, piece

itinerant adjective <u>wandering</u>, migratory, nomadic, peripatetic, roaming, roving, travelling, vagrant

► **Antonyms**
established, fixed, resident, rooted, settled

itinerary noun <u>schedule</u>, programme, route, timetable

J j

jab *verb, noun* poke, dig, lunge, nudge, prod, punch, stab, tap, thrust

jabber *verb* chatter, babble, blether, gabble, mumble, prate, rabbit (on) (*Brit. informal*), ramble, yap (*informal*)

jacket *noun* covering, case, casing, coat, sheath, skin, wrapper, wrapping

jackpot *noun* prize, award, bonanza, reward, winnings

jack up *verb* lift, elevate, hoist, lift up, raise

jaded *adjective* tired, exhausted, fatigued, spent, weary

► **Antonyms**
bright-eyed and bushy-tailed (*informal*), fresh, refreshed

jagged *adjective* uneven, barbed, craggy, indented, ragged, serrated, spiked, toothed

► **Antonyms**
level, regular, rounded, smooth

jail *noun* **1** prison, nick (*Brit. slang*), penitentiary (*U.S.*), reformatory, slammer (*slang*) ♦ *verb* **2** imprison, confine, detain, incarcerate, lock up, send down

jailer *noun* guard, keeper, warden, warder

jam *verb* **1** pack, cram, force, press, ram, squeeze, stuff, wedge **2** crowd, crush, throng **3** congest, block, clog, obstruct, stall, stick ♦ *noun* **4** predicament, deep water, fix (*informal*), hole (*slang*), hot water, pickle (*informal*), tight spot, trouble

jamboree *noun* festival, carnival, celebration, festivity, fête, revelry

jangle *verb* rattle, chime, clank, clash, clatter, jingle, vibrate

janitor *noun* caretaker, conci-erge, custodian, doorkeeper, porter

jar¹ *noun* pot, container, crock, jug, pitcher, urn, vase

jar² *verb* **1** irritate, annoy, get on one's nerves (*informal*), grate, irk, nettle, offend **2** jolt, bump, convulse, rattle, rock, shake, vibrate ♦ *noun* **3** jolt, bump, convulsion, shock, vibration

jargon *noun* parlance, argot, idiom, usage

jaundiced *adjective* **1** cynical, sceptical **2** bitter, envious, hostile, jealous, resentful, spiteful, suspicious

► **Antonyms**
≠cynical: credulous, naive ≠bitter: open-minded, trusting, unbiased

jaunt *noun* outing, airing, excursion, expedition, ramble, stroll, tour, trip

jaunty *adjective* sprightly, buoyant, carefree, high-spirited, lively, perky, self-confident, sparky

► **Antonyms**
dignified, dull, lifeless, sedate, serious, staid

jaw *Slang* ♦ *noun* **1** chat, chinwag (*Brit. informal*), gossip, natter, talk ♦ *verb* **2** talk, chat, chatter, gossip, spout

jaws *plural noun* opening, entrance, mouth

jazz up *verb* enliven, animate, enhance, improve

jazzy *adjective* flashy, fancy, gaudy, snazzy (*informal*)

jealous *adjective* **1** suspicious, mistrustful, possessive, protective, vigilant, wary, watchful **2** envious, covetous, desirous, green, grudging, resentful

► **Antonyms**
≠suspicious: trusting ≠envious: satisfied

jealousy *noun* envy, covetousness, mistrust, possessiveness, resentment, spite, suspicion

jeans *plural noun* denims, Levis (*Trademark*)

jeer *verb* **1** mock, barrack, deride, gibe, heckle, ridicule, scoff, taunt ♦ *noun* **2** <u>mockery</u>, abuse, boo, catcall, derision, gibe, ridicule, taunt

➤ **Antonyms**

verb ≠<u>mock</u>: acclaim, applaud, cheer, clap, praise ♦ *noun* ≠<u>mockery</u>: adulation, applause, cheers, encouragement, praise

jell *verb* **1** <u>take shape</u>, come together, crystallize, materialize **2** <u>solidify</u>, congeal, harden, set, thicken

jeopardize *verb* <u>endanger</u>, chance, expose, gamble, imperil, risk, stake, venture

jeopardy *noun* <u>danger</u>, insecurity, peril, risk, vulnerability

jerk *verb, noun* <u>tug</u>, jolt, lurch, pull, thrust, twitch, wrench, yank

jerky *adjective* <u>bumpy</u>, convulsive, jolting, jumpy, shaky, spasmodic, twitchy

➤ **Antonyms**

flowing, gliding, smooth

jerry-built *adjective* <u>ramshackle</u>, cheap, defective, flimsy, rickety, shabby, slipshod, thrown together

➤ **Antonyms**

sturdy, substantial, well-built, well-constructed

jest *noun* **1** <u>joke</u>, bon mot, crack (*slang*), jape, pleasantry, prank, quip, wisecrack (*informal*), witticism ♦ *verb* **2** <u>joke</u>, kid (*informal*), mock, quip, tease

jester *noun* <u>clown</u>, buffoon, fool, harlequin

jet¹ *noun* **1** <u>stream</u>, flow, fountain, gush, spout, spray, spring **2** <u>nozzle</u>, atomizer, sprayer, sprinkler ♦ *verb* **3** <u>fly</u>, soar, zoom

jet² *adjective* <u>black</u>, coal-black, ebony, inky, pitch-black, raven, sable

jettison *verb* <u>abandon</u>, discard, dump, eject, expel, scrap, throw overboard, unload

jetty *noun* <u>pier</u>, breakwater, dock, groyne, mole, quay, wharf

jewel *noun* **1** <u>gemstone</u>, ornament, rock (*slang*), sparkler (*informal*) **2** <u>rarity</u>, collector's find, gem, humdinger (*slang*),

jewellery *noun* <u>jewels</u>, finery, gems, ornaments, regalia, treasure, trinkets

jib *verb* <u>refuse</u>, balk, recoil, retreat, shrink, stop short

jibe *see* GIBE

jig *verb* <u>skip</u>, bob, bounce, caper, prance, wiggle

jingle *noun* **1** <u>song</u>, chorus, ditty, melody, tune **2** <u>rattle</u>, clang, clink, reverberation, ringing, tinkle ♦ *verb* **3** <u>ring</u>, chime, clatter, clink, jangle, rattle, tinkle

jinx *noun* **1** <u>curse</u>, hex (*U.S. & Canad. informal*), hoodoo (*informal*), nemesis ♦ *verb* **2** <u>curse</u>, bewitch, hex (*U.S. & Canad. informal*)

jitters *plural noun* <u>nerves</u>, anxiety, butterflies (in one's stomach) (*informal*), cold feet (*informal*), fidgets, nervousness, the shakes (*informal*)

jittery *adjective* <u>nervous</u>, agitated, anxious, fidgety, jumpy, shaky, trembling, twitchy (*informal*)

➤ **Antonyms**

calm, composed, laid-back (*informal*), relaxed, together (*slang*), unflustered

job *noun* **1** <u>occupation</u>, business, calling, career, employment, livelihood, profession, vocation **2** <u>task</u>, assignment, chore, duty, enterprise, errand, undertaking, venture, work

jobless *adjective* <u>unemployed</u>, idle, inactive, out of work, unoccupied

jocular *adjective* <u>humorous</u>, amusing, droll, facetious, funny, joking, jovial, playful, sportive, teasing, waggish

➤ **Antonyms**

earnest, humourless, serious, solemn

jog *verb* **1** <u>run</u>, canter, lope, trot **2** <u>nudge</u>, prod, push, shake, stir

joie de vivre *noun* <u>enthusiasm</u>, ebullience, enjoyment, gusto, relish, zest

➤ **Antonyms**

apathy, depression

join verb **1** enrol, enlist, enter, sign up **2** connect, add, append, attach, combine, couple, fasten, link, unite

➤ **Antonyms**

≠enrol: leave, quit, resign ≠connect: detach, disconnect, disengage, disentangle, divide, separate, sever, unfasten

joint adjective **1** shared, collective, combined, communal, cooperative, joined, mutual, united ♦ noun **2** junction, connection, hinge, intersection, nexus, node ♦ verb **3** divide, carve, cut up, dissect, segment, sever

jointly adverb collectively, as one, in common, in conjunction, in league, in partnership, mutually, together

➤ **Antonyms**

individually, separately, singly

joke noun **1** jest, gag (informal), jape, prank, pun, quip, wisecrack (informal), witticism **2** laughing stock, buffoon, clown ♦ verb **3** jest, banter, kid (informal), mock, play the fool, quip, taunt, tease

joker noun comedian, buffoon, clown, comic, humorist, jester, prankster, trickster, wag, wit

jolly adjective happy, cheerful, chirpy (informal), genial, jovial, merry, playful, sprightly, upbeat (informal)

➤ **Antonyms**

doleful, down in the dumps (informal), grave, lugubrious, miserable, morose, serious, solemn

jolt noun **1** surprise, blow, bolt from the blue, bombshell, setback, shock **2** jerk, bump, jar, jog, jump, lurch, shake, start ♦ verb **3** surprise, discompose, disturb, perturb, stagger, startle, stun **4** jerk, jar, jog, jostle, knock, push, shake, shove

jostle verb push, bump, elbow, hustle, jog, jolt, shake, shove

jot verb **1** note down, list, record, scribble ♦ noun **2** bit, fraction, grain, morsel, scrap, speck

journal noun **1** newspaper, daily, gazette, magazine, monthly, periodical, weekly **2** diary, chronicle, log, record

journalist noun reporter, broadcaster, columnist, commentator, correspondent, hack, journo (slang), newsman or newswoman, pressman

journey noun **1** trip, excursion, expedition, odyssey, pilgrimage, tour, trek, voyage ♦ verb **2** travel, go, proceed, roam, rove, tour, traverse, trek, voyage, wander

jovial adjective cheerful, animated, cheery, convivial, happy, jolly, merry, mirthful

➤ **Antonyms**

doleful, grumpy, morose, solemn, unfriendly

joy noun delight, bliss, ecstasy, elation, gaiety, glee, pleasure, rapture, satisfaction

➤ **Antonyms**

despair, grief, misery, sorrow, tribulation, unhappiness

joyful adjective delighted, elated, enraptured, glad, gratified, happy, jubilant, merry, pleased

joyless adjective unhappy, cheerless, depressed, dismal, dreary, gloomy, miserable, sad

joyous adjective joyful, festive, merry, rapturous

jubilant adjective overjoyed, elated, enraptured, euphoric, exuberant, exultant, thrilled, triumphant

➤ **Antonyms**

despondent, doleful, downcast, melancholy, sad, sorrowful

jubilation noun joy, celebration, ecstasy, elation, excitement, exultation, festivity, triumph

jubilee noun celebration, festival, festivity, holiday

judge noun **1** magistrate, beak (Brit. slang), justice **2** referee, adjudicator, arbiter, arbitrator, moderator, umpire **3** critic, arbiter, assessor, authority, connoisseur, expert ♦ verb **4** adjudicate, arbitrate, decide, mediate, referee, umpire **5** consider, appraise, assess, esteem, estimate, evaluate, rate, value

judgment noun **1** <u>opinion</u>, appraisal, assessment, belief, diagnosis, estimate, finding, valuation, view **2** <u>verdict</u>, arbitration, decision, decree, finding, ruling, sentence **3** <u>sense</u>, acumen, discernment, discrimination, prudence, shrewdness, understanding, wisdom

judicial adjective <u>legal</u>, official

judicious adjective <u>sensible</u>, astute, careful, discriminating, enlightened, prudent, shrewd, thoughtful, well-judged, wise

► **Antonyms**

imprudent, injudicious, thoughtless

jug noun <u>container</u>, carafe, crock, ewer, jar, pitcher, urn, vessel

juggle verb <u>manipulate</u>, alter, change, manoeuvre, modify

juice noun <u>liquid</u>, extract, fluid, liquor, nectar, sap

juicy adjective **1** <u>moist</u>, lush, succulent **2** Informal <u>interesting</u>, colourful, provocative, racy, risqué, sensational, spicy (informal), suggestive, vivid

jumble noun **1** <u>muddle</u>, clutter, confusion, disarray, disorder, mess, mishmash, mixture ♦ verb **2** <u>mix</u>, confuse, disorder, disorganize, mistake, muddle, shuffle

jumbo adjective <u>giant</u>, gigantic, huge, immense, large, oversized

► **Antonyms**

baby, dwarf, micro, mini, pocket, tiny, wee

jump verb **1** <u>leap</u>, bounce, bound, hop, hurdle, skip, spring, vault **2** <u>recoil</u>, flinch, jerk, start, wince **3** <u>increase</u>, advance, ascend, escalate, rise, surge **4** <u>miss</u>, avoid, evade, omit, skip ♦ noun **5** <u>leap</u>, bound, hop, skip, spring, vault **6** <u>rise</u>, advance, increase, increment, upsurge, upturn **7** <u>interruption</u>, break, gap, hiatus, lacuna, space

jumped-up adjective <u>conceited</u>, arrogant, insolent, overbearing, pompous, presumptuous

jumper noun <u>sweater</u>, jersey, pullover, woolly

jumpy adjective <u>nervous</u>, agitated, antsy (informal), anxious, apprehensive, fidgety, jittery (informal), on edge, restless, tense

► **Antonyms**

calm, composed, laid-back (informal), together (slang)

junction noun <u>connection</u>, coupling, linking, union

juncture noun <u>moment</u>, occasion, point, time

junior adjective <u>minor</u>, inferior, lesser, lower, secondary, subordinate, younger

► **Antonyms**

elder, higher-ranking, older, senior, superior

junk noun <u>rubbish</u>, clutter, debris, litter, odds and ends, refuse, scrap, trash, waste

jurisdiction noun **1** <u>authority</u>, command, control, influence, power, rule **2** <u>range</u>, area, bounds, compass, field, province, scope, sphere

just adverb **1** <u>recently</u>, hardly, lately, only now, scarcely **2** <u>merely</u>, by the skin of one's teeth, only, simply, solely **3** <u>exactly</u>, absolutely, completely, entirely, perfectly, precisely ♦ adjective **4** <u>fair</u>, conscientious, equitable, fair-minded, good, honest, upright, virtuous **5** <u>fitting</u>, appropriate, apt, deserved, due, justified, merited, proper, rightful

► **Antonyms**

adjective ≠fair: corrupt, devious, dishonest, inequitable, prejudiced, unfair, unjust ≠fitting: inappropriate, undeserved, unfit

justice noun **1** <u>fairness</u>, equity, honesty, integrity, law, legality, legitimacy, right **2** <u>judge</u>, magistrate

► **Antonyms**

≠fairness: dishonesty, favouritism, inequity, injustice, unfairness, wrong

justifiable adjective <u>reasonable</u>, acceptable, defensible, excusable, legitimate, sensible, understandable, valid, warrantable

► **Antonyms**
indefensible, inexcusable, unreasonable, unwarranted

justification noun 1 explanation, defence, excuse, rationalization, vindication 2 reason, basis, grounds, warrant

justify verb explain, defend, exculpate, excuse, exonerate, support, uphold, vindicate, warrant

justly adverb properly, correctly, equitably, fairly, lawfully

jut verb stick out, bulge, extend, overhang, poke, project, protrude

juvenile adjective 1 young, babyish, callow, childish, immature, inexperienced, infantile, puerile, youthful ♦ noun 2 child, adolescent, boy, girl, infant, minor, youth

► **Antonyms**
adjective ≠young: adult, grownup, mature ♦ noun ≠child: adult, grown-up

juxtaposition noun proximity, closeness, contact, nearness, propinquity, vicinity

K k

kamikaze adjective self-destructive, foolhardy, suicidal

keel over verb collapse, black out (informal), faint, pass out

keen adjective 1 eager, ardent, avid, enthusiastic, impassioned, intense, zealous 2 astute, canny, clever, perceptive, quick, shrewd, wise 3 sharp, cutting, incisive, razor-like

► **Antonyms**
≠eager: apathetic, half-hearted, indifferent, lukewarm, unenthusiastic, uninterested ≠astute: dull, obtuse, unperceptive ≠sharp: blunt, dull

keenness noun eagerness, ar-

dour, enthusiasm, fervour, intensity, passion, zeal, zest

keep verb 1 retain, conserve, control, hold, maintain, possess, preserve 2 look after, care for, guard, maintain, manage, mind, protect, tend, watch over 3 store, carry, deposit, hold, place, stack, stock 4 support, feed, maintain, provide for, subsidize, sustain 5 detain, delay, hinder, hold back, keep back, obstruct, prevent, restrain ♦ noun 6 board, food, living, maintenance 7 tower, castle

► **Antonyms**
verb ≠retain: abandon, discard, give up, lose ≠detain: free, liberate, release

keeper noun guardian, attendant, caretaker, curator, custodian, guard, preserver, steward, warden

keeping noun 1 care, charge, custody, guardianship, possession, protection, safekeeping 2 As in in keeping with agreement, accord, balance, compliance, conformity, correspondence, harmony, observance, proportion

keepsake noun souvenir, memento, relic, reminder, symbol, token

keep up verb maintain, continue, keep pace, preserve, sustain

keg noun barrel, cask, drum, vat

kernel noun essence, core, germ, gist, nub, pith, substance

key noun 1 opener, latchkey 2 answer, explanation, solution ♦ adjective 3 essential, crucial, decisive, fundamental, important, leading, main, major, pivotal, principal

► **Antonyms**
adjective ≠essential: minor, secondary, subsidiary

key in verb type, enter, input, keyboard

keynote noun heart, centre, core, essence, gist, substance, theme

kick verb 1 boot, punt 2 Informal give up, abandon, desist from, leave off, quit, stop ♦ noun 3 Informal <u>thrill</u>, buzz (slang), pleasure, stimulation

kick off verb Informal <u>begin</u>, commence, get the show on the road, initiate, open, start

kick out verb Informal <u>dismiss</u>, eject, evict, expel, get rid of, remove, sack (informal)

kid¹ noun Informal <u>child</u>, baby, bairn, infant, teenager, tot, youngster, youth

kid² verb <u>tease</u>, delude, fool, hoax, jest, joke, pretend, trick, wind up (Brit. slang)

kidnap verb <u>abduct</u>, capture, hijack, hold to ransom, seize

kill verb 1 <u>slay</u>, assassinate, butcher, destroy, execute, exterminate, liquidate, massacre, murder, slaughter 2 Informal <u>suppress</u>, extinguish, halt, quash, quell, scotch, smother, stifle, stop

killer noun <u>assassin</u>, butcher, cutthroat, executioner, exterminator, gunman, hit man (slang), murderer, slayer

killing adjective 1 Informal <u>tiring</u>, debilitating, exhausting, fatiguing, punishing 2 Informal <u>hilarious</u>, comical, ludicrous, uproarious ♦ noun 3 <u>slaughter</u>, bloodshed, carnage, extermination, homicide, manslaughter, massacre, murder, slaying 4 Informal <u>bonanza</u>, bomb (slang), cleanup (informal), coup, gain, profit, success, windfall

killjoy noun <u>spoilsport</u>, dampener, wet blanket (informal)

kin noun <u>family</u>, kindred, kinsfolk, relations, relatives

kind¹ adjective <u>considerate</u>, benign, charitable, compassionate, courteous, friendly, generous, humane, kindly, obliging, philanthropic, tender-hearted

► **Antonyms**

cruel, hard-hearted, harsh, heartless, merciless, severe, unkind

kind² noun <u>class</u>, brand, breed, family, set, sort, species, variety

kind-hearted adjective sympathetic, altruistic, compassionate, considerate, generous, good-

natured, helpful, humane, kind, tender-hearted

► **Antonyms**

cold-hearted, cruel, hard-hearted, harsh, heartless, unkind, unsympathetic

kindle verb 1 <u>set fire to</u>, ignite, inflame, light 2 <u>arouse</u>, awaken, induce, inspire, provoke, rouse, stimulate, stir

► **Antonyms**

extinguish, quench

kindliness noun <u>kindness</u>, amiability, benevolence, charity, compassion, friendliness, gentleness, humanity, kind-heartedness

kindly adjective 1 <u>benevolent</u>, benign, compassionate, good-natured, helpful, kind, pleasant, sympathetic, warm ♦ adverb 2 <u>benevolently</u>, agreeably, cordially, graciously, politely, tenderly, thoughtfully

► **Antonyms**

adjective ≠<u>benevolent</u>: cruel, harsh, malevolent, malicious, mean, spiteful, unsympathetic ♦ adverb ≠<u>benevolently</u>: cruelly, harshly, malevolently, maliciously, spitefully, unkindly

kindness noun <u>goodwill</u>, benevolence, charity, compassion, generosity, humanity, kindliness, philanthropy, understanding

► **Antonyms**

animosity, callousness, cold-heartedness, cruelty, hard-heartedness, heartlessness, ill will, inhumanity, malevolence, malice, misanthropy

kindred adjective 1 <u>similar</u>, akin, corresponding, like, matching, related ♦ noun 2 <u>family</u>, kin, kinsfolk, relations, relatives

king noun <u>ruler</u>, emperor, monarch, sovereign

kingdom noun <u>country</u>, nation, realm, state, territory

kink noun 1 <u>twist</u>, bend, coil, wrinkle 2 <u>quirk</u>, eccentricity, fetish, foible, idiosyncrasy, vagary, whim

kinky adjective 1 Slang <u>perverted</u>, depraved, deviant, pervy (slang), unnatural, warped **2** <u>twisted</u>, coiled, curled, tangled **3** *Slang* <u>weird</u>, eccentric, odd, outlandish, peculiar, queer, quirky, strange

kinship *noun* **1** <u>relation</u>, consanguinity, kin, ties of blood **2** <u>similarity</u>, affinity, association, connection, correspondence, relationship

kiosk *noun* <u>booth</u>, bookstall, counter, newsstand, stall, stand

kiss *verb* **1** <u>osculate</u>, neck (*informal*), peck (*informal*) **2** <u>brush</u>, glance, graze, scrape, touch ♦ *noun* **3** <u>osculation</u>, peck (*informal*), smacker (*slang*)

kit *noun* <u>equipment</u>, apparatus, gear, paraphernalia, tackle, tools

kit out *verb* <u>equip</u>, accoutre, arm, deck out, fit out, fix up, furnish, provide with, supply

knack *noun* <u>skill</u>, ability, aptitude, capacity, expertise, facility, gift, propensity, talent, trick

➤ **Antonyms**

awkwardness, clumsiness, ineptitude

knave *noun Archaic* <u>rogue</u>, blackguard, bounder (*old-fashioned Brit. slang*), rascal, rotter (*slang, chiefly Brit.*), scoundrel, villain

knead *verb* <u>squeeze</u>, form, manipulate, massage, mould, press, rub, shape, work

kneel *verb* <u>genuflect</u>, stoop

knell *noun* <u>ringing</u>, chime, peal, sound, toll

knickers *plural noun* <u>underwear</u>, bloomers, briefs, drawers, panties, smalls

knick-knack *noun* <u>trinket</u>, bagatelle, bauble, bric-a-brac, plaything, trifle

knife *noun* **1** <u>blade</u>, cutter ♦ *verb* **2** <u>cut</u>, lacerate, pierce, slash, stab, wound

knit *verb* **1** <u>join</u>, bind, fasten, intertwine, link, tie, unite, weave **2** <u>wrinkle</u>, crease, furrow, knot, pucker

knob *noun* <u>lump</u>, bump, hump, knot, projection, protrusion, stud

knock *verb* **1** <u>hit</u>, belt (*informal*),

cuff, punch, rap, smack, strike, thump **2** *Informal* <u>criticize</u>, abuse, belittle, censure, condemn, denigrate, deprecate, disparage, find fault, run down ♦ *noun* **3** <u>blow</u>, clip, clout (*informal*), cuff, rap, slap, smack, thump **4** *Informal* <u>setback</u>, defeat, failure, rebuff, rejection, reversal

knockabout *adjective* <u>boisterous</u>, farcical, riotous, rollicking, slapstick

knock about *or* **around** *verb* **1** <u>wander</u>, ramble, range, roam, rove, travel **2** <u>hit</u>, abuse, batter, beat up (*informal*), maltreat, manhandle, maul, mistreat, strike

knock down *verb* <u>demolish</u>, destroy, fell, level, raze

knock off *verb* **1** *Informal* <u>stop work</u>, clock off, clock out, finish **2** *Slang* <u>steal</u>, nick (*slang, chiefly Brit.*), pinch, rob, thieve

knockout *noun* **1** <u>killer blow</u>, coup de grâce, KO or K.O. (*slang*) **2** *Informal* <u>success</u>, hit, sensation, smash, smash hit, triumph, winner

➤ **Antonyms**

≠*success*: failure, flop (*informal*)

knot *noun* **1** <u>connection</u>, bond, joint, ligature, loop, tie **2** <u>cluster</u>, bunch, clump, collection ♦ *verb* **3** <u>tie</u>, bind, loop, secure, tether

know *verb* **1** <u>understand</u>, comprehend, feel certain, notice, perceive, realize, recognize, see **2** <u>be acquainted with</u>, be familiar with, have dealings with, have knowledge of, recognize

➤ **Antonyms**

≠*understand*: misunderstand ≠*be acquainted with*: be ignorant, be unfamiliar with

know-how *noun Informal* <u>capability</u>, ability, aptitude, expertise, ingenuity, knack, knowledge, savoir-faire, skill, talent

knowing *adjective* <u>meaningful</u>, expressive, significant

knowingly *adverb* <u>deliberately</u>, consciously, intentionally, on purpose, purposely, wilfully, wittingly

knowledge noun 1 learning, education, enlightenment, erudition, instruction, intelligence, scholarship, wisdom 2 acquaintance, familiarity, intimacy

➤ **Antonyms**

≠learning: ignorance, illiteracy ≠acquaintance: unfamiliarity

knowledgeable adjective 1 well-informed, au fait, aware, clued-up (informal), cognizant, conversant, experienced, familiar, in the know (informal), in the loop 2 intelligent, educated, erudite, learned, scholarly

known adjective famous, acknowledged, avowed, celebrated, noted, recognized, well-known

➤ **Antonyms**

concealed, hidden, secret, unknown, unrecognized

L l

label noun 1 tag, marker, sticker, ticket ♦ verb 2 tag, mark, stamp

laborious adjective hard, arduous, backbreaking, exhausting, onerous, strenuous, tiring, tough, wearisome

➤ **Antonyms**

easy, easy-peasy (slang), effortless, light

labour noun 1 work, industry, toil 2 workers, employees, hands, labourers, workforce 3 childbirth, delivery, parturition ♦ verb 4 work, endeavour, slave, strive, struggle, sweat (informal), toil 5 overemphasize, dwell on, elaborate, go on about, overdo, strain 6 usually with under be disadvantaged, be a victim of, be burdened by, suffer

➤ **Antonyms**

verb ≠work: relax, rest

laboured adjective difficult, awkward, forced, heavy, stiff, strained

labourer noun worker, blue-collar worker, drudge, hand, manual worker, navvy (Brit. informal)

labyrinth noun maze, intricacy, jungle, tangle

lace noun 1 netting, filigree, openwork 2 cord, bootlace, shoelace, string, tie ♦ verb 3 fasten, bind, do up, thread, tie 4 mix in, add to, fortify, spike 5 intertwine, interweave, twine

lacerate verb tear, claw, cut, gash, mangle, rip, slash, wound

laceration noun cut, gash, rent, rip, slash, tear, wound

lack noun 1 shortage, absence, dearth, deficiency, need, scarcity, want ♦ verb 2 need, be deficient in, be short of, be without, miss, require, want

➤ **Antonyms**

noun ≠shortage: abundance, adequacy, excess, plentifulness, sufficiency, surplus ♦ verb ≠need: enjoy, have, own, possess

lackadaisical adjective 1 lethargic, apathetic, dull, half-hearted, indifferent, languid, listless 2 lazy, abstracted, dreamy, idle, indolent, inert

➤ **Antonyms**

ambitious, diligent, excited, inspired, spirited

lackey noun 1 hanger-on, flatterer, minion, sycophant, toady, yes man 2 manservant, attendant, flunky, footman, valet

lacklustre adjective flat, drab, dull, leaden, lifeless, muted, prosaic, uninspired, vapid

laconic adjective terse, brief, concise, curt, monosyllabic, pithy, short, succinct

➤ **Antonyms**

long-winded, loquacious, rambling, verbose, voluble, wordy

lad noun boy, fellow, guy (informal), juvenile, kid (informal), youngster, youth

laden adjective loaded, burdened, charged, encumbered, full, weighed down

lady noun 1 gentlewoman, dame

2 **woman**, female

lady-killer *noun* womanizer, Casanova, Don Juan, heartbreaker, ladies' man, libertine, philanderer, rake, roué

ladylike *adjective* refined, elegant, genteel, modest, polite, proper, respectable, sophisticated, well-bred

► **Antonyms**
discourteous, ill-bred, ill-mannered, impolite, rude, uncultured, unladylike, unmannerly, unrefined

lag *verb* hang back, dawdle, delay, linger, loiter, straggle, tarry, trail

laggard *noun* straggler, dawdler, idler, loiterer, slowcoach (*Brit. informal*), sluggard, snail

laid-back *adjective* relaxed, casual, easy-going, free and easy, unflappable (*informal*), unhurried

► **Antonyms**
edgy, jittery (*informal*), jumpy, keyed-up, nervous, on edge, tense, uptight (*informal*), wound-up (*informal*)

lair *noun* nest, burrow, den, earth, hole

laissez faire *noun* nonintervention, free enterprise, free trade

lake *noun* pond, lagoon, loch (*Scot.*), lough (*Irish*), mere, reservoir, tarn

lame *adjective* 1 disabled, crippled, game, handicapped, hobbling, limping 2 unconvincing, feeble, flimsy, inadequate, pathetic, poor, thin, unsatisfactory, weak

lament *verb* 1 bemoan, bewail, complain, deplore, grieve, mourn, regret, sorrow, wail, weep ♦ *noun* 2 complaint, lamentation, moan, wailing 3 dirge, elegy, requiem, threnody

lamentable *adjective* regrettable, deplorable, distressing, grievous, mournful, tragic, unfortunate, woeful

lampoon *noun* 1 satire, burlesque, caricature, parody, send-up (*Brit. informal*), skit, takeoff (*informal*) ♦ *verb* 2 ridicule, caricature, make fun of, mock, parody, satirize, send up (*Brit. informal*), take off (*informal*)

land *noun* 1 ground, dry land, earth, terra firma 2 soil, dirt, ground, loam 3 countryside, farmland 4 *Law* property, estate, grounds, realty 5 country, district, nation, province, region, territory, tract ♦ *verb* 6 alight, arrive, come to rest, disembark, dock, touch down 7 *Informal* obtain, acquire, gain, get, secure, win

landlord *noun* 1 owner, freeholder, lessor, proprietor 2 innkeeper, host, hotelier

landmark *noun* 1 feature, monument 2 milestone, turning point, watershed

landscape *noun* scenery, countryside, outlook, panorama, prospect, scene, view, vista

landslide *noun* landslip, avalanche, rockfall

land up *verb* end up, turn up, wind up

lane *noun* road, alley, footpath, passageway, path, pathway, street, way

language *noun* 1 speech, communication, discourse, expression, parlance, talk 2 tongue, dialect, patois, vernacular

languid *adjective* 1 lazy, indifferent, lackadaisical, languorous, listless, unenthusiastic 2 lethargic, dull, heavy, sluggish, torpid

► **Antonyms**
active, alive and kicking, energetic, strong, tireless, vigorous

languish *verb* 1 *Literary* waste away, be abandoned, be neglected, rot, suffer 2 decline, droop, fade, fail, faint, flag, weaken, wilt, wither 3 often with **for** pine, desire, hanker, hunger, long, yearn

► **Antonyms**
≠waste away, decline: bloom, flourish, prosper, thrive

lank *adjective* 1 limp, lifeless, straggling 2 thin, emaciated, gaunt, lean, scrawny, skinny, slender, slim, spare

lanky *adjective* gangling, angular, bony, gaunt, rangy, spare, tall

➤ **Antonyms**

brawny, burly, chubby, fat, plump, portly, short, stocky, stout

lap¹ *noun* circuit, circle, loop, orbit, tour

lap² *verb* **1** ripple, gurgle, plash, purl, splash, swish, wash **2** drink, lick, sip, sup

lapse *noun* **1** mistake, error, failing, fault, indiscretion, negligence, omission, oversight, slip **2** interval, break, breathing space, gap, intermission, interruption, lull, pause **3** drop, decline, deterioration, fall ◆ *verb* **4** drop, decline, degenerate, deteriorate, fall, sink, slide, slip **5** end, expire, run out, stop, terminate

lapsed *adjective* expired, discontinued, ended, finished, invalid, out of date, run out

large *adjective* **1** big, considerable, enormous, gigantic, great, huge, immense, massive, monumental, sizable *or* sizeable, substantial, vast **2 at large: a** in general, as a whole, chiefly, generally, in the main, mainly **b** free, at liberty, on the loose, on the run, unconfined **c** at length, exhaustively, greatly, in full detail

➤ **Antonyms**

≠big: little, minute, short, slender, slight, slim, small, tiny

largely *adverb* mainly, as a rule, by and large, chiefly, generally, mostly, predominantly, primarily, principally, to a great extent

large-scale *adjective* wide-ranging, broad, extensive, far-reaching, global, sweeping, vast, wholesale, wide

lark *Informal* ◆ *noun* **1** prank, caper, escapade, fun, game, jape, mischief ◆ *verb* **2 lark about** play, caper, cavort, have fun, make mischief

lash¹ *noun* **1** blow, hit, stripe, stroke, swipe (*informal*) ◆ *verb* **2** whip, beat, birch, flog, scourge, thrash **3** pound, beat, buffet, dash, drum, hammer, smack, strike **4** censure, attack, blast, criticize, put down, scold, slate (*informal, chiefly Brit.*), tear into (*informal*), upbraid

lash² *verb* fasten, bind, make fast, secure, strap, tie

lass *noun* girl, damsel, lassie (*informal*), maid, maiden, young woman

last¹ *adjective* **1** hindmost, at the end, rearmost **2** most recent, latest **3** final, closing, concluding, terminal, ultimate ◆ *adverb* **4** in or at the end, after, behind, bringing up the rear, in the rear

➤ **Antonyms**

adjective ≠hindmost: first, foremost, leading ≠final: earliest, first, initial, introductory, opening

last² *verb* continue, abide, carry on, endure, keep on, persist, remain, stand up, survive

➤ **Antonyms**

cease, depart, die, end, expire, fade, fail, stop, terminate

lasting *adjective* continuing, abiding, durable, enduring, long-standing, long-term, perennial, permanent

➤ **Antonyms**

ephemeral, fleeting, momentary, passing, short-lived, transient, transitory

latch *noun* **1** fastening, bar, bolt, catch, hasp, hook, lock ◆ *verb* **2** fasten, bar, bolt, make fast, secure

late *adjective* **1** overdue, behind, behindhand, belated, delayed, last-minute, tardy **2** dead, deceased, defunct, departed, former, past **3** recent, advanced, fresh, modern, new ◆ *adverb* **4** belatedly, at the last minute, behindhand, behind time, dilatorily, tardily

➤ **Antonyms**

adjective ≠overdue: beforehand, early, prompt, punctual, seasoned, timely ≠dead: alive, existing ≠recent: old ♦ adverb ≠belatedly: beforehand, early, in advance

lately adverb recently, in recent times, just now, latterly, not long ago, of late

lateness noun delay, belatedness, tardiness

latent adjective hidden, concealed, dormant, invisible, potential, undeveloped, unrealized
➤ **Antonyms**
developed, manifest, realized

later adverb afterwards, after, by and by, in a while, in time, later on, subsequently, thereafter

lateral adjective sideways, edgeways, flanking

latest adjective up-to-date, current, fashionable, modern, most recent, newest, up-to-the-minute

lather noun 1 froth, bubbles, foam, soapsuds, suds 2 Informal fluster, dither (chiefly Brit.), flap (informal), fuss, state (informal), sweat, tizzy (informal) ♦ verb 3 froth, foam, soap

latitude noun scope, elbowroom, freedom, laxity, leeway, liberty, licence, play, space

latter adjective second, closing, concluding, last, last-mentioned
➤ **Antonyms**
antecedent, earlier, foregoing, former, preceding, previous, prior

latterly adverb recently, lately, of late

lattice noun grid, grating, grille, trellis

laudable adjective praiseworthy, admirable, commendable, creditable, excellent, meritorious, of note, worthy
➤ **Antonyms**
base, blameworthy, contemptible, ignoble, lowly, unworthy

laugh verb 1 chuckle, be in stitches, chortle, giggle, guffaw, snigger, split one's sides, titter ♦ noun 2 chuckle, chortle, giggle, guffaw, snigger, titter 3 Informal clown, card (informal), entertainer, hoot (informal), scream

(informal) 4 Informal joke, hoot (informal), lark, scream (informal)

laughable adjective ridiculous, absurd, derisory, farcical, ludicrous, nonsensical, preposterous, risible

laughing stock noun figure of fun, Aunt Sally (Brit.), butt, target, victim

laugh off verb disregard, brush aside, dismiss, ignore, minimize, pooh-pooh, shrug off

laughter noun amusement, glee, hilarity, merriment, mirth

launch verb 1 propel, discharge, dispatch, fire, project, send off, set in motion 2 begin, commence, embark upon, inaugurate, initiate, instigate, introduce, open, start

laurels plural noun glory, credit, distinction, fame, honour, praise, prestige, recognition, renown

lavatory noun toilet, bathroom, cloakroom (Brit.), latrine, loo (Brit. informal), powder room, privy, (public) washroom, water closet, W.C.

lavish adjective 1 plentiful, abundant, copious, profuse, prolific 2 generous, bountiful, free, liberal, munificent, open-handed, unstinting 3 extravagant, exaggerated, excessive, immoderate, prodigal, unrestrained, wasteful, wild ♦ verb 4 spend, deluge, dissipate, expend, heap, pour, shower, squander, waste
➤ **Antonyms**
adjective ≠plentiful: frugal, meagre, miserly, scanty, stingy ≠generous: cheap, miserly, parsimonious, stingy, tight-fisted ≠extravagant: sparing, thrifty ♦ verb ≠spend: begrudge, economize, stint, withhold

law noun 1 constitution, charter, code 2 rule, act, command, commandment, decree, edict, order, ordinance, regulation, statute 3 principle, axiom, canon, precept

law-abiding adjective obedient, compliant, dutiful, good, honest, honourable, lawful, orderly, peaceable

law-breaker noun criminal, convict, crook (informal), culprit, delinquent, felon (formerly criminal law), miscreant, offender, villain, wrongdoer

lawful adjective legal, authorized, constitutional, legalized, legitimate, licit, permissible, rightful, valid, warranted

► **Antonyms**
banned, forbidden, illegal, illegitimate, illicit, prohibited, unauthorized, unlawful

lawless adjective disorderly, anarchic, chaotic, rebellious, riotous, unruly, wild

► **Antonyms**
civilized, compliant, law-abiding, obedient, orderly

lawlessness noun anarchy, chaos, disorder, mob rule

lawsuit noun case, action, dispute, industrial tribunal, litigation, proceedings, prosecution, suit, trial

lawyer noun legal adviser, advocate, attorney, barrister, counsel, counsellor, solicitor

lax adjective slack, careless, casual, lenient, negligent, overindulgent, remiss, slapdash, slipshod

► **Antonyms**
conscientious, firm, scrupulous, severe, stern, strict, stringent

lay¹ verb 1 place, deposit, leave, plant, put, set, set down, spread 2 attribute, allocate, allot, ascribe, assign, impute 3 put forward, advance, bring forward, lodge, offer, present, submit 4 devise, concoct, contrive, design, hatch, plan, plot, prepare, work out 5 arrange, organize, position, set out 6 produce, bear, deposit 7 bet, gamble, give odds, hazard, risk, stake, wager

lay² adjective 1 nonclerical, secular 2 nonspecialist, amateur, inexpert, nonprofessional

layabout noun idler, couch potato (slang), good-for-nothing,

loafer, lounger, ne'er-do-well, skiver (Brit. slang), wastrel

layer noun tier, row, seam, stratum, thickness

layman noun nonprofessional, amateur, lay person, outsider

lay-off noun unemployment, discharge, dismissal

lay off verb dismiss, discharge, let go, make redundant, pay off

lay on verb provide, cater (for), furnish, give, purvey, supply

layout noun arrangement, design, format, formation, outline, plan

lay out verb 1 arrange, design, display, exhibit, plan, spread out 2 Informal spend, disburse, expend, fork out (slang), invest, pay, shell out (informal) 3 Informal knock out, knock for six (informal), knock unconscious, KO or K.O. (slang)

laziness noun idleness, inactivity, indolence, slackness, sloth, sluggishness

lazy adjective 1 idle, inactive, indolent, inert, slothful, slow, workshy 2 lethargic, drowsy, languid, languorous, sleepy, slow-moving, sluggish, somnolent, torpid

► **Antonyms**
active, assiduous, diligent, energetic, industrious, quick

leach verb extract, drain, filter, percolate, seep, strain

lead verb 1 guide, conduct, escort, pilot, precede, show the way, steer, usher 2 cause, dispose, draw, incline, induce, influence, persuade, prevail, prompt 3 command, direct, govern, head, manage, preside over, supervise 4 be ahead (of), blaze a trail, come first, exceed, excel, outdo, outstrip, surpass, transcend 5 live, experience, have, pass, spend, undergo 6 result in, bring on, cause, contribute, produce ► noun 7 first place, precedence, primacy, priority, supremacy, vanguard 8 example, direction, guidance, leadership, model **9** <u>advantage</u>, edge, margin, start **10** <u>clue</u>, hint, indication, suggestion **11** <u>leading role</u>, principal, protagonist, title role ◆ *adjective* **12** <u>main</u>, chief, first, foremost, head, leading, premier, primary, prime, principal

leader *noun* <u>principal</u>, boss (*informal*), captain, chief, chieftain, commander, director, guide, head, ringleader, ruler

➤ **Antonyms**
adherent, disciple, follower, hanger-on, henchman, sidekick (*slang*), supporter

leadership *noun* **1** <u>guidance</u>, direction, domination, management, running, superintendence **2** <u>authority</u>, command, control, influence, initiative, preeminence, supremacy

leading *adjective* <u>principal</u>, chief, dominant, first, foremost, greatest, highest, main, primary

➤ **Antonyms**
following, hindmost, lesser, minor, secondary, subordinate

lead on *verb* <u>entice</u>, beguile, deceive, draw on, lure, seduce, string along (*informal*), tempt

lead up to *verb* <u>introduce</u>, pave the way, prepare for

leaf *noun* **1** <u>frond</u>, blade **2** <u>page</u>, folio, sheet ◆ *verb* **3** <u>leaf through</u> skim, browse, flip, glance, riffle, thumb (through)

leaflet *noun* <u>booklet</u>, brochure, circular, pamphlet

leafy *adjective* <u>green</u>, shaded, shady, verdant

league *noun* **1** <u>association</u>, alliance, coalition, confederation, consortium, federation, fraternity, group, guild, partnership, union **2** *Informal* <u>class</u>, category, level

leak *noun* **1** <u>hole</u>, aperture, chink, crack, crevice, fissure, opening, puncture **2** <u>leakage</u>, drip, percolation, seepage **3** <u>disclosure</u>, divulgence ◆ *verb* **4** <u>escape</u>, drip, exude, ooze, pass, percolate, seep, spill, trickle **5** <u>disclose</u>, divulge, give away, let slip, make

known, make public, pass on, reveal, tell

leaky *adjective* <u>leaking</u>, cracked, holey, perforated, porous, punctured, split

lean [1] *verb* **1** <u>rest</u>, be supported, prop, recline, repose **2** <u>bend</u>, heel, incline, slant, slope, tilt, tip **3** <u>tend</u>, be disposed to, be prone to, favour, prefer **4** <u>lean on</u> <u>depend on</u>, count on, have faith in, rely on, trust

lean [2] *adjective* **1** <u>trim</u>, angular, bony, gaunt, rangy, skinny, slender, slim, spare, thin, wiry **2** <u>poor</u>, barren, meagre, scanty, unfruitful, unproductive

➤ **Antonyms**
≠trim: ample, brawny, burly, fat, full, obese, plump, portly ≠poor: abundant, fertile, plentiful, profuse, rich

leaning *noun* <u>tendency</u>, bent, bias, disposition, inclination, partiality, penchant, predilection, proclivity, propensity

leap *verb* **1** <u>jump</u>, bounce, bound, hop, skip, spring ◆ *noun* **2** <u>jump</u>, bound, spring, vault **3** <u>rise</u>, change, escalation, increase, surge, upsurge, upswing

learn *verb* **1** <u>master</u>, grasp, pick up **2** <u>memorize</u>, commit to memory, get off pat, learn by heart **3** <u>discover</u>, ascertain, detect, discern, find out, gather, hear, understand

learned *adjective* <u>scholarly</u>, academic, erudite, highbrow, intellectual, versed, well-informed, well-read

➤ **Antonyms**
ignorant, illiterate, uneducated, unlearned

learner *noun* <u>beginner</u>, apprentice, neophyte, novice, tyro

➤ **Antonyms**
adept, expert, master, virtuoso, wizard

learning *noun* <u>knowledge</u>, culture, education, erudition, information, lore, scholarship, study, wisdom

lease *verb* hire, charter, let, loan, rent

leash *noun* lead, rein, tether

least *adjective* smallest, fewest, lowest, meanest, minimum, poorest, slightest, tiniest

leathery *adjective* tough, hard, rough

leave¹ *verb* **1** depart, decamp, disappear, exit, go, go away, make tracks, move, pull out, quit, retire, slope off, withdraw **2** forget, leave behind, mislay **3** give up, abandon, drop, relinquish, renounce, surrender **4** cause, deposit, generate, produce, result in **5** entrust, allot, assign, cede, commit, consign, give over, refer **6** bequeath, hand down, will

➤ **Antonyms**

≠depart: appear, arrive, come, stay ≠give up: assume, continue, hold, persist, retain

leave² *noun* **1** permission, allowance, authorization, concession, consent, dispensation, freedom, liberty, sanction **2** holiday, furlough, leave of absence, sabbatical, time off, vacation **3** *As in* take one's leave of departure, adieu, farewell, goodbye, leavetaking, parting, retirement, withdrawal

➤ **Antonyms**

≠permission: denial, prohibition, refusal, rejection ≠holiday: duty ≠departure: arrival, stay

leave out *verb* omit, cast aside, disregard, exclude, ignore, neglect, overlook, reject

lecherous *adjective* lustful, lascivious, lewd, libidinous, licentious, prurient, randy (*informal, chiefly Brit.*), salacious

➤ **Antonyms**

prim, proper, prudish, puritanical, strait-laced, virginal, virtuous

lecture *noun* **1** talk, address, discourse, instruction, lesson, speech **2** telling off (*informal*), dressing-down (*informal*), rebuke, reprimand, reproof, scolding, talking-to (*informal*) ♦ *verb* **3**

talk, address, discourse, expound, hold forth, speak, spout, teach **4** tell off (*informal*), admonish, berate, castigate, censure, reprimand, reprove, scold

ledge *noun* shelf, mantle, projection, ridge, sill, step

leer *noun, verb* grin, gloat, goggle, ogle, smirk, squint, stare

lees *plural noun* sediment, deposit, dregs, grounds

leeway *noun* room, elbowroom, latitude, margin, play, scope, space

left *adjective* **1** left-hand, larboard (*Nautical*), port, sinistral **2** *Of politics* socialist, leftist, left-wing, radical

leftover *noun* remnant, oddment, scrap

left-wing *adjective* socialist, communist, radical, red (*informal*)

leg *noun* **1** limb, lower limb, member, pin (*informal*), stump (*informal*) **2** support, brace, prop, upright **3** stage, lap, part, portion, section, segment, stretch **4** pull someone's leg *Informal* tease, fool, kid (*informal*), make fun of, trick, wind up (*Brit. slang*)

legacy *noun* bequest, estate, gift, heirloom, inheritance

legal *adjective* **1** lawful, allowed, authorized, constitutional, legitimate, licit, permissible, sanctioned, valid **2** judicial, forensic, judiciary, juridical

legality *noun* lawfulness, legitimacy, rightfulness, validity

legalize *verb* permit, allow, approve, authorize, decriminalize, legitimate, legitimize, license, sanction, validate

legal tender *noun* currency, money

legation *noun* delegation, consulate, embassy, representation

legend *noun* **1** myth, fable, fiction, folk tale, saga, story, tale **2** celebrity, luminary, megastar (*informal*), phenomenon, prodigy **3** inscription, caption, motto

legendary *adjective* **1** famous, celebrated, famed, illustrious, immortal, renowned, well-known ≠ mythical, apocryphal, fabled, fabulous, fictitious, romantic, traditional

➤ **Antonyms**

≠famous: unknown ≠mythical: factual, genuine, historical

legibility noun readability, clarity, neatness

legible adjective readable, clear, decipherable, distinct, easy to read, neat

legion noun 1 army, brigade, company, division, force, troop 2 multitude, drove, horde, host, mass, myriad, number, throng

legislation noun 1 lawmaking, enactment, prescription, regulation 2 law, act, bill, charter, measure, regulation, ruling, statute

legislative adjective law-making, judicial, law-giving

legislator noun lawmaker, lawgiver

legislature noun parliament, assembly, chamber, congress, senate

legitimate adjective 1 lawful, authentic, authorized, genuine, kosher (informal), legal, licit, rightful 2 reasonable, admissible, correct, justifiable, logical, sensible, valid, warranted, well-founded ♦ verb 3 legitimize, authorize, legalize, permit, pronounce lawful, sanction

➤ **Antonyms**

adjective ≠lawful: false, fraudulent, illegal, illegitimate, unlawful ≠reasonable: unfair, unfounded, unjustified, unreasonable, unsound

legitimize verb legalize, authorize, permit, sanction

leisure noun spare time, ease, freedom, free time, liberty, recreation, relaxation, rest

➤ **Antonyms**

business, duty, employment, labour, occupation, work

leisurely adjective unhurried, comfortable, easy, gentle, lazy, relaxed, slow

➤ **Antonyms**

brisk, fast, hasty, hectic, hurried, quick, rapid, rushed

lend verb 1 loan, advance 2 give, add, bestow, confer, grant, impart, provide, supply 3 lend itself to be appropriate, be serviceable, suit

length noun 1 Of linear extent distance, extent, longitude, measure, reach, span 2 Of time duration, period, space, span, stretch, term 3 piece, measure, portion, section, segment 4 at length: a at last, at long last, eventually, finally, in the end b in detail, completely, fully, in depth, thoroughly, to the full c for a long time, for ages, for hours, interminably

lengthen verb extend, continue, draw out, elongate, expand, increase, prolong, protract, spin out, stretch

➤ **Antonyms**

abbreviate, abridge, curtail, cut, cut down, diminish, shorten, trim

lengthy adjective long, drawn-out, extended, interminable, long-drawn-out, long-winded, prolonged, protracted, tedious

➤ **Antonyms**

brief, concise, condensed, limited, short, succinct, terse, to the point

leniency noun mercy, clemency, compassion, forbearance, indulgence, moderation, pity, quarter, tolerance

lenient adjective merciful, compassionate, forbearing, forgiving, indulgent, kind, sparing, tolerant

➤ **Antonyms**

harsh, merciless, rigid, rigorous, severe, stern, strict, stringent

lesbian adjective homosexual, dykey (slang), gay, sapphic

less adjective 1 smaller, shorter ♦ preposition 2 minus, excepting, lacking, subtracting, without

lessen verb reduce, contract, decrease, diminish, ease, lower, minimize, narrow, shrink

➤ **Antonyms**

add to, augment, boost, enhance, enlarge, expand, increase, magnify, multiply, raise

lesser adjective <u>lower</u>, inferior, less important, minor, secondary

➤ **Antonyms**

greater, higher, major, primary, superior

lesson noun 1 <u>class</u>, coaching, instruction, period, schooling, teaching, tutoring 2 <u>example</u>, deterrent, message, moral

let¹ verb 1 <u>allow</u>, authorize, entitle, give permission, give the go-ahead, permit, sanction, tolerate 2 <u>lease</u>, hire, rent

let² noun <u>hindrance</u>, constraint, impediment, interference, obstacle, obstruction, prohibition, restriction

letdown noun <u>disappointment</u>, anticlimax, blow, comedown (informal), setback, washout (informal)

let down verb <u>disappoint</u>, disenchant, disillusion, dissatisfy, fail, fall short, leave in the lurch, leave stranded

lethal adjective <u>deadly</u>, dangerous, destructive, devastating, fatal, mortal, murderous, virulent

➤ **Antonyms**

harmless, healthy, innocuous, safe, wholesome

lethargic adjective <u>sluggish</u>, apathetic, drowsy, dull, languid, listless, sleepy, slothful

➤ **Antonyms**

active, alert, animated, energetic, responsive, spirited, stimulated, vigorous

lethargy noun <u>sluggishness</u>, apathy, drowsiness, inertia, languor, lassitude, listlessness, sleepiness, sloth

➤ **Antonyms**

animation, energy, life, liveliness, verve, vigour, vim, vitality, vivacity, zeal, zest

let off verb 1 <u>excuse</u>, absolve, discharge, exempt, exonerate, forgive, pardon, release, spare 2 <u>fire</u>, detonate, discharge, ex-

plode 3 <u>emit</u>, exude, give off, leak, release

let on verb Informal <u>reveal</u>, admit, disclose, divulge, give away, let the cat out of the bag (informal), make known, say

let out verb 1 <u>emit</u>, give vent to, produce 2 <u>release</u>, discharge, free, let go, liberate

letter noun 1 <u>message</u>, communication, dispatch, epistle, line, missive, note 2 <u>character</u>, sign, symbol

let-up noun Informal <u>lessening</u>, break, breathing space, interval, lull, pause, remission, respite, slackening

let up verb <u>stop</u>, abate, decrease, diminish, ease (up), moderate, relax, slacken, subside

level adjective 1 <u>horizontal</u>, flat 2 <u>even</u>, consistent, plain, smooth, uniform 3 <u>equal</u>, balanced, commensurate, comparable, equivalent, even, neck and neck, on a par, proportionate ♦ verb 4 <u>flatten</u>, even off or out, plane, smooth 5 <u>equalize</u>, balance, even up 6 <u>direct</u>, aim, focus, point, train 7 <u>destroy</u>, bulldoze, demolish, devastate, flatten, knock down, pull down, raze, tear down ♦ noun 8 <u>position</u>, achievement, degree, grade, rank, stage, standard, standing, status 9 **on the level** Informal <u>honest</u>, above board, fair, genuine, square, straight

➤ **Antonyms**

adjective ≠<u>horizontal</u>: slanted, tilted, vertical ≠<u>even</u>: bumpy, uneven ≠<u>equal</u>: above, below ♦ verb ≠<u>destroy</u>: build, erect, raise

level-headed adjective <u>calm</u>, balanced, collected, composed, cool, sensible, steady, unflappable (informal)

lever noun 1 <u>handle</u>, bar ♦ verb 2 <u>prise</u>, force

leverage noun <u>influence</u>, authority, clout (informal), pull (informal), weight

levity noun <u>light-heartedness</u>, facetiousness, flippancy, frivolity, silliness, skittishness, triviality

➤ **Antonyms**

earnestness, gravity, seriousness, solemnity

levy verb 1 impose, charge, collect, demand, exact 2 conscript, call up, mobilize, muster, raise ♦ noun 3 imposition, assessment, collection, exaction, gathering 4 tax, duty, excise, fee, tariff, toll

lewd adjective indecent, bawdy, lascivious, libidinous, licentious, lustful, obscene, pornographic, smutty, wanton

lewdness noun indecency, bawdiness, carnality, debauchery, depravity, lasciviousness, lechery, licentiousness, obscenity, pornography, wantonness

liability noun 1 disadvantage, burden, drawback, encumbrance, handicap, hindrance, inconvenience, millstone, nuisance 2 responsibility, accountability, answerability, culpability 3 debt, debit, obligation

liable adjective 1 likely, apt, disposed, inclined, prone, tending 2 vulnerable, exposed, open, subject, susceptible 3 responsible, accountable, answerable, obligated

liaise verb communicate, keep contact, link, mediate

liaison noun 1 communication, connection, contact, hook-up, interchange 2 affair, amour, entanglement, fling, intrigue, love affair, romance

liar noun falsifier, fabricator, fibber, perjurer

libel noun 1 defamation, aspersion, calumny, denigration, smear ♦ verb 2 defame, blacken, malign, revile, slur, smear, vilify

libellous adjective defamatory, derogatory, false, injurious, malicious, scurrilous, untrue

liberal adjective 1 progressive, libertarian, radical, reformist 2 generous, beneficent, bountiful, charitable, kind, open-handed, open-hearted, unstinting 3 tolerant, broad-minded, indulgent, permissive 4 abundant, ample, bountiful, copious, handsome, lavish, munificent, plentiful, profuse, rich

➤ **Antonyms**

≠progressive: conservative, reactionary, right-wing ≠generous: cheap, stingy ≠tolerant: biased, bigoted, intolerant, prejudiced ≠abundant: inadequate, limited, skimpy, small

liberality noun 1 generosity, beneficence, benevolence, bounty, charity, kindness, largesse or largess, munificence, philanthropy 2 broad-mindedness, latitude, liberalism, libertarianism, permissiveness, toleration

liberalize verb relax, ease, loosen, moderate, modify, slacken, soften

liberate verb free, deliver, emancipate, let loose, let out, release, rescue, set free

➤ **Antonyms**

confine, detain, imprison, incarcerate, jail, lock up

liberation noun freeing, deliverance, emancipation, freedom, liberty, release

liberator noun deliverer, emancipator, freer, redeemer, rescuer, saviour

libertine noun reprobate, debauchee, lecher, profligate, rake, roué, sensualist, voluptuary, womanizer

liberty noun 1 freedom, autonomy, emancipation, immunity, independence, liberation, release, self-determination, sovereignty 2 impertinence, impropriety, impudence, insolence, presumption 3 at liberty free, on the loose, unrestricted

➤ **Antonyms**

≠freedom: captivity, constraint, enslavement, imprisonment, restraint, slavery, tyranny

libidinous adjective lustful, carnal, debauched, lascivious, lecherous, randy (informal, chiefly Brit.), sensual, wanton

licence noun **1** certificate, charter, permit, warrant **2** permission, authority, authorization, blank cheque, carte blanche, dispensation, entitlement, exemption, immunity, leave, liberty, right **3** freedom, independence, latitude, leeway, liberty **4** laxity, excess, immoderation, indulgence, irresponsibility

➤ **Antonyms**
≠permission: denial, prohibition, restriction ≠freedom: constraint, restraint ≠laxity: moderation, strictness

license verb permit, accredit, allow, authorize, certify, empower, sanction, warrant

➤ **Antonyms**
ban, debar, disallow, forbid, outlaw, prohibit, proscribe, rule out, veto

licentious adjective promiscuous, abandoned, debauched, dissolute, immoral, lascivious, lustful, sensual, wanton

➤ **Antonyms**
chaste, moral, principled, virtuous

lick verb **1** taste, lap, tongue **2** Of flames flicker, dart, flick, play over, ripple, touch **3** Informal beat, defeat, master, outdo, outstrip, overcome, rout, trounce, vanquish ◆ noun **4** dab, bit, stroke, touch **5** Informal pace, clip (informal), rate, speed

lie[1] verb **1** fib, dissimulate, equivocate, fabricate, falsify, prevaricate, tell untruths ◆ noun **2** falsehood, deceit, fabrication, fib, fiction, invention, prevarication, untruth

lie[2] verb **1** recline, loll, lounge, repose, rest, sprawl, stretch out, be situated, be, be placed, exist, remain

life noun **1** being, sentience, vitality **2** existence, being, lifetime, span, time **3** behaviour, conduct, life style, way of life **4** biography, autobiography, confessions, history, life story, memoirs, story **5** liveliness, animation, energy, high spirits, spirit, verve, vigour, vitality, vivacity, zest

lifeless adjective **1** dead, deceased, defunct, extinct, inanimate **2** dull, colourless, flat, lacklustre, lethargic, listless, sluggish, wooden **3** unconscious, comatose, dead to the world (informal), insensible

➤ **Antonyms**
≠dead: alive, alive and kicking, animate, live, living, vital ≠dull: active, animated, lively, spirited

lifelike adjective realistic, authentic, exact, faithful, natural, true-to-life, vivid

lifelong adjective long-lasting, enduring, lasting, long-standing, perennial, persistent

lifetime noun existence, career, day(s), span, time

lift verb **1** raise, draw up, elevate, hoist, pick up, uplift, upraise **2** revoke, annul, cancel, countermand, end, remove, rescind, stop, terminate **3** disappear, be dispelled, disperse, dissipate, vanish ◆ noun **4** elevator (chiefly U.S.) **5** ride, drive, run **6** boost, encouragement, fillip, gee-up, pick-me-up, shot in the arm (informal)

➤ **Antonyms**
verb ≠raise: dash, descend, drop, fall, hang, lower ≠revoke: establish, impose ◆ noun ≠boost: blow, letdown

light[1] noun **1** brightness, brilliance, glare, gleam, glint, glow, illumination, luminosity, radiance, shine **2** lamp, beacon, candle, flare, lantern, taper, torch **3** aspect, angle, context, interpretation, point of view, slant, vantage point, viewpoint **4** match, flame, lighter ◆ adjective **5** bright, brilliant, illuminated, luminous, lustrous, shining, well-lit **6** pale, bleached, blond, faded, fair, pastel ◆ verb **7** ignite, inflame, kindle **8** illuminate, brighten, light up

➤ **Antonyms**
noun ≠brightness: cloud, dark,

darkness, dusk, shade, shadow ♦ *adjective* ≠bright: dark, dim, dusky, gloomy ≠pale: dark, deep ♦ *verb* douse, extinguish, put out, quench ≠illuminate: cloud, darken, dull

light² *adjective* **1** insubstantial, airy, buoyant, flimsy, portable, slight, underweight **2** weak, faint, gentle, indistinct, mild, moderate, slight, soft **3** insignificant, inconsequential, inconsiderable, scanty, slight, small, trifling, trivial **4** light-hearted, amusing, entertaining, frivolous, funny, humorous, witty **5** nimble, agile, graceful, lithe, sprightly, sylphlike **6** digestible, frugal, modest ♦ *verb* **7** settle, alight, land, perch **8 light on** *or* **upon** come across, chance upon, discover, encounter, find, happen upon, hit upon, stumble on

► **Antonyms**

adjective ≠insubstantial: heavy ≠weak: forceful, strong ≠insignificant: deep, profound, serious, weighty ≠light-hearted: serious, sombre ≠nimble: clumsy ≠digestible: rich, substantial

lighten¹ *verb* brighten, become light, illuminate, irradiate, light up

lighten² *verb* **1** ease, allay, alleviate, ameliorate, assuage, lessen, mitigate, reduce, relieve **2** cheer, brighten, buoy up, lift, perk up, revive

► **Antonyms**

≠ease: aggravate, heighten, increase, intensify, make worse, worsen ≠cheer: depress, oppress, sadden, weigh down

light-headed *adjective* faint, dizzy, giddy, hazy, vertiginous, woozy (*informal*)

light-hearted *adjective* carefree, blithe, cheerful, happy-go-lucky, jolly, jovial, playful, upbeat (*informal*)

► **Antonyms**

cheerless, dejected, depressed, despondent, gloomy, heavy-hearted, low, melancholy, morose, sad

lightly *adverb* **1** moderately, sparingly, sparsely, thinly **2** gently, delicately, faintly, slightly, softly **3** easily, effortlessly, readily, simply **4** carelessly, breezily, flippantly, frivolously, heedlessly, thoughtlessly

► **Antonyms**

≠moderately: abundantly, heavily, thickly ≠gently: firmly, forcefully, heavily ≠easily: arduously, awkwardly, slowly, with difficulty ≠carelessly: carefully, earnestly, seriously

lightweight *adjective* unimportant, inconsequential, insignificant, paltry, petty, slight, trifling, trivial, worthless

► **Antonyms**

important, momentous, serious, significant, substantial, weighty

likable, likeable *adjective* attractive, agreeable, amiable, appealing, charming, engaging, nice, pleasant, sympathetic

like¹ *adjective* similar, akin, alike, analogous, corresponding, equivalent, identical, parallel, same

► **Antonyms**

contrasted, different, dissimilar, divergent, diverse, opposite, unlike

like² *verb* **1** enjoy, be fond of, be keen on, be partial to, delight in, go for, love, relish, revel in **2** admire, appreciate, approve, cherish, esteem, hold dear, prize, take to **3** wish, care to, choose, desire, fancy, feel inclined, prefer, want

► **Antonyms**

≠enjoy, admire: abominate, despise, detest, dislike, hate, loathe

likelihood *noun* probability, chance, possibility, prospect

likely *adjective* **1** inclined, apt, disposed, liable, prone, tending **2** probable, anticipated, expected, odds-on, on the cards, to be expected **3** plausible, believable, credible, feasible, possible, reasonable **4** promising, hopeful, up-and-coming

liken *verb* compare, equate,

match, parallel, relate, set beside

likeness noun **1** <u>resemblance</u>, affinity, correspondence, similarity **2** <u>portrait</u>, depiction, effigy, image, picture, representation

likewise adverb <u>similarly</u>, in like manner, in the same way

liking noun <u>fondness</u>, affection, inclination, love, partiality, penchant, preference, soft spot, taste, weakness

➤ **Antonyms**

abhorrence, aversion, dislike, hatred, loathing, repugnance

limb noun **1** <u>part</u>, appendage, arm, extremity, leg, member, wing **2** <u>branch</u>, bough, offshoot, projection, spur

limelight noun <u>publicity</u>, attention, celebrity, fame, prominence, public eye, recognition, stardom, the spotlight

limit noun **1** <u>end</u>, breaking point, deadline, ultimate **2** <u>boundary</u>, border, edge, frontier, perimeter ♦ verb **3** <u>restrict</u>, bound, check, circumscribe, confine, curb, ration, restrain

limitation noun <u>restriction</u>, check, condition, constraint, control, curb, qualification, reservation, restraint

limited adjective <u>restricted</u>, bounded, checked, circumscribed, confined, constrained, controlled, curbed, finite

➤ **Antonyms**

boundless, limitless, unlimited, unrestricted

limitless adjective <u>infinite</u>, boundless, countless, endless, inexhaustible, unbounded, unlimited, untold, vast

limp[1] verb **1** <u>hobble</u>, falter, hop, shamble, shuffle ♦ noun **2** <u>lameness</u>, hobble

limp[2] adjective <u>floppy</u>, drooping, flabby, flaccid, pliable, slack, soft

➤ **Antonyms**

firm, hard, rigid, solid, stiff

line noun **1** <u>stroke</u>, band, groove, mark, score, scratch, streak, stripe **2** <u>wrinkle</u>, crease, crow's foot, furrow, mark **3** <u>boundary</u>, border, borderline, edge, frontier, limit **4** <u>string</u>, cable, cord, rope, thread, wire **5** <u>trajectory</u>, course, direction, path, route, track **6** <u>occupation</u>, area, business, calling, employment, field, job, profession, specialization, trade **7** <u>row</u>, column, file, procession, queue, rank **8** in line for due for, in the running for ♦ verb **9** <u>mark</u>, crease, furrow, rule, score **10** <u>border</u>, bound, edge, fringe

lineaments plural noun <u>features</u>, countenance, face, physiognomy

lined adjective **1** <u>ruled</u>, feint **2** <u>wrinkled</u>, furrowed, wizened, worn

lines plural noun <u>words</u>, part, script

line-up noun <u>arrangement</u>, array, row, selection, team

linger verb **1** <u>stay</u>, hang around, loiter, remain, stop, tarry, wait **2** <u>delay</u>, dally, dawdle, drag one's feet or heels, idle, take one's time

link noun **1** <u>component</u>, constituent, element, member, part, piece **2** <u>connection</u>, affinity, association, attachment, bond, relationship, tie-up ♦ verb **3** <u>connect</u>, attach, bind, couple, fasten, join, tie, unite **4** <u>associate</u>, bracket, connect, identify, relate

➤ **Antonyms**

verb ≠<u>connect</u>: detach, disconnect, divide, separate, sever, split, sunder

lip noun **1** <u>edge</u>, brim, brink, margin, rim **2** Slang <u>impudence</u>, backchat (informal), cheek (informal), effrontery, impertinence, insolence

liquid noun **1** <u>fluid</u>, juice, solution ♦ adjective **2** <u>fluid</u>, aqueous, flowing, melted, molten, running, runny **3** Of assets <u>convertible</u>, negotiable

liquidate verb **1** <u>pay</u>, clear, discharge, honour, pay off, settle, square **2** <u>dissolve</u>, abolish, annul, cancel, terminate **3** <u>kill</u>, destroy, dispatch, eliminate, exterminate, get rid of, murder, wipe out (*informal*)

liquor noun **1** <u>alcohol</u>, booze (*informal*), drink, hard stuff (*informal*), spirits, strong drink **2** <u>juice</u>, broth, extract, liquid, stock

list¹ noun **1** <u>inventory</u>, catalogue, directory, index, record, register, roll, series, tally ◆ verb **2** <u>itemize</u>, catalogue, enter, enumerate, record, register, tabulate

list² verb **1** <u>lean</u>, careen, heel over, incline, tilt, tip ◆ noun **2** <u>tilt</u>, cant, leaning, slant

listen verb **1** <u>hear</u>, attend, lend an ear, prick up one's ears **2** <u>pay attention</u>, heed, mind, obey, observe, take notice

listless adjective <u>languid</u>, apathetic, indifferent, indolent, lethargic, sluggish

➤ **Antonyms**

active, alert, energetic, full of beans (*informal*), lively, spirited

literacy noun <u>education</u>, knowledge, learning

literal adjective **1** <u>exact</u>, accurate, close, faithful, strict, verbatim, word for word **2** <u>actual</u>, bona fide, genuine, plain, real, simple, true, unvarnished

literally adverb <u>exactly</u>, actually, faithfully, precisely, really, strictly, to the letter, truly, verbatim, word for word

literary adjective <u>well-read</u>, bookish, erudite, formal, learned, scholarly

literate adjective <u>educated</u>, informed, knowledgeable

literature noun <u>writings</u>, letters, lore

lithe adjective <u>supple</u>, flexible, limber, lissom(e), loose-limbed, pliable

litigant noun <u>claimant</u>, party, plaintiff

litigate verb <u>sue</u>, go to court, press charges, prosecute

litigation noun <u>lawsuit</u>, action, case, prosecution

litter noun **1** <u>rubbish</u>, debris, detritus, garbage (*chiefly U.S.*), muck, refuse, trash **2** <u>brood</u>, offspring, progeny, young ◆ verb **3** <u>clutter</u>, derange, disarrange, disorder, mess up **4** <u>scatter</u>, strew

little adjective **1** <u>small</u>, diminutive, miniature, minute, petite, short, tiny, wee **2** <u>young</u>, babyish, immature, infant, junior, undeveloped ◆ adverb **3** <u>hardly</u>, barely **4** <u>rarely</u>, hardly ever, not often, scarcely, seldom ◆ noun **5** <u>bit</u>, fragment, hint, particle, speck, spot, touch, trace

➤ **Antonyms**

adjective ≠small: big, colossal, considerable, enormous, giant, great, huge, immense, large ◆ adverb ≠hardly: certainly, much, surely ≠rarely: always, much ◆ noun ≠bit: lot, many, much

live¹ verb **1** <u>exist</u>, be, be alive, breathe **2** <u>persist</u>, last, prevail **3** <u>dwell</u>, abide, inhabit, lodge, occupy, reside, settle **4** <u>survive</u>, endure, get along, make ends meet, subsist, support oneself **5** <u>thrive</u>, flourish, prosper

live² adjective **1** <u>living</u>, alive, animate, breathing **2** <u>topical</u>, burning, controversial, current, hot, pertinent, pressing, prevalent **3** <u>burning</u>, active, alight, blazing, glowing, hot, ignited, smouldering

livelihood noun <u>occupation</u>, bread and butter (*informal*), employment, job, living, work

liveliness noun <u>energy</u>, animation, boisterousness, dynamism, spirit, sprightliness, vitality, vivacity

lively adjective **1** <u>vigorous</u>, active, agile, alert, brisk, energetic, keen, perky, quick, sprightly **2** <u>animated</u>, cheerful, chirpy (*informal*), sparky, spirited, upbeat (*informal*), vivacious **3** <u>vivid</u>, bright, colourful, exciting, forceful, invigorating, refreshing, stimulating

➤ **Antonyms**

≠vigorous: debilitated, inactive, slow, sluggish, torpid ≠animated: apathetic, dull, lifeless, listless ≠vivid: dull

liven up verb stir, animate, brighten, buck up (informal), enliven, perk up, rouse

liverish adjective 1 Informal sick, bilious, queasy 2 irritable, crotchety (informal), crusty, disagreeable, grumpy, ill-humoured, irascible, splenetic, tetchy

livery noun costume, attire, clothing, dress, garb, regalia, suit, uniform

livid adjective 1 Informal angry, beside oneself, enraged, fuming, furious, incensed, indignant, infuriated, outraged 2 discoloured, black-and-blue, bruised, contused, purple

► **Antonyms**
≠angry: content, delighted, happy, pleased

living adjective 1 alive, active, breathing, existing 2 current, active, contemporary, extant, in use ◆ noun 3 existence, being, existing, life, subsistence 4 lifestyle, way of life

► **Antonyms**
adjective ≠alive: dead, deceased, defunct ≠current: obsolescent, obsolete, out-of-date

load noun 1 cargo, consignment, freight, shipment 2 burden, albatross, encumbrance, millstone, onus, trouble, weight, worry ◆ verb 3 fill, cram, freight, heap, pack, pile, stack, stuff 4 burden, encumber, oppress, saddle with, weigh down, worry 5 Of firearms make ready, charge, prime

loaded adjective 1 tricky, artful, insidious, manipulative, prejudicial 2 biased, distorted, weighted 3 Slang rich, affluent, flush (informal), moneyed, wealthy, well-heeled (informal), well off, well-to-do

loaf[1] noun 1 lump, block, cake, cube, slab 2 Slang head, gumption (Brit. informal), nous (Brit. slang), sense

loaf[2] verb idle, laze, lie around, loiter, lounge around, take it easy

loan noun 1 advance, credit ◆ verb 2 lend, advance, let out

loath, loth adjective unwilling, averse, disinclined, opposed, reluctant

► **Antonyms**
anxious, avid, desirous, eager, enthusiastic, keen, willing

loathe verb hate, abhor, abominate, despise, detest, dislike

loathing noun hatred, abhorrence, antipathy, aversion, detestation, disgust, repugnance, repulsion, revulsion

loathsome adjective hateful, abhorrent, detestable, disgusting, nauseating, obnoxious, odious, offensive, repugnant, repulsive, revolting, vile

► **Antonyms**
adorable, attractive, charming, delightful, enchanting, engaging, fetching, likable or likeable, lovable, lovely

lobby noun 1 corridor, entrance hall, foyer, hallway, passage, porch, vestibule 2 pressure group ◆ verb 3 campaign, influence, persuade, press, pressure, promote, push, urge

local adjective 1 regional, provincial 2 restricted, confined, limited ◆ noun 3 resident, inhabitant, native

locality noun 1 neighbourhood, area, district, neck of the woods (informal), region, vicinity 2 site, locale, location, place, position, scene, setting, spot

localize verb restrict, circumscribe, confine, contain, delimit, limit

locate verb 1 find, come across, detect, discover, pin down, pinpoint, track down, unearth 2 place, establish, fix, put, seat, set, settle, situate

location noun site, locale, place, point, position, situation, spot, venue

lock[1] noun 1 fastening, bolt, clasp, padlock ◆ verb 2 fasten, bolt, close, seal, secure, shut 3 unite, clench, engage, entangle, entwine, join, link 4 embrace, clasp, clutch, encircle, enclose,

grasp, hug, press
lock[2] *noun* strand, curl, ringlet, tress, tuft
lockup *noun* prison, cell, jail or gaol
lock up *verb* imprison, cage, confine, detain, incarcerate, jail, put behind bars, shut up
lodge *noun* 1 cabin, chalet, cottage, gatehouse, hut, shelter 2 society, branch, chapter, club, group ♦ *verb* 3 stay, board, room 4 stick, come to rest, imbed, implant 5 register, file, put on record, submit
lodger *noun* tenant, boarder, paying guest, resident
lodging *noun, often plural* accommodation, abode, apartments, digs (*Brit. informal*), quarters, residence, rooms, shelter
lofty *adjective* 1 high, elevated, raised, soaring, towering 2 noble, dignified, distinguished, elevated, exalted, grand, illustrious, renowned 3 haughty, arrogant, condescending, disdainful, patronizing, proud, supercilious
► **Antonyms**
≠high: dwarfed, low, short, stunted ≠noble: debased, degraded, humble, low, lowly, mean ≠haughty: friendly, modest, unassuming, warm
log *noun* 1 stump, block, chunk, trunk 2 record, account, journal, logbook ♦ *verb* 3 chop, cut, fell, hew 4 record, chart, note, register, set down
loggerheads *plural noun* at loggerheads quarrelling, at daggers drawn, at each other's throats, at odds, feuding, in dispute, opposed
logic *noun* reason, good sense, sense
logical *adjective* 1 rational, clear, cogent, coherent, consistent, sound, valid, well-organized 2 reasonable, plausible, sensible, wise
► **Antonyms**
≠rational: illogical, instinctive, irrational, unorganized ≠reason-

able: illogical, implausible, unlikely, unreasonable
loiter *verb* linger, dally, dawdle, dilly-dally (*informal*), hang about or around, idle, loaf, skulk
loll *verb* 1 lounge, loaf, recline, relax, slouch, slump, sprawl 2 droop, dangle, drop, flap, flop, hang, sag
lone *adjective* solitary, one, only, single, sole, unaccompanied
loneliness *noun* solitude, desolation, isolation, seclusion
lonely *adjective* 1 abandoned, destitute, forlorn, forsaken, friendless, lonesome 2 solitary, alone, apart, companionless, isolated, lone, single, withdrawn 3 desolate, deserted, godforsaken, isolated, out-of-the-way, remote, secluded, unfrequented, uninhabited
► **Antonyms**
≠abandoned: befriended, popular ≠solitary: accompanied, together ≠desolate: bustling, crowded, frequented, populous, teeming
loner *noun Informal* individualist, lone wolf, maverick, outsider, recluse
lonesome *adjective Chiefly U.S. & Canad.* lonely, companionless, desolate, dreary, forlorn, friendless, gloomy
long[1] *adjective* 1 elongated, expanded, extended, extensive, far-reaching, lengthy, spread out, stretched 2 prolonged, interminable, lengthy, lingering, long-drawn-out, protracted, sustained
► **Antonyms**
≠elongated: compressed, contracted, little, short, small ≠prolonged: abbreviated, abridged, brief, momentary, short, short-lived
long[2] *verb* desire, crave, hanker, itch, lust, pine, want, wish, yearn
longing *noun* desire, ambition, aspiration, craving, hope, itch, thirst, urge, wish, yearning, yen (*informal*)
► **Antonyms**
abhorrence, antipathy, disgust,

loathing, revulsion

long-lived *adjective* <u>long-lasting</u>, enduring

long shot *noun* <u>outsider</u>, dark horse

long-standing *adjective* <u>established</u>, abiding, enduring, fixed, long-established, long-lasting, time-honoured

long-suffering *adjective* <u>uncomplaining</u>, easy-going, forbearing, forgiving, patient, resigned, stoical, tolerant

long-winded *adjective* <u>rambling</u>, lengthy, long-drawn-out, prolix, prolonged, repetitious, tedious, tiresome, verbose, wordy

➤ **Antonyms**

brief, concise, curt, laconic, pithy, short, succinct, terse, to the point

look *verb* **1** <u>see</u>, behold (*archaic*), examine, eye, gaze, glance, observe, scan, study, survey, view, watch **2** <u>consider</u>, contemplate **3** <u>seem</u>, appear, look like, strike one as **4** <u>face</u>, front, overlook **5** <u>search</u>, forage, hunt, seek **6** <u>hope</u>, anticipate, await, expect, reckon on ◆ *noun* **7** <u>glimpse</u>, examination, gaze, glance, inspection, observation, peek, sight, view **8** <u>appearance</u>, air, aspect, bearing, countenance, demeanour, expression, manner, semblance

look after *verb* <u>take care of</u>, attend to, care for, guard, keep an eye on, mind, nurse, protect, supervise, take charge of, tend

look down on *verb* <u>disdain</u>, contemn, despise, scorn, sneer, spurn

look forward to *verb* <u>anticipate</u>, await, expect, hope for, long for, look for, wait for

lookout *noun* **1** <u>watch</u>, guard, readiness, vigil **2** <u>watchman</u>, guard, sentinel, sentry **3** <u>watchtower</u>, observation post, observatory, post **4** *Informal* <u>concern</u>, business, worry

look out *verb* <u>be careful</u>, beware,

keep an eye out, pay attention, watch out

look up *verb* **1** <u>research</u>, find, hunt for, search for, seek out, track down **2** <u>improve</u>, get better, perk up, pick up, progress, shape up (*informal*) **3** <u>visit</u>, call on, drop in on (*informal*), look in on **4** **look up to** <u>respect</u>, admire, defer to, esteem, honour, revere

loom *verb* <u>appear</u>, bulk, emerge, hover, impend, menace, take shape, threaten

loop *noun* **1** <u>curve</u>, circle, coil, curl, ring, spiral, twirl, twist, whorl ◆ *verb* **2** <u>twist</u>, coil, curl, knot, roll, spiral, turn, wind round

loophole *noun* <u>let-out</u>, escape, excuse

loose *adjective* **1** <u>slack</u>, easy, relaxed, sloppy **2** <u>free</u>, insecure, unattached, unbound, unfastened, unfettered, unrestricted, untied **3** <u>vague</u>, ill-defined, imprecise, inaccurate, indistinct, inexact, rambling, random **4** *Old-fashioned* <u>promiscuous</u>, abandoned, debauched, dissipated, dissolute, fast, immoral, profligate ◆ *verb* **5** <u>free</u>, detach, disconnect, liberate, release, set free, unfasten, unleash, untie

➤ **Antonyms**

adjective ≠<u>slack</u>: tight ≠<u>free</u>: bound, curbed, fastened, fettered, restrained, secured, tethered, tied ≠<u>vague</u>: accurate, clear, concise, exact, precise ≠<u>promiscuous</u>: chaste, disciplined, moral, virtuous ◆ *verb* ≠<u>free</u>: bind, cage, capture, fasten, imprison

loosen *verb* **1** <u>free</u>, liberate, release, set free **2** <u>untie</u>, detach, separate, undo, unloose **3** **loosen up** <u>relax</u>, ease up or off, go easy (*informal*), let up, soften

loot *noun* **1** <u>plunder</u>, booty, goods, haul, prize, spoils, swag (*slang*) ◆ *verb* **2** <u>plunder</u>, despoil, pillage, raid, ransack, ravage, rifle, rob, sack

lopsided *adjective* <u>crooked</u>,

askew, asymmetrical, awry, cock-eyed, disproportionate, skew-whiff (*Brit. informal*), squint, unbalanced, uneven, warped

lord *noun* 1 <u>master</u>, commander, governor, leader, liege, overlord, ruler, superior 2 <u>nobleman</u>, earl, noble, peer, viscount 3 **Our Lord** *or* **the Lord** Jesus Christ, Christ, God, Jehovah, the Almighty ♦ *verb* 4 **lord it over** <u>order around</u>, boss around (*informal*), domineer, pull rank, put on airs, swagger

lordly *adjective* <u>proud</u>, arrogant, condescending, disdainful, domineering, haughty, high-handed, imperious, lofty, overbearing

lore *noun* <u>traditions</u>, beliefs, doctrine, sayings, teaching, wisdom

lose *verb* 1 <u>mislay</u>, be deprived of, drop, forget, misplace 2 <u>forfeit</u>, miss, pass up (*informal*), yield 3 <u>be defeated</u>, come to grief, lose out

loser *noun* <u>failure</u>, also-ran, dud (*informal*), flop (*informal*)

loss *noun* 1 <u>losing</u>, defeat, failure, forfeiture, mislaying, squandering, waste 2 <u>damage</u>, cost, destruction, harm, hurt, injury, ruin 3 *sometimes plural* <u>deficit</u>, debit, debt, deficiency, depletion 4 **at a loss** <u>confused</u>, at one's wits' end, baffled, bewildered, helpless, nonplussed, perplexed, puzzled, stumped

► **Antonyms**

≠<u>losing</u>: acquisition, finding, gain, preservation, saving, winning ≠<u>damage</u>: advantage, recovery, restoration ≠<u>deficit</u>: save

lost *adjective* 1 <u>missing</u>, disappeared, mislaid, misplaced, vanished, wayward 2 <u>off-course</u>, adrift, astray, at sea, disoriented, off-track

lot *noun* 1 <u>collection</u>, assortment, batch, bunch (*informal*), consignment, crowd, group, quantity, set 2 <u>destiny</u>, accident, chance, doom, fate, fortune 3 **a lot** *or* **lots** <u>plenty</u>, abundance, a great deal, heap(s), load(s) (*informal*),

masses (*informal*), piles (*informal*), scores, stack(s)

loth *see* LOATH

lotion *noun* <u>cream</u>, balm, embrocation, liniment, salve, solution

lottery *noun* 1 <u>raffle</u>, draw, sweepstake 2 <u>gamble</u>, chance, hazard, risk, toss-up (*informal*)

loud *adjective* 1 <u>noisy</u>, blaring, booming, clamorous, deafening, ear-splitting, forte (*Music*), resounding, thundering, tumultuous, vociferous 2 <u>garish</u>, brash, flamboyant, flashy, gaudy, glaring, lurid, showy

► **Antonyms**

≠<u>noisy</u>: quiet, silent, soft ≠<u>garish</u>: dull, sober, sombre

loudly *adverb* <u>noisily</u>, deafeningly, fortissimo (*Music*), lustily, shrilly, uproariously, vehemently, vigorously

lounge *verb* <u>relax</u>, laze, lie about, loaf, loiter, loll, sprawl, take it easy

lout *noun* <u>oaf</u>, boor, dolt, yob *or* yobbo (*Brit. slang*)

lovable, **loveable** *adjective* <u>endearing</u>, adorable, amiable, charming, cute, delightful, enchanting, likable *or* likeable, lovely, sweet

► **Antonyms**

abhorrent, abominable, detestable, hateful, loathsome, obnoxious, odious, offensive, revolting

love *verb* 1 <u>adore</u>, cherish, dote on, hold dear, idolize, prize, treasure, worship 2 <u>enjoy</u>, appreciate, delight in, like, relish, savour, take pleasure in ♦ *noun* 3 <u>passion</u>, adoration, affection, ardour, attachment, devotion, infatuation, tenderness, warmth 4 <u>liking</u>, devotion, enjoyment, fondness, inclination, partiality, relish, soft spot, taste, weakness 5 <u>beloved</u>, darling, dear, dearest, lover, sweetheart, truelove 6 **in love** <u>enamoured</u>, besotted, charmed, enraptured, infatuated, smitten

► **Antonyms**

verb ≠<u>adore</u>, <u>enjoy</u>: abhor,

abominate, detest, dislike, hate, scorn ♦ noun ≠**passion**, liking: abhorrence, abomination, animosity, antagonism, antipathy, aversion, detestation, disgust, dislike, hate, hatred, hostility, ill will, loathing, repugnance ≠**beloved**: enemy, foe

love affair noun <u>romance</u>, affair, amour, intrigue, liaison, relationship

lovely adjective **1** <u>beautiful</u>, adorable, attractive, charming, comely, exquisite, graceful, handsome, pretty **2** <u>enjoyable</u>, agreeable, delightful, engaging, nice, pleasant, pleasing

➤ **Antonyms**
≠**beautiful**: hideous, ugly, unattractive ≠**enjoyable**: abhorrent, detestable, hateful, loathsome, odious, repellent, repugnant, revolting

lover noun <u>sweetheart</u>, admirer, beloved, boyfriend or girlfriend, flame (informal), mistress, suitor

loving adjective <u>affectionate</u>, amorous, dear, devoted, doting, fond, tender, warm-hearted

➤ **Antonyms**
cold, hostile, indifferent, unloving

low adjective **1** <u>small</u>, little, short, squat, stunted **2** <u>inferior</u>, deficient, inadequate, poor, secondrate, shoddy **3** <u>coarse</u>, common, crude, disreputable, rough, rude, undignified, vulgar **4** <u>dejected</u>, depressed, despondent, disheartened, downcast, down in the dumps (informal), fed up, gloomy, glum, miserable **5** <u>ill</u>, debilitated, frail, stricken, weak **6** <u>quiet</u>, gentle, hushed, muffled, muted, soft, subdued, whispered

➤ **Antonyms**
≠**small**: tall, towering ≠**dejected**: cheerful, elated, happy, high ≠**ill**: energetic, strong ≠**quiet**: loud, noisy

lowdown noun Informal <u>information</u>, gen (Brit. informal), info (informal), inside story, intelligence

lower adjective **1** <u>under</u>, inferior,

junior, lesser, minor, secondary, second-class, smaller, subordinate **2** <u>reduced</u>, curtailed, decreased, diminished, lessened ♦ verb **3** <u>drop</u>, depress, fall, let down, sink, submerge, take down **4** <u>lessen</u>, cut, decrease, diminish, minimize, prune, reduce, slash

➤ **Antonyms**
adjective ≠**reduced**: enlarged, higher, increased ♦ verb ≠**drop**: elevate, hoist, lift, raise ≠**lessen**: augment, boost, enlarge, extend, increase, magnify, raise

low-key adjective <u>subdued</u>, muted, quiet, restrained, toned down, understated

lowly adjective <u>humble</u>, meek, mild, modest, unassuming

low-spirited adjective <u>depressed</u>, dejected, despondent, dismal, down, down-hearted, fed up, low, miserable, sad

loyal adjective <u>faithful</u>, constant, dependable, devoted, dutiful, staunch, steadfast, true, trustworthy, trusty, unwavering

➤ **Antonyms**
disloyal, false, perfidious, traitorous, treacherous, unfaithful, untrustworthy

loyalty noun <u>faithfulness</u>, allegiance, constancy, dependability, devotion, fidelity, staunchness, steadfastness, trustworthiness

lubricate verb <u>oil</u>, grease, smear

lucid adjective **1** <u>clear</u>, comprehensible, explicit, intelligible, transparent **2** <u>translucent</u>, clear, crystalline, diaphanous, glassy, limpid, pellucid, transparent **3** <u>clear-headed</u>, all there, compos mentis, in one's right mind, rational, sane

➤ **Antonyms**
≠**clear**: ambiguous, clear as mud (informal), confused, equivocal, incomprehensible, indistinct, muddled, unclear, unintelligible, vague ≠**translucent**: unclear ≠**clear-headed**: confused, irrational, muddled, unclear, vague

luck noun **1** <u>fortune</u>, accident, chance, destiny, fate **2** <u>good fortune</u>, advantage, blessing, godsend, prosperity, serendipity, success, windfall

luckily adverb <u>fortunately</u>, favourably, happily, opportunely, propitiously, providentially

luckless adjective <u>unlucky</u>, cursed, doomed, hapless, hopeless, ill-fated, jinxed, unfortunate

lucky adjective <u>fortunate</u>, advantageous, blessed, charmed, favoured, jammy (Brit. slang), serendipitous, successful

➤ **Antonyms**
bad, unfavourable, unfortunate, unhappy, unlucky

lucrative adjective <u>profitable</u>, advantageous, fruitful, productive, remunerative, well-paid

lucre noun Usually facetious <u>money</u>, gain, mammon, pelf, profit, riches, spoils, wealth

ludicrous adjective <u>ridiculous</u>, absurd, crazy, farcical, laughable, nonsensical, outlandish, preposterous, silly

➤ **Antonyms**
logical, sensible

luggage noun <u>baggage</u>, bags, cases, gear, impedimenta, paraphernalia, suitcases, things

lugubrious adjective <u>gloomy</u>, doleful, melancholy, mournful, sad, serious, sombre, sorrowful, woebegone

lukewarm adjective **1** <u>tepid</u>, warm **2** <u>half-hearted</u>, apathetic, cool, indifferent, unenthusiastic, unresponsive

lull verb **1** <u>calm</u>, allay, pacify, quell, soothe, subdue, tranquillize ♦ noun **2** <u>respite</u>, calm, hush, let-up (informal), pause, quiet, silence

lumber¹ noun **1** Brit. <u>junk</u>, clutter, jumble, refuse, rubbish, trash ♦ verb **2** Brit. informal <u>burden</u>, encumber, land, load, saddle

lumber² verb <u>plod</u>, shamble, shuffle, stump, trudge, trundle, waddle

lumbering adjective <u>awkward</u>, clumsy, heavy, hulking, ponderous, ungainly

luminous adjective <u>bright</u>, glowing, illuminated, luminescent, lustrous, radiant, shining

lump noun **1** <u>piece</u>, ball, chunk, hunk, mass, nugget **2** <u>swelling</u>, bulge, bump, growth, hump, protrusion, tumour ♦ verb **3** <u>group</u>, collect, combine, conglomerate, consolidate, mass, pool

lumpy adjective <u>bumpy</u>, knobbly, uneven

lunacy noun **1** <u>foolishness</u>, absurdity, craziness, folly, foolhardiness, madness, stupidity **2** <u>insanity</u>, dementia, derangement, madness, mania, psychosis

➤ **Antonyms**
≠foolishness: sense   ≠insanity: reason, sanity

lunatic adjective **1** <u>irrational</u>, crackbrained, crackpot (informal), crazy, daft, deranged, insane, mad ♦ noun **2** <u>madman</u>, maniac, nutcase (slang), psychopath

lunge noun **1** <u>thrust</u>, charge, jab, pounce, spring, swing ♦ verb **2** <u>pounce</u>, charge, dive, leap, plunge, thrust

lurch verb **1** <u>tilt</u>, heave, heel, lean, list, pitch, rock, roll **2** <u>stagger</u>, reel, stumble, sway, totter, weave

lure verb **1** <u>tempt</u>, allure, attract, draw, ensnare, entice, invite, seduce ♦ noun **2** <u>temptation</u>, allurement, attraction, bait, carrot (informal), enticement, incentive, inducement

lurid adjective **1** <u>sensational</u>, graphic, melodramatic, shocking, vivid **2** <u>glaring</u>, intense

➤ **Antonyms**
≠sensational: factual, light-hearted   ≠glaring: pale, pastel, watery

lurk verb <u>hide</u>, conceal oneself, lie in wait, prowl, skulk, slink, sneak

luscious adjective <u>delicious</u>, appetizing, juicy, mouth-watering, palatable, succulent, sweet, toothsome

lush *adjective* **1** <u>abundant</u>, dense, flourishing, green, rank, verdant **2** <u>luxurious</u>, elaborate, extravagant, grand, lavish, opulent, ornate, palatial, plush (*informal*), sumptuous

lust *noun* **1** <u>lechery</u>, lasciviousness, lewdness, sensuality **2** <u>desire</u>, appetite, craving, greed, longing, passion, thirst ♦ *verb* **3** <u>desire</u>, covet, crave, hunger for or after, want, yearn

lustre *noun* **1** <u>sparkle</u>, gleam, glint, glitter, gloss, glow, sheen, shimmer, shine **2** <u>glory</u>, distinction, fame, honour, prestige, renown

lusty *adjective* <u>vigorous</u>, energetic, healthy, hearty, powerful, robust, strong, sturdy, virile

luxurious *adjective* <u>sumptuous</u>, comfortable, expensive, lavish, magnificent, opulent, plush (*informal*), rich, splendid

➤ **Antonyms**

ascetic, austere, economical, plain, poor, sparing, Spartan, thrifty

luxury *noun* **1** <u>opulence</u>, affluence, hedonism, richness, splendour, sumptuousness **2** <u>extravagance</u>, extra, frill, indulgence, treat

➤ **Antonyms**

≠<u>opulence</u>: austerity, deprivation, destitution, poverty, privation, want ≠<u>extravagance</u>: necessity, need

lying *noun* **1** <u>dishonesty</u>, deceit, mendacity, perjury, untruthfulness ♦ *adjective* **2** <u>deceitful</u>, dishonest, false, mendacious, perfidious, treacherous, two-faced, untruthful

➤ **Antonyms**

adjective ≠<u>deceitful</u>: candid, forthright, frank, honest, reliable, sincere, straight, straightforward, truthful, veracious

lyrical *adjective* <u>enthusiastic</u>, effusive, impassioned, inspired, poetic, rhapsodic

M m

macabre *adjective* <u>gruesome</u>, dreadful, eerie, frightening, ghastly, ghostly, ghoulish, grim, grisly, morbid

➤ **Antonyms**

appealing, beautiful, charming, delightful, lovely, pleasant

machiavellian *adjective* <u>scheming</u>, astute, crafty, cunning, cynical, double-dealing, opportunist, sly, underhand, unscrupulous

machine *noun* **1** <u>appliance</u>, apparatus, contraption, contrivance, device, engine, instrument, mechanism, tool **2** <u>system</u>, machinery, organization, setup (*informal*), structure

machinery *noun* <u>equipment</u>, apparatus, gear, instruments, tackle, tools

macho *adjective* <u>manly</u>, chauvinist, masculine, virile

mad *adjective* **1** <u>insane</u>, crazy (*informal*), demented, deranged, non compos mentis, nuts (*slang*), of unsound mind, out of one's mind, psychotic, raving, unhinged, unstable **2** <u>foolish</u>, absurd, asinine, daft (*informal*), foolhardy, irrational, nonsensical, preposterous, senseless, wild **3** *Informal* <u>angry</u>, berserk, enraged, furious, incensed, livid (*informal*), pissed (*taboo slang*), pissed off (*taboo slang*), wild **4** <u>enthusiastic</u>, ardent, avid, crazy (*informal*), fanatical, impassioned, infatuated, wild **5** <u>frenzied</u>, excited, frenetic, uncontrolled, unrestrained, wild **6** like mad *Informal* <u>energetically</u>, enthusiastically, excitedly, furiously, rapidly, speedily, violently, wildly

➤ **Antonyms**

≠<u>insane</u>: rational, sane ≠<u>foolish</u>: sensible, sound ≠<u>angry</u>: calm, composed, cool ≠<u>enthusiastic</u>:

nonchalant, uncaring

madcap *adjective* <u>reckless</u>, crazy, foolhardy, hare-brained, imprudent, impulsive, rash, thoughtless

madden *verb* <u>infuriate</u>, annoy, enrage, drive one crazy, enrage, incense, inflame, irritate, upset

► **Antonyms**
appease, calm, mollify, pacify, soothe

madly *adverb* **1** <u>insanely</u>, crazily, deliriously, distractedly, frantically, frenziedly, hysterically **2** <u>foolishly</u>, absurdly, irrationally, ludicrously, senselessly, wildly **3** <u>energetically</u>, excitedly, furiously, like mad (*informal*), recklessly, speedily, wildly **4** *Informal* <u>passionately</u>, desperately, devotedly, intensely, to distraction

madman *or* **madwoman** *noun* <u>lunatic</u>, maniac, nutcase (*slang*), psycho (*slang*), psychopath

madness *noun* **1** <u>insanity</u>, aberration, craziness, delusion, dementia, derangement, distraction, lunacy, mania, mental illness, psychopathy, psychosis **2** <u>foolishness</u>, absurdity, daftness (*informal*), folly, foolhardiness, idiocy, nonsense, preposterousness, wildness

maelstrom *noun* **1** <u>whirlpool</u>, vortex **2** <u>turmoil</u>, chaos, confusion, disorder, tumult, upheaval

maestro *noun* <u>master</u>, expert, genius, virtuoso

magazine *noun* **1** <u>journal</u>, pamphlet, periodical **2** <u>storehouse</u>, arsenal, depot, store, warehouse

magic *noun* **1** <u>sorcery</u>, black art, enchantment, necromancy, witchcraft, wizardry **2** <u>conjuring</u>, illusion, legerdemain, prestidigitation, sleight of hand, trickery **3** <u>charm</u>, allurement, enchantment, fascination, glamour, magnetism, power ♦ *adjective* **4** *Also* **magical** <u>miraculous</u>, bewitching, charming, enchanting, entrancing, fascinating, marvellous, spellbinding

magician *noun* <u>sorcerer</u>, conjuror *or* conjuror, enchanter *or* en-

chantress, illusionist, necromancer, warlock, witch, wizard

magisterial *adjective* <u>authoritative</u>, commanding, lordly, masterful

► **Antonyms**
deferential, humble, servile, submissive, subservient

magistrate *noun* <u>judge</u>, J.P., justice, justice of the peace

magnanimity *noun* <u>generosity</u>, benevolence, big-heartedness, largesse *or* largess, nobility, selflessness, unselfishness

magnanimous *adjective* <u>generous</u>, big-hearted, bountiful, charitable, kind, noble, selfless, unselfish

► **Antonyms**
miserly, petty, resentful, selfish, small, unforgiving, vindictive

magnate *noun* <u>tycoon</u>, baron, big hitter (*informal*), captain of industry, heavy hitter (*informal*), mogul, plutocrat

magnetic *adjective* <u>attractive</u>, captivating, charismatic, charming, fascinating, hypnotic, irresistible, mesmerizing, seductive

► **Antonyms**
repellent, repulsive, unappealing, unattractive, unlikable *or* unlikeable, unpleasant

magnetism *noun* <u>charm</u>, allure, appeal, attraction, charisma, drawing power, magic, pull, seductiveness

magnification *noun* <u>increase</u>, amplification, enhancement, enlargement, expansion, heightening, intensification

magnificence *noun* <u>splendour</u>, brilliance, glory, grandeur, majesty, nobility, opulence, stateliness, sumptuousness

magnificent *adjective* **1** <u>splendid</u>, glorious, gorgeous, imposing, impressive, majestic, regal, sublime, sumptuous **2** <u>excellent</u>, brilliant, fine, outstanding, splendid, superb

► **Antonyms**
bad, humble, ignoble, lowly, mean, modest, ordinary, petty,

poor, trivial, undistinguished, unimposing

magnify verb 1 <u>enlarge</u>, amplify, blow up (informal), boost, dilate, expand, heighten, increase, intensify 2 <u>overstate</u>, exaggerate, inflate, overemphasize, overplay

➤ **Antonyms**

≠<u>enlarge</u>: decrease, diminish, lessen, lower, minimize, reduce, shrink ≠<u>overstate</u>: belittle, deflate, denigrate, deprecate, disparage, understate

magnitude noun 1 <u>importance</u>, consequence, greatness, moment, note, significance, weight 2 <u>size</u>, amount, amplitude, extent, mass, quantity, volume

➤ **Antonyms**

≠<u>importance</u>: insignificance, triviality, unimportance ≠<u>size</u>: meanness, smallness

maid noun 1 <u>servant</u>, housemaid, maidservant, serving-maid 2 Literary <u>girl</u>, damsel, lass, lassie (informal), maiden, wench

maiden noun 1 Literary <u>girl</u>, damsel, lass, lassie (informal), maid, virgin, wench ♦ adjective 2 <u>unmarried</u>, unwed 3 <u>first</u>, inaugural, initial, introductory

maidenly adjective <u>modest</u>, chaste, decent, decorous, demure, pure, virginal

➤ **Antonyms**

brazen, immodest, impure, indecent, loose, promiscuous, unchaste, wanton

mail noun 1 <u>letters</u>, correspondence, post ♦ verb 2 <u>post</u>, dispatch, forward, send

maim verb <u>cripple</u>, disable, hurt, injure, mutilate, wound

main adjective 1 <u>chief</u>, central, essential, foremost, head, leading, pre-eminent, primary, principal ♦ noun 2 <u>conduit</u>, cable, channel, duct, line, pipe 3 **in the main** <u>on the whole</u>, for the most part, generally, in general, mainly, mostly

➤ **Antonyms**

adjective ≠<u>chief</u>: auxiliary, least, lesser, minor, secondary, subordi-

nate, unimportant

mainly adverb <u>chiefly</u>, for the most part, in the main, largely, mostly, on the whole, predominantly, primarily, principally

mainstay noun <u>pillar</u>, anchor, backbone, bulwark, buttress, lynchpin, prop

mainstream adjective <u>conventional</u>, accepted, current, established, general, orthodox, prevailing, received

➤ **Antonyms**

marginal, peripheral, unconventional, unorthodox

maintain verb 1 <u>continue</u>, carry on, keep up, perpetuate, preserve, prolong, retain, sustain 2 <u>look after</u>, care for, provide for, supply, support, take care of 3 <u>assert</u>, avow, claim, contend, declare, insist, profess, state

➤ **Antonyms**

≠<u>continue</u>: conclude, discontinue, drop, end, finish, give up, relinquish, suspend, terminate ≠<u>assert</u>: disavow

maintenance noun 1 <u>continuation</u>, carrying-on, perpetuation, prolongation 2 <u>upkeep</u>, care, conservation, keeping, nurture, preservation, repairs 3 <u>allowance</u>, alimony, keep, support

majestic adjective <u>grand</u>, grandiose, impressive, magnificent, monumental, regal, splendid, stately, sublime, superb

➤ **Antonyms**

humble, lowly, modest, ordinary

majesty noun <u>grandeur</u>, glory, magnificence, nobility, pomp, splendour, stateliness

➤ **Antonyms**

meanness, triviality

major adjective 1 <u>main</u>, bigger, chief, greater, higher, leading, senior, supreme 2 <u>important</u>, critical, crucial, great, notable, outstanding, serious, significant

➤ **Antonyms**

≠<u>main</u>: auxiliary, lesser, minor, secondary, smaller, subordinate ≠<u>important</u>: inconsequential, insignificant, trivial, unimportant

majority noun 1 <u>most</u>, best part, bulk, greater number, mass, preponderance 2 <u>adulthood</u>, manhood or womanhood, maturity, seniority

make verb 1 <u>create</u>, assemble, build, construct, fashion, form, manufacture, produce, put together, synthesize 2 <u>force</u>, cause, compel, constrain, drive, impel, induce, oblige, prevail upon, require 3 <u>produce</u>, accomplish, bring about, cause, create, effect, generate, give rise to, lead to 4 <u>perform</u>, carry out, do, effect, execute 5 <u>amount to</u>, add up to, compose, constitute, form 6 <u>earn</u>, clear, gain, get, net, obtain, win 7 **make it** Informal <u>succeed</u>, arrive (informal), crack it (informal), get on, prosper ♦ noun 8 <u>brand</u>, kind, model, sort, style, type, variety

make-believe noun <u>fantasy</u>, imagination, play-acting, pretence, unreality

➤ Antonyms

actuality, fact, reality, truthfulness

make for verb <u>head for</u>, aim for, be bound for, head towards

make off verb 1 <u>flee</u>, bolt, clear out (informal), run away or off, take to one's heels 2 **make off with** <u>steal</u>, abduct, carry off, filch, kidnap, nick (slang, chiefly Brit.), pinch (informal), run away or off with

make out verb 1 <u>see</u>, detect, discern, discover, distinguish, perceive, recognize 2 <u>understand</u>, comprehend, decipher, fathom, follow, grasp, work out 3 <u>write out</u>, complete, draw up, fill in or out 4 <u>pretend</u>, assert, claim, let on, make as if or though 5 <u>fare</u>, get on, manage

maker noun <u>manufacturer</u>, builder, constructor, producer

makeshift adjective <u>temporary</u>, expedient, provisional, stopgap, substitute

make-up noun 1 <u>cosmetics</u>, face (informal), greasepaint (Theatre), paint (informal), powder 2 <u>structure</u>, arrangement, assembly, composition, configuration, constitution, construction, format, organization 3 <u>nature</u>, character, constitution, disposition, temperament

make up verb 1 <u>form</u>, compose, comprise, constitute 2 <u>invent</u>, coin, compose, concoct, construct, create, devise, dream up, formulate, frame, originate 3 <u>complete</u>, fill, supply 4 <u>settle</u>, bury the hatchet, call it quits, reconcile 5 **make up for** <u>compensate for</u>, atone for, balance, make amends for, offset, recompense

making noun <u>creation</u>, assembly, building, composition, construction, fabrication, manufacture, production

makings plural noun <u>beginnings</u>, capacity, ingredients, potential

maladjusted adjective <u>disturbed</u>, alienated, neurotic, unstable

maladministration noun <u>mismanagement</u>, corruption, dishonesty, incompetence, inefficiency, malpractice, misrule

maladroit adjective <u>clumsy</u>, awkward, cack-handed (informal), ham-fisted or ham-handed (informal), inept, inexpert, unskilful

malady noun <u>disease</u>, affliction, ailment, complaint, disorder, illness, infirmity, sickness

malaise noun <u>unease</u>, anxiety, depression, disquiet, melancholy

malcontent noun <u>troublemaker</u>, agitator, mischief-maker, rebel, stirrer (informal)

male adjective <u>masculine</u>, manly, virile

➤ Antonyms

camp (informal), effeminate, female, feminine, girlie, unmanly

malefactor noun <u>wrongdoer</u>, criminal, delinquent, evildoer, miscreant, offender, villain

malevolence noun <u>malice</u>, hate, hatred, ill will, nastiness, rancour, spite, vindictiveness

malevolent adjective <u>spiteful</u>, hostile, ill-natured, malicious, malign, vengeful, vindictive

➤ **Antonyms**

amiable, benevolent, benign, friendly, gracious, kind, warm-hearted

malformation *noun* <u>deformity</u>, distortion, misshapenness

malformed *adjective* <u>misshapen</u>, abnormal, crooked, deformed, distorted, irregular, twisted

malfunction *verb* **1** <u>break down</u>, fail, go wrong ♦ *noun* **2** <u>fault</u>, breakdown, defect, failure, flaw, glitch

malice *noun* <u>spite</u>, animosity, enmity, evil intent, hate, hatred, ill will, malevolence, vindictiveness

malicious *adjective* <u>spiteful</u>, ill-disposed, ill-natured, malevolent, rancorous, resentful, vengeful

➤ **Antonyms**

amiable, benevolent, friendly, kind, warm-hearted

malign *verb* **1** <u>disparage</u>, abuse, defame, denigrate, libel, run down, slander, smear, vilify ♦ *adjective* **2** <u>evil</u>, bad, destructive, harmful, hostile, injurious, malevolent, malignant, pernicious, wicked

➤ **Antonyms**

verb ≠<u>disparage</u>: commend, compliment, extol, praise ♦ *adjective* ≠<u>evil</u>: beneficial, benevolent, benign, friendly, good, harmless, kind, virtuous

malignant *adjective* **1** <u>hostile</u>, destructive, harmful, hurtful, malevolent, malign, pernicious, spiteful **2** *Medical* <u>uncontrollable</u>, cancerous, dangerous, deadly, fatal, irremediable

➤ **Antonyms**

≠<u>hostile</u>: amicable, benevolent, benign, friendly, kind

malleable *adjective* **1** <u>workable</u>, ductile, plastic, soft, tensile **2** <u>manageable</u>, adaptable, biddable, compliant, impressionable, pliable, tractable

malodorous *adjective* <u>smelly</u>, fetid, mephitic, nauseating, noi-

some, offensive, putrid, reeking, stinking

malpractice *noun* <u>misconduct</u>, abuse, dereliction, mismanagement, negligence

maltreat *verb* <u>abuse</u>, bully, harm, hurt, ill-treat, injure, mistreat

mammoth *adjective* <u>colossal</u>, enormous, giant, gigantic, huge, immense, massive, monumental, mountainous, prodigious

➤ **Antonyms**

diminutive, insignificant, little, miniature, minute, small, tiny, trivial

man *noun* **1** <u>male</u>, bloke (*Brit. informal*), chap (*informal*), gentleman, guy (*informal*) **2** <u>human</u>, human being, individual, person, soul **3** <u>mankind</u>, Homo sapiens, humanity, humankind, human race, people **4** <u>manservant</u>, attendant, retainer, servant, valet ♦ *verb* **5** <u>staff</u>, crew, garrison, occupy, people

manacle *noun* **1** <u>handcuff</u>, bond, chain, fetter, iron, shackle ♦ *verb* **2** <u>handcuff</u>, bind, chain, fetter, put in chains, shackle

manage *verb* **1** <u>succeed</u>, accomplish, arrange, contrive, effect, engineer **2** <u>administer</u>, be in charge (of), command, conduct, direct, handle, run, supervise **3** <u>handle</u>, control, manipulate, operate, use **4** <u>cope</u>, carry on, get by (*informal*), make do, muddle through, survive

➤ **Antonyms**

≠<u>succeed</u>: bodge (*informal*), botch, fail, make a mess of, make a nonsense of, mismanage, muff, spoil

manageable *adjective* **1** <u>easy</u>, handy, user-friendly **2** <u>docile</u>, amenable, compliant, submissive

➤ **Antonyms**

≠<u>easy</u>: demanding, difficult, hard ≠<u>docile</u>: disobedient, headstrong, obstinate, refractory, stubborn, unruly, wild

management *noun* **1** <u>directors</u>, administration, board, employers, executive(s) **2** administration, command, control, direction, handling, operation, running, supervision

manager noun supervisor, administrator, boss (informal), director, executive, governor, head, organizer

mandate noun command, commission, decree, directive, edict, instruction, order

mandatory adjective compulsory, binding, obligatory, required, requisite

➤ **Antonyms**
discretionary, nonbinding, noncompulsory, nonobligatory, optional, voluntary

manfully adverb bravely, boldly, courageously, determinedly, gallantly, hard, resolutely, stoutly, valiantly

mangle verb crush, deform, destroy, disfigure, distort, mutilate, ruin, spoil, tear, wreck

mangy adjective scruffy, dirty, moth-eaten, seedy, shabby, shoddy, squalid

➤ **Antonyms**
clean, fine, splendid, spotless, superb, tidy, well-dressed, well-kept

manhandle verb rough up, knock about or around, maul, paw (informal)

manhood noun manliness, masculinity, virility

mania noun **1** obsession, craze, fad (informal), fetish, fixation, passion, preoccupation, thing (informal) **2** madness, delirium, dementia, derangement, insanity, lunacy

maniac noun **1** madman or madwoman, headcase (informal), lunatic, psycho (slang), psychopath **2** fanatic, enthusiast, fan, fiend (informal), freak (informal)

manifest adjective **1** obvious, apparent, blatant, clear, conspicuous, evident, glaring, noticeable, palpable, patent ♦ verb **2** display, demonstrate, exhibit, expose, express, reveal, show

➤ **Antonyms**
adjective ≠obvious: concealed, disguised, hidden, inconspicuous, indistinct, masked, suppressed, unapparent, vague, veiled ♦ verb ≠display: conceal, cover, cover up, hide, mask, obscure

manifestation noun display, demonstration, exhibition, expression, indication, mark, show, sign, symptom

manifold adjective Formal numerous, assorted, copious, diverse, many, multifarious, multiple, varied, various

manipulate verb **1** work, handle, operate, use **2** influence, control, direct, engineer, manoeuvre

mankind noun people, Homo sapiens, humanity, humankind, human race, man

manliness noun virility, boldness, bravery, courage, fearlessness, masculinity, valour, vigour

manly adjective virile, bold, brave, courageous, fearless, manful, masculine, strapping, strong, vigorous

➤ **Antonyms**
camp (informal), delicate, effeminate, feeble, feminine, girlie, soft, unmanly, weak, wimpish or wimpy (informal), womanish, wussy (slang)

man-made adjective artificial, ersatz, manufactured, mock, synthetic

manner noun **1** behaviour, air, aspect, bearing, conduct, demeanour **2** style, custom, fashion, method, mode, way **3** type, brand, category, form, kind, sort, variety

mannered adjective affected, artificial, arty-farty (informal), pretentious, stilted

➤ **Antonyms**
genuine, honest, natural, real, sincere, unaffected, unpretentious

mannerism noun habit, characteristic, foible, idiosyncrasy, peculiarity, quirk, trait, trick

manners plural noun **1** behaviour, conduct, demeanour **2** politeness, courtesy, decorum, etiquette, p's and q's, refinement

manoeuvre verb **1** manipulate, contrive, engineer, machinate, pull strings, scheme, wangle (informal) **2** move, deploy, operation ♦ noun **3** movement, exercise, operation **4** stratagem, dodge, intrigue, machination, ploy, ruse, scheme, subterfuge, tactic, trick

mansion noun residence, hall, manor, seat, villa

mantle noun **1** cloak, cape, hood, shawl, wrap **2** covering, blanket, canopy, curtain, pall, screen, shroud, veil

manual adjective **1** handoperated, human, physical ♦ noun **2** handbook, bible, guide, instructions

manufacture verb **1** make, assemble, build, construct, create, mass-produce, produce, put together, turn out **2** concoct, cook up (informal), devise, fabricate, invent, make up, think up, trump up ♦ noun **3** making, assembly, construction, creation, production

manufacturer noun maker, builder, constructor, industrialist, producer

manure noun compost, droppings, dung, excrement, fertilizer, muck, ordure

many adjective **1** numerous, abundant, countless, innumerable, manifold, myriad, umpteen (informal), various ♦ noun **2** a lot, heaps (informal), lots (informal), plenty, scores

mar verb spoil, blemish, damage, detract from, disfigure, hurt, impair, ruin, scar, stain, taint, tarnish

➤ **Antonyms**
adorn, ameliorate, better, embellish, improve, ornament

maraud verb raid, forage, loot, pillage, plunder, ransack, ravage

marauder noun raider, bandit, brigand, buccaneer, outlaw, plunderer

march verb **1** walk, file, pace, parade, stride, strut ♦ noun **2** walk, routemarch, trek **3** progress, advance, development, evolution, progression

margin noun edge, border, boundary, brink, perimeter, periphery, rim, side, verge

marginal adjective **1** borderline, bordering, on the edge, peripheral **2** insignificant, minimal, minor, negligible, slight, small

marijuana noun cannabis, dope (slang), grass (slang), hemp, pot (slang)

marine adjective nautical, maritime, naval, seafaring, seagoing

mariner noun sailor, salt, sea dog, seafarer, seaman

marital adjective matrimonial, conjugal, connubial, nuptial

maritime adjective **1** nautical, marine, naval, oceanic, seafaring **2** coastal, littoral, seaside

mark noun **1** spot, blemish, blot, line, scar, scratch, smudge, stain, streak **2** sign, badge, device, emblem, flag, hallmark, label, symbol, token **3** criterion, measure, norm, standard, yardstick **4** target, aim, goal, object, objective, purpose ♦ verb **5** scar, blemish, blot, scratch, smudge, stain, streak **6** characterize, brand, flag, identify, label, stamp **7** distinguish, denote, exemplify, illustrate, show **8** observe, attend, mind, note, notice, pay attention, pay heed, watch **9** grade, appraise, assess, correct, evaluate

marked adjective noticeable, blatant, clear, conspicuous, decided, distinct, obvious, patent, prominent, pronounced, striking

➤ **Antonyms**
concealed, doubtful, dubious, hidden, imperceptible, inconspicuous, indistinct, insignificant, obscure, unclear, unnoticeable, vague

markedly adverb noticeably,

clearly, considerably, conspicuously, decidedly, distinctly, obviously, strikingly

market noun 1 <u>fair</u>, bazaar, mart ♦ verb 2 <u>sell</u>, retail, vend

marketable adjective <u>sought after</u>, in demand, saleable, wanted

marksman, markswoman noun <u>sharpshooter</u>, crack shot (informal), good shot

maroon verb <u>abandon</u>, desert, leave, leave high and dry (informal), strand

marriage noun <u>wedding</u>, match, matrimony, nuptials, wedlock

marry verb 1 <u>wed</u>, get hitched (slang), tie the knot (informal) 2 <u>unite</u>, ally, bond, join, knit, link, merge, unify, yoke

marsh noun <u>swamp</u>, bog, fen, morass, quagmire, slough

marshal verb 1 <u>arrange</u>, align, array, deploy, draw up, group, line up, order, organize 2 <u>conduct</u>, escort, guide, lead, shepherd, usher

marshy adjective <u>swampy</u>, boggy, quaggy, waterlogged, wet

martial adjective <u>military</u>, bellicose, belligerent, warlike

martinet noun <u>disciplinarian</u>, stickler

martyrdom noun <u>persecution</u>, ordeal, suffering

➤ **Antonyms**
bliss, ecstasy, happiness, joy

marvel verb 1 <u>wonder</u>, be amazed, be awed, gape ♦ noun 2 <u>wonder</u>, miracle, phenomenon, portent, prodigy

marvellous adjective 1 <u>excellent</u>, fabulous (informal), fantastic (informal), great (informal), splendid, superb, terrific (informal), wonderful 2 <u>amazing</u>, astonishing, astounding, breathtaking, brilliant, extraordinary, jaw-dropping, miraculous, phenomenal, prodigious, spectacular, stupendous

➤ **Antonyms**
≠excellent: awful, bad, terrible ≠amazing: believable, common-

place, credible, everyday, ordinary

masculine adjective <u>male</u>, manlike, manly, mannish, virile

mask noun 1 <u>disguise</u>, camouflage, cover, façade, front, guise, screen, veil ♦ verb 2 <u>disguise</u>, camouflage, cloak, conceal, cover, hide, obscure, screen, veil

masquerade verb 1 <u>pose</u>, disguise, dissemble, dissimulate, impersonate, pass oneself off, pretend (to be) ♦ noun 2 <u>pretence</u>, cloak, cover-up, deception, disguise, mask, pose, screen, subterfuge 3 <u>masked ball</u>, fancy dress party, revel

mass noun 1 <u>piece</u>, block, chunk, hunk, lump 2 <u>lot</u>, bunch, collection, heap, load, pile, quantity, stack 3 <u>size</u>, bulk, greatness, magnitude ♦ adjective 4 <u>large-scale</u>, extensive, general, indiscriminate, wholesale, widespread ♦ verb 5 <u>gather</u>, accumulate, assemble, collect, congregate, rally, swarm, throng

massacre noun 1 <u>slaughter</u>, annihilation, blood bath, butchery, carnage, extermination, holocaust, murder ♦ verb 2 <u>slaughter</u>, butcher, cut to pieces, exterminate, kill, mow down, murder, wipe out

massage noun 1 <u>rub-down</u>, manipulation ♦ verb 2 <u>rub down</u>, knead, manipulate

massive adjective <u>huge</u>, big, colossal, enormous, gigantic, hefty, immense, mammoth, monumental, whopping (informal)

➤ **Antonyms**
light, little, minute, slight, small, thin, tiny

master noun 1 <u>head</u>, boss (informal), chief, commander, controller, director, governor, lord, manager, ruler 2 <u>expert</u>, ace (informal), doyen, genius, maestro, past master, virtuoso, wizard 3 <u>teacher</u>, guide, guru, instructor, tutor ♦ adjective 4 <u>main</u>, chief, foremost, leading, predominant, prime, principal ♦ verb 5 <u>learn</u>, get the hang of (*informal*), grasp **6** <u>overcome</u>, conquer, defeat, tame, triumph over, vanquish

➤ **Antonyms**

noun ≠<u>head</u>: crew, servant, slave, subject ≠<u>expert</u>: amateur, novice ≠<u>teacher</u>: student ♦ adjective ≠<u>main</u>: lesser, minor ♦ verb ≠<u>overcome</u>: cave in (*informal*), give in, surrender, yield

masterful adjective **1** <u>skilful</u>, adroit, consummate, expert, fine, first-rate, masterly, superlative, supreme, world-class **2** <u>domineering</u>, arrogant, bossy (*informal*), high-handed, imperious, overbearing, overweening

➤ **Antonyms**

≠<u>skilful</u>: amateurish, clumsy, incompetent, inept, unaccomplished, unskilled, untalented ≠<u>domineering</u>: meek, spineless, weak, wimpish or wimpy (*informal*), wussy (*slang*)

masterly adjective <u>skilful</u>, consummate, crack (*informal*), expert, first-rate, masterful, supreme, world-class

mastermind verb **1** <u>plan</u>, conceive, devise, direct, manage, organize ♦ noun **2** <u>organizer</u>, architect, brain(s) (*informal*), director, engineer, manager, planner

masterpiece noun <u>classic</u>, jewel, magnum opus, *pièce de résistance*, tour de force

mastery noun **1** <u>expertise</u>, finesse, know-how (*informal*), proficiency, prowess, skill, virtuosity **2** <u>control</u>, ascendancy, command, domination, superiority, supremacy, upper hand, whip hand

match noun **1** <u>game</u>, bout, competition, contest, head-to-head, test, trial **2** <u>equal</u>, counterpart, peer, rival **3** <u>marriage</u>, alliance, pairing, partnership ♦ verb **4** <u>correspond</u>, accord, agree, fit, go with, harmonize, tally **5** <u>rival</u>, compare, compete, emulate, equal, measure up to

matching adjective <u>identical</u>, co-ordinating, corresponding, equivalent, like, twin

➤ **Antonyms**

different, dissimilar, distinct, diverse, other, unequal, unlike

matchless adjective <u>unequalled</u>, incomparable, inimitable, superlative, supreme, unmatched, unparalleled, unrivalled, unsurpassed

➤ **Antonyms**

average, common, commonplace, equalled, everyday, inferior, lesser, mediocre, ordinary, second-class

mate noun **1** Informal <u>friend</u>, buddy (*informal*), chum (*informal*), comrade, crony, pal (*informal*) **2** <u>colleague</u>, associate, companion **3** <u>partner</u>, husband or wife, spouse **4** <u>assistant</u>, helper, subordinate ♦ verb **5** <u>pair</u>, breed, couple

material noun **1** <u>substance</u>, matter, stuff **2** <u>cloth</u>, fabric **3** <u>information</u>, data, evidence, facts, notes ♦ adjective **4** <u>physical</u>, bodily, concrete, corporeal, palpable, substantial, tangible **5** <u>relevant</u>, applicable, apposite, apropos, germane, pertinent **6** <u>important</u>, essential, meaningful, momentous, serious, significant, vital, weighty

materialize verb <u>occur</u>, appear, come about, come to pass, happen, take shape, turn up

materially adverb <u>significantly</u>, essentially, gravely, greatly, much, seriously, substantially

➤ **Antonyms**

barely, hardly, insignificantly, little, scarcely, unsubstantially

maternal adjective <u>motherly</u>

maternity noun <u>motherhood</u>, motherliness

matey adjective Brit. informal <u>friendly</u>, chummy (*informal*), hail-fellow-well-met, intimate, pally (*informal*), sociable, thick (*informal*)

matrimonial adjective <u>marital</u>, conjugal, connubial, nuptial

matrimony noun <u>marriage</u>, nuptials, wedding ceremony, wedlock

matted adjective tangled, knotted, tousled, uncombed

matter noun 1 substance, body, material, stuff 2 situation, affair, business, concern, event, incident, proceeding, question, subject, topic 3 As in **what's the matter?** problem, complication, difficulty, distress, trouble, worry ♦ verb 4 be important, carry weight, count, make a difference, signify

matter-of-fact adjective unsentimental, deadpan, down-to-earth, emotionless, mundane, plain, prosaic, sober, unimaginative

mature adjective 1 grown-up, adult, full-grown, fully fledged, mellow, of age, ready, ripe, seasoned ♦ verb 2 develop, age, bloom, blossom, come of age, grow up, mellow, ripen

➤ Antonyms

adjective ≠grown-up: adolescent, childish, immature, juvenile, puerile, undeveloped, unripe, young

maturity noun adulthood, experience, manhood or womanhood, ripeness, wisdom

➤ Antonyms

childishness, immaturity, juvenility, youthfulness

maudlin adjective sentimental, icky (informal), mawkish, over-emotional, slushy (informal), soppy (Brit. informal), tearful, weepy (informal)

maul verb 1 tear, claw, lacerate, mangle 2 ill-treat, abuse, batter, manhandle, molest

maverick noun rebel, dissenter, eccentric, heretic, iconoclast, individualist, nonconformist, protester, radical ♦ adjective 2 rebel, dissenting, eccentric, heretical, iconoclastic, individualistic, nonconformist, radical

➤ Antonyms

noun ≠rebel: conventionalist, traditionalist, yes man

mawkish adjective sentimental, emotional, icky (informal), maudlin, schmaltzy (slang), slushy (informal), soppy (Brit. informal)

maxim noun saying, adage, aphorism, axiom, dictum, motto, proverb, rule

maximum noun 1 top, ceiling, height, peak, pinnacle, summit, upper limit, utmost, zenith ♦ adjective 2 greatest, highest, most, paramount, supreme, topmost, utmost

➤ Antonyms

noun ≠top: bottom, minimum ♦ adjective ≠greatest: least, lowest, minimal

maybe adverb perhaps, perchance (archaic), possibly

mayhem noun chaos, commotion, confusion, destruction, disorder, fracas, havoc, trouble, violence

maze noun 1 labyrinth 2 web, confusion, imbroglio, tangle

meadow noun field, grassland, lea (poetic), pasture

meagre adjective insubstantial, inadequate, measly, paltry, poor, puny, scanty, slight, small

mean¹ verb 1 intend, aim, aspire, design, desire, plan, set out, want, wish 2 signify, convey, denote, express, imply, indicate, represent, spell, stand for, symbolize

mean² adjective 1 miserly, mercenary, niggardly, parsimonious, penny-pinching, stingy, tight-fisted, ungenerous 2 dishonourable, callous, contemptible, despicable, hard-hearted, petty, shabby, shameful, sordid, vile

➤ Antonyms

≠miserly: big, bountiful, generous, munificent, prodigal, unselfish ≠dishonourable: good, honourable, praiseworthy

mean³ noun 1 average, balance, compromise, happy medium, middle, midpoint, norm ♦ adjective 2 average, middle, standard

meander verb 1 wind, snake, turn, zigzag 2 wander, ramble,

stroll ♦ *noun* **3** <u>curve</u>, bend, coil, loop, turn, twist, zigzag

meaning *noun* <u>sense</u>, connotation, drift, gist, message, significance, substance

meaningful *adjective* <u>significant</u>, important, material, purposeful, relevant, useful, valid, worthwhile

➤ **Antonyms**
inconsequential, insignificant, meaningless, trivial, unimportant, useless, worthless

meaningless *adjective* <u>pointless</u>, empty, futile, inane, inconsequential, insignificant, senseless, useless, vain, worthless

➤ **Antonyms**
consequential, deep, evident, important, meaningful, obvious, sensible, significant, useful, worthwhile

meanness *noun* **1** <u>miserliness</u>, niggardliness, parsimony, selfishness, stinginess **2** <u>pettiness</u>, disgracefulness, ignobility, narrowmindedness, shabbiness, shamefulness

means *noun* **1** <u>method</u>, agency, instrument, medium, mode, process, way ♦ *plural noun* **2** <u>money</u>, affluence, capital, fortune, funds, income, resources, wealth, wherewithal **3** by all means <u>certainly</u>, definitely, doubtlessly, of course, surely **4** by no means <u>in no way</u>, definitely not, not in the least, on no account

meantime, meanwhile *adverb* <u>at the same time</u>, concurrently, in the interim, simultaneously

measly *adjective* <u>meagre</u>, miserable, paltry, pathetic, pitiful, poor, puny, scanty, skimpy

measurable *adjective* <u>quantifiable</u>, assessable, perceptible, significant

measure *noun* **1** <u>quantity</u>, allotment, allowance, amount, portion, quota, ration, share **2** <u>gauge</u>, metre, rule, scale, yardstick **3** <u>action</u>, act, deed, expedient, manoeuvre, means, procedure, step **4** <u>law</u>, act, bill, resolution, statute **5** <u>rhythm</u>, beat, cadence, metre, verse ♦ *verb* **6** <u>quantify</u>, assess, calculate, calibrate, compute, determine, evaluate, gauge, weigh

measured *adjective* **1** <u>steady</u>, dignified, even, leisurely, regular, sedate, slow, solemn, stately, unhurried **2** <u>considered</u>, calculated, deliberate, reasoned, sober, studied, well-thought-out

measurement *noun* <u>calculation</u>, assessment, calibration, computation, evaluation, mensuration, valuation

measure up to *verb* <u>fulfil the expectations</u>, be equal to, be suitable, come up to scratch (*informal*), fit or fill the bill, make the grade (*informal*)

meat *noun* <u>food</u>, flesh

meaty *adjective* **1** <u>brawny</u>, beefy (*informal*), burly, heavily built, heavy, muscular, solid, strapping, sturdy **2** <u>interesting</u>, meaningful, profound, rich, significant, substantial

mechanical *adjective* **1** <u>automatic</u>, automated **2** <u>unthinking</u>, automatic, cursory, impersonal, instinctive, involuntary, perfunctory, routine, unfeeling

➤ **Antonyms**
≠automatic: manual ≠unthinking: conscious, genuine, sincere, thinking, voluntary, warm, wholehearted

mechanism *noun* **1** <u>machine</u>, apparatus, appliance, contrivance, device, instrument, tool **2** <u>process</u>, agency, means, method, methodology, operation, procedure, system, technique, way

meddle *verb* <u>interfere</u>, butt in, intervene, intrude, pry, tamper

meddlesome *adjective* <u>interfering</u>, intrusive, meddling, mischievous, officious, prying

mediate *verb* <u>intervene</u>, arbitrate, conciliate, intercede, reconcile, referee, step in (*informal*), umpire

mediation *noun* <u>arbitration</u>, conciliation, intercession, intervention, reconciliation

mediator noun <u>negotiator</u>, arbiter, arbitrator, go-between, honest broker, intermediary, middleman, peacemaker, referee, umpire

medicinal adjective <u>therapeutic</u>, curative, healing, medical, remedial, restorative

medicine noun <u>remedy</u>, cure, drug, medicament, medication, nostrum

mediocre adjective <u>second-rate</u>, average, indifferent, inferior, middling, ordinary, passable, pedestrian, run-of-the-mill, so-so (informal), undistinguished

➤ **Antonyms**
distinctive, distinguished, excellent, extraordinary, fine, incomparable, superb, superior, unexcelled, unique, unrivalled, unsurpassed

mediocrity noun <u>insignificance</u>, indifference, inferiority, ordinariness, unimportance

meditate verb 1 <u>reflect</u>, cogitate, consider, contemplate, deliberate, muse, ponder, ruminate, think 2 <u>plan</u>, have in mind, intend, purpose, scheme

meditation noun <u>reflection</u>, cogitation, contemplation, musing, pondering, rumination, study, thought

medium adjective 1 <u>average</u>, fair, intermediate, mean, median, mediocre, middle, middling, midway ♦ noun 2 <u>middle</u>, average, centre, compromise, mean, midpoint 3 <u>means</u>, agency, channel, instrument, mode, organ, vehicle, way 4 <u>spiritualist</u>, channeller 5 <u>environment</u>, atmosphere, conditions, milieu, setting, surroundings

➤ **Antonyms**
adjective ≠<u>average</u>: curious, distinctive, extraordinary, extreme, uncommon, unique, unusual

medley noun <u>mixture</u>, assortment, farrago, hotchpotch, jumble, mélange, miscellany, mish-mash, mixed bag (informal), potpourri

meek adjective <u>submissive</u>, acquiescent, compliant, deferential, docile, gentle, humble, mild, modest, timid, unassuming, unpretentious

➤ **Antonyms**
arrogant, bold, bossy, domineering, feisty (informal, chiefly U.S. & Canad.), forward, immodest, overbearing, presumptuous, pretentious, proud, self-assertive, spirited, wilful

meekness noun <u>submissiveness</u>, acquiescence, compliance, deference, docility, gentleness, humility, mildness, modesty, timidity

meet verb 1 <u>encounter</u>, bump into, chance on, come across, confront, contact, find, happen on, run across, run into 2 <u>converge</u>, come together, connect, cross, intersect, join, link up, touch 3 <u>gather</u>, assemble, collect, come together, congregate, convene, muster 4 <u>fulfil</u>, answer, come up to, comply with, discharge, match, measure up to, satisfy 5 <u>experience</u>, bear, encounter, endure, face, go through, suffer, undergo

➤ **Antonyms**
≠<u>encounter</u>: avoid, elude, escape, miss ≠<u>converge</u>: diverge ≠<u>gather</u>: adjourn, disperse, scatter ≠<u>fulfil</u>: fail, fall short, renege

meeting noun 1 <u>encounter</u>, assignation, confrontation, engagement, introduction, rendezvous, tryst 2 <u>conference</u>, assembly, conclave, congress, convention, gathering, get-together (informal), reunion, session

melancholy noun 1 <u>sadness</u>, dejection, depression, despondency, gloom, low spirits, misery, sorrow, unhappiness ♦ adjective 2 <u>sad</u>, depressed, despondent, dispirited, downhearted, gloomy, glum, miserable, mournful, sorrowful

➤ **Antonyms**
noun ≠<u>sadness</u>: delight, gladness, happiness, joy, pleasure

♦ adjective ≠<u>sad</u>: blithe, bright, cheerful, gay, glad, happy, jolly, joyful, joyous, light-hearted, lively, merry, sunny

melee, mêlée noun <u>fight</u>, brawl, fracas, free-for-all (informal), rumpus, scrimmage, scuffle, set-to (informal), skirmish, tussle

mellifluous adjective <u>sweet</u>, dulcet, euphonious, honeyed, silvery, smooth, soft, soothing, sweet-sounding

mellow adjective 1 <u>ripe</u>, delicate, full-flavoured, mature, rich, soft, sweet ♦ verb 2 <u>mature</u>, develop, improve, ripen, season, soften, sweeten

► **Antonyms**

adjective ≠<u>ripe</u>: green, immature, raw, sour, unripe

melodious adjective <u>musical</u>, dulcet, euphonious, harmonious, melodic, sweet-sounding, tuneful

► **Antonyms**

cacophonous, discordant, grating, harsh, unharmonious, unmelodic, unmelodious, unmusical, untuneful

melodramatic adjective <u>theatrical</u>, blood-and-thunder, extravagant, histrionic, overdramatic, overemotional, sensational

melody noun 1 <u>tune</u>, air, music, song, strain, theme 2 <u>tunefulness</u>, euphony, harmony, melodiousness, musicality

melt verb 1 <u>dissolve</u>, fuse, liquefy, soften, thaw 2 often with away <u>disappear</u>, disperse, dissolve, evanesce, evaporate, fade, vanish 3 <u>soften</u>, disarm, mollify, relax

member noun 1 <u>representative</u>, associate, fellow 2 <u>limb</u>, appendage, arm, extremity, leg, part

membership noun 1 <u>members</u>, associates, body, fellows 2 <u>participation</u>, belonging, enrolment, fellowship

memento noun <u>souvenir</u>, keepsake, memorial, relic, remembrance, reminder, token, trophy

memoir noun <u>account</u>, biography, essay, journal, life, monograph, narrative, record

memoirs plural noun <u>autobiography</u>, diary, experiences, journals, life story, memories, recollections, reminiscences

memorable adjective <u>noteworthy</u>, celebrated, famous, historic, momentous, notable, remarkable, significant, striking, unforgettable

► **Antonyms**

commonplace, forgettable, insignificant, ordinary, unmemorable

memorandum noun <u>note</u>, communication, jotting, memo, message, minute, reminder

memorial noun 1 <u>monument</u>, memento, plaque, record, remembrance, souvenir ♦ adjective 2 <u>commemorative</u>, monumental

memorize verb <u>remember</u>, commit to memory, learn, learn by heart, learn by rote

memory noun 1 <u>recall</u>, recollection, remembrance, reminiscence, retention 2 <u>commemoration</u>, honour, remembrance

menace verb 1 <u>threaten</u>, bully, frighten, intimidate, loom, lour or lower, terrorize ♦ noun 2 <u>threat</u>, intimidation, warning 3 Informal <u>nuisance</u>, annoyance, pest, plague, troublemaker

menacing adjective <u>threatening</u>, forbidding, frightening, intimidating, looming, louring or lowering, ominous

► **Antonyms**

auspicious, encouraging, favourable, promising

mend verb 1 <u>repair</u>, darn, fix, patch, refit, renew, renovate, restore, retouch 2 <u>heal</u>, convalesce, get better, recover, recuperate 3 <u>improve</u>, ameliorate, amend, correct, emend, rectify, reform, revise ♦ noun 4 <u>repair</u>, darn, patch, stitch 5 **on the mend** <u>convalescent</u>, getting better, improving, recovering, recuperating

mendacious adjective <u>lying</u>, deceitful, deceptive, dishonest, duplicitous, fallacious, false, fraudulent, insincere, untruthful

➤ **Antonyms**
genuine, honest, true, truthful

menial *adjective* **1** <u>unskilled</u>, boring, dull, humdrum, low-status, routine ♦ *noun* **2** <u>servant</u>, attendant, dogsbody *(informal)*, drudge, flunky, lackey, skivvy *(chiefly Brit.)*, underling

➤ **Antonyms**
noun ≠<u>servant</u>: boss, chief, commander, lord, master, superior

mental *adjective* **1** <u>intellectual</u>, cerebral **2** *Informal* <u>insane</u>, deranged, disturbed, mad, mentally ill, psychotic, unbalanced, unstable

mentality *noun* <u>attitude</u>, cast of mind, character, disposition, make-up, outlook, personality, psychology

mentally *adverb* <u>in the mind</u>, in one's head, intellectually, inwardly, psychologically

mention *verb* **1** <u>refer to</u>, bring up, declare, disclose, divulge, intimate, point out, reveal, state, touch upon ♦ *noun* **2** <u>reference</u>, allusion, indication, observation, remark **3** <u>acknowledgment</u>, citation, recognition, tribute

mentor *noun* <u>guide</u>, adviser, coach, counsellor, guru, instructor, teacher, tutor

menu *noun* <u>bill of fare</u>, *carte du jour*, tariff *(chiefly Brit.)*

mercantile *adjective* <u>commercial</u>, trading

mercenary *noun* **1** <u>hireling</u>, soldier of fortune ♦ *adjective* **2** <u>greedy</u>, acquisitive, avaricious, grasping, money-grubbing *(informal)*, sordid, venal

➤ **Antonyms**
adjective ≠<u>greedy</u>: altruistic, benevolent, generous, idealistic, liberal, munificent, philanthropic, unselfish

merchandise *noun* <u>goods</u>, commodities, produce, products, stock, wares

merchant *noun* <u>tradesman</u>, broker, dealer, purveyor, retailer, salesman, seller, shopkeeper, sup-

plier, trader, trafficker, vendor, wholesaler

merciful *adjective* <u>compassionate</u>, clement, forgiving, generous, gracious, humane, kind, lenient, sparing, sympathetic, tender-hearted

➤ **Antonyms**
cruel, hard-hearted, inhumane, merciless, pitiless, uncompassionate, unfeeling

merciless *adjective* <u>cruel</u>, barbarous, callous, hard-hearted, harsh, heartless, pitiless, ruthless, unforgiving

mercurial *adjective* <u>lively</u>, active, capricious, changeable, impulsive, irrepressible, mobile, quicksilver, spirited, sprightly, unpredictable, volatile

➤ **Antonyms**
consistent, constant, predictable, steady, unchanging

mercy *noun* **1** <u>compassion</u>, clemency, forbearance, forgiveness, grace, kindness, leniency, pity **2** <u>blessing</u>, boon, godsend

➤ **Antonyms**
≠<u>compassion</u>: brutality, cruelty, harshness, inhumanity, pitilessness, severity

mere *adjective* <u>simple</u>, bare, common, nothing more than, plain, pure, sheer

meretricious *adjective* <u>trashy</u>, flashy, garish, gaudy, gimcrack, showy, tawdry, tinsel

merge *verb* <u>combine</u>, amalgamate, blend, coalesce, converge, fuse, join, meet, mingle, mix, unite

➤ **Antonyms**
detach, diverge, divide, part, separate, sever

merger *noun* <u>union</u>, amalgamation, coalition, combination, consolidation, fusion, incorporation

merit *noun* **1** <u>worth</u>, advantage, asset, excellence, goodness, integrity, quality, strong point, talent, value, virtue ♦ *verb* **2** <u>deserve</u>, be entitled to, be worthy of, earn, have a right to, rate, warrant

meritorious *adjective* praise-worthy, admirable, commendable, creditable, deserving, excellent, good, laudable, virtuous, worthy

➤ **Antonyms**
discreditable, dishonourable, ignoble, undeserving, unpraiseworthy

merriment *noun* fun, amusement, festivity, glee, hilarity, jollity, joviality, laughter, mirth, revelry

merry *adjective* **1** cheerful, blithe, carefree, convivial, festive, happy, jolly, joyous **2** *Brit. informal* tipsy, happy, mellow, squiffy (*Brit. informal*), tiddly (*slang, chiefly Brit.*).

➤ **Antonyms**
≠cheerful: dejected, dismal, down in the dumps (*informal*), gloomy, miserable, sad, unhappy

mesh *noun* **1** net, netting, network, tracery, web ◆ *verb* **2** engage, combine, connect, coordinate, dovetail, harmonize, interlock, knit

mesmerize *verb* entrance, captivate, enthral, fascinate, grip, hold spellbound, hypnotize

mess *noun* **1** disorder, chaos, clutter, confusion, disarray, disorganization, hotchpotch, jumble, litter, shambles, untidiness **2** difficulty, deep water, dilemma, fix (*informal*), hole (*informal*), jam (*informal*), muddle, pickle (*informal*), plight, predicament, tight spot ◆ *verb* **3** *often with up* dirty, clutter, disarrange, dishevel, muck up (*Brit. slang*), muddle, pollute, scramble **4** *often with with* interfere, fiddle (*informal*), meddle, play, tamper, tinker

mess about *or* **around** *verb* potter, amuse oneself, dabble, fool (about *or* around), muck about (*informal*), play about *or* around, trifle

message *noun* **1** communication, bulletin, communiqué, dispatch, letter, memorandum, note, tidings, word **2** point,

idea, import, meaning, moral, purport, theme

messenger *noun* courier, carrier, delivery boy, emissary, envoy, errand-boy, go-between, herald, runner

messy *adjective* untidy, chaotic, cluttered, confused, dirty, dishevelled, disordered, disorganized, muddled, shambolic, sloppy (*informal*)

➤ **Antonyms**
clean, meticulous, neat, ordered, orderly, shipshape, smart, squeaky-clean, tidy

metamorphosis *noun* transformation, alteration, change, conversion, mutation, transmutation

metaphor *noun* figure of speech, allegory, analogy, image, symbol, trope

metaphorical *adjective* figurative, allegorical, emblematic, symbolic

mete *verb* distribute, administer, apportion, assign, deal, dispense, dole, portion

meteoric *adjective* spectacular, brilliant, dazzling, fast, overnight, rapid, speedy, sudden, swift

➤ **Antonyms**
gradual, lengthy, long, prolonged, slow, steady

method *noun* **1** manner, approach, mode, modus operandi, procedure, process, routine, style, system, technique, way **2** orderliness, order, organization, pattern, planning, purpose, regularity, system

methodical *adjective* orderly, businesslike, deliberate, disciplined, meticulous, organized, precise, regular, structured, systematic

➤ **Antonyms**
chaotic, confused, disorderly, haphazard, irregular, random, unmethodical

meticulous *adjective* thorough, exact, fastidious, fussy, painstaking, particular, precise, punctilious, scrupulous, strict

> ➤ **Antonyms**

careless, haphazard, imprecise, inexact, loose, negligent, slapdash, sloppy

mettle noun <u>courage</u>, bravery, fortitude, gallantry, life, nerve, pluck, resolution, spirit, valour, vigour

microbe noun <u>microorganism</u>, bacillus, bacterium, bug (informal), germ, virus

microscopic adjective <u>tiny</u>, imperceptible, infinitesimal, invisible, minuscule, minute, negligible

> ➤ **Antonyms**

enormous, gigantic, great, huge, immense, large, vast

midday noun <u>noon</u>, noonday, twelve o'clock

middle noun 1 <u>centre</u>, focus, halfway point, heart, midpoint, midsection, midst ◆ adjective 2 <u>central</u>, halfway, intermediate, intervening, mean, median, medium, mid

middle-class adjective <u>bourgeois</u>, conventional, traditional

middling adjective 1 <u>mediocre</u>, indifferent, run-of-the-mill, so-so (informal), tolerable, unexceptional, unremarkable 2 <u>moderate</u>, adequate, all right, average, fair, medium, modest, O.K. or okay (informal), ordinary, passable, serviceable

midget noun <u>dwarf</u>, pygmy or pigmy, shrimp (informal), Tom Thumb

midnight noun <u>twelve o'clock</u>, dead of night, middle of the night, the witching hour

midst noun in the midst of <u>among</u>, amidst, during, in the middle of, in the thick of, surrounded by

midway adjective, adverb <u>halfway</u>, betwixt and between, in the middle

might noun 1 <u>power</u>, energy, force, strength, vigour 2 **with might and main** <u>forcefully</u>, lustily, manfully, mightily, vigorously

mightily adverb 1 <u>very</u>, decidedly, exceedingly, extremely, greatly, highly, hugely, intensely, much 2 <u>powerfully</u>, energetically, forcefully, lustily, manfully, strongly, vigorously

mighty adjective <u>powerful</u>, forceful, lusty, robust, strapping, strong, sturdy, vigorous

> ➤ **Antonyms**

feeble, impotent, weak, weedy (informal), wimpish or wimpy (informal), wussy (slang)

migrant noun 1 <u>wanderer</u>, drifter, emigrant, immigrant, itinerant, nomad, rover, traveller ◆ adjective 2 <u>travelling</u>, drifting, immigrant, itinerant, migratory, nomadic, roving, shifting, transient, vagrant, wandering

migrate verb <u>move</u>, emigrate, journey, roam, rove, travel, trek, voyage, wander

migration noun <u>wandering</u>, emigration, journey, movement, roving, travel, trek, voyage

migratory adjective <u>nomadic</u>, itinerant, migrant, peripatetic, roving, transient

mild adjective 1 <u>bland</u>, smooth 2 <u>gentle</u>, calm, docile, easy-going, equable, meek, peaceable, placid 3 <u>temperate</u>, balmy, calm, moderate, tranquil, warm

> ➤ **Antonyms**

≠gentle: harsh, powerful, severe, sharp, strong, unkind, unpleasant, violent ≠temperate: bitter, cold, fierce, harsh, rough, stormy, violent, wild

mildness noun <u>gentleness</u>, calmness, clemency, docility, moderation, placidity, tranquillity, warmth

milieu noun <u>surroundings</u>, background, element, environment, locale, location, scene, setting

militant adjective <u>aggressive</u>, active, assertive, combative, vigorous

> ➤ **Antonyms**

pacific, pacifist, peaceful

military adjective 1 <u>warlike</u>, armed, martial, soldierly ◆ noun 2 <u>armed forces</u>, army, forces, services

militate *verb* **militate against** counteract, be detrimental to, conflict with, counter, oppose, resist, tell against, weigh against

milk *verb* exploit, extract, pump, take advantage of

mill *noun* **1** factory, foundry, plant, works **2** grinder, crusher ♦ *verb* **3** grind, crush, grate, pound, powder **4** swarm, crowd, throng

millstone *noun* **1** grindstone, quernstone, **2** burden, affliction, albatross, encumbrance, load, weight

mime *verb* act out, gesture, represent, simulate

mimic *verb* **1** imitate, ape, caricature, do (*informal*), impersonate, parody, take off (*informal*) ♦ *noun* **2** imitator, caricaturist, copycat (*informal*), impersonator, impressionist

mimicry *noun* imitation, burlesque, caricature, impersonation, mimicking, mockery, parody, take-off (*informal*)

mince *verb* **1** cut, chop, crumble, grind, hash **2** *As in* **mince one's words** tone down, moderate, soften, spare, weaken

mincing *adjective* affected, arty-farty (*informal*), camp (*informal*), dainty, effeminate, foppish, precious, pretentious, sissy

mind *noun* **1** intelligence, brain(s) (*informal*), grey matter (*informal*), intellect, reason, sense, understanding, wits **2** memory, recollection, remembrance **3** intention, desire, disposition, fancy, inclination, leaning, notion, urge, wish **4** sanity, judgment, marbles (*informal*), mental balance, rationality, reason, senses, wits **5** make up one's mind decide, choose, determine, resolve ♦ *verb* **6** take offence, be affronted, be bothered, care, disapprove, dislike, object, resent **7** pay attention, heed, listen to, mark, note, obey, observe, pay heed to, take heed of, keep an eye on, look af-

ter, take care of, tend, watch **9** be careful, be cautious, be on (one's) guard, be wary, take care, watch

mindful *adjective* aware, alert, alive to, careful, conscious, heedful, wary, watchful

► **Antonyms**
heedless, incautious, mindless, oblivious, unaware

mindless *adjective* unthinking, dumb-ass (*slang*), foolish, idiotic, inane, moronic, stupid, thoughtless, witless

► **Antonyms**
mindful, thinking

mine *noun* **1** pit, colliery, deposit, excavation, shaft **2** source, abundance, fund, hoard, reserve, stock, store, supply, treasury, wealth ♦ *verb* **3** dig up, dig for, excavate, extract, hew, quarry, unearth

miner *noun* coalminer, collier (*Brit.*), pitman (*Brit.*)

mingle *verb* **1** mix, blend, combine, intermingle, interweave, join, merge, unite **2** associate, consort, fraternize, hang about or around, hobnob, rub shoulders (*informal*), socialize

► **Antonyms**
≠mix: detach, dissolve, divide, part, separate ≠associate: avoid, dissociate, estrange

miniature *adjective* small, diminutive, little, minuscule, minute, scaled-down, tiny, toy

► **Antonyms**
big, enormous, giant, gigantic, great, huge, immense, large, oversize

minimal *adjective* minimum, least, least possible, nominal, slightest, smallest, token

minimize *verb* **1** reduce, curtail, decrease, diminish, miniaturize, prune, shrink **2** play down, belittle, decry, deprecate, discount, disparage, make light or little of, underrate

► **Antonyms**
≠reduce: enlarge, expand, extend, heighten, increase, magni-

fy ≠play down: boast about, exalt, praise, vaunt

minimum noun **1** least, lowest, nadir ♦ adjective **2** least, least possible, lowest, minimal, slightest, smallest

► Antonyms

adjective ≠least: greatest, highest, largest, maximum, most

minion noun follower, flunky, hanger-on, henchman, hireling, lackey, underling, yes man

minister noun **1** clergyman, cleric, parson, pastor, preacher, priest, rector, vicar ♦ verb **2** attend, administer, cater to, pander to, serve, take care of, tend

ministry noun **1** the priesthood, holy orders, the church **2** department, bureau, council, office, quango

minor adjective small, inconsequential, insignificant, lesser, petty, slight, trivial, unimportant

► Antonyms

appreciable, consequential, great, important, major, serious, significant, substantial, superior, vital

minstrel noun musician, bard, singer, songstress, troubadour

mint verb make, cast, coin, produce, punch, stamp, strike

minuscule adjective tiny, diminutive, infinitesimal, little, microscopic, miniature, minute

minute[1] noun moment, flash, instant, jiffy (informal), second, tick (Brit. informal), trice

minute[2] adjective **1** small, diminutive, infinitesimal, little, microscopic, miniature, minuscule, tiny **2** precise, close, critical, detailed, exact, exhaustive, meticulous, painstaking, punctilious

► Antonyms

≠small: enormous, gigantic, grand, great, huge, immense, monstrous ≠precise: careless, haphazard, imprecise, inexact, loose, quick, rough, superficial

minutes plural noun record, memorandum, notes, proceedings, transactions, transcript

minutiae plural noun details, finer points, ins and outs, niceties, particulars, subtleties, trifles, trivia

minx noun flirt, coquette, hussy

miracle noun wonder, marvel, phenomenon, prodigy

miraculous adjective wonderful, amazing, astonishing, astounding, extraordinary, incredible, phenomenal, prodigious, unaccountable, unbelievable

► Antonyms

awful, bad, common, commonplace, everyday, normal, ordinary, run-of-the-mill, terrible, unexceptional, unremarkable, usual

mirage noun illusion, hallucination, optical illusion

mire noun **1** swamp, bog, marsh, morass, quagmire **2** mud, dirt, muck, ooze, slime

mirror noun **1** looking-glass, glass, reflector ♦ verb **2** reflect, copy, echo, emulate, follow

mirth noun merriment, amusement, cheerfulness, fun, gaiety, glee, hilarity, jollity, joviality, laughter, revelry

mirthful adjective merry, blithe, cheerful, cheery, festive, happy, jolly, jovial, light-hearted, playful, sportive

► Antonyms

dejected, depressed, despondent, dismal, down in the dumps (informal), gloomy, grave, melancholy, miserable, morose, sad, serious, solemn, sombre, sorrowful, unhappy

misadventure noun misfortune, accident, bad luck, calamity, catastrophe, debacle, disaster, mishap, reverse, setback

misanthropic adjective antisocial, cynical, malevolent, unfriendly

misapprehend verb misunderstand, misconstrue, misinterpret, misread, mistake

misapprehension noun misunderstanding, delusion, error, fallacy, misconception, misinterpretation, mistake

misappropriate verb steal, embezzle, misspend, misuse,

peculate, pocket

miscalculate *verb* misjudge, blunder, err, overestimate, overrate, slip up, underestimate, underrate

miscarriage *noun* failure, breakdown, error, mishap, perversion

miscarry *verb* fail, come to grief, fall through, go awry, go pearshaped (*informal*), go wrong, misfire

miscellaneous *adjective* mixed, assorted, diverse, jumbled, motley, sundry, varied, various

miscellany *noun* assortment, anthology, collection, hotchpotch, jumble, medley, mélange, mixed bag, mixture, potpourri, variety

mischance *noun* misfortune, accident, calamity, disaster, misadventure, mishap

mischief *noun* 1 misbehaviour, impishness, monkey business (*informal*), naughtiness, shenanigans (*informal*), trouble, waywardness 2 harm, damage, evil, hurt, injury, misfortune, trouble

mischievous *adjective* 1 naughty, impish, playful, puckish, rascally, roguish, sportive, troublesome, wayward 2 malicious, damaging, destructive, evil, harmful, hurtful, spiteful, vicious, wicked

misconception *noun* delusion, error, fallacy, misapprehension, misunderstanding

misconduct *noun* immorality, impropriety, malpractice, mismanagement, wrongdoing

miscreant *noun* wrongdoer, blackguard, criminal, rascal, reprobate, rogue, scoundrel, sinner, vagabond, villain

misdeed *noun* offence, crime, fault, misconduct, misdemeanour, sin, transgression, wrong

misdemeanour *noun* offence, fault, infringement, misdeed, peccadillo, transgression

miser *noun* hoarder, cheapskate (*informal*), niggard, pennypincher (*informal*), Scrooge, skinflint

miserable *adjective* 1 unhappy, dejected, depressed, despondent, disconsolate, forlorn, gloomy, sorrowful, woebegone, wretched 2 despicable, deplorable, lamentable, shameful, sordid, sorry, squalid, wretched

▶ **Antonyms**

≠unhappy: cheerful, happy ≠despicable: admirable, good, respectable

miserly *adjective* mean, avaricious, grasping, niggardly, parsimonious, penny-pinching (*informal*), stingy, tightfisted, ungenerous

▶ **Antonyms**

extravagant, generous, prodigal, unselfish

misery *noun* 1 unhappiness, anguish, depression, desolation, despair, distress, gloom, grief, sorrow, suffering, torment, woe 2 *Brit. informal* moaner, killjoy, pessimist, prophet of doom, sourpuss (*informal*), spoilsport, wet blanket (*informal*)

▶ **Antonyms**

≠unhappiness: contentment, ease, enjoyment, happiness, joy, pleasure

misfire *verb* fail, fall through, go pear-shaped (*informal*), go wrong, miscarry

misfit *noun* nonconformist, eccentric, fish out of water (*informal*), oddball (*informal*), square peg (in a round hole) (*informal*)

misfortune *noun* 1 bad luck, adversity, hard luck, ill luck, infelicity 2 mishap, affliction, calamity, disaster, reverse, setback, tragedy, tribulation, trouble

▶ **Antonyms**

fortune, good luck, relief

misgiving *noun* unease, anxiety, apprehension, distrust, doubt, qualm, reservation, suspicion, trepidation, uncertainty, worry

misguided *adjective* unwise, deluded, erroneous, ill-advised, imprudent, injudicious, misplaced, mistaken, unwarranted

mishandle *verb* mismanage,

mishap 355 **mistrust**

botch, bungle, make a mess of, mess up (informal), muff

mishap noun <u>accident</u>, calamity, misadventure, mischance, misfortune

misinform verb <u>mislead</u>, deceive, misdirect, misguide

misinterpret verb <u>misunderstand</u>, distort, misapprehend, misconceive, misconstrue, misjudge, misread, misrepresent, mistake

misjudge verb <u>miscalculate</u>, overestimate, overrate, underestimate, underrate

mislay verb <u>lose</u>, lose track of, misplace

mislead verb <u>deceive</u>, delude, fool, hoodwink, misdirect, misguide, misinform, take in (informal)

misleading adjective <u>confusing</u>, ambiguous, deceptive, disingenuous, evasive, false

► **Antonyms**
candid, clear, direct, frank, honest, simple, straightforward

mismanage verb <u>mishandle</u>, botch, bungle, make a mess of, mess up, misconduct, misdirect, misgovern

misplace verb <u>lose</u>, lose track of, mislay

misprint noun <u>mistake</u>, corrigendum, erratum, literal, typo (informal)

misquote verb <u>misrepresent</u>, falsify, twist

misrepresent verb <u>distort</u>, disguise, falsify, misinterpret

misrule noun <u>disorder</u>, anarchy, chaos, confusion, lawlessness, turmoil

miss verb 1 <u>omit</u>, leave out, let go, overlook, pass over, skip 2 <u>long for</u>, pine for, yearn for 3 <u>avoid</u>, escape, evade ◆ noun 4 <u>mistake</u>, blunder, error, failure, omission, oversight

misshapen adjective <u>deformed</u>, contorted, crooked, distorted, grotesque, malformed, twisted, warped

missile noun <u>rocket</u>, projectile, weapon

missing adjective <u>absent</u>, astray, lacking, left out, lost, mislaid, misplaced, unaccounted-for

► **Antonyms**
accounted for, at hand, available, here, in attendance, on hand, present, there, to hand

mission noun <u>task</u>, assignment, commission, duty, errand, job, quest, undertaking, vocation

missionary noun <u>evangelist</u>, apostle, preacher

missive noun <u>letter</u>, communication, dispatch, epistle, memorandum, message, note, report

misspent adjective <u>wasted</u>, dissipated, imprudent, profitless, squandered

► **Antonyms**
fruitful, industrious, profitable, unwasted, useful, worthwhile

mist noun <u>fog</u>, cloud, film, haze, smog, spray, steam, vapour

mistake noun 1 <u>error</u>, blunder, erratum, fault, faux pas, gaffe, howler (informal), miscalculation, oversight, slip ◆ verb 2 <u>misunderstand</u>, misapprehend, misconstrue, misinterpret, misjudge, misread 3 <u>confuse with</u>, mix up with, take for

mistaken adjective <u>wrong</u>, erroneous, false, faulty, inaccurate, incorrect, misguided, unsound, wide of the mark

► **Antonyms**
accurate, correct, right, sound, true

mistakenly adverb <u>incorrectly</u>, by mistake, erroneously, fallaciously, falsely, inaccurately, misguidedly, wrongly

mistimed adjective <u>inopportune</u>, badly timed, ill-timed, untimely

mistreat verb <u>abuse</u>, harm, illtreat, injure, knock about or around, maltreat, manhandle, misuse, molest

mistress noun <u>lover</u>, concubine, girlfriend, kept woman, paramour

mistrust verb 1 <u>doubt</u>, be wary

of, distrust, fear, suspect ♦ *noun* **2** <u>suspicion</u>, distrust, doubt, misgiving, scepticism, uncertainty, wariness

mistrustful *adjective* <u>suspicious</u>, chary, cynical, distrustful, doubtful, fearful, hesitant, sceptical, uncertain, wary

➤ **Antonyms**

certain, definite, positive, sure

misty *adjective* <u>foggy</u>, blurred, cloudy, dim, hazy, indistinct, murky, obscure, opaque, overcast

➤ **Antonyms**

bright, clear, distinct, sunny, well-defined

misunderstand *verb* <u>misinterpret</u>, be at cross-purposes, get the wrong end of the stick, misapprehend, misconstrue, misjudge, misread, mistake

misunderstanding *noun* <u>mistake</u>, error, misconception, misinterpretation, misjudgment, mix-up

misuse *noun* **1** <u>waste</u>, abuse, desecration, misapplication, squandering ♦ *verb* **2** <u>waste</u>, abuse, desecrate, misapply, prostitute, squander

➤ **Antonyms**

verb ≠<u>waste</u>: appreciate, prize, treasure, use

mitigate *verb* <u>ease</u>, extenuate, lessen, lighten, moderate, soften, subdue, temper

➤ **Antonyms**

aggravate, augment, enhance, heighten, increase, intensify, strengthen

mitigation *noun* <u>relief</u>, alleviation, diminution, extenuation, moderation, remission

mix *verb* **1** <u>combine</u>, blend, cross, fuse, intermingle, interweave, join, jumble, merge, mingle **2** <u>socialize</u>, associate, consort, fraternize, hang out (*informal*), hobnob, mingle ♦ *noun* **3** <u>mixture</u>, alloy, amalgam, assortment, blend, combination, compound, fusion, medley

mixed *adjective* **1** <u>combined</u>,

amalgamated, blended, composite, compound, joint, mingled, united **2** <u>varied</u>, assorted, cosmopolitan, diverse, heterogeneous, miscellaneous, motley

➤ **Antonyms**

≠<u>combined</u>: pure, straight, unmixed   ≠<u>varied</u>: homogeneous, unmixed

mixed-up *adjective* <u>confused</u>, at sea, bewildered, distraught, disturbed, maladjusted, muddled, perplexed, puzzled, upset

mixture *noun* <u>blend</u>, amalgam, assortment, brew, compound, fusion, jumble, medley, mix, potpourri, variety

mix-up *noun* <u>confusion</u>, mess, mistake, misunderstanding, muddle, tangle

mix up *verb* **1** <u>combine</u>, blend, mix **2** <u>confuse</u>, confound, muddle

moan *noun* **1** <u>groan</u>, lament, sigh, sob, wail, whine **2** *Informal* <u>grumble</u>, complaint, gripe (*informal*), grouch (*informal*), grouse, protest, whine ♦ *verb* **3** <u>groan</u>, lament, sigh, sob, whine **4** *Informal* <u>grumble</u>, bleat, carp, complain, groan, grouse, whine, whinge (*informal*)

mob *noun* **1** <u>crowd</u>, drove, flock, horde, host, mass, multitude, pack, swarm, throng **2** *Slang* <u>gang</u>, crew (*informal*), group, lot, set ♦ *verb* **3** <u>surround</u>, crowd around, jostle, set upon, swarm around

mobile *adjective* <u>movable</u>, itinerant, moving, peripatetic, portable, travelling, wandering

mobilize *verb* <u>prepare</u>, activate, call to arms, call up, get *or* make ready, marshal, organize, rally, ready

mock *verb* **1** <u>laugh at</u>, deride, jeer, make fun of, poke fun at, ridicule, scoff, scorn, sneer, taunt, tease **2** <u>mimic</u>, ape, caricature, imitate, lampoon, parody, satirize, send up (*Brit. informal*) ♦ *adjective* **3** <u>imitation</u>, artificial, dummy, fake, false, feigned, phoney or phony (*informal*), pretended, sham, spurious

➤ Antonyms

verb ≠<u>laugh at</u>: praise, respect, revere ◆ *adjective* ≠<u>imitation</u>: authentic, genuine, natural, real, sincere, true, unfeigned

mockery *noun* 1 <u>derision</u>, contempt, disdain, disrespect, insults, jeering, ridicule, scoffing, scorn 2 <u>farce</u>, apology (*informal*), disappointment, joke, letdown

mocking *adjective* <u>scornful</u>, contemptuous, derisive, disdainful, disrespectful, sarcastic, sardonic, satirical, scoffing

mode *noun* 1 <u>method</u>, form, manner, procedure, process, style, system, technique, way 2 <u>fashion</u>, craze, look, rage, style, trend, vogue

model *noun* 1 <u>representation</u>, copy, dummy, facsimile, image, imitation, miniature, mock-up, replica 2 <u>pattern</u>, archetype, example, ideal, original, paradigm, paragon, prototype, standard 3 <u>sitter</u>, poser, subject ◆ *verb* 4 <u>shape</u>, carve, design, fashion, form, mould, sculpt 5 <u>show off</u>, display, sport (*informal*), wear

moderate *adjective* 1 <u>mild</u>, controlled, gentle, limited, middle-of-the-road, modest, reasonable, restrained, steady 2 <u>average</u>, fair, indifferent, mediocre, middling, ordinary, passable, so-so (*informal*), unexceptional ◆ *verb* 3 <u>lessen</u>, control, curb, ease, modulate, regulate, restrain, soften, subdue, temper, tone down

➤ Antonyms

adjective ≠<u>mild</u>: extreme, intemperate, unreasonable, wild ≠<u>average</u>: excessive, extreme, immoderate, inordinate, unusual ◆ *verb* ≠<u>lessen</u>: heighten, increase, intensify

moderately *adverb* <u>reasonably</u>, fairly, passably, quite, rather, slightly, somewhat, tolerably

moderation *noun* <u>restraint</u>, fairness, reasonableness, temperance

modern *adjective* <u>current</u>, con-

temporary, fresh, new, newfangled, novel, present-day, recent, up-to-date

➤ Antonyms

ancient, antiquated, archaic, former, obsolete, old, old-fashioned, old hat, outmoded, passé, past

modernity *noun* <u>novelty</u>, currency, freshness, innovation, newness

modernize *verb* <u>update</u>, make over, rebrand, rejuvenate, remake, remodel, renew, renovate, revamp

modest *adjective* 1 <u>unpretentious</u>, bashful, coy, demure, diffident, reserved, reticent, retiring, self-effacing, shy 2 <u>moderate</u>, fair, limited, middling, ordinary, small, unexceptional

modesty *noun* <u>reserve</u>, bashfulness, coyness, demureness, diffidence, humility, reticence, shyness, timidity

➤ Antonyms

arrogance, boastfulness, conceit, confidence, egotism, immodesty, pride, vanity

modicum *noun* <u>little</u>, bit, crumb, drop, fragment, scrap, shred, touch

modification *noun* <u>change</u>, adjustment, alteration, qualification, refinement, revision, variation

modify *verb* 1 <u>change</u>, adapt, adjust, alter, convert, reform, remodel, revise, rework 2 <u>tone down</u>, ease, lessen, lower, moderate, qualify, restrain, soften, temper

modish *adjective* <u>fashionable</u>, contemporary, current, in, smart, stylish, trendy (*Brit. informal*), up-to-the-minute, voguish

modulate *verb* <u>adjust</u>, attune, balance, regulate, tune, vary

mogul *noun* <u>tycoon</u>, baron, big hitter (*informal*), big noise (*informal*), big shot (*informal*), heavy hitter (*informal*), magnate, V.I.P.

moist *adjective* <u>damp</u>, clammy, dewy, humid, soggy, wet

moisten *verb* dampen, damp, moisturize, soak, water, wet

moisture *noun* damp, dew, liquid, water, wetness

molecule *noun* particle, jot, speck

molest *verb* **1** abuse, attack, harm, hurt, ill-treat, interfere with, maltreat **2** annoy, badger, beset, bother, disturb, harass, persecute, pester, plague, torment, worry

mollify *verb* pacify, appease, calm, conciliate, placate, quiet, soothe, sweeten

mollycoddle *verb* pamper, baby, cosset, indulge, spoil

moment *noun* **1** instant, flash, jiffy (*informal*), jot, second, split second, trice, twinkling **2** time, juncture, point, stage

momentarily *adverb* briefly, for a moment, temporarily

momentary *adjective* short-lived, brief, fleeting, passing, short, temporary, transitory

► **Antonyms**
lasting, lengthy, long-lived, permanent

momentous *adjective* significant, critical, crucial, fateful, historic, important, pivotal, vital, weighty

► **Antonyms**
inconsequential, insignificant, trifling, trivial, unimportant

momentum *noun* impetus, drive, energy, force, power, propulsion, push, strength, thrust

monarch *noun* ruler, emperor or empress, king, potentate, prince or princess, queen, sovereign

monarchy *noun* **1** sovereignty, autocracy, kingship, monocracy, royalism **2** kingdom, empire, principality, realm

monastery *noun* abbey, cloister, convent, friary, nunnery, priory

monastic *adjective* monkish, ascetic, cloistered, contemplative, hermit-like, reclusive, secluded, sequestered, withdrawn

monetary *adjective* financial, budgetary, capital, cash, fiscal, pecuniary

money *noun* cash, capital, coin, currency, hard cash, legal tender, readies (*informal*), riches, silver, wealth

mongrel *noun* **1** hybrid, cross, crossbreed, half-breed ♦ *adjective* **2** hybrid, crossbred

monitor *noun* **1** watchdog, guide, invigilator, prefect (*Brit.*), supervisor ♦ *verb* **2** check, follow, keep an eye on, keep tabs on, keep track of, observe, survey, watch

monk *noun* friar (*loosely*), brother

monkey *noun* **1** simian, primate **2** rascal, devil, imp, rogue, scamp ♦ *verb* **3** with around or about with fool, meddle, mess, play, tinker

monolithic *adjective* huge, colossal, impenetrable, intractable, massive, monumental, solid

monologue *noun* speech, harangue, lecture, sermon, soliloquy

monopolize *verb* control, corner the market in, dominate, hog (*slang*), keep to oneself, take over

monotonous *adjective* tedious, boring, dull, humdrum, mind-numbing, repetitive, tiresome, unchanging, wearisome

► **Antonyms**
entertaining, enthralling, exciting, exhilarating, interesting, lively, stimulating

monotony *noun* tedium, boredom, monotonousness, repetitiveness, routine, sameness, tediousness

monster *noun* **1** giant, colossus, mammoth, titan **2** brute, beast, demon, devil, fiend, villain **3** freak, monstrosity, mutant ♦ *adjective* **4** huge, colossal, enormous, gigantic, immense, mammoth, massive, stupendous, tremendous

monstrosity *noun* eyesore, freak, horror, monster

monstrous *adjective* **1** unnatural, fiendish, freakish, frightful, grotesque, gruesome, hideous, horrible **2** outrageous, diabolical, disgraceful, foul, inhuman, intolerable, scandalous, shocking **3** <u>huge</u>, colossal, enormous, immense, mammoth, massive, prodigious, stupendous, tremendous

➤ **Antonyms**

≠<u>unnatural</u>: attractive, beautiful, delightful, lovely, natural, normal, ordinary ≠<u>outrageous</u>: admirable, decent, fine, good, honourable ≠<u>huge</u>: diminutive, little, miniature, minute, small, tiny

monument *noun* <u>memorial</u>, cairn, cenotaph, commemoration, gravestone, headstone, marker, mausoleum, shrine, tombstone

monumental *adjective* **1** <u>important</u>, awesome, enormous, epoch-making, historic, majestic, memorable, significant, unforgettable **2** *Informal* <u>immense</u>, colossal, great, massive, staggering

➤ **Antonyms**

≠<u>important</u>: inconsequential, insignificant, trivial, unimportant, unremarkable ≠<u>immense</u>: average, insignificant, small, tiny, trivial

mood *noun* <u>state of mind</u>, disposition, frame of mind, humour, spirit, temper

moody *adjective* **1** <u>sulky</u>, ill-tempered, irritable, pissed *(taboo slang)*, pissed off *(taboo slang)*, temperamental, touchy **2** <u>gloomy</u>, glum, morose, sad, sullen **3** <u>changeable</u>, capricious, erratic, fickle, flighty, impulsive, mercurial, temperamental, unpredictable, volatile

➤ **Antonyms**

≠<u>sulky</u>, <u>gloomy</u>: amiable, cheerful, gay, happy, optimistic ≠<u>changeable</u>: constant, stable, steady

moon *noun* **1** <u>satellite</u> ◆ *verb* **2** idle, daydream, languish, mope, waste time

moor[1] *noun* <u>moorland</u>, fell *(Brit.)*, heath

moor[2] *verb* <u>tie up</u>, anchor, berth, dock, lash, make fast, secure

moot *adjective* **1** <u>debatable</u>, argu-

able, contestable, controversial, disputable, doubtful, undecided, unresolved, unsettled ◆ *verb* **2** <u>bring up</u>, broach, propose, put forward, suggest

mop *noun* **1** <u>squeegee</u>, sponge, swab **2** <u>mane</u>, shock, tangle, thatch

mope *verb* <u>brood</u>, fret, languish, moon, pine, pout, sulk

mop up *verb* <u>clean up</u>, soak up, sponge, swab, wash, wipe

moral *adjective* **1** <u>good</u>, decent, ethical, high-minded, honourable, just, noble, principled, right, virtuous ◆ *noun* **2** <u>lesson</u>, meaning, message, point, significance

➤ **Antonyms**

adjective ≠<u>good</u>: amoral, dishonourable, immoral, sinful, unethical, unjust, wrong

morale *noun* <u>confidence</u>, esprit de corps, heart, self-esteem, spirit

morality *noun* **1** <u>integrity</u>, decency, goodness, honesty, justice, righteousness, virtue **2** <u>standards</u>, conduct, ethics, manners, morals, mores, philosophy, principles

morals *plural noun* <u>morality</u>, behaviour, conduct, ethics, habits, integrity, manners, mores, principles, scruples, standards

morass *noun* **1** <u>marsh</u>, bog, fen, quagmire, slough, swamp **2** <u>mess</u>, confusion, mix-up, muddle, tangle

moratorium *noun* <u>postponement</u>, freeze, halt, standstill, suspension

morbid *adjective* **1** <u>unwholesome</u>, ghoulish, gloomy, melancholy, sick, sombre, unhealthy **2** <u>gruesome</u>, dreadful, ghastly, grisly, hideous, horrid, macabre

➤ **Antonyms**

≠<u>unwholesome</u>: bright, cheerful, happy, healthy, wholesome

mordant *adjective* <u>sarcastic</u>, biting, caustic, cutting, incisive, pungent, scathing, stinging, trenchant

more *adjective* **1** <u>extra</u>, added, additional, further, new, new-found, other, supplementary ◆ adverb **2** to a greater extent, better, further, longer

moreover adverb furthermore, additionally, also, as well, besides, further, in addition, too

morgue noun mortuary

moribund adjective declining, on its last legs, stagnant, waning, weak

morning noun dawn, a.m., break of day, daybreak, forenoon, morn (poetic), sunrise

moron noun fool, blockhead, cretin, dumb-ass (slang), dunce, dunderhead, halfwit, idiot, imbecile, oaf

moronic adjective idiotic, cretinous, dumb-ass (slang), foolish, halfwitted, imbecilic, mindless, stupid, unintelligent

morose adjective sullen, depressed, dour, gloomy, glum, ill-tempered, moody, sour, sulky, surly, taciturn

➤ **Antonyms**

blithe, cheerful, chirpy (informal), gay, genial, good-humoured, good-natured, happy, pleasant

morsel noun piece, bit, bite, crumb, mouthful, part, scrap, soupçon, taste, titbit

mortal adjective **1** human, ephemeral, impermanent, passing, temporal, transient, worldly **2** fatal, deadly, death-dealing, destructive, killing, lethal, murderous, terminal ◆ noun **3** human being, being, earthling, human, individual, man, person, woman

mortality noun **1** humanity, impermanence, transience **2** killing, bloodshed, carnage, death, destruction, fatality

mortification noun **1** humiliation, annoyance, chagrin, discomfiture, embarrassment, shame, vexation **2** discipline, abasement, chastening, control, denial, subjugation **3** Medical gangrene, corruption, festering

mortified adjective humiliated,

ashamed, chagrined, chastened, crushed, deflated, embarrassed, humbled, shamed

mortify verb **1** humiliate, chagrin, chasten, crush, deflate, embarrass, humble, shame **2** discipline, abase, chasten, control, deny, subdue **3** Of flesh putrefy, deaden, die, fester

mortuary noun morgue, funeral parlour

mostly adverb generally, as a rule, chiefly, largely, mainly, on the whole, predominantly, primarily, principally, usually

moth-eaten adjective decayed, decrepit, dilapidated, ragged, shabby, tattered, threadbare, worn-out

mother noun **1** parent, dam, ma (informal), mater, mum (Brit. informal), mummy (Brit. informal) ◆ adjective **2** native, inborn, innate, natural ◆ verb **3** nurture, care for, cherish, nurse, protect, raise, rear, tend

motherly adjective maternal, affectionate, caring, comforting, loving, protective, sheltering

motif noun **1** theme, concept, idea, leitmotif, subject **2** design, decoration, ornament, shape

motion noun **1** movement, flow, locomotion, mobility, move, progress, travel **2** proposal, proposition, recommendation, submission, suggestion ◆ verb **3** gesture, beckon, direct, gesticulate, nod, signal, wave

motionless adjective still, fixed, frozen, immobile, paralysed, standing, static, stationary, stock-still, transfixed, unmoving

➤ **Antonyms**

animated, lively, mobile, moving, restless

motivate verb inspire, arouse, cause, drive, induce, move, persuade, prompt, stimulate, stir

motivation noun incentive, incitement, inducement, inspiration, motive, reason, spur, stimulus

motive noun reason, ground(s),

incentive, inducement, inspiration, object, purpose, rationale, stimulus

motley *adjective* **1** miscellaneous, assorted, disparate, heterogeneous, mixed, varied **2** multicoloured, chequered, variegated

► **Antonyms**

≠miscellaneous: homogeneous, uniform ≠multicoloured: monochromatic, plain, self-coloured

mottled *adjective* blotchy, dappled, flecked, piebald, speckled, spotted, stippled, streaked

motto *noun* saying, adage, dictum, maxim, precept, proverb, rule, slogan, tag-line, watchword

mould[1] *noun* **1** cast, pattern, shape **2** design, build, construction, fashion, form, format, kind, pattern, shape, style **3** nature, calibre, character, kind, quality, sort, stamp, type ♦ *verb* **4** shape, construct, create, fashion, forge, form, make, model, sculpt, work **5** influence, affect, control, direct, form, make, shape

mould[2] *noun* fungus, blight, mildew

mouldy *adjective* stale, bad, blighted, decaying, fusty, mildewed, musty, rotten

mound *noun* **1** heap, drift, pile, rick, stack **2** hill, bank, dune, embankment, hillock, knoll, rise

mount *verb* **1** ascend, clamber up, climb, go up, scale **2** get (up) on, bestride, climb onto, jump on **3** increase, accumulate, build, escalate, grow, intensify, multiply, pile up, swell ♦ *noun* **4** backing, base, frame, setting, stand, support **5** horse, steed (*literary*)

► **Antonyms**

verb ≠ascend: descend, drop, go down ≠get (up) on: climb down from, climb off, dismount, get down from, get off, jump off ≠increase: contract, decline, decrease, diminish, dwindle, fall, lessen, lower, reduce, shrink

mountain *noun* **1** peak, alp, fell (*Brit.*), mount **2** heap, abun-

dance, mass, mound, pile, stack, ton

mountainous *adjective* **1** high, alpine, highland, rocky, soaring, steep, towering, upland **2** huge, daunting, enormous, gigantic, great, immense, mammoth, mighty, monumental

► **Antonyms**

≠huge: diminutive, little, minute, small, tiny

mourn *verb* grieve, bemoan, bewail, deplore, lament, rue, wail, weep

mournful *adjective* **1** sad, melancholy, piteous, plaintive, sorrowful, tragic, unhappy, woeful **2** dismal, disconsolate, downcast, gloomy, grieving, heavy-hearted, lugubrious, miserable, rueful, sombre

► **Antonyms**

≠sad: cheerful, happy ≠dismal: bright, cheerful, chirpy (*informal*), happy, jolly, joyful, light-hearted, sunny

mourning *noun* **1** grieving, bereavement, grief, lamentation, weeping, woe **2** black, sackcloth and ashes, widow's weeds

mouth *noun* **1** lips, gob (*slang, especially Brit.*), jaws, maw **2** opening, aperture, door, entrance, gateway, inlet, orifice

mouthful *noun* taste, bit, bite, little, morsel, sample, spoonful, swallow

mouthpiece *noun* spokesperson, agent, delegate, representative, spokesman *or* spokeswoman

movable *adjective* portable, detachable, mobile, transferable, transportable

move *verb* **1** go, advance, budge, proceed, progress, shift, stir **2** change, shift, switch, transfer, transpose **3** relocate, leave, migrate, pack one's bags (*informal*), quit, remove **4** drive, activate, operate, propel, shift, start, turn **5** prompt, cause, incite, induce, influence, inspire, motivate, persuade, rouse **6** touch, affect, excite, impress **7** propose, advocate, put forward, recommend, suggest, urge ♦ noun **8** action, manoeuvre, measure, ploy, step, stratagem, stroke, turn **9** transfer, relocation, removal, shift

➤ **Antonyms**

verb ≠prompt: deter, discourage, dissuade, prevent, stop

movement noun **1** motion, action, activity, change, development, flow, manoeuvre, progress, stirring **2** group, campaign, crusade, drive, faction, front, grouping, organization, party **3** Music section, division, part, passage **4** workings, action, machinery, mechanism, works

movie noun film, feature, flick (slang), picture

moving adjective **1** emotional, affecting, inspiring, pathetic, persuasive, poignant, stirring, touching **2** mobile, movable, portable, running, unfixed

➤ **Antonyms**

≠emotional: unemotional, unexciting, unimpressive, uninspiring ≠mobile: fixed, immobile, immovable, stationary, still, unmoving

mow verb cut, crop, scythe, shear, trim

mow down verb massacre, butcher, cut down, cut to pieces, shoot down, slaughter

much adjective **1** great, abundant, a lot of, ample, considerable, copious, plenty of, sizable or sizeable, substantial ♦ noun **2** a lot, a good deal, a great deal, heaps (informal), loads (informal), lots (informal), plenty ♦ adverb **3** greatly, a great deal, a ton, considerably, decidedly, exceedingly

➤ **Antonyms**

adjective ≠great: inadequate, insufficient, little, scant ♦ noun ≠a lot: hardly anything, little, next to nothing, not a lot, not much, practically nothing, very little ♦ adverb ≠greatly: barely, hardly, not a lot, not much, only just, scarcely, slightly

muck noun **1** dirt, filth, gunge (informal), mire, mud, ooze, slime, sludge **2** manure, dung, ordure

muck up verb ruin, blow (slang), botch, bungle, make a mess of, make a pig's ear of (informal), mess up, muff, spoil

mucky adjective dirty, begrimed, filthy, grimy, messy, muddy

mud noun dirt, clay, mire, ooze, silt, slime, sludge

muddle noun **1** confusion, chaos, disarray, disorder, disorganization, jumble, mess, mix-up, predicament, tangle ♦ verb **2** jumble, disarrange, disorder, disorganize, mess, mix up, scramble, spoil, tangle **3** confuse, befuddle, bewilder, confound, daze, disorient, perplex, stupefy

muddy adjective **1** dirty, bespattered, grimy, mucky, mudcaked, soiled **2** boggy, marshy, quaggy, swampy

muffle verb **1** deaden, muzzle, quieten, silence, soften, stifle, suppress **2** wrap up, cloak, cover, envelop, shroud, swaddle, swathe

muffled adjective indistinct, faint, muted, stifled, strangled, subdued, suppressed

mug[1] noun cup, beaker, pot, tankard

mug[2] noun **1** face, countenance, features, visage **2** fool, chump (informal), easy or soft touch (slang), simpleton, sucker (slang)

mug[3] verb attack, assault, beat up, rob, set about or upon

muggy adjective humid, clammy, close, moist, oppressive, sticky, stuffy, sultry

mug up verb study, bone up on (informal), burn the midnight oil (informal), cram (informal), swot (Brit. informal)

mull verb ponder, consider, contemplate, deliberate, meditate, reflect on, ruminate, think over, weigh

multifarious adjective diverse, different, legion, manifold, many, miscellaneous, multiple, numerous, sundry, varied

multiple *adjective* **many**, manifold, multitudinous, numerous, several, sundry, various

multiply *verb* **1** <u>increase</u>, build up, expand, extend, proliferate, spread **2** <u>reproduce</u>, breed, propagate

➤ **Antonyms**

≠<u>increase</u>: abate, decline, decrease, diminish, lessen, reduce

multitude *noun* <u>mass</u>, army, crowd, horde, host, mob, myriad, swarm, throng

munch *verb* <u>chew</u>, champ, chomp, crunch

mundane *adjective* **1** <u>ordinary</u>, banal, commonplace, day-to-day, everyday, humdrum, prosaic, routine, workaday **2** <u>earthly</u>, mortal, secular, temporal, terrestrial, worldly

➤ **Antonyms**

≠<u>ordinary</u>: dramatic, exciting, extraordinary, interesting, novel, original, special, uncommon, unusual ≠<u>earthly</u>: ethereal, heavenly, spiritual, unworldly

municipal *adjective* <u>civic</u>, public, urban

municipality *noun* <u>town</u>, borough, city, district, township

munificence *noun* <u>generosity</u>, beneficence, benevolence, bounty, largesse *or* largess, liberality, magnanimousness, philanthropy

munificent *adjective* <u>generous</u>, beneficent, benevolent, bountiful, lavish, liberal, magnanimous, open-handed, philanthropic, unstinting

➤ **Antonyms**

cheap, mean, miserly, parsimonious, small, stingy

murder *noun* **1** <u>killing</u>, assassination, bloodshed, butchery, carnage, homicide, manslaughter, massacre, slaying ♦ *verb* **2** <u>kill</u>, assassinate, bump off (*slang*), butcher, eliminate (*slang*), massacre, slaughter, slay

murderer *noun* <u>killer</u>, assassin, butcher, cut-throat, hit man

(*slang*), homicide, slaughterer, slayer

murderous *adjective* <u>deadly</u>, bloodthirsty, brutal, cruel, cut-throat, ferocious, lethal, savage

murky *adjective* <u>dark</u>, cloudy, dim, dull, gloomy, grey, misty, overcast

➤ **Antonyms**

bright, clear, sunny

murmur *verb* **1** <u>mumble</u>, mutter, whisper **2** <u>grumble</u>, complain, moan (*informal*) ♦ *noun* **3** <u>drone</u>, buzzing, humming, purr, rumble, whisper

muscle *noun* **1** <u>tendon</u>, sinew **2** <u>strength</u>, brawn, clout (*informal*), forcefulness, might, power, stamina, weight ♦ *verb* **3** <u>muscle in</u> *Informal* impose oneself, butt in, force one's way in

muscular *adjective* <u>strong</u>, athletic, powerful, robust, sinewy, strapping, sturdy, vigorous

muse *verb* <u>ponder</u>, brood, cogitate, consider, contemplate, deliberate, meditate, mull over, reflect, ruminate

mushy *adjective* **1** <u>soft</u>, pulpy, semi-solid, slushy, squashy, squelchy, squidgy (*informal*) **2** *Informal* <u>sentimental</u>, icky (*informal*), maudlin, mawkish, saccharine, schmaltzy (*slang*), sloppy (*informal*), slushy (*informal*)

musical *adjective* <u>melodious</u>, dulcet, euphonious, harmonious, lyrical, melodic, sweet-sounding, tuneful

➤ **Antonyms**

discordant, grating, harsh, unmelodious, unmusical

must *noun* <u>necessity</u>, essential, fundamental, imperative, prerequisite, requirement, requisite, sine qua non

muster *verb* **1** <u>assemble</u>, call together, convene, gather, marshal, mobilize, rally, summon ♦ *noun* **2** <u>assembly</u>, collection, congregation, convention, gathering, meeting, rally, roundup

musty *adjective* <u>stale</u>, airless, dank, fusty, mildewed, mouldy, old, smelly, stuffy

mutability *noun* <u>change</u>, alteration, evolution, metamorphosis, transition, variation, vicissitude

mutable *adjective* <u>changeable</u>, adaptable, alterable, fickle, inconsistent, inconstant, unsettled, unstable, variable, volatile

mutation *noun* <u>change</u>, alteration, evolution, metamorphosis, modification, transfiguration, transformation, variation

mute *adjective* <u>silent</u>, dumb, mum, speechless, unspoken, voiceless, wordless

mutilate *verb* 1 <u>maim</u>, amputate, cut up, damage, disfigure, dismember, injure, lacerate, mangle 2 <u>distort</u>, adulterate, bowdlerize, censor, cut, damage, expurgate

mutinous *adjective* <u>rebellious</u>, disobedient, insubordinate, insurgent, refractory, riotous, subversive, unmanageable, unruly

mutiny *noun* 1 <u>rebellion</u>, disobedience, insubordination, insurrection, revolt, revolution, riot, uprising ◆ *verb* 2 <u>rebel</u>, disobey, resist, revolt, rise up

mutter *verb* <u>grumble</u>, complain, grouse, mumble, murmur, rumble

mutual *adjective* <u>shared</u>, common, interchangeable, joint, reciprocal, requited, returned

muzzle *noun* 1 <u>jaws</u>, mouth, nose, snout 2 <u>gag</u>, guard ◆ *verb* 3 <u>suppress</u>, censor, curb, gag, restrain, silence, stifle

myopic *adjective* <u>short-sighted</u>, near-sighted

myriad *adjective* 1 <u>innumerable</u>, countless, immeasurable, incalculable, multitudinous, untold ◆ *noun* 2 <u>multitude</u>, army, horde, host, swarm

mysterious *adjective* 1 <u>strange</u>, arcane, enigmatic, inexplicable, inscrutable, mystifying, perplexing, puzzling, secret, uncanny, unfathomable, weird 2 <u>secretive</u>, cloak-and-dagger, covert, furtive

> **Antonyms**

apparent, clear, manifest, open, plain

mystery *noun* <u>puzzle</u>, conundrum, enigma, problem, question, riddle, secret, teaser

mystic, mystical *adjective* <u>supernatural</u>, inscrutable, metaphysical, mysterious, occult, otherworldly, paranormal, preternatural, transcendental

mystify *verb* <u>puzzle</u>, baffle, bewilder, confound, confuse, flummox, nonplus, perplex, stump

mystique *noun* <u>fascination</u>, awe, charisma, charm, glamour, magic, spell

myth *noun* 1 <u>legend</u>, allegory, fable, fairy story, fiction, folk tale, saga, story 2 <u>illusion</u>, delusion, fancy, fantasy, figment, imagination, superstition, tall story

mythical *adjective* 1 <u>legendary</u>, fabled, fabulous, fairy-tale, mythological 2 <u>imaginary</u>, fictitious, invented, made-up, make-believe, nonexistent, pretended, unreal, untrue

mythological *adjective* <u>legendary</u>, fabulous, mythic, mythical, traditional

mythology *noun* <u>legend</u>, folklore, lore, tradition

N n

nab *verb* <u>catch</u>, apprehend, arrest, capture, collar (*informal*), grab, seize, snatch

nadir *noun* <u>bottom</u>, depths, lowest point, minimum, rock bottom

> **Antonyms**

acme, apex, climax, high point, peak, pinnacle, zenith

naevus *noun* <u>birthmark</u>, mole

naff *adjective* Brit. slang <u>bad</u>, duff (*Brit. informal*), inferior, low-grade, poor, rubbishy, second-rate, shabby, shoddy, worthless

➤ **Antonyms**
excellent, fine, first-class, first-rate, high-quality, superior

nag¹ verb 1 scold, annoy, badger, harass, hassle (informal), henpeck, irritate, pester, plague, upbraid, worry ♦ noun 2 scold, harpy, shrew, tartar, virago

nag² noun horse, hack

nagging adjective irritating, persistent, scolding, shrewish, worrying

nail verb fasten, attach, fix, hammer, join, pin, secure, tack

naive adjective 1 gullible, callow, credulous, green, unsuspicious, wet behind the ears (informal) 2 innocent, artless, guileless, ingenuous, open, simple, trusting, unsophisticated, unworldly

➤ **Antonyms**
≠innocent: disingenuous, experienced, sly, sophisticated, urbane, worldly

naivety, naïveté noun 1 gullibility, callowness, credulity 2 innocence, artlessness, guilelessness, inexperience, ingenuousness, naturalness, openness, simplicity

naked adjective 1 nude, bare, exposed, starkers (informal), stripped, unclothed, undressed, without a stitch on (informal)

➤ **Antonyms**
clothed, covered, dressed

nakedness noun nudity, bareness, undress

namby-pamby adjective feeble, insipid, sentimental, spineless, vapid, weak, weedy (informal), wimpish or wimpy (informal), wishy-washy (informal), wussy (slang)

name noun 1 title, designation, epithet, handle (slang), moniker or monicker (slang), nickname, sobriquet, term 2 fame, distinction, eminence, esteem, honour, note, praise, renown, repute ♦ verb 3 call, baptize, christen, dub, entitle, label, style, term 4 nominate, appoint, choose, designate, select, specify

named adjective 1 called, baptized, christened, dubbed, entitled, known as, labelled, styled, termed 2 nominated, appointed, chosen, designated, mentioned, picked, selected, singled out, specified

nameless adjective 1 anonymous, unnamed, untitled 2 unknown, incognito, obscure, undistinguished, unheard-of, unsung 3 horrible, abominable, indescribable, unmentionable, unspeakable, unutterable

namely adverb specifically, to wit, viz.

nap¹ noun 1 sleep, catnap, forty winks (informal), kip (Brit. slang), rest, siesta ♦ verb 2 sleep, catnap, doze, drop off (informal), kip (Brit. slang), nod off (informal), rest, snooze (informal)

nap² noun weave, down, fibre, grain, pile

napkin noun serviette, cloth

narcissism noun egotism, self-love, vanity

narcotic noun 1 drug, anaesthetic, analgesic, anodyne, opiate, painkiller, sedative, tranquillizer ♦ adjective 2 sedative, analgesic, calming, hypnotic, painkilling, soporific

nark verb annoy, bother, exasperate, get on one's nerves (informal), irritate, nettle

narrate verb tell, chronicle, describe, detail, recite, recount, relate, report

narration noun telling, description, explanation, reading, recital, relation

narrative noun story, account, chronicle, history, report, statement, tale

narrator noun storyteller, author, chronicler, commentator, reporter, writer

narrow adjective 1 thin, attenuated, fine, slender, slim, spare, tapering 2 limited, close, confined, constricted, contracted, meagre, restricted, tight 3 insular, dogmatic, illiberal, intolerant,

narrow-minded, partial, prejudiced, small-minded ♦ *verb* **4** tighten, constrict, limit, reduce

▶ **Antonyms**

adjective ≠thin: broad, wide ≠limited: ample, big, broad, generous, open, spacious, wide ≠insular: broad-minded, generous, liberal, receptive, tolerant

narrowly *adverb* just, barely, by the skin of one's teeth, only just, scarcely

narrow-minded *adjective* intolerant, bigoted, hidebound, illiberal, opinionated, parochial, prejudiced, provincial, small-minded

▶ **Antonyms**

broad-minded, catholic, indulgent, open-minded, permissive, tolerant, unprejudiced

nastiness *noun* unpleasantness, malice, meanness, spitefulness

nasty *adjective* **1** objectionable, disagreeable, loathsome, obnoxious, offensive, unpleasant, vile **2** painful, bad, critical, dangerous, serious, severe **3** spiteful, despicable, disagreeable, distasteful, malicious, mean, unpleasant, vicious, vile

▶ **Antonyms**

≠objectionable: admirable, agreeable, enjoyable, nice, pleasant, sweet ≠spiteful: decent, kind, nice, pleasant, sweet

nation *noun* country, people, race, realm, society, state, tribe

national *adjective* **1** nationwide, countrywide, public, widespread ♦ *noun* **2** citizen, inhabitant, native, resident, subject

nationalism *noun* patriotism, allegiance, chauvinism, jingoism, loyalty

nationality *noun* race, birth, nation

nationwide *adjective* national, countrywide, general, widespread

native *adjective* **1** local, domestic, home, indigenous **2** inborn, congenital, hereditary, inbred, ingrained, innate, instinctive, intrinsic, natural ♦ *noun* **3** inhabitant, aborigine, citizen, countryman, dweller, national, resident

natter *verb* **1** gossip, blether, chatter, gabble, jaw (*slang*), prattle, rabbit (on) (*Brit. informal*), talk ♦ *noun* **2** gossip, chat, chinwag (*Brit. informal*), chitchat, conversation, gab (*informal*), jaw (*slang*), prattle, talk

natty *adjective* smart, dapper, elegant, fashionable, neat, snazzy (*informal*), spruce, stylish, trim

natural *adjective* **1** normal, common, everyday, legitimate, logical, ordinary, regular, typical, usual **2** unaffected, genuine, ingenuous, open, real, simple, spontaneous, unpretentious, unsophisticated **3** innate, characteristic, essential, inborn, inherent, instinctive, intuitive, native **4** pure, organic, plain, unrefined, whole

▶ **Antonyms**

≠normal: abnormal, irregular, out of the ordinary, strange, untypical ≠unaffected: affected, artificial, assumed, counterfeit, feigned, phoney or phony (*informal*), unnatural ≠pure: manufactured, processed, synthetic, unnatural

naturalist *noun* biologist, botanist, ecologist, zoologist

naturalistic *adjective* realistic, lifelike, true-to-life

naturally *adverb* **1** of course, certainly **2** genuinely, normally, simply, spontaneously, typically, unaffectedly, unpretentiously

nature *noun* **1** creation, cosmos, earth, environment, universe, world **2** make-up, character, complexion, constitution, essence **3** kind, category, description, sort, species, style, type, variety **4** temperament, disposition, humour, mood, outlook, temper

naughty *adjective* **1** disobedient, bad, impish, misbehaved, mischievous, refractory, wayward, wicked, worthless **2** obscene, improper, lewd, ribald, risqué, smutty, vulgar

➤ **Antonyms**

≠disobedient: good, obedient, polite, proper, well-behaved, well-mannered ≠obscene: polite, proper

nausea noun sickness, biliousness, queasiness, retching, squeamishness, vomiting

nauseate verb sicken, disgust, offend, repel, repulse, revolt, turn one's stomach

nauseous adjective sickening, abhorrent, disgusting, distasteful, nauseating, offensive, repugnant, repulsive, revolting

nautical adjective maritime, marine, naval

naval adjective nautical, marine, maritime

navigable adjective 1 passable, clear, negotiable, unobstructed 2 sailable, controllable, dirigible

navigate verb sail, drive, guide, handle, manoeuvre, pilot, steer, voyage

navigation noun sailing, helmsmanship, seamanship, voyaging

navigator noun pilot, mariner, seaman

navvy noun labourer, worker, workman

navy noun fleet, armada, flotilla

near adjective 1 close, adjacent, adjoining, nearby, neighbouring 2 forthcoming, approaching, imminent, impending, in the offing, looming, nigh, upcoming

➤ **Antonyms**

≠close: distant, far, faraway, far-flung, far-off, far-removed, outlying, out-of-the-way, remote, removed ≠forthcoming: distant, faraway, far-off, remote

nearby adjective neighbouring, adjacent, adjoining, convenient, handy

nearly adverb almost, approximately, as good as, just about, practically, roughly, virtually, well-nigh

nearness noun closeness, accessibility, availability, handiness,

proximity, vicinity

near-sighted adjective short-sighted, myopic

neat adjective 1 tidy, orderly, ship-shape, smart, spick-and-span, spruce, systematic, trim 2 elegant, adept, adroit, deft, dexterous, efficient, graceful, nimble, skilful, stylish 3 Of alcoholic drinks undiluted, pure, straight, unmixed

➤ **Antonyms**

≠tidy: clumsy, cluttered, disorderly, disorganized, messy, sloppy (informal), untidy ≠elegant: clumsy, incompetent, inefficient, inelegant

neatly adverb 1 tidily, daintily, fastidiously, methodically, smartly, sprucely, systematically 2 elegantly, adeptly, adroitly, deftly, dexterously, efficiently, expertly, gracefully, nimbly, skilfully

neatness noun 1 tidiness, daintiness, orderliness, smartness, spruceness, trimness 2 elegance, adroitness, deftness, dexterity, efficiency, grace, nimbleness, skill, style

nebulous adjective vague, confused, dim, hazy, imprecise, indefinite, indistinct, shadowy, uncertain, unclear

necessarily adverb certainly, automatically, compulsorily, incontrovertibly, inevitably, inexorably, naturally, of necessity, undoubtedly

necessary adjective 1 needed, compulsory, essential, imperative, indispensable, mandatory, obligatory, required, requisite, vital 2 certain, fated, inescapable, inevitable, inexorable, unavoidable

➤ **Antonyms**

≠needed: dispensable, expendable, inessential, nonessential, superfluous, unnecessary ≠certain: unnecessary

necessitate verb compel, call for, coerce, constrain, demand, force, impel, oblige, require

necessities plural noun essentials, exigencies, fundamentals, needs, requirements

necessity *noun* **1** inevitability, compulsion, inexorableness, obligation **2** essential, desideratum, fundamental, need, prerequisite, requirement, requisite, *sine qua non*

necromancy *noun* magic, black magic, divination, enchantment, sorcery, witchcraft, wizardry

necropolis *noun* cemetery, burial ground, churchyard, graveyard

need *verb* **1** require, call for, demand, entail, lack, miss, necessitate, want ♦ *noun* **2** lack, inadequacy, insufficiency, paucity, shortage **3** requirement, demand, desideratum, essential, necessity, requisite **4** emergency, exigency, necessity, obligation, urgency, want **5** poverty, deprivation, destitution, penury

needed *adjective* necessary, called for, desired, lacked, required, wanted

needful *adjective* necessary, essential, indispensable, needed, required, requisite, stipulated, vital

needle *verb* irritate, annoy, get on one's nerves (*informal*), goad, harass, nag, pester, provoke, rile, taunt

needless *adjective* unnecessary, gratuitous, groundless, pointless, redundant, superfluous, uncalled-for, unwanted, useless

► **Antonyms**

essential, obligatory, required, useful

needlework *noun* embroidery, needlecraft, sewing, stitching, tailoring

needy *adjective* poor, deprived, destitute, disadvantaged, impoverished, penniless, poverty-stricken, underprivileged

► **Antonyms**

affluent, prosperous, rich, wealthy, well-off

ne'er-do-well *noun* layabout, black sheep, good-for-nothing, idler, loafer, loser, skiver (*Brit. slang*), wastrel

nefarious *adjective* wicked, criminal, depraved, evil, foul, heinous, infernal, villainous

► **Antonyms**

admirable, good, honourable, noble, praiseworthy, upright, virtuous

negate *verb* **1** invalidate, annul, cancel, countermand, neutralize, nullify, obviate, reverse, wipe out **2** deny, contradict, disallow, disprove, gainsay (*archaic or literary*), oppose, rebut, refute

► **Antonyms**

≠deny: affirm, assert, confirm, declare, state, swear

negation *noun* **1** cancellation, neutralization, nullification **2** denial, contradiction, converse, disavowal, inverse, opposite, rejection, renunciation, reverse

negative *adjective* **1** contradictory, contrary, denying, dissenting, opposing, refusing, rejecting, resisting **2** pessimistic, cynical, gloomy, jaundiced, uncooperative, unenthusiastic, unwilling ♦ *noun* **3** contradiction, denial, refusal

► **Antonyms**

adjective ≠contradictory: affirmative, approving, assenting, concurring, positive ≠pessimistic: cheerful, enthusiastic, optimistic, positive

neglect *verb* **1** forget, be remiss, evade, omit, pass over, shirk, skimp **2** disregard, disdain, ignore, overlook, rebuff, scorn, slight, spurn ♦ *noun* **3** negligence, carelessness, dereliction, failure, laxity, oversight, slackness **4** disregard, disdain, inattention, indifference

► **Antonyms**

verb ≠disregard: appreciate, attend to, notice, observe, regard, remember, value ♦ *noun* ≠negligence, ≠disregard: attention, care, consideration, notice, regard, respect

neglected *adjective* **1** abandoned, derelict, overgrown **2** disregarded, unappreciated, underestimated, undervalued

neglectful adjective <u>careless</u>, heedless, inattentive, indifferent, lax, negligent, remiss, thoughtless, uncaring

negligence noun <u>carelessness</u>, dereliction, disregard, inattention, indifference, laxity, neglect, slackness, thoughtlessness

negligent adjective <u>careless</u>, forgetful, heedless, inattentive, neglectful, remiss, slack, slapdash, thoughtless, unthinking

➤ **Antonyms**
attentive, careful, considerate, mindful, painstaking, rigorous, thorough, thoughtful

negligible adjective <u>insignificant</u>, imperceptible, inconsequential, minor, minute, small, trifling, trivial, unimportant

➤ **Antonyms**
important, noteworthy, significant, vital

negotiable adjective <u>debatable</u>, variable

negotiate verb 1 <u>deal</u>, arrange, bargain, conciliate, cut a deal, debate, discuss, mediate, transact, work out 2 <u>get round</u>, clear, cross, get over, get past, pass, surmount

negotiation noun <u>bargaining</u>, arbitration, debate, diplomacy, discussion, mediation, transaction, wheeling and dealing (informal)

negotiator noun <u>mediator</u>, ambassador, delegate, diplomat, honest broker, intermediary, moderator

neighbourhood noun <u>district</u>, community, environs, locale, locality, quarter, region, vicinity

neighbouring adjective <u>nearby</u>, adjacent, adjoining, bordering, connecting, near, next, surrounding

➤ **Antonyms**
distant, far, far-off, remote

neighbourly adjective <u>helpful</u>, considerate, friendly, harmonious, hospitable, kind, obliging, sociable

nemesis noun <u>retribution</u>, desti-

ny, destruction, fate, vengeance

nepotism noun <u>favouritism</u>, bias, partiality, patronage, preferential treatment

nerd, nurd noun Slang <u>bore</u>, anorak (informal), dork (slang), geek (informal), obsessive, trainspotter (informal), wonk (informal)

nerve noun 1 <u>bravery</u>, bottle (Brit. slang), courage, daring, fearlessness, grit, guts (informal), pluck, resolution, will 2 Informal <u>impudence</u>, audacity, boldness, brazenness, cheek (informal), impertinence, insolence, temerity
♦ verb 3 nerve oneself <u>brace oneself</u>, fortify oneself, gee oneself up, steel oneself

nerveless adjective 1 <u>calm</u>, composed, controlled, cool, impassive, imperturbable, self-possessed, unemotional 2 <u>fearless</u>, brave, courageous, daring, gutsy (slang), plucky, unafraid

nerve-racking adjective <u>tense</u>, difficult, distressing, frightening, gut-wrenching, harrowing, stressful, trying, worrying

nerves plural noun <u>tension</u>, anxiety, butterflies (in one's stomach) (informal), cold feet (informal), fretfulness, nervousness, strain, stress, worry

nervous adjective <u>apprehensive</u>, antsy (informal), anxious, edgy, fearful, jumpy, on edge, tense, uneasy, uptight (informal), worried

➤ **Antonyms**
calm, confident, cool, laid-back (informal), relaxed, steady, unfazed (informal)

nervousness noun <u>anxiety</u>, agitation, antsiness (informal), disquiet, excitability, fluster, tension, touchiness, worry

nervy adjective <u>anxious</u>, agitated, fidgety, jittery (informal), jumpy, nervous, on edge, tense, twitchy (informal)

nest noun <u>refuge</u>, den, haunt, hideaway, retreat

nest egg noun <u>reserve</u>, cache, deposit, fall-back, fund(s), savings, store

nestle *verb* snuggle, cuddle, curl up, huddle, nuzzle

nestling *noun* chick, fledgling

net[1] *noun* **1** mesh, lattice, netting, network, openwork, tracery, web ♦ *verb* **2** catch, bag, capture, enmesh, ensnare, entangle, trap

net[2], **nett** *adjective* **1** take-home, after taxes, clear, final ♦ *verb* **2** earn, accumulate, bring in, clear, gain, make, realize, reap

nether *adjective* lower, below, beneath, bottom, inferior, under, underground

nettled *adjective* irritated, annoyed, exasperated, galled, harassed, incensed, peeved, put out, riled, vexed

network *noun* system, arrangement, complex, grid, labyrinth, lattice, maze, organization, structure, web

neurosis *noun* obsession, abnormality, affliction, derangement, instability, maladjustment, mental illness, phobia

neurotic *adjective* unstable, abnormal, antsy (*informal*), compulsive, disturbed, maladjusted, manic, nervous, obsessive, unhealthy

➤ **Antonyms**
normal, rational, sane, stable, well-adjusted

neuter *verb* castrate, doctor (*informal*), emasculate, fix (*informal*), geld, spay

neutral *adjective* **1** unbiased, disinterested, even-handed, impartial, nonaligned, nonpartisan, uncommitted, uninvolved, unprejudiced **2** indeterminate, dull, indistinct, intermediate, undefined

➤ **Antonyms**
≠unbiased: biased, interested, partial, prejudiced

neutrality *noun* impartiality, detachment, nonalignment, noninterference, noninvolvement, nonpartisanship

neutralize *verb* counteract, cancel, compensate for, counterbalance, frustrate, negate, nullify, offset, undo

never *adverb* at no time, not at all, on no account, under no circumstances

➤ **Antonyms**
always, constantly, continually, every time, forever, perpetually

nevertheless *adverb* nonetheless, but, even so, (even) though, however, notwithstanding, regardless, still, yet

new *adjective* **1** modern, contemporary, current, fresh, groundbreaking, latest, novel, original, recent, state-of-the-art, unfamiliar, up-to-date **2** extra, added, more, new-found, supplementary **3** changed, altered, improved, modernized, rebranded, redesigned, renewed, restored

➤ **Antonyms**
≠modern: aged, ancient, antiquated, antique, hackneyed, old, old-fashioned, outmoded, passé, stale, trite

newcomer *noun* novice, arrival, beginner, Johnny-come-lately (*informal*), parvenu

newfangled *adjective* new, contemporary, fashionable, gimmicky, modern, novel, recent, state-of-the-art

➤ **Antonyms**
antiquated, dated, obsolete, old-fashioned, outmoded, out-of-date, passé

newly *adverb* recently, anew, freshly, just, lately, latterly

newness *noun* novelty, freshness, innovation, oddity, originality, strangeness, unfamiliarity, uniqueness

news *noun* information, bulletin, communiqué, exposé, gossip, hearsay, intelligence, latest (*informal*), report, revelation, rumour, story

newsworthy *adjective* interesting, important, notable, noteworthy, remarkable, significant, stimulating

next *adjective* **1** following, consequent, ensuing, later, subsequent, succeeding **2** nearest, adjacent, adjoining, closest, neighbouring ♦ adverb **3** afterwards, following, later, subsequent, thereafter

nibble verb **1** bite, eat, gnaw, munch, nip, peck, pick at ♦ noun **2** snack, bite, crumb, morsel, peck, soupçon, taste, titbit

nice adjective **1** pleasant, agreeable, attractive, charming, delightful, good, pleasurable **2** kind, courteous, friendly, likable or likeable, polite, well-mannered **3** neat, dainty, fine, tidy, trim **4** subtle, careful, delicate, fastidious, fine, meticulous, precise, strict

➤ **Antonyms**

≠pleasant: awful, disagreeable, dreadful, miserable, unpleasant ≠kind: disagreeable, mean, unfriendly, unkind, unpleasant, vulgar ≠neat: coarse, crude, rough, shabby, sloppy (informal) ≠subtle: careless, rough, sloppy (informal), vague

nicely adverb **1** pleasantly, acceptably, agreeably, attractively, charmingly, delightfully, pleasurably, well **2** kindly, amiably, commendably, courteously, politely **3** neatly, daintily, finely, tidily, trimly

➤ **Antonyms**

≠pleasantly: unattractively, unpleasantly ≠neatly: sloppily (informal)

nicety noun subtlety, daintiness, delicacy, discrimination, distinction, nuance, refinement

niche noun **1** alcove, corner, hollow, nook, opening, recess **2** position, calling, pigeonhole (informal), place, slot (informal), vocation

nick verb **1** cut, chip, dent, mark, notch, scar, score, scratch, snick **2** Slang steal, pilfer, pinch (informal), swipe (slang) ♦ noun **3** cut, chip, dent, mark, notch, scar, scratch

nickname noun pet name, di-

minutive, epithet, label, moniker or monicker (slang), sobriquet

nifty adjective Informal neat, attractive, chic, deft, pleasing, smart, stylish

niggard noun miser, cheapskate (informal), Scrooge, skinflint

niggardly adjective stingy, avaricious, frugal, grudging, mean, miserly, parsimonious, tight-fisted, ungenerous

➤ **Antonyms**

generous, lavish, liberal, prodigal

niggle verb **1** worry, annoy, irritate, rankle **2** criticize, carp, cavil, find fault, fuss

niggling adjective **1** persistent, gnawing, irritating, troubling, worrying **2** petty, finicky, fussy, nit-picking (informal), pettifogging, picky (informal), quibbling

night noun darkness, dark, night-time

nightfall noun evening, dusk, sundown, sunset, twilight

➤ **Antonyms**

cockcrow, dawn, daybreak, daylight, morning, sunrise

nightly adjective **1** nocturnal, night-time ♦ adverb **2** every night, each night, night after night, nights (informal)

nightmare noun **1** bad dream, hallucination **2** ordeal, horror, torment, trial, tribulation

nil noun nothing, love, naught, none, zero

nimble adjective agile, brisk, deft, dexterous, lively, quick, sprightly, spry, swift

➤ **Antonyms**

awkward, clumsy, heavy, lethargic, slow

nimbly adverb quickly, briskly, deftly, dexterously, easily, readily, smartly, spryly, swiftly

nincompoop noun idiot, blockhead, chump, dumb-ass (slang), fool, nitwit (informal), numbskull or numskull, twit (informal, chiefly Brit.)

nip¹ verb pinch, bite, squeeze, tweak

nip² noun dram, draught, drop,

mouthful, shot (informal), sip, snifter (informal)

nipper noun Informal child, baby, boy, girl, infant, kid (informal), tot

nippy adjective 1 chilly, biting, sharp 2 Informal quick, active, agile, fast, nimble, spry

nirvana noun paradise, bliss, joy, peace, serenity, tranquillity

nit-picking adjective fussy, captious, carping, finicky, hairsplitting, pedantic, pettifogging, quibbling

nitty-gritty noun basics, brass tacks (informal), core, crux, essentials, fundamentals, gist, substance

nitwit noun Informal fool, dimwit (informal), dummy (slang), halfwit, nincompoop, oaf, simpleton

no interjection 1 never, nay, not at all, no way ♦ noun 2 refusal, denial, negation, rejection

► **Antonyms**
interjection ≠never: certainly, of course, yes ♦ noun ≠refusal: acceptance, assent, consent

nob noun Slang aristocrat, big hitter (informal), bigwig (informal), heavy hitter (informal), toff (Brit. slang), V.I.P.

nobble verb Brit. slang bribe, get at, influence, intimidate, win over

nobility noun 1 integrity, honour, incorruptibility, uprightness, virtue 2 aristocracy, elite, lords, nobles, patricians, peerage, upper class

noble adjective 1 worthy, generous, honourable, magnanimous, upright, virtuous 2 aristocratic, blue-blooded, highborn, lordly, patrician, titled 3 impressive, dignified, distinguished, grand, great, imposing, lofty, splendid, stately ♦ noun 4 lord, aristocrat, nobleman, peer

► **Antonyms**
adjective ≠worthy: contemptible, despicable, dishonest, selfish ≠aristocratic: humble, ignoble, lowborn, lowly, plebeian ≠impressive: humble, insignificant,

lowly, mean, modest, plain ♦ noun ≠lord: commoner, peasant, serf

nobody pronoun 1 no-one ♦ noun 2 nonentity, cipher, lightweight (informal), menial

► **Antonyms**
noun ≠nonentity: big shot (slang), celebrity, superstar, V.I.P.

nocturnal adjective nightly, nighttime

nod verb 1 acknowledge, bow, gesture, indicate, signal 2 sleep, doze, drowse, nap ♦ noun 3 gesture, acknowledgment, greeting, indication, sign, signal

noggin noun 1 Informal head, block (informal), nut (slang) 2 cup, dram, mug, nip, tot

no go adjective impossible, futile, hopeless, not on (informal), vain

noise noun sound, clamour, commotion, din, hubbub, racket, row, uproar

noiseless adjective silent, hushed, inaudible, mute, quiet, soundless, still

noisome adjective 1 offensive, disgusting, fetid, foul, malodorous, noxious, putrid, smelly, stinking 2 poisonous, bad, harmful, pernicious, pestilential, unhealthy, unwholesome

noisy adjective loud, boisterous, cacophonous, clamorous, deafening, ear-splitting, strident, tumultuous, uproarious, vociferous

► **Antonyms**
hushed, quiet, silent, subdued, tranquil

nomad noun wanderer, drifter, itinerant, migrant, rambler, rover, vagabond

nomadic adjective wandering, itinerant, migrant, peripatetic, roaming, roving, travelling, vagrant

nom de plume noun pseudonym, alias, assumed name, nom de guerre, pen name

nomenclature noun terminology, classification, codification, phraseology, taxonomy, vocabulary

nominal *adjective* **1** so-called, formal, ostensible, professed, puppet, purported, supposed, theoretical, titular **2** small, inconsiderable, insignificant, minimal, symbolic, token, trifling, trivial

nominate *verb* name, appoint, assign, choose, designate, elect, propose, recommend, select, suggest

nomination *noun* choice, appointment, designation, election, proposal, recommendation, selection, suggestion

nominee *noun* candidate, aspirant, contestant, entrant, protégé, runner

nonaligned *adjective* neutral, impartial, uncommitted, undecided

nonchalance *noun* indifference, calm, composure, equanimity, imperturbability, sang-froid, self-possession, unconcern

nonchalant *adjective* casual, blasé, calm, careless, indifferent, insouciant, laid-back (*informal*), offhand, unconcerned, unperturbed

► **Antonyms**
anxious, caring, concerned, involved, worried

noncombatant *noun* civilian, neutral, nonbelligerent

noncommittal *adjective* evasive, cautious, circumspect, equivocal, guarded, neutral, politic, temporizing, tentative, vague, wary

non compos mentis *adjective* insane, crazy, deranged, mentally ill, unbalanced, unhinged

► **Antonyms**
compos mentis, lucid, rational, sane

nonconformist *noun* maverick, dissenter, eccentric, heretic, iconoclast, individualist, protester, radical, rebel

► **Antonyms**
stick-in-the-mud (*informal*), traditionalist

nonconformity *noun* dissent, eccentricity, heresy, heterodoxy

nondescript *adjective* ordinary, commonplace, dull, featureless,

run-of-the-mill, undistinguished, unexceptional, unremarkable

► **Antonyms**
distinctive, extraordinary, memorable, remarkable, unique, unusual

none *pronoun* not any, nil, nobody, no-one, nothing, not one, zero

nonentity *noun* nobody, cipher, lightweight (*informal*), mediocrity, small fry

nonessential *adjective* unnecessary, dispensable, expendable, extraneous, inessential, peripheral, superfluous, unimportant

► **Antonyms**
essential, important, indispensable, vital

nonetheless *adverb* nevertheless, despite that, even so, however, in spite of that, yet

nonevent *noun* flop (*informal*), disappointment, dud (*informal*), failure, fiasco, washout

nonexistent *adjective* imaginary, chimerical, fictional, hypothetical, illusory, legendary, mythical, unreal

► **Antonyms**
actual, existing, genuine, real, true

nonsense *noun* rubbish, balderdash, claptrap (*informal*), double Dutch (*Brit. informal*), drivel, gibberish, hot air (*informal*), stupidity, tripe (*informal*), twaddle

► **Antonyms**
fact, reality, reason, sense, seriousness, truth, wisdom

nonsensical *adjective* senseless, absurd, crazy, foolish, inane, incomprehensible, irrational, meaningless, ridiculous, silly

nonstarter *noun* dead loss, dud (*informal*), lemon (*informal*), loser, no-hoper (*informal*), turkey (*informal*), washout (*informal*)

nonstop *adjective* **1** continuous, constant, endless, incessant, interminable, relentless, unbroken, uninterrupted ♦ *adverb* **2** continuously, ceaselessly, constantly, endlessly, incessantly, interminably, perpetually, relentlessly

➤ **Antonyms**

adjective ≠ <u>continuous</u>: fitful, intermittent, irregular, periodic, spasmodic, sporadic

nook *noun* <u>niche</u>, alcove, corner, cubbyhole, hide-out, opening, recess, retreat

noon *noun* <u>midday</u>, high noon, noonday, noontide, twelve noon

norm *noun* <u>standard</u>, average, benchmark, criterion, par, pattern, rule, yardstick

normal *adjective* **1** <u>usual</u>, average, common, conventional, natural, ordinary, regular, routine, standard, typical **2** <u>sane</u>, rational, reasonable, well-adjusted

➤ **Antonyms**

≠ <u>usual</u>: abnormal, exceptional, irregular, rare, uncommon, unnatural, unusual

normality *noun* **1** <u>regularity</u>, conventionality, naturalness **2** <u>sanity</u>, balance, rationality, reason

normally *adverb* <u>usually</u>, as a rule, commonly, generally, habitually, ordinarily, regularly, typically

north *adjective* **1** <u>northern</u>, Arctic, boreal, northerly, polar ♦ *adverb* **2** <u>northward(s)</u>, northerly

nose *noun* **1** <u>snout</u>, beak, bill, hooter (*slang*), proboscis ♦ *verb* **2** <u>ease forward</u>, nudge, nuzzle, push, shove **3** <u>pry</u>, meddle, snoop (*informal*)

nosegay *noun* <u>posy</u>, bouquet

nosey, nosy *adjective* <u>inquisitive</u>, curious, eavesdropping, interfering, intrusive, meddlesome, prying, snooping (*informal*)

nostalgia *noun* <u>reminiscence</u>, homesickness, longing, pining, regretfulness, remembrance, wistfulness, yearning

nostalgic *adjective* <u>sentimental</u>, emotional, homesick, longing, maudlin, regretful, wistful

nostrum *noun* <u>medicine</u>, cure, drug, elixir, panacea, potion, remedy, treatment

notability *noun* <u>fame</u>, celebrity,

distinction, eminence, esteem, renown

notable *adjective* **1** <u>remarkable</u>, conspicuous, extraordinary, memorable, noteworthy, outstanding, rare, striking, uncommon, unusual ♦ *noun* **2** <u>celebrity</u>, big name, dignitary, luminary, personage, V.I.P.

➤ **Antonyms**

adjective ≠ <u>remarkable</u>: anonymous, concealed, hidden, imperceptible, obscure, unknown, vague

notably *adverb* <u>particularly</u>, especially, outstandingly, strikingly

notation *noun* <u>signs</u>, characters, code, script, symbols, system

notch *noun* **1** <u>cut</u>, cleft, incision, indentation, mark, nick, score **2** *Informal* <u>level</u>, degree, grade, step ♦ *verb* **3** <u>cut</u>, indent, mark, nick, score, scratch

notch up *verb* <u>register</u>, achieve, gain, make, score

note *noun* **1** <u>message</u>, comment, communication, epistle, jotting, letter, memo, memorandum, minute, remark, reminder **2** <u>symbol</u>, indication, mark, sign, token ♦ *verb* **3** <u>see</u>, notice, observe, perceive **4** <u>mark</u>, denote, designate, indicate, record, register **5** <u>mention</u>, remark

notebook *noun* <u>jotter</u>, diary, exercise book, journal, notepad

noted *adjective* <u>famous</u>, acclaimed, celebrated, distinguished, eminent, illustrious, notable, prominent, renowned, well-known

➤ **Antonyms**

infamous, obscure, undistinguished, unknown

noteworthy *adjective* <u>remarkable</u>, exceptional, extraordinary, important, notable, outstanding, significant, unusual

➤ **Antonyms**

commonplace, insignificant, normal, ordinary, pedestrian, run-of-the-mill, unexceptional, unremarkable

nothing *noun* <u>nought</u>, emptiness, nil, nothingness, nullity, void, zero

nothingness *noun* **1** oblivion, nonbeing, nonexistence, nullity **2** insignificance, unimportance, worthlessness

notice *noun* **1** interest, cognizance, consideration, heed, note, observation, regard **2** attention, civility, respect **3** announcement, advice, communication, instruction, intimation, news, notification, order, warning ◆ *verb* **4** observe, detect, discern, distinguish, mark, note, perceive, see, spot

► **Antonyms**

noun ≠interest: disregard, ignorance, neglect, omission, oversight ◆ *verb* ≠observe: disregard, ignore, neglect, overlook

noticeable *adjective* obvious, appreciable, clear, conspicuous, evident, manifest, perceptible, plain, striking

notification *noun* announcement, advice, declaration, information, intelligence, message, notice, statement, warning

notify *verb* inform, advise, alert, announce, declare, make known, publish, tell, warn

notion *noun* **1** idea, belief, concept, impression, inkling, opinion, sentiment, view **2** whim, caprice, desire, fancy, impulse, inclination, wish

notional *adjective* speculative, abstract, conceptual, hypothetical, imaginary, theoretical, unreal

► **Antonyms**

actual, factual, genuine, real

notoriety *noun* scandal, dishonour, disrepute, infamy, obloquy, opprobrium

notorious *adjective* infamous, dishonourable, disreputable, opprobrious, scandalous

notoriously *adverb* infamously, dishonourably, disreputably, opprobriously, scandalously

notwithstanding *preposition* despite, in spite of

nought *noun* zero, nil, nothing

nourish *verb* **1** feed, nurse, nurture, supply, sustain, tend **2** encourage, comfort, cultivate, foster, maintain, promote, support

nourishing *adjective* nutritious, beneficial, nutritive, wholesome

nourishment *noun* food, nutriment, nutrition, sustenance

novel[1] *noun* story, fiction, narrative, romance, tale

novel[2] *adjective* new, different, fresh, innovative, original, strange, uncommon, unfamiliar, unusual

► **Antonyms**

common, familiar, habitual, old-fashioned, ordinary, run-of-the-mill, traditional, usual

novelty *noun* **1** newness, freshness, innovation, oddity, originality, strangeness, surprise, unfamiliarity, uniqueness **2** gimmick, curiosity, gadget **3** knick-knack, bauble, memento, souvenir, trifle, trinket

novice *noun* beginner, amateur, apprentice, learner, newcomer, probationer, pupil, trainee

► **Antonyms**

doyen, expert, guru, master, old hand, professional

now *adverb* **1** nowadays, any more, at the moment **2** immediately, at once, instantly, promptly, straightaway **3** now and again *or* then occasionally, from time to time, infrequently, intermittently, on and off, sometimes, sporadically

nowadays *adverb* now, any more, at the moment, in this day and age, today

noxious *adjective* harmful, deadly, destructive, foul, hurtful, injurious, poisonous, unhealthy, unwholesome

► **Antonyms**

innocuous, inoffensive, safe

nuance *noun* subtlety, degree, distinction, gradation, nicety, refinement, shade, tinge

nubile *adjective* marriageable, ripe (*informal*)

nucleus *noun* centre, basis, core,

focus, heart, kernel, nub, pivot

nude *adjective* <u>naked</u>, bare, disrobed, stark-naked, stripped, unclad, unclothed, undressed, without a stitch on (*informal*)

➤ **Antonyms**

attired, clothed, covered, dressed

nudge *verb, noun* <u>push</u>, bump, dig, elbow, jog, poke, prod, shove, touch

nudity *noun* <u>nakedness</u>, bareness, deshabille, nudism, undress

nugget *noun* <u>lump</u>, chunk, clump, hunk, mass, piece

nuisance *noun* <u>problem</u>, annoyance, bother, drag (*informal*), hassle (*informal*), inconvenience, irritation, pain in the neck, pest, trouble

➤ **Antonyms**

benefit, blessing, delight, happiness, joy, pleasure, satisfaction

null *adjective* <u>null and void</u>, <u>invalid</u>, inoperative, useless, valueless, void, worthless

nullify *verb* <u>cancel</u>, counteract, invalidate, negate, neutralize, obviate, render null and void, veto

➤ **Antonyms**

confirm, endorse, ratify, validate

nullity *noun* <u>nonexistence</u>, invalidity, powerlessness, uselessness, worthlessness

numb *adjective* 1 <u>unfeeling</u>, benumbed, dead, deadened, frozen, immobilized, insensitive, paralysed, torpid ◆ *verb* 2 <u>deaden</u>, benumb, dull, freeze, immobilize, paralyse

➤ **Antonyms**

adjective ≠<u>unfeeling</u>: feeling, responsive, sensitive, sentient

number *noun* 1 <u>numeral</u>, character, digit, figure, integer 2 <u>quantity</u>, aggregate, amount, collection, crowd, horde, multitude, throng 3 <u>issue</u>, copy, edition, imprint, printing ◆ *verb* 4 <u>calculate</u>, account, add, compute, count, enumerate, include, reckon, total

➤ **Antonyms**

noun ≠<u>quantity</u>: insufficiency, lack, scantiness, scarcity, short-

age, want ◆ *verb* ≠<u>calculate</u>: conjecture, guess, theorize

numberless *adjective* <u>infinite</u>, countless, endless, innumerable, multitudinous, myriad, unnumbered, untold

numbness *noun* <u>deadness</u>, dullness, insensitivity, paralysis, torpor

numbskull, numskull *noun* <u>fool</u>, blockhead, clot (*Brit. informal*), dolt, dummy (*slang*), dunce, oaf, twit (*informal*)

numeral *noun* <u>number</u>, digit, figure, integer

numerous *adjective* <u>many</u>, abundant, copious, plentiful, profuse, several, thick on the ground

➤ **Antonyms**

few, not many, scarcely any

nuncio *noun* <u>ambassador</u>, envoy, legate, messenger

nunnery *noun* <u>convent</u>, abbey, cloister, house

nuptial *adjective* <u>marital</u>, bridal, conjugal, connubial, matrimonial

nuptials *plural noun* <u>wedding</u>, marriage, matrimony

nurse *verb* 1 <u>look after</u>, care for, minister to, tend, treat 2 <u>breastfeed</u>, feed, nourish, nurture, suckle, wet-nurse 3 <u>foster</u>, cherish, cultivate, encourage, harbour, preserve, promote, succour, support

nursery *noun* <u>crèche</u>, kindergarten, playgroup

nurture *noun* 1 <u>development</u>, discipline, education, instruction, rearing, training, upbringing ◆ *verb* 2 <u>develop</u>, bring up, discipline, educate, instruct, rear, school, train

➤ **Antonyms**

verb ≠<u>develop</u>: deprive, disregard, ignore, neglect, overlook

nut *noun* 1 *Slang* <u>madman</u>, crank (*informal*), lunatic, maniac, nutcase (*slang*), psycho (*slang*) 2 *Slang* <u>head</u>, brain, mind, reason, senses

nutrition *noun* <u>food</u>, nourishment, nutriment, sustenance

nutritious *adjective* <u>nourishing</u>,

beneficial, health-giving, invigorating, nutritive, strengthening, wholesome

nuzzle *verb* snuggle, burrow, cuddle, fondle, nestle, pet

nymph *noun* sylph, dryad, girl, maiden, naiad

O o

oaf *noun* **1** dolt, blockhead, clod, dumb-ass (*slang*), dunce, fool, goon, idiot, lout, moron, numbskull or numskull

➤ **Antonyms**

brain (*informal*), egghead (*informal*), genius, intellect, smart aleck (*informal*)

oafish *adjective* stupid, dense, dim-witted (*informal*), doltish, dumb (*informal*), dumb-ass (*slang*), loutish, moronic, thick

➤ **Antonyms**

acute, brainy (*informal*), bright, clever, intelligent, quick-witted, sharp, smart

oath *noun* **1** promise, affirmation, avowal, bond, pledge, vow, word **2** swearword, blasphemy, curse, expletive, profanity

obdurate *adjective* stubborn, dogged, hard-hearted, immovable, implacable, inflexible, obstinate, pig-headed, unyielding

➤ **Antonyms**

amenable, biddable, compliant, flexible, submissive, tractable, yielding

obedience *noun* submissiveness, acquiescence, compliance, docility, observance, respect, reverence, subservience

➤ **Antonyms**

defiance, disobedience, insubordination, obstinacy, stubbornness, wilfulness

obedient *adjective* submissive, acquiescent, biddable, compliant, deferential, docile, dutiful, respectful, subservient, well-trained

➤ **Antonyms**

contrary, disobedient, disrespectful, obdurate, obstinate, rebellious, stubborn, undutiful, ungovernable, unmanageable, unruly, wayward

obelisk *noun* column, monolith, monument, needle, pillar, shaft

obese *adjective* fat, corpulent, gross, heavy, overweight, paunchy, plump, portly, rotund, stout, tubby

➤ **Antonyms**

emaciated, gaunt, lean, scraggy, skeletal, skinny, slender, thin

obesity *noun* fatness, bulk, corpulence, grossness, portliness, stoutness, tubbiness

➤ **Antonyms**

emaciation, gauntness, leanness, skinniness, slenderness, thinness

obey do what one is told, cave in (*informal*) *verb* carry out, abide by, act upon, adhere to, comply, conform, follow, heed, keep, observe

➤ **Antonyms**

≠carry out: contravene, defy, disobey, disregard, ignore, transgress, violate

obfuscate *verb* Formal confuse, befog, cloud, darken, muddy the waters, obscure, perplex

object[1] *noun* **1** thing, article, body, entity, item, phenomenon **2** target, focus, recipient, victim **3** purpose, aim, design, end, goal, idea, intention, objective, point

object[2] *verb* protest, argue against, demur, draw the line (at something), expostulate, oppose, take exception

➤ **Antonyms**

accept, acquiesce, agree, approve, assent, comply, concur, consent

objection *noun* protest, counterargument, demur, doubt, opposition, remonstrance, scruple

➤ **Antonyms**

acceptance, agreement, approbation, assent, support

objectionable *adjective* unpleasant, deplorable, disagreeable, intolerable, obnoxious, offensive, regrettable, repugnant, unseemly

▶ **Antonyms**

acceptable, agreeable, desirable, likable *or* likeable, pleasant, pleasing, welcome

objective *noun* **1** purpose, aim, ambition, end, goal, intention, mark, object, target ♦ *adjective* **2** unbiased, detached, disinterested, dispassionate, even-handed, fair, impartial, impersonal, open-minded, unprejudiced

▶ **Antonyms**

adjective ≠unbiased: biased, personal, prejudiced, subjective, unfair

objectively *adverb* impartially, disinterestedly, dispassionately, even-handedly, with an open mind

objectivity *noun* impartiality, detachment, disinterestedness, dispassion

▶ **Antonyms**

bias, partiality, predisposition, prejudice, subjectivity

obligation *noun* duty, accountability, burden, charge, compulsion, liability, requirement, responsibility

obligatory *adjective* compulsory, binding, *de rigueur*, essential, imperative, mandatory, necessary, required, requisite, unavoidable

▶ **Antonyms**

discretionary, noncompulsory, optional, voluntary

oblige *verb* **1** compel, bind, constrain, force, impel, make, necessitate, require **2** do (someone) a favour or a kindness, accommodate, benefit, gratify, indulge, please

▶ **Antonyms**

≠do (someone) a favour or a kindness: bother, discommode, disoblige, inconvenience, put out, trouble

obliged *adjective* **1** grateful, appreciative, beholden, indebted, in (someone's) debt, thankful **2** bound, compelled, forced, required

obliging *adjective* cooperative, accommodating, agreeable, considerate, good-natured, helpful, kind, polite, willing

▶ **Antonyms**

discourteous, disobliging, inconsiderate, rude, unaccommodating, uncooperative, unhelpful, unobliging

oblique *adjective* **1** slanting, angled, aslant, sloping, tilted **2** indirect, backhanded, circuitous, implied, roundabout, sidelong

▶ **Antonyms**

≠indirect: blunt, candid, direct, downright, forthright, frank, open, straightforward

obliterate *verb* destroy, annihilate, blot out, efface, eradicate, erase, expunge, extirpate, root out, wipe out

▶ **Antonyms**

build, construct, create, establish, form, formulate, make

obliteration *noun* annihilation, elimination, eradication, extirpation, wiping out

▶ **Antonyms**

building, construction, creation, establishment, formation, making

oblivion *noun* neglect, abeyance, disregard, forgetfulness **2** unconsciousness, insensibility, obliviousness, unawareness

▶ **Antonyms**

≠unconsciousness: awareness, consciousness, perception, realization, sensibility

oblivious *adjective* unaware, forgetful, heedless, ignorant, insensible, neglectful, negligent, regardless, unconcerned, unconscious, unmindful

▶ **Antonyms**

aware, conscious, heedful, mindful

obloquy *noun Formal* **1** abuse, aspersion, attack, blame, censure, criticism, invective, reproach, slander, vilification **2** disgrace,

obnoxious discredit, dishonour, humiliation, ignominy, infamy, shame, stigma

obnoxious *adjective* offensive, disagreeable, insufferable, loathsome, nasty, nauseating, objectionable, odious, repulsive, revolting, unpleasant

➤ **Antonyms**
agreeable, charming, delightful, likable *or* likeable, pleasant, pleasing

obscene *adjective* 1 indecent, dirty, filthy, immoral, improper, lewd, offensive, pornographic, salacious 2 disgusting, atrocious, evil, heinous, loathsome, outrageous, shocking, sickening, vile, wicked

➤ **Antonyms**
≠indecent: chaste, decent, decorous, inoffensive, proper, pure, respectable, seemly

obscenity *noun* 1 indecency, coarseness, dirtiness, impropriety, lewdness, licentiousness, pornography, smut 2 swearword, four-letter word, profanity, vulgarism 3 atrocity, abomination, affront, blight, evil, offence, outrage, wrong

➤ **Antonyms**
≠indecency: chastity, decency, decorum, innocence, propriety, purity

obscure *adjective* 1 little-known, humble, lowly, out-of-the-way, remote, undistinguished, unheard-of, unknown 2 vague, ambiguous, arcane, confusing, cryptic, enigmatic, esoteric, mysterious, opaque, recondite, unclear 3 dark, blurred, cloudy, dim, faint, gloomy, indistinct, murky, shadowy ◆ *verb* 4 conceal, cover, disguise, hide, obfuscate, screen, veil

➤ **Antonyms**
adjective ≠little-known: celebrated, distinguished, eminent, famous, illustrious, prominent, renowned, well-known, widely-known ≠vague: apparent, clear, definite, evident, explicit, lucid, obvious, plain, straightforward ≠dark: bright, clear, sharp, transparent, well-defined ◆ *verb* ≠conceal: clarify, disclose, explain, expose, reveal, show

obscurity *noun* 1 insignificance, lowliness, unimportance 2 darkness, dimness, dusk, gloom, haze, shadows

obsequious *adjective* sycophantic, cringing, deferential, fawning, flattering, grovelling, ingratiating, servile, submissive, unctuous

observable *adjective* noticeable, apparent, detectable, discernible, evident, obvious, perceptible, recognizable, visible

observance *noun* carrying out, compliance, fulfilment, honouring, performance

➤ **Antonyms**
disregard, evasion, neglect, nonobservance, omission, oversight

observant *adjective* attentive, alert, eagle-eyed, perceptive, quick, sharp-eyed, vigilant, watchful, wide-awake

➤ **Antonyms**
distracted, dreamy, heedless, inattentive, negligent, preoccupied, unobservant

observation *noun* 1 study, examination, inspection, monitoring, review, scrutiny, surveillance, watching 2 comment, note, opinion, pronouncement, reflection, remark, thought, utterance

observe *verb* 1 see, detect, discern, discover, note, notice, perceive, spot, witness 2 watch, check, keep an eye on (*informal*), keep track of, look at, monitor, scrutinize, study, survey, view 3 remark, comment, mention, note, opine, say, state 4 carry out, abide by, adhere to, comply, conform to, follow, heed, honour, keep, obey, respect

➤ **Antonyms**
≠carry out: disregard, ignore, miss, neglect, omit, overlook

observer *noun* spectator, beholder, bystander, eyewitness, fly on the wall, looker-on, onlooker, viewer, watcher, witness

obsessed *adjective* <u>preoccupied</u>, dominated, gripped, haunted, hung up on (*slang*), infatuated, troubled

➤ **Antonyms**

apathetic, detached, disinterested, impassive, indifferent, uncaring, unconcerned

obsession *noun* <u>preoccupation</u>, complex, fetish, fixation, hang-up (*informal*), infatuation, mania, phobia, thing (*informal*)

obsessive *adjective* <u>compulsive</u>, besetting, consuming, gripping, haunting

obsolescent *adjective* <u>becoming obsolete</u>, ageing, declining, dying out, on the wane, on the way out, past its prime, waning

obsolete *adjective* <u>out of date</u>, antiquated, archaic, discarded, disused, extinct, old, old-fashioned, outmoded, passé

➤ **Antonyms**

contemporary, current, fashionable, in, in vogue, modern, new, present day, trendy (*Brit. informal*), up-to-date

obstacle *noun* <u>difficulty</u>, bar, barrier, block, hindrance, hitch, hurdle, impediment, obstruction, snag, stumbling block

➤ **Antonyms**

advantage, aid, asset, benefit, help, support

obstinacy *noun* <u>stubbornness</u>, doggedness, inflexibility, intransigence, obduracy, persistence, pig-headedness, tenacity, wilfulness

➤ **Antonyms**

compliance, cooperativeness, docility, flexibility, meekness, submissiveness, tractability

obstinate *adjective* <u>stubborn</u>, determined, dogged, inflexible, intractable, intransigent, pig-headed, refractory, self-willed, strong-minded, wilful

➤ **Antonyms**

amenable, compliant, docile, flexible, manageable, obedient,

submissive, tractable

obstreperous *adjective* <u>unruly</u>, disorderly, loud, noisy, riotous, rowdy, turbulent, unmanageable, wild

➤ **Antonyms**

calm, controlled, disciplined, docile, gentle, peaceful, placid, quiet

obstruct *verb* <u>block</u>, bar, barricade, check, hamper, hinder, impede, restrict, stop, thwart

➤ **Antonyms**

abet, advance, aid, assist, encourage, further, gee up, help, promote, support

obstruction *noun* <u>obstacle</u>, bar, barricade, barrier, blockage, difficulty, hindrance, impediment

➤ **Antonyms**

aid, assistance, cooperation, encouragement, furtherance, geeing-up, help, support

obstructive *adjective* <u>unhelpful</u>, awkward, blocking, delaying, difficult, hindering, restrictive, stalling, uncooperative

➤ **Antonyms**

cooperative, encouraging, helpful, supportive

obtain *verb* **1** <u>get</u>, achieve, acquire, attain, earn, gain, land, procure, secure **2** *Formal* <u>exist</u>, be in force, be prevalent, be the case, hold, prevail

➤ **Antonyms**

≠get: forfeit, forgo, give up, hand over, lose, relinquish, renounce, surrender

obtainable *adjective* <u>available</u>, achievable, attainable, on tap (*informal*), to be had

obtrusive *adjective* <u>noticeable</u>, blatant, obvious, prominent, protruding, protuberant, sticking out

➤ **Antonyms**

concealed, covert, hidden, inconspicuous, unnoticeable, unobtrusive

obtuse *adjective* <u>stupid</u>, dense, dull, dumb (*informal*), dumb-ass (*informal*), slow, stolid, thick, uncomprehending

➤ **Antonyms**

astute, bright, clever, keen, quick, sharp, shrewd, smart

obviate verb Formal **preclude**, avert, prevent, remove

obvious adjective **evident**, apparent, clear, conspicuous, distinct, indisputable, manifest, noticeable, plain, self-evident, undeniable, unmistakable

➤ **Antonyms**

ambiguous, concealed, dark, hidden, inconspicuous, indistinct, obscure, unapparent, unclear, vague

obviously adverb **clearly**, manifestly, of course, palpably, patently, plainly, undeniably, unmistakably, unquestionably, without doubt

occasion noun 1 **time**, chance, moment, opening, opportunity, window 2 **reason**, call, cause, excuse, ground(s), justification, motive, prompting, provocation 3 **event**, affair, celebration, experience, happening, occurrence ◆ verb 4 Formal **cause**, bring about, engender, give rise to, give rise to, induce, inspire, lead to, produce, prompt, provoke

occasional adjective **infrequent**, incidental, intermittent, irregular, odd, rare, sporadic, uncommon

➤ **Antonyms**

constant, continual, frequent, habitual, incessant, regular, routine, usual

occasionally adverb **sometimes**, at times, from time to time, irregularly, now and again, once in a while, periodically

➤ **Antonyms**

constantly, continually, continuously, frequently, habitually, often, regularly, routinely

occult adjective **supernatural**, arcane, esoteric, magical, mysterious, mystical

occupancy noun **tenancy**, possession, residence, tenure, use

occupant noun **inhabitant**, incumbent, indweller, inmate, les-

see, occupier, resident, tenant

occupation noun 1 **profession**, business, calling, employment, job, line (of work), pursuit, trade, vocation, walk of life 2 **possession**, control, holding, occupancy, residence, tenancy, tenure 3 **invasion**, conquest, seizure, subjugation

occupied adjective 1 **busy**, employed, engaged, working 2 **in use**, engaged, full, taken, unavailable 3 **inhabited**, lived-in, peopled, settled, tenanted

➤ **Antonyms**

≠inhabited: deserted, empty, uninhabited, unoccupied, untenanted, vacant

occupy verb 1 **live in**, dwell in, inhabit, own, possess, reside in 2 often passive **take up**, divert, employ, engage, engross, involve, monopolize, preoccupy, tie up 3 **fill**, cover, permeate, pervade, take up 4 **invade**, capture, overrun, seize, take over

➤ **Antonyms**

≠live in: abandon, depart, desert, evacuate, quit, vacate ≠invade: retreat, withdraw

occur verb 1 **happen**, befall, come about, crop up (informal), take place, turn up (informal) 2 **exist**, appear, be found, be present, develop, manifest itself, show itself 3 occur to **come to mind**, cross one's mind, dawn on, enter one's head, spring to mind, strike one, suggest itself

occurrence noun 1 **incident**, adventure, affair, circumstance, episode, event, happening, instance 2 **existence**, appearance, development, manifestation, materialization

odd adjective 1 **unusual**, bizarre, extraordinary, freakish, irregular, peculiar, rare, remarkable, singular, strange 2 **occasional**, casual, incidental, irregular, periodic, random, sundry, various 3 **spare**, leftover, remaining, solitary, surplus, unmatched, unpaired

➤ **Antonyms**

≠<u>unusual</u>: common, customary, familiar, natural, normal, ordinary, regular, typical, unexceptional, unremarkable, usual ≠<u>oc-casional</u>: habitual, regular, steady ≠<u>spare</u>: even, matched, paired

oddity noun 1 <u>irregularity</u>, abnormality, anomaly, eccentricity, freak, idiosyncrasy, peculiarity, quirk 2 <u>misfit</u>, crank (informal), maverick, oddball (informal)

oddment noun <u>leftover</u>, bit, fag end, fragment, off cut, remnant, scrap, snippet

odds plural noun 1 <u>probability</u>, chances, likelihood 2 at odds <u>in conflict</u>, at daggers drawn, at loggerheads, at sixes and sevens, at variance, out of line

odds and ends plural noun <u>scraps</u>, bits, bits and pieces, debris, oddments, remnants

odious adjective <u>offensive</u>, detestable, horrid, loathsome, obnoxious, repulsive, revolting, unpleasant

➤ **Antonyms**

agreeable, charming, congenial, delightful, enchanting, enjoyable, pleasant, pleasing, winsome

odour noun <u>smell</u>, aroma, bouquet, essence, fragrance, perfume, redolence, scent, stench, stink

odyssey noun <u>journey</u>, crusade, pilgrimage, quest, trek, voyage

off adverb 1 <u>away</u>, apart, aside, elsewhere, out ◆ adjective 2 <u>cancelled</u>, finished, gone, postponed, unavailable 3 <u>bad</u>, mouldy, rancid, rotten, sour, turned

offbeat adjective <u>unusual</u>, eccentric, left-field (informal), novel, outré, strange, unconventional, unorthodox, way-out (informal)

➤ **Antonyms**

conventional, normal, ordinary, orthodox, run-of-the-mill, usual

off colour adjective <u>ill</u>, out of sorts, peaky, poorly (informal), queasy, run down, sick, under the weather (informal), unwell

offence noun 1 <u>crime</u>, fault, misdeed, misdemeanour, sin, transgression, trespass, wrongdoing 2 <u>annoyance</u>, anger, displeasure, indignation, pique, resentment, umbrage, wrath 3 <u>insult</u>, affront, hurt, indignity, injustice, outrage, slight, snub

offend verb 1 <u>insult</u>, affront, annoy, displease, hurt (someone's) feelings, outrage, slight, snub, upset, wound

➤ **Antonyms**

appease, assuage, delight, mollify, placate, please, soothe

offended adjective <u>resentful</u>, affronted, disgruntled, displeased, outraged, piqued, put out (informal), smarting, stung, upset

offender noun <u>criminal</u>, crook, culprit, delinquent, lawbreaker, miscreant, sinner, transgressor, villain, wrongdoer

offensive adjective 1 <u>disgusting</u>, disagreeable, nauseating, obnoxious, odious, repellent, revolting, unpleasant, vile 2 <u>insulting</u>, abusive, discourteous, disrespectful, impertinent, insolent, objectionable, rude 3 <u>attacking</u>, aggressive, invading ◆ noun 4 <u>attack</u>, campaign, drive, onslaught, push (informal)

➤ **Antonyms**

adjective ≠<u>disgusting</u>: agreeable, attractive, captivating, charming, delightful, pleasant ≠<u>insulting</u>: civil, courteous, deferential, polite, respectful ≠<u>attacking</u>: defensive

offer verb 1 <u>proffer</u>, bid, tender 2 <u>provide</u>, afford, furnish, present 3 <u>volunteer</u>, come forward, offer one's services 4 <u>propose</u>, advance, submit, suggest ◆ noun 5 <u>proposal</u>, bid, proposition, submission, suggestion, tender

➤ **Antonyms**

verb ≠<u>proffer</u>: refuse, retract, revoke, take back, withdraw, withhold

offering noun 1 <u>contribution</u>, donation, gift, hand-out, present, subscription **2** sacrifice

offhand *adjective* **1** casual, aloof, brusque, careless, curt, glib ♦ *adverb* **2** impromptu, ad lib, extempore, off the cuff (*informal*)

► **Antonyms**

adjective ≠casual: intent, serious, thoughtful

office *noun* post, function, occupation, place, responsibility, role, situation

officer *noun* official, agent, appointee, executive, functionary, office-holder, representative

official *adjective* **1** authorized, accredited, authentic, certified, formal, legitimate, licensed, proper, sanctioned ♦ *noun* **2** officer, agent, bureaucrat, executive, functionary, office bearer, representative

► **Antonyms**

adjective ≠authorized: casual, informal, unauthorized, unofficial

officiate *verb* preside, chair, conduct, manage, oversee, serve, superintend

officious *adjective* interfering, dictatorial, intrusive, meddlesome, obtrusive, overzealous, pushy (*informal*), self-important

► **Antonyms**

aloof, detached, indifferent

offing *noun* **in the offing** imminent, in prospect, on the horizon, upcoming

off-putting *adjective Informal* discouraging, daunting, disconcerting, dispiriting, disturbing, formidable, intimidating, unnerving, unsettling

offset *verb* cancel out, balance out, compensate for, counteract, counterbalance, make up for, neutralize

offshoot *noun* by-product, adjunct, appendage, development, spin-off

offspring *noun* **1** child, descendant, heir, scion, successor **2** children, brood, descendants, family, heirs, issue, progeny, young

► **Antonyms**

ancestor, forebear, forefather,

parent, predecessor

often *adverb* frequently, generally, repeatedly, time and again

► **Antonyms**

hardly ever, infrequently, irregularly, never, now and then, occasionally, rarely, scarcely, seldom

ogle *verb* leer, eye up (*informal*)

ogre *noun* monster, bogeyman, bugbear, demon, devil, giant, spectre

oil *verb* lubricate, grease

oily *adjective* greasy, fatty, oleaginous

ointment *noun* lotion, balm, cream, embrocation, emollient, liniment, salve, unguent

O.K., okay *Informal* ♦ *interjection* **1** all right, agreed, right, roger, very good, very well, yes ♦ *adjective* **2** fine, acceptable, adequate, all right, good, in order, permitted, satisfactory, up to scratch (*informal*) ♦ *verb* **3** approve, agree to, authorize, endorse, give the green light, rubber-stamp, sanction ♦ *noun* **4** approval, agreement, assent, authorization, consent, go-ahead (*informal*), green light, permission, sanction, say-so (*informal*), seal of approval

► **Antonyms**

adjective ≠fine: inadequate, not up to scratch (*informal*), poor, unacceptable, unsatisfactory, unsuitable

old *adjective* **1** aged, ancient, decrepit, elderly, mature, senile, venerable **2** out of date, antediluvian, antiquated, antique, dated, obsolete, superannuated, time-worn **3** former, earlier, erstwhile, one-time, previous

► **Antonyms**

≠aged: immature, juvenile, young, youthful ≠out of date: current, fashionable, modern, new, novel, recent, up-to-date

old-fashioned *adjective* out of date, behind the times, dated, obsolescent, obsolete, old hat, outdated, outmoded, passé, unfashionable

> **Antonyms**

chic, contemporary, current, fashionable, modern, trendy (*Brit. informal*), up-to-date

omen *noun* sign, foreboding, indication, portent, premonition, presage, warning

ominous *adjective* threatening, fateful, foreboding, inauspicious, portentous, sinister, unpromising, unpropitious

> **Antonyms**

auspicious, encouraging, favourable, promising, propitious

omission *noun* exclusion, failure, lack, neglect, oversight

omit *verb* leave out, drop, eliminate, exclude, forget, neglect, overlook, pass over, skip

> **Antonyms**

add, enter, include, incorporate, insert, put in

omnipotence *noun* supremacy, invincibility, mastery

> **Antonyms**

impotence, powerlessness, weakness

omnipotent *adjective* almighty, all-powerful, supreme

> **Antonyms**

impotent, inferior, powerless, weak

omniscient *adjective* all-knowing, all-wise

once *adverb* **1** at one time, formerly, long ago, once upon a time, previously ♦ *noun* **2** at once: **a** immediately, directly, forthwith, instantly, now, right away, straight away, this (very) minute **b** simultaneously, at the same time, together

oncoming *adjective* approaching, advancing, forthcoming, looming, onrushing

onerous *adjective* difficult, burdensome, demanding, exacting, hard, heavy, laborious, oppressive, taxing

> **Antonyms**

cushy (*informal*), easy, effortless,

light, painless, simple, undemanding, unexacting, untaxing

one-sided *adjective* biased, lopsided, partial, partisan, prejudiced, unfair, unjust

> **Antonyms**

equal, equitable, fair, impartial, just, unbiased, unprejudiced

ongoing *adjective* in progress, continuous, developing, evolving, progressing, unfinished, unfolding

onlooker *noun* observer, bystander, eyewitness, looker-on, spectator, viewer, watcher, witness

only *adjective* **1** sole, exclusive, individual, lone, single, solitary, unique ♦ *adverb* **2** merely, barely, just, purely, simply

onset *noun* beginning, inception, outbreak, start

> **Antonyms**

conclusion, culmination, end, ending, finish, outcome, termination

onslaught *noun* attack, assault, blitz, charge, offensive, onrush, onset

> **Antonyms**

defensive, retreat, rout, withdrawal

onus *noun* burden, liability, load, obligation, responsibility, task

> **Antonyms**

exemption, liberation, release, relief, remission

onward, onwards *adverb* ahead, beyond, forth, forward, in front, on

ooze[1] *verb* seep, drain, dribble, drip, escape, filter, leak

ooze[2] *noun* mud, alluvium, mire, silt, slime, sludge

opaque *adjective* cloudy, dim, dull, filmy, hazy, impenetrable, murky

> **Antonyms**

bright, clear, crystal clear, limpid, lucid, transparent

open *adjective* **1** unclosed, agape, ajar, gaping, uncovered, unfastened, unlocked, yawning **2** extended, unfolded, unfurled **3** accessible, available, free, public, unoccupied, unrestricted, vacant **4** unresolved, arguable, debatable, moot, undecided, unsettled **5** frank, candid, guileless, honest, sincere, transparent ♦ verb **6** unfasten, unblock, uncork, uncover, undo, unlock, untie, unwrap **7** unfold, expand, spread (out), unfurl, unroll **8** start, begin, commence, inaugurate, initiate, kick off (informal), launch, set in motion

➤ **Antonyms**

adjective ≠unclosed: closed, fastened, locked, sealed, shut ≠accessible: inaccessible, private, protected, restricted ≠frank: artful, cunning, secretive, sly ≠verb ≠unfasten: block, close, fasten, lock, obstruct, seal, shut ≠unfold: fold ≠start: close, conclude, end, finish, terminate

open-air adjective outdoor, alfresco

open-handed adjective generous, bountiful, free, lavish, liberal, munificent, unstinting

➤ **Antonyms**

avaricious, close-fisted, grasping, mean, miserly, parsimonious, penny-pinching (informal), stingy, tight-fisted

opening noun **1** beginning, commencement, dawn, inception, initiation, launch, outset, start **2** opportunity, chance, look-in (informal), occasion, vacancy **3** hole, aperture, chink, cleft, crack, fissure, gap, orifice, perforation, slot, space ♦ adjective **4** first, beginning, inaugural, initial, introductory, maiden, primary

➤ **Antonyms**

noun ≠beginning: cessation, close, completion, conclusion, culmination, ending, finale, finish, termination, winding up (informal) ≠hole: blockage, obstruction, occlusion, plug, seal, stoppage

openly adverb candidly, forthrightly, frankly, overtly, plainly, unhesitatingly, unreservedly

➤ **Antonyms**

covertly, furtively, privately, quietly, secretly, slyly, surreptitiously

open-minded adjective unprejudiced, broad-minded, impartial, liberal, reasonable, receptive, tolerant, unbiased, undogmatic

➤ **Antonyms**

biased, bigoted, dogmatic, intolerant, narrow-minded, opinionated, pig-headed, prejudiced, uncompromising

operate verb **1** work, act, function, go, perform, run **2** handle, be in charge of, manage, manoeuvre, use, work

➤ **Antonyms**

≠work: break down, conk out (informal), cut out (informal), fail, stall, stop

operation noun procedure, action, course, exercise, motion, movement, performance, process

operational adjective working, functional, going, operative, prepared, ready, up and running, usable, viable, workable

➤ **Antonyms**

broken, ineffective, inoperative, kaput (informal), nonfunctional, on the blink (slang), out of order

operative adjective **1** in force, active, effective, functioning, in operation, operational ♦ noun **2** worker, artisan, employee, labourer

➤ **Antonyms**

adjective ≠in force: ineffective, inoperative, nonfunctional

operator noun worker, conductor, driver, handler, mechanic, operative, practitioner, technician

opinion noun belief, assessment, feeling, idea, impression, judgment, point of view, sentiment, theory, view

opinionated adjective dogmatic, bigoted, cocksure, doctrinaire, overbearing, pig-headed, prejudiced, single-minded

➤ **Antonyms**

broad-minded, open-minded, receptive, tolerant, unbigoted, unprejudiced

opponent noun <u>adversary</u>, antagonist, challenger, competitor, contestant, enemy, foe, rival

➤ **Antonyms**

accomplice, ally, associate, colleague, friend, helper, supporter

opportune adjective Formal <u>timely</u>, advantageous, appropriate, apt, auspicious, convenient, favourable, fitting, suitable, well-timed

➤ **Antonyms**

inappropriate, inconvenient, inopportune, unfavourable, unsuitable, untimely

opportunism noun <u>expediency</u>, exploitation, pragmatism, unscrupulousness

opportunity noun <u>chance</u>, moment, occasion, opening, scope, time

oppose verb <u>fight</u>, block, combat, counter, defy, resist, take issue with, take on, thwart, withstand

➤ **Antonyms**

aid, back, defend, help, support

opposed adjective <u>against</u>, antagonistic, averse, clashing, conflicting, contrary, dissentient, hostile

opposing adjective <u>conflicting</u>, contrary, enemy, hostile, incompatible, opposite, rival

opposite adjective 1 <u>facing</u>, fronting 2 <u>different</u>, antithetical, conflicting, contrary, contrasted, reverse, unlike ♦ noun 3 <u>reverse</u>, antithesis, contradiction, contrary, converse, inverse

➤ **Antonyms**

adjective ≠different: alike, consistent, corresponding, identical, like, matching, same, similar, uniform

opposition noun 1 <u>hostility</u>, antagonism, competition, disapproval, obstruction, prevention, resistance, unfriendliness 2 <u>opponent</u>, antagonist, competition, foe, other side, rival

➤ **Antonyms**

≠hostility: agreement, approval, assent, collaboration, concurrence, cooperation, friendliness

oppress verb 1 <u>subjugate</u>, abuse, maltreat, persecute, subdue, suppress, wrong 2 <u>depress</u>, afflict, burden, dispirit, harass, sadden, torment, vex

➤ **Antonyms**

≠subjugate: deliver, emancipate, free, liberate, loose, release, set free ≠depress: unburden

oppressed adjective <u>downtrodden</u>, abused, browbeaten, disadvantaged, harassed, maltreated, tyrannized, underprivileged

➤ **Antonyms**

advantaged, favoured, honoured, liberated, privileged

oppression noun <u>subjugation</u>, abuse, brutality, cruelty, injury, injustice, maltreatment, persecution, subjection, tyranny

➤ **Antonyms**

benevolence, clemency, justice, kindness, mercy

oppressive adjective 1 <u>tyrannical</u>, brutal, cruel, despotic, harsh, inhuman, repressive, severe, unjust 2 <u>stifling</u>, airless, close, muggy, stuffy, sultry

➤ **Antonyms**

≠tyrannical: gentle, just, lenient, merciful, soft

oppressor noun <u>persecutor</u>, autocrat, bully, despot, scourge, slave-driver, tormentor, tyrant

opt verb, often with **for** <u>choose</u>, decide (on), elect, go for, plump for, prefer

➤ **Antonyms**

decide against, eliminate, exclude, preclude, reject, rule out, turn down

optimistic adjective <u>hopeful</u>, buoyant, cheerful, confident, encouraged, expectant, positive, rosy, sanguine

➤ **Antonyms**

bleak, cynical, despairing, despondent, downhearted, fatalistic, gloomy, glum, hopeless, pessimistic, resigned

optimum adjective <u>ideal</u>, best, highest, optimal, peak, perfect, superlative

> ➤ **Antonyms**

inferior, least, lowest, minimal, poorest, worst

option noun <u>choice</u>, alternative, preference, selection

optional adjective <u>voluntary</u>, discretionary, elective, extra, open, possible

> ➤ **Antonyms**

compulsory, de rigueur, mandatory, obligatory, required

opulence noun 1 <u>wealth</u>, affluence, luxuriance, luxury, plenty, prosperity, riches 2 <u>abundance</u>, copiousness, cornucopia, fullness, profusion, richness, superabundance

> ➤ **Antonyms**

≠wealth: impecuniousness, lack, penury, poverty, privation, want ≠abundance: dearth, lack, paucity, scantiness, scarcity, want

opulent adjective 1 <u>rich</u>, affluent, lavish, luxurious, moneyed, prosperous, sumptuous, wealthy, well-off, well-to-do 2 <u>abundant</u>, copious, lavish, luxuriant, plentiful, profuse, prolific

> ➤ **Antonyms**

≠rich: broke (informal), destitute, down and out, indigent, needy, on the rocks, penurious, poor, poverty-stricken

opus noun <u>work</u>, brainchild, composition, creation, oeuvre, piece, production

oracle noun 1 <u>prophecy</u>, divination, prediction, prognostication, revelation 2 <u>authority</u>, adviser, guru, mastermind, mentor, pundit, wizard

oral adjective <u>spoken</u>, verbal, vocal

oration noun <u>speech</u>, address, discourse, harangue, homily, lecture

orator noun <u>public speaker</u>, declaimer, lecturer, rhetorician, speaker

oratorical adjective <u>rhetorical</u>, bombastic, declamatory, eloquent, grandiloquent, highflown, magniloquent, sonorous

oratory noun <u>eloquence</u>, declamation, elocution, grandiloquence, public speaking, rhetoric, speech-making

orb noun <u>sphere</u>, ball, circle, globe, ring

orbit noun 1 <u>path</u>, circle, course, cycle, revolution, rotation, trajectory 2 <u>sphere of influence</u>, ambit, compass, domain, influence, range, reach, scope, sweep ♦ verb 3 <u>circle</u>, circumnavigate, encircle, revolve around

orchestrate verb 1 <u>score</u>, arrange 2 <u>organize</u>, arrange, coordinate, put together, set up, stage-manage

ordain verb 1 <u>appoint</u>, anoint, consecrate, invest, nominate 2 Formal <u>order</u>, decree, demand, dictate, fix, lay down, legislate, prescribe, rule, will

ordeal noun <u>hardship</u>, agony, anguish, baptism of fire, nightmare, suffering, test, torture, trial, tribulation(s)

> ➤ **Antonyms**

bliss, delight, enjoyment, joy, pleasure

order noun 1 <u>instruction</u>, command, decree, dictate, direction, directive, injunction, law, mandate, regulation, rule 2 <u>tidiness</u>, method, neatness, orderliness, organization, pattern, regularity, symmetry, system 3 <u>sequence</u>, arrangement, array, grouping, layout, line-up, progression, series, structure 4 <u>peace</u>, calm, control, discipline, law, law and order, quiet, tranquillity 5 <u>request</u>, application, booking, commission, requisition, reservation 6 <u>class</u>, caste, grade, position, rank, status 7 <u>kind</u>, class, family, genre, ilk, sort, type 8 <u>society</u>, association, brotherhood, community, company, fraternity, guild, organization ♦ verb 9 <u>command</u>, bid, charge, decree, demand, direct, instruct, require 10 <u>request</u>, apply for, book, reserve, send away for 11 <u>arrange</u>, catalogue, classify, group, marshal, organize, sort out, systematize

> ➤ **Antonyms**

noun ≠tidiness: chaos, clutter, confusion, disarray, disorder, jumble, mess, muddle, pandemonium, shambles ♦ ≠**arrange:** clutter, confuse, disarrange, disorder, disturb, jumble up, mess up, mix up, muddle, scramble

orderly *adjective* **1** well-organized, businesslike, in order, methodical, neat, regular, scientific, shipshape, systematic, tidy **2** well-behaved, controlled, disciplined, law-abiding, peaceable, quiet, restrained

➤ **Antonyms**

≠**well-organized:** chaotic, disorderly, disorganized, higgledy-piggledy (*informal*), messy, sloppy, unsystematic ≠**well-behaved:** disorderly, riotous, uncontrolled, undisciplined

ordinarily *adverb* usually, as a rule, commonly, customarily, generally, habitually, in general, normally

➤ **Antonyms**

hardly ever, infrequently, occasionally, rarely, scarcely, seldom, uncommonly

ordinary *adjective* **1** usual, common, conventional, everyday, normal, regular, routine, standard, stock, typical **2** commonplace, banal, humble, humdrum, modest, mundane, plain, run-of-the-mill, unremarkable, workaday

➤ **Antonyms**

≠**commonplace:** distinguished, exceptional, extraordinary, impressive, notable, outstanding, rare, superior, uncommon, unconventional, unique, unusual

organ *noun* **1** part, element, structure, unit **2** medium, forum, mouthpiece, vehicle, voice

organic *adjective* **1** natural, animate, biological, live, living **2** systematic, integrated, methodical, ordered, organized, structured

organism *noun* creature, animal, being, body, entity, structure

organization *noun* **1** group, association, body, company, confederation, corporation, institution, outfit (*informal*), syndicate **2**

management, construction, coordination, direction, organizing, planning, running, structuring **3** structure, arrangement, chemistry, composition, format, make-up, pattern, unity

organize *verb* **1** plan, arrange, co-ordinate, marshal, put together, run, set up, take care of **2** put in order, arrange, classify, group, systematize

➤ **Antonyms**

≠**plan:** confuse, disrupt, upset ≠**put in order:** disorganize, jumble, mix up, muddle, scramble

orgy *noun* **1** revel, bacchanalia, carousal, debauch, revelry, Saturnalia **2** spree, binge (*informal*), bout, excess, indulgence, overindulgence, splurge, surfeit

orient *verb* adjust, acclimatize, adapt, align, familiarize, get one's bearings, orientate

orientation *noun* **1** position, bearings, direction, location **2** adjustment, acclimatization, adaptation, assimilation, familiarization, introduction, settling in

orifice *noun* opening, aperture, cleft, hole, mouth, pore, rent, vent

origin *noun* **1** root, base, basis, derivation, fount, fountainhead, source, wellspring **2** beginning, birth, creation, emergence, foundation, genesis, inception, launch, start

➤ **Antonyms**

≠**beginning:** conclusion, culmination, death, end, expiry, finale, finish, outcome, termination

original *adjective* **1** first, earliest, initial, introductory, opening, primary, starting **2** new, fresh, ground-breaking, innovative, novel, seminal, unprecedented, unusual **3** creative, fertile, imaginative, ingenious, inventive, resourceful ♦ *noun* **4** prototype, archetype, master, model, paradigm, pattern, precedent, standard

➤ **Antonyms**

adjective ≠**first:** final, last, latest

≠**new**: normal, ordinary, standard, typical, unimaginative, unoriginal, usual ♦ *noun* ≠**prototype**: copy, imitation, replica, reproduction

originality *noun* novelty, creativity, freshness, imagination, ingenuity, innovation, inventiveness, newness, unorthodoxy

▶ **Antonyms**
conformity, orthodoxy, staleness, traditionalism

originally *adverb* initially, at first, first, in the beginning, to begin with

originate *verb* **1** begin, arise, come, derive, emerge, result, rise, spring, start, stem **2** introduce, bring about, create, formulate, generate, institute, launch, pioneer

▶ **Antonyms**
cease, conclude, end, finish, terminate, wind up

originator *noun* creator, architect, author, father *or* mother, founder, inventor, maker, pioneer

ornament *noun* **1** decoration, accessory, adornment, bauble, embellishment, festoon, knickknack, trimming, trinket ♦ *verb* **2** decorate, adorn, beautify, embellish, festoon, grace, prettify

ornamental *adjective* decorative, attractive, beautifying, embellishing, for show, showy

ornamentation *noun* decoration, adornment, elaboration, embellishment, embroidery, frills, ornateness

ornate *adjective* elaborate, baroque, busy, decorated, fancy, florid, fussy, ornamented, overelaborate, rococo

▶ **Antonyms**
austere, bare, basic, plain, severe, simple, spartan, stark, unadorned, unfussy

orthodox *adjective* established, accepted, approved, conventional, customary, official, received, traditional, well-established

▶ **Antonyms**
eccentric, nonconformist, novel, off-the-wall (*slang*), original, radical, unconventional, unorthodox, unusual

orthodoxy *noun* conformity, authority, conventionality, received wisdom, traditionalism

▶ **Antonyms**
heterodoxy, nonconformism, nonconformity, unconventionality

oscillate *verb* fluctuate, seesaw, sway, swing, vacillate, vary, vibrate, waver

▶ **Antonyms**
commit oneself, decide, resolve, settle

oscillation *noun* swing, fluctuation, instability, vacillation, variation, wavering

ossify *verb* harden, fossilize, solidify, stiffen

ostensible *adjective* apparent, outward, pretended, professed, purported, seeming, so-called, superficial, supposed

ostensibly *adverb* apparently, on the face of it, professedly, seemingly, supposedly

ostentation *noun* display, affectation, exhibitionism, flamboyance, flashiness, flaunting, parade, pomp, pretentiousness, show, showing off (*informal*)

▶ **Antonyms**
inconspicuousness, modesty, plainness, simplicity, unpretentiousness

ostentatious *adjective* pretentious, brash, conspicuous, flamboyant, flashy, gaudy, loud, obtrusive, showy

▶ **Antonyms**
conservative, inconspicuous, lowkey, modest, plain, reserved, simple

ostracism *noun* exclusion, banishment, exile, isolation, rejection

▶ **Antonyms**
acceptance, admission, approval, inclusion, reception, welcome

ostracize *verb* exclude, banish,

cast out, cold-shoulder, exile, give (someone) the cold shoulder, reject, send to Coventry, shun

➤ **Antonyms**
accept, admit, approve, embrace, greet, include, receive, welcome

other *adjective* **1** additional, added, alternative, auxiliary, further, more, spare, supplementary **2** different, contrasting, dissimilar, distinct, diverse, separate, unrelated, variant

otherwise *conjunction* **1** or else, if not, or then ◆ *adverb* **2** differently, any other way, contrarily

ounce *noun* shred, atom, crumb, drop, grain, scrap, speck, trace

oust *verb* expel, depose, dislodge, displace, dispossess, eject, throw out, topple, turn out, unseat

out *adjective* **1** away, abroad, absent, elsewhere, gone, not at home, outside **2** extinguished, at an end, dead, ended, exhausted, expired, finished, used up

outbreak *noun* eruption, burst, epidemic, explosion, flare-up, outburst, rash, upsurge

outburst *noun* outpouring, eruption, explosion, flare-up, outbreak, paroxysm, spasm, surge

outcast *noun* pariah, castaway, exile, leper, persona non grata, refugee, vagabond, wretch

outclass *verb* surpass, eclipse, excel, leave standing (*informal*), outdo, outshine, outstrip, overshadow, run rings around (*informal*)

outcome *noun* result, conclusion, consequence, end, issue, payoff (*informal*), upshot

outcry *noun* protest, clamour, commotion, complaint, hue and cry, hullabaloo, outburst, uproar

outdated *adjective* old-fashioned, antiquated, archaic, obsolete, outmoded, out of date, passé, unfashionable

➤ **Antonyms**
contemporary, current, fashion-

able, in vogue, modern, trendy (*Brit. informal*), up-to-date

outdo *verb* surpass, beat, best, eclipse, exceed, get the better of, outclass, outmanoeuvre, overcome, top, transcend

outdoor *adjective* open-air, alfresco, out-of-door(s), outside

➤ **Antonyms**
indoor, inside, interior, within

outer *adjective* external, exposed, exterior, outlying, outside, outward, peripheral, surface

➤ **Antonyms**
central, inner, inside, interior, internal, inward

outfit *noun* **1** costume, clothes, ensemble, garb, get-up (*informal*), kit, suit **2** *Informal* group, company, crew, organization, setup (*informal*), squad, team, unit

outgoing *adjective* **1** leaving, departing, former, retiring, withdrawing **2** sociable, approachable, communicative, expansive, extrovert, friendly, gregarious, open, warm

➤ **Antonyms**
≠leaving: arriving, entering, incoming ≠sociable: cold, reserved, retiring, withdrawn

outgoings *plural noun* expenses, costs, expenditure, outlay, overheads

outing *noun* trip, excursion, expedition, jaunt, spin (*informal*)

outlandish *adjective* strange, bizarre, exotic, fantastic, far-out (*slang*), freakish, outré, preposterous, unheard-of, weird

➤ **Antonyms**
banal, commonplace, everyday, familiar, humdrum, mundane, normal, ordinary, usual, well-known

outlaw *noun* **1** *History* bandit, brigand, desperado, fugitive, highwayman, marauder, outcast, robber ◆ *verb* **2** forbid, ban, bar, disallow, exclude, prohibit, proscribe **3** put a price on (someone's) head

> ➤ **Antonyms**

verb ≠<u>forbid</u>: allow, approve, authorize, legalise, sanction

outlay *noun* <u>expenditure</u>, cost, expenses, investment, outgoings, spending

outlet *noun* 1 <u>release</u>, vent 2 <u>shop</u>, market, store 3 <u>opening</u>, avenue, channel, duct, exit, release

outline *noun* 1 <u>summary</u>, recapitulation, résumé, rundown, synopsis, thumbnail sketch 2 <u>shape</u>, configuration, contour, delineation, figure, form, profile, silhouette ♦ *verb* 3 <u>summarize</u>, adumbrate, delineate, draft, plan, rough out, sketch (in), trace

outlive *verb* <u>survive</u>, outlast

outlook *noun* 1 <u>attitude</u>, angle, frame of mind, perspective, point of view, slant, standpoint, viewpoint 2 <u>prospect</u>, expectations, forecast, future

outlying *adjective* <u>remote</u>, distant, far-flung, out-of-the-way, peripheral, provincial

outmoded *adjective* <u>old-fashioned</u>, anachronistic, antiquated, archaic, obsolete, out-of-date, outworn, passé, unfashionable

> ➤ **Antonyms**

fashionable, fresh, in vogue, latest, modern, new, recent

out-of-date *adjective* <u>old-fashioned</u>, antiquated, dated, expired, invalid, lapsed, obsolete, outmoded, outworn, passé

> ➤ **Antonyms**

contemporary, current, fashionable, in, new, trendy (*Brit. informal*), up to date, valid

outpouring *noun* <u>stream</u>, cascade, effusion, flow, spate, spurt, torrent

output *noun* <u>production</u>, achievement, manufacture, productivity, yield

outrage *noun* 1 <u>indignation</u>, anger, fury, hurt, resentment, shock, wrath 2 <u>violation</u>, abuse, affront, desecration, indignity, insult, offence, sacrilege, violence ♦ *verb* 3 <u>offend</u>, affront, incense, infuriate, madden, scandalize, shock

outrageous *adjective* 1 <u>unreasonable</u>, exorbitant, extravagant, immoderate, preposterous, scandalous, shocking, steep (*informal*) 2 <u>atrocious</u>, disgraceful, flagrant, heinous, iniquitous, nefarious, offensive, shocking, unspeakable, villainous, wicked

> ➤ **Antonyms**

≠<u>unreasonable</u>: equitable, fair, moderate, reasonable ≠<u>atrocious</u>: mild, minor, tolerable, trivial

outré *adjective* <u>eccentric</u>, bizarre, fantastic, freakish, odd, off-the-wall (*slang*), outlandish, unconventional, weird

outright *adjective* 1 <u>absolute</u>, complete, out-and-out, perfect, thorough, thoroughgoing, total, unconditional, unmitigated, unqualified 2 <u>direct</u>, definite, flat, straightforward, unequivocal, unqualified ♦ *adverb* 3 <u>absolutely</u>, completely, straightforwardly, thoroughly, to the full 4 <u>openly</u>, overtly

outset *noun* <u>beginning</u>, commencement, inauguration, inception, kickoff (*informal*), onset, opening, start

> ➤ **Antonyms**

closing, completion, conclusion, consummation, end, finale, finish, termination

outshine *verb* <u>outdo</u>, eclipse, leave *or* put in the shade, outclass, outstrip, overshadow, surpass, transcend, upstage

outside *adjective* 1 <u>external</u>, exterior, extraneous, outer, outward 2 *As in* An outside re<u>mote</u>, distant, faint, marginal, slight, slim, small, unlikely ♦ *noun* 3 <u>exterior</u>, façade, face, front, skin, surface, topside

> ➤ **Antonyms**

adjective ≠<u>external</u>: in, indoor, inner, innermost, inside, interior, internal, inward

outsider *noun* interloper, incomer, intruder, newcomer, odd one out, stranger

outsize *adjective* extra-large, giant, gigantic, huge, jumbo (*informal*), mammoth, monster, oversized

► **Antonyms**
dwarf, micro, mini, tiny, undersized

outskirts *plural noun* edge, boundary, environs, periphery, suburbia, suburbs

outspoken *adjective* forthright, abrupt, blunt, explicit, frank, open, plain-spoken, unceremonious, unequivocal

► **Antonyms**
diplomatic, judicious, reticent, tactful

outstanding *adjective* **1** excellent, exceptional, great, important, impressive, great, superior, superlative **2** unpaid, due, payable, pending, remaining, uncollected, unsettled

► **Antonyms**
≠excellent: dull, inferior, mediocre, no great shakes (*informal*), ordinary, run-of-the-mill, unexceptional, unimpressive

outstrip *verb* surpass, better, eclipse, exceed, excel, outdo, overtake, transcend

outward *adjective* apparent, noticeable, observable, obvious, ostensible, perceptible, surface, visible

► **Antonyms**
inner, inside, interior, internal, invisible, inward, unnoticeable

outwardly *adverb* apparently, externally, on the face of it, on the surface, ostensibly, seemingly, superficially, to all intents and purposes

outweigh *verb* override, cancel (out), compensate for, eclipse, prevail over, take precedence over, tip the scales

outwit *verb* outsmart (*informal*), cheat, dupe, get the better of, outfox, outmanoeuvre, outthink,

put one over on (*informal*), swindle, take in (*informal*)

outworn *adjective* outdated, antiquated, discredited, disused, hackneyed, obsolete, outmoded, out-of-date, worn-out

► **Antonyms**
fresh, new, recent, up to date

oval *adjective* elliptical, egg-shaped, ovoid

ovation *noun* applause, acclaim, acclamation, big hand, cheers, clapping, plaudits, tribute

► **Antonyms**
abuse, booing, catcalls, derision, heckling, jeers, mockery, ridicule

over *preposition* **1** on top of, above, on, upon **2** more than, above, exceeding, in excess of ♦ *adverb* **3** above, aloft, on high, overhead **4** extra, beyond, in addition, in excess, left over ♦ *adjective* **5** finished, bygone, closed, completed, concluded, done (with), ended, gone, past

overact *verb* exaggerate, ham *or* ham up (*informal*), overdo, overplay

overall *adjective* **1** total, all-embracing, blanket, complete, comprehensive, general, global, inclusive, overarching ♦ *adverb* **2** in general, on the whole

overawe *verb* intimidate, abash, alarm, daunt, frighten, scare, terrify

► **Antonyms**
bolster, comfort, console, hearten, reassure

overbalance *verb* topple over, capsize, keel over, overturn, slip, tip over, tumble, turn turtle

overbearing *adjective* dictatorial, arrogant, bossy (*informal*), domineering, haughty, high-handed, imperious, supercilious, superior

► **Antonyms**
deferential, humble, modest, self-effacing, submissive, unassertive, unassuming

overblown *adjective* excessive, disproportionate, immoderate, inflated, overdone, over the top, undue

overcast *adjective* <u>cloudy</u>, dismal, dreary, dull, grey, leaden, louring *or* lowering, murky

➤ **Antonyms**

bright, brilliant, clear, cloudless, fine, sunny

overcharge *verb* <u>cheat</u>, diddle (*informal*), fleece, rip off (*slang*), short-change, sting (*informal*), surcharge

overcome *verb* 1 <u>conquer</u>, beat, defeat, master, overpower, overwhelm, prevail, subdue, subjugate, surmount, triumph over, vanquish ♦ *adjective* 2 <u>affected</u>, at a loss for words, bowled over (*informal*), overwhelmed, speechless, swept off one's feet

overconfident *adjective* <u>cocksure</u>, brash, foolhardy, overweening, presumptuous

➤ **Antonyms**

cautious, diffident, hesitant, uncertain, unsure

overcrowded *adjective* <u>packed (out)</u>, bursting at the seams, choked, congested, jam-packed, overloaded, overpopulated, swarming

➤ **Antonyms**

desolate, empty, unoccupied, vacant

overdo *verb* 1 <u>exaggerate</u>, belabour, gild the lily, go overboard (*informal*), overindulge, overreach, overstate 2 **overdo it** <u>overwork</u>, bite off more than one can chew, burn the candle at both ends (*informal*), overload oneself, strain *or* overstrain oneself, wear oneself out

➤ **Antonyms**

≠exaggerate: belittle, disparage, minimize, play down, underplay, understate

overdone *adjective* 1 <u>excessive</u>, exaggerated, fulsome, immoderate, inordinate, overelaborate, too much, undue, unnecessary 2 <u>overcooked</u>, burnt, charred, dried up, spoiled

➤ **Antonyms**

≠excessive: minimized, moderated, played down, underdone, underplayed, understated

overdue *adjective* <u>late</u>, behindhand, behind schedule, belated, owing, tardy, unpunctual

➤ **Antonyms**

ahead of time, beforehand, early, in advance, in good time, punctual

overeat *verb* <u>overindulge</u>, binge (*informal*), gorge, gormandize, guzzle, pig out (*slang*), stuff oneself

overemphasize *verb* <u>overstress</u>, belabour, blow up out of all proportion, make a mountain out of a molehill (*informal*), overdramatize

➤ **Antonyms**

belittle, downplay, make light of, minimize, play down, underplay, underrate, understate

overflow *verb* 1 <u>spill</u>, brim over, bubble over, pour over, run over, well over ♦ *noun* 2 <u>surplus</u>, overabundance, spilling over

overhang *verb* <u>project</u>, extend, jut, loom, protrude, stick out

overhaul *verb* 1 <u>check</u>, do up (*informal*), examine, inspect, recondition, repair, restore, service 2 <u>overtake</u>, catch up with, get ahead of, pass ♦ *noun* 3 <u>check-up</u>, check, examination, going-over (*informal*), inspection, reconditioning, service

overhead *adverb* 1 <u>above</u>, aloft, in the sky, on high, skyward, up above, upward ♦ *adjective* 2 <u>aerial</u>, overhanging, upper

➤ **Antonyms**

adverb ≠above: below, beneath, downward, underfoot, underneath

overheads *plural noun* <u>running costs</u>, operating costs

overindulgence *noun* <u>immoderation</u>, excess, intemperance, overeating, surfeit

overjoyed *adjective* <u>delighted</u>, cock-a-hoop, elated, euphoric, jubilant, on cloud nine (*informal*), over the moon (*informal*), thrilled

➤ **Antonyms**

crestfallen, dejected, disappointed, downcast, down in the dumps (*informal*), heartbroken, miserable, sad, unhappy, woebegone

overload *verb* overburden, burden, encumber, oppress, overtax, saddle (with), strain, weigh down

overlook *verb* **1** miss, disregard, forget, neglect, omit, pass **2** ignore, condone, disregard, excuse, forgive, make allowances for, pardon, turn a blind eye to, wink at **3** have a view of, look over or out on

➤ **Antonyms**

≠miss: discern, heed, mark, note, notice, observe, perceive, spot

overpower *verb* overwhelm, conquer, crush, defeat, master, overcome, overthrow, quell, subdue, subjugate, vanquish

overpowering *adjective* overwhelming, forceful, invincible, irrefutable, irresistible, powerful, strong

overrate *verb* overestimate, exaggerate, overvalue

override *verb* overrule, annul, cancel, countermand, nullify, outweigh, supersede

overriding *adjective* predominant, dominant, major, paramount, primary, supreme, ultimate

➤ **Antonyms**

insignificant, minor, negligible, trivial, unimportant

overrule *verb* reverse, alter, annul, cancel, countermand, override, overturn, repeal, rescind, veto

➤ **Antonyms**

allow, approve, consent to, endorse, pass, permit, sanction

overrun *verb* **1** overwhelm, invade, occupy, rout **2** spread over, choke, infest, inundate, permeate, ravage, swarm over **3** exceed, go beyond, overshoot, run over or on

overseer *noun* supervisor, boss (*informal*), chief, foreman, master, superintendent

overshadow *verb* **1** outshine, dominate, dwarf, eclipse, leave or put in the shade, surpass, tower above **2** spoil, blight, mar, put a damper on, ruin, temper

oversight *noun* mistake, blunder, carelessness, error, fault, lapse, neglect, omission, slip

overt *adjective* open, blatant, manifest, observable, obvious, plain, public, unconcealed, undisguised

➤ **Antonyms**

concealed, covert, disguised, hidden, secret, surreptitious, underhand

overtake *verb* **1** pass, catch up with, get past, leave behind, outdistance, outdo, outstrip, overhaul **2** befall, engulf, happen, hit, overwhelm, strike

overthrow *verb* **1** defeat, bring down, conquer, depose, dethrone, oust, overcome, overpower, topple, unseat, vanquish ♦ *noun* **2** downfall, defeat, destruction, dethronement, fall, ousting, undoing, unseating

➤ **Antonyms**

verb ≠defeat: defend, guard, keep, maintain, preserve, protect, support, uphold ♦ *noun* ≠downfall: defence, preservation, protection

overtone *noun, often plural* hint, connotation, implication, innuendo, intimation, nuance, sense, suggestion, undercurrent

overture *noun* **1** *Music* introduction, opening, prelude **2** overtures approach, advance, invitation, offer, proposal, proposition

➤ **Antonyms**

≠introduction: coda, finale ≠approach: rejection, withdrawal

overturn *verb* **1** tip over, capsize, keel over, overbalance, topple, upend, upturn **2** overthrow, bring down, depose, destroy, unseat

overweight *adjective* fat, bulky,

chubby, chunky, corpulent, heavy, hefty, obese, plump, portly, stout, tubby (*informal*)

➤ **Antonyms**

emaciated, gaunt, lean, scraggy, scrawny, skinny, thin, underweight

overwhelm *verb* 1 <u>overcome</u>, bowl over (*informal*), devastate, knock (someone) for six (*informal*), stagger, sweep (someone) off his *or* her feet, take (someone's) breath away 2 <u>destroy</u>, crush, cut to pieces, massacre, overpower, overrun, rout

overwhelming *adjective* <u>overpowering</u>, breathtaking, crushing, devastating, irresistible, shattering, stunning, towering

➤ **Antonyms**

insignificant, negligible, trivial, unimportant

overwork *verb* 1 <u>strain oneself</u>, burn the midnight oil, sweat (*informal*), work one's fingers to the bone 2 <u>overuse</u>, exhaust, exploit, fatigue, oppress, wear out, weary

overwrought *adjective* <u>agitated</u>, distracted, excited, frantic, keyed up, on edge, overexcited, tense, uptight (*informal*)

➤ **Antonyms**

calm, collected, controlled, cool, impassive

owe *verb* <u>be in debt</u>, be in arrears, be obligated *or* indebted

owing *adjective* <u>unpaid</u>, due, outstanding, overdue, owed, payable, unsettled

owing to *preposition* <u>because of</u>, as a result of, on account of

own *adjective* 1 <u>personal</u>, individual, particular, private ♦ *pronoun* 2 <u>hold one's own keep going</u>, compete, keep one's end up, keep one's head above water 3 **on one's own** <u>alone</u>, by oneself, independently, singly, unaided, unassisted, under one's own steam ♦ *verb* 4 <u>possess</u>, be in possession of, enjoy, have, hold, keep, retain 5 <u>acknowledge</u>, admit, allow, concede, confess,

grant, recognize 6 **own up** <u>confess</u>, admit, come clean, tell the truth

owner *noun* <u>possessor</u>, holder, landlord *or* landlady, proprietor

ownership *noun* <u>possession</u>, dominion, title

P p

pace *noun* 1 <u>step</u>, gait, stride, tread, walk 2 <u>speed</u>, rate, tempo, velocity ♦ *verb* 3 <u>stride</u>, march, patrol, pound 4 **pace out** <u>measure</u>, count, mark out, step

pacifist *noun* <u>peace lover</u>, conscientious objector, dove

pacify *verb* <u>calm</u>, allay, appease, assuage, mollify, placate, propitiate, soothe

pack *verb* 1 <u>package</u>, bundle, load, store, stow 2 <u>cram</u>, compress, crowd, fill, jam, press, ram, stuff 3 **pack off** <u>send away</u>, dismiss, send packing (*informal*) ♦ *noun* 4 <u>bundle</u>, back pack, burden, kitbag, knapsack, load, parcel, rucksack 5 <u>packet</u>, package 6 <u>group</u>, band, bunch, company, crowd, flock, gang, herd, mob, troop

package *noun* 1 <u>parcel</u>, box, carton, container, packet 2 <u>unit</u>, combination, whole ♦ *verb* 3 <u>pack</u>, box, parcel (up), wrap

packed *adjective* <u>full</u>, chock-a-block, chock-full, crammed, crowded, filled, jammed, jam-packed

➤ **Antonyms**

deserted, empty, uncongested, uncrowded

packet *noun* 1 <u>package</u>, bag, carton, container, parcel 2 *Slang* <u>fortune</u>, bomb (*Brit. slang*), king's ransom (*informal*), pile (*informal*), small fortune, tidy sum (*informal*)

pack in *verb Brit. informal* <u>stop</u>, cease, chuck (*informal*), give up or over, kick (*informal*)

pack up *verb* **1** put away, store **2** *Informal* stop, finish, give up, pack in (*Brit. informal*) **3** break down, conk out (*informal*), fail

pact *noun* agreement, alliance, bargain, covenant, deal, treaty, understanding

pad[1] *noun* **1** cushion, buffer, protection, stuffing, wad **2** notepad, block, jotter, writing pad **3** paw, foot, sole **4** *Slang* home, apartment, flat, place ◆ *verb* **5** pack, cushion, fill, protect, stuff **6** pad out lengthen, elaborate, fill out, flesh out, protract, spin out, stretch

pad[2] *verb* sneak, creep, go barefoot, steal

padding *noun* **1** filling, packing, stuffing, wadding **2** waffle (*informal, chiefly Brit.*), hot air (*informal*), verbiage, verbosity, wordiness

paddle[1] *noun* **1** oar, scull ◆ *verb* **2** row, propel, pull, scull

paddle[2] *verb* **1** wade, slop, splash (about) **2** dabble, stir

pagan *adjective* **1** heathen, idolatrous, infidel, polytheistic ◆ *noun* **2** heathen, idolater, infidel, polytheist

page[1] *noun* folio, leaf, sheet, side

page[2] *noun* **1** attendant, pageboy, servant, squire ◆ *verb* **2** call, send for, summon

pageant *noun* show, display, parade, procession, spectacle, tableau

pageantry *noun* spectacle, display, grandeur, parade, pomp, show, splendour, theatricality

pain *noun* **1** hurt, ache, discomfort, irritation, pang, soreness, tenderness, throb, twinge **2** suffering, agony, anguish, distress, heartache, misery, torment, torture ◆ *verb* **3** hurt, smart, sting, throb **4** distress, agonize, cut to the quick, grieve, hurt, sadden, torment, torture

pained *adjective* distressed, aggrieved, hurt, injured, offended, upset, wounded

painful *adjective* **1** distressing, disagreeable, distasteful, grievous, unpleasant **2** sore, aching, agonizing, smarting, tender **3** difficult, arduous, hard, laborious, troublesome, trying

► **Antonyms**

≠distressing: agreeable, enjoyable, pleasant, satisfying ≠sore: comforting, painless, relieving, soothing ≠difficult: a piece of cake (*informal*), easy, effortless, interesting, short, simple, straightforward, undemanding

painfully *adverb* distressingly, clearly, dreadfully, sadly, unfortunately

painkiller *noun* analgesic, anaesthetic, anodyne, drug

painless *adjective* simple, easy, effortless, fast, quick

pains *plural noun* trouble, bother, care, diligence, effort

painstaking *adjective* thorough, assiduous, careful, conscientious, diligent, meticulous, scrupulous

► **Antonyms**

careless, half-hearted, haphazard, heedless, lazy, negligent, slapdash, slipshod, thoughtless

paint *noun* **1** colouring, colour, dye, pigment, stain, tint ◆ *verb* **2** depict, draw, picture, portray, represent, sketch **3** coat, apply, colour, cover, daub

pair *noun* **1** couple, brace, duo, twins ◆ *verb* **2** couple, bracket, join, match (up), team, twin

pal *noun* *Informal* friend, buddy (*informal*), chum (*informal*), companion, comrade, crony, mate (*informal*)

palatable *adjective* delicious, appetizing, luscious, mouthwatering, tasty

► **Antonyms**

bland, flat, insipid, stale, tasteless, unappetizing, unpalatable

palate *noun* taste, appetite, stomach

palatial *adjective* magnificent, grand, imposing, majestic, opulent, regal, splendid, stately

palaver *noun* fuss, business (*informal), carry-on (*informal, chiefly Brit.*), pantomime (*informal, chiefly Brit.*), performance (*informal*), rigmarole, song and dance (*Brit. informal*), to-do

pale *adjective* **1** white, ashen, bleached, colourless, faded, light, pallid, pasty, wan ♦ *verb* **2** become pale, blanch, go white, lose colour, whiten

➤ **Antonyms**

adjective ≠white: blooming, florid, flushed, glowing, rosy-cheeked, ruddy

pall[1] *noun* **1** cloud, mantle, shadow, shroud, veil **2** gloom, check, damp, damper

pall[2] *verb* become boring, become dull, become tedious, cloy, jade, sicken, tire, weary

pallid *adjective* pale, anaemic, ashen, colourless, pasty, wan

pallor *noun* paleness, lack of colour, pallidness, wanness, whiteness

palm off *verb* fob off, foist off, pass off

palpable *adjective* obvious, clear, conspicuous, evident, manifest, plain, unmistakable, visible

palpitate *verb* beat, flutter, pound, pulsate, throb, tremble

paltry *adjective* insignificant, contemptible, despicable, inconsiderable, meagre, mean, measly, minor, miserable, petty, poor, puny, slight, small, trifling, trivial, unimportant, worthless

➤ **Antonyms**

considerable, grand, important, major, mega (*slang*), significant, valuable

pamper *verb* spoil, coddle, cosset, indulge, mollycoddle, pet

pamphlet *noun* booklet, brochure, circular, leaflet, tract

pan[1] *noun* **1** pot, container, saucepan ♦ *verb* **2** sift out, look for, search for **3** *Informal* criticize, censure, knock (*informal*), slam (*slang*), tear into (*informal*)

pan[2] *verb* move, follow, sweep, track

panacea *noun* cure-all, nostrum,

universal cure

panache *noun* style, dash, élan, flamboyance

pandemonium *noun* uproar, bedlam, chaos, confusion, din, hullabaloo, racket, rumpus, turmoil

➤ **Antonyms**

calm, hush, order, peace, peacefulness, stillness, tranquillity

pander *verb* **pander to** indulge, cater to, gratify, play up to (*informal*), please, satisfy

pang *noun* twinge, ache, pain, prick, spasm, stab, sting

panic *noun* **1** fear, alarm, fright, hysteria, scare, terror ♦ *verb* **2** go to pieces, become hysterical, lose one's nerve **3** alarm, scare, unnerve

panic-stricken *adjective* frightened, frightened out of one's wits, hysterical, in a cold sweat (*informal*), panicky, scared, scared stiff, terrified

panoply *noun* array, attire, dress, garb, regalia, trappings

panorama *noun* **1** view, prospect, vista **2** survey, overall picture, overview, perspective

panoramic *adjective* wide, comprehensive, extensive, overall, sweeping

pant *verb* puff, blow, breathe, gasp, heave, wheeze

pants *plural noun* **1** *Brit.* underpants, boxer shorts, briefs, drawers, knickers, panties **2** *U.S.* trousers, slacks

paper *noun* **1** newspaper, daily, gazette, journal **2** essay, article, dissertation, report, treatise **3** papers: **a** documents, certificates, deeds, records **b** letters, archive, diaries, documents, dossier, file, records ♦ *verb* **4** wallpaper, hang

par *noun* average, level, mean, norm, standard, usual

parable *noun* lesson, allegory, fable, moral tale, story

parade *noun* **1** procession, array, cavalcade, march, pageant **2** show, display, spectacle ♦ *verb* **3** flaunt, display, exhibit, show off (*informal*) **4** <u>march</u>, process

paradigm *noun* <u>model</u>, example, ideal, pattern

paradise *noun* **1** <u>heaven</u>, Elysian fields, Happy Valley (*Islam*), Promised Land **2** <u>bliss</u>, delight, felicity, heaven, utopia

paradox *noun* <u>contradiction</u>, anomaly, enigma, oddity, puzzle

paradoxical *adjective* <u>contradictory</u>, baffling, confounding, enigmatic, puzzling

paragon *noun* <u>model</u>, epitome, exemplar, ideal, nonpareil, pattern, quintessence

paragraph *noun* <u>section</u>, clause, item, part, passage, subdivision

parallel *adjective* **1** <u>equidistant</u>, alongside, side by side **2** <u>matching</u>, analogous, corresponding, like, resembling, similar ♦ *noun* **3** <u>equivalent</u>, analogue, counterpart, equal, match, twin **4** <u>similarity</u>, analogy, comparison, likeness, resemblance

➤ **Antonyms**

adjective ≠<u>matching</u>: different, dissimilar, divergent, unlike ♦ *noun* ≠<u>equivalent</u>: opposite, reverse ≠<u>similarity</u>: difference, dissimilarity, divergence

paralyse *verb* **1** <u>disable</u>, cripple, incapacitate, lame **2** <u>immobilize</u>, freeze, halt, numb, petrify, stun

paralysis *noun* **1** <u>immobility</u>, palsy **2** <u>standstill</u>, breakdown, halt, stoppage

paralytic *adjective* <u>paralysed</u>, crippled, disabled, incapacitated, lame, palsied

parameter *noun* *Informal* <u>limit</u>, framework, limitation, restriction, specification

paramount *adjective* <u>principal</u>, cardinal, chief, first, foremost, main, primary, prime, supreme

➤ **Antonyms**

inferior, insignificant, least, minor, negligible, secondary, slight, subordinate, unimportant

paranoid *adjective* **1** <u>mentally ill</u>, deluded, disturbed, manic, neurotic, paranoiac, psychotic **2** *Informal* <u>suspicious</u>, antsy (*infor-*

mal), fearful, nervous, worried

paraphernalia *noun* <u>equipment</u>, apparatus, baggage, belongings, effects, gear, stuff, tackle, things, trappings

paraphrase *noun* **1** <u>rewording</u>, rephrasing, restatement ♦ *verb* **2** <u>reword</u>, express in other words or one's own words, rephrase, restate

parasite *noun* <u>sponger</u> (*informal*), bloodsucker (*informal*), hangeron, leech, scrounger (*informal*)

parasitic, parasitical *adjective* <u>scrounging</u> (*informal*), bloodsucking (*informal*), sponging (*informal*)

parcel *noun* **1** <u>package</u>, bundle, pack ♦ *verb* **2** *often with* up <u>wrap</u>, do up, pack, package, tie up

parch *verb* <u>dry up</u>, dehydrate, desiccate, evaporate, shrivel, wither

parched *adjective* <u>dried out or up</u>, arid, dehydrated, dry, thirsty

pardon *verb* **1** <u>forgive</u>, absolve, acquit, excuse, exonerate, let off (*informal*), overlook ♦ *noun* **2** <u>forgiveness</u>, absolution, acquittal, amnesty, exoneration

➤ **Antonyms**

verb ≠<u>forgive</u>: admonish, blame, censure, chastise, condemn, discipline, penalize, punish, rebuke ♦ *noun* ≠<u>forgiveness</u>: condemnation, guilt, penalty, punishment, redress, retribution

pardonable *adjective* <u>forgivable</u>, excusable, minor, understandable, venial

pare *verb* **1** <u>peel</u>, clip, cut, shave, skin, trim **2** <u>cut back</u>, crop, cut, decrease, dock, reduce

parent *noun* <u>father or mother</u>, procreator, progenitor, sire

parentage *noun* <u>family</u>, ancestry, birth, descent, lineage, pedigree, stock

pariah *noun* <u>outcast</u>, exile, undesirable, untouchable

parish *noun* <u>community</u>, church, congregation, flock

parity *noun* <u>equality</u>, consistency, equivalence, uniformity, unity

park noun parkland, estate, garden, grounds, woodland

parlance noun language, idiom, jargon, phraseology, speech, talk, tongue

parliament noun assembly, congress, convention, council, legislature, senate

parliamentary adjective governmental, law-making, legislative

parlour noun Old-fashioned sitting room, drawing room, front room, living room, lounge

parlous adjective Archaic or humorous dangerous, hazardous, risky

parochial adjective provincial, insular, limited, narrow, narrow-minded, petty, small-minded

➤ **Antonyms**

broad, broad-minded, cosmopolitan, international, liberal, national, universal, world-wide

parody noun 1 takeoff (informal), burlesque, caricature, satire, send-up (Brit. informal), skit, spoof (informal) ♦ verb 2 take off (informal), burlesque, caricature, do a takeoff of (informal), satirize, send up (Brit. informal)

paroxysm noun outburst, attack, convulsion, fit, seizure, spasm

parrot verb repeat, copy, echo, imitate, mimic

parry verb 1 ward off, block, deflect, rebuff, repel, repulse 2 evade, avoid, dodge, sidestep

parsimonious adjective mean, close, frugal, miserly, niggardly, penny-pinching (informal), stingy, tightfisted

➤ **Antonyms**

extravagant, generous, lavish, munificent, open-handed, spendthrift, wasteful

parson noun clergyman, churchman, cleric, minister, pastor, preacher, priest, vicar

part noun 1 piece, bit, fraction, fragment, portion, scrap, section, share 2 component, branch, constituent, division, member, unit 3 Theatre role, character, lines 4 side, behalf, cause, concern, interest 5 often plural region, area, district, neighbourhood, quarter, vicinity 6 in good part good-naturedly, cheerfully, well, without offence 7 in part partly, a little, in some measure, partially, somewhat ♦ verb 8 divide, break, come apart, detach, rend, separate, sever, split, tear 9 leave, depart, go, go away, separate, split up, withdraw

➤ **Antonyms**

noun ≠piece: bulk, entirety, mass, totality, whole ♦ ≠divide: adhere, close, combine, hold, join, stick, unite ≠leave: appear, arrive, come, gather, remain, show up (informal), stay, turn up

partake verb 1 partake of consume, eat, take 2 partake in participate in, engage in, share in, take part in

partial adjective 1 incomplete, imperfect, uncompleted, unfinished 2 biased, discriminatory, one-sided, partisan, prejudiced, unfair, unjust

➤ **Antonyms**

≠incomplete: complete, entire, finished, full, total, whole ≠biased: impartial, objective, unbiased, unprejudiced

partiality noun 1 bias, favouritism, preference, prejudice 2 liking, fondness, inclination, love, penchant, predilection, taste, weakness

➤ **Antonyms**

≠bias: disinterest, equity, fairness, impartiality, objectivity ≠liking: abhorrence, antipathy, aversion, disgust, disinclination, dislike, distaste, loathing, revulsion

partially adverb partly, fractionally, incompletely, in part, not wholly, somewhat

participant noun participator, contributor, member, player, stakeholder

participate verb take part, be involved in, join in, partake, perform, share

➤ **Antonyms**

abstain, boycott, forgo, opt out, pass up, refrain from, take no part of

participation noun taking part, contribution, involvement, joining in, partaking, sharing in

particle noun bit, grain, iota, jot, mite, piece, scrap, shred, speck

particular adjective 1 specific, distinct, exact, peculiar, precise, special 2 special, especial, exceptional, marked, notable, noteworthy, remarkable, singular, uncommon, unusual 3 fussy, choosy (informal), demanding, fastidious, finicky, pernickety (informal), picky (informal) ♦ noun 4 usually plural detail, circumstance, fact, feature, item, specification 5 in particular especially, distinctly, exactly, particularly, specifically

➤ **Antonyms**

adjective ≠specific: general, imprecise, indefinite, indistinct, inexact, unspecified, vague ≠fussy: casual, easy, easy to please, indiscriminate, negligent, slack, sloppy, uncritical

particularly adverb 1 especially, exceptionally, notably, singularly, uncommonly, unusually 2 specifically, distinctly, especially, explicitly, expressly, in particular

parting noun 1 going, farewell, goodbye 2 division, breaking, rift, rupture, separation, split

partisan noun 1 supporter, adherent, devotee, upholder 2 underground fighter, guerrilla, resistance fighter ♦ adjective 3 prejudiced, biased, interested, one-sided, partial, sectarian

➤ **Antonyms**

noun ≠supporter: adversary, critic, detractor, foe, opponent, rival ♦ adjective ≠prejudiced: disinterested, impartial, non-partisan, unbiased, unprejudiced

partition noun 1 screen, barrier, wall 2 division, segregation, separation 3 allotment, apportionment, distribution ♦ verb 4 separate, divide, screen

partly adverb partially, slightly, somewhat

➤ **Antonyms**

completely, entirely, fully, in full, totally, wholly

partner noun 1 spouse, consort, husband or wife, mate, significant other (U.S. informal) 2 companion, ally, associate, colleague, comrade, helper, mate

partnership noun company, alliance, cooperative, firm, house, society, union

party noun 1 get-together (informal), celebration, do (informal), festivity, function, gathering, reception, social gathering 2 group, band, company, crew, gang, squad, team, unit 3 faction, camp, clique, coterie, league, set, side 4 Informal person, individual, someone

pass verb 1 go by or past, elapse, go, lapse, move, proceed, run 2 qualify, do, get through, graduate, succeed 3 spend, fill, occupy, while away 4 give, convey, deliver, hand, send, transfer 5 approve, accept, decree, enact, legislate, ordain, ratify 6 exceed, beat, go beyond, outdo, outstrip, overtake, surpass 7 end, blow over, cease, go ♦ noun 8 gap, canyon, gorge, ravine, route 9 licence, authorization, passport, permit, ticket, warrant

➤ **Antonyms**

verb ≠go by or past: bring or come to a standstill, cease, halt, pause, stop ≠qualify: be inadequate, be unsuccessful, fail, lose ≠approve: ban, disallow, invalidate, overrule, prohibit, refuse, reject, veto

passable adjective adequate, acceptable, all right, average, fair, mediocre, so-so (informal), tolerable

➤ **Antonyms**

A1 or A-one (informal), exceptional, extraordinary, first-class, inadequate, marvellous, outstanding, superb, unacceptable, unsatisfactory

passage noun **1** way, alley, avenue, channel, course, path, road, route **2** corridor, hall, lobby, vestibule **3** extract, excerpt, piece, quotation, reading, section, text **4** journey, crossing, trek, trip, voyage **5** safe-conduct, freedom, permission, right

passageway noun corridor, aisle, alley, hall, hallway, lane, passage

pass away verb Euphemistic die, expire, kick the bucket (slang), pass on, pass over, shuffle off this mortal coil, snuff it (informal)

passé adjective out-of-date, dated, obsolete, old-fashioned, old hat, outdated, outmoded, unfashionable

passenger noun traveller, fare, rider

passer-by noun bystander, onlooker, witness

passing adjective **1** momentary, brief, ephemeral, fleeting, short-lived, temporary, transient, transitory **2** superficial, casual, cursory, glancing, quick, short

passion noun **1** love, ardour, desire, infatuation, lust **2** emotion, ardour, excitement, energy, fervour, fire, heat, intensity, warmth, zeal **3** rage, anger, fit, frenzy, fury, outburst, paroxysm, storm **4** mania, bug (informal), craving, craze, enthusiasm, fascination, obsession

➤ **Antonyms**

≠emotion: apathy, calmness, coldness, coolness, indifference, unconcern

passionate adjective **1** loving, amorous, ardent, erotic, hot, lustful **2** emotional, ardent, eager, fervent, fierce, heartfelt, impassioned, intense, strong

➤ **Antonyms**

≠loving: cold, frigid, passionless, unloving, unresponsive ≠emotional: apathetic, calm, cold, half-hearted, indifferent, nonchalant,

unemotional, unenthusiastic

passive adjective submissive, compliant, docile, inactive, quiescent, receptive

➤ **Antonyms**

active, bossy (informal), defiant, domineering, energetic, feisty (informal, chiefly U.S. & Canad.), lively, rebellious, spirited

pass off verb fake, counterfeit, make a pretence of, palm off

pass out verb Informal faint, become unconscious, black out (informal), lose consciousness

pass over verb disregard, ignore, overlook, take no notice of

pass up verb Informal miss, abstain, decline, forgo, give (something) a miss (informal), let slip, neglect

password noun signal, key word, watchword

past adjective **1** former, ancient, bygone, early, olden, previous **2** over, done, ended, finished, gone ♦ noun **3** background, history, life, past life **4** the past former times, days gone by, long ago, olden days ♦ preposition **5** after, beyond, later than **6** beyond, across, by, over

➤ **Antonyms**

adjective ≠former: arrived, begun, coming, future, now, present ♦ noun ≠former times: future, now, present, time to come, today, tomorrow

paste noun **1** adhesive, cement, glue, gum ♦ verb **2** stick, cement, glue, gum

pastel adjective pale, delicate, light, muted, soft

➤ **Antonyms**

bright, deep, rich, strong, vibrant, vivid

pastiche noun medley, blend, hotchpotch, mélange, miscellany, mixture

pastime noun activity, amusement, diversion, entertainment, game, hobby, recreation

pastor noun clergyman, churchman, ecclesiastic, minister, parson, priest, rector, vicar

pastoral adjective **1** <u>rustic</u>, bucolic, country, rural **2** <u>ecclesiastical</u>, clerical, ministerial, priestly

pasture noun <u>grassland</u>, grass, grazing, meadow

pasty adjective <u>pale</u>, anaemic, pallid, sickly, wan

pat verb **1** <u>stroke</u>, caress, fondle, pet, tap, touch ♦ noun **2** <u>stroke</u>, clap, tap

patch noun **1** <u>reinforcement</u>, piece of material **3** <u>spot</u>, bit, scrap, shred, small piece **3** <u>plot</u>, area, ground, land, tract ♦ verb **4** <u>mend</u>, cover, reinforce, repair, sew up

patchwork noun <u>mixture</u>, hotchpotch, jumble, medley, pastiche

patchy adjective <u>uneven</u>, erratic, fitful, irregular, sketchy, spotty, variable

➤ **Antonyms**

constant, even, regular, unbroken, unvarying

patent noun **1** <u>copyright</u>, licence ♦ adjective **2** <u>obvious</u>, apparent, clear, evident, glaring, manifest

paternal adjective <u>fatherly</u>, concerned, protective, solicitous

paternity noun **1** <u>fatherhood</u>, fathership **2** <u>parentage</u>, descent, extraction, family, lineage

path noun **1** <u>way</u>, footpath, road, track, trail **2** <u>course</u>, direction, road, route, way

pathetic adjective <u>sad</u>, affecting, distressing, gut-wrenching, heartrending, moving, pitiable, plaintive, poignant, tender, touching

➤ **Antonyms**

amusing, comical, droll, entertaining, funny, laughable, ludicrous, ridiculous

pathos noun <u>sadness</u>, pitifulness, plaintiveness, poignancy

patience noun **1** <u>forbearance</u>, calmness, restraint, serenity, sufferance, tolerance **2** <u>endurance</u>, constancy, fortitude, longsuffering, perseverance, resignation, stoicism, submission

➤ **Antonyms**

≠forbearance: exasperation, im-

patience, irritation, nervousness, restlessness

patient adjective **1** <u>long-suffering</u>, calm, enduring, persevering, philosophical, resigned, stoical, submissive, uncomplaining **2** <u>forbearing</u>, even-tempered, forgiving, indulgent, lenient, mild, tolerant, understanding ♦ noun **3** <u>sick person</u>, case, invalid, sufferer

patriot noun <u>nationalist</u>, chauvinist, loyalist

patriotic adjective <u>nationalistic</u>, chauvinistic, jingoistic, loyal

patriotism noun <u>nationalism</u>, jingoism

patrol noun **1** <u>policing</u>, guarding, protecting, vigilance, watching **2** <u>guard</u>, patrolman, sentinel, watch, watchman ♦ verb **3** <u>police</u>, guard, inspect, keep guard, keep watch, safeguard

patron noun **1** <u>supporter</u>, backer, benefactor, champion, friend, helper, philanthropist, sponsor **2** <u>customer</u>, buyer, client, frequenter, habitué, shopper

patronage noun **1** <u>support</u>, aid, assistance, backing, help, promotion, sponsorship **2** <u>custom</u>, business, clientele, commerce, trade, trading, traffic

patronize verb **1** <u>talk down to</u>, look down on **2** <u>be a customer or client of</u>, do business with, frequent, shop at **3** <u>support</u>, back, fund, help, maintain, promote, sponsor

patronizing adjective <u>condescending</u>, disdainful, gracious, haughty, snobbish, supercilious, superior

➤ **Antonyms**

deferential, humble, obsequious, respectful, servile

patter[1] verb **1** <u>tap</u>, beat, pitter-patter **2** <u>walk lightly</u>, scurry, scuttle, skip, trip ♦ noun **3** <u>tapping</u>, pattering, pitter-patter

patter[2] noun **1** <u>spiel</u> (informal), line, pitch **2** <u>chatter</u>, gabble, jabber, nattering, prattle **3** <u>jargon</u>, argot, cant, lingo (informal), patois, slang, vernacular ♦ verb **4**

chatter, jabber, prate, rattle on, spout (informal)

pattern noun **1** design, arrangement, decoration, device, figure, motif **2** order, method, plan, sequence, system **3** plan, design, diagram, guide, original, stencil, template ♦ verb **4** model, copy, follow, form, imitate, mould, style

paucity noun Formal scarcity, dearth, deficiency, lack, rarity, scantiness, shortage, sparseness

paunch noun belly, pot, potbelly, spare tyre (Brit. slang)

pauper noun down-and-out, bankrupt, beggar, mendicant, poor person

pause verb **1** stop briefly, break, cease, delay, halt, have a breather (informal), interrupt, rest, take a break, wait ♦ noun **2** stop, break, breather (informal), cessation, gap, halt, interlude, intermission, interval, lull, respite, rest, stoppage

► Antonyms
verb ≠stop briefly: advance, continue, proceed, progress ♦ noun ≠stop: advancement, continuance, progression

pave verb cover, concrete, floor, surface, tile

paw verb Informal manhandle, grab, handle roughly, maul, molest

pawn¹ verb hock (informal, chiefly U.S.), deposit, mortgage, pledge

pawn² noun tool, cat's-paw, instrument, plaything, puppet, stooge (slang)

pay verb **1** reimburse, compensate, give, recompense, remit, remunerate, requite, reward, settle **2** give, bestow, extend, grant, hand out, present **3** benefit, be worthwhile, repay **4** be profitable, make a return, make money **5** yield, bring in, produce, return ♦ noun **6** wages, allowance, earnings, fee, income, payment, recompense, reimbursement, remuneration, reward, salary, stipend

payable adjective due, outstanding, owed, owing

pay back verb **1** repay, refund, reimburse, settle up, square **2** get even with (informal), get one's own back, hit back, retaliate

payment noun **1** paying, discharge, remittance, settlement **2** remittance, advance, deposit, instalment, premium **3** wage, fee, hire, remuneration, reward

pay off verb **1** settle, clear, discharge, pay in full, square **2** succeed, be effective, work

pay out verb spend, disburse, expend, fork out or over or up (slang), shell out (informal)

peace noun **1** stillness, calm, calmness, hush, quiet, repose, rest, silence, tranquillity **2** serenity, calm, composure, contentment, repose **3** harmony, accord, agreement, concord **4** truce, armistice, treaty

peaceable adjective peace-loving, conciliatory, friendly, gentle, mild, peaceful, unwarlike

peaceful adjective **1** at peace, amicable, friendly, harmonious, nonviolent **2** calm, placid, quiet, restful, serene, still, tranquil, undisturbed **3** peace-loving, conciliatory, peaceable, unwarlike

► Antonyms
≠at peace: antagonistic, hostile, unfriendly, violent, warring ≠calm: agitated, disturbed, loud, nervous, noisy, restless, upset ≠peace-loving: belligerent, warlike

peacemaker noun mediator, arbitrator, conciliator, pacifier

peak noun **1** point, apex, brow, crest, pinnacle, summit, tip, top **2** high point, acme, climax, crown, culmination, zenith ♦ verb **3** culminate, climax, come to a head

peal noun **1** ring, blast, chime, clang, clap, crash, reverberation, roar, rumble ♦ verb **2** ring, chime, crash, resound, roar, rumble

peasant noun rustic, countryman

peccadillo noun misdeed, error, indiscretion, lapse, misdemeanour, slip

peck verb, noun pick, dig, hit, jab, poke, prick, strike, tap

peculiar adjective **1** odd, abnormal, bizarre, curious, eccentric, extraordinary, freakish, funny, offbeat, outlandish, outré, quaint, queer, singular, strange, uncommon, unconventional, unusual, weird **2** specific, characteristic, distinctive, particular, special, unique

➤ **Antonyms**

≠odd: commonplace, conventional, expected, familiar, ordinary, usual ≠specific: common, general, indistinctive, unspecific

peculiarity noun **1** eccentricity, abnormality, foible, idiosyncrasy, mannerism, oddity, quirk **2** characteristic, attribute, feature, mark, particularity, property, quality, trait

pedagogue noun teacher, instructor, master or mistress, schoolmaster or schoolmistress

pedant noun hairsplitter, nitpicker (informal), quibbler

pedantic adjective hairsplitting, academic, bookish, donnish, formal, fussy, nit-picking (informal), particular, precise, punctilious

pedantry noun hairsplitting, punctiliousness, quibbling

peddle verb sell, flog (slang), hawk, market, push (informal), trade

pedestal noun support, base, foot, mounting, plinth, stand

pedestrian noun **1** walker, foot-traveller ♦ adjective **2** dull, banal, boring, commonplace, humdrum, mediocre, mundane, ordinary, prosaic, run-of-the-mill, uninspired

➤ **Antonyms**

noun ≠walker: driver, motorist ♦ adjective ≠dull: exciting, fascinating, noteworthy, outstanding, remarkable, significant

pedigree noun **1** lineage, ancestry, blood, breed, descent, extraction, family, family tree, genealogy, line, race, stock ♦ adjective **2** purebred, full-blooded, thoroughbred

pedlar noun seller, door-to-door salesman, hawker, huckster, vendor

peek verb **1** glance, eyeball (slang), look, peep ♦ noun **2** glance, glimpse, look, look-see (slang), peep

peel verb **1** skin, flake off, pare, scale, strip off ♦ noun **2** skin, peeling, rind

peep¹ verb **1** peek, eyeball (slang), look, sneak a look, steal a look ♦ noun **2** look, glimpse, look-see (slang), peek

peep² verb, noun tweet, cheep, chirp, squeak

peephole noun spyhole, aperture, chink, crack, hole, opening

peer¹ noun **1** noble, aristocrat, lord, nobleman **2** equal, compeer, fellow, like

peer² verb squint, gaze, inspect, peep, scan, snoop, spy

peerage noun aristocracy, lords and ladies, nobility, peers

peerless adjective unequalled, beyond compare, excellent, incomparable, matchless, outstanding, unmatched, unparalleled, unrivalled

➤ **Antonyms**

commonplace, inferior, mediocre, no great shakes (informal), ordinary, poor, second-rate

peevish adjective irritable, cantankerous, childish, churlish, cross, crotchety (informal), fractious, fretful, grumpy, petulant, querulous, snappy, sulky, sullen, surly

➤ **Antonyms**

cheerful, cheery, easy-going, even-tempered, genial, good-natured, happy, merry

peg verb fasten, attach, fix, join, secure

pejorative adjective derogatory, deprecatory, depreciatory, disparaging, negative, uncomplimentary, unpleasant

pelt¹ verb **1** throw, batter, bombard, cast, hurl, pepper, shower, sling, strike **2** rush, belt (slang), charge, dash, hurry, run fast, shoot, speed, tear **3** pour, bucket down (informal), rain cats and dogs (informal), rain hard, teem

pelt² noun coat, fell, hide, skin

pen¹ verb write, compose, draft, draw up, jot down

pen² noun **1** enclosure, cage, coop, fold, hutch, pound, sty ♦ verb **2** enclose, cage, confine, coop up, fence in, hedge, shut up or in

penal adjective disciplinary, corrective, punitive

penalize verb punish, discipline, handicap, impose a penalty on

penalty noun punishment, fine, forfeit, handicap, price

penance noun atonement, penalty, reparation, sackcloth and ashes

penchant noun leaning, bent, bias, fondness, inclination, leaning, partiality, predilection, proclivity, propensity, taste, tendency

pending adjective undecided, awaiting, imminent, impending, in the balance, undetermined, unsettled

penetrate verb **1** pierce, bore, enter, go through, prick, stab **2** grasp, comprehend, decipher, fathom, figure out (informal), get to the bottom of, suss (out) (slang), work out

penetrating adjective **1** sharp, carrying, harsh, piercing, shrill **2** perceptive, acute, astute, incisive, intelligent, keen, perspicacious, quick, sharp, sharp-witted, shrewd

► **Antonyms**
≠sharp: blunt, dull, mild ≠perceptive: dull, obtuse, stupid, uncomprehending, unperceptive

penetration noun **1** piercing, entrance, entry, incision, puncturing **2** perception, acuteness, astuteness, insight, keenness, sharpness, shrewdness

penitence noun repentance, compunction, contrition, regret, remorse, shame, sorrow

penitent adjective repentant, abject, apologetic, conscience-stricken, contrite, regretful, remorseful, sorry

► **Antonyms**
callous, impenitent, remorseless, unrepentant

pen name noun pseudonym, nom de plume

pennant noun flag, banner, ensign, pennon, streamer

penniless adjective poor, broke (informal), destitute, dirt-poor (informal), down and out, flat broke (informal), impecunious, impoverished, indigent, penurious, poverty-stricken, skint (Brit. slang), stony-broke (Brit. slang)

► **Antonyms**
affluent, loaded (slang), rich, wealthy, well-heeled (informal)

pension noun allowance, annuity, benefit, superannuation

pensioner noun senior citizen, O.A.P., retired person

pensive adjective thoughtful, contemplative, dreamy, meditative, musing, preoccupied, reflective, sad, serious, solemn, wistful

► **Antonyms**
carefree, cheerful, frivolous, gay, happy, joyous, light-hearted

pent-up adjective suppressed, bottled up, curbed, held back, inhibited, repressed, smothered, stifled

penury noun poverty, beggary, destitution, indigence, need, privation, want

people plural noun **1** persons, humanity, mankind, men and women, mortals **2** nation, citizens, community, folk, inhabitants, population, public **3** family, clan, race, tribe ♦ verb **4** inhabit, colonize, occupy, populate, settle

pepper noun **1** seasoning, flavour, spice ♦ verb **2** sprinkle, dot, fleck, spatter, speck **3** pelt, bombard, shower

perceive verb **1** see, behold, discern, discover, espy, make out, note, notice, observe, recognize, spot **2** understand, comprehend, gather, grasp, learn, realize, see, suss (out) (*slang*)

perceptible *adjective* <u>visible</u>, apparent, appreciable, clear, detectable, discernible, evident, noticeable, observable, obvious, recognizable, tangible

► **Antonyms**

concealed, hidden, imperceptible, indiscernible, invisible, unapparent, undetectable, unnoticeable

perception *noun* <u>understanding</u>, awareness, conception, consciousness, feeling, grasp, idea, impression, notion, sensation, sense

perceptive *adjective* <u>observant</u>, acute, alert, astute, aware, percipient, perspicacious, quick, sharp

► **Antonyms**

dull, obtuse, slow-witted, stupid, thick

perch *noun* 1 <u>resting place</u>, branch, pole, post ♦ *verb* 2 <u>sit</u>, alight, balance, land, rest, roost, settle

percussion *noun* <u>impact</u>, blow, bump, clash, collision, crash, knock, smash, thump

peremptory *adjective* 1 <u>imperative</u>, absolute, binding, compelling, decisive, final, obligatory 2 <u>imperious</u>, authoritative, bossy (*informal*), dictatorial, dogmatic, domineering, overbearing

perennial *adjective* <u>lasting</u>, abiding, constant, continual, enduring, incessant, persistent, recurrent

perfect *adjective* 1 <u>complete</u>, absolute, consummate, entire, finished, full, sheer, unmitigated, utter, whole 2 <u>faultless</u>, flawless, immaculate, impeccable, pure, spotless, unblemished 3 <u>excellent</u>, ideal, splendid, sublime, superb, superlative, supreme 4 <u>exact</u>, accurate, correct, faithful, precise, true, unerring ♦ *verb* 5 <u>improve</u>, develop, polish, refine 6 <u>accomplish</u>, achieve, carry out, complete, finish, fulfil, perform

adjective ≠<u>complete</u>: incomplete, partial, unfinished ≠<u>faultless</u>: damaged, defective, deficient, faulty, flawed, impaired, imperfect, impure, ruined, spoiled ≠<u>excellent</u>: bad, inferior, poor, unskilled, worthless ♦ *verb* ≠<u>improve</u>: mar

perfection *noun* 1 <u>completeness</u>, maturity 2 <u>purity</u>, integrity, perfectness, wholeness 3 <u>excellence</u>, exquisiteness, sublimity, superiority 4 <u>exactness</u>, faultlessness, precision

perfectionist *noun* <u>stickler</u>, precisionist, purist

perfectly *adverb* 1 <u>completely</u>, absolutely, altogether, fully, quite, thoroughly, totally, utterly, wholly 2 <u>flawlessly</u>, faultlessly, ideally, impeccably, superbly, supremely, wonderfully

► **Antonyms**

≠<u>completely</u>: inaccurately, incompletely, mistakenly, partially ≠<u>flawlessly</u>: badly, defectively, faultily, imperfectly, poorly

perfidious *adjective* *Literary* <u>treacherous</u>, disloyal, doubledealing, traitorous, two-faced, unfaithful

perforate *verb* <u>pierce</u>, bore, drill, penetrate, punch, puncture

perform *verb* 1 <u>carry out</u>, accomplish, achieve, complete, discharge, do, execute, fulfil, pull off, work 2 <u>present</u>, act, enact, play, produce, put on, represent, stage

performance *noun* 1 <u>carrying out</u>, accomplishment, achievement, act, completion, execution, fulfilment, work 2 <u>presentation</u>, acting, appearance, exhibition, gig (*informal*), play, portrayal, production, show

performer *noun* <u>artiste</u>, actor *or* actress, player, Thespian, trouper

perfume *noun* <u>fragrance</u>, aroma, bouquet, odour, scent, smell

perfunctory *adjective* <u>offhand</u>, cursory, heedless, indifferent, mechanical, routine, sketchy, superficial

➤ **Antonyms**

assiduous, attentive, careful, diligent, keen, thorough

perhaps *adverb* maybe, conceivably, feasibly, it may be, perchance (*archaic*), possibly

peril *noun* danger, hazard, jeopardy, menace, risk, uncertainty

➤ **Antonyms**

invulnerability, safety, security

perilous *adjective* dangerous, hazardous, precarious, risky, threatening, unsafe

perimeter *noun* boundary, ambit, border, bounds, circumference, confines, edge, limit, margin, periphery

➤ **Antonyms**

central part, centre, core, heart, hub, middle, nucleus

period *noun* time, interval, season, space, span, spell, stretch, term, while

periodic *adjective* recurrent, cyclical, intermittent, occasional, regular, repeated, sporadic

periodical *noun* publication, journal, magazine, monthly, paper, quarterly, weekly, zine (*informal*)

peripheral *adjective* **1** incidental, inessential, irrelevant, marginal, minor, secondary, unimportant **2** outermost, exterior, external, outer, outside

perish *verb* **1** die, be killed, expire, lose one's life, pass away **2** be destroyed, collapse, decline, disappear, fall, vanish **3** rot, decay, decompose, disintegrate, moulder, waste

perishable *adjective* short-lived, decaying, decomposable

➤ **Antonyms**

durable, lasting, long-life, long-lived, non-perishable

perjure *verb* **perjure oneself** *Criminal law* commit perjury, bear false witness, forswear, give false testimony, lie under oath, swear falsely

perjury *noun* lying under oath, bearing false witness, false state-

ment, forswearing, giving false testimony

perk *noun Brit. informal* bonus, benefit, extra, fringe benefit, perquisite, plus

permanence *noun* continuity, constancy, continuance, durability, endurance, finality, indestructibility, perpetuity, stability

permanent *adjective* lasting, abiding, constant, enduring, eternal, everlasting, immutable, perpetual, persistent, stable, steadfast, unchanging

➤ **Antonyms**

brief, changing, ephemeral, fleeting, impermanent, inconstant, momentary, passing, short-lived, temporary, transitory

permeate *verb* pervade, charge, fill, imbue, impregnate, infiltrate, penetrate, saturate, spread through

permissible *adjective* permitted, acceptable, allowable, all right, authorized, lawful, legal, legitimate, O.K. or okay (*informal*)

➤ **Antonyms**

banned, forbidden, illegal, illicit, prohibited, unauthorized, unlawful

permission *noun* authorization, allowance, approval, assent, consent, dispensation, go-ahead (*informal*), green light, leave, liberty, licence, sanction

permissive *adjective* tolerant, easy-going, forbearing, free, indulgent, lax, lenient, liberal

➤ **Antonyms**

authoritarian, rigid, strict

permit *verb* **1** allow, authorize, consent, enable, entitle, give leave or permission, give the green light to, grant, let, license, sanction ♦ *noun* **2** licence, authorization, pass, passport, permission, warrant

permutation *noun* transformation, alteration, change, transposition

pernicious *adjective Formal* wicked, bad, damaging, dangerous, deadly, destructive, detrimental, evil, fatal, harmful, hurtful, malign, poisonous

pernickety *adjective Informal* fussy, exacting, fastidious, finicky, overprecise, particular, picky *(informal)*

➤ **Antonyms**

careless, heedless, inattentive, lax, slack, slapdash, slipshod, sloppy, uncritical

perpendicular *adjective* upright, at right angles to, on end, plumb, straight, vertical

perpetrate *verb* commit, carry out, do, enact, execute, perform, wreak

perpetual *adjective* 1 everlasting, endless, eternal, infinite, lasting, never-ending, perennial, permanent, unchanging, unending 2 continual, constant, continuous, endless, incessant, interminable, never-ending, persistent, recurrent, repeated

➤ **Antonyms**

brief, ephemeral, fleeting, impermanent, momentary, passing, short-lived, temporary, transitory

perpetuate *verb* maintain, immortalize, keep going, preserve

➤ **Antonyms**

abolish, destroy, end, put an end to, stamp out, suppress

perplex *verb* puzzle, baffle, bewilder, confound, confuse, mystify, stump

perplexing *adjective* puzzling, baffling, bewildering, complex, complicated, confusing, difficult, enigmatic, hard, inexplicable, mystifying

perplexity *noun* 1 puzzlement, bafflement, bewilderment, confusion, incomprehension, mystification 2 puzzle, difficulty, fix *(informal)*, mystery, paradox

perquisite *noun Formal* bonus, benefit, dividend, extra, perk *(Brit. informal)*, plus

persecute *verb* 1 victimize, afflict, ill-treat, maltreat, oppress, pick on, torment, torture 2 harass, annoy, badger, bother, hassle *(informal)*, pester, tease

➤ **Antonyms**

coddle, cosset, humour, indulge, leave alone, let alone, mollycoddle, pamper, pet, spoil

perseverance *noun* persistence, determination, diligence, doggedness, endurance, pertinacity, resolution, tenacity

persevere *verb* keep going, carry on, continue, go on, hang on, persist, remain, stick at or to

➤ **Antonyms**

dither *(chiefly Brit.)*, falter, give in, give up, hesitate, quit, throw in the towel

persist *verb* 1 continue, carry on, keep up, last, linger, remain 2 persevere, continue, insist, stand firm

persistence *noun* determination, doggedness, endurance, grit, perseverance, pertinacity, resolution, tenacity, tirelessness

persistent *adjective* 1 continuous, continual, endless, incessant, never-ending, perpetual, repeated 2 determined, dogged, obdurate, obstinate, persevering, pertinacious, steadfast, steady, stubborn, tenacious, tireless, unflagging

➤ **Antonyms**

≠continuous: inconstant, intermittent, irregular, occasional, off-and-on, periodic ≠determined: changeable, flexible, irresolute, tractable, yielding

person *noun* 1 individual, being, body, human, soul 2 in person personally, bodily, in the flesh, oneself

personable *adjective* pleasant, agreeable, amiable, attractive, charming, good-looking, handsome, likable or likeable, nice

➤ **Antonyms**

disagreeable, sullen, surly, ugly, unattractive, unpleasant, unsightly

personage *noun* personality, big shot *(informal)*, celebrity, dignitary, luminary, megastar *(informal)*, notable, public figure, somebody, V.I.P.

personal *adjective* 1 private, exclusive, individual, intimate, own, particular, peculiar, true **2** offensive, derogatory, disparaging, insulting, nasty

personality noun **1** nature, character, disposition, identity, individuality, make-up, temperament **2** character, attraction, charisma, charm, magnetism **3** celebrity, famous name, household name, megastar (informal), notable, personage, star

personally adverb **1** by oneself, alone, independently, on one's own, solely **2** in one's opinion, for one's part, from one's own viewpoint, in one's books, in one's own view **3** individually, individualistically, privately, specially, subjectively

personification noun embodiment, epitome, image, incarnation, portrayal, representation

personify verb embody, epitomize, exemplify, represent, symbolize, typify

personnel noun employees, helpers, human resources, people, staff, workers, workforce

perspective noun **1** outlook, angle, attitude, context, frame of reference **2** objectivity, proportion, relation, relative importance, relativity

perspicacious adjective Formal perceptive, acute, alert, astute, discerning, keen, percipient, sharp, shrewd

perspiration noun sweat, moisture, wetness

perspire verb sweat, exude, glow, pour with sweat, secrete, swelter

persuade verb **1** talk into, bring round (informal), coax, entice, impel, incite, induce, influence, sway, urge, win over **2** convince, cause to believe, satisfy

► **Antonyms**

≠talk into: deter, discourage, dissuade, forbid, prohibit

persuasion noun **1** urging, cajolery, enticement, inducement, wheedling **2** persuasiveness, cogency, force, potency, power, pull (informal) **3** creed, belief, conviction, credo, faith, opinion, tenet, views **4** faction, camp, denomination, party, school, school of thought, side

persuasive adjective convincing, cogent, compelling, credible, effective, eloquent, forceful, influential, plausible, sound, telling, valid, weighty

► **Antonyms**

feeble, flimsy, implausible, incredible, ineffective, invalid, unconvincing, weak

pert adjective impudent, bold, cheeky, forward, impertinent, insolent, sassy (U.S. informal), saucy

pertain verb relate, apply, befit, belong, be relevant, concern, refer, regard

pertinent adjective relevant, applicable, apposite, appropriate, apt, fit, fitting, germane, material, proper, to the point

► **Antonyms**

immaterial, inappropriate, irrelevant, unfitting, unrelated

pertness noun impudence, audacity, cheek (informal), cheekiness, effrontery, forwardness, front, impertinence, insolence, sauciness

perturb verb disturb, agitate, bother, disconcert, faze, fluster, ruffle, trouble, unsettle, vex, worry

perturbed adjective disturbed, agitated, antsy (informal), anxious, disconcerted, flustered, shaken, troubled, uncomfortable, uneasy, worried

► **Antonyms**

at ease, comfortable, composed, cool, impassive, relaxed, unperturbed, unruffled

peruse verb read, browse, check, examine, eyeball (slang), inspect, scan, scrutinize, study

pervade verb spread through, charge, fill, imbue, infuse, penetrate, permeate, suffuse

pervasive adjective widespread, common, extensive, general, omnipresent, prevalent, rife, ubiquitous, universal

perverse *adjective* **1** abnormal, deviant, improper, unhealthy **2** stubborn, contrary, cussed (*informal*), disobedient, dogged, headstrong, intractable, intransigent, obdurate, obstinate, pig-headed, rebellious, refractory, stiff-necked, troublesome, wayward, wilful **3** ill-natured, churlish, cross, fractious, ill-tempered, peevish, stroppy (*Brit. slang*), surly

➤ **Antonyms**
≠stubborn: accommodating, agreeable, complaisant, cooperative, flexible, obedient, obliging ≠ill-natured: agreeable, amiable, good-natured

perversion *noun* **1** deviation, aberration, abnormality, debauchery, depravity, immorality, kink (*Brit. informal*), kinkiness (*slang*), unnaturalness, vice **2** distortion, corruption, falsification, misinterpretation, misrepresentation, twisting

perversity *noun* contrariness, contradictoriness, intransigence, obduracy, refractoriness, waywardness, wrong-headedness

pervert *verb* **1** distort, abuse, falsify, garble, misrepresent, misuse, twist, warp **2** corrupt, debase, debauch, degrade, deprave, lead astray ♦ *noun* **3** deviant, degenerate, sicko (*informal*), weirdo or weirdie (*informal*)

perverted *adjective* unnatural, abnormal, corrupt, debased, debauched, depraved, deviant, kinky (*slang*), pervy (*slang*), sick, twisted, unhealthy, warped

pessimism *noun* gloominess, dejection, depression, despair, despondency, distrust, gloom, hopelessness, melancholy

pessimist *noun* wet blanket (*informal*), cynic, defeatist, killjoy, prophet of doom, worrier

pessimistic *adjective* gloomy, bleak, cynical, dark, dejected, depressed, despairing, despondent, glum, hopeless, morose

➤ **Antonyms**
bright, cheerful, cheery, hopeful, in good heart, optimistic, sanguine

pest *noun* **1** nuisance, annoyance, bane, bother, drag (*informal*), irritation, pain (*informal*), thorn in one's flesh, trial, vexation **2** infection, blight, bug, epidemic, pestilence, plague, scourge

pester *verb* annoy, badger, bedevil, be on one's back (*slang*), bother, bug (*informal*), harass, harry, hassle (*informal*), nag, plague, torment

pestilence *noun* plague, epidemic, visitation

pestilent *adjective* **1** annoying, bothersome, irksome, irritating, tiresome, vexing **2** harmful, detrimental, evil, injurious, pernicious **3** contaminated, catching, contagious, diseased, disease-ridden, infected, infectious

pestilential *adjective* deadly, dangerous, destructive, detrimental, harmful, hazardous, injurious, pernicious

pet *noun* **1** favourite, darling, idol, jewel, treasure ♦ *adjective* **2** favourite, cherished, dearest, dear to one's heart, fave (*informal*), favoured ♦ *verb* **3** pamper, baby, coddle, cosset, mollycoddle, spoil **4** fondle, caress, pat, stroke **5** *Informal* cuddle, canoodle (*slang*), kiss, neck (*informal*), smooch (*informal*), snog (*Brit. slang*)

peter out *verb* die out, dwindle, ebb, fade, fail, run out, stop, taper off, wane

petite *adjective* small, dainty, delicate, elfin, little, slight

petition *noun* **1** appeal, entreaty, plea, prayer, request, solicitation, suit, supplication ♦ *verb* **2** appeal, adjure, ask, beg, beseech, entreat, plead, pray, solicit, supplicate

petrify *verb* **1** terrify, horrify, immobilize, paralyse, stun, stupefy, transfix **2** fossilize, calcify, harden, turn to stone

petty *adjective* **1** trivial, contemptible, inconsiderable, insignificant, little, measly (*informal*), negligible, paltry, slight, small, trifling, unimportant **2** small-minded, mean, mean-minded, shabby, spiteful, ungenerous

➤ **Antonyms**

≠ trivial: considerable, essential, important, major, momentous, significant ≠ small-minded: broad-minded, generous, liberal, magnanimous, open-minded, tolerant

petulance *noun* sulkiness, bad temper, ill humour, irritability, peevishness, pique, sullenness

petulant *adjective* sulky, bad-tempered, huffy, ill-humoured, moody, peevish, sullen

➤ **Antonyms**

affable, cheerful, easy-going, even-tempered, good-humoured, good-natured, happy

phantom *noun* **1** spectre, apparition, ghost, phantasm, shade (*literary*), spirit, spook (*informal*), wraith **2** illusion, figment of the imagination, hallucination, vision

phase *noun* stage, chapter, development, juncture, period, point, position, step, time

phase out *verb* wind down, close, ease off, eliminate, pull out, remove, run down, terminate, wind up, withdraw

➤ **Antonyms**

activate, begin, create, establish, form, initiate, open, set up, start

phenomenal *adjective* extraordinary, exceptional, fantastic, marvellous, miraculous, outstanding, prodigious, remarkable, unusual

➤ **Antonyms**

average, common, mediocre, ordinary, poor, run-of-the-mill, second-rate, unexceptional, unremarkable, usual

phenomenon *noun* **1** occurrence, circumstance, episode, event, fact, happening, incident **2** wonder, exception, marvel,

miracle, prodigy, rarity, sensation

philanderer *noun* womanizer (*informal*), Casanova, Don Juan, flirt, ladies' man, lady-killer (*informal*), Lothario, playboy, stud (*slang*), wolf (*informal*)

philanthropic *adjective* humanitarian, beneficent, benevolent, charitable, generous, humane, kind, kind-hearted, munificent, public-spirited

➤ **Antonyms**

egoistic, mean, miserly, niggardly, penurious, selfish, self-seeking, stingy

philanthropist *noun* humanitarian, benefactor, contributor, donor, giver, patron

philanthropy *noun* humanitarianism, almsgiving, beneficence, benevolence, brotherly love, charitableness, charity, generosity, kind-heartedness

philistine *noun* **1** boor, barbarian, ignoramus, lout, lowbrow, vulgarian, yahoo ◆ *adjective* **2** uncultured, boorish, ignorant, lowbrow, tasteless, uncultivated, uneducated, unrefined

philosopher *noun* thinker, logician, metaphysician, sage, theorist, wise man

philosophical, philosophic *adjective* **1** rational, abstract, logical, sagacious, theoretical, thoughtful, wise **2** stoical, calm, collected, composed, cool, serene, tranquil, unruffled

➤ **Antonyms**

≠ rational: factual, illogical, irrational, practical, pragmatic, scientific ≠ stoical: emotional, hot-headed, impulsive

philosophy *noun* **1** thought, knowledge, logic, metaphysics, rationalism, reasoning, thinking, wisdom **2** outlook, beliefs, convictions, doctrine, ideology, principles, tenets, thinking, values, viewpoint, world view **3** stoicism, calmness, composure, equanimity, self-possession, serenity

phlegmatic *adjective* unemotional, apathetic, impassive, indifferent, placid, stoical, stolid, undemonstrative, unfeeling

➤ **Antonyms**

animated, emotional, energetic, excited, lively, passionate

phobia noun <u>terror</u>, aversion, detestation, dread, fear, hatred, horror, loathing, repulsion, revulsion, thing (*informal*)

➤ **Antonyms**

bent, fancy, fondness, inclination, liking, love, partiality, passion, penchant, soft spot

phone noun 1 <u>telephone</u>, blower (*informal*) 2 <u>call</u>, ring (*informal, chiefly Brit.*), tinkle (*Brit. informal*) ♦ verb 3 <u>call</u>, get on the blower (*informal*), give someone a call, give someone a ring (*informal, chiefly Brit.*), give someone a tinkle (*Brit. informal*), make a call, ring (up) (*informal, chiefly Brit.*), telephone

phoney *Informal* ♦ *adjective* 1 <u>fake</u>, bogus, counterfeit, ersatz, false, imitation, pseudo (*informal*), sham ♦ noun 2 <u>fake</u>, counterfeit, forgery, fraud, impostor, pseud (*informal*), sham

➤ **Antonyms**

adjective ≠<u>fake</u>: authentic, bona fide, genuine, original, real, sincere

photograph noun 1 <u>picture</u>, photo (*informal*), print, shot, snap (*informal*), snapshot, transparency ♦ verb 2 <u>take a picture of</u>, film, record, shoot, snap (*informal*), take (someone's) picture

photographic *adjective* 1 <u>lifelike</u>, graphic, natural, pictorial, realistic, visual, vivid 2 *Of a person's memory* <u>accurate</u>, exact, faithful, precise, retentive

phrase noun 1 <u>expression</u>, group of words, idiom, remark, saying ♦ verb 2 <u>express</u>, put, put into words, say, voice, word

phraseology noun <u>wording</u>, choice of words, expression, idiom, language, parlance, phrase, phrasing, speech, style, syntax

physical *adjective* 1 <u>bodily</u>, cor-

poral, corporeal, earthly, fleshly, incarnate, mortal 2 <u>material</u>, natural, palpable, real, solid, substantial, tangible

physician noun <u>doctor</u>, doc (*informal*), doctor of medicine, general practitioner, G.P., M.D., medic (*informal*), medical practitioner

physique noun <u>build</u>, body, constitution, figure, form, frame, shape, structure

pick verb 1 <u>select</u>, choose, decide upon, elect, fix upon, hand-pick, opt for, settle upon, single out 2 <u>gather</u>, collect, harvest, pluck, pull 3 <u>nibble</u>, have no appetite, peck at, play or toy with, push the food round the plate 4 <u>provoke</u>, incite, instigate, start 5 <u>open</u>, break into, break open, crack, force ♦ noun 6 <u>choice</u>, decision, option, preference, selection 7 <u>the best</u>, crème de la crème, elect, elite, the cream

➤ **Antonyms**

verb ≠<u>select</u>: cast aside, decline, discard, dismiss, reject, spurn, turn down

picket noun 1 <u>protester</u>, demonstrator, picketer 2 <u>lookout</u>, guard, patrol, sentinel, sentry, watch 3 <u>stake</u>, pale, paling, post, stanchion, upright ♦ verb 4 <u>blockade</u>, boycott, demonstrate

pickle noun 1 *Informal* <u>predicament</u>, bind (*informal*), difficulty, dilemma, fix (*informal*), hot water (*informal*), jam (*informal*), quandary, scrape (*informal*), tight spot ♦ verb 2 <u>preserve</u>, marinade, steep

pick-me-up noun *Informal* <u>tonic</u>, bracer (*informal*), refreshment, restorative, shot in the arm (*informal*), stimulant

pick on verb <u>torment</u>, badger, bait, bully, goad, hector, tease

pick out verb <u>identify</u>, discriminate, distinguish, make out, perceive, recognize, tell apart

pick up verb 1 <u>lift</u>, gather, grasp, raise, take up, uplift 2 <u>obtain</u>, buy, come across, find, purchase 3 <u>recover</u>, be on the mend, get better, improve, mend, rally, take a turn for the better, turn the corner **4** learn, acquire, get the hang of (*informal*), master **5** collect, call for, get

pick-up *noun* improvement, change for the better, rally, recovery, revival, rise, strengthening, upswing, upturn

picnic *noun* excursion, outdoor meal, outing

pictorial *adjective* graphic, illustrated, picturesque, representational, scenic

picture *noun* **1** representation, drawing, engraving, illustration, image, likeness, painting, photograph, portrait, print, sketch **2** description, account, depiction, image, impression, report **3** double, carbon copy, copy, dead ringer (*slang*), duplicate, image, likeness, lookalike, replica, spitting image (*informal*), twin **4** personification, embodiment, epitome, essence **5** film, flick (*slang*), motion picture, movie (*U.S. informal*) ♦ *verb* **6** imagine, conceive of, envision, see, visualize **7** represent, depict, draw, illustrate, paint, photograph, show, sketch

picturesque *adjective* **1** interesting, attractive, beautiful, charming, pretty, quaint, scenic, striking **2** vivid, colourful, graphic

➤ **Antonyms**
≠interesting: commonplace, everyday, unattractive, uninteresting ≠vivid: drab, dull

piebald *adjective* pied, black and white, brindled, dappled, flecked, mottled, speckled, spotted

piece *noun* **1** bit, chunk, fragment, morsel, part, portion, quantity, segment, slice **2** work, article, composition, creation, item, study, work of art

piecemeal *adverb* bit by bit, by degrees, gradually, little by little

pier *noun* **1** jetty, landing place, promenade, quay, wharf **2** pillar, buttress, column, pile, post, support, upright

pierce *verb* penetrate, bore, drill, enter, perforate, prick, puncture, spike, stab, stick into

piercing *adjective* **1** *Usually of sound* penetrating, ear-splitting, high-pitched, loud, sharp, shrill **2** perceptive, alert, keen, penetrating, perspicacious, quick-witted, sharp, shrewd **3** *Usually of weather* cold, arctic, biting, bitter, freezing, nippy, wintry **4** sharp, acute, agonizing, excruciating, intense, painful, severe, stabbing

➤ **Antonyms**
≠penetrating: inaudible, low, low-pitched, quiet, soundless ≠perceptive: obtuse, slow, slow-witted, thick, unperceptive

piety *noun* holiness, faith, godliness, piousness, religion, reverence

pig *noun* **1** hog, boar, porker, sow, swine **2** *Informal* slob (*slang*), boor, brute, glutton, swine

pigeonhole *noun* **1** compartment, cubbyhole, locker, niche, place, section ♦ *verb* **2** classify, categorize, characterize, compartmentalize, ghettoize, label, slot (*informal*) **3** put off, defer, postpone, shelve

pig-headed *adjective* stubborn, contrary, inflexible, mulish, obstinate, self-willed, stiff-necked, unyielding

➤ **Antonyms**
complaisant, cooperative, flexible, obliging, open-minded, tractable

pigment *noun* colour, colouring, dye, paint, stain, tincture, tint

pile¹ *noun* **1** heap, accumulation, collection, hoard, mass, mound, mountain, stack **2** *often plural Informal* a lot, great deal, ocean, quantity, stacks **3** building, edifice, erection, structure ♦ *verb* **4** collect, accumulate, amass, assemble, gather, heap, hoard, stack **5** crowd, crush, flock, flood, jam, pack, rush, stream

pile² *noun* foundation, beam, column, pillar, post, support, up-right

pile³ noun <u>nap</u>, down, fibre, fur, hair, plush

pile-up noun Informal <u>collision</u>, accident, crash, multiple collision, smash, smash-up (informal)

pilfer verb <u>steal</u>, appropriate, embezzle, filch, knock off (slang), lift (informal), nick (slang, chiefly Brit.), pinch (informal), purloin, snaffle (Brit. informal), swipe (slang), take

pilgrim noun <u>traveller</u>, wanderer, wayfarer

pilgrimage noun <u>journey</u>, excursion, expedition, mission, tour, trip

pill noun 1 <u>tablet</u>, capsule, pellet 2 **the pill** <u>oral contraceptive</u>

pillage verb 1 <u>plunder</u>, despoil, loot, maraud, raid, ransack, ravage, sack ♦ noun 2 <u>plunder</u>, marauding, robbery, sack, spoliation

pillar noun 1 <u>support</u>, column, pier, post, prop, shaft, stanchion, upright 2 <u>supporter</u>, leader, leading light (informal), mainstay, upholder

pillory verb <u>ridicule</u>, brand, denounce, stigmatize

pilot noun 1 <u>airman</u>, aviator, flyer 2 <u>helmsman</u>, navigator, steersman ♦ adjective 3 <u>trial</u>, experimental, model, test ♦ verb 4 <u>fly</u>, conduct, direct, drive, guide, handle, navigate, operate, steer

pimple noun <u>spot</u>, boil, plook (Scot.), pustule, zit (slang)

pin verb 1 <u>fasten</u>, affix, attach, fix, join, secure 2 <u>hold fast</u>, fix, hold down, immobilize, pinion

pinch verb 1 <u>squeeze</u>, compress, grasp, nip, press 2 <u>hurt</u>, cramp, crush, pain 3 Informal <u>steal</u>, filch, knock off (slang), lift (informal), nick (slang, chiefly Brit.), pilfer, purloin, snaffle (Brit. informal), swipe (slang) ♦ noun 4 <u>squeeze</u>, nip 5 <u>dash</u>, bit, jot, mite, soupçon, speck 6 <u>hardship</u>, crisis, difficulty, emergency, necessity, plight, predicament, strait

pinched adjective <u>thin</u>, drawn,

gaunt, haggard, peaky, worn

➤ **Antonyms**

blooming, chubby, fat, hale and hearty, healthy, plump, well-fed

pin down verb 1 <u>force</u>, compel, constrain, make, press, pressurize 2 <u>determine</u>, identify, locate, name, pinpoint, specify

pine verb 1 often with **for** <u>long</u>, ache, crave, desire, eat one's heart out over, hanker, hunger for, thirst for, wish for, yearn for 2 <u>waste</u>, decline, fade, languish, sicken

pinion verb <u>immobilize</u>, bind, chain, fasten, fetter, manacle, shackle, tie

pink adjective <u>rosy</u>, flushed, reddish, rose, roseate, salmon

pinnacle noun <u>peak</u>, apex, crest, crown, height, summit, top, vertex, zenith

pinpoint verb <u>identify</u>, define, distinguish, locate

pioneer noun 1 <u>settler</u>, colonist, explorer 2 <u>founder</u>, developer, innovator, leader, trailblazer ♦ verb 3 <u>develop</u>, create, discover, establish, initiate, instigate, institute, invent, originate, show the way, start

pious adjective <u>religious</u>, devout, God-fearing, godly, holy, reverent, righteous, saintly

➤ **Antonyms**

impious, irreligious, irreverent, ungodly, unholy

pipe noun 1 <u>tube</u>, conduit, duct, hose, line, main, passage, pipeline ♦ verb 2 <u>whistle</u>, cheep, peep, play, sing, sound, warble 3 <u>convey</u>, channel, conduct

pipe down verb Informal <u>be quiet</u>, hold one's tongue, hush, quieten down, shush, shut one's mouth, shut up (informal)

pipeline noun <u>tube</u>, conduit, duct, passage, pipe

piquant adjective 1 <u>spicy</u>, biting, pungent, savoury, sharp, tangy, tart, zesty 2 <u>interesting</u>, lively, provocative, scintillating, sparkling, stimulating

pique

> **Antonyms**

≠spicy: bland, insipid, mild ≠interesting: banal, bland, boring, dull, insipid, tame, uninteresting, vapid

pique noun **1** resentment, annoyance, displeasure, huff, hurt feelings, irritation, offence, umbrage, wounded pride ♦ verb **2** displease, affront, annoy, get (informal), irk, irritate, nettle, offend, rile, sting **3** arouse, excite, rouse, spur, stimulate, stir, whet

piracy noun robbery, buccaneering, freebooting, stealing, theft

pirate noun **1** buccaneer, corsair, freebooter, marauder, raider **2** plagiarist, cribber (informal), infringer, plagiarizer ♦ verb **3** copy, appropriate, crib (informal), plagiarize, poach, reproduce, steal

pit noun **1** hole, abyss, cavity, chasm, crater, dent, depression, hollow ♦ verb **2** scar, dent, indent, mark, pockmark

pitch verb **1** throw, cast, chuck (informal), fling, heave, hurl, lob (informal), sling, toss **2** set up, erect, put up, raise, settle **3** fall, dive, drop, topple, tumble **4** toss, lurch, plunge, roll ♦ noun **5** sports field, field of play, ground, park (U.S. & Canad.) **6** level, degree, height, highest point, point, summit **7** slope, angle, dip, gradient, incline, tilt **8** tone, modulation, sound, timbre **9** sales talk, patter, spiel (informal)

pitch-black adjective jet-black, dark, inky, pitch-dark, unlit

pitch in verb help, chip in (informal), contribute, cooperate, do one's bit, join in, lend a hand, participate

pitch into verb Informal attack, assail, assault, get stuck into (informal), tear into (informal)

piteous adjective pathetic, affecting, distressing, gut-wrenching, harrowing, heartbreaking, heart-rending, moving, pitiable, pitiful, plaintive, poignant, sad

pitfall noun danger, catch, difficulty, drawback, hazard, peril, snag, trap

pith noun essence, core, crux, gist, heart, kernel, nub, point, quintessence, salient point

pithy adjective succinct, brief, cogent, concise, epigrammatic, laconic, pointed, short, terse, to the point, trenchant

> **Antonyms**

garrulous, long, long-winded, loquacious, verbose, wordy

pitiful adjective **1** pathetic, distressing, grievous, gut-wrenching, harrowing, heartbreaking, heart-rending, piteous, pitiable, sad, wretched **2** contemptible, abject, base, low, mean, miserable, paltry, shabby, sorry

> **Antonyms**

≠pathetic: amusing, cheerful, cheering, comical, funny, happy, laughable, merry ≠contemptible: adequate, admirable, laudable, praiseworthy

pitiless adjective merciless, callous, cold-blooded, coldhearted, cruel, hardhearted, heartless, implacable, relentless, ruthless, unmerciful

> **Antonyms**

caring, compassionate, kind, merciful, soft-hearted

pittance noun peanuts (slang), chicken feed (slang), drop, mite, slave wages, trifle

pity noun **1** compassion, charity, clemency, fellow feeling, forbearance, kindness, mercy, sympathy **2** shame, bummer (slang), crying shame, misfortune, sin ♦ verb **3** feel sorry for, bleed for, feel for, grieve for, have compassion for, sympathize with, weep for

> **Antonyms**

noun ≠compassion: brutality, cruelty, hard-heartedness, indifference, inhumanity, mercilessness, pitilessness, ruthlessness, severity

pivot noun **1** axis, axle, fulcrum, spindle, swivel **2** hub, centre, heart, hinge, kingpin ♦ verb **3**

turn, revolve, rotate, spin, swivel, twirl **4** <u>rely</u>, be contingent, depend, hang, hinge

pivotal *adjective* <u>crucial</u>, central, critical, decisive, vital

pixie *noun* <u>elf</u>, brownie, fairy, sprite

placard *noun* <u>notice</u>, advertisement, bill, poster

placate *verb* <u>calm</u>, appease, assuage, conciliate, humour, mollify, pacify, propitiate, soothe

place *noun* **1** <u>spot</u>, area, location, point, position, site, venue, whereabouts **2** <u>region</u>, district, locale, locality, neighbourhood, quarter, vicinity **3** <u>position</u>, grade, rank, station, status **4** <u>space</u>, accommodation, room **5** <u>home</u>, abode, domicile, dwelling, house, pad (*slang*), property, residence **6** <u>duty</u>, affair, charge, concern, function, prerogative, responsibility, right, role **7** <u>job</u>, appointment, employment, position, post **8** take place happen, come about, go on, occur, transpire (*informal*) ♦ *verb* **9** <u>put</u>, deposit, install, lay, locate, position, rest, set, situate, stand, station, stick (*informal*) **10** <u>classify</u>, arrange, class, grade, group, order, rank, sort **11** <u>identify</u>, know, put one's finger on, recognize, remember **12** <u>assign</u>, allocate, appoint, charge, entrust, give

placid *adjective* <u>calm</u>, collected, composed, equable, even-tempered, imperturbable, serene, tranquil, unexcitable, unruffled, untroubled

➤ **Antonyms**

agitated, disturbed, emotional, excitable, passionate, temperamental, tempestuous

plagiarism *noun* <u>copying</u>, borrowing, cribbing (*informal*), infringement, piracy, theft

plagiarize *verb* <u>copy</u>, borrow, crib (*informal*), lift (*informal*), pirate, steal

plague *noun* **1** <u>disease</u>, epidemic, infection, pestilence **2** <u>affliction</u>,

bane, blight, curse, evil, scourge, torment ♦ *verb* **3** <u>pester</u>, annoy, badger, bother, harass, harry, hassle (*informal*), tease, torment, torture, trouble, vex

plain *adjective* **1** <u>clear</u>, comprehensible, distinct, evident, manifest, obvious, overt, patent, unambiguous, understandable, unmistakable, visible **2** <u>straightforward</u>, blunt, candid, direct, downright, forthright, frank, honest, open, outspoken, upfront (*informal*) **3** <u>unadorned</u>, austere, bare, basic, severe, simple, Spartan, stark, unembellished, unfussy, unornamented **4** <u>ugly</u>, ill-favoured, no oil painting (*informal*), not beautiful, unattractive, unlovely, unprepossessing **5** <u>ordinary</u>, common, commonplace, everyday, simple, unaffected, unpretentious ♦ *noun* **6** <u>flatland</u>, grassland, plateau, prairie, steppe, veld

➤ **Antonyms**

adjective ≠clear: ambiguous, complex, difficult, incomprehensible, indistinct, obscure, vague, veiled ≠straightforward: circuitous, indirect, meandering, rambling, roundabout ≠unadorned: adorned, decorated, fancy, ornate ≠ugly: attractive, beautiful, comely, good-looking, gorgeous, handsome ≠ordinary: affected, ostentatious, pretentious, sophisticated, worldly

plain-spoken *adjective* <u>blunt</u>, candid, direct, downright, forthright, frank, outspoken

➤ **Antonyms**

diplomatic, discreet, evasive, guarded, indirect, reticent, subtle, tactful

plaintive *adjective* <u>sorrowful</u>, heart-rending, mournful, pathetic, piteous, pitiful, sad

plan *noun* **1** <u>scheme</u>, design, method, plot, programme, proposal, strategy, suggestion, system **2** <u>diagram</u>, blueprint, chart, drawing, layout, map, representation, sketch ♦ *verb* **3** <u>devise</u>, arrange, contrive, design, draft, formulate, organize, outline, plot, scheme, think out **4** intend, aim, mean, propose, purpose

plane noun **1** aeroplane, aircraft, jet **2** flat surface, level surface **3** level, condition, degree, position ♦ adjective **4** level, even, flat, horizontal, regular, smooth ♦ verb **5** skim, glide, sail, skate

plant noun **1** vegetable, bush, flower, herb, shrub, weed **2** factory, foundry, mill, shop, works, yard **3** machinery, apparatus, equipment, gear ♦ verb **4** sow, put in the ground, scatter, seed, transplant **5** place, establish, fix, found, insert, put, set

plaster noun **1** mortar, gypsum, plaster of Paris, stucco **2** bandage, adhesive plaster, dressing, Elastoplast (*Trademark*), sticking plaster ♦ verb **3** cover, coat, daub, overlay, smear, spread

plastic adjective **1** manageable, docile, malleable, pliable, receptive, responsive, tractable **2** pliant, ductile, flexible, mouldable, pliable, soft, supple

➤ **Antonyms**

≠manageable: intractable, rebellious, recalcitrant, refractory, unmanageable, unreceptive ≠pliant: brittle, hard, inflexible, rigid, stiff, unbending, unyielding

plate noun **1** platter, dish, trencher (*archaic*) **2** helping, course, dish, portion, serving **3** layer, panel, sheet, slab **4** illustration, lithograph, print ♦ verb **5** coat, cover, gild, laminate, overlay

plateau noun **1** upland, highland, table, tableland **2** levelling off, level, stability, stage

platform noun **1** stage, dais, podium, rostrum, stand **2** policy, manifesto, objective(s), party line, principle, programme

platitude noun cliché, banality, commonplace, truism

platoon noun squad, company, group, outfit (*informal*), patrol, squadron, team

platter noun plate, dish, salver, tray, trencher (*archaic*)

plaudits plural noun approval, acclaim, acclamation, applause, approbation, praise

plausible adjective **1** believable, conceivable, credible, likely, persuasive, possible, probable, reasonable, tenable **2** glib, smooth, smooth-talking, smooth-tongued, specious

➤ **Antonyms**

≠believable: genuine, illogical, implausible, impossible, improbable, inconceivable, incredible, real, unbelievable, unlikely

play verb **1** amuse oneself, entertain oneself, fool, have fun, revel, romp, sport, trifle **2** compete, challenge, contend against, participate, take on, take part **3** act, act the part of, perform, portray, represent ♦ noun **4** drama, comedy, dramatic piece, farce, pantomime, piece, show, stage show, tragedy **5** amusement, diversion, entertainment, fun, game, pastime, recreation, sport **6** fun, humour, jest, joking, lark (*informal*), prank, sport **7** space, elbowroom, latitude, leeway, margin, room, scope

playboy noun womanizer, ladies' man, lady-killer (*informal*), philanderer, rake, roué

play down verb minimize, play over, make light of, make little of, soft-pedal (*informal*), underplay, underrate

player noun **1** sportsman or sportswoman, competitor, contestant, participant **2** musician, artist, instrumentalist, performer, virtuoso **3** performer, actor or actress, entertainer, Thespian, trouper

playful adjective lively, frisky, impish, merry, mischievous, spirited, sportive, sprightly, vivacious

➤ **Antonyms**

despondent, gloomy, grave, morose, sedate, serious

playmate noun friend, chum (*informal*), companion, comrade, pal (*informal*), playfellow

play on or **upon** *verb* take advantage of, abuse, capitalize on, exploit, impose on, trade on

plaything *noun* toy, amusement, game, pastime, trifle

play up *verb* **1** emphasize, accentuate, highlight, stress, underline **2** *Brit. informal* be awkward, be disobedient, be stroppy (*Brit. slang*), give trouble, misbehave **3** *Brit. informal* hurt, be painful, be sore, bother, pain, trouble **4** *Brit. informal* malfunction, be on the blink (*slang*), not work properly

plea *noun* **1** appeal, entreaty, intercession, petition, prayer, request, suit, supplication **2** excuse, defence, explanation, justification

plead *verb* appeal, ask, beg, beseech, entreat, implore, petition, request

pleasant *adjective* **1** pleasing, agreeable, amusing, delightful, enjoyable, fine, lovely, nice, pleasurable **2** friendly, affable, agreeable, amiable, charming, congenial, engaging, genial, likable or likeable, nice

► **Antonyms**

≠pleasing: awful, disagreeable, distasteful, horrible, horrid, offensive, repulsive, unpleasant ≠friendly: cold, disagreeable, horrible, horrid, impolite, offensive, rude, unfriendly, unlikable or unlikeable

pleasantry *noun* joke, badinage, banter, jest, quip, witticism

please *verb* delight, amuse, entertain, gladden, gratify, humour, indulge, satisfy, suit

► **Antonyms**

anger, annoy, disgust, displease, dissatisfy, grieve, offend, sadden, vex

pleased *adjective* happy, chuffed (*Brit. slang*), contented, delighted, euphoric, glad, gratified, over the moon (*informal*), satisfied, thrilled

pleasing *adjective* enjoyable, agreeable, charming, delightful, engaging, gratifying, likable or likeable, pleasurable, satisfying

► **Antonyms**

boring, disagreeable, dull, monotonous, unattractive, unlikable or unlikeable, unpleasant

pleasurable *adjective* enjoyable, agreeable, delightful, fun, good, lovely, nice, pleasant

pleasure *noun* happiness, amusement, bliss, delectation, delight, enjoyment, gladness, gratification, joy, satisfaction

► **Antonyms**

displeasure, misery, pain, sadness, sorrow, suffering, unhappiness

plebeian *adjective* **1** common, base, coarse, low, lower-class, proletarian, uncultivated, unrefined, vulgar, working-class ♦ *noun* **2** commoner, common man, man in the street, pleb, prole (*derogatory slang, chiefly Brit.*), proletarian

► **Antonyms**

adjective ≠common: aristocratic, cultivated, highborn, high-class, patrician, polished, refined, upper-class, well-bred

pledge *noun* **1** promise, assurance, covenant, oath, undertaking, vow, warrant, word **2** guarantee, bail, collateral, deposit, pawn, security, surety ♦ *verb* **3** promise, contract, engage, give one's oath, give one's word, swear, vow

plentiful *adjective* abundant, ample, bountiful, copious, generous, lavish, liberal, overflowing, plenteous, profuse

► **Antonyms**

deficient, inadequate, insufficient, scant, scarce, skimpy, small, sparing, sparse, thin on the ground

plenty *noun* **1** lots (*informal*), abundance, enough, great deal, heap(s) (*informal*), masses, pile(s) (*informal*), plethora, quantity, stack(s) **2** abundance, affluence, copiousness, fertility, fruitfulness, plenitude, profusion, prosperity, wealth

plethora noun <u>excess</u>, glut, over-abundance, profusion, superabundance, surfeit, surplus

➤ **Antonyms**

dearth, deficiency, lack, scarcity, shortage, want

pliable adjective 1 <u>flexible</u>, bendable, bendy, malleable, plastic, pliant, supple 2 <u>compliant</u>, adaptable, docile, easily led, impressionable, pliant, receptive, responsive, susceptible, tractable

➤ **Antonyms**

≠<u>flexible</u>: rigid, stiff ≠<u>compliant</u>: headstrong, inflexible, intractable, obdurate, obstinate, stubborn, unadaptable, unbending, unyielding, wilful

pliant adjective 1 <u>flexible</u>, bendable, bendy, plastic, pliable, supple 2 <u>impressionable</u>, biddable, compliant, easily led, pliable, susceptible, tractable

plight noun <u>difficulty</u>, condition, jam (informal), predicament, scrape (informal), situation, spot (informal), state, trouble

plod verb 1 <u>trudge</u>, clump, drag, lumber, tramp, tread 2 <u>slog</u>, grind (informal), labour, persevere, plough through, plug away (informal), soldier on, toil

plot[1] noun 1 <u>plan</u>, cabal, conspiracy, intrigue, machination, scheme, stratagem 2 <u>story</u>, action, narrative, outline, scenario, story line, subject, theme ◆ verb 3 <u>plan</u>, collude, conspire, contrive, intrigue, machinate, manoeuvre, scheme 4 <u>devise</u>, conceive, concoct, contrive, cook up (informal), design, hatch, lay 5 <u>chart</u>, calculate, locate, map, mark, outline

plot[2] noun <u>patch</u>, allotment, area, ground, lot, parcel, tract

plough verb 1 <u>turn over</u>, cultivate, dig, till 2 usually with **through** <u>forge</u>, cut, drive, plunge, press, push, wade

ploy noun <u>tactic</u>, device, dodge, manoeuvre, move, ruse,

scheme, stratagem, trick, wile

pluck verb 1 <u>pull out or off</u>, collect, draw, gather, harvest, pick 2 <u>tug</u>, catch, clutch, jerk, pull at, snatch, tweak, yank 3 <u>strum</u>, finger, pick, twang ◆ noun 4 <u>courage</u>, backbone, boldness, bottle (Brit. slang), bravery, grit, guts (informal), nerve

plucky adjective <u>courageous</u>, bold, brave, daring, game, gutsy (slang), have-a-go (informal), intrepid

➤ **Antonyms**

afraid, chicken (slang), cowardly, scared, spineless, timid, yellow (informal)

plug noun 1 <u>stopper</u>, bung, cork, spigot 2 Informal <u>mention</u>, advert (Brit. informal), advertisement, hype, publicity, push ◆ verb 3 <u>seal</u>, block, bung, close, cork, fill, pack, stop, stopper, stop up, stuff 4 Informal <u>mention</u>, advertise, build up, hype, promote, publicize, push 5 <u>plug away</u> Informal <u>slog</u>, grind (informal), labour, peg away, plod, toil

plum adjective <u>choice</u>, best, first-class, prize

plumb verb 1 <u>delve</u>, explore, fathom, gauge, go into, penetrate, probe, unravel ◆ noun 2 <u>weight</u>, lead, plumb bob, plummet ◆ adverb 3 <u>exactly</u>, bang, precisely, slap, spot-on (Brit. informal)

plume noun <u>feather</u>, crest, pinion, quill

plummet verb <u>plunge</u>, crash, descend, dive, drop down, fall, nose-dive, tumble

plump adjective <u>chubby</u>, corpulent, dumpy, fat, podgy, roly-poly, rotund, round, stout, tubby

➤ **Antonyms**

anorexic, bony, emaciated, lanky, lean, scrawny, skinny, slender, slim, sylphlike, thin

plunder verb 1 <u>loot</u>, pillage, raid, ransack, rifle, rob, sack, strip ◆ noun 2 <u>loot</u>, booty, ill-gotten gains, pillage, prize, spoils, swag (slang)

plunge verb 1 <u>throw</u>, cast, pitch 2 <u>hurtle</u>, career, charge, dash, jump, rush, tear 3 <u>descend</u>, dip, dive, drop, fall, nose-dive, plummet, sink, tumble ♦ noun 4 <u>dive</u>, descent, drop, fall, jump

plus preposition 1 <u>and</u>, added to, coupled with, with ♦ adjective 2 <u>additional</u>, added, add-on, extra, supplementary ♦ noun 3 Informal <u>advantage</u>, asset, benefit, bonus, extra, gain, good point

plush adjective <u>luxurious</u>, de luxe, lavish, luxury, opulent, rich, sumptuous

➤ Antonyms

cheap, inexpensive, ordinary, plain

ply verb 1 <u>work at</u>, carry on, exercise, follow, practise, pursue 2 <u>use</u>, employ, handle, manipulate, wield

poach verb <u>encroach</u>, appropriate, infringe, intrude, trespass

pocket noun 1 <u>pouch</u>, bag, compartment, receptacle, sack ♦ verb 2 <u>steal</u>, appropriate, filch, lift (informal), pilfer, purloin, take ♦ adjective 3 <u>small</u>, abridged, compact, concise, little, miniature, portable

pod noun, verb <u>shell</u>, hull, husk, shuck

podgy adjective <u>tubby</u>, chubby, dumpy, fat, plump, roly-poly, rotund, stout

podium noun <u>platform</u>, dais, rostrum, stage

poem noun <u>verse</u>, lyric, ode, rhyme, song, sonnet

poet noun <u>bard</u>, lyricist, rhymer, versifier

poetic adjective <u>lyrical</u>, elegiac, lyric, metrical

poetry noun <u>verse</u>, poems, rhyme, rhyming

poignancy noun 1 <u>sadness</u>, emotion, feeling, pathos, sentiment, tenderness 2 <u>sharpness</u>, bitterness, intensity, keenness

poignant adjective <u>moving</u>, bitter, distressing, gut-wrenching, heart-rending, intense, painful, pathetic, sad, touching

point noun 1 <u>essence</u>, crux, drift, gist, heart, import, meaning, nub, pith, question, subject, thrust 2 <u>aim</u>, end, goal, intent, intention, motive, object, objective, purpose, reason 3 <u>item</u>, aspect, detail, feature, particular 4 <u>characteristic</u>, aspect, attribute, quality, respect, trait 5 <u>place</u>, location, position, site, spot, stage 6 <u>full stop</u>, dot, mark, period, stop 7 <u>end</u>, apex, prong, sharp end, spike, spur, summit, tip, top 8 <u>headland</u>, cape, head, promontory 9 <u>stage</u>, circumstance, condition, degree, extent, position 10 <u>moment</u>, instant, juncture, time, very minute 11 <u>unit</u>, score, tally ♦ verb 12 <u>indicate</u>, call attention to, denote, designate, direct, show, signify 13 <u>aim</u>, direct, level, train

point-blank adjective 1 <u>direct</u>, blunt, downright, explicit, express, plain ♦ adverb 2 <u>directly</u>, bluntly, candidly, explicitly, forthrightly, frankly, openly, plainly, straight

pointed adjective 1 <u>sharp</u>, acute, barbed, edged 2 <u>cutting</u>, acute, biting, incisive, keen, penetrating, pertinent, sharp, telling

pointer noun 1 <u>hint</u>, advice, caution, information, recommendation, suggestion, tip 2 <u>indicator</u>, guide, hand, needle

pointless adjective <u>senseless</u>, absurd, aimless, dumb-ass (slang), fruitless, futile, inane, irrelevant, meaningless, silly, stupid, useless

➤ Antonyms

appropriate, beneficial, desirable, fitting, fruitful, to the point, useful, worthwhile

point out verb <u>mention</u>, allude to, bring up, identify, indicate, show, specify

poise noun <u>composure</u>, aplomb, assurance, calmness, cool (slang), dignity, presence, sangfroid, self-possession

poised adjective 1 <u>ready</u>, all set, prepared, standing by, waiting 2 <u>composed</u>, calm, collected, dignified, self-confident, self-possessed, together (*informal*)

➤ **Antonyms**

≠composed: agitated, annoyed, discomposed, disturbed, irritated, ruffled, worked up

poison *noun* **1** toxin, bane, venom ◆ *verb* **2** murder, give (someone) poison, kill **3** contaminate, infect, pollute **4** corrupt, defile, deprave, pervert, subvert, taint, undermine, warp

poisonous *adjective* **1** toxic, deadly, fatal, lethal, mortal, noxious, venomous, virulent **2** evil, baleful, corrupting, malicious, noxious, pernicious

poke *verb* **1** jab, dig, nudge, prod, push, shove, stab, stick, thrust ◆ *noun* **2** jab, dig, nudge, prod, thrust

poky *adjective* small, confined, cramped, narrow, tiny

➤ **Antonyms**

capacious, commodious, large, open, roomy, spacious, wide

pole *noun* rod, bar, mast, post, shaft, spar, staff, stick

police *noun* **1** the law (*informal*), boys in blue (*informal*), constabulary, fuzz (*slang*), police force, the Old Bill (*slang*) ◆ *verb* **2** control, guard, patrol, protect, regulate, watch

policeman *noun* cop (*slang*), bizzy (*informal*), bobby (*informal*), constable, copper (*slang*), fuzz (*slang*), officer

policy *noun* procedure, action, approach, code, course, custom, plan, practice, rule, scheme

polish *verb* **1** shine, brighten, buff, burnish, rub, smooth, wax **2** perfect, brush up, enhance, finish, improve, refine, touch up ◆ *noun* **3** varnish, wax **4** sheen, brightness, finish, glaze, gloss, lustre **5** style, breeding, class (*informal*), elegance, finesse, finish, grace, refinement

polished *adjective* **1** accomplished, adept, expert, fine, masterly, professional, skilful, superlative **2** shining, bright, burnished, gleaming, glossy, smooth **3** el-

egant, cultivated, polite, refined, sophisticated, well-bred

➤ **Antonyms**

≠accomplished: amateurish, inept, inexpert, unaccomplished, unskilled ≠shining: dark, dull, matt, rough ≠elegant: inelegant, uncivilized, uncultivated, unrefined, unsophisticated

polite *adjective* **1** mannerly, civil, complaisant, courteous, gracious, respectful, well-behaved, well-mannered **2** refined, civilized, cultured, elegant, genteel, polished, sophisticated, well-bred

➤ **Antonyms**

≠mannerly: crude, discourteous, ill-mannered, impertinent, impolite, impudent, insulting, rude ≠refined: uncultured, unrefined

politeness *noun* courtesy, civility, courteousness, decency, etiquette, mannerliness

politic *adjective* wise, advisable, diplomatic, expedient, judicious, prudent, sensible

political *adjective* governmental, parliamentary, policy-making

politician *noun* statesman, legislator, Member of Parliament, M.P., office bearer, public servant

politics *noun* statesmanship, affairs of state, civics, government, political science

poll *noun* **1** canvass, ballot, census, count, sampling, survey **2** vote, figures, returns, tally, voting ◆ *verb* **3** tally, register **4** question, ballot, canvass, interview, sample, survey

pollute *verb* **1** contaminate, dirty, foul, infect, poison, soil, spoil, stain, taint **2** defile, corrupt, debase, debauch, deprave, desecrate, dishonour, profane, sully

➤ **Antonyms**

≠contaminate: clean, cleanse, decontaminate, disinfect, sanitize, sterilize ≠defile: esteem, honour

pollution *noun* contamination, corruption, defilement, dirtying, foulness, impurity, taint, uncleanness

pomp noun **1** ceremony, flourish, grandeur, magnificence, pageant, pageantry, splendour, state **2** show, display, grandiosity, ostentation

pomposity noun self-importance, affectation, airs, grandiosity, pompousness, portentousness, pretension, pretentiousness

pompous adjective **1** self-important, arrogant, grandiose, ostentatious, pretentious, puffed up, showy **2** grandiloquent, arty-farty (informal), boastful, bombastic, high-flown, inflated

➤ **Antonyms**

≠self-important: humble, modest, natural, self-effacing, simple, unpretentious ≠grandiloquent: direct, plain-spoken, simple, succinct

pond noun pool, duck pond, fish pond, millpond, small lake, tarn

ponder verb think, brood, cogitate, consider, contemplate, deliberate, meditate, mull over, muse, reflect, ruminate

ponderous adjective **1** dull, heavy, long-winded, pedantic, tedious **2** unwieldy, bulky, cumbersome, heavy, huge, massive, weighty **3** clumsy, awkward, heavy-footed, lumbering

➤ **Antonyms**

≠unwieldy: handy, light, little, small ≠clumsy: graceful, light, light-footed

pontificate verb expound, hold forth, lay down the law, preach, pronounce, sound off

pool[1] noun **1** pond, lake, mere, puddle, tarn **2** swimming pool, swimming bath

pool[2] noun **1** syndicate, collective, consortium, group, team, trust **2** kitty, bank, funds, jackpot, pot ◆ verb **3** combine, amalgamate, join forces, league, merge, put together, share

poor adjective **1** impoverished, broke (informal), destitute, down and out, hard up (informal), impecunious, indigent, needy, on the breadline, penniless, penurious, poverty-stricken, short, skint (Brit. slang), stony-broke (Brit. slang) **2** meagre, deficient, inadequate, incomplete, insufficient, lacking, measly, scant, scanty, skimpy **3** inferior, below par, low-grade, mediocre, no great shakes (informal), not much cop (Brit. slang), rotten (informal), rubbishy, second-rate, substandard, unsatisfactory **4** unfortunate, hapless, ill-fated, luckless, pitiable, unlucky, wretched

➤ **Antonyms**

≠impoverished: affluent, comfortable (informal), prosperous, rich, wealthy, well-heeled (informal), well-off ≠meagre: abundant, adequate, ample, plentiful, satisfactory, sufficient ≠inferior: excellent, exceptional, first-class, first-rate, satisfactory, superior, valuable ≠unfortunate: fortunate, happy, lucky, successful

poorly adverb **1** badly, inadequately, incompetently, inexpertly, insufficiently, unsatisfactorily, unsuccessfully ◆ adjective **2** Informal ill, below par, off colour, rotten (informal), seedy (informal), sick, under the weather (informal), unwell

➤ **Antonyms**

adverb ≠badly: acceptably, adequately, competently, expertly, satisfactorily, sufficiently, well ◆ adjective ≠ill: fit, hale and hearty, healthy, in good health, in the pink, well

pop verb **1** burst, bang, crack, explode, go off, snap **2** put, insert, push, shove, slip, stick, thrust, tuck ◆ noun **3** bang, burst, crack, explosion, noise, report

pope noun Holy Father, Bishop of Rome, pontiff, Vicar of Christ

populace noun people, general public, hoi polloi, masses, mob, multitude

popular adjective **1** well-liked, accepted, approved, fashionable, fave (informal), favourite, in, in demand, in favour, liked, sought-after **2** common, conventional, current, general, prevailing, prevalent, universal

▶ **Antonyms**

≠well-liked: despised, detested, disliked, hated, loathed, unaccepted, unpopular ≠common: infrequent, rare, uncommon, unusual

popularity noun favour, acceptance, acclaim, approval, currency, esteem, regard, vogue

popularize verb make popular, disseminate, give currency to, give mass appeal, make available to all, spread, universalize

popularly adverb generally, commonly, conventionally, customarily, ordinarily, traditionally, universally, usually, widely

populate verb inhabit, colonize, live in, occupy, settle

population noun inhabitants, community, denizens, folk, natives, people, residents, society

populous adjective populated, crowded, heavily populated, overpopulated, packed, swarming, teeming

pore[1] verb pore over study, examine, peruse, ponder, read, scrutinize

pore[2] noun opening, hole, orifice, outlet

pornographic adjective obscene, blue, dirty, filthy, indecent, lewd, salacious, smutty

pornography noun obscenity, dirt, filth, indecency, porn (informal), smut

porous adjective permeable, absorbent, absorptive, penetrable, spongy

▶ **Antonyms**

impenetrable, impermeable, impervious, nonporous

port noun harbour, anchorage, haven, seaport

portable adjective light, compact, convenient, easily carried, handy, manageable, movable

portend verb foretell, augur, betoken, bode, foreshadow, herald, indicate, predict, prognosticate, promise, warn of

portent noun omen, augury, forewarning, indication, prognostication, sign, warning

portentous adjective **1** significant, crucial, fateful, important, menacing, momentous, ominous **2** pompous, ponderous, self-important, solemn

porter[1] noun baggage attendant, bearer, carrier

porter[2] noun Chiefly Brit. doorman, caretaker, concierge, gatekeeper, janitor

portion noun **1** part, bit, fragment, morsel, piece, scrap, section, segment **2** share, allocation, allotment, allowance, lot, measure, quantity, quota, ration **3** helping, piece, serving **4** Literary destiny, fate, fortune, lot, luck ◆ verb **5** divide, allocate, allot, apportion, deal, distribute, dole out, share out

portly adjective stout, burly, corpulent, fat, fleshy, heavy, large, plump

portrait noun **1** picture, image, likeness, painting, photograph, representation **2** description, characterization, depiction, portrayal, profile, thumbnail sketch

portray verb **1** represent, depict, draw, figure, illustrate, paint, picture, sketch **2** describe, characterize, depict, put in words **3** play, act the part of, represent

portrayal noun representation, characterization, depiction, interpretation, performance, picture

pose verb **1** position, model, sit **2** put on airs, posture, show off (informal) **3** impersonate, masquerade as, pass oneself off as, pretend to be, profess to be ◆ noun **4** posture, attitude, bearing, position, stance **5** act, affectation, air, façade, front, mannerism, posturing, pretence

poser noun puzzle, enigma, problem, question, riddle

posh adjective Informal, chiefly Brit. upper-class, classy (slang), grand, high-class, luxurious, ritzy (*slang*), smart, stylish, swanky (*informal, chiefly Brit.*), up-market

posit *verb* put forward, advance, assume, postulate, presume, propound, state

position *noun* 1 place, area, bearings, locale, location, point, post, situation, spot, station, whereabouts 2 posture, arrangement, attitude, pose, stance 3 attitude, belief, opinion, outlook, point of view, slant, stance, view, viewpoint 4 status, importance, place, prestige, rank, reputation, standing, station, stature 5 job, duty, employment, occupation, office, place, post, role, situation ♦ *verb* 6 place, arrange, lay out, locate, put, set, stand

positive *adjective* 1 certain, assured, confident, convinced, sure 2 definite, absolute, categorical, certain, clear, conclusive, decisive, explicit, express, firm, real 3 helpful, beneficial, constructive, practical, productive, progressive, useful 4 *Informal* absolute, complete, consummate, downright, out-and-out, perfect, thorough, utter

► **Antonyms**

≠certain: not confident, uncertain, unconvinced, unsure ≠definite: contestable, disputable, doubtful, inconclusive, indecisive, indefinite, uncertain ≠helpful: detrimental, harmful, unhelpful, useless

positively *adverb* definitely, absolutely, assuredly, categorically, certainly, emphatically, firmly, surely, unequivocally, unquestionably

possess *verb* 1 have, enjoy, hold, own 2 seize, acquire, control, dominate, hold, occupy, take over

possessed *adjective* crazed, berserk, demented, frenzied, obsessed, raving

possession *noun* 1 ownership, control, custody, hold, occupation, tenure, title 2 possessions property, assets, belongings, chattels, effects, estate, things

possessive *adjective* jealous, controlling, covetous, dominating, domineering, overprotective, selfish

possibility *noun* 1 feasibility, likelihood, potentiality, practicability, workableness 2 likelihood, chance, hope, liability, odds, probability, prospect, risk 3 *often plural* potential, capabilities, potentiality, promise, prospects, talent

possible *adjective* 1 conceivable, credible, hypothetical, imaginable, likely, potential 2 likely, hopeful, potential, probable, promising 3 feasible, attainable, doable, practicable, realizable, viable, workable

► **Antonyms**

≠conceivable: impossible, inconceivable, incredible, unimaginable, unlikely, unthinkable ≠likely: impossible, improbable ≠feasible: impossible, impracticable, unfeasible, unobtainable, unreasonable

possibly *adverb* perhaps, maybe, perchance (*archaic*)

post[1] *noun* 1 mail, collection, delivery, postal service ♦ *verb* 2 send, dispatch, mail, transmit 3 **keep someone posted** notify, advise, brief, fill in on (*informal*), inform, report to

post[2] *noun* 1 support, column, picket, pillar, pole, shaft, stake, upright ♦ *verb* 2 put up, affix, display, pin up

post[3] *noun* 1 job, appointment, assignment, employment, office, place, position, situation 2 station, beat, place, position ♦ *verb* 3 station, assign, place, position, put, situate

poster *noun* notice, advertisement, announcement, bill, placard, public notice, sticker

posterity *noun* 1 future, succeeding generations 2 descendants, children, family, heirs, issue, offspring, progeny

postpone verb put off, adjourn, defer, delay, put back, put on the back burner (informal), shelve, suspend

► **Antonyms**

advance, bring forward, carry out, go ahead with

postponement noun delay, adjournment, deferment, deferral, stay, suspension

postscript noun P.S., addition, afterthought, supplement

postulate verb Formal presuppose, assume, hypothesize, posit, propose, suppose, take for granted, theorize

posture noun 1 bearing, attitude, carriage, disposition, set, stance ♦ verb 2 show off (informal), affect, pose, put on airs

pot noun container, bowl, pan, vessel

potency noun power, effectiveness, force, influence, might, strength

potent adjective 1 powerful, authoritative, commanding, dominant, dynamic, influential 2 strong, forceful, mighty, powerful, vigorous

► **Antonyms**

≠strong: impotent, weak

potential adjective 1 possible, dormant, future, hidden, inherent, latent, likely, promising ♦ noun 2 ability, aptitude, capability, capacity, possibility, potentiality, power, wherewithal

potion noun concoction, brew, dose, draught, elixir, mixture, philtre

potter verb mess about, dabble, footle (informal), tinker

pottery noun ceramics, earthenware, stoneware, terracotta

pouch noun bag, container, pocket, purse, sack

pounce verb 1 spring, attack, fall upon, jump, leap at, strike, swoop ♦ noun 2 spring, assault, attack, bound, jump, leap, swoop

pound¹ verb 1 beat, batter, belabour, clobber (slang), hammer, pummel, strike, thrash, thump 2 crush, powder, pulverize 3 pulsate, beat, palpitate, pulse, throb 4 stomp (informal), march, thunder, tramp

pound² noun enclosure, compound, pen, yard

pour verb 1 flow, course, emit, gush, run, rush, spew, spout, stream 2 let flow, decant, spill, splash 3 rain, bucket down (informal), pelt (down), teem 4 stream, crowd, swarm, teem, throng

pout verb 1 sulk, glower, look petulant, pull a long face ♦ noun 2 sullen look, glower, long face

poverty noun 1 pennilessness, beggary, destitution, hardship, indigence, insolvency, need, penury, privation, want 2 scarcity, dearth, deficiency, insufficiency, lack, paucity, shortage

► **Antonyms**

≠pennilessness: affluence, comfort, luxury, opulence, richness, wealth ≠scarcity: abundance, plethora, sufficiency

poverty-stricken adjective penniless, broke (informal), destitute, down and out, flat broke (informal), impecunious, impoverished, indigent, poor

powder noun 1 dust, fine grains, loose particles, talc ♦ verb 2 dust, cover, dredge, scatter, sprinkle, strew

powdery adjective fine, crumbly, dry, dusty, grainy, granular

power noun 1 ability, capability, capacity, competence, competency, faculty, potential 2 control, ascendancy, authority, command, dominance, domination, dominion, influence, mastery, rule 3 authority, authorization, licence, prerogative, privilege, right, warrant 4 strength, brawn, energy, force, forcefulness, intensity, might, muscle, potency, vigour

► **Antonyms**

≠ability: inability, incapability, incapacity, incompetence ≠strength:

feebleness, impotence, listlessness, weakness

powerful adjective **1** controlling, authoritative, commanding, dominant, influential, prevailing **2** strong, energetic, mighty, potent, strapping, sturdy, vigorous **3** persuasive, cogent, compelling, convincing, effectual, forceful, impressive, storming, striking, telling, weighty

powerless adjective **1** defenceless, dependent, ineffective, subject, tied, unarmed, vulnerable **2** weak, debilitated, disabled, feeble, frail, helpless, impotent, incapable, incapacitated, ineffectual

➤ **Antonyms**
≠ weak: able-bodied, fit, healthy, lusty, powerful, robust, strong, sturdy

practicability noun feasibility, advantage, possibility, practicality, use, usefulness, viability

practicable adjective feasible, achievable, attainable, doable, possible, viable

➤ **Antonyms**
impossible, out of the question, unachievable, unattainable, unfeasible

practical adjective **1** functional, applied, empirical, experimental, factual, pragmatic, realistic, utilitarian **2** sensible, businesslike, down-to-earth, hard-headed, matter-of-fact, realistic **3** feasible, doable, practicable, serviceable, useful, workable **4** skilled, accomplished, efficient, experienced, proficient

➤ **Antonyms**
≠ functional: impracticable, impractical, speculative, theoretical, unpractical, unrealistic ≠ sensible: impractical, unrealistic ≠ feasible: impossible, impractical, unpractical, unworkable, useless ≠ skilled: inefficient, inexperienced, unaccomplished, unskilled

practically adverb **1** almost, all but, basically, essentially, fundamentally, in effect, just about,

nearly, very nearly, virtually, well-nigh **2** sensibly, clearly, matter-of-factly, rationally, realistically, reasonably

practice noun **1** custom, habit, method, mode, routine, rule, system, tradition, usage, way, wont **2** rehearsal, drill, exercise, preparation, repetition, study, training **3** profession, business, career, vocation, work **4** use, action, application, exercise, experience, operation

practise verb **1** rehearse, drill, exercise, go over, go through, prepare, repeat, study, train **2** underline{do}, apply, carry out, follow, observe, perform **3** work at, carry on, engage in, pursue

practised adjective skilled, able, accomplished, experienced, expert, proficient, seasoned, trained

➤ **Antonyms**
amateurish, bungling, incompetent, inexperienced, inexpert, unqualified, unskilled, untrained

pragmatic adjective practical, businesslike, down-to-earth, hard-headed, realistic, sensible, utilitarian

➤ **Antonyms**
airy-fairy, idealistic, impractical, theoretical, unprofessional, unrealistic

praise verb **1** approve, acclaim, admire, applaud, cheer, compliment, congratulate, eulogize, extol, honour, laud **2** give thanks to, adore, bless, exalt, glorify, worship ♦ noun **3** approval, acclaim, acclamation, approbation, commendation, compliment, congratulation, eulogy, plaudit, tribute **4** thanks, adoration, glory, homage, worship

praiseworthy adjective creditable, admirable, commendable, laudable, meritorious, worthy

➤ **Antonyms**
condemnable, deplorable, despicable, discreditable, disgraceful, reprehensible

prance verb **1** dance, caper, cavort, frisk, gambol, romp, skip 2 **strut**, parade, show off (*informal*), stalk, swagger, swank (*informal*)

prank *noun* trick, escapade, jape, lark (*informal*), practical joke

prattle *verb* chatter, babble, blather, blether, gabble, jabber, rabbit (on) (*Brit. informal*), waffle (*informal, chiefly Brit.*), witter (*informal*)

pray *verb* 1 say one's prayers, offer a prayer, recite the rosary 2 **beg**, adjure, ask, beseech, entreat, implore, petition, plead, request, solicit

prayer *noun* 1 orison, devotion, invocation, litany, supplication 2 **plea**, appeal, entreaty, petition, request, supplication

preach *verb* 1 deliver a sermon, address, evangelize 2 lecture, advocate, exhort, moralize, sermonize

preacher *noun* clergyman, evangelist, minister, missionary, parson

preamble *noun* introduction, foreword, opening statement *or* remarks, preface, prelude

precarious *adjective* dangerous, dodgy (*Brit., Austral., & N.Z. informal*), hazardous, insecure, perilous, risky, shaky, tricky, unreliable, unsafe, unsure

▶ **Antonyms**

certain, dependable, reliable, safe, secure, stable, steady

precaution *noun* 1 safeguard, insurance, protection, provision, safety measure 2 forethought, care, caution, providence, prudence, wariness

precede *verb* go before, antedate, come first, head, introduce, lead, preface

precedence *noun* priority, antecedence, pre-eminence, primacy, rank, seniority, superiority, supremacy

precedent *noun* instance, antecedent, example, model, paradigm, pattern, prototype, standard

preceding *adjective* previous, above, aforementioned, aforesaid, earlier, foregoing, former, past, prior

precept *noun* rule, canon, command, commandment, decree, instruction, law, order, principle, regulation, statute

precinct *noun* 1 enclosure, confine, limit 2 area, district, quarter, section, sector, zone

precious *adjective* 1 valuable, costly, dear, expensive, fine, invaluable, priceless, prized 2 loved, adored, beloved, cherished, darling, dear, prized, treasured 3 affected, artificial, overnice, overrefined, twee (*Brit. informal*)

precipice *noun* cliff, bluff, crag, height, rock face

precipitate *verb* 1 quicken, accelerate, advance, bring on, expedite, hasten, hurry, speed up, trigger 2 throw, cast, fling, hurl, launch, let fly ♦ *adjective* 3 hasty, heedless, impetuous, impulsive, precipitous, rash, reckless 4 swift, breakneck, headlong, rapid, rushing 5 sudden, abrupt, brief, quick, unexpected, without warning

precipitous *adjective* 1 sheer, abrupt, dizzy, high, perpendicular, steep 2 hasty, heedless, hurried, precipitate, rash, reckless

précis *noun* 1 summary, abridgment, outline, résumé, synopsis ♦ *verb* 2 summarize, abridge, outline, shorten, sum up

precise *adjective* 1 exact, absolute, correct, definite, explicit, express, particular, specific, strict 2 strict, careful, exact, fastidious, finicky, formal, meticulous, particular, punctilious, rigid, scrupulous, stiff

▶ **Antonyms**

≠exact: ambiguous, equivocal, incorrect, indefinite, inexact, loose, vague ≠strict: careless, inexact, informal, relaxed

precisely *adverb* exactly, absolutely, accurately, correctly, just so, plumb (*informal*), smack (*informal*), square, squarely, strictly

precision *noun* <u>exactness</u>, accuracy, care, meticulousness, particularity, preciseness

preclude *verb* <u>prevent</u>, check, debar, exclude, forestall, inhibit, obviate, prohibit, rule out, stop

precocious *adjective* <u>advanced</u>, ahead, bright, developed, forward, quick, smart

► **Antonyms**

backward, dense, dull, retarded, slow, underdeveloped

preconceived *adjective* <u>presumed</u>, forejudged, prejudged, presupposed

preconception *noun* <u>preconceived idea or notion</u>, bias, notion, predisposition, prejudice, presupposition

precursor *noun* **1** <u>herald</u>, forerunner, harbinger, vanguard **2** <u>forerunner</u>, antecedent, forebear, predecessor

predatory *adjective* <u>hunting</u>, carnivorous, predacious, raptorial

predecessor *noun* **1** <u>previous job holder</u>, antecedent, forerunner, precursor **2** <u>ancestor</u>, antecedent, forebear, forefather

predestination *noun* <u>fate</u>, destiny, foreordainment, foreordination, predetermination

predestined *adjective* <u>fated</u>, doomed, meant, preordained

predetermined *adjective* <u>prearranged</u>, agreed, fixed, preplanned, set

predicament *noun* <u>fix</u> (*informal*), dilemma, hole (*slang*), jam (*informal*), mess, pinch, plight, quandary, scrape (*informal*), situation, spot (*informal*)

predict *verb* <u>foretell</u>, augur, divine, forecast, portend, prophesy

predictable *adjective* <u>likely</u>, anticipated, certain, expected, foreseeable, reliable, sure

► **Antonyms**

out of the blue, surprising, unexpected, unforeseen, unlikely, unpredictable

prediction *noun* <u>prophecy</u>, augu-

ry, divination, forecast, prognosis, prognostication

predilection *noun* <u>liking</u>, bias, fondness, inclination, leaning, love, partiality, penchant, preference, propensity, taste, weakness

predispose *verb* <u>incline</u>, affect, bias, dispose, influence, lead, prejudice, prompt

predisposed *adjective* <u>inclined</u>, given, liable, minded, ready, subject, susceptible, willing

predominant *adjective* <u>main</u>, ascendant, chief, dominant, leading, paramount, prevailing, prevalent, prime, principal

► **Antonyms**

inferior, minor, secondary, subordinate, unimportant

predominantly *adverb* <u>mainly</u>, chiefly, for the most part, generally, largely, mostly, primarily, principally

predominate *verb* <u>prevail</u>, be most noticeable, carry weight, hold sway, outweigh, overrule, overshadow

pre-eminence *noun* <u>superiority</u>, distinction, excellence, predominance, prestige, prominence, renown, supremacy

pre-eminent *adjective* <u>outstanding</u>, chief, distinguished, excellent, foremost, incomparable, matchless, predominant, renowned, superior, supreme

pre-empt *verb* <u>anticipate</u>, appropriate, assume, usurp

preen *verb* **1** *Of birds* <u>clean</u>, plume **2** <u>smarten</u>, dress up, spruce up, titivate **3** **preen oneself** <u>pride oneself</u>, congratulate oneself

preface *noun* <u>introduction</u>, foreword, preamble, preliminary, prelude, prologue ♦ *verb* **2** <u>introduce</u>, begin, open, prefix

prefer *verb* <u>like better</u>, be partial to, choose, desire, fancy, favour, go for, incline towards, opt for, pick

preferable *adjective* <u>better</u>, best, chosen, favoured, more desirable, superior

➤ **Antonyms**

inferior, mediocre, poor, second-rate, undesirable

preferably *adverb* <u>rather</u>, by choice, first, in *or* for preference, sooner

preference *noun* **1** <u>first choice</u>, choice, desire, favourite, option, partiality, pick, predilection, selection **2** <u>priority</u>, favoured treatment, favouritism, first place, precedence

preferential *adjective* <u>privileged</u>, advantageous, better, favoured, special

preferment *noun* <u>promotion</u>, advancement, elevation, exaltation, rise, upgrading

pregnant *adjective* **1** <u>expectant</u>, big *or* heavy with child, expecting (*informal*), in the club (*Brit. slang*), with child **2** <u>meaningful</u>, charged, eloquent, expressive, loaded, pointed, significant, telling, weighty

prehistoric *adjective* <u>earliest</u>, early, primeval, primitive, primordial

prejudge *verb* <u>jump to conclusions</u>, anticipate, presume, presuppose

prejudice *noun* **1** <u>bias</u>, partiality, preconceived notion, preconception, prejudgment **2** <u>discrimination</u>, bigotry, chauvinism, injustice, intolerance, narrow-mindedness, unfairness ♦ *verb* **3** <u>bias</u>, colour, distort, influence, poison, predispose, slant **4** <u>harm</u>, damage, hinder, hurt, impair, injure, mar, spoil, undermine

prejudiced *adjective* <u>biased</u>, bigoted, influenced, intolerant, narrow-minded, one-sided, opinionated, unfair

➤ **Antonyms**

fair, impartial, just, neutral, not bigoted, not prejudiced, open-minded, unbiased

prejudicial *adjective* <u>harmful</u>, damaging, deleterious, detrimental, disadvantageous, hurtful, injurious, unfavourable

preliminary *adjective* **1** <u>first</u>, initial, introductory, opening, pilot, prefatory, preparatory, prior, test, trial ♦ *noun* **2** <u>introduction</u>, beginning, opening, overture, preamble, preface, prelude, start

prelude *noun* <u>introduction</u>, beginning, foreword, overture, preamble, preface, prologue, start

premature *adjective* **1** <u>early</u>, forward, unseasonable, untimely **2** <u>hasty</u>, ill-timed, overhasty, previous (*informal*), rash, too soon, untimely

premeditated *adjective* <u>planned</u>, calculated, conscious, considered, deliberate, intentional, wilful

➤ **Antonyms**

accidental, inadvertent, unintentional, unplanned, unpremeditated

premeditation *noun* <u>planning</u>, design, forethought, intention, plotting, prearrangement, predetermination, purpose

premier *noun* **1** <u>head of government</u>, chancellor, chief minister, P.M., prime minister ♦ *adjective* **2** <u>chief</u>, first, foremost, head, highest, leading, main, primary, prime, principal

premiere *noun* <u>first night</u>, debut, opening

premise *noun* <u>assumption</u>, argument, assertion, hypothesis, postulation, presupposition, proposition, supposition

premises *plural noun* <u>building</u>, establishment, place, property, site

premium *noun* **1** <u>bonus</u>, bounty, fee, perk (*Brit. informal*), perquisite, prize, reward **2 at a premium** <u>in great demand</u>, hard to come by, in short supply, rare, scarce

premonition *noun* <u>feeling</u>, foreboding, hunch, idea, intuition, presentiment, suspicion

preoccupation *noun* **1** <u>obsession</u>, bee in one's bonnet, fixation **2** <u>absorption</u>, absent-mindedness, abstraction, daydreaming, engrossment, immersion, reverie, woolgathering

preoccupied *adjective* absorbed, absent-minded, distracted, engrossed, immersed, lost in, oblivious, rapt, wrapped up

preparation *noun* **1** groundwork, getting ready, preparing **2** *often plural* arrangement, measure, plan, provision **3** mixture, compound, concoction, medicine

preparatory *adjective* introductory, opening, prefatory, preliminary, primary

prepare *verb* make or get ready, adapt, adjust, arrange, practise, prime, train, warm up

prepared *adjective* **1** ready, arranged, in order, in readiness, primed, set **2** willing, disposed, inclined

preponderance *noun* predominance, dominance, domination, extensiveness, greater numbers, greater part, lion's share, mass, prevalence, supremacy

prepossessing *adjective* attractive, appealing, charming, engaging, fetching, good-looking, handsome, likable or likeable, pleasing

➤ **Antonyms**

displeasing, objectionable, offensive, repulsive, ugly, unattractive, unlikable or unlikeable

preposterous *adjective* ridiculous, absurd, crazy, incredible, insane, laughable, ludicrous, nonsensical, out of the question, outrageous, unthinkable

prerequisite *noun* **1** requirement, condition, essential, must, necessity, precondition, qualification, requisite, sine qua non ♦ *adjective* **2** required, essential, indispensable, mandatory, necessary, obligatory, requisite, vital

prerogative *noun* right, advantage, due, exemption, immunity, liberty, privilege

presage *verb* portend, augur, betoken, bode, foreshadow, foretoken, signify

prescience *noun* Formal foresight, clairvoyance, foreknowledge, precognition, second sight

prescribe *verb* order, decree, dictate, direct, lay down, ordain, recommend, rule, set, specify, stipulate

prescription *noun* **1** instruction, direction, formula, recipe **2** medicine, drug, mixture, preparation, remedy

presence *noun* **1** being, attendance, existence, inhabitance, occupancy, residence **2** personality, air, appearance, aspect, aura, bearing, carriage, demeanour, poise, self-assurance

presence of mind *noun* levelheadedness, calmness, composure, cool (*slang*), coolness, self-possession, wits

present[1] *adjective* **1** here, at hand, near, nearby, ready, there **2** current, contemporary, existent, existing, immediate, present-day ♦ *noun* **3** the present now, here and now, the present moment, the time being, today **4** at present just now, at the moment, now, right now **5** for the present for now, for the moment, for the time being, in the meantime, temporarily

present[2] *noun* **1** gift, boon, donation, endowment, grant, gratuity, hand-out, offering, prezzie (*informal*) ♦ *verb* **2** introduce, acquaint with, make known **3** put on, display, exhibit, give, show, stage **4** give, award, bestow, confer, grant, hand out, hand over

presentable *adjective* decent, acceptable, becoming, fit to be seen, O.K. or okay (*informal*), passable, respectable, satisfactory, suitable

➤ **Antonyms**

below par, not good enough, not up to scratch, poor, rubbishy, unacceptable, unpresentable, unsatisfactory

presentation *noun* **1** giving, award, bestowal, conferral, donation, offering **2** performance, demonstration, display, exhibition, production, show

presently adverb soon, anon (archaic), before long, by and by, shortly

preservation noun protection, conservation, maintenance, safeguarding, safekeeping, safety, salvation, support

preserve verb 1 protect, care for, conserve, defend, keep, safeguard, save, shelter, shield 2 maintain, continue, keep, keep up, perpetuate, sustain, uphold ◆ noun 3 area, domain, field, realm, sphere

▶ **Antonyms**

verb ≠protect: assail, assault, attack, leave unprotected ≠maintain: abandon, discontinue, drop, end, give up

preside verb run, administer, chair, conduct, control, direct, govern, head, lead, manage, officiate

press verb 1 compress, crush, depress, force down, jam, mash, push, squeeze 2 hug, clasp, crush, embrace, fold in one's arms, hold close, squeeze 3 smooth, flatten, iron 4 urge, beg, entreat, exhort, implore, petition, plead, pressurize 5 crowd, flock, gather, herd, push, seethe, surge, swarm, throng ◆ noun 6 the press: a newspapers, Fleet Street, fourth estate, news media, the papers b journalists, columnists, correspondents, newsmen, pressmen, reporters

pressing adjective urgent, crucial, high-priority, imperative, important, importunate, serious, vital

▶ **Antonyms**

regular, routine, unimportant, unnecessary

pressure noun 1 force, compressing, compression, crushing, squeezing, weight 2 power, coercion, compulsion, constraint, force, influence, sway 3 stress, burden, demands, hassle (informal), heat, load, strain, urgency

prestige noun status, credit, distinction, eminence, fame, honour, importance, kudos, renown, reputation, standing

prestigious adjective celebrated, eminent, esteemed, great, illustrious, important, notable, prominent, renowned, respected

▶ **Antonyms**

humble, lowly, minor, unimportant

presumably adverb it would seem, apparently, in all likelihood, in all probability, on the face of it, probably, seemingly

presume verb 1 believe, assume, conjecture, guess (informal, chiefly U.S. & Canad.), infer, postulate, suppose, surmise, take for granted, think 2 dare, go so far, make so bold, take the liberty, venture

presumption noun 1 cheek (informal), audacity, boldness, effrontery, gall (informal), impudence, insolence, nerve (informal) 2 probability, basis, chance, likelihood

presumptuous adjective pushy (informal), audacious, bold, forward, insolent, overconfident, too big for one's boots, uppish (Brit. informal)

▶ **Antonyms**

bashful, humble, modest, retiring, shy, timid, unassuming

presuppose verb presume, assume, imply, posit, postulate, take as read, take for granted

presupposition noun assumption, belief, preconception, premise, presumption, supposition

pretence noun 1 deception, acting, charade, deceit, falsehood, feigning, sham, simulation, trickery 2 show, affectation, artifice, display, façade, veneer

▶ **Antonyms**

≠deception: candour, frankness, honesty, openness ≠show: actuality, fact, reality

pretend verb 1 feign, affect, allege, assume, fake, falsify, impersonate, profess, sham, simulate 2 make believe, act, imagine, make up, suppose

pretended adjective feigned, bogus, counterfeit, fake, false, phoney or phony (informal), pretend (informal), pseudo (informal), sham, so-called

pretender noun <u>claimant</u>, aspirant

pretension noun 1 <u>claim</u>, aspiration, assumption, demand, pretence, profession 2 <u>affectation</u>, airs, conceit, ostentation, pretentiousness, self-importance, show, snobbery, vanity

pretentious adjective <u>affected</u>, arty-farty (informal), conceited, grandiloquent, grandiose, high-flown, inflated, mannered, ostentatious, pompous, puffed up, showy, snobbish

> **Antonyms**
modest, natural, plain, simple, unaffected, unassuming, unpretentious

pretext noun <u>guise</u>, cloak, cover, excuse, ploy, pretence, ruse, show

pretty adjective 1 <u>attractive</u>, beautiful, bonny, charming, comely, fair, good-looking, lovely ◆ adverb 2 Informal fairly, kind of (informal), moderately, quite, rather, reasonably, somewhat

> **Antonyms**
adjective ≠<u>attractive</u>: plain, ugly, unattractive, unsightly

prevail verb 1 <u>win</u>, be victorious, overcome, overrule, succeed, triumph 2 <u>be widespread</u>, abound, be current, be the prevalent, exist generally, predominate

prevailing adjective 1 <u>widespread</u>, common, current, customary, established, fashionable, general, in vogue, ordinary, popular, prevalent, usual 2 <u>predominating</u>, dominant, main, principal, ruling

prevalence noun <u>commonness</u>, currency, frequency, popularity, universality

prevalent adjective <u>common</u>, current, customary, established, frequent, general, popular, universal, usual, widespread

> **Antonyms**
confined, infrequent, limited, localized, rare, restricted, uncommon, unusual

prevaricate verb <u>evade</u>, beat about the bush, cavil, deceive, dodge, equivocate, flannel (Brit. informal), hedge

> **Antonyms**
be blunt, be direct, be frank, be straightforward, come straight to the point, not beat about the bush

prevent verb <u>stop</u>, avert, avoid, foil, forestall, frustrate, hamper, hinder, impede, inhibit, obstruct, obviate, preclude, thwart

> **Antonyms**
allow, encourage, help, permit

prevention noun <u>elimination</u>, avoidance, deterrence, precaution, safeguard, thwarting

preventive, preventative adjective 1 <u>hindering</u>, hampering, impeding, obstructive 2 <u>protective</u>, counteractive, deterrent, precautionary ◆ noun 3 <u>hindrance</u>, block, impediment, obstacle, obstruction 4 <u>protection</u>, deterrent, prevention, remedy, safeguard, shield

preview noun <u>sample</u>, advance showing, foretaste, sneak preview, taster, trailer

previous adjective <u>earlier</u>, erstwhile, foregoing, former, past, preceding, prior

> **Antonyms**
consequent, following, later, subsequent, succeeding

previously adverb <u>before</u>, beforehand, earlier, formerly, hitherto, in the past, once

prey noun 1 <u>quarry</u>, game, kill 2 <u>victim</u>, dupe, fall guy (informal), mug (Brit. slang), target

price noun 1 <u>cost</u>, amount, charge, damage (informal), estimate, expense, fee, figure, rate, value, worth 2 <u>consequences</u>, cost, penalty, toll ◆ verb 3 <u>evaluate</u>, assess, cost, estimate, rate, value

priceless adjective 1 <u>valuable</u>,

costly, dear, expensive, invaluable, precious **2** *Informal* hilarious, amusing, comic, droll, funny, rib-tickling, side-splitting

➤ **Antonyms**

≠**valuable**: cheap, inexpensive, worthless

pricey, pricy *adjective* expensive, costly, dear, high-priced, steep (*informal*)

prick *verb* **1** pierce, jab, lance, perforate, punch, puncture, stab **2** sting, bite, itch, prickle, smart, tingle ♦ *noun* **3** puncture, hole, perforation, pinhole, wound

prickle *noun* **1** spike, barb, needle, point, spine, spur, thorn ♦ *verb* **2** tingle, itch, smart, sting **3** prick, jab, stick

prickly *adjective* **1** spiny, barbed, bristly, thorny **2** itchy, crawling, scratchy, sharp, smarting, stinging, tingling

pride *noun* **1** satisfaction, delight, gratification, joy, pleasure **2** self-respect, dignity, honour, self-esteem, self-worth **3** conceit, arrogance, egotism, hubris, pretension, pretentiousness, self-importance, self-love, superciliousness, vanity **4** gem, jewel, pride and joy, treasure

➤ **Antonyms**

≠**conceit**: humility, meekness, modesty

priest *noun* clergyman, cleric, curate, divine, ecclesiastic, father, minister, pastor, vicar

prig *noun* goody-goody (*informal*), prude, puritan, stuffed shirt (*informal*)

priggish *adjective* self-righteous, goody-goody (*informal*), holier-than-thou, prim, prudish, puritanical

prim *adjective* prudish, demure, fastidious, fussy, priggish, prissy (*informal*), proper, puritanical, strait-laced

➤ **Antonyms**

carefree, casual, easy-going, informal, laid-back, relaxed

prima donna *noun* diva, leading lady, star

primarily *adverb* **1** chiefly, above all, essentially, fundamentally, generally, largely, mainly, mostly, principally **2** at first, at or from the start, first and foremost, initially, in the beginning, in the first place, originally

primary *adjective* **1** chief, cardinal, first, greatest, highest, main, paramount, prime, principal **2** elementary, introductory, rudimentary, simple

➤ **Antonyms**

≠**chief**: inferior, lesser, lowest, subordinate, unimportant ≠**elementary**: later, secondary, subsequent

prime *adjective* **1** main, chief, leading, predominant, pre-eminent, primary, principal **2** best, choice, excellent, first-class, first-rate, highest, quality, select, top ♦ *noun* **3** peak, bloom, flower, height, heyday, zenith ♦ *verb* **4** inform, brief, clue in (*informal*), fill in (*informal*), notify, tell **5** prepare, coach, get ready, make ready, train

primeval *adjective* earliest, ancient, early, first, old, prehistoric, primal, primitive, primordial

primitive *adjective* **1** early, earliest, elementary, first, original, primary, primeval, primordial **2** crude, rough, rudimentary, simple, unrefined

➤ **Antonyms**

≠**early**: advanced, later, modern ≠**crude**: elaborate, refined

prince *noun* ruler, lord, monarch, sovereign

princely *adjective* **1** regal, imperial, majestic, noble, royal, sovereign **2** generous, bounteous, gracious, lavish, liberal, munificent, open-handed, rich

principal *adjective* **1** main, cardinal, chief, essential, first, foremost, key, leading, paramount, pre-eminent, primary, prime ♦ *noun* **2** headmaster *or* headmistress, dean, head (*informal*), head teacher, master *or* mistress, rector **3** star, lead, leader **4** capital, assets, money

▶ **Antonyms**

adjective ≠**main**: auxiliary, inferior, minor, subordinate, subsidiary, supplementary

principally *adverb* mainly, above all, chiefly, especially, largely, mostly, predominantly, primarily

principle *noun* 1 rule, canon, criterion, doctrine, dogma, fundamental, law, maxim, precept, standard, truth 2 morals, conscience, integrity, probity, scruples, sense of honour 3 in principle in theory, ideally, theoretically

print *verb* 1 publish, engrave, impress, imprint, issue, mark, stamp ◆ *noun* 2 publication, book, magazine, newspaper, newsprint, periodical, printed matter, zine (*informal*) 3 reproduction, copy, engraving, photo (*informal*), photograph, picture

prior *adjective* 1 earlier, foregoing, former, preceding, preexistent, pre-existing, previous 2 prior to before, earlier than, preceding, previous to

priority *noun* precedence, preeminence, preference, rank, right of way, seniority

priory *noun* monastery, abbey, convent, nunnery, religious house

prison *noun* jail, clink (*slang*), confinement, cooler (*slang*), dungeon, jug (*slang*), lockup, nick (*Brit. slang*), penitentiary (*U.S.*), slammer (*slang*)

prisoner *noun* 1 convict, con (*slang*), jailbird, lag (*slang*) 2 captive, detainee, hostage, internee

prissy *adjective* prim, old-maidish (*informal*), prim and proper, prudish, strait-laced

pristine *adjective* new, immaculate, pure, uncorrupted, undefiled, unspoiled, unsullied, untouched, virginal

privacy *noun* seclusion, isolation, retirement, retreat, solitude

private *adjective* 1 exclusive, individual, intimate, own, personal,

reserved, special 2 secret, clandestine, confidential, covert, hush-hush (*informal*), off the record, unofficial 3 secluded, isolated, secret, separate, sequestered 4 solitary, withdrawn

▶ **Antonyms**

≠**exclusive**: common, general, open, public, unlimited, unrestricted ≠**secret**: disclosed, known, open, public, revealed ≠**secluded**: bustling, busy, frequented, unsecluded ≠**solitary**: outgoing, sociable

privilege *noun* right, advantage, claim, concession, due, entitlement, freedom, liberty, prerogative

privileged *adjective* special, advantaged, elite, entitled, favoured, honoured

privy *adjective* 1 *Archaic* secret, confidential, private 2 privy to informed of, apprised of, aware of, cognizant of, in on, in the know about (*informal*), in the loop, wise to (*slang*) ◆ *noun* 3 *Obsolete* lavatory, latrine, outside toilet

prize¹ *noun* 1 reward, accolade, award, honour, trophy 2 winnings, haul, jackpot, purse, stakes ◆ *adjective* 3 champion, award-winning, best, first-rate, outstanding, top, winning

prize² *verb* value, cherish, esteem, hold dear, treasure

probability *noun* likelihood, chance(s), expectation, liability, likeliness, odds, prospect

probable *adjective* likely, apparent, credible, feasible, plausible, possible, presumable, reasonable

▶ **Antonyms**

doubtful, improbable, not likely, unlikely

probably *adverb* likely, doubtless, maybe, most likely, perchance (*archaic*), perhaps, possibly, presumably

probation *noun* trial period, apprenticeship, trial

probe *verb* 1 examine, explore, go into, investigate, look into, scrutinize, search **2** <u>explore</u>, feel around, poke, prod ♦ *noun* **3** <u>examination</u>, detection, exploration, inquiry, investigation, scrutiny, study

problem *noun* **1** <u>difficulty</u>, complication, dilemma, dispute, predicament, quandary, trouble **2** <u>puzzle</u>, conundrum, enigma, poser, question, riddle

problematic *adjective* <u>tricky</u>, debatable, doubtful, dubious, problematical, puzzling

➤ **Antonyms**
beyond question, certain, clear, definite, indisputable, undebatable

procedure *noun* <u>method</u>, action, conduct, course, custom, modus operandi, policy, practice, process, routine, strategy, system

proceed *verb* **1** <u>go on</u>, carry on, continue, go ahead, move on, press on, progress **2** <u>arise</u>, come, derive, emanate, flow, issue, originate, result, spring, stem

➤ **Antonyms**
≠go on: break off, cease, discontinue, end, get behind, halt, leave off, pack in (*Brit. informal*), retreat, stop

proceeding *noun* **1** <u>action</u>, act, deed, measure, move, procedure, process, step **2 proceedings** <u>business</u>, account, affairs, archives, doings, minutes, records, report, transactions

proceeds *plural noun* <u>income</u>, earnings, gain, products, profit, returns, revenue, takings, yield

process *noun* **1** <u>procedure</u>, action, course, manner, means, measure, method, operation, performance, practice, system **2** <u>development</u>, advance, evolution, growth, movement, progress, progression ♦ *verb* **3** <u>handle</u>, deal with, fulfil

procession *noun* <u>parade</u>, cavalcade, cortege, file, march, train

proclaim *verb* <u>declare</u>, advertise, announce, circulate, herald, indicate, make known, profess, publish

➤ **Antonyms**
conceal, hush up, keep secret, suppress, withhold

proclamation *noun* <u>declaration</u>, announcement, decree, edict, notice, notification, pronouncement, publication

procrastinate *verb* <u>delay</u>, dally, drag one's feet (*informal*), gain time, play for time, postpone, put off, stall, temporize

➤ **Antonyms**
get on with, hasten, hurry (up), proceed, speed up

procure *verb* <u>obtain</u>, acquire, buy, come by, find, gain, get, pick up, purchase, score (*slang*), secure, win

prod *verb* **1** <u>poke</u>, dig, drive, jab, nudge, push, shove **2** <u>prompt</u>, egg on, goad, impel, incite, motivate, move, rouse, spur, stimulate, urge ♦ *noun* **3** <u>poke</u>, dig, jab, nudge, push, shove **4** <u>prompt</u>, cue, reminder, signal, stimulus

prodigal *adjective* <u>extravagant</u>, excessive, immoderate, improvident, profligate, reckless, spendthrift, wasteful

➤ **Antonyms**
economical, frugal, miserly, parsimonious, sparing, stingy, thrifty, tight

prodigious *adjective* **1** <u>huge</u>, colossal, enormous, giant, gigantic, immense, massive, monstrous, vast **2** <u>wonderful</u>, amazing, exceptional, extraordinary, fabulous, fantastic (*informal*), marvellous, phenomenal, remarkable, staggering

➤ **Antonyms**
≠huge: negligible, small, tiny ≠wonderful: normal, ordinary, unexceptional, unimpressive, unremarkable, usual

prodigy *noun* **1** <u>genius</u>, mastermind, talent, whizz (*informal*), wizard **2** <u>wonder</u>, marvel, miracle, phenomenon, sensation

produce *verb* **1** <u>cause</u>, bring about, effect, generate, give rise to **2** <u>show</u>, advance, demonstrate, exhibit, offer, present **3** yield, afford, give, render, supply **4** make, compose, construct, create, develop, fabricate, invent, manufacture **5** bring forth, bear, beget, breed, deliver **6** present, direct, do, exhibit, mount, put on, show, stage ♦ *noun* **7** fruit and vegetables, crop, greengrocery, harvest, product, yield

producer *noun* **1** director, impresario **2** maker, farmer, grower, manufacturer

product *noun* **1** goods, artefact, commodity, creation, invention, merchandise, produce, work **2** result, consequence, effect, outcome, upshot

production *noun* **1** producing, construction, creation, fabrication, formation, making, manufacture, manufacturing **2** presentation, direction, management, staging

productive *adjective* **1** fertile, creative, fecund, fruitful, inventive, plentiful, prolific, rich **2** useful, advantageous, beneficial, constructive, effective, profitable, rewarding, valuable, worthwhile

► **Antonyms**
≠fertile: barren, poor, sterile, unfertile, unfruitful, unproductive ≠useful: unproductive, unprofitable, useless

productivity *noun* output, production, work rate, yield

profane *adjective* **1** sacrilegious, disrespectful, godless, impious, impure, irreligious, irreverent, sinful, ungodly, wicked **2** crude, blasphemous, coarse, filthy, foul, obscene, vulgar ♦ *verb* **3** desecrate, commit sacrilege, debase, defile, violate

► **Antonyms**
adjective ≠sacrilegious: holy, proper, religious, respectful, reverent, sacred

profanity *noun* **1** sacrilege, blasphemy, impiety, profaneness **2** swearing, curse, cursing, irrever-

ence, obscenity

profess *verb* **1** claim, allege, fake, feign, make out, pretend, purport **2** state, admit, affirm, announce, assert, avow, confess, declare, proclaim, vouch

professed *adjective* **1** supposed, alleged, ostensible, pretended, purported, self-styled, so-called, would-be **2** declared, avowed, confessed, confirmed, proclaimed, self-acknowledged, self-confessed

profession *noun* **1** occupation, business, calling, career, employment, office, position, sphere, vocation **2** declaration, affirmation, assertion, avowal, claim, confession, statement

professional *adjective* **1** expert, adept, competent, efficient, experienced, masterly, proficient, qualified, skilled ♦ *noun* **2** expert, adept, guru, maestro, master, past master, pro (*informal*), specialist, virtuoso

► **Antonyms**
adjective ≠expert: amateurish, incompetent, inefficient, inept, inexperienced, unqualified, unskilled

professor *noun* don (*Brit.*), fellow (*Brit.*), prof (*informal*)

proficiency *noun* skill, ability, aptitude, competence, dexterity, expertise, knack, know-how (*informal*), mastery

proficient *adjective* skilled, able, accomplished, adept, capable, competent, efficient, expert, gifted, masterly, skilful

► **Antonyms**
bad, incapable, incompetent, inept, unaccomplished, unskilled

profile *noun* **1** outline, contour, drawing, figure, form, side view, silhouette, sketch **2** biography, characterization, sketch, thumbnail sketch, vignette

profit *noun* **1** *often plural* earnings, gain, proceeds, receipts, return, revenue, takings, yield **2** benefit, advancement, advantage, gain, good, use, value

♦ *verb* **3** benefit, be of advantage to, gain, help, improve, promote, serve **4** make money, earn, gain

profitable *adjective* **1** money-making, commercial, cost-effective, fruitful, lucrative, paying, remunerative, worthwhile **2** beneficial, advantageous, fruitful, productive, rewarding, useful, valuable, worthwhile

► **Antonyms**
disadvantageous, fruitless, unremunerative, unrewarding, useless, vain, worthless

profiteer *noun* **1** racketeer, exploiter ♦ *verb* **2** exploit, make a quick buck (*slang*), racketeer

profligate *adjective* **1** extravagant, immoderate, improvident, prodigal, reckless, spendthrift, wasteful **2** depraved, debauched, degenerate, dissolute, immoral, licentious, shameless, wanton, wicked, wild ♦ *noun* **3** spendthrift, squanderer, waster, wastrel **4** degenerate, debauchee, libertine, rake, reprobate, roué, swinger (*slang*)

► **Antonyms**
adjective ≠depraved: chaste, decent, moral, upright, virtuous

profound *adjective* **1** wise, abstruse, deep, learned, penetrating, philosophical, sagacious, sage **2** sincere, acute, deeply felt, extreme, great, heartfelt, intense, keen

► **Antonyms**
≠wise: imprudent, stupid, thoughtless, unwise ≠sincere: insincere, shallow

profuse *adjective* **1** plentiful, abundant, ample, bountiful, copious, luxuriant, overflowing, prolific

► **Antonyms**
deficient, inadequate, meagre, scanty, scarce, skimpy, sparse

profusion *noun* abundance, bounty, excess, extravagance, glut, plethora, quantity, surplus, wealth

progeny *noun* children, descendants, family, issue, lineage, off-spring, race, stock, young

prognosis *noun* forecast, diagnosis, prediction, prognostication, projection

programme *noun* **1** schedule, agenda, curriculum, line-up, list, listing, order of events, plan, syllabus, timetable **2** show, broadcast, performance, presentation, production

progress *noun* **1** development, advance, breakthrough, gain, growth, headway, improvement **2** movement, advance, course, passage, way **3 in progress** going on, being done, happening, occurring, proceeding, taking place, under way ♦ *verb* **4** develop, advance, gain, grow, improve **5** move on, advance, continue, go forward, make headway, proceed, travel

► **Antonyms**
noun ≠development: decline, failure, recession, regression, relapse, retrogression ≠movement: regression, retrogression ♦ *verb* ≠develop: decrease, get behind, lose, lose ground, regress, retrogress ≠move on: get behind, recede, regress, retrogress

progression *noun* **1** progress, advance, advancement, furtherance, gain, headway, movement forward **2** sequence, chain, course, cycle, series, string, succession

progressive *adjective* **1** enlightened, advanced, avant-garde, forward-looking, liberal, modern, radical, reformist, revolutionary **2** growing, advancing, continuing, developing, increasing, ongoing

prohibit *verb* **1** forbid, ban, debar, disallow, outlaw, proscribe, veto **2** prevent, hamper, hinder, impede, restrict, stop

► **Antonyms**
≠forbid: allow, authorize, consent to, give leave, let, license, permit, suffer, tolerate ≠prevent: allow, let, permit

prohibition noun **1** <u>prevention</u>, constraint, exclusion, obstruction, restriction **2** <u>ban</u>, bar, boycott, embargo, injunction, interdict, proscription, veto

prohibitive adjective <u>exorbitant</u>, excessive, extortionate, steep (informal)

project noun **1** <u>scheme</u>, activity, assignment, enterprise, job, occupation, plan, task, undertaking, venture, work ♦ verb **2** <u>forecast</u>, calculate, estimate, extrapolate, gauge, predict, reckon **3** <u>stick out</u>, bulge, extend, jut, overhang, protrude, stand out

projectile noun <u>missile</u>, bullet, rocket, shell

projection noun **1** <u>protrusion</u>, bulge, ledge, overhang, protuberance, ridge, shelf **2** <u>forecast</u>, calculation, computation, estimate, estimation, extrapolation, reckoning

proletarian adjective **1** <u>working-class</u>, common, plebeian ♦ noun **2** <u>worker</u>, commoner, man of the people, pleb, plebeian, prole (derogatory slang, chiefly Brit.)

proletariat noun <u>working class</u>, commoners, hoi polloi, labouring classes, lower classes, plebs, proles (derogatory slang, chiefly Brit.), the common people, the masses

➤ **Antonyms**

aristo (informal), aristocracy, gentry, nobility, peerage, ruling class, upper class, upper crust (informal)

proliferate verb <u>increase</u>, breed, expand, grow rapidly, multiply

proliferation noun <u>multiplication</u>, expansion, increase, spread

prolific adjective <u>productive</u>, abundant, copious, fecund, fertile, fruitful, luxuriant, profuse

➤ **Antonyms**

barren, fruitless, infertile, sterile, unfruitful, unproductive, unprolific

prologue noun <u>introduction</u>, foreword, preamble, preface, prelude

prolong verb <u>lengthen</u>, continue, delay, drag out, draw out, extend, perpetuate, protract, spin out, stretch

➤ **Antonyms**

abbreviate, abridge, curtail, cut, cut down, shorten

promenade noun **1** <u>walkway</u>, esplanade, parade, prom **2** <u>stroll</u>, constitutional, saunter, turn, walk ♦ verb **3** <u>stroll</u>, perambulate, saunter, take a walk, walk

prominence noun **1** <u>conspicuousness</u>, markedness **2** <u>fame</u>, celebrity, distinction, eminence, importance, name, prestige, reputation

prominent adjective **1** <u>noticeable</u>, conspicuous, eye-catching, obtrusive, obvious, outstanding, pronounced **2** <u>famous</u>, distinguished, eminent, foremost, important, leading, main, notable, renowned, top, well-known

➤ **Antonyms**

≠noticeable: inconspicuous, indistinct, insignificant, unnoticeable ≠famous: insignificant, minor, undistinguished, unimportant, unknown, unnotable

promiscuity noun <u>licentiousness</u>, debauchery, immorality, looseness, permissiveness, promiscuousness, wantonness

promiscuous adjective <u>licentious</u>, abandoned, debauched, fast, immoral, libertine, loose, wanton, wild

➤ **Antonyms**

chaste, decent, innocent, modest, moral, pure, undefiled, unsullied, vestal, virginal, virtuous

promise verb **1** <u>guarantee</u>, assure, contract, give an undertaking, give one's word, pledge, swear, take an oath, undertake, vow, warrant **2** <u>seem likely</u>, augur, betoken, indicate, look like, show signs of, suggest ♦ noun **3** <u>guarantee</u>, assurance, bond, commitment, oath, pledge, undertaking, vow, word **4** <u>potential</u>, ability, aptitude, capability, capacity, talent

promising adjective **1** encouraging, auspicious, bright, favourable, hopeful, likely, propitious, reassuring, rosy 2 talented, able, gifted, rising

➤ **Antonyms**

≠encouraging: discouraging, unauspicious, unfavourable, unpromising

promontory noun point, cape, foreland, head, headland

promote verb 1 help, advance, aid, assist, back, boost, encourage, forward, foster, gee up, support 2 raise, elevate, exalt, upgrade 3 advertise, hype, plug (informal), publicize, push, sell

➤ **Antonyms**

≠help: discourage, hinder, hold back, impede, obstruct, oppose, prevent ≠raise: demote, downgrade

promotion noun 1 rise, advancement, elevation, exaltation, honour, move up, preferment, upgrading 2 publicity, advertising, plugging (informal) 3 encouragement, advancement, boosting, furtherance, support

prompt verb 1 cause, elicit, give rise to, occasion, provoke 2 remind, assist, cue, help out ♦ adjective 3 immediate, early, instant, quick, rapid, speedy, swift, timely ♦ adverb 4 Informal exactly, on the dot, promptly, punctually, sharp

➤ **Antonyms**

adjective ≠immediate: hesitating, late, slow

promptly adverb immediately, at once, directly, on the dot, on time, punctually, quickly, speedily, swiftly

promptness noun swiftness, briskness, eagerness, haste, punctuality, quickness, speed, willingness

promulgate verb make known, broadcast, circulate, communicate, disseminate, make public, proclaim, promote, publish, spread

prone adjective 1 liable, apt, bent, disposed, given, inclined,

likely, predisposed, subject, susceptible, tending 2 face down, flat, horizontal, prostrate, recumbent

➤ **Antonyms**

≠liable: averse, disinclined, indisposed, not likely, unlikely ≠face down: erect, face up, perpendicular, supine, upright, vertical

prong noun point, spike, tine

pronounce verb 1 say, accent, articulate, enunciate, sound, speak 2 declare, affirm, announce, decree, deliver, proclaim

pronounced adjective noticeable, conspicuous, decided, definite, distinct, evident, marked, obvious, striking

➤ **Antonyms**

imperceptible, inconspicuous, unapparent, unnoticeable, vague

pronouncement noun announcement, declaration, decree, dictum, edict, judgment, proclamation, statement

pronunciation noun intonation, accent, articulation, diction, enunciation, inflection, speech, stress

proof noun 1 evidence, authentication, confirmation, corroboration, demonstration, substantiation, testimony, verification ♦ adjective 2 impervious, impenetrable, repellent, resistant, strong

prop verb 1 support, bolster, brace, buttress, hold up, stay, sustain, uphold ♦ noun 2 support, brace, buttress, mainstay, stanchion, stay

propaganda noun information, advertising, disinformation, hype, promotion, publicity

propagate verb 1 spread, broadcast, circulate, disseminate, promote, promulgate, publish, transmit 2 reproduce, beget, breed, engender, generate, increase, multiply, procreate, produce

➤ **Antonyms**

≠spread: cover up, hide, hush up, suppress, withhold

propel verb drive, force, impel,

launch, push, send, shoot, shove, thrust

► Antonyms

check, delay, hold back, pull, slow, stop

propensity noun tendency, bent, disposition, inclination, liability, penchant, predisposition, proclivity

proper adjective 1 suitable, appropriate, apt, becoming, befitting, fit, fitting, right 2 correct, accepted, conventional, established, formal, orthodox, precise, right 3 polite, decent, decorous, genteel, gentlemanly, ladylike, mannerly, respectable, seemly

► Antonyms

≠suitable: improper, inappropriate, unbecoming, unsuitable ≠correct: unconventional, unorthodox, wrong ≠polite: coarse, common, crude, discourteous, impolite, indecent, rude, ungentlemanly, unladylike, unrefined, unseemly

properly adverb 1 suitably, appropriately, aptly, fittingly, rightly 2 correctly, accurately 3 politely, decently, respectably

► Antonyms

≠suitably: improperly, inappropriately, inaptly, unfittingly, unsuitably, wrongly ≠correctly: improperly, inaccurately, incorrectly, wrongly ≠politely: impolitely, improperly, indecently

property noun 1 possessions, assets, belongings, capital, effects, estate, goods, holdings, riches, wealth 2 land, estate, freehold, holding, real estate 3 quality, attribute, characteristic, feature, hallmark, trait

prophecy noun prediction, augury, divination, forecast, prognostication, second sight, soothsaying

prophesy verb predict, augur, divine, forecast, foresee, foretell, prognosticate

prophet noun soothsayer, diviner, forecaster, oracle, prophesier, seer, sibyl

prophetic adjective predictive, oracular, prescient, prognostic, sibylline

propitious adjective favourable, auspicious, bright, encouraging, fortunate, happy, lucky, promising

proportion noun 1 relative amount, ratio, relationship 2 balance, congruity, correspondence, harmony, symmetry 3 part, amount, division, fraction, percentage, quota, segment, share 4 proportions dimensions, capacity, expanse, extent, size, volume

proportional, proportionate adjective balanced, commensurate, compatible, consistent, corresponding, equitable, even, in proportion

► Antonyms

different, disproportionate, dissimilar, incompatible, inconsistent, unequal

proposal noun suggestion, bid, offer, plan, presentation, programme, project, recommendation, scheme

propose verb 1 put forward, advance, present, submit, suggest 2 nominate, name, present, recommend 3 intend, design, plan, aim, have in mind, mean, scheme 4 offer marriage, ask for someone's hand (in marriage), pop the question (informal)

proposition noun 1 proposal, plan, recommendation, scheme, suggestion ♦ verb 2 make a pass at, accost, make an improper suggestion, solicit

propound verb put forward, advance, postulate, present, propose, submit, suggest

proprietor, proprietress noun owner, landlord or landlady, titleholder

propriety noun 1 correctness, aptness, fitness, rightness, seemliness 2 decorum, courtesy, decency, etiquette, manners, politeness, respectability, seemliness

> **Antonyms**

≠ <u>decorum</u>: impoliteness, indecency, indecorum, vulgarity

propulsion noun <u>drive</u>, impetus, impulse, propelling force, push, thrust

prosaic adjective <u>dull</u>, boring, everyday, humdrum, matter-of-fact, mundane, ordinary, pedestrian, routine, trite, unimaginative

> **Antonyms**

exciting, extraordinary, fascinating, imaginative, interesting, unusual

proscribe verb **1** <u>prohibit</u>, ban, embargo, forbid, interdict **2** <u>outlaw</u>, banish, deport, exclude, exile, expatriate, expel, ostracize

> **Antonyms**

≠ <u>prohibit</u>: allow, authorize, endorse, give permission, license, permit, sanction, warrant

prosecute verb Law <u>put on trial</u>, arraign, bring to trial, indict, litigate, sue, take to court, try

prospect noun **1** <u>expectation</u>, anticipation, future, hope, odds, outlook, probability, promise **2** sometimes plural <u>likelihood</u>, chance, possibility **3** <u>view</u>, landscape, outlook, scene, sight, spectacle, vista ♦ verb **4** <u>look for</u>, search for, seek

prospective adjective <u>future</u>, anticipated, coming, destined, expected, forthcoming, imminent, intended, likely, possible, potential

prospectus noun <u>catalogue</u>, list, outline, programme, syllabus, synopsis

prosper verb <u>succeed</u>, advance, do well, flourish, get on, progress, thrive

prosperity noun <u>success</u>, affluence, fortune, good fortune, luxury, plenty, prosperousness, riches, wealth

> **Antonyms**

adversity, depression, destitution, failure, misfortune, poverty, shortage, want

prosperous adjective **1** <u>wealthy</u>, affluent, moneyed, rich, well-heeled (informal), well-off, well-to-do **2** <u>successful</u>, booming, doing well, flourishing, fortunate, lucky, thriving

> **Antonyms**

≠ <u>wealthy</u>: impoverished, poor ≠ <u>successful</u>: defeated, failing, inauspicious, unfavourable, unfortunate, unlucky, unpromising, unsuccessful, untimely

prostitute noun **1** <u>whore</u>, call girl, fallen woman, harlot, hooker (U.S. slang), loose woman, pro (slang), scrubber (Brit. & Austral. slang), streetwalker, strumpet, tart (informal), trollop ♦ verb **2** <u>cheapen</u>, debase, degrade, demean, devalue, misapply, pervert, profane

prostrate adjective **1** <u>prone</u>, flat, horizontal **2** <u>exhausted</u>, dejected, depressed, desolate, drained, inconsolable, overcome, spent, worn out ♦ verb **3** <u>exhaust</u>, drain, fatigue, sap, tire, wear out, weary **4** <u>prostrate oneself</u> <u>bow down to</u>, abase oneself, fall at (someone's) feet, grovel, kneel, kowtow

protagonist noun **1** <u>supporter</u>, advocate, champion, exponent **2** <u>leading character</u>, central character, hero or heroine, principal

protect verb <u>keep safe</u>, defend, guard, look after, preserve, safeguard, save, screen, shelter, shield, stick up for (informal), support, watch over

> **Antonyms**

assail, assault, attack, endanger, expose, expose to danger, threaten

protection noun **1** <u>safety</u>, aegis, care, custody, defence, protecting, safeguard, safekeeping, security **2** <u>safeguard</u>, barrier, buffer, cover, guard, screen, shelter, shield

protective adjective <u>protecting</u>, defensive, fatherly, maternal, motherly, paternal, vigilant, watchful

protector noun <u>defender</u>, bodyguard, champion, guard, guardian, patron

protest noun **1** objection, complaint, dissent, outcry, protestation, remonstrance ♦ verb **2** object, complain, cry out, demonstrate, demur, disagree, disapprove, express disapproval, oppose, remonstrate **3** assert, affirm, attest, avow, declare, insist, maintain, profess

protestation noun Formal declaration, affirmation, avowal, profession, vow

protester noun demonstrator, agitator, rebel

protocol noun code of behaviour, conventions, customs, decorum, etiquette, manners, propriety

prototype noun original, example, first, model, pattern, standard, type

protracted adjective extended, dragged out, drawn-out, long-drawn-out, prolonged, spun out

protrude verb stick out, bulge, come through, extend, jut, obtrude, project, stand out

protrusion noun projection, bulge, bump, lump, outgrowth, protuberance

protuberance noun bulge, bump, excrescence, hump, knob, lump, outgrowth, process, prominence, protrusion, swelling

proud adjective **1** satisfied, content, glad, gratified, pleased, well-pleased **2** conceited, arrogant, boastful, disdainful, haughty, imperious, lordly, overbearing, self-satisfied, snobbish, supercilious

► Antonyms

≠satisfied: discontented, displeased, dissatisfied ≠conceited: humble, meek, modest

prove verb **1** verify, authenticate, confirm, demonstrate, determine, establish, justify, show, substantiate **2** test, analyse, assay, check, examine, try **3** turn out, come out, end up, result

► Antonyms

≠verify: discredit, disprove, refute

proven adjective established, attested, confirmed, definite, proved, reliable, tested, verified

proverb noun saying, adage, dictum, maxim, saw

proverbial adjective conventional, acknowledged, axiomatic, current, famed, famous, legendary, notorious, traditional, typical, well-known

provide verb **1** supply, cater, equip, furnish, outfit, purvey, stock up **2** give, add, afford, bring, impart, lend, present, produce, render, serve, yield **3** provide for or against take precautions, anticipate, forearm, plan ahead, plan for, prepare for **4** provide for support, care for, keep, maintain, sustain, take care of

► Antonyms

≠supply: deprive, keep back, refuse, withhold ≠take precautions: disregard, fail to notice, miss, neglect, overlook ≠support: neglect

providence noun fate, destiny, fortune

provident adjective **1** thrifty, economical, frugal, prudent **2** foresighted, careful, cautious, discreet, far-seeing, forearmed, shrewd, vigilant, well-prepared, wise

► Antonyms

≠thrifty: improvident, imprudent, prodigal, spendthrift, uneconomical, wasteful ≠foresighted: careless, heedless, improvident, negligent, reckless, short-sighted, thoughtless

providential adjective lucky, fortuitous, fortunate, happy, heaven-sent, opportune, timely

provider noun **1** supplier, donor, giver, source **2** breadwinner, earner, supporter, wage earner

providing, provided conjunction on condition that, as long as, given

province noun **1** region, colony, department, district, division, domain, patch, section, zone **2** area, business, capacity, concern, duty, field, function, line, responsibility, role, sphere

provincial *adjective* **1** rural, country, hick (*informal, chiefly U.S. & Canad.*), homespun, local, rustic **2** parochial, insular, inward-looking, limited, narrow, narrow-minded, small-minded, small-town (*chiefly U.S.*) unsophisticated ♦ *noun* **3** yokel, country cousin, hayseed (*U.S. & Canad. informal*), hick (*informal, chiefly U.S. & Canad.*), rustic

➤ **Antonyms**
adjective ≠rural: urban ≠parochial: cosmopolitan, sophisticated, urbane

provision *noun* **1** supplying, catering, equipping, furnishing, providing **2** condition, clause, demand, proviso, requirement, rider, stipulation, term

provisional *adjective* **1** temporary, interim **2** conditional, contingent, limited, qualified, tentative

➤ **Antonyms**
≠temporary: permanent ≠conditional: definite, fixed

provisions *plural noun* food, comestibles, eatables, edibles, fare, foodstuff, rations, stores, supplies, victuals

proviso *noun* condition, clause, qualification, requirement, rider, stipulation

provocation *noun* **1** cause, grounds, incitement, motivation, reason, stimulus **2** offence, affront, annoyance, challenge, dare, grievance, indignity, injury, insult, taunt

provocative *adjective* offensive, annoying, galling, goading, insulting, provoking, stimulating

provoke *verb* **1** anger, aggravate (*informal*), annoy, enrage, hassle (*informal*), incense, infuriate, irk, irritate, madden, rile **2** rouse, bring about, cause, elicit, evoke, incite, induce, occasion, produce, promote, prompt, stir

➤ **Antonyms**
≠anger: appease, calm, concili-

ate, mollify, pacify, placate, propitiate, quiet, soothe ≠rouse: abate, allay, assuage, blunt, curb, ease, lessen, mitigate, moderate, modify, relieve, temper

prowess *noun* **1** skill, ability, accomplishment, adeptness, aptitude, excellence, expertise, genius, mastery, talent **2** bravery, courage, daring, fearlessness, heroism, mettle, valiance, valour

➤ **Antonyms**
≠skill: clumsiness, inability, ineptitude, inexpertise ≠bravery: cowardice, faint-heartedness, fear, gutlessness, timidity

prowl *verb* move stealthily, skulk, slink, sneak, stalk, steal

proximity *noun* nearness, closeness

proxy *noun* representative, agent, delegate, deputy, factor, substitute

prudence *noun* common sense, care, caution, discretion, good sense, judgment, vigilance, wariness, wisdom

prudent *adjective* **1** sensible, careful, cautious, discerning, discreet, judicious, politic, shrewd, vigilant, wary, wise **2** thrifty, canny, careful, economical, farsighted, frugal, provident, sparing

➤ **Antonyms**
≠sensible: careless, heedless, impolitic, imprudent, indiscreet, injudicious, rash, thoughtless, unwise ≠thrifty: careless, extravagant, improvident, imprudent, wasteful

prudish *adjective* prim, old-maidish (*informal*), overmodest, priggish, prissy (*informal*), proper, puritanical, starchy (*informal*), strait-laced, stuffy, Victorian

➤ **Antonyms**
broad-minded, liberal, open-minded, permissive

prune *verb* cut, clip, dock, reduce, shape, shorten, snip, trim

pry *verb* be inquisitive, be nosy (*informal*), interfere, intrude, meddle, poke, snoop (*informal*)

prying *adjective* inquisitive, curious, interfering, meddlesome, meddling, nosy (*informal*), snooping (*informal*), spying

psalm *noun* hymn, chant

pseudo- *adjective* false, artificial, fake, imitation, mock, phoney or phony (*informal*), pretended, sham, spurious

> **Antonyms**

actual, authentic, bona fide, genuine, honest, real, sincere, true

pseudonym *noun* false name, alias, assumed name, incognito, nom de plume, pen name

psyche *noun* soul, anima, individuality, mind, personality, self, spirit

psychiatrist *noun* psychotherapist, analyst, headshrinker (*slang*), psychoanalyst, psychologist, shrink (*slang*), therapist

psychic *adjective* 1 supernatural, mystic, occult 2 mental, psychological, spiritual

psychological *adjective* 1 mental, cerebral, cognitive, intellectual 2 imaginary, all in the mind, irrational, psychosomatic, unreal

psychology *noun* 1 behaviourism, science of mind, study of personality 2 *Informal* way of thinking, attitude, mental makeup, mental processes, thought processes, what makes one tick

psychopath *noun* madman, headbanger (*informal*), headcase (*informal*), lunatic, maniac (*informal*), nutcase (*slang*), nutter (*Brit. slang*), psychotic, sociopath

psychotic *adjective* mad, certifiable, demented, deranged, insane, lunatic, mental (*slang*), non compos mentis, unbalanced

pub *or* **public house** *noun* tavern, bar, inn

puberty *noun* adolescence, pubescence, teens

public *adjective* 1 general, civic, common, national, popular, social, state, universal, widespread 2 open, accessible, communal, unrestricted 3 well-known, important, prominent, respected 4 known, acknowledged, obvious, open, overt, plain ♦ *noun* 5 people, citizens, community, electorate, everyone, nation, populace, society

> **Antonyms**

adjective ≠open: barred, closed, exclusive, inaccessible, personal, private, restricted, unavailable ≠known: hidden, secluded, secret, unknown, unrevealed

publication *noun* 1 pamphlet, brochure, issue, leaflet, magazine, newspaper, periodical, title, zine (*informal*) 2 announcement, broadcasting, declaration, disclosure, notification, proclamation, publishing, reporting

publicity *noun* advertising, attention, boost, hype, plug (*informal*), press, promotion

publicize *verb* advertise, hype, make known, play up, plug (*informal*), promote, push

> **Antonyms**

conceal, contain, cover up, keep dark, keep secret, suppress, withhold

public-spirited *adjective* altruistic, charitable, humanitarian, philanthropic, unselfish

publish *verb* 1 put out, issue, print, produce 2 announce, advertise, broadcast, circulate, disclose, divulge, proclaim, publicize, reveal, spread

pucker *verb* 1 wrinkle, contract, crease, draw together, gather, knit, purse, screw up, tighten ♦ *noun* 2 wrinkle, crease, fold

pudding *noun* dessert, afters (*Brit. informal*), pud (*informal*), sweet

puerile *adjective* childish, babyish, foolish, immature, juvenile, silly, trivial

> **Antonyms**

adult, grown-up, mature, sensible

puff *noun* 1 blast, breath, draught, gust, whiff 2 smoke, drag (*slang*), pull ♦ *verb* 3 blow, breathe, exhale, gasp, gulp, pant, wheeze **4** smoke, drag (*slang*), draw, inhale, pull at *or* on, suck **5** *usually with up* swell, bloat, dilate, distend, expand, inflate

puffy *adjective* swollen, bloated, distended, enlarged, puffed up

pugilist *noun* boxer, fighter, prizefighter

pugnacious *adjective* aggressive, belligerent, combative, hot-tempered, quarrelsome

➤ **Antonyms**
conciliatory, peaceful, peace-loving, placatory

pull *verb* **1** draw, drag, haul, jerk, tow, trail, tug, yank **2** strain, dislocate, rip, sprain, stretch, tear, wrench **3** extract, draw out, gather, pick, pluck, remove, take out, uproot **4** *Informal* attract, draw, entice, lure, magnetize ♦ *noun* **5** tug, jerk, twitch, yank **6** puff, drag (*slang*), inhalation **7** *Informal* influence, clout (*informal*), muscle, power, weight

➤ **Antonyms**
verb ≠draw: drive, nudge, push, ram, shove, thrust ≠extract: implant, insert, plant ≠attract: deter, discourage, put one off, repel ♦ *noun* ≠tug: nudge, push, shove, thrust

pull down *verb* demolish, bulldoze, destroy, raze, remove

➤ **Antonyms**
build, construct, erect, put up, raise, set up

pull off *verb* *Informal* succeed, accomplish, carry out, do the trick, manage

pull out *verb* withdraw, depart, evacuate, leave, quit, retreat

pull through *verb* survive, get better, rally, recover

pull up *verb* **1** stop, brake, halt **2** reprimand, admonish, bawl out (*informal*), rap over the knuckles, read the riot act, rebuke, reprove, slap on the wrist, tear (someone) off a strip (*Brit. informal*), tell off (*informal*)

pulp *noun* **1** paste, mash, mush **2** flesh, soft part ♦ *verb* **3** crush,

mash, pulverize, squash ♦ *adjective* **4** cheap, lurid, rubbishy, trashy

pulsate *verb* throb, beat, palpitate, pound, pulse, quiver, thump

pulse *noun* **1** beat, beating, pulsation, rhythm, throb, throbbing, vibration ♦ *verb* **2** beat, pulsate, throb, vibrate

pulverize *verb* **1** crush, granulate, grind, mill, pound **2** defeat, annihilate, crush, demolish, destroy, flatten, smash, wreck

pummel *verb* beat, batter, hammer, pound, punch, strike, thump

pump *verb* **1** *often with* **into** drive, force, inject, pour, push, send, supply **2** interrogate, cross-examine, probe, quiz

pun *noun* play on words, double entendre, quip, witticism

punch[1] *verb* **1** hit, belt (*informal*), bop (*informal*), box, pummel, smash, sock (*slang*), strike, swipe (*informal*) ♦ *noun* **2** blow, bop (*informal*), hit, jab, sock (*slang*), swipe (*informal*), wallop (*informal*) **3** *Informal* effectiveness, bite, drive, forcefulness, impact, verve, vigour

punch[2] *verb* pierce, bore, cut, drill, perforate, prick, puncture, stamp

punctilious *adjective* *Formal* particular, exact, finicky, formal, fussy, meticulous, nice, precise, proper, strict

punctual *adjective* on time, exact, on the dot, precise, prompt, timely

➤ **Antonyms**
behind, behindhand, belated, delayed, late, overdue, tardy, unpunctual

punctuality *noun* promptness, promptitude, readiness

punctuate *verb* **1** interrupt, break, intersperse, pepper, sprinkle **2** emphasize, accentuate, stress, underline

puncture *noun* **1** hole, break, cut, damage, leak, nick, opening, slit **2** <u>flat tyre</u>, flat ◆ *verb* **3** <u>pierce</u>, bore, cut, nick, penetrate, perforate, prick, rupture

pungent *adjective* <u>strong</u>, acrid, bitter, hot, peppery, piquant, sharp, sour, spicy, tart

➤ **Antonyms**

bland, dull, mild, moderate, tasteless, weak

punish *verb* <u>discipline</u>, castigate, chasten, chastise, correct, penalize, sentence

punishable *adjective* <u>culpable</u>, blameworthy, criminal, indictable

punishing *adjective* <u>hard</u>, arduous, backbreaking, exhausting, gruelling, strenuous, taxing, tiring, wearing

➤ **Antonyms**

cushy (*informal*), easy, effortless, light, simple, undemanding, unexacting, untaxing

punishment *noun* <u>penalty</u>, chastening, chastisement, correction, discipline, penance, retribution

punitive *adjective* <u>retaliatory</u>, in reprisal, retaliative

punt *verb* **1** <u>bet</u>, back, gamble, lay, stake, wager ◆ *noun* **2** <u>bet</u>, gamble, stake, wager

punter *noun* **1** <u>gambler</u>, backer, better **2** *Informal* <u>person</u>, man in the street

puny *adjective* <u>feeble</u>, frail, little, sickly, stunted, tiny, weak

➤ **Antonyms**

brawny, burly, healthy, husky (*informal*), powerful, robust, strong, sturdy

pupil *noun* <u>learner</u>, beginner, disciple, novice, schoolboy or schoolgirl, student

➤ **Antonyms**

coach, guru, instructor, master or mistress, schoolmaster or schoolmistress, schoolteacher, teacher, trainer, tutor

puppet *noun* **1** <u>marionette</u>, doll **2** <u>pawn</u>, cat's-paw, instrument, mouthpiece, stooge, tool

purchase *verb* **1** <u>buy</u>, acquire, come by, gain, get, obtain, pay for, pick up, score (*slang*) ◆ *noun* **2** <u>buy</u>, acquisition, asset, gain, investment, possession, property **3** <u>grip</u>, foothold, hold, leverage, support

➤ **Antonyms**

verb ≠<u>buy</u>: market, merchandise, peddle, retail, sell, trade in

pure *adjective* **1** <u>unmixed</u>, authentic, flawless, genuine, natural, neat, real, simple, straight, unalloyed **2** <u>clean</u>, germ-free, sanitary, spotless, squeaky-clean, sterilized, uncontaminated, unpolluted, untainted, wholesome **3** <u>innocent</u>, blameless, chaste, impeccable, modest, squeakyclean, uncorrupted, unsullied, virginal, virtuous **4** <u>complete</u>, absolute, outright, sheer, thorough, unmitigated, unqualified, utter

➤ **Antonyms**

≠<u>unmixed</u>: adulterated, alloyed, flawed, imperfect, mixed ≠<u>clean</u>: contaminated, dirty, filthy, impure, infected, polluted, tainted ≠<u>innocent</u>: contaminated, corrupt, guilty, immodest, immoral, impure, indecent, sinful, unchaste ≠<u>complete</u>: qualified

purely *adverb* <u>absolutely</u>, completely, entirely, exclusively, just, merely, only, simply, solely, wholly

purge *verb* **1** <u>get rid of</u>, do away with, eradicate, expel, exterminate, remove, wipe out ◆ *noun* **2** <u>removal</u>, ejection, elimination, eradication, expulsion

purify *verb* **1** <u>clean</u>, clarify, cleanse, decontaminate, disinfect, refine, sanitize, wash **2** <u>absolve</u>, cleanse, redeem, sanctify

➤ **Antonyms**

≠<u>clean</u>: contaminate, corrupt, defile, foul, infect, pollute, soil, taint ≠<u>absolve</u>: stain, sully, taint, vitiate

purist *noun* <u>stickler</u>, formalist, pedant

puritan *noun* **1** <u>moralist</u>, fanatic, prude, rigorist, zealot ◆ *adjective* **2** <u>strict</u>, ascetic, austere, moralistic, narrow-minded, prudish, severe, strait-laced

puritanical *adjective* **1** <u>strict</u>, ascetic, austere, narrow-minded, proper, prudish, puritan, severe, strait-laced

► **Antonyms**

broad-minded, indulgent, liberal, permissive, tolerant

purity *noun* **1** <u>cleanness</u>, cleanliness, faultlessness, immaculateness, pureness, wholesomeness **2** <u>innocence</u>, chasteness, chastity, decency, honesty, integrity, virginity, virtue

► **Antonyms**

≠<u>cleanness</u>: contamination, impurity ≠<u>innocence</u>: impurity, unchasteness, vice, wickedness

purloin *verb Formal* <u>steal</u>, appropriate, filch, nick (*slang, chiefly Brit.*), pilfer, pinch (*informal*), swipe (*slang*), thieve

purport *verb* **1** <u>claim</u>, allege, assert, profess ◆ *noun* **2** <u>significance</u>, drift, gist, idea, implication, import, meaning

purpose *noun* **1** <u>reason</u>, aim, idea, intention, object, point **2** <u>aim</u>, ambition, desire, end, goal, hope, intention, object, plan, wish **3** <u>determination</u>, firmness, persistence, resolution, resolve, single-mindedness, tenacity, will **4 on purpose** <u>deliberately</u>, designedly, intentionally, knowingly, purposely

purposeless *adjective* <u>pointless</u>, aimless, empty, motiveless, needless, senseless, uncalled-for, unnecessary

purposely *adverb* <u>deliberately</u>, consciously, expressly, intentionally, knowingly, on purpose, with intent

► **Antonyms**

accidentally, by accident, by chance, by mistake, inadvertently, unconsciously, unintentionally, unknowingly, unwittingly

purse *noun* **1** <u>pouch</u>, money-bag, wallet **2** <u>money</u>, exchequer, funds, means, resources, treasury, wealth ◆ *verb* **3** <u>pucker</u>, contract, pout, press together, tighten

pursue *verb* **1** <u>follow</u>, chase, dog, hound, hunt, hunt down, run after, shadow, stalk, tail (*informal*), track **2** <u>try for</u>, aim for, desire, seek, strive for, work towards **3** <u>engage in</u>, carry on, conduct, perform, practise **4** <u>continue</u>, carry on, keep on, maintain, persevere in, persist in, proceed

► **Antonyms**

≠<u>follow</u>: avoid, flee, give (someone or something) a wide berth, keep away from, run away from, shun, steer clear of ≠<u>try for</u>: eschew, fight shy of

pursuit *noun* **1** <u>pursuing</u>, chase, hunt, quest, search, seeking, trailing **2** <u>occupation</u>, activity, hobby, interest, line, pastime, pleasure

purvey *verb* <u>supply</u>, cater, deal in, furnish, provide, sell, trade in

push *verb* **1** <u>shove</u>, depress, drive, press, propel, ram, thrust **2** <u>make or force one's way</u>, elbow, jostle, move, shoulder, shove, squeeze, thrust **3** <u>urge</u>, encourage, gee up, hurry, impel, incite, persuade, press, spur ◆ *noun* **4** <u>shove</u>, butt, nudge, thrust **5** *Informal* <u>drive</u>, ambition, dynamism, energy, enterprise, go (*informal*), initiative, vigour, vitality **6 the push** *Informal, chiefly Brit.* <u>dismissal</u>, discharge, one's cards (*informal*), the boot (*slang*), the sack (*informal*)

► **Antonyms**

verb ≠<u>shove</u>: drag, draw, haul, jerk, pull, tow, trail, tug, yank ≠<u>urge</u>: deter, discourage, dissuade, put off ◆ *noun* ≠<u>shove</u>: jerk, pull, tug, yank

pushed *adjective* *Informal, often with* **for** <u>short of</u>, hurried, pressed, rushed, under pressure

pushover *noun* *Informal* **1** <u>piece of cake</u> (*Brit. informal*), breeze (*U.S. & Canad. informal*), child's play (*informal*), cinch (*slang*), doddle (*Brit. slang*), picnic (*informal*), plain sailing, walkover (*informal*) **2** <u>sucker</u> (*slang*), easy game (*informal*), easy or soft mark (*informal*), mug (*Brit.*

slang), soft touch (slang), walk-over (informal)

➤ **Antonyms**

≠**piece of cake:** challenge, hassle (informal), ordeal, test, trial, undertaking

pushy adjective <u>forceful</u>, ambitious, assertive, bold, brash, bumptious, obtrusive, presumptuous, self-assertive

➤ **Antonyms**

meek, quiet, reserved, retiring, self-effacing, shy, timid, unassertive, unassuming, unobtrusive

pussyfoot verb <u>hedge</u>, beat about the bush, be noncommittal, equivocate, flannel (Brit. informal), hum and haw, prevaricate, sit on the fence

put verb 1 <u>place</u>, deposit, lay, position, rest, set, settle, situate 2 <u>express</u>, phrase, state, utter, word 3 <u>throw</u>, cast, fling, heave, hurl, lob, pitch, toss

put across or **over** verb <u>communicate</u>, convey, explain, get across, make clear, make oneself understood

put aside or **by** verb <u>save</u>, deposit, lay by, stockpile, store

put away verb 1 <u>save</u>, deposit, keep, put by 2 Informal <u>commit</u>, certify, institutionalize, lock up 3 Informal <u>consume</u>, devour, eat up, gobble, wolf down 4 <u>put back</u>, replace, tidy away

put down verb 1 <u>record</u>, enter, set down, take down, write down 2 <u>repress</u>, crush, quash, quell, stamp out, suppress 3 usually with to <u>attribute</u>, ascribe, impute, set down 4 <u>put to sleep</u>, destroy, do away with, put out of its misery 5 Slang <u>humiliate</u>, disparage, mortify, shame, slight, snub

put forward verb <u>recommend</u>, advance, nominate, propose, submit, suggest, tender

put off verb 1 <u>postpone</u>, defer, delay, hold over, put on the back burner (informal), take a rain check on (U.S. & Canad. informal) 2 <u>disconcert</u>, confuse, dis-

comfit, dismay, faze, nonplus, perturb, throw (informal), unsettle 3 <u>discourage</u>, dishearten, dissuade

➤ **Antonyms**

≠**discourage:** egg on, encourage, gee up, incite, persuade, prompt, push, spur, urge

put on verb 1 <u>don</u>, change into, dress, get dressed in, slip into 2 <u>fake</u>, affect, assume, feign, pretend, sham, simulate 3 <u>present</u>, do, mount, produce, show, stage 4 <u>add</u>, gain, increase by

➤ **Antonyms**

≠**don:** cast off, doff, remove, shed, slip off, slip out of, take off, undress

put out verb 1 <u>annoy</u>, anger, exasperate, irk, irritate, nettle, vex 2 <u>extinguish</u>, blow out, douse, quench 3 <u>inconvenience</u>, bother, discomfit, discommode, impose upon, incommode, trouble

putrid adjective <u>rotten</u>, bad, decayed, decomposed, off, putrefied, rancid, rotting, spoiled

➤ **Antonyms**

fresh, pure, sweet, uncontaminated, wholesome

put up verb 1 <u>build</u>, construct, erect, fabricate, raise 2 <u>accommodate</u>, board, house, lodge, take in 3 <u>submit</u>, nominate, offer, present, propose, put forward, recommend 4 **put up with** Informal <u>stand</u>, abide, bear, endure, stand for, swallow, take, tolerate

➤ **Antonyms**

≠**build:** demolish, destroy, flatten, knock down, level, pull down, raze, tear down ≠**stand:** not stand for, object to, oppose, protest against, take exception to

puzzle verb 1 <u>perplex</u>, baffle, bewilder, confound, confuse, mystify, stump 2 <u>problem</u>, conundrum, enigma, mystery, paradox, poser, question, riddle

puzzled adjective <u>perplexed</u>, at a loss, at sea, baffled, bewildered, confused, lost, mystified

puzzlement noun perplexity, bafflement, bewilderment, confusion, doubt, mystification

puzzling adjective perplexing, abstruse, baffling, bewildering, enigmatic, incomprehensible, involved, mystifying

➤ **Antonyms**

clear, comprehensible, easy, obvious, patent, plain, simple, unambiguous, unequivocal

Q q

quack noun charlatan, fake, fraud, humbug, impostor, mountebank, phoney or phony (informal)

quaff verb drink, down, gulp, imbibe, swallow, swig (informal)

quagmire noun bog, fen, marsh, mire, morass, quicksand, slough, swamp

quail verb shrink, blanch, blench, cower, cringe, falter, flinch, have cold feet (informal), recoil, shudder

quaint adjective 1 unusual, bizarre, curious, droll, eccentric, fanciful, odd, old-fashioned, peculiar, queer, rum (Brit. slang), singular, strange 2 old-fashioned, antiquated, old-world, picturesque

➤ **Antonyms**

≠unusual: normal, ordinary ≠old-fashioned: fashionable, modern, new, up-to-date

quake verb shake, move, quiver, rock, shiver, shudder, tremble, vibrate

qualification noun 1 attribute, ability, aptitude, capability, eligibility, fitness, quality, skill, suitability 2 condition, caveat, limitation, modification, proviso, requirement, reservation, rider, stipulation

qualified adjective 1 capable, able, adept, competent, efficient, experienced, expert, fit, practised, proficient, skilful, trained 2 restricted, bounded, conditional, confined, contingent, limited, modified, provisional, reserved

➤ **Antonyms**

≠capable: amateur, apprentice, self-styled, self-taught, trainee, uncertificated, unqualified, untrained ≠restricted: categorical, outright, unconditional, unequivocal, whole-hearted

qualify verb 1 certify, empower, equip, fit, permit, prepare, ready, train 2 moderate, diminish, ease, lessen, limit, reduce, regulate, restrain, restrict, soften, temper

➤ **Antonyms**

≠certify: ban, debar, disqualify, forbid, preclude, prevent

quality noun 1 excellence, calibre, distinction, grade, merit, position, rank, standing, status 2 characteristic, aspect, attribute, condition, feature, mark, property, trait 3 nature, character, kind, make, sort

qualm noun misgiving, anxiety, apprehension, compunction, disquiet, doubt, hesitation, scruple, twinge or pang of conscience, uneasiness

quandary noun difficulty, cleft stick, dilemma, impasse, plight, predicament, puzzle, strait

quantity noun 1 amount, lot, number, part, sum, total 2 size, bulk, capacity, extent, length, magnitude, mass, measure, volume

quarrel noun 1 disagreement, argument, brawl, breach, contention, controversy, dispute, dissension, feud, fight, row, squabble, tiff ♦ verb 2 disagree, argue, bicker, brawl, clash, differ, dispute, fall out (informal), fight, row, squabble

➤ **Antonyms**

noun ≠disagreement: accord,

agreement, concord ♦ *verb* ≠dis-agree: agree, get on *or* along (with)

quarrelsome *adjective* argumentative, belligerent, combative, contentious, disputatious, pugnacious

➤ **Antonyms**
easy-going, equable, even-tempered, placid

quarry *noun* prey, aim, game, goal, objective, prize, victim

quarter *noun* **1** district, area, locality, neighbourhood, part, place, province, region, side, zone **2** mercy, clemency, compassion, forgiveness, leniency, pity ♦ *verb* **3** accommodate, billet, board, house, lodge, place, post, station

quarters *plural noun* lodgings, abode, barracks, billet, chambers, dwelling, habitation, residence, rooms

quash *verb* **1** annul, cancel, invalidate, overrule, overthrow, rescind, reverse, revoke **2** suppress, beat, crush, overthrow, put down, quell, repress, squash, subdue

quasi- *adjective* pseudo-, apparent, seeming, semi-, so-called, would-be

quaver *verb* **1** tremble, flicker, flutter, quake, quiver, shake, vibrate, waver ♦ *noun* **2** trembling, quiver, shake, tremble, tremor, vibration

queasy *adjective* **1** sick, bilious, green around the gills (*informal*), ill, nauseated, off colour, squeamish, upset **2** uneasy, anxious, fidgety, ill at ease, restless, troubled, uncertain, worried

queen *noun* **1** sovereign, consort, monarch, ruler **2** ideal, mistress, model, star

queer *adjective* **1** strange, abnormal, curious, droll, extraordinary, funny, odd, peculiar, uncommon, unusual, weird **2** faint, dizzy, giddy, light-headed, queasy

➤ **Antonyms**
≠strange: common, conventional, customary, normal, ordinary, orthodox, regular

quell *verb* **1** suppress, conquer, crush, defeat, overcome, overpower, put down, quash, subdue, vanquish **2** assuage, allay, appease, calm, mollify, pacify, quiet, soothe

quench *verb* **1** satisfy, allay, appease, sate, satiate, slake **2** put out, crush, douse, extinguish, smother, stifle, suppress

querulous *adjective* complaining, captious, carping, critical, discontented, dissatisfied, fault-finding, grumbling, peevish, whining

➤ **Antonyms**
contented, easy to please, equable, placid, uncomplaining, uncritical, undemanding

query *noun* **1** question, doubt, inquiry, objection, problem, suspicion ♦ *verb* **2** doubt, challenge, disbelieve, dispute, distrust, mistrust, suspect **3** ask, inquire *or* enquire, question

quest *noun* search, adventure, crusade, enterprise, expedition, hunt, journey, mission

question *noun* **1** issue, motion, point, point at issue, proposal, proposition, subject, theme, topic **2** difficulty, argument, contention, controversy, dispute, doubt, problem, query **3** inquiry, examination, interrogation, investigation **4 in question** under discussion, at issue, in doubt, open to debate **5 out of the question** impossible, inconceivable, unthinkable ♦ *verb* **6** ask, cross-examine, examine, inquire, interrogate, interview, probe, quiz **7** dispute, challenge, disbelieve, doubt, mistrust, oppose, query, suspect

➤ **Antonyms**
noun ≠inquiry: answer, reply ♦ *verb* ≠ask: answer, reply ≠dispute: accept, believe, buy (*slang*), swallow (*informal*), take

on board, take on trust

questionable *adjective* <u>dubious</u>, controversial, debatable, dodgy (*Brit., Austral., & N.Z. informal*), doubtful, iffy (*informal*), moot, suspect, suspicious

➤ **Antonyms**

certain, incontrovertible, indisputable, straightforward, unequivocal

queue *noun* <u>line</u>, chain, file, sequence, series, string, train

quibble *verb* 1 <u>split hairs</u>, carp, cavil ♦ *noun* 2 <u>objection</u>, cavil, complaint, criticism, nicety, niggle

quick *adjective* 1 <u>fast</u>, brisk, express, fleet, hasty, rapid, speedy, swift 2 <u>brief</u>, cursory, hasty, hurried, perfunctory 3 <u>sudden</u>, prompt 4 <u>intelligent</u>, acute, alert, astute, bright (*informal*), clever, perceptive, quick-witted, sharp, shrewd, smart 5 <u>deft</u>, adept, adroit, dexterous, skilful 6 <u>excitable</u>, irascible, irritable, passionate, testy, touchy

➤ **Antonyms**

≠<u>fast</u>: slow, sluggish ≠<u>brief</u>: gradual, long ≠<u>intelligent</u>, <u>deft</u>: inexpert, maladroit, stupid, unintelligent, unskilful ≠<u>excitable</u>: calm, deliberate, patient, restrained

quicken *verb* 1 <u>speed</u>, accelerate, expedite, hasten, hurry, impel, precipitate 2 <u>invigorate</u>, arouse, energize, excite, incite, inspire, revive, stimulate, vitalize

quickly *adverb* <u>swiftly</u>, abruptly, apace, briskly, fast, hastily, hurriedly, promptly, pronto (*informal*), rapidly, soon, speedily

➤ **Antonyms**

carefully, eventually, slowly, sluggishly, unhurriedly

quick-tempered *adjective* <u>hot-tempered</u>, choleric, fiery, irascible, irritable, quarrelsome, ratty (*Brit. & N.Z. informal*), testy, tetchy

➤ **Antonyms**

cool, dispassionate, phlegmatic, placid, tolerant

quick-witted *adjective* <u>clever</u>, alert, astute, bright (*informal*), keen, perceptive, sharp, shrewd, smart

➤ **Antonyms**

dull, obtuse, slow, stupid, thick (*informal*)

quiet *adjective* 1 <u>silent</u>, hushed, inaudible, low, noiseless, peaceful, soft, soundless 2 <u>calm</u>, mild, peaceful, placid, restful, serene, smooth, tranquil 3 <u>undisturbed</u>, isolated, private, secluded, sequestered, unfrequented 4 <u>reserved</u>, gentle, meek, mild, retiring, sedate, shy ♦ *noun* 5 <u>peace</u>, calmness, ease, quietness, repose, rest, serenity, silence, stillness, tranquillity

➤ **Antonyms**

adjective ≠<u>silent</u>: deafening, ear-splitting, high-volume, loud, noisy, stentorian ≠<u>calm</u>: agitated, alert, excitable, exciting, frenetic, troubled, turbulent, violent ≠<u>undisturbed</u>: bustling, busy, crowded, exciting, fashionable, lively, popular, vibrant ≠<u>reserved</u>: excitable, loquacious, passionate, talkative, verbose ♦ *noun* ≠<u>peace</u>: activity, bustle, commotion, din, disturbance, noise, racket

quieten *verb* 1 <u>silence</u>, compose, hush, muffle, mute, quell, quiet, stifle, still, stop, subdue 2 <u>soothe</u>, allay, appease, blunt, calm, deaden, dull

➤ **Antonyms**

≠<u>soothe</u>: aggravate, exacerbate, intensify, provoke, upset, worsen

quietly *adverb* 1 <u>silently</u>, in an undertone, inaudibly, in silence, mutely, noiselessly, softly 2 <u>calmly</u>, mildly, patiently, placidly, serenely

quietness *noun* <u>peace</u>, calm, hush, quiet, silence, stillness, tranquillity

quilt *noun* <u>bedspread</u>, continental quilt, counterpane, coverlet, duvet, eiderdown

quintessence *noun* <u>essence</u>, distillation, soul, spirit

quintessential *adjective* ultimate, archetypal, definitive, prototypical, typical

quip *noun* joke, gibe, jest, pleasantry, retort, riposte, sally, wisecrack (*informal*), witticism

quirk *noun* peculiarity, aberration, characteristic, eccentricity, foible, habit, idiosyncrasy, kink, mannerism, oddity, trait

quirky *adjective* odd, eccentric, idiosyncratic, offbeat, peculiar, unusual

quit *verb* 1 stop, abandon, cease, discontinue, drop, end, give up, halt 2 resign, abdicate, go, leave, pull out, retire, step down (*informal*) 3 depart, go, leave, pull out

➤ **Antonyms**
≠stop: complete, continue, finish, go on with, see through

quite *adverb* 1 somewhat, fairly, moderately, rather, reasonably, relatively 2 absolutely, completely, entirely, fully, perfectly, totally, wholly 3 truly, in fact, in reality, in truth, really

quiver *verb* 1 shake, oscillate, quake, quaver, shiver, shudder, tremble, vibrate ♦ *noun* 2 shake, oscillation, shiver, shudder, tremble, tremor, vibration

quixotic *adjective* unrealistic, dreamy, fanciful, idealistic, impractical, romantic

quiz *noun* 1 examination, investigation, questioning, test ♦ *verb* 2 question, ask, examine, interrogate, investigate

quizzical *adjective* mocking, arch, questioning, sardonic, teasing

quota *noun* share, allowance, assignment, part, portion, ration, slice, whack (*informal*)

quotation *noun* 1 passage, citation, excerpt, extract, quote (*informal*), reference 2 *Commerce* estimate, charge, cost, figure, price, quote (*informal*), rate, tender

quote *verb* repeat, cite, detail, instance, name, recall, recite, recollect, refer to

R r

rabble *noun* 1 mob, canaille, crowd, herd, horde, swarm, throng

rabid *adjective* 1 fanatical, extreme, fervent, irrational, narrow-minded, zealous 2 mad, hydrophobic

➤ **Antonyms**
≠fanatical: half-hearted, moderate, wishy-washy (*informal*)

race[1] *noun* 1 contest, chase, competition, dash, pursuit, rivalry ♦ *verb* 2 compete, contest, run 3 run, career, dart, dash, fly, gallop, hurry, speed, tear, zoom

race[2] *noun* people, blood, folk, nation, stock, tribe, type

racial *adjective* ethnic, ethnological, folk, genealogical, genetic, national, tribal

rack *noun* 1 frame, framework, stand, structure ♦ *verb* 2 torture, afflict, agonize, crucify, harrow, oppress, pain, torment

racket *noun* 1 noise, clamour, din, disturbance, fuss, outcry, pandemonium, row 2 fraud, scheme

racy *adjective* 1 risqué, bawdy, blue, naughty, near the knuckle (*informal*), smutty, suggestive 2 lively, animated, energetic, entertaining, exciting, sparkling, spirited

radiance *noun* 1 happiness, delight, gaiety, joy, pleasure, rapture, warmth 2 brightness, brilliance, glare, gleam, glow, light, lustre, shine

radiant *adjective* 1 happy, blissful, delighted, ecstatic, glowing, joyful, joyous, on cloud nine (*informal*), rapturous 2 bright, brilliant, gleaming, glittering, glowing, luminous, lustrous, shining

> ➤ Antonyms

≠<u>happy</u>: down in the dumps (*informal*), gloomy, miserable, sad, sombre, sorrowful ≠<u>bright</u>: black, dark, dull, gloomy, sombre

radiate *verb* **1** <u>spread out</u>, branch out, diverge, issue **2** <u>emit</u>, diffuse, give off *or* out, pour, scatter, send out, shed, spread

radical *adjective* **1** <u>revolutionary</u>, extremist, fanatical **2** <u>fundamental</u>, basic, deep-seated, innate, natural, profound **3** <u>extreme</u>, complete, drastic, entire, severe, sweeping, thorough ♦ *noun* **4** <u>extremist</u>, fanatic, militant, revolutionary

> ➤ Antonyms

adjective ≠<u>fundamental</u>: insignificant, minor, superficial, token, trivial ♦ *noun* ≠<u>extremist</u>: conservative, moderate, reactionary

raffle *noun* <u>draw</u>, lottery, sweep, sweepstake

ragamuffin *noun* <u>urchin</u>, guttersnipe

rage *noun* **1** <u>fury</u>, anger, frenzy, ire, madness, passion, rampage, wrath **2** <u>craze</u>, enthusiasm, fad (*informal*), fashion, latest thing, vogue ♦ *verb* **3** <u>be furious</u>, blow one's top, blow up (*informal*), fly off the handle (*informal*), fume, go ballistic (*slang, chiefly U.S.*), go up the wall (*slang*), lose it (*informal*), lose one's temper, lose the plot (*informal*), seethe, storm

> ➤ Antonyms

noun ≠<u>fury</u>: calmness, equanimity, good humour, joy, pleasure, resignation ♦ *verb* ≠<u>be furious</u>: accept, keep one's cool, remain unruffled, resign oneself to, stay calm

ragged *adjective* **1** <u>shabby</u>, in rags, in tatters, tatty, threadbare, torn, unkempt **2** <u>rough</u>, jagged, rugged, serrated, uneven, unfinished

> ➤ Antonyms

≠<u>shabby</u>: fashionable, smart, well-dressed

raging *adjective* <u>furious</u>, beside oneself, enraged, fuming, incensed, infuriated, mad, raving, seething

rags *plural noun* <u>old clothes</u>, cast-offs, tattered clothing, tatters

> ➤ Antonyms

finery, gladrags, Sunday best

raid *noun* **1** <u>attack</u>, foray, incursion, inroad, invasion, sally, sortie ♦ *verb* **2** <u>attack</u>, assault, foray, invade, pillage, plunder, sack

raider *noun* <u>attacker</u>, invader, marauder, plunderer, robber, thief

railing *noun* <u>fence</u>, balustrade, barrier, paling, rails

rain *noun* **1** <u>rainfall</u>, cloudburst, deluge, downpour, drizzle, fall, raindrops, showers ♦ *verb* **2** <u>pour</u>, bucket down (*informal*), come down in buckets (*informal*), drizzle, pelt (down), teem **3** <u>fall</u>, deposit, drop, shower, sprinkle

rainy *adjective* <u>wet</u>, damp, drizzly, showery

> ➤ Antonyms

arid, dry, fine, sunny

raise *verb* **1** <u>lift</u>, elevate, heave, hoist, rear, uplift **2** <u>increase</u>, advance, amplify, boost, enhance, enlarge, heighten, inflate, intensify, magnify, strengthen **3** <u>collect</u>, assemble, form, gather, mass, obtain, rally, recruit **4** <u>cause</u>, create, engender, occasion, originate, produce, provoke, start **5** <u>bring up</u>, develop, nurture, rear **6** <u>put forward</u>, advance, broach, introduce, moot, suggest **7** <u>build</u>, construct, erect, put up

> ➤ Antonyms

≠<u>increase</u>: cut, decrease, diminish, drop, lessen, lower, reduce, sink ≠<u>build</u>: demolish, destroy, level, ruin, wreck

rake¹ *verb* **1** <u>gather</u>, collect, remove **2** <u>search</u>, comb, scour, scrutinize

rake² *noun* <u>libertine</u>, debauchee, lecher, playboy, roué, swinger (*slang*)

> ➤ Antonyms

ascetic, celibate

rakish adjective underlined: dashing, dapper, debonair, devil-may-care, jaunty, natty (informal), raffish, smart

rally noun 1 gathering, assembly, congress, convention, meeting 2 recovery, improvement, recuperation, revival ♦ verb 3 reassemble, regroup, reorganize, unite 4 gather, assemble, collect, convene, marshal, muster, round up, unite 5 recover, get better, improve, recuperate, revive

➤ **Antonyms**

noun ≠recovery: collapse, deterioration, relapse, turn for the worse ♦ verb ≠gather: disband, disperse, separate, split up ≠recover: deteriorate, fail, get worse, relapse, take a turn for the worse, worsen

ram verb 1 hit, butt, crash, dash, drive, force, impact, smash 2 cram, crowd, force, jam, stuff, thrust

ramble verb 1 walk, range, roam, rove, saunter, stray, stroll, wander 2 babble, rabbit (on) (Brit. informal), waffle (informal, chiefly Brit.), witter on (informal) ♦ noun 3 walk, hike, roaming, roving, saunter, stroll, tour

rambler noun walker, hiker, rover, wanderer, wayfarer

rambling adjective long-winded, circuitous, digressive, disconnected, discursive, disjointed, incoherent, wordy

➤ **Antonyms**

coherent, concise, direct, to the point

ramification noun ramifications consequences, developments, results, sequel, upshot

ramp noun slope, gradient, incline, rise

rampage verb 1 go berserk, rage, run amok, run riot, storm ♦ noun 2 on the rampage berserk, amok, out of control, raging, riotous, violent, wild

rampant adjective 1 widespread, prevalent, profuse, rife, spreading like wildfire, unchecked, uncontrolled, unrestrained 2 Heraldry upright, erect, rearing, standing

rampart noun defence, bastion, bulwark, fence, fortification, wall

ramshackle adjective rickety, crumbling, decrepit, derelict, flimsy, shaky, tumbledown, unsafe, unsteady

➤ **Antonyms**

solid, stable, steady, well-built

rancid adjective rotten, bad, fetid, foul, off, putrid, rank, sour, stale, strong-smelling, tainted

➤ **Antonyms**

fresh, pure, undecayed

rancour noun hatred, animosity, bad blood, bitterness, hate, ill feeling, ill will

random adjective 1 chance, accidental, adventitious, casual, fortuitous, haphazard, hit or miss, incidental ♦ noun 2 at random haphazardly, arbitrarily, by chance, randomly, unsystematically, willy-nilly

➤ **Antonyms**

adjective ≠chance: definite, deliberate, intended, planned, premeditated, specific

randy adjective Informal lustful, amorous, aroused, horny (slang), hot, lascivious, turned-on (slang)

range noun 1 limits, area, bounds, orbit, province, radius, reach, scope, sphere 2 series, assortment, collection, gamut, lot, selection, variety ♦ verb 3 vary, extend, reach, run, stretch 4 roam, ramble, rove, traverse, wander

rangy adjective long-limbed, gangling, lanky, leggy, long-legged

rank[1] noun 1 status, caste, class, degree, division, grade, level, order, position, sort, type 2 row, column, file, group, line, range, series, tier ♦ verb 3 arrange, align, array, dispose, line up, order, sort

rank[2] adjective 1 absolute, arrant, blatant, complete, downright, flagrant, gross, sheer, thorough, total, utter 2 foul, bad, disgusting, noisome, noxious, offensive, rancid, revolting, stinking > abundant, dense, lush, luxuriant, profuse

rank and file noun general public, majority, mass, masses

rankle verb annoy, anger, gall, get on one's nerves (*informal*), irk, irritate, rile

ransack verb 1 search, comb, explore, go through, rummage, scour, turn inside out 2 plunder, loot, pillage, raid, strip

ransom noun payment, money, payoff, price

rant verb shout, cry, declaim, rave, roar, yell

rap verb 1 hit, crack, knock, strike, tap ♦ noun 2 blow, clout (*informal*), crack, knock, tap 3 *Slang* rebuke, blame, punishment, responsibility

rapacious adjective greedy, avaricious, grasping, insatiable, predatory, preying, voracious

rape verb 1 sexually assault, abuse, force, outrage, ravish, violate ♦ noun 2 sexual assault, outrage, ravishment, violation 3 desecration, abuse, defilement, violation

rapid adjective quick, brisk, express, fast, hasty, hurried, prompt, speedy, swift
> **Antonyms**
deliberate, gradual, leisurely, slow, tardy, unhurried

rapidity noun speed, alacrity, briskness, fleetness, haste, hurry, promptness, quickness, rush, swiftness, velocity

rapidly adverb quickly, briskly, fast, hastily, hurriedly, in haste, promptly, pronto (*informal*), speedily, swiftly

rapport noun bond, affinity, empathy, harmony, link, relationship, sympathy, tie, understanding

rapprochement noun reconciliation, detente, reunion
> **Antonyms**
dissension, falling-out, quarrel, schism

rapt adjective spellbound, absorbed, engrossed, enthralled, entranced, fascinated, gripped
> **Antonyms**
bored, detached, left cold, unaffected, uninterested, uninvolved, unmoved

rapture noun ecstasy, bliss, delight, euphoria, joy, rhapsody, seventh heaven, transport

rapturous adjective ecstatic, blissful, euphoric, in seventh heaven, joyful, overjoyed, over the moon (*informal*), transported

rare adjective 1 uncommon, few, infrequent, scarce, singular, sparse, strange, unusual 2 superb, choice, excellent, fine, great, peerless, superlative
> **Antonyms**
≠uncommon: abundant, bountiful, common, frequent, habitual, many, plentiful, profuse, regular

rarefied adjective exalted, elevated, high, lofty, noble, spiritual, sublime

rarely adverb seldom, hardly, hardly ever, infrequently
> **Antonyms**
commonly, frequently, often, regularly, usually

raring adjective As in raring to eager, desperate, enthusiastic, impatient, keen, longing, ready

rarity noun 1 curio, collector's item, find, gem, treasure 2 uncommonness, infrequency, scarcity, shortage, sparseness, strangeness, unusualness

rascal noun rogue, blackguard, devil, good-for-nothing, imp, ne'er-do-well, scamp, scoundrel, villain

rash[1] adjective reckless, careless, foolhardy, hasty, heedless, ill-advised, impetuous, imprudent, impulsive, incautious
> **Antonyms**
canny, careful, cautious, considered, premeditated, prudent, well-thought-out

rash[2] noun 1 outbreak, eruption 2 spate, flood, outbreak, plague, series, wave

rashness noun recklessness, carelessness, foolhardiness, hastiness, heedlessness, indiscretion, thoughtlessness

rate noun **1** degree, proportion, ratio, scale, standard **2** speed, pace, tempo, velocity **3** charge, cost, fee, figure, price **4 at any rate** in any case, anyhow, anyway, at all events ♦ verb **5** evaluate, consider, count, estimate, grade, measure, rank, reckon, value **6** deserve, be entitled to, be worthy of, merit

rather adverb **1** to some extent, a little, fairly, moderately, quite, relatively, somewhat, to some degree **2** preferably, more readily, more willingly, sooner

ratify verb approve, affirm, authorize, confirm, endorse, establish, sanction, uphold

► **Antonyms**

abrogate, annul, cancel, reject, repeal, repudiate, revoke

rating noun position, class, degree, grade, order, placing, rank, rate, status

ratio noun proportion, fraction, percentage, rate, relation

ration noun **1** allowance, allotment, helping, measure, part, portion, quota, share ♦ verb **2** limit, budget, control, restrict

rational adjective sensible, intelligent, logical, lucid, realistic, reasonable, sane, sound, wise

► **Antonyms**

insane, irrational, unreasonable, unsound

rationale noun reason, grounds, logic, motivation, philosophy, principle, raison d'être, theory

rationalize verb justify, account for, excuse, vindicate

rattle verb **1** clatter, bang, jangle **2** shake, bounce, jar, jolt, vibrate **3** Informal fluster, disconcert, disturb, faze, perturb, shake, upset

raucous adjective harsh, grating, hoarse, loud, noisy, rough, strident

► **Antonyms**

dulcet, mellifluous, quiet,
smooth, sweet

raunchy adjective Slang sexy, coarse, earthy, lusty, sexual, steamy (informal)

ravage verb **1** destroy, demolish, despoil, devastate, lay waste, ransack, ruin, spoil ♦ noun **2** ravages damage, destruction, devastation, havoc, ruin, ruination, spoliation ·

rave verb **1** rant, babble, be delirious, go mad (informal), rage, roar **2** Informal enthuse, be mad about (informal), be wild about (informal), gush, praise

ravenous adjective starving, famished, starved

► **Antonyms**

full, glutted, sated, satiated

ravine noun canyon, defile, gorge, gulch (U.S.), gully, pass

raving adjective mad, crazed, crazy, delirious, hysterical, insane, irrational, wild

ravish verb **1** enchant, captivate, charm, delight, enrapture, entrance, fascinate, spellbind **2** Literary rape, abuse, force, sexually assault, violate

ravishing adjective enchanting, beautiful, bewitching, charming, entrancing, gorgeous, lovely

raw adjective **1** uncooked, fresh, natural **2** unrefined, basic, coarse, crude, natural, rough, unfinished, unprocessed **3** inexperienced, callow, green, immature, new **4** chilly, biting, bitter, cold, freezing, parky (Brit. informal), piercing

► **Antonyms**

≠uncooked: baked, cooked, done ≠unrefined: finished, prepared, refined ≠inexperienced: experienced, practised, professional, skilled, trained

ray noun beam, bar, flash, gleam, shaft

raze verb destroy, demolish, flatten, knock down, level, pull down, ruin

re preposition concerning, about, apropos, regarding, with reference to, with regard to

reach verb 1 <u>arrive at</u>, attain, get to, make 2 <u>touch</u>, contact, extend to, grasp, stretch to 3 <u>contact</u>, communicate with, get hold of, get in touch with, get through to ♦ noun 4 <u>range</u>, capacity, distance, extension, extent, grasp, influence, power, scope, stretch

react verb 1 <u>act</u>, behave, function, operate, proceed, work 2 <u>respond</u>, answer, reply

reaction noun 1 <u>response</u>, answer, reply 2 <u>counteraction</u>, backlash, recoil 3 <u>conservatism</u>, the right

reactionary adjective 1 <u>conservative</u>, right-wing ♦ noun 2 <u>conservative</u>, die-hard, right-winger

> **Antonyms**

adjective, noun ≠<u>conservative</u>: progressive, radical, reformist, revolutionary

read verb 1 <u>look at</u>, peruse, pore over, scan, study 2 <u>understand</u>, comprehend, construe, decipher, discover, interpret, see 3 <u>register</u>, display, indicate, record, show

readable adjective 1 <u>enjoyable</u>, entertaining, enthralling, gripping, interesting 2 <u>legible</u>, clear, comprehensible, decipherable

> **Antonyms**

≠<u>enjoyable</u>: as dry as dust, boring, dull, heavy, turgid, unreadable ≠<u>legible</u>: illegible, incomprehensible, indecipherable, unintelligible, unreadable

readily adverb 1 <u>willingly</u>, eagerly, freely, gladly, quickly 2 <u>promptly</u>, easily, effortlessly, quickly, smoothly, speedily, unhesitatingly

> **Antonyms**

≠<u>willingly</u>: reluctantly, unwillingly ≠<u>promptly</u>: hesitatingly, slowly, with difficulty

readiness noun 1 <u>willingness</u>, eagerness, keenness 2 <u>promptness</u>, adroitness, dexterity, ease, facility

reading noun 1 <u>learning</u>, education, erudition, knowledge, schol-

arship 2 <u>perusal</u>, examination, inspection, scrutiny, study 3 <u>recital</u>, lesson, performance, sermon 4 <u>interpretation</u>, grasp, impression, version

ready adjective 1 <u>prepared</u>, arranged, fit, organized, primed, ripe, set 2 <u>willing</u>, agreeable, disposed, eager, glad, happy, inclined, keen, prone 3 <u>prompt</u>, alert, bright, clever, intelligent, keen, perceptive, quick, sharp, smart 4 <u>available</u>, accessible, convenient, handy, near, present

> **Antonyms**

≠<u>prepared</u>: immature, unequipped, unfit, unprepared ≠<u>willing</u>: disinclined, hesitant, loath, reluctant, unprepared, unwilling ≠<u>prompt</u>: slow ≠<u>available</u>: distant, inaccessible, late, unavailable

real adjective <u>genuine</u>, actual, authentic, factual, rightful, sincere, true, unfeigned, valid

> **Antonyms**

counterfeit, fake, false, feigned, imaginary, imitation, insincere

realistic adjective 1 <u>practical</u>, common-sense, down-to-earth, level-headed, matter-of-fact, real, sensible 2 <u>lifelike</u>, authentic, faithful, genuine, natural, true, true to life

> **Antonyms**

≠<u>practical</u>: fanciful, idealistic, impractical, unrealistic

reality noun <u>truth</u>, actuality, fact, realism, validity, verity

realization noun 1 <u>awareness</u>, cognizance, comprehension, conception, grasp, perception, recognition, understanding 2 <u>achievement</u>, accomplishment, fulfilment

realize verb 1 <u>become aware of</u>, comprehend, get the message, grasp, take in, understand 2 <u>achieve</u>, accomplish, carry out or through, complete, do, effect, fulfil, perform

really adverb <u>truly</u>, actually, certainly, genuinely, in actuality, indeed, in fact, positively, surely

realm noun 1 <u>kingdom</u>, country, domain, dominion, empire, land 2 <u>field</u>, area, branch, department, province, sphere, territory, world

reap verb 1 <u>collect</u>, bring in, cut, garner, gather, harvest 2 <u>get</u>, acquire, derive, gain, obtain

rear¹ noun 1 <u>back</u>, end, rearguard, stern, tail, tail end ◆ adjective 2 <u>back</u>, following, hind, last

➤ **Antonyms**

noun ≠<u>back</u>: bow, front, nose, stem, vanguard ◆ adjective ≠<u>back</u>: forward, front, leading

rear² verb 1 <u>bring up</u>, breed, educate, foster, nurture, raise, train 2 <u>rise</u>, loom, soar, tower

reason noun 1 <u>cause</u>, aim, goal, grounds, incentive, intention, motive, object, purpose 2 <u>sense</u>, intellect, judgment, logic, mind, rationality, sanity, soundness, understanding ◆ verb 3 <u>deduce</u>, conclude, infer, make out, think, work out 4 <u>reason with</u> or <u>persuade</u>, bring round (informal), prevail upon, talk into or out of, urge, win over

➤ **Antonyms**

noun ≠<u>sense</u>: emotion, feeling, instinct, sentiment

reasonable adjective 1 <u>sensible</u>, logical, plausible, practical, sane, sober, sound, tenable, wise 2 <u>fair</u>, equitable, fit, just, moderate, proper, right 3 <u>average</u>, fair, moderate, modest, O.K. or okay (informal)

➤ **Antonyms**

≠<u>sensible</u>: impossible, irrational, unintelligent, unreasonable, unsound ≠<u>fair</u>: unfair, unreasonable

reasoned adjective <u>sensible</u>, clear, logical, well-thought-out

reasoning noun <u>thinking</u>, analysis, logic, thought

reassure verb <u>encourage</u>, comfort, gee up, hearten, put or set one's mind at rest, restore confidence to

rebate noun <u>refund</u>, allowance, bonus, deduction, discount, reduction

rebel verb 1 <u>revolt</u>, mutiny, resist, rise up 2 <u>defy</u>, disobey, dissent ◆ noun 3 <u>revolutionist</u>, insurgent, revolutionist, secessionist 4 <u>nonconformist</u>, apostate, dissenter, heretic, schismatic ◆ adjective 5 <u>rebellious</u>, insurgent, insurrectionary, revolutionary

rebellion noun 1 <u>resistance</u>, mutiny, revolt, revolution, rising, uprising 2 <u>nonconformity</u>, defiance, heresy, schism

rebellious adjective 1 <u>revolutionary</u>, disloyal, disobedient, disorderly, insurgent, mutinous, rebel, seditious, unruly 2 <u>defiant</u>, difficult, refractory, resistant, unmanageable

➤ **Antonyms**

≠<u>revolutionary</u>: dutiful, loyal, obedient, patriotic, subordinate ≠<u>defiant</u>: dutiful, obedient, subservient

rebound verb 1 <u>bounce</u>, recoil, ricochet 2 <u>misfire</u>, backfire, boomerang, recoil

rebuff verb 1 <u>reject</u>, cold-shoulder, cut, knock back (slang), refuse, repulse, slight, snub, spurn, turn down ◆ noun 2 <u>rejection</u>, cold shoulder, kick in the teeth (slang), knock-back (slang), refusal, repulse, slap in the face (informal), slight, snub

➤ **Antonyms**

verb ≠<u>reject</u>: encourage, lead on (informal), submit to, welcome ◆ noun ≠<u>rejection</u>: come-on (informal), encouragement, thumbs up, welcome

rebuke verb 1 <u>scold</u>, admonish, castigate, censure, chide, dress down (informal), give a rocket (Brit. & N.Z. informal), haul (someone) over the coals (informal), reprimand, reprove, tear (someone) off a strip (informal), tell off (informal) ◆ noun 2 <u>scolding</u>, admonition, censure, dressing down (informal), reprimand, row, telling-off (informal)

➤ **Antonyms**

verb ≠<u>scold</u>: applaud, approve, commend, compliment, congratulate, praise ◆ noun ≠<u>scold</u>-

ing: commendation, compliment, praise

rebut *verb* <u>disprove</u>, confute, invalidate, negate, overturn, prove wrong, refute

rebuttal *noun* <u>disproof</u>, confutation, invalidation, negation, refutation

recalcitrant *adjective* <u>disobedient</u>, defiant, insubordinate, refractory, unmanageable, unruly, wayward, wilful

► **Antonyms**
amenable, compliant, docile, obedient, submissive

recall *verb* 1 <u>recollect</u>, bring or call to mind, evoke, remember 2 <u>annul</u>, cancel, countermand, repeal, retract, revoke, withdraw ♦ *noun* 3 <u>recollection</u>, memory, remembrance 4 <u>annulment</u>, cancellation, repeal, rescindment, retraction, withdrawal

recant *verb* <u>withdraw</u>, disclaim, forswear, renege, repudiate, retract, revoke, take back

► **Antonyms**
insist, maintain, profess, reaffirm, reiterate, repeat, restate, uphold

recapitulate *verb* <u>restate</u>, outline, recap (*informal*), recount, repeat, summarize

recede *verb* <u>fall back</u>, abate, ebb, regress, retire, retreat, return, subside, withdraw

receipt *noun* 1 <u>sales slip</u>, counterfoil, proof of purchase 2 <u>receiving</u>, acceptance, delivery, reception

receive *verb* 1 <u>get</u>, accept, acquire, be given, collect, obtain, pick up, take 2 <u>experience</u>, bear, encounter, suffer, sustain, undergo 3 <u>greet</u>, accommodate, admit, entertain, meet, welcome

recent *adjective* <u>new</u>, current, fresh, late, modern, novel, present-day, up-to-date

► **Antonyms**
ancient, antique, earlier, early, former, historical, old

recently *adverb* <u>newly</u>, currently, freshly, lately, latterly, not long

ago, of late

receptacle *noun* <u>container</u>, holder, repository

reception *noun* 1 <u>party</u>, function, levee, soirée 2 <u>response</u>, acknowledgment, greeting, reaction, treatment, welcome

receptive *adjective* <u>open</u>, amenable, interested, open-minded, open to suggestions, susceptible, sympathetic

► **Antonyms**
narrow-minded, prejudiced, unreceptive, unresponsive

recess *noun* 1 <u>alcove</u>, bay, corner, hollow, niche, nook 2 <u>break</u>, holiday, intermission, interval, respite, rest, vacation

recession *noun* <u>depression</u>, decline, drop, slump

► **Antonyms**
boom, upturn

recipe *noun* 1 <u>directions</u>, ingredients, instructions 2 <u>method</u>, formula, prescription, procedure, process, technique

reciprocal *adjective* <u>mutual</u>, alternate, complementary, correlative, corresponding, equivalent, exchanged, interchangeable

► **Antonyms**
one-way, unilateral, unreciprocated

reciprocate *verb* <u>return</u>, exchange, reply, requite, respond, swap, trade

recital *noun* 1 <u>performance</u>, rehearsal, rendering 2 <u>recitation</u>, account, narrative, reading, relation, statement, telling

recitation *noun* <u>recital</u>, lecture, passage, performance, piece, reading

recite *verb* <u>repeat</u>, declaim, deliver, narrate, perform, speak

reckless *adjective* <u>careless</u>, hasty, headlong, heedless, imprudent, mindless, precipitate, rash, thoughtless, wild

► **Antonyms**
careful, cautious, observant, responsible, thoughtful, wary

reckon *verb* 1 *Informal* <u>think</u>, assume, believe, guess (*informal,* chiefly U.S. & Canad.), imagine, suppose **2** <u>consider</u>, account, count, deem, esteem, judge, rate, regard **3** <u>count</u>, add up, calculate, compute, figure, number, tally, total

reckoning noun **1** <u>count</u>, addition, calculation, estimate **2** <u>bill</u>, account, calculation, charge, due, score

reclaim verb <u>regain</u>, recapture, recover, redeem, reform, retrieve, salvage

recline verb <u>lean</u>, lie (down), loll, lounge, repose, rest, sprawl
► **Antonyms**
get up, rise, sit up, stand, stand up, stand upright

recluse noun <u>hermit</u>, anchoress, anchorite, monk, solitary

reclusive adjective <u>solitary</u>, hermit-like, isolated, retiring, withdrawn
► **Antonyms**
gregarious, sociable

recognition noun **1** <u>identification</u>, discovery, recollection, remembrance **2** <u>acceptance</u>, admission, allowance, confession **3** As in in recognition of <u>appreciation</u>, notice, respect

recognize verb **1** <u>identify</u>, know, notice, place, recall, recollect, remember, spot **2** <u>acknowledge</u>, accept, admit, allow, concede, grant **3** <u>appreciate</u>, notice, respect
► **Antonyms**
≠<u>acknowledge</u>: be unaware of, forget, ignore, overlook

recoil verb **1** <u>jerk back</u>, kick, react, rebound, spring back **2** <u>draw back</u>, falter, quail, shrink **3** <u>backfire</u>, boomerang, go pear-shaped (informal), misfire, rebound ♦ noun **4** <u>reaction</u>, backlash, kick, rebound, repercussion

recollect verb <u>remember</u>, place, recall, summon up

recollection noun <u>memory</u>, impression, recall, remembrance, reminiscence

recommend verb **1** <u>advise</u>, advance, advocate, counsel, prescribe, propose, put forward,

suggest **2** <u>commend</u>, approve, endorse, praise
► **Antonyms**
≠<u>advise</u>: commend: argue against, disapprove of, reject, veto

recommendation noun **1** <u>advice</u>, counsel, proposal, suggestion **2** <u>commendation</u>, advocacy, approval, endorsement, praise, reference, sanction, testimonial

recompense verb **1** <u>reward</u>, pay, remunerate **2** <u>compensate</u>, make up for, pay for, redress, reimburse, repay, requite ♦ noun **3** <u>compensation</u>, amends, damages, payment, remuneration, reparation, repayment, requital, restitution **4** <u>reward</u>, payment, return, wages

reconcile verb **1** <u>resolve</u>, adjust, compose, put to rights, rectify, settle, square **2** <u>make peace between</u>, appease, conciliate, propitiate, reunite **3** <u>accept</u>, put up with (informal), resign oneself, submit, yield

reconciliation noun <u>pacification</u>, conciliation, reconcilement, reunion
► **Antonyms**
alienation, antagonism, breakup, estrangement, falling-out, separation

recondite adjective <u>obscure</u>, arcane, concealed, dark, deep, difficult, hidden, mysterious, occult, profound, secret
► **Antonyms**
simple, straightforward

recondition verb <u>restore</u>, do up (informal), overhaul, remodel, renew, renovate, repair, revamp

reconnaissance noun <u>inspection</u>, exploration, investigation, observation, recce (slang), scan, survey

reconnoitre verb <u>inspect</u>, case (slang), explore, investigate, observe, scan, spy out, survey

reconsider verb <u>rethink</u>, reassess, review, revise, think again

reconstruct verb **1** <u>rebuild</u>, recreate, regenerate, remake, remodel, renovate, restore **2** deduce, build up, piece together

record noun **1** document, account, chronicle, diary, entry, file, journal, log, register, report **2** evidence, documentation, testimony, trace, witness **3** disc, album, LP, single, vinyl **4** background, career, history, performance **5** off the record not for publication, confidential, private, unofficial ♦ verb **6** set down, chronicle, document, enter, log, minute, note, register, take down, write down **7** make a recording of, tape, tape-record, video, video-tape **8** register, give evidence of, indicate, say, show

recorder noun chronicler, archivist, clerk, diarist, historian, scribe

recording noun record, disc, tape, video

recount verb tell, depict, describe, narrate, recite, relate, repeat, report

recoup verb **1** regain, recover, retrieve, win back **2** compensate, make up for, refund, reimburse, repay, requite

recourse noun option, alternative, choice, expedient, remedy, resort, resource, way out

recover verb **1** get better, convalesce, get well, heal, improve, mend, rally, recuperate, revive **2** regain, get back, recapture, reclaim, redeem, repossess, restore, retrieve

► **Antonyms**

≠get better: deteriorate, go downhill, relapse, take a turn for the worse, weaken, worsen ≠regain: abandon, forfeit, lose

recovery noun **1** improvement, convalescence, healing, mending, recuperation, revival **2** retrieval, reclamation, repossession, restoration

recreation noun pastime, amusement, diversion, enjoyment, entertainment, fun, hobby, leisure activity, play, relaxation, sport

recrimination noun bickering, counterattack, mutual accusa-

tion, quarrel, squabbling

recruit verb **1** enlist, draft, enrol, levy, mobilize, muster, raise **2** win (over), engage, obtain, procure ♦ noun **3** beginner, apprentice, convert, helper, initiate, learner, novice, trainee

► **Antonyms**

verb ≠enlist: dismiss, fire, lay off, make redundant, sack (informal)

rectify verb correct, adjust, emend, fix, improve, redress, remedy, repair, right

rectitude noun morality, decency, goodness, honesty, honour, integrity, principle, probity, virtue

► **Antonyms**

baseness, corruption, dishonesty, dishonour, immorality, scandalousness

recuperate verb recover, convalesce, get better, improve, mend

recur verb happen again, come again, persist, reappear, repeat, return, revert

recurrent adjective periodic, continued, frequent, habitual, recurring

► **Antonyms**

isolated, one-off

recycle verb reprocess, reclaim, reuse, salvage, save

red adjective **1** crimson, carmine, cherry, coral, ruby, scarlet, vermilion **2** Of hair chestnut, carroty, flame-coloured, reddish, sandy, titian **3** flushed, blushing, embarrassed, florid, shamefaced ♦ noun **4** in the red Informal in debt, in arrears, insolvent, overdrawn **5** see red Informal lose one's temper, be or get pissed (off) (taboo slang), blow one's top, crack up (informal), fly off the handle (informal), go ballistic (slang, chiefly U.S.), go mad (informal), lose it (informal), lose the plot (informal)

red-blooded adjective Informal vigorous, lusty, robust, strong, virile

redden verb flush, blush, colour (up), crimson, go red

redeem verb 1 <u>make up for</u>, atone for, compensate for, make amends for 2 <u>reinstate</u>, absolve, restore to favour 3 <u>save</u>, deliver, emancipate, free, liberate, ransom 4 <u>buy back</u>, reclaim, recover, regain, repurchase, retrieve

redemption noun 1 <u>compensation</u>, amends, atonement, reparation 2 <u>salvation</u>, deliverance, emancipation, liberation, release, rescue 3 <u>repurchase</u>, reclamation, recovery, repossession, retrieval

red-handed adjective <u>in the act</u>, bang to rights (slang), (in) flagrante delicto

redolent adjective 1 <u>reminiscent</u>, evocative, suggestive 2 <u>scented</u>, aromatic, fragrant, odorous, perfumed, sweet-smelling

redoubtable adjective <u>formidable</u>, fearful, fearsome, mighty, powerful, strong

redress verb 1 <u>make amends for</u>, compensate for, make up for 2 <u>put right</u>, adjust, balance, correct, even up, rectify, regulate ♦ noun 3 <u>amends</u>, atonement, compensation, payment, recompense, reparation

reduce verb 1 <u>lessen</u>, abate, curtail, cut, cut down, decrease, diminish, lower, moderate, shorten, weaken 2 <u>degrade</u>, break, bring low, downgrade, humble

➤ **Antonyms**

≠<u>lessen</u>: augment, enhance, enlarge, extend, heighten, increase ≠<u>degrade</u>: elevate, enhance, exalt, promote

redundancy noun <u>unemployment</u>, joblessness, layoff, the axe (informal), the sack (informal)

redundant adjective <u>superfluous</u>, extra, inessential, supernumerary, surplus, unnecessary, unwanted

➤ **Antonyms**

essential, necessary, needed, vital

reek verb 1 <u>stink</u>, pong (Brit. informal), smell ♦ noun 2 <u>stink</u>, fetor, odour, pong (Brit. informal), smell, stench

reel verb 1 <u>stagger</u>, lurch, pitch, rock, roll, sway 2 <u>whirl</u>, revolve, spin, swirl

refer verb 1 <u>allude</u>, bring up, cite, mention, speak of 2 <u>relate</u>, apply, belong, be relevant to, concern, pertain 3 <u>consult</u>, apply, go, look up, turn to 4 <u>direct</u>, guide, point, send

referee noun 1 <u>umpire</u>, adjudicator, arbiter, arbitrator, judge, ref (informal) ♦ verb 2 <u>umpire</u>, adjudicate, arbitrate, judge, mediate

reference noun 1 <u>citation</u>, allusion, mention, note, quotation 2 <u>testimonial</u>, character, credentials, endorsement, recommendation 3 As in with reference to <u>relevance</u>, applicability, bearing, connection, relation

referendum noun <u>public vote</u>, plebiscite, popular vote

refine verb 1 <u>purify</u>, clarify, cleanse, distil, filter, process 2 <u>improve</u>, hone, perfect, polish

refined adjective 1 <u>cultured</u>, civilized, cultivated, elegant, polished, polite, well-bred 2 <u>purified</u>, clarified, clean, distilled, filtered, processed, pure 3 <u>discerning</u>, delicate, discriminating, fastidious, fine, precise, sensitive

➤ **Antonyms**

≠<u>cultured</u>: boorish, coarse, common, ill-bred, inelegant, uncultured, ungentlemanly, unladylike, unmannerly, unrefined ≠<u>purified</u>: coarse, impure, unrefined

refinement noun 1 <u>sophistication</u>, breeding, civility, courtesy, cultivation, culture, discrimination, gentility, good breeding, polish, taste 2 <u>subtlety</u>, fine point, nicety, nuance 3 <u>purification</u>, clarification, cleansing, distillation, filtering, processing

reflect verb 1 <u>throw back</u>, echo, mirror, reproduce, return 2 <u>show</u>, demonstrate, display, indicate, manifest, reveal 3 <u>consider</u>, cogitate, meditate, muse, ponder, ruminate, think, wonder

reflection noun 1 <u>image</u>, echo, mirror image 2 <u>consideration</u>, cogitation, contemplation, idea, meditation, musing, observation, opinion, thinking, thought

reflective *adjective* **1** thoughtful, contemplative, meditative, pensive

reform *noun* **1** improvement, amendment, betterment, rehabilitation ♦ *verb* **2** improve, amend, correct, mend, rectify, restore **3** mend one's ways, clean up one's act (*informal*), go straight (*informal*), pull one's socks up (*Brit. informal*), shape up (*informal*), turn over a new leaf

refractory *adjective* unmanageable, difficult, disobedient, headstrong, intractable, uncontrollable, unruly, wilful

refrain[1] *verb* stop, abstain, avoid, cease, desist, forbear, leave off, renounce

refrain[2] *noun* chorus, melody, tune

refresh *verb* **1** revive, brace, enliven, freshen, invigorate, revitalize, stimulate **2** stimulate, jog, prompt, renew

refreshing *adjective* **1** stimulating, bracing, fresh, invigorating **2** new, novel, original

➤ **Antonyms**
≠stimulating: enervating, exhausting, soporific, tiring, wearisome

refreshment *noun* **refreshments** food and drink, drinks, snacks, titbits

refrigerate *verb* cool, chill, freeze, keep cold

refuge *noun* shelter, asylum, haven, hide-out, protection, retreat, sanctuary

refugee *noun* exile, displaced person, émigré, escapee

refund *verb* **1** repay, pay back, reimburse, restore, return ♦ *noun* **2** repayment, reimbursement, return

refurbish *verb* renovate, clean up, do up (*informal*), mend, overhaul, repair, restore, revamp

refusal *noun* rejection, denial,

knock-back (*slang*), rebuff

refuse[1] *verb* reject, decline, deny, say no, spurn, turn down, withhold

➤ **Antonyms**
accept, agree, allow, approve, consent, give, permit

refuse[2] *noun* rubbish, garbage, junk (*informal*), litter, trash, waste

refute *verb* disprove, discredit, negate, overthrow, prove false, rebut

➤ **Antonyms**
confirm, prove, substantiate

regain *verb* **1** recover, get back, recapture, recoup, retrieve, take back, win back **2** get back to, reach again, return to

regal *adjective* royal, kingly *or* queenly, magnificent, majestic, noble, princely

regale *verb* **1** entertain, amuse, delight, divert **2** serve, ply

regalia *plural noun* trappings, accoutrements, decorations, emblems, finery, paraphernalia

regard *verb* **1** consider, believe, deem, esteem, judge, rate, see, suppose, think, view **2** look at, behold, check out (*informal*), clock (*Brit. slang*), eye, eyeball (*U.S. slang*), gaze at, observe, scrutinize, view, watch **3** heed, attend, listen to, mind, pay attention to, take notice of **4 as regards** concerning, pertaining to, regarding, relating to ♦ *noun* **5** respect, care, concern, consideration, esteem, thought **6** heed, attention, interest, mind, notice **7** look, glance, gaze, scrutiny, stare

regarding *preposition* concerning, about, as regards, in *or* with regard to, on the subject of, re, respecting, with reference to

regardless *adjective* **1** heedless, inconsiderate, indifferent, neglectful, negligent, rash, reckless, unmindful ♦ *adverb* **2** in spite of everything, anyway, in any case, nevertheless

➤ **Antonyms**
adjective ≠heedless: heedful, mindful, regardful

regards plural noun good wishes, best wishes, compliments, greetings, respects

regenerate verb renew, breathe new life into, invigorate, reawaken, reinvigorate, rejuvenate, restore, revive

➤ **Antonyms**
decline, degenerate, stagnate, stultify

regime noun government, leadership, management, reign, rule, system

regimented adjective controlled, disciplined, ordered, organized, regulated, systematized

region noun area, district, locality, part, place, quarter, section, sector, territory, tract, zone

regional adjective local, district, parochial, provincial, zonal

register noun 1 list, archives, catalogue, chronicle, diary, file, log, record, roll, roster ♦ verb 2 record, catalogue, chronicle, enlist, enrol, enter, list, note 3 show, display, exhibit, express, indicate, manifest, mark, reveal

regress verb revert, backslide, degenerate, deteriorate, fall away or off, go back, lapse, relapse, return

➤ **Antonyms**
advance, improve, progress, wax

regret verb 1 feel sorry about, bemoan, bewail, deplore, grieve, lament, miss, mourn, repent, rue ♦ noun 2 sorrow, bitterness, compunction, contrition, penitence, remorse, repentance, ruefulness

➤ **Antonyms**
verb ≠feel sorry about: be happy, be satisfied, feel satisfaction, have not looked back, rejoice ♦ noun ≠sorrow: callousness, contentment, impenitence, lack of compassion, pleasure, satisfaction

regretful adjective sorry, apologetic, contrite, penitent, remorseful, repentant, rueful, sad, sorrowful

regrettable adjective unfortunate, disappointing, distressing, lamentable, sad, shameful

regular adjective 1 normal, common, customary, habitual, ordinary, routine, typical, usual 2 even, balanced, flat, level, smooth, straight, symmetrical, uniform 3 systematic, consistent, constant, even, fixed, ordered, set, stated, steady, uniform

➤ **Antonyms**
≠normal: abnormal, exceptional, infrequent, irregular, occasional, rare, uncommon, unconventional, unusual ≠even: erratic, irregular, uneven ≠systematic: erratic, inconsistent, inconstant, irregular, varied

regulate verb 1 control, direct, govern, guide, handle, manage, rule, run, supervise 2 adjust, balance, fit, moderate, modulate, tune

regulation noun 1 rule, decree, dictate, edict, law, order, precept, statute 2 control, direction, government, management, supervision 3 adjustment, modulation, tuning

regurgitate verb vomit, disgorge, puke (slang), sick up (informal), spew (out or up), throw up (informal)

rehabilitate verb 1 reintegrate, adjust 2 redeem, clear, reform, restore, save

rehash verb 1 rework, refashion, rejig (informal), reuse, rewrite ♦ noun 2 reworking, new version, rearrangement, rewrite

rehearsal noun practice, drill, preparation, rehearsing, runthrough

rehearse verb practise, drill, go over, prepare, recite, repeat, run through, train

reign noun 1 rule, command, control, dominion, monarchy, power ♦ verb 2 rule, be in power, command, govern, influence 3 be supreme, hold sway, predominate, prevail

reimburse verb pay back, compensate, recompense, refund, remunerate, repay, return

rein noun 1 control, brake, bridle,

check, curb, harness, hold, restraint ◆ *verb* **2** control, check, curb, halt, hold sway, limit, restrain, restrict

reincarnation *noun* rebirth, transmigration of souls

reinforce *verb* support, bolster, emphasize, fortify, prop, strengthen, stress, supplement, toughen

➤ **Antonyms**
contradict, undermine, weaken

reinforcement *noun* **1** strengthening, augmentation, fortification, increase **2** support, brace, buttress, prop, stay **3** reinforcements reserves, additional or fresh troops, auxiliaries, support

reinstate *verb* restore, recall, reestablish, replace, return

reiterate *verb* *Formal* repeat, do again, restate, say again

reject *verb* **1** deny, decline, disallow, exclude, renounce, repudiate, veto **2** rebuff, jilt, refuse, repulse, say no to, spurn, turn down **3** discard, eliminate, jettison, scrap, throw away or out ◆ *noun* **4** castoff, discard, failure, second

➤ **Antonyms**
verb ≠deny: accept, agree, allow, approve, permit ≠rebuff: accept ≠discard: accept, receive, select ◆ *noun* ≠castoff: prize, treasure

rejection *noun* **1** denial, dismissal, exclusion, renunciation, repudiation, thumbs down, veto **2** rebuff, brushoff (*slang*), kick in the teeth (*slang*), knock-back (*slang*), refusal

➤ **Antonyms**
≠denial: acceptance, affirmation, approval ≠rebuff: acceptance, selection

rejig *verb* *Informal* rearrange, alter, juggle, manipulate, reorganize, tweak

rejoice *verb* be glad, be happy, be overjoyed, celebrate, exult, glory

➤ **Antonyms**
be sad, be unhappy, be upset, grieve, lament, mourn

rejoicing *noun* happiness, celebration, elation, exultation, gladness, joy, jubilation, merrymaking

rejoin *verb* reply, answer, respond, retort, riposte

rejoinder *noun* reply, answer, comeback (*informal*), response, retort, riposte

rejuvenate *verb* revitalize, breathe new life into, refresh, regenerate, reinvigorate, renew, restore

relapse *verb* **1** lapse, backslide, degenerate, fail, regress, revert, slip back **2** worsen, deteriorate, fade, fail, sicken, sink, weaken ◆ *noun* **3** lapse, backsliding, regression, retrogression **4** worsening, deterioration, turn for the worse, weakening

➤ **Antonyms**
verb ≠worsen: get better, improve, rally, recover ◆ *noun* ≠worsening: improvement, rally, recovery, turn for the better

relate *verb* **1** connect, associate, correlate, couple, join, link **2** concern, apply, be relevant to, have to do with, pertain, refer **3** tell, describe, detail, narrate, recite, recount, report

➤ **Antonyms**
≠connect: detach, disconnect, dissociate, divorce ≠concern: be irrelevant to, be unconnected, have nothing to do with

related *adjective* **1** akin, kindred **2** associated, affiliated, akin, connected, interconnected, joint, linked

➤ **Antonyms**
≠akin: unrelated ≠associated: separate, unconnected, unrelated

relation *noun* **1** connection, bearing, bond, comparison, correlation, link **2** relative, kin, kinsman or kinswoman **3** kinship, affinity, kindred

relations *plural noun* **1** dealings, affairs, connections, contact, interaction, intercourse, relationship **2** family, clan, kin, kindred, kinsfolk, kinsmen, relatives, tribe

relationship noun **1** <u>association</u>, affinity, bond, connection, kinship, rapport **2** <u>affair</u>, liaison **3** <u>connection</u>, correlation, link, parallel, similarity, tie-up

relative adjective **1** <u>dependent</u>, allied, associated, comparative, contingent, corresponding, proportionate, related **2** <u>relevant</u>, applicable, apposite, appropriate, apropos, germane, pertinent ◆ noun **3** <u>relation</u>, kinsman or kinswoman, member of one's or the family

relatively adverb <u>comparatively</u>, rather, somewhat

relax verb **1** <u>be or feel at ease</u>, calm, chill out (slang, chiefly U.S.), lighten up (slang), rest, take it easy, unwind **2** <u>lessen</u>, abate, ease, ebb, let up, loosen, lower, moderate, reduce, relieve, slacken, weaken

➤ **Antonyms**

≠<u>be or feel at ease</u>: be alarmed, be alert ≠<u>lessen</u>: heighten, increase, intensify, tense, tighten, work

relaxation noun <u>leisure</u>, enjoyment, fun, pleasure, recreation, rest

relaxed adjective <u>easy-going</u>, casual, comfortable, easy, free and easy, informal, laid-back (informal), leisurely

relay noun **1** <u>shift</u>, relief, turn **2** <u>message</u>, dispatch, transmission ◆ verb **3** <u>pass on</u>, broadcast, carry, communicate, send, spread, transmit

release verb **1** <u>set free</u>, discharge, drop, extricate, free, liberate, loose, unbridle, undo, unfasten **2** <u>acquit</u>, absolve, exonerate, let go, let off **3** <u>issue</u>, circulate, distribute, launch, make known, make public, publish, put out ◆ noun **4** <u>liberation</u>, deliverance, discharge, emancipation, freedom, liberty **5** <u>acquittal</u>, absolution, exemption, exoneration **6** <u>issue</u>, proclamation, publication

➤ **Antonyms**

verb ≠<u>set free</u>: detain, engage,

fasten, hold, imprison, incarcerate, keep ≠<u>issue</u>: suppress, withhold ◆ noun ≠<u>liberation</u>: detention, imprisonment, incarceration, internment

relegate verb <u>demote</u>, downgrade

relent verb <u>be merciful</u>, capitulate, change one's mind, come round, have pity, show mercy, soften, yield

➤ **Antonyms**

be unyielding, remain firm, show no mercy

relentless adjective **1** <u>unremitting</u>, incessant, nonstop, persistent, unrelenting, unrelieved **2** <u>merciless</u>, cruel, fierce, implacable, pitiless, remorseless, ruthless, unrelenting

➤ **Antonyms**

≠<u>merciless</u>: compassionate, forgiving, merciful, submissive, yielding

relevant adjective <u>significant</u>, apposite, appropriate, apt, fitting, germane, pertinent, related, to the point

➤ **Antonyms**

beside the point, immaterial, inapplicable, inappropriate, irrelevant, unconnected, unrelated

reliable adjective <u>dependable</u>, faithful, safe, sound, staunch, sure, true, trustworthy

➤ **Antonyms**

irresponsible, undependable, unreliable, untrustworthy

reliance noun <u>trust</u>, belief, confidence, dependence, faith

relic noun <u>remnant</u>, fragment, keepsake, memento, souvenir, trace, vestige

relief noun **1** <u>ease</u>, comfort, cure, deliverance, mitigation, release, remedy, solace **2** <u>rest</u>, break, breather (informal), relaxation, respite **3** <u>aid</u>, assistance, help, succour, support

relieve verb **1** <u>ease</u>, alleviate, assuage, calm, comfort, console, cure, mitigate, relax, soften, soothe **2** <u>help</u>, aid, assist, succour, support, sustain

> ➤ Antonyms

≠**ease:** aggravate, exacerbate, heighten, intensify, worsen

religious adjective 1 <u>devout</u>, devotional, godly, holy, pious, sacred, spiritual 2 <u>conscientious</u>, faithful, meticulous, punctilious, rigid, scrupulous

> ➤ Antonyms

≠**devout:** godless, irreligious, rational, secular, unbelieving

relinquish verb Formal <u>give up</u>, abandon, abdicate, cede, drop, forsake, leave, let go, renounce, surrender

relish verb 1 <u>enjoy</u>, delight in, fancy, like, revel in, savour ♦ noun 2 <u>enjoyment</u>, fancy, fondness, gusto, liking, love, partiality, penchant, predilection, taste 3 <u>condiment</u>, sauce, seasoning 4 <u>flavour</u>, piquancy, smack, spice, tang, taste, trace

> ➤ Antonyms

verb ≠**enjoy:** be unenthusiastic about, dislike, loathe ♦ noun ≠**enjoyment:** dislike, distaste, loathing

reluctance noun <u>unwillingness</u>, aversion, disinclination, dislike, distaste, loathing, repugnance

reluctant adjective <u>unwilling</u>, disinclined, hesitant, loath, unenthusiastic

> ➤ Antonyms

eager, enthusiastic, inclined, keen, willing

rely verb <u>depend</u>, bank, bet, count, trust

remain verb 1 <u>continue</u>, abide, dwell, endure, go on, last, persist, stand, stay, survive 2 <u>stay behind</u>, be left, delay, linger, wait

> ➤ Antonyms

≠**stay behind:** depart, go, leave

remainder noun <u>rest</u>, balance, excess, leavings, remains, remnant, residue, surplus

remaining adjective <u>left-over</u>, lingering, outstanding, persisting, surviving, unfinished

remains plural noun 1 <u>remnants</u>, debris, dregs, leavings, leftovers, relics, residue, rest 2 <u>corpse</u>, body, cadaver, carcass

remark verb 1 <u>comment</u>, declare, mention, observe, pass comment, reflect, say, state 2 <u>notice</u>, espy, make out, mark, note, observe, perceive, see ♦ noun 3 <u>comment</u>, observation, reflection, statement, utterance

remarkable adjective <u>extraordinary</u>, notable, outstanding, rare, singular, striking, surprising, uncommon, unusual, wonderful

> ➤ Antonyms

common, commonplace, everyday, insignificant, mundane, ordinary, unimpressive, usual

remedy noun 1 <u>cure</u>, medicine, nostrum, treatment ♦ verb 2 <u>put right</u>, correct, fix, rectify, set to rights

remember verb 1 <u>recall</u>, call to mind, commemorate, look back (on), recollect, reminisce, think back 2 <u>bear in mind</u>, keep in mind

> ➤ Antonyms

disregard, forget, ignore, neglect, overlook

remembrance noun 1 <u>memory</u>, recall, recollection, reminiscence, thought 2 <u>souvenir</u>, commemoration, keepsake, memento, memorial, monument, reminder, token

remind verb <u>call to mind</u>, jog one's memory, make (someone) remember, prompt

reminisce verb <u>recall</u>, hark back, look back, recollect, remember, think back

reminiscence noun <u>recollection</u>, anecdote, memoir, memory, recall, remembrance

reminiscent adjective <u>suggestive</u>, evocative, similar

remiss adjective Formal <u>careless</u>, forgetful, heedless, lax, neglectful, negligent, thoughtless

> ➤ Antonyms

attentive, careful, diligent, painstaking, scrupulous

remission noun 1 <u>pardon</u>, absolution, amnesty, discharge, exemption, release, reprieve **2** lessening, abatement, alleviation, ebb, lull, relaxation, respite

remit *verb* **1** send, dispatch, forward, mail, post, transmit **2** cancel, halt, repeal, rescind, stop **3** postpone, defer, delay, put off, shelve, suspend ♦ *noun* **4** instructions, brief, guidelines, orders

remittance *noun* payment, allowance, fee

remnant *noun* remainder, end, fragment, leftovers, remains, residue, rest, trace, vestige

remonstrate *verb Formal* protest, argue, dispute, dissent, object, take issue

remorse *noun* regret, anguish, compunction, contrition, grief, guilt, penitence, repentance, shame, sorrow

remorseful *adjective* regretful, apologetic, ashamed, consciencestricken, contrite, guilty, penitent, repentant, sorry

remorseless *adjective* **1** pitiless, callous, cruel, inhumane, merciless, ruthless **2** relentless, inexorable

remote *adjective* **1** distant, far, inaccessible, in the middle of nowhere, isolated, out-of-the-way, secluded **2** aloof, abstracted, cold, detached, distant, reserved, standoffish, uncommunicative, withdrawn **3** slight, doubtful, dubious, faint, outside, slender, slim, small, unlikely

► Antonyms

≠distant: adjacent, central, close, near, nearby, neighbouring ≠aloof: attentive, gregarious, interested, involved, outgoing, sociable ≠slight: considerable, good, likely, strong

removal *noun* **1** taking away or off or out, dislodgment, ejection, elimination, eradication, extraction, uprooting, withdrawal **2** dismissal, expulsion **3** move, departure, flitting (*Scot. & Northern English dialect*), relocation, transfer

remove *verb* **1** take away or off or out, abolish, delete, detach,

displace, eject, eliminate, erase, excise, extract, get rid of, wipe from the face of the earth, withdraw **2** dismiss, depose, dethrone, discharge, expel, oust, throw out **3** move, depart, flit (*Scot. & Northern English dialect*), relocate

► Antonyms

≠take away or off or out: insert, put back, put in, put on, replace ≠dismiss: appoint, install

remunerate *verb Formal* pay, compensate, recompense, reimburse, repay, requite, reward

remuneration *noun* payment, earnings, fee, income, pay, return, reward, salary, stipend, wages

remunerative *adjective* profitable, economic, lucrative, moneymaking, paying, rewarding, worthwhile

renaissance, renascence *noun* rebirth, reappearance, reawakening, renewal, restoration, resurgence, revival

rend *verb Literary* tear, rip, rupture, separate, wrench

render *verb* **1** make, cause to become, leave **2** provide, furnish, give, hand out, pay, present, submit, supply, tender **3** represent, act, depict, do, give, perform, play, portray

rendezvous *noun* **1** appointment, assignation, date, engagement, meeting, tryst (*archaic*) **2** meeting place, gathering point, venue ♦ *verb* **3** meet, assemble, come together, gather, join up

rendition *noun Formal* **1** performance, arrangement, interpretation, portrayal, presentation, reading, rendering, version **2** translation, interpretation, reading, transcription, version

renegade *noun* **1** deserter, apostate, defector, traitor, turncoat ♦ *adjective* **2** traitorous, apostate, disloyal, rebellious, unfaithful

renege *verb* break one's word, back out, break a promise, default, go back

renew verb 1 recommence, continue, extend, reaffirm, recreate, reopen, repeat, resume 2 restore, mend, modernize, overhaul, refit, refurbish, renovate, repair 3 replace, refresh, replenish, restock

renounce verb give up, abjure, deny, disown, forsake, forswear, quit, recant, relinquish, waive

► **Antonyms**

assert, avow, claim, maintain, reassert

renovate verb restore, do up (informal), modernize, overhaul, recondition, refit, refurbish, renew, repair

renown noun fame, distinction, eminence, note, reputation, repute

renowned adjective famous, celebrated, distinguished, eminent, esteemed, notable, noted, well-known

► **Antonyms**

forgotten, little-known, neglected, obscure, unknown

rent[1] verb 1 hire, charter, lease, let ◆ noun 2 hire, fee, lease, payment, rental

rent[2] noun tear, gash, hole, opening, rip, slash, slit, split

renunciation noun giving up, abandonment, abdication, abjuration, denial, disavowal, forswearing, rejection, relinquishment, repudiation

reorganize verb rearrange, reshuffle, restructure

repair verb 1 mend, fix, heal, patch, patch up, renovate, restore 2 put right, compensate for, make up for, rectify, redress ◆ noun 3 mend, darn, overhaul, patch, restoration 4 condition, form, shape (informal), state

► **Antonyms**

verb ≠mend: damage, destroy, harm, ruin, wreck

reparation noun compensation, atonement, damages, recompense, restitution, satisfaction

repartee noun wit, badinage, banter, riposte, wittiness, wordplay

repast noun meal, food

repay verb 1 pay back, compensate, recompense, refund, reimburse, requite, return, square 2 reciprocate, avenge, get even with (informal), get one's own back on (informal), hit back, retaliate, revenge

repeal verb 1 abolish, annul, cancel, invalidate, nullify, recall, reverse, revoke ◆ noun 2 abolition, annulment, cancellation, invalidation, rescindment

► **Antonyms**

verb ≠abolish: confirm, enact, introduce, pass, ratify, reaffirm, validate ◆ noun ≠abolition: confirmation, enactment, introduction, passing, ratification, reaffirmation, validation

repeat verb 1 reiterate, echo, replay, reproduce, rerun, reshow, restate, retell ◆ noun 2 repetition, echo, reiteration, replay, rerun, reshowing

repeatedly adverb over and over, frequently, many times, often

repel verb 1 disgust, gross out (U.S. slang), nauseate, offend, revolt, sicken 2 drive off, fight, hold off, parry, rebuff, repulse, resist, ward off

► **Antonyms**

≠disgust: attract, delight, draw, entrance, fascinate, invite, please ≠drive off: submit

repellent adjective 1 disgusting, abhorrent, hateful, horrid, loathsome, nauseating, noxious, offensive, repugnant, repulsive, revolting, sickening 2 proof, impermeable, repelling, resistant

repent verb regret, be sorry, feel remorse, rue

repentance noun regret, compunction, contrition, grief, guilt, penitence, remorse

repentant adjective regretful, contrite, penitent, remorseful, rueful, sorry

repercussion noun repercussions consequences, backlash, result, sequel, side effects

repertoire noun range, collection, list, repertory, stock, store, supply

repetition noun repeating, echo, recurrence, reiteration, renewal, replication, restatement, tautology

repetitious adjective long-winded, prolix, tautological, tedious, verbose, wordy

repetitive adjective monotonous, boring, dull, mechanical, recurrent, tedious, unchanging, unvaried

rephrase verb reword, paraphrase, put differently

repine verb Literary complain, fret, grumble, moan

replace verb 1 take the place of, follow, oust, substitute, succeed, supersede, supplant, take over from 2 put back, re-establish, reinstate, restore

replacement noun successor, double, proxy, stand-in, substitute, surrogate, understudy

replenish verb refill, fill, provide, reload, replace, restore, top up

► **Antonyms**

consume, drain, empty, exhaust, use up

replete adjective 1 sated, full, full up, gorged 2 filled, crammed, glutted, stuffed

► **Antonyms**

≠sated: empty, famished, hungry, starving ≠filled: bare, barren, empty, lacking, wanting

replica noun duplicate, carbon copy (informal), copy, facsimile, imitation, model, reproduction

► **Antonyms**

master, original, prototype

replicate verb copy, duplicate, mimic, recreate, reduplicate, reproduce

reply verb 1 answer, counter, reciprocate, rejoin, respond, retaliate, retort ♦ noun 2 answer, counter, counterattack, reaction, rejoinder, response, retaliation, retort

report verb 1 communicate, broadcast, cover, describe, detail, inform of, narrate, pass on, recount, relate, state, tell 2 present oneself, appear, arrive, come, turn up ♦ noun 3 account, communication, description, narrative, news, record, statement, word 4 article, piece, story, write-up 5 rumour, buzz, gossip, hearsay, talk 6 bang, blast, boom, crack, detonation, discharge, explosion, noise, sound

reporter noun journalist, correspondent, hack (derogatory), journo (slang), pressman, writer

repose noun 1 peace, ease, quietness, relaxation, respite, rest, stillness, tranquillity 2 composure, calmness, poise, self-possession 3 sleep, slumber ♦ verb 4 rest, lie, lie down, recline, rest upon

repository noun store, depository, storehouse, treasury, vault

reprehensible adjective blameworthy, bad, culpable, disgraceful, objectionable, shameful, unworthy

► **Antonyms**

acceptable, admirable, forgivable, laudable, pardonable, praiseworthy, unobjectionable

represent verb 1 stand for, act for, betoken, mean, serve as, speak for, symbolize 2 exemplify, embody, epitomize, personify, symbolize, typify 3 depict, denote, describe, illustrate, outline, picture, portray, show

representation noun 1 portrayal, account, depiction, description 2 picture, illustration, image, likeness, model, portrait

representative noun 1 delegate, agent, deputy, member, proxy, spokesman or spokeswoman 2 salesman, agent, commercial traveller, rep ♦ adjective 3 typical, archetypal, characteristic, exemplary, symbolic

► **Antonyms**

adjective ≠typical: atypical, extraordinary, uncharacteristic

repress verb 1 control, bottle up, check, curb, hold back, inhibit, restrain, stifle, suppress **2** sub-due, quell, subjugate

➤ **Antonyms**

≠control: encourage, express, give free rein to, let out, release ≠subdue: free, liberate

repression noun subjugation, constraint, control, despotism, domination, restraint, suppression, tyranny

repressive adjective oppressive, absolute, authoritarian, despotic, dictatorial, tyrannical

➤ **Antonyms**

democratic, liberal, libertarian

reprieve verb **1** grant a stay of execution to, let off the hook (slang), pardon **2** relieve, abate, allay, alleviate, mitigate, palliate ♦ noun **3** stay of execution, amnesty, deferment, pardon, postponement, remission **4** relief, alleviation, mitigation, palliation, respite

reprimand verb **1** blame, censure, dress down (informal), haul over the coals (informal), rap over the knuckles, rebuke, scold, tear (someone) off a strip (Brit. informal) ♦ noun **2** blame, censure, dressing-down (informal), rebuke, reproach, reproof, talking-to (informal)

➤ **Antonyms**

verb ≠blame: applaud, commend, compliment, congratulate, praise ♦ noun ≠blame: commendation, compliment, congratulations, praise

reprisal noun retaliation, retribution, revenge, vengeance

reproach noun **1** blame, censure, condemnation, disapproval, opprobrium, rebuke ♦ verb **2** blame, censure, condemn, criticize, lambast(e), read the riot act, rebuke, reprimand, scold, upbraid

reproachful adjective critical, censorious, condemnatory, disapproving, fault-finding, reproving

reprobate noun **1** scoundrel, bad egg (old-fashioned informal), blackguard, degenerate, evil-doer, miscreant, ne'er-do-well, profligate, rake, rascal, villain ♦ adjective **2** unprincipled, abandoned, bad, base, corrupt, degenerate, depraved, dissolute, immoral, sinful, wicked

reproduce verb **1** copy, duplicate, echo, imitate, match, mirror, recreate, repeat, replicate **2** Biology breed, multiply, procreate, propagate, spawn

reproduction noun **1** Biology breeding, generation, increase, multiplication **2** copy, duplicate, facsimile, imitation, picture, print, replica

➤ **Antonyms**

≠copy: master, original, prototype

reproof noun rebuke, blame, censure, condemnation, criticism, reprimand, scolding

➤ **Antonyms**

commendation, compliment, encouragement, praise

reprove verb rebuke, berate, blame, censure, condemn, read the riot act, reprimand, scold, tear into (informal), take (someone) off a strip (Brit. informal), tell off (informal)

➤ **Antonyms**

applaud, commend, compliment, encourage, praise

repudiate verb reject, deny, disavow, disclaim, disown, renounce

➤ **Antonyms**

accept, acknowledge, assert, avow, defend, proclaim

repugnance noun distaste, abhorrence, aversion, disgust, dislike, hatred, loathing

repugnant adjective distasteful, abhorrent, disgusting, loathsome, nauseating, offensive, repellent, revolting, sickening, vile

➤ **Antonyms**

agreeable, attractive, pleasant, unobjectionable

repulse verb **1** disgust, fill with loathing, gross out (U.S. Slang), nauseate, offend, put off, repel, revolt, sicken, turn one's stomach **2** drive back, beat off, fight off, rebuff, repel, ward off **3** reject, rebuff, refuse, snub, spurn, turn down

repulsion noun disgust, abhorrence, aversion, detestation, distaste, hatred, loathing, repugnance, revulsion

repulsive adjective disgusting, abhorrent, foul, loathsome, nauseating, repellent, revolting, sickening, vile

► **Antonyms**

appealing, attractive, delightful, enticing, lovely, pleasant

reputable adjective respectable, creditable, excellent, good, honourable, reliable, trustworthy, well-thought-of, worthy

► **Antonyms**

cowboy (informal), disreputable, fly-by-night, shady (informal), unreliable, untrustworthy

reputation noun name, character, esteem, estimation, renown, repute, standing, stature

repute noun reputation, celebrity, distinction, eminence, fame, name, renown, standing, stature

reputed adjective supposed, alleged, believed, considered, deemed, estimated, held, reckoned, regarded

reputedly adverb supposedly, allegedly, apparently, seemingly

request verb **1** ask (for), appeal for, demand, desire, entreat, invite, seek, solicit ♦ noun **2** asking, appeal, call, demand, desire, entreaty, suit

► **Antonyms**

verb ≠ask (for): command, order ♦ noun ≠asking: command, order

require verb **1** need, crave, desire, lack, miss, want, wish **2** order, ask, bid, call upon, command, compel, demand, exact, insist upon, oblige

required adjective needed, called for, essential, necessary, obligatory, requisite

► **Antonyms**

optional, unimportant, voluntary

requirement noun necessity, de-

mand, essential, lack, must, need, prerequisite, stipulation, want

requisite adjective **1** necessary, called for, essential, indispensable, needed, needful, obligatory, required ♦ noun **2** necessity, condition, essential, must, need, prerequisite, requirement

requisition verb **1** demand, call for, request ♦ noun **2** demand, call, request, summons

requital noun return, repayment

requite verb return, get even, give in return, pay (someone) back in his or her own coin, reciprocate, repay, respond, retaliate

rescind verb annul, cancel, countermand, declare null and void, invalidate, repeal, set aside

► **Antonyms**

enact, implement

rescue verb **1** save, deliver, get out, liberate, recover, redeem, release, salvage ♦ noun **2** liberation, deliverance, recovery, redemption, release, salvage, salvation, saving

► **Antonyms**

verb ≠save: abandon, desert, leave, leave behind, lose, strand

research noun **1** investigation, analysis, examination, exploration, probe, study ♦ verb **2** investigate, analyse, examine, explore, probe, study

resemblance noun similarity, correspondence, kinship, likeness, parallel, sameness, similitude

► **Antonyms**

difference, disparity, dissimilarity, variation

resemble verb be like, bear a resemblance to, be similar to, look like, mirror, parallel

resent verb be bitter about, begrudge, be pissed (off) about (taboo slang), grudge, object to, take exception to, take offence at

► **Antonyms**

accept, approve, like, welcome

resentful adjective bitter, angry,

embittered, grudging, indignant, miffed (*informal*), offended, piqued, pissed (*taboo slang*), pissed off (*taboo slang*)

➤ Antonyms

content, flattered, gratified, pleased, satisfied

resentment noun bitterness, animosity, bad blood, grudge, ill feeling, ill will, indignation, pique, rancour, umbrage

reservation noun 1 doubt, hesitancy, scruple 2 condition, proviso, qualification, rider, stipulation 3 reserve, preserve, sanctuary, territory

reserve verb 1 keep, hoard, hold, put by, retain, save, set aside, stockpile, store 2 book, engage, prearrange, secure ◆ noun 3 store, cache, fund, hoard, reservoir, savings, stock, supply 4 reservation, park, preserve, sanctuary, tract 5 shyness, constraint, restraint, reticence, secretiveness, silence, taciturnity ◆ adjective 6 substitute, auxiliary, extra, fall-back, secondary, spare

reserved adjective 1 uncommunicative, restrained, reticent, retiring, secretive, shy, silent, standoffish, taciturn, undemonstrative 2 set aside, booked, engaged, held, kept, restricted, retained, spoken for, taken

➤ Antonyms

≠uncommunicative: demonstrative, forward, open, sociable, uninhibited, unreserved, warm

reservoir noun 1 lake, basin, pond, tank 2 store, pool, reserves, source, stock, supply

reshuffle noun 1 reorganization, change, rearrangement, redistribution, regrouping, restructuring, revision ◆ verb 2 reorganize, change around, rearrange, redistribute, regroup, restructure, revise

reside verb Formal live, abide, dwell, inhabit, lodge, stay

➤ Antonyms

holiday in, visit

residence noun home, abode,

domicile, dwelling, flat, habitation, house, lodging, place

resident noun inhabitant, citizen, local, lodger, occupant, tenant

➤ Antonyms

nonresident, visitor

residual adjective remaining, leftover, unconsumed, unused, vestigial

residue noun remainder, dregs, excess, extra, leftovers, remains, remnant, rest, surplus

resign verb 1 quit, abdicate, give in one's notice, leave, step down (*informal*), vacate 2 give up, abandon, forgo, forsake, relinquish, renounce, surrender, yield 3 resign oneself accept, acquiesce, give in, submit, succumb, yield

resignation noun 1 leaving, abandonment, abdication, departure 2 acceptance, acquiescence, compliance, endurance, nonresistance, passivity, patience, submission, sufferance

➤ Antonyms

≠acceptance: defiance, dissent, protest, resistance

resigned adjective stoical, compliant, long-suffering, patient, subdued, unresisting

resilient adjective 1 tough, buoyant, hardy, irrepressible, strong 2 flexible, elastic, plastic, pliable, rubbery, springy, supple

➤ Antonyms

≠tough: delicate, effete, sensitive, sickly, weak ≠flexible: flaccid, inflexible, limp, rigid, stiff

resist verb 1 oppose, battle, combat, defy, hinder, stand up to 2 refrain from, abstain from, avoid, forbear, forgo, keep from 3 withstand, be proof against

➤ Antonyms

≠oppose: accept, acquiesce, cave in (*informal*), give in, submit, succumb, surrender, welcome, yield ≠refrain from: enjoy, give in to, indulge in, surrender to

resistance noun fighting, battle, defiance, fight, hindrance, impediment, obstruction, opposition, struggle

resistant adjective 1 impervious, hard, proof against, strong, tough, unaffected by 2 opposed, antagonistic, hostile, intractable, intransigent, unwilling

resolute adjective determined, dogged, firm, fixed, immovable, inflexible, set, steadfast, strong-willed, tenacious, unshakable, unwavering

► **Antonyms**

doubtful, irresolute, undecided, unsteady, weak

resolution noun 1 determination, doggedness, firmness, perseverance, purpose, resoluteness, resolve, steadfastness, tenacity, willpower 2 decision, aim, declaration, determination, intent, intention, purpose, resolve

resolve verb 1 decide, conclude, determine, fix, intend, purpose 2 break down, analyse, reduce, separate 3 work out, answer, clear up, crack, fathom ♦ noun 4 determination, firmness, resoluteness, resolution, steadfastness, willpower 5 decision, intention, objective, purpose, resolution

► **Antonyms**

noun ≠determination: cowardice, half-heartedness, indecision, vacillation, wavering

resonant adjective echoing, booming, resounding, reverberating, ringing, sonorous

resort verb 1 resort to have recourse to, employ, fall back on, turn to, use, utilize ♦ noun 2 holiday centre, haunt, retreat, spot, tourist centre 3 recourse, reference

resound verb echo, re-echo, resonate, reverberate, ring

resounding adjective echoing, booming, full, powerful, resonant, reverberating, ringing, sonorous

resource noun 1 ingenuity, ability, capability, cleverness, initia-

tive, inventiveness 2 means, course, device, expedient, resort

resourceful adjective ingenious, able, bright, capable, clever, creative, inventive

► **Antonyms**

unimaginative, uninventive

resources plural noun funds, assets, capital, holdings, money, reserves, riches, supplies, wealth

respect noun 1 regard, admiration, consideration, deference, esteem, estimation, honour, recognition 2 particular, aspect, characteristic, detail, feature, matter, point, sense, way 3 As in in respect of or with respect to relation, bearing, connection, reference, regard ♦ verb 4 think highly of, admire, defer to, esteem, have a good or high opinion of, honour, look up to, value 5 abide by, adhere to, comply with, follow, heed, honour, obey, observe, show consideration for

► **Antonyms**

noun ≠regard: contempt, disdain, disregard, disrespect, irreverence, scorn ♦ verb ≠abide by: abuse, disregard, disrespect, ignore, neglect, scorn

respectable adjective 1 honourable, decent, estimable, good, honest, reputable, upright, worthy 2 reasonable, ample, appreciable, considerable, decent, fair, sizable or sizeable, substantial

► **Antonyms**

≠honourable: dishonourable, disreputable, improper, indecent, unrefined, unworthy ≠reasonable: paltry, poor, small

respectful adjective polite, civil, courteous, deferential, mannerly, reverent, well-mannered

respective adjective specific, individual, own, particular, relevant

respite noun pause, break, cessation, halt, interval, lull, recess, relief, rest

resplendent adjective brilliant, bright, dazzling, glorious, radiant, shining, splendid

respond verb <u>answer</u>, counter, react, reciprocate, rejoin, reply, retort, return

➤ **Antonyms**
ignore, remain silent, turn a blind eye

response noun <u>answer</u>, counterattack, feedback, reaction, rejoinder, reply, retort, return

responsibility noun **1** <u>authority</u>, importance, power **2** <u>accountability</u>, answerability, liability **3** <u>fault</u>, blame, culpability, guilt, liability **4** <u>level-headedness</u>, conscientiousness, dependability, rationality, sensibleness, trustworthiness **5** <u>duty</u>, care, charge, liability, obligation, onus

responsible adjective **1** <u>in charge</u>, in authority, in control **2** <u>to blame</u>, at fault, culpable, guilty **3** <u>accountable</u>, answerable, liable **4** <u>sensible</u>, dependable, level-headed, rational, reliable, trustworthy

➤ **Antonyms**
≠<u>accountable</u>: unaccountable ≠<u>sensible</u>: irresponsible, unconscientious, undependable, unreliable, untrustworthy

responsive adjective <u>sensitive</u>, alive, impressionable, open, reactive, receptive, susceptible

➤ **Antonyms**
apathetic, impassive, insensitive, unresponsive

rest[1] noun **1** <u>relaxation</u>, leisure, repose **2** <u>inactivity</u> **3** <u>refreshment</u>, relief **4** <u>calm</u>, stillness, tranquillity **5** <u>pause</u>, break, cessation, halt, interlude, intermission, interval, lull, respite, stop **6** <u>support</u>, base, holder, prop, stand ♦ verb **7** <u>relax</u>, be at ease, put one's feet up, sit down, take it easy **8** <u>place</u>, be supported, lean, lie, prop, recline, repose, sit **9** <u>stop</u>, break off, cease, halt, have a break, take a breather (informal)

➤ **Antonyms**
noun ≠<u>relaxation</u>, <u>pause</u>: activity, bustle, work ♦ verb ≠<u>relax</u>, <u>stop</u>: keep going, slog away (informal), work

rest[2] noun <u>remainder</u>, balance, excess, others, remains, remnants, residue, surplus

restaurant noun <u>café</u>, bistro, cafeteria, diner (chiefly U.S. & Canad.), eatery or eaterie, tearoom

restful adjective <u>relaxing</u>, calm, calming, peaceful, quiet, relaxed, serene, soothing, tranquil

➤ **Antonyms**
agitated, busy, disturbing, restless, uncomfortable, unrelaxed

restitution noun **1** Law <u>compensation</u>, amends, recompense, reparation, requital **2** <u>return</u>, restoration

restive adjective <u>restless</u>, antsy (informal), edgy, fidgety, impatient, jumpy, nervous, on edge

➤ **Antonyms**
at ease, calm, content, peaceful, relaxed, satisfied, serene, tranquil

restless adjective **1** <u>moving</u>, nomadic, roving, transient, unsettled, unstable, wandering **2** <u>unsettled</u>, antsy (informal), edgy, fidgeting, fidgety, jumpy, nervous, on edge, restive

➤ **Antonyms**
≠<u>moving</u>: settled, stable, steady ≠<u>unsettled</u>: comfortable, composed, easy, quiet, relaxed, restful, undisturbed

restlessness noun **1** <u>movement</u>, activity, bustle, unrest, unsettledness **2** <u>restiveness</u>, edginess, jitters (informal), jumpiness, nervousness

restoration noun **1** <u>repair</u>, reconstruction, renewal, renovation, revitalization, revival **2** <u>reinstatement</u>, re-establishment, replacement, restitution, return

➤ **Antonyms**
≠<u>repair</u>: demolition, scrapping, wrecking ≠<u>reinstatement</u>: abolition, overthrow

restore verb **1** <u>repair</u>, fix, mend, rebuild, recondition, reconstruct, refurbish, renew, renovate **2** <u>revive</u>, build up, refresh, revitalize, strengthen **3** <u>return</u>, bring back, give back, hand back, recover, reinstate, replace, send back **4** reinstate, re-establish, reintroduce

➤ **Antonyms**

≠repair: demolish, scrap, wreck ≠revive: make worse, sicken, weaken ≠reinstate: abolish, abrogate, repeal, rescind

restrain verb hold back, check, constrain, contain, control, curb, curtail, hamper, hinder, inhibit, restrict

➤ **Antonyms**

assist, encourage, gee up, help, incite, urge on

restrained adjective **1** controlled, calm, mild, moderate, self-controlled, undemonstrative **2** unobtrusive, discreet, quiet, subdued, tasteful

➤ **Antonyms**

≠controlled: fiery, hot-headed, intemperate, unrestrained, wild ≠unobtrusive: garish, loud, over-the-top, self-indulgent, tasteless

restraint noun **1** limitation, ban, check, curb, embargo, interdict, limit, rein **2** self-control, control, inhibition, moderation, self-discipline, self-possession, self-restraint

➤ **Antonyms**

≠limitation: freedom, liberty ≠self-control: excess, immoderation, intemperance, licence, self-indulgence

restrict verb limit, bound, confine, contain, hamper, handicap, inhibit, regulate, restrain

➤ **Antonyms**

allow, broaden, encourage, foster, free, permit, promote, widen

restriction noun limitation, confinement, control, curb, handicap, inhibition, regulation, restraint, rule

result noun **1** consequence, effect, end, end result, outcome, product, sequel, upshot ♦ verb **2** arise, appear, derive, develop, ensue, follow, happen, issue, spring **3** result in end in, culminate in, finish with

noun ≠consequence: beginning, cause, origin, root, source

resume verb begin again, carry on, continue, go on, proceed, re-open, restart

➤ **Antonyms**

cease, discontinue, stop

résumé noun summary, précis, recapitulation, rundown, synopsis

resumption noun continuation, carrying on, re-establishment, renewal, reopening, restart, resurgence

resurgence noun revival, rebirth, re-emergence, renaissance, resumption, resurrection, return

resurrect verb **1** restore to life, raise from the dead **2** revive, bring back, reintroduce, renew

resurrection noun **1** raising or rising from the dead, return from the dead **2** revival, reappearance, rebirth, renaissance, renewal, restoration, resurgence, return

➤ **Antonyms**

≠raising or rising from the dead: burial, demise ≠revival: killing off

resuscitate verb revive, bring round, resurrect, revitalize, save

retain verb **1** keep, hold, hold back, maintain, preserve, reserve, save **2** hire, commission, employ, engage, pay, reserve

➤ **Antonyms**

≠keep: let go, lose, release, use up

retainer noun **1** fee, advance, deposit **2** servant, attendant, domestic

retaliate verb pay (someone) back, get even with (informal), get one's own back (informal), hit back, reciprocate, strike back, take revenge

➤ **Antonyms**

accept, submit, turn the other cheek

retaliation noun revenge, an eye for an eye, counterblow, reciprocation, repayment, reprisal, requital, vengeance

retard verb slow down, arrest,

check, delay, handicap, hinder, hold back *or* up, impede, set back

➤ **Antonyms**

accelerate, advance, hasten, speed up

retch *verb* gag, be sick, heave, puke (*slang*), regurgitate, spew, throw up (*informal*), vomit

reticence *noun* silence, quietness, reserve, taciturnity

reticent *adjective* uncommunicative, close-lipped, quiet, reserved, silent, taciturn, tight-lipped, unforthcoming

➤ **Antonyms**

candid, communicative, expansive, frank, open, talkative, voluble

retinue *noun* attendants, aides, entourage, escort, followers, servants

retire *verb* 1 stop working, give up work 2 withdraw, depart, exit, go away, leave 3 go to bed, hit the hay (*slang*), hit the sack (*slang*), turn in (*informal*)

retirement *noun* withdrawal, privacy, retreat, seclusion, solitude

retiring *adjective* shy, bashful, quiet, reserved, self-effacing, timid, unassertive, unassuming

➤ **Antonyms**

bold, brassy, forward, gregarious, outgoing, sociable

retort *verb* 1 reply, answer, come back with, counter, respond, return, riposte ◆ *noun* 2 reply, answer, comeback (*informal*), rejoinder, response, riposte

retract *verb* 1 withdraw, deny, disavow, disclaim, eat one's words, recant, renege, renounce, revoke, take back 2 draw in, pull back, pull in, sheathe

retreat *verb* 1 withdraw, back away, back off, depart, draw back, fall back, go back, leave, pull back ◆ *noun* 2 withdrawal, departure, evacuation, flight, retirement 3 refuge, haven, hideaway, sanctuary, seclusion, shelter

➤ **Antonyms**

verb ≠withdraw: advance, engage, move forward ◆ *noun* ≠withdrawal: advance, charge, entrance

retrench *verb* cut back, economize, make economies, save, tighten one's belt

retrenchment *noun* cutback, cost-cutting, cut, economy, tightening one's belt

➤ **Antonyms**

expansion, investment

retribution *noun* punishment, justice, Nemesis, reckoning, reprisal, retaliation, revenge, vengeance

retrieve *verb* get back, recapture, recoup, recover, redeem, regain, restore, save, win back

retrograde *adjective* deteriorating, backward, declining, degenerative, downward, regressive, retrogressive, worsening

retrogress *verb* deteriorate, backslide, decline, go back, go downhill (*informal*), regress, relapse, worsen

retrospect *noun* hindsight, re-examination, review

➤ **Antonyms**

anticipation, foresight

return *verb* 1 come back, go back, reappear, rebound, recur, retreat, revert, turn back 2 put back, re-establish, reinstate, replace, restore 3 give back, pay back, recompense, refund, reimburse, repay 4 reply, answer, respond, retort 5 elect, choose, vote in ◆ *noun* 6 retreat, rebound, recoil 7 restoration, re-establishment, reinstatement 8 reappearance, recurrence 9 profit, gain, income, interest, proceeds, revenue, takings, yield 10 statement, account, form, list, report, summary 11 reply, answer, comeback (*informal*), rejoinder, response, retort

➤ **Antonyms**

verb ≠come back: depart, disappear, go away, leave ≠put back: give back: hold, keep, leave, remove, retain ♦ *noun* ≠<u>restoration</u>: removal ≠<u>reappearance</u>: departure, leaving

revamp *verb* <u>renovate</u>, do up (*informal*), overhaul, recondition, refurbish, restore

reveal *verb* **1** <u>make known</u>, announce, disclose, divulge, give away, impart, let out, let slip, make public, proclaim, tell **2** <u>show</u>, display, exhibit, manifest, uncover, unearth, unmask, unveil

➤ **Antonyms**

≠<u>make known</u>: conceal, cover up, hide, keep quiet about, sweep under the carpet (*informal*) ≠<u>show</u>: conceal, cover up, hide

revel *verb* **1** **revel in** <u>enjoy</u>, delight in, indulge in, lap up, luxuriate in, relish, take pleasure in, thrive on **2** <u>celebrate</u>, carouse, live it up (*informal*), make merry ♦ *noun* **3** *often plural* <u>merrymaking</u>, carousal, celebration, festivity, party, spree

➤ **Antonyms**

verb ≠<u>enjoy</u>: abhor, be uninterested in, dislike, hate, have no taste for

revelation *noun* <u>disclosure</u>, exhibition, exposé, exposure, news, proclamation, publication, uncovering, unearthing, unveiling

reveller *noun* <u>merrymaker</u>, carouser, partygoer

revelry *noun* <u>merrymaking</u>, carousal, celebration, festivity, fun, jollity, party, spree

revenge *noun* **1** <u>retaliation</u>, an eye for an eye, reprisal, retribution, vengeance ♦ *verb* **2** <u>avenge</u>, get even, get one's own back for (*informal*), hit back, repay, retaliate, take revenge for

revenue *noun* <u>income</u>, gain, proceeds, profits, receipts, returns, takings, yield

➤ **Antonyms**

expenditure, expenses, outgoings

reverberate *verb* <u>echo</u>, re-echo, resound, ring, vibrate

revere *verb* <u>be in awe of</u>, exalt,

honour, look up to, respect, reverence, venerate, worship

➤ **Antonyms**

deride, despise, hold in contempt, scorn, sneer at

reverence *noun* <u>respect</u>, admiration, awe, high esteem, honour, veneration, worship

➤ **Antonyms**

contempt, derision, disdain, scorn

reverent *adjective* <u>respectful</u>, awed, deferential, humble, reverential

➤ **Antonyms**

disrespectful, impious, irreverent, mocking, sacrilegious

reverie *noun* <u>daydream</u>, abstraction, brown study, woolgathering

reverse *verb* **1** <u>turn round</u>, invert, transpose, turn back, turn over, turn upside down, upend **2** <u>go backwards</u>, back, back up, move backwards, retreat **3** *Law* <u>change</u>, annul, cancel, countermand, invalidate, overrule, overthrow, overturn, quash, repeal, rescind, revoke, undo ♦ *noun* **4** <u>opposite</u>, contrary, converse, inverse **5** <u>back</u>, other side, rear, underside, wrong side **6** <u>misfortune</u>, adversity, affliction, blow, disappointment, failure, hardship, misadventure, mishap, reversal, setback ♦ *adjective* **7** <u>opposite</u>, contrary, converse

➤ **Antonyms**

verb ≠<u>go backwards</u>: advance, go forward, move forward ≠<u>change</u>: carry out, enforce, implement, validate ♦ *noun* ≠<u>back</u>: forward side, front, obverse, recto, right side

revert *verb* <u>return</u>, come back, go back, resume

review *noun* **1** <u>critique</u>, commentary, criticism, evaluation, judgment, notice **2** <u>magazine</u>, journal, periodical, zine (*informal*) **3** <u>survey</u>, analysis, examination, scrutiny, study **4** <u>inspection</u>, march past, parade ♦ *verb* **5** <u>assess</u>, criticize, evaluate, judge, study **6** <u>reconsider</u>, reassess, re-

reviewer noun *critic*, commentator, judge

revile verb *malign*, abuse, badmouth (*slang, chiefly U.S. & Canad.*), denigrate, knock (*informal*), reproach, run down, slag (off) (*slang*), vilify

revise verb **1** *change*, alter, amend, correct, edit, emend, redo, review, rework, update **2** *study*, cram (*informal*), go over, run through, swot up (*Brit. informal*)

revision noun **1** *change*, amendment, correction, emendation, updating **2** *studying*, cramming (*informal*), homework, swotting (*Brit. informal*)

revival noun *renewal*, reawakening, rebirth, renaissance, resurgence, resurrection, revitalization

➤ **Antonyms**
disappearance, extinction, falling off, suppression

revive verb *revitalize*, awaken, bring round, come round, invigorate, reanimate, recover, refresh, rekindle, renew, restore

➤ **Antonyms**
die out, disappear, exhaust, tire out, weary

revoke verb *cancel*, annul, countermand, disclaim, invalidate, negate, nullify, obviate, quash, repeal, rescind, retract, reverse, set aside, withdraw

➤ **Antonyms**
confirm, endorse, implement, maintain, put into effect, uphold

revolt noun **1** *uprising*, insurgency, insurrection, mutiny, rebellion, revolution, rising ♦ verb **2** *rebel*, mutiny, resist, rise **3** *disgust*, gross out (*U.S. slang*), make one's flesh creep, nauseate, repel, repulse, sicken, turn one's stomach

revolting adjective *disgusting*, foul, horrible, horrid, nauseating, repellent, repugnant, repulsive, sickening, yucky or yukky (*slang*)

➤ **Antonyms**
agreeable, attractive, delightful, fragrant, palatable, pleasant

revolution noun **1** *revolt*, coup, insurgency, mutiny, rebellion, rising, uprising **2** *transformation*, innovation, reformation, sea change, shift, upheaval **3** *rotation*, circle, circuit, cycle, lap, orbit, spin, turn

revolutionary adjective **1** *rebel*, extremist, insurgent, radical, subversive **2** *innovative*, different, drastic, ground-breaking, new, novel, progressive, radical ♦ noun **3** *rebel*, insurgent, revolutionist

➤ **Antonyms**
adjective, noun ≠*rebel*: counterrevolutionary, loyalist, reactionary ♦ adjective ≠*innovative*: conservative, conventional, mainstream, traditional

revolutionize verb *transform*, modernize, reform

revolve verb *go round*, circle, orbit, rotate, spin, turn, twist, wheel, whirl

revulsion noun *disgust*, abhorrence, detestation, loathing, repugnance, repulsion

➤ **Antonyms**
attraction, desire, fascination, liking, pleasure

reward noun **1** *payment*, bonus, bounty, compensation, premium, prize, recompense, repayment, return, wages **2** *punishment*, comeuppance (*slang*), just deserts, retribution ♦ verb **3** *compensate*, pay, recompense, remunerate, repay

➤ **Antonyms**
noun ≠*payment*: fine, penalty, punishment ♦ verb ≠*compensate*: fine, penalize, punish

rewarding adjective *satisfying*, beneficial, enriching, fruitful, fulfilling, productive, profitable, valuable, worthwhile

➤ **Antonyms**
barren, boring, fruitless, unpro-

ductive, unprofitable, unrewarding, vain

rhapsodize *verb* enthuse, go into ecstasies, gush, rave (*informal*)

rhetoric *noun* **1** oratory, eloquence **2** hyperbole, bombast, grandiloquence, magniloquence, verbosity, wordiness

rhetorical *adjective* high-flown, arty-farty (*informal*), bombastic, declamatory, grandiloquent, magniloquent, oratorical, verbose

rhyme *noun* **1** poetry, ode, poem, song, verse ♦ *verb* **2** sound like, harmonize

rhythm *noun* beat, accent, cadence, lilt, metre, pulse, swing, tempo, time

rhythmic, rhythmical *adjective* cadenced, lilting, metrical, musical, periodic, pulsating, throbbing

ribald *adjective* coarse, bawdy, blue, broad, earthy, naughty, near the knuckle (*informal*), obscene, racy, rude, smutty, vulgar

➤ **Antonyms**

decent, decorous, inoffensive, polite, proper, refined, tasteful

rich *adjective* **1** wealthy, affluent, loaded (*slang*), moneyed, prosperous, well-heeled (*informal*), well-off, well-to-do **2** well-stocked, full, productive, well-supplied **3** fruitful, abounding, abundant, ample, copious, fertile, lush, luxurious, plentiful, productive, prolific **4** full-bodied, creamy, fatty, luscious, succulent, sweet, tasty

➤ **Antonyms**

≠**wealthy:** destitute, impoverished, needy, penniless, poor ≠**well-stocked:** lacking, poor, scarce, wanting ≠**fruitful:** barren, poor, unfertile, unfruitful, unproductive ≠**full-bodied:** bland, dull

riches *plural noun* wealth, affluence, assets, fortune, plenty, resources, substance, treasure

➤ **Antonyms**

lack, need, paucity, poverty,

scarcity, want

richly *adverb* **1** elaborately, elegantly, expensively, exquisitely, gorgeously, lavishly, luxuriously, opulently, splendidly, sumptuously **2** fully, amply, appropriately, properly, suitably, thoroughly, well

rickety *adjective* shaky, insecure, precarious, ramshackle, tottering, unsound, unsteady, wobbly

rid *verb* **1** free, clear, deliver, disburden, disencumber, make free, purge, relieve, unburden **2** get rid of dispose of, dump, eject, eliminate, expel, remove, throw away or out

riddle *noun* puzzle, conundrum, enigma, mystery, poser, problem

riddled *adjective* filled, damaged, infested, permeated, pervaded, spoilt

ride *verb* **1** control, handle, manage **2** travel, be carried, go, move ♦ *noun* **3** journey, drive, jaunt, lift, outing, trip

ridicule *noun* **1** mockery, chaff, derision, gibe, jeer, laughter, raillery, scorn ♦ *verb* **2** laugh at, chaff, deride, jeer, make fun of, mock, poke fun at, sneer

ridiculous *adjective* laughable, absurd, comical, farcical, funny, ludicrous, risible, silly, stupid

➤ **Antonyms**

logical, rational, reasonable, sane, sensible, serious

rife *adjective* widespread, common, frequent, general, prevalent, rampant, ubiquitous, universal

riffraff *noun* rabble, hoi polloi, ragtag and bobtail

rifle *verb* ransack, burgle, go through, loot, pillage, plunder, rob, sack, strip

rift *noun* **1** breach, disagreement, division, falling out (*informal*), quarrel, separation, split **2** split, break, cleft, crack, crevice, fault, fissure, flaw, gap, opening

rig *verb* **1** fix (*informal*), arrange, engineer, gerrymander, manipulate, tamper with **2** *Nautical* equip, fit out, furnish, kit out, outfit, supply ♦ *noun* **3** apparatus, equipment, fittings, fixtures, gear, tackle

right *adjective* **1** just, equitable, ethical, fair, good, honest, lawful, moral, proper **2** correct, accurate, exact, factual, genuine, precise, true, valid **3** proper, appropriate, becoming, desirable, done, fit, fitting, seemly, suitable ♦ *adverb* **4** correctly, accurately, exactly, genuinely, precisely, truly **5** suitably, appropriately, aptly, fittingly, properly **6** straight, directly, promptly, quickly, straightaway **7** exactly, precisely, squarely ♦ *noun* **8** prerogative, authority, business, claim, due, freedom, liberty, licence, permission, power, privilege **9** justice, fairness, lawfulness, legality, righteousness, truth ♦ *verb* **10** rectify, correct, fix, put right, redress, settle, sort out, straighten

➤ **Antonyms**

adjective ≠just: bad, dishonest, immoral, improper, indecent, unethical, unfair, unjust, wrong ≠correct: erroneous, false, inaccurate, incorrect, mistaken, untruthful, wrong ≠proper: inappropriate, undesirable, unfitting, unseemly, unsuitable, wrong ♦ *adverb* ≠correctly: inaccurately, incorrectly ≠suitably: improperly, incompletely ≠straight: indirectly, slowly ♦ *noun* ≠justice: evil, immorality, impropriety ♦ *verb* ≠rectify: make crooked, topple

right away *adverb* immediately, at once, directly, forthwith, instantly, now, pronto (*informal*), straightaway

righteous *adjective* virtuous, ethical, fair, good, honest, honourable, just, moral, pure, upright

➤ **Antonyms**

dishonourable, evil, immoral, improper, sinful, unjust, wicked

righteousness *noun* virtue, goodness, honesty, honour, integrity, justice, morality, probity, purity, rectitude, uprightness

rightful *adjective* lawful, due, just, legal, legitimate, proper, real, true, valid

rigid *adjective* **1** strict, exact, fixed, inflexible, rigorous, set, stringent, unbending, uncompromising **2** stiff, inflexible, unyielding

➤ **Antonyms**

≠strict: flexible, indulgent, lax, lenient, merciful, soft, tolerant ≠stiff: bending, elastic, flexible, pliable, pliant, yielding

rigmarole *noun* **1** procedure, bother, carry-on (*informal, chiefly Brit.*), fuss, hassle (*informal*), nonsense, palaver, pantomime (*informal*), performance (*informal*) **2** twaddle, gibberish

rigorous *adjective* strict, demanding, exacting, hard, harsh, inflexible, severe, stern, stringent, tough

➤ **Antonyms**

easy, gentle, lax, lenient, permissive, relaxed

rigour *noun* **1** hardship, ordeal, privation, suffering, trial **2** strictness, harshness, inflexibility, rigidity, sternness, stringency

rigout *noun Informal* outfit, costume, dress, garb, gear (*informal*), get-up (*informal*), togs

rig out *verb* **1** dress, array, attire, clothe, costume, kit out **2** equip, fit, furnish, kit out, outfit

rig up *verb* set up, arrange, assemble, build, construct, erect, fix up, improvise, put together, put up

rile *verb* anger, aggravate (*informal*), annoy, get or put one's back up, irk, irritate

rim *noun* edge, border, brim, brink, lip, margin, verge

rind *noun* skin, crust, husk, outer layer, peel

ring[1] *verb* **1** chime, clang, peal, reverberate, sound, toll **2** phone, buzz (*informal, chiefly Brit.*), call, telephone ♦ *noun* **3** chime, knell, peal **4** call, buzz (*informal, chiefly Brit.*), phone call

ring[2] *noun* **1** circle, band, circuit,

halo, hoop, loop, round **2** arena, circus, enclosure, rink **3** gang, association, band, cartel, circle, group, mob, syndicate ♦ *verb* **4** encircle, enclose, gird, girdle, surround

rinse *verb* **1** wash, bathe, clean, cleanse, dip, splash ♦ *noun* **2** wash, bath, dip, splash

riot *noun* **1** disturbance, anarchy, confusion, disorder, lawlessness, strife, tumult, turbulence, turmoil, upheaval **2** merrymaking, carousal, festivity, frolic, high jinks, revelry **3** display, extravaganza, profusion, show, splash **4** run riot: a rampage, be out of control, go wild **b** grow profusely, spread like wildfire ♦ *verb* **5** rampage, go on the rampage, run riot

riotous *adjective* **1** unrestrained, boisterous, loud, noisy, uproarious, wild **2** unruly, anarchic, disorderly, lawless, rebellious, rowdy, ungovernable, violent

➤ **Antonyms**

calm, civilized, disciplined, orderly, peaceful, quiet, restrained, well-behaved

rip *verb* **1** tear, burst, claw, cut, gash, lacerate, rend, slash, slit, split ♦ *noun* **2** tear, cut, gash, hole, laceration, rent, slash, slit, split

ripe *adjective* **1** mature, mellow, ready, ripened, seasoned **2** suitable, auspicious, favourable, ideal, opportune, right, timely

➤ **Antonyms**

≠mature: green, immature, undeveloped, unripe ≠suitable: inappropriate, inconvenient, inopportune, unfavourable, unsuitable, untimely

ripen *verb* mature, burgeon, develop, grow ripe, season

rip-off *noun Slang* cheat, con (*informal*), con trick (*informal*), fraud, scam (*slang*), swindle, theft

rip off *verb Slang* cheat, con (*informal*), defraud, fleece, rob, skin (*slang*), swindle

riposte *noun* **1** retort, answer, comeback (*informal*), rejoinder, reply, response, sally ♦ *verb* **2** retort, answer, come back, reply, respond

rise *verb* **1** get up, arise, get to one's feet, stand up **2** go up, ascend, climb **3** advance, get on, progress, prosper **4** get steeper, ascend, go uphill, slope upwards **5** increase, go up, grow, intensify, mount **6** rebel, mutiny, revolt **7** originate, happen, issue, occur, spring ♦ *noun* **8** upward slope, ascent, elevation, incline **9** pay increase, increment, raise (*U.S.*) **10** increase, upsurge, upswing, upturn **11** advancement, climb, progress, promotion **12** give rise to cause, bring about, effect, produce, result in

➤ **Antonyms**

verb ≠go up, get steeper: descend, drop, fall, plunge, sink ≠increase: decline, decrease, diminish, drop, dwindle, fall, lessen, reduce, sink ♦ *noun* ≠increase: decline, decrease, downswing, downturn, drop, fall

risk *noun* **1** danger, chance, gamble, hazard, jeopardy, peril, pitfall, possibility ♦ *verb* **2** dare, chance, endanger, gamble, hazard, imperil, jeopardize, venture

risky *adjective* dangerous, chancy (*informal*), dicey (*informal, chiefly Brit.*), dodgy (*Brit., Austral., & N.Z. informal*), hazardous, perilous, uncertain, unsafe

➤ **Antonyms**

certain, reliable, safe, secure, stable, sure

risqué *adjective* suggestive, bawdy, blue, improper, indelicate, naughty, near the knuckle (*informal*), racy, ribald

rite *noun* ceremony, custom, observance, practice, procedure, ritual

ritual *noun* **1** ceremony, observance, rite **2** custom, convention, habit, practice, procedure, protocol, routine, tradition ♦ *adjective* **3** ceremonial, conventional, customary, habitual, routine

ritzy adjective Slang luxurious, deluxe, grand, high-class, luxury, plush (informal), posh (informal, chiefly Brit.), sumptuous, swanky (informal)

rival noun 1 opponent, adversary, competitor, contender, contestant ◆ adjective 2 competing, conflicting, opposing ◆ verb 3 compete, be a match for, come up to, compare with, equal, match

► **Antonyms**

noun ≠opponent: ally, friend, helper, supporter ◆ verb ≠compete: aid, back, help, support

rivalry noun competition, conflict, contention, contest, opposition

river noun 1 stream, brook, burn (Scot.), creek, tributary, waterway 2 flow, flood, rush, spate, torrent

riveting adjective enthralling, absorbing, captivating, engrossing, fascinating, gripping, hypnotic, spellbinding

road noun way, course, highway, lane, motorway, path, pathway, roadway, route, track

roam verb wander, prowl, ramble, range, rove, stray, travel, walk

roar verb 1 cry, bawl, bay, bellow, howl, shout, yell 2 guffaw, hoot, laugh heartily, split one's sides (informal) ◆ noun 3 cry, bellow, howl, outcry, shout, yell 4 guffaw, hoot

rob verb steal from, burgle, cheat, con (informal), defraud, deprive, dispossess, do out of (informal), hold up, loot, mug (informal), pillage, plunder, raid

robber noun thief, bandit, brigand, burglar, cheat, con man (informal), fraud, looter, mugger (informal), plunderer, raider

robbery noun theft, burglary, hold-up, larceny, mugging (informal), pillage, plunder, raid, rip-off (slang), stealing, stick-up (slang, chiefly U.S.), swindle

robe noun 1 gown, costume, habit ◆ verb 2 clothe, dress, garb

robot noun machine, android, automaton, mechanical man

robust adjective strong, fit, hale, hardy, healthy, muscular, powerful, stout, strapping, sturdy, tough, vigorous

► **Antonyms**

delicate, feeble, frail, sickly, unhealthy, weak, weedy (informal)

rock¹ noun stone, boulder

rock² verb 1 sway, lurch, pitch, reel, roll, swing, toss 2 shock, astonish, astound, shake, stagger, stun, surprise

rocky¹ adjective rough, craggy, rugged, stony

rocky² adjective unstable, rickety, shaky, unsteady, wobbly

rod noun stick, bar, baton, cane, pole, shaft, staff, wand

rogue noun scoundrel, blackguard, crook (informal), fraud, rascal, scally (Northwest English dialect), scamp, villain

role noun 1 job, capacity, duty, function, part, position, post, task 2 part, character, portrayal, representation

roll verb 1 turn, go round, revolve, rotate, spin, swivel, trundle, twirl, wheel, whirl 2 wind, bind, enfold, envelop, furl, swathe, wrap 3 flow, run, undulate 4 level, even, flatten, press, smooth 5 toss, lurch, reel, rock, sway, tumble ◆ noun 6 turn, cycle, reel, revolution, rotation, spin, twirl, wheel, whirl 7 register, census, index, list, record 8 rumble, boom, reverberation, roar, thunder

rollicking adjective boisterous, carefree, devil-may-care, exuberant, hearty, jaunty, lively, playful

► **Antonyms**

dull, gloomy, lifeless, morose, sad, sedate, serious

roly-poly adjective plump, buxom, chubby, fat, podgy, rounded, tubby

romance noun 1 love affair, affair, amour, attachment, liaison, relationship 2 excitement, charm, colour, fascination, glamour, mystery **3** <u>story</u>, fairy tale, fantasy, legend, love story, melodrama, tale

romantic adjective **1** <u>loving</u>, amorous, fond, icky (informal), passionate, sentimental, tender **2** <u>idealistic</u>, dreamy, impractical, starry-eyed, unrealistic **3** <u>exciting</u>, colourful, fascinating, glamorous, mysterious ♦ noun **4** <u>idealist</u>, dreamer, sentimentalist

> ► **Antonyms**

adjective ≠<u>loving</u>: cold-hearted, insensitive, unaffectionate, unloving, unromantic, unsentimental ≠<u>idealistic</u>: practical, realistic ≠<u>exciting</u>: uninspiring

romp verb **1** <u>frolic</u>, caper, cavort, frisk, gambol, have fun, sport **2** <u>win easily</u>, walk it (informal), win by a mile (informal), win hands down ♦ noun **3** <u>frolic</u>, caper, lark (informal)

room noun **1** <u>chamber</u>, apartment, office **2** <u>space</u>, area, capacity, expanse, extent, leeway, margin, range, scope **3** <u>opportunity</u>, chance, occasion, scope

roomy adjective <u>spacious</u>, ample, broad, capacious, commodious, extensive, generous, large, sizable or sizeable, wide

> ► **Antonyms**

confined, cramped, narrow, small, tiny

root[1] noun **1** <u>stem</u>, rhizome, tuber **2** <u>source</u>, base, bottom, cause, core, foundation, heart, nucleus, origin, seat, seed **3** <u>roots</u> <u>sense of belonging</u>, birthplace, cradle, family, heritage, home, origins ♦ verb **4** <u>become established</u>, anchor, establish, fasten, fix, ground, implant, moor, set, stick

root[2] verb <u>dig</u>, burrow, ferret

rooted adjective <u>deep-seated</u>, confirmed, deep, deeply felt, entrenched, established, firm, fixed, ingrained

root out verb <u>get rid of</u>, abolish, do away with, eliminate, eradicate, exterminate, extirpate, remove, weed out

rope noun **1** <u>cord</u>, cable, hawser, line, strand **2** <u>know the ropes</u> <u>be experienced</u>, be an old hand, be knowledgeable

rope in verb Brit. <u>persuade</u>, engage, enlist, inveigle, involve, talk into

ropey, ropy adjective Informal **1** <u>inferior</u>, deficient, inadequate, of poor quality, poor, substandard **2** <u>unwell</u>, below par, off colour, under the weather (informal)

roster noun <u>rota</u>, agenda, catalogue, list, register, roll, schedule, table

rostrum noun <u>stage</u>, dais, platform, podium, stand

rosy adjective **1** <u>pink</u>, red **2** <u>glowing</u>, blooming, healthy-looking, radiant, ruddy **3** <u>promising</u>, auspicious, bright, cheerful, encouraging, favourable, hopeful, optimistic

> ► **Antonyms**

≠<u>glowing</u>: ashen, grey, pale, pallid, sickly, wan ≠<u>promising</u>: depressing, discouraging, dismal, gloomy, hopeless, unpromising

rot verb **1** <u>decay</u>, crumble, decompose, deteriorate, go bad, moulder, perish, putrefy, spoil **2** <u>deteriorate</u>, decline, waste away ♦ noun **3** <u>decay</u>, blight, canker, corruption, decomposition, mould, putrefaction **4** Informal <u>nonsense</u>, claptrap (informal), codswallop (Brit. slang), drivel, garbage (chiefly U.S.), hogwash, poppycock (informal), rubbish, stuff and nonsense, trash, tripe (informal), twaddle

rotary adjective <u>revolving</u>, rotating, spinning, turning

rotate verb **1** <u>revolve</u>, go round, gyrate, pivot, reel, spin, swivel, turn, wheel **2** <u>follow in sequence</u>, alternate, switch, take turns

rotation noun **1** <u>revolution</u>, orbit, reel, spin, spinning, turn, turning, wheel **2** <u>sequence</u>, alternation, cycle, succession, switching

rotten adjective **1** <u>decaying</u>, bad, corrupt, crumbling, decomposing, festering, mouldy, perished, putrescent, rank, sour, stinking **2** *Informal* despicable, base, contemptible, dirty, mean, nasty **3** *Informal* inferior, crummy (*slang*), duff (*Brit. informal*), inadequate, lousy (*slang*), poor, substandard, unsatisfactory **4** corrupt, crooked (*informal*), dishonest, dishonourable, immoral, perfidious

➤ Antonyms

≠decaying: fresh, good, pure, sweet, wholesome ≠corrupt: decent, honest, honourable, moral, scrupulous, trustworthy

rotter *noun* Old-fashioned scoundrel, blackguard, bounder (*old-fashioned Brit. slang*), cad (*Brit. informal*), rat (*informal*)

rotund *adjective* **1** round, globular, rounded, spherical **2** plump, chubby, corpulent, fat, fleshy, podgy, portly, stout, tubby

➤ Antonyms

≠plump: gaunt, lean, skinny, slender, slight, slim, thin

rough *adjective* **1** uneven, broken, bumpy, craggy, irregular, jagged, rocky, stony **2** ungracious, blunt, brusque, coarse, impolite, rude, unceremonious, uncivil, uncouth, unmannerly **3** unpleasant, arduous, difficult, hard, tough, uncomfortable **4** approximate, estimated, general, imprecise, inexact, sketchy, vague **5** stormy, choppy, squally, turbulent, wild **6** basic, crude, imperfect, incomplete, rudimentary, sketchy, unfinished, unpolished, unrefined **7** harsh, cruel, hard, nasty, tough, unfeeling, unpleasant, violent ♦ *verb* **8** rough out outline, draft, plan, sketch ♦ *noun* **9** outline, draft, mock-up, preliminary sketch

➤ Antonyms

adjective ≠uneven: even, level, regular, smooth, unbroken ≠ungracious: courteous, gracious, pleasant, polite, refined, sophisticated, urbane, well-mannered ≠unpleasant: comfortable, cushy (*informal*), easy, pleasant, soft ≠approximate: exact, perfected,

specific ≠stormy: calm, gentle, quiet, smooth, tranquil ≠basic: complete, detailed, finished, perfected, polished, refined, specific ≠harsh: gentle, just, kind, mild, pleasant, quiet, soft

rough-and-ready *adjective* makeshift, crude, improvised, provisional, sketchy, stopgap, unpolished, unrefined

round *adjective* **1** spherical, circular, curved, cylindrical, globular, rotund, rounded **2** plump, ample, fleshy, full, full-fleshed, rotund ♦ *verb* **3** go round, bypass, circle, encircle, flank, skirt, turn ♦ *noun* **4** sphere, ball, band, circle, disc, globe, orb, ring **5** series, cycle, sequence, session, succession **6** stage, division, lap, level, period, session, turn **7** course, beat, circuit, routine, schedule, series, tour

roundabout *adjective* indirect, circuitous, devious, discursive, evasive, oblique, tortuous

➤ Antonyms

direct, straight, straightforward

round off *verb* complete, close, conclude, finish off

➤ Antonyms

begin, commence, initiate, open, start

roundup *noun* gathering, assembly, collection, herding, marshalling, muster, rally

round up *verb* gather, collect, drive, group, herd, marshal, muster, rally

rouse *verb* **1** wake up, awaken, call, rise, wake **2** excite, agitate, anger, animate, incite, inflame, move, provoke, stimulate, stir

rousing *adjective* lively, exciting, inspiring, moving, spirited, stimulating, stirring

➤ Antonyms

boring, dreary, dull, wearisome

rout *noun* **1** defeat, beating, debacle, drubbing, overthrow, pasting (*slang*), thrashing ♦ *verb* **2** defeat, beat, conquer, crush, destroy, drub, overthrow, thrash, wipe the floor with (*informal*)

route noun way, beat, circuit, course, direction, itinerary, journey, path, road

routine noun 1 procedure, custom, method, order, pattern, practice, programme ♦ adjective 2 usual, customary, everyday, habitual, normal, ordinary, standard, typical 3 boring, dull, humdrum, predictable, tedious, tiresome

➤ **Antonyms**

adjective ≠usual: abnormal, different, exceptional, irregular, special, unusual

rove verb wander, drift, ramble, range, roam, stray, traipse (informal)

row[1] noun 1 line, bank, column, file, range, series, string 2 in a row consecutively, one after the other, successively

row[2] noun Informal 1 quarrel, brawl, dispute, squabble, tiff, trouble 2 disturbance, commotion, noise, racket, rumpus, tumult, uproar ♦ verb 3 quarrel, argue, dispute, fight, squabble, wrangle

rowdy adjective 1 disorderly, loud, noisy, rough, unruly, wild ♦ noun 2 hooligan, lout, ruffian, tearaway (Brit.), yob or yobbo (Brit. slang)

➤ **Antonyms**

adjective ≠disorderly: gentle, law-abiding, orderly, peaceful, refined

royal adjective 1 regal, imperial, kingly, princely, queenly, sovereign 2 splendid, grand, impressive, magnificent, majestic, stately

rub verb 1 stroke, caress, massage 2 polish, clean, scour, shine, wipe 3 chafe, abrade, fray, grate, scrape ♦ noun 4 massage, caress, kneading 5 polish, shine, stroke, wipe

rubbish noun 1 waste, garbage (chiefly U.S.), junk (informal), litter, lumber, refuse, scrap, trash 2 nonsense, claptrap (informal), codswallop (Brit. slang), garbage (chiefly U.S.), hogwash, hot air (informal), rot, tommyrot, trash, tripe (informal), twaddle

rub out verb erase, cancel, delete, efface, obliterate, remove, wipe out

ructions plural noun Informal row, commotion, disturbance, fracas, fuss, hue and cry, trouble, uproar

ruddy adjective 1 rosy, blooming, fresh, glowing, healthy, radiant, red, reddish, rosy-cheeked

➤ **Antonyms**

anaemic, ashen, grey, pale, pallid, sickly, wan

rude adjective 1 impolite, abusive, cheeky, discourteous, disrespectful, ill-mannered, impertinent, impudent, insolent, insulting, uncivil, unmannerly 2 vulgar, boorish, brutish, coarse, graceless, loutish, oafish, rough, uncivilized, uncouth, uncultured 3 unpleasant, abrupt, harsh, sharp, startling, sudden 4 roughly-made, artless, crude, inartistic, inelegant, makeshift, primitive, raw, rough, simple

➤ **Antonyms**

≠impolite: considerate, cordial, courteous, gracious, polite, respectful, well-bred ≠vulgar: cultured, educated, elegant, learned, polished, refined, sophisticated, urbane ≠roughly-made: finished, shapely, smooth, well-made

rudimentary adjective basic, early, elementary, fundamental, initial, primitive, undeveloped

➤ **Antonyms**

advanced, developed, mature, refined, sophisticated

rudiments plural noun basics, beginnings, elements, essentials, foundation, fundamentals

rue verb Literary regret, be sorry for, kick oneself for, lament, mourn, repent

rueful adjective regretful, contrite, mournful, penitent, remorseful, repentant, sorrowful, sorry

➤ **Antonyms**

cheerful, delighted, glad, happy, joyful, pleased, unrepentant

ruffian noun thug, brute, bully, heavy (slang), hoodlum, hooligan, rough (informal), tough

ruffle verb 1 disarrange, dishevel, disorder, mess up, rumple, tousle 2 annoy, agitate, fluster, irritate, nettle, peeve (informal), upset

► Antonyms

≠annoy: appease, calm, comfort, console, soothe

rugged adjective 1 rocky, broken, bumpy, craggy, difficult, irregular, jagged, ragged, rough, uneven 2 strong-featured, roughhewn, weather-beaten 3 tough, brawny, burly, husky (informal), muscular, robust, strong, sturdy, well-built

► Antonyms

≠rocky: even, gentle, level, regular, smooth, unbroken ≠strong-featured: delicate, pretty, refined, smooth, unmarked, youthful ≠tough: delicate, feeble, frail, infirm, sickly, soft, weak

ruin verb 1 destroy, crush, defeat, demolish, devastate, lay waste, smash, wreck 2 bankrupt, impoverish, pauperize 3 spoil, blow (slang), botch, damage, make a mess of, mess up, screw up (informal) ◆ noun 4 destruction, breakdown, collapse, defeat, devastation, downfall, fall, undoing, wreck 5 disrepair, decay, disintegration, ruination, wreckage 6 bankruptcy, destitution, insolvency

► Antonyms

verb ≠destroy: build, construct, create, keep, preserve, save ≠spoil: enhance, enrich, improve, mend, repair, restore, strengthen, support ◆ noun ≠destruction: creation, preservation, success, triumph, victory

ruinous adjective 1 destructive, calamitous, catastrophic, devastating, dire, disastrous, shattering 2 extravagant, crippling, immoderate, wasteful

rule noun 1 regulation, axiom, canon, decree, direction, guideline, law, maxim, precept, princi-

ple, tenet 2 custom, convention, habit, practice, procedure, routine, tradition 3 government, authority, command, control, dominion, jurisdiction, mastery, power, regime, reign 4 **as a rule** usually, generally, mainly, normally, on the whole, ordinarily ◆ verb 5 govern, be in authority, be in power, command, control, direct, reign 6 be prevalent, be customary, predominate, preponderate, prevail 7 decree, decide, judge, pronounce, settle

rule out verb exclude, ban, debar, dismiss, eliminate, leave out, preclude, prohibit, reject

► Antonyms

allow, approve, authorize, let, license, order, permit, sanction

ruler noun 1 governor, commander, controller, head of state, king or queen, leader, lord, monarch, potentate, sovereign 2 measure, rule, yardstick

ruling adjective 1 governing, commanding, controlling, reigning 2 predominant, chief, dominant, main, pre-eminent, preponderant, prevailing, principal ◆ noun 3 decision, adjudication, decree, judgment, pronouncement, verdict

► Antonyms

adjective ≠predominant: auxiliary, inferior, least, minor, secondary, subordinate, subsidiary, unimportant

ruminate verb ponder, cogitate, consider, contemplate, deliberate, mull over, muse, reflect, think, turn over in one's mind

rummage verb search, delve, forage, hunt, ransack, root

rumour noun story, buzz, dirt (U.S. slang), gossip, hearsay, news, report, talk, whisper, word

rump noun buttocks, backside (informal), bottom, bum (Brit. slang), buns (U.S. slang), butt (U.S. & Canad. informal), derrière (euphemistic), hindquarters, posterior, rear, rear end, seat

rumpus noun commotion, disturbance, furore, fuss, hue and cry, noise, row, uproar

run verb 1 race, bolt, dash, gallop, hare (*Brit. informal*), hurry, jog, leg it (*informal*), lope, rush, scurry, sprint 2 flee, beat a retreat, beat it (*slang*), bolt, do a runner (*slang*), escape, leg it (*informal*), make a run for it, take flight, take off (*informal*), take to one's heels 3 move, glide, go, pass, roll, skim 4 work, function, go, operate, perform 5 manage, administer, be in charge of, control, direct, handle, head, lead, operate 6 continue, extend, go, proceed, reach, stretch 7 flow, discharge, go, gush, leak, pour, spill, spout, stream 8 melt, dissolve, go soft, liquefy 9 publish, display, feature, print 10 *chiefly U.S. & Canad.* compete, be a candidate, contend, put oneself up for, stand, take part 11 smuggle, bootleg, traffic in ♦ noun 12 race, dash, gallop, jog, rush, sprint, spurt 13 ride, drive, excursion, jaunt, outing, spin (*informal*), trip 14 sequence, course, period, season, series, spell, stretch, string 15 enclosure, coop, pen 16 in the long run in the end, eventually, ultimately

> **Antonyms**

verb ≠race: crawl, creep, dawdle, walk ≠flee: remain, stay ≠continue: cease, stop

run across verb meet, bump into, come across, encounter, run into

runaway noun 1 fugitive, deserter, escapee, refugee, truant ♦ adjective 2 escaped, fleeing, fugitive, loose, wild

run away verb flee, abscond, bolt, do a runner (*slang*), escape, fly the coop (*U.S. & Canad. informal*), make a run for it, scram (*informal*), take to one's heels

run-down adjective 1 exhausted, below par, debilitated, drained, enervated, unhealthy, weak, weary, worn-out 2 dilapidated, broken-down, decrepit, ramshackle, seedy, shabby, worn-out

> **Antonyms**

≠exhausted: fine, fit, healthy, well

run down verb 1 criticize, badmouth (*slang, chiefly U.S. & Canad.*), belittle, decry, denigrate, disparage, knock (*informal*), rubbish (*informal*), slag (off) (*slang*) 2 reduce, curtail, cut, cut back, decrease, downsize, trim 3 knock down, hit, knock over, run into, run over 4 weaken, debilitate, exhaust

run into verb 1 meet, bump into, come across or upon, encounter, run across 2 collide with, hit, strike

runner noun 1 athlete, jogger, sprinter 2 messenger, courier, dispatch bearer, errand boy

running adjective 1 continuous, constant, incessant, perpetual, unbroken, uninterrupted 2 flowing, moving, streaming ♦ noun 3 management, administration, control, direction, leadership, organization, supervision 4 working, functioning, maintenance, operation, performance

runny adjective flowing, fluid, liquefied, liquid, melted, watery

run off verb 1 flee, bolt, do a runner (*slang*), escape, fly the coop (*U.S. & Canad. informal*), make off, run away, take flight, take to one's heels

run-of-the-mill adjective ordinary, average, bog-standard (*Brit. & Irish slang*), mediocre, middling, passable, tolerable, undistinguished, unexceptional

> **Antonyms**

excellent, exceptional, extraordinary, marvellous, splendid, unusual

run out verb 1 be used up, be exhausted, dry up, fail, finish, give out 2 expire, end, terminate

run over verb 1 knock down, hit,

knock over, run down **2** <u>review</u>, check, go over, go through, rehearse, run through

rupture noun **1** <u>break</u>, breach, burst, crack, fissure, rent, split, tear ♦ verb **2** <u>break</u>, burst, crack, separate, sever, split, tear

rural adjective <u>rustic</u>, agricultural, country, pastoral, sylvan

➤ **Antonyms**
city, cosmopolitan, town, urban

ruse noun <u>trick</u>, device, dodge, hoax, manoeuvre, ploy, stratagem, subterfuge

rush verb **1** <u>hurry</u>, bolt, career, dash, fly, hasten, race, run, shoot, speed, tear **2** <u>push</u>, hurry, hustle, press **3** <u>attack</u>, charge, storm ♦ noun **4** <u>hurry</u>, charge, dash, haste, race, scramble, stampede, surge **5** <u>attack</u>, assault, charge, onslaught ♦ adjective **6** <u>hasty</u>, fast, hurried, quick, rapid, swift, urgent

➤ **Antonyms**
verb ≠<u>hurry</u>: dally, dawdle, delay, procrastinate, slow down, tarry, wait ♦ adjective ≠<u>hasty</u>: careful, detailed, leisurely, slow, thorough, unhurried

rust noun **1** <u>corrosion</u>, oxidation **2** <u>mildew</u>, blight, mould, must, rot ♦ verb **3** <u>corrode</u>, oxidize

rustic adjective **1** <u>rural</u>, country, pastoral, sylvan **2** <u>uncouth</u>, awkward, coarse, crude, rough ♦ noun **3** <u>yokel</u>, boor, bumpkin, clod, clodhopper (informal), hick (informal, chiefly U.S. & Canad.), peasant

➤ **Antonyms**
adjective ≠<u>rural</u>: cosmopolitan, urban ≠<u>uncouth</u>: courtly, polished, refined, sophisticated, urbane ♦ noun ≠<u>yokel</u>: city slicker, sophisticate, townie, townsman

rustle verb **1** <u>crackle</u>, crinkle, whisper ♦ noun **2** <u>crackle</u>, crinkling, rustling, whisper

rusty adjective **1** <u>corroded</u>, oxidized, rust-covered, rusted **2** <u>reddish-brown</u>, chestnut, coppery, reddish, russet, rust-coloured **3** <u>out of practice</u>, stale, unpractised, weak

rut noun **1** <u>groove</u>, furrow, indentation, track, trough, wheel mark **2** <u>habit</u>, dead end, pattern, routine, system

ruthless adjective <u>merciless</u>, brutal, callous, cruel, harsh, heartless, pitiless, relentless, remorseless

➤ **Antonyms**
compassionate, forgiving, lenient, merciful, pitying, sparing

S s

sabotage noun **1** <u>damage</u>, destruction, disruption, subversion, wrecking ♦ verb **2** <u>damage</u>, destroy, disable, disrupt, incapacitate, subvert, vandalize, wreck

saccharine adjective <u>oversweet</u>, cloying, honeyed, icky (informal), nauseating, sickly

sack[1] noun **1 the sack** <u>dismissal</u>, discharge, the axe (informal), the boot (slang), the push (slang) ♦ verb **2** Informal <u>dismiss</u>, axe (informal), discharge, fire (informal), give (someone) the push (informal)

sack[2] noun **1** <u>plundering</u>, looting, pillage ♦ verb **2** <u>plunder</u>, loot, pillage, raid, rob, ruin, strip

sacred adjective **1** <u>holy</u>, blessed, divine, hallowed, revered, sanctified **2** <u>religious</u>, ecclesiastical, holy **3** <u>inviolable</u>, protected, sacrosanct

➤ **Antonyms**
≠<u>holy</u>, <u>religious</u>: lay, nonspiritual, profane, secular, temporal, worldly

sacrifice noun **1** <u>surrender</u>, loss, renunciation **2** <u>offering</u>, oblation ♦ verb **3** <u>give up</u>, forego, forfeit, let go, lose, say goodbye to, surrender **4** <u>offer</u>, immolate, offer up

sacrilege noun <u>desecration</u>, blasphemy, heresy, impiety, irreverence, profanation, violation

➤ **Antonyms**

piety, respect, reverence

sacrilegious *adjective* profane, blasphemous, desecrating, impious, irreligious, irreverent

sacrosanct *adjective* inviolable, hallowed, inviolate, sacred, sanctified, set apart, untouchable

sad *adjective* 1 unhappy, blue, dejected, depressed, doleful, down, low, low-spirited, melancholy, mournful, woebegone 2 tragic, depressing, dismal, grievous, harrowing, heart-rending, moving, pathetic, pitiful, poignant, upsetting 3 deplorable, bad, lamentable, sorry, wretched

➤ **Antonyms**

≠unhappy: blithe, cheerful, cheery, chirpy (*informal*), glad, happy, in good spirits, jolly, joyful, joyous, light-hearted, merry, pleased ≠deplorable: good

sadden *verb* upset, deject, depress, distress, grieve, make sad

saddle *verb* burden, encumber, load, lumber (*Brit. informal*)

sadistic *adjective* cruel, barbarous, brutal, ruthless, vicious

sadness *noun* unhappiness, dejection, depression, despondency, grief, melancholy, misery, poignancy, sorrow, the blues

safe *adjective* 1 secure, impregnable, in safe hands, out of danger, out of harm's way, protected, safe and sound 2 unharmed, all right, intact, O.K. *or* okay (*informal*), undamaged, unhurt, unscathed 3 risk-free, certain, impregnable, secure, sound ♦ *noun* 4 strongbox, coffer, deposit box, repository, safe-deposit box, vault

➤ **Antonyms**

adjective ≠secure: at risk, endangered, imperilled, insecure, jeopardized, put at risk, put in danger, threatened

safeguard *verb* 1 protect, defend, guard, look after, preserve ♦ *noun* 2 protection, defence, guard, security

safely *adverb* in safety, in one piece, safe and sound, with impunity, without risk

safety *noun* 1 security, impregnability, protection 2 shelter, cover, refuge, sanctuary

sag *verb* 1 sink, bag, dip, droop, fall, give way, hang loosely, slump 2 tire, droop, flag, wane, weaken, wilt

saga *noun* tale, epic, narrative, story, yarn

sage *noun* 1 wise man, elder, guru, master, philosopher ♦ *adjective* 2 wise, judicious, sagacious, sapient, sensible

sail *verb* 1 embark, set sail 2 pilot, steer 3 glide, drift, float, fly, skim, soar, sweep, wing

sailor *noun* mariner, marine, sea dog, seafarer, seaman

saintly *adjective* virtuous, godly, holy, pious, religious, righteous, saintlike

sake *noun* 1 As in *for someone's or one's own sake* benefit, account, behalf, good, interest, welfare 2 As in *for the sake of purpose, aim, end, motive, objective, reason

salacious *adjective* lascivious, carnal, erotic, lecherous, lewd, libidinous, lustful

salary *noun* pay, earnings, income, wage, wages

sale *noun* 1 selling, deal, disposal, marketing, transaction 2 for sale available, obtainable, on the market

salient *adjective* prominent, conspicuous, important, noticeable, outstanding, pronounced, striking

sallow *adjective* wan, anaemic, pale, pallid, pasty, sickly, unhealthy, yellowish

➤ **Antonyms**

glowing, healthy-looking, radiant, rosy, ruddy

salt *noun* 1 seasoning, flavour, relish, savour, taste 2 with a grain *or* pinch of salt sceptically, cynically, disbelievingly, suspiciously, with reservations ♦ *adjective* 3 salty, brackish, briny, saline

salty *adjective* salt, brackish, briny, saline

salubrious *adjective* health-giving, beneficial, good for one, healthy, wholesome

salutary *adjective* beneficial, advantageous, good for one, profitable, useful, valuable

salute *verb* **1** greet, acknowledge, address, hail, welcome **2** honour, acknowledge, pay tribute or homage to, recognize ♦ *noun* **3** greeting, address, recognition, salutation

salvage *verb* save, recover, redeem, rescue, retrieve

salvation *noun* saving, deliverance, escape, preservation, redemption, rescue

➤ **Antonyms**
condemnation, damnation, doom, downfall, hell, perdition, ruin

salve *noun* ointment, balm, cream, lotion

same *adjective* **1** aforementioned, aforesaid **2** identical, alike, corresponding, duplicate, equal, twin **3** unchanged, changeless, consistent, constant, invariable, unaltered, unvarying

➤ **Antonyms**
≠identical: different, dissimilar, diverse, miscellaneous, other ≠unchanged: altered, inconsistent, variable

sample *noun* **1** specimen, example, instance, model, pattern ♦ *verb* **2** test, experience, inspect, taste, try ♦ *adjective* **3** test, representative, specimen, trial

sanctify *verb* consecrate, cleanse, hallow

sanctimonious *adjective* holier-than-thou, hypocritical, pious, self-righteous, smug

sanction *noun* **1** permission, approval, authority, authorization, backing, O.K. or okay (*informal*), stamp or seal of approval **2** *often plural* ban, boycott, coercive measures, embargo, penalty ♦ *verb* **3** permit, allow, approve, authorize, endorse

➤ **Antonyms**
noun ≠permission: ban, disapproval, embargo, prohibition, proscription, refusal, veto ≠ban: approbation, approval, authority, authorization, dispensation, licence, permission ♦ *verb* ≠permit: ban, boycott, disallow, forbid, refuse, reject, veto

sanctity *noun* **1** sacredness, inviolability **2** holiness, godliness, goodness, grace, piety

sanctuary *noun* **1** shrine, altar, church, temple **2** protection, asylum, haven, refuge, retreat, shelter **3** reserve, conservation area, national park, nature reserve

sane *adjective* **1** rational, all there (*informal*), compos mentis, in one's right mind, mentally sound, of sound mind **2** sensible, balanced, judicious, level-headed, reasonable, sound

➤ **Antonyms**
≠rational: crazy, daft (*informal*), insane, loony (*slang*), mad, mentally ill, non compos mentis, off one's head (*slang*) ≠sensible: dumb-ass (*slang*), foolish, stupid, unreasonable, unsound, up the pole (*informal*), wacko or whacko (*informal*)

sanguine *adjective* cheerful, buoyant, confident, hopeful, optimistic

➤ **Antonyms**
despondent, dispirited, gloomy, pessimistic

sanitary *adjective* hygienic, clean, germ-free, healthy, wholesome

sanity *noun* **1** mental health, normality, rationality, reason, saneness **2** good sense, common sense, level-headedness, rationality, sense

➤ **Antonyms**
≠mental health: craziness, dementia, insanity, lunacy, madness, mental illness ≠good sense: folly, senselessness, stupidity

sap[1] *noun* **1** vital fluid, essence, lifeblood **2** *Slang* fool, idiot, jerk (*slang, chiefly U.S. & Canad.*), ninny, simpleton, twit (*informal*), wally (*slang*)

sap² *verb* 1 weaken, deplete, drain, exhaust, undermine

sarcasm *noun* irony, bitterness, cynicism, derision, mockery, ridicule, satire

sarcastic *adjective* ironical, acid, biting, caustic, cutting, cynical, mocking, sardonic, sarky (*Brit. informal*), satirical

sardonic *adjective* mocking, cynical, derisive, dry, ironical, sarcastic, sneering, wry

Satan *noun* The Devil, Beelzebub, Lord of the Flies, Lucifer, Mephistopheles, Old Nick (*informal*), Prince of Darkness, The Evil One

satanic *adjective* evil, black, demonic, devilish, diabolic, fiendish, hellish, infernal, wicked

➤ **Antonyms**

benevolent, benign, divine, godly, holy

satiate *verb* 1 glut, cloy, gorge, jade, nauseate, overfill, stuff, surfeit 2 satisfy, sate, slake

satire *noun* mockery, burlesque, caricature, irony, lampoon, parody, ridicule

satirical, satiric *adjective* mocking, biting, caustic, cutting, incisive, ironical

satirize *verb* ridicule, burlesque, deride, lampoon, parody, pillory

satisfaction *noun* 1 contentment, comfort, content, enjoyment, happiness, pleasure, pride, repletion, satiety 2 fulfilment, achievement, assuaging, gratification

➤ **Antonyms**

≠contentment: annoyance, discontent, displeasure, dissatisfaction, frustration, unhappiness

satisfactory *adjective* adequate, acceptable, all right, average, fair, good enough, passable, sufficient

➤ **Antonyms**

bad, inadequate, insufficient, mediocre, no great shakes (*informal*), poor, sub-standard, unac-

ceptable, unsatisfactory

satisfy *verb* 1 content, assuage, gratify, indulge, pacify, pander to, please, quench, sate, slake 2 be sufficient, answer, be enough, do, fulfil, meet, serve, suffice 3 convince, assure, persuade, reassure

➤ **Antonyms**

≠content: annoy, displease, dissatisfy, frustrate ≠be sufficient: fail to meet ≠convince: dissuade, fail to persuade

saturate *verb* soak, drench, imbue, souse, steep, suffuse, waterlog, wet through

saturated *adjective* soaked, drenched, dripping, soaking (wet), sodden, sopping (wet), waterlogged, wet through

saturnine *adjective* gloomy, dour, glum, grave, morose, sombre

saucy *adjective* 1 impudent, cheeky (*informal*), forward, impertinent, insolent, pert, presumptuous, rude 2 jaunty, dashing, gay, natty (*informal*), perky

saunter *verb* 1 stroll, amble, meander, mosey (*informal*), ramble, roam, wander ♦ *noun* 2 stroll, airing, amble, ramble, turn, walk

savage *adjective* 1 wild, feral, undomesticated, untamed 2 cruel, barbarous, bestial, bloodthirsty, brutal, ferocious, fierce, harsh, ruthless, sadistic, vicious 3 primitive, rude, unspoilt 4 uncultivated, rough, rugged, uncivilized ♦ *noun* 5 lout, boor, yahoo, yob (*Brit. slang*) ♦ *verb* 6 attack, lacerate, mangle, maul

➤ **Antonyms**

adjective ≠wild: domesticated, tame ≠cruel: gentle, humane, kind, merciful, mild ≠uncultivated: civilized, cultivated, refined

savagery *noun* cruelty, barbarity, brutality, ferocity, ruthlessness, viciousness

save *verb* 1 rescue, deliver, free, liberate, recover, redeem, salvage 2 protect, conserve, guard, keep safe, look after, preserve,

safeguard 3 keep, collect, gather, hoard, hold, husband, lay by, put by, reserve, set aside, store

➤ **Antonyms**

≠rescue, protect: abandon, endanger, expose, imperil, risk, threaten ≠keep: be extravagant (with), consume, fritter away, spend, squander, use, use up, waste

saving noun **1** economy, bargain, discount, reduction ♦ adjective **2** As in saving grace redeeming, compensatory, extenuating

savings plural noun nest egg, fund, reserves, resources, store

saviour noun rescuer, defender, deliverer, liberator, preserver, protector, redeemer

Saviour noun Christ, Jesus, Messiah, Redeemer

savoir-faire noun social knowhow (informal), diplomacy, discretion, finesse, poise, social graces, tact, urbanity

savour verb **1** enjoy, appreciate, delight in, luxuriate in, relish, revel in **2** savour of suggest, be suggestive of, show signs of, smack of ♦ noun **3** flavour, piquancy, relish, smack, smell, tang, taste **4** trace, distinctive quality

savoury adjective spicy, appetizing, full-flavoured, luscious, mouthwatering, palatable, piquant, rich, tasty

➤ **Antonyms**

insipid, tasteless, unappetizing, unpalatable, unpleasant

say verb **1** speak, affirm, announce, assert, declare, express, maintain, mention, pronounce, remark, state, utter, voice **2** suppose, assume, conjecture, estimate, guess, imagine, presume, surmise **3** express, communicate, convey, imply ♦ noun **4** chance to speak, voice, vote **5** influence, authority, clout (informal), power, weight

saying noun proverb, adage, aphorism, axiom, dictum, maxim

scale[1] noun flake, lamina, layer, plate

scale[2] noun **1** graduation, gradation, hierarchy, ladder, progression, ranking, sequence, series, steps **2** ratio, proportion **3** degree, extent, range, reach, scope ♦ verb **4** climb, ascend, clamber, escalade, mount, surmount **5** adjust, proportion, regulate

scamp noun rascal, devil, imp, monkey, rogue, scallywag (informal)

scamper verb run, dart, dash, hasten, hurry, romp, scoot, scurry, scuttle

scan verb **1** glance over, check, check out (informal), examine, eye, eyeball (slang), look through, run one's eye over, run over, skim **2** scrutinize, investigate, scour, search, survey, sweep

scandal noun **1** crime, disgrace, embarrassment, offence, sin, wrongdoing **2** shame, defamation, discredit, disgrace, dishonour, ignominy, infamy, opprobrium, stigma **3** gossip, aspersion, dirt, rumours, slander, talk, tattle

scandalize verb shock, affront, appal, horrify, offend, outrage

scandalous adjective **1** shocking, disgraceful, disreputable, infamous, outrageous, shameful, unseemly **2** slanderous, defamatory, libellous, scurrilous, untrue

➤ **Antonyms**

≠shocking: decent, reputable, respectable, seemly, upright

scant adjective meagre, barely sufficient, little, minimal, sparse

➤ **Antonyms**

abundant, ample, full, generous, plentiful, satisfactory

scanty adjective meagre, bare, deficient, inadequate, insufficient, poor, scant, short, skimpy, sparse, thin

scapegoat noun whipping boy, fall guy (informal)

scar noun **1** mark, blemish, injury, wound ♦ *verb* **2** mark, damage, disfigure

scarce *adjective* rare, few, few and far between, infrequent, in short supply, insufficient, uncommon

➤ **Antonyms**

abundant, ample, common, commonplace, frequent, numerous, plentiful, sufficient

scarcely *adverb* **1** hardly, barely **2** *often used ironically* definitely not, hardly

scarcity *noun* shortage, dearth, deficiency, insufficiency, lack, paucity, rareness, want

➤ **Antonyms**

abundance, excess, glut, superfluity, surfeit, surplus

scare *verb* **1** frighten, alarm, dismay, intimidate, panic, shock, startle, terrify ♦ *noun* **2** fright, panic, shock, start, terror

scared *adjective* frightened, fearful, panicky, panic-stricken, petrified, shaken, startled, terrified

scarper *verb Brit slang* run away, abscond, beat it (*slang*), clear off (*informal*), disappear, flee, run for it, scram (*informal*), take to one's heels

scary *adjective Informal* frightening, alarming, chilling, creepy (*informal*), horrifying, spine-chilling, spooky (*informal*), terrifying

scathing *adjective* critical, biting, caustic, cutting, harsh, sarcastic, scornful, trenchant, withering

scatter *verb* **1** throw about, diffuse, disseminate, fling, shower, spread, sprinkle, strew **2** disperse, disband, dispel, dissipate

➤ **Antonyms**

≠throw about: cluster, collect ≠disperse: assemble, congregate, converge, rally, unite

scatterbrain *noun* featherbrain, butterfly, flibbertigibbet

scenario *noun* story line, outline, résumé, summary, synopsis

scene *noun* **1** site, area, locality, place, position, setting, spot **2** setting, backdrop, background, location, set **3** show, display, drama, exhibition, pageant, picture, sight, spectacle **4** act, division, episode, part **5** view, landscape, panorama, prospect, vista **6** fuss, carry-on (*informal, chiefly Brit.*), commotion, exhibition, performance, row, tantrum, to-do **7** *Informal* world, arena, business, environment

scenery *noun* **1** landscape, surroundings, terrain, view, vista **2** *Theatre* set, backdrop, flats, setting, stage set

scenic *adjective* picturesque, beautiful, panoramic, spectacular, striking

scent *noun* **1** fragrance, aroma, bouquet, odour, perfume, smell **2** trail, spoor, track ♦ *verb* **3** detect, discern, nose out, sense, smell, sniff

scented *adjective* fragrant, aromatic, odoriferous, perfumed, sweet-smelling

sceptic *noun* doubter, cynic, disbeliever, doubting Thomas

sceptical *adjective* doubtful, cynical, disbelieving, dubious, incredulous, mistrustful, unconvinced

➤ **Antonyms**

believing, certain, convinced, credulous, free from doubt, sure, trusting, unquestioning

scepticism *noun* doubt, cynicism, disbelief, incredulity, unbelief

schedule *noun* **1** plan, agenda, calendar, catalogue, inventory, list, programme, timetable ♦ *verb* **2** plan, appoint, arrange, book, organize, programme

scheme *noun* **1** plan, programme, project, proposal, strategy, system, tactics **2** plot, conspiracy, intrigue, manoeuvre, ploy, ruse, stratagem, subterfuge **3** diagram, blueprint, chart, draft, layout, outline, pattern ♦ *verb* **4** plan, lay plans, project, work out **5** plot, collude, conspire, intrigue, machinate, manoeuvre

scheming *adjective* calculating,

artful, conniving, cunning, sly, tricky, underhand, wily

► **Antonyms**

above-board, artless, guileless, honest, straightforward, trustworthy

schism *noun* division, breach, break, rift, rupture, separation, split

scholar *noun* **1** intellectual, academic, savant **2** student, disciple, learner, pupil, schoolboy *or* schoolgirl

scholarly *adjective* learned, academic, bookish, erudite, intellectual, lettered, scholastic

► **Antonyms**

lowbrow, philistine, unacademic, uneducated, unintellectual, unlettered

scholarship *noun* **1** learning, book-learning, education, erudition, knowledge **2** bursary, fellowship

scholastic *adjective* learned, academic, lettered, scholarly

school *noun* **1** academy, college, faculty, institute, institution, seminary **2** group, adherents, circle, denomination, devotees, disciples, faction, followers, set ♦ *verb* **3** train, coach, discipline, drill, educate, instruct, tutor

schooling *noun* **1** teaching, education, tuition **2** training, coaching, drill, instruction

science *noun* **1** discipline, body of knowledge, branch of knowledge **2** skill, art, technique

scientific *adjective* systematic, accurate, controlled, exact, mathematical, precise

scientist *noun* inventor, boffin (*informal*), technophile

scintillating *adjective* brilliant, animated, bright, dazzling, exciting, glittering, lively, sparkling, stimulating

scoff¹ *verb* scorn, belittle, deride, despise, jeer, knock (*informal*), laugh at, mock, pooh-pooh, ridicule, sneer

scoff² *verb* gobble (up), bolt, devour, gorge oneself on, gulp down, guzzle, wolf

scold *verb* **1** reprimand, berate, castigate, censure, find fault with, give (someone) a dressing-down, lecture, rebuke, reproach, reprove, tell off (*informal*), tick off (*informal*), upbraid ♦ *noun* **2** nag, shrew, termagant (*rare*)

► **Antonyms**

verb ≠reprimand: acclaim, applaud, approve, commend, compliment, extol, laud, praise

scolding *noun* rebuke, dressing-down (*informal*), lecture, row, telling-off (*informal*), ticking-off (*informal*)

scoop *noun* **1** ladle, dipper, spoon **2** exclusive, exposé, revelation, sensation ♦ *verb* **3** often *with up* lift, gather up, pick up, take up **4** scoop out hollow, bail, dig, empty, excavate, gouge, shovel

scope *noun* **1** opportunity, freedom, latitude, liberty, room, space **2** range, area, capacity, orbit, outlook, reach, span, sphere

scorch *verb* burn, parch, roast, sear, shrivel, singe, wither

scorching *adjective* burning, baking, boiling, fiery, flaming, red-hot, roasting, searing

score *noun* **1** points, grade, mark, outcome, record, result, total **2** grounds, basis, cause, ground, reason **3** grievance, grudge, injury, injustice, wrong **4** scores lots, hundreds, masses, millions, multitudes, myriads, swarms ♦ *verb* **5** gain, achieve, chalk up (*informal*), make, notch up (*informal*), win **6** keep count, count, record, register, tally **7** cut, deface, gouge, graze, mark, scrape, scratch, slash **8** *with out or through* cross out, cancel, delete, obliterate, strike out **9** *Music* arrange, adapt, orchestrate, set

scorn *noun* **1** contempt, derision, disdain, disparagement, mockery, sarcasm ♦ *verb* **2** despise, be above, deride, disdain, flout, reject, scoff at, slight, spurn

> ► **Antonyms**

noun ≠<u>contempt</u>: admiration, esteem, high regard, respect, veneration, worship ♦ verb ≠<u>despise</u>: admire, esteem, respect, revere, venerate, worship

scornful adjective <u>contemptuous</u>, derisive, disdainful, haughty, jeering, mocking, sarcastic, sardonic, scathing, scoffing, sneering

scoundrel noun Old-fashioned <u>rogue</u>, bastard (offensive), blackguard, good-for-nothing, heel (slang), miscreant, ne'er-do-well, rascal, reprobate, rotter (slang, chiefly Brit.), scally (Northwest English dialect), scamp, swine, villain

scour[1] verb 1 <u>rub</u>, abrade, buff, clean, polish, scrub 2 <u>wash</u>, cleanse

scour[2] verb <u>search</u>, beat, comb, hunt, ransack

scourge noun 1 <u>affliction</u>, bane, curse, infliction, misfortune, pest, plague, terror, torment 2 <u>whip</u>, cat, lash, strap, switch, thong ♦ verb 3 <u>afflict</u>, curse, plague, terrorize, torment 4 <u>whip</u>, beat, cane, flog, horsewhip, lash, thrash

> ► **Antonyms**

noun ≠<u>affliction</u>: benefit, blessing, boon, favour, gift, godsend

scout noun 1 <u>vanguard</u>, advance guard, lookout, outrider, precursor, reconnoitrer ♦ verb 2 <u>reconnoitre</u>, investigate, observe, probe, recce (slang), spy, survey, watch

scowl verb 1 <u>glower</u>, frown, lour or lower ♦ noun 2 <u>glower</u>, black look, dirty look, frown

scrabble verb <u>scrape</u>, claw, scramble, scratch

scraggy adjective <u>scrawny</u>, angular, bony, lean, skinny

scram verb Informal <u>go away</u>, abscond, beat it (slang), clear off (informal), get lost (informal), leave, make oneself scarce (informal), make tracks, scarper (Brit. slang), vamoose (slang, chiefly U.S.)

scramble verb 1 <u>struggle</u>, climb, crawl, scrabble, swarm 2 <u>strive</u>, contend, jostle, push, run, rush, vie ♦ noun 3 <u>climb</u>, trek 4 <u>struggle</u>, commotion, competition, confusion, melee or mêlée, race, rush, tussle

scrap[1] noun 1 <u>piece</u>, bit, crumb, fragment, grain, morsel, part, particle, portion, sliver, snippet 2 <u>waste</u>, junk, off cuts 3 scraps <u>leftovers</u>, bits, leavings, remains ♦ verb 4 <u>get rid of</u>, abandon, discard, ditch (slang), drop, jettison, throw away or out, write off

> ► **Antonyms**

verb ≠<u>get rid of</u>: bring back, reestablish, reinstate, restore, return

scrap[2] Informal ♦ noun 1 <u>fight</u>, argument, battle, disagreement, dispute, quarrel, row, squabble, wrangle ♦ verb 2 <u>fight</u>, argue, row, squabble, wrangle

scrape verb 1 <u>rub</u>, bark, graze, scratch, scuff, skin 2 <u>scour</u>, clean, erase, remove, rub 3 <u>grate</u>, grind, rasp, scratch, squeak 4 <u>scrimp</u>, pinch, save, skimp, stint 5 <u>scrape through</u> <u>get by</u> (informal), just make it, struggle ♦ noun 6 Informal <u>predicament</u>, awkward situation, difficulty, dilemma, fix (informal), mess, plight, tight spot

scrapheap noun **on the scrapheap** <u>discarded</u>, ditched (slang), jettisoned, put out to grass (informal), redundant, written off

scrappy adjective <u>incomplete</u>, bitty, disjointed, fragmentary, piecemeal, sketchy, thrown together

scratch verb 1 <u>mark</u>, claw, cut, damage, etch, grate, graze, lacerate, score, scrape 2 <u>erase</u>, cancel, cross out, delete, eliminate 3 <u>withdraw</u>, pull out ♦ noun 4 <u>mark</u>, blemish, claw mark, gash, graze, laceration, scrape 5 **up to scratch** Informal <u>adequate</u>, acceptable, satisfactory, sufficient, up to standard ♦ adjective 6 <u>improvised</u>, impromptu, rough-and-ready

scrawl verb, noun <u>scribble</u>,

doodle, squiggle

scrawny adjective <u>thin</u>, bony, gaunt, lean, scraggy, skin-and-bones (informal), skinny, undernourished

scream verb 1 <u>cry</u>, bawl, screech, shriek, yell ♦ noun 2 <u>cry</u>, howl, screech, shriek, yell, yelp

screech noun, verb <u>cry</u>, scream, shriek

screen noun 1 <u>cover</u>, awning, canopy, cloak, guard, partition, room divider, shade, shelter, shield 2 <u>mesh</u>, net ♦ verb 3 <u>cover</u>, cloak, conceal, hide, mask, shade, veil 4 <u>protect</u>, defend, guard, shelter, shield 5 <u>vet</u>, evaluate, examine, filter, gauge, scan, sift, sort 6 <u>broadcast</u>, present, put on, show

screw verb 1 <u>turn</u>, tighten, twist 2 Informal, often with **out of** <u>extort</u>, extract, wrest, wring

screw up verb 1 Informal <u>bungle</u>, botch, make a hash of (informal), make a mess of (slang), mess up, mishandle, spoil 2 <u>contort</u>, distort, pucker, wrinkle

screwy adjective Informal <u>crazy</u>, crackpot (informal), eccentric, loopy (informal), nutty (slang), odd, off-the-wall (slang), out to lunch (informal), round the bend (Brit. slang), weird

scribble verb <u>scrawl</u>, dash off, jot, write

scribe noun <u>copyist</u>, amanuensis, writer

scrimp verb <u>economize</u>, be frugal, save, scrape, skimp, stint, tighten one's belt

script noun 1 <u>text</u>, book, copy, dialogue, libretto, lines, words 2 <u>handwriting</u>, calligraphy, penmanship, writing

Scripture noun <u>The Bible</u>, Holy Bible, Holy Scripture, Holy Writ, The Good Book, The Gospels, The Scriptures

scrounge verb Informal <u>cadge</u>, beg, blag (slang), bum (informal), freeload (slang), sponge (informal)

scrounger adjective <u>cadger</u>, free-

loader (slang), parasite, sponger (informal)

scrub verb 1 <u>scour</u>, clean, cleanse, rub 2 Informal <u>cancel</u>, abolish, call off, delete, drop, forget about, give up

scruffy adjective <u>tatty</u>, ill-groomed, mangy, messy, ragged, run-down, seedy, shabby, unkempt, untidy

► **Antonyms**

chic, dapper, natty, neat, spruce, tidy, well-dressed, well-groomed, well-turned-out

scrumptious adjective Informal <u>delicious</u>, appetizing, delectable, luscious, mouthwatering, succulent, yummy (slang)

scruple noun 1 <u>misgiving</u>, compunction, doubt, hesitation, qualm, reluctance, second thoughts, uneasiness ♦ verb 2 <u>have misgivings about</u>, demur, doubt, have qualms about, hesitate, think twice about

scrupulous adjective 1 <u>moral</u>, conscientious, honourable, principled, upright 2 <u>careful</u>, exact, fastidious, meticulous, precise, punctilious, rigorous, strict

► **Antonyms**

≠moral: amoral, dishonest, unconscientious, unprincipled, unscrupulous, without scruples ≠careful: careless, inexact, reckless, slapdash, superficial

scrutinize verb <u>examine</u>, explore, inspect, investigate, peruse, pore over, probe, scan, search, study

scrutiny noun <u>examination</u>, analysis, exploration, inspection, investigation, perusal, search, study

scuffle verb 1 <u>fight</u>, clash, grapple, jostle, struggle, tussle ♦ noun 2 <u>fight</u>, brawl, commotion, disturbance, fray, scrimmage, skirmish, tussle

sculpture verb <u>sculpt</u>, carve, chisel, fashion, form, hew, model, mould, shape

scum noun 1 <u>impurities</u>, dross, film, froth 2 <u>rabble</u>, dregs of society, riffraff, trash (chiefly U.S. & Canad.)

scupper verb Brit. slang <u>destroy</u>, defeat, demolish, put paid to, ruin, torpedo, wreck

scurrilous adjective <u>slanderous</u>, abusive, defamatory, insulting, scandalous, vituperative

➤ **Antonyms**

polite, respectful

scurry verb 1 <u>hurry</u>, dart, dash, race, scamper, scoot, scuttle, sprint ♦ noun 2 <u>flurry</u>, scampering, whirl

➤ **Antonyms**

verb ≠ hurry: amble, saunter, stroll

scuttle verb <u>run</u>, bustle, hasten, hurry, rush, scamper, scoot, scurry

sea noun 1 <u>ocean</u>, main, the deep, the waves 2 <u>expanse</u>, abundance, mass, multitude, plethora, profusion 3 at sea be<u>wildered</u>, baffled, confused, lost, mystified, puzzled

seafaring adjective <u>nautical</u>, marine, maritime, naval

seal noun 1 <u>authentication</u>, confirmation, imprimatur, insignia, ratification, stamp ♦ verb 2 <u>close</u>, bung, enclose, fasten, plug, shut, stop, stopper, stop up 3 <u>authenticate</u>, confirm, ratify, stamp, validate 4 <u>settle</u>, clinch, conclude, consummate, finalize 5 seal off <u>isolate</u>, put out of bounds, quarantine, segregate

seam noun 1 <u>joint</u>, closure 2 lay<u>er</u>, lode, stratum, vein 3 <u>ridge</u>, furrow, line, wrinkle

sear verb <u>scorch</u>, burn, sizzle

search verb 1 <u>look</u>, comb, examine, explore, hunt, inspect, investigate, ransack, scour, scrutinize ♦ noun 2 <u>look</u>, examination, exploration, hunt, inspection, investigation, pursuit, quest

searching adjective <u>keen</u>, close, intent, penetrating, piercing, probing, quizzical, sharp

➤ **Antonyms**

cursory, perfunctory, sketchy, superficial

season noun 1 <u>period</u>, spell, term, time ♦ verb 2 <u>flavour</u>, enliven, pep up, salt, spice

seasonable adjective <u>appropriate</u>, convenient, fit, opportune, providential, suitable, timely, well-timed

seasoned adjective <u>experienced</u>, hardened, practised, time-served, veteran

➤ **Antonyms**

callow, green, inexperienced, new, novice, unpractised, unseasoned

seasoning noun <u>flavouring</u>, condiment, dressing, relish, salt and pepper, sauce, spice

seat noun 1 <u>chair</u>, bench, pew, settle, stall, stool 2 <u>centre</u>, capital, heart, hub, place, site, situation, source 3 <u>mansion</u>, abode, ancestral hall, house, residence 4 <u>membership</u>, chair, constituency, incumbency, place ♦ verb 5 <u>sit</u>, fix, install, locate, place, set, settle 6 <u>hold</u>, accommodate, cater for, contain, sit, take

seating noun <u>accommodation</u>, chairs, places, room, seats

secede verb <u>withdraw</u>, break with, leave, pull out, quit, resign, split from

secluded adjective <u>private</u>, cloistered, cut off, isolated, lonely, out-of-the-way, sheltered, solitary

➤ **Antonyms**

busy, frequented, open, public

seclusion noun <u>privacy</u>, isolation, shelter, solitude

second[1] adjective 1 <u>next</u>, following, subsequent, succeeding 2 <u>additional</u>, alternative, extra, further, other 3 <u>inferior</u>, lesser, lower, secondary, subordinate ♦ noun 4 <u>supporter</u>, assistant, backer, helper ♦ verb 5 <u>support</u>, approve, assist, back, endorse, go along with

second[2] noun <u>moment</u>, flash, instant, jiffy (informal), minute, sec (informal), trice

secondary adjective 1 <u>subordinate</u>, inferior, lesser, lower, minor, unimportant 2 <u>resultant</u>, contingent, derived, indirect 3 <u>backup</u>, auxiliary, fall-back, reserve, subsidiary, supporting

➤ **Antonyms**

≠<u>subordinate</u>: cardinal, chief, head, larger, main, major, more important, prime, principal, superior ≠<u>resultant</u>: original, preceding ≠<u>backup</u>: only, primary

second-class adjective inferior, indifferent, mediocre, second-best, second-rate, undistinguished, uninspiring

second-hand adjective **1** used, hand-me-down (informal), nearly new ♦ adverb **2** indirectly

second in command noun <u>deputy</u>, number two, right-hand man

secondly adverb <u>next</u>, in the second place, second

second-rate adjective inferior, low-grade, low-quality, mediocre, poor, rubbishy, shoddy, substandard, tacky (informal), tawdry, two-bit (U.S. & Canad. slang)

➤ **Antonyms**

choice, de luxe, excellent, fine, first-class, first-rate, high-class, quality, superior

secrecy noun **1** <u>mystery</u>, concealment, confidentiality, privacy, silence **2** <u>secretiveness</u>, clandestineness, covertness, furtiveness, stealth

secret adjective **1** <u>concealed</u>, close, confidential, disguised, furtive, hidden, undercover, underground, undisclosed, unknown, unrevealed **2** <u>stealthy</u>, sly, underhand **3** <u>mysterious</u>, abstruse, arcane, clandestine, cryptic, occult ♦ noun **4** <u>mystery</u>, code, enigma, key **5** <u>in secret</u> secretly, slyly, surreptitiously

➤ **Antonyms**

adjective ≠<u>concealed</u>, <u>stealthy</u>: apparent, candid, disclosed, frank, manifest, obvious, open, overt, public, unconcealed, visible ≠<u>mysterious</u>: straightforward, well-known

secrete[1] verb <u>give off</u>, emanate, emit, exude

secrete[2] verb <u>hide</u>, cache, conceal, harbour, stash (informal), stow

➤ **Antonyms**

display, exhibit, reveal, show

secretive adjective <u>reticent</u>, close, deep, reserved, tight-lipped, uncommunicative

➤ **Antonyms**

candid, communicative, expansive, forthcoming, frank, open, unreserved

secretly adverb <u>in secret</u>, clandestinely, covertly, furtively, privately, quietly, stealthily, surreptitiously

sect noun <u>group</u>, camp, denomination, division, faction, party, schism

sectarian adjective **1** <u>narrow-minded</u>, bigoted, doctrinaire, dogmatic, factional, fanatical, limited, parochial, partisan ♦ noun **2** <u>bigot</u>, dogmatist, extremist, fanatic, partisan, zealot

➤ **Antonyms**

adjective ≠<u>narrow-minded</u>: broad-minded, liberal, non-sectarian, open-minded, tolerant, unbigoted, unprejudiced

section noun **1** <u>part</u>, division, fraction, instalment, passage, piece, portion, segment, slice **2** <u>district</u>, area, region, sector, zone

sector noun <u>part</u>, area, district, division, quarter, region, zone

secular adjective <u>worldly</u>, civil, earthly, lay, nonspiritual, temporal

➤ **Antonyms**

divine, holy, religious, sacred, spiritual, theological

secure adjective **1** <u>safe</u>, immune, protected, unassailable **2** <u>sure</u>, assured, certain, confident, easy, reassured **3** <u>fixed</u>, fast, fastened, firm, immovable, stable, steady ♦ verb **4** <u>obtain</u>, acquire, gain, get, procure, score (slang) **5** <u>fasten</u>, attach, bolt, chain, fix, lock, make fast, tie up

➤ **Antonyms**

adjective ≠<u>safe</u>: endangered, unprotected, unsafe ≠<u>sure</u>: ill-at-ease, insecure, unassured, uncertain, uneasy, unsure ≠fixed: insecure, loose, not fastened, precarious, unfixed, unsafe ♦ verb ≠obtain: give up, let (something) slip through (one's) fingers, lose ≠fasten: loosen, unloose, untie

security noun **1** precautions, defence, protection, safeguards, safety measures **2** safety, custody, protection, refuge, safekeeping, sanctuary **3** assurance, certainty, confidence, conviction, positiveness, reliance, sureness **4** pledge, collateral, gage, guarantee, hostage, insurance, pawn, surety

► **Antonyms**
≠safety: exposure, jeopardy, vulnerability ≠assurance: insecurity, uncertainty

sedate adjective **1** calm, collected, composed, cool, dignified, serene, tranquil **2** unhurried, deliberate, slow-moving

► **Antonyms**
≠calm: agitated, antsy (informal), excitable, excited, jumpy, nervous, undignified

sedative adjective **1** calming, anodyne, relaxing, soothing, tranquillizing ♦ noun **2** tranquillizer, anodyne, downer or down (slang)

sedentary adjective inactive, desk, desk-bound, seated, sitting

► **Antonyms**
active, mobile, moving, on the go (informal)

sediment noun dregs, deposit, grounds, lees, residue

sedition noun rabble-rousing, agitation, incitement to riot, subversion

seditious adjective revolutionary, dissident, mutinous, rebellious, refractory, subversive

seduce verb **1** corrupt, debauch, deflower, deprave, dishonour **2** tempt, beguile, deceive, entice, inveigle, lead astray, lure, mislead

seduction noun **1** corruption **2** temptation, enticement, lure, snare

seductive adjective alluring, attractive, bewitching, enticing, inviting, provocative, tempting

seductress noun temptress, enchantress, femme fatale, siren, vamp (informal)

see verb **1** perceive, behold, catch sight of, discern, distinguish, espy, eyeball (slang), glimpse, look, make out, notice, observe, sight, spot, witness **2** understand, appreciate, comprehend, fathom, feel, follow, get, grasp, realize **3** find out, ascertain, determine, discover, learn **4** make sure, ensure, guarantee, make certain, see to it **5** consider, decide, deliberate, reflect, think over **6** visit, confer with, consult, interview, receive, speak to **7** go out with, court, date (informal, chiefly U.S.), go steady with (informal) **8** accompany, escort, lead, show, usher, walk

seed noun **1** grain, egg, embryo, germ, kernel, ovum, pip, spore **2** origin, beginning, germ, nucleus, source, start **3** chiefly Biblical offspring, children, descendants, issue, progeny **4** go or run to seed decline, decay, degenerate, deteriorate, go downhill (informal), go to pot, let oneself go

seedy adjective **1** shabby, dilapidated, grotty (slang), grubby, mangy, run-down, scruffy, sleazy, squalid, tatty **2** Informal unwell, ill, off colour, out of sorts, poorly (informal), under the weather (informal)

► **Antonyms**
≠shabby: classy, elegant, posh (informal, chiefly Brit.), smart

seeing conjunction since, as, inasmuch as, in view of the fact that

seek verb **1** look for, be after, follow, hunt, pursue, search for **2** try, aim, aspire to, attempt, endeavour, strive

seem verb appear, assume, give the impression, look

seemly adjective fitting, appropriate, becoming, decent, decorous, fit, proper, suitable

➤ **Antonyms**
improper, inappropriate, indecorous, out of place, unbecoming, unseemly, unsuitable

seep verb <u>ooze</u>, exude, leak, permeate, soak, trickle, well

seer noun <u>prophet</u>, sibyl, soothsayer

seesaw verb <u>alternate</u>, fluctuate, oscillate, swing

seethe verb 1 <u>be furious</u>, be livid, be pissed (off) (*taboo slang*), fume, go ballistic (*slang, chiefly U.S.*), rage, see red (*informal*), simmer 2 <u>boil</u>, bubble, fizz, foam, froth

see through verb 1 <u>be undeceived by</u>, be wise to (*informal*), fathom, not fall for, penetrate 2 **see (something) through** <u>persevere (with)</u>, keep at, persist, stick out (*informal*) 3 **see (someone) through** <u>help out</u>, stick by, support

segment noun <u>section</u>, bit, division, part, piece, portion, slice, wedge

segregate verb <u>set apart</u>, discriminate against, dissociate, isolate, separate

➤ **Antonyms**
amalgamate, desegregate, join together, mix, unify, unite

segregation noun <u>separation</u>, apartheid, discrimination, isolation

seize verb 1 <u>grab</u>, catch up, clutch, grasp, grip, lay hands on, snatch, take 2 <u>confiscate</u>, appropriate, commandeer, impound, take possession of 3 <u>capture</u>, apprehend, arrest, catch, take captive

➤ **Antonyms**
≠<u>grab</u>: let go, loose ≠<u>confiscate</u>: hand back, relinquish ≠<u>capture</u>: free, release, set free, turn loose

seizure noun 1 <u>attack</u>, convulsion, fit, paroxysm, spasm 2 <u>capture</u>, apprehension, arrest 3 <u>taking</u>, annexation, commandeering, confiscation, grabbing

seldom adverb <u>rarely</u>, hardly ever, infrequently, not often

➤ **Antonyms**
again and again, frequently, much, often, over and over again, time after time, time and again

select verb 1 <u>choose</u>, opt for, pick, single out ♦ adjective 2 <u>choice</u>, excellent, first-class, hand-picked, special, superior, top-notch (*informal*) 3 <u>exclusive</u>, cliquish, elite, privileged

➤ **Antonyms**
verb ≠<u>choose</u>: eliminate, reject, turn down ♦ adjective ≠<u>choice</u>: cheap, inferior, ordinary, run-of-the-mill, second-rate, shoddy, substandard, unremarkable ≠<u>exclusive</u>: indiscriminate

selection noun 1 <u>choice</u>, choosing, option, pick, preference 2 <u>range</u>, assortment, choice, collection, medley, variety

selective adjective <u>particular</u>, careful, discerning, discriminating

➤ **Antonyms**
all-embracing, careless, indiscriminate, unselective

self-assurance noun <u>confidence</u>, assertiveness, positiveness, self-confidence, self-possession

self-centred adjective <u>selfish</u>, egotistic, narcissistic, self-seeking

self-confidence noun <u>self-assurance</u>, aplomb, confidence, nerve, poise

self-confident adjective <u>self-assured</u>, assured, confident, poised, sure of oneself

self-conscious adjective <u>embarrassed</u>, awkward, bashful, diffident, ill at ease, insecure, nervous, uncomfortable

self-control noun <u>willpower</u>, restraint, self-discipline, self-restraint

self-esteem noun <u>self-respect</u>, confidence, faith in oneself, pride, self-assurance, self-regard

self-evident adjective <u>obvious</u>, clear, incontrovertible, inescapable, undeniable

self-important adjective <u>conceited</u>, bigheaded, cocky, full of oneself, pompous, swollen-headed

self-indulgence noun intemperance, excess, extravagance

selfish adjective self-centred, egoistic, egoistical, egotistic, egotistical, greedy, self-interested, ungenerous

➤ Antonyms
altruistic, considerate, generous, magnanimous, selfless, self-sacrificing, unselfish

selfless adjective unselfish, altruistic, generous, self-denying, self-sacrificing

self-possessed adjective self-assured, collected, confident, cool, poised, unruffled

self-reliant adjective independent, capable, self-sufficient, self-supporting

➤ Antonyms
dependent, helpless, reliant, relying on

self-respect noun pride, dignity, morale, self-esteem

self-restraint noun self-control, self-command, self-discipline, willpower

self-righteous adjective sanctimonious, complacent, holier-than-thou, priggish, self-satisfied, smug, superior

self-sacrifice noun selflessness, altruism, generosity, self-denial

self-satisfied adjective smug, complacent, pleased with oneself, self-congratulatory

self-seeking adjective selfish, careerist, looking out for number one (informal), out for what one can get, self-interested, self-serving

sell verb 1 trade, barter, exchange 2 deal in, handle, market, peddle, retail, stock, trade in, traffic in

➤ Antonyms
≠trade, deal in: acquire, buy, get, invest in, obtain, pay for, procure, purchase

seller noun dealer, agent, merchant, purveyor, retailer, salesman or saleswoman, supplier, vendor

selling noun dealing, business,

trading, traffic

sell out verb 1 dispose of, be out of stock of, get rid of, run out of 2 Informal betray, double-cross (informal), sell down the river (informal), stab in the back

semblance noun appearance, aspect, façade, mask, pretence, resemblance, show, veneer

seminal adjective influential, formative, ground-breaking, important, innovative, original

send verb 1 dispatch, convey, direct, forward, remit, transmit 2 propel, cast, fire, fling, hurl, let fly, shoot

send for verb summon, call for, order, request

sendoff noun farewell, departure, leave-taking, start, valediction

send-up noun imitation, parody, satire, skit, spoof (informal), take-off (informal)

send up verb imitate, burlesque, lampoon, make fun of, mimic, mock, parody, satirize, spoof (informal), take off (informal)

senile adjective doddering, decrepit, doting, in one's dotage

senility noun dotage, decrepitude, infirmity, loss of one's faculties, senile dementia

senior adjective 1 higher ranking, superior 2 older, elder, major (Brit.)

➤ Antonyms
≠higher ranking: inferior, junior, lesser, lower, minor, subordinate ≠older: junior, younger

senior citizen noun pensioner, O.A.P., old age pensioner, old or elderly person, retired person

seniority noun superiority, precedence, priority, rank

sensation noun 1 feeling, awareness, consciousness, impression, perception, sense 2 excitement, commotion, furore, stir, thrill

sensational adjective 1 exciting, amazing, astounding, dramatic, melodramatic, shock-horror (facetious), shocking, thrilling 2 Informal excellent, fabulous (informal), impressive, marvellous, mean (*slang*), mind-blowing (*informal*), out of this world (*informal*), smashing (*informal*), superb

► **Antonyms**

≠**exciting**: boring, dull, humdrum, understated, undramatic, unexaggerated, unexciting ≠**excellent**: commonplace, mediocre, no great shakes (*informal*), ordinary, prosaic, run-of-the-mill, vanilla (*informal*)

sense noun 1 **faculty**, feeling, sensation 2 **feeling**, atmosphere, aura, awareness, consciousness, impression, perception 3 *sometimes plural* **intelligence**, brains (*informal*), cleverness, common sense, judgment, reason, sagacity, sanity, sharpness, understanding, wisdom, wit(s) 4 **meaning**, drift, gist, implication, import, significance ♦ *verb* 5 **perceive**, be aware of, discern, feel, get the impression, pick up, realize, understand

► **Antonyms**

noun ≠**intelligence**: folly, foolishness, idiocy, nonsense, silliness, stupidity ♦ *verb* ≠**perceive**: be unaware of, fail to grasp or notice, miss, misunderstand, overlook

senseless *adjective* 1 **stupid**, asinine, crazy, daft (*informal*), dumb-ass (*slang*), foolish, idiotic, illogical, inane, irrational, mad, mindless, nonsensical, pointless, ridiculous, silly 2 **unconscious**, insensible, out, out cold, stunned

► **Antonyms**

≠**stupid**: intelligent, meaningful, rational, reasonable, sensible, useful, valid, wise, worthwhile ≠**unconscious**: conscious, sensible

sensibility noun 1 *often plural* **feelings**, emotions, moral sense, sentiments, susceptibilities 2 **sensitivity**, responsiveness, sensitiveness, susceptibility

► **Antonyms**

≠**sensitivity**: deadness, insensibility, insensitivity, numbness, unresponsiveness

sensible *adjective* 1 **wise**, canny, down-to-earth, intelligent, judi-

cious, practical, prudent, rational, realistic, sage, sane, shrewd, sound 2 *Literary, usually with* **of** **aware**, conscious, mindful, sensitive to

► **Antonyms**

≠**wise**: daft (*informal*), dumb-ass (*slang*), foolish, idiotic, ignorant, injudicious, irrational, senseless, silly, stupid, unreasonable, unwise ≠**aware**: blind, ignorant, insensible, insensitive, unaware, unmindful

sensitive *adjective* 1 **easily hurt**, delicate, tender 2 **susceptible**, easily affected, impressionable, responsive, touchy-feely (*informal*) 3 **touchy**, easily offended, easily upset, thin-skinned 4 **precise**, acute, fine, keen, responsive

► **Antonyms**

≠**easily hurt**: insensitive, tough ≠**susceptible**, **touchy**: callous, hard, hardened, insensitive, thick-skinned, tough, uncaring, unfeeling ≠**precise**: approximate, imprecise, inexact

sensitivity noun **sensitiveness**, delicacy, receptiveness, responsiveness, susceptibility

sensual *adjective* 1 **physical**, animal, bodily, carnal, fleshly, luxurious, voluptuous 2 **erotic**, lascivious, lecherous, lewd, lustful, raunchy (*slang*), sexual

sensuality noun **eroticism**, carnality, lasciviousness, lecherousness, lewdness, sexiness (*informal*), voluptuousness

sensuous *adjective* **pleasurable**, gratifying, hedonistic, sybaritic

► **Antonyms**

abstemious, ascetic, celibate, self-denying, Spartan

sentence noun 1 **punishment**, condemnation, decision, decree, judgment, order, ruling, verdict ♦ *verb* 2 **condemn**, doom, penalize

sententious *adjective* **pompous**, canting, judgmental, moralistic, preachifying (*informal*), sanctimonious

sentient *adjective* feeling, conscious, living, sensitive

sentiment *noun* **1** emotion, sensibility, tenderness **2** *often plural* feeling, attitude, belief, idea, judgment, opinion, view **3** sentimentality, emotionalism, mawkishness, romanticism

sentimental *adjective* romantic, emotional, icky (*informal*), maudlin, nostalgic, overemotional, schmaltzy (*slang*), slushy (*informal*), soft-hearted, touching, weepy (*informal*)

➤ **Antonyms**
dispassionate, down-to-earth, hard-headed, practical, realistic, unemotional, unfeeling, unromantic, unsentimental

sentimentality *noun* romanticism, corniness (*slang*), emotionalism, mawkishness, nostalgia, schmaltz (*slang*)

sentinel *noun* guard, lookout, sentry, watch, watchman

separable *adjective* distinguishable, detachable, divisible

separate *verb* **1** divide, come apart, come away, detach, disconnect, disjoin, remove, sever, split, sunder **2** part, break up, disunite, diverge, divorce, estrange, part company, split up **3** isolate, segregate, single out ♦ *adjective* **4** unconnected, detached, disconnected, divided, divorced, isolated, unattached **5** individual, alone, apart, distinct, particular, single, solitary

➤ **Antonyms**
verb ≠divide, part, isolate: amalgamate, combine, connect, join, link, merge, mix, unite ♦ *adjective* ≠unconnected, individual: alike, connected, interdependent, joined, similar, unified, united

separated *adjective* disconnected, apart, disassociated, disunited, divided, parted, separate, sundered

separately *adverb* individually, alone, apart, severally, singly

➤ **Antonyms**
as a group, as one, collectively, in a body, in unison, jointly, together

separation *noun* **1** division, break, disconnection, dissociation, disunion, gap **2** split-up, break-up, divorce, parting, rift, split

septic *adjective* infected, festering, poisoned, putrefying, putrid, suppurating

sepulchre *noun* tomb, burial place, grave, mausoleum, vault

sequel *noun* **1** follow-up, continuation, development **2** consequence, conclusion, end, outcome, result, upshot

sequence *noun* succession, arrangement, chain, course, cycle, order, progression, series

serene *adjective* calm, composed, peaceful, tranquil, unruffled, untroubled

➤ **Antonyms**
agitated, anxious, disturbed, excitable, flustered, perturbed, troubled, uptight (*informal*)

serenity *noun* calmness, calm, composure, peace, peacefulness, quietness, stillness, tranquillity

series *noun* sequence, chain, course, order, progression, run, set, string, succession, train

serious *adjective* **1** grave, acute, critical, dangerous, severe **2** important, crucial, fateful, grim, momentous, no laughing matter, pressing, significant, urgent, worrying **3** solemn, grave, humourless, sober, unsmiling **4** sincere, earnest, genuine, honest, in earnest

➤ **Antonyms**
≠important: insignificant, minor, slight, trivial, unimportant ≠solemn: flippant, frivolous, jolly, joyful, light-hearted, smiling ≠sincere: flippant, frivolous, insincere

seriously *adverb* **1** gravely, acutely, badly, critically, dangerously, severely **2** sincerely, gravely, in earnest

seriousness *noun* **1** importance, gravity, significance, urgency **2**

solemnity, earnestness, gravitas, gravity

sermon noun **1** homily, address **2** Disparaging lecture, harangue, talking-to (informal)

servant noun attendant, domestic, help, maid, retainer, skivvy (chiefly Brit.), slave

serve verb **1** work for, aid, assist, attend to, help, minister to, wait on **2** perform, act, complete, discharge, do, fulfil **3** provide, deliver, dish up, present, set out, supply **4** be adequate, answer the purpose, be acceptable, do, function as, satisfy, suffice, suit

service noun **1** help, assistance, avail, benefit, use, usefulness **2** work, business, duty, employment, labour, office **3** overhaul, check, maintenance **4** ceremony, observance, rite, worship ♦ verb **5** overhaul, check, fine tune, go over, maintain, tune (up)

serviceable adjective useful, beneficial, functional, helpful, operative, practical, profitable, usable, utilitarian

➤ **Antonyms**

impractical, unserviceable, unusable, useless

servile adjective subservient, abject, fawning, grovelling, obsequious, sycophantic, toadying

serving noun portion, helping

session noun meeting, assembly, conference, congress, discussion, hearing, period, sitting

set¹ verb **1** put, deposit, lay, locate, place, plant, position, rest, seat, situate, station, stick **2** prepare, arrange, lay, make ready, spread **3** harden, cake, congeal, crystallize, solidify, stiffen, thicken **4** arrange, appoint, decide (upon), determine, establish, fix, fix up, resolve, schedule, settle, specify **5** assign, allot, decree, impose, ordain, prescribe, specify **6** go down, decline, dip, disappear, sink, subside, vanish ♦ noun **7** position, attitude, bearing, carriage, posture **8** scenery, scene, setting, stage set ♦ adjec-

tive **9** fixed, agreed, appointed, arranged, decided, definite, established, prearranged, predetermined, scheduled, settled **10** inflexible, hard and fast, immovable, rigid, stubborn **11** conventional, stereotyped, traditional, unspontaneous **12** set on or upon determined, bent, intent, resolute

➤ **Antonyms**

adjective ≠inflexible: flexible, free, open, open-minded, undecided

set² noun **1** series, assortment, batch, collection, compendium **2** group, band, circle, clique, company, coterie, crowd, faction, gang

setback noun hold-up, blow, check, defeat, disappointment, hitch, misfortune, reverse

set back verb hold up, delay, hinder, impede, retard, slow

set off verb **1** leave, depart, embark, start out **2** detonate, explode, ignite

setting noun surroundings, backdrop, background, context, location, scene, scenery, set, site

settle verb **1** put in order, adjust, order, regulate, straighten out, work out **2** land, alight, come to rest, descend, light **3** move to, dwell, inhabit, live, make one's home, put down roots, reside, set up home, take up residence **4** colonize, people, pioneer, populate **5** calm, lull, pacify, quell, quiet, quieten, reassure, relax, relieve, soothe **6** pay, clear, discharge, square (up) **7** resolve, clear up, decide, put an end to, reconcile **8** often with on or upon decide, agree, confirm, determine, establish, fix

➤ **Antonyms**

≠calm: agitate, bother, discompose, disquieten, disturb, trouble, unsettle, upset

settlement noun **1** agreement, arrangement, conclusion, confirmation, establishment, working out **2** payment, clearing, discharge **3** <u>colony</u>, community, encampment, outpost

settler noun <u>colonist</u>, frontiersman, immigrant, pioneer

setup noun Informal <u>arrangement</u>, conditions, organization, regime, structure, system

set up verb **1** <u>build</u>, assemble, construct, erect, put together, put up, raise **2** <u>establish</u>, arrange, begin, found, initiate, institute, organize, prearrange, prepare

sever verb **1** <u>cut</u>, cut in two, detach, disconnect, disjoin, divide, part, separate, split **2** <u>discontinue</u>, break off, dissociate, put an end to, terminate

➤ **Antonyms**
≠<u>cut</u>: attach, connect, fix together, join, link, unite ≠<u>discontinue</u>: continue, maintain, uphold

several adjective <u>some</u>, different, diverse, manifold, many, sundry, various

severe adjective **1** <u>strict</u>, austere, cruel, drastic, hard, harsh, oppressive, rigid, unbending **2** <u>grim</u>, forbidding, grave, serious, stern, tight-lipped, unsmiling **3** <u>plain</u>, austere, classic, restrained, simple, Spartan, unadorned, unembellished, unfussy **4** <u>intense</u>, acute, extreme, fierce

➤ **Antonyms**
≠<u>strict</u>: easy, lax, lenient, relaxed, tractable ≠<u>grim</u>: affable, genial ≠<u>plain</u>: embellished, fancy, ornamental, ornate, temperate ≠<u>intense</u>: gentle, mild, minor, moderate

severely adverb **1** <u>strictly</u>, harshly, sharply, sternly **2** <u>seriously</u>, acutely, badly, critically, gravely

severity noun <u>strictness</u>, hardness, harshness, severeness, sternness, toughness

sex noun **1** <u>gender</u> **2** Informal <u>(sexual) intercourse</u>, coition, coitus, copulation, fornication, lovemaking, sexual relations

sexual adjective **1** <u>carnal</u>, erotic, intimate, sensual, sexy **2** <u>reproductive</u>, genital, procreative, sex

sexual intercourse noun <u>copulation</u>, bonking (informal), carnal knowledge, coition, coitus, sex (informal), union

sexuality noun <u>desire</u>, carnality, eroticism, lust, sensuality, sexiness (informal)

sexy adjective <u>erotic</u>, arousing, naughty, provocative, seductive, sensual, sensuous, suggestive, titillating

shabby adjective **1** <u>tatty</u>, dilapidated, mean, ragged, run-down, scruffy, seedy, tattered, threadbare, worn **2** <u>mean</u>, cheap, contemptible, despicable, dirty, dishonourable, low, rotten (informal), scurvy

➤ **Antonyms**
≠<u>tatty</u>: in mint condition, neat, new, smart, well-dressed, well-kept ≠<u>mean</u>: fair, generous, honourable, praiseworthy, worthy

shack noun <u>hut</u>, cabin, shanty

shackle noun **1** often plural <u>fetter</u>, bond, chain, iron, leg-iron, manacle ♦ verb **2** <u>fetter</u>, bind, chain, manacle, put in irons

shade noun **1** <u>dimness</u>, dusk, gloom, gloominess, semidarkness, shadow **2** <u>screen</u>, blind, canopy, cover, covering, curtain, shield, veil **3** <u>hue</u>, colour, tinge, tint, tone **4** <u>dash</u>, hint, suggestion, trace **5** Literary <u>ghost</u>, apparition, phantom, spectre, spirit **6** put into the shade <u>outshine</u>, eclipse, outclass, overshadow ♦ verb **7** <u>cover</u>, conceal, hide, obscure, protect, screen, shield, veil **8** <u>darken</u>, cloud, dim, shadow

shadow noun **1** <u>dimness</u>, cover, darkness, dusk, gloom, shade **2** <u>trace</u>, hint, suggestion, suspicion **3** <u>cloud</u>, blight, gloom, sadness ♦ verb **4** <u>shade</u>, darken, overhang, screen, shield **5** <u>follow</u>, stalk, tail (informal), trail

shadowy adjective **1** <u>dark</u>, dim, dusky, gloomy, murky, shaded, shady **2** <u>vague</u>, dim, dreamlike, faint, ghostly, nebulous, phantom, spectral, unsubstantial

shady adjective **1** shaded, cool, dim **2** Informal crooked, disreputable, dodgy (Brit., Austral., & N.Z. informal), dubious, questionable, shifty, suspect, suspicious, unethical

➤ **Antonyms**

≠shaded: bright, exposed, open, out in the open, sunlit, sunny, unshaded ≠crooked: aboveboard, ethical, honest, honourable, reputable, respectable, straight, upright

shaft noun **1** handle, pole, rod, shank, stem **2** ray, beam, gleam

shaggy adjective unkempt, hairy, hirsute, long-haired, rough, tousled, unshorn

➤ **Antonyms**

close-cropped, cropped, short-haired, smooth

shake verb **1** vibrate, bump, jar, jolt, quake, quiver, rock, shiver, totter, tremble **2** wave, brandish, flourish **3** upset, distress, disturb, frighten, rattle (informal), shock, unnerve ◆ noun **4** vibration, agitation, convulsion, jerk, jolt, quaking, shiver, shudder, trembling, tremor

shake up verb **1** stir (up), agitate, churn (up), mix **2** reorganize, overturn, turn upside down **3** Informal upset, disturb, shock, unsettle

shaky adjective **1** unsteady, faltering, precarious, quivery, rickety, trembling, unstable, weak **2** uncertain, dubious, iffy (informal), questionable, suspect

➤ **Antonyms**

≠unsteady: firm, stable, steady, strong

shallow adjective **1** superficial, empty, slight, surface, trivial **2** unintelligent, foolish, frivolous, ignorant, puerile, simple

➤ **Antonyms**

≠superficial: analytical, comprehensive, deep, in-depth, profound, serious ≠unintelligent: serious, thoughtful

sham noun **1** phoney or phony (informal), counterfeit, forgery, fraud, hoax, humbug, imitation, impostor, pretence ◆ adjective **2** false, artificial, bogus, counterfeit, feigned, imitation, mock, phoney or phony (informal), pretended, simulated ◆ verb **3** fake, affect, assume, feign, pretend, put on, simulate

➤ **Antonyms**

noun ≠phoney or phony: master, original, the genuine article, the real McCoy (or McKay), the real thing ◆ adjective ≠false: authentic, bona fide, genuine, legitimate, natural, real, sound, true, unfeigned, veritable

shambles noun chaos, confusion, disarray, disorder, havoc, madhouse, mess, muddle

shame noun **1** embarrassment, abashment, humiliation, ignominy, mortification **2** disgrace, blot, discredit, dishonour, disrepute, infamy, reproach, scandal, smear ◆ verb **3** embarrass, abash, disgrace, humble, humiliate, mortify **4** dishonour, blot, debase, defile, degrade, smear, stain

➤ **Antonyms**

noun ≠embarrassment: brass neck (Brit. informal), brazenness, cheek, shamelessness ≠disgrace: credit, distinction, esteem, glory, honour, pride, renown, self-respect ◆ verb ≠embarrass: do credit to, make proud ≠dishonour: acclaim, credit, enhance the reputation of, honour

shamefaced adjective embarrassed, abashed, ashamed, humiliated, mortified, red-faced, sheepish

shameful adjective **1** embarrassing, cringe-making (Brit. informal), humiliating, mortifying **2** disgraceful, base, dishonourable, low, mean, outrageous, scandalous, wicked

➤ **Antonyms**

≠disgraceful: admirable, creditable, exemplary, honourable, laudable, right

shameless adjective brazen, audacious, barefaced, flagrant, hardened, insolent, unabashed, unashamed

shanty *noun* shack, cabin, hut, shed

shape *noun* 1 form, build, configuration, contours, figure, lines, outline, profile, silhouette 2 pattern, frame, model, mould 3 condition, fettle, health, state, trim ◆ *verb* 4 form, create, fashion, make, model, mould, produce 5 develop, adapt, devise, frame, modify, plan

shapeless *adjective* formless, amorphous, irregular, misshapen, unstructured

➤ **Antonyms**

well-formed, well-proportioned

shapely *adjective* well-formed, curvaceous, elegant, graceful, neat, trim, well-proportioned

share *noun* 1 part, allotment, allowance, contribution, due, lot, portion, quota, ration, whack (*informal*) ◆ *verb* 2 divide, assign, distribute, split 3 go halves, go fifty-fifty (*informal*) 4 partake, participate, receive

sharp *adjective* 1 keen, acute, jagged, pointed, serrated, spiky 2 sudden, abrupt, distinct, extreme, marked 3 clear, crisp, distinct, well-defined 4 quick-witted, alert, astute, bright, clever, discerning, knowing, penetrating, perceptive, quick 5 cunning, artful, crafty, dishonest, sly, unscrupulous, wily 6 cutting, barbed, biting, bitter, caustic, harsh, hurtful 7 sour, acid, acrid, hot, piquant, pungent, tart 8 acute, gut-wrenching, intense, painful, piercing, severe, shooting, stabbing ◆ *adverb* 9 promptly, exactly, on the dot, on time, precisely, punctually

➤ **Antonyms**

adjective ≠keen: blunt, dull, rounded, unsharpened ≠sudden: even, gentle, gradual ≠clear: blurred, fuzzy, ill-defined, indistinct, unclear ≠quick-witted: dim, dull-witted, dumb (*informal*), slow, stupid ≠cunning: artless, guileless, ingenuous, innocent, naive, simple ≠cutting: amicable, courteous, friendly, gentle, kindly ≠sour: bland, mild, tasteless ◆ *adverb* ≠promptly: approximately, more or less, roughly, round about

sharpen *verb* whet, edge, grind, hone

shatter *verb* 1 smash, break, burst, crack, crush, pulverize 2 destroy, demolish, ruin, torpedo, wreck

shattered *adjective Informal* 1 exhausted, all in (*slang*), dead beat (*informal*), done in (*informal*), drained, knackered (*slang*), ready to drop, tired out, worn out 2 devastated, crushed, gutted (*slang*)

shave *verb* trim, crop, pare, shear

shed[1] *noun* hut, outhouse, shack

shed[2] *verb* 1 give out, cast, drop, emit, give, radiate, scatter, shower, spill 2 cast off, discard, moult, slough

sheen *noun* shine, brightness, gleam, gloss, lustre, polish

sheepish *adjective* embarrassed, abashed, ashamed, mortified, self-conscious, shamefaced

➤ **Antonyms**

bold, brash, brazen, confident, unabashed, unapologetic, unembarrassed

sheer *adjective* 1 total, absolute, complete, downright, out-and-out, pure, unmitigated, utter 2 steep, abrupt, precipitous 3 fine, diaphanous, gauzy, gossamer, see-through, thin, transparent

➤ **Antonyms**

≠total: moderate ≠steep: gentle, gradual, horizontal, slanting, sloping ≠fine: coarse, heavy, opaque, thick

sheet *noun* 1 coat, film, lamina, layer, overlay, stratum, surface, veneer 2 piece, panel, plate, slab 3 expanse, area, blanket, covering, stretch, sweep

shell *noun* 1 case, husk, pod 2 frame, framework, hull, structure ◆ *verb* 3 bomb, attack, blitz, bombard, strafe

shell out verb pay out, fork out (slang), give, hand over

shelter noun 1 protection, cover, defence, guard, screen 2 safety, asylum, haven, refuge, retreat, sanctuary, security ♦ verb 3 take shelter, hide, seek refuge 4 protect, cover, defend, guard, harbour, hide, safeguard, shield

► **Antonyms**
verb ≠protect: expose, lay open, leave open

sheltered adjective protected, cloistered, isolated, quiet, screened, secluded, shaded, shielded

► **Antonyms**
exposed, open, unprotected, unsheltered

shelve verb postpone, defer, freeze, put aside, put on ice, put on the back burner (informal), suspend, take a rain check on (U.S. & Canad. informal)

shepherd noun 1 herdsman, drover, grazier, stockman ♦ verb 2 guide, conduct, herd, steer, usher

shield noun 1 protection, cover, defence, guard, safeguard, screen, shelter ♦ verb 2 protect, cover, defend, guard, safeguard, screen, shelter

shift verb 1 move, budge, displace, move around, rearrange, relocate, reposition ♦ noun 2 move, displacement, rearrangement, shifting

shiftless adjective lazy, aimless, good-for-nothing, idle, lackadaisical, slothful, unambitious, unenterprising

shifty adjective untrustworthy, deceitful, devious, evasive, furtive, slippery, sly, tricky, underhand

► **Antonyms**
dependable, honest, honourable, open, reliable, trustworthy

shimmer verb 1 gleam, glisten, scintillate, twinkle ♦ noun 2 gleam, iridescence

shine verb 1 gleam, beam, flash, glare, glisten, glitter, glow, radiate, sparkle, twinkle 2 polish,

brush, buff, burnish 3 be outstanding, be conspicuous, excel, stand out ♦ noun 4 brightness, glare, gleam, light, radiance, shimmer, sparkle 5 polish, gloss, lustre, sheen

shining adjective bright, beaming, brilliant, gleaming, glistening, luminous, radiant, shimmering, sparkling

shiny adjective bright, gleaming, glistening, glossy, lustrous, polished

ship noun vessel, boat, craft

shipshape adjective tidy, neat, orderly, spick-and-span, trim, wellordered, well-organized

shirk verb dodge, avoid, evade, get out of, skive (Brit. slang), slack

shirker noun slacker, clockwatcher, dodger, idler, skiver (Brit. slang)

shiver[1] verb 1 tremble, quake, quiver, shake, shudder ♦ noun 2 trembling, flutter, quiver, shudder, tremor

shiver[2] verb splinter, break, crack, fragment, shatter, smash, smash to smithereens

shivery adjective shaking, chilled, chilly, cold, quaking, quivery

shock verb 1 horrify, appal, disgust, nauseate, revolt, scandalize, sicken 2 astound, jolt, shake, stagger, stun, stupefy ♦ noun 3 impact, blow, clash, collision 4 upset, blow, bombshell, distress, disturbance, stupefaction, stupor, trauma, turn (informal)

shocking adjective dreadful, appalling, atrocious, disgraceful, disgusting, ghastly, horrifying, nauseating, outrageous, revolting, scandalous, sickening

► **Antonyms**
delightful, excellent, fine, firstrate, honourable, marvellous, pleasant, praiseworthy, wonderful

shoddy adjective inferior, cheap, poor, rubbishy, second-rate, slipshod, tawdry, trashy

► **Antonyms**
excellent, fine, first-rate, superlative, well-made

shoot *verb* **1** <u>hit</u>, blast (*slang*), bring down, kill, open fire, plug (*slang*) **2** <u>fire</u>, discharge, emit, fling, hurl, launch, project, propel **3** <u>speed</u>, bolt, charge, dart, dash, fly, hurtle, race, rush, streak, tear ◆ *noun* **4** <u>sprout</u>, branch, bud, offshoot, sprig

shop *noun* <u>store</u>, boutique, emporium, hypermarket, supermarket

shore *noun* <u>beach</u>, coast, sands, seashore, strand (*poetic*)

shore up *verb* <u>support</u>, brace, buttress, hold, prop, reinforce, strengthen, underpin

short *adjective* **1** <u>concise</u>, brief, compressed, laconic, pithy, succinct, summary, terse **2** <u>small</u>, diminutive, dumpy, little, petite, squat **3** <u>brief</u>, fleeting, momentary **4** *often with* **of** *or on* <u>lacking</u>, deficient, limited, low (on), scant, scarce, wanting **5** <u>abrupt</u>, brusque, curt, discourteous, impolite, sharp, terse, uncivil ◆ *adverb* **6** <u>abruptly</u>, suddenly, without warning

▶ **Antonyms**

adjective ≠<u>concise</u>: lengthy, long, long-drawn-out, long-winded, rambling ≠<u>small</u>: big, high, lanky, lofty, tall ≠<u>brief</u>: extended, long, long-term ≠<u>lacking</u>: abundant, adequate, ample, bountiful, copious, plentiful, sufficient ≠<u>abrupt</u>: civil, courteous, polite ◆ *adverb* ≠<u>abruptly</u>: bit by bit, gently, gradually, little by little, slowly

shortage *noun* <u>deficiency</u>, dearth, insufficiency, lack, paucity, scarcity, want

▶ **Antonyms**

abundance, adequate amount, excess, overabundance, profusion, sufficiency, surfeit, surplus

shortcoming *noun* <u>failing</u>, defect, fault, flaw, imperfection, weakness

shorten *verb* <u>cut</u>, abbreviate, abridge, curtail, decrease, diminish, lessen, reduce

▶ **Antonyms**

draw out, elongate, expand, extend, increase, lengthen, make longer, prolong, protract, stretch

shortly *adverb* <u>soon</u>, before long, in a little while, presently

short-sighted *adjective* **1** <u>nearsighted</u>, myopic **2** <u>unthinking</u>, ill-advised, ill-considered, impolitic, impractical, improvident, imprudent, injudicious

short-tempered *adjective* <u>quick-tempered</u>, hot-tempered, impatient, irascible, ratty (*Brit. & N.Z. informal*), testy

shot *noun* **1** <u>throw</u>, discharge, lob, pot shot **2** <u>pellet</u>, ball, bullet, lead, projectile, slug **3** <u>marksman</u>, shooter **4** *Informal* <u>attempt</u>, effort, endeavour, go (*informal*), stab (*informal*), try, turn **5** *Informal* <u>guess</u>, conjecture, surmise

shoulder *verb* **1** <u>bear</u>, accept, assume, be responsible for, carry, take on **2** <u>push</u>, elbow, jostle, press, shove

shout *noun* **1** <u>cry</u>, bellow, call, roar, scream, yell ◆ *verb* **2** <u>cry (out)</u>, bawl, bellow, call (out), holler (*informal*), roar, scream, yell

shout down *verb* <u>silence</u>, drown, drown out, overwhelm

shove *verb* <u>push</u>, drive, elbow, impel, jostle, press, propel, thrust

shovel *verb* <u>move</u>, dredge, heap, ladle, load, scoop, toss

shove off *verb Informal* <u>go away</u>, clear off (*informal*), depart, leave, push off (*informal*), scram (*informal*)

show *verb* **1** <u>be visible</u>, appear **2** <u>present</u>, display, exhibit **3** <u>prove</u>, clarify, demonstrate, elucidate, point out **4** <u>instruct</u>, demonstrate, explain, teach **5** <u>indicate</u>, demonstrate, display, manifest, register, reveal **6** <u>guide</u>, accompany, attend, conduct, escort, lead ◆ *noun* **7** <u>entertainment</u>, presentation, production **8** <u>exhibition</u>, array, display, fair, pageant, parade, sight, spectacle **9** <u>pretence</u>, affectation, air, appearance, display, illusion, parade, pose

➤ **Antonyms**

verb ≠be visible: be invisible ≠present, indicate: conceal, hide, keep secret, mask, obscure, suppress, veil, withhold ≠prove: deny, disprove, gainsay (archaic or literary), refute

showdown noun Informal confrontation, clash, face-off (slang)

shower noun 1 <u>deluge</u>, barrage, stream, torrent, volley ◆ verb 2 <u>inundate</u>, deluge, heap, lavish, pour, rain

showman noun <u>performer</u>, entertainer

show-off noun Informal <u>exhibitionist</u>, boaster, braggart, poseur

show off verb 1 <u>exhibit</u>, demonstrate, display, flaunt, parade 2 Informal <u>boast</u>, blow one's own trumpet, brag, swagger

show up verb 1 <u>stand out</u>, appear, be conspicuous, be visible 2 <u>reveal</u>, expose, highlight, lay bare 3 Informal <u>embarrass</u>, let down, mortify, put to shame 4 Informal <u>arrive</u>, appear, come, turn up

showy adjective 1 <u>ostentatious</u>, brash, flamboyant, flash (informal), flashy, over the top (informal) 2 <u>gaudy</u>, garish, loud

➤ **Antonyms**

discreet, low-key, quiet, restrained, tasteful, unobtrusive

shred noun 1 <u>strip</u>, bit, fragment, piece, scrap, sliver, tatter 2 <u>particle</u>, atom, grain, iota, jot, scrap, trace

shrew noun <u>nag</u>, harpy, harridan, scold, spitfire, vixen

shrewd adjective <u>clever</u>, astute, calculating, canny, crafty, cunning, intelligent, keen, perceptive, perspicacious, sharp, smart

➤ **Antonyms**

dull, gullible, ingenuous, naive, obtuse, slow-witted, stupid

shrewdness noun <u>cleverness</u>, astuteness, canniness, discernment, judgment, perspicacity, quick wits, sharpness, smartness

shriek verb, noun <u>cry</u>, scream, screech, squeal, yell

shrill adjective <u>piercing</u>, high, penetrating, sharp

➤ **Antonyms**

deep, dulcet, soft, soothing

shrink verb 1 <u>decrease</u>, contract, diminish, dwindle, grow smaller, lessen, narrow, shorten 2 <u>recoil</u>, cower, cringe, draw back, flinch, quail

➤ **Antonyms**

≠decrease: dilate, distend, enlarge, expand, increase, inflate, swell ≠recoil: confront, embrace, face

shrivel verb <u>wither</u>, dehydrate, desiccate, shrink, wilt, wizen

shroud noun 1 <u>winding sheet</u>, grave clothes 2 <u>covering</u>, mantle, pall, screen, veil ◆ verb 3 <u>conceal</u>, blanket, cloak, cover, envelop, hide, screen, veil

shudder verb 1 <u>shiver</u>, convulse, quake, quiver, shake, tremble ◆ noun 2 <u>shiver</u>, quiver, spasm, tremor

shuffle verb 1 <u>scuffle</u>, drag, scrape, shamble 2 <u>rearrange</u>, disarrange, disorder, jumble, mix

shun verb <u>avoid</u>, keep away from, steer clear of

shut verb <u>close</u>, fasten, seal, secure, slam

➤ **Antonyms**

open, throw wide, undo, unfasten

shut down verb 1 <u>stop</u>, halt, switch off 2 <u>close</u>, shut up

shut out verb <u>exclude</u>, bar, debar, keep out, lock out

shuttle verb <u>go back and forth</u>, alternate, commute, go to and fro

shut up verb 1 Informal <u>be quiet</u>, fall silent, gag, hold one's tongue, hush, silence 2 <u>confine</u>, cage, coop up, immure, imprison, incarcerate

shy¹ adjective 1 <u>timid</u>, bashful, coy, diffident, retiring, self-conscious, self-effacing, shrinking 2 shy of <u>cautious of</u>, chary of, distrustful of, hesitant about, suspicious of, wary of ◆ verb 3 sometimes with off or away <u>recoil</u>, balk, draw back, flinch, start

► **Antonyms**

adjective ≠timid: assured, bold, brash, cheeky, confident, fearless, forward, pushy (*informal*), self-assured, self-confident ≠cautious of: rash, reckless, unsuspecting, unwary

shy² *verb* throw, cast, fling, hurl, pitch, sling, toss

shyness *noun* timidness, bashfulness, diffidence, lack of confidence, self-consciousness, timidity, timorousness

sick *adjective* **1** nauseous, ill, nauseated, queasy **2** unwell, ailing, diseased, indisposed, poorly (*informal*), under the weather **3** *Informal* morbid, black, ghoulish, macabre, sadistic **4** sick of tired, bored, fed up, jaded, weary

► **Antonyms**

≠unwell: able-bodied, fine, fit, fit as a fiddle, hale and hearty, healthy, robust, well

sicken *verb* **1** disgust, gross out (*U.S. slang*), nauseate, repel, revolt, turn one's stomach **2** fall ill, ail, take sick

sickening *adjective* disgusting, distasteful, foul, gut-wrenching, loathsome, nauseating, offensive, putrid, repulsive, revolting, stomach-turning (*informal*), yucky or yukky (*slang*)

► **Antonyms**

delightful, inviting, marvellous, mouth-watering, pleasant, tempting, wholesome, wonderful

sickly *adjective* **1** unhealthy, ailing, delicate, faint, feeble, infirm, pallid, peaky, wan, weak **2** nauseating, cloying, icky (*informal*), mawkish

sickness *noun* **1** illness, affliction, ailment, bug (*informal*), complaint, disease, disorder, malady **2** nausea, queasiness, vomiting

side *noun* **1** border, boundary, division, edge, limit, margin, perimeter, rim, sector, verge **2** part, aspect, face, facet, flank, hand, surface, view **3** party, camp, cause, faction, sect, team

4 point of view, angle, opinion, position, slant, stand, standpoint, viewpoint **5** *Brit. slang* conceit, airs, arrogance ♦ *adjective* **6** subordinate, ancillary, incidental, lesser, marginal, minor, secondary, subsidiary ♦ *verb* **7** *usually with* with support, ally with, favour, go along with, take the part of

► **Antonyms**

noun ≠border: centre, core, heart, middle ♦ *adjective* ≠subordinate: central, essential, fundamental, key, main, middle, primary, principal ♦ *verb* ≠support: counter, oppose, stand against, withstand

sidelong *adjective* sideways, covert, indirect, oblique

sidestep *verb* avoid, circumvent, dodge, duck (*informal*), evade, skirt

sidetrack *verb* distract, deflect, divert

sideways *adverb* **1** obliquely, edgewise, laterally, sidelong, to the side ♦ *adjective* **2** oblique, sidelong

sidle *verb* edge, creep, inch, slink, sneak, steal

siesta *noun* nap, catnap, doze, forty winks (*informal*), sleep, snooze (*informal*)

sieve *noun* **1** strainer, colander ♦ *verb* **2** sift, separate, strain

sift *verb* **1** sieve, filter, separate **2** examine, analyse, go through, investigate, research, scrutinize, work over

sight *noun* **1** vision, eye, eyes, eyesight, seeing **2** view, appearance, perception, range of vision, visibility **3** spectacle, display, exhibition, pageant, scene, show, vista **4** *Informal* eyesore, mess, monstrosity **5** catch sight of, spot, espy, glimpse ♦ *verb* **6** spot, behold, discern, distinguish, make out, observe, perceive, see

sign *noun* **1** indication, clue, evidence, gesture, hint, mark, proof, signal, symptom, token **2**

notice, board, placard, warning **3** <u>symbol</u>, badge, device, emblem, logo, mark **4** <u>omen</u>, augury, auspice, foreboding, portent, warning ♦ verb **5** <u>autograph</u>, endorse, initial, inscribe **6** <u>gesture</u>, beckon, gesticulate, indicate, signal

signal noun **1** <u>sign</u>, beacon, cue, gesture, indication, mark, token ♦ verb **2** <u>gesture</u>, beckon, gesticulate, indicate, motion, sign, wave

significance noun **1** <u>importance</u>, consequence, moment, relevance, weight **2** <u>meaning</u>, force, implication(s), import, message, point, purport, sense

significant adjective **1** <u>important</u>, critical, material, momentous, noteworthy, serious, vital, weighty **2** <u>meaningful</u>, eloquent, expressive, indicative, suggestive

➤ **Antonyms**
≠<u>important</u>: immaterial, inconsequential, insignificant, irrelevant, petty, trivial, unimportant ≠<u>meaningful</u>: meaningless

signify verb **1** <u>indicate</u>, be a sign of, betoken, connote, denote, imply, intimate, mean, portend, suggest **2** Informal <u>matter</u>, be important, carry weight, count

silence noun **1** <u>quiet</u>, calm, hush, lull, peace, stillness **2** <u>muteness</u>, dumbness, reticence, taciturnity ♦ verb **3** <u>quieten</u>, cut off, cut short, deaden, gag, muffle, quiet, stifle, still, suppress

➤ **Antonyms**
noun ≠<u>quiet</u>: cacophony, din, noise, racket, sound, tumult, uproar ≠<u>muteness</u>: babble, chatter, garrulousness, hubbub, loquaciousness, prattle, speech, talking, verbosity ♦ verb ≠<u>quieten</u>: amplify, make louder

silent adjective **1** <u>quiet</u>, hushed, muted, noiseless, soundless, still **2** <u>mute</u>, dumb, speechless, taciturn, voiceless, wordless

silently adjective <u>quietly</u>, inaudibly, in silence, mutely, noiselessly, soundlessly, without a sound, wordlessly

silhouette noun **1** <u>outline</u>, form, profile, shape ♦ verb **2** <u>outline</u>, etch, stand out

silky adjective <u>smooth</u>, silken, sleek, velvety

silly adjective <u>foolish</u>, absurd, asinine, daft, dumb-ass (slang), fatuous, idiotic, inane, ridiculous, senseless, stupid, unwise

➤ **Antonyms**
bright, clever, intelligent, perceptive, profound, prudent, reasonable, sensible, smart, thoughtful, well-thought-out, wise

silt noun **1** <u>sediment</u>, alluvium, deposit, ooze, sludge ♦ verb **2** silt up <u>clog</u>, choke, congest

similar adjective <u>alike</u>, analogous, close, comparable, like, resembling

➤ **Antonyms**
contrary, different, disparate, dissimilar, diverse, opposite, unlike, varying

similarity noun <u>resemblance</u>, affinity, agreement, analogy, closeness, comparability, correspondence, likeness, sameness

➤ **Antonyms**
difference, disagreement, discrepancy, disparity, dissimilarity, diversity, unalikeness, variation

simmer verb <u>fume</u>, be angry, be pissed (off) (taboo slang), rage, seethe, smoulder

simmer down verb Informal <u>calm down</u>, control oneself, cool off or down

simper verb <u>smile coyly</u>, smile affectedly, smirk

simple adjective **1** <u>uncomplicated</u>, clear, easy, intelligible, lucid, plain, straightforward, understandable, uninvolved **2** <u>plain</u>, classic, natural, unembellished, unfussy **3** <u>pure</u>, elementary, unalloyed, uncombined, unmixed **4** <u>artless</u>, childlike, guileless, ingenuous, innocent, naive, natural, sincere, unaffected, unsophisticated **5** <u>honest</u>, bald, basic, direct, frank, naked, plain, sincere, stark **6** <u>unpretentious</u>, homely, humble, modest **7** Informal feeble-minded, dumb (*informal*), dumb-ass (*slang*), foolish, half-witted, moronic, slow, stupid

➤ **Antonyms**

≠uncomplicated: advanced, complex, complicated, difficult, elaborate, intricate, involved, refined, sophisticated ≠plain: contrived, elaborate, fussy, intricate, ornate ≠artless: artful, smart, sophisticated, worldly, worldly-wise ≠unpretentious: extravagant, fancy, flashy ≠feeble-minded: astute, bright, clever, intelligent, quick, quick-witted, sharp, smart, wise

simple-minded *adjective* feeble-minded, backward, dim-witted, foolish, idiot, idiotic, moronic, retarded, simple, stupid

simpleton *noun* halfwit, dullard, dumb-ass (*slang*), fool, idiot, imbecile (*informal*), moron, numskull or numbskull

simplicity *noun* **1** ease, clarity, clearness, straightforwardness **2** plainness, lack of adornment, purity, restraint **3** artlessness, candour, directness, innocence, naivety, openness

➤ **Antonyms**

≠ease: complexity, difficulty, intricacy, lack of clarity ≠plain-ness: decoration, elaborateness, embellishment, fanciness, fussiness, ornateness ≠artlessness: craftiness, cunning, deviousness, guile, slyness, worldliness

simplify *verb* make simpler, abridge, disentangle, dumb down, reduce to essentials, streamline

simply *adverb* **1** plainly, clearly, directly, easily, intelligibly, naturally, straightforwardly, unpretentiously **2** just, merely, only, purely, solely **3** totally, absolutely, completely, really, utterly, wholly

simulate *verb* pretend, act, affect, feign, put on, sham

simultaneous *adjective* coinciding, at the same time, coincident, concurrent, contemporaneous, synchronous

simultaneously *adverb* at the same time, concurrently, together

sin *noun* **1** wrongdoing, crime, error, evil, guilt, iniquity, misdeed, offence, transgression ♦ *verb* **2** transgress, err, fall, go astray, lapse, offend

sincere *adjective* honest, candid, earnest, frank, genuine, guileless, heartfelt, real, serious, true, unaffected

➤ **Antonyms**

affected, artificial, deceptive, dishonest, false, insincere, phoney or phony (*informal*), pretended, put on

sincerely *adverb* honestly, earnestly, genuinely, in earnest, seriously, truly, wholeheartedly

sincerity *noun* honesty, candour, frankness, genuineness, seriousness, truth

sinecure *noun* cushy number (*informal*), gravy train (*slang*), money for jam or old rope (*informal*), soft job (*informal*), soft option

sinful *adjective* wicked, bad, corrupt, criminal, erring, guilty, immoral, iniquitous

➤ **Antonyms**

free from sin, godly, holy, honourable, moral, pure, sinless, spotless, squeaky-clean, virtuous, without sin

sing *verb* **1** warble, carol, chant, chirp, croon, pipe, trill, yodel **2** hum, buzz, purr, whine

singe *verb* burn, char, scorch, sear

singer *noun* vocalist, balladeer, chorister, crooner, minstrel, soloist

single *adjective* **1** one, distinct, individual, lone, only, separate, sole, solitary **2** individual, exclusive, separate, undivided, unshared **3** unmarried, free, unattached, unwed **4** simple, unblended, unmixed ♦ *verb* **5** *usually with* out pick, choose, distinguish, fix on, pick on or out, select, separate, set apart

single-handed *adverb* unaided, alone, by oneself, independently, on one's own, solo, unassisted, without help

single-minded *adjective* determined, dedicated, dogged, fixed, unswerving

singly *adverb* one by one, individually, one at a time, separately

singular *adjective* **1** single, individual, separate, sole **2** remarkable, eminent, exceptional, notable, noteworthy, outstanding **3** unusual, curious, eccentric, extraordinary, odd, peculiar, queer, strange

> ➤ **Antonyms**

≠ remarkable, unusual: common, common or garden, commonplace, conventional, everyday, familiar, normal, routine, run-of-the-mill, unexceptional, unremarkable, usual

singularly *adverb* remarkably, especially, exceptionally, notably, outstandingly, particularly, uncommonly, unusually

sinister *adjective* threatening, dire, disquieting, evil, malign, menacing, ominous

> ➤ **Antonyms**

auspicious, benign, promising, propitious, reassuring

sink *verb* **1** descend, dip, drop, fall, founder, go down, go under, lower, plunge, submerge, subside **2** fall, abate, collapse, drop, lapse, slip, subside **3** stoop, be reduced to, lower oneself **4** decline, decay, decrease, deteriorate, diminish, dwindle, fade, fail, flag, lessen, weaken, worsen **5** dig, bore, drill, drive, excavate

> ➤ **Antonyms**

≠ descend: arise, ascend, climb, go up, move up, rise, rise up ≠ decline: go up, grow, improve, increase, intensify, rise, rise up

sink in *verb* be understood, get through to, penetrate, register (*informal*)

sinner *noun* wrongdoer, evildoer, malefactor, miscreant, offender, transgressor

sip *verb* **1** drink, sample, sup,

taste ♦ *noun* **2** swallow, drop, taste, thimbleful

sissy *or* **cissy** *noun* **1** wimp (*informal*), coward, jessie (*Scot. slang*), milksop, mummy's boy, namby-pamby, softie (*informal*), weakling, wet (*Brit. informal*), wuss (*slang*) ♦ *adjective* **2** wimpish *or* wimpy (*informal*), cowardly, effeminate, feeble, namby-pamby, soft (*informal*), unmanly, weak, wet (*Brit. informal*), wussy (*slang*)

sit *verb* **1** rest, perch, settle **2** convene, assemble, deliberate, meet, officiate, preside

site *noun* **1** location, place, plot, position, setting, spot ♦ *verb* **2** locate, install, place, position, set, situate

situation *noun* **1** state of affairs, case, circumstances, condition, equation, plight, state **2** location, place, position, setting, site, spot **3** status, rank, station **4** job, employment, office, place, position, post

sizable, sizeable *adjective* large, considerable, decent, goodly, largish, respectable, substantial

size *noun* dimensions, amount, bulk, extent, immensity, magnitude, mass, proportions, range, volume

size up *verb Informal* assess, appraise, evaluate, take stock of

sizzle *verb* hiss, crackle, frizzle, fry, spit

skeleton *noun* framework, bare bones, draft, frame, outline, sketch, structure

sketch *noun* **1** drawing, delineation, design, draft, outline, plan ♦ *verb* **2** draw, delineate, depict, draft, outline, represent, rough out

sketchy *adjective* incomplete, cursory, inadequate, perfunctory, rough, scrappy, skimpy, superficial

> ➤ **Antonyms**

complete, detailed, full, thorough

skilful *adjective* expert, able, adept, adroit, clever, competent, dexterous, masterly, practised, professional, proficient, skilled

➤ **Antonyms**

amateurish, awkward, bungling, clumsy, cowboy (informal), ham-fisted, incompetent, inept, inexperienced, inexpert, unskilful, unskilled

skill noun <u>expertise</u>, ability, art, cleverness, competence, craft, dexterity, facility, knack, proficiency, skilfulness, talent, technique

➤ **Antonyms**

awkwardness, clumsiness, ham-fistedness, inability, incompetence, ineptitude

skilled adjective <u>expert</u>, able, masterly, professional, proficient, skilful

➤ **Antonyms**

amateurish, cowboy (informal), inexpert, unprofessional, unskilled

skim verb 1 <u>separate</u>, cream 2 <u>glide</u>, coast, float, fly, sail, soar 3 usually with **through** <u>scan</u>, glance, run one's eye over

skimp verb <u>stint</u>, be mean with, be sparing with, cut corners, scamp, scrimp

➤ **Antonyms**

be extravagant, be generous with, be prodigal, fritter away, lavish, overspend, squander, throw money away

skin noun 1 <u>hide</u>, fell, pelt 2 <u>coating</u>, casing, crust, film, husk, outside, peel, rind ◆ verb 3 <u>peel</u>, flay, scrape

skinflint noun <u>miser</u>, meanie or meany (informal, chiefly Brit.), niggard, penny-pincher (informal), Scrooge

skinny adjective <u>thin</u>, emaciated, lean, scrawny, undernourished

➤ **Antonyms**

fat, fleshy, heavy, obese, plump, podgy, portly, stout, tubby

skip verb 1 <u>hop</u>, bob, bounce, caper, dance, flit, frisk, gambol, prance, trip 2 <u>pass over</u>, eschew, give (something) a miss, leave out, miss out, omit

skirmish noun 1 <u>fight</u>, battle,

brush, clash, conflict, encounter, fracas, scrap (informal) ◆ verb 2 <u>fight</u>, clash, collide

skirt verb 1 <u>border</u>, edge, flank 2 often with **around** or **round** <u>avoid</u>, circumvent, evade, steer clear of

skit noun <u>parody</u>, burlesque, sketch, spoof (informal), takeoff (informal)

skittish adjective <u>lively</u>, antsy (informal), excitable, fidgety, highly strung, jumpy, nervous, restive

➤ **Antonyms**

calm, composed, placid, relaxed, steady, unexcitable

skive verb Brit. informal <u>slack</u>, idle, malinger, shirk, swing the lead

skulduggery noun Informal <u>trickery</u>, double-dealing, duplicity, machinations, underhandedness

skulk verb 1 <u>sneak</u>, creep, prowl, slink 2 <u>lurk</u>, lie in wait, loiter

sky noun <u>heavens</u>, firmament

slab noun <u>piece</u>, chunk, lump, portion, slice, wedge

slack adjective 1 <u>loose</u>, baggy, lax, limp, relaxed 2 <u>negligent</u>, idle, inactive, lax, lazy, neglectful, remiss, slapdash, slipshod 3 <u>slow</u>, dull, inactive, quiet, slow-moving, sluggish ◆ noun 4 <u>room</u>, excess, give (informal), leeway ◆ verb 5 <u>shirk</u>, dodge, idle, skive (Brit. slang)

➤ **Antonyms**

adjective ≠<u>loose</u>: inflexible, rigid, stiff, strained, stretched, taut, tight ≠<u>negligent</u>: concerned, diligent, exacting, hard-working, meticulous ≠<u>slow</u>: active, bustling, busy, fast-moving, hectic

slacken verb, often with **off** <u>lessen</u>, abate, decrease, diminish, drop off, moderate, reduce, relax

slacker noun <u>layabout</u>, dodger, idler, loafer, shirker, skiver (Brit. slang)

slag verb Slang, often with **off** <u>criticize</u>, abuse, deride, insult, malign, mock, slander, slate

slake verb <u>satisfy</u>, assuage, quench, sate

slam verb 1 <u>bang</u>, crash, smash 2

throw, dash, fling, hurl

slander noun 1 <u>defamation</u>, calumny, libel, scandal, smear ♦ verb 2 <u>defame</u>, blacken (someone's) name, libel, malign, smear

> **Antonyms**

noun ≠<u>defamation</u>: acclaim, acclamation, approval, praise ♦ verb ≠<u>defame</u>: acclaim, applaud, approve, compliment, praise, sing the praises of

slanderous adjective defamatory, damaging, libellous, malicious

slant verb 1 <u>slope</u>, bend, bevel, cant, heel, incline, lean, list, tilt 2 <u>bias</u>, angle, colour, distort, twist ♦ noun 3 <u>slope</u>, camber, gradient, incline, tilt 4 <u>bias</u>, angle, emphasis, one-sidedness, point of view, prejudice

slanting adjective sloping, angled, at an angle, bent, diagonal, inclined, oblique, tilted, tilting

slap noun 1 <u>smack</u>, blow, cuff, spank, swipe ♦ verb 2 <u>smack</u>, clap, cuff, spank, swipe

slapdash adjective careless, clumsy, hasty, hurried, messy, slipshod, sloppy (informal), untidy

> **Antonyms**

careful, conscientious, meticulous, painstaking, precise, punctilious, tidy

slap-up adjective Brit. informal luxurious, lavish, magnificent, splendid, sumptuous, superb

slash verb 1 <u>cut</u>, gash, hack, lacerate, rend, rip, score, slit 2 <u>reduce</u>, cut, drop, lower ♦ noun 3 <u>cut</u>, gash, incision, laceration, rent, rip, slit

slate verb Informal, chiefly Brit. criticize, censure, rebuke, scold, tear into (informal)

slaughter noun 1 <u>slaying</u>, bloodshed, butchery, carnage, killing, massacre, murder ♦ verb 2 <u>slay</u>, butcher, kill, massacre, murder

slaughterhouse noun abattoir, butchery

slave noun 1 <u>servant</u>, drudge, serf, skivvy (chiefly Brit.), vassal

♦ verb 2 toil, drudge, slog

slavery noun enslavement, bondage, captivity, servitude, subjugation

> **Antonyms**

emancipation, freedom, liberty, release

slavish adjective 1 <u>servile</u>, abject, base, cringing, fawning, grovelling, obsequious, submissive, sycophantic 2 <u>imitative</u>, secondhand, unimaginative, unoriginal

> **Antonyms**

≠<u>servile</u>: domineering, masterful, rebellious, self-willed, wilful ≠<u>imitative</u>: creative, imaginative, inventive, original

slay verb Archaic or literary <u>kill</u>, butcher, massacre, mow down, murder, slaughter

sleaze noun Informal <u>corruption</u>, bribery, dishonesty, extortion, fraud, unscrupulousness, venality

sleazy adjective <u>sordid</u>, disreputable, low, run-down, seedy, squalid

sleek adjective <u>glossy</u>, lustrous, shiny, smooth

> **Antonyms**

dishevelled, rough, shaggy, unkempt

sleep noun 1 <u>slumber(s)</u>, doze, forty winks (informal), hibernation, nap, siesta, snooze (informal), zizz (Brit. informal) ♦ verb 2 <u>slumber</u>, catnap, doze, drowse, hibernate, snooze (informal), take a nap

sleepless adjective <u>wakeful</u>, insomniac, restless

sleepy adjective <u>drowsy</u>, dull, heavy, inactive, lethargic, sluggish

> **Antonyms**

active, alert, awake, energetic, lively, wide-awake

slender adjective 1 <u>slim</u>, lean, narrow, slight, willowy 2 <u>faint</u>, poor, remote, slight, slim, tenuous, thin 3 <u>meagre</u>, little, scant, scanty, small

> **Antonyms**

≠<u>slim</u>: bulky, chubby, fat, heavy, large, podgy, stout, tubby, well-built ≠<u>faint</u>: good, strong ≠<u>mea-gre</u>: ample, appreciable, considerable, generous, large, substantial

sleuth noun Informal <u>detective</u>, private eye (informal), (private) investigator

slice noun 1 <u>piece</u>, cut, helping, portion, segment, share, sliver, wedge ♦ verb 2 <u>cut</u>, carve, divide, sever

slick adjective 1 <u>glib</u>, plausible, polished, smooth, specious 2 <u>skilful</u>, adroit, deft, dexterous, polished, professional ♦ 3 <u>smooth</u>, plaster down, sleek

➤ **Antonyms**

adjective ≠<u>skilful</u>: amateur, amateurish, clumsy, crude, unpolished, unprofessional, unskilful

slide verb <u>slip</u>, coast, glide, skim, slither

slight adjective 1 <u>small</u>, feeble, insignificant, meagre, measly, minor, paltry, scanty, trifling, trivial, unimportant 2 <u>slim</u>, delicate, feeble, fragile, lightly-built, small, spare ♦ verb 3 <u>snub</u>, affront, disdain, ignore, insult, scorn ♦ noun 4 <u>insult</u>, affront, neglect, rebuff, slap in the face (informal), snub, (the) cold shoulder

➤ **Antonyms**

adjective ≠<u>small</u>: appreciable, considerable, great, important, large, significant ≠<u>slim</u>: muscular, solid, strong, sturdy, well-built ♦ verb ≠<u>snub</u>: compliment, flatter, praise, speak well of ♦ noun ≠<u>insult</u>: compliment, flattery, praise

slightly adverb <u>a little</u>, somewhat

slim adjective 1 <u>slender</u>, lean, narrow, slight, svelte, thin, trim 2 <u>slight</u>, faint, poor, remote, slender ♦ verb 3 <u>lose weight</u>, diet, reduce

➤ **Antonyms**

adjective ≠<u>slender</u>: broad, bulky, chubby, fat, heavy, obese, overweight, tubby, thick ≠<u>slight</u>: good, strong ♦ verb ≠<u>lose weight</u>: build oneself up,

put on weight

slimy adjective 1 <u>viscous</u>, clammy, glutinous, oozy 2 Chiefly Brit. <u>obsequious</u>, creeping, grovelling, oily, servile, smarmy (Brit. informal), unctuous

sling verb 1 Informal <u>throw</u>, cast, chuck (informal), fling, heave, hurl, lob (informal), shy, toss 2 <u>hang</u>, dangle, suspend

slink verb <u>creep</u>, prowl, skulk, slip, sneak, steal

slinky adjective <u>figure-hugging</u>, clinging, close-fitting, skintight

slip verb 1 <u>fall</u>, skid 2 <u>slide</u>, glide, skate, slither 3 <u>sneak</u>, conceal, creep, hide, steal 4 sometimes with up <u>make a mistake</u>, blunder, err, miscalculate 5 let slip <u>give away</u>, disclose, divulge, leak, reveal ♦ noun 6 <u>mistake</u>, blunder, error, failure, fault, lapse, omission, oversight 7 give (someone) the slip <u>escape from</u>, dodge, elude, evade, get away from, lose (someone)

slippery adjective 1 <u>smooth</u>, glassy, greasy, icy, slippy (informal or dialect), unsafe 2 <u>untrust-worthy</u>, crafty, cunning, devious, dishonest, evasive, shifty, tricky

slipshod adjective <u>careless</u>, casual, slapdash, sloppy (informal), slovenly, untidy

slit noun 1 <u>cut</u>, gash, incision, opening, rent, split, tear ♦ verb 2 <u>cut (open)</u>, gash, knife, lance, pierce, rip, slash

slither verb <u>slide</u>, glide, slink, slip, snake, undulate

sliver noun <u>shred</u>, fragment, paring, shaving, splinter

slob noun Informal <u>layabout</u>, couch potato (slang), good-for-nothing, idler, loafer, lounger

slobber verb <u>drool</u>, dribble, drivel, salivate, slaver

slobbish adjective <u>messy</u>, slovenly, unclean, unkempt, untidy

slog verb 1 <u>work</u>, labour, plod, plough through, slave, toil 2 <u>trudge</u>, tramp, trek 3 <u>hit</u>, punch, slug, sock (slang), strike, thump, wallop (informal) ♦ noun 4 <u>la-</u>

bour, effort, exertion, struggle 5 trudge, hike, tramp, trek

slogan noun catch phrase, catchword, motto, tag-line

slop verb spill, overflow, slosh (informal), splash

slope noun 1 inclination, gradient, incline, ramp, rise, slant, tilt ◆ verb 2 slant, drop away, fall, incline, lean, rise, tilt 3 slope off or away Informal slink away, creep away, slip away

sloping adjective slanting, inclined, leaning, oblique

sloppy adjective 1 Informal careless, messy, slipshod, slovenly, untidy 2 Informal sentimental, gushing, icky (informal), mawkish, slushy (informal), soppy (Brit. informal)

slot noun 1 opening, aperture, groove, hole, slit, vent 2 Informal place, opening, position, space, time, vacancy ◆ verb 3 fit in, fit, insert

sloth noun laziness, idleness, inactivity, inertia, slackness, sluggishness, torpor

slothful adjective Formal lazy, idle, inactive, indolent, skiving (Brit. slang), workshy

slouch verb slump, droop, loll, stoop

slovenly adjective 1 untidy, disorderly 2 careless, negligent, slack, slapdash, slipshod, sloppy (informal)

➤ **Antonyms**

≠untidy: clean, neat, smart, tidy, well-groomed ≠careless: careful, conscientious, methodical, meticulous

slow adjective 1 prolonged, gradual, lingering, long-drawn-out, protracted 2 unhurried, dawdling, lackadaisical, laggard, lazy, leisurely, ponderous, sluggish 3 late, backward, behind, delayed, tardy 4 stupid, braindead (informal), dense, dim, dozy (Brit. informal), dull-witted, obtuse, retarded, thick ◆ verb 5 often with up or down reduce speed, brake, decelerate, handi-

cap, hold up, retard, slacken (off)

➤ **Antonyms**

adjective ≠unhurried: brisk, fast, hectic, hurried, prompt, quick, sharp, speedy, swift ≠stupid: bright, clever, intelligent, perceptive, quick, quick-witted, sharp, smart ◆ verb ≠reduce speed: accelerate, pick up speed, quicken, speed up

slowly adverb gradually, leisurely, unhurriedly

sludge noun sediment, mire, muck, mud, ooze, residue, silt, slime

sluggish adjective inactive, dull, heavy, indolent, inert, lethargic, slothful, slow, torpid

➤ **Antonyms**

animated, brisk, dynamic, energetic, fast, lively, swift

slum noun hovel, ghetto

slumber verb sleep, doze, drowse, nap, snooze (informal), zizz (Brit. informal)

slump verb 1 fall, collapse, crash, plunge, sink, slip 2 sag, droop, hunch, loll, slouch ◆ noun 3 fall, collapse, crash, decline, downturn, drop, reverse, trough 4 recession, depression

➤ **Antonyms**

verb ≠fall: boom, develop, expand, flourish, grow, increase, prosper, thrive ◆ noun ≠fall: boom, development, expansion, growth, improvement, increase, upsurge, upturn

slur noun insult, affront, aspersion, calumny, innuendo, insinuation, smear, stain

slut noun Offensive tart, scrubber (Brit. & Austral. slang), slag (Brit. slang), slapper (Brit. slang), trollop

sly adjective 1 cunning, artful, clever, crafty, devious, scheming, secret, shifty, stealthy, subtle, underhand, wily 2 roguish, arch, impish, knowing, mischievous ◆ noun 3 on the sly secretly, covertly, on the quiet, privately, surreptitiously

➤ **Antonyms**

adjective ≠*cunning*: above-board, artless, direct, frank, guileless, honest, ingenuous, open, straightforward, trustworthy

smack *verb* 1 <u>slap</u>, clap, cuff, hit, spank, strike, swipe ♦ *noun* 2 <u>slap</u>, blow, swipe ♦ *adverb* 3 *Informal* <u>directly</u>, exactly, precisely, right, slap (*informal*), squarely, straight

small *adjective* 1 <u>little</u>, diminutive, mini, miniature, minute, petite, pygmy *or* pigmy, teeny, teeny-weeny, tiny, undersized, wee 2 <u>unimportant</u>, insignificant, minor, negligible, petty, trifling, trivial 3 <u>petty</u>, base, mean, narrow 4 <u>modest</u>, humble, unpretentious

➤ **Antonyms**

≠*little*: big, colossal, enormous, great, huge, immense, massive, mega (*slang*), sizable *or* sizeable, vast ≠*unimportant*: important, major, significant, urgent, vital ≠*modest*: grand, large-scale

small-minded *adjective* <u>petty</u>, bigoted, intolerant, mean, narrow-minded, ungenerous

➤ **Antonyms**

broad-minded, generous, liberal, open, open-minded, tolerant, unbigoted

small-time *adjective* <u>minor</u>, insignificant, of no account, petty, unimportant

smarmy *adjective Informal* <u>obsequious</u>, crawling, ingratiating, servile, smooth, suave, sycophantic, toadying, unctuous

smart *adjective* 1 <u>chic</u>, elegant, natty (*informal*), neat, snappy, spruce, stylish, trim 2 <u>clever</u>, acute, astute, bright, canny, ingenious, intelligent, keen, quick, sharp, shrewd 3 <u>brisk</u>, lively, quick, vigorous ♦ *verb* 4 <u>sting</u>, burn, hurt ♦ *noun* 5 <u>sting</u>, pain, soreness

➤ **Antonyms**

adjective ≠*chic*: dowdy, dull, old-fashioned, scruffy, sloppy, unfashionable ≠*clever*: daft (*infor-*

mal), dense, dim-witted (*informal*), dumb (*informal*), dumb-ass (*slang*), foolish, idiotic, moronic, slow, stupid, thick, unintelligent

smart aleck *noun Informal* <u>know-all</u> (*informal*), clever-clogs (*informal*), smarty pants (*informal*), wise guy (*informal*)

smarten *verb* <u>tidy</u>, groom, put in order, put to rights, spruce up

smash *verb* 1 <u>break</u>, crush, demolish, pulverize, shatter 2 <u>collide</u>, crash 3 <u>destroy</u>, lay waste, ruin, trash (*slang*), wreck ♦ *noun* 4 <u>destruction</u>, collapse, downfall, failure, ruin 5 <u>collision</u>, accident, crash

smashing *adjective Informal, chiefly Brit.* <u>excellent</u>, awesome (*slang*), brilliant (*informal*), cracking (*Brit. informal*), fabulous (*informal*), fantastic (*informal*), great (*informal*), magnificent, marvellous, mean (*slang*), sensational (*informal*), super (*informal*), superb, terrific (*informal*), wonderful

➤ **Antonyms**

abysmal, appalling, average, awful, bad, crap (*slang*), disappointing, disgraceful, dreadful, horrible, mediocre, no great shakes (*informal*), ordinary, rotten, run-of-the-mill, terrible, vile

smattering *noun* <u>modicum</u>, bit, rudiments

smear *verb* 1 <u>spread over</u>, bedaub, coat, cover, daub, rub on 2 <u>dirty</u>, smudge, soil, stain, sully 3 <u>slander</u>, besmirch, blacken, malign ♦ *noun* 4 <u>smudge</u>, blot, blotch, daub, splotch, streak 5 <u>slander</u>, calumny, defamation, libel

smell *verb* 1 <u>sniff</u>, scent 2 <u>stink</u>, pong (*Brit. informal*), reek ♦ *noun* 3 <u>odour</u>, aroma, bouquet, fragrance, perfume, scent 4 <u>stink</u>, fetor, pong (*Brit. informal*), stench

smelly *adjective* <u>stinking</u>, fetid, foul, foul-smelling, malodorous, noisome, reeking

smirk *noun* <u>smug look</u>, simper

smitten *adjective* 1 <u>afflicted</u>, laid

low, plagued, struck **2** <u>infatuated</u>, beguiled, bewitched, captivated, charmed, enamoured

smooth *adjective* **1** <u>even</u>, flat, flush, horizontal, level, plane **2** <u>sleek</u>, glossy, polished, shiny, silky, soft, velvety **3** <u>easy</u>, effortless, well-ordered **4** <u>flowing</u>, regular, rhythmic, steady, uniform **5** <u>mellow</u>, agreeable, mild, pleasant **6** <u>suave</u>, facile, glib, persuasive, slick, smarmy (*Brit. informal*), unctuous, urbane ♦ *verb* **7** <u>flatten</u>, iron, level, plane, press **8** <u>ease</u>, appease, assuage, calm, mitigate, mollify, soften, soothe **9** <u>facilitate</u>, ease

➤ **Antonyms**

adjective ≠<u>even</u>: bumpy, irregular, lumpy, rough, uneven ≠<u>sleek</u>: coarse, rough ♦ *verb* ≠<u>ease</u>: aggravate, exacerbate, intensify, make worse

smother *verb* **1** <u>extinguish</u>, snuff **2** <u>suffocate</u>, choke, stifle, strangle **3** <u>suppress</u>, conceal, hide, muffle, repress, stifle

smoulder *verb* <u>seethe</u>, boil, fume, rage, simmer

smudge *verb* **1** <u>smear</u>, daub, dirty, mark, smirch ♦ *noun* **2** <u>smear</u>, blemish, blot

smug *adjective* <u>self-satisfied</u>, complacent, conceited, superior

smuggler *noun* <u>trafficker</u>, bootlegger, runner

smutty *adjective* <u>obscene</u>, bawdy, blue, coarse, crude, dirty, indecent, indelicate, suggestive, vulgar

snack *noun* <u>light meal</u>, bite, refreshment(s)

snag *noun* **1** <u>difficulty</u>, catch, complication, disadvantage, downside, drawback, hitch, obstacle, problem ♦ *verb* **2** <u>catch</u>, rip, tear

snap *verb* **1** <u>break</u>, crack, separate **2** <u>crackle</u>, click, pop **3** <u>bite at</u>, bite, nip, snatch **4** <u>speak sharply</u>, bark, jump down (someone's) throat, lash out at ♦ *noun* **5** <u>crackle</u>, pop **6** <u>bite</u>, grab, nip ♦ *adjective* **7** <u>instant</u>,

immediate, spur-of-the-moment, sudden

snappy *adjective* **1** <u>smart</u>, chic, dapper, fashionable, natty (*informal*), stylish **2** <u>irritable</u>, cross, edgy, pissed (*taboo slang*), pissed off (*taboo slang*), ratty (*Brit. & N.Z. informal*), testy, tetchy, touchy

snap up *verb* <u>take advantage of</u>, grab, pounce upon, seize

snare *noun* **1** <u>trap</u>, gin, net, noose, wire ♦ *verb* **2** <u>trap</u>, catch, entrap, net, seize, wire

snarl *verb*, *often with* **up** <u>tangle</u>, entangle, entwine, muddle, ravel

snarl-up *noun* <u>tangle</u>, confusion, entanglement, muddle

snatch *verb* **1** <u>seize</u>, clutch, grab, grasp, grip ♦ *noun* **2** <u>bit</u>, fragment, part, piece, snippet

sneak *verb* **1** <u>slink</u>, lurk, pad, skulk, slip, steal **2** <u>slip</u>, smuggle, spirit **3** *Informal, chiefly Brit.* <u>inform on</u>, grass on (*Brit. slang*), shop (*slang, chiefly Brit.*), tell on (*informal*), tell tales ♦ *noun* **4** <u>informer</u>, telltale

sneaking *adjective* **1** <u>nagging</u>, persistent, uncomfortable, worrying **2** <u>secret</u>, hidden, private, undivulged, unexpressed, unvoiced

sneaky *adjective* <u>sly</u>, deceitful, devious, dishonest, double-dealing, furtive, low, mean, shifty, untrustworthy

sneer *noun* **1** <u>scorn</u>, derision, gibe, jeer, mockery, ridicule ♦ *verb* **2** <u>scorn</u>, deride, disdain, jeer, laugh, mock, ridicule

snide *or* **snidey** *adjective* <u>nasty</u>, cynical, disparaging, hurtful, ill-natured, malicious, sarcastic, scornful, sneering, spiteful

sniff *verb* <u>inhale</u>, breathe, smell

snigger *noun*, *verb* <u>laugh</u>, giggle, snicker, titter

snip *verb* **1** <u>cut</u>, clip, crop, dock, shave, trim ♦ *noun* **2** *Informal, chiefly Brit.* <u>bargain</u>, giveaway, good buy, steal (*informal*) **3** <u>bit</u>, clipping, fragment, piece, scrap, shred

snipe verb <u>criticize</u>, carp, denigrate, disparage, jeer, knock (informal), put down

snippet noun <u>piece</u>, fragment, part, scrap, shred

snivel verb <u>whine</u>, cry, grizzle (informal, chiefly Brit.), moan, sniffle, whimper, whinge (informal)

snob noun <u>elitist</u>, highbrow, prig

snobbery noun <u>arrogance</u>, airs, pretension, pride, snobbishness

snobbish adjective <u>superior</u>, arrogant, patronizing, pretentious, snooty (informal), stuck-up (informal)

➤ **Antonyms**

humble, modest, natural, unassuming, unpretentious, without airs

snoop verb <u>pry</u>, interfere, poke one's nose in (informal), spy

snooper noun <u>nosy parker</u> (informal), busybody, meddler, snoop (informal)

snooze Informal ◆ verb 1 <u>doze</u>, catnap, nap, take forty winks (informal) ◆ noun 2 <u>doze</u>, catnap, forty winks (informal), nap, siesta

snub verb 1 <u>insult</u>, cold-shoulder, cut (informal), humiliate, put down, rebuff, slight ◆ noun 2 <u>insult</u>, affront, put-down, slap in the face

snug adjective <u>cosy</u>, comfortable, comfy (informal), warm

snuggle verb <u>nestle</u>, cuddle, nuzzle

soak verb 1 <u>wet</u>, bathe, damp, drench, immerse, moisten, saturate, steep 2 <u>penetrate</u>, permeate, seep 3 <u>soak up</u> <u>absorb</u>, assimilate

soaking adjective <u>soaked</u>, drenched, dripping, saturated, sodden, sopping, streaming, wet through, wringing wet

soar verb 1 <u>ascend</u>, fly, mount, rise, wing 2 <u>rise</u>, climb, escalate, rocket, shoot up

➤ **Antonyms**

descend, dive, drop, fall, nosedive, plummet, plunge

sob verb <u>cry</u>, howl, shed tears, weep

sober adjective 1 <u>abstinent</u>, abstemious, moderate, temperate 2 <u>serious</u>, composed, cool, grave, level-headed, rational, reasonable, sedate, solemn, staid, steady 3 <u>plain</u>, dark, drab, quiet, sombre, subdued

➤ **Antonyms**

≠abstinent: bevvied (dialect), blitzed (slang), drunk, flying (slang), inebriated, intoxicated, merry (Brit. informal), paralytic (informal), pissed (taboo slang), plastered, rat-arsed (taboo slang), sloshed (slang), smashed (slang), tiddly (slang, chiefly Brit.), tight (informal), tipsy, wasted (slang), wrecked (slang) ≠serious: frivolous, happy, immoderate, imprudent, injudicious, irrational, lighthearted, unrealistic ≠plain: bright, flamboyant, flashy, garish, gaudy, light

sobriety noun 1 <u>abstinence</u>, abstemiousness, moderation, nonindulgence, soberness, temperance 2 <u>seriousness</u>, gravity, level-headedness, solemnity, staidness, steadiness

so-called adjective <u>alleged</u>, pretended, professed, self-styled, supposed

sociable adjective <u>friendly</u>, affable, companionable, convivial, cordial, genial, gregarious, outgoing, social, warm

➤ **Antonyms**

antisocial, cold, distant, formal, standoffish, unfriendly, unsociable, withdrawn

social adjective 1 <u>communal</u>, collective, common, community, general, group, public ◆ noun 2 <u>get-together</u> (informal), gathering, party

socialize verb <u>mix</u>, fraternize, get about or around, go out

society noun 1 <u>civilization</u>, humanity, mankind, people, the community, the public 2 <u>organization</u>, association, circle, club, fellowship, group, guild, institute, league, order, union 3 <u>upper classes</u>, beau monde, elite, gentry, high society 4 Old-

fashioned <u>companionship</u>, company, fellowship, friendship

sodden *adjective* <u>soaked</u>, drenched, saturated, soggy, sopping, waterlogged

sofa *noun* <u>couch</u>, chaise longue, divan, settee

soft *adjective* **1** <u>pliable</u>, bendable, elastic, flexible, malleable, mouldable, plastic, supple **2** <u>yielding</u>, elastic, gelatinous, pulpy, spongy, squashy **3** <u>velvety</u>, downy, feathery, fleecy, silky, smooth **4** <u>quiet</u>, dulcet, gentle, murmured, muted, softtoned **5** <u>pale</u>, bland, light, mellow, pastel, subdued **6** <u>dim</u>, dimmed, faint, restful **7** <u>mild</u>, balmy, temperate **8** <u>lenient</u>, easygoing, indulgent, lax, overindulgent, permissive, spineless **9** <u>out of condition</u>, effeminate, flabby, flaccid, limp, weak **10** *Informal* <u>easy</u>, comfortable, cushy (*informal*), undemanding **11** <u>kind</u>, compassionate, gentle, sensitive, sentimental, tender, tenderhearted, touchy-feely (*informal*)

► **Antonyms**
≠<u>pliable</u>, <u>yielding</u>: firm, hard, inflexible, rigid, solid, stiff, tough, unyielding ≠<u>velvety</u>: abrasive, coarse, grating, hard, rough ≠<u>quiet</u>: harsh, loud, noisy, strident ≠<u>pale</u>: bright, garish, gaudy, glaring, harsh ≠<u>dim</u>: bright, glaring, harsh ≠<u>lenient</u>: austere, harsh, no-nonsense, stern, strict

soften *verb* <u>lessen</u>, allay, appease, cushion, ease, mitigate, moderate, mollify, still, subdue, temper

softhearted *adjective* <u>kind</u>, charitable, compassionate, sentimental, sympathetic, tender, tenderhearted, warm-hearted

► **Antonyms**
callous, cold, cruel, hard, hardhearted, heartless, insensitive, uncaring, unkind, unsympathetic

soggy *adjective* <u>sodden</u>, dripping, moist, saturated, soaked, sopping, waterlogged

soil[1] *noun* **1** <u>earth</u>, clay, dirt, dust, ground **2** <u>land</u>, country

soil[2] *verb* <u>dirty</u>, befoul, besmirch, defile, foul, pollute, spot, stain, sully, tarnish

solace *noun* **1** <u>comfort</u>, consolation, relief ♦ *verb* **2** <u>comfort</u>, console

soldier *noun* <u>fighter</u>, man-atarms, serviceman, squaddie or squaddy (*Brit. slang*), trooper, warrior

sole *adjective* <u>only</u>, alone, exclusive, individual, one, single, solitary

solely *adverb* <u>only</u>, alone, completely, entirely, exclusively, merely

solemn *adjective* **1** <u>formal</u>, ceremonial, dignified, grand, grave, momentous, stately **2** <u>serious</u>, earnest, grave, sedate, sober, staid

► **Antonyms**
≠<u>formal</u>: informal, relaxed, unceremonious ≠<u>serious</u>: bright, cheerful, chirpy (*informal*), frivolous, light-hearted, merry

solemnity *noun* **1** <u>formality</u>, grandeur, impressiveness, momentousness **2** <u>seriousness</u>, earnestness, gravity

solicitous *adjective* <u>concerned</u>, anxious, attentive, careful

solicitude *noun* <u>concern</u>, anxiety, attentiveness, care, consideration, regard

solid *adjective* **1** <u>firm</u>, compact, concrete, dense, hard **2** <u>strong</u>, stable, sturdy, substantial, unshakable **3** <u>reliable</u>, dependable, trusty, upright, upstanding, worthy **4** <u>sound</u>, genuine, good, pure, real, reliable

► **Antonyms**
≠<u>firm</u>: gaseous, hollow, liquid, unsubstantial ≠<u>strong</u>: crumbling, decaying, flimsy, precarious, shaky, unstable, unsteady ≠<u>reliable</u>: flighty, irresponsible, unreliable, unsound, unstable, unsteady ≠<u>sound</u>: impure, unreliable, unsound

solidarity *noun* <u>unity</u>, accord, co-

solidify verb harden, cake, coagulate, cohere, congeal, jell, set

solitary adjective 1 unsociable, cloistered, isolated, reclusive, unsocial 2 single, alone, lone, sole 3 lonely, companionless, friendless, lonesome 4 isolated, hidden, out-of-the-way, remote, unfrequented

➤ **Antonyms**
≠unsociable: companionable, convivial, cordial, gregarious, outgoing, sociable, social ≠isolated: bustling, busy, frequented, public, well-frequented

solitude noun isolation, loneliness, privacy, retirement, seclusion

solution noun 1 answer, explanation, key, result 2 Chemistry mixture, blend, compound, mix, solvent

solve verb answer, clear up, crack, decipher, disentangle, get to the bottom of, resolve, suss (out) (slang), unravel, work out

sombre adjective 1 gloomy, dismal, doleful, grave, joyless, lugubrious, mournful, sad, sober 2 dark, dim, drab, dull, gloomy, sober

➤ **Antonyms**
≠gloomy: bright, cheerful, chirpy (informal), happy, lively, sunny, upbeat (informal) ≠dark: bright, colourful, dazzling, garish, gaudy

somebody noun celebrity, dignitary, household name, luminary, megastar (informal), name, notable, personage, star

➤ **Antonyms**
also-ran, lightweight (informal), nobody, nonentity, nothing (informal)

someday adverb eventually, one day, one of these (fine) days, sooner or later

somehow adverb one way or another, by fair means or foul, by hook or (by) crook, by some means or other, come hell or high water (informal), come what may

sometimes adverb occasionally, at times, now and then

➤ **Antonyms**
always, constantly, continually, eternally, forever, perpetually

song noun ballad, air, anthem, carol, chant, chorus, ditty, hymn, number, psalm, tune

soon adverb before long, in the near future, shortly

soothe verb 1 calm, allay, appease, hush, lull, mollify, pacify, quiet, still 2 relieve, alleviate, assuage, ease

➤ **Antonyms**
≠calm: aggravate (informal), agitate, annoy, disturb, excite, irritate, rouse, upset ≠relieve: exacerbate, increase, irritate, stimulate

soothing adjective 1 calming, relaxing, restful 2 emollient, palliative

soothsayer noun prophet, diviner, fortune-teller, seer, sibyl

sophisticated adjective 1 cultured, cosmopolitan, cultivated, refined, urbane, worldly 2 complex, advanced, complicated, delicate, elaborate, intricate, refined, subtle

➤ **Antonyms**
≠cultured: naive, unrefined, unsophisticated, unworldly ≠complex: basic, plain, primitive, simple, uncomplicated, unrefined, unsophisticated, unsubtle

sophistication noun savoir-faire, finesse, poise, urbanity, worldliness, worldly wisdom

soporific adjective 1 sleepinducing, sedative, somnolent, tranquillizing ◆ noun 2 sedative, narcotic, opiate, tranquillizer

soppy adjective Brit. informal sentimental, icky (informal), overemotional, schmaltzy (slang), slushy (informal), weepy (informal)

sorcerer or **sorceress** noun magician, enchanter, necromancer, warlock, witch, wizard

sorcery noun black magic, black art, enchantment, magic, necromancy, witchcraft, wizardry

sordid adjective 1 dirty, filthy, foul, mean, seedy, sleazy, squalid, unclean 2 base, debauched, degenerate, low, shabby, shameful, vicious, vile 3 mercenary, avaricious, covetous, grasping, selfish

▶ Antonyms

≠dirty: clean, fresh, pure, spotless, squeaky-clean ≠base: blameless, decent, honourable, noble, pure, upright

sore adjective 1 painful, angry, burning, inflamed, irritated, raw, sensitive, smarting, tender 2 annoying, severe, sharp, troublesome 3 annoyed, aggrieved, angry, cross, hurt, irked, irritated, pained, pissed (taboo slang), pissed (off) (taboo slang), resentful, stung, upset 4 Literary urgent, acute, critical, desperate, dire, extreme, pressing

sorrow noun 1 grief, anguish, distress, heartache, heartbreak, misery, mourning, regret, sadness, unhappiness, woe 2 affliction, hardship, misfortune, trial, tribulation, trouble, woe ♦ verb grieve, agonize, bemoan, be sad, bewail, lament, mourn

▶ Antonyms

noun ≠grief: bliss, delight, elation, gladness, happiness, joy, pleasure ≠affliction: good fortune, lucky break ♦ verb ≠grieve: celebrate, delight, exult, rejoice

sorrowful adjective sad, dejected, dismal, doleful, grieving, miserable, mournful, sorry, unhappy, woebegone, woeful, wretched

sorry adjective 1 regretful, apologetic, conscience-stricken, contrite, penitent, remorseful, repentant, shamefaced 2 sympathetic, commiserative, compassionate, full of pity, moved 3 wretched, deplorable, mean, miserable, pathetic, pitiful, poor, sad

▶ Antonyms

≠regretful: impenitent, not contrite, shameless, unapologetic, unashamed, unremorseful, unrepentant ≠sympathetic: heartless, indifferent, uncompassionate, unconcerned, unmoved, unpitying, unsympathetic

sort noun 1 kind, brand, category, class, ilk, make, nature, order, quality, style, type, variety ♦ verb 2 arrange, categorize, classify, divide, grade, group, order, put in order, rank

sort out verb 1 resolve, clarify, clear up 2 organize, tidy up

soul noun 1 spirit, essence, life, vital force 2 essence, embodiment, epitome, personification, quintessence, type 3 person, being, body, creature, individual, man or woman

sound¹ noun 1 noise, din, report, reverberation, tone 2 impression, drift, idea, look ♦ verb 3 resound, echo, reverberate 4 seem, appear, look 5 pronounce, announce, articulate, declare, express, utter

sound² adjective 1 perfect, fit, healthy, intact, solid, unhurt, unimpaired, uninjured, whole 2 sensible, correct, logical, proper, prudent, rational, reasonable, right, trustworthy, valid, wellfounded, wise 3 deep, unbroken, undisturbed, untroubled

▶ Antonyms

≠perfect: ailing, damaged, frail, weak ≠sensible: fallacious, faulty, flawed, irrational ≠deep: broken, fitful, shallow, troubled

sound³ verb fathom, plumb, probe

sound out verb probe, canvass, pump, question, see how the land lies

sour adjective 1 sharp, acetic, acid, bitter, pungent, tart 2 gone off, curdled, gone bad, turned 3 ill-natured, acrimonious, disagreeable, embittered, illtempered, peevish, tart, ungenerous, waspish

➤ **Antonyms**

≠<u>sharp</u>: agreeable, bland, mild, pleasant, savoury, sugary, sweet ≠<u>gone off</u>: fresh, unimpaired, unspoiled ≠<u>ill-natured</u>: affable, amiable, congenial, friendly, genial, good-humoured, good-natured, good-tempered, pleasant

source noun **1** <u>origin</u>, author, beginning, cause, derivation, fount, originator **2** <u>informant</u>, authority

souvenir noun <u>keepsake</u>, memento, reminder

sovereign noun **1** <u>monarch</u>, chief, emperor or empress, king or queen, potentate, prince or princess, ruler ◆ adjective **2** <u>supreme</u>, absolute, imperial, kingly or queenly, principal, royal, ruling **3** <u>excellent</u>, effectual, efficacious, efficient

sovereignty noun <u>supreme power</u>, domination, kingship, primacy, supremacy

sow verb <u>scatter</u>, implant, plant, seed

space noun **1** <u>room</u>, capacity, elbowroom, expanse, extent, leeway, margin, play, scope **2** <u>gap</u>, blank, distance, interval, omission **3** <u>time</u>, duration, interval, period, span, while

spacious adjective <u>roomy</u>, ample, broad, capacious, commodious, expansive, extensive, huge, large, sizable or sizeable

➤ **Antonyms**

close, confined, cramped, crowded, limited, narrow, poky, restricted, small

spadework noun <u>preparation</u>, donkey-work, groundwork, labour

span noun **1** <u>extent</u>, amount, distance, length, reach, spread, stretch **2** <u>period</u>, duration, spell, term ◆ verb **3** <u>extend across</u>, bridge, cover, cross, link, traverse

spank verb <u>smack</u>, cuff, slap

spar verb <u>argue</u>, bicker, row, scrap (informal), squabble, wrangle

spare adjective **1** <u>extra</u>, additional, free, leftover, odd, over, superfluous, surplus, unoccupied, unused, unwanted **2** <u>thin</u>, gaunt, lean, meagre, wiry ◆ verb **3** <u>have mercy on</u>, be merciful to, go easy on (informal), leave, let off (informal), pardon, save from **4** <u>afford</u>, do without, give, grant, let (someone) have, manage without, part with

➤ **Antonyms**

adjective ≠<u>extra</u>: in use, necessary, needed, set aside, spoken for ≠<u>thin</u>: corpulent, fat, flabby, fleshy, generous, heavy, large, plump ◆ verb ≠<u>have mercy on</u>: condemn, damn, hurt, punish, show no mercy to

spare time noun <u>leisure</u>, free time, odd moments

sparing adjective <u>economical</u>, careful, frugal, prudent, saving, thrifty

➤ **Antonyms**

extravagant, lavish, liberal, open-handed, prodigal, spendthrift

spark noun **1** <u>flicker</u>, flare, flash, gleam, glint **2** <u>trace</u>, atom, hint, jot, scrap, vestige ◆ verb **3** often with off <u>start</u>, inspire, precipitate, provoke, set off, stimulate, trigger (off)

sparkle verb **1** <u>glitter</u>, dance, flash, gleam, glint, glisten, scintillate, shimmer, shine, twinkle ◆ noun **2** <u>glitter</u>, brilliance, flash, flicker, gleam, glint, twinkle **3** <u>vivacity</u>, dash, élan, life, liveliness, spirit, vitality

sparse adjective <u>scattered</u>, few and far between, meagre, scanty, scarce

➤ **Antonyms**

dense, lavish, lush, luxuriant, numerous, plentiful, thick

spartan adjective <u>austere</u>, ascetic, disciplined, frugal, plain, rigorous, self-denying, severe, strict

spasm noun **1** <u>convulsion</u>, contraction, paroxysm, twitch **2** <u>burst</u>, eruption, fit, frenzy, outburst, seizure

spasmodic adjective <u>sporadic</u>, convulsive, erratic, fitful, intermittent, irregular, jerky

spate noun <u>flood</u>, deluge, flow, outpouring, rush, torrent

speak verb 1 <u>talk</u>, articulate, converse, express, pronounce, say, state, tell, utter 2 <u>lecture</u>, address, declaim, discourse, hold forth

speaker noun <u>orator</u>, lecturer, public speaker, spokesman or spokeswoman, spokesperson

speak up or **out** verb <u>speak one's mind</u>, have one's say, make one's position plain

spearhead verb <u>lead</u>, head, initiate, launch, pioneer, set in motion, set off

special adjective 1 <u>exceptional</u>, extraordinary, important, memorable, significant, uncommon, unique, unusual 2 <u>specific</u>, appropriate, distinctive, individual, particular, precise

► Antonyms

≠exceptional: common, everyday, humdrum, mediocre, normal, ordinary, routine, run-of-the-mill, unexceptional, usual

specialist noun <u>expert</u>, authority, buff (informal), connoisseur, consultant, guru, master, professional

speciality noun <u>forte</u>, bag (slang), métier, pièce de résistance, specialty

species noun <u>kind</u>, breed, category, class, group, sort, type, variety

specific adjective 1 <u>particular</u>, characteristic, distinguishing, special 2 <u>precise</u>, clear-cut, definite, exact, explicit, express, unequivocal

► Antonyms

≠particular: common, general ≠precise: approximate, general, hazy, imprecise, non-specific, unclear, vague, woolly

specification noun <u>requirement</u>, condition, detail, particular, qualification, stipulation

specify verb <u>state</u>, define, designate, detail, indicate, mention, name, stipulate

specimen noun <u>sample</u>, example, exemplification, instance, model, pattern, representative, type

speck noun 1 <u>mark</u>, blemish, dot, fleck, mote, speckle, spot, stain 2 <u>particle</u>, atom, bit, grain, iota, jot, mite, shred

speckled adjective <u>flecked</u>, dappled, dotted, mottled, spotted, sprinkled

spectacle noun 1 <u>sight</u>, curiosity, marvel, phenomenon, scene, wonder 2 <u>show</u>, display, event, exhibition, extravaganza, pageant, performance

spectacular adjective 1 <u>impressive</u>, dazzling, dramatic, grand, magnificent, sensational, splendid, striking, stunning (informal) ♦ noun 2 <u>show</u>, display, spectacle

► Antonyms

adjective ≠impressive: everyday, modest, ordinary, plain, run-of-the-mill, simple, unimpressive, unostentatious, unspectacular

spectator noun <u>onlooker</u>, bystander, looker-on, observer, viewer, watcher

► Antonyms

participant, participator, party, player

spectre noun <u>ghost</u>, apparition, phantom, spirit, vision, wraith

speculate verb 1 <u>conjecture</u>, consider, guess, hypothesize, suppose, surmise, theorize, wonder 2 <u>gamble</u>, hazard, risk, venture

speculation noun 1 <u>conjecture</u>, guess, guesswork, hypothesis, opinion, supposition, surmise, theory 2 <u>gamble</u>, hazard, risk

speculative adjective <u>hypothetical</u>, academic, conjectural, notional, suppositional, theoretical

speech noun 1 <u>communication</u>, conversation, dialogue, discussion, talk 2 <u>talk</u>, address, discourse, homily, lecture, oration, spiel (informal) 3 <u>language</u>, articulation, dialect, diction, enunciation, idiom, jargon, parlance, tongue

speechless *adjective* **1** mute, dumb, inarticulate, silent, wordless **2** astounded, aghast, amazed, dazed, shocked

speed *noun* **1** swiftness, haste, hurry, pace, quickness, rapidity, rush, velocity ♦ *verb* **2** race, career, gallop, hasten, hurry, make haste, rush, tear, zoom **3** help, advance, aid, assist, boost, expedite, facilitate

► **Antonyms**

noun ≠swiftness: delay, slowness, sluggishness, tardiness ♦ *verb* ≠race: crawl, creep, dawdle, delay, take one's time ≠help: delay, hamper, hinder, hold up, retard, slow

speed up *verb* accelerate, gather momentum, increase the tempo

► **Antonyms**

brake, decelerate, reduce speed, slow down

speedy *adjective* quick, express, fast, hasty, headlong, hurried, immediate, precipitate, prompt, rapid, swift

► **Antonyms**

leisurely, lingering, long-drawn-out, plodding, slow, sluggish, tardy, unhurried

spell¹ *verb* indicate, augur, imply, mean, point to, portend, signify

spell² *noun* **1** incantation, charm **2** enchantment, allure, bewitchment, fascination, glamour, magic

spell³ *noun* period, bout, course, interval, season, stretch, term, time

spellbound *adjective* entranced, bewitched, captivated, charmed, enthralled, fascinated, gripped, mesmerized, rapt

spend *verb* **1** pay out, disburse, expend, fork out (*slang*) **2** pass, fill, occupy, while away **3** use up, consume, dissipate, drain, empty, exhaust, run through, squander, waste

► **Antonyms**

≠pay out, use up: hoard, invest, keep, put aside, put by, save, store

spendthrift *noun* **1** squanderer, big spender, profligate, spender, waster ♦ *adjective* **2** wasteful, extravagant, improvident, prodigal, profligate

► **Antonyms**

noun ≠squanderer: miser, penny-pincher (*informal*), Scrooge, skinflint ♦ *adjective* ≠wasteful: careful, economical, frugal, parsimonious, provident, prudent, sparing, thrifty

spew *verb* vomit, disgorge, puke (*slang*), regurgitate, throw up (*informal*)

sphere *noun* **1** ball, circle, globe, globule, orb **2** field, capacity, department, domain, function, patch, province, realm, scope, territory, turf (*U.S. slang*)

spherical *adjective* round, globe-shaped, globular, rotund

spice *noun* **1** seasoning, relish, savour **2** excitement, colour, pep, piquancy, zest, zing (*informal*)

spicy *adjective* **1** hot, aromatic, piquant, savoury, seasoned **2** *Informal* scandalous, hot (*informal*), indelicate, racy, ribald, risqué, suggestive, titillating

spike *noun* **1** point, barb, prong, spine ♦ *verb* **2** impale, spear, spit, stick

spill *verb* **1** pour, discharge, disgorge, overflow, slop over ♦ *noun* **2** *Informal* fall, tumble

spin *verb* **1** revolve, gyrate, pirouette, reel, rotate, turn, twirl, whirl **2** reel, swim, whirl ♦ *noun* **3** revolution, gyration, roll, whirl **4** *Informal* drive, joy ride (*informal*), ride

spine *noun* **1** backbone, spinal column, vertebrae, vertebral column **2** barb, needle, quill, ray, spike, spur

spine-chilling *adjective* frightening, bloodcurdling, eerie, horrifying, scary (*informal*), spooky (*informal*), terrifying

spineless *adjective* weak, cowardly, faint-hearted, feeble, gutless (*informal*), lily-livered, soft, weak-kneed (*informal*)

➤ **Antonyms**

bold, brave, courageous, gritty, strong, strong-willed

spin out *verb* prolong, amplify, delay, drag out, draw out, extend, lengthen

spiral *noun* **1** coil, corkscrew, helix, whorl ♦ *adjective* **2** coiled, helical, whorled ♦ *adjective* **2** coiled, helical, whorled, winding

spirit *noun* **1** life force, life, soul, vital spark **2** feeling, atmosphere, gist, tenor, tone **3** temperament, attitude, character, disposition, outlook, temper **4** liveliness, animation, brio, energy, enthusiasm, fire, force, life, mettle, vigour, zest **5** courage, backbone, gameness, grit, guts (*informal*), spunk (*informal*) **6** intention, essence, meaning, purport, purpose, sense, substance **7** ghost, apparition, phantom, spectre **8** spirits mood, feelings, frame of mind, morale ♦ *verb* **9** with *away* or *off* remove, abduct, abstract, carry, purloin, seize, steal, whisk

spirited *adjective* lively, active, animated, energetic, feisty (*informal, chiefly U.S. & Canad.*), mettlesome, vivacious

➤ **Antonyms**

apathetic, dispirited, dull, feeble, half-hearted, lacklustre, lifeless, spiritless, unenthusiastic, weary

spiritual *adjective* **1** nonmaterial, immaterial, incorporeal **2** sacred, devotional, divine, holy, religious

➤ **Antonyms**

≠nonmaterial: concrete, corporeal, material, nonspiritual, physical, substantial, tangible

spit *verb* **1** eject, expectorate, splutter, throw out ♦ *noun* **2** saliva, dribble, drool, slaver, spittle

spite *noun* **1** malice, animosity, hatred, ill will, malevolence, spitefulness, spleen, venom **2** in spite of despite, (even) though, notwithstanding, regardless of

♦ *verb* **3** annoy, harm, hurt, injure, vex

➤ **Antonyms**

noun ≠malice: benevolence, goodwill, kindness, love ♦ *verb* ≠annoy: benefit, help

spiteful *adjective* malicious, bitchy (*informal*), ill-natured, malevolent, nasty, vindictive

splash *verb* **1** scatter, shower, slop, spatter, spray, sprinkle, wet **2** publicize, broadcast, tout, trumpet ♦ *noun* **3** dash, burst, patch, spattering, touch **4** *Informal* display, effect, impact, sensation, stir

splash out *verb Informal* spend, be extravagant, push the boat out (*Brit. informal*), spare no expense, splurge

splendid *adjective* **1** excellent, cracking (*Brit. informal*), fantastic (*informal*), first-class, glorious, great (*informal*), marvellous, wonderful **2** magnificent, costly, gorgeous, grand, impressive, lavish, luxurious, ornate, resplendent, rich, sumptuous, superb

➤ **Antonyms**

≠excellent: mediocre, miserable, no great shakes (*informal*), ordinary, pathetic, poor, rotten, run-of-the-mill, undistinguished, unexceptional ≠magnificent: beggarly, drab, dull, low, mean, plain, poor, poverty-stricken, sordid, squalid

splendour *noun* magnificence, display, grandeur, pomp, richness, show, spectacle, sumptuousness

➤ **Antonyms**

ordinariness, plainness, poverty, simplicity, squalor, tawdriness

splinter *noun* **1** sliver, chip, flake, fragment ♦ *verb* **2** shatter, disintegrate, fracture, split

split *verb* **1** break, burst, come apart, come undone, crack, give way, open, rend, rip **2** separate, branch, cleave, disband, disunite, diverge, fork, part **3** share out, allocate, allot, apportion, distribute, divide, halve, partition ♦ *noun* **4** crack, breach, division, fissure, gap, rent, rip, separation, slit, tear **5** division, breach, break-up, discord, dissension, estrangement, rift, rupture, schism ♦ *adjective* **6** divided, broken, cleft, cracked, fractured, ruptured

split up *verb* separate, break up, divorce, part

spoil *verb* **1** ruin, damage, destroy, disfigure, harm, impair, injure, mar, mess up, trash (*slang*), wreck **2** overindulge, coddle, cosset, indulge, mollycoddle, pamper **3** go bad, addle, curdle, decay, decompose, go off (*Brit. informal*), rot, turn

➤ **Antonyms**

≠ruin: improve, keep, preserve, save ≠overindulge: be strict with, deprive, treat harshly

spoils *plural noun* booty, loot, plunder, prey, swag (*slang*)

spoilsport *noun Informal* killjoy, damper, dog in the manger, misery (*Brit. informal*), wet blanket (*informal*)

spoken *adjective* said, expressed, oral, told, unwritten, uttered, verbal, viva voce, voiced

spokesperson *noun* speaker, mouthpiece, official, spin doctor (*informal*), spokesman *or* spokeswoman, voice

spongy *adjective* porous, absorbent

sponsor *noun* **1** backer, patron, promoter ♦ *verb* **2** back, finance, fund, patronize, promote, subsidize

spontaneous *adjective* unplanned, impromptu, impulsive, instinctive, natural, unprompted, voluntary, willing

➤ **Antonyms**

arranged, calculated, deliberate, forced, planned, prearranged, premeditated, preplanned

spoof *noun Informal* parody, burlesque, caricature, mockery, satire, send-up (*Brit. informal*), take-off (*informal*)

spooky *adjective* eerie, chilling,

creepy (*informal*), frightening, scary (*informal*), spine-chilling, uncanny, unearthly, weird

sporadic *adjective* intermittent, irregular, occasional, scattered, spasmodic

➤ **Antonyms**

consistent, frequent, recurrent, regular, steady

sport *noun* **1** game, amusement, diversion, exercise, pastime, play, recreation **2** fun, badinage, banter, jest, joking, teasing ♦ *verb* **3** *Informal* wear, display, exhibit, show off

sporting *adjective* fair, game (*informal*), sportsmanlike

➤ **Antonyms**

unfair, unsporting, unsportsmanlike

sporty *adjective* athletic, energetic, outdoor

spot *noun* **1** mark, blemish, blot, blotch, scar, smudge, speck, speckle, stain **2** place, location, point, position, scene, site **3** pimple, pustule, zit (*slang*) **4** *Informal* predicament, difficulty, hot water (*informal*), mess, plight, quandary, tight spot, trouble ♦ *verb* **5** see, catch sight of, detect, discern, espy, make out, observe, recognize, sight **6** mark, dirty, fleck, mottle, smirch, soil, spatter, speckle, splodge, splotch, stain

spotless *adjective* clean, flawless, gleaming, immaculate, impeccable, pure, shining, unblemished, unstained, unsullied, untarnished

➤ **Antonyms**

blemished, defiled, dirty, filthy, flawed, impure, messy, soiled, spotted, stained, sullied, tarnished

spotlight *noun* **1** attention, fame, limelight, public eye ♦ *verb* **2** highlight, accentuate, draw attention to

spotted *adjective* speckled, dappled, dotted, flecked, mottled

spouse *noun* partner, consort, husband *or* wife, mate, significant other (*U.S. informal*)

spout verb <u>stream</u>, discharge, gush, shoot, spray, spurt, surge

sprawl verb **1** <u>loll</u>, flop, lounge, slouch, slump **2** <u>spread</u>, ramble, straggle, trail

spray¹ noun **1** <u>droplets</u>, drizzle, fine mist **2** <u>aerosol</u>, atomizer, sprinkler ♦ verb **3** <u>scatter</u>, diffuse, shower, sprinkle

spray² noun <u>sprig</u>, branch, corsage, floral arrangement

spread verb **1** <u>open (out)</u>, broaden, dilate, expand, extend, sprawl, stretch, unfold, unroll, widen **2** <u>proliferate</u>, escalate, multiply **3** <u>circulate</u>, broadcast, disseminate, make known, propagate ♦ noun **4** <u>increase</u>, advance, development, dispersal, dissemination, expansion, proliferation **5** <u>extent</u>, span, stretch, sweep

➤ **Antonyms**

verb ≠<u>circulate</u>: contain, control, repress, restrain, stifle

spree noun <u>binge</u> (*informal*), bacchanalia, bender (*informal*), carousal, fling, orgy, revel

sprightly adjective <u>lively</u>, active, agile, brisk, energetic, nimble, spirited, spry, vivacious

➤ **Antonyms**

dull, inactive, lethargic, sedentary, sluggish, torpid, unenergetic

spring verb **1** <u>jump</u>, bounce, bound, leap, vault **2** *often with* from <u>originate</u>, arise, come, derive, descend, issue, proceed, start, stem **3** *often with* up <u>appear</u>, develop, mushroom, shoot up ♦ noun **4** <u>jump</u>, bound, leap, vault **5** <u>elasticity</u>, bounce, buoyancy, flexibility, resilience

springy adjective <u>elastic</u>, bouncy, buoyant, flexible, resilient

sprinkle verb <u>scatter</u>, dredge, dust, pepper, powder, shower, spray, strew

sprinkling noun <u>scattering</u>, dash, dusting, few, handful, sprinkle

sprint verb <u>race</u>, dart, dash, hare (*Brit. informal*), shoot, tear

sprite noun <u>spirit</u>, brownie, elf, fairy, goblin, imp, pixie

sprout verb <u>grow</u>, bud, develop, shoot, spring

spruce adjective <u>smart</u>, dapper, natty (*informal*), neat, trim, well-groomed, well turned out

➤ **Antonyms**

bedraggled, dishevelled, messy, rumpled, unkempt, untidy

spruce up verb <u>smarten up</u>, tidy, titivate

spry adjective <u>active</u>, agile, nimble, sprightly, supple

➤ **Antonyms**

awkward, doddering, inactive, lethargic, slow, sluggish, stiff

spur noun **1** <u>stimulus</u>, impetus, impulse, incentive, incitement, inducement, motive **2** <u>goad</u>, prick **3** on the spur of the moment <u>on impulse</u>, impromptu, impulsively, on the spot, without planning ♦ verb **4** <u>incite</u>, animate, drive, goad, impel, prick, prod, prompt, stimulate, urge

spurious adjective <u>false</u>, artificial, bogus, fake, phoney *or* phony (*informal*), pretended, sham, specious, unauthentic

➤ **Antonyms**

authentic, bona fide, genuine, honest, legitimate, real

spurn verb <u>reject</u>, despise, disdain, rebuff, repulse, scorn, slight, snub

➤ **Antonyms**

embrace, welcome

spurt verb **1** <u>gush</u>, burst, erupt, shoot, squirt, surge ♦ noun **2** <u>burst</u>, fit, rush, spate, surge

spy noun **1** <u>undercover agent</u>, mole, nark (*Brit., Austral., & N.Z. slang*) ♦ verb **2** <u>catch sight of</u>, espy, glimpse, notice, observe, spot

squabble verb **1** <u>quarrel</u>, argue, bicker, dispute, fight, row, wrangle ♦ noun **2** <u>quarrel</u>, argument, disagreement, dispute, fight, row, tiff

squad noun <u>team</u>, band, company, crew, force, gang, group, troop

squalid adjective <u>dirty</u>, filthy,

seedy, sleazy, slummy, sordid, unclean

➤ **Antonyms**

clean, hygienic, salubrious, spotless

squalor noun <u>filth</u>, foulness, sleaziness, squalidness

➤ **Antonyms**

cleanliness

squander verb <u>waste</u>, blow (slang), expend, fritter away, misspend, misuse, spend

➤ **Antonyms**

be frugal, be thrifty, economize, keep, save, store

square adjective 1 <u>honest</u>, above board, ethical, fair, genuine, kosher (informal), on the level (informal), straight ♦ verb 2 <u>even up</u>, adjust, align, level 3 sometimes with up <u>pay off</u>, settle 4 often with with <u>agree</u>, correspond, fit, match, reconcile, tally

squash verb 1 <u>crush</u>, compress, distort, flatten, mash, press, pulp, smash 2 <u>suppress</u>, annihilate, crush, humiliate, quell, silence

squashy adjective <u>soft</u>, mushy, pulpy, spongy, yielding

squawk verb <u>cry</u>, hoot, screech

squeak verb <u>peep</u>, pipe, squeal

squeal noun, verb <u>scream</u>, screech, shriek, wail, yell

squeamish adjective 1 <u>fastidious</u>, delicate, prudish, strait-laced 2 <u>queasy</u>, nauseous, sick

➤ **Antonyms**

≠<u>fastidious</u>: bold, brazen, coarse, earthy ≠<u>queasy</u>: strong-stomached

squeeze verb 1 <u>press</u>, clutch, compress, crush, grip, pinch, squash, wring 2 <u>cram</u>, crowd, force, jam, pack, press, ram, stuff 3 <u>hug</u>, clasp, cuddle, embrace, enfold 4 <u>extort</u>, milk, pressurize, wrest ♦ noun 5 <u>hug</u>, clasp, embrace 6 <u>crush</u>, congestion, crowd, jam, press, squash

squint adjective Informal <u>crooked</u>, askew, aslant, awry, cockeyed, skew-whiff (informal)

➤ **Antonyms**

even, in line, level, square, straight

squirm verb <u>wriggle</u>, twist, writhe

stab verb 1 <u>pierce</u>, impale, jab, knife, spear, stick, thrust, transfix, wound ♦ noun 2 <u>wound</u>, gash, incision, jab, puncture, thrust 3 <u>twinge</u>, ache, pang, prick 4 Informal <u>attempt</u>, endeavour, go, try

stability noun <u>firmness</u>, solidity, soundness, steadiness, strength

➤ **Antonyms**

changeableness, inconstancy, instability, unsteadiness

stable adjective 1 <u>firm</u>, constant, established, fast, fixed, immovable, lasting, permanent, secure, sound, strong 2 <u>steady</u>, reliable, staunch, steadfast, sure

➤ **Antonyms**

≠<u>firm</u>: erratic, inconstant, insecure, shaky, uncertain, unpredictable, unreliable, unstable, volatile ≠<u>steady</u>: unsteady, unsure

stack noun 1 <u>pile</u>, heap, load, mass, mound, mountain ♦ verb 2 <u>pile</u>, accumulate, amass, assemble, heap up, load

staff noun 1 <u>workers</u>, employees, personnel, team, workforce 2 <u>stick</u>, cane, crook, pole, rod, sceptre, stave, wand

stage noun <u>step</u>, division, juncture, lap, leg, level, period, phase, point

stagger verb 1 <u>totter</u>, lurch, reel, sway, wobble 2 <u>astound</u>, amaze, astonish, confound, overwhelm, shake, shock, stun, stupefy 3 <u>alternate</u>, overlap, step

stagnant adjective <u>stale</u>, quiet, sluggish, still

➤ **Antonyms**

clear, flowing, fresh, pure, running

stagnate verb <u>vegetate</u>, decay, decline, idle, languish, rot, rust

staid adjective <u>sedate</u>, calm, composed, grave, serious, sober, solemn, steady

➤ **Antonyms**

exuberant, lively, wild

stain verb **1** mark, blemish, blot, dirty, discolour, smirch, soil, spot, tinge **2** dye, colour, tint ♦ noun **3** mark, blemish, blot, discoloration, smirch, spot **4** stigma, disgrace, dishonour, shame, slur **5** dye, colour, tint

stake¹ noun pole, pale, paling, palisade, picket, post, stick

stake² noun **1** bet, ante, pledge, wager **2** interest, concern, investment, involvement, share ♦ verb **3** bet, chance, gamble, hazard, risk, venture, wager

stale adjective **1** old, decayed, dry, flat, fusty, hard, musty, sour **2** unoriginal, banal, hackneyed, overused, stereotyped, threadbare, trite, worn-out

➤ **Antonyms**

≠old: crisp, fresh ≠unoriginal: different, imaginative, innovative, new, novel, original

stalk verb pursue, follow, haunt, hunt, shadow, track

stall verb play for time, hedge, temporize

stalwart adjective **1** strong, stout, strapping, sturdy **2** loyal, dependable, reliable, staunch

➤ **Antonyms**

≠strong: feeble, frail, infirm, namby-pamby, puny, weak

stamina noun staying power, endurance, energy, force, power, resilience, strength

stammer verb stutter, falter, hesitate, pause, stumble

stamp noun **1** imprint, brand, earmark, hallmark, mark, signature ♦ verb **2** trample, crush **3** identify, brand, categorize, label, mark, reveal, show to be **4** imprint, impress, mark, print

stampede noun rush, charge, flight, rout

stamp out verb eliminate, crush, destroy, eradicate, put down, quell, scotch, suppress

stance noun **1** attitude, position, stand, standpoint, viewpoint **2** posture, bearing, carriage, deportment

stanch see STAUNCH¹

stand verb **1** be upright, be erect, be vertical, rise **2** put, mount, place, position, set **3** exist, be valid, continue, hold, obtain, prevail, remain **4** tolerate, abide, allow, bear, brook, countenance, endure, handle, put up with (informal), stomach, take ♦ noun **5** stall, booth, table **6** position, attitude, determination, opinion, stance **7** support, base, bracket, dais, platform, rack, stage, tripod

standard noun **1** level, gauge, grade, measure **2** criterion, average, benchmark, example, guideline, model, norm, yardstick **3** often plural principles, ethics, ideals, morals **4** flag, banner, ensign ♦ adjective **5** usual, average, basic, customary, normal, orthodox, regular, typical **6** accepted, approved, authoritative, definitive, established, official, recognized

➤ **Antonyms**

adjective ≠usual: abnormal, atypical, exceptional, extraordinary, irregular, singular, strange, uncommon, unusual ≠accepted: unauthorised, unconventional, unofficial

standardize verb bring into line, institutionalize, regiment

stand by verb **1** be prepared, wait **2** support, back, be loyal to, champion, take (someone's) part

stand for verb **1** represent, betoken, denote, indicate, mean, signify, symbolize **2** Informal tolerate, bear, brook, endure, put up with

stand-in noun substitute, deputy, locum, replacement, reserve, stopgap, surrogate, understudy

stand in for verb be a substitute for, cover for, deputize for, represent, take the place of

standing adjective **1** permanent, fixed, lasting, regular **2** upright, erect, vertical ♦ *noun* **3** status, eminence, footing, position, rank, reputation, repute **4** duration, continuance, existence

standoffish *adjective* reserved, aloof, cold, distant, haughty, remote, unapproachable, unsociable

➤ **Antonyms**

affable, approachable, congenial, cordial, friendly, open, sociable, warm

stand out *verb* be conspicuous, be distinct, be obvious, be prominent

standpoint *noun* point of view, angle, position, stance, viewpoint

stand up for *verb* support, champion, defend, stick up for (*informal*), uphold

staple *adjective* principal, basic, chief, fundamental, key, main, predominant

star *noun* **1** heavenly body **2** celebrity, big name, luminary, main attraction, megastar (*informal*), name ♦ *adjective* **3** leading, brilliant, celebrated, major, prominent, well-known

stare *verb* gaze, eyeball (*slang*), gape, gawk, gawp (*Brit. slang*), goggle, look, watch

stark *adjective* **1** harsh, austere, bare, barren, bleak, grim, hard, plain, severe **2** absolute, blunt, downright, out-and-out, pure, sheer, unmitigated, utter ♦ *adverb* **3** absolutely, altogether, completely, entirely, quite, utterly, wholly

start *verb* **1** begin, appear, arise, commence, issue, originate **2** set about, embark upon, make a beginning, take the first step **3** set in motion, activate, get going, initiate, instigate, kick-start, open, originate, trigger **4** jump, flinch, jerk, recoil, shy **5** establish, begin, create, found, inaugurate, initiate, institute, launch, pioneer, set up ♦ *noun* **6** beginning, birth, dawn, foundation, inception, initiation, onset, opening, outset **7** advantage,

edge, head start, lead **8** jump, convulsion, spasm

➤ **Antonyms**

verb ≠begin, set about, set in motion: abandon, bring to an end, call it a day (*informal*), cease, conclude, delay, desist, end, finish, give up, put aside, put off, quit, stop, switch off, terminate, wind up ♦ *noun* ≠beginning: cessation, conclusion, end, finish, stop, termination, wind-up

startle *verb* surprise, frighten, make (someone) jump, scare, shock

starving *adjective* hungry, famished, ravenous, starved

state *noun* **1** condition, circumstances, equation, position, predicament, shape, situation **2** frame of mind, attitude, humour, mood, spirits **3** country, commonwealth, federation, government, kingdom, land, nation, republic, territory **4** ceremony, display, glory, grandeur, majesty, pomp, splendour, style ♦ *verb* **5** express, affirm, articulate, assert, declare, expound, present, say, specify, utter, voice

stately *adjective* grand, august, dignified, lofty, majestic, noble, regal, royal

➤ **Antonyms**

common, humble, lowly, modest, simple, undignified

statement *noun* account, announcement, communication, communiqué, declaration, proclamation, report

state-of-the-art *adjective* latest, newest, up-to-date, up-to-the-minute

➤ **Antonyms**

obsolescent, obsolete, old-fashioned, outdated, out of date

static *adjective* stationary, fixed, immobile, motionless, still, unmoving

➤ **Antonyms**

active, dynamic, kinetic, mobile, moving

station *noun* **1** headquarters, base, depot **2** position, post, rank, situation, standing, status **3** occupation, business, calling, employment **4** place, location, position, post, seat, situation ♦ verb **5** assign, establish, install, locate, post, set

stationary adjective motionless, fixed, parked, standing, static, stock-still, unmoving

➤ **Antonyms**

changeable, mobile, moving, shifting, travelling

statuesque adjective well-proportioned, imposing, Juno-esque

stature noun importance, eminence, prestige, prominence, rank, standing

status noun position, condition, consequence, eminence, grade, prestige, rank, standing

staunch[1], **stanch** verb stop, check, dam, halt, stay, stem

staunch[2] adjective loyal, faithful, firm, sound, stalwart, steadfast, true, trusty

stay verb **1** remain, abide, continue, halt, linger, loiter, pause, stop, tarry, wait ♦ noun **2** visit, holiday, sojourn, stop, stopover **3** postponement, deferment, delay, halt, stopping, suspension

➤ **Antonyms**

verb ≠remain: abandon, depart, exit, go, leave, move on, pass through, quit, withdraw

steadfast adjective firm, faithful, fast, fixed, intent, loyal, resolute, stalwart, staunch, steady, unswerving, unwavering

➤ **Antonyms**

fickle, half-hearted, irresolute, wavering

steady adjective **1** firm, fixed, safe, secure, stable **2** continuous, ceaseless, consistent, constant, incessant, nonstop, persistent, regular, unbroken, uninterrupted **3** dependable, balanced, calm, equable, level-headed, reliable, sensible, sober ♦ verb **4** stabilize, brace, secure, support

➤ **Antonyms**

adjective ≠firm: insecure, unset-

tled, unstable, unsteady ≠continuous: changeable, inconsistent, infrequent, intermittent, irregular, occasional, sporadic ≠dependable: undependable, unpredictable, unreliable ♦ verb ≠stabilize: agitate, shake, tilt, upset

steal verb **1** take, appropriate, embezzle, filch, lift (informal), misappropriate, nick (slang, chiefly Brit.), pilfer, pinch (informal), purloin, thieve **2** sneak, creep, slink, slip, tiptoe

stealth noun secrecy, furtiveness, slyness, sneakiness, stealthiness, surreptitiousness, unobtrusiveness

stealthy adjective secret, furtive, secretive, sneaking, surreptitious

steep[1] adjective **1** sheer, abrupt, precipitous **2** Informal high, exorbitant, extortionate, extreme, overpriced, unreasonable

➤ **Antonyms**

≠sheer: easy, gentle, gradual, moderate, slight ≠high: fair, moderate, reasonable

steep[2] verb **1** soak, drench, immerse, marinate (Cookery), moisten, souse, submerge **2** saturate, fill, imbue, infuse, permeate, pervade, suffuse

steer verb drive, control, direct, guide, handle, pilot

stem[1] noun **1** stalk, axis, branch, shoot, trunk ♦ verb **2** stem from originate from, arise from, be caused by, derive from

stem[2] verb stop, check, curb, dam, hold back, staunch

stench noun stink, foul smell, pong (Brit. informal), reek, whiff (Brit. slang)

step noun **1** footstep, footfall, footprint, pace, print, stride, track **2** stage, move, phase, point **3** action, act, deed, expedient, means, measure, move **4** degree, level, rank ♦ verb **5** walk, move, pace, tread

step in verb Informal intervene, become involved, take action

step up verb Informal increase, intensify, raise

stereotype noun **1** <u>formula</u>, pattern ♦ verb **2** <u>categorize</u>, pigeonhole, standardize, typecast

sterile adjective **1** <u>germ-free</u>, aseptic, disinfected, sterilized **2** <u>barren</u>, bare, dry, empty, fruitless, unfruitful, unproductive

➤ **Antonyms**

≠<u>germ-free</u>: contaminated, dirty, germ-ridden, infected, insanitary, unhygienic, unsterile ≠<u>barren</u>: fecund, fertile, fruitful, productive, prolific

sterilize verb <u>disinfect</u>, fumigate, purify

sterling adjective <u>excellent</u>, fine, genuine, sound, superlative, true

stern adjective **1** <u>strict</u>, austere, grim, hard, harsh, inflexible, rigid **2** <u>severe</u>, forbidding, serious

➤ **Antonyms**

≠<u>strict</u>: flexible, gentle, kind, lenient, soft ≠<u>severe</u>: approachable, friendly, warm

stick¹ noun **1** <u>cane</u>, baton, crook, pole, rod, staff, twig **2** Slang <u>abuse</u>, criticism, flak (informal)

stick² verb **1** <u>poke</u>, dig, jab, penetrate, pierce, prod, puncture, spear, stab, thrust, transfix **2** <u>fasten</u>, adhere, affix, attach, bind, bond, cling, fix, glue, hold, join, paste, weld **3** with out, up, etc. <u>protrude</u>, bulge, extend, jut, obtrude, poke, project, show **4** Informal <u>put</u>, deposit, lay, place, set **5** <u>stay</u>, linger, persist, remain **6** Slang <u>tolerate</u>, abide, stand, stomach, take

stickler noun <u>fanatic</u>, fusspot (Brit. informal), perfectionist, purist

stick up for verb Informal <u>defend</u>, champion, stand up for, support

sticky adjective **1** <u>tacky</u>, adhesive, clinging, gluey, glutinous, gooey (informal), gummy, icky (informal), viscid, viscous **2** Informal <u>difficult</u>, awkward, delicate, embarrassing, nasty, tricky, unpleasant **3** <u>humid</u>, clammy, close, muggy, oppressive, sultry, sweltering

stiff adjective **1** <u>inflexible</u>, firm, hard, inelastic, rigid, solid, taut, tense, tight, unbending, unyielding **2** <u>awkward</u>, clumsy, graceless, inelegant, jerky (informal), ungainly, ungraceful **3** <u>difficult</u>, arduous, exacting, hard, tough **4** <u>severe</u>, drastic, extreme, hard, harsh, heavy, strict **5** <u>unrelaxed</u>, constrained, forced, formal, stilted, unnatural

➤ **Antonyms**

≠<u>inflexible</u>: bendable, ductile, elastic, flexible, pliable, pliant, yielding ≠<u>unrelaxed</u>: casual, easy, informal, laid-back, natural, relaxed, spontaneous

stiffen verb **1** <u>brace</u>, reinforce, tauten, tense **2** <u>set</u>, congeal, crystallize, harden, jell, solidify, thicken

stifle verb **1** <u>suppress</u>, check, hush, repress, restrain, silence, smother, stop **2** <u>suffocate</u>, asphyxiate, choke, smother, strangle

stigma noun <u>disgrace</u>, dishonour, shame, slur, smirch, stain

still adjective **1** <u>motionless</u>, calm, peaceful, restful, serene, stationary, tranquil, undisturbed **2** <u>silent</u>, hushed, quiet ♦ verb **3** <u>quieten</u>, allay, calm, hush, lull, pacify, quiet, settle, silence, soothe ♦ conjunction **4** <u>however</u>, but, nevertheless, notwithstanding, yet

➤ **Antonyms**

adjective ≠<u>motionless</u>: active, agitated, lively, moving, restless ≠<u>silent</u>: noisy ♦ verb ≠<u>quieten</u>: aggravate, agitate, increase, rouse, stir up

stilted adjective <u>stiff</u>, constrained, forced, unnatural, wooden

➤ **Antonyms**

free, natural, spontaneous

stimulant noun <u>pick-me-up</u> (informal), restorative, tonic, upper (slang)

➤ **Antonyms**

depressant, downer (slang), sedative, tranquilliser

stimulate verb <u>encourage</u>, arouse, fire, gee up, impel, incite, inspire, prompt, provoke, rouse, spur

stimulating adjective exciting, exhilarating, inspiring, provocative, rousing, stirring

► **Antonyms**

boring, dull, mind-numbing, unexciting, uninspiring, uninteresting, unstimulating

stimulus noun incentive, encouragement, fillip, geeing-up, goad, impetus, incitement, inducement, spur

sting verb 1 hurt, burn, pain, smart, tingle, wound 2 Informal cheat, defraud, do (slang), fleece, overcharge, rip off (slang), swindle

stingy adjective mean, miserly, niggardly, parsimonious, penny-pinching (informal), tightfisted, ungenerous

stink noun 1 stench, fetor, foul smell, pong (Brit. informal) ♦ verb 2 reek, pong (Brit. informal)

stint verb 1 be mean, be frugal, be sparing, hold back, skimp on ♦ noun 2 share, period, quota, shift, spell, stretch, term, time, turn

stipulate verb specify, agree, contract, covenant, insist upon, require, settle

stipulation noun condition, agreement, clause, precondition, proviso, qualification, requirement, specification

stir verb 1 mix, agitate, beat, shake 2 stimulate, arouse, awaken, excite, incite, move, provoke, rouse, spur ♦ noun 3 commotion, activity, bustle, disorder, disturbance, excitement, flurry, fuss

► **Antonyms**

verb ≠stimulate: check, curb, dampen, inhibit, restrain, stifle, suppress

stock noun 1 goods, array, choice, commodities, merchandise, range, selection, variety, wares 2 supply, fund, hoard, reserve, stockpile, store 3 property, assets, capital, funds, invest-

ment 4 livestock, beasts, cattle, domestic animals ♦ adjective 5 standard, conventional, customary, ordinary, regular, routine, usual 6 hackneyed, banal, overused, trite ♦ verb 7 sell, deal in, handle, keep, supply, trade in 8 provide with, equip, fit out, furnish, supply 9 stock up (up), accumulate, amass, gather, hoard, lay in, put away, save

stocky adjective thickset, chunky, dumpy, solid, stubby, sturdy

stodgy adjective 1 heavy, filling, leaden, starchy 2 dull, boring, fuddy-duddy (informal), heavy going, staid, stuffy, tedious, unexciting

► **Antonyms**

≠heavy: appetizing, fluffy, light ≠dull: exciting, fresh, interesting, lively, stimulating

stoical adjective resigned, dispassionate, impassive, long-suffering, philosophic, phlegmatic, stoic, stolid

stoicism noun resignation, acceptance, forbearance, fortitude, impassivity, long-suffering, patience, stolidity

stolid adjective apathetic, dull, lumpish, unemotional, wooden

► **Antonyms**

animated, bright, emotional, energetic, lively, sharp

stomach noun 1 belly, abdomen, gut (informal), pot, tummy (informal) 2 inclination, appetite, desire, relish, taste ♦ verb 3 bear, abide, endure, swallow, take, tolerate

stony adjective cold, blank, chilly, expressionless, hard, hostile, icy, unresponsive

stoop verb 1 bend, bow, crouch, duck, hunch, lean 2 stoop to to lower oneself by, descend to, resort to, sink to ♦ noun 3 slouch, bad posture, round-shoulderedness

stop verb 1 halt, cease, conclude, cut short, desist, discontinue, end, finish, pause, put an end to, quit, refrain, shut down, terminate **2** <u>prevent</u>, arrest, forestall, hinder, hold back, impede, repress, restrain **3** <u>plug</u>, block, obstruct, seal, staunch, stem **4** <u>stay</u>, lodge, rest ♦ *noun* **5** <u>end</u>, cessation, finish, halt, standstill **6** <u>stay</u>, break, rest **7** <u>station</u>, depot, terminus

► **Antonyms**

verb ≠<u>halt</u>: advance, begin, commence, continue, get going, get under way, go, keep going, keep on, proceed, set in motion, set off, start ≠<u>prevent</u>: assist, boost, encourage, facilitate, further, gee up, hasten, promote, push ♦ *noun* ≠<u>end</u>: beginning, commencement, kick-off (*informal*), start

stopgap *noun* <u>makeshift</u>, improvisation, resort, substitute

stoppage *noun* <u>stopping</u>, arrest, close, closure, cutoff, halt, hindrance, shutdown, standstill

store *verb* **1** <u>put by</u>, deposit, garner, hoard, keep, put aside, reserve, save, stockpile ♦ *noun* **2** <u>shop</u>, market, mart, outlet **3** <u>supply</u>, accumulation, cache, fund, hoard, quantity, reserve, stock, stockpile **4** <u>repository</u>, depository, storeroom, warehouse

storm *noun* **1** <u>tempest</u>, blizzard, gale, hurricane, squall **2** <u>outburst</u>, agitation, commotion, disturbance, furore, outbreak, outcry, row, rumpus, strife, tumult, turmoil ♦ *verb* **3** <u>attack</u>, assail, assault, charge, rush **4** <u>rage</u>, bluster, rant, rave, thunder **5** <u>rush</u>, flounce, fly, stamp

stormy *adjective* <u>wild</u>, blustery, inclement, raging, rough, squally, turbulent, windy

story *noun* **1** <u>tale</u>, account, anecdote, history, legend, narrative, romance, yarn **2** <u>report</u>, article, feature, news, news item, scoop

stout *adjective* **1** <u>fat</u>, big, bulky, burly, corpulent, fleshy, heavy, overweight, plump, portly, rotund, tubby **2** <u>strong</u>, ablebodied, brawny, muscular, robust, stalwart, strapping, sturdy **3** <u>brave</u>, bold, courageous, fearless, gallant, intrepid, plucky, resolute, valiant

► **Antonyms**

≠<u>fat</u>: lanky, lean, skin-and-bones (*informal*), skinny, slender, slight, slim ≠<u>strong</u>: feeble, flimsy, frail, puny ≠<u>brave</u>: cowardly, fainthearted, fearful, soft, spineless, timid, weak

stow *verb* <u>pack</u>, bundle, load, put away, stash (*informal*), store

straight *adjective* **1** <u>direct</u>, near, short **2** <u>level</u>, aligned, even, horizontal, right, smooth, square, true **3** <u>upright</u>, erect, plumb, vertical **4** <u>accurate</u>, fair, honest, true **5** <u>frank</u>, blunt, bold, candid, forthright, honest, outright, plain, straightforward **6** <u>successive</u>, consecutive, continuous, nonstop, running, solid **7** <u>undiluted</u>, neat, pure, unadulterated, unmixed **8** <u>orderly</u>, arranged, in order, neat, organized, shipshape, tidy **9** <u>honest</u>, above board, fair, honourable, just, law-abiding, reliable, respectable, trustworthy, upright **10** *Slang* <u>conventional</u>, bourgeois, conservative ♦ *adverb* **11** <u>directly</u>, at once, immediately, instantly

► **Antonyms**

adjective ≠<u>direct</u>: circuitous, indirect, roundabout, winding, zigzag ≠<u>level</u>: askew, bent, crooked, curved, skewwhiff (*Brit. informal*), twisted, uneven ≠<u>frank</u>: ambiguous, cryptic, equivocal, evasive, indirect, vague ≠<u>successive</u>: broken, discontinuous, interrupted, non-consecutive ≠<u>orderly</u>: confused, disorderly, disorganized, in disarray, messy, untidy ≠<u>honest</u>: bent (*slang*), crooked (*informal*), dishonest, dishonourable, shady (*informal*), unlawful ≠<u>conventional</u>: cool, fashionable, trendy (*Brit. informal*)

straight away *adverb* <u>immediately</u>, at once, directly, instantly, now, right away

straighten *verb* <u>neaten</u>, arrange, order, put in order, tidy (up)

straightforward *adjective* **1** honest, candid, direct, forthright, genuine, open, sincere, truthful, upfront (*informal*) **2** *Chiefly Brit.* simple, easy, easy-peasy (*slang*), elementary, routine, uncomplicated

➤ **Antonyms**

≠honest: devious, roundabout, shady, sharp, unscrupulous ≠simple: complex, complicated, confused, convoluted, unclear

strain[1] *noun* **1** stress, anxiety, burden, pressure, tension **2** exertion, effort, force, struggle **3** injury, pull, sprain, wrench ♦ *verb* **4** strive, bend over backwards (*informal*), endeavour, give it one's best shot (*informal*), go for it (*informal*), knock oneself out (*informal*), labour, struggle **5** overexert, injure, overtax, overwork, pull, sprain, tax, tear, twist, wrench **6** sieve, filter, purify, sift **7** stretch, distend, draw tight, tauten, tighten

➤ **Antonyms**

noun ≠stress, exertion: ease, effortlessness, lack of tension, relaxation ♦ *verb* ≠strive, overexert: idle, relax, rest, slacken, take it easy

strain[2] *noun* **1** breed, ancestry, blood, descent, extraction, family, lineage, race **2** trace, streak, suggestion, tendency

strained *adjective* **1** forced, artificial, false, put on, unnatural **2** tense, awkward, difficult, embarrassed, stiff, uneasy

➤ **Antonyms**

≠forced: natural ≠tense: comfortable, relaxed

strait *noun* **1** *often plural* channel, narrows, sound **2** straits difficulty, dilemma, extremity, hardship, plight, predicament

strait-laced *or* **straight-laced** *adjective* puritanical, moralistic, narrow-minded, prim, proper, prudish, strict

➤ **Antonyms**

broad-minded, immoral, loose, relaxed, uninhibited, unreserved

strand *noun* filament, fibre, string, thread

stranded *adjective* **1** beached, aground, ashore, grounded, marooned, shipwrecked **2** helpless, abandoned, high and dry

strange *adjective* **1** odd, abnormal, bizarre, curious, extraordinary, peculiar, queer, uncommon, weird, wonderful **2** unfamiliar, alien, exotic, foreign, new, novel, unknown, untried

➤ **Antonyms**

≠odd: common, commonplace, ordinary, regular, routine, usual ≠unfamiliar: accustomed, familiar, habitual

stranger *noun* newcomer, alien, foreigner, guest, incomer, outlander, visitor

strangle *verb* **1** throttle, asphyxiate, choke, strangulate **2** suppress, inhibit, repress, stifle

strap *noun* **1** belt, thong, tie ♦ *verb* **2** fasten, bind, buckle, lash, secure, tie

strapping *adjective* well-built, big, brawny, husky (*informal*), powerful, robust, sturdy

stratagem *noun* trick, device, dodge, manoeuvre, plan, ploy, ruse, scheme, subterfuge

strategic *adjective* **1** tactical, calculated, deliberate, diplomatic, planned, politic **2** crucial, cardinal, critical, decisive, important, key, vital

strategy *noun* plan, approach, policy, procedure, scheme

stray *verb* **1** wander, drift, err, go astray **2** digress, deviate, diverge, get off the point ♦ *adjective* **3** lost, abandoned, homeless, roaming, vagrant **4** random, accidental, chance

streak *noun* **1** band, layer, line, slash, strip, stripe, stroke, vein **2** trace, dash, element, strain, touch, vein ♦ *verb* **3** speed, dart, flash, fly, hurtle, sprint, tear, whizz (*informal*), zoom

stream *noun* **1** river, bayou, beck, brook, burn (*Scot.*), rivulet, tributary **2** flow, course, current, drift, run, rush, surge, tide, torrent ♦ *verb* **3** flow, cascade, flood, gush, issue, pour, run, spill, spout

streamlined *adjective* efficient, organized, rationalized, slick, smooth-running

street *noun* road, avenue, lane, roadway, row, terrace

strength *noun* **1** might, brawn, courage, fortitude, muscle, robustness, stamina, sturdiness, toughness **2** strong point, advantage, asset **3** power, effectiveness, efficacy, force, intensity, potency, vigour

► **Antonyms**

≠might: feebleness, infirmity, powerlessness, weakness ≠strong point: Achilles heel, chink in one's armour, defect, failing, flaw, shortcoming, weakness ≠power: feebleness, powerlessness, weakness

strengthen *verb* **1** fortify, brace up, consolidate, gee up, harden, invigorate, restore, stiffen, toughen **2** reinforce, augment, bolster, brace, build up, buttress, harden, intensify, support

► **Antonyms**

debilitate, enervate, sap, subvert, undermine, weaken

strenuous *adjective* demanding, arduous, hard, laborious, taxing, tough, uphill

► **Antonyms**

easy, effortless, relaxing, undemanding, untaxing

stress *noun* **1** strain, anxiety, burden, pressure, tension, trauma, worry **2** emphasis, force, significance, weight **3** accent, accentuation, beat, emphasis ♦ *verb* **4** emphasize, accentuate, dwell on, underline

stretch *verb* **1** extend, cover, put forth, reach, spread, unroll **2** pull, distend, draw out, elongate, expand, strain, tighten ♦ *noun* **3** expanse, area, distance, extent, spread, tract **4** period, space, spell, stint, term, time

strict *adjective* **1** severe, authoritarian, firm, harsh, stern, stringent **2** exact, accurate, close, faithful, meticulous, precise, scrupulous, true **3** absolute, total, utter

► **Antonyms**

≠severe: easy-going, flexible, laid-back (*informal*), lax, mild, soft, tolerant

strident *adjective* harsh, discordant, grating, jarring, raucous, screeching, shrill

► **Antonyms**

dulcet, gentle, harmonious, mellifluous, mellow, quiet, soothing, sweet

strife *noun* conflict, battle, clash, discord, dissension, friction, quarrel

strike *verb* **1** walk out, down tools, mutiny, revolt **2** hit, beat, clobber (*slang*), clout (*informal*), cuff, hammer, knock, punch, slap, smack, swipe, thump, wallop (*informal*) **3** collide with, bump into, hit, run into **4** affect, hit, register (*informal*) **5** occur to, come to, dawn on or upon, hit, register (*informal*) **6** strike at attack, assail, assault, hit

striking *adjective* impressive, conspicuous, dramatic, jaw-dropping, noticeable, outstanding

► **Antonyms**

undistinguished, unexceptional, unimpressive, uninteresting

string *noun* **1** cord, fibre, twine **2** series, chain, file, line, procession, row, sequence, succession

stringent *adjective* strict, inflexible, rigid, rigorous, severe, tight, tough

► **Antonyms**

flexible, lax, loose, relaxed, slack, unrigorous

stringy *adjective* fibrous, gristly, sinewy, tough

strip[1] *verb* **1** undress, disrobe, unclothe **2** plunder, despoil, divest, empty, loot, pillage, ransack, rob, sack

strip[2] *noun* piece, band, belt, shred

strive *verb* **1** <u>try</u>, attempt, bend over backwards (*informal*), break one's neck (*informal*), do one's best, give it one's best shot (*informal*), go all out (*informal*), knock oneself out (*informal*), labour, make an all-out effort (*informal*), struggle, toil

stroke *verb* **1** <u>caress</u>, fondle, pet, rub ♦ *noun* **2** <u>apoplexy</u>, attack, collapse, fit, seizure **3** <u>blow</u>, hit, knock, pat, rap, swipe, thump

stroll *verb* **1** <u>walk</u>, amble, promenade, ramble, saunter ♦ *noun* **2** <u>walk</u>, breath of air, constitutional, promenade, ramble

strong *adjective* **1** <u>powerful</u>, athletic, brawny, burly, hardy, lusty, muscular, robust, strapping, sturdy, tough **2** <u>durable</u>, hardwearing, heavy-duty, sturdy, substantial, well-built **3** <u>distinct</u>, clear, marked, overpowering, unmistakable **4** <u>persuasive</u>, compelling, convincing, effective, potent, sound, telling, weighty, well-founded **5** <u>intense</u>, acute, deep, fervent, fervid, fierce, firm, keen, vehement, violent, zealous **6** <u>extreme</u>, drastic, forceful, severe **7** <u>bright</u>, bold, brilliant, dazzling

➤ **Antonyms**

≠powerful: delicate, feeble, frail, ineffectual, namby-pamby, puny, weak ≠bright: dull, insipid, pale, pastel, washed-out

stronghold *noun* <u>fortress</u>, bastion, bulwark, castle, citadel, fort

stroppy *adjective* *Brit. informal* <u>awkward</u>, bloody-minded (*Brit. informal*), difficult, obstreperous, quarrelsome, uncooperative

structure *noun* **1** <u>building</u>, construction, edifice, erection **2** <u>arrangement</u>, configuration, construction, design, form, formation, make-up, organization ♦ *verb* **3** <u>arrange</u>, assemble, build up, design, organize, shape

struggle *verb* **1** <u>strive</u>, exert oneself, give it one's best shot (*informal*), go all out (*informal*), knock oneself out (*informal*), labour, make an all-out effort (*informal*), strain, toil, work **2** <u>fight</u>, battle, compete, contend, grapple, wrestle ♦ *noun* **3** <u>effort</u>, exertion, labour, pains, scramble, toil, work **4** <u>fight</u>, battle, brush, clash, combat, conflict, contest, tussle

strut *verb* <u>swagger</u>, parade, peacock, prance

stub *noun* **1** <u>butt</u>, dog-end (*informal*), end, remnant, stump, tail, tail end **2** <u>counterfoil</u>

stubborn *adjective* <u>obstinate</u>, dogged, headstrong, inflexible, intractable, obdurate, persistent, pig-headed, recalcitrant, tenacious, unyielding

➤ **Antonyms**

compliant, docile, flexible, irresolute, manageable, pliable, pliant, tractable, yielding

stubby *adjective* <u>stocky</u>, chunky, dumpy, short, squat, thickset

stuck *adjective* **1** <u>fastened</u>, cemented, fast, fixed, glued, joined **2** *Informal* <u>baffled</u>, beaten, stumped

stuck-up *adjective* *Informal* <u>snobbish</u>, arrogant, bigheaded (*informal*), conceited, haughty, proud, snooty (*informal*), toffeenosed (*slang, chiefly Brit.*)

stud *verb* <u>ornament</u>, bejewel, dot, spangle, spot

student *noun* <u>learner</u>, apprentice, disciple, pupil, scholar, trainee, undergraduate

studied *adjective* <u>planned</u>, conscious, deliberate, intentional, premeditated

➤ **Antonyms**

impulsive, natural, spontaneous, spur-of-the-moment, unplanned, unpremeditated

studio *noun* <u>workshop</u>, atelier

studious *adjective* <u>scholarly</u>, academic, assiduous, bookish, diligent, hard-working, intellectual

➤ **Antonyms**

idle, lazy, unacademic, unintellectual, unscholarly

study *verb* **1** <u>learn</u>, cram (*informal*), mug up (*Brit. slang*), read up, swot (up) (*Brit. informal*) **2**

contemplate, consider, examine, go into, ponder, pore over, read **3** *examine*, analyse, investigate, look into, research, scrutinize, survey ♦ *noun* **4** *learning*, application, lessons, reading, research, school work, swotting (*Brit. informal*) **5** *examination*, analysis, consideration, contemplation, inquiry, inspection, investigation, review, scrutiny, survey

stuff *noun* **1** substance, essence, matter **2** things, belongings, effects, equipment, gear, kit, objects, paraphernalia, possessions, tackle **3** material, cloth, fabric, textile ♦ *verb* **4** cram, crowd, fill, force, jam, pack, push, ram, shove, squeeze

stuffing *noun* filling, packing, wadding

stuffy *adjective* **1** airless, close, frowsty, heavy, muggy, oppressive, stale, stifling, sultry, unventilated **2** *Informal* staid, dreary, dull, pompous, priggish, prim, stodgy

➤ Antonyms
≠airless: airy, breezy, cool, draughty, fresh, gusty, well-ventilated

stumble *verb* **1** trip, fall, falter, lurch, reel, slip, stagger **2** with **across**, **on** or **upon** discover, chance upon, come across, find

stump *verb* baffle, bewilder, confuse, flummox, mystify, nonplus, perplex, puzzle

stumpy *adjective* stocky, dumpy, short, squat, stubby, thickset

stun *verb* **1** overcome, astonish, astound, bewilder, confound, confuse, overpower, shock, stagger, stupefy **2** knock out, daze

stunning *adjective Informal* wonderful, beautiful, dazzling, gorgeous, impressive, jaw-dropping, lovely, marvellous, sensational (*informal*), spectacular, striking

➤ Antonyms
average, dreadful, horrible, mediocre, no great shakes (*informal*), ordinary, plain, poor, rot-

ten, run-of-the-mill, ugly, unattractive, unimpressive

stunt *noun* feat, act, deed, exploit, trick

stunted *adjective* undersized, diminutive, little, small, tiny

stupefy *verb* astound, amaze, daze, dumbfound, shock, stagger, stun

stupendous *adjective* **1** wonderful, amazing, astounding, breathtaking, jaw-dropping, marvellous, overwhelming, sensational (*informal*), staggering, superb **2** huge, colossal, enormous, gigantic, mega (*slang*), vast

➤ Antonyms
≠wonderful: average, mediocre, modest, ordinary, unexciting, unimpressive, unremarkable, unsurprising ≠huge: diminutive, puny, tiny

stupid *adjective* **1** unintelligent, brainless, dense, dim, dumb-ass (*slang*), half-witted, moronic, obtuse, simple, simple-minded, slow, slow-witted, thick **2** silly, asinine, daft (*informal*), foolish, idiotic, imbecilic, inane, nonsensical, pointless, rash, senseless, unintelligent **3** dazed, groggy, insensate, semiconscious, stunned, stupefied

➤ Antonyms
≠unintelligent: astute, brainy, bright, brilliant, clever, intelligent, quick-witted, sensible, smart, wise ≠silly: astute, prudent, realistic, reasonable, sensible, thoughtful, well-thought-out, wise

stupidity *noun* **1** lack of intelligence, brainlessness, denseness, dimness, dullness, imbecility, obtuseness, slowness, thickness **2** silliness, absurdity, fatuousness, folly, foolishness, idiocy, inanity, lunacy, madness

stupor *noun* daze, coma, insensibility, stupefaction, unconsciousness

sturdy *adjective* **1** robust, athletic, brawny, hardy, lusty, muscular, powerful **2** substantial, durable, solid, well-built, well-made

➤ **Antonyms**

≠robust: feeble, infirm, puny, skinny, weak ≠substantial: flimsy, frail, rickety, unsubstantial

stutter verb stammer, falter, hesitate, stumble

style noun 1 design, cut, form, manner 2 manner, approach, method, mode, technique, way 3 elegance, chic, élan, flair, panache, polish, smartness, sophistication, taste 4 type, category, genre, kind, sort, variety 5 fashion, mode, rage, trend, vogue 6 luxury, affluence, comfort, ease, elegance, grandeur ✦ verb 7 design, adapt, arrange, cut, fashion, shape, tailor 8 call, designate, dub, entitle, label, name, term

stylish adjective smart, chic, dressy (informal), fashionable, modish, trendy (Brit. informal), voguish

➤ **Antonyms**

naff (Brit. slang), old-fashioned, outmoded, scruffy, shabby, tacky, tawdry, unfashionable, unstylish

suave adjective smooth, charming, courteous, debonair, polite, sophisticated, urbane

subconscious adjective hidden, inner, intuitive, latent, repressed, subliminal

➤ **Antonyms**

aware, conscious, knowing, sensible, sentient

subdue verb 1 overcome, break, conquer, control, crush, defeat, master, overpower, quell, tame, vanquish 2 moderate, mellow, quieten down, soften, suppress, tone down

➤ **Antonyms**

≠moderate: agitate, arouse, awaken, incite, provoke, stir up, waken

subdued adjective 1 quiet, chastened, crestfallen, dejected, downcast, down in the mouth, sad, serious 2 soft, dim, hushed,

muted, quiet, subtle, toned down, unobtrusive

➤ **Antonyms**

≠quiet: cheerful, happy, lively, vivacious ≠soft: bright, loud, strident

subject noun 1 topic, affair, business, issue, matter, object, point, question, substance, theme 2 citizen, national, subordinate ✦ adjective 3 subordinate, dependent, inferior, satellite 4 subject to: a liable to, prone to b vulnerable to, exposed to, in danger of, open to, susceptible to c conditional on, contingent on, dependent on ✦ verb 5 put through, expose, lay open, submit, treat

subjective adjective personal, biased, nonobjective, prejudiced

➤ **Antonyms**

detached, disinterested, impartial, impersonal, objective, open-minded, unbiased

subjugate verb conquer, enslave, master, overcome, overpower, quell, subdue, suppress, vanquish

sublime adjective noble, elevated, exalted, glorious, grand, great, high, lofty

➤ **Antonyms**

bad, lowly, ordinary, poor, ridiculous

submerge verb immerse, deluge, dip, duck, engulf, flood, inundate, overflow, overwhelm, plunge, sink, swamp

submission noun 1 surrender, assent, capitulation, cave-in (informal), giving in, yielding 2 presentation, entry, handing in, tendering 3 meekness, compliance, deference, docility, obedience, passivity, resignation

submissive adjective meek, accommodating, acquiescent, amenable, compliant, docile, obedient, passive, pliant, tractable, unresisting, yielding

➤ **Antonyms**

awkward, difficult, disobedient, headstrong, intractable, obstinate, stubborn, uncooperative, unyielding

submit *verb* **1** surrender, accede, agree, capitulate, cave in (*informal*), comply, endure, give in, succumb, tolerate, yield **2** present, hand in, proffer, put forward, table, tender

subordinate *adjective* **1** lesser, dependent, inferior, junior, lower, minor, secondary, subject ♦ *noun* **2** inferior, aide, assistant, attendant, junior, second

➤ **Antonyms**

adjective ≠lesser: central, greater, higher, key, main, necessary, predominant, senior, superior ♦ *noun* ≠inferior: boss (*informal*), captain, chief, commander, head, leader, senior, superior

subordination *noun* inferiority, inferior *or* secondary status, servitude, subjection

subscribe *verb* **1** contribute, donate, give **2** support, advocate, endorse

subscription *noun* **1** Chiefly Brit. membership fee, annual payment, dues **2** contribution, donation, gift

subsequent *adjective* following, after, ensuing, later, succeeding, successive

➤ **Antonyms**

antecedent, earlier, erstwhile, former, one-time, past, preceding, previous, prior

subsequently *adverb* later, afterwards

subservient *adjective* servile, abject, deferential, obsequious, slavish, submissive, sycophantic

➤ **Antonyms**

bossy, disobedient, domineering, overbearing, rebellious, wilful

subside *verb* **1** decrease, abate, diminish, ease, ebb, lessen, quieten, slacken, wane **2** collapse, cave in, drop, lower, settle, sink

➤ **Antonyms**

≠decrease: grow, heighten, increase, intensify, mount, rise, soar

subsidence *noun* **1** decrease, abatement, easing off, lessening, slackening **2** sinking, collapse, settling

subsidiary *adjective* lesser, ancillary, auxiliary, minor, secondary, subordinate, supplementary

➤ **Antonyms**

central, chief, head, key, leading, main, major, primary, principal

subsidize *verb* fund, finance, promote, sponsor, support

subsidy *noun* aid, allowance, assistance, grant, help, support

substance *noun* **1** material, body, fabric, stuff **2** meaning, essence, gist, import, main point, significance **3** reality, actuality, concreteness **4** wealth, assets, estate, means, property, resources

substantial *adjective* big, ample, considerable, important, large, significant, sizable *or* sizeable

➤ **Antonyms**

inconsiderable, insignificant, insubstantial, poor, small

substantiate *verb* support, authenticate, confirm, establish, prove, verify

➤ **Antonyms**

contradict, disprove, negate, prove false, rebut, refute

substitute *verb* **1** replace, change, exchange, interchange, swap, switch ♦ *noun* **2** replacement, agent, deputy, locum, proxy, reserve, sub, surrogate ♦ *adjective* **3** replacement, alternative, fall-back, proxy, reserve, second, surrogate

substitution *noun* replacement, change, exchange, swap, switch

subterfuge *noun* trick, deception, dodge, manoeuvre, ploy, ruse, stratagem

subtle *adjective* **1** faint, delicate, implied, slight, understated **2** crafty, artful, cunning, devious, ingenious, shrewd, sly, wily **3** sophisticated, delicate, refined

➤ **Antonyms**

≠faint: overwhelming, strong ≠crafty: artless, blunt, direct, downright, guileless, obvious, simple, straightforward ≠sophisticated: crass, tactless, unsophisticated, unsubtle

subtlety noun 1 <u>fine point</u>, delicacy, refinement, sophistication 2 <u>cunning</u>, artfulness, cleverness, craftiness, deviousness, ingenuity, slyness, wiliness

subtract verb <u>take away</u>, deduct, diminish, remove, take from, take off

➤ **Antonyms**
add, add to, increase by

subversive adjective 1 <u>seditious</u>, riotous, treasonous ♦ noun 2 <u>dissident</u>, fifth columnist, saboteur, terrorist, traitor

subvert verb <u>overturn</u>, sabotage, undermine

succeed verb 1 <u>make it</u> (informal), be successful, crack it (informal), do well, flourish, make good, make the grade (informal), prosper, thrive, triumph, work 2 <u>follow</u>, come next, ensue, result 3 <u>take over</u>, accede, assume the office of, come into, come into possession of, inherit

➤ **Antonyms**
≠make it: be unsuccessful, fail, fall flat, fall short, flop (informal), not make the grade, not manage ≠follow: be a precursor of, come before, go ahead of, go before, precede

success noun 1 <u>favourable outcome</u>, fame, fortune, happiness, luck, prosperity, triumph 2 <u>hit</u> (informal), celebrity, megastar (informal), sensation, smash (informal), star, winner

➤ **Antonyms**
≠favourable outcome: collapse, disaster, downfall, failure, misfortune ≠hit: fiasco, flop (informal), loser, nobody, washout

successful adjective 1 <u>thriving</u>, booming, flourishing, fortunate, fruitful, lucky, profitable, rewarding, top, victorious 2 <u>prosperous</u>, wealthy

➤ **Antonyms**
≠thriving: defeated, failed, luck-

less, uneconomic, unprofitable, unsuccessful

successfully adverb <u>well</u>, favourably, victoriously, with flying colours

succession noun 1 <u>series</u>, chain, course, cycle, order, progression, run, sequence, train 2 <u>taking over</u>, accession, assumption, inheritance

successive adjective <u>consecutive</u>, following, in succession

succinct adjective <u>brief</u>, compact, concise, laconic, pithy, terse

➤ **Antonyms**
circuitous, long-winded, rambling, verbose, wordy

succour noun 1 <u>help</u>, aid, assistance ♦ verb 2 <u>help</u>, aid, assist

succulent adjective <u>juicy</u>, luscious, lush, moist

succumb verb 1 <u>surrender</u>, capitulate, cave in (informal), give in, submit, yield 2 <u>die</u>, fall

➤ **Antonyms**
≠surrender: beat, conquer, get the better of, master, overcome

sucker noun Slang <u>fool</u>, dupe, mug (Brit. slang), pushover (slang), victim

sudden adjective <u>quick</u>, abrupt, hasty, hurried, rapid, rash, swift, unexpected

➤ **Antonyms**
expected, gentle, gradual, slow

suddenly adverb <u>abruptly</u>, all of a sudden, unexpectedly

sue verb Law <u>take (someone) to court</u>, charge, indict, prosecute, summon

suffer verb 1 <u>undergo</u>, bear, endure, experience, go through, sustain 2 <u>tolerate</u>, put up with (informal)

suffering noun <u>pain</u>, agony, anguish, discomfort, distress, hardship, misery, ordeal, torment

suffice verb <u>be enough</u>, be adequate, be sufficient, do, meet requirements, serve

sufficient adjective <u>adequate</u>, enough, satisfactory

➤ **Antonyms**
deficient, inadequate, insuffi-

cient, not enough, short

suffocate *verb* choke, asphyxiate, smother, stifle

suggest *verb* **1** recommend, advise, advocate, prescribe, propose **2** bring to mind, evoke **3** hint, imply, indicate, intimate

suggestion *noun* **1** recommendation, motion, plan, proposal, proposition **2** hint, breath, indication, intimation, trace, whisper

suggestive *adjective* smutty, bawdy, blue, indelicate, provocative, racy, ribald, risqué, rude

suit *noun* **1** outfit, clothing, costume, dress, ensemble, habit **2** lawsuit, action, case, cause, proceeding, prosecution, trial ♦ *verb* **3** befit, agree, become, go with, harmonize, match, tally **4** be acceptable to, do, gratify, please, satisfy

suitability *noun* appropriateness, aptness, fitness, rightness

suitable *adjective* appropriate, apt, becoming, befitting, fit, fitting, proper, right, satisfactory

➤ **Antonyms**

inappropriate, incorrect, jarring, unbecoming, unfitting, unsuitable

suite *noun* rooms, apartment

suitor *noun* Old-fashioned admirer, beau, young man

sulk *verb* be sullen, be in a huff, pout

sulky *adjective* huffy, cross, disgruntled, in the sulks, moody, petulant, querulous, resentful, sullen

sullen *adjective* morose, cross, dour, glowering, moody, sour, sulky, surly, unsociable

➤ **Antonyms**

bright, cheerful, cheery, good-humoured, good-natured, pleasant, sociable, sunny

sully *verb* **1** dishonour, besmirch, disgrace, ruin, smirch **2** defile, stain, tarnish

sultry *adjective* **1** humid, close, hot, muggy, oppressive, sticky, stifling **2** seductive, provocative, sensual, sexy (*informal*)

➤ **Antonyms**

≠humid: cool, fresh, invigorating, refreshing

sum *noun* total, aggregate, amount, tally, whole

summarize *verb* sum up, abridge, condense, encapsulate, epitomize, précis

summary *noun* synopsis, abridgment, outline, précis, résumé, review, rundown

summit *noun* peak, acme, apex, head, height, pinnacle, top, zenith

➤ **Antonyms**

base, bottom, depths, foot, lowest point, nadir

summon *verb* **1** send for, bid, call, invite **2** *often with* up gather, draw on, muster

sumptuous *adjective* luxurious, gorgeous, grand, lavish, opulent, splendid, superb

➤ **Antonyms**

austere, basic, cheap, mean, plain, shabby, wretched

sum up *verb* summarize, put in a nutshell, recapitulate, review

sunburnt *adjective* tanned, bronzed, brown, burnt, peeling, red

sundry *adjective* various, assorted, different, miscellaneous, several, some

sunken *adjective* **1** hollow, drawn, haggard **2** lower, buried, recessed, submerged

sunny *adjective* **1** bright, clear, fine, radiant, summery, sunlit, unclouded **2** cheerful, buoyant, cheery, happy, joyful, lighthearted

➤ **Antonyms**

≠bright: cloudy, depressing, dreary, dreich (*Scot.*), dull, gloomy, murky, overcast, rainy, shaded, shadowy, sunless, wet, wintry ≠cheerful: doleful, down in the dumps (*informal*), gloomy, miserable

sunrise *noun* dawn, break of day, cockcrow, daybreak

sunset *noun* nightfall, close of (the) day, dusk, eventide

super *adjective Informal* excellent, cracking (*Brit. informal*), glorious, magnificent, marvellous, outstanding, sensational (*informal*), smashing (*informal*), superb, terrific (*informal*), wonderful

superb *adjective* splendid, excellent, exquisite, fine, first-rate, grand, magnificent, marvellous, superior, superlative, world-class

➤ **Antonyms**

abysmal, awful, bad, dreadful, inferior, mediocre, pathetic, poor quality, run-of-the-mill, terrible, third-rate

supercilious *adjective* scornful, arrogant, contemptuous, disdainful, haughty, lofty, snooty (*informal*), stuck-up (*informal*)

➤ **Antonyms**

deferential, humble, meek, modest, self-effacing, unassuming

superficial *adjective* **1** hasty, casual, cursory, desultory, hurried, perfunctory, sketchy, slapdash **2** shallow, empty-headed, frivolous, silly, trivial **3** surface, exterior, external, on the surface, slight

➤ **Antonyms**

≠hasty: complete, comprehensive, detailed, exhaustive, in depth, thorough ≠shallow: earnest, serious ≠surface: deep, profound

superfluous *adjective* excess, extra, left over, redundant, remaining, spare, supernumerary, surplus

➤ **Antonyms**

essential, indispensable, vital

superhuman *adjective* **1** heroic, phenomenal, prodigious **2** supernatural, paranormal

superintendence *noun* supervision, charge, control, direction, government, management

superintendent *noun* supervisor, chief, controller, director, governor, inspector, manager, overseer

superior *adjective* **1** better, grander, greater, higher, surpassing, unrivalled **2** supercilious, condescending, disdainful, haughty, lofty, lordly, patronizing, pretentious, snobbish **3** first-class, choice, de luxe, excellent, exceptional, exclusive, first-rate ♦ *noun* **4** boss (*informal*), chief, director, manager, principal, senior, supervisor

➤ **Antonyms**

adjective ≠better: inferior, less, lesser, lower, not as good, worse ≠first-class: average, inferior, mediocre, ordinary, second-class, second-rate, substandard, unremarkable ♦ *noun* ≠boss: assistant, inferior, junior, subordinate

superiority *noun* supremacy, advantage, ascendancy, excellence, lead, predominance

superlative *adjective* supreme, excellent, outstanding, unparalleled, unrivalled, unsurpassed

➤ **Antonyms**

average, inferior, ordinary, run-of-the-mill, unexceptional

supernatural *adjective* paranormal, ghostly, miraculous, mystic, occult, psychic, spectral, uncanny, unearthly

supersede *verb* replace, displace, oust, supplant, take the place of, usurp

supervise *verb* oversee, control, direct, handle, look after, manage, run, superintend

supervision *noun* superintendence, care, charge, control, direction, guidance, management

supervisor *noun* boss (*informal*), administrator, chief, foreman, inspector, manager, overseer

supplant *verb* replace, displace, oust, supersede, take the place of

supple *adjective* **1** flexible, limber, lissom(e), lithe **2** pliant, pliable

➤ **Antonyms**

≠flexible: inflexible, stiff, unsupple ≠pliant: firm, inflexible, rigid, stiff

supplement *noun* **1** addition, add-on, appendix, extra, insert, postscript, pull-out ♦ *verb* **2** add, augment, extend, reinforce

supplementary *adjective* additional, add-on, ancillary, auxiliary, extra, secondary

supplication noun Formal plea, appeal, entreaty, petition, prayer, request

supply verb **1** provide, contribute, endow, equip, furnish, give, grant, produce, stock, yield ◆ noun **2** store, cache, fund, hoard, quantity, reserve, source, stock **3** **supplies** provisions, equipment, food, materials, necessities, rations, stores

support verb **1** bear, brace, buttress, carry, hold, prop, reinforce, sustain **2** provide for, finance, fund, keep, look after, maintain, sustain **3** help, aid, assist, back, champion, defend, second, side with **4** bear out, confirm, corroborate, substantiate, verify ◆ noun **5** help, aid, assistance, backing, encouragement, loyalty **6** prop, brace, foundation, pillar, post **7** supporter, backer, mainstay, prop, second, tower of strength **8** upkeep, keep, maintenance, subsistence, sustenance

► **Antonyms**
verb ≠provide for: live off, sponge off ≠help: go against, hinder, oppose, stab in the back, turn one's back on, undermine ≠bear out: challenge, contradict, deny, refute ◆ noun ≠help: burden, encumbrance, hindrance, impediment ≠supporter: antagonist

supporter noun follower, adherent, advocate, champion, fan, friend, helper, patron, sponsor, well-wisher

► **Antonyms**
adversary, antagonist, foe, opponent, rival

supportive adjective helpful, encouraging, sympathetic, understanding

suppose verb **1** presume, assume, conjecture, expect, guess (informal, chiefly U.S. & Canad.), imagine, think **2** imagine, conjecture, consider, hypothesize, postulate, pretend

supposed adjective **1** presumed, accepted, alleged, assumed, professed **2** usually with **to** meant, expected, obliged, required

supposedly adverb presumably, allegedly, hypothetically, ostensibly, theoretically

► **Antonyms**
actually, certainly, in fact, really, truly, undoubtedly

supposition noun guess, conjecture, hypothesis, presumption, speculation, surmise, theory

suppress verb **1** stop, check, conquer, crush, overpower, put an end to, quash, quell, subdue **2** restrain, conceal, contain, curb, hold in or back, repress, silence, smother, stifle

► **Antonyms**
encourage, foster, further, gee up, incite, inflame, promote, rouse, spread, stimulate, stir up

suppression noun **1** elimination, check, crushing, quashing **2** inhibition, smothering

supremacy noun domination, mastery, predominance, primacy, sovereignty, supreme power, sway

supreme adjective highest, chief, foremost, greatest, head, leading, paramount, pre-eminent, prime, principal, top, ultimate

► **Antonyms**
least, lowest, most inferior, worst

supremo noun Brit. informal head, boss (informal), commander, director, governor, leader, master, principal, ruler

sure adjective **1** certain, assured, confident, convinced, decided, definite, positive **2** reliable, accurate, dependable, foolproof, infallible, undeniable, undoubted, unerring, unfailing **3** inevitable, assured, bound, guaranteed, inescapable

► **Antonyms**
≠certain: distrustful, doubtful, dubious, sceptical, unassured, uncertain, unconvinced, unsure ≠reliable: dubious, fallible, undependable, unreliable ≠inevitable:

touch-and-go, unsure

surely *adverb* <u>undoubtedly</u>, certainly, definitely, doubtlessly, indubitably, unquestionably, without doubt

surface *noun* **1** <u>outside</u>, covering, exterior, face, side, top, veneer ♦ *verb* **2** <u>appear</u>, arise, come to light, come up, crop up (*informal*), emerge, materialize, transpire

surfeit *noun* <u>excess</u>, glut, plethora, superfluity
➤ **Antonyms**
deficiency, insufficiency, lack, scarcity, shortage, want

surge *noun* **1** <u>rush</u>, flood, flow, gush, outpouring **2** <u>wave</u>, billow, roller, swell ♦ *verb* **3** <u>rush</u>, gush, rise **4** <u>roll</u>, heave

surly *adjective* <u>ill-tempered</u>, churlish, cross, grouchy (*informal*), morose, sulky, sullen, uncivil, ungracious
➤ **Antonyms**
cheerful, cheery, genial, good-natured, happy, pleasant, sunny

surmise *verb* **1** <u>guess</u>, conjecture, imagine, presume, speculate, suppose ♦ *noun* **2** <u>guess</u>, assumption, conjecture, presumption, speculation, supposition

surpass *verb* <u>outdo</u>, beat, eclipse, exceed, excel, outshine, outstrip, transcend

surpassing *adjective* <u>supreme</u>, exceptional, extraordinary, incomparable, matchless, outstanding, unrivalled

surplus *noun* **1** <u>excess</u>, balance, remainder, residue, surfeit ♦ *adjective* **2** <u>extra</u>, excess, odd, remaining, spare, superfluous
➤ **Antonyms**
noun ≠<u>excess</u>: deficiency, deficit, insufficiency, lack, shortage, shortfall ♦ *adjective* ≠<u>extra</u>: deficient, inadequate, insufficient, lacking, scarce

surprise *noun* **1** <u>shock</u>, bombshell, eye-opener (*informal*), jolt, revelation **2** <u>amazement</u>, astonishment, incredulity, wonder ♦ *verb* **3** <u>amaze</u>, astonish, stag-

ger, stun, take aback **4** <u>catch unawares *or* off-guard</u>, discover, spring upon, startle

surprised *adjective* **1** <u>amazed</u>, astonished, speechless, thunderstruck **2** <u>taken by surprise</u>

surprising *adjective* <u>amazing</u>, astonishing, extraordinary, incredible, jaw-dropping, remarkable, staggering, unexpected, unusual

surrender *verb* **1** <u>give in</u>, capitulate, cave in (*informal*), give way, submit, succumb, yield **2** <u>give up</u>, abandon, cede, concede, part with, relinquish, renounce, waive, yield ♦ *noun* **3** <u>submission</u>, capitulation, cave-in (*informal*), relinquishment, renunciation, resignation
➤ **Antonyms**
verb ≠<u>give in</u>: defy, fight (on), oppose, resist, stand up to, withstand

surreptitious *adjective* <u>secret</u>, covert, furtive, sly, stealthy, underhand
➤ **Antonyms**
blatant, conspicuous, open, overt, unconcealed, undisguised

surrogate *noun* <u>substitute</u>, proxy, representative, stand-in

surround *verb* <u>enclose</u>, encircle, encompass, envelop, hem in, ring

surroundings *plural noun* <u>environment</u>, background, location, milieu, setting

surveillance *noun* <u>observation</u>, inspection, scrutiny, supervision, watch

survey *verb* **1** <u>look over</u>, contemplate, examine, eyeball (*slang*), inspect, observe, scrutinize, view **2** <u>estimate</u>, appraise, assess, measure, plan, plot, size up ♦ *noun* **3** <u>examination</u>, inspection, scrutiny **4** <u>study</u>, inquiry, review

survive *verb* <u>remain alive</u>, endure, last, live on, outlast, outlive

susceptible *adjective* **1** *usually with* **to** <u>liable</u>, disposed, given, inclined, prone, subject, vulnerable **2** <u>impressionable</u>, receptive, responsive, sensitive, suggestible

➤ **Antonyms**

≠<u>liable</u>: immune, insusceptible, invulnerable, resistant, unaffected by ≠<u>impressionable</u>: insensitive, unaffected by, unmoved by, unresponsive

suspect verb **1** <u>believe</u>, consider, feel, guess, speculate, suppose **2** <u>distrust</u>, doubt, mistrust ♦ adjective **3** <u>dubious</u>, doubtful, iffy (informal), questionable

➤ **Antonyms**

verb ≠<u>believe</u>: accept, be certain, be confident of, believe, know ≠<u>distrust</u>: have faith in, think innocent, trust ♦ adjective ≠<u>dubious</u>: above suspicion, reliable, trustworthy

suspend verb **1** <u>hang</u>, attach, dangle **2** <u>postpone</u>, cease, cut short, defer, discontinue, interrupt, put off, shelve

➤ **Antonyms**

≠<u>postpone</u>: carry on, continue, resume

suspense noun <u>uncertainty</u>, anxiety, apprehension, doubt, expectation, insecurity, irresolution, tension

suspension noun <u>postponement</u>, abeyance, break, breaking off, deferment, discontinuation, interruption

suspicion noun **1** <u>distrust</u>, doubt, dubiety, misgiving, mistrust, qualm, scepticism, wariness **2** <u>idea</u>, guess, hunch, impression, notion **3** <u>trace</u>, hint, shade, soupçon, streak, suggestion, tinge, touch

suspicious adjective **1** <u>suspect</u>, dodgy (Brit., Austral., & N.Z. informal), doubtful, dubious, fishy (informal), questionable **2** <u>distrustful</u>, doubtful, sceptical, unbelieving, wary

➤ **Antonyms**

≠<u>suspect</u>: above board, beyond suspicion, straight, straightforward, unquestionable ≠<u>distrustful</u>: believing, credulous, gullible, trusting, unsuspicious

sustain verb **1** <u>maintain</u>, continue, keep up, prolong, protract **2** <u>keep alive</u>, aid, assist, help, nourish **3** <u>suffer</u>, bear, endure, experience, feel, undergo, withstand **4** <u>support</u>, bear, uphold

sustained adjective <u>continuous</u>, constant, nonstop, perpetual, prolonged, steady, unremitting

➤ **Antonyms**

broken, discontinuous, intermittent, irregular, periodic, spasmodic, sporadic

swagger verb <u>show off</u> (informal), boast, brag, parade

swallow verb <u>gulp</u>, consume, devour, drink, eat, swig (informal)

swamp noun **1** <u>bog</u>, fen, marsh, mire, morass, quagmire, slough ♦ verb **2** Naut. <u>flood</u>, capsize, engulf, inundate, sink, submerge **3** <u>overwhelm</u>, engulf, flood, inundate, overload, submerge

swap, swop verb <u>exchange</u>, barter, interchange, switch, trade

swarm noun **1** <u>multitude</u>, army, crowd, flock, herd, horde, host, mass, throng ♦ verb **2** <u>crowd</u>, flock, mass, stream, throng **3** <u>teem</u>, abound, bristle, crawl

swarthy adjective <u>dark-skinned</u>, black, brown, dark, dark-complexioned, dusky

swashbuckling adjective <u>dashing</u>, bold, daredevil, flamboyant

swathe verb <u>wrap</u>, bundle up, cloak, drape, envelop, shroud

sway verb **1** <u>bend</u>, lean, rock, roll, swing **2** <u>influence</u>, affect, guide, induce, persuade ♦ noun **3** <u>power</u>, authority, clout (informal), control, influence

swear verb **1** <u>curse</u>, be foul-mouthed, blaspheme **2** <u>vow</u>, attest, promise, testify **3** <u>declare</u>, affirm, assert

swearing noun <u>bad language</u>, blasphemy, cursing, foul language, profanity

swearword noun <u>oath</u>, curse, expletive, four-letter word, obscenity, profanity

sweat noun **1** <u>perspiration</u> **2**

Slang labour, chore, drudgery, toil **3** *Informal* worry, agitation, anxiety, distress, panic, strain ♦ *verb* **4** perspire, glow **5** *Informal* worry, agonize, fret, suffer, torture oneself

sweaty *adjective* perspiring, clammy, sticky

sweep *verb* **1** clear, brush, clean, remove **2** sail, fly, glide, pass, skim, tear, zoom ♦ *noun* **3** arc, bend, curve, move, stroke, swing **4** extent, range, scope, stretch

sweeping *adjective* **1** wide-ranging, all-embracing, all-inclusive, broad, comprehensive, extensive, global, overarching, wide **2** indiscriminate, blanket, exaggerated, overstated, unqualified, wholesale

► **Antonyms**

≠wide-ranging: constrained, limited, minor, narrow, restricted

sweet *adjective* **1** sugary, cloying, icky (*informal*), saccharine **2** charming, agreeable, kind **3** delightful, appealing, cute, engaging, likable *or* likeable, lovable, winning **4** melodious, dulcet, harmonious, mellow, musical **5** fragrant, aromatic, clean, fresh, pure ♦ *noun* **6** *usually plural* confectionery, bonbon, candy (*U.S.*) **7** *Brit.* dessert, pudding

► **Antonyms**

adjective ≠sugary: acid, bitter, savoury, sharp, sour, tart, vinegary ≠charming: bad-tempered, disagreeable, grouchy (*informal*), grumpy, ill-tempered, nasty, obnoxious ≠delightful: loathsome, nasty, objectionable, obnoxious, unappealing, unattractive, unlovable, unpleasant ≠melodious: cacophonous, discordant, grating, harsh, shrill, strident, unharmonious, unmusical ≠fragrant: fetid, foul, rank, stinking

sweeten *verb* **1** sugar **2** mollify, appease, pacify, soothe

sweetheart *noun* love, beloved, boyfriend *or* girlfriend, darling, dear, lover

swell *verb* **1** expand, balloon, bloat, bulge, dilate, distend, enlarge, grow, increase, rise **2** increase, heighten, intensify, mount, surge ♦ *noun* **3** wave, billow, surge

► **Antonyms**

verb ≠expand: become smaller, contract, deflate, shrink ≠increase: decrease, diminish, ebb, fall, go down, lessen, reduce, wane

swelling *noun* enlargement, bulge, bump, distension, inflammation, lump, protuberance

sweltering *adjective* hot, boiling, burning, oppressive, scorching, stifling

swerve *verb* veer, bend, deflect, deviate, diverge, stray, swing, turn, turn aside

swift *adjective* quick, fast, hurried, prompt, rapid, speedy

► **Antonyms**

plodding, ponderous, slow, sluggish, tardy, unhurried

swiftly *adverb* quickly, fast, hurriedly, promptly, rapidly, speedily

swiftness *noun* speed, promptness, quickness, rapidity, speediness, velocity

swindle *verb* **1** cheat, con, defraud, do (*slang*), fleece, rip (someone) off (*slang*), skin (*slang*), sting (*informal*), trick ♦ *noun* **2** fraud, con trick (*informal*), deception, fiddle (*Brit. informal*), racket, rip-off (*slang*), scam (*slang*)

swindler *noun* cheat, con man (*informal*), fraud, rogue, shark, trickster

swing *verb* **1** sway, oscillate, rock, veer, wave **2** *usually with* round turn, curve, pivot, rotate, swivel **3** hang, dangle, suspend ♦ *noun* **4** swaying, oscillation

swingeing *adjective* *Chiefly Brit.* severe, drastic, excessive, harsh, heavy, punishing, stringent

swipe *verb* **1** *Informal* hit, lash out at, slap, strike, wallop (*informal*) **2** *Slang* steal, appropriate, filch, lift (*informal*), nick (*slang*, chiefly *Brit*.), pinch (*informal*), purloin ♦ *noun* **3** blow, clout (*informal*), cuff, slap, smack, thump, wallop (*informal*)

swirl *verb* whirl, churn, eddy, spin, twist

switch *noun* **1** change, reversal, shift **2** exchange, substitution, swap ♦ *verb* **3** change, deflect, deviate, divert, shift **4** exchange, substitute, swap

swivel *verb* turn, pivot, revolve, rotate, spin

swollen *adjective* enlarged, bloated, distended, inflamed, puffed up

swoop *verb* **1** pounce, descend, dive, rush, stoop, sweep ♦ *noun* **2** pounce, descent, drop, lunge, plunge, rush, stoop, sweep

swop *see* SWAP

swot *verb Informal* study, cram (*informal*), mug up (*Brit. slang*), revise

sycophant *noun* crawler, bootlicker (*informal*), fawner, flatterer, toady, yes man

sycophantic *adjective* obsequious, crawling, fawning, flattering, grovelling, ingratiating, servile, smarmy (*Brit. informal*), toadying, unctuous

syllabus *noun* course of study, curriculum

symbol *noun* sign, badge, emblem, figure, image, logo, mark, representation, token

symbolic *adjective* representative, allegorical, emblematic, figurative

symbolize *verb* represent, denote, mean, personify, signify, stand for, typify

symmetrical *adjective* balanced, in proportion, regular

► Antonyms

asymmetrical, irregular, lopsided, unbalanced, unequal, unsymmetrical

symmetry *noun* balance, evenness, order, proportion, regularity

sympathetic *adjective* **1** caring, compassionate, concerned, interested, kind, pitying, supportive, understanding, warm **2** like-minded, agreeable, companionable, compatible, congenial, friendly

► Antonyms

≠caring: apathetic, callous, disinterested, indifferent, insensitive, uncaring, uncompassionate, uninterested, unmoved, unsympathetic ≠like-minded: uncongenial, unresponsive

sympathize *verb* **1** feel for, commiserate, condole, pity **2** agree, side with, understand

► Antonyms

≠feel for: have no feelings for, mock, scorn ≠agree: disagree, fail to understand, misunderstand, oppose

sympathizer *noun* supporter, partisan, well-wisher

sympathy *noun* **1** compassion, commiseration, pity, understanding **2** affinity, agreement, fellow feeling, rapport

► Antonyms

≠compassion: callousness, hardheartedness, indifference, insensitivity, lack of feeling or understanding or sympathy, pitilessness ≠affinity: antagonism, hostility, opposition

symptom *noun* sign, expression, indication, mark, token, warning

symptomatic *adjective* indicative, characteristic, suggestive

synthetic *adjective* artificial, fake, man-made

► Antonyms

authentic, genuine, natural, pure, real

system *noun* **1** method, practice, procedure, routine, technique **2** arrangement, classification, organization, scheme, structure

systematic *adjective* methodical, efficient, orderly, organized

► Antonyms

arbitrary, disorderly, disorganized, haphazard, random, unmethodical, unsystematic

table 553 **tail**

T t

table noun 1 counter, bench, board, stand 2 list, catalogue, chart, diagram, record, register, roll, schedule, tabulation ♦ verb 3 Brit. submit, enter, move, propose, put forward, suggest

tableau noun picture, representation, scene, spectacle

taboo noun 1 prohibition, anathema, ban, interdict, proscription, restriction ♦ adjective 2 forbidden, anathema, banned, outlawed, prohibited, proscribed, unacceptable, unmentionable

➤ **Antonyms**

adjective ≠forbidden: acceptable, allowed, permitted, sanctioned

tacit adjective implied, implicit, inferred, undeclared, understood, unexpressed, unspoken, unstated

➤ **Antonyms**

explicit, express, spoken, stated

taciturn adjective uncommunicative, quiet, reserved, reticent, silent, tight-lipped, unforthcoming, withdrawn

➤ **Antonyms**

communicative, forthcoming, garrulous, loquacious, outgoing, talkative, voluble

tack¹ noun 1 nail, drawing pin, pin ♦ verb 2 fasten, affix, attach, fix, nail, pin 3 Brit. stitch, baste, sew 4 tack on append, add, attach, tag

tack² noun course, approach, direction, heading, line, method, path, plan, procedure, way

tackle verb 1 deal with, attempt, come or get to grips with, embark upon, get stuck into (informal), have a go or stab at (informal), set about, undertake 2 confront, challenge, grab, grasp, halt, intercept, seize, stop

♦ noun 3 challenge, block 4 equipment, accoutrements, apparatus, gear, paraphernalia, tools, trappings

tacky¹ adjective sticky, adhesive, gluey, gummy, icky (informal), wet

tacky² adjective Informal 1 vulgar, cheap, naff (Brit. slang), sleazy, tasteless 2 shabby, seedy, shoddy, tatty

tact noun diplomacy, consideration, delicacy, discretion, sensitivity, thoughtfulness, understanding

➤ **Antonyms**

awkwardness, clumsiness, gaucherie, indiscretion, insensitivity, tactlessness

tactful adjective diplomatic, considerate, delicate, discreet, polite, politic, sensitive, thoughtful, understanding

➤ **Antonyms**

awkward, clumsy, gauche, indiscreet, insensitive, tactless, thoughtless, undiplomatic

tactic noun 1 policy, approach, manoeuvre, method, move, ploy, scheme, stratagem 2 tactics strategy, campaigning, generalship, manoeuvres, plans

tactical adjective strategic, cunning, diplomatic, shrewd, smart

➤ **Antonyms**

blundering, clumsy, gauche, impolitic, inept

tactician noun strategist, general, mastermind, planner, schemer

tactless adjective insensitive, impolite, impolitic, inconsiderate, indelicate, indiscreet, thoughtless, undiplomatic, unsubtle

➤ **Antonyms**

considerate, diplomatic, discreet, polite, subtle, tactful

tag noun 1 label, flap, identification, mark, marker, note, slip, tab, ticket ♦ verb 2 label, mark 3 with along or on accompany, attend, follow, shadow, tail (informal), trail

tail noun 1 extremity, appendage, end, rear end, tailpiece 2

turn tail run away, cut and run, flee, retreat, run off, take to one's heels ◆ verb **3** Informal follow, shadow, stalk, track, trail

tailor noun **1** outfitter, clothier, costumier, couturier, dressmaker, seamstress ◆ verb **2** adapt, adjust, alter, customize, fashion, modify, mould, shape, style

taint verb **1** spoil, blemish, contaminate, corrupt, damage, defile, pollute, ruin, stain, sully, tarnish ◆ noun **2** stain, black mark, blemish, blot, defect, demerit, fault, flaw, spot

► **Antonyms**
verb ≠spoil: clean, cleanse, decontaminate, disinfect, purify

take verb **1** accompany, bring, conduct, convoy, escort, guide, lead, usher **2** carry, bear, bring, convey, ferry, fetch, haul, transport **3** obtain, acquire, catch, get, grasp, grip, secure, seize **4** steal, appropriate, misappropriate, pinch (informal), pocket, purloin **5** capture, seize **6** require, call for, demand, necessitate, need **7** tolerate, abide, bear, endure, put up with (informal), stand, stomach, withstand **8** have room for, accept, accommodate, contain, hold **9** subtract, deduct, eliminate, remove **10** assume, believe, consider, perceive, presume, regard, understand

► **Antonyms**
≠carry: send ≠steal: give, give back, hand over, restore, return, surrender, yield ≠capture: free, let go, release ≠tolerate: avoid, dodge, give in, give way ≠subtract: add, put

take in verb **1** understand, absorb, assimilate, comprehend, digest, get the hang of (informal), grasp **2** deceive, cheat, con (informal), dupe, fool, hoodwink, mislead, swindle, trick

takeoff noun **1** departure, launch, liftoff **2** Informal parody, caricature, imitation, lampoon, satire, send-up (Brit. informal),

spoof (informal)

take off verb **1** remove, discard, peel off, strip off **2** lift off, take to the air **3** Informal depart, abscond, decamp, disappear, go, leave, slope off **4** Informal parody, caricature, imitate, lampoon, mimic, mock, satirize, send up (Brit. informal)

takeover noun merger, coup, corporation

take up verb **1** occupy, absorb, consume, cover, extend over, fill, use up **2** start, adopt, become involved in, engage in

taking adjective charming, attractive, beguiling, captivating, enchanting, engaging, fetching (informal), likable or likeable, prepossessing

► **Antonyms**
abhorrent, loathsome, offensive, repulsive, unattractive, unpleasant

takings plural noun revenue, earnings, income, proceeds, profits, receipts, returns, take

tale noun story, account, anecdote, fable, legend, narrative, saga, yarn (informal)

talent noun ability, aptitude, capacity, flair, genius, gift, knack

talented adjective gifted, able, brilliant

talisman noun charm, amulet, fetish, lucky charm, mascot

talk verb **1** speak, chat, chatter, communicate, converse, gossip, natter, utter **2** discuss, confabulate, confer, negotiate, parley **3** inform, blab, give the game away, grass (Brit. slang), let the cat out of the bag, tell all ◆ noun **4** speech, address, discourse, disquisition, lecture, oration, sermon

talkative adjective loquacious, chatty, effusive, garrulous, gossipy, long-winded, mouthy, verbose, voluble, wordy

► **Antonyms**
quiet, reserved, silent, taciturn, tight-lipped, uncommunicative, unforthcoming

talker noun speaker, chatterbox, conversationalist, lecturer, orator

talking-to noun Informal reprimand, criticism, dressing-down (informal), lecture, rebuke, reproach, reproof, scolding, telling-off (informal), ticking-off (informal)

➤ **Antonyms**

commendation, encouragement, praise

tall adjective **1** high, big, elevated, giant, lanky, lofty, soaring, towering **2** As in tall story Informal ≠implausible, absurd, cock-and-bull (informal), exaggerated, far-fetched, incredible, preposterous, unbelievable **3** As in tall order difficult, demanding, hard, unreasonable, well-nigh impossible

➤ **Antonyms**

≠high: short, small, squat, stumpy, tiny, wee ≠implausible: accurate, believable, plausible, realistic, reasonable, true, unexaggerated

tally verb **1** agree, accord, coincide, concur, conform, correspond, fit, harmonize, match, square **2** record ♦ noun **2** record, count, mark, reckoning, running total, score, total

➤ **Antonyms**

verb ≠agree: clash, conflict, contradict, differ, disagree

tame adjective **1** domesticated, amenable, broken, disciplined, docile, gentle, obedient, tractable **2** submissive, compliant, docile, manageable, meek, obedient, subdued, unresisting **3** unexciting, bland, boring, dull, humdrum, insipid, uninspiring, uninteresting, vapid ♦ verb **4** domesticate, break in, house-train, train **5** subdue, conquer, discipline, humble, master, subjugate, suppress

➤ **Antonyms**

adjective ≠domesticated: aggressive, feral, ferocious, savage, undomesticated, untamed, wild ≠submissive: aggressive, argumentative, obdurate, strong-

willed, stubborn, unmanageable ≠unexciting: exciting, frenzied, hot, interesting, lively, stimulating ♦ verb ≠domesticate: make fiercer ≠subdue: arouse, incite, intensify

tamper verb interfere, alter, fiddle (informal), fool about (informal), meddle, mess about, tinker

tangible adjective definite, actual, concrete, material, palpable, perceptible, positive, real

➤ **Antonyms**

abstract, immaterial, imperceptible, indiscernible, insubstantial, intangible, theoretical, unreal

tangle noun **1** knot, coil, entanglement, jungle, twist, web **2** confusion, complication, entanglement, fix (informal), imbroglio, jam, mess, mix-up ♦ verb **3** twist, coil, entangle, interweave, knot, mat, mesh, ravel **4** often with come come into conflict, come up against, contend, contest, cross swords, dispute, lock horns

➤ **Antonyms**

verb ≠twist: disentangle, extricate, free, straighten out, unravel, untangle

tangled adjective **1** twisted, entangled, jumbled, knotted, matted, messy, snarled, tousled **2** complicated, complex, confused, convoluted, involved, knotty, messy, mixed-up

tangy adjective sharp, piquant, pungent, spicy, tart

tantalize verb torment, frustrate, lead on, taunt, tease, torture

tantamount adjective tantamount to equivalent to, commensurate with, equal to, synonymous with

tantrum noun outburst, fit, flare-up, hysterics, temper

tap¹ verb **1** knock, beat, drum, pat, rap, strike, touch ♦ noun **2** knock, pat, rap, touch

tap² noun **1** valve, stopcock **2 on tap:** a Informal available: at hand, in reserve, on hand, ready **b on draught** ♦ verb **3** listen in on, bug (*informal*), eavesdrop on **4** draw off, bleed, drain, siphon off

tape *noun* **1** strip, band, ribbon ♦ *verb* **2** record, tape-record, video **3** bind, seal, secure, stick, wrap

taper *verb* **1** narrow, come to a point, thin **2** taper off decrease, die away, dwindle, fade, lessen, reduce, subside, wane, wind down

➤ **Antonyms**

≠decrease: grow, increase, intensify, step up, strengthen, swell, widen

target *noun* **1** goal, aim, ambition, end, intention, mark, object, objective **2** victim, butt, scapegoat

tariff *noun* **1** tax, duty, excise, levy, toll **2** price list, menu, schedule

tarnish *verb* **1** stain, blemish, blot, darken, discolour **2** damage, blacken, smirch, sully, taint ♦ *noun* **3** stain, blemish, blot, discoloration, spot, taint

➤ **Antonyms**

verb ≠stain: brighten, enhance, polish up, shine ≠damage: enhance

tart[1] *noun* pie, pastry, tartlet

tart[2] *adjective* sharp, acid, piquant, pungent, sour, tangy, vinegary

➤ **Antonyms**

honeyed, sugary, sweet, syrupy, toothsome

tart[3] *noun* slut, call girl, floozy (*slang*), prostitute, trollop, whore

task *noun* **1** job, assignment, chore, duty, enterprise, exercise, mission, undertaking **2** take to task criticize, blame, censure, rebuke, reprimand, reproach, reprove, scold, tell off (*informal*), upbraid

taste *noun* **1** flavour, relish, savour, smack, tang **2** bit, bite, dash, morsel, mouthful, sample, soupçon, spoonful, titbit **3** liking, appetite, fancy, fondness, inclination, partiality, penchant, predi-

lection, preference **4** refinement, appreciation, discernment, discrimination, elegance, judgment, sophistication, style ♦ *verb* **5** distinguish, differentiate, discern, perceive **6** sample, savour, sip, test, try **7** have a flavour of, savour of, smack of **8** experience, encounter, know, meet with, partake of, undergo

➤ **Antonyms**

noun ≠flavour: blandness, insipidity, tastelessness ≠liking: disinclination, dislike, distaste, hatred, loathing ≠refinement: lack of discernment, lack of judgment, mawkishness, tackiness, tastelessness ♦ *verb* ≠distinguish: fail to discern ≠experience: fail to achieve, miss, remain ignorant of

tasteful *adjective* refined, artistic, cultivated, cultured, discriminating, elegant, exquisite, in good taste, polished, stylish

➤ **Antonyms**

garish, gaudy, loud, showy, tacky (*informal*), tasteless, tawdry, vulgar

tasteless *adjective* **1** insipid, bland, boring, dull, flat, flavourless, mild, thin, weak **2** vulgar, crass, crude, gaudy, gross, inelegant, naff (*Brit. slang*), tacky (*informal*), tawdry

➤ **Antonyms**

≠insipid: appetizing, delicious, flavoursome, savoury, scrumptious (*informal*), tasty ≠vulgar: elegant, graceful, refined, tasteful

tasty *adjective* delicious, appetizing, delectable, full-flavoured, luscious, palatable, savoury, scrumptious (*informal*), toothsome

➤ **Antonyms**

bland, flavourless, insipid, tasteless, unappetizing, unsavoury

tatters *plural noun* in tatters ragged, down at heel, in rags, in shreds, ripped, tattered, threadbare, torn

tatty *adjective* Chiefly Brit. shabby, bedraggled, dilapidated, down at heel, neglected, ragged, run-

down, scruffy, threadbare, worn
➤ **Antonyms**
new, smart, well-preserved

taunt verb 1 jeer, deride, insult, mock, provoke, ridicule, tease, torment ♦ noun 2 jeer, derision, dig, gibe, insult, provocation, ridicule, sarcasm, teasing

taut adjective tight, flexed, rigid, strained, stressed, stretched, tense
➤ **Antonyms**
loose, relaxed, slack

tavern noun inn, alehouse (archaic), bar, hostelry, pub (informal, chiefly Brit.), public house

tawdry adjective vulgar, cheap, gaudy, gimcrack, naff (Brit. slang), tacky (informal), tasteless, tatty
➤ **Antonyms**
elegant, stylish, tasteful

tax noun 1 charge, duty, excise, levy, tariff, tithe, toll ♦ verb 2 charge, assess, rate 3 strain, burden, exhaust, load, stretch, test, try, weaken, weary

taxing adjective demanding, exacting, onerous, punishing, sapping, stressful, tiring, tough, trying
➤ **Antonyms**
easy, effortless, light, undemanding

teach verb instruct, coach, drill, educate, enlighten, guide, inform, show, train, tutor

teacher noun instructor, coach, educator, guide, lecturer, master or mistress, mentor, schoolteacher, trainer, tutor

team noun 1 group, band, body, bunch, company, gang, line-up, set, side, squad ♦ verb 2 often with up join, band together, cooperate, couple, get together, link, unite, work together

teamwork noun cooperation, collaboration, coordination, esprit de corps, fellowship, harmony, unity

tear verb 1 rip, rend, rupture, scratch, shred, split 2 pull apart, claw, lacerate, mangle, mutilate

3 rush, bolt, charge, dash, fly, hurry, race, run, speed, sprint, zoom ♦ noun 4 hole, laceration, rent, rip, rupture, scratch, split

tearaway noun Brit. hooligan, delinquent, good-for-nothing, rowdy, ruffian

tearful adjective weeping, blubbering, crying, in tears, lachrymose, sobbing, weepy (informal), whimpering

tears plural noun 1 crying, blubbering, sobbing, wailing, weeping 2 in tears weeping, blubbering, crying, distressed, sobbing

tease verb 1 mock, goad, provoke, pull someone's leg (informal), taunt, torment 2 tantalize, lead on

technical adjective scientific, hitech or high-tech, skilled, specialist, specialized, technological

technique noun 1 method, approach, manner, means, mode, procedure, style, system, way 2 skill, artistry, craft, craftsmanship, execution, performance, proficiency, touch

tedious adjective boring, drab, dreary, dull, humdrum, irksome, laborious, mind-numbing, monotonous, tiresome, wearisome
➤ **Antonyms**
enthralling, exciting, exhilarating, inspiring, interesting, stimulating

tedium noun boredom, drabness, dreariness, dullness, monotony, routine, sameness, tediousness
➤ **Antonyms**
excitement, exhilaration, fascination, interest, liveliness, stimulation

teeming¹ adjective full, abundant, alive, brimming, bristling, bursting, crawling, overflowing, swarming, thick
➤ **Antonyms**
deficient, lacking, short, wanting

teeming² adjective pouring, bucketing down (informal), pelting

teenager noun youth, adolescent, boy, girl, juvenile, minor

teeter verb wobble, rock, seesaw,

stagger, sway, totter, waver

teetotaller noun <u>abstainer</u>, non-drinker

telepathy noun <u>mind-reading</u>, sixth sense

telephone noun **1** <u>phone</u>, dog and bone (slang), handset, line, mobile (phone) ♦ verb **2** <u>call</u>, dial, phone, ring (chiefly Brit.)

telescope noun **1** <u>glass</u>, spyglass ♦ verb **2** <u>shorten</u>, abbreviate, abridge, compress, condense, contract, shrink

➤ **Antonyms**
verb ≠<u>shorten</u>: amplify, draw out, elongate, extend, lengthen, protract, spread out

television noun <u>TV</u>, small screen (informal), telly (Brit. informal), the box (Brit. informal), the tube (slang)

tell verb **1** <u>inform</u>, announce, communicate, disclose, divulge, express, make known, notify, proclaim, reveal, state **2** <u>instruct</u>, bid, call upon, command, direct, order, require, summon **3** <u>describe</u>, chronicle, depict, narrate, portray, recount, relate, report **4** <u>distinguish</u>, differentiate, discern, discriminate, identify **5** <u>have or take effect</u>, carry weight, count, make its presence felt, register, take its toll, weigh

telling adjective <u>effective</u>, considerable, decisive, forceful, impressive, influential, marked, powerful, significant, striking

➤ **Antonyms**
inconsequential, ineffectual, insignificant, minor, negligible, slight, trivial, unimportant

telling-off noun <u>reprimand</u>, criticism, dressing-down (informal), lecture, rebuke, reproach, reproof, scolding, talking-to, ticking-off (informal)

tell off verb <u>reprimand</u>, berate, censure, chide, haul over the coals (informal), lecture, read the riot act, rebuke, reproach, scold

temerity noun <u>audacity</u>, boldness, cheek, chutzpah (U.S. & Canad. informal), effrontery,

front, impudence, nerve (informal), rashness, recklessness

temper noun **1** <u>rage</u>, bad mood, fury, passion, tantrum **2** <u>irritability</u>, hot-headedness, irascibility, passion, petulance, resentment, surliness **3** <u>self-control</u>, calmness, composure, cool (slang), equanimity **4** <u>frame of mind</u>, constitution, disposition, humour, mind, mood, nature, temperament ♦ verb **5** <u>moderate</u>, assuage, lessen, mitigate, mollify, restrain, soften, soothe, tone down **6** <u>strengthen</u>, anneal, harden, toughen

➤ **Antonyms**
noun ≠<u>irritability</u>: contentment, goodwill ≠<u>self-control</u>: anger, excitability, irascibility, wrath ♦ verb ≠<u>moderate</u>: aggravate, arouse, excite, heighten, intensify, provoke, stir ≠<u>strengthen</u>: soften

temperament noun **1** <u>nature</u>, bent, character, constitution, disposition, humour, make-up, outlook, personality, temper **2** <u>excitability</u>, anger, hot-headedness, moodiness, petulance, volatility

temperamental adjective **1** <u>moody</u>, capricious, emotional, excitable, highly strung, hypersensitive, irritable, sensitive, touchy, volatile **2** Informal <u>unreliable</u>, erratic, inconsistent, inconstant, unpredictable

➤ **Antonyms**
≠<u>moody</u>: easy-going, even-tempered, level-headed, phlegmatic, unexcitable, unflappable, unperturbable ≠<u>unreliable</u>: constant, dependable, reliable, stable, steady

temperance noun **1** <u>moderation</u>, continence, discretion, forbearance, restraint, self-control, self-discipline, self-restraint **2** <u>teetotalism</u>, abstemiousness, abstinence, sobriety

➤ **Antonyms**
≠<u>moderation</u>: excess, immoderation, intemperance, overindulgence, prodigality

temperate adjective **1** <u>mild</u>,

calm, cool, fair, gentle, moderate, pleasant **2** moderate, calm, composed, dispassionate, even-tempered, mild, reasonable, self-controlled, self-restrained, sensible

► **Antonyms**

≠mild: extreme, harsh, inclement, intemperate, severe, torrid ≠moderate: intemperate, uncontrolled, undisciplined, unreasonable, unrestrained, wild

tempest noun Literary storm, cyclone, gale, hurricane, squall, tornado, typhoon

tempestuous adjective **1** stormy, blustery, gusty, inclement, raging, squally, turbulent, windy **2** passionate, boisterous, emotional, furious, heated, intense, stormy, turbulent, violent, wild

► **Antonyms**

≠passionate: calm, peaceful, quiet, serene, still, tranquil, undisturbed, unruffled

temple noun shrine, church, sanctuary

temporarily adverb briefly, fleetingly, for the time being, momentarily, pro tem

temporary adjective impermanent, brief, ephemeral, fleeting, interim, momentary, provisional, short-lived, transitory

► **Antonyms**

durable, enduring, eternal, everlasting, long-lasting, long-term, permanent

tempt verb **1** entice, coax, invite, lead on, lure, seduce, tantalize **2** attract, allure

► **Antonyms**

≠entice: deter, discourage, dissuade, hinder, inhibit, put off

temptation noun **1** enticement, allurement, inducement, lure, pull, seduction, tantalization **2** appeal, attraction

tempting adjective inviting, alluring, appetizing, attractive, enticing, mouthwatering, seductive, tantalizing

► **Antonyms**

off-putting (Brit. informal), unap-

petizing, unattractive, undesirable, uninviting, untempting

tenable adjective sound, arguable, believable, defensible, justifiable, plausible, rational, reasonable, viable

► **Antonyms**

indefensible, insupportable, unjustifiable, untenable

tenacious adjective **1** firm, clinging, forceful, immovable, iron, strong, tight, unshakable **2** stubborn, adamant, determined, dogged, obdurate, obstinate, persistent, resolute, steadfast, unswerving, unyielding

► **Antonyms**

≠stubborn: changeable, flexible, irresolute, vacillating, wavering, yielding

tenacity noun perseverance, application, determination, doggedness, obduracy, persistence, resolve, steadfastness, stubbornness

tenancy noun lease, occupancy, possession, renting, residence

tenant noun leaseholder, inhabitant, lessee, occupant, occupier, renter, resident

tend¹ verb **1** be inclined, be apt, be liable, gravitate, have a tendency, incline, lean **2** go, aim, bear, head, lead, make for, move, point

tend² verb take care of, attend, cultivate, keep, look after, maintain, manage, nurture, watch over

► **Antonyms**

disregard, ignore, neglect, overlook, shirk

tendency noun inclination, disposition, leaning, liability, proclivity, proneness, propensity, susceptibility

tender¹ adjective **1** gentle, affectionate, caring, compassionate, considerate, kind, loving, sympathetic, tenderhearted, warm-hearted **2** vulnerable, immature, impressionable, inexperienced, raw, sensitive, young, youthful **3** sensitive, bruised, inflamed, painful, raw, sore

➤ **Antonyms**
≠gentle: cruel, hard, insensitive, pitiless, tough, uncaring, unkind, unsympathetic ≠vulnerable: experienced, grown-up, mature, seasoned, sophisticated, worldly, worldly-wise

tender² verb **1** offer, give, hand in, present, proffer, propose, put forward, submit, volunteer ✦ noun **2** offer, bid, estimate, proposal, submission

tenderness noun **1** gentleness, affection, care, compassion, consideration, kindness, love, sentimentality, sympathy, warmth **2** soreness, inflammation, pain, sensitivity

➤ **Antonyms**
≠gentleness: cruelty, hardness, harshness, indifference, insensitivity, unkindness

tense adjective **1** nervous, antsy (informal), anxious, apprehensive, edgy, jumpy, keyed up, on edge, on tenterhooks, strained, uptight (informal) **2** exciting, nerve-racking, stressful, worrying **3** tight, rigid, strained, stretched, taut ✦ verb **4** tighten, brace, flex, strain, stretch

➤ **Antonyms**
adjective ≠nervous: calm, collected, easy-going, self-possessed, serene, unconcerned, unruffled, unworried ≠exciting: boring, dull, uninteresting ≠tight: flaccid, flexible, limp, loose, pliant, relaxed ✦ verb ≠tighten: loosen, relax, slacken

tension noun **1** strain, anxiety, apprehension, hostility, nervousness, pressure, stress, suspense, unease **2** tightness, pressure, rigidity, stiffness, stress, stretching, tautness

➤ **Antonyms**
≠strain: calmness, peacefulness, relaxation, restfulness, serenity, tranquillity

tentative adjective **1** unconfirmed, conjectural, experimental, indefinite, provisional, speculative, unsettled **2** hesitant, cautious, diffident, doubtful, faltering, timid, uncertain, undecided, unsure

➤ **Antonyms**
≠unconfirmed: conclusive, confirmed, decisive, definite, final, fixed, resolved, settled ≠hesitant: assured, bold, certain, confident, unhesitating

tenuous adjective slight, doubtful, dubious, flimsy, insubstantial, nebulous, shaky, sketchy, weak

➤ **Antonyms**
significant, solid, sound, strong, substantial

tepid adjective **1** lukewarm, warmish **2** half-hearted, apathetic, cool, indifferent, lukewarm, unenthusiastic

➤ **Antonyms**
≠half-hearted: animated, eager, enthusiastic, excited, keen, passionate, vibrant, zealous

term noun **1** word, expression, name, phrase, title **2** period, duration, interval, season, span, spell, time, while ✦ verb **3** call, designate, dub, entitle, label, name, style

terminal adjective **1** fatal, deadly, incurable, killing, lethal, mortal **2** final, concluding, extreme, last, ultimate, utmost ✦ noun **3** terminus, depot, end of the line, station

➤ **Antonyms**
adjective ≠final: beginning, commencing, first, initial, introductory, opening

terminate verb end, abort, cease, close, complete, conclude, discontinue, finish, stop

➤ **Antonyms**
begin, commence, inaugurate, initiate, instigate, introduce, open, start

termination noun ending, abortion, cessation, completion, conclusion, discontinuation, end, finish

➤ **Antonyms**
beginning, commencement, inauguration, initiation, opening, start

terminology noun language, jargon, nomenclature, phraseology, terms, vocabulary

terminus noun end of the line, depot, garage, last stop, station

terms plural noun 1 conditions, particulars, provisions, provisos, qualifications, specifications, stipulations 2 relationship, footing, relations, standing, status

terrain noun ground, country, going, land, landscape, topography

terrestrial adjective 1 earthly, global, worldly

terrible adjective 1 serious, dangerous, desperate, extreme, severe 2 *Informal* bad, abysmal, awful, dire, dreadful, poor, rotten (*informal*) 3 fearful, dreadful, frightful, horrendous, horrible, horrifying, monstrous, shocking, terrifying

➤ Antonyms

≠serious: harmless, insignificant, mild, moderate, paltry, small ≠bad: brilliant, excellent, fine, great, remarkable, superb, terrific, wonderful ≠fearful: calming, comforting, encouraging, reassuring, settling, soothing

terribly adverb extremely, awfully (*informal*), decidedly, desperately, exceedingly, seriously, thoroughly, very

terrific adjective 1 great, enormous, fearful, gigantic, huge, intense, tremendous 2 *Informal* excellent, amazing, brilliant, fantastic (*informal*), magnificent, marvellous, outstanding, sensational (*informal*), stupendous, superb, wonderful

➤ Antonyms

≠great: insignificant, mild, moderate, paltry ≠excellent: appalling, awful, bad, dreadful, terrible

terrified adjective frightened, alarmed, appalled, horrified, horror-struck, panic-stricken, petrified, scared

terrify verb frighten, alarm, appal, horrify, make one's hair stand on end, scare, shock, terrorize

territory noun district, area, country, domain, land, patch, province, region, zone

terror noun 1 fear, alarm, anxiety, dread, fright, horror, panic, shock 2 scourge, bogeyman, bugbear, devil, fiend, monster

terrorize verb oppress, browbeat, bully, coerce, intimidate, menace, threaten

terse adjective 1 concise, brief, condensed, laconic, monosyllabic, pithy, short, succinct 2 curt, abrupt, brusque, short, snappy

➤ Antonyms

≠concise: discursive, lengthy, long-winded, rambling, roundabout, vague, verbose, wordy ≠curt: chatty, polite

test verb 1 check, analyse, assess, examine, experiment, investigate, put to the test, research, try out ◆ noun 2 examination, acid test, analysis, assessment, check, evaluation, investigation, research, trial

testament noun 1 proof, demonstration, evidence, testimony, tribute, witness 2 will, last wishes

testify verb bear witness, affirm, assert, attest, certify, corroborate, state, swear, vouch

➤ Antonyms

belie, contradict, controvert, disprove, dispute, gainsay (*archaic or literary*), oppose

testimonial noun tribute, commendation, endorsement, recommendation, reference

testimony noun 1 evidence, affidavit, deposition, statement, submission 2 proof, corroboration, demonstration, evidence, indication, manifestation, support, verification

testing adjective difficult, arduous, challenging, demanding, exacting, rigorous, searching, strenuous, taxing, tough

➤ Antonyms

easy, friendly, gentle, simple, straightforward, undemanding

tether noun 1 rope, chain, fetter, halter, lead, leash 2 at the end

of one's tether exasperated, at one's wits' end, exhausted
♦ *verb* **3** tie, chain, bind, fasten, fetter, secure

text *noun* **1** contents, body **2** words, wording

texture *noun* feel, consistency, grain, structure, surface, tissue

thank *verb* say thank you, show one's appreciation

thankful *adjective* grateful, appreciative, beholden, indebted, in (someone's) debt, obliged, pleased, relieved

➤ **Antonyms**
thankless, unappreciative, ungrateful

thankless *adjective* unrewarding, fruitless, unappreciated, unprofitable, unrequited

➤ **Antonyms**
fruitful, productive, profitable, rewarding, useful, worthwhile

thanks *plural noun* **1** gratitude, acknowledgment, appreciation, credit, gratefulness, recognition **2 thanks to** because of, as a result of, due to, owing to, through

thaw *verb* melt, defrost, dissolve, liquefy, soften, unfreeze, warm

➤ **Antonyms**
chill, congeal, freeze, harden, solidify, stiffen

theatrical *adjective* **1** dramatic, Thespian **2** exaggerated, affected, dramatic, histrionic, mannered, melodramatic, ostentatious, showy, stagy

➤ **Antonyms**
≠exaggerated: natural, plain, straightforward, unaffected, unassuming, unexaggerated, unpretentious

theft *noun* stealing, embezzlement, fraud, larceny, pilfering, purloining, robbery, thieving

theme *noun* **1** subject, idea, keynote, subject matter, topic **2** motif, leitmotif

theological *adjective* religious, doctrinal, ecclesiastical

theoretical *adjective* abstract, academic, conjectural, hypothetical,

notional, speculative

➤ **Antonyms**
applied, experiential, factual, practical, realistic

theorize *verb* speculate, conjecture, formulate, guess, hypothesize, project, propound, suppose

theory *noun* hypothesis, assumption, conjecture, presumption, speculation, supposition, surmise, thesis

➤ **Antonyms**
certainty, experience, fact, practice, reality

therapeutic *adjective* beneficial, corrective, curative, good, healing, remedial, restorative, salutary

➤ **Antonyms**
adverse, damaging, destructive, detrimental, harmful

therapist *noun* healer, physician

therapy *noun* remedy, cure, healing, treatment

therefore *adverb* consequently, accordingly, as a result, ergo, hence, so, then, thence, thus

thesis *noun* **1** dissertation, essay, monograph, paper, treatise **2** proposition, contention, hypothesis, idea, opinion, proposal, theory, view

thick *adjective* **1** wide, broad, bulky, fat, solid, substantial **2** dense, close, compact, concentrated, condensed, heavy, impenetrable, opaque **3** full, brimming, bristling, bursting, covered, crawling, packed, swarming, teeming **4** *Informal* stupid, brainless, dense, dopey (*informal*), dumb-ass (*informal*), moronic, obtuse, slow, thickheaded **5** *As in* **thick as thieves** *Informal* friendly, close, devoted, familiar, inseparable, intimate, pally (*informal*) **6** **a bit thick** *Brit. informal* unreasonable, unfair, unjust

➤ **Antonyms**
≠wide: narrow, slight, slim, thin ≠dense: clear, diluted, runny, thin, watery, weak ≠full: bare, clear, devoid of, empty, free

from, sparse, thin ≠stupid: bright, clever, intellectual, intelligent, quick-witted, smart ≠friendly: antagonistic, distant, hostile, unfriendly

thicken verb set, clot, coagulate, condense, congeal, jell

➤ **Antonyms**
dilute, thin, water down, weaken

thicket noun wood, brake, coppice, copse, covert, grove

thickset adjective stocky, bulky, burly, heavy, muscular, strong, sturdy, well-built

➤ **Antonyms**
gangling, gaunt, scrawny, weedy (informal)

thief noun robber, burglar, embezzler, housebreaker, pickpocket, pilferer, plunderer, shoplifter, stealer

thieve verb steal, filch, nick (slang, chiefly Brit.), pilfer, pinch (informal), purloin, rob, swipe (slang)

thin adjective 1 narrow, attenuated, fine 2 slim, bony, emaciated, lean, scrawny, skeletal, skinny, slender, slight, spare, spindly 3 meagre, deficient, scanty, scarce, scattered, skimpy, sparse, wispy 4 fine, delicate, diaphanous, filmy, flimsy, gossamer, sheer, unsubstantial 5 unconvincing, feeble, flimsy, inadequate, lame, poor, superficial, weak

➤ **Antonyms**
≠narrow: heavy, thick ≠slim: bulky, corpulent, fat, heavy, obese, stout ≠meagre: abundant, adequate, plentiful, profuse ≠fine: bulky, dense, heavy, strong, substantial, thick ≠unconvincing: adequate, convincing, strong, substantial

thing noun 1 object, article, being, body, entity, something, substance 2 Informal obsession, bee in one's bonnet, fetish, fixation, hang-up (informal), mania, phobia, preoccupation 3 things possessions, belongings, clobber (Brit. slang), effects, equipment, gear, luggage, stuff

think verb 1 believe, consider, deem, estimate, imagine, judge, reckon, regard, suppose 2 ponder, cerebrate, cogitate, contemplate, theory, deliberate, meditate, muse, obsess, reason, reflect, ruminate

thinker noun philosopher, brain (informal), intellect (informal), mastermind, sage, theorist, wise man

thinking noun 1 reasoning, conjecture, idea, judgment, opinion, position, theory, view ◆ adjective 2 thoughtful, contemplative, intelligent, meditative, philosophical, rational, reasoning, reflective

think up verb devise, come up with, concoct, contrive, create, dream up, invent, visualize

thirst noun 1 thirstiness, drought, dryness 2 craving, appetite, desire, hankering, keenness, longing, passion, yearning

➤ **Antonyms**
≠craving: apathy, aversion, disinclination, dislike, distaste, loathing, revulsion

thirsty adjective 1 parched, arid, dehydrated, dry 2 with for eager, avid, craving, desirous, greedy, hungry, itching, longing, yearning

thorn noun prickle, barb, spike, spine

thorny adjective prickly, barbed, bristly, pointed, sharp, spiky, spiny

thorough adjective 1 careful, assiduous, conscientious, efficient, exhaustive, full, in-depth, intensive, meticulous, painstaking, sweeping 2 complete, absolute, out-and-out, outright, perfect, total, unmitigated, unqualified, utter

➤ **Antonyms**
≠careful: careless, cursory, half-hearted, haphazard, lackadaisical, sloppy ≠complete: imperfect, incomplete, partial, superficial

thoroughbred adjective purebred, pedigree

> ➤ **Antonyms**
crossbred, hybrid, mongrel

thoroughfare noun <u>road</u>, avenue, highway, passage, passageway, street, way

thoroughly adverb 1 <u>carefully</u>, assiduously, conscientiously, efficiently, exhaustively, from top to bottom, fully, intensively, meticulously, painstakingly, scrupulously 2 <u>completely</u>, absolutely, downright, perfectly, quite, totally, to the hilt, utterly

> ➤ **Antonyms**
≠<u>carefully</u>: carelessly, cursorily, half-heartedly, haphazardly, lackadaisically, sloppily ≠<u>completely</u>: imperfectly, incompletely, in part, partly, somewhat, superficially

though conjunction 1 <u>although</u>, even if, even though, notwithstanding, while ♦ adverb 2 <u>nevertheless</u>, for all that, however, nonetheless, notwithstanding, still, yet

thought noun 1 <u>thinking</u>, brainwork, cogitation, consideration, deliberation, meditation, musing, reflection, rumination 2 <u>idea</u>, concept, judgment, notion, opinion, view 3 <u>consideration</u>, attention, heed, regard, scrutiny, study 4 <u>intention</u>, aim, design, idea, notion, object, plan, purpose 5 <u>expectation</u>, anticipation, aspiration, hope, prospect

thoughtful adjective 1 <u>considerate</u>, attentive, caring, helpful, kind, kindly, solicitous, unselfish 2 <u>well-thought-out</u>, astute, canny, prudent 3 <u>reflective</u>, contemplative, deliberative, meditative, pensive, ruminative, serious, studious

> ➤ **Antonyms**
≠<u>considerate</u>: impolite, inconsiderate, insensitive, neglectful, selfish, uncaring ≠<u>well-thought-out</u>: irresponsible, rash, thoughtless, unthinking ≠<u>reflective</u>: extrovert, shallow, superficial

thoughtless adjective <u>inconsiderate</u>, impolite, insensitive, rude, selfish, tactless, uncaring, undiplomatic, unkind

> ➤ **Antonyms**
attentive, considerate, diplomatic, tactful, thoughtful, unselfish

thrash verb 1 <u>beat</u>, belt (informal), cane, flog, give (someone) a (good) hiding (informal), scourge, spank, whip 2 <u>defeat</u>, beat, crush, drub, rout, run rings around (informal), slaughter (informal), trounce, wipe the floor with (informal) 3 <u>thresh</u>, flail, jerk, toss and turn, writhe

thrashing noun 1 <u>beating</u>, belting (informal), flogging, hiding (informal), punishment, whipping 2 <u>defeat</u>, beating, drubbing, hammering (informal), hiding (informal), rout, trouncing

thrash out verb <u>settle</u>, argue out, debate, discuss, have out, resolve, solve, talk over

thread noun 1 <u>strand</u>, fibre, filament, line, string, yarn 2 <u>theme</u>, direction, drift, plot, story line, train of thought ♦ verb 3 <u>string</u> 4 <u>pass</u>, ease, pick (one's way), squeeze through

threadbare adjective 1 <u>shabby</u>, down at heel, frayed, old, ragged, scruffy, tattered, tatty, worn 2 <u>hackneyed</u>, commonplace, conventional, familiar, overused, stale, stereotyped, tired, trite, well-worn

> ➤ **Antonyms**
≠<u>shabby</u>: brand-new, new, smart, unused, well-preserved ≠<u>hackneyed</u>: different, fresh, new, novel, original, unconventional, unfamiliar, unusual

threat noun 1 <u>menace</u>, threatening remark 2 <u>warning</u>, foreboding, foreshadowing, omen, portent, presage, writing on the wall 3 <u>danger</u>, hazard, menace, peril, risk

threaten verb 1 <u>intimidate</u>, browbeat, bully, lean on (slang), menace, pressurize, terrorize 2 <u>endanger</u>, imperil, jeopardize, put at risk, put in jeopardy, put on the line 3 <u>foreshadow</u>, forebode, impend, portend, presage

➤ **Antonyms**

≠intimidate, endanger: defend, guard, protect, safeguard, shelter, shield

threatening _adjective_ **1** menacing, bullying, intimidatory **2** ominous, forbidding, grim, inauspicious, sinister

➤ **Antonyms**

≠ominous: auspicious, comforting, encouraging, favourable, promising, reassuring

threshold _noun_ **1** entrance, door, doorstep, doorway **2** start, beginning, brink, dawn, inception, opening, outset, verge **3** minimum, lower limit

➤ **Antonyms**

≠start: close, decline, end, finish, twilight

thrift _noun_ economy, carefulness, frugality, parsimony, prudence, saving, thriftiness

➤ **Antonyms**

carelessness, extravagance, prodigality, profligacy, recklessness, squandering, waste

thrifty _adjective_ economical, careful, frugal, parsimonious, provident, prudent, saving, sparing

➤ **Antonyms**

extravagant, free-spending, generous, improvident, prodigal, spendthrift, wasteful

thrill _noun_ **1** pleasure, buzz (_slang_), kick (_informal_), stimulation, tingle, titillation ◆ _verb_ **2** excite, arouse, electrify, move, stimulate, stir, titillate

➤ **Antonyms**

noun ≠pleasure: boredom, dreariness, dullness, ennui, monotony, tedium

thrilling _adjective_ exciting, electrifying, gripping, riveting, rousing, sensational, stimulating, stirring

➤ **Antonyms**

boring, dreary, dull, monotonous, tedious, tiresome, uninteresting

thrive _verb_ prosper, boom, develop, do well, flourish, get on,

grow, increase, succeed

➤ **Antonyms**

decline, languish, stagnate, wane, wither

thriving _adjective_ successful, blooming, booming, burgeoning, flourishing, healthy, prosperous, well

➤ **Antonyms**

ailing, failing, languishing, on the rocks, unsuccessful

throb _verb_ **1** pulsate, beat, palpitate, pound, pulse, thump, vibrate ◆ _noun_ **2** pulse, beat, palpitation, pounding, pulsating, thump, thumping, vibration

throng _noun_ **1** crowd, crush, horde, host, mass, mob, multitude, pack, swarm ◆ _verb_ **2** crowd, congregate, converge, flock, mill around, pack, swarm around

➤ **Antonyms**

verb ≠crowd: disband, disperse, scatter, separate, spread out

throttle _verb_ strangle, choke, garrotte, strangulate

through _preposition_ **1** from one side to the other of, between, by, past **2** because of, by means of, by way of, using, via **3** during, in, throughout ◆ _adjective_ **4** completed, done, ended, finished ◆ _adverb_ **5** through and through completely, altogether, entirely, fully, thoroughly, totally, utterly, wholly

throughout _preposition_ **1** through the whole of, all over, everywhere in, right through ◆ _adverb_ **2** from start to finish, right through

throw _verb_ **1** hurl, cast, chuck (_informal_), fling, launch, lob (_informal_), pitch, send, sling, toss **2** _Informal_ confuse, astonish, baffle, confound, disconcert, dumbfound, faze ◆ _noun_ **3** toss, fling, heave, lob (_informal_), pitch, sling

throwaway _adjective_ _Chiefly Brit._ casual, careless, offhand, passing, understated

throw away _verb_ discard, dispense with, dispose of, ditch

thrust *(slang)*, dump *(informal)*, get rid of, jettison, reject, scrap, throw out

➤ **Antonyms**

conserve, keep, preserve, retain, retrieve, salvage, save

thrust *verb* **1** push, drive, force, jam, plunge, propel, ram, shove ◆ *noun* **2** push, drive, lunge, poke, prod, shove, stab **3** momentum, impetus

thud *noun, verb* thump, crash, knock, smack

thug *noun* ruffian, bruiser *(informal)*, bully boy, gangster, heavy *(slang)*, hooligan, tough

thump *noun* **1** thud, bang, clunk, crash, thwack **2** blow, clout *(informal)*, knock, punch, rap, smack, swipe, wallop *(informal)*, whack ◆ *verb* **3** strike, beat, clobber *(slang)*, clout *(informal)*, hit, knock, pound, punch, smack, swipe, wallop *(informal)*, whack

thunder *noun* **1** rumble, boom, crash, explosion ◆ *verb* **2** rumble, boom, crash, peal, resound, reverberate, roar **3** shout, bark, bellow, roar, yell

thunderous *adjective* loud, booming, deafening, ear-splitting, noisy, resounding, roaring, tumultuous

thunderstruck *adjective* amazed, astonished, astounded, dumbfounded, flabbergasted *(informal)*, open-mouthed, shocked, staggered, stunned, taken aback

thus *adverb* **1** therefore, accordingly, consequently, ergo, for this reason, hence, on that account, so, then **2** in this way, as follows, like this, so

thwart *verb* frustrate, foil, hinder, obstruct, outwit, prevent, snooker, stymie

➤ **Antonyms**

aid, assist, encourage, facilitate, help, support

tick¹ *noun* **1** mark, dash, stroke **2** tapping, clicking, ticktock **3** *Brit. informal* moment, flash, instant, minute, second, split second, trice, twinkling ◆ *verb* **4** mark, check off, indicate **5** tap, click, ticktock

tick² *noun Brit. informal* credit, account, the slate *(Brit. informal)*

ticket *noun* **1** voucher, card, certificate, coupon, pass, slip, token **2** label, card, docket, marker, slip, sticker, tab, tag

tide *noun* **1** current, ebb, flow, stream, tideway, undertow **2** tendency, direction, drift, movement, trend

tidy *adjective* **1** neat, clean, methodical, orderly, shipshape, spruce, well-kept, well-ordered **2** *Informal* considerable, ample, generous, goodly, handsome, healthy, large, sizable or sizeable, substantial ◆ *verb* **3** neaten, clean, groom, order, spruce up, straighten

➤ **Antonyms**

adjective ≠neat: disordered, in disarray, messy, unkempt, unmethodical, unsystematic, untidy ≠considerable: inconsiderable, insignificant, little, small, tiny ◆ *verb* ≠neaten: dirty, dishevel, disorder, mess, mess up

tie *verb* **1** fasten, attach, bind, connect, join, knot, link, secure, tether **2** restrict, bind, confine, hamper, hinder, limit, restrain **3** draw, equal, match ◆ *noun* **4** bond, affiliation, allegiance, commitment, connection, liaison, relationship **5** fastening, bond, cord, fetter, knot, ligature, link **6** draw, dead heat, deadlock, stalemate

➤ **Antonyms**

verb ≠fasten: free, loose, release, separate, undo, unfasten, untie ≠restrict: free, release

tier *noun* row, bank, layer, level, line, rank, storey, stratum

tight *adjective* **1** taut, rigid, stretched **2** close-fitting, close, constricted, cramped, narrow, snug **3** secure, fast, firm, fixed **4** *Informal* miserly, grasping, mean, niggardly, parsimonious, stingy, tightfisted **5** close, even, evenly-balanced, well-matched **6** *Infor-*

mal <u>drunk</u>, inebriated, intoxicated, paralytic (*informal*), plastered (*slang*), tipsy, under the influence (*informal*)

➤ **Antonyms**

≠<u>taut</u>: relaxed, slack ≠<u>close-fitting</u>: loose, slack ≠<u>miserly</u>: abundant, extravagant, generous, lavish, open, prodigal, profuse, spendthrift ≠<u>close</u>: easy, landslide, overwhelming, runaway, uneven ≠<u>drunk</u>: sober

tighten *verb* <u>squeeze</u>, close, constrict, narrow

➤ **Antonyms**

ease off, let out, slacken

till[1] *verb* <u>cultivate</u>, dig, plough, work

till[2] *noun* <u>cash register</u>, cash box

tilt *verb* **1** <u>slant</u>, heel, incline, lean, list, slope, tip ♦ *noun* **2** <u>slope</u>, angle, inclination, incline, list, pitch, slant **3** *Medieval history* <u>joust</u>, combat, duel, fight, lists, tournament **4** (at) <u>full tilt</u> <u>full speed</u>, for dear life, headlong

timber *noun* **1** <u>wood</u>, beams, boards, logs, planks **2** <u>trees</u>, forest

timbre *noun* <u>tone</u>, colour, resonance, ring

time *noun* **1** <u>period</u>, duration, interval, season, space, span, spell, stretch, term **2** <u>occasion</u>, instance, juncture, point, stage **3** <u>tempo</u>, beat, measure, rhythm ♦ *verb* **4** <u>schedule</u>, set

timeless *adjective* <u>eternal</u>, ageless, changeless, enduring, everlasting, immortal, lasting, permanent

➤ **Antonyms**

ephemeral, momentary, passing, temporary, transitory

timely *adjective* <u>opportune</u>, appropriate, convenient, judicious, propitious, seasonable, suitable, well-timed

➤ **Antonyms**

ill-timed, inconvenient, inopportune, late, tardy, unseasonable, untimely

timetable *noun* <u>schedule</u>, agenda, calendar, curriculum, diary,

list, programme

timid *adjective* <u>fearful</u>, apprehensive, bashful, coy, diffident, faint-hearted, shrinking, shy, timorous

➤ **Antonyms**

aggressive, bold, brave, confident, daring, fearless, forceful, self-confident

timorous *adjective Literary* <u>timid</u>, apprehensive, bashful, coy, diffident, faint-hearted, fearful, shrinking, shy

➤ **Antonyms**

assertive, assured, audacious, bold, confident, courageous, daring, fearless

tinge *noun* **1** <u>tint</u>, colour, shade **2** <u>bit</u>, dash, drop, smattering, sprinkling, suggestion, touch, trace ♦ *verb* **3** <u>tint</u>, colour, imbue, suffuse

tingle *verb* **1** <u>prickle</u>, have goose pimples, itch, sting, tickle ♦ *noun* **2** <u>quiver</u>, goose pimples, itch, pins and needles (*informal*), prickling, shiver, thrill

tinker *verb* <u>meddle</u>, dabble, fiddle (*informal*), mess about, play, potter

tint *noun* **1** <u>shade</u>, colour, hue, tone **2** <u>dye</u>, rinse, tincture, tinge, wash ♦ *verb* **3** <u>dye</u>, colour

tiny *adjective* <u>small</u>, diminutive, infinitesimal, little, microscopic, miniature, minute, negligible, petite, slight

➤ **Antonyms**

colossal, enormous, gigantic, great, huge, immense, massive, vast

tip[1] *noun* **1** <u>end</u>, extremity, head, peak, pinnacle, point, summit, top ♦ *verb* **2** <u>cap</u>, crown, finish, surmount, top

tip[2] *noun* **1** <u>gratuity</u>, gift **2** <u>hint</u>, pointer, suggestion ♦ *verb* **3** <u>reward</u>, remunerate **4** <u>advise</u>, suggest

tip[3] *verb* **1** <u>tilt</u>, incline, lean, list, slant **2** *Brit.* <u>dump</u>, empty, pour out, unload ♦ *noun* **3** *Brit.* <u>dump</u>, refuse heap, rubbish heap

tip-off *noun* <u>hint</u>, clue, pointer, suggestion, warning

tip off verb <u>advise</u>, caution, forewarn, suggest, warn

tipple verb 1 <u>drink</u>, imbibe, indulge (*informal*), quaff, swig, tope ♦ noun 2 <u>alcohol</u>, booze (*informal*), drink, liquor

tirade noun <u>outburst</u>, diatribe, fulmination, harangue, invective, lecture

tire verb 1 <u>exhaust</u>, drain, fatigue, wear out, weary 2 <u>flag</u>, fail 3 *usually passive* <u>bore</u>, exasperate, irk, irritate, weary

► **Antonyms**

≠exhaust: energize, enliven, invigorate, liven up, refresh, restore, revive

tired adjective 1 <u>exhausted</u>, drained, drowsy, fatigued, flagging, sleepy, weary, worn out 2 <u>bored</u>, fed up, sick, weary 3 <u>hackneyed</u>, clichéd, corny (*slang*), old, outworn, stale, threadbare, trite, well-worn

► **Antonyms**

≠exhausted: energetic, fresh, full of beans (*informal*), lively, refreshed, rested, wide-awake ≠bored: enthusiastic about, fond of, keen on ≠hackneyed: innovative, original

tireless adjective <u>energetic</u>, indefatigable, industrious, resolute, unflagging, untiring, vigorous

► **Antonyms**

drained, exhausted, fatigued, flagging, tired, weak, weary, worn out

tiresome adjective <u>boring</u>, dull, irksome, irritating, tedious, trying, vexatious, wearing, wearisome

► **Antonyms**

exhilarating, inspiring, interesting, refreshing, rousing, stimulating

tiring adjective <u>exhausting</u>, arduous, demanding, exacting, laborious, strenuous, tough, wearing

titbit noun <u>delicacy</u>, dainty, morsel, snack, treat

titillate verb <u>excite</u>, arouse, interest, stimulate, tantalize, tease, thrill

titillating adjective <u>exciting</u>, arousing, interesting, lurid, provocative, stimulating, suggestive, teasing

title noun 1 <u>name</u>, designation, handle (*slang*), moniker or monicker (*slang*), term 2 *Sport* <u>championship</u>, crown 3 *Law* <u>ownership</u>, claim, entitlement, prerogative, privilege, right

titter verb <u>snigger</u>, chortle (*informal*), chuckle, giggle, laugh

toady noun 1 <u>sycophant</u>, bootlicker (*informal*), crawler (*slang*), creep (*slang*), flatterer, flunkey, hanger-on, lackey, minion, yes man ♦ verb 2 <u>fawn on</u>, crawl, creep, cringe, flatter, grovel, kowtow to, pander to, suck up to (*informal*)

► **Antonyms**

verb ≠fawn on: defy, oppose, rebel, resist, stand against, withstand

toast[1] verb 1 <u>brown</u>, grill, roast 2 <u>warm</u>, heat

toast[2] noun 1 <u>tribute</u>, compliment, health, pledge, salutation, salute 2 <u>favourite</u>, darling, hero or heroine ♦ verb 3 <u>drink to</u>, drink (to) the health of, salute

together adverb 1 <u>collectively</u>, as one, hand in glove, in concert, in unison, jointly, mutually, shoulder to shoulder, side by side 2 <u>at the same time</u>, at one fell swoop, concurrently, contemporaneously, simultaneously ♦ adjective 3 *Slang* <u>self-possessed</u>, composed, well-adjusted, well-balanced

► **Antonyms**

adverb ≠collectively: alone, apart, independently, individually, one at a time, one by one, separately, singly

toil noun 1 <u>hard work</u>, application, drudgery, effort, elbow grease (*informal*), exertion, graft (*informal*), slog, sweat ♦ verb 2 <u>labour</u>, drudge, graft (*informal*), slave, slog, strive, struggle, sweat (*informal*), work, work one's fingers to the bone

> ➤ Antonyms

noun ≠hard work: idleness, inactivity, indolence, inertia, laziness, sloth, torpor

toilet noun lavatory, bathroom, convenience, gents or ladies (Brit. informal), ladies' room, latrine, loo (Brit. informal), privy, urinal, water closet, W.C.

token noun 1 symbol, badge, expression, indication, mark, note, representation, sign ✦ adjective 2 nominal, hollow, minimal, perfunctory, superficial, symbolic

tolerable adjective 1 bearable, acceptable, allowable, endurable, sufferable, supportable 2 Informal fair, acceptable, adequate, all right, average, O.K. or okay (informal), passable

> ➤ Antonyms

≠bearable: insufferable, intolerable, unacceptable, unbearable, unendurable ≠fair: awful, bad, dreadful, rotten

tolerance noun 1 broad-mindedness, forbearance, indulgence, open-mindedness, permissiveness 2 endurance, fortitude, hardiness, resilience, resistance, stamina, staying power, toughness

> ➤ Antonyms

≠broad-mindedness: bigotry, discrimination, intolerance, narrow-mindedness, prejudice, sectarianism

tolerant adjective, broad-minded, catholic, forbearing, liberal, long-suffering, open-minded, understanding, unprejudiced

> ➤ Antonyms

biased, bigoted, dogmatic, illiberal, intolerant, narrow-minded, prejudiced, sectarian

tolerate verb 1 allow, accept, brook, condone, permit, put up with (informal), take 2 endure, put up with (informal), stand, stomach, take

> ➤ Antonyms

≠allow: ban, disallow, disapprove, forbid, outlaw, preclude, prohibit, veto

toleration noun acceptance, allowance, endurance, indulgence, permissiveness, sanction

toll[1] verb 1 ring, chime, clang, knell, peal, sound, strike ✦ noun 2 ringing, chime, clang, knell, peal

toll[2] noun 1 charge, duty, fee, levy, payment, tariff, tax 2 damage, cost, loss, penalty

tomb noun grave, catacomb, crypt, mausoleum, sarcophagus, sepulchre, vault

tombstone noun gravestone, headstone, marker, memorial, monument

tomfoolery noun foolishness, buffoonery, clowning, fooling around (informal), horseplay, shenanigans (informal), silliness, skylarking (informal), stupidity

> ➤ Antonyms

gravity, seriousness, sobriety, solemnity

tone noun 1 pitch, inflection, intonation, modulation, timbre 2 character, air, attitude, feel, manner, mood, spirit, style, temper 3 colour, hue, shade, tinge, tint ✦ verb 4 harmonize, blend, go well with, match, suit

tone down verb moderate, play down, reduce, restrain, soften, subdue, temper

tongue noun language, dialect, parlance, speech

tonic noun stimulant, boost, fillip, pick-me-up (informal), restorative, shot in the arm (informal)

too adverb 1 also, as well, besides, further, in addition, likewise, moreover, to boot 2 excessively, extremely, immoderately, inordinately, overly, unduly, unreasonably, very

tool noun 1 implement, appliance, contraption, contrivance, device, gadget, instrument, machine, utensil 2 puppet, cat's-paw, creature, flunkey, hireling, lackey, minion, pawn, stooge (slang)

top noun 1 peak, apex, crest, crown, culmination, head,

height, pinnacle, summit, zenith **2** first place, head, lead **3** lid, cap, cover, stopper ♦ *adjective* **4** leading, best, chief, elite, finest, first, foremost, head, highest, pre-eminent, principal, uppermost ♦ *verb* **5** cover, cap, crown, finish, garnish **6** lead, be first, head **7** surpass, beat, better, eclipse, exceed, excel, outstrip, transcend

➤ **Antonyms**

noun ≠peak: base, bottom, foot, nadir, underneath, underside ♦ *adjective* ≠leading: inferior, second-rate ♦ *verb* ≠surpass: fail to equal, fall short of, not be as good as

topic *noun* subject, issue, matter, point, question, subject matter, theme

topical *adjective* current, contemporary, newsworthy, popular, up-to-date, up-to-the-minute

topmost *adjective* highest, dominant, foremost, leading, paramount, principal, supreme, top, uppermost

➤ **Antonyms**

bottom, bottommost, last, lowest

topple *verb* **1** fall over, collapse, fall, keel over, overbalance, overturn, totter, tumble **2** overthrow, bring down, bring low, oust, overturn, unseat

topsy-turvy *adjective* confused, chaotic, disorderly, disorganized, inside-out, jumbled, messy, mixed-up, upside-down

➤ **Antonyms**

neat, ordered, orderly, organized, shipshape, systematic, tidy

torment *verb* **1** torture, crucify, distress, rack **2** tease, annoy, bother, harass, hassle (*informal*), irritate, nag, pester, vex ♦ *noun* **3** suffering, agony, anguish, distress, hell, misery, pain, torture

➤ **Antonyms**

verb ≠torture: comfort, delight, ease, encourage, make happy, put at ease, reassure, soothe ♦ *noun* ≠suffering: bliss, comfort, ease, ecstasy, happiness, joy

torn *adjective* **1** cut, lacerated, ragged, rent, ripped, slit, split **2** undecided, in two minds (*informal*), irresolute, uncertain, unsure, vacillating, wavering

tornado *noun* whirlwind, cyclone, gale, hurricane, squall, storm, tempest, typhoon

torpor *noun* inactivity, apathy, drowsiness, indolence, laziness, lethargy, listlessness, sloth, sluggishness

➤ **Antonyms**

animation, energy, get-up-and-go (*informal*), go, liveliness, pep, vigour

torrent *noun* stream, cascade, deluge, downpour, flood, flow, rush, spate, tide

torrid *adjective* **1** arid, dried, parched, scorched **2** passionate, ardent, fervent, intense, steamy (*informal*)

tortuous *adjective* **1** winding, circuitous, convoluted, indirect, mazy, meandering, serpentine, sinuous, twisting, twisty **2** complicated, ambiguous, convoluted, devious, indirect, involved, roundabout, tricky

➤ **Antonyms**

≠complicated: direct, honest, open, reliable, straightforward

torture *verb* **1** torment, afflict, crucify, distress, persecute, put on the rack, rack ♦ *noun* **2** agony, anguish, distress, pain, persecution, suffering, torment

➤ **Antonyms**

verb ≠torment: comfort, console, ease, mollify, salve, soothe ♦ *noun* ≠agony: bliss, delight, enjoyment, happiness, joy, pleasure, well-being

toss *verb* **1** throw, cast, fling, flip, hurl, launch, lob (*informal*), pitch, sling **2** thrash, rock, roll, shake, wriggle, writhe ♦ *noun* **3** throw, lob (*informal*), pitch

tot *noun* **1** infant, baby, child, mite, toddler **2** measure, dram, finger, nip, shot (*informal*), slug, snifter (*informal*)

total *noun* **1** whole, aggregate,

entirety, full amount, sum, totality ♦ *adjective* **2** complete, absolute, comprehensive, entire, full, gross, overarching, thoroughgoing, undivided, utter, whole ♦ *verb* **3** amount to, come to, mount up to, reach **4** add up, reckon, tot up

➤ **Antonyms**

noun ≠whole: part, subtotal ♦ *adjective* ≠complete: fragmentary, incomplete, partial, qualified, restricted ♦ *verb* ≠add up: deduct, subtract

totalitarian *adjective* dictatorial, authoritarian, despotic, oppressive, tyrannous, undemocratic

➤ **Antonyms**

autonomous, democratic, egalitarian, popular, self-governing

totality *noun* whole, aggregate, entirety, sum, total

totally *adverb* completely, absolutely, comprehensively, entirely, fully, one hundred per cent, thoroughly, utterly, wholly

➤ **Antonyms**

incompletely, in part, partially, partly, somewhat, to a certain extent

totter *verb* stagger, falter, lurch, reel, stumble, sway, wobble

tot up *verb* add up, calculate, count up, reckon, tally, total

touch *verb* **1** handle, brush, caress, contact, feel, finger, fondle, stroke **2** tap **3** come into contact, abut, adjoin, be in contact, border, contact, graze, impinge upon, meet **4** affect, impress, influence, inspire **5** move, disturb, stir **6** consume, drink, eat, partake of **7** match, compare with, equal, hold a candle to (*informal*), parallel, rival **8** touch on refer to, allude to, bring in, cover, deal with, mention, speak of ♦ *noun* **9** feeling, handling, physical contact **10** contact, brush, caress, stroke **11** tap, pat **12** bit, dash, drop, jot, small amount, smattering, soupçon, spot, trace **13** style, manner, method, technique, trademark, way

touch and go *adjective* risky, close, critical, near, nerve-racking, precarious

touching *adjective* moving, affecting, emotive, pathetic, pitiable, poignant, sad, stirring

touchstone *noun* standard, criterion, gauge, measure, norm, par, yardstick

touchy *adjective* oversensitive, irascible, irritable, querulous, quick-tempered, testy, tetchy, thin-skinned

➤ **Antonyms**

affable, easy-going, genial, good-humoured, insensitive, thick-skinned

tough *adjective* **1** resilient, durable, hard, inflexible, leathery, resistant, rugged, solid, strong, sturdy **2** strong, hardy, seasoned, stout, strapping, sturdy, vigorous **3** rough, hard-bitten, pugnacious, ruthless, violent **4** strict, firm, hard, merciless, resolute, severe, stern, unbending **5** difficult, arduous, exacting, hard, laborious, strenuous, troublesome, uphill **6** *As in* tough luck! *Informal* unlucky, lamentable, regrettable, unfortunate ♦ *noun* **7** ruffian, bruiser (*informal*), bully, hooligan, roughneck (*slang*), thug

➤ **Antonyms**

adjective ≠resilient: delicate, flexible, flimsy, fragile, soft, tender, weak ≠strong: delicate, soft, weak ≠rough: civilized, gentle, humane, soft, tender ≠strict: accommodating, compassionate, flexible, indulgent, lenient, merciful, soft, sympathetic ≠difficult: easy, easy-peasy (*slang*), unexacting

tour *noun* **1** journey, excursion, expedition, jaunt, outing, trip ♦ *verb* **2** visit, explore, go round, journey, sightsee, travel through

tourist *noun* traveller, excursionist, globetrotter, holiday-maker, sightseer, tripper, voyager

tournament *noun* competition, contest, event, meeting, series

tow verb <u>drag</u>, draw, haul, lug, pull, tug, yank

towards preposition 1 <u>in the direction of</u>, en route for, for, on the way to, to 2 <u>regarding</u>, about, concerning, for, with regard to, with respect to

tower noun <u>column</u>, belfry, obelisk, pillar, skyscraper, steeple, turret

towering adjective 1 <u>tall</u>, colossal, elevated, high, lofty, soaring 2 <u>impressive</u>, imposing, magnificent

toxic adjective <u>poisonous</u>, deadly, harmful, lethal, noxious, pernicious, pestilential, septic

➤ **Antonyms**
harmless, non-poisonous, non-toxic, safe

toy noun 1 <u>plaything</u>, doll, game ◆ verb **toy with** 2 <u>play</u>, amuse oneself with, dally with, fool (about or around) with, trifle 3 <u>fiddle</u> (informal), play

trace verb 1 <u>find</u>, detect, discover, ferret out, hunt down, track, unearth 2 <u>copy</u> 3 <u>outline</u>, draw, sketch ◆ noun 4 <u>track</u>, footmark, footprint, footstep, path, spoor, trail 5 <u>bit</u>, drop, hint, shadow, suggestion, suspicion, tinge, touch, whiff 6 <u>remnant</u>, evidence, indication, mark, record, sign, survival, vestige

track noun 1 <u>path</u>, course, line, orbit, pathway, road, trajectory, way 2 <u>trail</u>, footmark, footprint, footstep, mark, path, spoor, trace, wake 3 <u>line</u>, permanent way, rails ◆ verb 4 <u>follow</u>, chase, hunt down, pursue, shadow, stalk, tail (informal), trace, trail

track down verb <u>find</u>, dig up, discover, hunt down, run to earth or ground, sniff out, trace, unearth

tract¹ noun <u>area</u>, district, expanse, extent, plot, region, stretch, territory

tract² noun <u>treatise</u>, booklet, dissertation, essay, homily, monograph, pamphlet

tractable adjective Formal <u>man-</u> <u>ageable</u>, amenable, biddable, compliant, docile, obedient, submissive, tame, willing, yielding

➤ **Antonyms**
defiant, headstrong, obstinate, refractory, stubborn, unruly, wilful

traction noun 1 <u>pulling</u>, pull 2 <u>grip</u>, friction, purchase, resistance

trade noun 1 <u>commerce</u>, barter, business, dealing, exchange, traffic, transactions, truck 2 <u>job</u>, business, craft, employment, line of work, métier, occupation, profession ◆ verb 3 <u>deal</u>, bargain, cut a deal, do business, have dealings, peddle, traffic, transact, truck 4 <u>exchange</u>, barter, swap, switch

trader noun <u>dealer</u>, merchant, purveyor, seller, supplier

tradesman noun 1 <u>craftsman</u>, artisan, journeyman, workman 2 <u>shopkeeper</u>, dealer, merchant, purveyor, retailer, seller, supplier, vendor

tradition noun <u>custom</u>, convention, folklore, habit, institution, lore, ritual

traditional adjective <u>customary</u>, accustomed, conventional, established, old, time-honoured, usual

➤ **Antonyms**
avant-garde, contemporary, innovative, modern, new, novel, original, revolutionary, unconventional

traffic noun 1 <u>transport</u>, freight, transportation, vehicles 2 <u>trade</u>, business, commerce, dealings, exchange, peddling, truck ◆ verb 3 <u>trade</u>, bargain, cut a deal, deal, do business, exchange, have dealings, peddle

tragedy noun <u>disaster</u>, adversity, calamity, catastrophe, misfortune

➤ **Antonyms**
fortune, happiness, joy, prosperity, success

tragic adjective 1 <u>distressing</u>, appalling, calamitous, catastrophic, deadly, dire, disastrous, dreadful, sad, unfortunate 2 <u>sad</u>, miserable, mournful, pathetic

➤ **Antonyms**

≠*distressing*: beneficial, fortunate, lucky, satisfying, worthwhile ≠*sad*: cheerful, comic, happy, joyful

trail noun **1** path, footpath, road, route, track, way **2** tracks, footprints, marks, path, scent, spoor, trace, wake ♦ verb **3** drag, dangle, draw, haul, pull, tow **4** follow, chase, hunt, pursue, shadow, stalk, tail (*informal*), trace, track **5** lag, dawdle, follow, hang back, linger, loiter, straggle, traipse (*informal*)

train verb **1** instruct, coach, drill, educate, guide, prepare, school, teach, tutor **2** exercise, prepare, work out **3** aim, direct, focus, level, point ♦ noun **4** sequence, chain, progression, series, set, string, succession

trainer noun coach, handler

training noun **1** instruction, coaching, discipline, education, grounding, schooling, teaching, tuition **2** exercise, practice, preparation, working out

traipse verb *Informal* trudge, drag oneself, footslog, slouch, trail, tramp

trait noun characteristic, attribute, feature, idiosyncrasy, mannerism, peculiarity, quality, quirk

traitor noun betrayer, apostate, back-stabber, defector, deserter, Judas, quisling, rebel, renegade, turncoat

➤ **Antonyms**

defender, loyalist, patriot, supporter

trajectory noun path, course, flight path, line, route, track

tramp verb **1** hike, footslog, march, ramble, roam, rove, slog, trek, walk **2** trudge, plod, stump, toil, traipse (*informal*) ♦ noun **3** vagrant, derelict, down-and-out, drifter **4** hike, march, ramble, slog, trek **5** tread, footfall, footstep, stamp

trample verb often with **on** crush, flatten, run over, squash, stamp,

tread, walk over

trance noun daze, abstraction, dream, rapture, reverie, stupor, unconsciousness

tranquil adjective calm, peaceful, placid, quiet, restful, sedate, serene, still, undisturbed

➤ **Antonyms**

agitated, busy, confused, disturbed, excited, hectic, restless, troubled

tranquillity noun calm, hush, peace, placidity, quiet, repose, rest, serenity, stillness

➤ **Antonyms**

agitation, commotion, confusion, disturbance, excitement, noise, restlessness, turmoil

tranquillize verb calm, lull, pacify, quell, quiet, relax, sedate, settle one's nerves, soothe

➤ **Antonyms**

agitate, confuse, distress, disturb, harass, perturb, ruffle, trouble, upset

tranquillizer noun sedative, barbiturate, bromide, downer (*slang*), opiate

transaction noun deal, bargain, business, enterprise, negotiation, undertaking

transcend verb surpass, eclipse, exceed, excel, go beyond, outdo, outstrip, rise above

transcendent adjective unparalleled, consummate, incomparable, matchless, pre-eminent, sublime, unequalled, unrivalled

transcribe verb write out, copy out, reproduce, take down, transfer

transcript noun copy, duplicate, manuscript, record, reproduction, transcription

transfer verb **1** move, change, convey, hand over, pass on, relocate, shift, transplant, transport, transpose ♦ noun **2** move, change, handover, relocation, shift, transference, translation, transmission, transposition

transfix verb **1** stun, engross, fascinate, hold, hypnotize, mesmerize, paralyse **2** pierce, impale, puncture, run through, skewer, spear

➤ **Antonyms**

≠ stun: bore, fatigue, tire, weary

transform verb change, alter, convert, remodel, revolutionize, transmute

transformation noun change, alteration, conversion, metamorphosis, revolution, sea change, transmutation

transgress verb Formal **1** break, break the law, contravene, disobey, infringe, offend, sin, trespass, violate **2** go beyond, encroach, exceed, overstep

transgression noun crime, contravention, encroachment, infraction, infringement, misdeed, misdemeanour, offence, sin, trespass, violation

transgressor noun criminal, culprit, lawbreaker, miscreant, offender, sinner, trespasser, villain, wrongdoer

transient adjective brief, ephemeral, fleeting, impermanent, momentary, passing, short-lived, temporary, transitory

➤ **Antonyms**

durable, enduring, eternal, long-lasting, permanent, perpetual, persistent, undying

transit noun movement, carriage, conveyance, crossing, passage, transfer, transport, transportation

transition noun change, alteration, conversion, development, metamorphosis, passing, progression, shift, transmutation

transitional adjective changing, developmental, fluid, intermediate, passing, provisional, temporary, unsettled

transitory adjective short-lived, brief, ephemeral, fleeting, impermanent, momentary, passing, short, temporary, transient

➤ **Antonyms**

enduring, eternal, lasting, long-term, permanent, perpetual, persistent, undying

translate verb interpret, con-

strue, convert, decipher, decode, paraphrase, render

translation noun interpretation, decoding, paraphrase, rendering, rendition, version

transmission noun **1** transfer, conveyance, dissemination, sending, shipment, spread, transference **2** broadcasting, dissemination, putting out, relaying, sending, showing **3** programme, broadcast, show

transmit verb **1** pass on, bear, carry, convey, disseminate, hand on, impart, send, spread, transfer **2** broadcast, disseminate, radio, relay, send out

transparency noun **1** clarity, clearness, limpidity, pellucidness, translucence **2** photograph, slide

➤ **Antonyms**

≠ clarity: cloudiness, murkiness, opacity, unclearness

transparent adjective **1** clear, crystalline, diaphanous, limpid, lucid, see-through, sheer, translucent **2** obvious, evident, explicit, manifest, patent, plain, recognizable, unambiguous, undisguised

➤ **Antonyms**

≠ clear: cloudy, muddy, opaque, thick, turbid, unclear ≠ obvious: hidden, mysterious, opaque, uncertain, unclear, vague

transpire verb **1** become known, come out, come to light, emerge **2** not universally accepted happen, arise, befall, chance, come about, occur, take place

transplant verb transfer, displace, relocate, remove, resettle, shift, uproot

transport verb **1** convey, bear, bring, carry, haul, move, take, transfer **2** History exile, banish, deport **3** enrapture, captivate, delight, enchant, entrance, move, ravish ◆ noun **4** vehicle, conveyance, transportation **5** transference, conveyance, shipment, transportation **6** ecstasy, bliss, delight, enchantment, euphoria, heaven, rapture, ravishment

> ➤ **Antonyms**

noun ≠*ecstasy*: depression, despondency, doldrums, dumps (*informal*), melancholy

transpose *verb* <u>interchange</u>, alter, change, exchange, move, reorder, shift, substitute, swap, switch, transfer

trap *noun* **1** <u>snare</u>, ambush, gin, net, noose, pitfall **2** <u>trick</u>, ambush, deception, ruse, stratagem, subterfuge, wile ♦ *verb* **3** <u>catch</u>, corner, enmesh, ensnare, entrap, snare, take **4** <u>trick</u>, ambush, beguile, deceive, dupe, ensnare, inveigle

trappings *plural noun* <u>accessories</u>, accoutrements, equipment, finery, furnishings, gear, panoply, paraphernalia, things, trimmings

trash *noun* **1** <u>nonsense</u>, drivel, hogwash, moonshine, poppycock (*informal*), rot, rubbish, tripe (*informal*), twaddle **2** *Chiefly U.S. & Canad.* <u>litter</u>, dross, garbage, junk (*informal*), refuse, rubbish, waste

> ➤ **Antonyms**

≠*nonsense*: logic, reason, sense, significance

trashy *adjective* <u>worthless</u>, cheap, inferior, rubbishy, shabby, shoddy, tawdry

> ➤ **Antonyms**

excellent, exceptional, first-class, first-rate, outstanding, superlative

trauma *noun* **1** <u>shock</u>, anguish, ordeal, pain, suffering, torture **2** <u>injury</u>, agony, damage, hurt, wound

traumatic *adjective* **1** <u>shocking</u>, disturbing, painful, scarring, upsetting **2** <u>wounding</u>, agonizing, damaging, hurtful, injurious

> ➤ **Antonyms**

≠*shocking*: calming, relaxing, therapeutic ≠*wounding*: healing, helpful, therapeutic, wholesome

travel *verb* **1** <u>go</u>, journey, move, progress, roam, tour, trek, voyage, wander ♦ *noun* **2** *usually plural* <u>journey</u>, excursion, expedi-

tion, globetrotting, tour, trip, voyage, wandering

traveller *noun* <u>voyager</u>, explorer, globetrotter, <u>gypsy</u>, holidaymaker, tourist, wanderer, wayfarer

travelling *adjective* <u>itinerant</u>, migrant, mobile, nomadic, peripatetic, roaming, roving, touring, wandering, wayfaring

traverse *verb* <u>cross</u>, go over, span, travel over

travesty *noun* **1** <u>mockery</u>, burlesque, caricature, distortion, lampoon, parody, perversion ♦ *verb* **2** <u>mock</u>, burlesque, caricature, distort, lampoon, make a mockery of, parody, ridicule

treacherous *adjective* **1** <u>disloyal</u>, deceitful, double-dealing, duplicitous, faithless, false, perfidious, traitorous, unfaithful, untrustworthy **2** <u>dangerous</u>, deceptive, hazardous, icy, perilous, precarious, risky, slippery, unreliable, unsafe, unstable

> ➤ **Antonyms**

≠*disloyal*: dependable, faithful, loyal, reliable, true, trustworthy ≠*dangerous*: reliable, safe

treachery *noun* <u>betrayal</u>, disloyalty, double-dealing, duplicity, faithlessness, infidelity, perfidy, treason

> ➤ **Antonyms**

allegiance, dependability, faithfulness, fidelity, loyalty, reliability

tread *verb* **1** <u>crush underfoot</u>, squash, trample **2** <u>step</u>, hike, march, pace, stamp, stride, walk ♦ *noun* **3** <u>step</u>, footfall, footstep, gait, pace, stride, walk

treason *noun* <u>disloyalty</u>, duplicity, lese-majesty, mutiny, perfidy, sedition, traitorousness, treachery

> ➤ **Antonyms**

allegiance, faithfulness, fidelity, loyalty, patriotism

treasonable *adjective* <u>disloyal</u>, mutinous, perfidious, seditious, subversive, traitorous, treacherous

> ➤ **Antonyms**

dependable, faithful, loyal, patriotic, reliable, trustworthy

treasure noun 1 riches, cash, fortune, gold, jewels, money, valuables, wealth 2 Informal darling, apple of one's eye, gem, jewel, nonpareil, paragon, pride and joy ♦ verb 3 prize, adore, cherish, esteem, hold dear, idolize, love, revere, value

treasury noun storehouse, bank, cache, hoard, repository, store, vault

treat verb 1 behave towards, act towards, consider, deal with, handle, look upon, manage, regard, use 2 take care of, attend to, care for, nurse 3 provide, entertain, lay on, regale, stand (informal) ♦ noun 4 entertainment, banquet, celebration, feast, gift, party, refreshment 5 pleasure, delight, enjoyment, fun, joy, satisfaction, surprise, thrill

treatise noun paper, dissertation, essay, monograph, pamphlet, study, thesis, tract, work

treatment noun 1 care, cure, healing, medication, medicine, remedy, surgery, therapy 2 handling, action, behaviour, conduct, dealing, management, manipulation

treaty noun agreement, alliance, compact, concordat, contract, convention, covenant, entente, pact

trek noun 1 journey, expedition, hike, march, odyssey, safari, slog, tramp ♦ verb 2 journey, footslog, hike, march, rove, slog, traipse (informal), tramp, trudge

tremble verb 1 shake, quake, quiver, shiver, shudder, totter, vibrate, wobble ♦ noun 2 shake, quake, quiver, shiver, shudder, tremor, vibration, wobble

tremendous adjective 1 huge, colossal, enormous, formidable, gigantic, great, immense, stupendous, terrific 2 excellent, amazing, brilliant, exceptional, extraordinary, fantastic (informal), great, marvellous, sensational (informal), wonderful

> **Antonyms**

≠huge: diminutive, little, minuscule, minute, small, tiny ≠excellent: abysmal, appalling, awful, dreadful, rotten, terrible

tremor noun 1 shake, quaking, quaver, quiver, shiver, trembling, wobble 2 earthquake, quake (informal), shock

trench noun ditch, channel, drain, excavation, furrow, gutter, trough

trenchant adjective 1 scathing, acerbic, caustic, cutting, incisive, penetrating, pointed, pungent 2 effective, energetic, forceful, potent, powerful, strong, vigorous

> **Antonyms**

≠scathing: appeasing, kind, mollifying, soothing

trend noun 1 tendency, bias, current, direction, drift, flow, inclination, leaning 2 fashion, craze, fad (informal), mode, rage, style, thing, vogue

trendy adjective Brit. informal fashionable, in fashion, in vogue, modish, stylish, voguish, with it (informal)

trepidation noun Formal anxiety, alarm, apprehension, consternation, disquiet, dread, fear, nervousness, uneasiness, worry

> **Antonyms**

aplomb, calm, composure, confidence, coolness, equanimity, self-assurance

trespass verb 1 intrude, encroach, infringe, invade, obtrude ♦ noun 2 intrusion, encroachment, infringement, invasion, unlawful entry

trespasser noun intruder, interloper, invader, poacher

trial noun 1 Law hearing, litigation, tribunal 2 test, audition, dry run (informal), experiment, probation, test-run 3 hardship, adversity, affliction, distress, ordeal, suffering, tribulation, trouble

tribe noun race, clan, family, people

tribunal noun hearing, court, trial

tribute noun **1** <u>accolade</u>, commendation, compliment, eulogy, panegyric, recognition, testimonial **2** <u>tax</u>, charge, homage, payment, ransom

► **Antonyms**

≠<u>accolade</u>: blame, complaint, condemnation, criticism, disapproval, reproach, reproof

trick noun **1** <u>deception</u>, fraud, hoax, manoeuvre, ploy, ruse, stratagem, subterfuge, swindle, trap, wile **2** <u>joke</u>, antic, jape, legpull (*Brit. informal*), practical joke, prank, stunt **3** <u>secret</u>, hang (*informal*), knack, know-how (*informal*), skill, technique **4** <u>sleight of hand</u>, legerdemain **5** <u>mannerism</u>, characteristic, foible, habit, idiosyncrasy, peculiarity, practice, quirk, trait ◆ verb **6** <u>deceive</u>, cheat, con (*informal*), dupe, fool, hoodwink, kid (*informal*), mislead, swindle, take in (*informal*), trap

trickery noun <u>deception</u>, cheating, chicanery, deceit, dishonesty, guile, jiggery-pokery (*informal, chiefly Brit.*), monkey business (*informal*)

► **Antonyms**

candour, directness, frankness, honesty, openness, straightforwardness

trickle verb **1** <u>dribble</u>, drip, drop, exude, ooze, run, seep, stream ◆ noun **2** <u>dribble</u>, drip, seepage

tricky adjective **1** <u>difficult</u>, complicated, delicate, knotty, problematic, risky, thorny, ticklish **2** <u>crafty</u>, artful, cunning, deceitful, devious, scheming, slippery, sly, wily

► **Antonyms**

≠<u>difficult</u>: clear, easy, obvious, simple, straightforward, uncomplicated ≠<u>crafty</u>: genuine, honest, ingenuous, open, sincere, truthful

trifle¹ noun <u>knick-knack</u>, bagatelle, bauble, plaything, toy

trifle² verb <u>toy</u>, dally, mess about, play

trifling adjective <u>insignificant</u>,

measly, negligible, paltry, trivial, unimportant, worthless

► **Antonyms**

considerable, crucial, important, large, major, serious, significant, vital, weighty

trigger verb <u>set off</u>, activate, cause, generate, produce, prompt, provoke, spark off, start

► **Antonyms**

block, hinder, impede, inhibit, obstruct, prevent, repress, stop

trim adjective **1** <u>neat</u>, dapper, natty (*informal*), shipshape, smart, spruce, tidy, well-groomed **2** <u>slender</u>, fit, shapely, sleek, slim, streamlined, svelte, willowy ◆ verb **3** <u>cut</u>, clip, crop, even up, pare, prune, shave, tidy **4** <u>decorate</u>, adorn, array, beautify, deck out, dress, embellish, ornament ◆ noun **5** <u>decoration</u>, adornment, border, edging, embellishment, frill, ornamentation, piping, trimming **6** <u>condition</u>, fettle, fitness, health, shape (*informal*), state, wellness **7** <u>cut</u>, clipping, crop, pruning, shave, shearing, tidying up

► **Antonyms**

adjective ≠<u>neat</u>: disorderly, messy, scruffy, shabby, sloppy, ungroomed, unkempt, untidy

trimming noun **1** <u>decoration</u>, adornment, border, edging, embellishment, frill, ornamentation, piping **2** <u>trimmings</u> extras, accessories, accompaniments, frills, ornaments, paraphernalia, trappings

trinity noun <u>threesome</u>, triad, trio, triumvirate

trinket noun <u>ornament</u>, bagatelle, bauble, knick-knack, toy, trifle

trio noun <u>threesome</u>, triad, trilogy, trinity, triumvirate

trip noun **1** <u>journey</u>, errand, excursion, expedition, foray, jaunt, outing, run, tour, voyage **2** <u>stumble</u>, fall, misstep, slip ◆ verb **3** <u>stumble</u>, fall, lose one's footing, misstep, slip, tumble **4** <u>catch out</u>, trap **5** <u>skip</u>, dance, gambol, hop

triple adjective **1** threefold, three-way, tripartite ♦ verb **2** treble, increase threefold

trite adjective unoriginal, banal, clichéd, commonplace, hackneyed, stale, stereotyped, threadbare, tired

➤ **Antonyms**
exciting, fresh, interesting, novel, original, uncommon, unexpected, unfamiliar

triumph noun **1** joy, elation, exultation, happiness, jubilation, pride, rejoicing **2** success, accomplishment, achievement, attainment, conquest, coup, feat, victory ♦ verb **3** often with **over** succeed, overcome, prevail, prosper, vanquish, win **4** rejoice, celebrate, crow, exult, gloat, glory, revel

➤ **Antonyms**
noun ≠**success**: catastrophe, defeat, disaster, failure, fiasco, flop (informal), washout (informal) ♦ verb ≠**succeed**: come a cropper (informal), fail, fall, flop (informal), lose

triumphant adjective **1** victorious, cock-a-hoop, conquering, elated, exultant, proud, successful, winning **2** celebratory, jubilant

➤ **Antonyms**
≠**victorious**: beaten, defeated, embarrassed, humbled, humiliated, shamed, unsuccessful

trivia noun minutiae, details, trifles, trivialities

➤ **Antonyms**
basics, brass tacks (informal), core, essentials, fundamentals, nitty-gritty (informal), rudiments

trivial adjective unimportant, incidental, inconsequential, insignificant, meaningless, minor, petty, small, trifling, worthless

➤ **Antonyms**
crucial, essential, important, serious, significant, vital, weighty, worthwhile

triviality noun insignificance, meaninglessness, pettiness, unimportance, worthlessness

➤ **Antonyms**
consequence, importance, significance, value, worth

trivialize verb undervalue, belittle, laugh off, make light of, minimize, play down, scoff at, underestimate, underplay

troop noun **1** group, band, body, company, crowd, horde, multitude, squad, team, unit **2** troops soldiers, armed forces, army, men, servicemen, soldiery ♦ verb **3** flock, march, stream, swarm, throng, traipse (informal)

trophy noun prize, award, booty, cup, laurels, memento, souvenir, spoils

tropical adjective hot, steamy, stifling, sultry, sweltering, torrid

➤ **Antonyms**
arctic, chilly, cold, cool, freezing, frosty

trot verb **1** run, canter, jog, lope, scamper ♦ noun **2** run, canter, jog, lope

trouble noun **1** distress, anxiety, disquiet, grief, misfortune, pain, sorrow, torment, woe, worry **2** ailment, complaint, defect, disease, disorder, failure, illness, malfunction **3** disorder, agitation, bother (informal), commotion, discord, disturbance, strife, tumult, unrest **4** effort, care, exertion, inconvenience, labour, pains, thought, work ♦ verb **5** bother, disconcert, distress, disturb, pain, perturb, plague, sadden, upset, worry **6** take pains, exert oneself, make an effort, take the time **7** inconvenience, bother, burden, disturb, impose upon, incommode, put out

➤ **Antonyms**
noun ≠**distress**: comfort, contentment, good fortune, happiness, pleasure, tranquillity ≠**disorder**: agreement, contentment, harmony, peace, tranquillity, unity ≠**effort**: convenience, ease, facility ♦ verb ≠**bother**: appease, calm, mollify, please, relieve, soothe ≠**take pains**: avoid, dodge ≠**inconvenience**: relieve

troublesome *adjective* **1** <u>bothersome</u>, annoying, demanding, difficult, inconvenient, irksome, taxing, tricky, trying, vexatious, worrying **2** <u>disorderly</u>, rebellious, rowdy, turbulent, uncooperative, undisciplined, unruly, violent

➤ **Antonyms**

≠<u>bothersome</u>: agreeable, calming, congenial, easy, pleasant, simple, soothing, undemanding ≠<u>disorderly</u>: disciplined, eager-to-please, obedient, well-behaved

trough *noun* **1** <u>manger</u>, water trough **2** <u>channel</u>, canal, depression, ditch, duct, furrow, gully, gutter, trench

trounce *verb* <u>defeat heavily or utterly</u>, beat, crush, drub, give a hiding (*informal*), hammer (*informal*), rout, slaughter (*informal*), thrash, wipe the floor with (*informal*)

troupe *noun* <u>company</u>, band, cast

truancy *noun* <u>absence</u>, absence without leave, malingering, shirking, skiving (*Brit. slang*)

truant *noun* <u>absentee</u>, malingerer, runaway, shirker, skiver (*Brit. slang*)

truce *noun* <u>ceasefire</u>, armistice, cessation, let-up (*informal*), lull, moratorium, peace, respite

truculent *adjective* <u>hostile</u>, aggressive, bellicose, belligerent, defiant, ill-tempered, obstreperous, pugnacious

➤ **Antonyms**

amiable, co-operative, gentle, good-natured, peaceable, placid

trudge *verb* **1** <u>plod</u>, footslog, lumber, slog, stump, traipse (*informal*), tramp, trek ◆ *noun* **2** <u>tramp</u>, footslog, hike, march, slog, traipse (*informal*), trek

true *adjective* **1** <u>correct</u>, accurate, authentic, factual, genuine, precise, real, right, truthful, veracious **2** <u>faithful</u>, dedicated, devoted, dutiful, loyal, reliable, staunch, steady, trustworthy **3** <u>exact</u>, accurate, on target, perfect, precise, spot-on (*Brit. informal*), unerring

➤ **Antonyms**

≠<u>correct</u>: bogus, erroneous, fake, false, fictitious, incorrect, made-up, untrue ≠<u>faithful</u>: deceitful, disloyal, faithless, false, treacherous, unreliable, untrue, untrustworthy ≠<u>exact</u>: askew, awry, inaccurate, incorrect

truism *noun* <u>cliché</u>, axiom, bromide, commonplace, platitude

truly *adverb* **1** <u>correctly</u>, authentically, exactly, factually, genuinely, legitimately, precisely, rightly, truthfully **2** <u>faithfully</u>, devotedly, dutifully, loyally, sincerely, staunchly, steadily **3** <u>really</u>, extremely, greatly, indeed, of course, very

➤ **Antonyms**

≠<u>correctly</u>: falsely, fraudulently, inaccurately, incorrectly, mistakenly

trumpet *noun* **1** <u>horn</u>, bugle, clarion ◆ *verb* **2** <u>proclaim</u>, advertise, announce, broadcast, shout from the rooftops, tout (*informal*)

➤ **Antonyms**

verb ≠<u>proclaim</u>: hide, hush up, keep secret, make light of, play down

trump up *verb* <u>invent</u>, concoct, contrive, cook up (*informal*), create, fabricate, fake, make up

truncate *verb* <u>shorten</u>, abbreviate, curtail, cut short, dock, lop, pare, prune, trim

➤ **Antonyms**

drag out, draw out, extend, lengthen, prolong, protract, spin out, stretch

truncheon *noun Chiefly Brit.* <u>club</u>, baton, cudgel, staff

trunk *noun* **1** <u>stem</u>, bole, stalk **2** <u>chest</u>, box, case, casket, coffer, crate **3** <u>body</u>, torso **4** <u>snout</u>, proboscis

truss *verb* **1** <u>tie</u>, bind, fasten, make fast, secure, strap, tether ◆ *noun* **2** *Medical* <u>support</u>, bandage **3** <u>joist</u>, beam, brace, buttress, prop, stanchion, stay, strut, support

trust *verb* **1** <u>believe in</u>, bank on,

count on, depend on, have faith in, rely upon **2** <u>entrust</u>, assign, commit, confide, consign, delegate, give **3** <u>expect</u>, assume, hope, presume, suppose, surmise ◆ *noun* **4** <u>confidence</u>, assurance, belief, certainty, conviction, credence, credit, expectation, faith, reliance

➤ **Antonyms**

verb ≠<u>believe in</u>: be sceptical of, beware, distrust, doubt, lack confidence in, lack faith in, mistrust, suspect ◆ *noun* ≠<u>confidence</u>: distrust, doubt, fear, mistrust, scepticism, suspicion, uncertainty, wariness

trustful, trusting *adjective* <u>unsuspecting</u>, credulous, gullible, naive, unsuspicious, unwary

➤ **Antonyms**

cagey (*informal*), cautious, chary, distrustful, guarded, on one's guard, suspicious, wary

trustworthy *adjective* <u>dependable</u>, honest, honourable, principled, reliable, reputable, responsible, staunch, steadfast, trusty

➤ **Antonyms**

deceitful, dishonest, disloyal, irresponsible, treacherous, unprincipled, unreliable, untrustworthy

trusty *adjective* <u>reliable</u>, dependable, faithful, solid, staunch, steady, strong, trustworthy

➤ **Antonyms**

dishonest, irresolute, irresponsible, unfaithful, unreliable

truth *noun* <u>truthfulness</u>, accuracy, exactness, fact, genuineness, legitimacy, precision, reality, validity, veracity

➤ **Antonyms**

error, falsity, inaccuracy

truthful *adjective* **1** <u>honest</u>, candid, frank, sincere, straight, true, trustworthy **2** <u>true</u>, accurate, correct, precise

➤ **Antonyms**

≠<u>honest</u>: deceptive, dishonest, false, insincere, lying, untruthful ≠<u>true</u>: false, fictitious, inaccurate, incorrect, untrue, untruthful

try *verb* **1** <u>attempt</u>, aim, endeav-

our, have a go, make an effort, seek, strive, struggle **2** <u>test</u>, appraise, check out, evaluate, examine, investigate, put to the test, sample, taste ◆ *noun* **3** <u>attempt</u>, crack (*informal*), effort, go (*informal*), shot (*informal*), stab (*informal*), whack (*informal*)

trying *adjective* <u>annoying</u>, bothersome, difficult, exasperating, hard, stressful, taxing, tiresome, tough, wearisome

➤ **Antonyms**

simple, undemanding

tubby *adjective* <u>fat</u>, chubby, corpulent, obese, overweight, plump, portly, stout

tuck *verb* **1** <u>push</u>, fold, gather, insert ◆ *noun* **2** <u>fold</u>, gather, pinch, pleat **3** *Brit. informal* <u>food</u>, grub (*slang*), nosh (*slang*)

tuft *noun* <u>clump</u>, bunch, cluster, collection, knot, tussock

tug *verb* **1** <u>pull</u>, jerk, wrench, yank ◆ *noun* **2** <u>pull</u>, jerk, yank

tuition *noun* <u>training</u>, education, instruction, lessons, schooling, teaching, tutelage, tutoring

tumble *verb* **1** <u>fall</u>, drop, flop, plummet, stumble, topple ◆ *noun* **2** <u>fall</u>, drop, plunge, spill, stumble, trip

tumbledown *adjective* <u>dilapidated</u>, crumbling, decrepit, ramshackle, rickety, ruined

➤ **Antonyms**

solid, sound, stable, sturdy, well-kept

tumour *noun* <u>growth</u>, cancer, carcinoma (*Pathology*), lump, sarcoma (*Medical*), swelling

tumult *noun* <u>commotion</u>, clamour, din, hubbub, pandemonium, riot, row, turmoil, upheaval, uproar

➤ **Antonyms**

calm, hush, peace, quiet, repose, serenity, silence, stillness

tumultuous *adjective* **1** <u>turbulent</u>, stormy **2** <u>wild</u>, boisterous, excited, noisy, riotous, rowdy, unruly, uproarious

➤ **Antonyms**

calm, hushed, peaceful, quiet,

restful, serene, still, tranquil

tune *noun* **1** <u>melody</u>, air, song, strain, theme **2** <u>concord</u>, consonance, euphony, harmony, pitch ♦ *verb* **3** <u>adjust</u>, adapt, attune, harmonize, pitch, regulate

➤ **Antonyms**

noun ≠<u>concord</u>: conflict, discord, disharmony

tuneful *adjective* <u>melodious</u>, catchy, euphonious, harmonious, mellifluous, melodic, musical, pleasant

➤ **Antonyms**

cacophonous, clashing, discordant, dissonant, harsh, tuneless

tuneless *adjective* <u>discordant</u>, atonal, cacophonous, dissonant, harsh, unmusical

➤ **Antonyms**

harmonious, melodious, musical, pleasing, sonorous, symphonic, tuneful

tunnel *noun* **1** <u>passage</u>, burrow, channel, hole, passageway, shaft, subway, underpass ♦ *verb* **2** <u>dig</u>, burrow, excavate, mine, scoop out

turbulence *noun* <u>confusion</u>, agitation, commotion, disorder, instability, tumult, turmoil, unrest, upheaval

➤ **Antonyms**

calm, peace, quiet, repose, rest, stillness

turbulent *adjective* <u>agitated</u>, blustery, choppy, foaming, furious, raging, rough, tempestuous, tumultuous

➤ **Antonyms**

calm, glassy, peaceful, quiet, smooth, still, unruffled

turf *noun* **1** <u>grass</u>, sod, sward **2 the turf** <u>horse-racing</u>, racing, the flat

turmoil *noun* <u>confusion</u>, agitation, chaos, commotion, disarray, disorder, tumult, upheaval, uproar

➤ **Antonyms**

calm, peace, quiet, repose, rest, serenity, stillness, tranquillity

turn *verb* **1** <u>change course</u>, move, shift, swerve, switch, veer, wheel

2 <u>rotate</u>, circle, go round, gyrate, pivot, revolve, roll, spin, twist, whirl **3** <u>change</u>, alter, convert, mould, mutate, remodel, shape, transform **4** <u>shape</u>, fashion, frame, make, mould **5** <u>go bad</u>, curdle, go off (*Brit. informal*), sour, spoil, taint ♦ *noun* **6** <u>rotation</u>, circle, cycle, gyration, revolution, spin, twist, whirl **7** <u>change of direction</u>, departure, deviation, shift **8** <u>opportunity</u>, chance, crack (*informal*), go, stint, time, try **9** <u>direction</u>, drift, heading, tendency, trend **10** *As in* **good turn** <u>act</u>, action, deed, favour, gesture, service

turncoat *noun* <u>traitor</u>, apostate, backslider, defector, deserter, renegade

turn down *verb* **1** <u>lower</u>, lessen, muffle, mute, quieten, soften **2** <u>refuse</u>, decline, rebuff, reject, repudiate, spurn

➤ **Antonyms**

≠<u>lower</u>: amplify, augment, boost, increase, raise, strengthen, swell, turn up ≠<u>refuse</u>: accede, accept, acquiesce, agree, receive, take

turn in *verb Informal* **1** <u>go to bed</u>, go to sleep, hit the sack (*slang*) **2** <u>hand in</u>, deliver, give up, hand over, return, submit, surrender, tender

turning *noun* <u>turn-off</u>, bend, crossroads, curve, junction, side road, turn

turning point *noun* <u>crossroads</u>, change, crisis, crux, moment of truth

turn off *verb* <u>stop</u>, cut out, put out, shut down, switch off, turn out, unplug

turn on *verb* **1** <u>start</u>, activate, ignite, kick-start, start up, switch on **2** <u>attack</u>, assail, assault, fall on, round on **3** *Informal* <u>arouse</u>, attract, excite, please, stimulate, thrill, titillate

➤ **Antonyms**

≠<u>start</u>: put out, shut off, stop, switch off, turn off

turnout *noun* <u>attendance</u>, assembly, audience, congregation, crowd, gate, number, throng

turnover noun **1** output, business, productivity **2** movement, change, coming and going

turn up verb **1** arrive, appear, attend, come, put in an appearance, show one's face, show up (*informal*) **2** find, dig up, disclose, discover, expose, reveal, unearth **3** come to light, crop up (*informal*), pop up **4** increase, amplify, boost, enhance, intensify, raise

➤ **Antonyms**

≠find: hide ≠come to light: disappear, evaporate, fade, vanish ≠increase: diminish, lessen, lower, reduce, soften, turn down

tussle noun **1** fight, battle, brawl, conflict, contest, scrap (*informal*), scuffle, struggle ◆ verb **2** fight, battle, grapple, scrap (*informal*), scuffle, struggle, vie, wrestle

tutor noun **1** teacher, coach, educator, guardian, guide, guru, instructor, lecturer, mentor ◆ verb **2** teach, coach, drill, educate, guide, instruct, school, train

twaddle noun nonsense, claptrap (*informal*), drivel, garbage (*informal*), gobbledegook (*informal*), poppycock (*informal*), rubbish, waffle (*informal, chiefly Brit.*)

tweak verb, noun twist, jerk, pinch, pull, squeeze

twig noun branch, shoot, spray, sprig, stick

twilight noun dusk, dimness, evening, gloaming (*Scot. or poetic*), gloom, half-light, sundown, sunset

➤ **Antonyms**

dawn, daybreak, morning, sunrise

twin noun **1** double, clone, counterpart, duplicate, fellow, likeness, lookalike, match, mate ◆ verb **2** pair, couple, join, link, match, yoke

twine noun **1** string, cord, yarn ◆ verb **2** coil, bend, curl, encircle, loop, spiral, twist, wind

twinge noun pain, pang, prick, spasm, stab, stitch

twinkle verb **1** sparkle, blink, flash, flicker, gleam, glint, glisten, glitter, shimmer, shine ◆ noun **2** sparkle, flash, flicker, gleam, glimmer, shimmer, spark

twirl verb **1** turn, pirouette, pivot, revolve, rotate, spin, twist, wheel, whirl, wind ◆ noun **2** turn, pirouette, revolution, rotation, spin, twist, wheel, whirl

twist verb **1** distort, contort, screw up **2** wind, coil, curl, screw, spin, swivel, wrap, wring ◆ noun **3** wind, coil, curl, spin, swivel **4** development, change, revelation, slant, surprise, turn, variation **5** curve, arc, bend, meander, turn, undulation, zigzag **6** distortion, defect, deformation, flaw, imperfection, kink, warp

➤ **Antonyms**

verb ≠distort: straighten, untwist ≠wind: straighten, uncoil, unravel, unroll, untwist, unwind

twit noun *Informal, chiefly Brit.* fool, ass, chump (*informal*), dumb-ass (*slang*), halfwit, idiot, nincompoop, numbskull or numskull, prat (*slang*), twerp or twirp (*informal*)

twitch verb **1** jerk, flutter, jump, squirm **2** pull, pluck, tug, yank ◆ noun **3** jerk, flutter, jump, spasm, tic

two-faced adjective hypocritical, deceitful, dissembling, duplicitous, false, insincere, treacherous, untrustworthy

➤ **Antonyms**

candid, frank, genuine, honest, sincere, trustworthy

tycoon noun magnate, baron, capitalist, fat cat (*slang, chiefly U.S.*), financier, industrialist, mogul, plutocrat

type noun kind, category, class, genre, group, order, sort, species, style, variety

typhoon noun storm, cyclone, squall, tempest, tornado

typical adjective characteristic, archetypal, average, model, normal, orthodox, representative, standard, stock, usual

➤ **Antonyms**

atypical, exceptional, singular, uncharacteristic, unconventional, unique, unrepresentative, unusual

typify *verb* represent, characterize, embody, epitomize, exemplify, illustrate, personify, sum up, symbolize

tyrannical *adjective* oppressive, authoritarian, autocratic, cruel, despotic, dictatorial, domineering, high-handed, imperious, overbearing, tyrannous

➤ **Antonyms**

democratic, liberal, tolerant

tyranny *noun* oppression, absolutism, authoritarianism, autocracy, cruelty, despotism, dictatorship, high-handedness, imperiousness

➤ **Antonyms**

democracy, liberality, tolerance

tyrant *noun* dictator, absolutist, authoritarian, autocrat, bully, despot, martinet, oppressor, slave-driver

U u

ubiquitous *adjective* everywhere, ever-present, omnipresent, pervasive, universal

ugly *adjective* 1 unattractive, homely (*chiefly U.S.*), ill-favoured, plain, unlovely, unprepossessing, unsightly 2 unpleasant, disagreeable, distasteful, horrid, objectionable, shocking, terrible 3 ominous, baleful, dangerous, menacing, sinister

➤ **Antonyms**

≠unattractive: attractive, beautiful, good-looking, gorgeous, handsome, lovely, pretty ≠unpleasant: agreeable, pleasant ≠ominous: auspicious, promising

ulcer *noun* sore, abscess, boil, gumboil, peptic ulcer, pustule

ulterior *adjective* hidden, concealed, covert, secret, undisclosed

➤ **Antonyms**

declared, manifest, obvious, overt, plain

ultimate *adjective* 1 final, end, last 2 supreme, extreme, greatest, highest, paramount, superlative, utmost

ultimately *adverb* 1 finally, after all, at last, eventually, in due time, in the end, sooner or later 2 fundamentally, basically

umpire *noun* 1 referee, arbiter, arbitrator, judge ◆ *verb* 2 referee, adjudicate, arbitrate, judge

unabashed *adjective* unembarrassed, blatant, bold, brazen

➤ **Antonyms**

abashed, embarrassed, mortified, shamefaced, sheepish

unable *adjective* incapable, impotent, ineffectual, powerless, unfit, unqualified

➤ **Antonyms**

able, capable, competent, effective, powerful

unabridged *adjective* uncut, complete, full-length, unexpurgated, whole

unacceptable *adjective* unsatisfactory, displeasing, objectionable

➤ **Antonyms**

acceptable, delightful, pleasing

unaccompanied *adjective* 1 alone, by oneself, lone, on one's own, solo, unescorted 2 *Music* a cappella

unaccountable *adjective* 1 inexplicable, baffling, mysterious, odd, puzzling, unexplainable, unfathomable 2 not answerable, exempt, not responsible

➤ **Antonyms**

≠inexplicable: explicable, understandable

unaccustomed *adjective* 1 unfamiliar, new, strange, unwonted 2 unaccustomed to not used to, inexperienced at, unfamiliar with, unused to

> **Antonyms**

≠<u>unfamiliar</u>: accustomed, familiar, ordinary ≠<u>not used to</u>: experienced at, used to

unaffected[1] adjective <u>natural</u>, artless, genuine, plain, simple, sincere, unpretentious

> **Antonyms**

affected, assumed, insincere, mannered, pretentious, put-on

unaffected[2] adjective <u>impervious</u>, proof, unmoved, unresponsive, untouched

> **Antonyms**

affected, hard-hit, influenced, responsive, touched

unafraid adjective <u>fearless</u>, daring, dauntless, intrepid

> **Antonyms**

afraid, alarmed, anxious, fearful, frightened, scared

unalterable adjective <u>unchangeable</u>, fixed, immutable, permanent

> **Antonyms**

alterable, changeable, flexible, mutable

unanimity noun <u>agreement</u>, accord, assent, concord, concurrence, consensus, harmony, like-mindedness, unison

> **Antonyms**

difference, disagreement, discord, division, variance

unanimous adjective <u>agreed</u>, common, concerted, harmonious, in agreement, like-minded, united

> **Antonyms**

disunited, divided, split

unanimously adverb <u>without exception</u>, nem. con., with one accord

unanswerable adjective <u>conclusive</u>, absolute, incontestable, incontrovertible, indisputable

unanswered adjective <u>unresolved</u>, disputed, open, undecided

unappetizing adjective <u>unpleasant</u>, distasteful, off-putting (Brit. informal), repulsive, unappealing, unattractive, unpalatable

> **Antonyms**

appealing, appetizing, attractive, delicious, mouthwatering, palatable, savoury, scrumptious (informal), succulent, tempting

unapproachable adjective **1** <u>unfriendly</u>, aloof, chilly, cool, distant, remote, reserved, standoffish **2** <u>inaccessible</u>, out of reach, remote

> **Antonyms**

≠<u>unfriendly</u>: affable, approachable, congenial, cordial, friendly

unarmed adjective <u>defenceless</u>, exposed, helpless, open, unprotected, weak

> **Antonyms**

armed, fortified, protected, strengthened

unassailable adjective <u>impregnable</u>, invincible, invulnerable, secure

unassuming adjective <u>modest</u>, humble, quiet, reserved, retiring, self-effacing, unassertive, unobtrusive, unpretentious

> **Antonyms**

conceited, overconfident, presumptuous, pretentious

unattached adjective **1** <u>free</u>, independent **2** <u>single</u>, available, not spoken for, unengaged, unmarried

> **Antonyms**

≠<u>free</u>: attached, committed, dependent, involved

unattended adjective **1** <u>abandoned</u>, unguarded, unwatched **2** <u>alone</u>, on one's own, unaccompanied

unauthorized adjective <u>illegal</u>, unlawful, unofficial, unsanctioned

> **Antonyms**

authorized, lawful, legal, official, sanctioned

unavoidable adjective <u>inevitable</u>, certain, fated, inescapable

unaware adjective <u>ignorant</u>, not in the loop (informal), oblivious, unconscious, uninformed, unknowing

> **Antonyms**

aware, conscious, informed, in the loop (informal), knowing

unawares *adverb* **1** by surprise, off guard, suddenly, unexpectedly **2** unknowingly, accidentally, by accident, inadvertently, unwittingly

➤ **Antonyms**

≠*by surprise*: forewarned, prepared ≠*unknowingly*: deliberately, knowingly, on purpose

unbalanced *adjective* **1** shaky, lopsided, uneven, unstable, wobbly **2** biased, one-sided, partial, partisan, prejudiced, unfair **3** deranged, crazy, demented, disturbed, eccentric, insane, irrational, mad, *non compos mentis*, not all there, unhinged, unstable

➤ **Antonyms**

≠*shaky*: balanced, even, stable

unbearable *adjective* intolerable, insufferable, too much (*informal*), unacceptable

➤ **Antonyms**

acceptable, bearable, endurable, tolerable

unbeatable *adjective* invincible, indomitable

unbeaten *adjective* undefeated, triumphant, victorious

unbecoming *adjective* **1** unattractive, unbefitting, unflattering, unsightly, unsuitable **2** unseemly, discreditable, improper, offensive

➤ **Antonyms**

≠*unseemly*: becoming, decent, proper, seemly

unbelievable *adjective* **1** incredible, astonishing, far-fetched, implausible, impossible, improbable, inconceivable, jaw-dropping, preposterous, unconvincing **2** wonderful, excellent, fabulous (*informal*), fantastic (*informal*), great (*informal*), splendid, superb, terrific (*informal*)

➤ **Antonyms**

≠*incredible*: believable, credible, likely, plausible, possible, probable ≠*wonderful*: awful, bad, terrible

unbending *adjective* inflexible, firm, intractable, resolute, rigid,

severe, strict, stubborn, tough, uncompromising

unbiased *adjective* fair, disinterested, equitable, impartial, just, neutral, objective, unprejudiced

➤ **Antonyms**

biased, bigoted, partial, prejudiced, unfair, unjust

unblemished *adjective* spotless, flawless, immaculate, impeccable, perfect, pure, untarnished

➤ **Antonyms**

blemished, imperfect, impure, tarnished

unborn *adjective* expected, awaited, embryonic

unbreakable *adjective* indestructible, durable, lasting, rugged, strong

➤ **Antonyms**

breakable, brittle, delicate, flimsy, fragile

unbridled *adjective* unrestrained, excessive, intemperate, licentious, riotous, unchecked, unruly, wanton

unbroken *adjective* **1** intact, complete, entire, whole **2** continuous, constant, incessant, uninterrupted

➤ **Antonyms**

≠*intact*: broken, cracked, damaged, fragmented, in pieces, shattered ≠*continuous*: erratic, fitful, intermittent, interrupted, occasional

unburden *verb* confess, confide, disclose, get (something) off one's chest (*informal*), reveal

uncalled-for *adjective* unnecessary, gratuitous, needless, undeserved, unjustified, unwarranted

➤ **Antonyms**

deserved, justified, necessary, needed, warranted

uncanny *adjective* **1** weird, mysterious, strange, supernatural, unearthly, unnatural **2** extraordinary, astounding, exceptional, incredible, miraculous, remarkable, unusual

unceasing *adjective* continual, constant, continuous, endless, incessant, nonstop, perpetual

> **Antonyms**

fitful, intermittent, irregular, occasional, periodic, spasmodic, sporadic

uncertain *adjective* **1** unpredictable, doubtful, indefinite, questionable, risky, speculative **2** unsure, dubious, hazy, irresolute, unclear, unconfirmed, undecided, vague

> **Antonyms**

≠unpredictable: certain, definite, fixed, known, predictable ≠unsure: certain, positive, resolute, sure, unhesitating

uncertainty *noun* **1** unpredictability, ambiguity **2** doubt, confusion, dubiety, hesitancy, indecision

> **Antonyms**

≠unpredictability: conclusiveness, predictability ≠doubt: assurance, certainty, decision, sureness, trust

unchangeable *adjective* unalterable, constant, fixed, immutable, invariable, irreversible, permanent, stable

> **Antonyms**

changeable, inconstant, mutable, unstable, variable

unchanging *adjective* constant, continuing, enduring, eternal, immutable, lasting, permanent, perpetual, unvarying

uncharitable *adjective* unkind, cruel, hardhearted, unfeeling, ungenerous

> **Antonyms**

charitable, feeling, generous, kind

uncharted *adjective* unexplored, strange, undiscovered, unfamiliar, unknown

uncivil *adjective* impolite, bad-mannered, discourteous, ill-mannered, rude, unmannerly

> **Antonyms**

civil, courteous, mannerly, polite, well-mannered

uncivilized *adjective* **1** primitive, barbarian, savage, wild **2** uncouth, boorish, coarse, philistine, uncultivated, uneducated

unclean *adjective* dirty, corrupt, defiled, evil, filthy, foul, impure, polluted, soiled, stained

> **Antonyms**

clean, pure, spotless, unstained

unclear *adjective* **1** indistinct, blurred, dim, faint, fuzzy, hazy, obscure, shadowy, undefined, vague **2** doubtful, ambiguous, indefinite, indeterminate, vague

> **Antonyms**

≠indistinct: clear, distinct ≠doubtful: evident

uncomfortable *adjective* **1** painful, awkward, cramped, rough **2** uneasy, awkward, discomfited, disturbed, embarrassed, troubled

> **Antonyms**

≠uneasy: at ease, at home, comfortable, easy, relaxed, untroubled

uncommitted *adjective* uninvolved, floating, free, neutral, nonaligned, not involved, unattached

uncommon *adjective* **1** rare, infrequent, novel, odd, peculiar, queer, scarce, strange, unusual **2** extraordinary, distinctive, exceptional, notable, outstanding, remarkable, special

> **Antonyms**

≠rare: common, frequent, regular, routine, usual ≠extraordinary: average, commonplace, everyday, humdrum, mundane, ordinary, run-of-the-mill

uncommonly *adverb* **1** rarely, hardly ever, infrequently, occasionally, seldom **2** exceptionally, particularly, very

uncommunicative *adjective* reticent, close, reserved, secretive, silent, taciturn, tight-lipped, unforthcoming

> **Antonyms**

chatty, communicative, forthcoming, garrulous, loquacious, talkative

uncompromising *adjective* inflexible, firm, inexorable, intransigent, rigid, strict, tough, unbending

unconcern *noun* indifference, aloofness, apathy, detachment, lack of interest, nonchalance

unconcerned *adjective* indifferent, aloof, apathetic, cool, detached, dispassionate, distant, uninterested, unmoved

➤ **Antonyms**
avid, eager, interested

unconditional *adjective* absolute, complete, entire, full, outright, positive, total, unlimited, unqualified, unreserved

➤ **Antonyms**
conditional, limited, partial, qualified, reserved

unconnected *adjective* **1** separate, detached, divided **2** incoherent, disjointed, illogical, irrelevant, meaningless

➤ **Antonyms**
≠incoherent: coherent, connected, logical, relevant

unconscious *adjective* **1** senseless, insensible, knocked out, out, out cold, stunned **2** unaware, ignorant, oblivious, unknowing **3** unintentional, accidental, inadvertent, unwitting

➤ **Antonyms**
≠senseless: awake, conscious, sensible ≠unaware: alert, aware, conscious ≠unintentional: calculated, conscious, deliberate, intentional, planned

uncontrollable *adjective* wild, frantic, furious, mad, strong, unruly, violent

uncontrolled *adjective* unrestrained, rampant, riotous, unbridled, unchecked, undisciplined

➤ **Antonyms**
contained, controlled, disciplined, restrained

unconventional *adjective* unusual, eccentric, individual, irregular, nonconformist, odd, offbeat, original, outré, unorthodox

➤ **Antonyms**
conventional, normal, ordinary, orthodox, regular, usual

unconvincing *adjective* implausible, dubious, feeble, flimsy, improbable, lame, questionable, suspect, thin, unlikely, weak

➤ **Antonyms**
believable, convincing, credible, likely, plausible, probable

uncooperative *adjective* unhelpful, awkward, difficult, disobliging, obstructive

➤ **Antonyms**
cooperative, helpful, obliging

uncoordinated *adjective* clumsy, awkward, bungling, graceless, lumbering, maladroit, ungainly, ungraceful

uncouth *adjective* coarse, barbaric, boorish, crude, graceless, ill-mannered, loutish, oafish, rough, rude, vulgar

➤ **Antonyms**
elegant, graceful, well-mannered

uncover *verb* **1** open, bare, show, strip, unwrap **2** reveal, disclose, divulge, expose, make known

➤ **Antonyms**
≠reveal: conceal, cover, cover up, hide, suppress

uncritical *adjective* undiscriminating, indiscriminate, undiscerning

➤ **Antonyms**
critical, discerning, discriminating

undecided *adjective* **1** unsure, dithering (*chiefly Brit.*), hesitant, in two minds, irresolute, torn, uncertain **2** unsettled, debatable, iffy (*informal*), indefinite, moot, open, unconcluded, undetermined

➤ **Antonyms**
≠unsure: certain, decided, resolute, sure ≠unsettled: decided, definite, determined, resolved, settled

undefined *adjective* **1** unspecified, imprecise, inexact, unclear **2** indistinct, formless, indefinite, vague

➤ **Antonyms**
≠unspecified: clear, defined, exact, precise, specified ≠indistinct: clear, defined, definite

undeniable *adjective* certain, clear, incontrovertible, indisputable, obvious, sure, unquestionable

> ➤ **Antonyms**

debatable, deniable, doubtful, dubious, questionable, uncertain

under *preposition* **1** below, beneath, underneath **2** subject to, governed by, secondary to, subordinate to ♦ *adverb* **3** below, beneath, down, lower

> ➤ **Antonyms**

preposition ≠below: above, over, up, upper, upward ♦ *adverb* ≠below: above, over, up, upward

underclothes *plural noun* underwear, lingerie, undergarments, undies (*informal*)

undercover *adjective* secret, concealed, covert, hidden, private

> ➤ **Antonyms**

open, overt, plain, unconcealed, visible

undercurrent *noun* **1** undertow, riptide **2** undertone, atmosphere, feeling, hint, overtone, sense, suggestion, tendency, tinge, vibes (*slang*)

underdog *noun* weaker party, little fellow (*informal*), outsider

underestimate *verb* underrate, belittle, minimize, miscalculate, undervalue

> ➤ **Antonyms**

exaggerate, inflate, overdo, overestimate, overrate, overstate

undergo *verb* experience, bear, endure, go through, stand, suffer, sustain

underground *adjective* **1** subterranean, buried, covered **2** secret, clandestine, covert, hidden ♦ *noun* **3** the underground: **a** the Resistance, partisans **b** the tube (*Brit.*), the metro, the subway

undergrowth *noun* scrub, bracken, briars, brush, underbrush

underhand *adjective* sly, crafty, deceitful, devious, dishonest, furtive, secret, sneaky, stealthy

> ➤ **Antonyms**

above board, frank, honest, open

underline *verb* **1** underscore, mark **2** emphasize, accentuate, highlight, stress

> ➤ **Antonyms**

≠emphasize: gloss over, make

light of, minimize, play down

underlying *adjective* fundamental, basic, elementary, intrinsic, primary, prime

undermine *verb* weaken, disable, sabotage, sap, subvert

> ➤ **Antonyms**

fortify, reinforce, strengthen

underprivileged *adjective* disadvantaged, deprived, destitute, impoverished, needy, poor

underrate *verb* underestimate, belittle, discount, undervalue

> ➤ **Antonyms**

exaggerate, overestimate, overrate, overvalue

undersized *adjective* stunted, dwarfish, miniature, pygmy or pigmy, small

> ➤ **Antonyms**

big, colossal, giant, huge, massive, oversized

understand *verb* **1** comprehend, conceive, fathom, follow, get, grasp, perceive, realize, see, take in **2** believe, assume, gather, presume, suppose, think

understandable *adjective* reasonable, justifiable, legitimate, natural, to be expected

understanding *noun* **1** perception, appreciation, awareness, comprehension, discernment, grasp, insight, judgment, knowledge, sense **2** interpretation, belief, idea, judgment, notion, opinion, perception, view **3** agreement, accord, pact ♦ *adjective* **4** sympathetic, compassionate, considerate, kind, patient, sensitive, tolerant

> ➤ **Antonyms**

noun ≠perception: ignorance, incomprehension, misapprehension, misunderstanding, obtuseness ≠agreement: disagreement, dispute ♦ *adjective* ≠sympathetic: inconsiderate, insensitive, intolerant, unfeeling, unsympathetic

understood *adjective* **1** implied, implicit, inferred, tacit, unspoken, unstated **2** assumed, accepted, taken for granted

understudy *noun* stand-in, re-

undertake *verb* agree, bargain, contract, engage, guarantee, pledge, promise

undertaking *noun* **1** task, affair, attempt, business, effort, endeavour, enterprise, operation, project, venture **2** promise, assurance, commitment, pledge, vow, word

undertone *noun* **1** murmur, whisper **2** undercurrent, hint, suggestion, tinge, touch, trace

undervalue *verb* underrate, depreciate, hold cheap, minimize, misjudge, underestimate

➤ **Antonyms**
exaggerate, overestimate, overrate, overvalue

underwater *adjective* submerged, submarine, sunken

under way *adjective* in progress, begun, going on, started

underwear *noun* underclothes, lingerie, undergarments, underthings, undies (*informal*)

underweight *adjective* skinny, emaciated, half-starved, puny, skin and bone (*informal*), undernourished, undersized

underworld *noun* **1** criminals, gangland (*informal*), gangsters, organized crime **2** nether world, Hades, nether regions

underwrite *verb* **1** finance, back, fund, guarantee, insure, sponsor, subsidize **2** sign, endorse, initial

undesirable *adjective* objectionable, disagreeable, distasteful, unacceptable, unattractive, unsuitable, unwanted, unwelcome

➤ **Antonyms**
acceptable, agreeable, appealing, attractive, desirable, inviting, welcome

undeveloped *adjective* **1** immature, embryonic **2** potential, latent

undignified *adjective* unseemly, improper, indecorous, inelegant, unbecoming, unsuitable

➤ **Antonyms**
becoming, decorous, dignified,

elegant, proper, seemly, suitable

undisciplined *adjective* uncontrolled, obstreperous, unrestrained, unruly, wayward, wild, wilful

➤ **Antonyms**
controlled, disciplined, restrained

undisguised *adjective* obvious, blatant, evident, explicit, open, overt, patent, unconcealed

➤ **Antonyms**
concealed, covert, disguised, hidden, secret

undisputed *adjective* acknowledged, accepted, certain, indisputable, recognized, unchallenged, undeniable, undoubted

➤ **Antonyms**
deniable, disputed, doubtful, dubious, uncertain

undistinguished *adjective* ordinary, everyday, mediocre, run-of-the-mill, unexceptional, unimpressive, unremarkable

➤ **Antonyms**
distinguished, exceptional, extraordinary, impressive, notable, outstanding, remarkable, striking

undisturbed *adjective* **1** quiet, calm, peaceful, restful, serene, still, tranquil **2** calm, collected, composed, placid, sedate, serene, tranquil, unfazed (*informal*), unperturbed, untroubled

➤ **Antonyms**
≠calm: disturbed, excited, flustered, nervous, perturbed, troubled, upset

undivided *adjective* **1** complete, entire, exclusive, full, thorough, total, undistracted, whole **2** united, entire, solid, whole

undo *verb* **1** open, disentangle, loose, unbutton, unfasten, untie **2** reverse, annul, cancel, invalidate, neutralize, offset **3** ruin, defeat, destroy, overturn, quash, shatter, subvert, undermine, upset, wreck

undoing *noun* ruin, collapse, defeat, disgrace, downfall, overthrow, reversal, shame

undone *adjective* unfinished, left,

neglected, omitted, unfulfilled, unperformed

➤ **Antonyms**

accomplished, done, finished, fulfilled, performed

undoubted adjective certain, acknowledged, definite, indisputable, indubitable, sure, undisputed, unquestioned

undoubtedly adverb certainly, assuredly, definitely, doubtless, surely, without doubt

undress verb **1** strip, disrobe, shed, take off one's clothes ◆ noun **2** nakedness, nudity

undue adjective excessive, extreme, improper, inappropriate, needless, uncalled-for, unnecessary, unwarranted

➤ **Antonyms**

appropriate, due, necessary, proper

unduly adverb excessively, overly, unnecessarily, unreasonably

➤ **Antonyms**

duly, reasonably

undying adjective eternal, constant, deathless, everlasting, infinite, permanent, perpetual, unending

➤ **Antonyms**

ephemeral, finite, fleeting, impermanent, inconstant, short-lived

unearth verb **1** discover, expose, find, reveal, uncover **2** dig up, dredge up, excavate, exhume

unearthly adjective eerie, ghostly, phantom, spectral, spooky (informal), strange, supernatural, uncanny, weird

uneasiness noun anxiety, disquiet, doubt, misgiving, qualms, trepidation, worry

➤ **Antonyms**

calm, composure, cool, ease, serenity

uneasy adjective **1** anxious, antsy (informal), disturbed, edgy, nervous, on edge, perturbed, troubled, twitchy (informal), uncomfortable, worried **2** precarious, awkward, insecure, shaky, strained, tense, uncomfortable

➤ **Antonyms**

≠anxious: at ease, calm, comfortable, relaxed, unperturbed

uneconomic adjective unprofitable, loss-making, nonpaying

➤ **Antonyms**

economic, money-making, productive, profitable

uneducated adjective **1** ignorant, illiterate, unschooled, untaught **2** lowbrow, uncultivated, uncultured

➤ **Antonyms**

≠ignorant: educated, literate, schooled, taught

unemotional adjective impassive, apathetic, cold, cool, phlegmatic, reserved, undemonstrative, unexcitable

➤ **Antonyms**

demonstrative, emotional, excitable

unemployed adjective out of work, idle, jobless, laid off, redundant

unending adjective perpetual, continual, endless, eternal, everlasting, interminable, unceasing

unendurable adjective unbearable, insufferable, insupportable, intolerable

➤ **Antonyms**

bearable, endurable, sufferable, tolerable

unenthusiastic adjective indifferent, apathetic, half-hearted, nonchalant

➤ **Antonyms**

enthusiastic, excited, interested, keen

unenviable adjective unpleasant, disagreeable, uncomfortable, undesirable

➤ **Antonyms**

agreeable, attractive, desirable, enviable, pleasant

unequal adjective **1** different, differing, disparate, dissimilar, unlike, unmatched, varying **2** disproportionate, asymmetrical, illmatched, irregular, unbalanced, uneven

➤ **Antonyms**

≠different: equal, equivalent,

identical, like, matched, similar

unequalled *adjective* incomparable, matchless, paramount, peerless, supreme, unparalleled, unrivalled

unequivocal *adjective* clear, absolute, certain, definite, explicit, incontrovertible, indubitable, manifest, plain, unambiguous

➤ **Antonyms**
ambiguous, doubtful, equivocal, evasive, noncommittal, vague

unerring *adjective* accurate, exact, infallible, perfect, sure, unfailing

unethical *adjective* immoral, dishonest, disreputable, illegal, improper, shady (*informal*), unprincipled, unscrupulous, wrong

➤ **Antonyms**
ethical, honest, legal, moral, proper, scrupulous

uneven *adjective* 1 rough, bumpy 2 variable, broken, fitful, irregular, jerky, patchy, spasmodic 3 unbalanced, lopsided, odd 4 unequal, ill-matched, unfair

➤ **Antonyms**
≠rough: even, flat, level, plane, smooth

uneventful *adjective* humdrum, boring, dull, ho-hum (*informal*), monotonous, routine, tedious, unexciting

➤ **Antonyms**
eventful, exciting

unexceptional *adjective* ordinary, commonplace, conventional, mediocre, normal, pedestrian, run-of-the-mill, undistinguished, unremarkable

➤ **Antonyms**
distinguished, exceptional, notable, noteworthy, outstanding, remarkable

unexpected *adjective* unforeseen, abrupt, chance, fortuitous, sudden, surprising, unanticipated, unlooked-for, unpredictable

➤ **Antonyms**
anticipated, expected, foreseen, predictable

unfailing *adjective* 1 continuous, boundless, endless, persistent,

unflagging 2 reliable, certain, dependable, faithful, loyal, staunch, sure, true

➤ **Antonyms**
≠reliable: disloyal, uncertain, unfaithful, unreliable, unsure

unfair *adjective* 1 biased, bigoted, one-sided, partial, partisan, prejudiced, unjust 2 unscrupulous, dishonest, unethical, unsporting, wrongful

➤ **Antonyms**
≠unscrupulous: ethical, fair, honest, just, scrupulous

unfaithful *adjective* 1 faithless, adulterous, inconstant, two-timing (*informal*), untrue 2 disloyal, deceitful, faithless, false, traitorous, treacherous, untrustworthy

➤ **Antonyms**
≠faithless: constant, faithful ≠disloyal: faithful, loyal, steadfast, true, trustworthy

unfamiliar *adjective* strange, alien, different, new, novel, unknown, unusual

➤ **Antonyms**
average, everyday, familiar, normal, unexceptional, usual

unfashionable *adjective* passé, antiquated, dated, obsolete, old-fashioned, old hat

➤ **Antonyms**
fashionable, modern, stylish, trendy (*Brit. informal*)

unfasten *verb* undo, detach, let go, loosen, open, separate, untie

unfathomable *adjective* 1 baffling, deep, impenetrable, incomprehensible, indecipherable, inexplicable, profound 2 immeasurable, bottomless, unmeasured

unfavourable *adjective* 1 adverse, contrary, inauspicious, unfortunate, unlucky, unpropitious 2 hostile, inimical, negative, unfriendly

➤ **Antonyms**
≠hostile: amicable, favourable, friendly, positive

unfeeling *adjective* 1 callous, apathetic, cold, cruel, hardhearted, heartless, insensitive, pitiless, uncaring **2** numb, insensate, insensible

➤ **Antonyms**

≠callous: benevolent, caring, gentle, humane, kind, sensitive, sympathetic

unfinished *adjective* **1** incomplete, half-done, uncompleted, undone **2** rough, bare, crude, natural, raw, unrefined

➤ **Antonyms**

≠rough: finished, perfected, refined

unfit *adjective* **1** incapable, inadequate, incompetent, no good, unqualified, useless **2** unsuitable, inadequate, ineffective, unsuited, useless **3** out of shape, feeble, flabby, in poor condition, unhealthy

➤ **Antonyms**

≠incapable: able, capable, competent, qualified ≠unsuitable: acceptable, adequate, suitable ≠out of shape: fit, healthy, in good condition, strong, well

unflappable *adjective Informal* imperturbable, calm, collected, composed, cool, impassive, level-headed, self-possessed

➤ **Antonyms**

antsy (*informal*), excitable, hot-headed, nervous, volatile

unflattering *adjective* **1** blunt, candid, critical, honest **2** unattractive, plain, unbecoming

unflinching *adjective* determined, firm, immovable, resolute, staunch, steadfast, steady, unfaltering

➤ **Antonyms**

faltering, scared

unfold *verb* **1** open, expand, spread out, undo, unfurl, unravel, unroll, unwrap **2** reveal, disclose, divulge, make known, present, show, uncover

unforeseen *adjective* unexpected, accidental, sudden, surprising, unanticipated, unpredicted

➤ **Antonyms**

anticipated, expected, foreseen, predicted

unforgettable *adjective* memo-

rable, exceptional, impressive, notable

unforgivable *adjective* inexcusable, deplorable, disgraceful, shameful, unpardonable

➤ **Antonyms**

excusable, forgivable, pardonable, venial

unfortunate *adjective* **1** disastrous, adverse, calamitous, ill-fated **2** unlucky, cursed, doomed, hapless, unhappy, unsuccessful, wretched **3** regrettable, deplorable, lamentable, unsuitable

➤ **Antonyms**

≠disastrous: auspicious, felicitous, fortunate ≠unlucky: fortunate, happy, lucky, successful ≠regrettable: unsuitable

unfounded *adjective* groundless, baseless, false, idle, spurious, unjustified

➤ **Antonyms**

factual, justified

unfriendly *adjective* **1** hostile, aloof, chilly, cold, distant, uncongenial, unsociable **2** unfavourable, alien, hostile, inhospitable

➤ **Antonyms**

≠hostile: affable, amiable, convivial, friendly, sociable, warm ≠unfavourable: congenial, hospitable

ungainly *adjective* awkward, clumsy, inelegant, lumbering, ungraceful

➤ **Antonyms**

elegant, graceful

ungodly *adjective* **1** wicked, corrupt, depraved, godless, immoral, impious, irreligious, profane, sinful **2** *Informal* unreasonable, dreadful, intolerable, outrageous, unearthly

ungracious *adjective* bad-mannered, churlish, discourteous, impolite, rude, uncivil, unmannerly

➤ **Antonyms**

affable, civil, courteous, gracious, mannerly, polite, well-mannered

ungrateful *adjective* unappreciative, unmindful, unthankful

➤ **Antonyms**
appreciative, grateful, mindful, thankful

unguarded *adjective* **1** unprotected, defenceless, undefended, vulnerable **2** careless, heedless, ill-considered, imprudent, incautious, rash, thoughtless, unthinking, unwary

➤ **Antonyms**
≠careless: cagey (*informal*), careful, cautious, guarded, prudent, wary

unhappiness *noun* sadness, blues, dejection, depression, despondency, gloom, heartache, low spirits, melancholy, misery, sorrow, wretchedness

unhappy *adjective* **1** sad, blue, dejected, depressed, despondent, downcast, melancholy, miserable, mournful, sorrowful **2** unlucky, cursed, hapless, ill-fated, unfortunate, wretched

➤ **Antonyms**
≠sad: cheerful, exuberant, happy, joyful, light-hearted, overjoyed ≠unlucky: fortunate, lucky

unharmed *adjective* unhurt, intact, safe, sound, undamaged, unscathed, whole

➤ **Antonyms**
damaged, harmed, hurt, injured

unhealthy *adjective* **1** harmful, detrimental, insalubrious, insanitary, unwholesome **2** sick, ailing, delicate, feeble, frail, infirm, invalid, sickly, unwell

➤ **Antonyms**
≠harmful: beneficial, good, healthy, salubrious, wholesome ≠sick: fit, healthy, robust, well

unheard-of *adjective* **1** unprecedented, inconceivable, new, novel, singular, unique **2** shocking, disgraceful, outrageous, preposterous **3** obscure, unfamiliar, unknown

unhesitating *adjective* **1** instant, immediate, prompt, ready **2** wholehearted, resolute, unfaltering, unquestioning, unreserved

➤ **Antonyms**
≠wholehearted: diffident, hesi-

tant, irresolute, tentative, uncertain, unsure

unholy *adjective* evil, corrupt, profane, sinful, ungodly, wicked

➤ **Antonyms**
godly, holy, saintly, virtuous

unhurried *adjective* leisurely, easy, sedate, slow

➤ **Antonyms**
brief, cursory, hasty, hectic, hurried, quick, rushed, speedy, swift

unidentified *adjective* unnamed, anonymous, nameless, unfamiliar, unrecognized

➤ **Antonyms**
familiar, identified, named, recognized

unification *noun* union, alliance, amalgamation, coalescence, coalition, confederation, federation, uniting

uniform *noun* **1** outfit, costume, dress, garb, habit, livery, regalia, suit ♦ *adjective* **2** unvarying, consistent, constant, even, regular, smooth, unchanging **3** alike, equal, like, same, similar

➤ **Antonyms**
adjective ≠unvarying: changing, inconsistent, irregular, uneven, varying

uniformity *noun* **1** regularity, constancy, evenness, invariability, sameness, similarity **2** monotony, dullness, flatness, sameness, tedium

unify *verb* unite, amalgamate, combine, confederate, consolidate, join, merge

➤ **Antonyms**
disconnect, disjoin, disunite, divide, separate, split

unimaginable *adjective* inconceivable, fantastic, impossible, incredible, unbelievable

unimaginative *adjective* unoriginal, banal, derivative, dull, hackneyed, ordinary, pedestrian, predictable, prosaic, uncreative, uninspired

➤ **Antonyms**
creative, different, fresh, groundbreaking, imaginative, innovative, inventive, original

unimportant *adjective* insignificant, inconsequential, irrelevant, minor, paltry, petty, trifling, trivial, worthless

➤ **Antonyms**
essential, grave, important, major, significant, urgent, vital

uninhabited *adjective* deserted, barren, desolate, empty, unpopulated, vacant

uninhibited *adjective* **1** unselfconscious, free, liberated, natural, open, relaxed, spontaneous, unrepressed, unreserved **2** unrestrained, free, unbridled, unchecked, unconstrained, uncontrolled, unrestricted

➤ **Antonyms**
≠unselfconscious: bashful, inhibited, modest, self-conscious, shy, uptight (*informal*) ≠unrestrained: checked, constrained, controlled, hampered, inhibited, restrained

uninspired *adjective* unexciting, banal, dull, humdrum, ordinary, prosaic, unimaginative, unoriginal

➤ **Antonyms**
different, exciting, imaginative, inspired, original

unintelligent *adjective* stupid, braindead (*informal*), brainless, dense, dull, dumb-ass (*slang*), foolish, gormless (*Brit. informal*), obtuse, slow, thick

➤ **Antonyms**
bright, clever, intelligent, sharp, smart

unintelligible *adjective* incomprehensible, inarticulate, incoherent, indistinct, jumbled, meaningless, muddled

➤ **Antonyms**
clear, coherent, comprehensible, intelligible, lucid, understandable

unintentional *adjective* accidental, casual, inadvertent, involuntary, unconscious, unintended

➤ **Antonyms**
conscious, deliberate, intended, intentional, wilful

uninterested *adjective* indifferent, apathetic, blasé, bored, listless, unconcerned

➤ **Antonyms**
concerned, enthusiastic, interested, keen

uninteresting *adjective* boring, drab, dreary, dry, dull, flat, humdrum, monotonous, tedious, unexciting

➤ **Antonyms**
absorbing, compelling, exciting, gripping, interesting, intriguing, stimulating

uninterrupted *adjective* continuous, constant, nonstop, steady, sustained, unbroken

union *noun* **1** joining, amalgamation, blend, combination, conjunction, fusion, mixture, uniting **2** alliance, association, coalition, confederacy, federation, league **3** agreement, accord, concord, harmony, unanimity, unison, unity

unique *adjective* **1** single, lone, only, solitary **2** unparalleled, matchless, unequalled, unmatched, without equal

unison *noun* agreement, accord, concert, concord, harmony, unity

➤ **Antonyms**
disagreement, discord, disharmony, dissension, dissidence, dissonance

unit *noun* **1** item, entity, whole **2** part, component, constituent, element, member, section, segment **3** section, detachment, group **4** measure, measurement, quantity

unite *verb* **1** join, amalgamate, blend, combine, couple, fuse, link, merge, unify **2** cooperate, ally, band, collaborate, join forces, pool

➤ **Antonyms**
≠join: break, detach, disunite, divide, part, separate, sever, split ≠cooperate: break, part, separate, split

united *adjective* **1** combined, affiliated, allied, banded together, collective, concerted, pooled, unified **2** in agreement, agreed, of one mind, of the same opinion, unanimous

unity noun **1** wholeness, entity, integrity, oneness, singleness, union **2** agreement, accord, assent, concord, consensus, harmony, solidarity, unison

➤ **Antonyms**

≠wholeness: disunity, division, heterogeneity, multiplicity, separation ≠agreement: disagreement, discord, disunity, division, in-fighting, strife

universal adjective widespread, common, general, overarching, total, unlimited, whole, world-wide

universally adverb everywhere, always, invariably, without exception

universe noun cosmos, creation, macrocosm, nature

unjust adjective unfair, biased, one-sided, partial, partisan, prejudiced, wrong, wrongful

➤ **Antonyms**

fair, impartial, just, right, unbiased

unjustifiable adjective inexcusable, indefensible, outrageous, unacceptable, unforgivable, unpardonable, wrong

unkempt adjective **1** uncombed, shaggy, tousled **2** untidy, dishevelled, disordered, messy, scruffy, slovenly, ungroomed

➤ **Antonyms**

≠untidy: neat, spruce, tidy, trim, well-groomed

unkind adjective cruel, hard-hearted, harsh, malicious, mean, nasty, spiteful, uncharitable, unfeeling, unfriendly, unsympathetic

➤ **Antonyms**

benevolent, charitable, generous, kind, soft-hearted, sympathetic

unknown adjective **1** hidden, concealed, dark, mysterious, secret, unrevealed **2** strange, alien, new **3** unidentified, anonymous, nameless, uncharted, undiscovered, unexplored, unnamed **4**

obscure, humble, unfamiliar

➤ **Antonyms**

≠obscure: celebrated, familiar, known, renowned, well-known

unlawful adjective illegal, banned, criminal, forbidden, illicit, outlawed, prohibited

unleash verb release, free, let go, let loose

unlike adjective different, dissimilar, distinct, diverse, not alike, opposite, unequal

➤ **Antonyms**

equal, like, matched, similar

unlikely adjective **1** improbable, doubtful, faint, remote, slight **2** unbelievable, implausible, incredible, questionable

unlimited adjective **1** infinite, boundless, countless, endless, extensive, great, immense, limitless, unbounded, vast **2** total, absolute, complete, full, unqualified, unrestricted

➤ **Antonyms**

≠infinite: bounded, finite, limited ≠total: constrained, limited, restricted

unload verb empty, discharge, dump, lighten, relieve, unpack

unlock verb open, release, undo, unfasten, unlatch

unlooked-for adjective unexpected, chance, fortuitous, surprising, unanticipated, unforeseen, unpredicted

unloved adjective uncared-for, forsaken, loveless, neglected, rejected, spurned, unpopular, unwanted

➤ **Antonyms**

adored, beloved, cherished, loved, popular, precious, wanted

unlucky adjective **1** unfortunate, cursed, hapless, luckless, miserable, unhappy, wretched **2** ill-fated, doomed, inauspicious, ominous, unfavourable

➤ **Antonyms**

≠unfortunate: blessed, fortunate, happy, lucky, prosperous

unmarried adjective single, bachelor, maiden, unattached, unwed

unmask verb reveal, disclose, discover, expose, lay bare, uncover

unmentionable *adjective* taboo, forbidden, indecent, obscene, scandalous, shameful, shocking, unspeakable

unmerciful *adjective* merciless, brutal, cruel, hard, implacable, inhumane, pitiless, remorseless, ruthless

➤ **Antonyms**
humane, merciful, pitying, tender-hearted

unmistakable *adjective* clear, certain, distinct, evident, manifest, obvious, plain, sure, unambiguous

➤ **Antonyms**
ambiguous, dim, doubtful, hidden, mistakable, obscure, uncertain, unclear, unsure

unmitigated *adjective* **1** unrelieved, intense, persistent, unalleviated, unbroken, undiminished **2** complete, absolute, arrant, downright, outright, sheer, thorough, utter

unmoved *adjective* unaffected, cold, impassive, indifferent, unimpressed, unresponsive, untouched

➤ **Antonyms**
affected, impressed, moved, touched

unnatural *adjective* **1** strange, extraordinary, freakish, outlandish, queer **2** abnormal, anomalous, irregular, odd, perverse, perverted, unusual **3** false, affected, artificial, feigned, forced, insincere, phoney *or* phony (*informal*), stiff, stilted

➤ **Antonyms**
≠strange, abnormal: normal, ordinary, typical ≠false: genuine, honest, natural, sincere, unaffected, unfeigned

unnecessary *adjective* needless, expendable, inessential, redundant, superfluous, unneeded, unrequired

➤ **Antonyms**
essential, necessary, needed, required, vital

unnerve *verb* intimidate, demor-

alize, discourage, dishearten, dismay, faze, fluster, frighten, psych out (*informal*), rattle (*informal*), shake, upset

➤ **Antonyms**
brace, encourage, gee up, hearten, nerve, steel, strengthen, support

unnoticed *adjective* unobserved, disregarded, ignored, neglected, overlooked, unheeded, unperceived, unrecognized, unseen

➤ **Antonyms**
heeded, noted, noticed, observed, perceived, recognized

unobtrusive *adjective* inconspicuous, low-key, modest, quiet, restrained, retiring, self-effacing, unassuming, unnoticeable

➤ **Antonyms**
bold, conspicuous, eye-catching, noticeable, obtrusive, prominent

unoccupied *adjective* empty, uninhabited, vacant

unofficial *adjective* unauthorized, informal, private, unconfirmed

unorthodox *adjective* unconventional, abnormal, irregular, off-the-wall (*slang*), unusual

➤ **Antonyms**
conventional, customary, established, orthodox, traditional, usual

unpaid *adjective* **1** voluntary, honorary, unsalaried **2** owing, due, outstanding, overdue, payable, unsettled

unpalatable *adjective* unpleasant, disagreeable, distasteful, horrid, offensive, repugnant, unappetizing, unsavoury

➤ **Antonyms**
agreeable, appetizing, palatable, pleasant, savoury, tasty

unparalleled *adjective* unequalled, incomparable, matchless, superlative, unique, unmatched, unprecedented, unsurpassed

unpardonable *adjective* unforgivable, deplorable, disgraceful, indefensible, inexcusable

unperturbed *adjective* calm, as cool as a cucumber, composed, cool, placid, unfazed (*informal*), unruffled, untroubled, unworried

➤ **Antonyms**

anxious, perturbed, ruffled, troubled, worried

unpleasant *adjective* nasty, bad, disagreeable, displeasing, distasteful, horrid, objectionable

➤ **Antonyms**

agreeable, likable or likeable, lovely, nice, pleasant

unpopular *adjective* disliked, rejected, shunned, unwanted, unwelcome

➤ **Antonyms**

favoured, liked, loved, popular, wanted, welcome

unprecedented *adjective* extraordinary, abnormal, new, novel, original, remarkable, singular, unheard-of

unpredictable *adjective* inconstant, chance, changeable, doubtful, erratic, random, unforeseeable, unreliable, variable

➤ **Antonyms**

constant, foreseeable, predictable, reliable, unchanging

unprejudiced *adjective* impartial, balanced, fair, just, objective, open-minded, unbiased

➤ **Antonyms**

biased, bigoted, narrow-minded, partial, prejudiced, unfair, unjust

unprepared *adjective* 1 taken off guard, surprised, unaware, unready 2 improvised, ad-lib, off the cuff (*informal*), spontaneous

unpretentious *adjective* modest, humble, plain, simple, straightforward, unaffected, unassuming, unostentatious

➤ **Antonyms**

affected, arty-farty (*informal*), conceited, ostentatious, pretentious, showy

unprincipled *adjective* dishonest, amoral, crooked, devious, dishonourable, immoral, underhand, unethical, unscrupulous

➤ **Antonyms**

decent, ethical, honest, honourable, moral, righteous, scrupulous, upright, virtuous

unproductive *adjective* 1 useless, fruitless, futile, idle, ineffective, unprofitable, unrewarding, vain 2 barren, fruitless, sterile

➤ **Antonyms**

≠useless: effective, fruitful, profitable, rewarding, useful ≠barren: abundant, fertile, fruitful, productive

unprofessional *adjective* 1 unethical, improper, lax, negligent, unprincipled 2 amateurish, cowboy (*informal*), incompetent, inefficient, inexpert

➤ **Antonyms**

≠amateurish: adept, competent, efficient, expert, professional, skilful

unprotected *adjective* vulnerable, defenceless, helpless, open, undefended

➤ **Antonyms**

defended, immune, protected, safe, secure

unqualified *adjective* 1 unfit, ill-equipped, incapable, incompetent, ineligible, unprepared 2 total, absolute, complete, downright, outright, thorough, utter

unquestionable *adjective* certain, absolute, clear, conclusive, definite, incontrovertible, indisputable, sure, undeniable, unequivocal, unmistakable

➤ **Antonyms**

doubtful, dubious, inconclusive, questionable, uncertain, unclear

unravel *verb* 1 undo, disentangle, free, separate, untangle, unwind 2 solve, explain, figure out (*informal*), resolve, work out

unreal *adjective* 1 imaginary, dreamlike, fabulous, fanciful, illusory, make-believe, visionary 2 insubstantial, immaterial, intangible, nebulous 3 fake, artificial, false, insincere, mock, pretended, sham

➤ **Antonyms**

≠fake: authentic, bona fide, genuine, real, realistic, sincere, true, veritable

unrealistic *adjective* impractical, impracticable, improbable, romantic, unworkable

➤ **Antonyms**

practical, probable, realistic, sensible, unromantic, workable

unreasonable *adjective* **1** <u>excessive</u>, extortionate, immoderate, undue, unfair, unjust, unwarranted **2** <u>biased</u>, blinkered, opinionated

➤ **Antonyms**

≠<u>excessive</u>: fair, just, justified, moderate, reasonable, warranted ≠<u>biased</u>: fair-minded, flexible, open-minded

unrelated *adjective* **1** <u>unconnected</u>, different, unlike **2** <u>irrelevant</u>, extraneous, inapplicable, inappropriate, unconnected

unreliable *adjective* **1** <u>undependable</u>, irresponsible, treacherous, untrustworthy **2** <u>uncertain</u>, deceptive, fallible, false, implausible, inaccurate, unsound

➤ **Antonyms**

≠<u>undependable</u>: dependable, reliable, responsible, trustworthy ≠<u>uncertain</u>: accurate, infallible

unrepentant *adjective* <u>impenitent</u>, abandoned, callous, hardened, incorrigible, shameless, unremorseful

➤ **Antonyms**

ashamed, contrite, penitent, remorseful, repentant, rueful, sorry

unreserved *adjective* **1** <u>total</u>, absolute, complete, entire, full, unlimited, wholehearted **2** <u>uninhibited</u>, demonstrative, extrovert, free, open, outgoing, unrestrained

➤ **Antonyms**

≠<u>uninhibited</u>: inhibited, reserved, restrained, shy, undemonstrative

unresolved *adjective* <u>undecided</u>, doubtful, moot, unanswered, undetermined, unsettled, unsolved, vague

unrest *noun* <u>discontent</u>, agitation, discord, dissension, protest, rebellion, sedition, strife

➤ **Antonyms**

calm, contentment, peace, relaxation, rest, stillness, tranquillity

unrestrained *adjective* <u>uncontrolled</u>, abandoned, free, immoderate, intemperate, unbounded, unbridled, unchecked, uninhibited

➤ **Antonyms**

checked, inhibited, restrained

unrestricted *adjective* **1** <u>unlimited</u>, absolute, free, open, unbounded, unregulated **2** <u>open</u>, public

unrivalled *adjective* <u>unparalleled</u>, beyond compare, incomparable, matchless, supreme, unequalled, unmatched, unsurpassed

unruly *adjective* <u>uncontrollable</u>, disobedient, mutinous, rebellious, wayward, wild, wilful

➤ **Antonyms**

amenable, biddable, docile, obedient

unsafe *adjective* <u>dangerous</u>, hazardous, insecure, perilous, risky, unreliable

➤ **Antonyms**

harmless, reliable, safe, secure

unsatisfactory *adjective* <u>not good enough</u>, deficient, disappointing, inadequate, insufficient, not up to scratch (*informal*), poor, unacceptable

➤ **Antonyms**

acceptable, adequate, passable, satisfactory, sufficient

unsavoury *adjective* **1** <u>unpleasant</u>, distasteful, nasty, obnoxious, offensive, repellent, repulsive, revolting **2** <u>unappetizing</u>, nauseating, sickening, unpalatable

➤ **Antonyms**

≠<u>unappetizing</u>: appetizing, palatable, pleasant, savoury, tasty

unscathed *adjective* <u>unharmed</u>, safe, unhurt, uninjured, unmarked, whole

unscrupulous *adjective* <u>unprincipled</u>, corrupt, dishonest, dishonourable, immoral, improper, unethical

➤ **Antonyms**

ethical, honest, honourable, moral, principled, proper, scrupulous, upright

unseat *verb* **1** throw, unhorse, unsaddle **2** depose, dethrone, displace, oust, overthrow, remove

unseemly *adjective* improper, inappropriate, indecorous, unbecoming, undignified, unsuitable

► **Antonyms**

appropriate, becoming, decorous, fitting, proper, seemly, suitable

unseen *adjective* **1** hidden, concealed, invisible, obscure **2** unobserved, undetected, unnoticed

unselfish *adjective* generous, altruistic, kind, magnanimous, noble, selfless, self-sacrificing

unsettle *verb* disturb, agitate, bother, confuse, disconcert, faze, fluster, perturb, ruffle, trouble, upset

unsettled *adjective* **1** unstable, disorderly, insecure, shaky, unsteady **2** restless, agitated, anxious, confused, disturbed, flustered, restive, shaken, tense **3** inconstant, changing, uncertain, variable

unshakable *adjective* firm, absolute, fixed, immovable, secure, staunch, steadfast, sure, unswerving, unwavering

► **Antonyms**

insecure, shaky, unsure, wavering, wobbly

unsightly *adjective* ugly, disagreeable, hideous, horrid, repulsive, unattractive

► **Antonyms**

agreeable, attractive, beautiful, handsome, pretty

unskilled *adjective* unprofessional, amateurish, cowboy (*informal*), inexperienced, unqualified, untrained

► **Antonyms**

adept, expert, masterly, professional, qualified, skilled

unsociable *adjective* unfriendly, chilly, cold, distant, hostile, retiring, unforthcoming, withdrawn

► **Antonyms**

friendly, gregarious, outgoing, sociable

unsolicited *adjective* unasked for, gratuitous, uncalled-for, uninvited, unrequested, unsought

unsophisticated *adjective* **1** natural, artless, childlike, guileless, ingenuous, unaffected **2** simple, plain, uncomplicated, unrefined, unspecialized

► **Antonyms**

≠simple: advanced, complicated, intricate, sophisticated

unsound *adjective* **1** unhealthy, ailing, defective, diseased, ill, unbalanced, unstable, unwell, weak **2** invalid, defective, fallacious, false, flawed, illogical, shaky, specious, unreliable, weak

unspeakable *adjective* **1** indescribable, inconceivable, unbelievable, unimaginable **2** dreadful, abominable, appalling, awful, heinous, horrible, monstrous, shocking

unspoiled, unspoilt *adjective* **1** undamaged, intact, perfect, preserved, unchanged, untouched **2** natural, artless, innocent, unaffected

► **Antonyms**

≠undamaged: changed, damaged, imperfect, spoilt, touched

unspoken *adjective* tacit, implicit, implied, understood, unexpressed, unstated

► **Antonyms**

clear, explicit, expressed, spoken, stated

unstable *adjective* **1** insecure, precarious, shaky, tottering, unsettled, unsteady, wobbly **2** changeable, fitful, fluctuating, inconstant, unpredictable, variable, volatile **3** unpredictable, capricious, changeable, erratic, inconsistent, irrational, temperamental

► **Antonyms**

≠changeable: constant, predictable, stable ≠unpredictable: consistent, level-headed, rational, stable

unsteady *adjective* **1** unstable, infirm, insecure, precarious, shaky, unsafe, wobbly **2** erratic, changeable, inconstant, temperamental, unsettled, volatile

unsuccessful adjective **1** useless, failed, fruitless, futile, unavailing, unproductive, vain **2** unlucky, hapless, luckless, unfortunate

➤ **Antonyms**

≠useless: flourishing, fruitful, productive, successful, thriving, useful, worthwhile ≠unlucky: fortunate, lucky

unsuitable adjective inappropriate, improper, inapposite, inapt, ineligible, unacceptable, unbecoming, unfit, unfitting, unseemly

➤ **Antonyms**

acceptable, apposite, appropriate, apt, eligible, fitting, proper, suitable

unsure adjective **1** lacking in confidence, insecure, unassured, unconfident **2** doubtful, distrustful, dubious, hesitant, mistrustful, sceptical, suspicious, unconvinced

➤ **Antonyms**

assured, certain, confident, convinced, decided, persuaded, resolute, sure

unsuspecting adjective unconscious, credulous, gullible, trustful, trusting, unwary

unswerving adjective constant, firm, resolute, single-minded, staunch, steadfast, steady, true, unwavering

unsympathetic adjective hard, callous, cold, cruel, harsh, heartless, insensitive, unfeeling, unkind, unmoved

➤ **Antonyms**

caring, kind, sensitive, sympathetic, understanding

untangle verb **1** disentangle, extricate, unravel, unsnarl **2** solve, clear up, explain, straighten out

➤ **Antonyms**

≠disentangle: enmesh, entangle, snarl, tangle

untenable adjective unsustainable, groundless, illogical, indefensible, insupportable, shaky, unsound, weak

➤ **Antonyms**

defensible, logical, sensible, sound, supportable, valid, well-grounded

unthinkable adjective **1** impossible, absurd, out of the question, unreasonable **2** inconceivable, implausible, incredible, unimaginable

untidy adjective messy, chaotic, cluttered, disarrayed, disordered, jumbled, littered, muddled, shambolic, unkempt

➤ **Antonyms**

methodical, neat, orderly, shipshape, spruce, tidy, well-kept

untie verb undo, free, loosen, release, unbind, unfasten, unlace

untimely adjective **1** early, premature, unseasonable **2** ill-timed, awkward, inappropriate, inconvenient, inopportune, mistimed

➤ **Antonyms**

≠early: seasonable, timely ≠ill-timed: appropriate, convenient, opportune, well-timed

untiring adjective tireless, constant, determined, dogged, persevering, steady, unflagging, unremitting

untold adjective **1** indescribable, inexpressible, undreamed of, unimaginable, unthinkable, unutterable **2** countless, incalculable, innumerable, myriad, numberless, uncountable

untouched adjective unharmed, intact, undamaged, unhurt, uninjured, unscathed

untoward adjective **1** troublesome, annoying, awkward, inconvenient, irritating, unfortunate **2** unfavourable, adverse, inauspicious, inopportune, unlucky

untrained adjective amateur, green, inexperienced, raw, uneducated, unqualified, unschooled, unskilled, untaught

➤ **Antonyms**

educated, experienced, expert, qualified, schooled, skilled, taught, trained

untroubled adjective undisturbed, calm, cool, peaceful,

placid, tranquil, unconcerned, unfazed (*informal*), unperturbed, unworried

> ► **Antonyms**

agitated, anxious, concerned, disturbed, perturbed, troubled, worried

untrue *adjective* **1** false, deceptive, dishonest, erroneous, inaccurate, incorrect, lying, mistaken, wrong **2** unfaithful, deceitful, disloyal, faithless, false, inconstant, treacherous, untrustworthy

> ► **Antonyms**

≠false: accurate, correct, factual, right, true ≠unfaithful: constant, dependable, faithful, loyal

untrustworthy *adjective* unreliable, deceitful, devious, dishonest, disloyal, false, slippery, treacherous, tricky, undependable

> ► **Antonyms**

dependable, honest, loyal, reliable, trustworthy

untruth *noun* lie, deceit, falsehood, fib, pork pie (*Brit. slang*), porky (*Brit. slang*), story

untruthful *adjective* dishonest, deceitful, deceptive, false, lying, mendacious

> ► **Antonyms**

candid, honest, true, truthful, veracious

unusual *adjective* extraordinary, curious, different, exceptional, odd, queer, rare, remarkable, singular, strange, uncommon, unconventional

> ► **Antonyms**

average, banal, commonplace, conventional, everyday, familiar, normal, routine, traditional, typical, unremarkable, usual

unveil *verb* reveal, disclose, divulge, expose, make known, uncover

> ► **Antonyms**

cloak, conceal, cover, disguise, hide, mask, obscure, veil

unwanted *adjective* undesired, outcast, rejected, uninvited, unneeded, unsolicited, unwelcome

> ► **Antonyms**

desired, necessary, needed, wanted, welcome

unwarranted *adjective* unnecessary, gratuitous, groundless, indefensible, inexcusable, uncalled-for, unjustified, unprovoked

unwavering *adjective* steady, consistent, determined, immovable, resolute, staunch, steadfast, unshakable, unswerving

unwelcome *adjective* **1** unwanted, excluded, rejected, unacceptable, undesirable **2** disagreeable, displeasing, distasteful, undesirable, unpleasant

> ► **Antonyms**

acceptable, agreeable, desirable, pleasant, pleasing, popular, wanted, welcome

unwell *adjective* ill, ailing, sick, sickly, under the weather (*informal*), unhealthy

> ► **Antonyms**

fine, healthy, robust, sound, well

unwholesome *adjective* **1** harmful, deleterious, noxious, poisonous, unhealthy **2** wicked, bad, corrupting, degrading, demoralizing, evil, immoral

> ► **Antonyms**

≠harmful: beneficial, healthy, wholesome ≠wicked: moral

unwieldy *adjective* **1** awkward, cumbersome, inconvenient, unmanageable **2** bulky, clumsy, clunky (*informal*), hefty, massive, ponderous

unwilling *adjective* reluctant, averse, disinclined, grudging, indisposed, loath, resistant, unenthusiastic

> ► **Antonyms**

amenable, compliant, disposed, eager, enthusiastic, inclined, willing

unwind *verb* **1** unravel, slacken, uncoil, undo, unroll, untwine, untwist **2** relax, loosen up, take it easy, wind down

unwise *adjective* foolish, foolhardy, improvident, imprudent, inadvisable, injudicious, rash, reckless, senseless, silly, stupid

➤ Antonyms

judicious, prudent, sensible, shrewd, wise

unwitting adjective **1** unintentional, accidental, chance, inadvertent, involuntary, unplanned **2** unknowing, ignorant, innocent, unaware, unconscious, unsuspecting

➤ Antonyms

≠ unintentional: deliberate, intentional, planned ≠ unknowing: conscious, deliberate, knowing, witting

unworldly adjective **1** spiritual, metaphysical, nonmaterialistic **2** naive, idealistic, innocent, unsophisticated

unworthy adjective **1** undeserving, not fit for, not good enough **2** dishonourable, base, contemptible, degrading, discreditable, disgraceful, disreputable, ignoble, shameful **3** unworthy of unbefitting, beneath, inappropriate, unbecoming, unfitting, unseemly, unsuitable

➤ Antonyms

≠ undeserving: deserving, fit, meritorious, worthy ≠ dishonourable: commendable, creditable, honourable

unwritten adjective **1** oral, vocal **2** customary, accepted, tacit, understood

unyielding adjective firm, adamant, immovable, inflexible, obdurate, obstinate, resolute, rigid, stiff-necked, stubborn, tough, uncompromising

➤ Antonyms

compliant, compromising, flexible, movable, yielding

upbeat adjective Informal cheerful, cheery, encouraging, hopeful, optimistic, positive

upbraid verb scold, admonish, berate, rebuke, reprimand, reproach, reprove

upbringing noun education, breeding, raising, rearing, training

update verb bring up to date, amend, modernize, rebrand, renew, revise

upgrade verb promote, advance, better, elevate, enhance, improve, raise

➤ Antonyms

degrade, demote, downgrade, lower

upheaval noun disturbance, disorder, disruption, revolution, turmoil

uphill adjective **1** ascending, climbing, mounting, rising **2** arduous, difficult, exhausting, gruelling, hard, laborious, strenuous, taxing, tough

➤ Antonyms

≠ ascending: descending, downhill, lowering

uphold verb support, advocate, aid, back, champion, defend, endorse, maintain, promote, sustain

upkeep noun **1** maintenance, keep, repair, running, subsistence **2** running costs, expenditure, expenses, overheads

uplift verb **1** raise, elevate, hoist, lift up **2** improve, advance, better, edify, inspire, raise, refine ◆ noun **3** improvement, advancement, edification, enhancement, enlightenment, enrichment, refinement

upper adjective **1** higher, high, loftier, superior, top, topmost **2** superior, eminent, greater, important

➤ Antonyms

≠ higher: bottom, inferior, low, lower ≠ superior: inferior, junior, low, lower

upper-class adjective aristocratic, blue-blooded, highborn, highclass, noble, patrician

upper hand noun control, advantage, ascendancy, edge, mastery, supremacy

uppermost adjective **1** top, highest, loftiest, topmost **2** supreme, chief, dominant, foremost, greatest, leading, main, principal

➤ Antonyms

≠ top: bottom, lowermost, lowest ≠ supreme: humblest, least, lowliest, slightest

uppity adjective Informal conceited, bumptious, cocky, full of oneself, impertinent, self-important, uppish (Brit. informal)

upright adjective 1 vertical, erect, perpendicular, straight 2 honest, conscientious, ethical, good, honourable, just, principled, righteous, virtuous

➤ **Antonyms**

≠vertical: flat, horizontal, prone, prostrate, supine ≠honest: dishonest, dishonourable, unethical, unjust, wicked

uprising noun rebellion, disturbance, insurgence, insurrection, mutiny, revolt, revolution, rising

uproar noun commotion, din, furore, mayhem, noise, outcry, pandemonium, racket, riot, turmoil

uproarious adjective 1 hilarious, hysterical, killing (informal), ribtickling, rip-roaring (informal), side-splitting, very funny 2 boisterous, loud, rollicking, unrestrained

➤ **Antonyms**

≠hilarious: mournful, sad, serious, tragic ≠boisterous: quiet

uproot verb 1 pull up, dig up, rip up, root out, weed out 2 displace, exile

upset adjective 1 distressed, agitated, bothered, dismayed, disturbed, grieved, hurt, put out, troubled, worried 2 sick, ill, queasy 3 disordered, chaotic, confused, disarrayed, in disarray, muddled 4 overturned, capsized, spilled, upside down ♦ verb 5 tip over, capsize, knock over, overturn, spill 6 mess up, change, disorder, disorganize, disturb, spoil 7 distress, agitate, bother, disconcert, disturb, faze, fluster, grieve, perturb, ruffle, trouble ♦ noun 8 reversal, defeat, shake-up (informal) 9 distress, agitation, bother, disturbance, shock, trouble, worry 10 illness, bug (informal), complaint, disorder, malady, sickness

upshot noun result, culmination, end, end result, finale, outcome, sequel

upside down adjective 1 inverted, overturned, upturned 2 Informal confused, chaotic, disordered, higgledy-piggledy (informal), muddled, topsy-turvy

upstanding adjective honest, ethical, good, honourable, incorruptible, moral, principled, upright

➤ **Antonyms**

bad, corrupt, dishonest, immoral, unethical, unprincipled

upstart noun social climber, arriviste, nouveau riche, parvenu

uptight adjective Informal tense, anxious, edgy, on edge, uneasy, wired (slang)

up-to-date adjective modern, current, fashionable, in vogue, stylish, trendy (Brit. informal), up-to-the-minute

➤ **Antonyms**

dated, old fashioned, outmoded, out of date, passé

upturn noun rise, advancement, improvement, increase, recovery, revival, upsurge, upswing

urban adjective civic, city, metropolitan, municipal, town

urbane adjective sophisticated, cultivated, cultured, debonair, polished, refined, smooth, suave, well-bred

➤ **Antonyms**

boorish, gauche, uncouth, uncultured

urchin noun ragamuffin, brat, gamin, waif

urge noun 1 impulse, compulsion, desire, drive, itch, longing, thirst, wish, yearning ♦ verb 2 beg, beseech, entreat, exhort, implore, plead 3 advocate, advise, counsel, recommend, support 4 drive, compel, encourage, force, gee up, goad, impel, incite, induce, press, push, spur

➤ **Antonyms**

noun ≠impulse: aversion, disinclination, distaste, indisposition, reluctance, repugnance ≠verb ≠advocate, drive: caution, deter, discourage, dissuade, warn

urgency noun <u>importance</u>, extremity, gravity, hurry, necessity, need, pressure, seriousness

urgent adjective <u>crucial</u>, compelling, critical, immediate, imperative, important, pressing, top-priority

➤ **Antonyms**

low-priority, minor, trivial, unimportant

usable adjective <u>serviceable</u>, available, current, functional, practical, utilizable, valid, working

usage noun **1** <u>use</u>, control, employment, handling, management, operation, running **2** <u>practice</u>, convention, custom, habit, method, mode, procedure, regime, routine

use verb **1** <u>employ</u>, apply, exercise, exert, operate, practise, utilize, work **2** <u>take advantage of</u>, exploit, manipulate **3** <u>consume</u>, exhaust, expend, run through, spend ♦ noun **4** <u>usage</u>, application, employment, exercise, handling, operation, practice, service **5** <u>good</u>, advantage, avail, benefit, help, point, profit, service, usefulness, value **6** <u>purpose</u>, end, object, reason

used adjective <u>second-hand</u>, cast-off, nearly new, shopsoiled

➤ **Antonyms**

brand-new, fresh, new, pristine, unused

used to adjective <u>accustomed to</u>, familiar with

useful adjective <u>helpful</u>, advantageous, beneficial, effective, fruitful, practical, profitable, serviceable, valuable, worthwhile

➤ **Antonyms**

inadequate, ineffective, unhelpful, unproductive, useless, vain, worthless

usefulness noun <u>helpfulness</u>, benefit, convenience, effectiveness, efficacy, practicality, use, utility, value, worth

useless adjective **1** <u>worthless</u>, fruitless, futile, impractical, ineffectual, pointless, unproductive, vain, valueless **2** Informal <u>inept</u>, hopeless, incompetent, ineffectual, no good

➤ **Antonyms**

≠<u>worthless</u>: advantageous, fruitful, practical, productive, useful, valuable, worthwhile

use up verb <u>consume</u>, absorb, drain, exhaust, finish, run through

usher noun **1** <u>attendant</u>, doorkeeper, doorman, escort, guide ♦ verb **2** <u>escort</u>, conduct, direct, guide, lead

usual adjective <u>normal</u>, common, customary, everyday, general, habitual, ordinary, regular, routine, standard, typical

➤ **Antonyms**

exceptional, extraordinary, new, novel, off-beat, rare, singular, uncommon, unique, unusual

usually adverb <u>normally</u>, as a rule, commonly, generally, habitually, mainly, mostly, on the whole

usurp verb <u>seize</u>, appropriate, assume, commandeer, take, take over, wrest

utility noun <u>usefulness</u>, benefit, convenience, efficacy, practicality, serviceableness

utilize verb <u>use</u>, avail oneself of, employ, make use of, put to use, take advantage of, turn to account

utmost adjective **1** <u>greatest</u>, chief, highest, maximum, paramount, pre-eminent, supreme **2** <u>farthest</u>, extreme, final, last ♦ noun **3** <u>greatest</u>, best, hardest, highest

Utopia noun <u>paradise</u>, bliss, Eden, Garden of Eden, heaven, Shangri-la

Utopian adjective <u>perfect</u>, dream, fantasy, ideal, idealistic, imaginary, romantic, visionary

utter[1] verb <u>express</u>, articulate, pronounce, say, speak, voice

utter[2] adjective <u>absolute</u>, complete, downright, outright, sheer, thorough, total, unmitigated

utterance noun <u>speech</u>, announcement, declaration, expression, remark, statement, words

utterly adverb <u>totally</u>, absolutely, completely, entirely, extremely, fully, perfectly, thoroughly

V v

vacancy noun <u>job</u>, opening, opportunity, position, post, situation

vacant adjective 1 <u>unoccupied</u>, available, empty, free, idle, unfilled, untenanted, void 2 <u>blank</u>, absent-minded, abstracted, dreamy, idle, inane, vacuous, vague

➤ **Antonyms**
≠<u>unoccupied</u>: busy, engaged, full, inhabited, in use, occupied, taken ≠<u>blank</u>: animated, engrossed, expressive, lively, reflective, thoughtful

vacate verb <u>leave</u>, evacuate, quit

vacuous adjective <u>unintelligent</u>, blank, inane, stupid, uncomprehending, vacant

vacuum noun <u>emptiness</u>, gap, nothingness, space, vacuity, void

vagabond noun <u>vagrant</u>, beggar, down-and-out, itinerant, rover, tramp

vagrant noun 1 <u>tramp</u>, drifter, hobo (U.S.), itinerant, rolling stone, wanderer ♦ adjective 2 <u>itinerant</u>, nomadic, roaming, rootless, roving, unsettled, vagabond

➤ **Antonyms**
adjective ≠<u>itinerant</u>: established, fixed, purposeful, rooted, settled

vague adjective 1 <u>unclear</u>, hazy, imprecise, indefinite, loose, uncertain, unspecified, woolly 2 <u>indistinct</u>, hazy, ill-defined, indeterminate, nebulous, unclear

➤ **Antonyms**
≠<u>unclear</u>: clear, clear-cut, definite, distinct, exact, explicit, precise, specific ≠<u>indistinct</u>: clear,

distinct, well-defined

vain adjective 1 <u>proud</u>, arrogant, conceited, egotistical, narcissistic, self-important, swaggering 2 <u>futile</u>, abortive, fruitless, idle, pointless, senseless, unavailing, unprofitable, useless, worthless ♦ noun 3 **in vain** <u>to no avail</u>, fruitless(ly), ineffectual(ly), unsuccessful(ly), useless(ly), vain(ly)

➤ **Antonyms**
adjective ≠<u>proud</u>: bashful, humble, meek, modest, self-deprecating ≠<u>futile</u>: fruitful, profitable, serious, successful, useful, valid, worthwhile, worthy

valiant adjective <u>brave</u>, bold, courageous, fearless, gallant, heroic, intrepid, lion-hearted

➤ **Antonyms**
cowardly, craven, fearful, shrinking, spineless, timid, weak

valid adjective 1 <u>sound</u>, cogent, convincing, good, logical, telling, well-founded, well-grounded 2 <u>legal</u>, authentic, bona fide, genuine, lawful, legitimate, official

➤ **Antonyms**
≠<u>sound</u>: bogus, false, sham, spurious, unfounded, unrecognized ≠<u>legal</u>: illegal, inoperative, invalid, unlawful, unofficial

validate verb 1 <u>confirm</u>, certify, corroborate, prove, substantiate 2 <u>authorize</u>, authenticate, endorse, ratify

validity noun 1 <u>soundness</u>, cogency, force, power, strength, weight 2 <u>legality</u>, authority, lawfulness, legitimacy, right

valley noun <u>hollow</u>, dale, dell, depression, glen, vale

valour noun <u>bravery</u>, boldness, courage, fearlessness, gallantry, heroism, intrepidity, spirit

➤ **Antonyms**
cowardice, dread, fear, timidity, trepidation, weakness

valuable adjective 1 <u>precious</u>, costly, dear, expensive, high-priced 2 <u>useful</u>, beneficial, helpful, important, prized, profitable, worthwhile ♦ noun 3 **valuables**

treasures, heirlooms
► **Antonyms**
adjective ≠<u>precious</u>: cheap, inexpensive, worthless ≠<u>useful</u>: insignificant, pointless, trivial, unimportant, useless, worthless

value *noun* **1** <u>importance</u>, advantage, benefit, desirability, merit, profit, usefulness, utility, worth **2** <u>cost</u>, market price, rate **3** <u>values</u> <u>principles</u>, ethics, (moral) standards ♦ *verb* **4** <u>evaluate</u>, appraise, assess, estimate, price, rate, set at **5** <u>regard highly</u>, appreciate, cherish, esteem, hold dear, prize, respect, treasure
► **Antonyms**
noun ≠<u>importance</u>: insignificance, unimportance, uselessness, worthlessness ♦ *verb* ≠<u>regard highly</u>: disregard, have no time for, hold a low opinion of, underestimate, undervalue

vandal *noun* <u>hooligan</u>, delinquent, rowdy, yob or yobbo (*Brit. slang*)

vanguard *noun* <u>forefront</u>, cutting edge, forerunners, front line, leaders, spearhead, trailblazers, trendsetters, van
► **Antonyms**
rearguard, tail end

vanish *verb* <u>disappear</u>, dissolve, evanesce, evaporate, fade (away), melt (away)
► **Antonyms**
appear, arrive, materialize, pop up

vanity *noun* <u>pride</u>, arrogance, conceit, conceitedness, egotism, narcissism
► **Antonyms**
humility, meekness, modesty, self-deprecation

vanquish *verb Literary* <u>defeat</u>, beat, conquer, crush, master, overcome, overpower, overwhelm, triumph over

vapid *adjective* <u>dull</u>, bland, boring, flat, insipid, tame, uninspiring, uninteresting, weak, wishy-washy (*informal*)

vapour *noun* <u>mist</u>, exhalation, fog, haze, steam

variable *adjective* <u>changeable</u>, flexible, fluctuating, inconstant, mutable, shifting, temperamental, uneven, unstable, unsteady
► **Antonyms**
constant, fixed, settled, stable, steady, unalterable, unchanging

variance *noun* <u>at variance</u> <u>in disagreement</u>, at loggerheads, at odds, at sixes and sevens (*informal*), conflicting, out of line

variant *adjective* **1** <u>different</u>, alternative, divergent, modified ♦ *noun* **2** <u>variation</u>, alternative, development, modification

variation *noun* <u>difference</u>, change, departure, deviation, diversity, innovation, modification, novelty, variety
► **Antonyms**
monotony, sameness, uniformity

varied *adjective* <u>different</u>, assorted, diverse, heterogeneous, miscellaneous, mixed, motley, sundry, various
► **Antonyms**
homogeneous, repetitive, similar, standardized, uniform, unvarying

variety *noun* **1** <u>diversity</u>, change, difference, discrepancy, diversification, multifariousness, variation **2** <u>range</u>, array, assortment, collection, cross section, medley, miscellany, mixture **3** <u>type</u>, brand, breed, category, class, kind, sort, species, strain
► **Antonyms**
≠<u>diversity</u>: homogeneity, monotony, similarity, uniformity

various *adjective* <u>different</u>, assorted, disparate, distinct, diverse, miscellaneous, several, sundry, varied
► **Antonyms**
alike, equivalent, matching, same, similar, uniform

varnish *noun, verb* <u>lacquer</u>, glaze, gloss, polish

vary *verb* **1** <u>change</u>, alter, fluctuate **2** <u>differ</u>, disagree, diverge **3** <u>alternate</u>

vast *adjective* <u>huge</u>, boundless, colossal, enormous, gigantic, great, immense, massive, monumental, wide

➤ **Antonyms**

microscopic, negligible, paltry, puny, small, tiny

vault[1] *noun* **1** strongroom, depository, repository **2** crypt, catacomb, cellar, charnel house, mausoleum, tomb, undercroft

vault[2] *verb* jump, bound, clear, hurdle, leap, spring

vaulted *adjective* arched, cavernous, domed

veer *verb* change direction, change course, sheer, shift, swerve, turn

vegetate *verb* stagnate, deteriorate, go to seed, idle, languish, loaf

➤ **Antonyms**

develop, grow

vehemence *noun* forcefulness, ardour, emphasis, energy, fervour, force, intensity, passion, vigour

➤ **Antonyms**

coolness, indifference, lethargy, stoicism

vehement *adjective* strong, ardent, emphatic, fervent, fierce, forceful, impassioned, intense, passionate, powerful

➤ **Antonyms**

calm, cool, dispassionate, half-hearted, lukewarm

vehicle *noun* **1** transport, conveyance, transportation **2** medium, apparatus, channel, means, mechanism, organ

veil *noun* **1** cover, blind, cloak, curtain, disguise, film, mask, screen, shroud ◆ *verb* **2** cover, cloak, conceal, disguise, hide, mask, obscure, screen, shield

➤ **Antonyms**

verb ≠cover: disclose, display, divulge, expose, lay bare, reveal, uncover, unveil

veiled *adjective* disguised, concealed, covert, hinted at, implied, masked, suppressed

vein *noun* **1** blood vessel **2** seam, course, current, lode, stratum, streak, stripe **3** mood, mode, note, style, temper, tenor, tone

velocity *noun* speed, pace, quickness, rapidity, swiftness

velvety *adjective* soft, delicate, downy, smooth

vendetta *noun* feud, bad blood, quarrel

veneer *noun* **1** layer, finish, gloss **2** mask, appearance, façade, front, guise, pretence, semblance, show

venerable *adjective* respected, august, esteemed, honoured, revered, sage, wise, worshipped

➤ **Antonyms**

discredited, disgraced, ignominious, inglorious, scorned

venerate *verb* respect, adore, esteem, honour, look up to, revere, reverence, worship

➤ **Antonyms**

dishonour, execrate, mock, scorn

vengeance *noun* revenge, reprisal, requital, retaliation, retribution

➤ **Antonyms**

absolution, acquittal, exoneration, forbearance, forgiveness, mercy, pardon, remission

venom *noun* **1** malice, acrimony, bitterness, hate, rancour, spite, spleen, virulence **2** poison, bane, toxin

➤ **Antonyms**

≠malice: benevolence, charity, compassion, favour, goodwill, kindness, love, mercy

venomous *adjective* **1** malicious, hostile, malignant, rancorous, savage, spiteful, vicious, vindictive **2** poisonous, mephitic, noxious, toxic, virulent

➤ **Antonyms**

≠malicious: affectionate, benevolent, compassionate, forgiving, harmless, loving, magnanimous ≠poisonous: harmless, nonpoisonous, nontoxic, nonvenomous

vent *noun* **1** outlet, aperture, duct, opening, orifice ◆ *verb* **2** express, air, discharge, emit, give vent to, pour out, release, utter, voice

➤ **Antonyms**

verb ≠express: bottle up, curb,

hold back, inhibit, repress, stifle

venture noun **1** undertaking, adventure, endeavour, enterprise, gamble, hazard, project, risk ♦ verb **2** risk, chance, hazard, speculate, stake, wager **3** go, embark on, plunge into, set out **4** dare, hazard, make bold, presume, take the liberty, volunteer

verbal adjective spoken, oral, unwritten, word-of-mouth

verbatim adverb word for word, exactly, precisely, to the letter

verbose adjective long-winded, circumlocutory, diffuse, periphrastic, prolix, tautological, windy, wordy

► **Antonyms**
brief, concise, curt, short, succinct, terse

verbosity noun long-windedness, loquaciousness, prolixity, verboseness, wordiness

verdant adjective Literary green, flourishing, fresh, grassy, leafy, lush

verdict noun decision, adjudication, conclusion, finding, judgment, opinion, sentence

verge noun **1** border, boundary, brim, brink, edge, limit, margin, threshold ♦ verb **2** verge on come near to, approach, border

verification noun proof, authentication, confirmation, corroboration, substantiation, validation

verify verb **1** check **2** prove, authenticate, bear out, confirm, corroborate, substantiate, support, validate

► **Antonyms**
≠prove: deny, invalidate, nullify

vernacular noun dialect, idiom, parlance, patois, speech

versatile adjective adaptable, adjustable, all-purpose, all-round, flexible, multifaceted, resourceful, variable

► **Antonyms**
fixed, inflexible, invariable, limited, one-sided

versed adjective knowledgeable, acquainted, conversant, experienced, familiar, practised, profi-

cient, seasoned, well informed

► **Antonyms**
ignorant, inexperienced, unpractised, unschooled, unversed

version noun **1** form, design, model, style, variant **2** account, interpretation **3** adaptation, portrayal, rendering

vertical adjective upright, erect, on end, perpendicular

► **Antonyms**
flat, horizontal, level, plane, prone

vertigo noun dizziness, giddiness, light-headedness

verve noun enthusiasm, animation, energy, gusto, liveliness, sparkle, spirit, vitality

► **Antonyms**
apathy, half-heartedness, indifference, inertia, languor, lethargy, torpor

very adverb **1** extremely, acutely, decidedly, deeply, exceedingly, greatly, highly, profoundly, really, uncommonly, unusually ♦ adjective **2** exact, precise, selfsame

vessel noun **1** ship, boat, craft **2** container, pot, receptacle, utensil

vest verb, with in or with place, bestow, confer, consign, endow, entrust, invest, settle

vestibule noun hall, anteroom, foyer, lobby, porch, portico

vestige noun trace, glimmer, indication, remnant, scrap, suspicion

vet verb check, appraise, examine, investigate, review, scrutinize

veteran noun **1** old hand, old stager, past master, warhorse (informal) ♦ adjective **2** long-serving, battle-scarred, old, seasoned

► **Antonyms**
noun ≠old hand: apprentice, beginner, initiate, novice

veto noun **1** ban, boycott, embargo, interdict, prohibition ♦ verb **2** ban, boycott, disallow, forbid, prohibit, reject, rule out, turn down

► **Antonyms**
noun ≠ban: approval, endorsement, go-ahead (informal), ratifi-

cation ♦ *verb* ≠ban: approve, endorse, O.K. or okay (*informal*), pass, ratify

vex *verb* annoy, bother, distress, exasperate, irritate, plague, trouble, upset, worry

➤ **Antonyms**

appease, comfort, console, mollify, please, soothe

vexation *noun* **1** annoyance, chagrin, displeasure, dissatisfaction, exasperation, frustration, irritation, pique **2** problem, bother, difficulty, hassle (*informal*), headache (*informal*), nuisance, trouble, worry

viable *adjective* workable, applicable, feasible, operable, practicable, usable

➤ **Antonyms**

impossible, impracticable, inconceivable, out of the question, unthinkable, unworkable

vibrant *adjective* energetic, alive, animated, dynamic, sparkling, spirited, storming, vigorous, vivacious, vivid

vibrate *verb* shake, fluctuate, judder (*informal*), oscillate, pulsate, quiver, reverberate, sway, throb, tremble

vibration *noun* shake, judder (*informal*), oscillation, pulsation, quiver, reverberation, throbbing, trembling, tremor

vicarious *adjective* **1** indirect, at one remove **2** substituted, surrogate **3** delegated, deputed

vice *noun* **1** wickedness, corruption, depravity, evil, immorality, iniquity, sin, turpitude **2** fault, blemish, defect, failing, imperfection, shortcoming, weakness

➤ **Antonyms**

≠wickedness: honour, morality, virtue ≠fault: gift, good point, strong point, talent

vice versa *adverb* conversely, contrariwise, in reverse, the other way round

vicinity *noun* neighbourhood, area, district, environs, locality, neck of the woods (*informal*), proximity

vicious *adjective* **1** savage, barbarous, cruel, ferocious, violent **2** malicious, cruel, mean, spiteful, venomous, vindictive

➤ **Antonyms**

≠savage: docile, friendly, gentle, good, honourable, kind, playful, tame, upright, virtuous

victim *noun* casualty, fatality, martyr, sacrifice, scapegoat, sufferer

➤ **Antonyms**

survivor

victimize *verb* persecute, discriminate against, have it in for (someone) (*informal*), pick on

victor *noun* winner, champion, conqueror, prizewinner, vanquisher

➤ **Antonyms**

also-ran, dud (*informal*), failure, flop (*informal*), loser, vanquished

victorious *adjective* winning, champion, conquering, first, prizewinning, successful, triumphant, vanquishing

➤ **Antonyms**

beaten, conquered, defeated, failed, losing, overcome, unsuccessful, vanquished

victory *noun* win, conquest, success, triumph

➤ **Antonyms**

defeat, failure, loss

vie *verb* compete, contend, strive, struggle

view *noun* **1** *sometimes plural* opinion, attitude, belief, conviction, feeling, impression, point of view, sentiment **2** scene, landscape, outlook, panorama, perspective, picture, prospect, spectacle, vista **3** vision, sight ♦ *verb* **4** regard, consider, deem, look on

viewer *noun* watcher, observer, onlooker, spectator

vigilance *noun* watchfulness, alertness, attentiveness, carefulness, caution, circumspection, observance

vigilant *adjective* watchful, alert, attentive, careful, cautious, circumspect, on one's guard, on the lookout, wakeful

► **Antonyms**

careless, inattentive, lax, neglectful, negligent, remiss, slack

vigorous *adjective* energetic, active, dynamic, forceful, lively, lusty, powerful, spirited, strenuous, strong

► **Antonyms**

apathetic, feeble, inactive, lethargic, lifeless, weak, wishy-washy

vigorously *adverb* energetically, forcefully, hard, lustily, strenuously, strongly

vigour *noun* energy, animation, dynamism, forcefulness, gusto, liveliness, power, spirit, strength, verve, vitality

► **Antonyms**

apathy, inactivity, inertia, lethargy, sluggishness, weakness

vile *adjective* **1** wicked, corrupt, degenerate, depraved, evil, nefarious, perverted **2** disgusting, foul, horrid, nasty, nauseating, offensive, repugnant, repulsive, revolting, sickening

► **Antonyms**

≠wicked: honourable, noble, pure, refined, righteous, worthy ≠disgusting: agreeable, delicate, lovely, marvellous, pleasant, splendid, sublime

vilify *verb* malign, abuse, berate, denigrate, disparage, revile, slander, smear

► **Antonyms**

commend, esteem, exalt, glorify, honour, praise

villain *noun* **1** evildoer, blackguard, criminal, miscreant, reprobate, rogue, scoundrel, wretch **2** antihero, baddy (*informal*)

► **Antonyms**

≠antihero: goody, hero, heroine

villainous *adjective* wicked, bad, cruel, degenerate, depraved, evil, fiendish, nefarious, vicious, vile

► **Antonyms**

angelic, good, heroic, noble, righteous, saintly, virtuous

villainy *noun* wickedness, delin-

quency, depravity, devilry, iniquity, turpitude, vice

vindicate *verb* **1** clear, absolve, acquit, exculpate, exonerate, rehabilitate **2** justify, defend, excuse

► **Antonyms**

≠clear: accuse, blame, condemn, convict, incriminate, punish, reproach

vindication *noun* **1** exoneration, exculpation **2** justification, defence, excuse

vindictive *adjective* vengeful, implacable, malicious, resentful, revengeful, spiteful, unforgiving, unrelenting

► **Antonyms**

forgiving, generous, magnanimous, merciful

vintage *adjective* best, choice, classic, prime, select, superior

violate *verb* **1** break, contravene, disobey, disregard, encroach upon, infringe, transgress **2** desecrate, abuse, befoul, defile, dishonour, pollute, profane **3** rape, abuse, assault, debauch, ravish

► **Antonyms**

≠break: honour, obey, respect, uphold ≠desecrate: defend, honour, protect, respect, revere, set on a pedestal

violation *noun* **1** infringement, abuse, breach, contravention, encroachment, infraction, transgression, trespass **2** desecration, defilement, profanation, sacrilege, spoliation

violence *noun* **1** force, bloodshed, brutality, cruelty, ferocity, fighting, savagery, terrorism **2** intensity, abandon, fervour, force, severity, vehemence

violent *adjective* destructive, brutal, cruel, hot-headed, murderous, riotous, savage, uncontrollable, unrestrained, vicious

► **Antonyms**

calm, composed, gentle, mild, peaceful, placid, quiet, rational, sane, serene, unruffled, well-behaved

V.I.P. *noun* celebrity, big hitter

virgin noun 1 maiden (archaic), girl ♦ adjective 2 pure, chaste, immaculate, uncorrupted, undefiled, vestal, virginal

➤ **Antonyms**

adjective ≠pure: corrupted, defiled, impure

virginity noun chastity, maidenhood

virile adjective manly, lusty, macho, manlike, masculine, red-blooded, strong, vigorous

➤ **Antonyms**

effeminate, feminine, girlie, impotent, unmanly, weak

virility noun masculinity, machismo, manhood, vigour

➤ **Antonyms**

effeminacy, femininity, impotence, unmanliness

virtual adjective practical, essential, in all but name

virtually adverb practically, almost, as good as, in all but name, in effect, in essence, nearly

virtue noun 1 goodness, incorruptibility, integrity, morality, probity, rectitude, righteousness, uprightness, worth 2 merit, advantage, asset, attribute, credit, good point, plus (informal), strength

➤ **Antonyms**

≠goodness: corruption, debauchery, depravity, dishonesty, evil, immorality, sinfulness, vice ≠merit: drawback, failing, shortcoming, weak point

virtuosity noun mastery, brilliance, craft, expertise, flair, panache, polish, skill

virtuoso noun master, artist, genius, maestro, magician

virtuous adjective good, ethical, honourable, incorruptible, moral, praiseworthy, righteous, upright, worthy

➤ **Antonyms**

corrupt, debauched, depraved,

dishonest, evil, immoral, sinful, wicked

virulent adjective deadly, lethal, pernicious, poisonous, toxic, venomous

➤ **Antonyms**

harmless, innocuous, nonpoisonous, nontoxic

viscous adjective thick, gelatinous, icky (informal), sticky, syrupy

visible adjective apparent, clear, discernible, evident, in view, manifest, observable, perceptible, unconcealed

➤ **Antonyms**

concealed, hidden, imperceptible, invisible, obscured, unnoticeable, unseen

vision noun 1 sight, eyesight, perception, seeing, view 2 image, concept, conception, daydream, dream, fantasy, idea, ideal 3 hallucination, apparition, chimera, delusion, illusion, mirage, revelation 4 foresight, discernment, farsightedness, imagination, insight, intuition, penetration, prescience

visionary adjective 1 idealistic, impractical, quixotic, romantic, speculative, starry-eyed, unrealistic, unworkable, utopian 2 prophetic, mystical ♦ noun 3 idealist, daydreamer, dreamer, romantic 4 prophet, mystic, seer

➤ **Antonyms**

adjective ≠idealistic: pragmatic, realistic ♦ noun ≠idealist: cynic, pessimist, pragmatist, realist

visit verb 1 call on, drop in on (informal), look (someone) up, stay with, stop by ♦ noun 2 call, sojourn, stay, stop

visitation noun 1 inspection, examination, visit 2 catastrophe, blight, calamity, cataclysm, disaster, ordeal, punishment, scourge

visitor noun guest, caller, company

vista noun view, panorama, perspective, prospect

visual adjective 1 optical, ocular, optic 2 observable, discernible, perceptible, visible

➤ **Antonyms**

≠<u>observable</u>: imperceptible, indiscernible, invisible, out of sight, unnoticeable

visualize *verb* <u>picture</u>, conceive of, envisage, imagine

vital *adjective* **1** <u>essential</u>, basic, fundamental, imperative, indispensable, necessary, requisite **2** <u>important</u>, critical, crucial, decisive, key, life-or-death, significant, urgent **3** <u>lively</u>, animated, dynamic, energetic, spirited, vibrant, vigorous, vivacious, zestful

➤ **Antonyms**

≠<u>essential</u>: dispensable, inessential, nonessential, unnecessary ≠<u>important</u>: minor, trivial, unimportant ≠<u>lively</u>: apathetic, lethargic, listless

vitality *noun* <u>energy</u>, animation, exuberance, life, liveliness, strength, vigour, vivacity

➤ **Antonyms**

apathy, inertia, lethargy, listlessness, sluggishness, weakness

vitriolic *adjective* <u>bitter</u>, acerbic, caustic, envenomed, sardonic, scathing, venomous, virulent, withering

vivacious *adjective* <u>lively</u>, bubbling, ebullient, high-spirited, sparkling, spirited, sprightly, upbeat (*informal*), vital

➤ **Antonyms**

dull, languid, lifeless, listless, unenthusiastic

vivacity *noun* <u>liveliness</u>, animation, ebullience, energy, gaiety, high spirits, sparkle, spirit, sprightliness

➤ **Antonyms**

apathy, ennui, inertia, languor, lethargy, listlessness, weariness

vivid *adjective* **1** <u>bright</u>, brilliant, clear, colourful, glowing, intense, rich **2** <u>clear</u>, dramatic, graphic, lifelike, memorable, powerful, realistic, stirring, telling, true to life

➤ **Antonyms**

≠<u>bright</u>: drab, dull, pale, pastel,

sombre ≠<u>clear</u>: unclear, vague

vocabulary *noun* <u>words</u>, dictionary, glossary, language, lexicon

vocal *adjective* **1** <u>spoken</u>, oral, said, uttered, voiced **2** <u>outspoken</u>, articulate, eloquent, expressive, forthright, frank, plainspoken, strident, vociferous

➤ **Antonyms**

≠<u>outspoken</u>: inarticulate, quiet, reserved, reticent, retiring, shy, silent, uncommunicative

vocation *noun* <u>profession</u>, calling, career, job, mission, pursuit, trade

vociferous *adjective* <u>noisy</u>, clamorous, loud, outspoken, strident, uproarious, vehement, vocal

➤ **Antonyms**

hushed, muted, noiseless, quiet, silent, still

vogue *noun* **1** <u>fashion</u>, craze, custom, mode, style, trend, way **2** *As in* **in vogue** <u>popularity</u>, acceptance, currency, favour, prevalence, usage, use

voice *noun* **1** <u>sound</u>, articulation, tone, utterance **2** <u>say</u>, view, vote, will, wish ♦ *verb* **3** <u>express</u>, air, articulate, declare, enunciate, utter

void *noun* **1** <u>emptiness</u>, blankness, gap, lack, space, vacuity, vacuum ♦ *adjective* **2** <u>invalid</u>, ineffective, inoperative, null and void, useless, vain, worthless **3** *Old-fashioned* <u>empty</u>, bare, free, tenantless, unfilled, unoccupied, vacant ♦ *verb* **4** <u>invalidate</u>, cancel, nullify, rescind **5** <u>empty</u>, drain, evacuate

➤ **Antonyms**

adjective ≠<u>empty</u>: abounding, complete, filled, full, occupied, replete, tenanted

volatile *adjective* **1** <u>changeable</u>, explosive, inconstant, unsettled, unstable, unsteady, variable **2** <u>temperamental</u>, erratic, fickle, mercurial, up and down (*informal*)

➤ **Antonyms**

≠<u>changeable</u>: constant, inert, settled, stable, steady ≠<u>tempera-

<u>mental</u>: calm, consistent, cool-headed, dependable, reliable, self-controlled, sober

volition noun <u>free will</u>, choice, choosing, discretion, preference, will

volley noun <u>barrage</u>, blast, bombardment, burst, cannonade, fusillade, hail, salvo, shower

voluble adjective <u>talkative</u>, articulate, fluent, forthcoming, glib, loquacious

➤ **Antonyms**
inarticulate, reticent, succinct, taciturn, terse, unforthcoming

volume noun 1 <u>capacity</u>, compass, dimensions 2 <u>amount</u>, aggregate, body, bulk, mass, quantity, total 3 <u>book</u>, publication, title, tome, treatise

voluminous adjective <u>large</u>, ample, capacious, cavernous, roomy, vast

➤ **Antonyms**
skimpy, slight, small, tiny

voluntarily adverb <u>willingly</u>, by choice, freely, off one's own bat, of one's own accord

voluntary adjective <u>unforced</u>, discretionary, free, optional, spontaneous, willing

➤ **Antonyms**
automatic, forced, instinctive, involuntary, obligatory, unintentional

volunteer verb <u>offer</u>, step forward

➤ **Antonyms**
begrudge, deny, keep, refuse, retain, withdraw, withhold

voluptuous adjective 1 <u>buxom</u>, ample, curvaceous (informal), enticing, seductive, shapely 2 <u>sensual</u>, epicurean, hedonistic, licentious, luxurious, self-indulgent, sybaritic

➤ **Antonyms**
≠<u>sensual</u>: abstemious, ascetic, celibate, rigorous, self-denying, Spartan

vomit verb <u>be sick</u>, disgorge, emit, heave, regurgitate, retch,

spew out or up, throw up (informal)

voracious adjective 1 <u>gluttonous</u>, greedy, hungry, insatiable, omnivorous, ravenous 2 <u>avid</u>, hungry, insatiable, rapacious, unquenchable

➤ **Antonyms**
≠<u>avid</u>: moderate, sated, satisfied, temperate

vortex noun <u>whirlpool</u>, eddy, maelstrom

vote noun 1 <u>poll</u>, ballot, franchise, plebiscite, referendum, show of hands ♦ verb 2 <u>cast one's vote</u>, elect, opt

voucher noun <u>ticket</u>, coupon, token

vouch for verb 1 <u>guarantee</u>, answer for, certify, give assurance of, stand witness, swear to 2 <u>confirm</u>, affirm, assert, attest to, support, uphold

vow noun 1 <u>promise</u>, oath, pledge ♦ verb 2 <u>promise</u>, affirm, pledge, swear

voyage noun <u>journey</u>, crossing, cruise, passage, trip

vulgar adjective <u>crude</u>, coarse, common, impolite, indecent, ribald, risqué, rude, tasteless, uncouth, unrefined

➤ **Antonyms**
elegant, genteel, high-brow, refined, sophisticated, tasteful, urbane

vulgarity noun <u>crudeness</u>, bad taste, coarseness, indelicacy, ribaldry, rudeness, tastelessness

➤ **Antonyms**
gentility, good manners, good taste, refinement, sensitivity, sophistication, tastefulness

vulnerable adjective 1 <u>susceptible</u>, sensitive, tender, thin-skinned, weak 2 <u>exposed</u>, accessible, assailable, defenceless, unprotected, wide open

➤ **Antonyms**
≠<u>susceptible</u>: immune, impervious, insensitive, thick-skinned ≠<u>exposed</u>: guarded, invulnerable, unassailable, well-protected

W w

wad noun <u>mass</u>, bundle, hunk, roll

waddle verb <u>shuffle</u>, sway, toddle, totter, wobble

wade verb 1 <u>walk through</u>, ford, paddle, splash 2 **wade through** <u>plough through</u>, drudge at, labour at, peg away at, toil at, work one's way through

waffle verb 1 <u>prattle</u>, blather, jabber, prate, rabbit (on) (*Brit. informal*), witter on (*informal*) ◆ noun 2 <u>verbosity</u>, padding, prolixity, verbiage, wordiness

waft verb <u>carry</u>, bear, convey, drift, float, transport

wag verb 1 <u>wave</u>, bob, nod, quiver, shake, stir, vibrate, waggle, wiggle ◆ noun 2 <u>wave</u>, bob, nod, quiver, shake, vibration, waggle, wiggle

wage noun 1 *Also* **wages** <u>payment</u>, allowance, emolument, fee, pay, recompense, remuneration, reward, stipend ◆ verb 2 <u>engage in</u>, carry on, conduct, practise, proceed with, prosecute, pursue, undertake

wager noun 1 <u>bet</u>, flutter (*Brit. informal*), gamble, punt (*chiefly Brit.*) ◆ verb 2 <u>bet</u>, chance, gamble, lay, risk, speculate, stake, venture

waggle verb <u>wag</u>, flutter, oscillate, shake, wave, wiggle, wobble

waif noun <u>stray</u>, foundling, orphan

wail verb 1 <u>cry</u>, bawl, grieve, howl, lament, weep, yowl ◆ noun 2 <u>cry</u>, complaint, howl, lament, moan, weeping, yowl

wait verb 1 <u>remain</u>, hang fire, hold back, linger, pause, rest, stay, tarry ◆ noun 2 <u>delay</u>, halt, hold-up, interval, pause, rest, stay

> **Antonyms**
verb ≠<u>remain</u>: depart, go, go away, leave, move off, quit, set off, take off (*informal*)

waiter, waitress noun <u>attendant</u>, server, steward *or* stewardess

wait on *or* **upon** verb <u>serve</u>, attend, minister to, tend

waive verb <u>set aside</u>, abandon, dispense with, forgo, give up, relinquish, remit, renounce

> **Antonyms**
claim, demand, insist, maintain, press, profess, pursue, uphold

wake[1] verb 1 <u>awaken</u>, arise, awake, bestir, come to, get up, rouse, stir 2 <u>activate</u>, animate, arouse, excite, fire, galvanize, kindle, provoke, stimulate, stir up ◆ noun 3 <u>vigil</u>, deathwatch, funeral, watch

> **Antonyms**
verb ≠<u>awaken</u>: doze, drop off (*informal*), nod off (*informal*), sleep, snooze (*informal*)

wake[2] noun <u>slipstream</u>, aftermath, backwash, path, track, trail, train, wash, waves

wakeful adjective 1 <u>sleepless</u>, insomniac, restless 2 <u>watchful</u>, alert, alive, attentive, observant, on guard, vigilant, wary

> **Antonyms**
≠<u>sleepless</u>: asleep, dormant, dozing ≠<u>watchful</u>: dreamy, drowsy, heedless, inattentive, off guard, sleepy

waken verb <u>awaken</u>, activate, arouse, awake, rouse, stir

> **Antonyms**
doze, nap, repose, sleep, slumber, snooze (*informal*)

walk verb 1 <u>go</u>, amble, hike, march, move, pace, step, stride, stroll 2 <u>escort</u>, accompany, convoy, take ◆ noun 3 <u>stroll</u>, hike, march, promenade, ramble, saunter, trek, trudge 4 <u>gait</u>, carriage, step 5 <u>path</u>, alley, avenue, esplanade, footpath, lane, promenade, trail 6 <u>walk of life</u> <u>profession</u>, calling, career, field, line, trade, vocation

walker noun <u>pedestrian</u>, hiker,

rambler, wayfarer

walkout noun strike, industrial action, protest, stoppage

walkover noun pushover (slang), breeze (U.S. & Canad. informal), cakewalk (informal), child's play (informal), doddle (Brit. slang), picnic (informal), piece of cake (informal)

➤ Antonyms

effort, ordeal, strain, struggle, trial

wall noun **1** partition, enclosure, screen **2** barrier, fence, hedge, impediment, obstacle, obstruction

wallet noun holder, case, pocketbook, pouch, purse

wallop verb **1** hit, batter, beat, clobber (slang), pound, pummel, strike, swipe, thrash, thump, whack ◆ noun **2** blow, bash, punch, slug, smack, swipe, thump, thwack, whack

wallow verb **1** revel, bask, delight, glory, luxuriate, relish, take pleasure **2** roll about, splash around

➤ Antonyms

≠revel: abstain, avoid, do without, eschew, forgo, give up, refrain

wan adjective pale, anaemic, ashen, pallid, pasty, sickly, washed out, white

➤ Antonyms

glowing, healthy, rosy, ruddy

wand noun stick, baton, rod

wander verb **1** roam, drift, meander, ramble, range, rove, stray, stroll **2** deviate, depart, digress, diverge, err, go astray, swerve, veer ◆ noun excursion, cruise, meander, ramble

➤ Antonyms

verb ≠deviate: comply, conform, fall in with, follow, run with the pack, toe the line

wanderer noun traveller, drifter, gypsy, nomad, rambler, rover, vagabond, voyager

wandering adjective nomadic, itinerant, migratory, peripatetic, rootless, roving, travelling, vagrant, wayfaring

wane verb **1** decline, decrease, diminish, dwindle, ebb, fade, fail, lessen, subside, taper off, weaken **2** on the wane declining, dwindling, ebbing, fading, obsolescent, on the decline, tapering off, weakening

➤ Antonyms

verb ≠decline: expand, grow, improve, increase, rise, strengthen, wax

wangle verb contrive, arrange, engineer, fiddle (informal), fix (informal), manipulate, manoeuvre, pull off

want verb **1** desire, covet, crave, hanker after, hope for, hunger for, long for, thirst for, wish, yearn for **2** need, call for, demand, lack, miss, require ◆ noun **3** wish, appetite, craving, desire, longing, need, requirement, yearning **4** lack, absence, dearth, deficiency, famine, insufficiency, paucity, scarcity, shortage **5** poverty, destitution, neediness, penury, privation

➤ Antonyms

verb ≠desire: detest, dislike, hate, loathe, reject, spurn ≠need: be sated, have, own, possess ◆ noun ≠lack: abundance, adequacy, excess, plenty, sufficiency, surfeit, surplus ≠poverty: comfort, ease, luxury, wealth

wanting adjective **1** lacking, absent, incomplete, missing, short, shy **2** inadequate, defective, deficient, faulty, imperfect, poor, substandard, unsound

➤ Antonyms

≠lacking: complete, full ≠inadequate: adequate, enough, satisfactory, sufficient

wanton adjective **1** unprovoked, arbitrary, gratuitous, groundless, motiveless, needless, senseless, uncalled-for, unjustifiable, wilful **2** promiscuous, dissipated, dissolute, immoral, lecherous, libidinous, loose, lustful, shameless, unchaste

➤ **Antonyms**

≠<u>unprovoked</u>: excusable, justified, legitimate, provoked, warranted ≠<u>promiscuous</u>: priggish, prim, prudish, puritanical, strait-laced, stuffy

war noun 1 <u>fighting</u>, battle, combat, conflict, enmity, hostilities, struggle, warfare ♦ verb 2 <u>fight</u>, battle, campaign against, clash, combat, take up arms, wage war

➤ **Antonyms**

noun ≠<u>fighting</u>: ceasefire, harmony, peace, treaty, truce ♦ verb ≠<u>fight</u>: call a ceasefire, make peace

warble verb <u>sing</u>, chirp, trill, twitter

ward noun 1 <u>room</u>, apartment, cubicle 2 <u>district</u>, area, division, precinct, quarter, zone 3 <u>dependant</u>, charge, minor, protégé, pupil

warden noun <u>keeper</u>, administrator, caretaker, curator, custodian, guardian, ranger, superintendent

warder, wardress noun <u>jailer</u>, custodian, guard, prison officer, screw (slang)

ward off verb <u>repel</u>, avert, avoid, deflect, fend off, parry, stave off

➤ **Antonyms**

accept, admit, allow, embrace, permit, receive, take in, welcome

wardrobe noun 1 <u>clothes cupboard</u>, closet 2 <u>clothes</u>, apparel, attire

warehouse noun <u>store</u>, depository, depot, stockroom, storehouse

wares plural noun <u>goods</u>, commodities, merchandise, produce, products, stock, stuff

warfare noun <u>war</u>, arms, battle, combat, conflict, fighting, hostilities

➤ **Antonyms**

ceasefire, harmony, peace, truce

warily adverb <u>cautiously</u>, carefully, charily, circumspectly, distrustfully, gingerly, suspiciously, vigilantly, watchfully, with care

➤ **Antonyms**

carelessly, hastily, heedlessly, irresponsibly, rashly, recklessly, thoughtlessly

warlike adjective <u>belligerent</u>, aggressive, bellicose, bloodthirsty, hawkish, hostile, martial, warmongering

➤ **Antonyms**

conciliatory, friendly, pacific, peaceable, peaceful, placid

warlock noun <u>magician</u>, conjuror, enchanter, sorcerer, wizard

warm adjective 1 <u>heated</u>, balmy, lukewarm, pleasant, sunny, tepid, thermal 2 <u>affectionate</u>, amorous, cordial, friendly, hospitable, kindly, loving, tender ♦ verb 3 <u>heat</u>, heat up, melt, thaw, warm up

➤ **Antonyms**

adjective ≠<u>heated</u>: chilly, cold, cool, freezing, icy ≠<u>affectionate</u>: aloof, distant, stand-offish, unenthusiastic, unfriendly, unwelcoming ♦ verb ≠<u>heat</u>: chill, cool, cool down, freeze

warmonger noun <u>hawk</u>, belligerent, militarist, sabre-rattler

warmth noun 1 <u>heat</u>, hotness, warmness 2 <u>affection</u>, amorousness, cordiality, heartiness, kindliness, love, tenderness

➤ **Antonyms**

≠<u>heat</u>: chill, cold, coldness, coolness, iciness ≠<u>affection</u>: aloofness, hard-heartedness, hostility, indifference

warn verb <u>notify</u>, advise, alert, apprise, caution, forewarn, give notice, inform, make (someone) aware, tip off

warning noun <u>caution</u>, advice, alarm, alert, notification, omen, sign, tip-off

warp verb 1 <u>twist</u>, bend, contort, deform, distort ♦ noun 2 <u>twist</u>, bend, contortion, distortion, kink

warrant noun 1 <u>authorization</u>, authority, licence, permission, permit, sanction ♦ verb 2 <u>call for</u>, demand, deserve, excuse, justify, license, necessitate, permit, require, sanction 3 <u>guarantee</u>, affirm, attest, certify, declare, pledge, vouch for

warranty noun <u>guarantee</u>, assurance, bond, certificate, contract, covenant, pledge

warrior noun <u>soldier</u>, combatant, fighter, gladiator, man-at-arms

wary adjective <u>cautious</u>, alert, careful, chary, circumspect, distrustful, guarded, suspicious, vigilant, watchful

➤ **Antonyms**
careless, foolhardy, imprudent, negligent, rash, reckless, unsuspecting, unwary

wash verb **1** <u>clean</u>, bathe, cleanse, launder, rinse, scrub **2** <u>sweep away</u>, bear away, carry off, move **3** Informal <u>be plausible</u>, bear scrutiny, be convincing, carry weight, hold up, hold water, stand up, stick ♦ noun **4** <u>cleaning</u>, cleansing, laundering, rinse, scrub **5** <u>coat</u>, coating, film, layer, overlay **6** <u>swell</u>, surge, wave

washout noun <u>failure</u>, disappointment, disaster, dud (informal), fiasco, flop (informal)

➤ **Antonyms**
conquest, feat, success, triumph, victory, winner

waste verb **1** <u>squander</u>, blow (slang), dissipate, fritter away, lavish, misuse, throw away **2** <u>waste away</u> <u>decline</u>, atrophy, crumble, decay, dwindle, fade, wane, wear out, wither ♦ noun **3** <u>squandering</u>, dissipation, extravagance, frittering away, misuse, prodigality, wastefulness **4** <u>rubbish</u>, debris, dross, garbage, leftovers, litter, refuse, scrap, trash **5** <u>wastes</u> <u>desert</u>, wasteland, wilderness ♦ adjective **6** <u>unwanted</u>, leftover, superfluous, supernumerary, unused, useless, worthless **7** <u>uncultivated</u>, bare, barren, desolate, empty, uninhabited, unproductive, wild

➤ **Antonyms**
verb ≠<u>squander</u>: conserve, economize, husband, preserve, protect, save ≠<u>decline</u>: build, devel-

op, increase, rally, strengthen ♦ noun ≠<u>squandering</u>: economy, frugality, good housekeeping, saving, thrift ♦ adjective ≠<u>unwanted</u>: necessary, needed, utilized ≠<u>uncultivated</u>: arable, in use, productive

wasteful adjective <u>extravagant</u>, lavish, prodigal, profligate, spendthrift, thriftless, uneconomical

➤ **Antonyms**
economical, frugal, money-saving, parsimonious, sparing, thrifty

waster noun <u>layabout</u>, good-for-nothing, idler, loafer, ne'er-do-well, shirker, skiver (Brit. slang), wastrel

watch verb **1** <u>look at</u>, contemplate, eye, eyeball (slang), observe, regard, see, view **2** <u>guard</u>, keep, look after, mind, protect, superintend, take care of, tend ♦ noun **3** <u>wristwatch</u>, chronometer, timepiece **4** <u>lookout</u>, observation, surveillance, vigil

watchdog noun **1** <u>guard dog</u> **2** <u>guardian</u>, custodian, monitor, protector, scrutineer

watchful adjective <u>alert</u>, attentive, observant, on the lookout, suspicious, vigilant, wary, wide awake

➤ **Antonyms**
careless, inattentive, reckless, thoughtless, unaware, unobservant, unwary

watchman noun <u>guard</u>, caretaker, custodian, security guard

watchword noun <u>motto</u>, battle cry, byword, catch phrase, catchword, maxim, rallying cry, slogan, tag-line

water noun **1** <u>liquid</u>, H_2O ♦ verb **2** <u>moisten</u>, dampen, douse, drench, hose, irrigate, soak, spray

water down verb <u>dilute</u>, thin, weaken

➤ **Antonyms**
purify, strengthen, thicken

waterfall noun <u>cascade</u>, cataract, fall

waterlogged adjective <u>soaked</u>,

drenched, dripping, saturated, sodden, sopping, streaming, wet through, wringing wet

watertight *adjective* **1** waterproof, sound **2** foolproof, airtight, flawless, impregnable, sound, unassailable

➤ **Antonyms**
≠waterproof: leaky ≠foolproof: defective, flawed, questionable, shaky, tenuous, uncertain, unsound, weak

watery *adjective* **1** wet, aqueous, damp, fluid, liquid, moist, soggy **2** diluted, runny, thin, washy, watered-down, weak

➤ **Antonyms**
≠diluted: concentrated, condensed, strong, thick

wave *verb* **1** signal, beckon, direct, gesticulate, gesture, indicate, sign **2** brandish, flap, flourish, flutter, oscillate, shake, stir, swing, wag ◆ *noun* **3** ripple, billow, breaker, ridge, roller, swell, undulation **4** outbreak, flood, rash, rush, stream, surge, upsurge

waver *verb* **1** hesitate, dither (*chiefly Brit.*), falter, fluctuate, hum and haw, seesaw, vacillate **2** tremble, flicker, quiver, shake, totter, wobble

➤ **Antonyms**
≠hesitate: be decisive, be determined, be resolute, resolve, stand firm

wax *verb* increase, develop, enlarge, expand, grow, magnify, swell

➤ **Antonyms**
decline, decrease, diminish, dwindle, fade, shrink, wane

way *noun* **1** method, fashion, manner, means, mode, procedure, process, system, technique **2** style, custom, habit, manner, nature, personality, practice, wont **3** route, channel, course, direction, path, pathway, road, track, trail **4** journey, approach, march, passage **5** distance, length, stretch

wayfarer *noun* traveller, gypsy,

itinerant, nomad, rover, voyager, wanderer

wayward *adjective* erratic, capricious, inconstant, ungovernable, unmanageable, unpredictable, unruly

➤ **Antonyms**
dependable, manageable, obedient, obliging, predictable, reliable

weak *adjective* **1** feeble, debilitated, effete, fragile, frail, infirm, puny, sickly, unsteady **2** unsafe, defenceless, exposed, helpless, unguarded, unprotected, vulnerable **3** unconvincing, feeble, flimsy, hollow, lame, pathetic, unsatisfactory **4** tasteless, diluted, insipid, runny, thin, watery

➤ **Antonyms**
≠feeble: energetic, hardy, healthy, hefty, mighty, strong, tough ≠unsafe: invulnerable, safe, secure, well-defended ≠unconvincing: conclusive, convincing, forceful, powerful, valid ≠tasteless: flavoursome, intoxicating, potent, tasty

weaken *verb* **1** lessen, diminish, dwindle, fade, flag, lower, moderate, reduce, sap, undermine, wane **2** dilute, thin out, water down

➤ **Antonyms**
≠lessen: boost, enhance, grow, improve, increase, invigorate, revitalize, strengthen

weakling *noun* sissy, drip (*informal*), wet (*Brit. informal*), wimp (*informal*), wuss (*slang*)

weakness *noun* **1** frailty, decrepitude, feebleness, fragility, infirmity, powerlessness, vulnerability **2** failing, blemish, defect, deficiency, fault, flaw, imperfection, lack, shortcoming **3** liking, fondness, inclination, partiality, passion, penchant, soft spot

➤ **Antonyms**
≠frailty: potency, power, sturdiness, vigour, vitality ≠failing: vantage, forte, strength, strong point ≠liking: aversion, dislike, hatred, loathing

wealth *noun* **1** riches, affluence,

capital, fortune, money, opulence, prosperity **2** plenty, abundance, copiousness, cornucopia, fullness, profusion, richness

➤ **Antonyms**

≠riches: destitution, penury, poverty ≠plenty: dearth, lack, need, paucity, poverty, scarcity, shortage, want

wealthy adjective rich, affluent, flush (informal), moneyed, opulent, prosperous, well-heeled (informal), well-off, well-to-do

➤ **Antonyms**

broke (informal), destitute, down and out, impoverished, needy, penniless, poor

wear verb **1** be dressed in, don, have on, put on, sport (informal) **2** show, display, exhibit **3** deteriorate, abrade, corrode, erode, fray, grind, rub ♦ noun **4** clothes, apparel, attire, costume, dress, garb, garments, gear (informal), things **5** damage, abrasion, attrition, corrosion, deterioration, erosion, wear and tear

➤ **Antonyms**

noun ≠damage: conservation, maintenance, preservation, repair, upkeep

weariness noun tiredness, drowsiness, exhaustion, fatigue, languor, lassitude, lethargy, listlessness

➤ **Antonyms**

drive, energy, stamina, vigour, vitality, zeal, zest

wearing adjective tiresome, exasperating, fatiguing, irksome, oppressive, trying, wearisome

➤ **Antonyms**

easy, effortless, painless, refreshing, stimulating, undemanding

wearisome adjective tedious, annoying, boring, exhausting, fatiguing, irksome, oppressive, tiresome, troublesome, trying, wearing

➤ **Antonyms**

agreeable, delightful, enjoyable, exhilarating, interesting, invigorating, pleasurable, refreshing, stimulating

wear off verb subside, decrease, diminish, disappear, dwindle, fade, peter out, wane

➤ **Antonyms**

grow, increase, intensify, magnify, persist, strengthen

weary adjective **1** tired, done in (informal), drained, drowsy, exhausted, fatigued, flagging, jaded, sleepy, worn out **2** tiring, arduous, laborious, tiresome, wearisome ♦ verb **3** tire, drain, enervate, fatigue, sap, take it out of (informal), tax, tire out, wear out

➤ **Antonyms**

adjective ≠tired: energetic, fresh, invigorated, lively, refreshed, stimulated ≠tiring: exciting, invigorating, original, refreshing ♦ verb ≠tire: enliven, invigorate, refresh, revive, stimulate

weather noun **1** climate, conditions ♦ verb **2** withstand, brave, come through, endure, overcome, resist, ride out, stand, survive

➤ **Antonyms**

verb ≠withstand: cave in, collapse, go under, succumb, surrender, yield

weave verb **1** knit, braid, entwine, interlace, intertwine, plait **2** create, build, construct, contrive, fabricate, make up, put together, spin **3** zigzag, crisscross, wind

web noun **1** spider's web, cobweb **2** network, lattice, tangle

wed verb **1** marry, get married, take the plunge (informal), tie the knot (informal) **2** unite, ally, blend, combine, interweave, join, link, merge

➤ **Antonyms**

≠unite: break up, disunite, divide, divorce, part, separate, sever, split

wedding noun marriage, nuptials, wedlock

wedge noun **1** block, chunk, lump ♦ verb **2** squeeze, cram, crowd, force, jam, lodge, pack, ram, stuff, thrust

wedlock noun <u>marriage</u>, matrimony

weed out verb <u>eliminate</u>, dispense with, eradicate, get rid of, remove, root out, uproot

weedy adjective <u>weak</u>, feeble, frail, ineffectual, namby-pamby, puny, skinny, thin

weep verb <u>cry</u>, blubber, lament, mourn, shed tears, snivel, sob, whimper

➤ **Antonyms**

be glad, celebrate, delight, exult, make merry, rejoice, revel, triumph

weigh verb **1** <u>have a weight of</u>, tip the scales at (*informal*) **2** <u>consider</u>, contemplate, deliberate upon, evaluate, examine, meditate upon, ponder, reflect upon, think over **3** <u>matter</u>, carry weight, count

weight noun **1** <u>heaviness</u>, load, mass, poundage, tonnage **2** <u>importance</u>, authority, consequence, impact, import, influence, power, value ◆ verb **3** <u>load</u>, freight **4** <u>bias</u>, load, slant, unbalance

weighty adjective **1** <u>important</u>, consequential, crucial, grave, momentous, portentous, serious, significant, solemn **2** <u>heavy</u>, burdensome, cumbersome, hefty (*informal*), massive, ponderous

➤ **Antonyms**

≠<u>important</u>: frivolous, incidental, inconsequential, insignificant, minor, petty, trivial, unimportant

weird adjective <u>strange</u>, bizarre, creepy (*informal*), eerie, freakish, mysterious, odd, queer, spooky (*informal*), unnatural

➤ **Antonyms**

common, mundane, natural, normal, ordinary, regular, typical, usual

welcome verb **1** <u>greet</u>, embrace, hail, meet, receive ◆ noun **2** <u>greeting</u>, acceptance, hospitality, reception, salutation ◆ adjective **3** <u>acceptable</u>, agreeable, appreciated, delightful, desirable, gratifying, pleasant, refreshing **4**

free, under no obligation

➤ **Antonyms**

verb ≠<u>greet</u>: exclude, rebuff, refuse, reject, slight, snub, spurn, turn away ◆ noun ≠<u>greeting</u>: cold shoulder, exclusion, ostracism, rebuff, rejection, slight, snub ◆ adjective ≠<u>acceptable</u>: disagreeable, unacceptable, undesirable, unpleasant, unwanted, unwelcome

weld verb <u>join</u>, bind, bond, connect, fuse, link, solder, unite

welfare noun <u>wellbeing</u>, advantage, benefit, good, happiness, health, interest, prosperity

well[1] adverb **1** <u>satisfactorily</u>, agreeably, nicely, pleasantly, smoothly, splendidly, successfully **2** <u>skilfully</u>, ably, adeptly, adequately, admirably, correctly, efficiently, expertly, proficiently, properly **3** <u>prosperously</u>, comfortably **4** <u>suitably</u>, fairly, fittingly, justly, properly, rightly **5** <u>intimately</u>, deeply, fully, profoundly, thoroughly **6** <u>favourably</u>, approvingly, glowingly, highly, kindly, warmly **7** <u>considerably</u>, abundantly, amply, fully, greatly, heartily, highly, substantially, thoroughly, very much ◆ adjective **8** <u>healthy</u>, fit, in fine fettle, sound **9** <u>satisfactory</u>, agreeable, fine, pleasing, proper, right, thriving

➤ **Antonyms**

adverb ≠<u>satisfactorily</u>: badly, inadequately, poorly, wrongly ≠<u>skilfully</u>: badly, ham-fistedly, incompetently, incorrectly, ineptly, inexpertly, sloppily, unskilfully ≠<u>suitably</u>: unfairly, unjustly, unsuitably ≠<u>intimately</u>: slightly, somewhat, vaguely ≠<u>favourably</u>: coldly, disapprovingly, gracelessly, unkindly, unsympathetically ◆ adjective ≠<u>healthy</u>: ailing, frail, ill, infirm, poorly, sick, unwell, weak ≠<u>satisfactory</u>: going badly, unsatisfactory, unsuccessful, wrong

well[2] noun **1** <u>hole</u>, bore, pit, shaft ◆ verb **2** <u>flow</u>, gush, jet, pour, spout, spring, spurt, surge

well-known adjective <u>famous</u>, celebrated, familiar, noted, popular, renowned

well-off adjective <u>rich</u>, affluent, comfortable, moneyed, prosperous, wealthy, well-heeled (informal), well-to-do

➤ **Antonyms**

badly off, broke (informal), destitute, hard up (informal), impoverished, penniless, poor, poverty-stricken

well-to-do adjective <u>rich</u>, affluent, comfortable, moneyed, prosperous, wealthy, well-heeled (informal), well-off

➤ **Antonyms**

down at heel, hard up (informal), needy, poor

well-worn adjective <u>stale</u>, banal, commonplace, hackneyed, overused, stereotyped, trite

welt noun <u>mark</u>, contusion, streak, stripe, wale, weal

welter noun <u>jumble</u>, confusion, hotchpotch, mess, muddle, tangle, web

wet adjective 1 <u>damp</u>, dank, moist, saturated, soaking, sodden, soggy, sopping, waterlogged, watery 2 <u>rainy</u>, drizzling, pouring, raining, showery, teeming 3 Informal <u>feeble</u>, effete, ineffectual, namby-pamby, soft, spineless, timorous, weak, weedy (informal), wussy (slang) ♦ noun 4 <u>rain</u>, drizzle 5 Informal <u>weakling</u>, drip (informal), weed (informal), wimp (informal), wuss (slang) 6 <u>moisture</u>, condensation, damp, dampness, humidity, liquid, water, wetness ♦ verb 7 <u>moisten</u>, dampen, douse, irrigate, saturate, soak, spray, water

➤ **Antonyms**

adjective ≠<u>damp</u>: bone-dry, dried, dry, hardened, parched, set ≠<u>rainy</u>: arid, dry, fine, sunny ♦ noun ≠<u>rain</u>: dry weather, fine weather ♦ ≠<u>moisture</u>: dryness ♦ verb ≠<u>moisten</u>: dehydrate, desiccate, dry, parch

whack verb 1 <u>strike</u>, bang, belt (informal), clobber (slang), hit,

smack, swipe, thrash, thump, thwack, wallop (informal) ♦ noun 2 <u>blow</u>, bang, belt (informal), hit, smack, stroke, swipe, thump, thwack, wallop (informal) 3 Informal <u>share</u>, bit, cut (informal), part, portion, quota 4 As in have a whack <u>attempt</u>, bash (informal), crack (informal), go (informal), shot (informal), stab (informal), try, turn

wharf noun <u>dock</u>, jetty, landing stage, pier, quay

wheedle verb <u>coax</u>, cajole, entice, inveigle, persuade

wheel noun 1 <u>circle</u>, gyration, pivot, revolution, rotation, spin, turn ♦ verb 2 <u>turn</u>, gyrate, pirouette, revolve, rotate, spin, swing, swivel, twirl, whirl

wheeze verb 1 <u>gasp</u>, cough, hiss, rasp, whistle ♦ noun 2 <u>gasp</u>, cough, hiss, rasp, whistle 3 Brit. slang <u>trick</u>, idea, plan, ploy, ruse, scheme, stunt

whereabouts noun <u>position</u>, location, site, situation

wherewithal noun <u>resources</u>, capital, funds, means, money, supplies

whet verb 1 As in whet someone's appetite <u>stimulate</u>, arouse, awaken, enhance, excite, kindle, quicken, rouse, stir 2 <u>sharpen</u>, hone

➤ **Antonyms**

≠<u>stimulate</u>: blunt, dampen, depress, dull, numb, stifle, subdue, suppress ≠<u>sharpen</u>: blunt, dull

whiff noun <u>smell</u>, aroma, hint, odour, scent, sniff

whim noun <u>impulse</u>, caprice, fancy, notion, urge

whimper verb 1 <u>cry</u>, moan, snivel, sob, weep, whine, whinge (informal), snivel, whine ♦ noun 2 <u>sob</u>, moan, snivel, whine

whimsical adjective <u>fanciful</u>, curious, eccentric, freakish, funny, odd, playful, quaint, unusual

whine noun 1 <u>cry</u>, moan, sob, wail, whimper 2 <u>complaint</u>, gripe (informal), grouch (informal), grouse, grumble, moan,

whinge (*informal*) ♦ verb 3 <u>cry</u>, moan, sniffle, snivel, sob, wail, whimper 4 <u>complain</u>, gripe (*informal*), grizzle (*informal*, *chiefly Brit.*), grouch (*informal*), grouse, grumble, moan, whinge (*informal*)

whinge *Informal* ♦ verb 1 <u>complain</u>, bleat, carp, gripe (*informal*), grouse, grumble, moan ♦ noun 2 <u>complaint</u>, gripe (*informal*), grouch, grouse, grumble, moan, whine

whip noun 1 <u>lash</u>, birch, cane, cat-o'-nine-tails, crop, scourge ♦ verb 2 <u>lash</u>, beat, birch, cane, flagellate, flog, scourge, spank, strap, thrash 3 *Informal* <u>dash</u>, dart, dive, fly, rush, shoot, tear, whisk 4 <u>whisk</u>, beat 5 <u>incite</u>, agitate, drive, foment, goad, spur, stir, work up

whirl verb 1 <u>spin</u>, pirouette, revolve, roll, rotate, swirl, turn, twirl, twist 2 <u>feel dizzy</u>, reel, spin ♦ noun 3 <u>revolution</u>, pirouette, roll, rotation, spin, swirl, turn, twirl, twist 4 <u>bustle</u>, flurry, merry-go-round, round, series, succession 5 <u>confusion</u>, daze, dither (*chiefly Brit.*), giddiness, spin

whirlwind noun 1 <u>tornado</u>, waterspout ♦ adjective 2 <u>rapid</u>, hasty, quick, short, speedy, swift

➤ **Antonyms**

adjective ≠<u>rapid</u>: calculated, cautious, considered, deliberate, measured, prudent, slow, unhurried

whisk verb 1 <u>flick</u>, brush, sweep, whip 2 <u>beat</u>, fluff up, whip ♦ noun 3 <u>flick</u>, brush, sweep, whip 4 <u>beater</u>

whisper verb 1 <u>murmur</u>, breathe 2 <u>rustle</u>, hiss, sigh, swish ♦ noun 3 <u>murmur</u>, undertone 4 *Informal* <u>rumour</u>, gossip, innuendo, insinuation, report 5 <u>rustle</u>, hiss, sigh, swish

➤ **Antonyms**

verb ≠<u>murmur</u>: bawl, bellow, roar, shout, thunder, yell

white adjective <u>pale</u>, ashen, pallid, pasty, wan

➤ **Antonyms**

black, dark

white-collar adjective <u>clerical</u>, nonmanual, professional, salaried

whiten verb <u>pale</u>, blanch, bleach, fade

➤ **Antonyms**

blacken, colour, darken

whitewash noun 1 <u>cover-up</u>, camouflage, concealment, deception ♦ verb 2 <u>cover up</u>, camouflage, conceal, gloss over, suppress

➤ **Antonyms**

verb ≠<u>cover up</u>: disclose, expose, lay bare, reveal, uncover, unmask, unveil

whittle verb 1 <u>carve</u>, cut, hew, pare, shape, shave, trim 2 <u>whittle down</u> or <u>away</u> <u>reduce</u>, consume, eat away, erode, wear away

whole adjective 1 <u>complete</u>, entire, full, total, unabridged, uncut, undivided 2 <u>undamaged</u>, in one piece, intact, unbroken, unharmed, unscathed, untouched ♦ noun 3 <u>totality</u>, ensemble, entirety 4 **on the whole**: **a** <u>all in all</u>, all things considered, by and large **b** <u>generally</u>, as a rule, in general, in the main, mostly, predominantly

➤ **Antonyms**

adjective ≠<u>complete</u>: cut, divided, fragmented, incomplete, in pieces, partial ≠<u>undamaged</u>: broken, damaged ♦ noun ≠<u>totality</u>: bit, component, constituent, element, fragment, part, piece, portion

wholehearted adjective <u>sincere</u>, committed, dedicated, determined, devoted, enthusiastic, unstinting, zealous

➤ **Antonyms**

grudging, half-hearted, insincere, qualified, reserved

wholesale adjective 1 <u>extensive</u>, broad, comprehensive, far-reaching, indiscriminate, mass, sweeping, wide-ranging ♦ adverb 2 <u>extensively</u>, comprehensively, indiscriminately

> **Antonyms**

adjective ≠<u>extensive</u>: limited, partial, restricted, selective

wholesome adjective 1 <u>healthy</u>, beneficial, good, nourishing, nutritious, salubrious 2 <u>moral</u>, decent, edifying, improving, respectable

> **Antonyms**

≠<u>healthy</u>: rotten, unhealthy, unhygienic, unwholesome ≠<u>moral</u>: immoral, lewd, pernicious, trashy, unwholesome

wholly adverb <u>completely</u>, altogether, entirely, fully, in every respect, perfectly, thoroughly, totally, utterly

> **Antonyms**

incompletely, in part, moderately, partially, partly, relatively, slightly, somewhat

whopper noun 1 <u>giant</u>, colossus, crackerjack (informal), jumbo (informal), leviathan, mammoth, monster 2 <u>big lie</u>, fabrication, falsehood, tall story (informal), untruth

whopping adjective <u>gigantic</u>, big, enormous, giant, great, huge, mammoth, massive

whore noun <u>prostitute</u>, call girl, streetwalker, tart (informal)

wicked adjective 1 <u>bad</u>, corrupt, depraved, devilish, evil, fiendish, immoral, sinful, vicious, villainous 2 <u>mischievous</u>, impish, incorrigible, naughty, rascally, roguish

> **Antonyms**

≠<u>bad</u>: ethical, good, honourable, good, moral, noble, principled, virtuous ≠<u>mischievous</u>: good, obedient, well-behaved

wide adjective 1 <u>broad</u>, expansive, extensive, far-reaching, immense, large, overarching, sweeping, vast 2 <u>spacious</u>, baggy, capacious, commodious, full, loose, roomy 3 <u>expanded</u>, dilated, distended, outspread, outstretched 4 <u>distant</u>, off course, off target, remote ♦ adverb 5 <u>fully</u>, completely 6 <u>off target</u>,

astray, off course, off the mark, out

> **Antonyms**

adjective ≠<u>broad</u>: narrow, strict, tight ≠<u>spacious</u>: confined, constricted, cramped, tight ≠<u>expanded</u>: closed, limited, restricted, shut ♦ adverb ≠<u>fully</u>: narrowly, partially, partly

widen verb <u>broaden</u>, dilate, enlarge, expand, extend, spread, stretch

> **Antonyms**

constrict, contract, diminish, narrow, reduce, shrink, tighten

widespread adjective <u>common</u>, broad, extensive, far-reaching, general, pervasive, popular, universal

> **Antonyms**

confined, exclusive, limited, local, narrow, rare, sporadic, uncommon

width noun <u>breadth</u>, compass, diameter, extent, girth, scope, span, thickness

wield verb 1 <u>brandish</u>, employ, flourish, handle, manage, manipulate, ply, swing, use 2 As in **wield power** <u>exert</u>, exercise, have, maintain, possess

wife noun <u>spouse</u>, better half (humorous), bride, mate, partner

wiggle verb, noun <u>jerk</u>, jiggle, shake, shimmy, squirm, twitch, wag, waggle, writhe

wild adjective 1 <u>untamed</u>, feral, ferocious, fierce, savage, unbroken, undomesticated 2 <u>uncultivated</u>, free, natural 3 <u>uncivilized</u>, barbaric, barbarous, brutish, ferocious, fierce, primitive, savage 4 <u>uncontrolled</u>, disorderly, riotous, rowdy, turbulent, undisciplined, unfettered, unmanageable, unrestrained, unruly, wayward 5 <u>stormy</u>, blustery, choppy, raging, rough, tempestuous, violent 6 <u>excited</u>, crazy (informal), enthusiastic, hysterical, raving ♦ noun 7 **wilds** <u>wilderness</u>, back of beyond (informal), desert, middle of nowhere (informal), wasteland

> **Antonyms**

adjective ≠untamed: broken, domesticated, tame ≠uncultivated: cultivated, farmed, planted ≠uncivilized: advanced, civilized ≠uncontrolled: calm, controlled, disciplined, orderly, peaceful, quiet, restrained, well-behaved ≠excited: unenthusiastic, uninterested

wilderness *noun* desert, jungle, wasteland, wilds

wiles *plural noun* trickery, artfulness, chicanery, craftiness, cunning, guile, slyness

wilful *adjective* **1** obstinate, determined, headstrong, inflexible, intransigent, obdurate, perverse, pig-headed, stubborn, uncompromising **2** intentional, conscious, deliberate, intended, purposeful, voluntary

> **Antonyms**

≠obstinate: biddable, docile, flexible, good-natured, obedient, pliant, tractable, yielding ≠intentional: accidental, involuntary, unconscious, unintentional, unplanned, unwitting

will *noun* **1** determination, purpose, resolution, resolve, willpower **2** wish, desire, fancy, inclination, mind, preference, volition **3** testament, last wishes ♦ *verb* **4** wish, desire, prefer, see fit, want **5** bequeath, confer, give, leave, pass on, transfer

willing *adjective* ready, agreeable, amenable, compliant, consenting, game (*informal*), inclined, prepared

> **Antonyms**

averse, disinclined, grudging, indisposed, loath, reluctant, unenthusiastic, unwilling

willingly *adverb* readily, by choice, cheerfully, eagerly, freely, gladly, happily, of one's own accord, voluntarily

> **Antonyms**

grudgingly, hesitantly, involuntarily, reluctantly, unwillingly

willingness *noun* inclination, agreement, consent, volition, will, wish

> **Antonyms**

aversion, disinclination, hesitation, reluctance, unwillingness

willowy *adjective* slender, graceful, lithe, slim, supple, svelte, sylphlike

willpower *noun* self-control, determination, drive, grit, resolution, resolve, self-discipline, single-mindedness

> **Antonyms**

indecision, irresolution, uncertainty, weakness

wilt *verb* **1** droop, sag, shrivel, wither **2** weaken, fade, flag, languish, wane

wily *adjective* cunning, artful, astute, crafty, guileful, sharp, shrewd, sly, tricky

> **Antonyms**

artless, guileless, honest, ingenuous, naive, simple, straightforward

wimp *noun* Informal weakling, coward, drip (*informal*), mouse, sissy, softy or softie, wuss (*slang*)

win *verb* **1** triumph, come first, conquer, overcome, prevail, succeed, sweep the board **2** gain, achieve, acquire, attain, earn, get, land, obtain, procure, secure ♦ *noun* **3** victory, conquest, success, triumph

> **Antonyms**

verb ≠triumph: fail, fall ≠gain: forfeit, lose, miss ♦ *noun* ≠victory: beating, defeat, downfall, failure, loss

wince *verb* **1** flinch, blench, cower, cringe, draw back, quail, recoil, shrink, start ♦ *noun* **2** flinch, cringe, start

wind[1] *noun* **1** air, blast, breeze, draught, gust, zephyr **2** breath, puff, respiration **3** flatulence, gas **4** talk, babble, blather, bluster, boasting, hot air, humbug **5** As in get wind of hint, inkling, notice, report, rumour, suggestion, warning, whisper

wind[2] *verb* **1** coil, curl, encircle, loop, reel, roll, spiral, twist **2** meander, bend, curve, ramble, snake, turn, twist, zigzag

windfall noun godsend, bonanza, find, jackpot, manna from heaven

➤ **Antonyms**

misadventure, mischance, misfortune, mishap

wind up verb 1 end, close, conclude, finalize, finish, settle, terminate, wrap up 2 end up, be left, finish up 3 Informal excite, put on edge, work up

➤ **Antonyms**

≠end: begin, commence, embark on, initiate, instigate, institute, open, start

windy adjective breezy, blowy, blustery, gusty, squally, stormy, wild, windswept

➤ **Antonyms**

becalmed, calm, motionless, smooth, still, windless

wing noun 1 faction, arm, branch, group, section ♦ verb 2 fly, glide, soar 3 wound, clip, hit

wink verb 1 blink, bat, flutter 2 twinkle, flash, gleam, glimmer, sparkle ♦ noun 3 blink, flutter

winkle out verb extract, dig out, dislodge, draw out, extricate, force out, prise out

winner noun victor, champ (informal), champion, conqueror, master

winning adjective 1 victorious, conquering, successful, triumphant 2 charming, alluring, attractive, cute, disarming, enchanting, endearing, engaging, likable or likeable, pleasing

➤ **Antonyms**

≠charming: disagreeable, offensive, repellent, tiresome, unappealing, unattractive, unpleasant

winnings plural noun spoils, gains, prize, proceeds, profits, takings

winnow verb separate, divide, select, sift, sort out

win over verb convince, bring or talk round, convert, influence, persuade, prevail upon, sway

wintry adjective cold, chilly, freezing, frosty, frozen, icy, snowy

➤ **Antonyms**

balmy, bright, mild, pleasant, summery, sunny, warm

wipe verb 1 clean, brush, mop, rub, sponge, swab 2 erase, remove ♦ noun 3 rub, brush

wipe out verb destroy, annihilate, eradicate, erase, expunge, exterminate, massacre, obliterate

wiry adjective lean, sinewy, strong, tough

➤ **Antonyms**

fat, flabby, fleshy, podgy

wisdom noun understanding, discernment, enlightenment, erudition, insight, intelligence, judgment, knowledge, learning, sense

➤ **Antonyms**

folly, idiocy, nonsense, senselessness, stupidity

wise adjective sensible, clever, discerning, enlightened, erudite, intelligent, judicious, perceptive, prudent, sage

➤ **Antonyms**

daft (informal), foolish, rash, silly, stupid, unintelligent, unwise

wisecrack noun 1 joke, jest, jibe, quip, witticism ♦ verb 2 joke, jest, jibe, quip

wish verb 1 want, aspire, crave, desire, hanker, hope, long, yearn ♦ noun 2 desire, aspiration, hope, intention, urge, want, whim, will

➤ **Antonyms**

noun ≠desire: aversion, disinclination, dislike, distaste, loathing, reluctance, repulsion, revulsion

wispy adjective thin, attenuated, delicate, fine, flimsy, fragile, frail

wistful adjective melancholy, contemplative, dreamy, longing, meditative, pensive, reflective, thoughtful

wit noun 1 humour, badinage, banter, drollery, jocularity, raillery, repartee, wordplay 2 humorist, card (informal), comedian, joker, wag 3 cleverness, acumen, brains, common sense, ingenuity, intellect, sense, wisdom

> **Antonyms**

≠<u>humour</u>: dullness, humourlessness, seriousness, sobriety, solemnity ≠<u>cleverness</u>: folly, foolishness, ignorance, obtuseness, silliness, stupidity

witch noun <u>enchantress</u>, crone, hag, magician, sorceress

witchcraft noun <u>magic</u>, black magic, enchantment, necromancy, occultism, sorcery, the black art, voodoo, wizardry

withdraw verb <u>remove</u>, draw back, extract, pull out, take away, take off

withdrawal noun <u>removal</u>, extraction

withdrawn adjective <u>uncommunicative</u>, distant, introverted, reserved, retiring, shy, taciturn, unforthcoming

> **Antonyms**

extrovert, forward, friendly, gregarious, open, outgoing, sociable

wither verb <u>wilt</u>, decay, decline, disintegrate, fade, perish, shrivel, waste

> **Antonyms**

bloom, blossom, flourish, prosper, succeed, thrive

withering adjective <u>scornful</u>, devastating, humiliating, hurtful, mortifying, snubbing

withhold verb <u>keep back</u>, conceal, hide, hold back, refuse, reserve, retain, suppress

> **Antonyms**

give, grant, hand over, let go, release, relinquish, reveal

withstand verb <u>resist</u>, bear, cope with, endure, hold off, oppose, stand up to, suffer, tolerate

> **Antonyms**

capitulate, falter, give in, give way, relent, succumb, surrender, weaken, yield

witless adjective <u>foolish</u>, dumbass (slang), halfwitted, idiotic, inane, moronic, senseless, silly, stupid

witness noun 1 <u>observer</u>, beholder, bystander, eyewitness, looker-on, onlooker, spectator, viewer, watcher 2 <u>testifier</u>, corroborator

♦ verb 3 <u>see</u>, note, notice, observe, perceive, view, watch 4 <u>sign</u>, countersign, endorse

wits plural noun <u>intelligence</u>, acumen, brains (informal), cleverness, comprehension, faculties, ingenuity, reason, sense, understanding

witter verb <u>chatter</u>, babble, blather, chat, gabble, jabber, prate, prattle, waffle (informal, chiefly Brit.)

witticism noun <u>quip</u>, bon mot, one-liner (slang), pun, riposte

witty adjective <u>humorous</u>, amusing, clever, droll, funny, piquant, sparkling, waggish, whimsical

> **Antonyms**

boring, dull, humourless, tiresome, uninteresting, witless

wizard noun <u>magician</u>, conjuror, magus, necromancer, occultist, shaman, sorcerer, warlock, witch

wizardry noun <u>magic</u>, sorcery, voodoo, witchcraft

wizened adjective <u>wrinkled</u>, dried up, gnarled, lined, shrivelled, shrunken, withered

> **Antonyms**

bloated, plump, rounded, smooth, swollen, turgid

wobble verb 1 <u>shake</u>, rock, sway, teeter, totter, tremble ♦ noun 2 <u>unsteadiness</u>, shake, tremble, tremor

wobbly adjective <u>unsteady</u>, rickety, shaky, teetering, tottering, uneven

woe noun <u>grief</u>, agony, anguish, distress, gloom, misery, sadness, sorrow, unhappiness, wretchedness

> **Antonyms**

bliss, elation, happiness, joy, jubilation, pleasure, rapture

woeful adjective 1 <u>sad</u>, deplorable, dismal, distressing, grievous, lamentable, miserable, pathetic, tragic, wretched 2 <u>pitiful</u>, abysmal, appalling, bad, deplorable, dreadful, feeble, pathetic, poor, sorry

> **Antonyms**

≠<u>sad</u>: carefree, cheerful, glad,

happy, jolly, joyful, light-hearted ≠*pitiful*: ample, enviable, extensive, generous, lavish, luxurious, profuse

woman noun <u>lady</u>, female, girl
➤ **Antonyms**
boy, gentleman, male, man

womanizer noun <u>philanderer</u>, Casanova, Don Juan, lady-killer, lecher, seducer

womanly adjective <u>feminine</u>, female, ladylike, matronly, motherly, tender, warm

wonder verb 1 <u>think</u>, conjecture, meditate, ponder, puzzle, query, question, speculate 2 <u>be amazed</u>, be astonished, gape, marvel, stare ◆ noun 3 <u>phenomenon</u>, curiosity, marvel, miracle, prodigy, rarity, sight, spectacle 4 <u>amazement</u>, admiration, astonishment, awe, bewilderment, fascination, surprise, wonderment

wonderful adjective 1 <u>excellent</u>, brilliant, fabulous (*informal*), fantastic (*informal*), great (*informal*), magnificent, marvellous, outstanding, superb, terrific, tremendous 2 <u>remarkable</u>, amazing, astonishing, extraordinary, incredible, jaw-dropping, miraculous, phenomenal, staggering, startling, unheard-of
➤ **Antonyms**
≠*excellent*: abysmal, appalling, awful, bad, dreadful, miserable, rotten, terrible ≠*remarkable*: common, commonplace, ordinary, run-of-the-mill, uninteresting, unremarkable, usual

wonky adjective <u>shaky</u>, unsteady, wobbly

woo verb <u>court</u>, cultivate, pursue

wood noun 1 <u>timber</u>, planks 2 <u>woodland</u>, coppice, copse, forest, grove, thicket

wooded adjective <u>tree-covered</u>, forested, sylvan (*poetic*), timbered, tree-clad

wooden adjective 1 <u>woody</u>, ligneous, timber 2 <u>expressionless</u>, deadpan, lifeless, unresponsive

wool noun <u>fleece</u>, hair, yarn

woolly adjective 1 <u>fleecy</u>, hairy,

shaggy, woollen 2 <u>vague</u>, confused, hazy, ill-defined, indefinite, indistinct, muddled, unclear
➤ **Antonyms**
≠*vague*: clear, definite, distinct, exact, obvious, precise, sharp, well-defined

word noun 1 <u>term</u>, expression, name 2 <u>chat</u>, confab (*informal*), consultation, discussion, talk, tête-à-tête 3 <u>remark</u>, comment, utterance 4 <u>message</u>, communiqué, dispatch, information, intelligence, news, notice, report 5 <u>promise</u>, assurance, guarantee, oath, pledge, vow 6 <u>command</u>, bidding, decree, mandate, order 7 last word: a <u>final say</u>, summation, ultimatum b <u>epitome</u>, best, crème de la crème, perfection, quintessence, ultimate c <u>vogue</u>, latest, rage ◆ verb 8 <u>express</u>, couch, phrase, put, say, state, utter

wording noun <u>phraseology</u>, language, phrasing, terminology, words

wordy adjective <u>long-winded</u>, diffuse, prolix, rambling, verbose, windy
➤ **Antonyms**
brief, concise, laconic, pithy, short, succinct, terse, to the point

work noun 1 <u>effort</u>, drudgery, elbow grease (*facetious*), exertion, industry, labour, sweat, toil 2 <u>employment</u>, business, duty, job, livelihood, occupation, profession, trade 3 <u>task</u>, assignment, chore, commission, duty, job, stint, undertaking 4 <u>creation</u>, achievement, composition, handiwork, opus, piece, production ◆ verb 5 <u>labour</u>, drudge, exert oneself, peg away, slave, slog (away), sweat, toil 6 <u>be employed</u>, be in work 7 <u>operate</u>, control, drive, handle, manage, manipulate, move, use 8 <u>function</u>, go, operate, run 9 <u>cultivate</u>, dig, farm, till 10 <u>manipulate</u>, fashion, form, knead, mould, shape

➤ **Antonyms**

noun ≠<u>effort</u>: ease, leisure, relaxation, rest ≠<u>employment</u>: hobby, holiday, play, recreation, unemployment ♦ *verb* ≠<u>labour</u>: have fun, play, relax, skive (*Brit. slang*), take it easy ≠<u>function</u>: be broken, be out of order

workable *adjective* <u>viable</u>, doable, feasible, possible, practicable, practical

➤ **Antonyms**

impossible, impractical, unattainable, unworkable

worker *noun* <u>employee</u>, artisan, craftsman, hand, labourer, tradesman, workman

working *adjective* 1 <u>employed</u>, active, in work 2 <u>functioning</u>, going, operative, running

workman *noun* <u>labourer</u>, artisan, craftsman, employee, hand, journeyman, mechanic, operative, tradesman, worker

workmanship *noun* <u>skill</u>, artistry, craftsmanship, expertise, handiwork, technique

work out *verb* 1 <u>solve</u>, calculate, figure out, find out 2 <u>happen</u>, develop, evolve, result, turn out 3 <u>exercise</u>, practise, train, warm up

works *plural noun* 1 <u>factory</u>, mill, plant, workshop 2 <u>writings</u>, canon, *oeuvre*, output 3 <u>mechanism</u>, action, machinery, movement, parts, workings

workshop *noun* <u>studio</u>, factory, mill, plant, workroom

world *noun* 1 <u>earth</u>, globe 2 <u>mankind</u>, everybody, everyone, humanity, humankind, man, the public 3 <u>sphere</u>, area, domain, environment, field, realm

worldly *adjective* 1 <u>earthly</u>, physical, profane, secular, temporal, terrestrial 2 <u>materialistic</u>, grasping, greedy, selfish 3 <u>worldly-wise</u>, blasé, cosmopolitan, experienced, knowing, sophisticated, urbane

➤ **Antonyms**

≠<u>earthly</u>: divine, ethereal, heavenly, immaterial, spiritual, transcendental, unworldly ≠<u>materialistic</u>: moral, unworldly ≠<u>worldly-wise</u>: ingenuous, innocent, naive, unsophisticated, unworldly

worldwide *adjective* <u>global</u>, general, international, omnipresent, pandemic, ubiquitous, universal

➤ **Antonyms**

limited, local, national, parochial, provincial

worn *adjective* <u>ragged</u>, frayed, shabby, tattered, tatty, the worse for wear, threadbare

worn-out *adjective* 1 <u>run-down</u>, on its last legs, ragged, shabby, threadbare, used-up, useless, worn 2 <u>exhausted</u>, all in (*slang*), done in (*informal*), fatigued, fit to drop, spent, tired out, weary

➤ **Antonyms**

≠<u>exhausted</u>: fresh, refreshed, rested, restored, revived, strengthened

worried *adjective* <u>anxious</u>, afraid, antsy (*informal*), apprehensive, concerned, fearful, frightened, nervous, perturbed, tense, troubled, uneasy

➤ **Antonyms**

calm, tranquil, unafraid, unconcerned, unfazed (*informal*), unworried

worry *verb* 1 <u>be anxious</u>, agonize, brood, fret, obsess 2 <u>trouble</u>, annoy, bother, disturb, perturb, pester, unsettle, upset, vex ♦ *noun* 3 <u>anxiety</u>, apprehension, concern, fear, misgiving, trepidation, trouble, unease 4 <u>problem</u>, bother, care, hassle (*informal*), trouble

➤ **Antonyms**

verb ≠<u>be anxious</u>: be apathetic, be unconcerned, be unperturbed ≠<u>trouble</u>: calm, comfort, console, soothe ♦ *noun* ≠<u>anxiety</u>: calm, comfort, consolation, peace of mind, reassurance, serenity, solace, tranquillity

worsen *verb* 1 <u>aggravate</u>, damage, exacerbate 2 <u>deteriorate</u>, decay, decline, degenerate, get worse, go downhill (*informal*), sink

➤ Antonyms

≠aggravate: ameliorate, enhance, improve, mend, rectify, upgrade ≠deteriorate: be on the mend, improve, mend, recover

worship verb **1** praise, adore, exalt, glorify, honour, pray to, revere, venerate **2** love, adore, idolize, put on a pedestal ◆ noun **3** praise, adoration, adulation, devotion, glory, honour, regard, respect, reverence

➤ Antonyms

verb ≠praise: blaspheme, deride, dishonour, mock, revile, ridicule, scoff at ≠love: despise, disdain, spurn

worth noun **1** value, cost, price, rate, valuation **2** importance, excellence, goodness, merit, quality, usefulness, value, worthiness

➤ Antonyms

≠importance: futility, insignificance, triviality, unworthiness, uselessness, worthlessness

worthless adjective **1** useless, ineffectual, rubbishy, unavailing, valueless **2** good-for-nothing, contemptible, despicable, vile

➤ Antonyms

≠useless: effective, important, precious, useful, valuable, worthwhile ≠good-for-nothing: decent, honourable, noble, upright, worthy

worthwhile adjective useful, beneficial, constructive, expedient, helpful, productive, profitable, valuable

➤ Antonyms

pointless, trivial, unimportant, useless, vain, worthless

worthy adjective praiseworthy, admirable, creditable, deserving, laudable, meritorious, valuable, virtuous, worthwhile

➤ Antonyms

disreputable, ignoble, unworthy, useless

would-be adjective budding, self-appointed, self-styled, unfulfilled, wannabe (informal)

wound noun **1** injury, cut, gash, hurt, laceration, lesion, trauma

(Pathology) **2** insult, offence, slight ◆ verb **3** injure, cut, gash, hurt, lacerate, pierce, wing **4** offend, annoy, cut (someone) to the quick, hurt, mortify, sting

wrangle verb **1** argue, bicker, contend, disagree, dispute, fight, quarrel, row, squabble ◆ noun **2** argument, altercation, bickering, dispute, quarrel, row, squabble, tiff

wrap verb **1** cover, bind, bundle up, encase, enclose, enfold, pack, package, shroud, swathe ◆ noun **2** cloak, cape, mantle, shawl, stole

➤ Antonyms

verb ≠cover: open, unpack, unwrap

wrapper noun cover, case, envelope, jacket, packaging, wrapping

wrap up verb **1** giftwrap, bundle up, pack, package **2** Informal end, conclude, finish off, polish off, round off, terminate, wind up

wrath noun anger, displeasure, fury, indignation, ire, rage, resentment, temper

➤ Antonyms

contentment, delight, happiness, joy, pleasure

wreath noun garland, band, chaplet, crown, festoon, ring

wreck verb **1** destroy, break, demolish, devastate, ruin, shatter, smash, spoil ◆ noun **2** shipwreck, hulk

➤ Antonyms

verb ≠destroy: build, conserve, create, preserve, reconstruct, salvage, save

wreckage noun remains, debris, fragments, pieces, rubble, ruin

wrench verb **1** twist, force, jerk, pull, rip, tear, tug, yank **2** sprain, rick, strain ◆ noun **3** twist, jerk, pull, rip, tug, yank **4** sprain, strain, twist **5** blow, pang, shock, upheaval **6** spanner, adjustable spanner

wrest verb seize, extract, force, take, win, wrench

wrestle verb fight, battle, combat, grapple, scuffle, struggle, tussle

wretch noun scoundrel, good-for-nothing, miscreant, rascal, rogue, swine, worm

wretched adjective **1** unhappy, dejected, depressed, disconsolate, downcast, forlorn, hapless, miserable, woebegone **2** worthless, inferior, miserable, paltry, pathetic, poor, sorry

► **Antonyms**

≠unhappy: carefree, cheerful, contented, happy, jovial, lighthearted, untroubled ≠worthless: excellent, flourishing, great, splendid, successful, thriving

wriggle verb **1** twist, jerk, jiggle, squirm, turn, waggle, wiggle, writhe **2** crawl, slink, snake, worm, zigzag **3** As in wriggle out of manoeuvre, dodge, extricate oneself ♦ noun **4** twist, jerk, jiggle, squirm, turn, waggle, wiggle

wring verb twist, extract, force, screw, squeeze

wrinkle noun **1** crease, corrugation, crinkle, crow's-foot, crumple, fold, furrow, line ♦ verb **2** crease, corrugate, crumple, fold, furrow, gather, pucker, rumple

► **Antonyms**

verb ≠crease: even out, flatten, smooth, straighten

writ noun summons, court order, decree, document

write verb record, draft, draw up, inscribe, jot down, pen, scribble, set down

writer noun author, hack, novelist, penpusher, scribbler, scribe, wordsmith

writhe verb squirm, jerk, struggle, thrash, thresh, toss, twist, wiggle, wriggle

writing noun **1** script, calligraphy, hand, handwriting, penmanship, scrawl, scribble **2** document, book, composition, opus, publication, work

wrong adjective **1** incorrect, erroneous, fallacious, false, inaccurate, mistaken, untrue, wide of the mark **2** bad, criminal, dishonest, evil, illegal, immoral, sinful, unjust, unlawful, wicked, wrongful **3** inappropriate, incongruous, incorrect, unacceptable, unbecoming, undesirable, unseemly, unsuitable **4** defective, amiss, askew, awry, faulty ♦ adverb **5** incorrectly, badly, erroneously, inaccurately, mistakenly, wrongly **6** amiss, askew, astray, awry ♦ noun **7** offence, crime, error, injury, injustice, misdeed, sin, transgression ♦ verb **8** mistreat, abuse, cheat, dishonour, harm, hurt, malign, oppress, take advantage of

► **Antonyms**

adjective ≠incorrect: accurate, correct, precise, right, true ≠bad: ethical, fair, honourable, just, lawful, legal, moral ≠inappropriate: appropriate, apt, correct, fitting, proper, suitable ♦ adverb ≠incorrectly: accurately, correctly, exactly, precisely, properly, squarely, truly ♦ noun ≠offence: favour, good deed, good turn ♦ verb ≠mistreat: aid, do a favour, help, support

wrongdoer noun offender, criminal, culprit, delinquent, lawbreaker, miscreant, sinner, villain

wrongful adjective improper, criminal, evil, illegal, illegitimate, immoral, unethical, unjust, unlawful, wicked

► **Antonyms**

fair, just, lawful, legal, legitimate, proper, rightful

wry adjective **1** ironic, droll, dry, mocking, sarcastic, sardonic **2** contorted, crooked, twisted, uneven

► **Antonyms**

≠contorted: even, level, smooth, straight

Xx, Yy, Zz

Xmas noun <u>Christmas</u>, Noel, Yule (archaic), Yuletide (archaic)

X-rays plural noun <u>Röntgen rays</u> (old name)

yank verb, noun <u>pull</u>, hitch, jerk, snatch, tug, wrench

yardstick noun <u>standard</u>, benchmark, criterion, gauge, measure, par, touchstone

yarn noun 1 <u>thread</u>, fibre 2 Informal <u>story</u>, anecdote, cock-and-bull story (informal), fable, tale, tall story, urban legend, urban myth

yawning adjective <u>gaping</u>, cavernous, vast, wide

yearly adjective 1 <u>annual</u> ♦ adverb 2 <u>annually</u>, every year, once a year, per annum

yearn verb <u>long</u>, ache, covet, crave, desire, hanker, hunger, itch

yell verb 1 <u>scream</u>, bawl, holler (informal), howl, screech, shout, shriek, squeal ♦ noun 2 <u>scream</u>, cry, howl, screech, shriek, whoop

► **Antonyms**

verb, noun ≠<u>scream</u>: mumble, murmur, mutter, whisper

yelp verb <u>cry</u>, yap, yowl

yen noun <u>longing</u>, ache, craving, desire, hankering, hunger, itch, passion, thirst, yearning

yes man noun <u>sycophant</u>, bootlicker (informal), crawler (slang), minion, timeserver, toady

yet conjunction 1 <u>nevertheless</u>, however, notwithstanding, still ♦ adverb 2 <u>so far</u>, as yet, thus far, until now, up to now 3 <u>still</u>, besides, in addition, into the bargain, to boot 4 <u>now</u>, just now, right now, so soon

yield verb 1 <u>produce</u>, bear, bring forth, earn, generate, give, net, provide, return, supply 2 <u>surrender</u>, bow, capitulate, cave in (informal), give in, relinquish, resign, submit, succumb ♦ noun 3 <u>profit</u>, crop, earnings, harvest, income, output, produce, return, revenue, takings

► **Antonyms**

verb ≠<u>produce</u>: consume, use, use up ≠<u>surrender</u>: hold out, keep, maintain, retain, seize, struggle ♦ noun ≠<u>profit</u>: consumption, input, loss

yielding adjective 1 <u>submissive</u>, accommodating, acquiescent, biddable, compliant, docile, flexible, obedient, pliant 2 <u>soft</u>, elastic, pliable, spongy, springy, supple, unresisting

► **Antonyms**

≠<u>submissive</u>: dogged, headstrong, obstinate, wilful

yob, yobbo noun <u>thug</u>, hooligan, lout, roughneck (slang), ruffian

yokel noun <u>peasant</u>, (country) bumpkin, countryman, hick (informal, chiefly U.S. & Canad.), hillbilly, rustic

young adjective 1 <u>immature</u>, adolescent, callow, green, infant, junior, juvenile, little, youthful 2 <u>new</u>, early, fledgling, recent, undeveloped ♦ plural noun 3 <u>offspring</u>, babies, brood, family, issue, litter, progeny

► **Antonyms**

adjective ≠<u>immature</u>: adult, aged, elderly, full-grown, grown-up, mature, old, senior ≠<u>new</u>: advanced, developed, old ♦ plural noun ≠<u>offspring</u>: adults, grown-ups, parents

youngster noun <u>youth</u>, boy, girl, juvenile, kid (informal), lad, lass, teenager

youth noun 1 <u>immaturity</u>, adolescence, boyhood or girlhood, girlhood, salad days 2 <u>boy</u>, adolescent, kid (informal), lad, stripling, teenager, young man, youngster

➤ **Antonyms**

≠*immaturity*: adulthood, age, manhood *or* womanhood, maturity, old age ≠*boy*: adult, grown-up, OAP, pensioner, senior citizen

youthful *adjective* <u>young</u>, boyish, childish, girlish, immature, inexperienced, juvenile

➤ **Antonyms**

adult, aged, ageing, elderly, grown-up, mature, old

zany *adjective* <u>comical</u>, clownish, crazy, eccentric, goofy (*informal*), madcap, wacky (*slang*)

zeal *noun* <u>enthusiasm</u>, ardour, eagerness, fanaticism, fervour, gusto, keenness, passion, spirit, verve, zest

➤ **Antonyms**

apathy, indifference, passivity, unresponsiveness

zealot *noun* <u>fanatic</u>, bigot, enthusiast, extremist, militant

zealous *adjective* <u>enthusiastic</u>, ardent, devoted, eager, fanatical, fervent, impassioned, keen, passionate

➤ **Antonyms**

apathetic, half-hearted, indifferent, lackadaisical, lacklustre, unenthusiastic, unimpassioned

zenith *noun* <u>height</u>, acme, apex,

apogee, climax, crest, high point, peak, pinnacle, summit, top

➤ **Antonyms**

base, bottom, depths, lowest point, nadir

zero *noun* **1** <u>nothing</u>, nil, nought **2** <u>bottom</u>, nadir, rock bottom

zest *noun* **1** <u>enjoyment</u>, appetite, gusto, keenness, relish, zeal **2** <u>flavour</u>, charm, interest, piquancy, pungency, relish, spice, tang, taste

➤ **Antonyms**

≠*enjoyment*: abhorrence, apathy, aversion, disinclination, distaste, indifference, lack of enthusiasm, loathing, repugnance, weariness

zip *noun* **1** *Informal* <u>energy</u>, drive, gusto, liveliness, verve, vigour, zest ♦ *verb* **2** <u>speed</u>, flash, fly, shoot, whizz (*informal*), zoom

➤ **Antonyms**

noun ≠*energy*: apathy, indifference, inertia, laziness, lethargy, listlessness, sloth, sluggishness

zone *noun* <u>area</u>, belt, district, region, section, sector, sphere

zoom *verb* <u>speed</u>, dash, flash, fly, hurtle, pelt, rush, shoot, whizz (*informal*)